Human–Computer Interaction
INTERACT '99

IFIP — The International Federation for Information Processing

IFIP was founded in 1960 under the auspices of UNESCO, following the First World Computer Congress held in Paris the previous year. An umbrella organization for societies working in information processing, IFIP's aim is two-fold: to support information processing within its member countries and to encourage technology transfer to developing nations. As its mission statement clearly states:

> IFIP's mission is to be the leading, truly international, apolitical organization which encourages and assists in the development, exploitation and application of information technology for the benefit of all people.

IFIP is a non-profitmaking organization, run almost solely by 2,500 volunteers. It operates through a number of technical committees, which organize events and publications. IFIP's events range from an international congress to local seminars, but the most important are:

- the IFIP World Computer Congress, held every second year;

- open conferences;

- working conferences.

The flagship event is the IFIP World Computer Congress, at which both invited and contributed papers are presented. Contributed papers are rigorously refereed and the rejection rate is high.

As with the Congress, participation in open conferences is open to all and papers may be invited or submitted. Again, submitted papers are stringently refereed.

The working conferences are structured differently. They are usually run by a working group and attendance is small and by invitation only. Their purpose is to create an atmosphere conducive to innovation and development. Refereeing is less rigorous and papers are subjected to extensive group discussion.

Publications arising from IFIP events vary. The papers presented at the IFIP World Computer Congress and at open conferences are published as conference proceedings, while the results of the working conferences are often published as collections of selected and edited papers.

Any national society whose primary activity is in information may apply to become a full member of IFIP, although full membership is restricted to one society per country. Full members are entitled to vote at the Annual General Assembly. National societies preferring a less committed involvement may apply for associate or corresponding membership. Associate members enjoy the same benefits as full members, but without voting rights. Corresponding members are not represented in IFIP bodies. Affiliated membership is open to non-national societies, and individual and honorary membership schemes are also offered.

Human–Computer Interaction
INTERACT '99

IFIP TC.13 International Conference
on Human–Computer Interaction,
30th August – 3rd September 1999, Edinburgh, UK

Edited by

M. Angela Sasse
University College London
UK

Chris Johnson
Glasgow University
UK

**Published by IOS Press on behalf of the
International Federation for Information Processing (IFIP)**

IOS
Press

Ohmsha

Amsterdam • Berlin • Oxford • Tokyo • Washington, DC

ISBN 0 9673355 0 7 (IOS Press)
ISBN 4 274 90308 7 C3000 (Ohmsha)
Library of Congress Catalog Card Number: 99-64705

Publisher
IOS Press
Van Diemenstraat 94
1013 CN Amsterdam
The Netherlands
fax: +31 20 620 3419
email: order@iospress.nl

Distributor in the UK and Ireland
IOS Press/Lavis Marketing
73 Lime Walk
Headington
Oxford OX3 7AD
UK
fax: +44 1865 75 0079

Distributor in Germany
IOS Press
Spandauer Strasse 2
D-10178 Berlin
Germany
fax: +49 30 242 3113

Distributor in the USA and Canada
IOS Press, Inc.
5795-G Burke Centre Parkway
Burke, VA 22015
USA
fax: +1 703 323 3668
email: iosbooks@iospress.com

Distributor in Japan
Ohmsha, Ltd.
3-1 Kanda Nishiki-cho
Chiyoda-ku, Tokyo 101
Japan
fax: +81 3 3233 2426

Printed in The Netherlands.

Typeset by *Winder.*✍

Contents

Next Generation Office Systems

Novel Interaction

Accessibility

Interruptions and Coordination

Communities and Language

Part Three   Doctoral Consortium   661

The following Parts of these proceedings are contained in Volume 2:

IFIP TC.13 Preface

Fifteen years ago the first INTERACT Conference was held in the United Kingdom. It set out the main areas of study which made up the discipline at that time. One hundred and fifty two papers addressed issues under the headings: user aspects, hardware interface, software interface, cognitive aspects, design and implementation, wider issues and application. Additional components of the conference focussed on an application emphasis devoted to behavioural issues in the system life cycle and usage aspects of electronic mail, conferencing and journals.

Professor Brian Shackel, the conference chair, drew attention to four general aspects of HCI research. He considered that hardware ergonomics was well covered and did not need to be enlarged; that software human factors and cognitive ergonomics were important areas needing growth; that the basic issue of human cognitive characteristics and performance when interacting with computing and IT systems needed to become better known and a sound theoretical basis established; that the inter-relationship of computing and IT systems with job and organisational structure and functioning was a large and complex gap in HCI research.

He concluded that "at last we are beginning to recognise and understand just how much we do not know and how much still needs to be studied" and made a plea for larger funds to allow the reduction of "...the extent to which our knowledge about computer technology exceeds our knowledge about human usage of that technology."

In the intervening years technological development has been exponential. Technologies have come and gone, some have persisted. The social and work environment has changed dramatically. Most applications developed today pay little heed of HCI and the need to integrate it into the development life cycle. Has Shackel's prediction been realised?

INTERACT '99 provides an opportunity for some response to these issues. It can be seen that learning, design and evaluation tools and techniques, organisation issues and social psychology are still active fields of research. It is also clear that new phenomena such as the Web and its applications, 3-dimensional and virtual environments, mobile systems, and emerging forms of applications, such as electronic commerce, are current, vibrant grounds for the application of HCI research.

Today, one of the most written and spoken about impacts of computing and IT is communication and the easy accessibility to information. Geography is no longer a constraint. With these advances in first and second world nations, and slower introduction to the third world, an enlarging proportion of the world population is encountering computer based systems. This brings a changing basis of approach, as issues such as cultural, political and economic differences must be accommodated in ways that have not existed before.

HCI researchers and practitioners have a responsibility to propose scientifically, socially and environmentally sustainable solutions that will help ease the burden that current new technologies impose on people and organisations. The goal must be to achieve benefit from technological advances, for it should match the skills, needs and expectations of users of those technologies.

This volume of proceedings is a permanent record of the paper presentations and the doctoral consortium that were part of INTERACT '99. Other components of the conference — panels, posters, videos, interactive experiences, tutorials and workshops, laboratory and organisational overviews and professional practice and experience — are recorded in Volume 2 of the INTERACT '99 Proceedings, published by the British Computer Society and available from the British Computer Society and IFIP TC.13. The sum reveals the growth of international HCI in terms of facets and the depth of examination that has occurred since the 1984 INTERACT.

Its internationality is reflected by the number of countries represented by presenters and by IFIP's determination, through the Developing Countries Support Committee scheme, to support HCI scientists from Africa, China, India and South America so that they can participate in this INTERACT conference.

IFIP TC.13 provides quality activities and publications that promote and advance HCI in all regions of the world associated with IFIP. INTERACT '99 is a major part of this undertaking and I thank the British Computer Society, through the British HCI Group, for inviting the conference to Edinburgh. The Group has incorporated its annual conference within INTERACT '99 — a gesture that is warmly acknowledged by IFIP TC.13. This joint activity will refresh the HCI community nationally as well as internationally.

IFIP TC.13 thanks most sincerely the conference chair, Professor Alistair Kilgour, and all the members making up the INTERACT '99 committees for their substantial efforts in creating this conference. Dedication is the facilitator of a conference such as INTERACT '99. This conference organisation has once again shown that spirit. It is reflected in the work of the various professional societies which are co-operating societies whose active support brings the international theme to the fore. Corporate sponsors have also played a significant role in making the conference possible. IFIP TC.13 is strengthened through these alliances which demonstrate a common goal — the advancement of HCI around the world.

Special recognition goes to those who helped in the creation of the technical programme and proceedings, particularly the Editors, the International Programme Committee and those undertaking organisational aspects that are integral to covering the diversity and complexity of such a conference. Their names are recorded in this volume.

The International Conference Committee has provided unstinting support and advice to the INTERACT '99 committee during the long period of planning. Their involvement is much appreciated, especially that of the INTERACT Conference Advisor, Professor Brian Shackel, whose substantial knowledge and experience of all preceding INTERACT conferences has been invaluable.

With members of committees being geographically disbursed, the organisation of this conference has been made possible by technology. Email and the World Wide Web were employed at all stages and for most processes — something that could not have been done in earlier conferences in the series.

Achieving a high standard is the continuing goal of IFIP TC.13. This publication is a new development aimed at achieving that goal. We are indebted to Professor Russel Winder for his tireless, meticulous effort in typesetting this volume. The style and format is now set for subsequent conference proceedings. He has collaborated for many weeks on an almost daily basis (by email with attachments) with Professor Brian Shackel and me, the editors, the conference chair and the publisher to create this volume.

Unfortunately it is not possible, at the time of publication, to identify the paper which has been awarded the initial Brian Shackel Award for the most outstanding contribution in the form of a refereed paper submitted to and delivered at each INTERACT conference. Reference to the IFIP TC.13 Web site will do that, as the paper will be mounted there. The Award marks the contribution of Professor Brian Shackel to the establishment of HCI as an international discipline, and is intended to draw attention to the need for a comprehensive human-centred approach in the design and use of information technology in which the human and social implications have been taken into account.

Without the submission of papers, a conference cannot occur. IFIP TC.13 sincerely thanks all those who spent much effort in developing their papers and making their presentations. The role of the world-wide reviewers is also acknowledged as their judgements made possible the assembly of a diverse set of papers and so have enabled the sharing of HCI knowledge and advances both at the conference and in the Proceedings.

Judy Hammond
IFIP TC.13 Chair
University of Technology, Sydney
Australia

Editors' Preface: A Perspective on Failure

The English philosopher Bertrand Russell is said to have remarked that

> "One of the symptoms of an approaching nervous breakdown is the belief that one's work is terribly important"

Many people at this conference will be looking back with justifiable pride at twenty years of achievement in HCI. This preface deliberately takes an alternative view and poses some deeper questions about our future. The submissions to this conference reflected 'the good, the bad and the ugly' sides of HCI. At the end of the reviewing process, it is perhaps easier to remember the problems that affect our research than the achievements that can be built upon. These problems are easy to identify. Many submissions began with a motivational section that stresses the general importance of their HCI research to the public good. Who are they kidding? Large areas of industry and the general public, in particular, are unaffected by the products of our research. Our argument can be summarised by citing McClintock's foreword to Beyer and Holtzblatt's Contextual Design (1998):

> "Computer interaction has come a long way since punched cards. Moreover, in the process, we have learned much about Human–Computer Interaction, much of which HCI research has substantiated. However, designing computer software still remains a rather mysterious art. Newspapers and magazines abound with stories of computer systems and products that are delivered late and over budget and that do not perform as expected. Anyone who has had to wait while a store clerk struggles with a new 'easy to use' computer system can attest to this."

As McClintock states, HCI research substantiates observations of interaction with existing systems. This is bad news. We may end by simply explaining the success or failure of existing commercial products. This focus upon explanation and substantiation gives many HCI researchers the academic high-ground. However, it may also abandon the market place to the technologists and marketing managers.

Many people have spoken about the 'lag' or delay that exists between innovation in the market place and the HCI research that explains or validates that success. This lag was certainly apparent in many of the submissions that we received. Several papers focussed on usability problems with obsolete databases and word-processors. Of course, these results may still inform the development of future systems. However, in many cases their findings were simply irrelevant as technological advances, for instance in indexing and retrieval techniques, change the way in which we interact with these systems.

Conversely, we were eagerly awaiting papers that provide empirical guidance to support the design of 'leading-edge' technology, for example in the area of mobile telecommunications. Of course, there are some valuable papers in the conference, such as Kiljander's study of prototyping methods for mobile handsets. However, many of the submissions focussed narrowly on surface level issues. They ignored the more fundamental, and perhaps more technically challenging, infrastructure changes that will have a profound effect on what users can and cannot access over distributed, mobile networks. Perhaps more significantly for the 'public good', nobody addressed the usability issues that stem from the different charging mechanisms associated with these resources.

It can be argued that INTERACT ought not to focus on short-term preoccupations with emerging technology. In contrast, it should explore longer-term opportunities for inter-disciplinary research. It is difficult to argue with this utopian view. It is reminiscent, however, of a paper entitled "Sociologists Can be Surprisingly Useful in Interactive System Design" by Sommerville et al. (1992):

> "The fact that sociologists have a role to play in the design of complex computer systems is becoming more widely accepted although we believe that it will be many years before the participation of a sociologist in a requirements team is normal practice."

The key point here is that the same sentiments could be expressed about most of the techniques that have been presented at recent conferences. Their usefulness has been demonstrated in small case studies but few have achieved their promise of widespread commercial acceptance. Perhaps the Sommerville et al. paper ought to be re-titled "Sociologists can be Surprisingly Useful but Not Yet".

There was a CSCW panel at CHI'90. Bob Kraut argued that the only successful application of CSCW was email. Nobody at the meeting objected. Even new developments in CSCW, such as the World Wide Web, have emerged in spite of the browser's interface design rather than because of it. If we assume that HCI is an applied subject then it must be remembered that many industries remain sceptical about even the most basic tenets of HCI research. The situation varies from country to country. Even in the USA, however, there is considerable debate about whether empirical techniques provide any insights about the context of use for office-based products, far less the continual metamorphosis that we see on the Web.

As things stand, HCI research has had its greatest impact in the interpretation of technological change. HCI research has had almost no impact in the development or direction of that technological change. This role of interpretation, of explaining what does and what does not work from a users' perspective, is the critical skill that we must teach the next generation of interface designers.

Russell's opening quotation is important:

> "One of the symptoms of an approaching nervous breakdown is the belief that one's work is terribly important."

HCI research is much less important than many people would have us believe. What is important is that we educate our software engineers how to think critically about user needs. We need to train our psychologists to consider the interruptions, the spontaneity and the dynamism that characterises everyday working environments. We need to train our sociologists to ask questions that will guide the pragmatics of systems development. Above everything, we need to get more closely involved in the industrial research and development labs that are producing tomorrow's products. If we ignore these issues then there is a bleak future for HCI.

M. Angela Sasse
University College London
UK

Chris Johnson
University of Glasgow
UK

References

Beyer, H. & Holtzblatt, K. (1998), *Contextual Design: Defining Customer-centered Systems*, Morgan-Kaufmann.

Sommerville, I., Rodden, T., Sawyer, P. & Bentley, R. (1992), Sociologists Can be Surprisingly Useful in Interactive System Design, *in* A. Monk, D. Diaper & M. Harrison (eds.), *People and Computers VII (Proceedings of HCI'92)*, Cambridge University Press.

Editors' Note

The proceedings contain 77 full papers that were accepted for presentation at INTERACT '99 following an open call for participation. Submissions and the reviewing process reflect the international nature of INTERACT. 227 full papers were submitted from 27 countries by the deadline. Each submission was reviewed blind by 4 referees drawn from the IPC of 123 HCI experts from 22 countries (chaired by Michael Tauber and M. Angela Sasse), and the members of the Conference Committee. The final conference technical programme, as represented in this volume, was selected on the basis of referees' ratings and comments, and programme balance.

IFIP TC.13

Established in 1989, the International Federation for Information Processing Technical Committee on Human–Computer Interaction (IFIP TC.13) is an international committee of 23 member national societies and 5 Working Groups, representing specialists in human factors, ergonomics, cognitive science, computer science, design and related disciplines.

IFIP TC.13 aims to develop a science and technology of human–computer interaction by encouraging empirical research, promoting the use of knowledge and methods from the human sciences in design and evaluation of computer systems; promoting better understanding of the relation between formal design methods and system usability and acceptability; developing guidelines, models and methods by which designers may provide better human-oriented computer systems; and, co-operating with other groups, inside and outside IFIP, to promote user-orientation and 'humanization' in system design. Thus, TC.13 seeks to improve interactions between people and computers, encourage the growth of HCI research and disseminate these benefits world-wide.

The main orientation is towards users, especially the non-computer professional users, and how to improve human–computer relations between them. Areas of study include: the problems people have with computers; the impact on people in individual and organizational contexts; the determinants of utility, usability and acceptability; the appropriate allocation of tasks between computers and users; modelling the user to aid better system design; and harmonizing the computer to user characteristics and needs.

While the scope is thus set wide, with a tendency towards general principles rather than particular systems, it is recognized that progress will only be achieved through both general studies to advance theoretical understanding and specific studies on practical issues (e.g. interface design standards, software system consistency, documentation, appropriateness of alternative communication media, human factors guidelines for dialogue design, the problems of integrating multimedia systems to match system needs and organizational practices, etc.).

IFIP TC.13 stimulates working events and activities through its Working Groups. WGs consist of HCI experts from many countries, who seek to expand knowledge and find solutions to HCI issues and concerns within their domains, as outlined below:

WG13.1 (*Education in HCI and HCI Curricula*) aims to improve HCI education at all levels of higher education, coordinate and unite efforts to develop HCI curricula and promote HCI teaching.

WG13.2 (*Methodology for User-centred System Design*) aims to foster research, dissemination of information and good practice in the methodical application of HCI to software engineering.

WG13.3 (*HCI and People with Special Needs*) aims to make HCI designers aware of the special needs of disabled and elderly people and encourage development of systems, hardware and software tools permitting adaptation of interfaces to individual users.

WG13.4 (also WG2.7) (*User Interface Engineering*) investigates the nature, concepts and construction of user interfaces for software systems, using a framework for reasoning about interactive systems and an engineering model for developing user interfaces.

WG13.5 (*Human Error, Safety and System Development*) seeks a framework for studying human factors relating to systems failure, develops leading edge techniques in hazard analysis and safety engineering of computer-based systems, and guides international accreditation activities for safety-critical systems.

New Working Groups are formed as areas of significance to HCI arise. Further information is available at the IFIP TC.13 Web site: http://www.csd.uu.se/ifip_tc13/

IFIP TC.13 Members

Australia
Judy Hammond (IFIP TC.13
Chair)
Australian Computer Society

Austria
Michael Tauber
Austrian Computer Society

Belgium
Monique Noirhomme-Fraiture
*Federation des Associations
Informatiques de Belgique*

Canada
Mary Frances Laughton
*Canadian Information Processing
Society*

China
Liu Zhengjie
Chinese Institute of Electronics

Czech Republic
Václav Matoušek
*Czech Society for Cybernetics &
Informatics*

Denmark
Leif Lovborg
*Danish Federation for
Information Processing*

Finland
Pekka Lehtio
*Finnish Information Processing
Association*

Germany
Peter Gorny
Gesellschaft für Informatik eV

Greece
John Darzentas
Greek Computer Society

Italy
Fabio Paternò
Italian Computer Society

Japan
Masaaki Kurosu
*Information Processing Society of
Japan*

The Netherlands
Gerrit van der Veer
*Nederlands Genootschap voor
Informatica*

Norway
Svein Arnesen
Norwegian Computer Society

Poland
Julius Kulikowski
Polish Academy of Sciences

Portugal
Mário Rui Gomes
*Associacão Portuguesa de
Informática*

Spain
Julio Abascal
*Federacion Española de
Sociedades de Informática*

Sweden
Lars Oestreicher (IFIP TC.13
Vice-chair)
*Swedish Interdisciplinary Society
for Human–Computer Interaction*

Switzerland
Matthias Rauterberg
*Swiss Federation of Information
Processing Societies*

UK
Brian Shackel (IFIP TC.13
Secretary)
British Computer Society

USA
John Karat (IFIP TC.13
Vice-chair)
*Association for Computing
Machinery*

Affiliate Member
Andrew Westlake
*International Association for
Statistical Computing*

Corresponding Member
José A. Pino
*Centro Latinoamericano de
Estudios Informatica*

Working Group Chairmen

WG 13.1
(Education in HCI and HCI Curriculum)
Matthias Rauterberg

WG 13.2
(Methodology for User-Centred System Design)
Alistair Sutcliffe

WG 13.3
(HCI and People with Special Needs)
Geoff Busby

WG 2.7/13.4
(User Interface Engineering)
Rick Kazman

WG 13.5
(Human Error, Safety, and System Development)
Chris Johnson

Cooperating Societies

All IFIP Member Societies
British Psychological Society (BPS)
Institution of Electrical Engineers (IEE)
British HCI Group
The Ergonomics Society
AFIHM
Association for Artificial Intelligence of Russia (RAAI)
CEPIS
CHISIG
ACM SIGCHI
EUROGRAPHICS
IMAS

International Programme Committee

Co-chairs

M. Angela Sasse, *UK*
Michael Tauber, *Germany*

Members

J. Abascal, *Spain*
A. Adams, *Australia*
C. Allwood, *Sweden*
J. Alty, *UK*
G. Andrienko, *Germany*
N. Andrienko, *Germany*
M. Apperley, *New Zealand*
W. Ark, *USA*
S. Arnesen, *Norway*
M. Atyeo, *USA*
C. Baber, *UK*
S. Balakrishan, *USA*
S. Balbo, *Australia*
M. Beaudouin-Lafon, *France*
D. Benyon, *UK*
J. Bonner, *UK*
S. Brewster, *UK*
D. Busse, *UK*
J. Carroll, *USA*
A. Cawsey, *UK*
J. Cañas, *Spain*
L. Clark, *UK*
G. Cockton, *UK*
I. Connell, *UK*
M. Costabile, *Italy*
J. Coutaz, *France*
J. Darzentas, *Greece*
F. Détienne, *France*
D. Diaper, *UK*
A. Dix, *UK*
C. Dormann, *Denmark*
P. Dourish, *USA*
J. Dowell, *UK*
S. Dray, *USA*
J. Earthy, *UK*
D. England, *UK*
P. Faraday, *USA*
M. Gomes, *Portugal*
D. Gorgan, *Romania*
P. Gorny, *Germany*

P. Gray, *UK*
S. Greenberg, *Canada*
T. Gross, *Austria*
J. Grundy, *New Zealand*
S. Guest, *USA*
K. Gunn, *USA*
J. Hammond, *Australia*
M. Harrison, *UK*
H. Hasan, *Australia*
T. Hewett, *USA*
P. Holt, *UK*
J. Horton, *UK*
I. Ismail, *UK*
N. Iwayama, *Japan*
R. Jacob, *USA*
C. Johnson, *UK*
L. Johnston, *Australia*
S. Jones, *Australia*
J. Jorge, *USA*
A. Jorgensen, *Denmark*
V. Kaptelinin, *Sweden*
J. Karat, *USA*
J. Kay, *Australia*
R. Kazman, *USA*
R. Keil-Slawik, *Germany*
A. Kilgour, *UK*
M. Kurosu, *Japan*
E. Kuwana, *Japan*
A. Lantz, *Sweden*
L. Larsen, *Denmark*
M. Laughton, *Canada*
D. Lavery, *UK*
A. Lee, *USA*
P. Lehtiö, *Finland*
H. Lowe, *UK*
L. Loevborg, *Denmark*
A. MacLean, *France*
V. Matoušek, *Czech Republic*
I. McClelland, *The Netherlands*
A. Monk, *UK*
M. Montgomery Masters, *UK*
M. Muller, *USA*

J. Newman, *UK*
L. Nigay, *France*
J. Noble, *USA*
M. Noirhomme-Fraiture, *Belgium*
L. Oestreicher, *Sweden*
N. Ozkan, *Australia*
P. Palanque, *France*
F. Paternò, *Italy*
J. Pino, *Chile*
R. Procter, *UK*
H. Reiterer, *Germany*
D. Rigas, *UK*
C. Roast, *UK*
M. Rosson, *USA*
V. Ruvinskaia, *Ukraine*
D. Scapin, *France*
A. Sears, *USA*
B. Shackel, *UK*
M. Sikorski, *Poland*
C. Stary, *Austria*
A. Sutcliffe, *UK*
G. Szwillus, *Germany*
A. Takeuchi, *Japan*
J. Tanaka, *Japan*
J. Tang, *USA*
B. Thomas, *Australia*
R. Thomas, *Australia*
M. Tscheligi, *Austria*
S. Turner, *UK*
C. Unger, *Germany*
C. van der Mast, *The Netherlands*
G. van der Veer, *The Netherlands*
J. Vanderdonckt, *Belgium*
A. Watson, *UK*
J. Whittle, *UK*
P. Wild, *UK*
C. Wolf, *USA*
W. Wong, *New Zealand*
V. Wulf, *Germany*
J. Ziegler, *Germany*
N. Zin, *UK*

INTERACT '99 Committees

International Conference Committee

INTERACT '99 Conference Chair
Alistair Kilgour, *Heriot-Watt University, UK*

INTERACT Conference Adviser
Brian Shackel, *HUSAT Research Institute, UK*

Members
David Gilmore (IPC Chair, INTERACT '95), *IDEO Product Development, USA*
Judy Hammond (Conference Chair, INTERACT '97), *University of Technology, Sydney, Australia*
Masaaki Kurosu (Conference Chair, INTERACT 2001), *Shizuoka University, Japan*

Technical Programme Committee

Chair
Chris Johnson, *University of Glasgow, UK*

Papers
M. Angela Sasse, *University College London, UK*
Michael Tauber, *University of Paderborn, Germany*

Tutorials
Janet Finlay, *University of Huddersfield, UK*

Workshops
Alistair Sutcliffe, *City University, UK*
Alan Newell, *University of Dundee, UK*

Doctoral Consortium
James Alty, *Loughborough University, UK*
John Karat, *IBM, USA*

Panels
David Benyon, *Napier University, UK*
Dianne Murray, *King's College London, UK*

Posters
Gilbert Cockton, *University of Sunderland, UK*
Alison Cawsey, *Heriot-Watt University, UK*

Professional Practice and Experience
Graham Johnson, *NCR, UK*
Alistair Kilgour, *Heriot-Watt University, UK*

Interactive Experience
Julian Newman, *Glasgow Caledonian University, UK*
Stephen Brewster, *University of Glasgow, UK*

Laboratory and Organisational Overviews
Rob Procter, *University of Edinburgh, UK*

Videos
Richard Coyne, *University of Edinburgh, UK*

Organizing Committee

Press
Tom McEwan, *Napier University, UK*

Publicity
Phil Gray, *University of Glasgow, UK*

Treasurer
Ian Benest, *University of York, UK*

Sponsorship
Alistair Kilgour, *Heriot-Watt University, UK*
Brian Shackel, *HUSAT Research Institute, UK*
Richard Wilson, *University of Glasgow, UK*

Exhibition
Richard Wilson, *University of Glasgow, UK*

Social Programme
Lachlan Mackinnon, *Heriot-Watt University, UK*

Student Volunteers
Alison Cawsey, *Heriot-Watt University, UK*

Web
Mark Dunlop, *University of Glasgow, UK*

Conference Manager
Christian Jones, *Heriot-Watt University, UK*

Internet Access
Patrick McAndrew, *Heriot-Watt University, UK*

Invited Speakers
Chris Brotherton, *Heriot-Watt University, UK*
Patrik Holt, *Heriot-Watt University, UK*

Proceedings
Brian Shackel, *HUSAT Research Institute, UK*

British HCI Group Adviser
Chris Roast, *Sheffield Hallam University, UK*

Asia-Pacific Liaison
Richard Thomas, *University of Western Australia, Australia*

Scholarships
Fabio Paternò, *CNUCE, Italy*

Reviewing Support
Ismail Ismail, *University College London, UK*
Nadav Zin, *University College London, UK*
Louise Clark, *University College London, UK*
Ann Watson, *University College London, UK*

Secretariat
Vicki Grant, *Meeting Makers Ltd, UK*
Elaine King, *Meeting Makers Ltd, UK*
Yvonne Prager, *Meeting Makers Ltd, UK*

Part One

Keynote Speakers

Human–Computer Interaction — INTERACT '99
M. Angela Sasse and Chris Johnson (Editors)
Published by IOS Press, © IFIP TC.13, 1999

Customer Centred Design as Discipline

Karen Holtzblatt

InContext Enterprises, Inc., 249 Ayer Road, Suite 304, Harvard, MA 01451, USA.

karen@incent.com

Abstract: Over the last 12 years companies in the high tech industry have come to recognize that engineering-driven system design is just bad business. Commercial companies and internal software departments have increasingly accepted that the power position for creating successful products and systems is customer-centred front-end systems design: using data about how people work and live to drive product direction, definition and structure. Over the years we have tried various techniques and learned much to move ourselves toward a more customer-centred way of working. This paper calls for instituting a discipline of customer-centred front-end systems design: a set of skills which work to help designers understand the way technology will impact human practice; procedures which people shipping systems explicitly share and follow; and a body of knowledge about human practice to support these activities. Examples and recommendations for actions and directions illustrate what a discipline of customer-centred front end design might look like.

Keywords: style, guide, millennium, Edinburgh.

1 The Central Problem of Design

Some years ago AT&T announced a new innovation which would revolutionize the world of communication as we knew it: the picture phone. This product was a dismal failure. For every product, failure can come from many individual and combined causes. The company can fail to market properly. The technology can be too unstable and buggy. The product can ship so late that the company loses credibility. The company can be distracted by internal fires and never ship the right things. But the picture phone was going to fail no matter what — and this failure could have been avoided or at least predicted.

The picture phone story is symptomatic of many stories in our industry. We invest people's time and company money in hopeful new ventures. Products fail. Projects are cancelled without ever shipping. This is, one may argue, the simple cost of doing business. But is there a better way? Can we increase the odds of success?

In many ways we are a young industry. The whole field of software development has grown up in my life-time. The field was formed by people who love technology, making technology for other people who love technology. But today's challenge is to make technology for people that want to get on with their work and lives. More and more the people who build the technology are not and will not be using the technology. It doesn't work reliably any more to: "think up cool things", "put smart guys in a room and let them go", "make skunk projects in basements", "start 5 competing projects hoping one will succeed". The success of these ventures is all too expensive and unpredictable. Even companies like Nokia who have initially benefited from early adopters of such inventions recognize that broad market adoption depends on fit with the world of the user (Ruuska & Väänänen-Vainio-Mattila, n.d.). In other words, engineering driven product definition and design is just bad business.

Some years ago at a keynote address at CHI, the speaker called for moving our industry from art to engineering: from haphazard development practice to reliable and repeatable procedure. Such was and is the mission of the Software Engineering Institute. For the past 12 years I have watched us, as an industry, introduce customer data into software development. We started with usability testing in the tail end of the process. But increasingly we recognize that the power position for creating successful products and systems is *customer-centred* front end systems design: using data about how people work and live to drive product direction, definition and structure. Increasingly we understand that we can avoid failed products and identify lucrative and transformative new technology directions through understanding how people work and live and deliberately designing technology to enhance that work. What would it mean to move our industry to a *discipline* of customer-centred front-end systems design: a set of skills which work, procedures which people explicitly share and follow, and a body of knowledge to support these activities?

1.1   Understanding Practice as the Core Competency of Design: The Picture Phone

So how might customer-centred front end design have helped AT&T? Because of telephone technology person-to-person communication has been transformed. The first phones were in post-offices and central town places. People got dressed, hitched up their horses and rode to town to make a call. Making a call was an event. With the new telephone technology person-to-person communication was still point-to-point much like the telegraph, focusing on simple communication and emergencies, both of which could be better communicated and discussed with synchronous talk. Telephone use was certainly not a way to chit-chat with a friend. Imagine the scene: standing in the centre of the busiest place in town shouting into the mouthpiece, the user nailed to the wall, perhaps standing on a box for height, trying to get the ear and mouthpieces next to the right body parts. This is a public communication event, not the context or comfort needed to share feelings about a mid-life crisis!

When the phone moved to the home, use was more frequent and, with the removal of the operator, more private. The first stop in homes was the hallway, still not a good place for chat. But when the phone moved into the living room people could sit down on the couch to talk. The social context on the phone started to imitate the friendship visit: come have a cup of tea, talk with me. Like a formal visit invitation, we focused only on our guests, talked with them and gave them our attention. As the phones moved into the bedrooms and studies the practice of intimate talk and the prolonged telephone visit was born.

Next came what I consider to be the single most powerful innovation in phone technology from the point of view of human contact: the long cord. As soon as a the headset could be separated reliably from the body of the phone and moved a distance from the base, the first instance of the 'cell' phone was created. Using the wall phone as an anchor, and chucking the head-piece under the chin, we could move around the kitchen doing the work of life while chatting to a friend. This informality of communication came along with the overall informality of social relationship in the 60's which was particularly strong in the USA where this form of telephone contact seems dominant. "Drop in" we told our friends. "Come live our lives with us". "Talk with us while we cook, fold laundry, care for our kids. Let's do life together". With the long cord we could be with our friends while we did the work of family life. As the formality of face-to-face entertainment gave way to the informality of dropping in, 'sitting and chatting' by phone was joined by 'dropping in' by phone. The cordless phone simply extended this relationship into the garage, the downstairs and, yes, the bathroom.

So AT&T announced the picture phone. The picture phone had to fail in the consumer market. Given the 'dropping in' relationship that was now supported by the long cord telephone, the picture phone was a throwback. It would again lock people to the wall. To see the faces of the caller we would have to stay in one place. It would again lock people into a formal relationship. To be seen we would have to be dressed! Seated looking at the picture we could not race around doing things, making it much too clear how fragmented our attention really was. The picture phone had to fail because it implied a model of use that did not extend and support the existing *practice** of talking in the context of life.

So why does desktop video have a chance? Because we are already at work, dressed and in a formal relationship. And the culture of office work accepts the notion that workers are supposed to be at their desks. (Ah, watch out, tele-commuting!)

Certainly usage models both push and are pushed by technology. Direct dial, faster cheaper wiring systems, wiring throughout the house and across the country, cheaper phones all make new ways of living with phones possible. But technology will fit into and be bent by the existing practice. If we want to design successful products and systems, we must become skilled at seeing, understanding and using knowledge about human practice. The core of the problem of front-end design is how technology will impact practice. The core competence of a discipline of customer-centred design is how to see human practice, understand its structure and apply that understanding to a design problem.

---

*I will use the word practice throughout this paper to mean both life and work practice.

2   What Makes a Discipline?

In many ways this is a frenzied time in product and system development. We know we need to really understand our customers to compete and to just do the right thing. The competition on our heels, or the internal customer breathing down our throats wanting the next version their way, or simply the demand to keep delivering another release or announced product — all cause intense pressure to ship. A hot new idea that we 'know' will be the key to unlock the market; a board of directors meeting to account for our milestones, creates a culture of 'do — don't think'. The internet has encouraged development at a breathtaking clip as we try to 'figure out' what it all means, what we can take advantage of and how not to be last. We are pushed ever faster to decide what to make and get it out there before 'they' do. Do we think we have time for discipline in front-end design?

Discipline is what we put in place to move fast. Discipline, as learned from any martial art, is what keeps us centred so we can think quickly and react quickly to any offensive. Discipline is the tool of smart strategy and quick decision-making.

Discipline is about *skill*. If understanding customer practice is the centre of successful design, we need skill in seeing — we need to learn how to see both the structure of human practice and its implications for design.

But discipline is about having *procedure*. Skill is exercised inside of a process, a set of steps which taken together allow action. Skill to see alone, without a shared and explicit way to work together to produce a result that supports the customer, will not let us move fast.

And discipline is about producing a body of *knowledge*. The knowledge of how people work and live with and without new technology is the jumping off point for design action. Procedures, like Contextual Design, tell teams what to do. But with no or not enough shared knowledge in common domains of human practice, every project has to start by itself from scratch. As a field, we have produced various writing about the procedures for collecting customer data. And we have produced writing about principles of software and user interface design. But the knowledge of the practices themselves, describing key characteristics and structures and their implications for design for human use are sparse at best.

In this time of frenzy, we need the discipline of seeing, of knowledge and of procedure.

3   Seeing Human Practice

If we are going to see human practice, we have go look at it. If we really want to see what is going on with technology in people's lives we have to be situated in the context of their lives. The idea that we need field data for design is increasingly accepted as we embrace methods such as Contextual Inquiry, ethnography, participatory design and other user-centred processes as a necessary part of the design process. We certainly can't see practice if we aren't in the right place to see it unfold and if we don't have basic field interviewing skills to watch and talk with customers.

But seeing work practice is also about how we look. Whether we like it or not, we enter into any data collection situation with preconceived notions — what works and what doesn't, what we believe people value and want, what we think we need to find out. These entering assumptions may or may not be true and they need to be shaped by the real situation. But we can enter with other more conscious lenses that let us see more of what is there and relevant to design. *Work models* and *metaphors* are two kinds of lenses that help us know how to look. By looking through the multiple perspectives of work models and metaphors we take different vantage points on the same customer data. We see more than we would without them. Interestingly, without any lens we would be like newborns, looking at everything and discerning nothing — attracted by light and contrast, movement and noise indiscriminately. But when we have structure, concepts, pattern and meaning, when we have a clear way to look, we can see more.

Lenses, like work models and metaphors, are like the brain behind the eye, making us creative and giving real sight. But they also limit what is seen. In a funny way we see what we know to look for. So how can we see what we don't know to look for? Real seeing is not only about having lenses, it is also about being committed to continuous paradigm shift, to continuous and deliberated de-stabilization in what we believe to be true about practice. Creativity and insight come from the dynamic tension between having a way to look and challenging the very paradigms through which we look. This dialectic is a core skill for a customer centred front end design process.

3.1   Work Models

Contextual Design has 5 work models which structure seeing. They represent the 'five faces of work', five points of view on the field data being collected on any customer (see Figures 1–5). Practice is complex and detailed and as a result, overwhelming. Work models, captured in an interpretation session (Beyer

& Holtzblatt, 1998, p.128) focused on one user's field data, give teams a way to handle the detail and complexity without 'simplifying' data in an effort to get on top of the overwhelm.

Because work models break practice down into five points of view, they make seeing and capturing the data possible without losing all the richness and complexity of the practice. Work models say pay attention to 'this' stuff. So for example, teams that know they will draw a flow model during the interpretation session, pay attention to communication and coordination between people and the roles people play. Teams that know they will draw a cultural model, look for underlying influences, feelings, power issues and policy that affect the work. Because the models organize what to look at, they tell teams what to see. Work models help teams see the difference between aspects of practice that will have design relevance and aspects that will not.

And here the dialectic emerges. Using work models enhance the skill of seeing in the field. But what if we miss something important? The principle of vigilance is critical. If the data has to be twisted to fit the models, if the models don't drive the distinctions important to the design problem, a vigilant self-reflective team will see the mismatch- and invent new, more appropriate work models. Model thinking begets model thinking. A team used to separating the complexities of practice into clean points of view through models will naturally modify and invent new models to fit the data and problem. This invention happens in the context of dealing with the data — when the existing tools of seeing are not working. A commitment to challenging paradigms of seeing enhances the seeing and ensures that a breadth of practice is seen.

Whatever work models you use, the skill of using work models is part of the skill of seeing what matters in human practice for the purpose of design.

Consolidated Work Models Drive Design Thinking

Consolidated work models[†] bring the data of the individual work models into one view of the customer population showing underlying work structure, pattern, concept and values. Because each model is consolidated separately, the team can talk about each point of view on the practice separately. They can identify population trends and design implications driven by that model's way of looking

at the population. Moving from consolidated model to consolidated model, the team integrates their understanding of the practice and design solutions begin to emerge. If teams have the skill to build and then use consolidated data, they can see key issues, and patterns of work to account for in new designs and even implications for future business directions.

Role consolidation is the central organizing concept of the flow model. A role is a coherent set of responsibilities to get a job done. To consolidate the data across people teams look beneath the way responsibilities are structured by organizational title to see the multiple hats, or roles, that people play when doing their work. By looking at roles, not titles, teams can see how different people across the customer population play the same role. Using the consolidated flow model to drive design, teams can target key roles to support, discuss which 'jobs' to enhance with automation or identify roles whose technology support is a challenge because they are shared by people of different levels of skill.

But when teams look at the consolidated flow from the point of view of understanding organizational or business practice, something else is revealed (see Figure 6). Let's look at a section of a consolidated flow model that I put together in '97. I was exploring the ways people were using the Web in a preliminary study[‡]of internet usage which became the basis for our current work on e-commerce. The selling site has responsibilities: to sell product or services from all over the company including buying incentives and product information; to be responsive to customer requests about availability; to manage the corporate face, communicating corporate strategy, controlling the appearance of the company, highlighting press releases and protecting the confidence in the brand name; and as a result to help competitors gather competitive information. Content for the Web page is coming in from all over the organization. Also, the key role of the buying stimulator is being played by multiple job titles in different departments at both high and low levels within the organization: company president or CEO, affiliated third party marketing company, internal sales person. But the PR group role is also monitoring and putting pieces up on the selling site to contribute to the overall package. The business Web site creator is pulling all the pieces together during site construction. What does all this mean?

[†]For a description of how to consolidate individual models see (Beyer & Holtzblatt, 1998).

[‡]All data presented in this paper is derived from studies using the contextual design methodology for data collection, interpretation and consolidation.

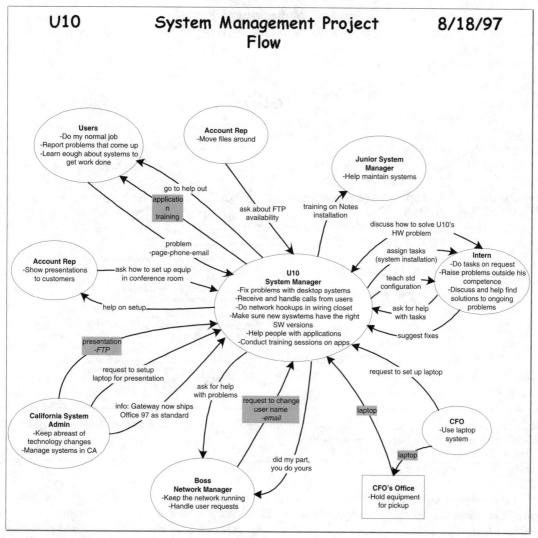

U10   **System Management Project Flow**   **8/18/97**

Users
-Do my normal job
-Report problems that come up
-Learn eough about systems to get work done

Account Rep
-Move files around

Junior System Manager
-Help maintain systems

go to help out

applicatio n training

ask about FTP availability

training on Notes installation

discuss how to solve U10's HW problem

problem -page-phone-email

assign tasks (system installation)

Account Rep
-Show presentations to customers

ask how to set up equip in conference room

U10 System Manager
-Fix problems with desktop systems
-Receive and handle calls from users
-Do network hookups in wiring closet
-Make sure new syswtems have the right SW versions
-Help people with applications
-Conduct training sessions on apps

teach std configuration

Intern
-Do tasks on request
-Raise problems outside his competence
-Discuss and help find solutions to ongoing problems

help on setup

ask for help with tasks

presentation -FTP

suggest fixes

request to setup laptop for presentation

request to set up laptop

ask for help with problems

request to change user name -email

laptop

California System Admin
-Keep abreast of technology changes
-Manage systems in CA

info: Gateway now ships Office 97 as standard

CFO
-Use laptop system

did my part, you do yours

laptop

Boss Network Manager
-Keep the network running
-Handle user requests

CFO's Office
-Hold equipment for pickup

Figure 1: The *flow model* focuses a design team on communication and coordination between people. The bubbles show the people and their responsibilities; the lines show how they coordinate. Shaded text on the lines indicates that an artefact is passed between people; unshaded text shows coordination.

The Web site was becoming the coordinator of all buying stimuli and communications about the company. The concept of selling included not just presenting 'what was for sale' but also building confidence in the company policy and direction. Rather than multiple communications to the public from multiple sources using multiple media targeted at particular customer segments, the Web pushed all the different intents and points of view relative to selling into one mechanism and created single point of communication for all customers.

This data reflects the practice that people put in place unreflectively as they scrambled to get onto the Web. If we look at its implications we can see the

seeds of the problems and issues being played out today. The Web page creators receive contributions and requests from all over the company and affiliated organizations like PR. Without knowing it, the Web site creators were becoming coordinators of content not just software coders. Content was harvested from different people, created in different tools and formats marching to a time schedule driven by the needs of sales, PR and the shipping release schedule. The dominance of content in the site challenged software process: a different kind of coordination between people building the product was needed. Developers were not the only ones responsible for the deliverable — the whole organization was. And because the

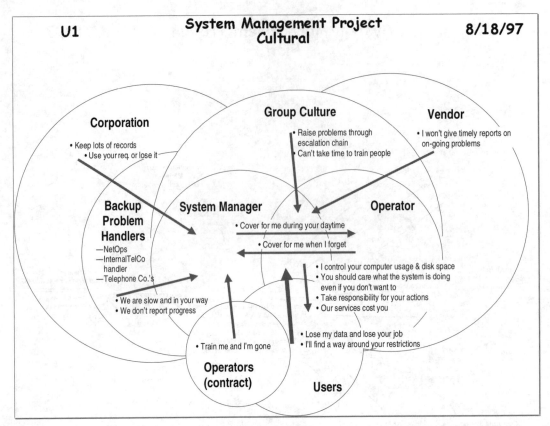

Figure 2: The *cultural model* reveals how the culture constrains the work or life practice. Bubbles show who is influencing or constraining who; arrows show what the constraints are.

culture of the Web was different than expectations for brochures and sales talks, content was expected to be updated very frequently.

Without knowing it department members were becoming 'reporters' and Web site creators the 'news' coordinators. Software was no longer a tool and content was no longer presented in a known paper or television media delivered through a known process. The two had merged inside of a model of daily update becoming more like a newspaper organization than a software, advertising or publishing organization. But a newspaper organization whose delivery mechanism is now software. A forward looking tool company, seeing this trend in the data, would be able to predict that coordination and writing tools would become hot in the future. A forward looking business manager in a publishing or advertising company would see that quality software process would distinguish them from the crowd and allow fast and predictable action.

Overall the challenge was and is one of coordination, not only in the production of the site but in its design and content. The Web site was becoming the corporate communication mechanism and way to

manage customer relationships for the lower level salesperson *and* the CEO communicating corporate strategy. In a big company the high level manager and the sales person could see the full stimulus package letting each monitor and build on each other's attack — or reveal the inconsistency. Different departments and business units put up their own products and communications. As more departments posted to the Web would the site come to reflect the organizational structure rather than be a coherent communication mechanism? In 1997 I foresaw a *potential* role, Selling Site Coordinator, responsible for the coherent design and coordination process needed to realize the design and ensure corporate wide coordination. Two years ago there were no VP's responsible for coordinating e-commerce. The role did not exist then, but a forward thinking business manager could have read this data and also predicted this potential role. A forward thinking business manager could see how the company needed to manage itself to be ahead of the organizational game.

Work models, because they separate the complexities of human practice into different key

U1	**System Management Project — Sequence**	8/18/97

Trigger: Time for scheduled installation
Intent: Get needed software (PCSA) installed on machines

- Goes to machine to install PCSA on
- Has plan for what to do
- Start installation of PCSA
- Opens documentation — enters part number — enters LAT node
- Phone rings: Urgetn request for account to runa demo

Intent: Provide ongoing support to users even while doing other tasks

- U3 thinks this account may be against policy
- Asks another system manager about rules for creating accounts
- Tells caller about rules an about a form they need to fill out
- Helps caller fill out form
- Hangs up
- Phone rings: System manager from U3's old job wants to know how to use a VMS command

Intent: Provide ongoing support to other system managers

- U3 looks at DCL HELP to see options
- The discuss if the other system manager's tape is big enough for what he wants to do
- U3 suggests a short cut
- Hangs up
- Goes back to interrupted PCSA installation
- Cant' find his place — looking up information blew away his installation

Figure 3: The *sequence model* shows the steps of a task ordered in time. *Triggers* reveal the event that caused the task to be started. *Intents* make explicit the motivation for different steps.

conversations about the practice, help teams both see what is in the data originally and later the implications for design and business direction. They provide the power of vision. Coupled with the commitment to challenging assumptions and ways of representing the data, work models let teams see more than they could without these organizing lenses. Using work models as part of front-end design help teams who are not used to looking at human practice learn useful ways of looking, and structure discussions to ensure that the customer data is being used to drive design action.

3.2 Metaphor

Seeing work is much about seeing pattern, seeing the relationships between people's roles, actions, values and motivations. Work models allow teams to see this pattern in an organized way. Often people gathering contextual data do not know how to look for pattern and focus primarily on problems and solutions. If teams only gather data on how a tool is used, it is easy to focus on what works and what does not. But if teams take a wider focus and try to characterize

the work itself, seeing the structure of the work, different kinds of issues and possibilities will reveal themselves. Work models help reveal the structure of the work. Finding analogous metaphors of work reveal what is going on with the work holistically. This is particularly important when trying to understand a new work domain or grasp the fundamental issue in the domain under inquiry.

As I said, we see through a 'paradigm' of the work. Seeing is about relating new data to what is already known. In a funny way, to see what is going on in any work domain we must already be able to see what is going on in the work domain. Once we see something the principle of vigilance pushes us to pay attention to mismatches and drives us to challenge our existing way of seeing until we change our paradigm accordingly. But what happens when teams have no paradigm or need to get out of their preexisting paradigm to see something new? Using and finding a metaphorical work practice or related work practice provides an initial scaffolding of

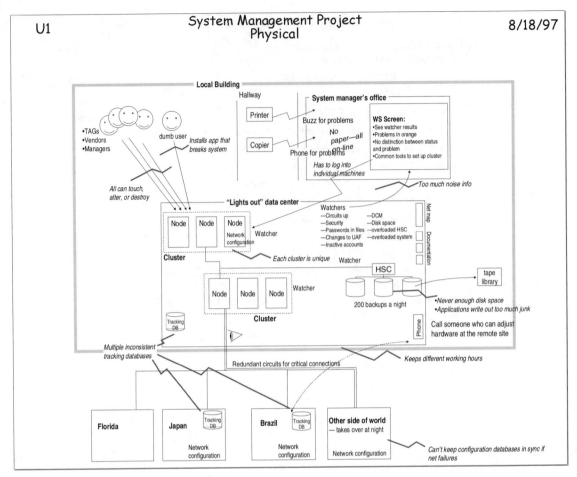

Figure 4: The *physical model* shows the aspects of the physical environment that affect practice. The team uses it to highlight the constraints, implications and opportunities of the physical environment.

understanding. Metaphors simultaneously provide a way to see and a structure to iterate with the real data until it shifts and becomes a proper reflection of what is going on in the actual work domain. How does this work?

Drug Discovery: Seeing the Data

I was looking at drug discovery for the first time. "You can't understand all of drug discovery in two hours" my client challenged "You can't understand without any background in the field. It takes years to become a research scientist." This is, after all, very complex science. Watching the work of the scientists I asked myself "What work is this work like?" Like a computer searching a data base for known cases I looked for a work practice I knew about to get a handle on what might be going on — and landed on experimental psychology. At the level of intention and manipulation of chemicals and data the scientists were using the same principles for variable

isolation and hypothesis testing that I had used in psychology experiments. The variables were different, the substances were different, the conditions of the study were different and the language was different — but the basic way of thinking and working was parallel. Once I formed this hypothesis I started talking to the participant/scientist in terms of my hypothesis. "I see that you seem to be adding this reagent systematically so you can tell what its effects will be" "Your spread sheet seems to be tracking all the changes in variation you introduced with each chemical change" "The biological component is the disease, the rest of the solution is what you think will affect the disease". Using the outlines of experimental psychology allowed me to start talking about what was going on. Then the customer could correct my thinking and fill in the details. Within two hours I had understood enough for my client to turn to me and say "I'm a convert, you really can find out a lot in

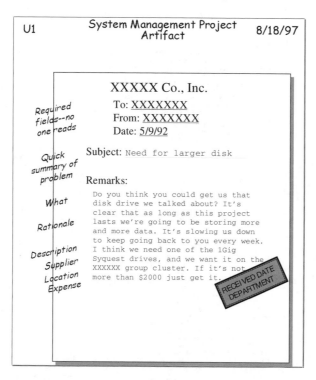

Figure 5: The *artefact model* shows the intent and usage of physical things that support the practice. The team annotates them to show how parts of the artefacts are used and what they are intended for.

___

only two hours!" Finding the related work metaphor coupled with a commitment to vigilance, in this case in the form of checking the interpretation with the user, gives teams a way of seeing that allows for quick and accurate understanding of a work domain.

Software Support: Seeing Design Implication

Metaphor also plays a key role in seeing design implications in the consolidated data. If teams can relate the domain of work under study to a completely different domain of work, that re-framing reveals design possibilities. Figure 7 is part of a consolidated flow representing software support. But all the role names sound like the emergency room in a hospital. The team had the insight that the intents and strategies of the software support professionals were similar to those of doctors and nurses. (To use a metaphorical work practice the team has to have a reasonable understanding of what it does.) In software support, hardware problems were separated by role from software problems thus the psychiatrist took care of software and the physician took care of hardware. Like with medicine, different skills were needed to address the different problems. Naming the roles this way emphasizes the difference in function and content

and pushed the team away from merging the function in the design interface.

What about the role of triage nurse? The triage nurse assesses the patient's problem quickly. The patient is dealt with immediately. Not by routing the patient to someone else to determine the real problem — but by having such a deep and broad knowledge of presenting symptoms that a preliminary diagnosis can identify the right solution provider as fast as possible. The concept of triage suggests the need: quick action, immediate diagnosis, prioritization, pushing the problem on to the right role to apply the solution. This is a deep knowledge worker.

When applied to software support, the team could see that the traditional help-desk worker who sits in the triage role has some but not all of the knowledge and tools necessary to support the role possibility suggested by the triage metaphor. The team's contribution could be to put a support environment in place embodying knowledge and tools to quickly help those in the first contact position assess the problem and correctly route the customer to the 'psychiatrist' or 'physician' as appropriate, or solve the problem on the spot. Although the help-desk job exists in the software support environment today, its role definition is not as powerful as that of triage nurse. The creation

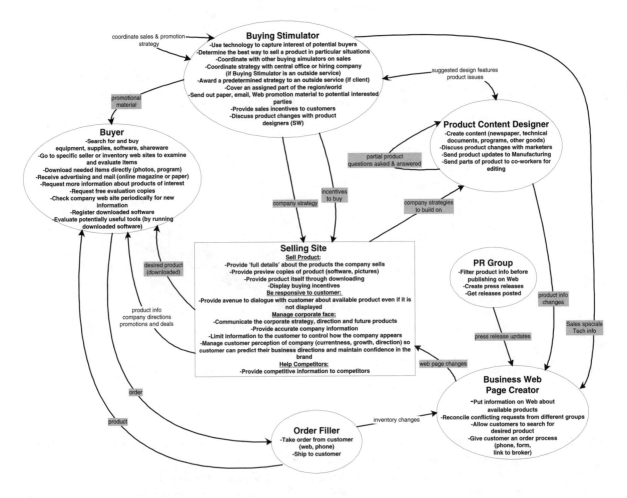

Figure 6: Partial consolidated flow model showing some key roles and responsibilities in managing corporate Web sites.

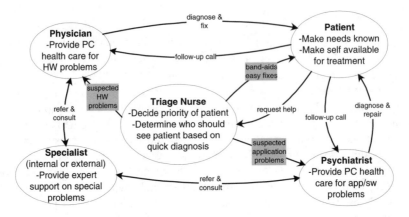

Figure 7: Partial consolidated flow model showing the role of the Triage Nurse — an interesting metaphor for any kind of problem handling.

of software to support triage of software problems is re-framed by the triage metaphor and suggests both design possibility for tools and the limitations of automatic routing which cannot do quick and dirty but accurate diagnosis.

In design, teams reinvent practice by stealing good practice ideas from their customers and other work domains and twisting them to fit the issues revealed in the consolidated data. Using a very different metaphor that is nevertheless parallel in structure allows for this creative invention. Using metaphors on consolidated data lets teams see design possibility. The more domains designers work in, the more metaphors they have to help see the domain they are trying to understand.

3.3 Seeing Requires a Lens

What we see in field data (or any data!) is dependent on what lens we look through. We see through our past experiences, our assumptions, and our skill set. Work models and metaphors, when used systematically and jointly with a team, help teams see. They help reveal problems *and* solutions, the structure of the work *and* ways to restructure the work with technology. Both of these techniques keep teams focused on the big picture and patterns of customer work, not just a set of problems and requests to be fixed and fulfilled. The big picture of practice drives innovative and useful design. And as long as teams apply the principal of vigilance — that they are not married to one way of looking, that power comes from looking from multiple perspectives and challenging and changing each to fit the data- they will be able to see what they need to see for the purpose of designing customer centred systems.

Knowing how to see customer data and its design implications is a basic skill for customer-centred front-end design. It is the core of any discipline of systems design.

4 A Body of Knowledge: Creating a Discipline

The central problem of front-end design is understanding how technology will impact human practice. Design-for-people implies, as I have said, understanding and knowing human practice in the domain a design will address. Across the high-tech industry and within individual companies, multiple companies and multiple departments within one company create tools that support aspects of the same domain of practice (for example, office work, system management, mobility). In vertical

industries, pharmaceuticals for example, multiple software companies support the specific needs of each industry. Within IT departments, multiple teams support the same type of work (getting data reports for marketing, for management, for ...). In other words, although some teams are supporting practice that is very esoteric many teams are supporting common practice domains. And when technology pushes a new domain like e-commerce everyone wants to know what is going on with customers.

As an industry, we want to be customer-centred and we want to design from data, but we want to do it quickly. Having every company and every team in the same company collect and organize its own data on the same domain is simply inefficient. It is inefficient because wide data on human practice — fundamental intents, strategies, roles and values — is stable over years. It is inefficient because technology changes, from the point of view of impact on practice, look like revisions to an existing theme not radical new ways of working. The cell phone is an extension of the long cord.

Against my recommendations I have helped teams in the same company gather data on the same topic because "We don't share", "Our problem is different", "This is a new technology" only to have the teams later admit that the data was common, the solutions were common, and the changes due to technology added a subset of points to a larger common data set. If teams started with that larger common data set they could focus their own data gathering on the particular dimension of the work relevant to their product or version. They would have the big common picture to contextualize their own inquiry. With the common context, the work of the team would be situated in the whole and the likelihood of fragmenting the user's practice by taking too narrow a focus would be reduced. Front-end design time can be significantly reduced if *as an industry* we create and maintain stable, reusable, current data on our key work domains.

I am calling for books and journals specifically focused on descriptions, models and discussions of practice with implications for design. Currently we do publish widely on good user interface, usability, and customer-centred design process. Occasionally we write articles on work like Sellen & Harper's (1997, p.319) article on the use of paper or Sachs' (1995, p.36) article describing a trouble ticketing system. Certainly ethnographic studies are going on and publications from these emerge (Suchman, 1987). And as an industry we can buy special reports such as Seybolt's work on office products. But we do not have what I would call continuing bodies of knowledge dedicated to a deep understanding of the key human practices which dominate design within and across industries. What might this look like?

4.1 The Stability of System Management

I have been collecting data on system management on behalf of our clients and for our own use for 11 years. The lack of change in the data over that time is remarkable. Indeed when I do multiple system management studies for the same client, convinced that the change in focus will reveal new work structure, teams are astonished at how much of the old data is relevant to the new problem. Changes in the technology being managed don't fundamentally change the structure of the system manager's work or even the questions they ask. Indeed the differences between system management, network management, telephone network management and software support are so minimal that they could be considered a single domain of practice. A journal on complex system's management would provide teams both data on their own domain and a way to learn from work in these related fields. Let's look at some data.

Figure 8 is a partial consolidated flow model from my generic data on system management. Here are some of the core roles that continuously repeat in complex system management. The work is characterized by a set of 'problem solvers'. The first line help is primarily a standard answer giver and traffic cop directing the problem to real solution owners. The solution owner solves and tracks the problem. The experts (internal and vender) are called in to help when the solution owner can't solve the problem alone. The remote system management group takes over the problems at their site during their daytime but ownership reverts to the solution owners at night. What does this mean?

No problem is handled by one person alone. When problems re-occur they are distributed anew to different solution owners. Since problems are also similar, reuse of diagnostic knowledge becomes critical. In other words, there is a community of people who together diagnose and keep systems running. What does this mean for design?

Context of systems and problems must be carried between solution owners and across time. The trouble ticket system which is often in place attempts to do this by requiring text input and history. The problems I have seen over and over in the sequence and affinity data is that system managers either avoid entry of history or history is entered in text fields which can not be easily searched or accessed. In other words,

carrying context between the players is a critical design challenge which current system management tools do not yet solve.

This is just one example of design challenges that are continuing and unsolved in this domain. Others which re-occur and also remain unsolved include:

- Management of 'remote hands': All the remote caretakers and field service that touch the physical hardware and tapes that keep things going at the work site must be coordinated and directed.

- Alarms: Too many alarms go off and flash at the system manager from internal monitors shipped by vendors. The alarms clutter the screen, are often not at all alarming, and have no action tied to them.

- Customer Contact: The system management group is a charge back group. They need to walk around and talk to their customers. Invisible automatic fixes to systems make their work invisible and can be resisted

- The need for standards: System managers push users to use standard configurations and users want their favourite tools. How can we help both?

The patterns and issues that I have talked about here recur for any management of complex technical systems. A body of knowledge collected by the industry and published together would be a great contribution to the many companies designing solutions in this space. Then they could take their particular focus, collect additional data, and apply their unique design ideas to the problem. Knowledge is a competitive advantage but the global knowledge describing the larger structure of work within a domain will not impede creativity or competition. It is what a team does with the knowledge and how they extend it that counts.

4.2 Directions for Domain Knowledge Creation

System management is only one of many such domains of practice that could be useful to a large segment of the industry. Many products address the generic work practice of creation: documents, slides, greeting cards, even code. All products care about how people learn and different approaches to learning how to use software. I have studied finding and report writing almost every year of my career at many companies and with many teams. Self-organization

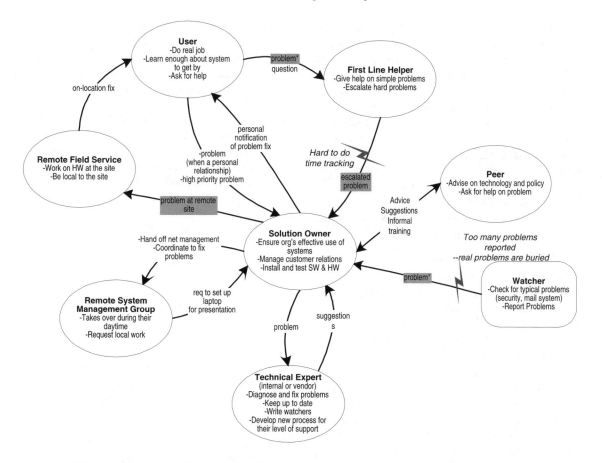

Figure 8: Partial consolidated flow model showing some of the key roles in system management.

and communication between people with and without mobility has implications for many product teams.

Because the basic paradigms of practice are stable, because each team will take what is relevant to their problem and design from their unique focus and skill, insight and speed in customer-centred front end design would be greatly enhanced if as an industry, we deliberately grew bodies of knowledge on human practice.

5 Design as Procedure

As the developer of Contextual Design I would be remiss if I did not talk about design as a discipline of procedure. There is no successful martial art, development process, engineering task, or science without rules of the game. People need simple knowledge of what they need to do to do their work. Today we have an agreed upon way of doing usability lab testing. Lab testing has a set of procedures and expectations which can be taught and followed. We also have procedures and standards for good coding

and testing. We have no such agreed upon procedures for front end design.

As reported by my clients, typical instructions for defining a product might be: "Go write specs" alone in your office or together with other 'smart guys' but without customer data; or "go talk to the customer and find out what they want" with no knowledge of how to do that effectively; or "marketing tells us to make X features but what does that mean and why do people need it."; or "what features should we pick off the enhancement database"; or "you used to do the work, you know it already"; or, finally, "*I* used to do the work, *you* don't need to talk to customers." Team members learning and using Contextual Design have thanked me for simply giving them the direction they need to get their job done in a way that lets them believe in the results.

Systems engineering programs in information systems and industrial design departments teach a more organized set of procedures than software development. Contextual Design, user centred design, participatory design and ethnography are now being taught in pieces, in design, human factors and requirements courses at universities all over the world. But as an industry, we do not have an agreed upon set of procedures which is accepted and required in standard software projects. We do not have a discipline of procedure for front end design.

For the 12 years that I have been participating in this industry we have moved step by step toward a procedure of customer-centred front end design. We have recognized the need for field data during requirements gathering and clear processes to analyse it and use its implications in design. I believe that we are ready for a discipline of procedure as standard practice in product development.

5.1   A Discipline of Procedure

Contextual Design is a procedure. It takes a cross-functional team from customer data to design action leaving the team clear about what to do to define their design. For many, Contextual Design has become a scaffolding of stable procedure on which other processes (usability, creativity, existing design and testing expectation) can be hung. For others, Contextual Design becomes a way to walk into front end work with customers. Using Contextual Design as a set of techniques, they adapt their existing practices adding one technique at a time. Other companies have instituted procedures similar to Contextual Design which work for them. As an industry we are all trying to put something stable and reliable in place to make customer centred front end design a real step in the development process.

But we should start to have hard expectations for ourselves about implementing good practices. What might these expectations be? Here are my recommendations based on what has worked, has been adopted and seems critical to successful customer-centred front end design:

Have an agreed upon process: Never start any technology development project without knowing exactly how you will do the front end design piece. Make sure it is shared, agreed upon and discussed by all who will be any part of the process. This of course is the basics of SEI.

Gather field data: In the last 12 years we have come to understand that field data is the best way to find out about the customer. Institutionalize it.

Get everyone who matters into the field: Make sure all designers and product definers have contact with customers in the field. There is no way to design a product when designers have never even seen the setting where their product will be used or when they have never spoken to a single customer. If everyone can't be sent to the field at least once, make sure the field is brought to them in some poignant way.

Have a way to represent qualitative data: Have a standard way to interpret and represent the data, preferably work models. Email, white papers and slide shows do not guarantee that the findings and implications of the data are really understood and used. If there is no way to deal with the data, no one can use it. If there is no way to roll up the data to see market issues no one can use it. Teach people how to understand data. *Make having data a milestone in the process.*

Make sure anyone who invents the system knows the data: Invention always comes from our internalization of the customer and the problem. If people invent and they don't know the data they will invent from their own assumptions and experiences. Data tailors and shapes technological possibility. Data filters those 'hot ideas' to which designers are too attached.

Represent the system in a implementation independent way: Contextual Design's user environment design lets designers see the impact of the system on the user. It lets designers run scenarios of use through the potential system. What ever representation you use, designers need a way to support talking about how to structure the system to support the customer's practice. And the linear text of a thick specification with no reference to impact on customer work doesn't do it.

Iterate the design with the customer: Any design, even those derived initially through the implications of field data, must be honed through iteration. Create paper mockups of the potential design and take them out to the field so people can try them out. Invention is a leap away from the data and must be tested. Testing in the field where people try to do their real work tasks in the mockup is a powerful way to see the impact of a future design. (Kyng, 1988b)

I consider these to be the basics for a discipline of procedure for customer centred front end design. I invite others to join me in defining these basics. But I challenge us to dialogue toward action. It is time to expect ourselves to operate on and with customer data at the front end of our design processes. It is past time to discuss whether or not we have to.

As an industry, we suffer from a lack of clear procedures. My fencing instructor said. "This is how you move your feet. We have learned, after hundreds of years, that this works. Don't reinvent it. Just do what I tell you." We haven't been designing software yet for hundreds of years. But for the past 12 years, we have been moving in the direction of processes I have outlined above. It is time to come forward with a single voice and push these basic principles into our organizations and classrooms until we have a true discipline of action.

6 Customer-centred Design as Discipline

For some people, including myself, the word discipline is scary. It implies constraint and lack of creativity — holding us down and back from going in our own direction. But if we look at any field of creativity we see that it includes fundamental skills that must be learned, ways of working that have proven themselves over time, bodies of history and knowledge to call upon and teachers and practitioners that make it all real.

I have been proud to be a part of the many people who have moved this industry toward the use of customer field data to drive front end design. Having gotten this far, I am thankful for the industry luminaries who have influenced and shared my work. But the real heroes are the developers, usability professionals, UI designers, marketers and managers who introduced these processes into their organizations drop by drop. Because of them we are ready to create a discipline of customer-centred front end design.

As an industry we are ready for and we need discipline. The kind of discipline that fosters fast action when we embody the skills we need. The kind of academic discipline that provides us domain knowledge at our fingertips. The kind of disciplined procedures that helps teams know what to do Monday morning when they design. As an industry, it is time to move to customer centred design as a discipline.

References

Beyer, H. & Holtzblatt, K. (1998), *Contextual Design: Defining Customer-centered Systems*, Morgan-Kaufmann.

Kyng, M. (1988), Designing for a Dollar a Day, *in* D. G. Tatar (ed.), *Proceedings of CSCW'88: Conference on Computer Supported Cooperative Work*, ACM Press, pp.178–88.

Ruuska, S. & Väänänen-Vainio-Mattila, K. (n.d.), Contextual Research for Technological Innovation — Satisfying User Needs in the Design of Mobile Communication Devices, Pre-print.

Sachs, P. (1995), "Transforming Work: Collaboration, Learning and Design", *Communications of the ACM* **38**(9).

Sellen, A. & Harper, R. (1997), Paper as an Analytic Resource for the Design of New Technologies, *in* S. Pemberton (ed.), *Proceedings of CHI'97: Human Factors in Computing Systems*, ACM Press.

Suchman, L. A. (1987), *Plans and Situated Actions — The Problem of Human–Machine Communication*, Cambridge University Press.

Human–Computer Interaction — INTERACT '99
M. Angela Sasse and Chris Johnson (Editors)
Published by IOS Press, © IFIP TC.13, 1999

HCI in the Next Millennium: Supporting the World Mind

Brian R. Gaines

Knowledge Science Institute, University of Calgary,
Alberta T2N 1N4, Canada.

gaines@cpsc.ucalgary.ca

Abstract: This presentation uses *three worlds, collective stance* and *learning curves* perspectives to analyse developments in human–computer interaction. It argues from historic data that the human interests have remained unchanged over at least five millennia, and may be expected to have the same basis during the next millennium. It concludes that we are still at a very early stage in the development of HCI, and that the major impact of the technology on our societies is yet to come. To understand the issues involved we will need greater understanding of the operation of our societies, their economies, politics and cultures, and how these evolve under the influence of environmental factors including advances in information technologies.

1 Introduction

INTERACT'99 falls in a year which is the 50th anniversary of EDSAC, the first stored program digital computer (Williams, 1985); the 40th of the first paper on HCI (Shackel, 1959); the 30th of the first issue of the *International Journal of Man–Machine Studies* (Chaplin et al., 1969); the 20th of Visicalc, the first spread-sheet program (VisiCalc, 1984); and the 10th of the proposal for a World Wide Web of hypertext documents (Berners-Lee, 1989). In another decade what will we remember of 1999, what will be the issues of 2009, and what will be the challenges and opportunities of computing and HCI in the next millennium?

I welcome this opportunity to look back on the evolution of computing and HCI, and forward to the growing role of computing in human society. The editor of a journal is an impresario continually seeking new 'acts', the innovative performers of tomorrow who will challenge the envelope, surprise us with their ideas and achievements, and create the cultures of the future. In this article I will share with you perspectives on the future of computing and HCI that drive my anticipations of what will be reported in the *International Journal of Human–Computer Studies* in the next millennium.

As one browses through the first three decades of IJHCS and later journals that developed in its wake, it is apparent that the HCI literature to date has been largely focused on the interaction between the individual person and the computer system. In recent years the development of group-ware has led to papers on systems in which the technology mediates the activities of a team, but the focus is still largely on individual cognitive issues such as situational awareness. Similarly, the development of the Internet and World Wide Web has led to papers on various aspects of computer-mediated communication, but the focus is largely on supporting the individual to interface to community resources.

My argument in this presentation is that these foci of attention must, and will, change to model the larger unit as a composite human entity whose processes interact with computing technologies. The *team*, the *special-interest community*, and *humanity at large*, are the relevant systems to consider in designing, modelling and understanding the next generation of human–computer interaction (Gaines et al., 1997). Studies of individual interaction will continue but they will be greatly enriched by situating that interaction in the social, organizational, political, economic and cultural situations within which that interaction plays a role.

2 Background and Issues

There are many papers that address the role of information technology in organizations, particularly in the management literature, but they tend do so on the basis of organizational design rather than organizational emergence. They assume that the structure of the organization is pre-defined as are the roles within it, and the focus of interest is on the application of information technology to support those roles and that organization.

This is a valid approach to organizational analysis but it does not address some of the most important impacts of computing in recent years where organizational structures have emerged that did not previously exist, or where the operation of existing communities has changed through the effective use of the Internet and Web. What is needed is a framework for the emergence of social structures through the process of interaction where the definition and maintenance of an organization is an ongoing process embedded in the interaction, not an externally defined precursor of that interaction.

The framework exists in various literatures, such as: philosophy of *three worlds* (Popper, 1968); the *group mind* (Bar-Tal, 1990); *reflexive sociology* (Bourdieu & Wacquant, 1992); *economic sociology* (Granovetter & Swedberg, 1992); *social network theory* (Burt, 1992); but not in what are normally regarded as the foundations of HCI.

I suggested in a keynote address at the 1978 System, Man and Cybernetics conference in Tokyo (Gaines, 1978) that the distinctions made by Popper in defining '3 Worlds', the physical, the mental, and the mediating products of the mental, were fundamental to the analysis of HCI. I later used that framework to analyse person–computer interaction in distributed systems (Gaines, 1988), computer-aided knowledge acquisition (Gaines, 1989), and the support of scholarly communities on the Internet (Gaines et al., 1997).

The original presentation focused on computers as vehicles to explore Popper's 'World 3', the mediating products of the human mind, and is useful in modelling developments in simulation, artificial intelligence and electronic journals (Gaines, 1993). However, the massive growth of discourse on the Internet may be viewed as computer networks providing vehicles to explore Popper's 'World 2' of mental processes, and draws attention to the need for deeper models of communities of discourse. A useful perspective from which to examine such communities is a *collective stance* (Gaines, 1994) in which humanity is viewed as a single adaptive agent recursively partitioned in space and time into sub-systems that are similar to the whole. In human terms, these parts include societies, organizations, groups, individuals, roles, and neurological functions (Gaines, 1987).

A third framework is needed for computers as a physical technology in 'World 1'. For this I will use a model of the generational infrastructure of information

technology as a set of tiered learning curves (Gaines & Shaw, 1986) that was developed as an outcome of the studies of 5th generation computing (Gaines, 1984b) underlying my INTERACT'84 presentation (Gaines, 1984a). In particular, it can be used to model the convergence of communications and computer technologies and the growth of the Web (Gaines, 1998).

This presentation will make use of the *three worlds, collective stance* and *learning curves* perspectives to explore potential future development in human–computer interaction. In particular, I shall argue from historic data that the human interests and resultant collective dynamics underlying socio-cultural phenomena have remained unchanged over at least five millennia, and hence may reasonably be expected to continue to operate during the next millennium.

In HCI studies it is the 'C' that is changing rapidly while the 'H' remains fundamentally unchanged although the 'I' may lead to the emergence of variant socio-cultural configurations.

I will conclude that we are still at a very early stage in the development of HCI, that the major impact of the technology on society is yet to come, and that to understand the design issues involved we will need much greater overt understanding of the operation of our societies, their economies, politics and cultures, and how these evolve under the influence of environmental factors including the development of information technologies.

Let me pause in this rather dry academic discussion and give an experiential perspective that serves to illustrate the major issues. While preparing this presentation in early April 1999 I attended a performance of Brahms' *German Requiem* and reflected on how many of the issues noted above were instantiated through that experience:

- First, there were no computers involved in the performance. There are many major aspects of our lives that are yet unaffected by computer technology.

- Second, the capability of people to coordinate a complex activity involving the skilled activities of a large team of individuals was very apparent. The choir, soloists, and orchestra came together in a social unity constructed for a particular task that only existed for this performance.

- Third, the social activity involved a wider socio-economic context of an audience paying to attend, the payment of those taking part, payment for the hall and associated staff, marketing activities, and so on. It was situated in an even wider social environment that provided for the building and management of the concert hall, car park, associated transportation facilities, paid employment for the audience that left them with the disposable income to attend, and so on.

- Fourth, the basis of the performance was the product of a long-dead composer from another country who had composed it as a response to the death of his mother. There were links across space and time to another social unit.

- Fifth, the words of the requiem were themselves reminders of the essential short-term embeddedness of the individual in the collective, "*the grass withereth and the flower fadeth*". The components of humanity are short-lived and fragile, and much of our socio-cultural system derives from this.

- Sixth, a requiem was appropriate to a time when planes from my countries were currently bombing buildings in the capital city of another country and fellow humans who might have been friends and colleagues were dying. Warfare has played a major role in human interests throughout recorded history.

- Seventh, the troops of the country being bombed were reported to be robbing the refugees fleeing their homes. Crime has played a major role in human interests throughout recorded history.

- Eighth, the media that was now full of war reports had recently been equally full of reports of the puerile sexual behaviours of the leader of the nation leading the bombing. Sexual desires have played an equally major role in human interests throughout recorded history.

- Ninth, as a scholar I could model all this and see its relevance to related social phenomena involving the Internet, including its use to support hate literature, criminal activities, pornography and scholarship. Reflection on its own nature has been one of the most distinctive features of human life throughout recorded history. Modelling and designing human–computer interaction on a social scale requires an understanding of issues that go far beyond the cognitive psychology of the individual.

3   Looking Back to INTERACT'84

What were the HCI issues 15 years ago when Brian Shackel and I had the pleasure of providing the two keynote addresses at INTERACT'84, the first major IFIP conference on human–computer interaction? Five more INTERACT conferences have been held in the UK, Germany, The Netherlands, Norway and Australia, with attendance at INTERCHI'93 in Amsterdam exceeding 1,500 participants from 32 countries. It is fitting to pay tribute to IFIP Technical Committee 13 on Human–Computer Interaction which, under the leadership of Brian Shackel, has supported HCI activities world-wide. We owe a profound debt of gratitude to those who have worked in IFIP and TC13 on our behalf.

My presentation at INTERACT'84 was entitled *from ergonomics to the fifth generation* (Gaines, 1984a) and focused on HCI within the context of the Japanese 5G initiative. It is salutary in this presentation concerned with forecasting trends in HCI to note how few outcomes have resulted from that initiative, or from the others it stimulated in other countries, despite the enthusiasm at the time. One lesson from a life of research, and from the study of the history of scholarship, is that the majority of what any of us do is evanescent and will have no lasting impact. Each of us plays a minor role in the accumulation of knowledge and would not be missed if we did not play that role.

However, the *community* of scholarship of which we are part does generate lasting outcomes, and some members of that community will be remembered for their parts through a fairly erratic process of attribution (Brannigan, 1981). History tends to focus on the 'breakthroughs', neglecting the majority of research activity, which was fun, challenging, frustrating and rewarding, but had little dramatic impact. However, major changes arise out of that amorphous soup of forgotten research, often through a serendipitous process, and it is important to model this in forecasting. I will exemplify this through significant cases in this presentation.

Brian Shackel's presentation at INTERACT'84 was entitled *designing for people in the age of information* (Shackel, 1984) and posed some interesting questions about the expected state of the art by the end of the millennium: *the passing of paper; the reduction of writing; the victory of voice; the wired society; the expert in the system?*

The evidence of my ever-expanding bookcases and piles of documents is that paper is not yet obsolete. However, major changes are occurring. In my role as a university bureaucrat the majority of communication is through email, and when I receive the rare written memo I reply by email. One impact of this is upon filing systems where electronic archives of email provide a readily searchable corporate memory. Last year also I dropped most of my paper journal subscriptions by subscribing to the electronic versions, achieving major reductions in costs and needs for filing and storage.

Handwriting has been largely replaced by keyboarding but voice entry has had singularly little impact despite continuing research efforts dating from the 1950's. James Martin's (1978) *wired society* has arrived in the late 1990's and is having a major impact on our lives. In my day to day research I am continuously connected to a range of information resources on the Internet including library catalogues, abstracting services, electronic journals, bookstores and an ongoing flow of email from various list servers. One reason the use of paper has not stopped for me is that, with thousands of bookstores on the Web, it is often quicker to order a book through the Web than to request it through inter-library loan. The digitization of the entire corpus of written literature will be a major undertaking in the next millennium. The major impediments are issues of copyright and effective mechanisms for electronic commerce rather than the technologies of digitization *per se*.

Expert systems development was another exciting research area in the 1980's, stemming from the promise of artificial intelligence in the fifth generation era but failing to achieve its apparent potential. The social need that such systems targeted in terms of access to expert knowledge has been addressed instead by the access to human expert knowledge through the Internet. The *wired society* has to large extent obviated the need for the *expert in the system* by providing access to a network of human experts through list servers and newsgroups.

I can claim to have foreseen the significance of Internet communities some 28 years ago:

> "If fifty percent of the world's population are connected through terminals, then questions from one location may be answered not by access to an internal data-base but by routing them to users elsewhere — who better to answer a question on abstruse Chinese history than an abstruse Chinese historian." (Gaines, 1971).

This remark arose out of my experience with developing operating systems for time-shared computers where a common bug was for console buffers to be switched and for one user to receive material intended for another. In the days before the widespread usage of email, it struck me that such serendipitous communication might not be entirely a bad thing!

4 Computers in Three Worlds

In 1968, as we planned the first issue of IJHCS, Karl Popper was publishing his seminal paper proposing that:

> "thoughts in the sense of contents or statements in themselves and thoughts in the sense of thought processes belong to two entirely different 'worlds' ... If we call the world of 'things' — of physical objects — the first world and the world of subjective experience the second world we may call the world of statements in themselves the third world (... world 3) ... I regard books and journals and letters as typically third-world objects, especially if they develop and discuss a theory ... I regard the third world as being essentially the product of the human mind. It is we who create third-world objects. That these objects have their own inherent or autonomous laws which create unintended and unforeseeable consequences is only an instance of a more general rule, the rule that all our actions have such consequences." (Popper, 1968)

Popper later included the computer in this framework, noting that:

> "human evolution proceeds, largely, by developing new organs outside our bodies or persons ... instead of growing better memories and brains we grow paper, pens, pencils, typewriters, dictaphones, the printing press, and libraries ... the latest development (used mainly in the support of argumentative abilities) is the growth of computers." (Popper, 1972)

Human agents interact with each of the three worlds through: *perception* and *action* to predict and control the reality of the physical World 1; through *comprehension* and *explanation* to understand and persuade the community of the mental World 2; through *derivation* and *creation* to use and create representations in the mediational World 3.

Computers, like books, span all three worlds: depending on major developments of physical technologies in World 1; involving the expression of human intentions in World 2 as programs represented in World 3; and storing and managing products in World 3 (Gaines, 1988). Unlike books, computational products can be active, supporting dynamic processes that *generate* presentations rather than merely store them. Computers add data processing, modelling, simulation, hypertext links, and so on, to the repertoire of World 3 products.

Computers amplify human capabilities in World 1 through their instrumentation/control capabilities. Galison (1997) documents modern science's dependence on technologies to explore World 1. We have noted the dependence of developments in genetic engineering on the learning curves of computer technologies (Gaines & Shaw, 1986).

Computers amplify human capabilities in World 2 through their communication capabilities. The convergence of computer and communications technologies to the Internet and World Wide Web is a technological advance with major social impact (Gaines, 1998), and governments have recognized it as a major economic driver (Gore, 1995).

Computers amplify human capabilities in World 3 through their mediational capabilities. The digital media is able to encode any arbitrary entity so that it can be represented, processed and communicated in a computer system (Negroponte, 1995).

5   A Collective Stance

Popper also models the evolution of the agent as taking place in all three worlds through the same process of inwardly developed trial and the elimination of error.

> "On all three levels — genetic adaptation, adaptive behaviour, and scientific discovery — the mechanism of adaptation is fundamentally the same ... inherited structures are exposed to certain pressures, or challenges, or problems ... variations of the genetically inherited or traditionally inherited instructions are produced by methods which are at least partly random. On the genetic level, these are mutations and recombinations of the coded instructions. On the behavioural level, they are tentative variations and recombinations within the repertoire. On the scientific level, they are new and

revolutionary tentative theories ... The next stage is that of selecting from the available mutations and variations: those of the new tentative trials which are badly adapted are eliminated." (Popper, 1994)

These notions of how changes occur in the worlds are critical to understanding and forecasting human developments including the evolution of computers and their applications. Learning is a directed process based on presuppositions that can block progress (Gaines, 1976). However, the introduction of randomness can bypass the blocks (Gaines, 1971), and the resultant product will be selected not only in terms of the originating intention but also for any other value it may have-that is, serendipity is rife (Roberts, 1989).

Such phenomena have fascinated me through my career. The first computer I developed at ITT in 1965 was a *stochastic computer* that simulated an analogue computer digitally by using random pulse trains in the manner of neurons (Gaines, 1967). It interested me thereafter to find problems that could be solved simply through random processes compared with insolubility or complexity with deterministic processes (Gaines, 1969b). My experience with using linear describing functions to model the highly nonlinear human controller and the artifacts this produced (Gaines, 1969a) led to an interest in the distortions of empirical theories caused by incorrect presuppositions (Gaines, 1976). I also became interested in the intrinsic positive feedback processes of learning processes, that one advance tended to lead to another and that exponential growth was common until curtailed by some limiting process (Gaines, 1988b).

In recent years I have integrated these concepts in a model of Worlds 2 and 3 which adopts a *collective stance* to World 2 and models the human species as a single adaptive organism recursively partitioned in space and time into sub-organisms that are similar to the whole (Gaines, 1994). These parts include societies, organizations, groups, individuals, roles, and neurological functions.

The organism adapts as a whole through adaptation of its interacting parts, leading to distribution of tasks and functional differentiation of the parts. The mechanism is one of positive feedback from parts of the organism allocating resources for action to other parts on the basis of those latter parts' past performance of similar activities. Distribution and differentiation follow if performance is rewarded, and low performers of tasks, being excluded by the feedback mechanism from the performance of those tasks, seek out alternative tasks where there is less competition.

World 3 phenomena, such as meaning and its representation in language and overt knowledge, arise as byproducts of the communication, coordination and modelling processes associated with the basic exchange-theoretic behavioural model. The model links to existing analyses of human action and knowledge in biology, psychology, sociology and philosophy, and is used to analyse the role of information technology in supporting activities in the life-world of World 2.

6 Human Interests

Human interests is the term conventionally used to capture the underlying dynamics of World 2. In general, technology will play a significant role if it supports these collective interests. I will first provide evidence for my sweeping statement in Section 2 that human interests have not changed throughout recorded history by a series of anecdotes that illustrate how the phenomena of the Internet have been instantiated in various past societies.

Let us commence with the intellectual experiments of the Greek enlightenment around 500BC that gave us: *argumentation; persuasion; utopian wishes; Greek language; empirical psychology*; and *rational reconstruction* as foundations for our own knowledge processes (Solmsen, 1975). We have come to idealize Pericles and Athens at that time as providing the foundations for democracy and scientific thought. However, detailed social histories of the period tell a story of *hetaireiai*, special-interest groups based on kinship, religion, military affiliation, employment, pleasures, and so on, that vied in the assembly to present their interests in developing the law (Connor, 1971). Legal, financial and marital corruption were rife, and the intellectual tools that we value were developed as ways of both managing and manipulating it as well as for more idealistic purposes. These are the same phenomena and same interests that the Internet and Web address today.

Greek language is of particular interest because the written form was developed to allow the works of Homer to be transcribed (Powell, 1991). Writing technology substituted for an oral technology based on formulaic use of hexameters that provided communal storage for stories in the society of bards (Hobart & Schiffman, 1998). We see the mediation of Internet technology providing similar written capture for discourse in the special-interest communities using list servers. What was previously *cultural software* (Balkin, 1998) becomes captured in the archives of those servers, and newcomers can attune to the group through the archives without having to participate in the discourse.

The invention of writing led to a major industry in books. Around 250AD Origen was reckoned to have published some 6,000 books in his attempt to recreate accurate copies of Christian literature from the many versions extant. His extensive annotations and cross-references may be the earliest examples of hypertext linkage. His tracing the texts not only to biblical sources but also to earlier pagan literature led to Pope Anastasius condemning his works in 400AD, and the Council of Constantinople pronouncing them anathema in 533AD — censorship took longer to operate in those days! Nevertheless much of his work survives and is a basis for modern biblical scholarship (Constable, 1995).

The printing press revolutionized book production in the mid 15th century, having not only the intended effect of making it easier to propagate the bible and the established order, but also the serendipitous effect of making it easier to publish texts attacking that order. Eisenstein (1979) sees the book as a foundation for modern scholarship supporting *standardization*, *dissemination* and *fixity*. However, Johns' (1998) detailed studies of the book during the scientific revolution shows otherwise, that it was a very difficult to obtain a definitive copy of a book and that piracy of incorrect editions was rife. The issues of spurious and incorrect materials on the Internet today were problems with books then, and Johns gives modern examples suggesting they continue in scholarly publications today.

Writing also led to massive use of correspondence. Jardine (1996) notes that Datini, a Renaissance Venetian merchant, exchanged 125,549 letters with his factors or agents between 1364 and 1410. She also gives interesting examples of early pornography, that the works of Titian were sold for sexual titillation in the bedroom, and that the owners wanted to ensure that they were anonymous. She documents the commercial aspects of the book trade as a major business for both authors and printers, who were often at loggerheads. Hampson (1968) throws further light on the book trade during the Enlightenment, noting that book prices increased by a factor of five or more when they were banned.

One of the most interesting correspondents during the scientific revolution was Henry Oldenburg who came over as an ambassador from Bremen to Oliver Cromwell and stayed in London through the Restoration becoming a confidant of Robert Boyle and the first secretary to the Royal Society. Much of his massive correspondence survives (Hall & Hall, 1965) and has been the foundation of a range of studies of the scientific revolution and the role of the Royal Society. His world-wide correspondence with scholars of the seventeenth century can be mode-led as if he were a human list server and shows patterns of discourse similar to those on the Internet today. The main different is in the time scales since his correspondence with Europe had a cycle time of some 6 months and that with America some 6 years.

Oldenburg used correspondence to support himself financially. He concludes a letter to Boyle in 1664 with the postscript:

> "Sr, give me leave to entreat you, yt in case you should meet with any curious persons, yt would be willing to receave weekly intelligence, both of state and litterary news, you would doe me the favour of engaging them to me for it. The Expences cannot be considerable to persons yt have but a mediocrity; Ten lb. A yeare will be the most will be expected; 8. or 6. will also do the business."

His newsy letters became the *Transactions of the Royal Society* which he hoped would bring him £100 a year but, as he complains to Boyle, brought in rather less. What we see as the first scientific journal started as a commercial newsletter, driven by similar economic issues to those of how to charge for Internet information.

Shapin (1994) provides one of the most profound analyses of the Oldenburg correspondence and other documents and activities of that time in terms of the networks of trust underlying scholarship and science. His model generalizes not only to the modern scholarly community but also to communities in general on the Internet. The basis of trust in the intentions of those participating, how it is monitored and managed, is one of the most important issues for any communications technology supporting human communities.

7   Advances in Technology

Information technology is a recent invention whose rapid growth has had a major impact on age-old human interests. In 1959, as Brian Shackel at EMI published his paper on computer ergonomics, I was changing a semiconductor diffusion furnace at ITT to operate with boron rather than phosphorus in order to experiment with the new Bell Laboratory process for making planar transistors. Production processes for silicon transistors at that point involved etching the silicon away from the transistor. The new process created the transistor as an island in an area of non-conducting silicon so that we could put multiple coupled transistors on the same slice of silicon and create integrated circuits.

The number of transistors on an integrated circuit chip has increased exponentially by nine orders of magnitude since the first planar transistor in 1959, a growth curve commonly termed Moore's law after a joking prediction made by Gordon Moore, a co-founder of Fairchild Semiconductor. In 1964 when he made the prediction, 20 on a chip allowed the first flip-flop to be integrated; in 1972, 5,000 allowed the first 1 Kilobit memory (Intel 1103) and microcomputer (Intel 4004) to be integrated; in 1980, 500,000 allowed major central processing units to be integrated. The projected limit as we enter the next millennium is some 10,000,000,000 devices on a chip as quantum mechanical effects become a barrier to further packing density on silicon planar chips.

The substitution of integrated circuits for discrete components radically accelerated the evolution of computers. The decrease in costs and increase in reliability made it possible to develop computers with greater storage capacity and processing power that also had mean times between failures that allowed them to be used in an interactive mode. For example, in 1968 I was able to develop the MINIC I computer using 74N TTL circuits to a full commercial product in some 6 months. In those days as well as the circuit design one also developed the microcode, wrote the operating system, developed the compilers and programmed the early applications.

My first interactive system on MINIC was a 12-bed patient monitoring system for the intensive care ward at University College Hospital. It had 1Kbyte of main memory, a 64Kbyte storage drum, and provided graphic output on temperature, respiratory rate and heart rate, over a period of time for a patient selected by the physician. The major market for MINIC, however, was not this type of intended application but rather the programmed control of machine tools where its microprogram allowed cost-effective control of the servo loops. This success in an area of which I knew nothing is another example of the serendipity that is prevalent in the development of technology and ideas.

The mention of computer architectures, programming and interaction in the example above is a reminder that the learning curve of integrated circuits was not the only factor in the evolution of computing. The nine orders of magnitude increase in the number of transistors on a chip has depended on the use of the computer to support the design and fabrication of such circuits. This is an example of a positive feedback loop within the evolution of computers, that the computer industry has achieved a learning curve that is unique in its sustained exponential growth because each advance in computer technology has been able to support further advances in computer technology.

Such positive feedback is known to give rise to emergent phenomena in biology (Ulanowicz, 1991) whereby systems exhibit major new phenomena in their behaviour. The history of computing shows the emergence of major new industries concerned with activities that depend upon, and support, the basic circuit development but which are qualitatively different in their conceptual frameworks and applications impacts from that development. For example, programming has led to a software industry, human–computer interaction has led to an interactive applications industry, document representation has led to a desktop publishing industry, and so on.

Each of these emergent areas of computing has had its own learning curve (Linstone & Sahal, 1976), and the growth of information systems technology overall may be seen as the cumulative impact of a tiered succession of learning curves. Each curve is triggered by advances at lower levels, and each supports further advances at lower levels and the eventual triggering of new advances at higher levels (Gaines, 1991).

It has also been noted in many disciplines that the qualitative phenomena during the growth of the learning curve vary from stage to stage (Gaines & Shaw, 1986). The era before the learning curve takes off, when too little is known for planned progress, is that of the inventor having very little chance of success but continuing a search based on intuition and faith. When an inventor makes a *breakthrough*, his or her work is *replicated* at research institutions world-wide. Experience gained leads to *empirical* design rules with little foundation except successes and failures. As enough empirical experience is gained it becomes possible to model the basis of success and failure and develop *theories*. The theoretical models make it possible to *automate* the manufacturing processes. Once automaton has been put in place effort can focus on cost reduction and quality improvements in a *mature* technology.

Figure 1 left shows a tiered succession of learning curves for information technologies in which a breakthrough in one technology is triggered by a supporting technology as it moves from its research to its empirical stage. The initial sequence of technologies is those of *computer science*: digital

circuits; computer architecture; software engineering; and human–computer interaction; followed by those of *knowledge science*: knowledge representation; knowledge acquisition; autonomous agents; and socially organized agents.

Also shown are trajectories for the eras of *invention, research, product innovation, long-life product lines, low-cost products*, and *throw-away products*. One phenomenon not shown on this diagram is that the new industries can sometimes themselves be supportive of further development in the industries on which they depend. Thus, in the later stages of the development of an industrial sector there will be a tiered structure of interdependent industries at different stages along their learning curves.

8 The Growth of the Internet

The *Request for Comments* (RFC) that answers the question "What is the Internet?", offers three different definitions (Krol, 1993): *a network of networks based on the TCP/IP protocols; a community of people who use and develop those networks; a collection of resources that can be reached from those networks* — which nicely characterizes the net in Worlds 1, 2 and 3.

The Internet came into being through serendipity rather than design in that the intentions and aspirations of their originators had little relation to what they have become. The Eisenhower administration reacted to the USSR launch of Sputnik, the first artificial earth satellite, in 1957 with the formation of the Advanced Research Projects Agency (ARPA) within the Department of Defense to regain a lead in advanced technology. In 1969 ARPANET (Salus, 1995) was commissioned for research into networking with nodes at UCLA, UCSB and the University of Utah. By 1971 ARPANET had 15 nodes connecting 23 computers and by 1973 international connections to the UK and Norway had been created.

Use of ARPANET by the scientific and engineering communities grew through the 1970s and in 1984 the National Science Foundation funded a program to create a national academic infrastructure connecting university computers in a network, NSFNET. In 1987 the net had grown to such an extent that NSF subcontracted its operation to Merit and other commercial providers, and in 1993/1994 the network was privatized and its operation taken over by a group of commercial service providers.

Email on the Internet commenced in 1972, news distribution in 1979, gopher in 1991, and Web browsers with multimedia capabilities in 1993. Existing use encouraged further use leading to exponential growth in the number of connected

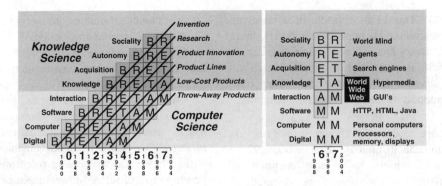

Figure 1: The infrastructure of information technology (left) and its role in the World Wide Web (right).

machines of 100% a year. The growth to over one million nodes, the growing commercial usage of the Internet, and the multimedia capabilities of the Web in the 1993/1994 period combined to persuade government and industry that the Internet was a new commercial force comparable to the telephone and television industries, and the concept of an *information highway* came into widespread use.

9   The Growth of the Web

The need for better technologies to manage the growth of human knowledge was recognized before the advent of the computer. Wells promoted the concept of a '*world brain/mind*':

> "Encyclopaedic enterprise has not kept pace with material progress. These observers realize that the modern facilities of transport, radio, photographic reproduction and so forth are rendering practicable a much more fully succinct and accessible assembly of facts and ideas than was ever possible before." (Wells, 1938)

Bush proposed a technological solution based on his concept of memex, a multimedia personal computer:

> "There is a growing mountain of research. But there is increased evidence that we are being bogged down today as specialization extends … The difficulty seems to be not so much that we publish unduly in view of the extent and variety of present-day interests, but rather that publication has been extended far beyond our present ability to make real use of the record." (Bush, 1945)

Martin's model of a '*wired society*' in 1978 comes closest to forecasting many aspects and impacts of the information highway:

> "The technology of communications is changing in ways which will have impact on the entire fabric of society in both developed and developing nations." (Martin, 1978)

However, attempts to make available the wired society at the time of Martin's seminal work were presented in terms of greatly exaggerated expectations. For example, Fedida & Malik presented Viewdata as having the potential to have major social and economic impacts:

> "We believe that Viewdata is a major new medium according to the McLuhan definition; one comparable with print, radio, and television, and which could have as significant effects on society and our lives as those did and still do." (Fedida & Malik, 1979)

Ten years after Viewdata, in 1989 Tim Berners-Lee presented CERN with a proposal for managing its documents effectively that over the next decade became through a series of serendipitous processes the World Wide Web as we know it today:

> "We should work toward a universal linked information system, in which generality and portability are more important than fancy graphics techniques and complex extra facilities." (Berners-Lee, 1989)

The Web was slow to emerge as a viable technology and in the early 1990's the gopher protocol that had been developed for campus-wide information services was rapidly coming into use as a way of sharing structured databases of documents (Anklesaria et al., n.d.). However, in November 1992 Marc Andreessen joined the *www-talk* list server that Berners-Lee had established in October 1991 asking:

> "Anyone written code to construct HTML files in Emacs? I'm hacking something up; let me know if you're interested",

and the development of the Web began to change as Marc moved into the development of what became the Mosaic browser and eventually *Netscape* and *Internet Explorer*.

Tracking the development of the Web is simple since the email correspondence that Marc used to discuss the design of Mosaic remains available through the email archives of the *www-talk* list — the modern equivalent of Oldenburg's correspondence.

Unfortunately, librarians have been slow to realize the value of archiving list servers and data is being lost that is invaluable to the study of the significant human activities now taking place through the Internet. The Web provides a reflexive technology through which we can understand not only the growth of the Web but also the wide range of human knowledge processes it now mediates.

Examination of the *www-talk* archives illustrates serendipity in the design of Mosaic. Features incorporated for one purpose proved even more valuable for unforeseen purposes. A major example is the discussion about where the search terms text box should be placed in the browser window. Marc got annoyed with all the suggestions and complaints and decided to embed it in the document being viewed. At 3am on 19th August 1993 he mailed to the list:

> "You may be happy to know that I have before me a Mosaic running a quite revised HTML widget, thanks to Eric's kamikaze work ethic, that includes the following features ... (BTW, this also means that putting widgets — e.g. Motif text entry fields, etc. — inside the HTML widget suddenly got a lot simpler and therefore should be arriving soon.)"

The embedding of HCI widgets in documents was revolutionary in allowing them to be used as graphic user interfaces and radically changed the nature of the Web as Web browsers became universal interface.

The BRETAM tiered learning curves infrastructure of Figure 1 brings together the various phenomena of convergence in an integrated model which has the potential both to explain the past and forecast the future of the Web. The relevant learning curves in Figure 1 are the lower four: digital electronics; computer architecture; software; and interaction. The *product innovation* trajectory passes through the last of these in the fourth generation, 1972–1980, and led to the premature development of Viewdata and to Martin's detailed forecasts of the potential for a wired society. However, the mass market potential for wired society technology at costs comparable to other mass media such as the telephone and television is dependent on the cost reductions possible in the post-maturity phase of the learning curves leading to *throw-away products*. This trajectory passes through the interaction learning curve in the current seventh generation era, 1996–2004, and it is this that has made the information highway economically feasible.

The analysis of product opportunities arising from the existence of the information highway involves the upper learning curves of the BRETAM model — knowledge representation and acquisition, autonomy and sociality. Knowledge representation and processing encompasses all the media that can be passed across the Web, not just the symbolic logic considered in artificial intelligence studies but also typographic text, pictures, sounds, movies, and the massive diversity of representations of specific material to be communicated.

The significance of discourse in the human communities collaborating through the Internet has been underestimated in the stress on 'artificial' intelligence in computer research. Knowledge need not be machine-interpretable to be useful, and it can often be machine-processed, indexed and enhanced without a depth of interpretation one might associate with artificial intelligence.

There are socio-economic problems with the Web in that much represented knowledge is owned by copyright holders who seek some financial reward. Technologically it is important to develop ways of charging for access to knowledge at a low enough rate to encourage widespread use at a high enough volume to compensate the knowledge provider. The knowledge-level problem for the information highway is not so much representation and processing but rather effective trading.

10 Conclusions — The Future

Those of us who can no longer function without access to the resources of the Internet may sympathize with an earlier insight into human relations with the previous generation of technology:

"Leave us to ourselves, without our books, and at once we get into a muddle and lose our way — we don't know whose side to be on or where to give our allegiance, what to love and what to hate, what to respect and what to despise. We even find it difficult to be human beings ... and are always striving to be some unprecedented kind of generalized human being ... Soon we shall invent a method of being born from an idea."
(Dostoyevsky, 1864)

How prophetic this seems today, but also how one sided — the *underground man* has surrendered to despair, to be an unwilling passenger in World 3, not an architect, a builder, or even a free-wheeling traveller. The positive side of Dostoyevsky's insight is that technology may play a role in enriching our humanity, particularly in extending our access to the network of ideas since much of what we value has always been 'born from an idea'.

In this article I have shared with you perspectives on the future of computing and HCI that drive my anticipations of what will be reported in the *International Journal of Human–Computer Studies* in the next millennium. Whereas the foundations of HCI for the past 30 years have been cognitive psychology, I would see the future as having a broader basis in sociology, economics, anthropology, politics, and other models of the life-world. Perhaps cognitive psychology will come to encompass these communal aspects of humanity. However, I doubt that any systematic framework is possible that captures the nature of humanity.

We are essentially open systems, open to experience and open to our own processes of redesign. We can choose to exhibit whatever social theories interest us, although some may be rather more comfortable than others. I sympathize with Castoriadis' (1987) emphasis on the *imaginary institution of society*, and with Bourdieu's emphasis that reflexive sociology is not a system because its fundamental postulate is that no system can describe the life-world (Bourdieu & Wacquant, 1992).

Let me conclude with another quotation:

"It is our duty to remain optimistic ... The future is open. It is not predetermined and thus cannot be predicted — except by accident. The possibilities that lie in the future are infinite ... all of us contribute to it by everything we do: we are all responsible for what the future holds in store." (Popper, 1994)

This is a nice prescription on which to end.

There is joy and creativity in being optimistic, and it is a state of mind, not a response to circumstances. All interesting developments in HCI were created in a spirit of optimism (as were many of the failures, but they were the stepping stones to success). This quotation also makes my title and theme a tautology — you and your systems will not be able to avoid contributing to the world mind. What matters is how effectively you and others learn from the experience of making that contribution.

Acknowledgements

Financial assistance for this work has been made available by the Natural Sciences and Engineering Research Council of Canada. My thanks to Mildred Shaw for criticism of this paper.

References

Anklesaria, F., McCahill, M., Lindner, P., Johnson, D., Torrey, D. & Alberti, B. (n.d.), "The Internet Gopher Protocol (A Distributed Document Search and Retrieval Protocol)", Internet RFC 1436.

Balkin, J. M. (1998), *Cultural Software: A Theory of Ideology*, Yale University Press.

Bar-Tal, D. (1990), *Group Beliefs: A Conception for Analyzing Group Structure Processes, and Behavior*, Springer-Verlag.

Berners-Lee, T. (1989), "Information Management: A Proposal". http://www.w3.org/History/1989/proposal.html.

Bourdieu, P. & Wacquant, L. J. D. (1992), *An Invitation to Reflexive Sociology*, University of Chicago Press.

Brannigan, A. (1981), *The Social Basis of Scientific Discoveries*, Cambridge University Press.

Burt, R. S. (1992), *Structural Holes: The Social Structure of Competition*, Harvard University Press.

Bush, V. (1945), "As We May Think", *Atlantic Monthly* **176**, 101–8.

Castoriadis, C. (1987), *The Imaginary Institution of Society*, MIT Press.

Chaplin, G. B. B., Gaines, B. R. & Gedye, J. L. (1969), "Editorial", *International Journal of Man–Machine Studies* **1**(1), i–ii.

Connor, W. R. (1971), *The New Politicians of Fifth-Century Athens*, Princeton University Press.

Constable, G. (1995), *Three Studies in Medieval Religious and Social Thought*, Cambridge University Press.

Dostoyevsky, F. (1864), *Notes from the Underground*, Penguin.

Eisenstein, E. L. (1979), *The Printing Press as Agent of Change: Communications Cultural Transformations in Early Modern Europe*, Cambridge University Press.

Fedida, S. & Malik, R. (1979), *The Viewdata Revolution*, Associated Business Press.

Gaines, B. R. (1967), Stochastic Computing, *in Spring Joint Computer Conference*, pp.149–56.

Gaines, B. R. (1969a), "Linear and Nonlinear Models of the Human Controller", *International Journal of Man–Machine Studies* **1**(4), 333–60.

Gaines, B. R. (1969b), Stochastic Computing Systems, *in* J. Tou (ed.), *Advances in Information Systems Science*, Vol. 2, Plenum Press, pp.37–172.

Gaines, B. R. (1971), "Memory Minimization in Control with Stochastic Automata", *Electronics* **7**(24), 710–1.

Gaines, B. R. (1976), "On the Complexity of Causal Models", *IEEE Transactions in Systems, Man and Cybernetics* **6**(1), 56–9.

Gaines, B. R. (1978), Computers in World Three, *in Proceedings of the International Conference on Cybernetics and Society*, IEEE Publications, pp.1515–21.

Gaines, B. R. (1984a), From Ergonomics to the Fifth Generation: 30 Years of Human–Computer Interaction Studies, *in* B. Shackel (ed.), *Proceedings of INTERACT '84 — First IFIP Conference on Human–Computer Interaction*, Elsevier Science, pp.3–7.

Gaines, B. R. (1984b), "Perspectives on Fifth Generation Computing", *Oxford Surveys in Information Technology* **1**, 1–53.

Gaines, B. R. (1987), Positive Feedback Processes Underlying Functional Differentiation, *in* M. Caudhill & C. Butler (eds.), *Proceedings of IEEE First International Conference on Neural Networks*, pp.387–94.

Gaines, B. R. (1988), "A Conceptual Framework for Person–Computer Interaction in Distributed Systems", *IEEE Transactions in Systems, Man and Cybernetics* **18**(4), 532–41.

Gaines, B. R. (1988b), "Positive Feedback Processes Underlying the Formation of Expertise", *IEEE Transactions in Systems, Man and Cybernetics* **18**(6), 1016–20.

Gaines, B. R. (1989), "Social and Cognitive Processes in Knowledge Acquisition", *Knowledge Acquisition* **1**(1), 251–80.

Gaines, B. R. (1991), "Modeling and Forecasting the Information Sciences", *Information Sciences* **57-8**, 3–22.

Gaines, B. R. (1993), "An Agenda for Digital Journals: The Socio-Technical Infrastructure of Knowledge Dissemination", *Journal of Organizational Computing* **3**(2), 135–93.

Gaines, B. R. (1994), "The Collective Stance in Modeling Expertise in Individuals and Organizations", *International Journal of Expert Systems* **7**(1), 21–51.

Gaines, B. R. (1998), "The Learning Curves Underlying Convergence", *Technological Forecasting and Social Change* **57**(1), 7–34.

Gaines, B. R. & Shaw, M. L. G. (1986), "A Learning Model for Forecasting the Future of Information Technology", *Future Computing Systems* **1**(1), 31–69.

Gaines, B. R., Chen, L. L.-J. & Shaw, M. L. G. (1997), "Modeling the Human Factors of Scholarly Communities supported through the Internet and World Wide Web", *Journal American Society Information Science* **48**(11), 987–1003.

Galison, P. L. (1997), *Image and Logic: A Material Culture of Microphysics*, University of Chicago Press.

Gore, A. (1995), Speech to National Press Club, *in* R. Goldsborough (ed.), *Straight Talk about the Information Superhighway*, MacMillan.

Granovetter, M. S. & Swedberg, R. (1992), *The Sociology of Economic Life*, Westview Press.

Hall, A. R. & Hall, M. B. (1965), *Correspondence of Henry Oldenburg*, University of Wisconsin Press.

Hampson, N. (1968), *The Enlightenment*, Harmondsworth (Penguin).

Hobart, M. E. & Schiffman, Z. S. (1998), *Information Ages: Literacy, Numeracy, and the Computer Revolution*, Johns Hopkins University Press.

Jardine, L. (1996), *Worldly Goods: A New History of the Renaissance*, Nan A. Talese.

Johns, A. (1998), *The Nature of the Book: Print and Knowledge in the Making*, University of Chicago Press.

Krol, E. (1993), "FYI on "What is the Internet?"", Internet. RFC 1462.

Linstone, H. A. & Sahal, D. (eds.) (1976), *Technological Substitution: Forecasting Techniques and Applications*, Elsevier Science.

Martin, J. (1978), *The Wired Society: A Challenge for Tomorrow*, Prentice–Hall.

Negroponte, N. (1995), *Being Digital*, Alfred A. Knopf.

Popper, K. R. (1968), Epistemology Without a Knowing Subject, *in* B. van Rootselaar (ed.), *Logic, Methodology and Philosophy of Science III*, North-Holland, pp.333–73.

Popper, K. R. (1972), *Objective Knowledge: An Evolutionary Approach*, Clarendon Press.

Popper, K. R. (1994), *The Myth of the Framework: In Defence of Science and Rationality*, Routledge.

Powell, B. B. (1991), *Homer and the Origin of the Greek Alphabet*, Cambridge University Press.

Roberts, R. M. (1989), *Serendipity: Accidental Discoveries in Science*, John Wiley & Sons.

Salus, P. (1995), *Casting the Net: From ARPANET to INTERNET and Beyond*, Addison–Wesley.

Shackel, B. (1959), "Ergonomics for a Computer", *Design* **120**, 36–9.

Shackel, B. (1984), Designing for People in the Age of Information, *in* B. Shackel (ed.), *Proceedings of INTERACT '84 — First IFIP Conference on Human–Computer Interaction*, Elsevier Science, pp.9–18.

Shapin, S. (1994), *A Social History of Truth: Civility and Science in Seventeenth-Century England*, University of Chicago Press.

Solmsen, F. (1975), *Intellectual Experiments of the Greek Enlightenment*, Princeton University Press.

Ulanowicz, R. E. (1991), Formal Agency in Ecosystem Development, *in* M. Higashi & T. P. Burns (eds.), *Theoretical Studies of Ecosystems: The Network Perspective*, Cambridge University Press, pp.58–70.

VisiCalc (1984), "VisiCalc '79", *Creative Computing* **10**, 122–34.

Wells, H. G. (1938), *World Brain*, Doubleday.

Williams, M. R. (1985), *A History of Computing Technology*, Prentice–Hall.

Human–Computer Interaction — INTERACT '99
M. Angela Sasse and Chris Johnson (Editors)
Published by IOS Press, © IFIP TC.13, 1999

Understanding Cognitive Complexity

Véronique De Keyser & Denis Javaux

University of Liège, Faculty of Psychology and Educational Sciences — Work Psychology Department, bd. du Rectorat 5-B32, B-4000 Liège, Belgium.

vdekeyser@ulg.ac.be, d.javaux@ulg.ac.be

Abstract: Different authors have tried to grasp the concept of cognitive complexity. This paper presents some of their approaches, with an original and predictive methodology, applied to the autopilot of the Boeing B737-300. This methodology could be used in the design and certification process of modern flight decks.

Keywords: automation, cognitive complexity, aviation, design, certification.

1 Introduction

The growing complexity of technical systems is causing more and more problems for operators who are supposed to master them. This is especially true for the control of dynamic situations, and in the case of an unexpected incidents or events. Far from finding the assistance expected from the numerous computerized aids at their disposition, the operators, to the contrary, see in them an extra source of complexity and one more risk. This is exactly the problem of *clumsy automation* brought up by Woods (1988), or the ironies of automation that Bainbridge denounced in a famous article (Bainbridge, 1987). However, the problem of complexity disarms the researcher. By nature, it is difficult to evaluate since it brings in so many variables. For all we know, anything could be a source of complexity: the environment, the operator, artefacts, the process to control and numerous variables which are impossible to enumerate. Moreover, it is less the variables themselves than their combination that makes them become critical. The more the researcher becomes exhaustive, the less he masters his object; and the more reductive he is, the more the validity of his research is called into question.

In this presentation, we will remain very pragmatic by attempting to see how it is possible to understand and to predict the complexity associated with certain technical systems and to reduce it at its conception. We will take aviation as an application case, where human error and the catastrophes that it can bring on are critical. Aviation is no doubt one of the areas where the human–computer interaction

has been pushed the furthest, and this is done not to eliminate the human being, but to harmoniously combine him with highly advanced devices. It is the dream of a 'joint cognitive system' which has always been welcomed by designers, which seems to find its concretization here. Indeed, the new-generation airplanes are widely computerized, and the automatic pilot has become the required partner of the crew in the management of the flight. The number of variables to take into account is so high, and the economic constraints such that a strictly manual piloting can only be conceived of on an ad hoc basis. But it must be possible to do so, especially in critical situations. It is here that the dream of joint cognitive system seems to fall apart. Investigations, feedback returns and the analyses of certain recent accidents indicates a real difficulty among pilots to understand the logic of certain technical devices, to have an exact situation awareness in which they locate themselves and to predict the behaviour of the plane. In a recent study carried out on different airline companies, Gras et al. (1994) shows that man–machine interactions are at the top of the list of fears expressed by pilots, and this even comes before weather or environmental disturbances. Moreover, a whole series of authors, based on field observations, have stigmatized these computerized modes, specifically Wiener (1985), Sarter & Woods (1992; 1994; 1995a), Billings (1997) and Amalberti (1996). Sarter & Woods' research in particular has had a deep impact because it shows very clearly that highly qualified and proficient pilots have obvious lacks in their understanding of automation. The difficulties are situated both at declarative (erroneous or incomplete mental models) and procedural (limits in the ability to modify automation status and behaviour) levels. The same type of observation has been made by Amalberti who recognizes the impossibility for the pilot to understand everything today.   But this approximative knowledge becomes a risk when the context is modified, and de facto the pilot is led to act within an environment that he has poorly mastered. The context thus appears like a terrifying activator of the effects of the complexity inherent in technical devices.

2   The Different Approaches to Cognitive Complexity

2.1   The Notion of Complexity

Complexity, in its current meaning, constitutes a blurry notion with a wide spectrum which is difficult to define. It is the same thing in the area of human sciences and, in particular, that of human factors. Numerous authors have studied the question, but a literature review shows that the subject was first approached in a very diverse manner. Few authors agree on the meaning that should be given to this notion (De Keyser & Javaux, 1998). Amalberti (1996) considers, for example, in his work on the conduct of high-risk systems, that the factors that make up the complexity of a situation correspond to:

> "traits or dimensions of the situation which require a non-nominal execution of the task, to added constraints and different behaviours of those which are defined by reference to a nominal situation (where the complexity is minimal and the behaviours stereotypical)."

As for Van Daele (1993), she extends the notion and dissociates complexity of situations, or of the environment, from the complexity of tasks and goals assigned to operators. Pedersen (1990), who is a mathematician by training, also considers that there are several forms of complexity in man–machine interactions: objective complexity and subjective complexity, complexity of the system, representational complexity and complexity linked to the agent. Pedersen also describes the computational complexity, a form of complexity measurement that stems from theoretical computer science, which he dissociates into algorithmic complexity and informational complexity. We noticed that among these different authors there is a real diversity of viewpoints and of forms of complexity envisioned. We cannot speak about a common and integrated vision of complexity on which the scientific community agrees unequivocally.

On of the most interesting, and probably the most heuristic for our purpose, is that of elicitation attempts or description of factors that make up the complexity in man–machine interaction situations. Amalberti (1996) identifies the characteristics of the system, of agents and of representations (in doing so taking up the ideas proposed by Woods in 1988), the dynamic of the process, temporal pressure, irreversibility of acts, the non-predictability of the process, the number of temporal reference systems to manage simultaneously, the risk, certain factors stemming from the insertion of high-risk systems into cooperative macro-systems (influence of hierarchical, functional and temporal structures) and finally the factors tied to the man–machine interface (direct or indirect access, retro-action delays, . . .). Van Daele (1993) describes the factors that influence the different forms of complexity that she had identified earlier: constraints preventing the normal realization of the task (complexity of the task), faraway character of goals (complexity tied to goals), dynamicity of the environment, multi-determination, uncertainty and risks (complexity linked to the environment). These lists of factors are interesting. However, they are only slightly operational because none of them leads to a method of measurement or characterization of the complexity that can be used in the operational context, in particular in the context of design and certification. They lack a precise explicative model of the genesis of complexity. Such models that do exist are based on the notion of *cognitive complexity*. They start from the idea that the complexity of the man–machine interaction situation is reflected in the complexity of the cognitive processes underlying the realization of the tasks. *Cognitive complexity, as it is studied in this case is thus that of the cognitive processes that reflect the complexity of the man–machine interaction situation in which they are submerged.*

2.2   The Forms of Study of Cognitive Complexity

The study of the complexity of situations can thus be reduced to that of the cognitive processes that take place there. In order to study the complexity of a specific situation, it is necessary, according to this approach, to elicit the cognitive processes that appear there and to characterize their computational complexity.   This is one of the biases of this approach: it is indeed not possible to study cognitive processes. These are part of what psychologists call 'covert behaviours', behaviours which are not directly observable. In order for the study of the cognitive complexity of situations to be viable, we must find a way to get around this methodological breach. Therefore, four forms of study — indirect ones — of cognitive processes and of their complexity have been envisioned.

The first form of study of the cognitive complexity is part of a *theoretical* approach. The models of cognitive processing are not explicitly described; they are implicit. The theoretical approach focuses on the structural aspects of situations and tasks. The complexity measured is thus that of the formal structures. We will thus study the complexity of the situation in terms of the measurement of the indeterminism, of the reactive or interruptive character and of branching factors, etc. (Javaux, 1996). Equally implicit within the theoretical approach in certain cases is the idea of 'universal' agent. It is considered that certain cognitive tasks or some information processing are difficult or heavy by nature, whatever agent carries them out. Access to specific information is for example simpler (fewer operations to carry out) if the information has been sorted beforehand (e.g. looking for a name in a phone book). This is true for whatever agent carries out the task, whether it is a machine or a human being.

The approach by *computational models* could be said to constitute a specialized form of the theoretical approach. The models of cognitive processing are explicit. They are described with enough precision to allow their implementation on the computer, and consequently the cognitive simulation of information processing in situation. The traditional models such as KLM, GOMS or CCT are part of the approach by computational models applied to the area of human–computer interaction (HCI). In the area of control of dynamic processes, we find such models as the EPIC (Kieras & Meyer, 1995), MIDAS, developed at NASA (Corker & Smith, 1993; Pisanich & Corker, 1995), Aide (Amalberti & Deblon, 1992) and Cosimo (Cacciabue et al., 1992). The approach by computational models is based in a more or less explicit fashion (depending on the models) on the experiences of cognitive psychology. Cognitive psychology itself proposes theories and models — the very essence of a science — but these are generally not formalized and implementable. They do not allow us to directly characterize the complexity of cognitive processes, even if certain notions, such as attentional load and quantitative information in work memory, are undoubtedly linked to them. We could turn to Wickens (1992) for what probably represents today's best text on cognitive psychology applied to situations of man–machine interaction. We will finish up by pointing out that the choice — or the construction

— of a specific computational model to study the complexity of a man–machine interaction situation largely depends on the specific characteristics of the situation and of the tasks. Models such as KLM, GOMS and CCT lend themselves better to static situations of human–computer interaction (HCI) than to more dynamic ones such as those to which such models as EPIC or MIDAS are applied.

The approach by *experimentation and performance measurements* constitutes a primary form of non-theoretical study of cognitive complexity. While the first two approaches are characterized more by their predictive capacities and the possibility of an intervention at the beginning of the design process, here we have a form of study which presupposes the existence of an implementation — prototypical or final — of the man–machine interaction situation to be evaluated. With the help of different experimental protocols, there is an attempt to bring to light the elements of the man–machine interaction situations that pose a problem and break down the performance of pilots. The approach is thus more descriptive than predictive and explicative. The research of Sarter & Woods (1992; 1994; 1995b) and the work carried out at MIT (Johnson & Pritchett, 1995) are especially representative of the approach by experimentation. We will also point out that this approach requires the precise definition of performance criteria, generally based on the executions of tasks, on the rate of error, on the precision of the flight or on the maintenance of situation awareness.

The operational approach *by feedback* includes accidents, incidents, problems and 'reporting systems'. It constitutes the final form of operationalization of the cognitive complexity. When we use the term final form, we mean that it is only possible at the end of the design phase, when the man–machine interaction situation exists and is introduced into a real operational context. Like the preceding approach, it reveals in a descriptive manner the points which pose problems. However, it differs from it by the nature of the performance indexes used (rate and nature of problems, incidents or accidents) and by the way in which information comes back to designers (incidents, accidents, reporting systems). It is also the most ecologically valid form of operationalization since it focuses on the exploitation system itself.

We noticed that when passing from the theoretical form to the operational form we evolve from a predictive evaluation to a descriptive evaluation of the complexity. This way we situate ourselves early on or late in the design process. The primary forms are also more integrated, bringing together numerous aspects of the man–machine interaction in a unique framework, while the latter forms describe problems in a punctual manner without necessarily being able to explain them. In practice, it is fitting to combine the different forms of approach, the theoretical forms and by models which allow a better understanding of the nature of the problems revealed by the experimental and operational approaches. Finally, we must point out that to just state the forms of study of complexity is not enough. For each one, it is fitting to define a series of observable markers. These markers directly inform us about the complexity of cognitive processes, which are in essence not observable. The performance indicators used in the framework of an experimental approach must, for example, be chosen precisely in order to give information on these points. It is not always possible — and moreover not always necessary — to obtain a measure of cognitive complexity in a metric form, like those proposed by Kieras & Polson's CCT. Other forms of operationalization of cognitive complexity also exist. Although they are less powerful, they are also more often less costly to obtain.

3   Evaluation of the Cognitive Complexity of the Computerized Modes of B737-EFIS

In order to evaluate the cognitive complexity of the computerized modes of the B737-EFIS, we used a combination of theoretical and computational approaches. We draw on the theoretical approach because a large part of the evaluation is based on the formal description of technical characteristics of computerized modes. We draw on a computational approach because minimal cognitive hypotheses were formulated, allowing us to predict how a human operator apprehends the functioning of the modes. The procedure was carried out in three phases:

3.1   Characterization of the State Transitions of the Computerized Modes

The analysis was limited to four vertical modes on the automatic pilot: ALT HOLD, ALT ACQ, LVL CHG and V/S. Since no description of these modes existed in the state, it was necessary to reconstitute them starting from the operation manual — which was sometimes missing items or was erroneous — and from interviews of instructors and pilots.

The following structure, made up of five information fields, was used for the description of the rules of mode transition. The examples concern the devVS$_2$ rule (voluntary engagement of V/S mode):

A unique identifier: It describes the type of transition (e.g. an engagement), its voluntary or autonomous character and the mode it concerns. A numerical index is added to the description if a possible confusion exists with another rule.

The identifier devVS$_2$ concerns the rule which describes a voluntary transition (v) of the V/S mode (vs.) from the disengaged state (d) to the engaged state (e). This is the second rule (2) which presents these characteristics for V/S.

A description in natural language: It describes when and how the transition is carried out.

V/S is engaged when the ALT ACQ mode is engaged and a new MCP altitude is selected by rotating the altitude selector. The amplitude of the altitude change must be greater than 100ft.

Extracts of the Operation Manual (if they are available): They confirm the description of the rule in natural language. Moreover, they help to localize the source of information, in particular when it is distributed between different sections of the Operation Manual.

V/S is (automatically) activated (engaged) by pressing the V/S mode switch or when a new altitude is selected when ALT ACQ is annunciated (07.10.02B, 5). The V/S mode automatically engages when the ALT ACQ mode is engaged and a new altitude is selected which differs by more than 100ft. from the previously selected altitude (07.20.05,1)

A Boolean description of the rule: The rule is described in the language of propositional logic. The different conditions necessary to activate the rule are determined and organized with the help of classical Boolean operators AND, OR and NOT. This is a format of representation that is very similar to the one used by Leveson & Palmer (1997) in their study of modes.

(ALT ACQ engaged) AND (MCP altitude changed) AND (amplitude of change > 100)

A procedural description of the rule: This is a very important part of the characterization. The procedural description adds the temporal dimension to the Boolean description. In order for the transition to be carried out, the conditions must be verified in a specific order, with a sequential, partial or concurrent (parallelism) order of conditions. Accounting for the temporal dimension is essential for the comprehension and prediction of certain types of errors. Figure 1 represents an example of procedural description. It concerns the $deaLC_1$, which is better known under the name of 'performance limit reversion'. It is a particularly important transition which is not always known by the pilots. It carries out an autonomous transition from the V/S mode towards the LVL CHG mode. This transition only arises in certain rare and potentially dangerous situations: the V/S mode must be engaged during the ascent (with a constant specified airspeed and ascent rate) and the real airspeed of the plane decreases at the point it reaches a value inferior by 5 kts to the target airspeed (if this mode reversion is not carried out, the speed of the plane could continue to decrease, until it reaches the minimum airspeed at which the apparatus is close to stalling). The figure describes the three conditions necessary for the transition to be carried out in a richer form than the Boolean form would make. The V/S engaged condition must, for example, be carried out first. This is the context of rule application. The two conditions on the non-increase of the airspeed and the surpassing of 5 kts in relation to the target airspeed will be carried out after this first condition, and in an order that is not specified. The order is partial: the two conditions can be carried out simultaneously (parallelism) or in sequence but according to an order which is not constrained (non-constrained sequentiality). The transition (engagement of the LVL CHG mode) is carried out when conditions are carried out in a specified order.

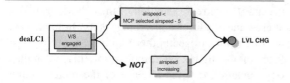

Figure 1: Performance limit reversion (autonomous substitution of the LVL CHG mode for the V/S mode).

3.2 Local Evaluation of Cognitive Complexity through a Metrical Index

Formulating a hypothesis close to that of the CCT on the limits of human work memory, we calculated an index of syntactical complexity starting from the description of transition rules.

The measurement of the syntactical complexity is an approximation of the global cost linked to the logical expression: it evaluates the quantity of cognitive resources to put in play by the average number of elementary argument evaluations to carry out in order to determine if the expression is true. The calculation of syntactical complexity is not carried out on the expression itself but on the syntactical tree which is directly derived from it, which explains the name of the measurement.

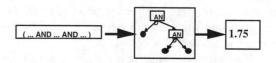

Figure 2: The Syntactical complexity (of the Boolean form) of the devVS2 rule.

According to this method, the syntactical complexity of the $devVS_2$ rule is 1.75: on average, 1.75 argument evaluations must be carried out (e.g. is the ALT ACQ engaged?) in order to determine whether the transition will be carried out or not in the current context. The complete development of the mathematical method of calculation of the syntactical complexity is presented in (De Keyser & Javaux, 1998). A software called C-Plex was developed to make possible the automatic processing of these Boolean expressions. It is capable of applying this calculation method to each of the transition rules that characterize a machine. C-Plex was thus used to calculate the syntactical complexity of the forty-four transition rules associated with the modes ALT HOLD, ALT ACQ, LVL CHG and V/S of the B737-EFIS.

3.2.1 Global Evaluation of the Cognitive Complexity of Simplification Mechanisms

The following cognitive hypotheses were formulated to predict the pilots' risk of error based on procedural descriptions of transition rules:

- A 'frequential simplification', where we will postulate that the mnemonic trace is directly linked to the frequency of rule confrontation.

- A simplification of abstraction and of generalization of rules, such as what we find in analogical reasoning.

- A mechanisms of rule linking, which will conflict with the reduced capacity of work memory.

3.2.2 *Frequential Simplification*

A first hypothesis is that one of the main factors contributing to errors and to incomplete mental models observed in the pilots is the *frequency* of exposure to the transition rules. The pilots are confronted with rules and with their conditions with diverse frequencies, both during their normal operational life as well as during the recurrent training sessions on the simulator. Certain rules are rarely activated (e.g. most rules concerning the GA mode, rarely used in normal operational conditions) while others are used during most flights (e.g. the engagement of ALT HOLD). For an interesting study on the frequency of mode use (Degani et al., 1995).

The effects of the rule frequencies and the conditional frequencies are differential. They have a different impact on the rules and their traces in memory. The main effect of the *rules frequency* is to weaken or fortify the trace of rules in long-term memory. The rules that are frequently activated have strong traces while the rules rarely used have weak traces. Rules whose traces are weak are particularly susceptible to being affected by inferential simplification, the second error mechanism. The main effect of the *conditional frequencies* is to lead to the *simplification* of rules stored in long-term memory. The rule is stored there in a simplified or prototypical form. The differences between the prototypical form and the correct representation accounts for certain alterations observed at the level of the mental models of pilots.

Our first example deals with the reversions of automatic modes. It concerns the *effects of low frequency of rules*. The reversions are autonomous transitions which are put in place by the auto-pilot in order to keep the plane out of certain risky or dangerous situations. They are related to the active protections found on most of the planes of the Airbus family.

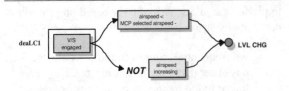

Figure 3: Performance limit reversion.

The frequency of the deaLC₁ is low. Fortunately, the 'performance limit reversions' are rare in normal operational conditions because the two internal conditions are rarely carried out together (the frequency of their conjunction is extremely low). The trace of the rule in long-term memory is thus weak,

the rule is not well known (i.e. the detail of the internal conditions cannot be recalled with exactness) and sometimes not known by certain pilots. The transition can thus be triggered in an operational situation without being detected because it was not expected (and that the p-feedback on the final state is weak). And when detection does occur, it produces an 'automation surprise' such as those described in the literature (Palmer, 1995).

The second example concerns the effects of the *conditional frequencies*. They lead to a simplification of the representation stored in long-term memory. A remarkable example of simplification concerns the voluntary engagement of the ALT HOLD to stabilize itself at the current barometric altitude. The conditions for the engagement of the ALT HOLD are simple: the G/S mode must not be engaged and the ALT HOLD button on the MCP panel must be pushed.

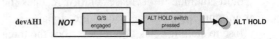

Figure 4: The complete representation of the devAH1 rule.

The frequency of the devAH₁ rule is high (the rule is activated several times during a normal flight). The frequency of the condition 'NOT (G/S engaged)' is particularly high. This condition is indeed generally true — G/S is not engaged — when the pilot tries to stabilize at the current altitude (a stabilization at the current altitude with G/S engaged can arise during the final approach in response to a request by the ATC but it is not a common event). The high frequency of the precondition relative to G/S leads to the following representation of the devAH₁ rule: the ALT HOLD button only has to be pressed down to engage the ALT HOLD mode. This simplified rule is correct as long as G/S is not engaged (which is indeed the case most of the time). The representation of the conditions is thus altered, the condition concerning G/S is eliminated and the rule is memorized in the simplified or prototypical form of the figure. The effects of this incomplete representation (i.e. the absence of the representation of the condition concerning G/S) is observed when the pilots seek to use the rule while G/S is indeed engaged: we see them press the ALT HOLD button repeatedly and without success. The transition is not carried out.

Figure 5: The prototypical or simplified representation of the devAH1 rule.

3.2.3 Simplification by Abstraction and Generalization

A second simplification mechanism is equally responsible for the gaps observed at the level of the mental models. It derives from the capacity of the human cognitive system to abstract patterns through a mechanism of abstraction and generalization. As we have seen, the pilot is confronted with a vast set of transition rules that he must store in long-term memory. The number of rules is high: forty-four rules for the four modes studied. Since the B737-EFIS presents numerous modes, we can estimate that it is necessary to integrate between one hundred and two hundred rules in order to master the set of modes on this machine. The function of the inferential mechanism or the abstraction mechanism is to seek out regularities that exist at the level of the rules. We can interpret it, within the classic symbolic framework, like an improvement of the storage of rules that minimizes the mnemonic load. The inferential mechanism thus seems to reduce the cognitive complexity of the material to be memorized: the rules that share characteristics or conditions with rules already stored in long-term memory appear to be easier to learn. But other interpretations are possible, because we can also model these abstraction and generalization mechanisms in a connectionist form; this was carried out by our team in the framework of analogical reasoning (French, 1995). But we will not differ here with the underlying cognitive model. Whatever its origin, the mechanism is not without inconvenience: the rules which do not conform to the general scheme are learned with more difficulty and are expressed in a simplified or distorted form, derived from structures which are already abstract (over-generalization of abstract rules). We will see an example of this.

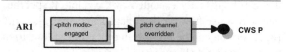

Figure 6: AR1: the abstract rule for pitch override.

Several abstract rules can be inferred on the transition rules of the Boeing 737-EFIS. The AR_1 rule is one of them. This voluntary abstract transition specifies that any pitch mode can be disengaged if enough force is exerted on the handle (in the vertical plane). The current pitch mode is then replaced by the neutral mode CWS P. AR_1 is indeed an abstraction of the individual rules $edvAH_3$, $edvAA_3$, $edvLC_3$ and $edvVS3$ which correspond to the disengagement by pitch override of the ALT HOLD, ALT ACQ, LVL CHG

and V/S modes. The benefit of an abstract rule is obvious: the engagement of CWS P can be carried out by the same action, whatever prior pitch mode had been engaged. The advantage in terms of storage is equally clear: one single rule (abstract) is enough whereas four were necessary without the inferential mechanism.

Abstract rules exist equally for the autonomous transitions. One example concerns the capacity of the G/S mode to disengage the pitch modes. Thus, in the abstract rule AR_2, G/S will engage as soon as the conditions necessary for its engagement are realized, whatever the pitch mode engaged prior to it. But although this is very useful, the abstraction mechanism can be misleading and contribute to the introduction of errors into the mental models and the production of errors. The following example clearly demonstrates this. It concerns the ending of vertical modes by the autonomous engagement of ALT ACQ. The abstract rule AR_3 specifies that the vertical modes can be disengaged and replaced by ALT ACQ when the ALT ACQ condition (which is not described in the Operation Manual) is realized. As for the AR_2 rule and the G/S mode, the nature of the prior pitch mode engaged has no impact on the realization of the transition.

Figure 7: The abstract rule for the engagement of ALT ACQ.

The difficulties appear here because the AR_3 rule is in fact only partially correct. Contrary to the AR_1 and AR_2 rules, AR_3 is only true for the subset of pitch modes: LVL CHG, V/S and TO. The substitution of the <pitch mode> variable by any of these modes in AR_3 will indeed produce a rule that belongs to the set of transition rules of the B737-EFIS. The problems — and the errors — appear when the pilots erroneously apply AR_3 to the GA mode and obtain the form described in Figure 7. The explanation of this over-generalization of the AR_3 rule is found in the similarities that exist between GA and the modes to which AR_3 really does apply: GA is a pitch mode, it is very similar to the TO mode (from the point of view of its external behaviours) and it can indeed end by a transition towards ALT ACQ.

3.2.4 The Generation of the Action Plan and Rule Linking

The third mechanism produces no simplifications of the representation of rules. It concerns the mechanism of generation by which a plan of action is produced by the pilot, either to set off a voluntary transition or to monitor the execution of an autonomous transition. In order to better understand this mechanism, let us consider the following situation (rather frequent).

The apparatus is stabilized (with ALT HOLD engaged) at the altitude (selected on the MCP) of 6000ft. when it receives a request from the ATC enjoining it to descend to 4000ft.

Figure 8 describes the cognitive processes which make it possible to respond to this request. The first stage consists of determining what transition rule must be applied. This is the *rule selection*. In the specific context of this example, it was decided to use LVL CHG mode and the devLC$_1$ voluntary transition which substitutes this mode for ALT HOLD (Figure 8). The second step consists of producing an instantiation of the devLC$_1$ rule in the current context. This is the *contextual instantiation* of the rule. Here, the context, called Ca, is made up of two clauses, both of which are true, that can be inferred from the description of the situation provided above: 'ALT HOLD engaged' and 'current altitude= MCP selected altitude'. In order to produce a contextual instance of devLC$_1$, all conditions that are already true in the Ca context are eliminated. Only 'ALT HOLD engaged' responds to this criteria: it is at once part of the Ca context and the devLC1 conditions. By eliminating it from devLC$_1$, one gets the contextual instance devLC$_1$ (Ca). It only contains false conditions (Figure 8). The third and last step — the *generation of the plan of action* — aims to define which actions can be placed in order to carry out these remaining conditions (i.e. make them true) and thus carry out the transition. They involve the consideration of the dependent or independent character of the conditions. Some can be carried out without any direct action from the pilot. Others can only be carried out in an autonomous manner, and the action of the pilot will consist, in this case, of monitoring their evolution, an operation either facilitated or not facilitated by their associated p-feedback and n-feedback values. In the devLC$_1$ instance (Ca) of Figure 8, the two remaining conditions are dependent on the pilot. Two specific actions correspond to them: changing the target altitude on the MCP panel and pushing the LVL CHG button. These two actions define the *plan of action* that must be executed in order to engage the LVL CHG mode in the current context. It corresponds exactly to the action sequence that the pilots execute when they respond to a request of this type.

We have seen that the mechanism of generation of the plan of action was dissociated into three relatively

simple application steps. However, there are cases in which the cognitive complexity of these operations is greatly increased. They arise in contexts in which the conditions present in the contextual instance of the rule are not terminal conditions. We will see an example of this with the devAH1 rule already mentioned several times. Let us consider the following context:

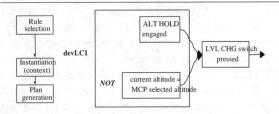

Figure 8: The mechanism of generation of a plan of action.

The plane has established itself on the glide-slope. The G/S mode is engaged. The ATC requires maintenance at the current barometric altitude (level-off).

This corresponds to a classic example from Sarter & Woods (1992). Figure 8 describes the process of generation of the plan of action. The rule to apply here is the devAH$_1$ rule. Let us recall that this rule is already weakened by the frequential simplification mechanism, which tends to produce a simplified version of it. The current context, called Cb, contains a single true clause — 'G/S engaged'— that can be inferred from the description of the situation. The contextual instantiation devAH$_1$ (Cb) — not represented in figure — is in fact identical to the devAH$_1$ rule. Indeed, none of the conditions of devAH$_1$ belongs to the Cb context and consequently, conditions are not eliminated during the process of contextual instantiation. Like in the preceding example, the two remaining conditions are dependent on the pilot: the plan of action contains only actions that can be directly executed by the pilot. It specifies that G/S must first be disengaged and then the ALT HOLD button can be pressed in order for the transition to be carried out (Figure 9).

The problems characteristic of the plan generation appear here: the action that aims to disengage G/S is not *terminal*. This action is itself a mode transition! Consequently, it involves the application of a second transition rule and the satisfaction of a series of other conditions (Figure 9). In the Cb context, the plan of action to engage ALT HOLD presents two hierarchical levels and it involves the manipulation of two transition rules. We are talking about *rule linking*. The cognitive complexity of plan generation is increased since it is necessary to coordinate (link) the execution of two rules and maintain a higher quantity of information in working memory (i.e. pushing on ALT HOLD after the disengagement of G/S). The rule linking involved in this particular context, and the weakening of the representation of the rule by the mechanism of frequential simplification explains why a great number of pilots experience difficulties and show the incomplete knowledge on the devAH$_1$ rule, just as Sarter & Woods had pointed out in 1992.

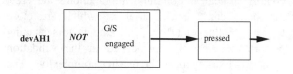

Figure 9: The mechanism of action plan generation in the case of rule linking.

This particularly demonstrative example shows all the importance of the context in which the rules are instantiated. The linking of rules only shows up in certain contexts, those that produce contextual instances containing non-terminal conditions. Here is an area of study particularly interesting for the designer, the certifier and the trainer. It consists of systematically exploring the set (finite) of the contexts of a rule in order to determine if there are any situations in which the rule linking mechanism is invoked and the cognitive complexity increased.

4 Discussion

The procedure proposed presents certain characteristics — and at least until now, certain limits — which must be discussed.

First, it is based on a strong postulate, that which psychologists or ergonomists must penetrate at the very heart of technique if they want to be credible or just simply useful to the world of work. To penetrate into the heart of the technique is to first train in an intensive manner, as our researcher Javaux did in the present case in relation to aeronautics, or already in our department, Nyssen (1997) did in relation to very similar works on human error prevention in anaesthesia. These researchers are a little bit like homologues of Sarter in aeronautics, or Cook in anaesthesia, at the Woods Laboratory in Columbus, Ohio. This intense training will not transform the researcher into an expert in the field, but it is a necessary condition for a strict inter-disciplinarity which alone can guarantee the efficiency and the relevance of the results. The second postulate on which we rely is inscribed on the heels of Hollnagel's (1998) manifesto for a cognitive model, but a minimal

and contextual one. That is, one which accounts for the way in which the individual re-appropriates and reconstructs the surrounding environment for himself, for the mechanisms brought into play, for certain well-known cognitive limits — but without going further in the exploration of the cognitive model. Some may hold this against us. This is why we have never made any formal statement on the mode of acquisition and the cognitive modelling subtending the learning of rules. It is clear that different symbolic and connectionist models, or those that call on genetic algorithms, could answer for this; work in this area is presently being carried out in our laboratory, but it will not, for the moment, bring anything new to the debate. On the contrary, it seems to slow down the advancement of a research project focused on concrete results, research which is of burning relevance today and which brings up serious safety problems. However, as such, the research is still incomplete and must be carried out on different fronts.

4.1 Design and Certification

The interest of Airbus, Sabena, NASA and Honeywell in the finished work completely justifies the efforts put forth. Indeed, a collaboration was started in 1998 with Honeywell in Phoenix, Arizona, and they have shown a deep interest in the frequential and abstraction/generalization simplification mechanisms. Honeywell is the major manufacturer of autopilots in the world (70% of recent commercial airliners are equipped with Honeywell airpilots). Honeywell will provide us the detailed specification of the autopilot of the McDonnell Douglas MD-11, and the simplification mechanisms will be applied to predict the knowledge possessed by the pilots and the errors they are likely to produce. A collaboration has also been started with the NASA Ames Research Center in Mountain View, California: again the simplification mechanisms will be exploited. As for Airbus and Aerospatiale, the research project will be extended in a contractual form very shortly, with the objective of evaluating the A340-200/30 autopilot, and to apply the concepts of the procedure to a very early stage of the design of the new A340-50/600.

4.2 Generalization

The study was performed on the B737-EFIS, and it shows, as already demonstrated by Sarter & Woods (1992), that this aircraft presents some examples of the difficulties of pilot-automation interactions. This is not limited to this aircraft nor to this manufacturer. Similar results would be found on commercial aircraft made by other manufacturers (e.g. Airbus and McDonnell Douglas). Sarter & Woods (1995b) report, for example, similar automation problems on the A320 Airbus. In the very near future, we intend to carry out a more intense study with Airbus Industry on the cognitive complexity of the mode transitions in their future aircrafts. Up to now, we have only analysed four modes of the B737-EFIS: a possible expansion of the study would be to extend the Boolean and procedural descriptions to the other modes.

4.3   Validation

A set of experiments has already been carried out at Sabena in order to validate the methodology. Subjective complexity assessed by pilots was compared to a metrical measurement of the syntactical complexity (local measurement) for voluntary and autonomous transitions of modes. The results found were expected, that is, the autonomous transitions are systematically considered as more complex than the voluntary transitions.

Figures 10a & b present the results obtained on the B737-EFIS for these four modes. Figure 10a describes the syntactical complexity for the individual rules, and Figure 10b, grouped by modes. Three specific rules get a high score. They correspond to the voluntary transitions for engaging ALT HOLD, LVL CHG and V/S, with complex conditions and actions to verify in case of prior engagement of the APP mode. These three measurements agree with the results obtained by Sarter & Woods in 1992 on the disengagement of the APP mode. The explanation of the greatest complexity of these three transitions holds for the mechanism of rule linking which have been described above. Research is being pursued regarding the prediction of errors stemming from simplification and rule-linking mechanisms described in the method. Indeed, the theoretical results obtained with the aid of this methodology have until now been supported by three sources: the data in the literature on the difficulties and incidents encountered by pilots, and in particular those described by Sarter & Woods (1992; 1994); the interviews with the Sabena instructors on the difficulties encountered by their novices; our own observations on the Sabena simulator during training sessions. However, these results are not sufficient and must be backed up by a more rigorous experimental plan. Negotiations are underway and it is mainly economic considerations connected to the use of a costly simulator for strictly experimental ends that has until now slowed down its realization.

4.4   Extension of the Notion of Context

Up until now, we have limited the notion of objective context to the description of certain computerized modes and to particular situations in which these modes could appear. This is a purposely reductionist vision of the context, but which can be explained by a concern about operation. It was necessary to deal with variables at the very heart of the technical design of apparatuses, knowing that as the design progresses, and as soon as the aircraft is put into circulation, other elements of complexity intervene which will influence performance: pilots' expertise and meta-knowledge, unexpected flight circumstances, pilots' control strategies, communication among the crew members, etc. Such variables, which are close to what Hollnagel (1998) calls the factors shaping performance, can be introduced in the validation scenarios like layers of increasing complexity. The objective is to end up, through the design, avoiding certain black spots of reliability (that is to say, certain rule modalities of high cognitive complexity) or to temper them through interfaces which make them intelligible and salient. The ambitious hypothesis is that the design will then be more robust compared to other sources of complexity which may be added. The joining of these levels of complexity to test the robustness and the design would make it possible to slowly move towards the analysis of pilots' activities in real work situations. It thus wraps up the initial project of the research: to conjugate a top-down type research to the traditional bottom-up approach of francophone work psychology and ergonomics.

4.5   Training

The analysis of the instruction manual for the Boeing 737-EFIS showed that it was incomplete and sometimes erroneous in the explanation of modes. Although the ultimate objective of the work is directed towards the design of modes and interfaces, it is clear that at the present time, and for the airplanes already constructed, it is the role of training to palliate these 'latent failures'. Instructors have an intuitive knowledge of the difficulties that pilots can encounter, but the research makes this clearer to them and for this reason could be an excellent training aid. Extensions in this direction have been planned for the future.

Acknowledgement

To carry this research I benefited from specific circumstances. First, from a solid research team within the University of Liege and specially from one researcher, D. Javaux, who was not only excellent, but also very enthusiastic about this area. But I also benefited from scientific subsidies which allowed a research groove to be slowly carved over time. My gratitude goes out to la Politique Scientifique Belge, which supported studies within the framework of its

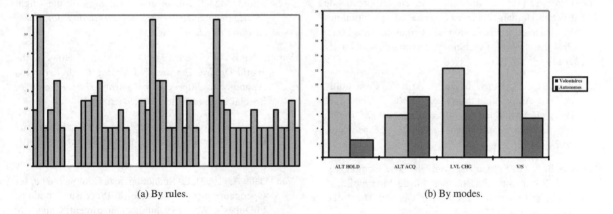

(a) By rules.   (b) By modes.

Figure 10: Syntactical complexity.

PAI program, to la Direction Generale de l'Aviation Civile of France which did the same, and to the Industrie Airbus and to Sabena for their constant confidence and cooperation.

References

Amalberti, R. (1996), *La Conduite des Systèmes à Risques. Le Travail Humain*, Presses Universitaires de France.

Amalberti, R. & Deblon, F. (1992), "Cognitive Modelling of Fighter Aircraft Process Control: A Step Towards an Intelligent Onboard Assistance System", *International Journal of Man–Machine Studies* **36**(5), 639–773.

Bainbridge, L. (1987), Ironies of Automation, *in* J. Rasmussen, K. Duncan & J. Leplat (eds.), *New Technology and Human Error*, John Wiley & Sons, pp.271–84.

Billings, C. E. (1997), *Aviation Automation. The Search for a Human-centered Approach*, Lawrence Erlbaum Associates.

Cacciabue, P. C., Decortis, F., Drozdowicz, B., Masson, M. & Nordvik, J. P. (1992), "COSIMO: A Cognitive Simulation Model of Human Decision Making and Behaviour in Complex Work Environments", *IEEE Transactions in Systems, Man and Cybernetics* **22**(5), 1–17.

Corker, K. M. & Smith, B. (1993), An Architecture and Model for Cognitive Engineering Simulation Analysis: Application to Advanced Aviation Analysis, *in Proceedings of AIAA Conference on Computing in Aerospace*.

De Keyser, V. & Javaux, D. (1998), Convention SFACT — Prédictibilité des États du Système et Conscience de la Situation pour les Équipages Glass-cockpit,

Technical Report final, Ministère de l'Equipement, des Transports et du Tourisme Français.

Degani, A., Shafto, M. & Kirlik, A. (1995), Mode Usage in Automated Cockpits: Some Initial Observations, *in* T. B. Sheridan (ed.), *Proceedings of the International Federation of Automatic Control; Man-Machine Systems (IFAC-MMS) Conference*.

French, B. (1995), *The Subtlety of Sameness. A Theory and Computer Model of Analogy-making*, MIT Press.

Gras, A., Moricot, C., Poirot-Delpech, S. & Scardigli, V. (1994), *Face à l'Automate*, Publications de la Sorbonne.

Hollnagel, E. (1998), *Cognitive Reliability and Error Analysis Method*, Elsevier Science.

Javaux, D. (1996), La Formalisation des Tâches. Temporelle, *in* J.-M. Cellier, V. De Keyser & C. Valot (eds.), *Gestion du Temps dans les Environnements Dynamiques*, Presses Universitaires de France, pp.122–58.

Johnson, E. N. & Pritchett, A. R. (1995), Experimental Study of Vertical Flight Path Mode Awareness, Technical Report ASL-93-3, Department of Aeronautics and Astronautics, MIT.

Kieras, D. E. & Meyer, D. E. (1995), An Overview of the EPIC Architecture for Cognition and Performance with Application to Human–Computer Interaction, Technical Report TR 95/ONR - EPIC-5, University of Michigan.

Leveson, N. G. & Palmer, E. A. (1997), Designing Automation to Reduce Operator Errors, *in Proceedings of IEEE International Conference on Systems, Man, and Cybernetics*.

Nyssen, A. S. (1997), Vers une Nouvelle Approche de l'Erreur Humaine dans les Systèmes, Exploration des Mécanismes de Production de l'Erreur en Anesthésie, PhD thesis, Work Psychology Department, University of Liège.

Palmer, E. (1995), Oops, It Didn't Arm. A Case Study of Two Automation Surprises, *in* R. S. Jensen & L. A. Rakovan (eds.), *Proceedings of the Eighth International Symposium on Aviation Psychology*, pp.24–7.

Pedersen, S. A. (1990), Coping with Objective Complexity, *in* J. Rasmussen, B. Brehmer, M. de Montmollin & J. Leplat (eds.), *Proceedings of the first MOHAWC workshop*, Risoe National Laboratory.

Pisanich, G. M. & Corker, K. M. (1995), Predictive Model of Flight Crew Performance Automated Air Traffic Control and Flight Management Operations, *in* R. S. Jensen & L. A. Rakovan (eds.), *Proceedings of the 8th International Symposium on Aviation Psychology*.

Sarter, N. & Woods, D. D. (1992), "Pilot Interaction with Cockpit Automation. I. Operational Experiences with the Flight Management System", *International Journal of Aviation Psychology* **2**, 303–21.

Sarter, N. & Woods, D. D. (1994), "Pilot Interaction with Cockpit Automation. II. An Experimental of Pilot's Mental Model and Awareness of the Flight Management System (FMS)", *International Journal of Aviation Psychology* **4**(1), 1–28.

Sarter, N. B. & Woods, D. D. (1995a), ""How in the World Did We Get into that Mode? Mode Error and Awareness in Supervisory Control", *Human Factors* . Special Issue on Situation Awareness.

Sarter, N. B. & Woods, D. D. (1995b), Strong, Silent, and Out-of-the-Loop, Technical Report Report 95-TR-01, CSEL.

Van Daele, A. (1993), La Réduction de la Complexité par les Opérateurs dans le Contrôle de Processus Continus, PhD thesis, Work Psychology Department, University of Liège.

Wickens, C. D. (1992), *Engineering Psychology and Human Performance*, Harper Collins.

Wiener, E. L. (1985), Human Factors of Cockpit Automation: A Field Study of Flight Crew Transition, Technical Report 177333, NASA-Ames Research Center.

Woods, D. D. (1988), Coping with Complexity: the Human Behavior in Complex Systems, *in* L. P. Goodstein, H. B. Andersen & S. E. Olsen (eds.), *Tasks, Errors and Mental Models*, Taylor & Francis.

Part Two

Technical Sessions

Human–Computer Interaction — INTERACT '99
M. Angela Sasse and Chris Johnson (Editors)
Published by IOS Press, © IFIP TC.13, 1999

Comparative Study of Analytical Product Selection Support Mechanisms

Markus Stolze

IBM Research Division, Zurich Research Laboratory, Saumerstrasse 4,
CH-8803 Ruschlikon, Switzerland.

mrs@zurich.ibm.com

Abstract: Electronic commerce and the buying of goods electronically on the Internet is gaining momentum. An important step when buying products online is the selection process. A wide variety of mechanisms supporting this step can be found in commercial online catalogues and research prototypes. However, it is often difficult to assess how users will use these selection support mechanisms. In this paper we want to contribute to a better understanding of mechanisms that support analytical product selection: filtering, visualization, and evaluation. We will report results of a study in which the usage of three catalogues that employ different combinations of these selection support mechanisms is compared.

Keywords: empirical study (qualitative), evaluation, Internet, intelligent system, comparison shopping.

1 Introduction

The number of Internet users and the volume of online business is growing rapidly. An important step when buying products online is the selection of products from a catalogue (Schmid, 1997; Maes et al., 1999). A wide variety of mechanisms to support this step are currently used in commercial electronic catalogues and research prototypes. This creates a challenge to designers of electronic catalogues to understand which selection support mechanisms to use for specific electronic catalogues and to anticipate how these mechanisms will be used by customers.

In this paper we want to contribute to a better understanding of support mechanisms for product selection and how these mechanisms are used. We propose a classification of selection support mechanisms, and we present the results of a study in which the usage of three catalogues that employ different combinations of analytical selection support mechanisms is compared.

2 Product Selection Support

Product selection support mechanisms can be classified into three top-level categories (Figure 1): Information collection mechanisms, analytical product selection support mechanisms, and support mechanisms for emotional selection and networking.

Information collection mechanisms deal with the problem of collecting, normalizing, and pre-filtering product information that might reside in various distributed databases. Mechanisms in this class (Genesereth et al., 1997) are an important ingredient for electronic catalogues, but will not be discussed further in this paper. The paper also omits mechanisms geared towards supporting *emotional and networking-based product selection* (Steiger et al., 1999) and instead investigates in detail support mechanisms for analytical product selection.

Analytical product selection support mechanisms support buyers in making buying decisions in an analytical way. These mechanisms can be divided into three subtypes: filtering mechanisms, visualization mechanisms, and evaluation mechanisms. Systems supporting product selection will usually offer users one or more product selection mechanisms. *Filtering* mechanisms let users express constraints to determine whether a product (or a group of products) is of interest to the user. Depending on the concrete mechanisms used, only products of interest are shown, or different markings are used to distinguish them from products not within the established constraints. A typical example of a filtering mechanism is the retrieval mechanism used in the VISA online catalogue (http://shopguide.yahoo.com/shopguide/). For example, when looking for a new computer, users can specify such constraints as minimal speed, memory, and disk size. Based on these constraints the VISA catalogue searches its database and returns the matching computers.

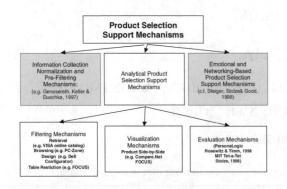

Figure 1: Classification of product selection support mechanisms.

Other popular support mechanisms for product selection can also be classified as filtering mechanisms (Stolze, 1998). These include hierarchical browsing (used in virtually all online shops, see e.g. PC-Zone, http://www.pc-zone.com), interactive configuration (for example, DELL online shop, http://commerce.us.dell.com/), and includes product table restriction as used by the IBM advanced catalogue tool (http://www.software.ibm.com/commerce/net.comerce/cattools.html), and the GMD Focus tool (Spenke et al., 1996).

A second class of analytic selection support mechanisms is *product information visualization*. The most popular visualization mechanism is to present products in side-by-side comparison tables. This is done, for example, by the comparison tool of Compare. Net (www.compare.net). The above-mentioned IBM advanced catalogue tool and GMD Focus also support this kind of visualization.

A number of research systems have explored how to combine filtering and visualization mechanisms. The Dynamic HomeFinder (Williamson & Shneiderman, 1992) lets users construct filtering queries interactively using sliders for feature value restriction. The filtered set of remaining homes is visualized interactively on a map that updates while the user is moving the sliders. The Attribute Explorer (Tweedie et al., 1996) uses Parallel Coordinates to display product features and their values. Each product is represented as a dot on each of the feature coordinates. Users can enter filtering constraints by selecting values on the coordinates. Products fulfilling

all constraints are highlighted. The Influence Explorer (Tweedie et al., 1996) extends this work for the domain of engineering design. It not only shows the products that fulfill all constraints, it also uses colour coding to indicate how many constraints a product fulfils. In the context of this paper we will not investigate these more advanced visualization techniques, and focus on product side-by-side tables as the current state-of-the-practice mechanism for product visualization.

The third class of analytical selection support mechanisms is *evaluation mechanisms*. Typically these mechanisms use an additive value function to compute a numerical measure of utility for each product and rank products according to this measure (Stolze, 1998; Clemen, 1996). Evaluation mechanisms have been explored in the context of engi-neering design (Bradley, 1994; Sykes & White, 1991), but only recently have such mechanisms been used in the context of electronic consumer catalogues. A commercial tool that employs numerical evaluation is the cataloguing tool of PersonaLogic (http://www.personalogic.com/home/demo/demo.stm). This CGI-based cataloguing tool engages users in a dialogue to elicit preferences and requirements. The cataloguing tool uses the elicited data to compile an ordered list of matching products, with the best match first. PersonaLogic tools have been created for various domains including cars, computers and camcorders. A similar cataloguing tool for which the details of the evaluation mechanisms are known is the Sales Assistant for TV selection developed by Rosewitz, M. (1998) at FORWIS. Their tool uses fuzzy functions for computing the product evaluations. A third evaluation catalogue was developed at the MIT Media Lab as part of the Tete-a-Tete project (Maes et al., 1999), http://ecommerce.media.mit.edu/tete-a-tete/.

The problem with the three above-mentioned evaluation catalogues is that they do not provide users with a sensitivity analysis to ensure that the top-ranked product is really the one that best matches their needs. An alternative Java-based cataloguing tool that offers improved support for sensitivity analysis was proposed recently (Stolze, 1998).

3   Study of Analytical Product Selection Support

The goal of our study is to contribute to a better understanding of three mechanisms that support analytical product selection: filtering mechanisms, visualization mechanisms, and evaluation mechanisms. Our general hypothesis was that evaluation mechanisms can contribute to better consumer selection support. In particular we wanted to investigate the following questions:

Q1: Quality of selection: Decision theory (Payene et al., 1993) predicts that evaluation is a more reliable analytical selection support mechanism than filtering. In particular, Steiger & Stolze (1997) observed in their study of users of a filtering catalogue that suboptimal performance can be caused by premature commitment to constraints of low importance. Can we reproduce these findings and do we find objective (Q1a) and subjective (Q1b) improvements of selection quality if evaluation mechanisms are used in addition to filtering and visualization mechanisms?

Q2: Effect of preference pre-setting: Evaluation mechanisms can be primed by pre-setting preference rules. Does this pre-setting influence the selection process and the final selection?

Q3: Time on task: Decision theory predicts that evaluation requires four times more effort than attribute-based filtering (Payene et al., 1993). Can we find experimental support of this?

Q4: Naturalness of evaluation: Does the numerical evaluation of products match users' thinking about product selection?

Q5: Catalogue usability: How usable are the three catalogues that provide different combinations of filtering, visualization, and evaluation mechanisms?

3.1 Test Elements

In our study, a total of 16 test persons were given the task of selecting a notebook computer from a set of 23 anonymized notebook computers. Depending on the test conditions, they had to use one or more of the following three electronic cataloguing tools: a Product Scoring Catalogue ('EvalCat') including a visualization window ('EvalVis'), a Product Selection Catalogue ('FilterCat'), and GMD FOCUS ('FilterVis').

EvalCat (Figure 2) uses filtering, side-by-side product visualization, and evaluation mechanisms. The product table on the left shows the list of anonymized notebook computers currently sorted by the highlighted 'Pts/$' column. The 'Point Sum' and the 'Pts/$' column show values as numbers and as bars. EvalCat does not remove excluded products, but the bars of the 'Point Sum' and 'Pts/$' ofrejected products are drawn in magenta instead of red, and the

rejected products are sorted to the bottom of the table. The rightmost column in the table lists all the values of the attributes selected in the attribute table on the right.

The attribute table has a row for each attribute and displays the attribute values for the product selected in the left product table (UUUUU in this case). Attribute values are listed in the second column and their evaluation in the third column. The evaluation of each attribute A of product X is determined by applying the respective attribute preference rule (see below) to the attribute value of X. A more detailed explanation of the evaluation scheme is described by Stolze (1998).

The fourth column allows users to set the importance of attributes. The rightmost column shows the points that the selected notebook computer receives for each of the attributes. The points are computed by multiplying the attribute evaluation and the attribute importance. The sum of all points is the 'Point Sum' value displayed in the left-hand table. The lower right part of the window always displays an editor for the preference rule of the currently selected attribute (Calculation Performance in this case). Various editors are available for continuous and discrete attributes. Rule editors support the specification of preferences (i.e. the setting of attribute value utilities). They also support the specification of filtering constraints (i.e. the rejection of specific values or value ranges). Users can change the column that sorts the left-hand product table by clicking on the column header. They can also change the importance of attributes by manipulating the slider in the right-hand attributes table, and can edit the attribute preference rule in the rule-editor at the lower right.

The Product Scoring Catalogue tool also includes a 'side-by-side' view window — 'EvalVis', see Figure 3. This window lists all the products that are checked in the first column of the product table. All attribute values are displayed for each product, with attribute evaluations shown as underlying bars.

The second cataloguing tool used in our study was FilterCat (Figure 4). *FilterCat* is a stripped-down version of EvalCat that uses only filtering and does not include visualization and evaluation mechanisms. As in EvalCat the left-hand product table lists all products and their prices. The third and rightmost column lists for each product the values of the attribute selected in the right-hand attribute table. The other columns, which are only relevant to product evaluation, are omitted. Excluded products are indicated by magenta colouring. The attribute table on the right in Figure 4 lists all the attributes and displays their values of the

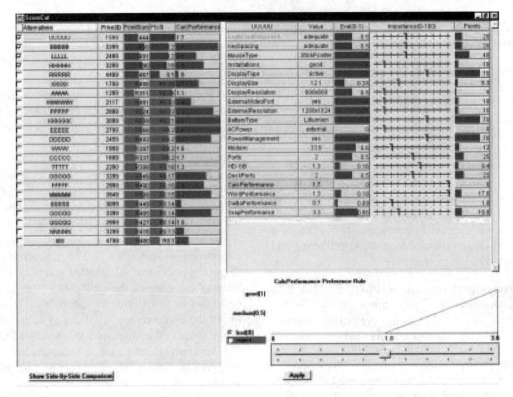

Figure 2: Screen shot of EvalCat from one of the tests performed under condition B (see text for details).

product that was selected in the product table on the left. At the lower right, users can edit the preference rule for the selected attribute. The editor allows only the specification of constraints. Users can only define which attribute values they are willing to accept, and which values they reject.

![The side-by-side comparison window of EvalVis.]

Figure 3: The side-by-side comparison window of EvalVis.

The third tool we used in our study, 'FilterVis', was the FOCUS cataloguing tool developed at the GMD FIT institute (Spenke et al., 1996). FilterVis uses product filtering and visualization mechanisms

(Figure 5). FilterVis lists products and their attributes in a table that is made to fit a full page. Users set requirements for attributes by selecting attribute values and pushing the 'set' or the 'exclude' buttons at the top of the window to exclude the products that do (or do not) have the selected attribute values. Table 1 summarizes the cataloguing tools used in our study and the selection support mechanisms they employ.

	Filtering	Side-by-side Visualization	Evaluation
FilterCat	+		
FilteVis	+	+	
EvalCat	+		+
EvalVis		+	

Table 1: Tested cataloguing tools and their selection support mechanisms.

In our study each of the 16 test persons had to work under one of the following four conditions (Table 2) to allow the investigation of questions Q1 to Q5 described above.

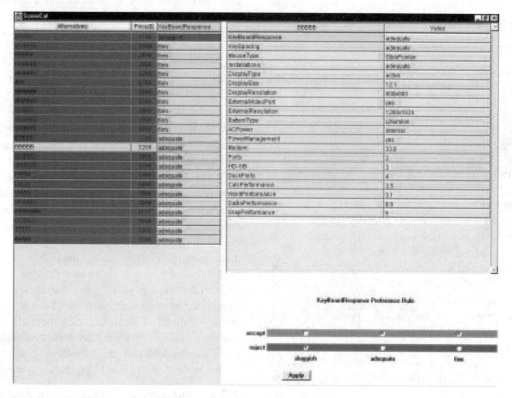

Figure 4: Screen shot of FilterCat (see text for details).

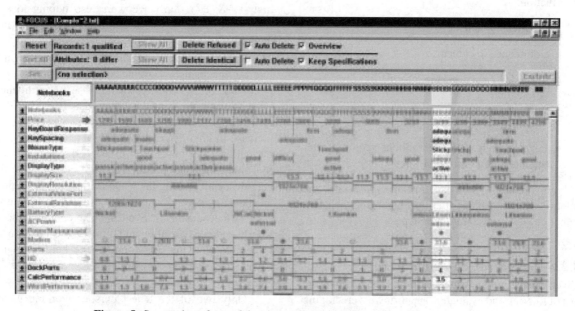

Figure 5: Screen shot of one of the views offered by FilterVis (see text for details).

	FilterCat	FilterVis	EvalCat pre-set	EvalCat not set	EvalVis
E+	Step 1	Step 2	Step 3		Step 4
E-	Step 1	Step 2		Step 3	Step 4
F+		Step 2a	Step 1		Step 2b
F-		Step 2a		Step 1	Step 2b

Table 2: Summary of test conditions.

Test persons working under *condition F-* first had to use FilterCat to make a choice, then FilterVis to validate their choice, and then EvalCat with preset preference rules and attribute importance as another way to validate their choice. Finally, in the fourth step they had to use the EvalCat Product Side-by-Side window for a final validation of their choice.

Condition F+ involved the same steps as condition F-, but the attribute preference rules and the attribute importance were not preset in EvalCat.

Test persons working under *condition E-* first had to use EvalCat with preset preference rules and attribute importance and without the EvalVis Window to make a choice. They then had to use one of the visualization tools (FilterVis or EvalVis) to validate their choice.

Condition E+ involved the same steps as condition E-, but the attribute preference rules and the attribute importance were not preset in EvalCat.

For all test steps we recorded the following information:

- Product selected.

- Confidence in choice.

- Surprised reaction to information not seen before.

- Time needed to make the selection.

- Level of help and interventions required after the initial demonstration.

In addition, we had test persons rate the importance of attributes after they had made their first selection (i.e. worked through Step 1).

3.2 Results
3.2.1 Quality of Selection (Q1a)
Given our interest in finding differences between the use of filtering and evaluation support, we were hoping to see differences among the selections made after the first step by members of the groups using FilterCat first (F- & F+) and the groups using EvalCat first (E- & E+). We were also hoping to see people in groups

F- and F+ revise their initial selection when using the visualization and evaluation support.

In the study, most test persons chose computer 'P' after the first step (10 of 16). It is interesting to note that almost all of the test persons who first used a version of EvalCat under conditions E- and E+ (7 of 8) selected 'P', and that only 3 of the 8 test persons who used FilterCat in the first step in conditions F- and F+ selected 'P'. In fact, all four test persons working under condition E+ with EvalCat with preset preference values selected 'P'.

Although this result might be interpreted such that the use of evaluation mechanisms led to better selections, this cannot be proved from the data. Only one of the test persons using FilterCat in the first step initially selected a product different from 'P' but then, using FilterEval, settled on P. For the five test persons who selected a product different from 'P' and did not change their mind, the choice could be considered as consistent with the data they specified on the independent attribute rating sheet after the first test step. However, their selection behaviour would also be consistent with the hypothesis that they were misled in their choice due to premature commitment.

3.2.2 Subjective Confidence in Selection (Q1b)
As in Q1a we were hoping to find differences in confidence after the first step between the groups using FilterCat first (F- & F+) and the groups using EvalCat first (E- & E+) step. We were also hoping to see confidence increase for these groups when working with more than one tool.

Half of the test persons who first used a pure filtering mechanism working under condition F- and F+ (4 out of 8) reported an increase in confidence after using the additional product visualization of the FilterVis tool. All four persons also reported an increase in confidence after using additional product evaluation mechanisms (EvalCat). Of the remaining four persons, one person reported no increase in confidence after using the visualization, but did report an increase in confidence after using the evaluation support mechanisms in EvalCat. The combination of side-by-side visualization and numerical evaluation as offered by EvalVis was found to be helpful by all except one test person working under conditions F- and F+.

Only two of the 8 test persons working under condition E- and E+, who first used the combined filtering and evaluation support mechanisms offered by EvalCat, reported an increase in confidence after using additional product side-by-side visualization.

3.2.3 Effect of Preference Pre-setting (Q2)

To investigate this question we split the group using EvalCat first (group F) and the group using FilterCat first (group F) into two each, where half of each group always worked with the evaluation setting preset and the other half without preset evaluation settings. This was the reason why we ended up having the four groups (F+, F-, E+, and E-).

In our study we did not observe that pre-setting preferences had a significant influence on the final product selection, the confidence in the selection, or the time required to perform the task. However, test persons working under condition E- who used the combined filtering and evaluation mechanisms without pre-setting required the most help in using the tool to perform filtering and preference setting actions. It can be assumed that without the direct help and intervention of the experimenter, the selection process would have taken considerably longer, or would have been aborted altogether.

3.2.4 Time on Task (Q3)

Consistent with decision theory (Payene et al., 1993) we were expecting people using EvalCat first (E+ & E-) to take longer for the first experimental step than test persons using FilterCat first (F- & F+). Our main interest was on how much longer evaluation takes.

Our study supports the fact that use of pure filtering mechanisms is the quickest product selection method. Persons working under conditions F+ and F- took an average of 15 minutes to complete a task, with times ranging from 10 to 28 minutes. The use of filtering and evaluation mechanisms in combination, as available in EvalCat under conditions E+ and E-, was generally slower with an average time of 25 minutes until the final choice was made. Surprisingly, however, the shortest time to select a computer (8 minutes) was taken by a test person working under condition E+. The maximum time taken was 30 minutes.

3.2.5 'Naturalness' of Evaluation (Q4)

To answer this question we collected from our experiment logs comments that had been spontaneously volunteered by test persons using the various tools. Our focus here was on comments regarding the usefulness and problems experienced in connection with evaluation support mechanisms.

We observed reactions to product evaluation support mechanisms that ranged from very positive to very negative. Some of the test persons who reacted positively reported that they had used similar evaluation methods for recent buying decisions —

for example when buying a car or a new kitchen installation. Those who reacted negatively usually implied that they do not like to assign numerical values to express attribute importance because the concrete values seem very arbitrary. Some of these test persons related negative experiences with the numerical evaluation or described a non-numerical strategy they had used recently for product selection. Similar negative reactions during tests with an earlier version of EvalCat, which supported only numerical evaluation (Stolze, 1998), led us to combine a filtering and an evaluation mechanism in the version of EvalCat that was used in the study reported here.

3.2.6 Catalogue Usability (Q5)

To investigate this question we collected information about the situations in which test subjects had problems using the different tools and intervention of the experimenter was necessary.

As reported under Q2, the number of explanations and interventions required after the initial catalogue demonstration was highest when working with EvalCat under condition E-. Test persons working with EvalCat under condition E+ also required a fair amount of help. The most frequent problems were that test persons had to be reminded which computer corresponded to the data in the attribute table, how the data of a particular computer can be displayed, and how the value distribution for a particular attribute can be inspected. Some test persons working with EvalCat became confused because the sliders for setting attribute value preferences and relative attribute importance have similar but not equivalent functions. Some test persons would have liked to sort attributes by their importance.

With FilterVis, test persons had to be reminded how to read the rich visualization and how to manipulate the display on the screen. In particular in the initial selection phases, when all product information was displayed in parallel, users expressed problems reading the display.

FilterCat, the stripped-down version of EvalCat, required the least intervention and help. Many test persons found FilterCat the easiest of the three tools to use. Some persons using FilterCat had to be reminded how to inspect the distribution of an attribute value over all products. A repeated request made by test persons using FilterCat was to see which constraints they had already entered. Many test persons also asked for a view that allowed them to compare computers side-by-side.

4 Implications

Interpreting results from experiments with small sample sizes is a delicate issue. This study is clearly a qualitative study in that, from a purely statistical perspective, almost all the interpretations presented in this section have to be understood as plausible hypotheses and not as statistically significant facts.

The results from our comparative study of analytical product selection support mechanisms indicate that catalogues that only use filtering mechanisms are likely to be easier to understand and take less time until a decision is reached, but that also the objective and subjective quality of the resulting selection is likely to be lower.

In our study we found that the use of evaluation mechanisms took longer, but only about twice the time, not four times the time of filtering. The use of evaluation mechanisms often raised the confidence of users in their choice — even if they had already used filtering and visualization. In our opinion the inclusion of evaluation and visualization mechanisms should be considered for catalogues of higher priced goods for which the feeling of having made the 'right' decision is an important part of customer satisfaction. Especially the use of evaluation as the first method appears to be very useful to reduce the chances of prematurely committing to a set of products with suboptimal overall performance.

Although these results favour evaluation and visualization mechanisms, we also found that offering only evaluation mechanisms is usually not accepted by users and that offering a combination of filtering, evaluation and visualization mechanisms can be very demanding. More work is needed to make catalogues like EvalCat, that offer multiple mechanisms for product selection support that are as easy to use as catalogues that only support filtering. However, care has to taken that the resulting tools leave users as confident about their decision as if they had used multiple mechanisms. A guided process that offers only one selection mechanism at a time might be the appropriate approach towards this goal for walk-up-and-use catalogues. Collaborative filtering mechanisms used in recommender systems (Resnick & Varian, 1997) could provide additional means to reach this goal. Catalogues like EvalCat, which offer less guidance and more freedom to react to the needs of the situation, will probably be most useful for frequent users such as sales personnel, who can use such a tool in a sales dialogue to identify 'objectively' the product that best matches the needs expressed by the client.

References

Bradley, S. A. (1994), Intelligent Engineering Component Catalogs, *in* J. S. Gero & F. Sudweeks (eds.), *Artificial Intelligence in Design*, Kluwer, pp.641–58.

Clemen, R. T. (1996), *Making Hard Decisions: An Introduction to Decision Analysis*, Wadsworth Publishing Company.

Genesereth, M. R., Keller, A. M. & Duschka, O. M. (1997), Infomaster: An Information Integration System, *in Proceedings of the ACM SIGMOD International Conference on Management of Data*, *ACM SIGMOD Record* **26**(2), ACM Press, pp.539–42.

Maes, P., Guttman, R. & Moukas, A. (1999), "Agents That Buy and Sell", *Communications of the ACM* **42**(3), 81–91.

Payene, J., Bettman, J. & Johnson, E. (1993), *The Adaptive Decision Maker*, Cambridge University Press.

Resnick, P. & Varian, H. R. (1997), "Recommender Systems", *Communications of the ACM* **40**(3), 56–8.

Rosewitz, M. (1998), "Electronic Sales Assistance", Proceedings CHI'98 Workshop on Beyond Internet Business-as-Usual.   http://www.forwiss.uni-erlangen.de/ rosewitz/chi98/paper.htm.

Schmid, B. F. (1997), "Requirements for Electronic Markets Architecture", *Electronic Markets* **7**(1), 3–6.

Spenke, M., Beilken, C. & Berlage, T. (1996), FOCUS: The Interactive Table for Product Comparison and Selection, *in Proceedings of the ACM Symposium on User Interface Software and Technology, UIST'96*, ACM Press, pp.41–50.

Steiger, P. & Stolze, M. (1997), Effective Product Selection in Electronic Catalogs, *in* S. Pemberton (ed.), *Proceedings of CHI'97: Human Factors in Computing Systems*, ACM Press, pp.291–2.

Steiger, P., Stolze, M. & Good, M. (1999), "Beyond Internet Business-as-Usual: Report about a CHI'98 Workshop", *ACM SIGCHI Bulletin* **30**(4), 48–52. http://www.zurich.ibm.com/ pst/chi98/report.html.

Stolze, M. (1998), Soft Navigation in Product Catalogs, *in* C. Nikolaou & C. Stephanidis (eds.), *Proceedings of the Second European Conference on Research and Advanced Technology for Electronic Libraries*, Springer-Verlag, pp.385–96.

Sykes, E. A. & White, C. C. (1991), "Multiobjective Intelligent Computer-Aided Design", *IEEE Transactions in Systems, Man and Cybernetics* **21**(6), 1498–511.

Tweedie, L., Spence, R., Dawkes, H. & Su, J. (1996), Externalising Abstract Mathematical Models, *in* G. van der Veer & B. Nardi (eds.), *Proceedings of CHI'96: Human Factors in Computing Systems*, ACM Press, pp.406–12.

Williamson, C. & Shneiderman, B. (1992), The Dynamic HomeFinder: Evaluating Dynamic Queries in a Real-estate Information Exploration System, *in* N. Belkin, P. Ingwersen & A. M. Pejtersen (eds.), *SIGIR'92 Proceedings of the Fifteenth Annual International ACM SIGIR Conference on Research and Development in Information Retrieval*, ACM Press, pp.338–46.

Human–Computer Interaction — INTERACT '99
M. Angela Sasse and Chris Johnson (Editors)
Published by IOS Press, © IFIP TC.13, 1999

A Case Study in the Development of Collaborative Customer Care: Concept and Solution

Catherine G. Wolf, Alison Lee, Maroun Touma & Shahrokh Daijavad

IBM T. J. Watson Research Center, Hawthorne, NY 10532, USA.
{cwolf,alisonl,touma,shahrokh}@us.ibm.com

Abstract: We describe the concept of Web-based collaborative customer care and our experience designing a proof of concept solution for a real-world customer. The paper describes the requirements for collaborative customer care and the features of the implemented system. They differ from the requirements for work-group collaboration due to differences in users, tasks and goals, and context of use. We also discuss the design process with a focus on how particular design activities revealed key requirements for integrating collaborative customer care into the business' organizational and information systems infrastructures. We found the use of concrete methods and artifacts to be effective techniques for discovering design requirements for this new technology.

Keywords: collaboration, customer care, QOC, system design, scenarios, World Wide Web.

1 Introduction

Synchronous collaboration tools have typically been designed to support work-groups. For example, consider shared writing tools (Ellis et al., 1991; Olson et al., 1993) and shared whiteboard tools (Bly, 1988; Greenberg et al., 1995). However, as more consumers gain access to the World Wide Web and as businesses increasingly use the Web as a channel for commerce, the Web has become a potential medium for collaboration between a business and its customers. As the Web offerings become more complex, there is a need to supplement Web-based self-service with human assistance on demand. Furthermore, businesses are beginning to realize the importance of human assistance in establishing and maintaining a relationship with customers, and are exploring ways of doing this over the Web (Conway, 1998).

For the past several years, we have been developing a system to support collaborative customer care over the Web. We have worked with several customers in a joint research relationship to better understand the business, technical and usability requirements for collaborative customer care. These requirements differ from those for work-group collaboration due to differences in users, tasks and business goals, the organizational context and the information technology infrastructure.

This paper focuses on the design of collaborative customer care based on our experience doing joint research with several real-world customers. We will draw heavily on our experience with one customer, mbanx — a division of Bank of Montreal, with whom we worked with for about 15 months. We will describe several aspects of our experience:

- The design process — System design involves more than technology design. It involves understanding the business, organizational, and social context into which the technology is integrated with the customer. In addition, the design process includes many shareholders, and needs to employ methods that are accessible and comprehensible to all of them. We found the use of concrete methods and artifacts to be effective techniques for discovering design requirements.

- The requirements for collaborative customer care — We describe the features of the implemented system, as well as the requirements that could not be implemented within the project time-frame. The description of the requirements focuses on the functionality from the users' and organization's perspectives. A detailed technical description appears in (Kobayashi et al., 1998).

The next section provides the background for the development of the collaborative customer care concept, a scenario of use that illustrates many of the capabilities of the resulting solution and overview of the solution's components. This is followed by a discussion of the design process and the resulting requirements and features. We conclude with 'lessons learned' that can be applied more generally.

2 Customer Care

We developed the key elements of the vision for collaborative customer care in 1995–96. They were encapsulated in a nice demonstration that was used to convey the vision to businesses. We used an approach similar to the one described in (Wolf & Zadrozny, 1998) for bringing research technology to the marketplace. In order to understand the real requirements for collaborative customer care and to evaluate the technology, its usability and potential value to businesses, we entered into a joint research agreement with mbanx, a direct banking division of Bank of Montreal. As part of this arrangement, we agreed to deliver a working prototype solution that would be used in a limited pilot with real bank customers.

From the initial seed of the demonstration prototype, the joint research and business team identified goals, requirements, and applications of the collaborative customer care solution for online banking (Fischer et al., 1994). The following scenario illustrates the result of our efforts. It gives an idea of what we mean by collaborative customer care over the Web and illustrates the main features of the technology (see Figure 1). Then, we summarize the components and framework of the solution deployed within the bank's environment (see Figure 2).

2.1 Scenario of Use

Iris Cashman opened a bank account two months ago. From home, she connects to the Internet and to the bank Web site with her modem. She looks at the Credit Card page to see what the online bank has of interest. She notices an icon labelled 'Ask us about our Magic MasterCards'. She remembers the last time she looked at the MasterCard choices; it was hard to figure out which one was best for her so she didn't apply for any of them.

Iris clicks on the icon and this pops up a new page asking her to wait until a customer service representative (CSR) is found to handle the call. Behind the scenes, this search process is initiated. Within seconds, Iris is connected to Marianne Banks, the bank's credit card specialist. The 'Waiting for a CSR' page is minimized and Iris sees the original page from which she initiated her call. Marianne's

Web browser displays the same document. She and Iris are also able to talk over a voice channel carried on the same telephone line as the Internet connection. She asks how she can help. Iris explains that she was thinking about getting a MasterCard, but was confused by all the choices.

Marianne takes Iris to the MasterCard choices page. She asks Iris a few questions to determine her credit needs. Marianne shows Iris the Midas MasterCard plan. Using the remote pointer, Marianne points out the interest rate and annual fee. She underlines the special frequent flyer mileage option, leaving a red trail of digital ink. Iris uses her remote pointer as she asks a question about the cost of the frequent flyer option of the card.

Iris is convinced the Midas MasterCard is the one for her so Marianne now takes Iris to the online application form. Since Marianne is connected to the Web server by a high speed Intranet connection, she is likely to see the page before the customer. Marianne glances at a synchronization indicator embedded in the browser's title bar to see if it has turned green. Once this indicator has turned green, Marianne is assured that the two sides are synchronized. As Iris speaks, Marianne clicks a field in the form to begin entering information. When she clicks in the field, a corner turns red, providing feedback to Iris that Marianne is about to type in the field. Iris notices that Marianne has misspelled her mother's maiden name. She clicks in that field (a corner of the field turns blue) and corrects the spelling. While filling in the address information, Iris mentions that she is saving to move from her apartment to her own home. Marianne makes a note in Iris's customer record to follow up with a call from a mortgage consultant next month to suggest ways Iris might be able to finance a home.

2.2 Technology Description

The collaborative customer care technology (known as CLIVE) allows a customer connected via a modem to speak and share data with a CSR located behind the bank's electronic firewall (see Figure 2).

Customers connect to the Internet using IBM's Internet access service. They run software that transmits voice and data over a single dialup line to the Internet access point (Zhang et al., 1998). There, the voice and data are split apart. The data portion is routed over the Internet and redirected to the collaboration server while the voice portion is routed over the telephone network. The collaboration server filters all bank Web page requests and forwards them to the bank's Web server. Both of these servers are on the Internet. The collaboration

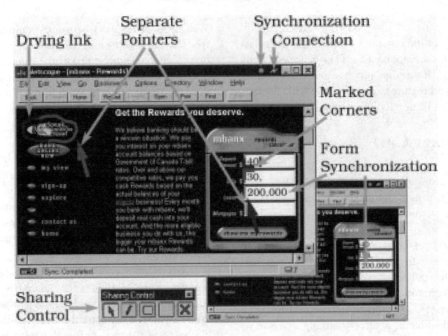

Figure 1: User interface features of CLIVE.

server scans the retrieved Web pages for CLIVE comment tags and substitutes them with appropriate text and icons to show CLIVE information and functionality.

When the user clicks the CLIVE icon or text to collaborate with a CSR, the collaboration server communicates with the call handling process, located at the computer-telephony integration server to find an available representative. Once one is found, the two voice portions of the call are connected by software running at the Internet access point. At the same time, the collaboration server sends the CSR a copy of the page that the customer was looking at just before initiating the call. Both parties can collaborate on this and any other pages.

During the session, the collaboration server replicates Web page requests from one party to the other (URL synchronization). Static and dynamic pages are shared through a proxy-like process managed by the collaboration server (Barrett & Maglio, 1998). This process forwards only one request for the page to the bank's Web server and on behalf of the customer. When the response returns, the process forwards it to the customer. It also caches the response on the collaboration server so that it can forward a copy to the CSR. Secure Web pages are handled in a similar fashion except that secure sessions are established to process the request.

While collaborating on a page, a CLIVE plug-in, hidden in the Web page, replicates form inputs,

cursor positions, inking data, mouse clicks, and page scrolling actions to the other CLIVE plug-in. The plug-ins support the page synchronization and form synchronization features of CLIVE.

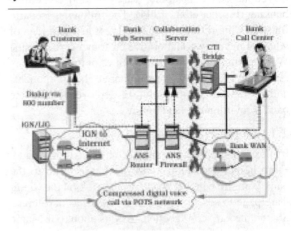

Figure 2: CLIVE solution architecture.

3   Design Process

The research agreement was made between the information systems (IS) organization of the bank and our research lab. The actual project team involved people from several organizations of the bank, organized into two overlapping teams, the business team and the technical team. These teams met every other week for discussion and decision-making.

Since this paper is concerned with design requirements from the user and organizational perspective, we will focus on the design process within the business team. The business team included representatives from the bank's information systems organization, marketing, call centre operations, market research and training, as well as, the authors and a project manager from our organization.

This section gives several examples of methods used to understand the requirements for collaborative customer care in the bank's environment. The process was an iterative one, as the developers' understanding of the bank's operations and the bank's understanding of the technology evolved. The design process involved many other activities not discussed here. Our discussion has two main themes:

- There are requirements for the effective *use* of CLIVE technology beyond those features that directly support customer-CSR interactions. Many of these are needed to integrate a new way of doing business into the existing organizational and information systems infrastructure.

- Given the differing backgrounds and knowledge of the team members, it was both effective and productive to use techniques that allow all participants to develop a common understanding and a means to brainstorm jointly. The techniques involved the use of concrete methods and artifacts as vehicles for team members to think and communicate about the uses of novel technology and to discover requirements.

3.1 Setting Objectives with QOC

The first task in the design process was to understand and agree on the objectives of the project. It was assumed that the system would deliver functionality similar to that illustrated by the demo system. In order to determine how the technology should be modified and how it would be applied, we needed to come to an agreement on the project goals. However, it proved difficult to move the discussion of goals beyond high level statements such as "test the viability of the technology and the value of the technology to the Bank".

We made better progress in identifying goals and also functionality requirements when we focused on the applications to be supported. We adopted a modified version of the QOC (Questions, Options, Criteria) method to structure the discussion (MacLean et al., 1991). We used a tabular format in which

potential application options or tasks to which the collaborative technology might be applied were listed vs. selection criteria. The cells of the table were filled in with the group's evaluation of the applications on each criterion. The QOC method had the benefit of making the selection criteria explicit and caused the evaluation discussion to proceed in an orderly way. While more elaborate methods for representing design rationale exist (Jarczyk et al., 1992), this approach was easy for all team members to understand without training.

The process of determining the criteria for application selection and the discussion evaluating the applications on the criteria produced a more specific set of goals for the technology and project. The vague concept of 'value' was translated into the more specific application selection criteria of increasing sales, market share, customer retention, satisfaction, and CSR productivity. When thinking about the specific candidate bank applications, the team was able to articulate the goals for the use of the technology. These criteria, thus, became business goals for the CLIVE technology.

The selected applications include the following:

Customer acquisition: The goal was to enhance the self-service function with collaborative assistance on-demand (i.e. *customer support*). Collaboration would be used to make the process easier and speedier for the customer, to reduce input errors due to misunderstandings, and to increase the completion rate for the process, thereby increasing market share.

Determining the pay-back for doing various types of business with the bank: This consisted of what-if calculations that determined a customer's pay-back for having a mortgage, savings account, loan or other types of relationships with the bank (see Figure 1). Collaboration would facilitate *sales and marketing* as the CSR discussed the pay-back for different services and products.

Overview of bank services: This consisted of pages containing text and graphics information describing the products and services. Collaboration would *generate leads* and *open opportunities for cross selling* (i.e. selling a customer who called about one product an additional product).

Adding billers for electronic bill payment: With collaboration, customers could view and point to a list of billers while talking to the CSR.

Without collaboration, customers needed to specify billers in a separate telephone call; perhaps, disconnecting from their session to do so. CLIVE was expected to facilitate *customer service* by making biller registration easier to use and more convenient.

Many of the end-user collaboration features in these applications had been incorporated in the demonstration and the challenge was to implement them in a working system. However, the business team discussions suggested that a number of changes and additions would be needed for the technology, the Web pages and the bank work practices in order to meet the bank's business goals for collaborative customer care. Some examples of these and the design processes used to elucidate the requirements are described in the following sections. Many implementation issues were also uncovered in the course of the technical team's work, but these are discussed in (Kobayashi et al., 1998).

3.2   Call Centre Observations

In order to understand the Call Centre environment and work practices, we observed the customer service representatives in action and followed up with discussions with the Call Centre manager. This led us to formulate recommendations for changes to the environment and work practices to effectively utilize collaboration. We give an example for impact on the environment and impact on work practices based on our Call Centre observations.

We observed the CSR wearing telephone headsets and using two desktop computers (for access to different systems). To maintain CSR productivity, it was necessary for them to handle Web collaboration calls as well as telephone calls. The introduction of CLIVE technology would add another system and also an independent audio channel. Clearly, CSR productivity would be adversely affected if they had to constantly change headsets and shift from system to system. While we were not able to solve the multiple computer problem, we introduced some hardware which allowed the CSRs to switch between the two sources of audio without changing headsets.

Also, we observed that in the self-service mode of customer acquisition, customers would fill out several forms containing substantial explanatory materials. A few days later, they received a telephone call from a customer service representative to gather additional information needed to complete the process. Before calling the customer, the CSR typically did a credit check. With the introduction of collaboration, several modifications to the process were desirable so that

collaboration would enhance CSR productivity and sales. One modification would be to eliminate the explanatory material in the forms and to collapse several forms when the CSR was assisting the customer. This would reduce the number of pages required and thus the wait time while the next page was retrieved from the server. The bank did not adopt this proposal because this would require either maintaining two sets of pages or developing a different approach to page creation that allowed the appropriate pages to be dynamically generated depending on whether self-service or collaboration mode was used. Another desirable modification was to enable the CSR to perform the credit check in real time while collaborating with the customer in order to complete the process in one interaction. This was expected to be possible to do in most cases.

The Call Centre observations gave us a concrete understanding of the environment and work practices into which Web collaboration was to be integrated. Although we were unable to implement all of the proposed optimizations to take best advantage of Web-based collaborative customer care, the team gained insights into the work practice and technology requirements that could be applied in the future.

3.3   Scenarios

We used scenarios to envision how business might be conducted using the CLIVE technology. We describe two effects of using scenarios. One effect was to illustrate how the collaboration technology could improve an existing process, such as customer acquisition. A second effect was to show how the technology could radically transform the business.

Scenarios were used to determine where the CLIVE icon or text link would be placed for the various applications. Initially, some team members assumed an icon should be placed only on the top-level page for each application. This assumption was motivated in part by a desire to minimize the number of pages that would need to be changed. In order to meet the goal of improving ease of use for the customer, however, the icon had to be offered wherever the customer would be likely to need help. In the case of the customer acquisition application, one could imagine a customer starting to fill in the form in self-service mode, but then needing assistance at some point in the process beyond the top level page. We created detailed scenarios of use that concretely illustrated the need for collaboration at particular points in the applications. These scenarios succeeded in convincing other team members of the need for the multiple access points.

Scenarios were also used to illustrate how CLIVE could be used to sell more products and services to customers. The QOC discussions revealed the goal to increase sales to customers. We suggested that Web-based collaboration had the potential to turn service interactions (e.g. pay-back application) into sales opportunities by enabling the CSR to propose new products and to show the information to the customer. To illustrate this potential value, we presented several detailed scenarios using the bank's Web pages. However, the Call Centre observations revealed that sales and marketing operations were largely separated from service and support operations (handling customer problems and inquiries). In fact, to implement some of these scenarios, it would be necessary to retrain Call Centre personnel, change work practices, and support session transfer to another bank specialist. This was beyond the scope of the project. Instead, the team decided that the CSR should use information gathered while collaborating with the customer to generate leads for referral. Looking beyond the research project, the scenarios revealed valuable insights into the technology, work practice and organizational requirements for future business transformations.

4 Requirements

Three sets of requirements surfaced from the design meetings and the observations at the Call Centre. They correspond to the user, organizational, and task-specific elements of integrating Web collaboration into a self-service banking Web site. A number of the end user features differ from those required for work-group collaboration due to the characteristics of the users and the activities to be supported. The organizational and task-specific elements of collaborative customer care raised requirements not found for work-group collaboration.

4.1 End User: Features

Our conception of collaborative customer care supplements a bank's existing self-service Web site with human assistance on demand. The object of the collaboration is the content of the Web browser. This is different from generic application sharing for work-groups. First, full screen sharing is not required as only the browser's content needs to be shared. Second, sharing the browser content means sharing a small number of application objects (i.e. URL for a page, page's contents including form fields) but not a bitmap of the browser window. This makes sharing more efficient due to lower bandwidth requirements. Third, the operations that the users would perform

in a collaboration are few in number (i.e. navigation and form submission) but quite powerful in their effect (e.g. sign-up online, what-if calculations, make purchases). Thus, optimizing collaboration on Web browser contents resulted in a powerful yet simple and comprehensible tool for customer care.

Ease of use and ease of comprehension were important for other reasons. Collaborative customer care is a novel service for customers. Unlike work-group members, who may be willing to invest some time in mastering a powerful collaboration tool, bank customers have little motivation to learn a tool that they will use casually and infrequently. In view of this, simplicity rather than power was an important goal in the design of the customer interface. Instead of having only a single pointer or requiring users to use a turn-taking protocol to attain floor control as in NetMeeting, each party has their own coloured pointer which they individually controlled; red for the CSR and blue for the customer. Each party is able to see the other party's pointer. The voice channel could also be used to allow the two parties to negotiate their actions. When either or both parties are interacting with a form field, both parties are aware of this because coloured marked corners appear in the form field that they are working with. As well, we did not provide the customer with the sharing control panel which provided options for switching between pen and pointer, clearing ink, refreshing ink, or to disconnect from a session. We decided that it was better to let the CSR act as the control surrogate for the user because the CSR received formal training on the technology and would be more familiar with the technology through frequent use of CLIVE.

Another requirement was to make system constraints transparent to users (Beaudouin-Lafon & Karsenty, 1992). Latency and asymmetry in the users' connections existed due to differences in the way the customer and CSR were connected. To ensure that collaboration proceeds naturally, awareness tools were provided. The synchronization indicator on the browser title bar (see Figure 1) kept each party abreast of when their pages synchronized. A message box popped up when one party navigated to another page to remind them to wait until both sides were synchronized. Finally, when the CSR highlighted things to the customer with a pen, the ink trail would change colour as it was echoed to the customer. Latency and asymmetry in users' connections may also exist in some work-group environments, and similar feedback may be desirable.

The last end-user requirement was to design for casual use and errors. This was particularly important for customers because of their infrequent interactions with CLIVE. We describe two instances where this was necessary. The first instance occurred when the user clicked to collaborate with a CSR. A 'Waiting for CSR' page popped up and remained up until a CSR was found. This page gave guidance to the customer about what was happening, what they should and should not do, the hours of service and disconnecting from the call. The second instance occurred when either party inadvertently clicked on a CLIVE link or icon in the midst of a session. If this occurred, a message popped up to remind both sides that they were already in a collaborative session. We found this to be a necessary precaution because there was no special visual appearance on the hyperlink or image icon to indicate the collaborative session. The bank did not want to maintain separate appearances for being in and not being in a session.

4.2   Organizational: Call Centre and Work Practices Integration

One of the bank goals revealed in the QOC discussions was to improve CSR productivity. They wanted the CLIVE CSR to handle Web collaboration calls as well as regular telephone calls. This way, the CSR did not idly wait for CLIVE calls when regular calls were waiting. CLIVE calls were routed through a call handling system independent of the one used to route telephone calls. In order for the two systems to know about the availability of a CLIVE CSR, it was necessary to link the status information and call handling capabilities of the two systems. This way, productive and efficient use of CLIVE service representatives were ensured.

This requirement necessitated that the CLIVE CSR login before they could handle CLIVE calls. They did this through the Call Control and Status panel that appeared on a third computer provided to handle CLIVE calls. This panel provided information about the CSR call status (e.g. unavailable). As well, it provided controls for allowing the CSR to become available/unavailable to take a call and to logout.

4.3   Task: Web Site Integration

At the outset of the joint research project, it was understood that the integration of CLIVE into the bank's Web site would minimally impact its operation. More importantly, CLIVE capabilities had to be integrated into the Web pages in a way that resulted in only one set of pages that would work for CLIVE and non-CLIVE bank customers. As well, the Web page changes had to be cost-effective since this was contracted to a third party. These requirements were met by embedding comment tags and attributes into

the relevant Web pages. The collaboration server substitutes the tag with HTML code that displays text and/or images to CLIVE customers. Non-CLIVE customers went directly to the bank's Web server and did not have the additions made.

Scenarios were also effective in surfacing the bank's Web design goals. Initially, we had created explanatory text for CLIVE that integrated with the text in the bank's Web pages. However, on seeing the text, team members from the bank declared it too lengthy. In their experience, users were unlikely to read it all. In fact, they preferred a consistent identifying 'catch phrase' similar to an identifying image button for CLIVE. The image button appeared in the same location, alongside the main menu located in a standard place on the pages. Using one of their own design goals (to provide information about bank services), we were able to convince them to add several CLIVE application-specific information pages. The additional Web pages explained, for instance, the collaborative customer care service and listed the bank applications supported by the service.

5   Concluding Remarks

In this paper, we presented the concept and business solution for Web-based collaborative customer care. They were developed through a joint design process with a real-world bank, seeded by a demonstration prototype. We used concrete methods and artifacts, like QOC and scenarios, during the design process to flesh out user, task, and organizational requirements for collaborative customer care. The use of concrete design methodologies was instrumental in helping the design team develop a common understanding and a means to brainstorm jointly. The team needed to consider not only technology issues, but also to understand the business, organizational, and social context into which the technology was to be integrated. Only when technology and work practices co-evolve do we create a solution that will integrate effectively into the business' organizational and information systems infrastructures. We discussed the requirements for collaborative customer care and how they differ from work-group requirements.

The insights obtained in an extensive joint research partnership are being incorporated into a product offering being developed by our customer care organization. In addition, our work with other business partners has shown strong support for the requirements presented here. These engagements have hinted at other requirements (e.g. call transfer, three-way conferencing) and issues to pursue in the future (e.g. limiting collaboration to segments of a Web site, sharing applets, requiring form input by the customer).

Acknowledgements

We gratefully acknowledge the contributions of the Bank of Montreal/mbanx project team, and in particular the project leader, Cathy Lee.

References

Barrett, R. & Maglio, P. P. (1998), "Intermediaries: New Places for Producing and Manipulating Web Content", *Computer Networks and ISDN Systems* **30**, 509–18.

Beaudouin-Lafon, M. & Karsenty, A. (1992), Transparency and Awareness in Real-time Groupware System, *in* M. Green (ed.), *Proceedings of the ACM Symposium on User Interface Software and Technology, UIST'92*, ACM Press, pp.171–80.

Bly, S. (1988), Use of Drawing Surfaces in Different Collaborative Settings, *in* D. G. Tatar (ed.), *Proceedings of CSCW'88: Conference on Computer Supported Cooperative Work*, ACM Press, pp.250–6.

Conway, K. D. (1998), *Building Customer Relationships in the Electronic Age*, Technology Solutions Company.

Ellis, C. A., Gibbs, S. J. & Rein, G. L. (1991), "Groupware: Some Issues and Experiences", *Communications of the ACM* **34**(1), 39–58.

Fischer, G., McCall, R., Ostwald, J., Reeves, B. & Shipman, F. (1994), Seeding, Evolutionary Growth and Reseeding: Supporting the Incremental Development of Design Environments, *in* B. Adelson, S. Dumais & J. Olson (eds.), *Proceedings of CHI'94: Human Factors in Computing Systems*, ACM Press, pp.292–8.

Greenberg, S., Hayne, S. & Rada, R. (1995), *Groupware for Real-time Drawing: A Designer's Guide*, McGraw-Hill.

Jarczyk, A., Loeffler, P. & Shipman, F. (1992), Design Rationale for Software Engineering: A Survey, *in* V. Milutinovic & B. D. Shriber (eds.), *Proceedings of the Twenty-Fifth Annual Hawaii International Conference on System Sciences*, IEEE Publications, pp.577–86.

Kobayashi, M., Shinozaki, M., Sakairi, T., Touma, M., Daijavad, S. & Wolf, C. G. (1998), Collaborative Customer Services using Synchronous Web Browser Sharing, *in Proceedings of CSCW'98: Conference on Computer Supported Cooperative Work*, ACM Press, pp.99–108.

MacLean, A., Young, R. M., Bellotti, V. M. E. & Moran, T. P. (1991), "Questions, Options and Criteria: Elements of Design Space Analysis", *Human–Computer Interaction* **6**(3-4), 201–50.

Olson, J. S., Olson, G. M., Storrosten, M. & Carter, M. (1993), "Groupwork Close Up: A Comparison of the Group Design Process With and Without a Simple Group Editor", *ACM Transactions on Office Information Systems* **11**(4), 321–48.

Wolf, C. G. & Zadrozny, W. (1998), Evolution of the Conversation Machine: A Case Study of Bringing Advanced Technology to the Marketplace, *in* C.-M. Karat, A. Lund, J. Coutaz & J. Karat (eds.), *Proceedings of CHI'98: Human Factors in Computing Systems*, ACM Press, pp.488–95.

Zhang, Q., Wolf, C. G., Daijavad, S. & Touma, M. (1998), Talking to Customers on the Web: A Comparison of Three Voice Alternatives, *in Proceedings of CSCW'98: Conference on Computer Supported Cooperative Work*, ACM Press, pp.109–17.

Human–Computer Interaction — INTERACT '99
M. Angela Sasse and Chris Johnson (Editors)
Published by IOS Press, © IFIP TC.13, 1999

Pushing All The Right Buttons: Lessons From Two Case Studies of Touch-screen Kiosks

David Martin[1], Jacki O'Neill[2], R. Varey[2] & D. Wastell[1]

[1] Department of Computer Science, University of Manchester, Manchester, UK.

[2] Corporate Communications Research Unit , University of Salford, Salford, UK.

martind@cs.man.ac.uk, J.Oneill@man-school.salford.ac.uk

Abstract: With touch-screen kiosks becoming increasingly prevalent in retail environments this paper reports the results from two case studies of commercial applications. One, PhotoKiosk, provides for photographic film drop-off for processing. The other, ShoppingKiosk, is a supermarket information and service kiosk. PhotoKiosk was evaluated by users as largely being a success while Shopping Kiosk was negatively evaluated. The reasons for these outcomes are discussed in detail. Then, from these case studies a number of issues relating to the design, look and environment are raised and discussed leading to some general design suggestions for such applications in retail environments.

Keywords: design, ethnography, kiosks, retail, touch-screen, user trials.

1 Introduction

Touch-screen kiosks are becoming increasingly popular in retail and public service environments. A kiosk can be defined as a:

> "...computer-based information system in a publicly accessible place, offering access to information or transactions for an anonymous, constantly varying group of users, with typically short dialogue times and a simple user interface" (Holfelder & Hehmann, 1994).

Nearly all kiosk systems use touch-screens as these are well suited to naïve users (Totty, 1995; Wehrer, 1997).

The interest in kiosks stems from the belief that they:

- help reduce the burden on staff by dealing with simple queries and transactions;

- provide a high-tech profile for the company; and

- are 'user friendly'.

A growing number of companies are developing and using touch-screen kiosks. In the UK these currently include BT, the British Council, Manchester Central Library and Microsoft. For example, British Telecom is currently running a large-scale trial of its 'Touchpoint' information kiosk at locations such as station platforms and Microsoft has recently installed an information and advertising kiosk in several computer retailers.

There are several reviews of kiosks in trade journal articles taken from an industry standpoint. These show a mixed response depending on the individual application. For example, some suggest that kiosks provide poor customer service in banking applications, whereas some information and sales kiosks such as those at CarShop are considered a success (Whybrow, 1996). Some of these reviews also provide general classifications and a few very basic design ideas.

Academic research also suggests some important features of design. For example, layout has been shown to be crucial to information kiosks, and should be clearer than on systems where the user can spend some time (Borchers et al., 1995). However, to our knowledge, there seems to be little in-depth research into the design issues involved in successful kiosk development as a whole, tending to centre instead on more specific aspects of design (Wehrer, 1997; Scott & Conzala, 1997).

This paper provides a report of research into two actual commercial projects for retail kiosks, considering their differing design approaches and their consequent evaluation during user trials. Its aim is to highlight some potentially important issues in the design of successful kiosks.

2 Background

The first project we shall call PhotoKiosk. A leading UK high street retailer was seeking to develop a touch-screen kiosk that would enable customers to place their photographic films in for development themselves. Our involvement in this project was to undertake user trials with three levels of prototype and use these to evaluate the application and feed back into design. Although the final application is not fully up and running in store yet, the trials have been very successful.

The second project, which we shall call ShoppingKiosk, was undertaken by a large UK conglomerate, and varied considerably from the first, in purpose, design method and our involvement. The company had developed a touch-screen kiosk that would present information about its range of businesses, its policies and ethics. On-line services were also available. This touch-screen kiosk was piloted at one of the companies new supermarkets in the South of England. Our involvement was to carry out user trials, observation and interviews in-store, in order to evaluate the application. Our research indicated a number of problems with this kiosk.

The user trials of the three PhotoKiosk prototypes were carried out in the same way as outlined in the paper "Ethnographically Informed System Design (EISD)", (Martin et al., 1998) which draws on the approach to prototype evaluation outlined in "Principles for Co-operative Prototyping" (Bødker & Grønbæk, 1991). These trials have an ethnographic flavour, and are conducted with potential users. The trialist is given control of the application, being encouraged to fully explore it while actually envisioning using it. They are asked to comment on any aspect of the application at any time. In this way we try to create a situation which will be closer to the natural situation of user interacting with application. Our materials are detailed notes on what occurs and what is said. The proximity one can gain to a natural setting during these trials depends on the type of prototype. For example, with PhotoKiosk the first trial, of a paper prototype, was not in-store, while the final trial, of an almost full working prototype, was.

The aim of progressing through trials of increasingly functional prototypes is to try to discover usability issues early on while acknowledging certain problems will only be revealed at later stages of testing.

The evaluation of ShoppingKiosk combined similar in-store user trials to those of PhotoKiosk, with unstructured interviews and observation in a five day, 'quick and dirty' ethnography (COMIC, 1994). Due to the size and complexity of the application, compared to PhotoKiosk, shoppers in these trials could not always be expected to thoroughly explore the application. Therefore this part of the evaluation did not have the same comprehensive detail of the PhotoKiosk trials. Overall this study, while short, provided a detailed ethnography of the usability, usefulness, use and opinions on ShoppingKiosk.

The evaluations of these two projects suggest that at this stage PhotoKiosk is a much more successful, usable and useful application than ShoppingKiosk. PhotoKiosk went live in April 1999 while ShoppingKiosk has been withdrawn and is currently being redesigned. What are the reasons for this? There are many reasons. However, by examining such features of the applications as the design methods used to build them, the actual design of the screens, their relevancy and so on, we should be better able to understand the reasons for project success or failure. In this paper we describe each project separately, from the design, through to the testing and evaluation. From this we outline some of the issues that contribute to the different outcomes, and make comparisons between the two where possible. It is not our contention that they can be systematically compared but rather that PhotoKiosk illustrates mainly 'good' design and ShoppingKiosk 'bad', and together they can provide some useful guidelines for the design of touch-screen kiosks for retail environments and even in general.

3 PhotoKiosk Project

3.1 Background

The PhotoKiosk Project involved the development and evaluation of a touch-screen kiosk to provide an express film drop-off service for customers. The kiosk was to be placed in the photographic section of the store, close to the film processing counter. The main aim of the kiosk was to allow customers to put their own films in for processing in an attempt to reduce queuing time and the burden on staff.

Only 35mm and Advanced Photo System (APS) films could be dropped off at the kiosk. This decision was made to keep the process simple; these are the most popular film types and mostly can be processed with straightforward developing instructions. The kiosk would allow customers to select the developing options they wanted, for example, size of print and processing time and deposit their film/s for developing.

The kiosk design was based on a model derived from two days of observation of staff filling out the film processing envelopes and from the options listed on the envelopes themselves. The process developed from this model is outlined below.

3.2   The Process and Initial Screen Design

An 'Attractor Screen', consisting of a moving image, demonstrating the steps of the process, is used to attract the customers attention. To begin the process customers insert the stores Loyalty Card, containing details of their name and address. This takes them to the 'Film Type Screen'. Here the user chooses between APS and 35mm. Following the 35mm route, the next screen, 'Number of Exposures Screen' allows the user to select between 12, 24 and 36 exposures, leading to the 'Processing Time Screen' where they choose between 1, 24 and 48 hours. On the 'Print Size Screen' users get to choose between two or three print sizes depending on the processing time selected.

Apart from the 'Attractor Screen' the previous screens consist of large, blue oval buttons and illustrative graphics, for example, showing a roll of film with the number of exposures highlighted. The following screens consist of text and buttons.

Following the 'Print Size Screen' is the 'Summary and Extra Set Of Prints? Screen', this summarises the choices made so far, including price, and offers the chance to order extra sets of prints. Depending on their choice users either progress to the 'Extra Set Screen' or straight to the following screens which allow them to finish the process or drop-off more films. The APS process is similar, apart from a few differences in developing procedure and therefore in options, for example, each APS film has an ID number which must be entered.

Navigation occurs by selecting options which then move the user through the process to the next screen. Additional navigation is provided by the 'Back' button, taking the user to the previous screen, and the 'Cancel' button, which ends the process. These buttons are consistently placed on all screens.

The process finishes with an envelope being printed for each film, into which the film/s are placed. Once posted through a drop-off slot a receipt is printed and the card returned. The final screen provides the instructions for these activities.

3.3   The Prototypes

There were three iterations of prototyping. These were the paper-based prototype, the electronic prototype and the beta prototype.

The paper-based prototype consisted of paper representations of the graphical application flow chart of the process described above, as well as screen and housing designs. 15 trialists were asked to follow the flow chart step-by-step and were shown the screen designs for each stage. They were asked to act as though the paper-based prototype was actually a touch-screen, that is to touch the 'screens' as they would if using the application. Trialists were also asked to comment on the housing and the name of the kiosk.

The information gathered from these trials was reported back to the developers. Discussions between the store and the developers, in the light of the research, decided what would be fed into the development of the electronic prototype. Some of the research would not be acted on due to technical complexity, politics and the need to find a balance between keeping the process simple and offering enough flexibility and choice to the customer.

The electronic prototype consisted of a lap-top version of the application. This version was not touch-screen or fully operational, for example, there was no 'Attractor Screen'. 15 user trials were undertaken and the results fed into the development of the next iteration, the beta prototype.

The beta prototype was a touch-screen kiosk in which the process was almost fully implemented, except for the envelope and receipt printing. It was situated in-store near the film processing counter, although not in its housing. Trials were carried out with customers in the photography department, and the findings were fed back to the developers for the development of the finished PhotoKiosk.

3.4   Analysis of User Trials

Overall the analysis was positive. The trials of each prototype produced progressively less comments and problems. The up and running version appears to be well received as was suggested by the in-store trial where trialists generally liked the application and found few problems using it. From the beginning trialists found the process simple and easy to use and they thought the buttons were clear and obvious. Importantly, there was a strong favourable response in-store with the majority of customers stating they were looking forward to actually using the application. A number of changes however were made to the process from how it was initially conceived, some examples of these are given below:

1. Name of application. The original name suggested was 'Express Drop-Off', however trialists did not feel that that would express the purpose clearly. It was thought that this name could indicate a number of functions, although its location by the film processing counter might reduce confusion. To ensure that its purpose was clear and obvious the name was changed to 'Express Film Drop-Off'.

2. Screen alterations. Trials indicated a number of confusing features of the original screens which were subsequently changed. One example is the 'Print Size Screen'. On this screen users choose between three print sizes, small, medium and large, illustrated by pictures of photos of different sizes. Originally trialists wanted to know which was 'standard' size, so 'small', being the standard size was changed to 'standard'. Users also wanted to know if the illustrations were actual size or not, so 'actual size' was included on the screen.

In this project it was through the process of repeated testing and feeding back into design that many potential problems, such as those above, with usability and usefulness were revealed at earlier stages of the design allowing for them to be tackled. Overall the research indicates there should be few problems with the PhotoKiosk final version.

4 ShoppingKiosk

4.1 Design Method

The conglomerate that developed ShoppingKiosk consists of a wide range of businesses. These vary from retail, to banking, travel and manufacturing. Recently they have begun to try to present themselves as a united set of businesses. Some of the branches of the organization, for example, banking and travel, already have a strong electronic presence, offering information and on-line services through the Internet. Now a Web site has been set up, providing information on the group of businesses also with links to Web pages of the parts of the organization with a pre-existing presence. This provides a general corporate feel and presence, if one that is more comprehensive for some parts than others. For example, clicking on the banking icon allows the user access to a series of pages and services, while clicking on the farming icon accesses half a page of text.

Since the Internet is only accessible to a portion of their customers the organization is keen to provide the services available on their Web site to the wider public. For this reason they developed ShoppingKiosk, which is comprised of a personal computer linked to access only their Web pages, live, via the Internet. Access is through a touch-screen interface configured to allow the user to operate it through finger presses instead of keyboard and mouse clicks.

4.2 Actual Design

The pages have not been altered to cater for the touch-screen interface. As with the Internet, commands are actioned by pressing on buttons, icons, text and pictures. Most have been reduced to a single press rather than a double click, however there is no 'little hand' icon to indicate what is and what is not a button.

There is no Internet navigator control panel available. Navigation can only be achieved through pressing buttons on the actual pages or by two control buttons located beneath the pages. On the left-hand side is a button with a left-facing arrow on it, which takes you back to the previous page. On the right-hand side is a button labelled 'home' allowing the user to return to the first screen. Beside the 'home' button is a final control button, not used for navigation, the 'keyboard' button. Some of the screens require input of text, for example name and address. This is achieved through using an on-screen, touch-screen keyboard. This is activated by pressing 'keyboard', which leads to the appearance of an alphabetical keyboard that takes up half the screen. When the user has finished using it, pressing 'keyboard' again removes it.

The screen is about chest height and sits within a housing about two and a half metres high. Above the screen is a sign saying 'touch-screen', while on the housing is information indicating the interactive services available on the kiosk, for example travel, as well as the Web site address. In the store in which it was piloted it was situated side on, against a wall, just inside the main door. As one walked into the store one could see a cigarette counter just across from it, a red post box beside it and the first main isle behind it.

4.3 Evaluation

The idea behind the ShoppingKiosk was, as one company representative said, to "ship it out and see what happened". Little research went into its design, and testing consisted of making sure it worked. Customers were not consulted during the design.

Evaluation, as previously mentioned, consisted of a five day 'quick and dirty' ethnography. This research was conducted opportunistically combining observation, unstructured interviews and user trials. For periods of time customers were observed as they walked past the application to determine their reaction, if any, to it — whether they used it, what for and so forth. Both spontaneous users and those who walked past were interviewed, usually while viewing or using the application. Finally, a variety of customers were asked to explore the application in the manner of a user trial. The ethnography was recorded as detailed hand-written notes. Other materials were drawings and a number of photographs of the location. Unfortunately to maintain anonymity we cannot show any screen shots or photographs within this paper.

4.4 Analysis

Our analysis provided a negative evaluation of ShoppingKiosk. Sustained observation indicated that only a small percentage of shoppers actually noticed the kiosk. Fewer still stopped to look at it, less actually used it. Those who used ShoppingKiosk did so for no more than a few minutes.

Problematically for the kiosk, if so few people even noticed it, whether it was useful and usable might be unimportant. Shoppers who appeared to glance at it were questioned as to what they thought it was and why they had not used it. This provided a range of answers. Although some shoppers indicated that they thought it was about information on the organization, the variety of responses indicated ambiguity. Some suggested it was *"information about the store"*, *"something to do with computers"* or simply that *"they did not know"*. Apparently ShoppingKiosk needs to better self-advertise itself. There were many reasons for not wanting to try and use it. The main reason was customers were busy *"doing their shopping"* with other comments indicating a perceived lack of benefit or relevance.

A particular picture was building up. Few customers were noticing ShoppingKiosk, of those that did many were unsure as to what its purpose was. Of those who knew its purpose or found out only some suggested they would use it. Often saying it would depend on other features of their shopping trip and the store such as how much time they had or how busy the store was.

Interestingly, customers who actually spent time with ShoppingKiosk gave, if anything, a more favourable impression of its usefulness. A number stated that various features were interesting or useful. However, when customers tried to use the application many usability problems became clear:

Buttons: People had problems working out what were buttons, either asking directly what to press or just trying different areas of the screen. This was compounded by the fact that some areas of text and some icons that were buttons were hard to press.

Feedback: The sometimes slow speed of the Internet meant that customers did not get the required feedback, of the page changing, quickly enough. This lead to them pressing buttons twice or more.

Menus and Scrollbars: Some pages contained pop-up, scroll down menus which users found almost impossible to use. When they popped up, if they tried to scroll down, the menu would often disappear. The scroll bars down the sides of pages were similarly difficult to operate. Few users understood the left-facing arrow 'back' button.

Keyboard: Only a portion of users realised that pressing keyboard at the appropriate time would bring up an on-screen keyboard. When the keyboard was up on screen the alphabetical rather than qwerty letter arrangement confused people. Many complained that it was difficult to type with.

Structure and navigation: The structure was complicated. For example, with the group of businesses listed on a central page the impression might be that similar information would be available for each. Instead there was a great variety in amount of information and style of presentation. Navigation through the application was limited therefore customers had trouble finding information or got lost. An index was available but in a large and diverse application the limited number of index entries proved little use in finding specific information.

Overall ShopppingKiosk was a very problematic application. Apart from the usability difficulties customers encountered there are questions over its usefulness and relevancy. However, the organization appears to be willing to take ShoppingKiosk as a first version prototype, therefore the pilot can be taken as a learning experience, although this was not their original intention.

5   Discussion

Existing trade journal and academic work mostly centres on success/failure with little discussion of the reasons for this or provides only very basic design considerations (Corcoran, 1994; Borchers et al., 1995).

This paper provides an in-depth evaluation of two kiosks and attempts to provide more detailed design considerations. In this section several features that can potentially explain the outcomes of their evaluations are discussed.

5.1   Design Method

The applications were designed according to very different design principles. PhotoKiosk was designed with strong reference to users throughout. The current activities and artifact involved were analysed. This was undertaken because it was thought that understanding the current process would give insight into what might be important for developing an electronic version. Another important feature of this method was that users were involved directly in the process of testing and feeding back into design throughout.

There were two parts to the design of ShoppingKiosk. The content was predetermined as the organizations' Web pages, originally meant to be accessed via keyboard and mouse from a personal computer. There may be good reasons for wanting to link kiosks to Web pages, such as to update information centrally (Brousseau, 1997), however, either the GUI of the kiosk or the Web pages themselves need to be designed with this dual purpose in mind. In this case the Web pages were neither designed for touch-screen nor kiosk use. Instead a very basic interface was designed to allow the kiosk to access the Web pages. This new interface was not user trialed, nor was the whole concept. Therefore ShoppingKiosk was designed without any user involvement. It has often been shown that user involvement is an important factor in leading to successful application design (Newman & Robey, 1992). We may tentatively conclude that this may have been a factor that affected project outcome.

5.2   Screen Design

The design of the screens for the kiosks was radically different. PhotoKiosk employed a simple layout with few functions (five at most) on screen at one time. This ensured uncluttered screens with the functions clearly differentiated. Buttons were large and consistently presented in the same shape and colour. They were clearly labelled and all the text was tested to ensure it could be easily read. Feedback was consistently shown — when a button was pressed it would be seen to depress and the screen would change. The process was a simple series of steps and navigation

was basic. Trialists found that these design features all contributed to ease of use. ShoppingKiosk had a much more complex layout often with a lot of information and functions on the screen at one time. One screen contained about 50 choices. Buttons were presented in a variety of ways and sizes causing identification problems, especially as they were not clearly labelled. There was a particular problem pressing small buttons designed for use with a mouse. Slow and inconsistent feedback caused interaction problems. The complex structure of the pages and lack of usable index made navigation difficult. Activating and using the keyboard caused many problems. All these factors made ShoppingKiosk's usability poor.

The simple, clear and consistent screen design and process personified by PhotoKiosk made it a readily usable application for a wide variety of users. The screen design for ShoppingKiosk, in many ways was the antithesis of this. If a large section of kiosk users are naïve users (Totty, 1995) ShoppingKiosk certainly did not appear to cater for them. These evaluations stress the need for basic interface design, with PhotoKiosk being a good example of this.

5.3   Housing and Placement

It was not possible to test the impact of the housing of PhotoKiosk however ShoppingKiosk demonstrates that this is an important issue. The housing for ShoppingKiosk did not seem to attract the attention of customers in the store. When their attention was drawn to the kiosk few could tell exactly what it was for. The labelling did not indicate the exact purpose of the kiosk. It was also placed side on, meaning customers did not immediately see the screen, and placed amongst other distractions. These factors made it hard to notice.

The look of the kiosk is important in attracting peoples attention. It also appears important to place a kiosk in a position where it will stand out from other distractions. Its purpose needs to be clearly identified from a distance, at-a-glance. If people do not notice the application and what it does only a few can be expected to take the time to find out its purpose.

5.4   Purpose and Benefits

The purpose and potential benefits of PhotoKiosk were obvious to the trialists. They indicated that they would be prepared to spend the time to try the application because of its obvious perceived benefits. It also allows them to carry out an activity they already intend do. The purpose of ShoppingKiosk was confusing for the trialists. Different trialists assumed it had different purposes. Few perceived an obvious benefit. As one trialist said:

"why spend time looking up information when you can pick up a leaflet to take home".

A kiosk, like PhotoKiosk, designed with a clear purpose and to provide obvious benefits is more likely to make these clear to the users and contribute to their willingness to use it. An application like ShoppingKiosk, designed with a number of purposes in mind, is more likely to confuse the customer. It is even questionable as to how well diverse purposes sit on this type of retail kiosk and if the designers are not clear about how they are communicating themselves through their artifact it is likely to be a failure. There is also no particular benefit to simply presenting information, already in the environment, electronically. Especially with no printing facility. As is there little point in allowing customers to order goods electronically when they can do this face-to-face in store. A clear benefit seems important in diverting people from the activity they are engaged in onto the kiosk.

5.5   Relevancy

Trialists indicated that they wanted and would expect PhotoKiosk to be situated close to the film processing desk. This would help indicate its purpose and mean that it would be relevant to their current activity. Customers questioned the relevancy of ShoppingKiosk to its surroundings and the activity they were currently engaged in. They were shopping and did not see it as related to that activity. Customers instead asked if, for example, it showed the shop layout or gave out vouchers.

The research suggests that people expect a kiosk in a given environment to be relevant to the other features of that environment. This helps give meaning to these artifacts. If people are in a supermarket they expect a kiosk in that environment to be related to that shop, food and so forth.

6   Conclusions

These two studies illustrate a number of issues that appear to be important for the successful design of touch-screen kiosks for retail environments. The issues of user involvement in the design method and of screen design can be seen to relate to system design as a whole and as such have been discussed in previous work. However we would suggest that they are particularly important in kiosk design because kiosks have a particularly wide range of users with typically short interaction times and no guarantee of repeated use. When they are understood alongside the

specific findings from these studies they can add to a more comprehensive list for successful design.

Once again these studies emphasise that there is a need to carry out some research into users wants and needs when designing a computer application. Indeed, the positive evaluation of the electronic prototype of PhotoKiosk would appear to present the case for the study of the activity to be modelled electronically, and for user involvement in the actual testing and design process. Although PhotoKiosk is a simpler application than ShoppingKiosk this does not mean that the user involvement was not an important aspect of good design.

The Web pages that comprise ShoppingKiosk were originally meant to be read in an environment where the user would most likely have privacy, time, a seat and a keyboard and mouse. Moving this to a supermarket, presenting it on a touch-screen kiosk in a busy part of the store with no seat proved too great a shift of environment. PhotoKiosk was developed especially for its environment.

If a kiosk is to be successful it must *initially attract* potential users. This involves paying attention to where it is to be placed and what it should look like. It must *stand out* from its surroundings and *clearly state* its purpose. In a retail environment potential users are shoppers. If this is their interest it is likely a kiosk which has *relevance to that activity* will gain more users. If the kiosk has done its job in attracting the customers attention, if it offers an *obvious benefit* they are more likely to actually try and use it. Again, being in a retail environment the customer is unlikely to want to spend a long amount of time learning how to use the kiosk so the application must be *easy to use*. A complex structure, a lot of information and a complicated and inconsistent interface are liable to put people off using the kiosk in such an environment.

While ShoppingKiosk is a much more complex application than PhotoKiosk this is precisely a reason why it is a poor application for both a retail environment and a touch-screen. The obvious lessons to be learnt are that *generally* both the nature of a retail environment and that of touch-screen technology need to be catered for in design, and *specifically* the purpose of the touch-screen, the users and the environment it will be placed in need to be investigated in detail.

Currently a simpler and more appropriate version of ShoppingKiosk is being developed, based on user-centred design methods. It will include a two layered hierarchy, fewer screens and services relevant to the supermarket environment.

References

Bødker, S. & Grønbæk, K. (1991), Cooperative Prototyping Studies, *in* J. Bowers & S. Benford (eds.), *Studies in CSCW*, Elsevier Science, pp.68–74.

Borchers, J., Deussan, O. & Knorzer, C. (1995), "Getting it Across: Layout Issues for Kiosk Systems", *ACM SIGCHI Bulletin* **27**(4), 68–74.

Brousseau, M. (1997), "Kiosks Let Dealers Touch People they Wouldn't Ordinarily Reach", *Automotive News* **5697**, 33.

COMIC (1994), "Deliverable 2.1 of COMIC project: Computer-based Mechanisms of Interaction in Cooperative Work". ESPRIT III, project 6225. http//www.comp.lancs.ac.uk/computing/research/cseg/comic/docs/intro.html.

Corcoran, C. T. (1994), "Employment Agency gets a Grip on its Workload", *Infoworld* **16**(46), 122.

Holfelder, W. & Hehmann, D. (1994), A Networked Multimedia Retrieval Management System for Distributed Kiosk Applications, *in Proceedings of the 1994 IEEE International Conference on Multimedia Computing and Systems*, IEEE Computer Society Press.

Martin, D., Wastell, D. & Bowers, J. (1998), Ethnographically Informed System Design (EISD), *in* W. R. J. Baets (ed.), *Proceedings of European Conference on Information Systems*, Vol. 2, Euro-Arab Management School, pp.513–27.

Newman, M. & Robey, D. (1992), "A Social Process Model of User Analyst Relationships", *MIS Quarterly* **16**(2), 249–66.

Scott, B. & Conzala, V. (1997), Designing Touch-screen Numeric Keypads: Effects of Finger Size, Key Size, and Key Spacing, *in "Designing for Diversity; Proceedings of the 41st Annual Meeting*, Vol. 1, Human Factors and Ergonomics Society, pp.360–4.

Totty, J. A. (1995), "Mid-Band Public Multimedia Kiosks", *BT Technology Journal* **13**(4), 97–104.

Wehrer, W. (1997), "Developing Effective Touch System Interfaces", *I&CS* **70**(5), 47–51.

Whybrow, M. (1996), "Nipped in the Bud", *Banking Technology* **13**(6), 34–36.

Human–Computer Interaction — INTERACT '99
M. Angela Sasse and Chris Johnson (Editors)
Published by IOS Press, © IFIP TC.13, 1999

Usability Test Results for Information Visualizations: Determinants of Usefulness for Complex Business Problems

Barbara Mirel

Lucent Technologies, Visual Insights Group, 263 Shuman 1C-512, Naperville, Illinois 60566, USA.

bmirel@visualinsights.com

Abstract: Designers know too little about how users conduct realistic business analyses with interactive graphics. This article reports the results of two usability tests that assessed visualizations for use-in-context and realistic tasks. Results show that meanings in visualized displays are socially negotiated and that users — even novices — do ad hoc analysis for any inquiries that are the least bit unstructured. Results also show that users have integrated views of core problem-solving activities that they expect the visualizations to support. These results suggest a user model and designs for utility that would address it. To support ad hoc analysis, visualizations need to make it easy for users to create variables and new fields on the fly and to help users learn the right graphics to use for specific types of problems. For users' concepts of tasks, programs have to provide feedback on interactions and display states so that users may weave discrete actions into an integrated whole. Programs also have to offer memory aids and reporting capabilities to help users keep track of where they have been, what they know, and what they still need to discover. Only contextual and scenario-based testing can uncover these utility-based issues, all of which are crucial to users' mastery of visual querying.

Keywords: information visualization, data visualization, contextual usability testing, usability, scenario-based testing, interactive graphics.

1 Introduction

At present, analysts in industry use graphics — such as those in *Crystal Reports* or *Excel* — in two ways: either to present results from an analysis or to conduct the analysis itself. Presenting results graphically is easy. Using graphics for analysis, however, is not. Each step of inquiry calls for flipping back and forth between spreadsheet and graphic data which is time consuming and tedious.

Yet business analysts want to discover insights through graphics. In studies that I am conducting with retail market analysts, they estimate that 60% to 80% of their analytical time is taken up formatting data and moving back and forth between spreadsheets and graphics. That leaves only 20% for the crux of data analysis — interpreting, concluding, and developing new strategies. Business analysts need better ways to visually analyse data.

Interactive visualizations offer this improvement. (See Figure 1.) They are dynamic, letting users interact with multiple, linked views at once to see the same data from different perspectives. They are interactive, allowing users to bring in and change additional dimensions through such visual cues as colour, size, and position. Finally, they let users query by directly manipulating data in graphics — selecting, deleting, sorting, filtering, zooming. In visualizations, users almost simultaneously search for, retrieve, and interpret data.

Because visual analysis is new to business environments and because visualizations may be used for complex problem-solving, users need help in adapting them to their work-related purposes, domains, contexts, and problem-solving practices. This help should be built into the software and interfaces.

This article examines empirically the support that visualization software needs to provide in order to be coherent with users' actual visual analysis for complex business problems. My focus is on complex data analysis because this use of interactive graphics is the most uncharted territory in visualization design today. I am the usability specialist on a design and development team that is creating interactive visualizations for business analysis and problem-solving. Based on findings from my scenario-based testing and contextual usability testing (in progress), I argue that for complex problem-solving, visualization software must address three high level aspects of an end-user model — aspects that currently receive scant attention in design. These aspects are:

1. users' scope in actual complex inquiries, including ad hoc analysis;

2. the program interactions that users integrate into a single task; and

3. the social and situated dimensions of data analysis.

Results from my studies reveal user traits associated with each of these three aspects, and they have implications for software design.

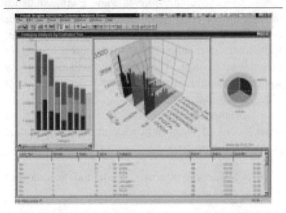

Figure 1: Linked and interactive bar chart, 3D table, pie chart and data sheet showing customer sales by brand, store, time, gender.

2 Background: Current Research

Users' approaches to solving complex problems are highly varied, contextually determined, and often unpredictable. Architecturally, visualizations for complex problem-solving usually provide two or more dynamically linked workspaces to let users view and manipulate their data from many angles at once. For complex problem-solving, designers need to attend to users' high level inquiry tasks which have cognitive and perceptual demands that differ in kind not just degree from well-structured, more formulaic problem-solving. In focusing on these tasks, designers give high priority to utility — that is, to making software coherent with users' actual work practices.

Designing for high utility requires knowing and supporting the core activities of open-ended visual querying. These core activities are enumerated and discussed in the Results and Discussion section below. Few usability studies in interactive graphics focus on these core activities in context, the user model they imply, or on designing for this user model. My usability studies strive to fill this gap.

Extensive research and product information on information visualizations can be found in On-line Library of Information Visualization Environments (OLIVE) http://www.otal.umd.edu/Olive). Most empirical testing focuses on program features, user interface controls, or perceptual processing load, asking users either to operate various features or controls or to follow the steps of a pre-defined structured task. Studies have compared, for example, different designs for features such as zooming to find the most intuitive, accessible and spatially orienting design (Johnson, 1995). Researchers also have tested the structures for data display — such as folding lists for large data sets — to identify the ones that best facilitate meaning and interactivity (Furnas, 1997). They have examined the combinations of text and visuals that help users accurately interpret graphics that may be coded in multiple ways — by colour, size, shape and position (Kitajima & Polson, 1996; Yazici, 1995); and they have comparatively evaluated various devices for setting up and conducting queries – sliders, drag-and-drop routines, select-by-sweeping options and fish-eye lenses (Fishkin & Stone, 1995; Kumar et al., 1997). Studies have also examined the information that flows from the screen, finding, for instance that if screen text is overly technical or otherwise obtuse, compensating with improved terms and language in online Help will not improve users' understanding or performance (Terwilliger & Polson, 1997).

A minority of studies do diverge from this focus on features and controls and from a bias toward structured problems. They test the ways in which program and UI designs correspond to a broader concept of users' tasks, for instance the tasks of troubleshooting and strategic planning and the 'meta-tasks' of setting up tasks and switching task environments.

Tweedie et al. (1996), for instance, find that using sliders to filter data is not an effective design when queries are complex. These researchers also find that when users have pressing questions — as in troubleshooting tasks — they want only a few colours in the colour-coding scheme, but when they do more nuanced work such as strategic planning they value a full spectrum of colours. Kandogan & Shneiderman (1997) argue that users benefit from different window management schemes according to their immediate task purpose (setting up a task, executing it, switching task environments) but that for most tasks elastic windows are best. And investigators have found that users master querying better when they control what fields are displayed, how results are sequenced, and how they are clustered (Pirolli et al., 1996).

Strikingly, none of these more task-oriented studies takes a contextual and social view of visual querying. Contextual testing and scenario-based testing are common in human factors but sorely lacking in the specific area of visualization software. As important as the task-oriented studies discussed above are, they neither address the same questions as contextual and scenario-based testing nor do they produce as comprehensive a set of traits for a user model. It is toward this end — the start of a comprehensive user model for complex visual querying — that I have conducted my usability studies.

3 Methods

To develop a user model for visually solving complex problems I have conducted a scenario-based user test and various contextual assessments in two different work domains — intranet management and consumer package goods marketing. My methods for each follow.

3.1 Scenario-based User Testing

I created a rich scenario drawn from managers' actual analyses in call centres when they evaluate agent performance. The scenario asked users to find agents with the most worrisome performance, using visualizations for the entire inquiry. Users worked with pre-scripted sets of graphics that had a week's worth of data on performance metrics read into them (for instance, time spent on a call, time spent entering data, time spent taking personal incoming calls).

The problem of worrisome agent performance was semi structured. It does not have one right answer nor can it be performed using a foolproof formulaic method. Test participants made judgements throughout their inquiry. The scenario gave participants criteria to guide their judgements based on actual call centre standards and provided participants with a suggested method for analysis. Test users, however, pursued any methods and paths of inquiry that fit their evolving interpretations and insights.

Ten users participated in this study. In an effort to control for factors that influence users' performance with visualizations, my human factors colleague and I screened participants to include people with roughly the same amounts and types of knowledge and experience in data analysis, software graphics, and performance metrics. We also gave all of the participants the same training. For all test users data analysis was a core aspect of their job, and 70% of them had extensive experience evaluating performance metrics. All of the participants were novices to visualizations though they all had used static graphics to conduct analysis and to present findings. Independent variables for which we did not control include users' problem-solving approaches, learning styles, vision, gender, and age.

The data set comprises 2,816 records for 36 call centre agents. For this problem-solving activity, users interacted with six different graphics: A bar chart, a data sheet, a scatter-plot, a view giving statistics for metrics for each agent, and two special graphics created by Bell Labs researchers — a parallel box-plot and a trends over time view. At times users had all six graphics up at once. They managed windows as they wanted and could create new graphics, visual cues or bring in new data as needed.

To gather data, my colleague and I recorded our observations of users at work and their think-aloud protocols, focusing on:

- Sequences, patterns, speed, and accuracy of actions and accessing of features.

- Impasses or errors requiring Help, when and why errors were detected or not, methods and speed of error recovery, reasons for not recovering.

- Number of times referencing Help, time in Help, searches, keywords, and success rates.

- Conceptions/misconceptions due to conventions, prior mental models of querying, assumptions about the software.

In analysing the test data, we tabulated times, accuracy counts, and other patterns in behaviour relevant to gauging whether program and UI design and Help were coherent with users' actual approaches to this problem.

3.2 Contextual Testing

In my contextual studies, I examined visualizations for complex problem-solving in two domains:

1. the management of corporate intranet performance; and

2. category management and customer behaviour.

Users respectively included Information Technology analysts responsible for troubleshooting slow response times in their company networks and market analysts responsible for developing new product strategies. In both domains, users interacted with alpha or beta versions.

In the intranet troubleshooting study, I observed two users in two different work settings as they interacted with visualizations to find the cause of slow response times. Visualizations were one of many network management tools open on the users' desktops for troubleshooting. I was careful not to gear them toward using visualizations more than they needed for troubleshooting.

My on-site testing with market analysts is still in progress. By the time of the conference, I will have completed a study of five retail analysts in four different work sites. These analysts have at least three years of experience with *Excel*-based analyses; they all had to make a transition to visual querying.

In contextual assessments, I spent one to two hours a day for two to four days shadowing users as they conducted their ongoing work. They thought aloud as they worked, and I interrupted only to clarify variables with which they were working or to identify other tools that they brought into their analyses. Users conducted their work as if I were not there — taking phone calls, getting interrupted by co-workers, multi-tasking, taking breaks. Users also filled out logs each time they visually queried without me there. My choices of methods reflect my working in a different state from users.

In my observations, I recorded the same issues as in the scenario testing. In addition, I focused on the tools and other information that users integrated with the visualizations and on the organizational purpose for analysis and its role in a system of work and communication. I also examined the ways in which organizational mandates shaped the paths of users' inquiry; the effects of physical office arrangements on users' processes of inquiry; the effects of users' roles and authority on the depth and strategy of their problem-solving; users' patterns of work and interruptions; instances of individual and collective problem-solving; and the ways that users negotiated meaning alone and jointly.

4   Results and Discussion

Broadly, results show two things:

1. the analyses that users conduct with visualizations for real world problems; and

2. user traits relevant to a user model.

I will look at each type of result in turn.

4.1   Problems and Analyses in Context

Only the findings from contextual testing reveal users' actual problems in context and their corresponding visual querying practices. I present one instance from each work domain and context.

1 An intranet manager analyses network data to find the source of slow response time.

This user is notified by her beeper through a network monitoring tool that an alarm fired for a slow transaction in the network. She acts immediately. She responds quickly because her IT department has contracted service level agreements with users. Any response times that exceed the guaranteed level — indicated by an alarm — incur costs for the IT department.

To inquire into this problem, the user checks the screen of her network monitoring tool to see where the alarm fired. It fired on an Accounts/Receivables (A/R) user's machine for a transaction sent to the Sybase server. Focusing on this machine, she pulls up a pre-scripted view in the visualization software that shows every transaction for users' machines over the course of the day (see Figure 2).

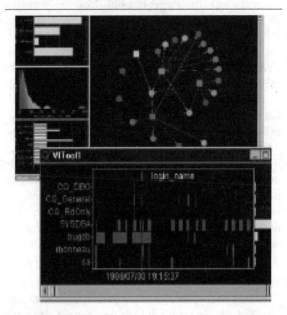

Figure 2: In the bottom graph, each mark is a transaction sent by a PC plotted over time. In the top graph, PCs are linked to the servers to which they sent transactions.

Transactions coloured red show high response times — some alarming, some close to it. The user selects red transactions and deletes the others. She now drills down for details on just these transactions to characterize the problem.

In these transactions, she looks in the data sheet for details about transactions that had high response times and few rows sent to the server, an indication that something is askew. It shouldn't take a long time to transmit a small number of rows. She sorts the data table, finds the subset she's looking for, and selects it.

She now drills down further to examine if this subset of transactions is slow because of the network or the server. She examines the two times that comprise response time:

1. time sent from a PC to a server; and

2. time returning back from the server to the PC.

For this part of the analysis, she switches to the top pre-scripted perspective shown in Figure 2. The links show transactions sent from a PC to a server. She colour-codes the links by send time; red indicates a long time. Then she switches the colour-coding to return time.

This colour-coding doesn't give her the comparison between high send and return times that she wants. Therefore, she uses different visual codings. She codes the colour of the links by send time and codes the size of the links by return time (the wider the link, the longer it took). Now she sees that all red links are also wide, assuring her of a network problem.

Convinced that the network is slow, she now switches to her network troubleshooting tools to diagnose and resolve the problem. She wants a simple way to export information on transaction times from her visualizations to her network tool but it does not exist. Therefore, she spends time jotting down the information on a pad of paper and is about to enter it into the network tool when a co-worker comes in and asks her to help him. She leaves for about five minutes. When she returns she spends several minutes re-orienting herself. She has to re-interpret the last display in the visualizations and her notes for the network tool.

2   A grocery analyst wants to discover what pasta sauce he should introduce into his store.

This user looked at many brands and items and weighed and compared dollar sales, market share and percent gain or loss. He does this type of analysis frequently but the angles he takes vary by retail category. Categories, he notes, each have their own

'character'. Pasta sauce's 'character' is that a limited number of vendors and brands have the top 75% of the market with wide variation in tier (up-scale, mainstream, and canned); flavour; and size.

For this analysis, the user first identifies the brands within pasta sauce that his retail store does not carry but that are doing well nationwide. He looks at dollar and volume sales in the national market (excluding his own market) and compares them with his market. He identifies a promising brand.

He now examines this brand nationwide. He finds the items doing well in this brand, and they become potential new products to introduce in his grocery. To find these products, he looks at the market share and growth of items in this brand and compares them to other brands.

Then he narrows down within items to the best tier, flavours, and sizes. He looks for high market share and growth but considers lower market share if growth is dramatically high.

From his inquiry, he sees that it looks promising to introduce an up-scale, garlic and vegetable, 26 ounce pasta sauce. He prints and saves the outcomes of this visual querying. He now starts analysing anew, examining the same questions but now only for his market. He hopes to find that the same combined tier, flavour and size that are successful nationwide are successful in his market but under-stocked in his own stores. He comes close to this conclusion, varying only by flavour. In his market garlic is doing better than garlic and vegetable, and his store carries little of either flavour. He saves and prints the results of this portion of his inquiry.

To decide about flavour, he now compares only the brands that comprise 75% of the national market nation to his market. To get this 75%, he needs to create new variables — aggregating data to get averages for only these top brands for sales, market share and average growth for each item, tier, flavour, and size.

He has a hard time doing these transformations in the visualization software. He therefore, exits the program, does the aggregations in his data file, and returns to the visualizations now reloaded with the new variables. Fortunately, the visualizations let him save the state of his analysis so that when he resumes his work with the new aggregated variables he does not have to start from scratch. He does, however, take some time re-orienting after interrupting his analysis.

He compares his market to the rest of the market for sales, growth, and share and gets strong evidence that he should stick with the garlic and vegetable flavour. This flavour, introduced only a short while ago into the market, is the clear winner in 75% of the market; he believes it is due to take off soon in his market.

He prints and saves the last display in the visualizations in its current state. He tries to annotate it for later reference but is confused about how to annotate. He wants to annotate the other saved sessions, as well. In his mind, the analysis is not over until he completes these actions for communicating findings.

4.2 Traits for a User Model

1 Scope. Users who are experienced data analysts go into ad hoc analysis for problems that are the least bit unstructured even if they are visualization novices.

This finding is critical because if users cannot do ad hoc analysis sufficiently — if they cannot create (calculate) new variables as they work and display them — their problem-solving falters. This ad hoc tendency flies in the face of many visualization designers' assumptions that pre-structured graphics and parameters for specific domain questions will satisfy users' problem-solving needs.

One user in the scenario test, for example, reached a point in which he could not decide on worrisome agents unless he summed the values of two columns to create a new variable. Unfortunately the software did not provide easy ways to transform variables on the fly. Without a solution, this user's plans and goals fell apart. The one-to-one correspondence between intentions and program interactions crumbled.

2 Task definition. Users define core problem-solving activities at a higher level than program operations and expect visualizations to support their integrated concepts of an activity.

Results reveal the ways in which users define the following core activities:

1. preparing data;

2. choosing the right graphics for a question;

3. interpreting data;

4. managing inquiry;

5. communicating results; and

6. selecting data.

I discuss selecting data last because scenario test results about it are extensive.

2.1 Preparing data takes place before inquiry and during data selection.

Users started inquiries by preparing and transforming their data in their spreadsheets or text files. But they also prepared data in the midst of inquiry when exploratory analysis raised the need to create a new field or calculate a new variable. Having to exit the program to do so broke their train of thought, slowed down querying, and detracted from problem-solving.

2.2 Knowing the right graphic for a question requires a good deal of experience but users want to have this skill almost as soon as they start using visualizations.

This competence develops late in a novice's learning curve. But without it users are hampered in ad hoc analysis which they want to do right away. Users reported frustration that they were not developing it more readily.

2.3 Interpreting graphics for complex problems requires multiple views of the same data and leveraging the value of one view to another.

Complex problem solving is more complicated than the overview-zoom-details mantra that works for structured problems. Rarely if ever did descriptive (fact) findings satisfy users. They sought to answer 'why' questions by comparing cross-sectionally and longitudinally, by analysing changes over time, by drilling down for detail, and in hierarchical data by relating several measures across multiple dimensions.

2.4 Managing inquiry requires memory aids to ease users' cognitive and perceptual load.

Users held a lot of data and inferences in mind at once, compounded by interrupting and resuming their work. If the program did not supply adequate information aids or easy annotation capabilities, they used paper and pen to mark where they were and what they knew.

2.5 Communicating findings requires complementing graphics with text.

To present findings, users demanded the ability to supplement graphics with explanations and captions, not simply capture screen displays.

2.6 Users define selecting data at a higher level than the couple program operations used for sweeping (selecting) data. To users, selecting included these integrated actions:

Setting up a display for selection — Selecting data with the right mode — Verifying that one selected what one thought one selected — Deciding what to do next.

When any one of these unified actions for selection became uncertain, the whole selection task was threatened. These instances of uncertainty contribute to a user model by revealing user expectations about the integrated selection task. Findings on uncertainties follow:

- In selection, users expect overt feedback on the values that they select during and after selection. 20% of the users said that without feedback, they weren't confident of their selection or of their overall inquiry.

- Users expect results of selection to match their intentions and may neglect to verify if, in fact, they do. When mismatches occured and users noticed them, they expected ample indications from the program about the results of selection and the program state so that they could figure out what went wrong. 33% of the users did not recognize incomplete selections. Due to scanty feedback, users who did notice the disparity rarely tied it to its rightful cause.

- Users expect to manipulate data for selecting without having their attention diverted from their task to the tool. Sorting two or more columns in the data table to prepare for selection took on average six minutes. Users lost their place and had to return to the start of the selection task, probably due to their integrated concept of selection.

- Users expect the formalisms of written queries to guide them sufficiently in visual querying. When they don't, users need help in pictorially thinking about selection. Users understood intersections and joins from written query and search statements but had difficulty transforming these notions into visual interactions. When they experienced errors, users backed up almost to the start of their querying to shift from thinking formalistically to pictorially.

- Users expect to be able to transform variables into whatever content makes sense to their aims for selecting subsets. As one user's inability to recover shows, not being able to transform data threatens querying more than any other unmet expectation.

3 Social and situated queries. Users' analyses are shaped by their job roles, status, workplace incentives, collaborations, relations with stakeholders, and norms and practices.

Only the contextual findings reveal social and situated dimensions as follows:

3.1 For the same question, different analysts dig deeply or superficially based on job role, status, and incentives for strategic analysis.

The retail analysts who had status as 'resident experts' or who were being groomed for managerial roles spent long times examining many angles of the data. Another analyst who did not have 'stellar' status considered inventive angles but did not implement them because they were not 'part of her job'.

3.2 Users' methods and depth of analysis are shaped by relationships with stakeholders and the inherently persuasive purposes of analysis.

At times, retail analysts examined product opportunities based on a priori notions about persuasive success. They had longstanding relations with clients and knew what was needed to persuade these clients.

3.3 Organizational crises incite new analyses and reporting that users must learn and implement immediately.

In one network management case, when an operations unit introduced a new application, network performance suffered. An organizational crisis emerged, and no one was willing to own the application causing the problems. The IT manager escalated the troubleshooting analysis that his staff conducted and introduced new reporting requirements. Findings on causes of poor performance were critical for showing who owned both the problem and its costs.

3.4 Users' negotiated meanings may differ from the inferences a user draws alone, prompting users to do more collaborative work.

In the IT user's case, she saw a discrepancy between the network management tools and the visualizations. She asked a co-worker to help her determine which view was valid. Discussions made her see the visualization differently from how she first had interpreted it. This experience motivated her to negotiate visual meaning with co-workers more often. It also led to more inventive uses of colour-coding to accord with the users' schemes for classifying the problem and data.

3.5 Users confer over the phone and need to call up the visualizations at a distance.

Distance collaboration requires calling up the exact same visualizations in the exact same state. Lacking this coordination, users cannot jointly solve a problem visually.

3.6 Users inevitably interrupt and resume their visual querying.

Analysts multi-task and work jointly with others. They need to mark their places and thoughts as they move through visual querying.

5 Design Implications

Findings show a multifaceted user model for complex problem-solving with visualizations. Users pursue their own ad hoc approaches. They respond in speed and depth based on organizational crisis. They expect to be able to create whatever variables they need to answer their questions. They collaborate at least partially to discover meanings from the graphics. They move so quickly through questions and displays that they need memory aids to mark where they are and where they've been, and they lose confidence when their analysis falters or diverts them too long from their task to the tool.

Based on findings, the following program and UI designs are critical for high utility:

- Architecturally, provide users with multiple, linked graphics that they can leverage for insights and answers to 'why' questions.

- For ad hoc analysis, aid users in learning to create the right graphs for their questions, new variables, innovative visual encodings.

- Support users' integrated notions of core activities through adequate feedback on what they just did, what program state they are in, what state the data is in (colouring, ordering), what data is showing or hidden. This feedback may legitimately require using screen real estate for text, not data.

- Ease perceptual and cognitive overload by giving users ways to write comments about displays during inquiry and ways to feed outcomes into other tools for further inquiry.

- Include at least basic reporting capabilities — titles, captions, labels, textual explanations.

- Let users make perceptual cues accord with their notions of the data and problem by giving them easy ways to control colour mappings and the positioning of data.

- Provide preference settings that make distance coordination easy and quick.

These utility issues do not supplant the need to make visualizations easy to use in terms of navigation and access. But it is utility improvements such as these that enhance the likelihood of users succeeding in both their inquiries and their persuasive ends.

References

Fishkin, K. & Stone, M. (1995), Enhanced Dynamic Queries via Movable Filters, *in* I. Katz, R. Mack, L. Marks, M. B. Rosson & J. Nielsen (eds.), *Proceedings of CHI'95: Human Factors in Computing Systems*, ACM Press. http://www.acm.org/sigchi/chi95/proceedings/papers/kpf_bdy.htm.

Furnas, G. W. (1997), Effective View Navigation, *in* S. Pemberton (ed.), *Proceedings of CHI'97: Human Factors in Computing Systems*, ACM Press, pp.367–74.

Johnson, J. (1995), A Comparison of User Interfaces for Panning on a Touch-controlled Display, *in* I. Katz, R. Mack, L. Marks, M. B. Rosson & J. Nielsen (eds.), *Proceedings of CHI'95: Human Factors in Computing Systems*, ACM Press, pp.218–25.

Kandogan, E. & Shneiderman, B. (1997), Elastic Windows: Evaluation of Multi-window Operations, *in* S. Pemberton (ed.), *Proceedings of CHI'97: Human Factors in Computing Systems*, ACM Press. http://www.acm.org/sigchi/chi97/proceedings/paper/ek.htm.

Kitajima, M. & Polson, P. G. (1996), A Comprehension-based Model of Exploration, *in* G. van der Veer & B. Nardi (eds.), *Proceedings of CHI'96: Human Factors in Computing Systems*, ACM Press, pp.324–31. http://www.acm.org/sigchi/chi96/proceedings/paper/kitajima/mk_txt.htm.

Kumar, H., Plaisant, C. & Shneiderman, B. (1997), "Browsing Hierarchical Data with Multi-level Dynamic Queries and Pruning", *International Journal of Human–Computer Studies* **46**, 103–24.

Pirolli, P., Pikow, J. & Rao, R. (1996), Silk From a Sow's Ear: Extracting Usable Structures From the Web, *in* G. van der Veer & B. Nardi (eds.), *Proceedings of CHI'96: Human Factors in Computing Systems*, ACM Press. http://www.acm.org/sigchi/chi96/proceedings/paper/Pirolli_2/ppp2.html.

Terwillinger, R. & Polson, P. (1997), Relationships Between Users' and Interfaces, *in* S. Pemberton (ed.), *Proceedings of CHI'97: Human Factors in Computing Systems*, ACM Press. http://www.acm.org/sigchi/chi97/proceedings/paper/pol.htm.

Tweedie, L., Spence, R., Dawkes, H. & Su, J. (1996), Externalising Abstract Mathematical Models, *in* G. van der Veer & B. Nardi (eds.), *Proceedings of CHI'96: Human Factors in Computing Systems*, ACM Press, pp.406–12.

Yazici, H. (1995), A Cognitive Approach to the Influence of Graphics on Decision-Making, *in* J. Carey (ed.), *Human Factors in Information Systems*, Ablex, pp.101–12.

Human–Computer Interaction — INTERACT '99
M. Angela Sasse and Chris Johnson (Editors)
Published by IOS Press, © IFIP TC.13, 1999

Register-domain Separation as a Methodology for Development of Natural Language Interfaces to Databases

Serge Sharoff & Vlad Zhigalov

Russian Research Institute for Artificial Intelligence, PO Box 111, 103001 Moscow, Russia.

{sharoff,zhigalov}@aha.ru

Abstract: Wider application of interfaces to access databases in natural language is hindered by the problem of portability, i.e. customization of a general-purpose language-processing component to a particular database. In this paper we propose a methodology which is based on a separation of the domain model of a database from the register of database queries, i.e. a system of meanings employed by natural language for making queries. The paper describes basic concepts of the domain model, the procedure required for tuning the parsing engine to a database and the semantic-oriented approach for parsing queries. The described methodology is implemented as InBase, a system which allows easy and efficient development of interfaces to arbitrary SQL databases.

Keywords: natural language, database, portability, domain model, parsing, vocabulary content.

1 Introduction

A recent introduction to the field of natural language interfaces to databases (NLIDBs) states that it is no longer a fashionable topic of academic research (Androutsopoulos et al., 1995). However, this still does not undermine the practical importance of this task, which is aimed at extraction of data from a database using a natural language (NL) as the universal medium for human communication instead of learning a formal query language with its artificial and rigid syntax. The second thing to be learned by a user is the data model of a database: a user usually knows a database problem domain, however, arrangement of this knowledge in tables, attributes and values of a corresponding (typically relational) database can be completely strange. These two types of problems are presented by a simple query in English *Average salary of managers in support services?* which corresponds to an SQL statement:

```
select AVG(Personnel.Salary)
from Personnel, Departments
where (Personnel.DeptID =
Departments.DeptID)
and (Departments.Name = "Service")
and (Personnel.Category ¡ 2)
```

Thus, structures of natural language expressions are mapped into SQL statements keeping the following conventions:

- Keeping the formal syntax of SQL, for example, the averaging operation is expressed as AVG(Personnel.Salary).

- Department names are not stored in the same table as information on personnel (so the join operation between two tables is necessary).

- The department of support services is stored under the title 'Service'.

- Categories of personnel are encoded by integers; in particular, managers are denoted by numbers 0 and 1.

All these conventions are hard to be kept in mind for a computer-illiterate user. Often, command-line interfaces, which input is based on a formal language, are replaced by graphical user interfaces (GUIs). This achieves both simplification of formal syntax (the user chooses a respective label, like AVG, from a list of options) and simplification of data presentation (data distributed over several tables are combined in a single screen object). However, GUIs require skills in interaction, thus constituting an interface language, which sometimes is more tedious to use than a formal language proper (in MS Access, for example, formulation of the expression AVG(Personnel.Salary) requires a sequence of 15 mouse clicks and very deliberate choices from appeared options). On the other hand, expression of queries in user-oriented representations, like Seeheim model applications (Olsen, Jr, 1992), (Wegener, 1995), is hindered by contextual dependency of what user treats as objects and their slots. For example, a country may be treated as an object in such queries as *Which countries supply products costing above twenty pounds?*, while the domain model treats Country as an attribute of Supplier, which is an attribute of the Product. In contrast, the system of meanings encoded in natural language with its relations and induced metaphors is by far the most natural system of meanings for a naïve user.

By such reasons development of NLIDBs has been one of the most popular directions of computational linguistics research since late sixties, scored close to machine translation. However, modern reviews of the state of the art, for example, (Androutsopoulos et al., 1995), (Copestake & Sparck Jones, 1990) admit that NLIDBs are not wide-spread and existing systems for development of them are far from commercial applications. Obstacles for wider application of NLIDBs are partly related to the principal incompleteness of existing technologies for parsing queries (this is also related to the problem of user's false negative and positive expectations about queries acceptable by the system). However, portability issues are of the same importance, relating to amount of efforts required for tuning a general analyser to a particular database.

The technology described in this paper mostly addresses the latter problem; it allows semi-automatic creation of a simple interface to user's database. In several person-days or weeks this interface can be improved to handle complex queries.

The basic design principles of InBase are discussed in Section 2; Section 3 is devoted to the Domain Model and its relation to the Database Model; Section 4 describes operations required for customization of InBase for a new database. Section 5 gives an overview of a parsing engine used for analysis of NL queries. Throughout this paper, examples refer to a database for the personnel of a sample company. The database consists of two tables: Personnel and Departments, first of which consists of attributes of Name, BirthDate, HireDate, Post, Category, DeptId, Sex, ChildNum, Marriage, Salary, Telephone. The second table consists of attributes of DeptId, Name, Chief, Operations.

2   Design Principles of InBase

The need for a separation of the core processing engine from the database-specific component is widely accepted in design of modern NLIDBs (Alshawi, 1992). However, the core engine mostly deals with syntactic analysis, which results are hard to map into database query statements, thus increasing the amount of efforts for customization. In contrast, the core parsing engine of InBase operates in terms of functions (language-oriented meanings) and follows the notion of register, which, according to Halliday (1978), describes a functional variation engendered by language use in a problem domain, cf. an analysis of the register of mathematics in Ch.11 of (Halliday, 1978). The register of the database queries differs from a problem domain, which is represented by a database: the register is a semiotic system of functions and means, which express these functions. Functions of the register of database queries include, for example, *Attribute, Value, Aggregate-Value*, etc.; configurations of functions are *Predicate, Interval, Class-Instance*, etc. The notion of register in InBase provides possibility to reuse semantic knowledge expressed in linguistic structures across different domains

Basically, tuning of the parsing engine of InBase to a user's database consists in development of a vocabulary (which domain-dependent part is extracted from the database automatically), mapping it onto domain model resources, including functional classes, which are included in the system, and testing for a proper mapping of register-based functions into database statements (the procedure is described in greater detail in Section 4).

Methods for analysis of user's queries also follows the classification of functions using, in the first place, semantic and pragmatic components of the communication as well as its context, instead of complete syntactic parsing of a query. The background of this original semantic-oriented approach (Narin'yani, 1980) is close to such approaches as Wilks' preferential semantics (Wilks, 1968), which was also applied to analysis of database queries by Boguraev & Sparck Jones (1981). So, instead of looking into syntactic constructions and lexical meanings (thus slipping into notorious problems like attachment of prepositional phrases or meanings of nominal compounds), the parsing engine determines "What function can be denoted by this particular lexical item?", "Which configurations of functions are possible?" and "What are linguistic constructions for their expression?". Another advantage of using functions is a greater congruence of their system across languages which are even not closely related typologically (the work reported in this paper has been done primarily for Russian and English with experiments for French, German, Georgian, and Czech, which happened to have relatively minor differences in their registers of database queries).

Analysis of a query results in a partial specification of an object requested (cf. Figure 1). Conceptually this partial specification is represented as a typed-feature structure constraining a set of objects that conform to this query. Structures of the intermediate representation language (Q) for partial specifications correspond to user's expectations for meanings encoded in the database.

From the user's viewpoint, a retrieved set of objects corresponding to this specification is either presented as a list (using forms corresponding to the class of retrieved objects and some conditions of the query) or mapped into a value (when an aggregate value, like *average* or *how many* is requested). A value returned from an aggregate value can be used in embedded queries, as in the query shown in Figure 1.

The Q-level corresponds to notions at the level of problem domain and is independent from the internal organization of a database. For example, it is natural for the database to store the birth date, as a constant value instead of person's age, while in the NL-query it is more natural to refer to this date from the current moment perspective (*Who is older than 40?* instead of *Who was born earlier than 01/01/59?*). A partial specification in Q-language is translated into an SQL query using joint operations for virtual attributes and substitution rules for such values as 'engineers' (which is a set of different positions) and '40 years' using information from the domain model of a database.

3   Domain Model

The core structure of a domain model (DM) in InBase is based on entity-relationship diagrams (ERDs). A DM consists of elements (including classes, attributes, values of attributes), and relations between them. Structural relations (the inheritance relation between classes, the slot relation between a class and its attributes) define a set of types of user's DM; they assemble entities in terms of ERD. Other relations may be defined between entities; they are whole-part and class-instance. The latter relation is of particular importance in relational databases, since often one table defines types (for example, goods) and another one — instances (for example, sold items). This distinction and its implications for the content of a formal query are rarely understood by a naïve

user (*Who deals with spare parts?*   vs. *Who sold spare parts to John Smith?*). The methodology for DM development in InBase significantly differs from other DM methodologies, like (Prieto-Diaz & Arango, 1991) due to the static nature of DMs in InBase. Such DM encodes only meanings pertaining to user's database, so it lacks some elements typical for CHI DMs, like tasks and scripts for interaction. DMs in InBase are represented using Resource Description Framework, RDF (W3C, 1999). Though RDF was designed as a language to describe meta-data of Web documents, it captures all the DM semantics necessary for the InBase. The Figure 2 shows the ERD for our database and fragments of its RDF-description. Note that the class Employee inherits the class Person, which belongs to the library of InBase classes facilitating development of user's DMs. This class belongs to built-in classes, since data about persons and their standard attributes (like name, age, etc.)   are often stored in databases and NL-queries employ specific constructions referring to them, so this knowledge facilitates understanding of such queries. Other classes in this library are locations, units of measurements, and so on.

Partially an ERD maps onto the relational schema of a database (database tables correspond to classes, and attributes to properties of classes). In many cases, however, some semantically significant features of the DM are not reflected in the database model, and even in its content. For example, instances of classes Employee and Chief are stored in a single table; some attributes of the class Employee are virtual; they represent relations to other objects (Department is stored in another table). The database model also defines no relation between values of Education, but in user's terms, types of education constitute a scale, so in order to answer such questions as *Who has no higher education?*, the education scale should be modelled in the DM. The RDF representation of the education scale is the following:

```
<ib:Class ID="Education"/>
<dm:Education ID="Primary"/>

<dm:Education ID="Secondary"/>
<dm:Education ID="Higher_Ed"/>
<dm:Higher_Ed ID="BA"/>
<dm:Higher_Ed ID="MS"/>
<dm:Higher_Ed ID="PhD"/>
<ib:Seq><dm:Primary/><dm:Secondary/>
<dm:Higher/></ib:Seq>
<ib:Seq><dm:BA/><dm:MS/><dm:PhD/>
</ib:Seq>
```

In SQL the condition:

```
Employee[Education < higher_ed]
```

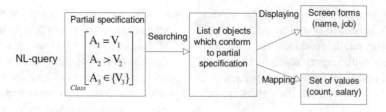

Who has the maximum salary among engineers employed for more than 10 years.

$$EMPLOYEE \left[salary = MAX \left(salary \leftarrow \begin{array}{c} {}_{EMPLOYEE} \end{array} \left[\begin{array}{c} job\_title \supseteq 'engineer' \\ duty\_duration > 10years \end{array} \right] \right) \right]$$

Figure 1: The query processing scheme.

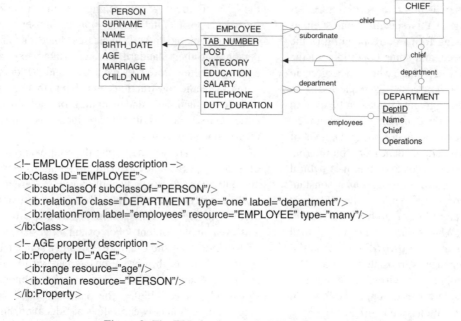

```
<!- EMPLOYEE class description ->
<ib:Class ID="EMPLOYEE">
  <ib:subClassOf subClassOf="PERSON"/>
  <ib:relationTo class="DEPARTMENT" type="one" label="department"/>
  <ib:relationFrom label="employees" resource="EMPLOYEE" type="many"/>
</ib:Class>
<!- AGE property description ->
<ib:Property ID="AGE">
  <ib:range resource="age"/>
  <ib:domain resource="PERSON"/>
</ib:Property>
```

Figure 2: The ERD for the sample DM and a part of its RDF description.

is represented using an 'or' clause:

    (Education="primary" or Education="secondary")

4   Customization

Customization of a new NLIDB consists in:

- Development of the domain model.

- Stuffing the vocabulary.

- Debugging the newly created NLIDB.

The DM is created from the relational schema of the database semi-automatically; initially DM classes with their properties are created from database tables.

Then the user can customize the DM by changing, adding and deleting classes and properties and binding them by relations (including virtual attributes, which are linked to other tables). This procedure is facilitated by inheriting classes from the library of predefined classes. Also the NLIDB designer specifies rules for presentation of objects retrieved by search. One more type of information to be specified upon customization is used for handling meta-questions about the DM, for example, *Which information is known about employees? What are the possible job titles?*

The content of the vocabulary of the constructed NLIDB consists of three parts. The first part includes the general-purpose lexicon, which forms the initial vocabulary content of any L-processor (*list, find, more than, not, except, average,* etc., approximately 600 words). The second part, which is also the largest one, is extracted automatically by scanning the database. Such words and phrases are added to the vocabulary as values with corresponding semantic descriptions referring to attributes of the DM classes ('orientations' of words). The third part of the lexicon is formed during the NLIDB tuning stage and consists of words specific for the database problem domain. This includes words and phrases referring to attributes (*salary, wage, date of issue*), synonyms to values taken from the database (for example, *woman* for *female* denoting sex in the database).

New words to the vocabulary are also added from the built-in vocabulary in the course of customization, when built-in classes and their attributes are added to user's DM. For example, adding a class inheriting the class **Person** results in a prompt for adding specific lexical items referring to possible attributes of a human being (*who, name, born, sex,* etc.); presence of dates in the DM adds names of months and rules for assembling complex dates (*during November 25–29*), and so on.

Another type of information to be specified for the vocabulary of InBase is rarely addressed in NLIDBs, but is often encountered in applications. These are regular expressions (templates), which do not belong to a lexicon, but are meaningful in a problem domain. Examples of templates are standard identifiers (ISBN 0–465–05154–5), telephone numbers, which may be expressed in several ways: 255 4530, 255–4530, or 2554530, etc. Regular expressions for templates and their orientations are defined automatically by scanning the database. Additional templates and rules for their conversion to a standard representation stored in user's database are added upon customization.

Reliability of the created NLIDB and completeness of its lexicon are evaluated by the designer issuing test queries, which may be collected in a special list to save user's time for typing typical queries. A screen shot of InBase processing a query is shown in Figure 3.

5   Analysis of Queries

The parsing engine of InBase operates in terms of the register of database queries using entities, their attributes, values, and relations between entities as defined in the DM. In itself the parsing engine is implemented in a special language for development of L-processors, SNOOP (Sharoff, 1993), which integrates object-oriented approach with network representations and a production rule control

mechanism, so entities of the domain model in SNOOP are represented as nodes of a semantic network.

According to the semantic-oriented approach (Narin'yani, 1980), lexical semantics of words and phrases at the surface level is represented by the 'orientation' referring to a number of DM concepts that could be related to these words, for example, date in this database has two orientations: birth and hire dates. Several types of semantic units that appear in queries (attributes, values, comparisons, etc.) are combined into semantic structures on the basis of their orientations (so a date in a predicate with a value larger than 01/01/1980 in this database receives the only orientation of a hire date). Also analysis uses information about semantic classes, for example, existential predicates (like *has children, without higher education*) are interpreted according to types of their arguments (respectively, a numerical attribute, which value is greater than zero, or a non-numerical value, which represents a sequence).

Morphological and syntactic analyses are locally involved in cases of structural and semantic ambiguity, for example, local syntactic analysis is used for the recovery of ellipsis, when comparative and coordinate constructions are processed. The local top-down syntactic procedure may be supported by the bottom-up analysis in the case of more than one candidate for the role of the noun phrase nucleus. Detection of syntactic relations (government and agreement) is useful for solving the problem of the influence region of the negation, degree/modality modifiers, and certain locative units in elliptic constructions. Application of this technology to understanding of short texts and representing their domain model is described in (Kononenko & Sharoff, 1996).

6   Conclusion

The principles of the semantic-oriented analysis used in InBase have been developed by the end of 70s (Narin'yani, 1980), when several NLIDBs were developed manually. These experiments have led to InterBASE, a prototype system for development of NLIDBs to dBase-type databases in Russian and English (Narin'yani, 1991), (Trapeznikov et al., 1993). The system presented in this paper has extended capabilities of InterBASE by achieving a proper separation between the register and the domain model. Now the system operates with arbitrary SQL-access databases using the Borland Database Engine in Microsoft Windows. Currently the parsing engine of InBase has some evident limitations:

- A static world model, it has no support of databases designed to store information

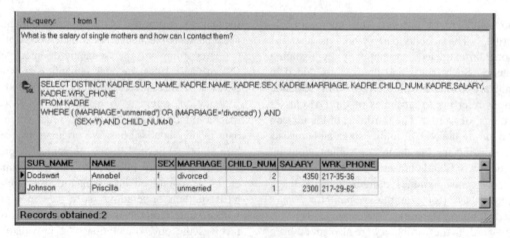

Figure 3: Data access in natural language.

about changes (Tansel et al., 1993), temporal databases require extensions in domain and linguistic models.

- No dialogue handling, the system answers to queries separately, being not able to resolve anaphoric links (like *Has he a PhD?* following the question in Figure 1).

- No handling of complex quantification (in such queries as *In which departments every employee has higher education?*).

- Results are presented in tables or screen forms (no NL-response generation component).

These limitations are topics for further developments. An advantage of the proposed technology is that it allows rapid development of NLIDBS by an inexperienced user and robustness of analysis. As Palmer & Finin (1990) note, evaluation of an NLP system is based on complex criteria, primarily involving its success in accomplishing user's goals. Despite of evident gaps in parsing, InBase addresses much of the real questions arising in interaction with databases. Experiments with several databases show that our interfaces analyse more than 85% of queries. Even in the case of false understanding the final SQL representation of a query provides a feedback which helps in detection of an error in analysis, so that either the source NL query or its SQL representation can be corrected to improve results of analysis. Alterations of the DM and the vocabulary of the NLIDB provide a way to reduce this error for further queries. The crucial questions for application of computational linguistics to HCI are: "For what and under what conditions is NL access effective for interaction of the end user with computer?" NLIDBs enable the end user with easy and efficient access to data stored in a database without mastery in artificial query languages and knowledge of precise relations between its tables. At present, our abilities in modelling NL features used for information delivery are inadequate for complete and correct understanding of all user queries. By this reason, the methodology adopted in InBase is based on customization of the general-purpose system of functions to the DM of a particular database.

One of the most promising research directions in NLIDBs is an interface to voice processing. The semantic-oriented approach described in this paper facilitates voice recognition, since in speech a syntactic norm is often violated, morphological information contained in flexions is missed during recognition, semantically insignificant words are not stressed, so they are often recognized with errors. Because the DM is represented using object notions, another research direction for InBase consists in development of interfaces to object-oriented DBMSs; this also helps in mapping the intermediate representation language to a database query language.

Access to WWW using NL queries as a prospective extension of this technology would dramatically increase precision and recall ratios in comparison to keyword-search facilities offered by the modern search engines. NL interface for a restricted problem domain can analyse a query taking into account its topic, such linguistic relations as synonymy, part-whole, generic-specific, and so on, in order to search documents with RDF-meta-data conforming to the content of the query.

References

Alshawi, H. (1992), *The Core Language Engine*, MIT Press.

Androutsopoulos, I., Ritchie, G. D. & Thanisch, P. (1995), "Natural Language Interfaces to Databases: An Introduction", *Natural Language Engineering* 1(1), 29–81.

Boguraev, B. & Sparck Jones, K. (1981), A General Semantic Analyzer for Database Access, *in Proceedings of the Seventh International Joint Conference on Artificial Intelligence (IJCAI'81)*, pp.443–5.

Copestake, A. & Sparck Jones, K. (1990), "Natural Language Interfaces to Databases", *Knowledge Engineering Review* 5(4), 225–49.

Halliday, M. A. K. (1978), *Language as a Social Semiotic: The Social Interpretation of Language and Meaning*, Edward Arnold.

Kononenko, I. & Sharoff, S. (1996), Understanding Short Texts with Integration of Knowledge Representation Methods, *in* D. Bjorner, M. Broy & I. V. Pottosin (eds.), *Perspectives of System Informatics*, Vol. 1181 of *Lecture Notes in Computer Science*, Springer-Verlag, pp.111–121.

Narin'yani, A. S. (1980), Interaction with a Limited Object Domain — ZAPSIB Project, *in Proceedings of COLING-1980*.

Narin'yani, A. S. (1991), "Intelligent Software Technology for the New Decade", *Communications of the ACM* 34(6), 60–7.

Olsen, Jr, D. R. (1992), *User Interface Management Systems: Models and Algorithms*, Morgan-Kaufmann.

Palmer, M. & Finin, T. (1990), "Workshop on the Evaluation of Natural Language Processing Systems", *Computational Linguistics* 16(3), 175–81.

Prieto-Diaz, R. & Arango, G. (1991), *Domain Analysis and Software Systems Modeling*, Vol. 1(1) of *IEEE Computer Society Press Tutorial*, IEEE Computer Society Press. ISBN 0 8186 8996 X.

Sharoff, S. (1993), SNOOP: A System for Development of Linguistic Processors, *in Proceedings of the East–West Conference on Artificial Intelligence*, pp.184–8.

Tansel, A., Clifford, J., Gadia, S. K., Jajodia, S., Segev, A. & Snodgrass, R. T. (1993), *Temporal Databases — Theory, Design, and Implementation*, Benjamin/Cummings (Addison–Wesley).

Trapeznikov, S., Dinenberg, F. & Kuchin, S. (1993), InterBase: A Natural Language Interface System for Popular Commercial DBMSs, *in Proeedings of the East–West Conference on Artificial Intelligence*, pp.189–93.

W3C (1999), Resource Description Framework (RDF) Model and Syntax Specification, Technical Report, W3C. http://www.w3.org/TR/PR-rdf-syntax.

Wegener, H. (1995), The Myth of the Separable Dialogue: Software Engineering vs. User Models, *in* K. Nordby, P. H. Helmersen, D. J. Gilmore & S. A. Arnessen (eds.), *Human–Computer Interaction — INTERACT '95: Proceedings of the Fifth IFIP Conference on Human–Computer Interaction*, Chapman & Hall, pp.169–72.

Wilks, Y. A. (1968), "On-line Semantic Analysis of English Texts", *Machine Translation* 11(3-4), 59–72.

Human–Computer Interaction — INTERACT '99
M. Angela Sasse and Chris Johnson (Editors)
Published by IOS Press, © IFIP TC.13, 1999

Data Abstractions and Their Use: An Experimental Study of User Productivity

Ananth Srinivasan & Gretchen Irwin

University of Auckland, Department of Management Science & Information Systems School of Business and Economics, Auckland, New Zealand.

{a.srinivasan,ga.irwin}@auckland.ac.nz

Abstract: The design of effective user–database interfaces is an important issue that must be based on an understanding of how users interact with technology to solve problems. This paper describes an in-depth verbal protocol study of users engaged in two tasks: data model construction and data model manipulation. The objectives of the research are twofold: to identify successful strategies for constructing data models with high-level abstractions (HLAs); and to determine whether models with HLAs facilitate subsequent query formulation. Results show that: a successful strategy for modelling with HLAs involves the systematic transition between higher and lower levels of abstraction; and users who successfully incorporate HLAs into their data models have an easier time with the predicate portion of their queries than users who did not incorporate HLAs. There is some evidence that modelling with HLAs has a 'productivity payoff' in subsequent data manipulation tasks.

Keywords: data abstractions, data modelling, query formulation, user–database interface, verbal protocols.

1 Introduction

As information systems become more pervasive in organizations, end users are confronted with new and complex technologies that they must use to be effective in their work. An important issue is the design of user-technology interfaces that effectively and efficiently support the user.

In the database arena, there is a discernible trend in research and practice toward interfaces that are user-oriented rather than computer-oriented. Early hierarchical and network systems required the user to interact with the database at a low level of abstraction, understanding details of how the data was physically stored and organized on computer devices. Relational databases, with the SQL data manipulation language, provide a user interface at a higher level of abstraction, based on the fundamental construct of a relation. This logical view of the database hides some of the physical computer storage details from the user, although a considerable amount of database-related knowledge (e.g. primary keys, foreign keys, join conditions) is needed for effective use. Subsequent efforts continue to elevate the level of abstraction in the user–database interface. For example, the Entity-Relationship (ER) model provides a representation of data based on the fundamental construct of an entity with associated properties. Extensions to the ER model and more recently, the Object-Oriented (OO) model provide higher-level abstractions that allow collections of entities to be treated as single constructs.

At each step in this evolution, the constructs of the user–database interface move closer toward the semantics of the user and further away from the semantics of the computer. The underlying premise is that this evolution will enhance productivity by allowing users to focus on accomplishing their tasks (Batra et al., 1990; Chan et al., 1993).

The theoretical arguments for higher levels of abstraction in the user–database interface are compelling and intuitive. However, empirical evidence on the usability of various database environments is far from conclusive. Further research is needed to understand the difficulties and complexities users face when constructing a representation of data (data modelling) and manipulating this representation (query formulation). The current study experimentally examines users engaged in data modelling and query formulation tasks. Such an understanding will enable the design of more effective user–database interfaces.

This paper describes an in-depth verbal protocol study of ten users. The objectives of this study are twofold. First, we investigate the cognitive processes and outcomes of data modelling. In particular, we examine successful and unsuccessful strategies for modelling with high level abstractions (HLAs) such as those included in Extended ER (EER) and OO models. Second, we explore the impact of HLAs on query formulation. Specifically, we assess whether there is a 'productivity payoff' from modelling with HLAs that is realised in query formulation. We argue that queries based on a design with HLAs are easier to formulate than those based on a design without HLAs (such as a pure relational design). This follows from embedding domain-specific semantics in the modelling environment.

Results of the study reveal that a successful strategy for modelling with HLAs involves the systematic transition from higher levels of abstraction to lower levels of abstraction and back again. This strategy differentiated the best from the worst performers on the data modelling task. There are also indications that the effort expended in successfully modelling with HLAs does have a payoff in data retrieval tasks. Users who were successful at modelling with HLAs then spent less of their time formulating the predicate portion of the query. This was particularly true as the query tasks became more complex.

2   Prior Work

Users' interaction with a database consists primarily of a representation or model of the database's underlying structure and a language for manipulating that structure to answer real-world questions. Thus, the data model and the query language are the primary components of the user–database interface. Chan et al. (1993) classify user–database interfaces into three broad abstraction levels: physical, logical, and conceptual. These levels differ in terms of how 'close' the semantics of the interface are to the user's world, with conceptual level interfaces being the closest of the three.

Currently, the most prevalent and popular database environments are based on the relational data model and the query language SQL. These environments provide a logical level user–database interface. While the user may not need to know physical file organization and storage details, he or she does need to understand specific relational database constructs. These constructs are still removed from the user's semantic world and can be difficult for users to learn and use (Smelcer, 1995).

user–database interfaces that use domain-level semantics should theoretically provide improved usability over logical level interfaces such as the relational model and SQL. The premise is that since the conceptual level deals with objects in the user's world, such as entities and relationships, users can design and manipulate data without being forced to translate conceptual-level constructs into artificial computer-oriented constructs Batra & Srinivasan (1992; Chan et al., 1993).

Many prior studies have investigated specific aspects of the user–database interface. However, there are very few studies that directly examine the underlying claims in support of higher levels of user–database interaction. The following sections briefly review research in three areas related to the current study: data model usability, query language usability, and user behaviour in data representation and manipulation tasks.

2.1   Data Model Usability

Several studies examine data models at the conceptual and logical levels. For example, Batra et al. (1990) compared design correctness for relational and EER models and found greater accuracy for some but not all tasks with the EER model. Leitheiser & March (1996) compared several variations on relational and ER model representations and found limited support for the superiority of entity-based representations for data structure comprehension tasks.

Other studies investigate competing models at the conceptual level, such as the EER and Object-Oriented (OO) models. Proponents of the OO model argue that it is semantically richer and closer to the user's world than other data models. However, empirical evidence has not supported this argument and has instead found that the OO model was more difficult to learn than data- or process-oriented models (Vessey & Conger, 1994) and the OO model resulted in less accurate designs than the EER model (Bock & Ryan, 1993).

2.2   Query Language Usability

Several studies investigate query formulation tasks at the logical and conceptual levels. Jih et al. (1989) and Leitheiser & March (1996) examined performance using SQL with relational and ER-based representations of the data structure. Neither study found convincing evidence that ER-based representations facilitate better query performance. However, these results are not surprising if we consider that users' performance should qualitatively improve when the semantics of the data model closely match the semantics of the query language. Since the logical level query language SQL was used in both studies, we might expect users to have difficulty with conceptual level representations of the data structure.

This argument motivated the Chan et al. (1993) study, which compared user performance on query tasks at the logical and conceptual levels. In their study, the logical level included a relational data model and SQL and the conceptual level included an ER model and an ER query language called KQL. Users at the conceptual level clearly outperformed their counterparts at the logical level in terms of query accuracy, user confidence, and time. We are aware of no other study that shows such strong support user–database interfaces at the conceptual level over the logical level.

2.3   User Behaviour in Data Modelling and Query Formulation Tasks

There are many reasons for the lack of consistent findings across studies of user–database interfaces. One of the reasons is that data modelling and query formulation are examples of design tasks and as such can be characterised as unstructured and complex problems (Simon, 1973).   Most of the studies described above treat these tasks as black boxes and examine the impact of the experimental treatment on outcomes such as model or query accuracy.   These studies can be complemented by research that opens the black box and explores the cognitive processes of data modelling and query formulation. A few studies have explored the modelling process using ER or OO representations (Vessey & Conger, 1994; Pennington et al., 1995;   Srinivasan & Te'eni, 1995) and the query formulation process using SQL (Smelcer, 1995). These studies reveal various difficulties that users encounter and indicate possible strategies for overcoming the difficulties. However, we found no process studies that investigated both data modelling and query formulation at the conceptual level. The current study begins to fill this research void on user–database interfaces.

3   Research Questions

As stated earlier, the objectives of this research are twofold:

1. to examine the cognitive processes of modelling with HLAs; and

2. to investigate the impact of HLAs on subsequent query formulation tasks.

With respect to the first objective, there are intuitive and theoretical reasons to believe that modelling with HLAs should be easier or more natural

for users than modelling at lower levels of abstraction. On the other hand, modelling with HLAs may prove challenging for users because of the need to articulate and integrate less concrete objects (Duncker, 1945; Schroder et al., 1967).   Thus, our first research question explores user behaviour to identify successful strategies for modelling with HLAs.

- What problem-solving strategies do more and less successful data modellers employ?

With respect to the second research objective, we are interested in how data models with HLAs impact subsequent query formulation. If the query language supports the same level of abstraction as the data model, then models at higher levels of abstraction should facilitate subsequent query formulation. HLAs allow a collection of entities to be manipulated as a single object, and thus hide some of the complexity that would otherwise be needed in the query.   This is particularly true for queries with complex predicate clauses involving join conditions. The second set of research questions explores this premise:

- Is query formulation easier when the data model includes HLAs than when the data model does not include HLAs? Does the ease or difficulty of query formulation vary as the task increases in complexity?

4   Research Method

Our research questions focus primarily on problem-solving processes.   Consequently, the research methodology rests heavily on concurrent verbal reports (Ericsson & Simon, 1993) to trace participants' cognitive processes. This section outlines the research method employed. The task and technology below were used in a pilot study (Srinivasan & Te'eni, 1995). In the present study, subjects were asked to think aloud and were videotaped as they worked on a data modelling task followed by several query formulation tasks.

4.1   Subjects and Procedure

Ten subjects were recruited to take part in the experiment from a graduate level course in database management. They were familiar with the concepts of logical database design, normalization, relational systems, and the structure and syntax of SQL. They had implemented a fairly complex database system as part of the course requirement. Participation in the experiment was entirely voluntary and involved two training sessions of approximately three hours each, followed by the experimental task. The whole process required a time commitment of about ten hours spread over a two-week period. These subjects represented a fairly uniform skill level. There were no rewards offered to the subjects for participation in the experiments.

4.2 The Technology: High Level Abstractions

The experimental task required an environment that allowed users to represent a given problem using HLAs. Specifically, we focused on two abstraction mechanisms — generalization and composition (Smith & Smith, 1977). These are the most commonly discussed extensions to the ER model and also are core OO modelling constructs. These two HLAs allow collections of entities to be viewed at a more abstract level as a single object.

Generalizations allow for the definition of an entity type along with its associated subtypes. While all subtypes share a common set of properties, each one may have a unique property subset that is different from other subtypes of the same parent. The generalization abstraction is constructed as a cluster that contains the supertype with its associated subtypes. Further, subtypes inherit properties from their supertype.

Compositions allow a group of related yet distinct entities to be treated as a 'molecule'. The composite object abstraction captures the relationship concept from ER modelling as well as more complicated situations where the composite object in turn is associated with another entity. A composite object is declared in terms of its component entities. A component entity may be another composite object; in such cases it is meaningful to refer to a chain of related objects.

4.3 Experimental Tasks

Subjects completed two tasks of comparable complexity. The first task was used for learning purposes during two training sessions held one week apart. Subjects were taught how to construct data models with HLAs and how to use these abstractions in data retrieval tasks.

The second task was the experimental task. This task included several generalization and composition HLAs, including one composite object that represented a chain of objects (some of which were also composite objects). Subjects were asked to read the narrative and construct a model of the situation using HLAs. They were asked to 'think aloud' as they developed their representation. This session was videotaped for later analysis.

Subjects were then asked to construct queries based on their representations for a set of ten tasks. The tasks varied in complexity from simple to complex. We used an approach that roughly follows the complexity metric proposed by (Cardenas, 1985) to characterise the queries. This metric examines the predicate component of a query and enumerates the number of item value specifications (M1), conjunction specifications (M2), and join conditions (M3). We characterised each of the ten tasks by a vector of three values to indicate the complexity of the task. This complexity profile was based on a design that incorporates HLAs. Table 1 shows the complexity profile for the ten queries under this design scenario and compares this to a complexity profile based on a pure relational design.

Query	Relational Model <M1, M2, M3>	Model with HLAs <M1, M2, M3>
1	<0,0, 0>	<0,0, 0>
2	<1,1, 1>	<1,0, 0>
3	<1,0, 0>	<1,0, 0>
4	<2,3, 2>	<2,2, 0>
5	<3,3, 1>	<3,2, 0>
6	<1,2, 2>	<1,0, 0>
7	<1,1, 1>	<1,0, 0>
8	<1,2, 2>	<1,0, 0>
9	<2,3, 2>	<2,1, 0>
10	<1,2, 2>	<1,1, 1>

Table 1: Complexity profiles for queries based on relational design and design with HLAs.

As Table 1 shows, queries based on the relational design are generally more complex than their counterparts based on the design with HLAs. This observation becomes more pronounced as the tasks become more complex. For example, query 3 is a simple query (no conjunction or join conditions) whose complexity profile is the same for both design alternatives. However, when query 6 is based on a relational design, the predicate clause requires two conjunction conditions and two join conditions. The same query based on a design with HLAs requires no conjunction or join conditions. This illustrates the motivation for the second research question about the 'productivity payoff' to modelling with HLAs.

4.4 Coding of the Data: Data Modelling Task

A coding scheme for characterising the data modelling process was defined and then applied to the videotapes. The primary focus of the coding scheme was to capture the user's cognitive movement across various levels of modelling abstraction. (Other aspects of the data modelling process were coded as well. For more details on these aspects of the coding, see (Srinivasan & Te'eni, 1995).) The coding scheme consisted of five levels of abstraction, as described below:

Level 0: Focus on individual properties of an object.

Level 1: Focus on basic entities.   These were entities that had no subtypes; usually they were components of composite objects.

Level 2: Focus on a supertype/subtypes cluster.

Level 3: Focus on basic composite objects.

Level 4: Focus on composite object chains.

This coding scheme was applied to the videotapes on the basis of the level at which the subject dealt with the problem at a particular point in time. Simple time stamping was used to track the points at which a subject moved from one level of abstraction to another.   This coding scheme and time stamping procedure allowed us to generate a transition graph for each subject (Figure 1). The graph shows a process description of the user's data modelling activity over time and clearly shows the shifts between levels of abstraction in the order in which they occurred.

In addition to the process description, we used the quality of the data model as a measure of performance.   The strategy that we used to assess data model quality was similar to previous empirical studies of this nature — e.g. (Batra et al., 1990). Quality was assessed as deviations of the data model from a complete solution.   Counts of the following measures of representation quality were obtained: missing elements, mis-specified elements, and redundant elements. While there may be several alternative 'correct' model formulations, the approach that we used stressed the capture of all relevant linkages between the problem elements.

4.5   Coding of the Data: Query Formulation Tasks

Subjects were asked to represent three essential components for each querying task: the target list (attributes to be displayed in the result), the source list (objects that will provide the data) and the predicate condition (restrictions that specify exactly what is to be retrieved).   This representation was familiar to subjects due to their prior knowledge of SQL, and was also flexible enough to support HLAs. A data model using HLAs would affect the structure of the query since source lists could contain higher level abstract

objects.   As with the model construction, the query construction activity was videotaped.   The data was coded by time stamping segments of the query tasks depending on whether the subject was generating a target list, a source list, or a predicate condition. This enabled us to obtain a distribution of time spent on each component of a query for all subjects.

5   Results

Figure 1 shows the transition graphs for four subjects working on the data modelling task. The distribution of time spent at the various levels of abstraction by subject is shown in Table 2.   The times shown are proportions of total development time spent by the subject at each level. The distributions are different for the different subjects.   While some tended to devote relatively more time to lower levels of abstraction, others did the reverse.

Table 3 shows the quality of the data models produced by the ten subjects.   The quality of a data model decreases with the number of missing elements, mis-specified elements, and redundant elements.   In trying to interpret relationships between the modelling behaviour and the performance of the subjects, some interesting observations are stated below. We isolated the behaviour of Subjects A, C, F and G in order to look at extreme cases in terms of performance. While Subjects C and F have completely and correctly specified their models (no errors as per our error-coding scheme), Subjects A and G have poorly specified models (relative to the pool of subjects). Our intention is to study the pairs that are on either end of the performance spectrum to examine the existence of interesting process-related phenomena that might be related to their performance.

5.1   Distribution of Modelling Effort

The transition graphs in Figure 1 demonstrate most clearly the dynamic behaviour in terms of shifts in the levels of abstraction.   Shifts to a higher level of abstraction occur when the subject gets lost in detail and needs the broader context to understand the details or to decide how to proceed. Shifts to a lower level of abstraction occur when the subject feels that the higher level can no longer guide him on how to proceed or understand the problem.   This is in concert with findings on general problem solving Duncker (1945). In general, the higher levels of abstraction are more difficult to process because they require the subject to think of less concrete entities and integrate such entities into a composite object.

For example, Subject A spent more time on the lower abstraction levels, (i.e. the attributes and objects)

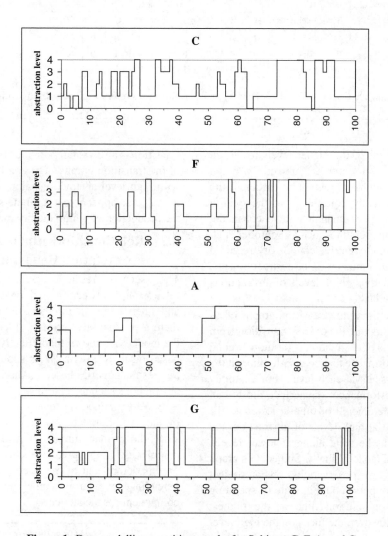

Figure 1: Data modelling transition graphs for Subjects C, F, A, and G.

Abstr	Subject									
	A	B	C	D	E	F	G	H	I	J
Level	**(5: 54)**	(12: 27)	**(14: 56)**	(14: 58)	(17: 50)	**(33: 11)**	**(27: 44)**	(16: 00)	(9: 53)	(14: 47)
0	**20**	3	**6**	22	5	**32**	**10**	15	0	15
1	**44**	31	**49**	36	28	**35**	**46**	32	36	39
2	**13**	10	**8**	7	13	**11**	**16**	8	18	12
3	**7**	31	**18**	4	18	**6**	**5**	13	11	2
4	**16**	25	**19**	31	36	**16**	**23**	32	35	32

Table 2: Distribution of time spent on each abstraction level. (Entries are percentages of total time (shown in parentheses) spent by subject — bold entries refer to subjects discussed in the paper.)

Model elements	Subject									
	A	B	**C**	D	E	**F**	**G**	H	I	J
Missing	**2**	0	**0**	1	0	**0**	**0**	0	0	0
Redundant	**2**	0	**0**	0	0	**0**	**1**	0	0	0
Misspecified	**3**	1	**0**	1	2	**0**	**2**	1	3	2

Table 3: Frequency Counts of Errors in Data Models. (Bold entries refer to subjects discussed in the paper.)

and deferred treatment of the higher levels to late in the solution process. In contrast, Subject C's graph shows treatment of higher levels much earlier in the process. This apparently contributed to the quality of the model. This phenomenon is also consistent with problem solving literature, such as Schroder et al. (1967) findings on the cognitive complexity required for the articulation and integration of abstract objects. Working early at relatively high levels of abstractions appears to be beneficial.

Further, in examining the transition graphs of all the subjects, it appears that the orderly transition from higher to lower levels of abstraction is far more crucial in determining performance than merely looking at the proportion of time spent at each level. For example, Subject F whose performance was perfect, did in fact spend a considerable amount of time at lower levels. However, he started at high levels of abstraction and built clarifications as he went along at lower levels, thus yielding a good model. Finally, Subject G's graph yields some interesting observations. This subject provided a relatively poor model in spite of spending a fair proportion of solution time at the highest abstraction level. However, the focus on the high level abstractions seemed to have occurred primarily during the earlier part of the model building process. The latter stages of the process show an emphasis on the lower levels. This is in contrast with Subjects C and F where the focus on higher levels occurred throughout the process with the subjects coming back to these levels constantly till the model was completed.

When one examines the transitions across the various levels, the intensity of transitions is revealing. The transition counts (number of transitions from any level to another) for the four subjects are as follows: Subjects A and G have 13 and 30 transitions respectively; Subjects C and F have 41 and 37 transitions respectively. The difference in these counts between the better and poorer performers suggests that it is vital for users to relate higher level abstract objects to the details at a sustained rate. This back-and-forth activity is what leads to fit between the more abstract end and the details that underlay the abstraction in the representation of the problem. The intensity of

transition is also visually obvious from an examination of the transition graphs. The combination of working with high level abstractions along with relating them with details appears to contribute significantly toward the production of a high quality model.

5.2 Relationship with Query Formulation Behaviour

The second research question addresses the relationship between model construction behaviour and query construction behaviour. Specifically, is there a productivity payoff in incorporating HLAs in the model? As shown theoretically in Table 1, queries based on models with HLAs should be less complex queries than queries based on models with lower level abstractions such as relations.

We examined the query construction behaviour of the four Subjects A, C, F, and G. Specifically, since the primary impact of using HLAs is on the complexity of the predicate condition, we focussed on this component of the query. Figure 2 shows the percentage of querying time spent on the predicate component for the subjects.

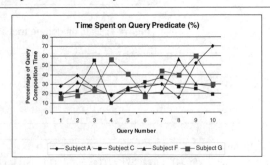

Figure 2: Time spent on the predicate clause of each query for Subjects A, C, F, and G.

Subjects C and F spent less of their time on the predicate component than did Subjects A and G, on average. What is more striking is that for complex queries (e.g. 4, 5, 9, and 10), the percentage of time spent by A and G on the predicate component is almost uniformly higher. This data provides some evidence for the payoff obtained by using HLAs in model construction: queries become easier to construct. We restrict our attention to time spent on various query components and not the correctness of the query itself. We did this since the quality issues were dealt with when we characterised the model in terms of various error counts. Further error classifications of queries constructed against possibly imperfect models would confound the measures rendering the results difficult to interpret.

6 Implications and Conclusions

The understanding of how users cope when confronted with demanding tasks is important in the design of appropriate interfaces to support the use of technology. Results of this study suggest several avenues for improving user–database interfaces. It is clear, for example, that users ought to be encouraged to work at high levels of abstraction until a broad picture of the problem is at hand, and to systematically transition back and forth between levels of abstraction. The interface should provide mechanisms by which users are inclined to proceed with their design activity along these directions.

There is some evidence of a productivity payoff to modelling with HLAs. We recognise that the accurate use of these abstractions during model construction is cognitively demanding. However, model construction is typically done once followed by incremental changes as domain specifications change. The payoff occurs during subsequent use of the model. Use of the model for query formulation is a frequent activity that is performed against a relatively stable representation. Thus, the additional effort invested in constructing a model with HLAs should be quickly offset by reduced effort in query formulation tasks. However, interfaces at the conceptual level must support HLAs for this opportunity to be feasible. Currently, the dominant query language is SQL which does not support HLAs.

Finally, this study examined the productivity payoff associated with HLAs for users who both develop the data model and formulate queries against their model. Clearly, some users do engage in both these activities. However, in many other situations, users formulate queries based on a data model created by someone else. In these cases, the issue changes from data model *creation* to data model *comprehension*. It is reasonable to expect that the nature of our findings would not change for a comprehension vs. a modelling task, since model creation, in some sense, requires comprehension of the model. However, future studies are needed that examine the usability and productivity payoff of HLAs in different user task settings.

References

Batra, D. & Srinivasan, A. (1992), "A Review and Analysis of the Usability of Data Management Environments", *International Journal of Man–Machine Studies* **36**, 395–417.

Batra, D., Hoffer, J. A. & Bostrom, R. P. (1990), "Comparing Representations with Relational and EER Models", *Communications of the ACM* **33**(2), 126–39.

Bock, D. B. & Ryan, T. (1993), "Accuracy in Modeling with Extended Entity Relationship and Object-Oriented Data Models", *Journal of Database Management* **4**(4), 30–9.

Cardenas, A. F. (1985), *Data Base Management Systems*, Boston, Allyn and Bacon.

Chan, H. C., Wei, K. K. & Siau, K. L. (1993), "User-Database Interface: The Effect of Abstraction Levels on Query Performance", *Management Information Systems Quarterly* **17**(4), 441–464.

Duncker, K. (1945), *On Problem Solving*, Psychological Monographs, The American Psychological Association.

Ericsson, K. A. & Simon, H. A. (1993), *Protocol Analysis: Verbal Reports as Data*, third edition, MITP.

Jih, W. J. K., Bradbard, D. A., Snyder, C. A. & Thompson, N. G. (1989), "The Effects of Relational and Entity-Relationship Data Models on Query Performance of End Users", *International Journal of Man–Machine Studies* **31**, 257–67.

Leitheiser, R. L. & March, S. T. (1996), "The Influence of Database Structure Representation on Database System Learning and Use", *Journal of Management Information Systems* **12**(4), 187–213.

Pennington, N., Lee, A. & Rehder, B. (1995), "Cognitive Activities and Levels of Abstraction in Procedural and Object-Oriented Design", *Human–Computer Interaction* **10**, 171–226.

Schroder, H. M., Driver, M. J. & Streufert, S. (1967), *Human Information Processing*, Holt, Rinehart and Winston.

Simon, H. A. (1973), "The Structure of Ill-Structured Problems", *Artificial Intelligence* **4**, 181–201.

Smelcer, J. B. (1995), "User Errors in Database Query Composition", *International Journal of Human–Computer Studies* **42**, 353–81.

Smith, J. M. & Smith, D. C. P. (1977), "Database Abstractions: Aggregation and Generalization", *ACM Transactions on Database Systems* **2**, 105–133.

Srinivasan, A. & Te'eni, D. (1995), "Modeling as Constrained Problem Solving: An Empirical Study of the Data Modeling Process", *Management Science* **41**(3), 419–34.

Vessey, I. & Conger, S. A. (1994), "Requirements Specification: Learning Object, Process, and Data Methodologies", *Communications of the ACM* **37**(5), 102–13.

Human–Computer Interaction — INTERACT '99
M. Angela Sasse and Chris Johnson (Editors)
Published by IOS Press, © IFIP TC.13, 1999

Consulting Search Engines as Conversation

Noboru Iwayama, Masahiko Murakami & Masahiro Matsuda

Fujitsu Laboratories Ltd., Okubo Nishiwaki 64, Akashi 674–8555, Japan.

iwayama@flab.fujitsu.co.jp

Abstract: We describe a chat environment that allows people to issue commands to search engines as chat utterances. This Chat-and-Search environment is proposed as a new way supplementing the use of search engines with socially-mediated search, that is, information seeking using one's social network. Embedding the use of search engines in the Chat-and-Search environment is promising because it reduces feelings of social obligation which both the command observer and issuer may have. An 18 month field study shows a variety of collaborative conversational behaviours. This work is an example of an organizational interface defined by T.W.Malone, a system that connects users to one another and to the capabilities provided by computers.

Keywords: IRC (Internet Relay Chat), information seeking, technically-mediated search, socially-mediated search, search engine, collaborative information retrieval, CSCW

1 Introduction

1.1 Problems in Information Seeking

People search for information in two different ways:

1. Technically-mediated search: people use artifacts to find information.

2. Socially-mediated search: people consult other people.

By technically-mediated search, we refer to activities using information artifacts. Typical examples of information artifacts include dictionaries, encyclopedias, and telephone books. In this paper, we focus on the artifacts implemented on computer systems, especially those distributed across computer networks. This is the reason why we say 'technically'-mediated Search. The Internet contains a huge amount of information and we find it by using information artifacts such as directory services or search engines.

Each type of information search has tradeoffs. We discuss the pros and cons of technically-mediated search and socially-mediated search, which are related to definition and evaluation of search and social cost.

Definition and evaluation of search: The definition and evaluation of the search are examples of the gulf of execution and evaluation in (Norman, 1988). Defining a search means that a seeker must map his information needs to a specific search action, such as selecting a search engine and keywords. The evaluation of the search means that a seeker has to consider the reliability of the result. It is not easy to estimate whether results from search engines are good enough.

In technically-mediated search, much effort is needed to define the search and to evaluate the results of the search, although less effort is needed in socially-mediated search because of the intelligence of people.

Social cost: Two types of people, questioners and recipients, are involved in socially-mediated search; the questioners are seeking information from other people, and the recipients are those who are addressed and may possibly answer the questions. In socially-mediated search, there are social costs for each type of person. For example, recipients may be interrupted by questions. On the other hand, questioners, recognizing this, may hesitate to ask. Also, directly asking someone a question creates a sense of obligation for both parties, and the questioner may wish to avoid this.

In technically-mediated search, there is no need to communicate other people. It is enough to fill out the forms of search engines and hit the enter key to obtain retrieval results from search engines.

1.2   A Possible Solution

We want to explore ways of combining these two types of information search. In particular, we want to supplement the use of search engines with socially-mediated search. We hope that socially-mediated search will compensate for the shortcomings of technically-mediated search.

This approach, however, leads to a new problem: how do information seekers engaged in technically-mediated search make others aware of what they are searching for? Explicitly consulting others has all the shortcomings of socially-mediated search.

In this paper, we provide a chat environment that allows people to issue commands to search engines. The information seekers by issuing search commands do not need to consult other people directly; the commands may be observed by others. This lessens the social cost of information seeking because those who observe the search commands issued in the chat environment are not being directly asked but can still volunteer to help.

The structure of this paper is as follows: in the next two sections, we describe the details of our system, the Chat-and-Search environment, and its design goals. In the succeeding sections we describe the results of field trial of the Chat-and-Search environment and discussion about the results. We then refer to related work and conclude this paper with several remarks.

2   The Chat-and-Search Environment

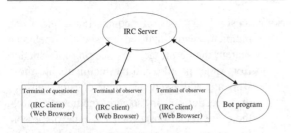

Figure 1: System configuration of Chat-and-Search environment.

In this section, we describe how search engine consultation has been integrated in chat. The Chat-and-Search environment is built upon IRC (Internet Relay Chat), which is specified in RFC1459 (Oikarinen & Reed, 1993), and consists of a robot program handling search commands, an IRC user client software, and a WWW (World Wide Web) browser coupled to the IRC client. These are connected

as shown in Figure 1 (the arrows represent IRC connections between the server and each client).

In IRC, users can chat privately (on a one-to-one basis), or in a space (or room) as in other text chat systems. A channel in IRC corresponds to the space, in which a group of participants share the same conversation. A user can be involved in multiple chats (one-to-one or group) simultaneously. Both one-to-one chats and group chats (in channels) are used in the Chat-and-Search environment.

2.1   IRC Client

Before showing details of the Chat-and-Search, we should mention our IRC client, which constitutes the Chat-and-Search environment.

Since we can share knowledge as topics of chat conversation by means of presenting URLs, chat communication may be initiated and supplemented by the presentation of URLs. In order to improve the usefulness of URLs for chat, we closely integrate the Web browser with our IRC client. The integration is comprised of three functions to work with the Web browser: URL identification in chat, automatic transfer of the identified URL to the Web browser, and URL transfer from the Web browser to our IRC client. Figure 2 show our IRC client CHOCOA (CHat Oriented COoperative work Augment).

Every URL in the chat conversation is identified so the identified URL is transferred automatically to the Web browser and the appropriate Web page is displayed in the browser. Our users can simply send the identified URLs to the Web browser even when the automatic URL transfer is turned off. The identified URL can be displayed as a live (underlined) URL in the conversation window (the upper left window in Figure 2). If the live URL in the conversation window is mouse-clicked, the live URL is transferred to the browser whether the automatic URL transfer is turned on or off.

In addition, the URL of any Web page shown in the browser can be captured by clicking URL button of the client (top middle, Figure 2); the URL then sent to our client and is inserted into the chat input buffer so that it may be used when the user would like to chat.

We have observed chat participants using URLs as new topics for conversation, using URLs to answer questions, and using URLs to expand topics in ongoing conversations. The browser integration with our IRC client is similar to the MOO client system Juggler described in (Dieberger, 1997).

2.2   Issuing Search Commands in Chat

The following outlines how Chat-and-Search works:

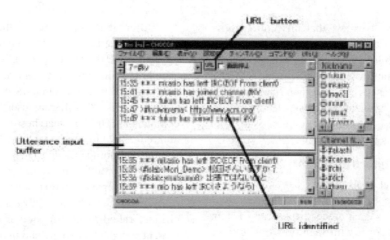

Figure 2: The IRC client CHOCOA.

A search command is issued in an IRC channel as an ordinary chat utterance as follows:

navi ACM

This command is used to consult a search engine *(navi)* about the keyword 'ACM'. To consult a different search engine, it is enough to assign the search engine to a different search command; for AltaVista (http://altavista.digital.com/) we use the command *alta*, for Lycos (http://www.lycos.com/) *lycos*, for example.

An IRC robot program (called a 'bot') interprets the character strings intended as a search command issued in a chat channel. The robot program translates the character string to a CGI URL (Common Gateway Interface Uniform Resource Locator) representing a search for the specified keyword. For the above example, the following CGI URL will be returned (the URL is an imaginary one):

http://engine.search.org/s.cgi?key=ACM

The translated CGI URL is returned via chat to the person issuing the command. The result returned from the search engine, such as a list of the top 10 hits for the keyword, is shown in the Web browser of the person issuing the command. So far, we can think of this as technically-mediated search, which is performed by the command issuer. In addition to the one-to-one reply of the CGI URL, the URL is sent to the channel in which the original search command was issued. See the next example conversation in some channel:

```
<p1>navi ACM
<bot>http://engine.search.org/s.cgi?key=ACM
```

The first line shows that user p1 issues a command and the second line that robot program, named bot, returns the CGI URL into the channel. All participants in the channel observe the command and the reply issued as seen above. The CGI URL is not automatically transferred to their browser because it is sent as a special IRC message so that the participants are not disturbed by results of the command shown in their browsers. But participants can send the URL to browser by clicking on the URL and can see the result if they want.

Participants in the chat channel can observe the search command being issued, and thus may volunteer their help — this is socially-mediated search.

In our Chat-and-Search environment, we hope that being able to observe search commands can lead to collaborative conversations. In fact, our 18-month field trial of Chat-and-Search shows that participants do help each other on search tasks. There were cases in which information seekers on chat were told the exact answers to their queries.

3   Design Goals

We expect that the use of search engines in chat results in socially-mediated search, which means a kind of collaboration among chat participants. In this section, we describe which kind of collaboration we are expecting as goals of designing the Chat-and-Search environment.

3.1   Reciprocity among Users

Our primary goal is that chat participants actively help each other with Chat-and-Search. The collaboration among users will include telling not only which search engines or keywords be chosen but also exact answers to searches. We will expect that this collaborative behaviour is reciprocal in the long term.

In order to archive this active collaboration, it will play an important role that participants in a chat room are acquaintances. Background information, like personalities, organizational position, and current status of others, is helpful for volunteers to infer searchers' intentions more precisely.

3.2 Sharing Search Process

One of the technical goals of the Chat-and-Search is that we would like to equip a mechanism to share search process. The search process is a series of steps in which a searcher copes with an information artifact. (Twindale et al., 1997) states that the sharing of the search product and the search process are important for collaborative activities.

In Chat-and-Search, we implement our system so that the first step of the search process, that is the selection of a search engine and a keyword, is shared among chat participants.

3.3 Judging Possibilities for Socially-mediated Search

Another technical goal of the Chat-and-Search environment is that a command issuer can easily judge whether socially-mediated search has been triggered successfully or has failed. Since chat is a kind of computer mediated medium, which depends on real time text sharing, if no chat utterance occurs after the search command is issued, the issuer could conclude that there is no volunteer to help him at that time.

4 Field Trial

The Chat-and-Search environment has been tested as a part of our Intranet IRC network for 18 months. Our IRC network has been operated for several years, and currently (July 1998) has over 1000 users connected simultaneously and about 500 channels on normal business days. In the following, we show analysis of usage patterns of Chat-and-Search.

During the first 14 days (in February 1997) just after Chat-and-Search was released into the IRC network, the first author did 34 searches in the largest channel in the network as demonstration with explaining Chat-and-Search itself in chat. That is because the first author does not know real identities of 95% participants in the channel and we thought that demonstrating Chat-and-Search was the best way of instruction. In the 14 days, 18 users did 115 Chat-and-Search, which does not include the 34 demonstration search. Only one user did 62 searches among the 115 search.

After this initial trial, the Chat-and-Search function was gradually released into 14 channels of the Intranet network. The trial is still going on.

In the following analysis we have investigated a period of 15 weeks (March 1998 to June 1998). In the 15 weeks, 88 different users issued 202 search commands. The 202 searches consist of 88 searches at *navi* and 114 *goo* searches; *navi* is an engine for Fujitsu company-wide Web resources, and *goo* (http://www.goo.ne.jp/) is one of the most popular engines for Japanese Web resources.

Of the 202 searches, 79 searches were done in a channel called #dict. In another normal channel, 55 searches of 202 were done and in other 12 channels 10 or less searches were.

The channel #dict was established to provide English and Japanese dictionary services by a dictionary robot program. Participants in a ordinary channel (#F) built the channel #dict to consult dictionaries and to issue the Chat-and-Search commands. About 20 users in the ordinary channel #F also joins #dict.

We have examined all conversations in #dict to clarify effects of Chat-and-Search, because the largest number of searches was carried out here. We could not investigate conversation logging in the second-most searched channel because of privacy.

4.1 Usage Patterns for the Channel #dict

Search With Chat	search-chat	10	18
	chat-search-chat	7	
	chat-search	1	
Search Without Chat	search		61

Table 1: Occurrences of conversation patterns with Chat-and-Search in #dict.

The 79 searches in the channel #dict are classified under the following 4 categories according to conversation patterns before or after search command issued (as summarized in Table 1):

Search – Chat: Search command issued is followed by chat conversation. 10 turns of conversational chunks belong to this category.

Chat – Search – Chat: Search command is issued in the flow of chat conversation. 7 turns belong to this category.

Chat – Search: Search command closes chat conversation. 1 turn belongs to this category.

Search: There is no conversation before or after the search command. 61 of the 79 searches belong to this category.

4.2 Examples of Conversations

In addition to this quantitative usage pattern, we have found interesting examples of conversation in the channel #dict.*

Description of the number of Web pages retrieved by the search engine (just after search command Issued):

> <p1> Only 2 pages are hit
>
> <p2> Ohh, 17 pages are found!

Discussion of the subjects dealt with in Web pages retrieved by the search engine (just after command issued):

> <p3> Those pages look like problematic.
>
> <p4> goo Estragon
> <bot> [returned CGI URL for goo search]
> <p4> Pages show delicious menus.
> <p5> Estragon is food, isn't it?

Answer to search engine queries from other participants:

> <p6> navi CSP
> <bot>[returned CGI URL for navi search]
> <p7> Chip Size Package
> <p6> OHHH, that's it!

Conversations about how to use the search engine:

> <p9> goo Philippe Candeloro
> <bot> [returned CGI URL for goo search]
> <p9> this spelling is correct?
> <p10> Correct > the spelling.
>
> <p7> goo chik Korea
> <bot> [returned CGI URL for goo search]
> <p8> you'd better say Chik Corea
> <p7> goo Chik Corea
> <bot> [returned CGI URL for goo search]
> <p7> So many pages are found!

Conversation on status of search engine:

> <p9> goo Philippe Candeloro
> <bot> [returned CGI URL for goo search]
> <p9> is this engine available now?
> <p10> Errors on the engine

4.3 Users' Opinions

Users' opinions about Chat-and-Search were gathered by email at the end of the 18 months. Seven frequent users of Chat-and-Search answered our email questionnaires. Four of the seven users said that they have issued search commands with the intention

that someone would provide the answers. Three of the seven said that they have used Chat-and-Search because they would like others to know about their search activities.

One frequent user said that she issued a search command even though she didn't think that anyone would answer her question. She said that she thought that her query would start a discussion. Another frequent user said that he wanted to share the results of search without disturbing those who have little interest in it. Another said that he would issue search commands to demonstrate ways of searching when he was asked for some information.

Users felt social costs even when issuing the search command. One of seven users said that she hesitated to issue search commands in other channels than #dict. Since users were aware that participants in the channel #dict had the intention of consulting a dictionary and search engines and that they didn't complain about the utterance of search command, she thought that she could issue search commands without scruples in the channel. We discuss about this point in the next section.

5 Discussion

Chat-and-Search seems to be accepted as a useful tool, because users said the new functionality helped to convey their search intentions to others. However, quantitative data does not support that, because 202 searches were done in 15 weeks on 14 channels and only 18 (23%) of 79 search commands were accompanied by conversation in one of the 14 channels.

In addition to the low involvement, we do not think that we can generalize the result of the field study, because data are mostly from the special channel #dict. But we identified the following issues from the field study, which will be useful for further research.

5.1 Social Cost

We have introduced the Chat-and-Search facility to reduce social costs which both the questioner and recipient may have. However, as described in the previous section, Chat-and-Search reveals another dimension of social cost: command issuers fear that they might interrupt chat conversations. In fact, this is the reason why the channel #dict is separated from the original channel #F.

This might be because search commands and their replies are different from ordinary conversational utterances. A possible solution to reduce this

---

*All of the following examples are originally in Japanese.

dimension of social cost is that the commands and replied URLs are displayed in a different part of the ordinary conversation window in the user chat client.

5.2   Interface to Issue Command

In the Chat-and-Search environment, a search is done by issuing the corresponding command as a chat utterance. This implies that command issuers must know the name of the command and its arguments. In other words, users may forget the usage syntax of Chat-and-Search.

This might be one reason why so few searches were done. This drawback is also resolved by modifying the user client (commands are able to be issued by menu selection, for example). Since the modification may introduce new complexity to the chat client, we need more consideration to do that.

5.3   Role of Information Transferred by Search Commands

Although in the channel #dict, 23% of the search commands were accompanied by conversation, we do not think that the rest (61) of the search commands had no meaning in socially-mediated search. Rather we may conclude that this result is a reasonable one, because every search command issued does not always have those who correspond on the command as ordinary socially-mediated search does not succeed every time. Plenty of search commands with no conversation would seem to be evidence that command issuers do not worry about failure of socially-mediated search. Ease in judging the failure of socially-mediated search is one of the design goal as we described in Section 3.3. We need more experiments to confirm this.

Independently of whether the search commands are accompanied by conversation, we think that search commands play a certain role in the social relation among chat participants. The commands (and their arguments) transfer some aspect of intentional information of the command issuer to the chat participants, because keywords in the commands reflect current interests or problems of the issuers more or less. The information will provide command observers social clues. From this perspective awareness (Dourish & Bellotti, 1992) and other research directions are related, which deal with mechanisms to make digital activity of users visible to others (Erickson et al., 1999).

6   Related Work

6.1   Enhanced Real Time Text Communication Systems

There is previous work on chat-like communication systems enhanced by accessibility to network resources. In Workingman's MOO (Guzdial, 1997), a MOO (a multiuser, text-based virtual environment) is enhanced by a command transferring mechanism. Examples in the Workingman's MOO show how the desktop applications of MOO users are controlled by transferred commands, although in our case search engines (not on any user's desktop) are controlled. The effects of others observing issued command is not mentioned.

Other important MOO related work is the ability to access Gopher from a MOO (Masinter & Ostrom, 1993). They developed several ways of navigating Gopher space from the MOO. They had snapshots of Gopher navigation kept as MOO objects and referred in MOO commands. Any users can continue navigating Gopher from the points captured in the snapshots by issuing MOO commands. Gopher access from the MOO is closely related to our work, as users are able to observe how others navigate in network by watching commands issued in chat. However, this way of sharing Gopher navigation contrasts to our way of sharing search engine consultations. Users in the MOO can share Gopher page transitions, that is, who proceeds to which Gopher page. In the Chat-and-Search environment, users can share selections of search engines and keywords, namely, who searches for what keyword by which engine.

6.2   Answer Garden

Answer Garden (Ackerman, 1994), an organizational memory system, extends the standard information retrieval model so as to include socially-mediated search. Answer Garden has two primary mechanisms for handling an organization's knowledge: a retrieval system to access archived knowledge and an email facility for routing user questions to an appropriate human expert when user is not satisfied with the results from the retrieval system.

In comparison with our work, chat is used as the underlying communication medium for socially-mediated search, whereas electronic mail is used in the Answer Garden system. Chat provides us with real time response, so command issuers are able to immediately understand that their search effort results in success or failure. The difference in the underlying medium is important from the viewpoint of design principles of two systems.

In the design of Answer Garden, a clear-cut separation of experts and users is established because the email containing the user's question is sent to the expert anonymously to reduce status implications (having to do with the personalities and organizational positions of the users and experts). The clear-cut separation is intended to reduce need for reciprocity. This principle keeps users from hesitating to submit questions. However, there is no possibility of that users can help each other by observing others to have emailed to the Answer Garden experts. On the other hand, reciprocity among chat participants was our primary concern on designing Chat-and-Search environment. Since participants are able to infer the status of others from their chat conversations, Chat-and-Search encourages reciprocity and collaboration.

7 Concluding Remarks

In this paper, we have described the Chat-and-Search environment which allows people to issue commands to search engines as chat utterances. The environment is our attempt to supplement the use of search engines with socially-mediated search. The intent is that socially-mediated search will reduce the problems of search engine use, and that embedding the search engine use in Chat-and-Search environment (where others can observe the technically-mediated search) will result in socially-mediated search but reduce social costs. We have carried out an 18 month field study and found a variety of collaborative interactions among Chat-and-Search users.

We claim that this work demonstrates not only a new style of human computer interaction between services and multiple users over network, but also a possibility of a new human-human interaction style based on the human computer interaction. In this sense, this work is an instance of an organizational interface (Malone, 1985), which is defined by Malone as:

> "the parts of a computer system that connect human users to each other and to the capabilities provided by computers."

Our experience with the Chat-and-Search environment leaves us very optimistic about the usefulness of this approach. Our future work will be to explore embedding other capabilities into the chat environment.

Acknowledgements

We thank Thomas Erickson and Akihiko Obata for helpful comments. We also thank Noah Kanzaki and Naoshi Koki for development and operation of Fujitsu Intranet search engine. We wish to thank all support and staff who operate Fujitsu Intranet (IRC) network.

References

Ackerman, M. (1994), Augmenting the Organizational Memory: A Field Study of Answer Garden, *in* R. Furuta & C. Neuwirth (eds.), *Proceedings of CSCW'94: Conference on Computer Supported Cooperative Work*, ACM Press, pp.243–253.

Dieberger, A. (1997), "Supporting Social Navigation on the World Wide Web", *International Journal of Human–Computer Studies* **46**(6), 805–29. Special Issue on Innovative Applications of the WWW.

Dourish, P. & Bellotti, V. (1992), Awareness and Coordination in Shared Workspaces, *in* J. Turner & R. Kraut (eds.), *Proceedings of CSCW'92: Conference on Computer Supported Cooperative Work*, ACM Press, pp.107–114.

Erickson, T., Smith, D. N., Kellogg, W. A., Laff, M., Richards, J. T. & Brandnerl, E. (1999), Socially Translucent Systems: Social Proxies, Persistent Conversation, and the Design of "Babble", *in* M. G. Williams, M. W. Altom, K. Ehrlich & W. Newman (eds.), *Proceedings of CHI'99: Human Factors in Computing Systems*, ACM Press, pp.72–9.

Guzdial, M. (1997), A Shared Command Line in a Virtual Space: The Workingman's MOO, *in* D. Fay (ed.), *Proceedings of the ACM Symposium on User Interface Software and Technology, UIST'97*, ACM Press, pp.73–4.

Malone, T. W. (1985), Designing Organizational Interfaces, *in* L. Borman & B. Curtis (eds.), *Proceedings of CHI'85: Human Factors in Computing Systems*, ACM Press, pp.66–71.

Masinter, L. & Ostrom, E. (1993), "Collaborative Information Retrieval: Gopher from MOO", Proceedings of INET'93, ftp://ftp.lambda.moo.mud.org/pub/MOO/papers/MOOGopher.html.

Norman, D. A. (1988), *The Psychology of Everyday Things*, Basic Books.

Oikarinen, J. & Reed, D. (1993), "Internet Relay Chat Protocol". RFC1459.

Twindale, M. B., Nichols, D. M., & Paice, C. D. (1997), "Browsing is a Collaborative Process, in Information Processing and Management", *Information Processing and Management* **33**(6), 761–83.

Human–Computer Interaction — INTERACT '99
M. Angela Sasse and Chris Johnson (Editors)
Published by IOS Press, © IFIP TC.13, 1999

Complementary Menu System Combining Document Structure and Taxonomic Hierarchy

Yasuko Senda, Yasusi Sinohara & Kozo Bannai

Communication and Information Research Laboratory, Central Research Institute of Electric Power Industry, 2-11-1 Iwado Kita, Komae-shi, Tokyo 201, Japan.

senda@denken.or.jp

Abstract: The users of conventional menu systems for information retrieval, sometimes choose wrong items or hesitate to choose one menu item among the items listed. To suppress these faulty actions, we propose a menu system named "Complementary Menu System" which combines two different types of menu systems, one based on the compositional structure of the document and the other based on based on the taxonomic hierarchy of a thesaurus. We have developed this menu system and conducted an experiment to evaluate the effects of the combination. The experiments showed that the complementary menu system achieves higher precision than the component menu systems. The interview of users and the log analysis suggest the combination gives different clues and more useful information for retrieval for users because each component menu system compensates the lack of information of the other with one's information.

Keywords: taxonomic hierarchy, compositional structure of document, menu-based interface.

1 Introduction

With the spread of personal computers and inter/intra-networking, people have increasing opportunities to access various kind of on-line documents, such as computer software manuals, online books, and online business documents.

However, users face growing problems in finding the text segments they want to read in a given document. A typical method of retrieving the necessary text segments is keyword-based retrieval (Salton, 1989) as used in full-text retrieval systems. Another typical retrieval method is menu-based retrieval, such as a structured table of contents, or an index of keywords referring to the text segments each keyword appears in (Noerr & Noerr, 1985; Lee, 1986), as is often used with commercial online software manuals.

The keyword-based retrieval systems are difficult for novice users, who are unfamiliar with (technical) terms in the given document and who are unable to think of suitable keywords to retrieve the target text segments. In a menu-based system, on the other hand, the clues to retrieving the target text segments are listed in a menu. The user however sometimes hesitates in choosing a menu item or chooses the wrong item. These problems occur in two typical situations:

Incomprehensible Categorization:
The categorization used in the menu system is based on knowledge that the user doesn't have, or the categorization doesn't match the user's purpose. For example, an alphabetically-ordered command list, which is a case of the latter, is not helpful for the user who is looking for the command to carry out a specific function (Card, 1982).

Ambiguous Categorization and Unsuitable Titles:
Several menu items seem to refer to similar things and the user lacks the knowledge needed to distinguish between them. Or the title of a menu item is misleading or ambiguous and the user is unable to guess the content.

Recently the research by Rennison (1994) and Lamping et al. (1995) in information visualization proposed how to present large and complicated categorization. But these researches didn't discuss the above problems. The research of (Tweedie et al., 1994) proposed a system which combines several histograms categorizing for example 'houses' according to their attributes in order to search for the house that meets the user's conditions. In this system, because the user can select and use the preferred histogram (which is a kind of menu system), the problem of "Incomprehensible Categorization" is solved to some extent. And further, because the system shows the relationships between attributes (histograms) and selecting a value on one histogram immediately affects the other histograms, users can understand the meaning of their selecting. Therefore the problem "Ambiguous Categorization & Unsuitable Titles" is solved to some extent. However, the histograms can only categorize a kind of article like houses, but cannot categorize the contents of document. Therefore the idea cannot be easily applied to document retrieval, which we are discussing here.

To remedy this situation of document retrieval, we propose a menu system that we call a "Complementary Menu System", which combines and correlates two types of menu systems. One is based on the structure of a given document, and the other is based on the general taxonomic hierarchy used in a thesaurus. Taxonomic hierarchy of a thesaurus categorizes terms according to the similarity of the meaning of terms. Each taxonomic categorization has a title which corresponds to the meaning of the terms.

The organization of a document structure-based menu system is specific to the given document and each menu item is a heading of a text segment (just like an entry in a table of contents). Usually a heading summarizes the topic concisely, but the description is based on domain-specific knowledge.

On the other hand, the structure of a taxonomy-based menu system is general and is not specific to the document. It is a hierarchical index to terms used in a given document. The menu titles are the titles of taxonomic categories. Unlike the usual index of keywords, indexed terms are categorized according to the similarity of the meaning of the terms.

We believe that combining these two types of menu systems will achieve the following improvements.

Different Clues: Both domain/document-specific and general clues are available. Even when the user lacks sufficient domain/document-specific knowledge, he/she can use the taxonomy-based menu system as a clue to retrieving the target text segments using only general knowledge. The user can choose the menu system that is more understandable to them.

Compensation of Information: Each heading of the document structure-based menu system suggests the major topic of the corresponding text segment, but doesn't necessarily show the information which is important to the user. The terms in the categories of the taxonomy-based menu system point to both major and subsidiary topics. The complementary menu system can therefore compensate for the information that is missing from one system with information from the other.

This paper first describes the document structure-based, taxonomy-based, and complementary menu systems, and then describes experiments to evaluate the effectiveness of the complementary menu system.

2 Document Structure and Taxonomy

This section describes the document structure-based and taxonomy-based menu systems and discusses their problems.

2.1 Document Structure-based Menu System

Most documents are organized hierarchically into sections and subsections, sub-subsections, and so on. The document structure-based menu system is a set of menus that are based on this hierarchical structure of a given document. A menu contains a list of the headings of corresponding text segments (e.g. section titles), just like in a table of contents. By selecting an item on a non-terminal menu, the user is shown a new menu for the text segment corresponding to the selected menu item (e.g. a list of subsections in a section). The user can read the text segment by selecting a menu item from a terminal menu in the hierarchy.

An example of the document structure-based menu system is the right-half of Figures 1 & 2. The document structure used in the examples of these figures is extracted from office regulations for a research institute. (Though all the text in the real menu system is in Japanese, these figures use English for case of understanding). This menu system has the following three windows layers.

Position window at the top, shows the position of the currently selectable text segments in the document structure. In other words, this window lists the headings of the higher nodes of the selectable text segments from the top of

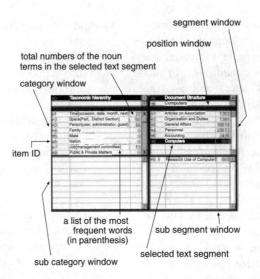

segment window

position window

total numbers of the noun
terms in the selected text segment

category window

item ID

a list of the most
frequent words
(in parenthesis)

sub category window

sub segment window

selected text segment

Figure 1: In case an item of a document structure-based menu is selected.

The numbers changed by the selecting
a menu item in the opposite menu system.

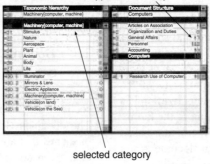

selected category

Figure 2: In case an item of a taxonomy-based menu is selected (this is a case of following on Figure 1.)

the document structure. By selecting a heading on this window, the following segment window lists the headings of its sub text segments.

Segment window in the middle, is a menu of selectable text segments. When a segment on this window is selected, it is highlighted and the position window is updated, and then the menu for the selected segment is shown in the bottom window.

Sub-segment window at the bottom, is a menu for the selected segment. Selecting a menu item on this window highlights the item and updates the position window. Then the segment window shows the content of the current subsegment window and the sub-segment window shows the menu for the selected segment.

2.2 Taxonomy-based Menu System

The taxonomy-based menu system is a hierarchical index of terms used in a given document, whose hierarchy is based on of the taxonomy used in a thesaurus. The thesaurus taxonomy is a tree-like categorization of ordinary words according to the similarity in the general sense of the words. The hierarchy is modified by the deletion of categories for which there are no terms in the document, and then the top categories are reordered by their concreteness/abstractness. The method is reported in another paper (Senda et al., 1997). Further, we use a Japanese taxonomy (The National Language Research Institute, 1964) because the document is written in Japanese. However this is a difference only in the language, and there is no difference in form between Japanese taxonomy and the other language's taxonomy. Therefore the taxonomy of other languages can also be used in the same way.

The indexed terms are (compound) nouns found by automatic morphological analysis, and the terms are linked to terminal categories of the taxonomy which categorizes a noun in the term. A menu for a non-terminal category shows a list of a taxonomic category name of its subcategories. By selecting a menu item, the user is shown the menu for the selected category. The menu for a terminal category is a list of terms used in the document belonging to that category. By selecting a term, the user is shown a list of KWICs (keywords in context) which shows lines of texts from the document around the selected term.

The taxonomy-based menu system also has the same window layers: a position window, a category window and a sub-category window. Their roles are the same of those in the document structure-based menu system. An example of the taxonomy-based menu system is the left-half of Figures 1 & 2.

2.3 Problems of the Menu Systems

In this section, we discuss the problems of the above menu systems and the remedy to these problems. The problems are incomprehensive categorization and ambiguous categorization/unsuitable titles, which are described in Section 1.

These problems are fundamental in all hierarchical menu systems. Every hierarchical menu system can be viewed as a categorization. They classify items into classes according to some criterion. To use the menu system, the user has to guess the criterion and decide which menu item is more closely related to the required information based on the criterion. However, it is generally difficult to classify items without hesitation because the criterion needs interpretation which depends on the knowledge of the classifier or environments related to the items (e.g. contexts of terms).

Incomprehensible categorization occurs when the user cannot understand the criterion because of lack of knowledge, or when the criterion is not directly related to the purpose of the retrieval. Ambiguous categorization occurs when there is uncertainty about which menu item has to be chosen because of lack of information related to the interpretation. The uncertainty will increase when the title of each menu item is unsuitable or misleading. But, those cases sometimes occur because it is difficult to make a title which concisely summarizes all the lower items.

As for the document structure-based menu system, its menu gives information on the major topics and the context of the text segment by its heading

and its position in the menu hierarchy. These pieces of information are useful for finding items closely related to the topics in the document. However, the criterion used in the menu system strongly depends on the compositional rules of documents and domain-specific knowledge. Therefore, for the user without domain-specific knowledge, the criterion might be incomprehensible or ambiguous. For example, when the user wants to retrieve items which are described in the document but are not major topics, the user may have troubles because the title of a menu item i.e. the heading, describes only the major topics (this is a case of "Unsuitable Titles".)

As for the taxonomy-based menu system, its menu gives information on the concrete description (i.e. indexed terms) used in the document and the general semantic categories which index the terms. The criterion is general and is useful for the user with only minimum domain-specific knowledge because it requests from the user only general knowledge (e.g. similarity of word's sense). The criterion is also effective to find text segments which are subsidiary topics in the document, but are important to the user. But the taxonomy lacks the specific major topics and the context. Therefore the user doesn't understand what context the terms of each category are used in, and then it is difficult to guess whether each category is related to the target text segment in the menu system.

Table 1 summarizes the above discussion. Document structure-based menu suggests the topics and contexts but not concrete descriptions and semantic categories in the document. It also requests domain-specific knowledge. On the other hand, taxonomy-based menus give concrete descriptions in the document (e.g. terms) as well as general semantic keys (categories) which don't request rich domain-specific knowledge. However, the taxonomy doesn't provide enough information on the topics of the document or the context of concrete descriptions in the document, which are essential to make a proper interpretation.

We note that each menu system has information required to disambiguate or to increase the understandability of the other menu system and thus the combination of these menu systems will be useful to make more effective retrieval.

3 Complementary Menu System

In this section, we propose a menu system we have called the "Complementary Menu System" which combines two different types of menu systems, that is, the document structure-based menu system and the taxonomy-based menu system.

Category	Document Structure	Taxonomy
Sufficient	Major Topics & Context	Concrete Description & Semantic Category
Insufficient	Concrete Description Topics & Semantic Category	Specific Major & Context
Basis	Domain-dependent Knowledge	General Knowledge (Similarity of Word's Sense)

Table 1: The menu system's features.

3.1   Correlating the Menu Systems

The complementary menu system not only arranges the two menu systems in a row, but it also correlates them. The menu item on each menu consists of more than just the name of a category or the heading of a text segment.

A menu item, in the document structure-based menu, consists of the total numbers of noun terms in the text segment and the headings. If an item is selected in the taxonomy-based menu, the terms are restricted to the terms belonging to the selected taxonomic category in the text segment. The third column of the the right-half of Figures 1 & 2 is for the total number of terms. In the taxonomy-based menu, a menu item consists of the category name and the total number of occurrences of terms in the category in the selected text segment and a list of the most frequent terms. The third column of the left-half of Figures 1 & 2 is for the total number of terms and the terms in parenthesis in the second column are a list of the most frequent terms. If an item is selected in the document structure-based menu, the terms are also restricted to the terms within the text segment selected in the document structure-based menu subsystem.

The numbers and lists of the most frequent terms in a menu system change when you select a menu item in the other menu system.

3.2   How to Compensate

Here we explain how to use the two subsystems and the above correlation mechanism to find the target text segment.

At first, users can use either menu subsystem depending on their initial knowledge. It is better to use the document structure-based menu subsystem for the user who has domain/document-specific knowledge or who cannot find a suitable category in the taxonomy-based menus. On the other hand, the taxonomy-based menus subsystem is better for the user who doesn't have enough knowledge to use the document structure-based menus.

When a user selects an item from a document structure-based menu, the total numbers of terms and the lists of the most frequent terms on the taxonomy-based menu subsystem change to lists of the terms within the text segment corresponding to the selection. From the numbers, the user can become familiar with the categories frequently mentioned in the selected text segment and from the lists, he/she can become familiar with the specific terms which belong to the category and are used in the selected text. From these categories and specific terms, the user can guess the items described in the selected text segment but not in the heading. It will be helpful in order to decide whether the text segment is worth pursuing or not. Moreover, they can narrow down the terms belonging to each category from the list of terms. This will be useful for selecting a suitable category in the taxonomy-based menu.

The same kind of situations occur when the user selects taxonomy-based menu items. The number in each menu item in the document structure-based menu changes to the numbers of terms which are within the corresponding text segment and belong to the selected category. Through these numbers, the user can make an assumption about which text segment is closely related to the selected category, or what kind of topics are closely related to the selected category. These are useful to select the appropriate text segment listed in the document structure-based menus.

However, the effect of correlation will be greater when using subsystems alternately. For example, consider the case that a user selects an item A in the document structure-based menu although he cannot decide with confidence which text segment A or B is suitable. By selecting A, the user can narrow down the range of terms belonging to each category in the taxonomy-based menu and he/she can decide more precisely which category will be suitable for the purpose, as explained above. When he/she selects category C as the suitable category, this causes a change in the numbers in the document structure-based menus. If the number of text segment B is greater than the number of text segment A, the user can assume that text segment B will be more suitable. The selection of text segment B will change the most frequent terms in category C. If the user finds a specific term closely related to the required information in the list of frequent terms, it will reinforce the assumption and it will also be helpful in selecting a subcategory of category C.

We believe this kind of compensation of information by the correlation mechanism is very useful to avoid wrong selections or to make suitable selections with confidence.

4 Experimental Method

We conducted experiments to evaluate the complementary menu system, especially the effect of combining menu systems to compensate for lack of information.

4.1 Document and Taxonomy and Menu Systems

The document used in the experiment was a book on office regulations for a research institute with a file of about 250K bytes, which has 6 parts consisting of 44 regulations. The regulations contains 53 chapters and 208 sections in total, and some regulations have only sections. We used this document structure for the document structure-based menus. The parts are "Articles of Association", "Organization and Duties", "General affairs", "Personnel", "Accounting" and "Computers", and each of them corresponds to an administrative section that covers a wide variety of activities in the office.

We generated our taxonomy from the genus of nouns in the "Word List by Semantic Principles" thesaurus developed by the National Language Research Institute of Japan, which contains over 32,600 Japanese words. The taxonomy we used in the taxonomy-based menu system has 28 top categories and 193 subcategories (non-terminal 15, terminal 178), 195 terminal sub-subcategories and 3597 terms in the book indexed under its terminal categories.

The following four menu systems were tested.

COMPLEMENTARY: the complementary menu system using the document structure and the taxonomy described above.

STRUCTURE-BASED: the document structure-based menu system shown on the right in the above complementary system. The left-half of the complementary system was shadowed.

TAXONOMY-BASED: the taxonomy-based menu system shown on the left of the complementary system. The right-half of the complementary system is shadowed.

TAXONOMY-BASED2: another taxonomy-based menu system, which has a different structure.

We don't discuss this system because the comparison with the TAXONOMY-BASED system is reported in another paper (Senda et al., 1997).

Eight members of the company (7 researchers, 1 assistant) who have worked there for several years but none of whom have read the book through, were used as subjects for the experiments.

We prepared a total of 24 questions for the experiment and the correct answers to each question were defined as terminals of the document structure. We carefully avoided any overlap between the answers to different questions.

After an (oral and document-based) introduction to the task, the experimental procedure and how to use each system, each subject was asked to retrieve all answers within 10 minutes for each of the 24 questions (6 questions for each of the 4 systems). When the subject believes they have reached an answer, they click the "OK" button on the screen. Each action, that is, selection of menu-items and clicking on buttons were automatically logged with time stamps. After completing all the tasks for each subject, the subject was asked to fill out a questionnaire indicating the preference of systems and other factors, and we interviewed them to review the user's retrieval process.

In addition, we designed the experiment to be balanced in subjects and systems, and we used the analysis of variance to confirm the results.

5 Experimental Results

5.1 Precision and Coverage

We define the precision of a subject's answers as the percentage of correct answers among subject's answers. We also define the coverage of the subject's answers as the percentage of correct answers found in the predefined right answers for a given question.

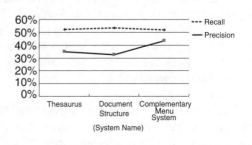

Figure 3: Precision and coverage.

Figure 3 depicts the average of the two indices for the three systems. ANOVA (analysis of variance) and other detailed analyses showed the primary factor in each index is the 'questions'. But the precision of the complementary system is significantly 10% higher than the other two systems at a significance level of 30%. On the other hand, the coverage of the three systems did not make much difference.

This result indicates that the complementary menu system is more effective in suppressing wrong choices of menu items than the usage of either the document-based or taxonomy-based menu systems alone.

5.1.1   Interviews

Six subjects found the complementary menu system to be preferable. Five of the six subjects gave their reason as being that selection in one sub menu system gives a clue to selecting the proper item in the other menu system.

5.1.2   Case Analysis

We also analysed the cases for which the difference in performance is significant among the systems tested. The analysis also revealed the effect of compensation for missing information by combining the menu subsystems. One example is given below.

The question was "What documents/forms are computerized?" The answers lie in "Chapter 4: Kinds of Vouchers" and "Chapter 7: Voucher Processing in the Account Section" of "Regulation: Accounting" of "Part: Financial Affairs."

The first subject who used the document STRUCTURE-BASED menu system, chose "Part: Computers" at first, which seemed most closely related. However, it only includes the regulations on research uses of computers. This demonstrates the "Unsuitable Titles" problem described in Section 1.

He also selected "Part: General Affairs" and others which seemed to him related indirectly to the question. However, the subject thought "Part: Financial Affairs" is irrelevant to the question. Here is another example of the "Incomprehensible Categorization" problem described in Section 1. The structure of the document is mainly related to the duties of the administrative sections, but the relation between the document structure (or duties) and the question isn't understandable to a subject without knowledge.

The second subject used the TAXONOMY-BASED menu system, and chose many top categories after hesitating for a long time in selecting "Tool", "Social", "Space", "Article", etc. However, she failed to reach any right answers because the names of the

subcategories seemed to her irrelevant to the question and quit the search. This is another case of 'unsuitable titles'.

The third subject who used the COMPLEMENTARY menu system first chose "Part: Computers" on the document structure-based menu subsystem, like the first subject. However, in the complementary menu system, the selection of "Part: Computers" changes the numbers and the term list of each category in the taxonomy-based menus to the total number of occurrences and the list of the most frequent terms in "Part: Computers". So he selected the top category "Machinery&Instruments" from the taxonomy-based menu which occurs most frequently among the top categories, although the associated frequent word list didn't contain 'computer' (Stage 1). The selection also changes the numbers of each part/regulation in the document structure-based menus to the number of terms belonging in the category "Machinery&Instruments." In this way, he became aware that "Part: Computers" and "Part: Financial Affairs" are related to the category (Stage 2). In the end, he selected "Part: Financial Affairs" and succeeded in reaching the right answers guided by the numbers of terms related to "Machinery&Instruments".

The last retrieval sequence demonstrates the effect of mutual compensation of information between the document structure-based menu subsystem and the taxonomy-based menu subsystem. At Stage 1, the user gains information on what kind of categories are related to the current question by selecting a text segment, while he gaining information on which parts of the document are related to the question more specifically by selecting a category at Stage 2.

However, the combination was not always effective. In some cases, the users were confused by the amount of information supplied by the two subsystems, or they depended on either one of the subsystems. A more effective guide to avoid these situations will be helpful in improving the system's performance.

6   Summary and Future Works

In this paper, we proposed a complementary menu system combining document structure-based and taxonomy-based menu systems to reduce erroneous selections or hesitation in selecting menu items in a single use of the menu systems. The experiments showed a better performance for complementary use of the two menu systems compared with using either one on its own. The case analysis and interviews provided evidence that one of the main reasons for this is the correlation and mutual compensation of information that is not provided by a single menu system.

We believe that this technique is effective in reducing the number of erroneous selections and is applicable to more general applications. We think that this combination is appropriate for tasks, like expert systems or menu-based retrieval systems, which use a kind of ontology. Most ontologies are incomplete and defective for users but this combination may compensate for this. We are currently investigating what kind of ontologies are appropriate for combining.

We are currently investigating the situation where the user is confronted with multiple ontologies to reach the information that they want, and what kind of ontologies are appropriate for combining.

References

Card, S. K. (1982), User Perceptual Mechanisms in the Search of Computer Command Menus, *in Proceedings of CHI'82: Human Factors in Computing Systems*, ACM Press, pp.190–6.

Lamping, J., Rao, R. & Pirolli, P. (1995), A Focus+Context Technique Based on Hyperbolic Geometry for Visualizing Large Hierarchies, *in* I. Katz, R. Mack, L. Marks, M. B. Rosson & J. Nielsen (eds.), *Proceedings of CHI'95: Human Factors in Computing Systems*, ACM Press, pp.401–8.

Lee, E. (1986), "Keyword-menu Retrieval: An Effective Alternative to Menu Indexes", *Ergonomics* **29**(1), 115–30.

Noerr, P. L. & Noerr, K. T. B. (1985), "Browse and Novigate: An Advance in Database Access Methods", *Information Processing & Management* **21**(3), 205–13.

Rennison, E. (1994), Galaxy of News — An Approach to Visualizing and Understanding Expansive News Landscapes, *in Proceedings of the ACM Symposium on User Interface Software and Technology, UIST'94*, ACM Press, pp.3–12.

Salton, G. (1989), *Automatic Text Processing: The Transformation, Analysis and Retrieval of Information by Computer*, Addison–Wesley.

Senda, Y., Sinohara, Y. & Bannai, K. (1997), Menu Systems for Information Retrieval Using Taxonomy of Thesaurus: The Use of Japanese Thesaurus 'Bunrui Goihyo', *in Proceedings of the (Japanese) National Language Research Institute Fifth International Symposium Session 1 Language Study and Thesaurus*, pp.127–35.

The National Language Research Institute (ed.) (1964), *Word List by Semantic Principles(Bunrui Goi Hyou)*, Dai Nihon Tosho. in Japanese.

Tweedie, L. A., Spence, B., Williams, D. & Bhogal, R. (1994), "The Attribute Explorer". Video presentation at CHI'94.

Human–Computer Interaction — INTERACT '99
M. Angela Sasse and Chris Johnson (Editors)
Published by IOS Press, © IFIP TC.13, 1999

Plasticity of User Interfaces: Framework and Research Agenda

David Thevenin & Joëlle Coutaz

CLIPS-IMAG, BP 53, 38041 Grenoble Cedex 9, France.

{david.thevenin,joelle.coutaz}@imag.fr

Abstract: This paper introduces the notion of plasticity, a new property of interactive systems that denotes a particular type of user interface adaptation. Plasticity is the capacity of a user interface to withstand variations of both the system physical characteristics and the environment while preserving usability. Typically, a 'plastic' electronic agenda would run both on a workstation and on a hand-held computer without requiring a complete system redesign and re-implementation. We present a generic framework inspired by the model-based approach, for supporting the development of plastic user interfaces. Within this framework, a plastic user interface is specified once and serves multiple sources of physical variations. The goal is to guarantee usability continuity under variations in physical constraints while minimizing development and maintenance costs. This framework is illustrated with two simple case studies. Preliminary results and the state of the art in HCI open a new research agenda for the design and development of plastic user interfaces.

Keywords: user interface adaptation, plasticity, user interface, development process, usability.

1 Introduction

The need for ubiquitous access to information processing, the success of new consumer devices such as pocket computers and wireless networks, the availability of large electronic boards as well as the development of immersive caves, offer new challenges to the HCI software community. In particular, user interfaces need to accommodate the variability of a large set of interactional devices without leading to costly development efforts. For example, an electronic agenda should run both on a workstation and on a hand-held computer without requiring a complete system redesign and re-implementation. In this article, we introduce the notion of plasticity to denote this particular type of user interface adaptation.

In the next section, we define the coverage of plasticity within the problem space of adaptation. We then present a generic framework inspired from a model-based approach, for supporting the development of plastic user interfaces. This framework is illustrated with simple case studies. Preliminary results and the state of the art in HCI open a new research agenda for the design and development of plastic user interfaces.

2 Adaptation and Plasticity

2.1 Adaptation

In HCI, adaptation is modeled as two complementary system properties: adaptability and adaptivity (Browne et al., 1990; IFIP WG2.7, 1996). Adaptability is the capacity of the system to allow users to customize their system from a predefined set of parameters. Adaptivity is the capacity of the system to perform adaptation automatically without deliberate action from the user's part. Whether adaptation is performed on human requests or automatically, the design space for adaptation includes three additional orthogonal axes (see Figure 1): target, means, and time.

The target for adaptation: This axis denotes the entities for which adaptation is intended: adaptation to users, adaptation to the environment, and adaptation to the physical characteristics of the system (e.g. interactional devices such as a mouse).

The means of adaptation: This axis denotes the software components of the system involved in adaptation: typically, the system task model, the rendering techniques, and the help subsystems, may be modified to adapt to the targeted entities. The system task model is the system implementation of the user task model specified by experts on human factors. The rendering techniques denote the observable presentation and behaviour of the system. The help subsystems include help about the system and help about the task domain.

The temporal dimension of adaptation: Adaptation may be static (i.e. effective between sessions) and/or dynamic (i.e. occurring at run time).

A more comprehensive classification scheme can be found in (Dieterich et al., 1994) motivated by the detailed analysis of intelligent user interfaces

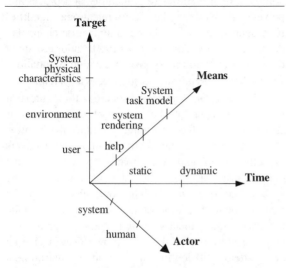

Figure 1: A design space for adaptation at a high level of reasoning.

2.2 Plasticity

The term 'plasticity' is inspired from the property of materials that expand and contract under natural constraints without breaking, thus preserving continuous usage. By analogy, *plasticity* is the capacity of a user interface to *withstand variations* of both the system physical characteristics and the environment while *preserving usability*. In addition, a plastic user interface is specified once to serve multiple sources of physical variations, thus *minimizing development and maintenance costs*. Plasticity may be static and/or dynamic. It may be achieved automatically and/or manually.

Within the design space of adaptation presented in Figure 1, plasticity is characterized in the following way:

1. Along the *target* axis, plasticity is concerned with the variations of the system physical

characteristics and/or the environment. It does not, therefore, cover adaptation to users' variations.

2. Along the *means* axis, plasticity involves the modification of the system task model and/or of the rendering techniques.

3. The *temporal* and *automaticity* axes are left opened.

Technically, platform independence of code execution is not a sufficient condition to support plasticity. Virtual toolkits, such as the Java abstract machine, offer very limited mechanisms for the automatic reconfiguration of a user interface in response to variations of interactional devices. All of the current tools for developing user interfaces embed an implicit model of a single class of target computers (typically, a keyboard, a mouse and at least a 640×480 colour screen). As a result, the rendering and responsiveness of a Java applet may be satisfactory on the developer's workstation but not necessarily usable for a remote Internet user. Therefore, platform independence is not sufficient to guarantee *usability continuity*. In addition, the iterative nature of the user interface development process, as well as code maintenance, make it difficult to maintain consistency between the multiple target versions.

In the absence of appropriate software tools, we need a framework for reasoning about the design and development of plastic user interfaces.

3 A Framework for Plasticity

Going one step further than the slogan for portability (i.e. "write it once and run it multiple times"), a framework for supporting plasticity should allow developers to *specify it usable and produce it multiple times*.

Model-based user interface generators, which promote the specification of high level models, provide an approach consistent with our requirements: they aim at usability while stressing computational reification. Our framework, inspired from such generators, should be viewed as an added-value to the models and methodological guides provided by the seminal design methods in HCI — e.g. MUSE (Dowell & Long, 1989), ADEPT (Johnson et al., 1993), or MAD (Scapin & Pierret-Golbreich, 1990). Our framework is not intended as a substitute to the models advocated by the design methods. Instead:

- It builds upon the models that work well in user interface design and user interface development.

- It improves existing models to satisfy the requirements imposed by plasticity.

- It explicitly introduces new models that have been overlooked or ignored so far.

Figure 2 shows the seven components of our framework. A detailed description is given in (Thevenin, 1998).

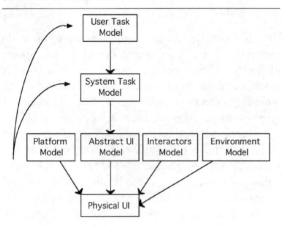

Figure 2: A framework for the development of plastic. Arrows denote models dependencies.

The *User Task Model* is a formal or semi-formal transcription of the real world activities. It results from the activity analysis performed by human factor specialists.

The *System Task Model* describes how the work tasks could be achieved with the introduction of the designed system. This model is informed by the User Task Model. The rules that govern the derivation of the User Task Model into a System Task Model are not well formalized yet. One can find in (Gamboa Rodriguez & Scapin, 1997) some early attempts at making the transformation explicit.

The *Abstract User Interface* is the canonical expression of an abstract rendering of the domain concepts and domain functions in conformance to the System Task Model. At this level of abstraction, rendering is interactor independent. It is similar in spirit to the notion of common information representation proposed in (Hüther & Rist, 1998). The notion of Abstract User Interface will be discussed further in Section 5.

The *Interactors Model* describes the interactors available for the physical rendering of a particular user interface. An interactor is an independent communicating agent characterized by an internal state and a perceivable state. It is capable of producing events and processing events caused by a user or by any component of the system. Graphical user interface

widgets, speech sentences are examples of interactors. The interactor model has been used in a variety of ways including system architecture modeling (Coutaz et al., 1996), presentation mapping validity (Doherty & Harrison, 1997), and user interface conformity with system task modeling (Markopoulos et al., 1997).

The *Platform Model* describes the physical characteristics of the target platforms. To our knowledge, platform modeling has been considered implicitly as the pervasive workstation. Plasticity needs the explicit expression of the target platforms in terms of quantified physical resources. A platform model should include the interactional devices available (e.g. mouse, screen, video cameras), the computational facilities (e.g. memory and processing power), as well as the communicational facilities (e.g. bandwidth rate of the communication channels). Although Mackinlay et al. (1990) address input devices only, their theory provides sound foundations for modeling the physical resources of a system.

The *Environment Model* specifies the context of use. The scope of the notion of environment is still unclear in the literature. Within the context of our framework, the environment roughly covers objects, persons and events that are peripheral to the current task but that may have an impact on the system and/or the user's behaviour. For example, a mobile phone that knows that it has entered a public area will automatically switch ringing signal from sonic to vibrating. Salber & Abowd (1999) give an early attempt at defining the notion of environment along with software components that support the development of 'context sensitive' interactive systems.

The *Physical User Interface* results from the constraints resolution and/or constraints propagation expressed in the Platform Model, the Abstract User Interface Model, the Interactors and the Environment Models.

Finally, the models in relation to the physical world (i.e. the Platform, the Interactors, and the Environments Models) may in turn have an impact on the System Task and the User Task models. For example, users needs for reading email from a mobile phone may not be different from the requirements for processing email on a standard workstation. Therefore, the derivation of a plastic user interface (as any user interface) does not necessarily follow a pure top-down design process.

The framework of Figure 2 sets the foundations for the development of plastic user interfaces. To be operational, the models it involves must be structured and formalized. Next section provides preliminary requirements and heuristics in that direction.

4   Requirements and Heuristics

An early analysis of an electronic agenda has led us to formulate a number of requirements and heuristics in relation to the User Task Model, the System Task Model, and the Interactors Model. The electronic agenda runs both on a Palm Pilot and personal workstations (i.e. PC and Macintosh).

4.1   The User Task Model

With regard to the User Task Model, we advocate the following recommendation:

> "Domain concepts involved in a task should be ranked according to their level of importance in the task domain as well as according to their degree of centrality for this particular interaction point."

For example, in the agenda application, the day of the month and the month of the year are *first class objects*. Conversely, the day of the week (e.g. whether the 15th of October is a Wednesday or a Friday) is not necessary to carry most frequent tasks. It is a second class object. The *degree of centrality* of a concept denotes the extent to which that concept is part of the environment for that particular task or is used as a central item for carrying the task. Typically, the location of use of an agenda is not central for executing the task but may modify the way the task is carried out.

User and system task models and notations have no provision for specifying the relative importance and periphery of domain concepts. A notable exception, however, is the task-related information analysis presented in Sutcliffe (1997) and in TKS (Johnson et al., 1995). The authors make an explicit distinction between "the information required" and "the information needed" by the user to carry a task.

The availability of *first class and second class concepts*, as well as the *centrality* of concepts can help the rendering process using general heuristics. An example of such a heuristic is:

> "First class objects should be observable whereas second class objects may be browsable if observability cannot be guaranteed due to the lack of physical resources."

Another example is:

> "Peripheral objects may be browsable whereas central objects should be observable."

Observability is the capacity of the system to make perceivable the concepts relevant for carrying a particular task. Browsability allows the user to make a concept perceivable when this concept is not directly observable (IFIP WG2.7, 1996). In the agenda example, a date is displayed as "Wednesday October 15,1998" on a workstation. It is rendered as "15 Oct 98" on the Palm Pilot whose screen resources are scarce. Here, the day of the week, which is a second class object, is not observable.

4.2   The System Task Model

The System Task Model, which describes how the work tasks are achieved with the system, includes domain-dependent tasks and articulatory tasks. An *articulatory task* is domain independent. As such, it does not appear in the User Task Model and it does not modify the values of the domain concepts. In general, an articulatory task is induced by the physical apparatus and the rendering techniques of the system. For example, the lack of screen space may introduce extraneous tasks for accessing a sequence of screen contents that would otherwise be presented at once on a large display. Scrolling and navigating are typical articulatory tasks.

In the context of plasticity, browsability, when used for accessing second class objects, generates articulatory tasks. For example, opening the agenda at a certain date requires selecting the month and the day in the calendar. On the PC version, the calendar is always visible whereas on the Palm Pilot, the calendar must be opened on demand. The 'GoTo' command is an articulatory task introduced in the System Task Model of the Palm Pilot version to access the calendar, a browsable domain concept.

Our early analysis of simple case studies calls for the following recommendation:

> "Generic articulatory tasks should be identified in a systematic way and inserted appropriately in the System Task Model."

4.3   The Interactors Model

As mentioned in Section 3, interactors have been used for addressing distinct issues and purposes. As a result, a multiplicity of formal representations has been developed for specifying interactors. Although these modeling techniques are convenient for their particular context of use, none of them addresses the problem of plasticity explicitly. This leads us to formulate the following additional recommendation:

"Interactors should specify the abstract data types they are able to handle. They should also be able to evaluate their appropriateness as well as their rendering cost."

The abstract data type description provides the information necessary to perform the mapping between a domain concept and a set of candidate interactors. The modeling techniques of Mackinlay (1986) and Roth & Mattis (1990) have paved the way in this direction but for graphical non interactive presentation only. Fischer (1998) addresses a similar problem for direct manipulation without considering multi-modal interaction.

The appropriateness of an interactor denotes its user-centered effectiveness at rendering a particular concept for a particular task. Because of constraints imposed by the lack of physical resources, a concept may not be rendered optimally with regard to the designer's intent or to the user's requirements. A number of mapping rules may be found in Vanderdonckt (1995) for graphics user interfaces and in Sutcliffe (1997) and Bernsen (1994) for multimedia and multi-modal interaction. The capacity of an interactor to evaluate its appropriateness serves two purposes: It guides the selection process for concept rendering and it permits to quantify the continuity or the degradation of the system usability.

The rendering cost of an interactor expresses the quantity of physical resources needed for its instantiation. As discussed in Coutaz et al. (1995), an interactor belongs to a modality. A modality m is defined as the couple $m = < r, d >$ where r denotes a representational system, and d the physical I/O device used to convey expressions of the representational system. Both r and d can be characterized with a rendition cost Cr and Cd. For example, the display footprint is a way to express the rendition cost of a graphical interactor. Temporal footprint, i.e. the time to enunciate a vocal output message, expresses the rendition cost of a speech output interactor. The rendering cost drives the selection of the final interactors set for presenting domain concepts.

Figure 3 shows the thumb index interactor used on the PC for setting the visualization mode of the agenda, whereas the Palm Pilot version deploys a tiny set of three icons. The visualization mode is an enumerated data type (day, month, and year) that can be mapped to a set of three icon interactors. Both sets use the same physical output device (i.e. the screen) but two different representational systems (text and graphics) whose rendition costs Cr (their display footprint) are different. In the example of

the date ("October 1998" vs. "Oct 98") the same representational system is used (text) using distinct pragmatic values that convey the same semantics at a lower footprint cost.

Having presented general requirements and heuristics for the components of our framework, we now discuss the principles for producing a Physical User Interface from an Abstract User Interface and an Interactors model.

Figure 3: On the left, the thumb index used for the workstation. On the right, the icons set for the Palm Pilot.

5 From Abstract to Physical User Interfaces

5.1 Overall Principles

The notion of Presentation Unit (PU) used in TRIDENT (Vanderdonckt, 1995) sets the foundations of a canonical representation for the Abstract Interface Model. A PU is a hierarchical structure that models information containers such as workspaces, as well as elementary units that correspond to domain concepts at the appropriate level of granularity. In addition to the structural static description of a PU, PU's have a behaviour and are linked by navigational relationships. These relationships reify task ordering as expressed in the System Task Model. The Physical User Interface is obtained by associating an interactor to every PU. Additionally, an interactors configuration is performed for PU's composed of sub-PU's.

For the selection of interactors, we advocate a two step process:

Step 1: Correspondence matching between PU's and interactors.

Step 2: Correspondence matching between the interactors selected in Step 1 and the physical resources provided by the system.

Correspondence matching between PU's and Interactors is based on consistency checking between the information flows that the PU's and the Interactors support respectively. An information flow is characterized with attributes including:

Direction of information: one way input, one way output, two ways input and output,

Information data type: type, domain of values, cardinality, etc. ((Mackinlay, 1986; Roth &

(a)

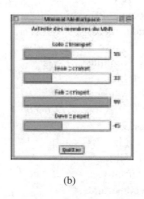

(b)

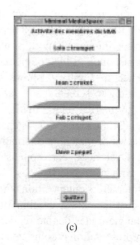

(c)

Rendering of MMS when using a small window. Only users' name and their level of activiy are observable using an integer value. Since workstation names are second class objects, they are not observable.

Rendering of MMS using bar charts when using a medium range window size.

Rendering of MMS when using a window large enough to accommodate plot interactors.

Figure 4: Dynamic rendering of MMS in response to screen space variations.

Mattis, 1990) for additional attributes). For a PU, the information data type corresponds to the domain concept supported by the PU. For an interactor, the information data type denotes the abstract domain the interactor is able to render.

For example, the graphic thermometer and the bar chart interactors, the graphic and the audio real number, all support information flows that are compatible with PU Temperature. Interactors, such as the check box and the radio button, are not consistent with this PU. They are discarded in Step 1 of the selection process.

Correspondence matching between the interactors selected in Step 1 and the physical resources of the system, is based on constraints resolution between the rendering costs of the interactors ($< Cr, Cd >$) and the availability of the physical resources of the computer system. For example, the thermometer and the bar chart interactors both require a screen ($Cd =$ Screen) whereas, for the real number, $Cd =$ (Screen or Loudspeaker). In addition, their representational cost Cr ($Cr =$ Screen footprint) is higher than that of the graphic real number. On a mobile phone with no screen or with a small screen, the audio/graphic real number satisfies the constraints.

We have applied this simple process to MMS, a simple media space.

5.2 MMS

MMS conveys the level of activity of the community members of our lab. It currently runs on standard workstations but with varying window sizes as a means to simulate different physical screen sizes. The activity level is computed from the use of the mouse and the keyboard. Image differences from video cameras could also have been used as a source of input.

In this example, a single compound PU contains three elementary PU's: the purpose of the system, a quit command, the list of users currently connected to MMS, their activity level and the name of their workstation. All of the concepts are first class objects except the name of the workstation the user is currently connected to. Table 1 shows the information flow of the elementary PU's.

Concept	Direction	Data Type	Card	Domain
Person name	Out	ASCII	1	Undefined
Workstation name	Out	ASCII	1	Undefined
Level of activity	Out	Integer	1	[0, 10] Step 1
Quit command	In	ASCII	1	{Quitter}
System Purpose	Out	ASCII	1	Undefined

Table 1: Information flow of the PU's for MMS.

The interactors that satisfy the PU's information flow include: the string interactor for the purpose of the system, as well as for the users and workstations names; the button interactor fits the quit command; the integer, the bar chart and the plot interactors match the level of activity. In our system, interactors are selected dynamically according to the size of the window. This window which, in the current implementation, simulates a physical screen, corresponds to the compound workspace PU. The sequence in Figure 4 shows the rendering of MMS according to screen space variations. Figure 5 illustrates the internal representation used to compute the final rendering. Each node is characterized with a cost and the set of matching alternatives for rendering a PU. An Oval node corresponds to an interactor decorated with its rendering cost. Diamond nodes represent interactors composition with layout rules. Its rendering cost is a linear combination of its siblings cost. Rectangle nodes denote rendering Alternatives. The final representation is computed using a constraint resolution algorithm based the rendering costs and physical resource availability.

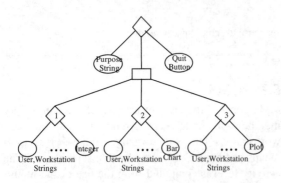

Figure 5: Internal representation of the solution space for rendering MMS.

6   Conclusion

In this paper, we have introduced the notion of plasticity for addressing the portability of interactive systems in relation to usability continuity. Building on the model-based approach, we propose a framework that structures the problem space and provides the foundations for a solution space using high level specifications. Such descriptions trigger the appropriate design questions and open the way to the automatic or semi-automatic generation of plastic user interfaces. We have illustrated the feasibility of the approach with simple case studies: an off-the shelf electronic agenda, and MMS a media-space that conveys the level of activity of the community members of our lab. These preliminary results need to be completed with a more thorough analysis and formalization in order to make our framework operational.

References

Bernsen, N. O. (1994), "Foundations of Multimodal Representations: A Taxonomy of Representational Modalities", *Interacting with Computers* **6**(4), 347–71.

Browne, D., Totterdell, P. & Norman, M. (eds.) (1990), *Adaptive User Interfaces*, Computer and People Series, Academic Press.

Coutaz, J., Nigay, L. & Salber, D. (1996), Agent-based Architecture Modeling for Interactive Systems, *in* D. Benyon & P. Palanque (eds.), *Critical Issues in User Interface Engineering*, Springer-Verlag, pp.191–209.

Coutaz, J., Nigay, L., Salber, D., Blandford, A., May, J. & Young, R. (1995), Four Easy Pieces for Assessing the Usability of Multimodal Interaction: The CARE Properties, *in* K. Nordby, P. H. Helmersen, D. J. Gilmore & S. A. Arnessen (eds.), *Human–Computer Interaction — INTERACT '95: Proceedings of the Fifth IFIP Conference on Human–Computer Interaction*, Chapman & Hall, pp.115–20.

Dieterich, H., Malinowski, U., Kühme, T. & Schneider-Hufschmidt, M. (1994), "State of the Art in Adaptive User Interfaces". http://www.cc.gatech.edu/computing/classes/cs8113d_94_fall/homepage.html.

Doherty, G. & Harrison, M. (1997), A Representational Approach to the Specification of Presentations, *in* M. Harrison & J. Torres (eds.), *Design, Specification and Verification of Interactive Systems'97*, Springer-Verlag, pp.273–90.

Dowell, J. & Long, J. (1989), "Towards a Conception for an Engineering Discipline of Human Factors", *Ergonomics* **32**(11), 1513–35.

Fischer, M. (1998), A Framework for Generating Spatial Configurations in User Interfaces, *in* P. Markopoulos & P. Johnson (eds.), *Design, Specification and Verification of Interactive Systems'98*, Springer-Verlag, pp.225–41.

Gamboa Rodriguez, F. & Scapin, D. (1997), Editing MAD* Task Descriptions for Specifying User Interfaces at both Semantic and Presentation Levels, *in* M. Harrison & J. Torres (eds.), *Design, Specification and Verification of Interactive Systems'97*, Springer-Verlag, pp.193–208.

Hüther, M. & Rist, T. (1998), "Entering a shared Information Space through Heterogeneous Communication Devices", http://www.dfki.uni-sb.de/imedia/workshops/ecai98/#Program.

IFIP WG2.7 (1996), *Design Principles for Interactive Software*, Chapman & Hall.

Johnson, P., Johnson, H. & Wilson, S. (1995), Rapid Prototyping of User Interfaces Driven by Task Models, *in* J. M. Carroll (ed.), *Scenario-Based Design: Envisioning Work and Technology in System Development*, John Wiley & Sons, pp.209–46.

Johnson, P., S., W., P., M. & Pycock, Y. (1993), ADEPT — Advanced Design Environment for Prototyping with Task Models, *in* S. Ashlund, K. Mullet, A. Henderson, E. Hollnagel & T. White (eds.), *Proceedings of INTERCHI'93*, ACM Press/IOS Press, p.66.

Mackinlay, J. (1986), "Automating the Design of Graphical Presentations of Relational Information", *ACM Transactions on Graphics* **5**(2), 110–141.

Mackinlay, J., Card, S. K. & Robertson, G. (1990), "A Semantic Analysis of the Design Space of Input Devices", *Human–Computer Interaction* **5**, 145–90.

Markopoulos, P., Johnson, P., & Rowson, J. (1997), Formal Aspects of Task-based Design, *in* M. Harrison & J. Torres (eds.), *Design, Specification and Verification of Interactive Systems'97*, Springer-Verlag, pp.209–24.

Roth, S. & Mattis, J. (1990), Data Characterization for Intelligent Graphics Presentation, *in* J. C. Chew & J. Whiteside (eds.), *Proceedings of CHI'90: Human Factors in Computing Systems*, ACM Press, pp.193–200.

Salber, D. & Abowd, G. (1999), The Context Toolkit, *in* M. G. Williams, M. W. Altom, K. Ehrlich & W. Newman (eds.), *Proceedings of CHI'99: Human Factors in Computing Systems*, ACM Press, pp.434–41.

Scapin, D. & Pierret-Golbreich, C. (1990), Towards a Method for Task Description: MAD, *in* L. Berlinguet & D. Berthelette (eds.), *Proceedings of Work with Display Unit '89*, Elsevier Science, pp.371–80.

Sutcliffe, A. (1997), "Task-Related Information Analysis", *International Journal of Human–Computer Studies* **47**(2), 223–57.

Thevenin, D. (1998), *Interfaces Homme — Machine Autoconfigurables*, DEA Informatique, UJF.

Vanderdonckt, J. (1995), Knowledge-Based Systems for Automated User Interface Generation; The TRIDENT Experience, Technical Report RP-95-010, Fac. Univ. de N-D de la Paix, Inst. d'Informatique, Namur.

Human–Computer Interaction — INTERACT '99
M. Angela Sasse and Chris Johnson (Editors)
Published by IOS Press, © IFIP TC.13, 1999

User Interface Prototyping Methods in Designing Mobile Handsets

Harri Kiljander

Nokia Mobile Phones, 6000 Connection Drive, Irving, TX 75039, USA.

harri.kiljander@nmp.nokia.com

Abstract: This paper describes the experiences of using different user interface (UI) prototyping methods and tools in designing user interfaces for mobile handsets at Nokia.

Creating and evaluating prototypes is one of the cornerstones in human-centred design. Designing mobile handset user interfaces requires various user interface prototyping methods: scenarios, state transition diagrams, paper prototypes, CAD models, solid models, hardware prototypes, computer simulations and even virtual reality prototypes. The different methods have different capabilities. As the cost of a design change increases when the design moves from the initial UI concepts to detailed UI specifications, so does also the complexity of the UI prototypes. The lower fidelity methods — e.g. paper prototyping — are efficient tools to support rapid design iterations and to answer major design questions in the early phases of the design process. The more expensive higher fidelity methods — such as computer simulations — are necessary in addressing the more detailed design issues later in the process.

Keywords: mobile phones, communicators, smart phones, prototyping, scenarios, state transition diagrams, simulations, models, virtual reality, interaction design, design process

1 Introduction

1.1 Objectives

Nokia has a long history of applying human-centred design methods when designing and developing mobile handsets, i.e. mobile phones and communicators. During the last couple of years there has been a continuous effort to improve the user interface design and usability processes in the company. The findings described in this paper are results of an internal study the author conducted at Nokia Research Center and Nokia Mobile Phones during 1997 and 1998. The objective of the study was to gain a better understanding of the capabilities of the UI prototyping methods that were used in the UI design process so that possible deficiencies in the process could be improved. UI prototyping is one of the cornerstones in human-centred design and significant resources are spent in UI prototyping activities for mobile handsets like the vision prototype shown in Figure 1. Knowing the applicability of the different UI prototyping methods and their strengths and weaknesses in various design and development tasks assists the designers in selecting the best methods in

different phases of the design and development process.

Figure 1: Mobile handset UI prototype.

1.2 Previous Research

As the name implies, most human–computer interaction (HCI) research focuses on traditional human–*computer* interaction. The interest in interaction research for mobile computing and mobile handsets has emerged quite recently (e.g. (Bonner, 1996; Grace & Schneider-Hufschmidt,

1997; Kiljander, 1997; van Leeuwen & Thomas, 1997; Petrie et al., 1998; Väänänen-Vainio-Mattila & Ruuska, 1998). According to Brouwer-Janse (1997), most HCI research is devoted to applications for which target users are known or can reasonably well be defined. In contrast, consumer products — such as mobile phones — have no explicitly defined users. These users do not expect to operate a computer system but use the product in their daily lives without any or with just a minimal training. Thus the problem settings in mobile handset UI design are somewhat different than in human–computer interaction.

Bonner (1996) describes the challenges related to designing intelligent consumer and domestic product interfaces. Among the research questions is the applicability of incomplete prototypes: how easy is it to evaluate prototype intelligent interfaces without developing all the functionality?

Virzi et al. (1996) compare the usability problems uncovered using low- and high-fidelity prototypes. They conclude that the use of low-fidelity prototypes can be effective throughout the product development cycle and not just during the early phases of design.

Kespohl & Szwillus (1996) present the KAP tool for prototyping user interfaces of 'technical devices' such as video cassette recorders, CD players, alarm clocks, answering machines, telephones, etc. They claim that KAP has significant advantages over programming-based environments since the KAP user needs to know only about states and rule-based state transitions.

Grace & Schneider-Hufschmidt (1997) report on the development of a prototyping environment for telephone user interfaces. At Siemens they have implemented a user interface prototyping environment for designers and product managers with little or no experience with programming or knowledge of the internal software architecture of the actual phones. Although the prototypes developed with the tool were able to satisfy their needs, the prototyping environment itself was not accepted by the non-expert user interface developers. Their analysis suggests that the inherent complexity of communicating devices cannot be hidden from the user interface designers without sacrificing the required functionality.

van Leeuwen & Thomas (1997) report on the interaction design process of the Philips Fizz GSM phone user interface. They consider the full integration of the various disciplines involved — product management, hardware developers, software developers, interaction designers, and human factors specialists — being a major key to the success of the user interface design. They conclude that an ideal product creation process is probably an illusion since numerous changes in direction are usually commonplace throughout the development process.

Kerttula et al. (1997) describe their experiences and further plans to develop virtual reality design tools for the electronics and telecommunications industry.

Petrie et al. (1998) report on the design of wearable and mobile computers for people with visual disabilities. They found cardboard and plastic prototypes — the wearable answer to paper prototypes for 2D interfaces — a useful method for potential users and the design team in clarifying the design.

2 User Interface Design

2.1 Mobile Handset User Interfaces

Depending on the viewpoint, mobile handsets are consumer electronics products or embedded systems. Their user interfaces consist of both the physical device that the users hold in their hands when using the product — sometimes in very mobile circumstances — and the immaterial product, i.e. the dynamic user interface software that the users interact with and view through the product's small display. This dualistic combination of hardware and software together with the mobility requirements can make the user interface, interaction, and industrial design more interdisciplinary and challenging than traditional HCI work.

2.2 Prototyping in the UI Design Process

The UI design process is part of the overall product development process that, e.g. Ulrich & Eppinger (1995) divide into the five consecutive phases of Concept Development, System-Level Design, Detail Design, Testing and Refinement, and Production Ramp-Up and Launch. Nokia's mobile handset UI design activities are based on a human-centred design methodology and they overlap these product development phases. UI prototyping is one of the cornerstones of human-centred design and it involves the following ISO-standardized (ISO 1996) activities at Nokia:

1. Using existing knowledge to develop a proposed design solution.

2. Making that design solution more concrete.

3. Showing the prototype to users and allowing them to perform tasks.

4. Using this feedback to improve design.

5. Iterating this process until design objectives are met.

2.3 Why Prototype

The experiences from Nokia and other sources — e.g. (ISO, 1996; Isensee & Rudd, 1996; Petrie et al., 1998) point out at least the following benefits of applying UI prototyping methods and tools:

- Better collection of customer requirements.

- Evaluation of new interface techniques and functions.

- Demonstration of feasibility.

- Improved user participation and satisfaction.

- Early testing and evaluating.

- A clear specification.

- Cost savings in development and maintenance.

- Increased quality assurance and control.

- Improved productivity.

- Demonstration of early progress.

- Sales and marketing tool (internal & external).

- Vision spreading.

- Early prototypes are usually inexpensive.

- Prototypes can be used for (sales force) training.

- Products that are prototyped have better user interfaces than those that are not.

3   UI Prototyping Methods

The various UI prototyping methods used in designing mobile handsets at Nokia are briefly described in this section.

3.1 Scenarios

Scenarios help in specifying the functionality of a new product. Scenarios describe in detail an interaction session — i.e. a set of related tasks — with no or limited flexibility for the user. A scenario forces the designers to think about the users who eventually will use the product and also the activities they will perform with the product. According to Nielsen (1993), a scenario is an encapsulated description of:

1. An individual *user*.

2. Using a specific set of computer (or any product) *facilities*.

3. To achieve a specific *outcome*.

4. Under specified *circumstances*.

5. Over a certain *time interval*.

Scenarios are usually made for usability evaluations; a test scenario constitutes a major part of a usability test plan at Nokia. Scenarios can be created through brainstorming or, e.g. using the Contextual Inquiry method (Väänänen-Vainio-Mattila & Ruuska, 1998).

3.2 State Transition Diagrams

An interaction chain of events can be presented through a sequence of display images of the mobile handset. A state transition diagram, UI map or a storyboard connects these static displays or screen shots together. It conveys the dynamic aspects of the system to the users more easily than written UI specifications or separate static screen shots.

Finite state machines are commonly used in real-time system design. Informal UI state transition diagrams — often called *storyboards* — are often the basis for UI style guides that are the initial UI documents before the actual UI specifications are prepared. The boundaries between storyboarding and paper prototyping are often blurred since some interactivity is easily added to the state transition diagrams.

3.3 Paper Prototypes

Paper prototyping — Isensee & Rudd (1996) use the term *paper-and-pencil* — is one of the archetypes of the prototyping techniques used in interaction design (Isensee & Rudd, 1996; Keinonen et al., 1996). Display images and elements are quickly sketched on paper and diagrams of control flow are defined; the difference between paper prototypes and storyboards being that the former are interactive while the latter are not. The usage of paper prototypes in usability testing is sometimes called the 'Wizard-of-Oz' technique. One of the designers is playing the product, i.e. operating the bunch of paper by flipping the pages, writing down the user input in input fields etc. while the user is interacting with the paper prototype.

Paper prototypes are normally used in the initial usability evaluations in product development projects at Nokia. Both internal and external test users are conducting predefined tasks with the UI prototypes while the UI design team is monitoring the situation to learn about the design defects.

3.4 3D Paper Prototypes

Paper prototypes are two-dimensional by nature. However, when used to prototype user interfaces of three-dimensional products such as mobile phones, the designers face the need to evaluate their ideas in all three dimensions. 3D paper prototyping (Keinonen et al., 1996) is an extension to conventional paper prototyping for this purpose.

3D mock-ups of concept ideas are quickly built from paper, cardboard, rigid foam, or even children's clay. These models are used to experiment with product shape, weight (distribution), placement of controls and display elements. The 3D mock-up contains the static elements of the user interface: the casing, keypad, display element, etc. The changing elements — such as different screens to be displayed on the display element — can be printed on paper and glued on cardboard. When the dynamic part of the user interface is very complex, like, e.g. in mobile phones, the swapping of cardboard elements becomes tedious. In occasions like this it may be more convenient to keep the 3D model purely static and present the dynamic interaction through an interactive computer simulation prototype. Then the test-wizard follows the user and operates the computer prototype accordingly.

A 3D paper prototype realizes the three-dimensional experience so that the product can be evaluated as a whole instead of focusing only on the UI software seen through the display. It is also possible to evaluate the ergonomics aspects.

3.5 2D & 3D Drawings and CAD Models

Concept drawings or CAD models are usually not regarded as prototypes. However, any entity that exhibits some aspect of the product that is of interest to the design team can be viewed as a prototype.

In the conceptualization phase the industrial designers make simple sketches — *thumbnail sketches* — of the concepts. These sketches are a fast and inexpensive medium for expressing ideas and evaluating possibilities. Later in the process the industrial and mechanical designers further refine the designs with 3D CAD solid modelling systems; most contemporary systems can be used in conjunction with *rapid prototyping* machines. Creating photo-realistically rendered images of the 3D models is also a relatively inexpensive method to produce futuristic vision prototypes that can be used for internal and external PR purposes.

3.6 Computer Simulations

Computer simulations are interactive computer software applications that often closely resemble the user interface — both the appearance and behaviour — of a product. The user of a computer simulation can experience the user interface by operating the on-screen prototype with a mouse, finger or other pointing device.

According to Grace & Schneider-Hufschmidt (1997) the most important reason for building computer simulation prototypes of, e.g. mobile phone user interfaces is that the user interface is becoming so complicated that it is difficult to envision how usable a new interface design or modification will be without a simulated UI.

Computer simulations have proved to be an efficient tool that is currently widely used in UI design work at Nokia. In many cases test users interacting with a simulated mobile phone almost forget they are using a simulation and actually believe they are using a real wireless handset.

3.7 Hard Models

Hard models (sometimes *physical product models, solid(s) models or visual models*) are normally used by industrial designers in the design and development process. Hard models are usually technically non-functional but still close replicas of the proposed design. However, functional high-fidelity hard models are also produced depending on the product and the design phase. A small product with a clamshell-type casing incorporating various buttons, knobs and hinge mechanisms requires smoothly working detailed models to let the designers and engineers evaluate the design.

Hard models are made from wood, rigid foam, clay, plastics, silicone rubber or metal. High-fidelity models usually incorporate several materials: plastics in the casing, rubber in the keypad, metal in the case opening mechanism, and glass in the display. *Rapid prototyping* systems use digital cross-section data from a 3D CAD model of the product to produce the prototype layer by layer through a sterolithography, selective laser sintering, solid ground curing, laminating, or ink-jet printing.

3.8 Virtual Reality Prototypes

Virtual (reality) prototypes are digital product models. They are computer-based simulations of a product with a degree a functional realism that is comparable to that of a physical prototype. However, instead of simulating only the physical aspects of a product they can also simulate the 'immaterial product'; e.g. the user interface software of a communicator. Typically the simulated features include the visual outlook of a product, its acoustic properties, the functionality of the user interface software, the functionality and behaviour of the product, and the tactile and force feedback present in user-to-product interactions.

Nokia is currently participating in an experimental research program to investigate the use of virtual prototyping technologies in the electronics and telecommunications industry (Kerttula et al., 1997). The pilot case of the project is a wireless pen phone.

3.9 Hardware Prototypes

The first hardware prototypes are hand-crafted by a prototype shop or factory when the prototype hardware and software modules are mature enough to be integrated. Many features of the final product have not yet been implemented in this phase and the complete prototype is usually implemented with 'chewing gum' technology.

The previous product generation often serves as the baseline for the next, enhanced product; quite often the hardware of an existing handset is taken as the platform onto which an experimental version of the new user interface is implemented. The wireless infrastructure plays a major part in using mobile handsets; it is not possible to get realistic feedback from users if they cannot use the prototype for call making or, e.g. accessing the internet. Incorporating a next generation user interface into an existing product is a good way to speed up the design and evaluation process since there is no need to wait for the next generation hardware to be available before initial user testing can be conducted.

4   Classifying the Methods

There are several ways to categorize user interface prototypes. Isensee & Rudd (1996) classify (computer) UI software prototypes into *low-fidelity* and *high-fidelity* ones. Low-fidelity prototypes are generally limited-function, limited-interaction prototyping efforts. In contrast, high-fidelity prototypes are fully interactive and represent the functionality of the product's user interface.

Nielsen (1993) and others divide prototyping activities and prototypes to *horizontal vs. vertical*. In horizontal prototyping only specific layers of the system or product are built. The main advantages of horizontal prototypes are that they can often be implemented fast with the use of various prototyping and screen design tools and that they can be used to assess how well the entire interface operates and feels as a whole. In vertical prototyping a chosen part of the target system is implemented completely. With a vertical prototype a feature can be evaluated in depth under realistic circumstances with real user tasks.

Prototypes can be further classified as *throw-away prototypes, incremental prototypes* or *evolutionary prototypes* depending on how they are utilized when implementing the final product.

The UI prototyping methods described above are often applied in several ways at Nokia; a low-fidelity horizontal storyboard is first sketched and when the design seems to be working decently, a higher-fidelity vertical storyboard is used to design the specific features in more detail. A rough ordering of the methods using the *physical/analytical* vs. *comprehensive/focused* dimensions presented by Ulrich & Eppinger (1995) is shown in Figure 2.

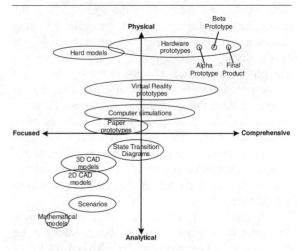

Figure 2: Prototyping methods.

5   Applicability of the Methods

The different user interface prototyping methods can be characterized by several attributes: do the tools facilitate teamwork, can screen layouts be designed, can ergonomics be evaluated, or is it possible to reuse prototype software in the real product, etc. No single prototyping method or tool is uniformly best at satisfying all the requirements of the user interface design process.

Based on the experiences acquired in UI design work at Nokia, Table 1 summarizes the applicability of the different prototyping methods — Scenarios (S), State Transition Diagrams (STD), Paper Prototypes (PP), 3D Paper Prototypes (3DP), 2D/3D Drawings and CAD models (CAD), Computer Simulations (CS), Hard Models (HM), Virtual Reality Prototypes (VR), Hardware Prototypes (HW) — for specific UI design tasks in the design process (the glyph scale –, •, ••, •••, •••• translates to '*not applicable*, ..., *very well suited*'). The different prototyping methods are ordered in 'fidelity order', i.e. according to the average level of detail they support in representing the actual product. The individual design process or prototyping aspects are also ordered in 'fidelity order' so that the relative strengths and weaknesses between the methods become more apparent.

6 Conclusions

Prototyping is one of the core activities in human-centred design for mobile handsets. User interface prototypes are created, evaluated and enhanced iteratively in order to involve users in the design work and get feedback from them. Several different prototyping methods and tools are available and used in designing and developing user interfaces for mobile phones and communicators.

There is no single silver bullet among these prototyping methods. Thus, the major question should not be the choice between methods or tools in general but instead how to fit them into the overall product design and development process in the most effective way. The most resource-friendly prototyping methods — i.e. the low-fidelity ones — should be applied in the early phases of the design process, when major design issues need to be addressed and major design changes will be likely regarding metaphor, content or navigation. Later, the more expensive higher-fidelity methods are required to address smaller design issues, and smaller changes are made regarding, e.g. layout or terminology.

The UI design process and the prototyping methods should be viewed as a continuum from low fidelity to high fidelity as illustrated in Figure 3.

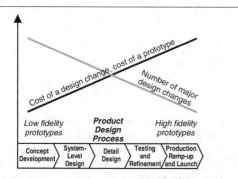

Figure 3: Prototyping in the UI design process.

7 Further Research

Although there is a shared understanding that human-centred design with appropriate prototyping activities is a prerequisite of good UI design we still lack thorough knowledge on the design process; more research would be needed to, e.g. define the transition

points between different UI prototyping methods. Petrie et al. (1998) conclude that there is a need to develop appropriate iterative user-centred design lifecycles for wearable technologies. These can build on mainstream HCI, but need to consider the particular characteristics of wearables.

More efficient and easy-to-use prototyping software tools are required to bring the interaction design possibilities to the non-programmers such as human factors specialists and graphic designers. There is active research work going on at Nokia to make this happen.

Acknowledgements

The author wishes to thank Dr Turkka Keinonen and Miika Silfverberg from Nokia Research Center and the anonymous reviewers for their constructive criticism and valuable comments to improve the manuscript.

References

Bonner, J. (1996), The Challenge to Design Intelligent Consumer and Domestic Product Interfaces, *in Proceedings of the IEEE Colloquium on Artificial Intelligence in Consumer and Domestic Products*, IEEE Publications.

Brouwer-Janse, M. (1997), "User Interfaces for Young and Old: Introduction", *Interactions* **4**(2), 36.

Grace, G. & Schneider-Hufschmidt, M. (1997), Prototyping Environments for Telephone User Interfaces — Development Results and Experiences, *in Proceedings of the 16th International Symposium of Human Factors in Telecommunications '97*, Løren Grafish, pp.347–54. ISBN 82-994236-0-0.

Isensee, S. & Rudd, J. (1996), *The Art of Rapid Prototyping*, International Thomson Press. ISBN 1-85032-215-5.

ISO (1996), Ergonomic Requirements for Office Work with VDTs — Dialogue Principles, Technical Report 9241-10, ISO.

Keinonen, T., Nieminen, M., Riihiaho, S. & Säde, S. (1996), *Designing Usable Smart Products*, Helsinki University of Technology / University of Art and Design Helsinki. ISBN 951-22-3188-3.

Kerttula, M., Salmela, M. & Heikkinen, M. (1997), Virtual Reality Prototyping — A Framework for the Development of Electronics and Telecommunication Products, *in Proceedings of the 8th IEEE International Workshop on Rapid Systems Prototyping*, pp.24–6.

Design Process or Prototyping Aspects	S	STD	PP	3DP	CAD	CS	HM	VR	HW
Low-cost prototypes	••••	••••	••••	•••	••	••	•	•	•
Method and tools are easy to use	••••	••••	••••	•••	•••	••	••	•	•
Prototypes are fast to create and update	••••	••••	•••	•••	•••	••	••	•	•
Portability of prototyping tools	••••	•••	••••	•••	••	•••	•	••	•
Supports participatory design	••••	•••	•••	•••	•••	•	••	•	•
Low-cost design iterations	••••	••••	••••	•••	••	•••	••	••	••
Supports team design	••••	••••	••••	••••	••	••	••	•••	••
Portability of prototypes	••••	•••	••••	••••	••	•••	••	•	•••
2D prototypes	–	•	••	•	••••	••••	–	–	–
An established method	••••	••••	••••	••	••••	••••	••••	•	••••
Facilitator-driven usability testing	•	•	•••	•	•••	•	••	•	•
Interaction design method	•••	•••	•••	••	•	•••	–	•••	••••
Screen layout design tool	•	••	••	••	•••	••••	•	•••	••
Prototypes as proof of concept and to investigate concept feasibility	–	•	•••	•••	•••	•••	•••	•••	••
Supports usability testing	•	•	•••	•••	•	•••	•	•••	••••
Prototypes in focus groups to, e.g. gather and specify requirements	•	–	•	••	••	••	••••	••	•••
Fidelity of the prototypes	•	•	••	••	••	•••	•••	••••	••••
User-driven usability testing	•	•	•	••	•	•••	••	•••	•••
Prototypes as UI specification or documentation	–	••	•	•	•••	•••	•••	••••	••••
Mimics the interaction, navigation and functionality of product UI	–	•	••	••	–	••••	–	••••	••••
Mimics the look of product UI	–	•	•	••	••••	•••	••••	••••	••••
Industrial design method	–	–	•	••	••••	•	••••	•••	••
Supports different UI languages	–	•	•	•	•	••••	•	••••	••••
Prototypes as internal demonstrators	–	–	•	•	••	•••	••••	•••	••••
3D prototypes	–	–	–	•••	••	•	•	•••	••••
Runnable prototypes	–	–	•	••	–	•••	–	•••	••••
Usage data can be collected	–	–	•	••	•	•••	–	•••	•••
Supports automatic version control	–	•	•	–	•	•	•	•	•••
Supports error checking	–	–	•	•	•	•••	•	•••	•••
Mimics the feel of product UI	–	–	–	•••	•	•	••••	•••	••••
Ergonomics can be evaluated	–	–	–	••	••	•	••••	•••	••••
Materials and finishing can be evaluated	–	–	–	•	••	–	••••	••	•••
Design tooling	–	–	–	–	•••	–	••••	••	•••
Assess production feasibility	–	–	–	–	•••	–	•••	••	•••
Marketing and sales tool	–	–	–	–	••	•••	••	••	••••
Estimate manufacturing costs	–	–	–	–	•••	–	•••	••	••••
Prototypes as trade show demonstrators	–	–	–	–	•	•••	••	••	••••
Prototypes for sales people training	–	–	–	–	–	•••	–	•	••••
Prototyping tools can generate C code for the product platform	–	–	–	–	–	••	–	••	••••
Do reliability, life and performance testing	–	–	–	–	–	•	•	•	••••
Supports field usability testing	–	–	–	–	–	–	–	•	••••

Table 1: Applicability of UI prototyping methods.

Kespohl, K. & Szwillus, G. (1996), A Prototyper for Technical Device Interfaces, *in* M. Tauber (ed.), *Companion Proceedings of CHI'96: Human Factors in Computing Systems (CHI'96 Conference Companion)*, ACM Press, pp.3–4.

Kiljander, H. (1997), Interactive Computer Simulation Prototypes in Mobile Phone User Interface Design, *in* G. Szwillus (ed.), *Tagungsband — PB'97: Prototypen für Benutzungsschnittstellen*, pp.74–9.

Nielsen, J. (1993), *Usability Engineering*, Academic Press.

Petrie, H., Furner, S., Strothotte, T. & von Guericke, O. (1998), Design Lifecycles and Wearable Computers for Users with Disabilities, *in* C. Johnson (ed.), *Proceedings of the First Workshop on Human Computer Interaction with Mobile Devices*, Department of Computing Science, University of Glasgow, pp.31–7. GIST Technical Report G98-1. http://www.dcs.gla.ac.uk/˜johnson/mobile.html.

Ulrich, K. T. & Eppinger, S. D. (1995), *Product Design and Development*, McGraw-Hill. ISBN 0-07-065811-0.

Väänänen-Vainio-Mattila, K. & Ruuska, S. (1998), User Needs for Mobile Communication Devices: Requirements Gathering and Analysis through Contextual Inquiry, *in* C. Johnson (ed.), *Proceedings of the First Workshop on Human–Computer Interaction with Mobile Devices*, Department of Computing Science, University of Glasgow, pp.113–20. GIST Technical Report G98-1. http://www.dcs.gla.ac.uk/~johnson/mobile.html.

van Leeuwen, M. & Thomas, B. (1997), The Integration of Interaction Design and Human Factors in the Product Creation Process: A Case Study, *in* K. Nordby (ed.), *Proceedings of the 16th International Symposium of*

Human Factors in Telecommunications 1997, Løren Grafish, pp.355–62. ISBN 82-994236-0-0.

Virzi, R. A., Sokolov, J. L. & Karis, D. (1996), Usability Problem Identification Using Both Low- and High-Fidelity Prototypes, *in* G. van der Veer & B. Nardi (eds.), *Proceedings of CHI'96: Human Factors in Computing Systems*, ACM Press, pp.236–43.

Human–Computer Interaction — INTERACT '99
M. Angela Sasse and Chris Johnson (Editors)
Published by IOS Press, © IFIP TC.13, 1999

A Wearable Computer for Paramedics: Studies in Model-based, User-centred and Industrial Design

Chris Baber, Theodoros N. Arvanitis, David J. Haniff & Robert Buckley[1]

School of Electronic and Electrical Engineering, The University of Birmingham, Birmingham, UK.
[1] Birmingham Institute of Art and Design, University of Central England, Corporation Street, Birmingham, UK.

c.baber@bham.ac.uk

Abstract: In this paper, we report work into wearable computers for paramedics. The paper begins with an overview of the design using Unified Modelling Language (UML). This demonstrates the information flow and task activity in typical paramedic work. A demonstrator system was described using such UML models. The second part of the paper reports a user trial of a working prototype wearable computer, involving experienced paramedics, at a training school. The results of this study suggest that the wearable computer might slow collection of baseline data, although this finding does not apply to all tasks. On the basis of the trial findings and the positive comments received from the paramedics, it is proposed that a wearable computer may offer benefits over current work practice. The paramedics did complain about the design of current technology which led to an industrial design project to develop a new concept. The third section presents the new design concept for a wearable computer for paramedics. This design relies on the distribution of the equipment around the body in order to increase the wearability of the design.

Keywords: wearable computers, paramedics, speech recognition.

1 Introduction

In the past decade, there has been a rapid growth in the development of wearable computers. The technology is now at a stage where commercial products are available (e.g. InterVision, Xybernaut, Mentis). A goal of the work reported in this paper is to examine the feasibility of wearable computers for the emergency services. In this particular study, the concern is with paramedics (although other work in progress focuses on applications for fire-fighters and police officers). For each of the emergency services, there is a requirement to produce communications and information technologies that can be fully integrated into the users' work activity.

This means that the focus of the work is on the design of wearable computers as 'information appliances' (Norman, 1998) which could form part of the uniform of personnel in the emergency services. The notion of 'computer as uniform' has been considered by Bass et al. (1997), Smith et al. (1995) and Esposito (1997) amongst others, and can be contrasted with the notion of 'computer as clothing', being pursued by Mann (1997; 1998). The notion of 'information appliance' leads to the proposal that wearable computers ought not to be seen as miniaturised versions of the multi-functional Personal Computer (PC), so much as limited-function products which provide useful information and access to useful functionality when the user requires. To this end, we have been developing a methodology which allows us to design wearable computers which offer limited-functions, present useful information and which can be incorporated into workaday activity. Initially, the design method followed broad principles of object-oriented software engineering (Baber et al., to appear). However, this approach has been expanded for two reasons. First, the initial approach was not particularly formal or easy to audit, and we required a method which would allow us to generate designs which could be proven to be sound. Second, it was felt that methods couched in software engineering approaches might force design decisions along purely software routes and wearable computer design needs to combine both software and hardware — e.g. (Bass et al., 1997). Consequently, we employed Unified Modelling Language (UML), which although it clearly has its roots in software engineering, can be adapted to model objects in terms of actors and functions; which can be human, hardware or software.

2   Model-based Design

The modelling process followed in this project draws upon the Unified Modelling Language (UML) of Rumbaugh, Booch and Jacobson — see (Alhir, 1998; Pooley & Stevens, 1999). UML is a standardised notation for the documentation of object-oriented design. It contains a repertoire of notation techniques, taken from Booch, OMT, Objectory, etc. methods, which are formulated into a single framework. In our work, UML is the primary focus for object-oriented design activity. In this section, we describe the use of UML as a means of representing paramedic work activity in order to demonstrate the development of our wearable, paramedic protocol patient reporting computer (Baber et al., to appear). At the first level, Figure 1 shows an extract from the use-case model.

One of the attractions of UML is that it begins (like many other object-oriented approaches) with scenario-based descriptions. The user-centred approach that we follow also relies heavily on notions relating to scenario-based design (Carroll, 1995), and the methodology used allows for the development and refinement of scenarios, particularly through the definition of UML use-cases. The description shown in Figure 1 focuses on the initial stages of the paramedic work activity.

The main function of use-case diagrams is to show the actors within a system (shown by the stick figures in boxes) and the functionality of that system (shown by the connections between actors). In particular, functionality is indicated by use-cases, which are specific ways in which the system is used. Figure 1 shows the activities performed by actors within the system and the technology used, i.e. radio links and mobile data terminals. This represents a view of the current system. The paramedic in the ambulance receives sufficient information to allow travel to the scene of the incident and some background information relating to the incident. However, the paramedic will need to collect additional information at the scene in order to formulate a diagnosis, and also to verify the original incident details. It is not uncommon for paramedics to revise the diagnosis

provided by the caller on the basis of information collected at the scene.

The use-case description is based on a set of scenarios collected through discussion with paramedics and dispatch staff. The aim is to present, in as concise a diagram as possible, the typical operation of a given system. Following development of use-case diagrams, the next stage is to develop specific sequence diagrams for the system. A sequence diagram represents the flow of activity performed by actors in the system; usually time is represented from top to bottom of the diagram and actors are represented by horizontal columns.

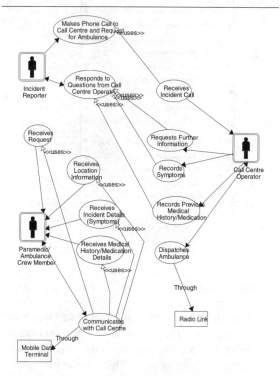

Figure 1: Use-case diagram for incident reporting and ambulance dispatch.

Figure 2 shows the sequence diagram for collecting a set of initial, i.e. baseline, observations from the patient. Baseline observations are typically taken when the patient is conscious and in order to support diagnosis. On encountering unconscious patients, the paramedic's first response is to run through an Advanced Trauma Life Support (ATLS) protocol and to perform sufficient actions to stabilise the patient. For the purposes of the current description, the baseline observations are assumed to be made on a conscious patient.

The paramedic's main tasks in this instance are concerned with verbal communication with the patient, particularly to reassure the patient but also to collect relevant information, which might support diagnosis. Typically, the verbal communication consists of an initial discussion of symptoms and history, followed by explanation of treatment. Usually, verbal communication is performed throughout recording of baseline observations.

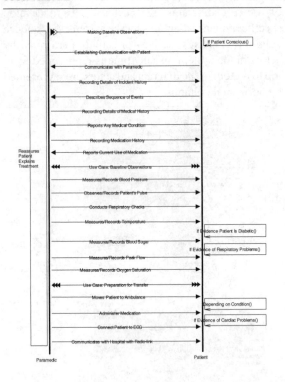

Figure 2: Sequence diagram for baseline observations.

The sequence diagram in Figure 2 assumes some linearity in the course of treatment. Our observations lead us to suspect that this linearity is largely true. Furthermore, a number of health authorities have been investigating the potential for standardising baseline observations in order to ensure that all relevant material is recorded at the scene.

The sequence diagram allows us to further expand the scenario, in terms of specifying activities for the actors. In one sense, this is a form of task analysis, in that we can demonstrate the flow of tasks and their interactions. However, sequence diagrams also provide insight into flow of information and the provision of information storage / retrieval, together with notes on the conditions under which tasks are performed. The description produced so far can be traced back to the scenarios (and we typically present the scenarios verbally for confirmation by users).

For the baseline observations phase, the sequence of activities can be further represented in terms of a state diagram (Figure 3). Each state in this diagram

represents a specific parameter which the paramedic needs to measure and record.

Notice that there are two main sets of activity: set A is concerned with communicating with the patient; set B is concerned with collection of background information. The background information comes from several sources, e.g. the incident details, any relatives or bystanders who have witnessed the incident or know the patient's history, and initial observations. The initial observations are used to establish a 'baseline' against which the efficacy of treatments can be assessed, and also as an aid to developing a diagnosis. The current prototype that we have developed concentrates on the collection of quantitative data as these can be readily captured and forwarded to hospitals.

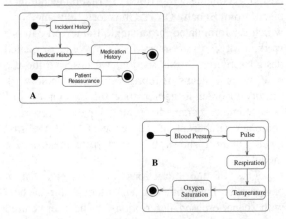

Figure 3: State diagram for baseline observations.

Baseline observation requires the paramedic to record basic physiological information while treating the patient. This leads to the requirement to have some form of hands-free interaction with the computer (in order to support parallel activity), and we have used speech recognition. The speech recognition system can access the data entry fields sequentially (initiated by the word 'next') or directly by the field name (for example 'pulse'). One could envisage alternative designs which employ, say, a 'temperature' object capable of recording and entering specific data to the computer. In our design, we opted for speech recognition in order to allow the paramedic to remain in the data entry loop, i.e. by requiring the paramedic to speak information to the computer, it is assumed that this will allow checking and retention of these baseline values.

3 User-centred Design

When we use the term 'user-centred design' our primary concerns are whether a technology matches the task and cognitive requirements associated with its intended application domain. In order to address this issue, we conduct an end-user trial. The target user group will be trained paramedics. Consequently, the user trial was designed to involve paramedics. The target application domain was recording of patient details during collection of baseline observations. In order to explore this domain in a way which was both amenable to study and ethically acceptable, it was decided to use a simulated task rather than real patients in real distress. The simulated task needed to be acceptable to paramedics, needed to exhibit as many characteristics of real situations as possible (i.e. to have some level of ecological validity), and needed to have some aspects which could be measured. The task selected was the collection of baseline observations from a training dummy in a paramedic training centre. This is an accepted paradigm for paramedic training, and hence, is assumed to have sufficient validity to represent 'real' tasks for the purposes of training and evaluation. The task was also amenable to time measurement, e.g. how long the overall activity took, and how long it took to record each observation.

3.1 Participants

The user trials were carried out with trained paramedics. The trials took place over the course of three days in a paramedic training centre.

Paramedics were recruited on a voluntary basis and within the constraints of their shift patterns and call activity, e.g. one trial had to be abandoned because the paramedics were called to attend a road traffic accident. Given these constraints we were not able to exercise complete control over the selection of participants, nor were we able to recruit as many paramedics as we would have liked in the time period. On the one hand, we were able to specify that we use experienced paramedics (with between one month and twenty years experience; mean of around ten years), rather than either trainees or technicians. On the other hand, it is possible that the paramedics were self-selecting on the basis of their interest in the project; this might be reflected in the fact that we found little resistance or hostility to the design, either during the trials or during debriefing.

In total we ran trials with 10 paramedics over the course of three days. Each trial lasted approximately 45 minutes, including preparation, trials and debriefing. The first two trials were used to finalise the experimental design and the data of these participants are not used. The tenth trial was abandoned, as mentioned above. Consequently, in this paper we will only report data from seven paramedics

who participated in all trials. Obviously, one must be cautious about extrapolating from such a small sample size. One must also note that paramedics throughout the UK might differ in terms of the procedures followed, the drugs they can administer, and type of activity most frequently performed. However, we feel that the study is reportable because it examines the impact of a wearable computer in an environment which is both ecologically valid and controlled.

3.2 Equipment

A Pentium II computer was used to run the software. A Seattle Sight monocular, monochrome head-mounted display was used to present information to participants. An AURIX speech recognizer (developed by the Speech Research Unit at DERA, Malvern) was used for speech input. The trials were conducted using a MediCode training dummy. The paramedics used oral thermometers and stethoscopes, together with equipment for measuring oxygen saturation and blood pressure.

3.3 Procedure

After an initial introduction to the project, the paramedics were given the following scenario:

> "You have been called out to a male, aged 45–50, complaining of mild chest pains. The pains started suddenly, around 20 minutes ago, while the patient was watching television. The patient appears to be pale and his skin is slightly clammy to the touch. The patient has no history of heart problems."

Following this introduction, the paramedic approaches the 'patient', reassures him and describes the course of treatment. Speaking to the patient and observers / relatives / bystanders is an important means of acquiring additional patient / incident history and we were interested in seeing whether the kit would impair this activity. The paramedic then took a series of baseline observations. Given that we were using a dummy, the baseline observations were defined previously and passed to the paramedic during treatment (blood pressure 140/90; pulse 80; respiration rate 15; temperature 37; SaO_2 98).

In one condition, the paramedic treated the patient whilst wearing the headset and speaking to the speech recognizer, and in the other condition, the paramedic followed normal practice. The main difference between conditions (in addition to the wearing of unusual kit) was the manner in which patient details were recorded. In the 'computer' condition, patient details are spoken to the computer as they are taken, and in the 'normal' condition, patient details are remembered and spoken at hand-over. We simulated the hand-over phase by asking the paramedic to recall the baseline observations taken at the end of the trial, using a surprise, i.e. unexpected, recall test.

3.4   Results

The main results to be reported in this paper concern performance time. Performance times are considered in terms of overall performance and time to make each baseline observation. The mean time for the normal condition was 97.4s. and the mean time for the 'computer' condition was 114.1s.

Observation of performance suggested that the longer time recorded for the 'computer' condition resulted from additional activity (rather than speaking to the computer). For example, paramedics wearing the headset would adjust the headset between taking baseline observations. If one considered the performance for collecting each observation, then there was little difference between conditions. A further point to note is that there were marked individual differences between participants (as one might anticipate given such a small sample size). However, one typically found that performance with the computer was either as good or slower than 'normal'. In addition to time data, we also observed variation in procedure following (which had not been anticipated). In the normal condition, there was marked variation between the paramedics in terms of the order in which baseline observations were collected, e.g. for some paramedics the first observation was to take the pulse and check respiration, while some took heart rate, some attached the oxygen saturation meter etc. In the computer condition, the collection of observations was dictated by the layout of the fields on the screen. It is, of course, not surprising that the paramedics followed the procedure laid out on the screen, but the variation in 'normal' condition was interesting.

3.5   Conclusions

The results from this study suggest that there is an impact on total task performance time when wearing a monocular headset and using speech recognition. This supports the findings from previous, laboratory- based studies (Baber et al., 1998). However, when individual tasks were considered, the differences become less apparent and performance is more affected by task content than technology used. The presence of a strong between-subjects effect means that the results from such a small sample should be treated with caution, but on the basis of these results, we believe

that wearable computers need not adversely affect performance of routine paramedic tasks.

Discussion with paramedics during debriefing suggested broad acceptance of the concept, with reservations as to the technology used. The paramedics who participated in this trial agreed that wearable computers could offer benefits in their work, particularly in terms of direct data capture. This benefit would be significant if the technology allowed direct transmission of information to a hospital. The paramedics felt that the wearable computer was not unduly intrusive into task performance, and several commented that the provision of data fields on the baseline observations screen was useful. It is interesting to note that in the 'computer' condition, all seven paramedics followed the order presented on the display, whereas in the 'normal' condition there was an observable variation in the order in which baseline observations were taken. This suggests that the wearable computer would modify task sequence. When asked about the possibility of such a modification, i.e. to standardise collection of baseline observations rather than allow individual discretion, the paramedics were cautiously in favour.

The main complaint against the technology was the bulkiness of the headset and the weight of the processor (which the paramedics did not wear in this trial, but which they examined and commented upon). The speech recognition system employed produce few problems during this study.

There are, of course, caveats to bear in mind regarding the interpretation of the results obtained. The use of a dummy rather than a patient, the fact that the study was being observed, the fact that the paramedics were asked to work singly (rather than in pairs) all contributed to the 'unrealistic' nature of the task. However, the aim of the study was not so much to 'prove' the technology in a field trial as to assess paramedics' acceptance of wearable computers, and whether such technology impaired tasks in a standard training environment. In broad terms, the results suggest that performance is not severely affected, and that paramedics were receptive of the concept. This latter point is further supported by the responses received during demonstrations of the equipment at exhibitions in the UK and we are currently in discussion with commercial developers regarding a fully functioning system.

4   Industrial Design

The principle complaint that the paramedics had against the equipment used in the study was the bulkiness of the headset. The final part of this paper concerns an industrial design project carried out to develop concept designs which deal with this problem. We examined the design of commercially available wearable computers, and several prototypes developed by other universities. Our conclusion is that most of these products comprise four parts: core systems components (processor, RAM, hard disk etc.), power, display, input device. From an ergonomics perspective, the individual parts might be somewhat bulky and could restrict movement.

Weight is becoming less of an issue in wearable computing, with the reducing size of individual components. From this perspective, dividing the computer into sections and placing these around the body makes sense; not only will this distribute load and bulk, it could also allow novel forms of 'functional' grouping of controls. For instance, CPU and radio are placed on the hips (on the assumption that the wearer is able to support more weight here than on the chest or shoulders), power units are held on the shoulders, controls are located around the chest. The bandoleer design means that the computer becomes part of the paramedics uniform (see Figure 4).

The first part of the paper is concerned with the use of UML to relate scenario-based designs to the development of user interfaces. While the limited space available precludes a fully worked example, the intention was to present sufficient information to allow readers to see how the different stages of UML progressed to a final design concept. The second part of the paper concerned an initial set of user trials. The aim of the trials was to evaluate the acceptability of wearable computers for paramedic, both in terms of user acceptance and in terms of performance. In general, the outcome of this study was positive and it is proposed that wearable computers could be beneficial to paramedic work. The final section reported a design project which sought to develop the notion of distributed computing for wearable technology. This section brings the paper back to the concept of object-oriented computing discussed in the introduction. By considering objects as being both hardware and software, the final design concept distributes computing objects ('information appliances') about the body in order to distribute load, but also as a means of producing a network solution to wearable computers.

Acknowledgements

The work reported in this paper has been partly supported by EPSRC grant GR/L 48508 (Human Factors of Wearable Computers).

References

Alhir, S. S. (1998), *UML in a Nutshell*, O'Reilly.

Baber, C., Haniff, D. & Woolley, S. (to appear), "Contrasting Design Paradigms for Wearable Computers", *IBM Systems Journal* **38**(4), 1–15.

Baber, C., Haniff, D., Cooper, L., Knight, J. & Mellor, B. A. (1998), Preliminary Investigations into the Human Factors of Wearable Computers, *in* H. Johnson, L. Nigay & C. Roast (eds.), *People and Computers XIII (Proceedings of HCI'98)*, Springer-Verlag, pp.313–26.

Bass, L., Kasabach, C., Martin, R., Siewiork, D., Smailagic, A. & Stivoric, J. (1997), The Design of a Wearable Computer, *in* S. Pemberton (ed.), *Proceedings of CHI'97: Human Factors in Computing Systems*, ACM Press, pp.139–46.

Carroll, J. M. (ed.) (1995), *Scenario-Based Design: Envisioning Work and Technology in System Development*, John Wiley & Sons.

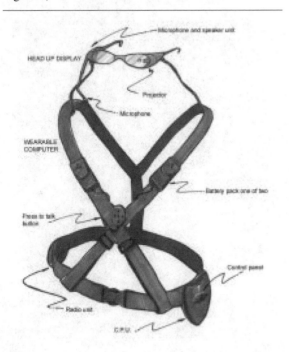

Figure 4: Concept sketch of 'distributed' wearable computer for paramedics.

5 Discussion

In this paper, we have reported three aspects of the design of a wearable computer for paramedics.

Esposito, C. (1997), "Wearable Computers: Field-test Observations and System Design Guidelines", *Personal Technologies* **1**(2), 81–8.

Mann, S. (1997), "Wearable Computing: A First Step Towards Personel Imaging", *IEEE Computer* **30**(2), 25–32.

Mann, S. (1998), "Humanistic Computing: 'Wear-Comp' as a New Framework and Application for Intelligent Signal Processing", *Proceedings of the IEEE* **86**(11), 2123–51.

Norman, D. A. (1998), *The Invisable Computer*, MIT Press.

Pooley, R. & Stevens, P. (1999), *Using UML: Software Engineering with Objects and Components*, Addison–Wesley.

Smith, B., Bass, L. & Siegel, J. (1995), On-site Maintenance Using a Wearable Computer System, *in* I. Katz, R. Mack, L. Marks, M. B. Rosson & J. Nielsen (eds.), *Proceedings of CHI'95: Human Factors in Computing Systems*, ACM Press, pp.119–20.

Human–Computer Interaction — INTERACT '99
M. Angela Sasse and Chris Johnson (Editors)
Published by IOS Press, © IFIP TC.13, 1999

The Beauty of Errors: Patterns of Error Correction in Desktop Speech Systems

Christine A. Halverson[1], Daniel B. Horn[2], Clare-Marie Karat[3] & John Karat[3]

[1] SRI International, 333 Ravenswood Ave, Menlo Park, CA 94025, USA.
[2] University of Michigan, CREW, 701 Tappan Street,
Ann Arbor, MI 48109, USA.
[3] IBM T J Watson, Research Center, 30 Saw Mill River Road,
Hawthorne, NY 10532, USA.

krys@speech.sri.com, danhorn@umich.edu, {ckarat,jkarat}@us.ibm.com

Abstract: Automatic Speech Recognition (ASR) systems have improved greatly over the last three decades. However, even with 98% reported accuracy, error correction still consumes a significant portion of user effort in text creation tasks. We report on data collected during a study of three commercially available ASR systems that show how initial users of speech systems tend to fixate on a single strategy for error correction. This tendency coupled with application assumptions about how error correction features will be used, combine to make a very frustrating, and unsatisfying user experience. We observe two distinct error correction patterns: spiral depth (Oviatt & VanGent, 1996) and cascades. In contrast, users with more extensive experience learn to switch correction strategies more quickly.

Keywords: speech recognition, error correction, speech user interfaces, analysis methods.

1 Introduction

Recent announcements of speech software focus on the speed of using speech input. However, in a recent study we found that users experienced a great deal of difficulty correcting errors, and that these difficulties had a strong influence on user satisfaction (Karat et al., 1999). In our study subjects used commercially available continuous speech recognition systems to complete a set of text creation tasks. Our focus was to compare speech and keyboard as input modalities and measure user performance and satisfaction. One part of the study (Initial Use) involved 24 users who enrolled, received training, carried out practice tasks, and then completed a set of transcription and composition tasks in a single session. In the other part of the study (Extended Use), four researchers used speech recognition to carry out real work tasks over 10 sessions each with three speech recognition software products.

What stood out, during both the execution of the study and subsequent analysis, was the frequency and variety of error correction patterns that were attempted, despite generally good recognition. Attempts to correct an error often set off a *cascade* of additional errors, which then needed to be corrected. We know that poor error handling is a significant problem for the successful commercialization of recognition-based technologies (Rhyne & Wolf, 1993), so understanding the process of error correction would be of great assistance for future designs.

This paper delves deeply into users' experiences with error correction. User strategies for error correction differed between the Initial and Extended Use groups, pointing out important lessons for developing desktop speech applications. We present data about user error correction strategies gleaned primarily from the Initial Use subjects. We compare this with diagnostic data from preliminary analysis of the Extended Use subjects.

We begin by providing some background about automatic speech recognition (ASR) systems and the role of error correction in them. Next, we outline the systems we studied, as well as the experimental design and procedure. (This is reported in depth in Karat et al. (1999).) With this as foundation we discuss the differences in error correction between the keyboard and mouse interface people are used to and ASR systems. After briefly discussing how we coded errors we present our findings about the error correction patterns that users developed and compare them with preliminary data about the patterns that more experienced users display. Finally, we conclude with suggestions for the development of future ASR systems.

2   Background

The last three decades of research and development of automatic speech recognition (ASR) technology is beginning to pay off. ASR systems translate speech input into character strings or commands, and the last two years have seen the introduction of several commercial applications for dictation and navigating the desktop which rely on ASR technology for input.

While ASR technology has come a long way, there are some fundamental factors that distinguish the use of speech as an input modality. First, speech recognition technology involves errors that are fundamentally different from user errors with other input techniques (Danis & Karat, 1995). When users press keys on a keyboard, they can feel quite certain of the result. When users say words to an ASR system, they may experience system errors — errors in which the system output does not match their input — that they do not experience with other devices. Imagine how user behaviour might be different if keyboards occasionally entered a random letter whenever you typed the 'a' key. While there is ongoing development of speech recognition technology aimed at lowering error rates, we cannot expect the sort of error free system behaviour we experience with keyboards in the near future. How we go from an acoustic signal to some useful translation of the signal remains technically challenging, and error rates in the 1–5% range are the best for which anyone should hope.

Second, speech as an input modality for computers is not as 'natural' as we might like to think. Many of today's computer users have been typing for quite some time and refer to it as a 'natural experience'. In addition, it takes time and practice to develop a new form of interaction (Karat, 1995; Lai & Vergo, 1997). Speech user interfaces (SUIs) will evolve as we learn about problems users face with current designs and work to remedy them. While the systems studied in this paper represent the state-of-the-art in large vocabulary speech recognition systems, they still have areas that could stand improvement.

3   Method

3.1   Systems

We investigated three commercially available ASR systems that shipped as products in 1998. These systems are IBM ViaVoice98 Executive, Dragon Naturally Speaking Preferred 2.0, and L&H Voice Xpress Plus, referred to as IBM, Dragon and L&H below. (Philips released their Free Speech system during the course of the study and was therefore not included.) All three products share some important features. First, they all recognize continuous speech as opposed to forcing the user to speak 'discretely' with pauses between words.

Second, all are considered *modeless systems*. Each application has integrated command recognition into the dictation so that the user does not need to explicitly identify an utterance as text or command. To do this the user must learn a command grammar (a list of specific command phrases), and sometimes a keyword that is uttered to indicate what follows as a command. In general, commands must be spoken together as a phrase, without pausing between words, in order to be recognized. Otherwise, the words are treated as text.

In principle, all three systems are *speaker independent*. This means that the system should recognize text without specific training to a user's voice. However, we found the speaker independent recognition performance insufficiently accurate for the purposes of our study. To improve recognition performance, we had all users carry out the standard speaker enrolment. During enrolment, the user reads a predetermined text to the system and the system processes the users' speech to develop a speaker-specific speech model.

3.2   Experimental Procedure

Different procedures were used for the Initial Use and the Extended Use subjects in the study. Although the Initial Use study was designed to allow for statistical comparisons between the three systems, we reported on general patterns observed across the systems as they are of more general interest to the design of successful ASR systems (Karat et al., 1999). We provide a synopsis of the design and procedure here.

3.3 Initial Use

Twenty-four native English speakers, balanced for gender and with an age range from 20–55 years, participated as paid volunteers. Participants were IBM employees from a broad spectrum of occupational backgrounds.

We assigned subjects to one of three speech recognition products: IBM, Dragon, or L&H. Each subject performed two kinds of text creation tasks using each of the input modalities. The order of modality was varied, as was the task order within each modality. All text was created with the assigned product's dictation application. Similar to Windows95 WordPad they provided basic editing functions but did not include advanced functions such as spelling or grammar checking.

Immediately before the speech tasks all participants had a training session with the experimenter. This session was standardized across the three systems to cover basic areas such as text entry and correction. Each subject dictated a body of text supplied by the experimenter, composed a brief document, learned how to correct mistakes, and was given free time to explore the functions of the system. During the training session, each subject was shown how to make corrections both during and after dictation. Subjects were also taught the different ways to make corrections, including text selection by voice, re-dictation, and use of application specific correction dialogues. Subjects were not trained for keyboard-mouse text creation tasks.

3.4 Extended Use

In contrast, the subjects in the Extended Use study were the four co-authors of this paper. Each subject used each of the three speech recognition products for ten sessions of approximately one-hour duration; for 30 sessions across the products. During seven of the ten sessions the subjects used speech recognition software to carry out actual work related correspondence. The first, sixth and tenth sessions were used for benchmark tasks. Similar to Initial Use subjects, we completed one transcription task and one email composition task. We expected our performance to improve so the tasks were considerably longer than in the Initial Use experiment to prevent ceiling effects. All sessions were videotaped. In addition, after completing at least 20 sessions, subjects completed the same set of transcription tasks used in the Initial Use study. We limit the presentation of the results of the Extended Use phase of the study to some general comparisons with the Initial Use data.

3.5 Analysis

For the Initial Use sessions, we performed a detailed analysis of the videotapes of the text creation tasks. This included coding of all of the pertinent actions carried out by subjects in the study. A taxonomy of approximately 100 codes was constructed. Over 6500 individual events were coded for 12 subjects covering speech and keyboard text creation tasks (Halverson et al., 1999). Coding included misrecognitions of commands, along with a range of usability and system problems. We paid particular attention to the interplay of text entry and correction segments during a task, as well as strategies used to make corrections. Because of the extensive time required to do this, we completed the this detailed analysis for 12 of the 24 subjects in the Initial Use phase of the study (four randomly selected subjects from each of the three systems, maintaining gender balance). Our findings here are based on detailed data from those 12 subjects. Additionally, we report selected data from the four subjects in the Extended Use phase. Data from each of the three speech recognition systems are collapsed together.

4 Results

Elsewhere we compared task performance by modality (Karat et al., 1999). For this study, we introduced a measure that allowed us to compare speech and keyboard input in terms of entry time. This measure, corrected words per minute (CWPM) is the number of words in the final document divided by the time the subject took to enter the text and make corrections, and is equivalent to typing speed reported as WPM. Speech input took significantly longer than keyboard and mouse when corrections were factored into throughput. Table 1 summarizes the data for the transcription tasks by juxtaposing speech and keyboard measures for Initial Use as well as comparisons to Extended Use performance.

Transcription	Initial Use		Extended Use
	Speech	Keyboard & mouse	Speech
CWPM	13.6	32.5	25.1
Time (min)	7.52	2.64	3.10

Table 1: Mean corrected words per minute and time per task by entry modality and task type ($n = 12$).

After 20 sessions Extended Use subjects' mean task time is beginning to approach the task time for keyboard and mouse input. In addition, the measure of corrected words per minute is also nearing the rate associated with keyboard and mouse interaction.

We wanted to take a closer look at why. This improvement, albeit after 20 hours of experience, led us to look more closely at the effort going into error correction. We began by defining correction episodes as an effort to correct one or more words through actions that 1) identified the error, and 2) corrected it. Thus, if a subject selected one or more words using a single select action and retyped or re-dictated their correction, we scored this as a single correction episode. Each action taken during an episode counted as a step. In the previous example, the episode consists of two steps — the select action and the re-dictation.

Identifying episodes and their steps allowed us to quantify and compare the number of episodes between the modalities and between Initial and Extended Use. Table 2 summarizes the data for transcription tasks.

Transcription	Initial Use		Extended Use
	Speech	Keyboard & mouse	Speech
# Episodes	11.3	8.4	8.8
Steps/Episode	7.3	2.2	3.5

Table 2: Mean number of correction episodes and steps per task by entry modality ($n = 12$ for Initial Use, $n = 4$ for Extended Use).

Surprisingly, we found that the number of episodes was not significantly different between Initial Use and Extended Use. However, the number of steps per episode *was* significantly reduced for Extended Use subjects. Our impression was that the pattern of what happened during the correction episode was was different.

To confirm this we further segmented the data into correction 'primitives'. A primitive is defined as whatever is necessary to identify the error, get to it, and act on it. The difference from our definition of an episode is that the steps in a correction primitive are not necessarily successful, thus requiring multiple primitives per episode. In the example we gave above one episode did equal one primitive. That is, 1) the select both moved to and selected the error, and 2) the re-dictate acted on it. Because the re-dictate was successful, this was the end of the correction. However, in most cases this was not so.

4.1 Inside a Correction Episode

In general, there are three types of errors. First is when the user means to do one thing and physically does the wrong thing. This is a *direct* error. On a keyboard this is a typo — actually pressing one sequence of keys when another was intended. In speech one can mis-speak or stutter. In both cases, there is immediate physical feedback that an error has been made. The second phenomenon that can be classified as a direct error is when you change your mind. When you first write something you may intend to say it one way; on rereading you decide to say it another way. While no real error has been made, we call this an *intent* error. For the rest of this paper, we will not distinguish this kind of error from other direct errors, precisely because we are more interested in how users recover from errors.

The third type of error is one that appears in speech but not keyboard modality. Speech induced errors are fundamentally different than keyboard errors because they are produced by the operation of the system not the user. Thus, we call this an *indirect* error. When the speech engine mis-recognizes what the user says the output is a valid word. This means that tools designed for keyboard and mouse systems, like spell checkers, will not 'catch the error', because the word is properly spelled. This also means that errors are difficult to detect during proofreading.

Even with stellar speech engine accuracy this kind of error will occur. For example, 95% accuracy means there will be 5 errors per 100 words (on average). One hundred words is roughly the length of a paragraph, and for an 8 page paper, like this one with approximately 65 paragraphs, that's 325 errors that need to be corrected. Once you begin to create additional errors during the correction process this can become truly overwhelming.

4.2 Techniques and Strategies

During tasks in the keyboard modality users predominately used a technique of deleting text (usually by backspacing over it) and retyping (73% of all corrections). The alternate technique was to select the word to be corrected and type over it (27%). Performance in the speech conditions was more varied, as it included options not available in keyboard conditions. While there are parallels to keyboard methods of error correction in ASR systems there are also important differences.

An important distinction is the many ways the user can get rid of a prior action. Systems have some combination of two or three commands that handle "undo what I just said" and "undo my last action". For example, SCRATCH THAT and UNDO. (For the remainder of the paper we will indicate a command by using all caps.) Some subtle issues arise in speech input because what the user last said may be dictated text or a command. In most cases SCRATCH THAT will cover both. In the case of just dictated text SCRATCH THAT will delete the last

Basic Stages	Keyboard/	Speech	Examples	
in a correction	Mouse	2 step episode	3 step episode	5 step episode
episode	example	BEST CASE	MOST COMMON	Correction Dialog
Locate/move to	Use mouse to move and click to relocate		**MOVE LEFT ONE WORD**	**MOVE LEFT ONE WORD**
Select so can operate	Keyboard select	**SELECT** *Kiss*	**SELECT THAT**	**SELECT THAT**
Operate on-- i.e. Correct	Retype over	*Keep*	*Keep*	**CORRECT THAT**
				SELECT three
				CLICK OK

Figure 1: Actions are represented in regular type. Spoken is in bold, command are all capitals and text is in italics. This is an example of changing the phrase "Kiss the dog" to the intended "keep the dog".

---

word or phrase said. If the user had selected text and was correcting it, SCRATCH THAT will delete the new text and restore the previously selected text, still selected. In some cases if the user just performed a command, such as a formatting command, SCRATCH THAT will also undo the formatting. On the other hand, UNDO is the method of choice if you've just done an unintended command, for example one that deletes your entire document, and you want to recover quickly. Because the exact command varies across products, we combined these into one code: SCRUNDO, short for scratch plus undo.

Each application provides several different ways to correct errors. During training we taught users five techniques and had them practice each one. These included:

1. undoing the immediately previous action and continuing dictation (SCRUNDO);

2. selecting a word by voice and re-dictating the word (correcting by *re-dictation*);

3. selecting a word by voice, opening the error correction dialogue; and

    (a) picking from an alternates list of words (not supported by L&H);

    (b) spelling the word out loud; and

    (c) typing in the correction in the dialogue box.

We told them they could use any of these techniques at any time, as well as use keyboard and mouse to correct if desired. We did not suggest any particular technique was better than another, nor did we suggest any strategies. (By strategy, we mean both what techniques they use to correct an error and when they use them.)

There are three main patterns of *when* an error is corrected. *Inline* refers to correcting an error immediately or almost as soon as it happens. For example, typographical errors (typos) are often corrected by immediately backspacing and retyping the information. In contrast, some people do not make corrections as they go along. Rather they wait until they have all their text on the page and then take a *post-entry* or *proofreading* pass (or several) and make corrections. Finally, these strategies are not mutually exclusive so a mixed strategy, of in-line correction and then a proofreading pass, is possible.

While early speech recognition products varied in the strategies of error correction strategies that they encouraged for users, the systems in the current study all accommodate in-line correction and post-entry correction equally well. Earlier, discrete speech systems, such as IBM's VoiceType, encouraged users (in documentation and online help) to dictate first and then switch to correction mode, while Dragon Dictate encouraged users to make corrections immediately after an error was dictated. These strategies were encouraged to accommodate system designs and limitations, and not because of a user driven reason.

4.3 What We Expected and What We Saw

Ideally, correction should be a straightforward process. What we expect to see is a pattern of detecting the error, locating and selecting the word to be corrected, and then making the correction. Given the variety of correction methods in speech this could be at best a 2-step process (select, re-dictate). This is possible because the command SELECT <word> locates the word and highlights it. (All three products have an algorithm that cycles through selections if there is more than one in the document, although each product makes different choices about which direction to search from the current cursor position.) Using the correction dialogue, it could be a 4-step process, or at most a 5-step process (move, select, open correction dialogue, choose from list, close dialogue). (Figure 1 summarizes some common patterns.)

While using the correction dialogue may take more steps, it can be the least error prone because the word does not need to be re-dictated. With the correct information in the alternates list the user can select the word, open the correction dialogue, and pick the word — replacing the selected word and closing the dialogue — in just three steps. Because of this efficiency we might expect to see the correction dialogue used frequently. Instead, we see it invoked in only 8% of all correction primitives.

Instead, the most common correction technique is to re-dictate the incorrect word. Initial Use subjects chose this technique 40% of the time. This makes sense when you consider two things. First, it is a two step process: Select the word and re-dictate. Second, if there is a problem the user can just undo the last dictation and try again. This is a lot like typing where users have gotten used to typing, immediately backspacing and retyping. However, there is a significant problem with this technique. One problem is that the accuracy for re-dictation is considerably lower than for initial dictation (47% averaged across all systems, vs. reported accuracy of 95% or better).

There is another problem with correction: when speech is used, there is still a chance of error — not only with re-dictation, but also with mis-recognition of commands. In fact, 22% of the correction primitives were about undoing the effect of incorrect commands. This is the tip of the iceberg however. When this occurs we often see several errors, expanding a correction episode to as many as twenty-five steps with five or more correction primitives. In short, we see a *cascade* of errors.

While it might have been faster, none of the subjects analysed switched to an all keyboard strategy for correction. (Only one subject reliably integrated keyboard and mouse with speech during correction.)

In fact, subjects tended to stay in the speech modality much longer during a correction than we expected or was efficient. In later comments they reported that they knew there must be a better way to do it, and figured that integrating speech with keyboard would be more efficient, but they had no idea how to go about it. They may have been biased to correcting with speech because they knew the experiment was to evaluate speech systems. Nonetheless, their tenacity was despite experimenters' instructions to use keyboard and mouse whenever they wished.

In sum, we see two distinct patterns. First, Initial Use subjects' fixated on re-dictation, in spite of reduced recognition accuracy. This pattern is what Oviatt & VanGent (1996) refer to as *spiral depths*: the number of times a subject continues to re-dictate the same word, despite incorrect recognition. Second, across all systems commands were sometimes mis-recognized as either dictation or other commands. During error correction, these mis-recognitions caused a new error that must be corrected before the original error can be dealt with. The result is a *cascade* of errors where apparent user frustration increased with the depth.

These two patterns — cascades and spirals — and how users handle them, are behind the difference in the number of steps in a correction episode of Initial Use and Extended Use.

4.4 Spiral Depths of Re-dictation

Oviatt & van Gent designed their experiment to understand the potential benefits of multi-modal input for error resolution. To this end, they simulated the equivalent of serial mis-recognitions to a spiral depth of 6. They found, as we did, that "on the first repetition following an error, an initial *no-switch strategy*, is evident in which users tend to repeat the same lexical content within the same mode" (p.207). On subsequent repetitions they found an increasing likelihood to switch either modality or lexical expression or both.

In our study, a little over 50% of the time we saw subjects continue to re-dictate to a spiral depth of 3. One quarter of the time they continued to a depth of 4. Slightly less than one quarter of the time they gave up after level two. We rarely saw changing to a synonym in the composition tasks, which is the only place they could have changed the lexical expression.

Unlike Oviatt & van Gent we did not see an increasing likelihood to switch modalities with the depth. Correcting with the keyboard, was equally as likely as successfully re-dictating the correction or a switch to the correction dialogue (which usually maintains modality). Almost as likely was giving up on the error completely. While a switch in modality did result in correcting the error, opening the correction dialogue usually meant more frustration.

Unfortunately, the correction dialogues appear to be designed with the assumption that they will be invoked first not last. Thus, by the time the user invokes a correction dialogue *the speech engine data has been lost or discarded and the alternates list is empty!* One subject explicitly reselected the word each time rather than undoing the previous action. Her reward was finding the alternates list still full of words. However, the majority of subjects used one of the SCRUNDO commands, and as a result find it empty. (One of the products does not provide an alternates list in the correction dialogue, so subjects invoked the dialogue only in order to spell.)

4.5 Cascades of Errors

Five times more often than isolated spirals we observed cascades. One quarter of these contained embedded spirals, within which other errors regularly intervened. In these spirals, the picture was different than with the isolated spirals. Just under half of these ended in correction dialogues, with a quarter ending in successful re-dictations and another 20% were corrected on the keyboard. (Less than 1% gave up without correcting.) Correcting phrases sometimes meant two embedded spirals in a cascade.

What predominantly characterizes cascades is what we might think of as "commands gone wrong". These may be because the speech engine mis-recognized a command — either as another command or as dictation — or because the subject used the wrong command or said a command in the wrong way. In each of these cases an additional error may be created that must also be corrected. Error cascades seem to have 'depth' similar to spirals, but are in fact different. To see this we need to look at a specific error.

Take the following case. The subject is trying to correct the composition he has just dictated. (We have diagrammed this in Figure 2. The top line is a running commentary of the 'plot' of the correction. In the diagram, moving across the page indicates length while moving down the page indicates levels.)

He begins by moving into position. The first command is successful, but the second command is mis-recognized and inserted in the text as dictation. His immediate response is an almost involuntary *back*, quickly cut off. This mis-speak is also inserted in the text and creates a second error. Then, trying to correct that error, the command is again mis-recognized and inserted in the text as dictation. He now has three levels separating him from the actual correction.

To reset the level he must correct each of these errors. Because these products all have multiple levels of undo, he uses the "undo what I just said" command (symbolized here as SCRUNDO) repeatedly to undo the effects of each problem.

Now he again tries to move ahead in the document, and again his command is mis-recognized as dictation. Again using undo, he is finally successful at the move and dictates the word he wants to insert.

This example shows the difficulty subjects get into because of command mis-recognitions. While this example is many levels deep, most cascades are only one level down but many more long. Figure 2 is only 11 steps long, while twice that number was not uncommon.

What we also see is evidence of subjects' lack of knowledge about the commands and lack of facility using them. Command mis-recognitions are dramatic because they have unexpected effects, while command misuse often has no discernible effect at all. Nonetheless, the effort, and steps required for the subject to recover from these errors is just as significant.

5 Discussion

While we only present a detailed example from one subject, these patterns are pervasive across the 12 subjects analysed. Initial Use subjects have a lot to contend with — spirals, cascades, and cascades with embedded spirals. They create these with help from the design of the speech products — and their frustration shows.

This is in contrast to the observed behaviour of the Extended Use subjects. While we have not completed an in-depth video analysis like that for Initial Use we do have diagnostic evidence of very different behaviour. After 20 sessions, all four Extended Use subjects have learned two things. They cut off re-dictation spirals at level 2 and they cut cascades very quickly. They do both of these by switching to different techniques more rapidly.

In the case of mis-recognized commands, the Extended Use subjects switch modalities, using their facility with the keyboard and mouse to manipulate text, make selections, and close dialogue boxes. These two strategies appear to account for the significant decrease in the number of steps in a correction episode between Initial and Extended Use subjects.

In sum, the increasing speed and facility of more experienced users appears related to the patterns of error correction experienced by first time users. While designers of ASR systems have developed correction aids, like the correction dialogue with its alternates list, users' patterns of use often make it unusable. Instead, novice users predominantly use one method of error correction — staying with the speech modality and re-dictating the same word three or four times before switching techniques. This arises because of reduced recognition accuracy with re-dictation. The result is a spiral. In addition, we saw a pattern of cascading errors due to problems with using commands. The primary culprit was mis-recognized

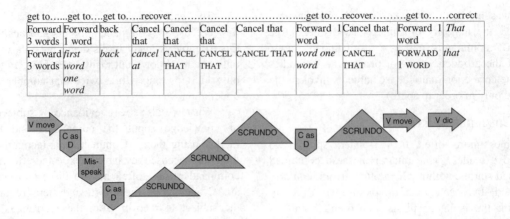

Figure 2: Diagram of cascade, showing levels, and length. 'V' is the abbreviation for voice, while 'C as D' represents command mis-recognized as dictation. The first line is what the subject is trying to do, the second line is what he says, while the third line is what is recognized. Recognized commands are in caps. Text inserted into the document is in italic.

commands, although not knowing the right command, or being able to say it properly was also a factor.

Based on the observed errors there are some design recommendations we can suggest. First, increase recognition accuracy for re-dictation. Second, recognize novice users' tendency to use the SCRATCH THAT (or comparable) command. In current ASR systems this appears to discard information saved from the speech engine that is necessary to populate the alternates list in the correction dialogue. Third, recognize that novices' tendency to fixate on one technique may mean they stick with a strategy past its optimum. We saw this despite explicit training on a variety of techniques. This tendency contributes to the spiral and cascade error patterns that mark Initial Use error correction.

Learning to do things differently takes a significant amount of time. The snapshot we have of the Extended Use subjects after 20 hours shows that these lessons are being learned. We will be looking in more depth at Extend Use sessions to see exactly how long it takes to learn to switch strategies quickly.

Acknowledgements

We would like to thank John Vergo, Tom Erickson, Robert Bowdidge, Wendy Stimpson, John Alcock, and Bill Rubin and the 24 participants we subjected to ASR.

References

Danis, C. & Karat, J. (1995), Technology-Driven-Design of Speech Recognition Systems, *in* G. Olson & S. Schuon (eds.), *Proceedings of the Symposium on Designing Interactive Systems: Processes, Practices, Methods and Techniques (DIS'95)*, ACM Press, pp.17–24.

Halverson, C., Horn, D., Karat, C., & Karat, J. (1999), Understanding What Speech Recognition Can't: A Language to Understand Your Users Behaviour, *in Proceedings of AVIOS'99: Speech Developers Conference*, American Voice Input/Output Society, pp.267–76.

Karat, C., Halverson, C., Horn, D. & Karat, J. (1999), Patterns of Entry and Correction in Large Vocabulary Continuous Speech Recognition Systems, *in* M. G. Williams, M. W. Altom, K. Ehrlich & W. Newman (eds.), *Proceedings of CHI'99: Human Factors in Computing Systems*, ACM Press, pp.568–75.

Karat, J. (1995), Scenario Use in the Design of a Speech Recognition System, *in* J. M. Carroll (ed.), *Scenario-Based Design: Envisioning Work and Technology in System Development*, John Wiley & Sons, pp.109–34.

Lai, J. & Vergo, J. (1997), MedSpeak: Report Creation with Continuous Speech Recognition, *in* S. Pemberton (ed.), *Proceedings of CHI'97: Human Factors in Computing Systems*, ACM Press, pp.431–38.

Oviatt, S. & VanGent, R. (1996), Error Resolution During Multimodal Human–Computer Interaction, *in* T. Bunnell & W. Idsardi (eds.), *Proceedings of the Fourth International Conference on Spoken Language Processing*, University of Delaware and AI DuPont Institute, New York, pp.204–7.

Rhyne, J. & Wolf, C. (1993), Recognition-Based User Interfaces, *in* H. R. Hartson & D. Hix (eds.), *Advances in Human–Computer Interaction*, Vol. 4, Ablex, pp.191–250.

Human–Computer Interaction — INTERACT '99
M. Angela Sasse and Chris Johnson (Editors)
Published by IOS Press, © IFIP TC.13, 1999

Managing Spoken Dialogues in Information Services

Jana Ocelíková & Václav Matoušek

University of West Bohemia in Pilsen, Univerzitní 22, CZ-306 14 Plzeň, Czech Republic.

{jnetrval,matousek}@kiv.zcu.cz

Abstract: This paper presents an approach to managing spoken dialogues in information service systems. We briefly describe how the approach based upon a tri-partite model of interaction addresses the problems of cooperativeness and portability across language and task domains as well as the semantic interpretation of utterances in a spoken dialogue system answering the train timetable inquiries. The described approach has been implemented in the generic dialogue manager of the SQEL multi-lingual information retrieval dialogue system.

Keywords: information retrieval dialogue system, dialogue manager, dialogue history, natural language ambiguity resolution.

1 Introduction

The main problem of human–machine interaction can be seen in the fact, that we assume, that both in the dialogue participating subjects have approximately equal knowledge and experience in the dialogue domain; speaking human need not express some essential information, because it results directly from the receiver's knowledge and the dialogue context. Therefore, the used dialogue model have to take the dialogue context into account, using particular knowledge base (*a dialogue history*), which is build during the dialogue, and simple types of references (anaphora, ellipses) can be processed. The dialogue system gains then the features of natural reasoning, of incoherence detection and internal correction, and of anticipation and prediction.

The main components of the developed system prototype are following (see Figure 1): the speech input/output interface, the acoustic-phonetic recognizer, the linguistic processor, and the dialogue manager. The acoustic-phonetic recognizer, the linguistic processor and a part of the dialogue manager are integrated into the subsystem of a spoken dialogue interface. The interface of the developed system provides three principal functions: the interpretation of user (customer) utterances, the generation of system utterances (answers containing required data and/or clarifying question) and the user-friendly management of a coherent and natural dialogue.

2 Dialogue System Architecture

An in-house telephone and/or input microphone is connected to the standard multimedia module of the workstation, with the help of which the input speech signal is sampled and digitized. A set of cepstral features and their derivatives are processed in the speech signal preprocessing module. Input to the acoustic-phonetic analysis module (word recognizer) is a preprocessed (into feature vectors transformed and quantized) utterance, output is the best fitting chain of word hypotheses. The principal phonetic sub-word unit is the polyphone (Schukat-Talamazzini & Niemann, 1994), representing a generalized context-dependent sub-word unit surrounded by an arbitrarily large context. In contrast to triphones, the context is not artificially restricted to one symbol to the left and to the right; the context items may also include suprasegmental markers or even word boundaries. This ensures that large scaled contextual effects are properly statistically modelled. Design of the models and training of the HMM parameters are performed by the ISADORA system (Schukat-Talamazzini & Niemann, 1994).

The Czech word recognizer was evaluated on microphone and telephone quality of speech, the results of experiments are summarized in the following table:

quality of speech	microphone	telephone
word rec. accuracy	82–87%	67–78%
sentence rec. accuracy	45–49%	27–46%

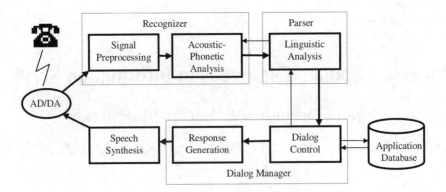

Figure 1: Functional structure of the dialogue system.

The recognition accuracy rates of the telephone speech recognition were surely caused by the low quality of the analogue telephone exchange being at disposal.

The linguistic processor was designed as an extended Tomita parser (Tomita, 1986) operating left-to-right and bottom-up on the best word sequence returned by the recognizer.

Operating on recognized words, the linguistic processor is responsible to generate a semantic description of the user utterance. Primarily the success of the linguistic processor is caused by the use of partial descriptions, the so called *utterance field objects* (UFOs), whenever a complete parse is not possible. These partial parses are used for further pragmatic analysis in the dialogue manager in order to find an adequate context dependent interpretation. Processing partial information is the normal mode in our system, not just a backup strategy.

Inside the linguistic processor a chart parser using a *unification categorial grammar* (UCG) is analysing the word string returned from the acoustic phonetic recognizer. Syntactic and semantic structures are built in parallel by unifying complex feature structures during parsing. Thus, beginning with isolated word interpretations, the spanning edges are extended into a consistent maximal description of the utterance.

A principal demand for the system to withstand an arbitrary (naïve) user is *robustness*. We argue, that for successful speech understanding systems the principle of partial information processing is vital. This paper describes the approach to the robust analysis of semantic information in spoken dialogues.

Well known problems of spontaneous speech are, e.g. *unknown or mispronounced words, filled pauses* (ah, uh, um, ...), *restarts* — repeating a word or phrase, *interjections* — extraneous phrases,

ellipses, ungrammatical constructions. While the first of them is 'just' a problem of the recognizer, the others are to be handled in the semantic interpretation process. Identification and proper processing of those phenomena is a difficult problem causing every traditional parser to fail to provide a single closed interpretation. There are two principal approaches to overcome such inconveniences: the grammar of the parser is extended by modelling those phenomena, or the linguistic analysis itself is designed robustly.

Our approach to the semantic analysis is the second one. Based on UCG which encodes grammatical correct expressions and their combination, the key to robust analysis is to use partial descriptions for ungrammatical (or incorrectly recognized) utterances. Two typical examples observed in our collection inquires are:

> *I want to go from — at nine from Prague.*

or

> *...night train from Berlin — ah — from — from...*

Usually, parts of the utterance are built properly, but the combination of them is out of coverage of the linguistic grammar. In these cases robust interpretation is performed by using partial results, the UFOs.

Given a best string (or word graph) as the result of the recognizer, the linguistic processor's task is to produce a proper semantic representation. In spontaneous speech the case of incomplete parses is the regular case; dealing with complete and coherent descriptions is the exception. A chart parser is best suited for supplying partial parses, because all previous combinations of partial instances are represented as edges in the chart.

In our current experiments, the syntactic and semantic scores are weighted extremely high, so every UFO must be syntactically and semantically well formed.

The pragmatic interpretation process of the semantic information is using the concept of UFOs to find the task relevant parts of information pieces. The results of the parser an their elaboration are represented using the Semantic Interface Language — SIL (Eckert & Niemann, 1994).

The semantic interface language (SIL) provides a simple but flexible representation of utterances in terms of structured objects (Netrvalova, 1997).

The dialogue manager was designed and implemented with partners from the countries participating in the Copernicus project resulting in a language independent, multi-lingual system. Several different dialogue strategies were implemented to allow a wide variety of different system reactions. Management of spoken dialogues requires the interpretation of the user utterances and the generation of system responses coherent with user utterances. The underlying interaction model consists of the semantic, the task and the dialogue models (Netrvalova, 1997). Semantic descriptions of user utterances are processed dealing with ambiguity, context dependence and the hypothetical nature of the linguistic representation.

The response, or message generator — a language dependent part of the dialogue manager — produces then an appropriate answer or a clarifying question corresponding to the recognized input sentence (inquire). The output sentence is finally converted to the speech signal by the text-to-speech module implemented on the basis of concatenation of segments of compressed (by an original compression method) real speech signal of possible answers and/or additional questions prepared in advance.

3 Dialogue Manager

The task oriented subsystem of dialogue control and management (*dialogue manager*) accepts the semantic representation of the user's utterance and performs its interpretation within the current dialogue context. Dialogue manager was designed by the way, that it incorporates pragmatic interpretation formation, formulas describing the access to the database relating to the required application, interpretation rules of earlier history of the current dialogue and their relationships (*dialogue model*), as well as a set of dialogue goals representing intentions of the system (Krutisova et al., 1998). The following basic program modules were incorporated into the dialogue manager:

Linguistic interface module: providing the communication with the parser.

Interpretation module: setting user utterance interpretation in the current dialogue context.

Task module: handling with database query and language adaptation task performance.

Dialogue module: planning system utterance formulation within the pragmatic information context and interpretation.

Message planning module: generating the system message and protocols.

Postie: managing the queue of internal messages.

The structure of the dialogue manager was made full open to enable the system extension by new modules. Their incorporation is performed under control of the dialogue control module in which the message passing protocol was used to provide the communication among the modules. With the help of this subsystem we demonstrate the language and application independence of the dialogue manager and its possible adaptation to the Czech language and to the required application only by the adaptation or simple modification of message planning and task modules as well.

3.1 Dialogue Features

In dyadic dialogue communication between humans, conversation among speakers is characterized by turn-taking: in general, one participant, A, talks, stops; another, B, talks, stops, and so we obtain an A-B-A-B-A-B distribution of talk across two participants. This transition from one speaker to another has been shown to be orderly, with precise timing and with less than 5% overlap.

Sacks et al. (1974) suggest that the mechanism that governs turn-taking, and accounts for the properties noted, is a set of rules with ordered options which operates on a turn-by-turn basis, and can thus be termed a 'local management system'. One way of looking at the participant is to see him as a sharing device operating over a scare resource, namely control of the 'floor'. Such an allocational system will require minimum units over which it will operate. These units are, in this model, determined by various features of linguistic surface structure: they are syntactic units (sentences, clauses, noun phrases, and so on) identified as turn-units in part by prosodic means. Other psychologists working on conversation have suggested a different solution to how turn-taking works. According to this other view, turn-taking is regulated primarily by signals, and not by opportunity assignment rules at all. In Gibbon et al. (1997) we can find three basic signals for the turn-taking mechanism:

- Turn-yielding signals by the speaker.

- Attempt-suppressing signals by the speaker.

- Back-channel signals by the auditor.

These signals are used and responded to in a relatively structured manner. On a such view, the current speaker will signal when he intends to hand over the floor, and other participants may bid by recognized signals for the right to speak.

3.2   Dialogue Design

A kernel module of the developed interactive dialogue system, *dialogue manager*, completely monitoring the dialogue, may be able to handle several input and output devices in parallel: a user may be interact with the dialogue system using multi-modal input and output (in our case via telephone or a classical microphone/loudspeaker), and several input devices may be used in transferring the same message to the system. Users communicate with the system in a number of transactions. A transaction consist of a number of message exchanges, each of which consist of the input utterance or the corresponding system response being put out by means of the synthetic or scanned and compressed speech. The dialogue strategy of the interactive dialogue system changes in a sequence of turns (Sadek & de Mori, 1997).

A developed dialogue system can be considered as a kind of interface which performs communication between a human being and an application database. Such dialogue system must process two kinds of information: that coming from the user and that coming from the task itself through specialized database interface, one for the speech technologies, one for the application. One of the dialogue system's main activities is to maintain coherence between both. Therefore, the connection between a human being's action (e.g. a natural language utterance) and the response of the system is not direct: the dialogue system must achieve a number internal actions in order to give a response which is not unique but depends on the internal state of the system and on the context of the interaction. This form of communication is referred to as the *agent metaphor* or the *adviser metaphor*.

One important component of the dialogue leading is the *dialogue history* which keeps track of the previous information exchanges. The different

modules and their associated knowledge bases allow the dialogue manager to perform internal actions including the following:

- Verify the coherence of the user's request with the system.

- Knowledge concerning the linguistic analysis and generation modules, etc.

- Negotiate with the user.

- Resolve problems of reference (anaphoras, ellipses, etc.).

- Generate a relevant response.

- Draw reasonable inferences.

- Predict the user's most probable reaction.

The different comprehension levels involved (acoustic, phonetic, lexical, syntactic, semantico-pragmatic) may be addressed sequentially. Alternatively, information transfers may take place in parallel between different levels in a non-hierarchical fashion, depending on the dialogue situation.

The interaction is reduced to a question/answer user interface. The dialogue model is merged into the task model (Phillips et al., 1988) from which it cannot be distinguished. dialogues of this kind are here represented by branching tree structures. The dialogue have to be strictly guided, leaving very little initiative to the user. Several exchanges may be necessary to provoke one action or to obtain information from the system.

The dialogue model takes context into account, using particular knowledge base (a dialogue history), which is build during dialogue. Multiple types of references (anaphora, ellipses, ...) may be processed. The system may be capable of reasoning, of incoherence detection and internal correction, and of anticipation and prediction.

At each stage in each possible dialogue, the designer attempts to answer question *"What could happen next?"*. This question can be answered at multiple levels. For example: In a classical human dialogue the earlier understood information is often modified, specified and reversed later. A human has no problem with this situation, he accepts it and the effect of this situation too. But the system 'doesn't understand', therefore it must generate a clarifying question. In the dialogue interpretation process the semantic interpretations and the dialogue model are matched, deciding the subsequent steps of cooperative user interaction in the structured dialogue model.

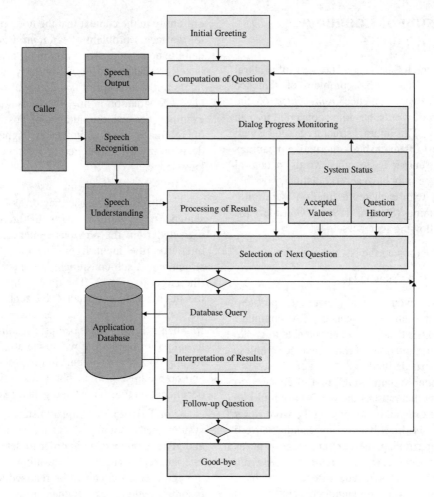

Figure 2: Simplified scheme of the dialogue control.

Using this partitioned interactional model, dialogue management is independent on the language and of the information service domain. By automatic production there is necessary to save dialogue's history.

The main steps of the dialogue control are shown in Figure 2 and the significant tasks of dialogue leading can be summarized in the following list:

- Initial greeting.

- Generation of a first question.

- Output of the question to the text-to-speech component.

- Passing control to speech recognition and speech understanding.

- Modifying these components according to the current system status.

- Processing of the results obtained from speech understanding.

- Combining this information with the current system status.

- Selection of the next question based on the new system status.

- Generation of the exact form of this question.

- Verification of previously obtained results.

- Access to the application database.

- Output of the query results, possibly after converting them into a suitable form.

- Dealing with special situations during the dialogue, like errors from the database, repetition of a question, repetition of results.

- Monitoring of the dialogue progress.

4 Processing of Language Ambiguities

Each system which analyses sentences of natural language has to deal with a problem of sentence representation. Every sentence, *represented* on the input by a string of words, has to be converted into an internal structure. This internal structure has to be well defined and must distinguish all alternative meanings of the original sentence. In other words, a natural language sentence may have several distinct, possible representations, with each representation identifying a different meaning (Stetina, 1997). Consider, for example, the following sentences:

1. The conductor sold the last ticket to Prague.

2. He sold it to a young lady.

A human would not have a problem understanding the above sequence. A computer system, on the other hand, would not be able to create an internal representation of this sentence, unless several issues were clarified.

The computer system would, first of all, have to deal with the fact that most of the words have multiple meanings. For example, if we look up the word *ticket* in a dictionary, we find that it can be either a verb or a noun. Determining the correct category poses a problem of *lexical syntactic ambiguity*. Having determined the correct syntactic category, we have to further decide, what semantic concept a word represents. The meaning behind the noun *conductor*, for example, can be either a person who sells tickets on a bus, a person who conducts an orchestra, or a substance that passes heat or electricity. Deciding which of these meanings is correct constitutes the goal of the *lexical semantic ambiguity* resolution.

Secondly, the system would to determine the relations between the individual words. Was the ticket in (1) *sold to Prague* or was *it a ticket to Prague* that was sold? The syntactic knowledge defines all possible structural representations, i.e. there are two different corresponding syntactic trees they can be generated in above mentioned cases.

The identification of the relations among the words is based on our knowledge of the concepts they represent. Without this knowledge, the system would incorrectly take into consideration the inappropriate structure, leaving us with a structural ambiguity of two possible syntactic structures.

Every noun phrase is either indefinite or definite. While indefinite noun phrases evoke new discourse entities, the definite noun phrases refer to entities already established in context. If there is more than one entity in the context that the noun phrase can refer to, we face a problem of *referential ambiguity*. The definite noun phrase *the ticket* in (2) refers to the same ticket established in (1). Similarly, the pronoun *he* refers to the concept of *conductor* also established in (1). The situation is not always as simple as in this example, because the number of possible candidates of reference is usually much higher, and/or the decision involves complicated inference with general knowledge.

Ellipsis involves the use of sentences that appear ill-formed because they do not form complete sentences. Typically the parts that are missing can be extracted from the previous sentence. An *elliptical* utterance (the input fragment) must correspond in structure to a sub-constituent in the previous sentence (the target fragment). The final syntactic structure of the utterance is constructed by replacing the target fragment in the previous sentence with the input fragment. In this sense, ellipsis resolution is similar to *anaphora* resolution, where we also have to search for appropriate constituents in the previous sentences, and both ellipsis and anaphora resolution are heavily dependent on the context and general knowledge.

Similarly to the human listener, the computer system needs to apply syntactic, semantic, pragmatic and general knowledge in order to determine the final internal representation of meaning. Unfortunately, this representation cannot be realized solely from the incoming utterance. Rather, it is a result of the utterance itself, the context of the previous utterances, the context in which the communication takes place, and the general knowledge on the listener's, i.e. system's side. Intuitively, we can envisage this representation as a semantic network of concepts that the words represent, connected by the corresponding semantic relations. But, it is only an usual graphical representation to visualize the semantic relations of the sentence. The 'real understanding' system have to combine the incomplete semantic information extracted from the analysed utterance with the previous 'data' stored in the dialogue history path. This is provided in the developed dialogue system by the module of the *dialogue history*, which is designed as an one-purpose rule oriented knowledge system with rules derived from the comprehensive set of training sentences. The created rules are internal represented (and implemented) as a hierarchical structure of frames containing at least three contextual elements. The frames are implemented by using dynamic data structures to obtain the efficient implementation and to save the memory space.

The functional features of the developed dialogue manager involving the program module of the dialogue history processing were tested and evaluated by the group of 'semi-naïve' users (students and laboratory staff), the results of this evaluation are presented at the end of the last paragraph.

5   Implementation

The processing of sentences of all kinds, including the incomplete sentences, is controlled by the dialogue module of the dialogue manager.   The meaning of analysed sentences is internal represented (and implemented) as a chained hierarchical structure of sentence frames containing at most seven contextual elements.   The frames are implemented by using dynamic data structures to obtain the efficient implementation and to save the memory space.

To preserve the dialogue history, all analysed and step by step completed semantic frames are stored to the special temporary storage area of the dialogue module. If the last analysed sentence is classified as an incomplete one, its representing frame is compared with all temporary stored frames of previously analysed sentences, the frame is 'overlapped' with the most corresponding 'elder' frame and completed for all missing data. If no corresponding frame is found in the temporary storage (in the dialogue history), i.e. the analysed sentence is the anaphoric one, the dialogue module hands over the sentence analysis to the interpretation module, which attempts to complete the missing data with the help of a set of especially created and organized domain dependent knowledge bases. If this second analysis phase is unsuccessful too, only then the clarifying question is uttered.

All stored sentence frames representing the saved dialogue history are immediately cleared after the ceremony closing the sequence of dialogue acts.

The structure of the dialogue manager is made full open to enable the system extension form new modules and its incorporation under control by the dialogue control module in which the message passing protocol to communicate among the modules was used.   With help of this subsystem the dialogue manager is language and application independent and can be possibly adapted for the required application only by the modification of message planning and task modules.

The dialogue control module was written in the C programming language and it cooperates with a number of modules written in the Quintus Prolog programming language.

6   Conclusion

It is widely accepted that, alone, (spoken or written) natural language processing, or mere integration of communication media, is not sufficient for building systems that can engage in a truly cooperative dialogue with humans. Moreover, improving system ergonomy can only be a place-holder for the fundamental requirement, which is system intelligence.

Many of the prototypes that have been developed so far, especially those based on simple finite-state diagrams, are too rigid and do not exhibit the degree of 'intelligence' that makes them appear as cooperative as a normal user would expect. An important question that needs to me addressed is "What should be the basis for system intelligence?".

Some of important issues that need to be explored in the future with rigorous experimentation are the following:

- Effective procedures for default reasoning; in particular, defining methods for establishing priorities between inference alternatives in interpretation and planning.

- Tractable belief revision models that are compatible with the formal framework, in particular for managing the dialogue history in a generic way.

- Tractable, relevant-for-communication formal models of plan recognition.

- Formal models for complex planning methods (conjunctive goals, hierarchical planning, etc.).

- More sophisticated logical systems for handling uncertainty as a mental attitude, and dealing with plausible inference.

- Building application models (e.g. semantic networks) automatically, starting from non-structured data.

- Computational methods that enable rational agents (and therefore dialogue systems) to learn users' profiles and behaviours.

- Techniques for learning from examples how some components of communicative acts can be determined from utterances).

- Heuristics and decision procedures for determining when to attempt to infer new information from the current dialogue state or when it is more convenient to switch to a question/answering interaction.

- Methodologies and techniques for the testing, evaluation, and validation of advanced dialogue system.

The first version of the 'Czech natural speaking' dialogue system was designed and successfully implemented. Looking back to the designing process we can formulate following steps of this process, taking both human linguistic behaviours and speech technology performance into account:

- Carefully formulate the dialogue task based on an ergonomic analysis of needs or requirements of potential users.

- Analyse an adequate account of all kinds of possible dialogues recorded in real life, making objectives explicit.

- Transcribe the dialogues recorded in real life using a standard transcription scheme if possible.

- Draw up a specification of the interactive dialogue system.

- Design and implement a first version of the dialogue system.

- Conduct laboratory tests using corpora recorded in dialogue simulations provided by laboratory staff simulating users, recording new data.

- Conduct field tests with real users, recording new corpora.

- 'Tune' the system by iterative modifying, then testing it.

- Design a revised version of the dialogue strategy and implement a new version of the dialogue system.

- Carry out new laboratory and field tests with real users.

- Repeat the previous two steps until all reasonable requests of real users are satisfied.

The last six design steps of development of the interactive dialogue system had to be performed in close collaboration with a professional organization which have ordered the dialogue system and takes the system into its services. First functional tests were provided only by the group of 'semi-naïve' users, their results are summarized in the following table:

Number of users	15
Number of dialogues	150
Excellent dialogues	32
Dialogues with troubles [†]	61
Unsuccessful dialogues	57
Successful dialogues total	93
%	62.0

[†] Dialogue with troubles means the dialogue with information repeats, corrections, misunderstandings, additions, etc.

References

Eckert, W. & Niemann, H. (1994), Semantic Analysis in a Robust Spoken Dialog System, *in Proceedings of the International Conference on Spoken Language Processing*, pp.107–110.

Gibbon, D., Moore, R. & Winski, R. (1997), *Handbook of Standards and Resources for Spoken Language Systems*, Mouton de Gruyter Verlag.

Krutisova, J., Matoušek, V. & Ocelíková, J. (1998), Development of an One-purpose Dialog Manager, *in Proceedings of the International Workshop SPECOM 1998,*, pp.131–4.

Netrvalova, J. (1997), Representation and Interpretation of Continuous Utterances, *in Proceedings of the 2nd SQEL Workshop on Multi-Lingual Information Retrieval Dialogs*, pp.28–31.

Phillips, M. D., Bashinski, H. S., Ammerman, H. L. & Fligg, C. M. (1988), A Task Analytic Approach to Dialogue Design, *in* M. Helander (ed.), *Handbook of Human–Computer Interaction*, North-Holland, pp.835–57.

Sacks, H., Schlegloff, E. & Jefferson, G. (1974), "A Simplest Systematics for the Organization of Turn-taking in Conversation", *Language* **50**, 697–735.

Sadek, D. & de Mori, R. (1997), Dialogue Systems, *in* R. de Mori (ed.), *Spoken Dialogues with Computers*, Academic Press, pp.523–61.

Schukat-Talamazzini, E. G. & Niemann, H. (1994), Speech Recognition for Spoken Dialog Systems, *in* H. Niemann, R. de Mori & G. Hannrieder (eds.), *Progress and Prospects of Speech Research and Technology, Proceedings of CRIM/FORWISS Workshop*, Infix, pp.110–20.

Stetina, J. (1997), Corpus Based Natural Language Ambiguity Resolution, PhD thesis, CTU Prague.

Tomita, M. (1986), *Efficient Parsing for Natural Language*, Kluwer.

Human–Computer Interaction — INTERACT '99
M. Angela Sasse and Chris Johnson (Editors)
Published by IOS Press, © IFIP TC.13, 1999

Speech Interaction Can Support Problem Solving

David Golightly[1], Kate S. Hone[2] & Frank E. Ritter[1]

[1] School of Psychology; [2] Informatics Institute of Information Technology
University of Nottingham, University Park, Nottingham NG7 2RD, UK.
{David.Golightly,Kate.Hone,Frank.Ritter}@nottingham.ac.uk

Abstract: Speech can lead to increased performance in computer-based problem solving. Studies of complex interaction styles — such as command-line or system-delayed interaction — have found that complex interaction styles can lead to savings in the number of actions users take to reach a solution for certain tasks compared with direct manipulation. Speech can be viewed a complex interaction style because it requires users to reference objects symbolically, rather than through deictic reference, and often involves a system delay. We compared speech interaction with two previously studied interaction styles — delayed interaction and direct manipulation — on the 8-puzzle task. The results show that speech leads to significant savings in moves to solution. Importantly, these savings are not at the expense of greater overall solution times. Savings through speech can be primarily attributed to the effects of system delay. These results suggest the potential for speech interfaces to be used as a tool to support problem solving.

Keywords: direct manipulation, system delay, speech recognition, display-based problem solving.

1 Introduction

Speech, the primary and most natural form of human communication, can be used as a mode of interaction. Speech can be used in hands-free situations or as an extra input mechanism, and is used in an increasingly diverse range of applications.

What are the advantages of speech for computer-based problem solving? This paper discusses the cognitive implications of using speech in display-based problem solving. Using speech is not always a neutral interaction style, and can potentially enhance problem solving in certain tasks.

2 Background and Predictions

Display-based problem solving relies on the relationship between represented objects to convey information about the state of the problem (Larkin, 1989). The relationship between interaction-style and display-based problem solving is complex. The common assumption is that the interaction should be made as easy as possible, as interacting using complex interface styles is a drain on cognitive resources. This drain reduces the cognitive resources available to devote to task-related problem solving.

However, anecdotal and experimental evidence suggest that complex interaction is not always disruptive. This introduction reviews the evidence and underlying theory, before presenting the argument that speech, a complex form of interaction, can support problem solving.

2.1 Does Direct Manipulation Suit All Tasks?

Direct manipulation is currently the most pervasive form of interaction. Its success is due to the perceived ease with which users can interact with the display and interpret their actions. Such interfaces reduce the gulfs of execution and evaluation (Norman, 1986) that the user must cross in order to achieve their task goals. Direct manipulation systems accept an input that closely maps to the user's own goal structure, and gives an output that can be easily interpreted in terms of the users own goal structure.

As an example, the user may want to throw away an old text document. The system uses a direct manipulation desktop metaphor. The user can 'pick up' (i.e. point-and-click on) a document and move it into a trash can. The gulf of execution is reduced because the system lets the user act in a way that maps to the user's goal structure. The user acts as if physically manipulating the object. Also, the act of putting it in a 'trashcan' holds a semantic link for the user with the action of discarding an actual paper file in a waste bin.

The gulf of evaluation is also reduced as the state of the system is immediately interpretable by the user. When the user carries out the action the system gives immediate feedback by moving the file — normally simultaneously with the pointer movement — into the trashcan and removing it visually from the previous file space.

The trashcan example serves to highlight two key aspects of Direct Manipulation. First, direct manipulation uses deictic reference (Ziegler & Fahnrich, 1988). Rather than referencing the objects symbolically by typing a file name, for example, the user points and interacts directly with a representation of the object. The user has a sense of engagement with objects within the system rather than using the interface as an intermediary. The second key aspect of direct manipulation is that it naturally supports reversible actions (Shneiderman, 1992). Errors can be easily undone. In the example above the user can take their file out of the trashcan folder and move it back to its original file space and so the user can try out actions without fear of irreversible consequences.

Overall, the interaction features of direct manipulation are assumed to allow novice or occasional users to understand and explore the functionality of the interface, while allowing expert users to operate quickly. However, there are some situations where direct manipulation may not provide these benefits. Observations from the educational community suggest that the user may be so engaged in the interaction itself, that the learning experience of the interaction becomes marginalized (Moore, 1993). There are many personal accounts of users who feel that command-line languages allow greater flexibility and control of the system or that using command-line enforces a certain degree of 'rigour' on interaction as opposed to almost aimless action with direct manipulation (J. Clarke, 1998, personal communication). This is not to imply that Direct Manipulation is disruptive *per se*, but it may be the case that, for certain tasks and users, direct manipulation may not be the ideal form of interaction.

A body of work has empirically compared interface styles. Svendsen (1991) and O'Hara & Payne (1998) compared command-line interaction and direct manipulation for problem solving tasks. Svendsen compared the two interaction styles for the Tower of Hanoi task; O'Hara & Payne compared interfaces over the 8-puzzle task (shown in Figure 1). In both cases the command-line users showed significant savings in the number of moves taken to reach the solution state.

The command-line participants took longer between moves, indicating greater reflection on the task (i.e. cognitive activity). These longer move times were not so great that it took longer overall to complete the puzzles.

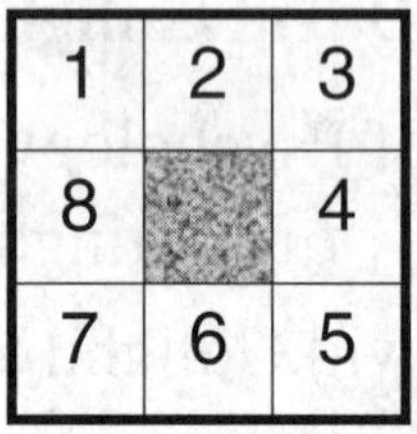

Figure 1: The 8-puzzle. Each tile is moved by sliding the tile into the space (greyed in the figure). The solver starts the puzzle with the tiles randomised and must move the tiles until they match the goal configuration, shown here.

Similar results have been found for an interaction style that was fundamentally Direct Manipulation but with increased complexity. The interaction style used point-and-click interaction, but required the user to click on buttons that represented the tiles rather the tiles themselves (Golightly & Gilmore, 1997). Again, users who solved the 8-puzzle with this style of interaction showed significant problem solving savings over conventional Direct Manipulation users.

These findings can be brought under the heading of Manipulation Supported Problem Solving (MSPS) effects. MSPS is the phenomena of more complex interaction leading to better styles of problem solving. The key elements of MSPS are:

- Problem solving move savings are found with complex interaction styles in comparison with direct manipulation interfaces.

- Longer intervals are taken between moves with a complex interaction style indicating greater cognitive activity.

The following section introduces the mechanism by which complexity leads to shorter solution paths.

2.2   The Cost of an Action Leads to Manipulation Supported Problem Solving

O'Hara & Payne (1998) describe an explanation of why the complex interfaces support problem solving. When the user is faced with a complex interface they carry out a cost-benefit analysis. With the complex interface, executing an action is perceived as having a high cost. Therefore, the user chooses a problem solving strategy that does not require a high number of costly actions. The strategy the user takes is to plan actions in advance to check that the next move — or sequence of moves — to be executed will move the user towards the goal state.

Consider the case of a command-line interaction style for the 8-puzzle. With a command-line interaction style (or with the interaction style used by Golightly and Gilmore) the user has to refer to each object symbolically rather than by pointing at it. The user perceives a high-cost to having to type in each command many times (or having to click on the button). This encourages the user to plan their actions in advance so that the moves will be effective. Planning results in the longer inter-move times seen with MSPS, but ensures that the user need to take fewer high-cost steps to reach their goal.

On the other hand, Direct Manipulation users perceive a low cost to their actions. As each move is easily executed, the user is prepared to carry out a trail-and-error problem solving strategy. Take the case of a direct manipulation interface for the 8-puzzle. Each move can be made with very little effort, so the user is prepared to explore sequences of moves on the display rather than planning them in advance. The result is that users expend less cognitive effort on each move but take more moves to reach a solution.

There is further support for the 'cost' explanation of MSPS from studies of system delay. The common belief is that system delay has a disruptive effect on interaction. This is often the case with delay leading to reductions in productivity. However, delay has been found to lead to an increase in productivity in some situations — specifically tasks which involve problem solving (see Teal & Rudnicky (1992), for a short review of system delay studies). In such cases users perceive actions that take an extended period to occur in the system as having a high-cost. Rather than having to execute many actions that involve a delay, the user plans moves in advance in order to reduce the number of actions required. O'Hara & Payne (1998) reported that long system delays do indeed lead to fewer moves to solution than short system delays for the 8-puzzle task.

Overall, MSPS occurs when there is some form of interface complexity. The user perceives a cost to their actions. The user tries to reduce the number of actions required by planning actions in advance. This planning leads to longer times between actions but ultimately reduces the number of actions that have to be executed.

The following section introduces the prediction that MSPS should occur with speech-driven interaction.

2.3 Can Speech Interfaces Support Problem Solving?

There have been some studies comparing direct manipulation interaction with speech interaction e.g. (Schmandt et al., 1990) though none have looked directly at problem solving tasks. However, there is good reason for believing that speech could support problem solving. Speech has two types of cost that have lead to MSPS in the past — speech requires the user to symbolically reference objects and speech interaction involves a system delay.

Speech is the ability to symbolically reference objects in the world using sound. It is inherent that speech involves symbolic reference. Work on protocol analysis (Ericsson & Simon, 1993) has found that talking aloud can influence problem solving. Having to refer to objects by name, rather than simply pointing at them, increases the gulf of execution. The user must articulate the name of the object. As Svendsen, O'Hara & Payne and Golightly & Gilmore have shown, symbolically referencing objects when carrying out display-based problem solving invokes a cost. This cost leads to MSPS for the right tasks. Speech should invoke a similar cost, and therefore lead to MSPS for those tasks.

The second source of cost in speech systems is delay. Although increasing processor speed continues to reduce the delay, and continuous speech recognizers reduces it further, the delay is still apparent. Current speech recognition systems still require some time to process speech input. As discussed above, delay disrupts the interaction. In order to minimise this disruption, users plan their actions. Therefore, the cost due to the delay in speech recognition should also lead to MSPS.

Overall, speech requires symbolic reference and objects and incurs a system delay. Combined, these two sources of cost should encourage planning and support problem solving. The following experiment tested this prediction. A direct manipulation interface was compared against a speech interface. The task was the 8-puzzle — a task where MSPS effect had been found in the past. The prediction was that the speech interface should lead to:

- Longer intervals between moves.

- Fewer moves to solution.

A third interaction style, delayed interaction, was also implemented. This was a direct manipulation interface with an equivalent delay to that expected due to the delay due speech recognition. If performance with the delay was comparable to performance with the speech recognition then this would indicate the problem solving savings through the speech interface were primarily due to system delay. If not, savings are due to the need to symbolically reference objects.

3   Method

3.1   Participants

39 participants (21 women, 18 men) took part in the study. Each participant was paid £5.

3.2   Apparatus

The three interfaces were implemented on a PC with Pentium 166 processor running Visual Basic 5.0. The display had a representation of the 8-puzzle (approximately 10cm × 10cm) in the centre of the screen. To the right was a smaller example representation of the 8-puzzle already in the goal configuration (shown in Figure 1). On-screen instructions, specific to each interface, told the user how to control the puzzle and that they should get the puzzle to the same state as the example goal configuration.

The Direct Manipulation (Direct) interface required the participant to click on the tile they wished to move. If the tile was next to the space (i.e. the move was legal) the tile would move into the space.

The Speech Recognition interface (Speech) was implemented using Dragon Dictate recognition software. Dragon Dictate is speaker dependent recognition software, primarily for dictation, but was integrated with the Visual Basic project through the Dragon X-tools scripting tool. Instead of clicking on the tile participants said the tile they wished to move by stating the digit on the tile. All participants in the speech recognition condition were trained on the 'intense' setting with the necessary vocabulary (the digits from '1' to '8') before the study. Mean recognition level during the task was 90%.

The Delay (Delay) condition was implemented with a 0.8 seconds delay between the system receiving a mouse click and the tile moving. Testing (by one of the authors) showed that the speech recognition software could be optimised to respond with a minimum system delay of 0.8 seconds. This time included the time required to verbalise the speech input.

There were ten different starting configurations for the 8-puzzle. All participants received the configurations in the same order

3.3   Procedure

Each participant was given a brief introduction to the task. If the participant was in the Speech condition then they trained the recognition software on the task vocabulary.

All the participants were given time to familiarise themselves with the equipment. The participant then read the task instructions, which were clarified by the experimenter, and the participant then started the experimental session in their own time.

The session ended when the participant either completed all 10 puzzles or had worked for 55 minutes, whichever came first. 3 participants in the Delay condition timed-out and were dropped from the analysis.

3.4   Design

The study had a 1 × 3 between-subjects design varying by interaction style (Direct, Speech, Delay; $n = 12$ for each group). Three measurements were taken from participants:

- Mean move intervals (including the 0.8 second delay for the Delay group). This score was log (ln) transformed to remove the influence of interval peaks in the data. When solution paths are short then a few interval peaks can distort the mean.

- Average extra moves to solution. The minimum number of moves for each puzzle was deducted from the number of moves taken to solve each puzzle. The total for the ten puzzles was then averaged for each participant.

- Total task time.

4   Results

The average move intervals are shown in Table 1. As predicted, both Delay and Speech conditions showed longer move intervals than Direct condition. A 1 × 3 ANOVA showed an overall effect for interface ($F(2,33) = 30.6$). Post-hoc Scheffé tests confirmed that the Delay and Speech groups had shorter move intervals than the Direct group. Figure 2 shows the move intervals for each puzzle.

The average extra moves are shown in Table 1. As predicted both the Delay and the Speech took fewer extra moves to solution than the Direct condition. A 1 × 3 ANOVA showed an overall effect for interface ($F(2,33) = 5.7$). Post-hoc Scheffé tests confirmed that the Delay and Speech groups took fewer extra moves to solution than the Direct group. Figure 3 shows the extra moves for each puzzle.

	Delay ($n = 12$)		Direct ($n = 12$)		Speech ($n = 12$)		Significant Differences $*p < 0.05; **p < 0.01$	Overall F (2,33)
	Mean	Std Dev	Mean	Std Dev	Mean	Std Dev		
Mean move intervals ln(secs)	0.4	0.1	-0.1	0.15	0.27	0.33	** Delay > Direct ** Speech > Direct	** 30.6
Average extra moves (moves)	60.0	25.2	109.8	68.2	53.7	26.2	* Delay < Direct * Speech < Direct	** 5.7
Total time (secs)	1372	416	1522	752	1613	583		0.6

Table 1: Means for each of the conditions across the interactions style (standard deviations given in brackets). Group differences (using a Scheffé test) are given along with overall ANOVA interactions.

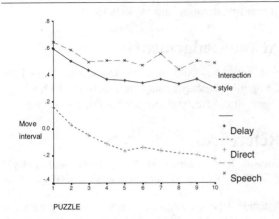

Figure 2: Move latency (ln(secs)) over puzzle

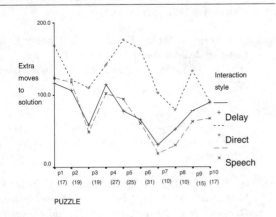

Figure 3: Extra (i.e. extra to the minimum solution path) moves to solution. Numbers in brackets show the minimum solution path for that puzzle.

The total task times are shown in Table 1. There were no differences between conditions. A 1×3 ANOVA showed no overall effect for interface ($F(2,33) = 0.6$). Post-hoc Scheffé tests revealed no group differences.

5 Interpretation and Implications

The results and analysis can be interpreted as follows:

- Delay and Speech interaction users show longer move intervals than Direct Manipulation users. This result indicates that extra cognitive reflection is taking place.

- Delay and Speech users show a saving in the number of moves taken to reach solution.

- There are no reliable differences between the interfaces in the total time to completion for this task.

The results show a significant saving for speech interaction, over direct manipulation, in the number of actions to reach solution for this problem solving task. Though Speech Interaction led to longer move intervals, their cumulative effect was not sufficient to influence total task time. The delay interface user showed a comparable problem solving saving.

Participants are sensitive to the types of puzzles they are solving. Figure 3 shows the extra moves to solution for the series of puzzles given to participants. Changes in the length of the minimum solution path (shown on the abscissa) influences participants behaviour. However, despite this influence, the series of means for Delay and Speech show very similar trajectories. It would appear that the advantage of Speech may be closely related to system delay.

The interpretation that Speech savings are primarily caused by delay is worthy of further investigation. As speech (and CPU) technology improves, the delay inherent in recognition software will decrease. If delay is the primary source of MSPS, then problem solving savings will decrease as recognition speed increases. On the other hand, if the necessity to symbolically reference objects is the primary source of MSPS, then problem solving savings will remain constant as recognition speed increases. An alternative mechanism for MSPS, Svendsen's 'learning mode' hypothesis (see Svendsen (1991) for an explanation of this mechanism) would predict that savings would remain constant. Clearly, it would be a powerful finding if speech at any speed of recognition supported problem solving.

Whatever the exact cause of MSPS, the effect has occurred here with current technology. The results show that speech interaction can, under the right circumstances, enhance problem solving.

There are several implications to these findings. First, if one is designing an interface for display-based problem solving, and speech is to be used, then speech may have some influence on how the tasks are performed. For some applications — hands-free situations or by disabled users — there is no option but to use speech. The designer should be aware there is a potential for speech to affect how an application is used.

A more powerful implication is that speech can support the user in carrying out tasks. MSPS effects are most potent for display-based 'transfer' tasks. Transfer tasks are tasks that require many operations to move the problem display through many problem states. If the problem only moves through a few problem states, then there would be no cumulative advantage in extra planning seen in problems such as the 8-puzzle.

Several tasks fall into the category of transfer problems. One category is navigation, either through hypertext systems or through virtual environments. Navigation is carried out by making a series of moves through an information space — particularly in immersive virtual environments. Choices of where to go next are made on assessing the current state of the information space. The information space is equivalent to the problem space. MSPS involves the user reflecting in order to take the shortest path through the problem space. So speech could be utilised, while a user is navigating, to encourage reflection to take the shortest path through the information space.

Another situation akin to transformation problems is process control. In process control the user may have to constantly alter the state of the system to keep it within certain parameters. MSPS, and therefore speech interaction, would encourage the user to plan before applying an input to the system. The input would be more effective at moving the user towards the goal state, thus requiring fewer inputs.

These are two example applications. Clearly, an important line of research is to verify the advantages of speech and identify the range of applications in which this advantage holds. It is also worth remembering these results indicate that problem solving savings can occur without increasing overall task time. Speech could be of particular value in situations where the number of actions the user can execute is at a premium.

To conclude, speech interaction should not be considered a neutral interaction style. Speech interaction can influence display-based problem solving. Speech can lead to a saving in the number actions taken to reach a goal. This saving is not always at the expense of longer total time spent on the task. There is a potential for speech to support problem solving tasks if the task is right. This potential needs further investigation and exploitation.

Acknowledgements

The authors would like to thank the School of Computer Science and Information Technology, University of Nottingham, for funding this project.

References

Ericsson, K. A. & Simon, H. A. (1993), *Protocol Analysis: Verbal Reports as Data*, third edition, MITP.

Golightly, D. & Gilmore, D. J. (1997), Breaking the Rules of Direct Manipulation, *in* S. Howard, J. Hammond & G. K. Lindgaard (eds.), *Human–Computer Interaction — INTERACT '97: Proceedings of the Sixth IFIP Conference on Human–Computer Interaction*, Chapman & Hall, pp.156–63.

Larkin, J. (1989), Display Based Problem Solving, *in Complex Information Processing: The Impact of Herbert A. Simon*, Lawrence Erlbaum Associates, pp.319–41.

Moore, A. (1993), Siuli's Maths Lesson: Autonomy or Control, *in* J. Benyon & H. Mackay (eds.), *Computers in the Classroom. More Questions than Answers*, The Falmer Press.

Norman, D. A. (1986), Cognitive Engineering, *in* D. A. Norman & S. W. Draper (eds.), *User Centered Systems Design: New Perspectives on Human–Computer Interaction*, Lawrence Erlbaum Associates, pp.31–62.

O'Hara, K. & Payne, S. J. (1998), "Effects of Operator Implementation Cost on Performance of Problem Solving and Learning", *Cognitive Psychology* **35**(1), 34–70.

Schmandt, C., Ackerman, M. S. & Hindus, D. (1990), "Augmenting a Window System with Speech Input", *Computer* **23**(8), 50–6.

Shneiderman, B. (1992), *Designing the User Interface: Strategies for Effective Human–Computer Interaction*, second edition, Addison–Wesley.

Svendsen, G. B. (1991), "The Influence of Interface Style on Problem Solving", *International Journal of Man–Machine Studies* **35**(3), 379–97.

Teal, S. L. & Rudnicky, A. I. (1992), A Performance Model of System Delay and User Selection Strategy, *in* P. Bauersfeld, J. Bennett & G. Lynch (eds.), *Proceedings of CHI'92: Human Factors in Computing Systems*, ACM Press, pp.295–306.

Ziegler, J. E. & Fahnrich, K. P. (1988), Direct Manipulation., *in* M. Helander (ed.), *Handbook of Human–Computer Interaction*, North-Holland, pp.123–33.

Human–Computer Interaction — INTERACT '99
M. Angela Sasse and Chris Johnson (Editors)
Published by IOS Press, © IFIP TC.13, 1999

The Explorer Bar: Unifying and Improving Web Navigation

Scott Berkun

Microsoft Research, One Microsoft Way, Redmond, WA 98052, USA.

scottber@microsoft.com

Abstract: The Explorer Bar is a component of the Internet Explorer Web browser that provides a unified model for Web navigation activities. The user tasks of searching for new sites, visiting favourite sites, and accessing previously viewed sites are simplified and enhanced by using a single user interface element.

Keywords: navigation, bookmark, design, hypertext, searching, browsing.

1 Introduction

The World Wide Web provides access to an enormous amount of information and resources. The primary usability issues with using the Web involve insufficient support for helping users find and return to individual Web pages. The Explorer Bar was designed to improve these usability problems by providing a single well designed user interface model for the most common set of Web navigation tasks.

2 The Design Problem

Three of the most problematic common end user tasks on the Web are: searching for new Web pages, returning to a bookmarked/favourite page, and returning to a particular non bookmarked page (Abrahms, 1997; Pitkow, 1996). For users with existing Web browsers these tasks were often cumbersome, and sometimes impossible.

Bookmarks or Favourites lists do help the user by providing a mechanism for remembering pages, but as that list grows the value of the mechanism decreases (Abrahms, 1997). It is also known that users frequently need to return to pages that are relatively close in chronological order but browsers may not be designed to support these needs (Tauscher, 1996).

3 The Design Solution

We separated the entire set of Web documents into more digestible groups that users would understand. We settled on three groupings: Web pages the user had not seen before, Web pages the user was interested in, and Web pages the user had visited before. We gave these groupings the names Search, Favourites and History for easier reference. As we sketched

out different ideas for solutions to the most common navigation problems, we recognized that there were strong similarities for how users might interact with these sets of information.

For example, when searching the Web using a search engine, users received a long list of search results. In formal and informal usability studies, we observed many users click on a result link which took them to a new site, click on several links on that site, and then recognize it was not the site they wanted. They would then use the back button repeatedly to return to the list of results and repeat the process with the next search result. We observed similar behaviour when users were trying to find a particular item in their Favourites or history lists. The critical problem was a loss of context. There was no easy way for the user to return to an important page during a searching process, or skip between multiple items in their Favourites list to find the one they needed. This behaviour is often referred to as spoke and hub navigation (Tauscher, 1996).

This indicated significant value in representing these different groups of Web pages in a similar way. The user could then learn a set of concepts once, and apply it to all of these different types of Web pages. We felt if we developed the right general model for navigating through lists of items, we could improve the usability of the most common navigation tasks performed with a Web browser.

4 General Model

We started by looking at existing mechanisms (Egan et al., 1989) for navigating through lists or hierarchies of information. In particular, we examined the Windows95 file management utility called Windows

Explorer. It displayed a hierarchical view on the leftmost 20% section of the screen, and a viewing area comprising the remaining 80%. The left area acted as a map or overview for what was viewed on the right. Clicking on an item in the left section caused the main area to navigate to the selected item. This was useful for advanced users who were familiar with the file system hierarchy.

In the context of Web browsing, we found several problems with Windows Explorer design. The hierarchical view on the left never displayed folder contents. If the user clicked on a folder, it would navigate the main window to show a list of the items in that folder. This behaviour was useful for file system maintenance, where the detailed information of each file is important. However, it forced the user to frequently navigate away from whatever you were viewing before.

This problem helped us recognize that we needed to help the user keep track of the relationship between the current page they were on, and the page they were trying to locate. We established a general principle: for Web navigation: the Explorer Bar should have it's own context. The bar would only navigate the main window if the user clicked on a specific page. If the user clicked on a folder or group of pages, it would open the folder in place to show the available pages. This allowed the user to view potential navigation targets without losing their current place in the Web browser.

5   Search

Helping users find new Web pages was a particularly problematic area (Pitkow, 1996). Search results are provided by the user's choice of Web search provider and each provider had control over how results were presented to the user. We knew that we were restricted to providing a framework for searching to work in, and that to a degree we were dependent on the providers to do a good job with much of the searching experience. We worked with the providers to develop a set of guidelines for search bar content that they would follow to obtain some level of consistency.

The first step was to figure out how to compress search results pages down to a size that would fit in the bar. We started with a design that could fit 10 search results inside the Explorer Bar, which approximated the number found on regular search results pages. During our exploratory tests of a prototype in the usability labs, all five intermediate participants were able to complete basic search tasks on the first try using the Explorer Bar. Tasks included generating a new query, looking through multiple results pages,

and clicking on different result links. The limited real estate forced us to leave out result information such as the URL or sample text. This caused problems in cases where there were poorly titled pages, and the user had no way to even guess which page was the best one without trying them all.

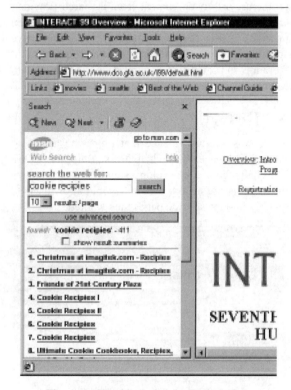

Figure 1: Searching using the Explorer Bar.

In response to this problem, we enabled an unused HyperText Markup Language (HTML) attribute called TITLE, to set the tool-tip property for a search result link. When the user moved their mouse pointer over a search link, a small window would appear that provided additional information, such as file size, Internet address, or text abstract. This helped offset the small screen real estate available to the bar, and helped users decide what link to use before clicking on it. We saw evidence that when noticed, the tool-tips improved user performance, however 2 of the 8 subjects did not even notice the tool-tips. In all cases users were still able to complete their tasks, but without discovering the tool-tips some tasks took longer. We accepted this as a reasonable tradeoff since we needed to balance the number of results we could fit, with how much information we could expose for each result. Tool-tips were the only option we knew of that didn't consume more real estate.

The tool-bar area of the search bar provided a 'next provider' button that allows the user to recast the current query to a different search provider without retyping, increasing the speed of using multiple sources. We also provided a 'new search' button that when clicked showed the user a list of available types of searches, grouped by task instead of by provider. This gave the user a way to recover from server problems, or broken content from a search provider. One special item in this list was a display of the ten previous queries they had entered. We did not have specific data on the recurrence of search queries, but Abrahms indicated that bookmark lists often contain references to searches.

6   History

There was strong evidence that improved access to viewed Web pages would help users (Tauscher, 1996). The challenge was to develop a simple way to organize the large lists of history data that would allow users to quickly find the specific pages they wanted.

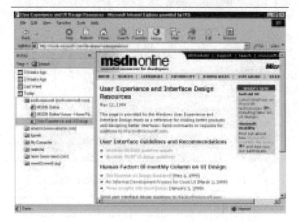

Figure 2: History using the Explorer Bar.

We started with a simple structure for the history list, organizing the data chronologically and then by site. This made it possible for a user to access a site simply by knowing when they visited, and then walking through the sites visited on that day. Figure 2 shows the History Bar in use, with the time and site fields visible. In addition, the history list intelligently groups visited Web pages based on their second level domain name, which would help speed locating a specific site from a list. We added this feature in response to watching users struggle to find sites with non-standard domain names (www1.microsoft.com) in a list that was alphabetized by the entire URL.

In the second usability study for history, seven participants with beginner to intermediate level Web experience were given navigation tasks that required returning to pages previously visited at different time periods. All of the users were able to complete

the navigation tasks using a combination of the History Bar, the back button, and on occasion some of the navigation assistance provided by the site's themselves.

We also designed the history list to act as constant indicator for where the user is currently located on the Web. By showing the list of Web domains, and indicating in the list where the user was with a gray bar, we were able to give the user some context for where they were on the Web. In the future we want to measure how effective this mechanism is for expediting use of the History Bar, and in reducing the user symptom of feeling lost in cyber-space.

To cover cases where a strict chronology was useless, such as when a user remembers the site they were on, but not when they went there, we added the ability to change the history list. A drop-down menu in the History Bar called 'view' allows the user to change the ordering to be sorted by date, by site, by frequency, or by the exact chronological order each individual pages was visited. To support scenarios where only text from the page is remembered, a searching feature is provided that searches the text of every page the user has visited that is still in the user's cache. For any page that has a match, its title is displayed conveniently in the History Bar allowing the user to easily try out different result hits.

7   Favourites

The user behaviour of navigating through existing favourites showed many of the same issues as navigating through a large history list (Abrahms, 1997). Even though the user created the Favourites hierarchy, the larger list grew the harder it became to find an individual item. We used the same general model for Favourites as we had for History. This made it possible to easily navigate from one favourite to another, and open or close folders without losing the current Web page in the main window. We also provided in place organization of favourites: the user could drag and drop items between folders, add items to favourites, and remove favourites items while viewing particular Web pages. This was mostly of value to intermediate and advanced who were familiar with the drag and drop convention.

Unfortunately, most novice and intermediate users were not aware that this convention could be used in the Explorer Bar. Nearly half of the 8 beginner and intermediate users tested on favourites tasks would open the favourites bar and fail to find a way to create folders or move items into existing folders. To improve access to these commands from the Explorer

Bar, we used a tool-bar strip underneath the title of the Explorer Bar to display command buttons.

We experimented with different visual elements, and text descriptions using an informal paper prototype with users of different experience levels. The simple approach of using the text label for each command was most effective, provided that the text labels for the commands would fit in the available space. In the final design, clicking on the Add button displayed the add to favourites dialogue, and clicking on the organize button displayed the organize favourites dialogue. We verified the success of these buttons in a smaller usability test after the tool-bar had been added. All of the participants were able to get to the add and organize dialogues through the Favourites bar.

Figure 3: Favourites using the Explorer Bar.

8   Conserving Real Estate

The Explorer Bar forced users to choose between maximizing the screen area for the Web page they are viewing, and maximizing their ability to navigate using the Explorer Bar. We experimented with different sized bars, and found 200 pixels to be a balanced tradeoff between effective page viewing and Web navigation. If we made the bar larger, many Web sites could not be viewed easily without horizontal scrolling. If we made the bar smaller, it was impossible to view lists of sites without horizontal scrolling. We knew based on survey data (Pitkow, 1996) that the majority of the population that could report resolution was using 800 × 600 or better screen resolution. The Explorer Bar used 200 pixels allowing 600 for page viewing. Users with larger resolutions would have a full 800 or greater pixel width for Web pages. We also made the Explorer Bar resizable to allow the user to customize the size to account for particularly troublesome pages.

To increase the user's control over available real estate, we provided a mode of the browser called full-screen. This removed all secondary menus, status and cosmetic elements, thereby maximizing the screen real estate for the content of the page. When in full-screen mode, the Explorer Bar assumes a special behaviour called auto-hide. The bar slides away off the left edge of the screen. The user can bring the bar back by moving her mouse to the left most edge of the screen. The bar then slides back onto the screen and can be used to navigate the browser to another page. As soon as the user has clicked on an item, or moved his mouse away from the bar, the bar slides back off the left edge of the screen. A tool-bar button and a menu command were provided to toggle in and out of full-screen mode.

For some tasks, such as moving between multiple search results or history items, it is useful for the bar to remain visible even while in full-screen mode. To enable this, we added a small pushpin button to the title area of the Explorer Bar. This button allowed the user to pin the bar in place for as long as necessary. When depressed, the bar would stay visible. If pressed a second time, it would return to auto-hide behaviour. Figure 5 shows the pushpin button.

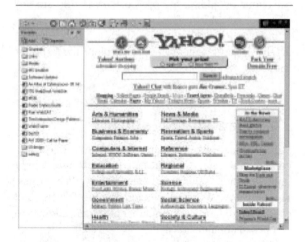

Figure 4: Full-screen mode in Internet Explorer.

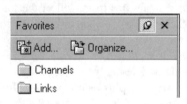

Figure 5: The pushpin button in full-screen mode.

9   Activating and Closing the Bar

There was a conflict between providing a single user interface element, and making sure that the critical features of the browser were easily discoverable. We experimented in sketches with having one tool-bar button for activating the entire set of bars, one button with a drop down list for each bar, and relying purely on the menus for activation of each bar. We could not think of one button label that could describe all of these functions in a way that would be sensible to users. The best compromise we found was to allow each function that used the bar to have it's own tool-bar button. The buttons would be mutually exclusive of each other, allowing the user to switch from one bar to another. Each button also acted as a toggle switch, turning a particular bar on or off.

In usability tests of initial designs we found that users often had trouble discovering how to close the Explorer Bar. Nearly half of the 8 intermediate users failed on their first few attempts to make the bar go away. They would complete the task of finding a specific page, but would not recognize that the active tool-bar button in the tool-bar worked as a toggle switch. We reinforced the discoverability of the toggle behaviour by adding a close box to the title area of the Explorer Bar. This provided a distinct visual affordance for closing the bar, and in follow up tests nearly all participants were able to close the Explorer Bar.

10   Problems with the Hierarchy View and Scrollbars

We examined the standard Windows95 tree view control and saw two places where changes might improve the usability of navigating Web pages. Removing the plus element for opening folders, and changing the limit on the number of folders allowed to be opened simultaneously.

Since the most common action users applied to a folder in the Explorer Bar was opening or closing, it followed that the largest visual target on the folder should provide those actions. The standard tree view design has a small plus to the left of the folder name that was the only way to open or close the folder. We modified the tree view in the Explorer Bar so that if a folder name was clicked, it opened. To select a folder for renaming or deleting, you needed to right click on it. We removed the plus element to simplify the tree view and make the most frequent task the easiest to perform.

Once we had a working prototype of the Favourites and History Bars, we discovered in our own usage that it was easy to get bogged down in the number of open folders. The user would either have to manually go back to close folders they were no longer using, or use the scrollbar repeatedly to maneuver around them. We accounted for this by automatically closing unused folders. If the user opened folder A, and then opened folder B, we would automatically close folder A for them. This did create some negative side effects. For advanced users, this behaviour made it more cumbersome to move items from one folder to another. Since advanced users were the minority, we decided to default to auto-closing folders. We added a switch to the program options for advanced users to turn this feature off.

We needed a user interface element inside the Explorer Bar to allow it to scroll. Large lists of bookmarks are common and cause obvious problems (Abrahms, 1997). We found that the standard scroll box consumed a large amount of real estate and was visually unappealing inside the Explorer Bar. We copied the scrolling affordances used elsewhere in Internet Explorer 4.0's tool-bars and menus, which provided a simple arrow at the top and bottom of the list whenever it was necessary.

Figure 6: The new scrollbar style.

After usability testing, we discovered that this new scrolling model had many problems. Unlike the standard scrollbar, this new affordance did now allow for easy paging of long lists, or for granular control over the pace at which items were scrolled. We reverted back to using the standard scrollbar control in version 5.0 of Internet Explorer.

11   Usability Testing Summary

Over the course of two versions of Internet Explorer (4.0 and 5.0), 6 different usability studies were conducted on different aspects of the Explorer Bar. In some tests only specific features were examined, such as favourites or Search feature, or specific concerns were examined such as the ability for users to close the Explorer Bar. In many instances usability tests for other aspects of the product touched on Explorer Bar issues and provided additional, though often more anecdotal, information.

Each usability study used from 5 to 10 participants, depending on the sophistication of the test design. The studies used a mixture of user backgrounds, ranging from Windows95 users with beginning Web experience (little or no experience with Internet), to advanced (high experience with internet). Verbal protocol was used as one of the primary methods of data collection, except in cases where we performed benchmarking or performance comparison tests between two different prototypes. In those cases time on task and error frequency were the only primary measures.

12 Future Applications

After our initial success with the Explorer Bar, we did some limited explorations into potential other uses. We added the ability to create horizontal Explorer Bars, than ran across the top or bottom of the browser. We expected that communication tasks such as chats or reading news information would work better in the horizontal form factor.

The major roadblock to other uses of the Explorer Bar is the mutual exclusion rule for each kind of bar (vertical or horizontal). To keep the interface simple, we allowed only one vertical Explorer Bar to be active at any time. For example, if the Favourites Bar is active, and the user clicks on the History button, the Favourites Bar goes away and is replaced by the History Bar. Horizontal bars follow the same rule when other horizontal bars are involved. However, the user is allowed to have one vertical bar and one horizontal bar at the same time. In general, mutual exclusion was the only design we could think of to keep turning individual bars on and off from becoming a complex task. Search, Favourites and History were critical parts of the user experience and we did not want to complicate those core functions in the name of enabling less frequent user tasks.

The vertical bar is most useful for navigation tasks. Any time the user needs to pick from a list of items, and move between them frequently, the vertical bar provides value. The ability to keep a separate context is likely to help the user stay on task and keep useful context. Good examples are table of contents lists, troubleshooting information, or help content. We considered moving Internet Explorer's help system to use the Explorer Bar, but hit the mutual exclusion problem: you couldn't view the help information for the favourites bar, and the actual favourites bar at the same time. Site maps for Web sites could work well in an Explorer Bar as well, provided there were guidelines or conventions for how sites design them. We experimented with site maps during Internet Explorer 4.0 but removed the feature for schedule and other reasons (Berkun, 1996).

We provided the ability for other software developers to add their own Explorer Bars to Internet Explorer. We expected that certain Web sites that are used as launching points, such as portals, could use an Explorer Bar to speed the user's access to specific pages or parts of the portal.

13 Conclusions

In working on the Explorer Bar we recognized four themes:

- There is value in applying the same user interface to diverse data sets provided the usage patterns for each are similar.

- Using a large percentage of real estate is acceptable to users if you are solving an immediate problem and providing discoverable ways to customize or deactivate items.

- History can be a very effective tool for Web navigation if you provide users with ways to mine useful data out of the large pile of history information.

- Standard user interface elements often have been thoroughly designed. Do not stray from them unless you have exceptional and well understood reasons. For example, reusing the standard scrollbar was the best choice for the Explorer Bar. However, in the case of the tree view, we had strong evidence that something different was required for the user tasks we were designing for.

Acknowledgements

There were many critical people that made this work possible: Steve Capps, Walter Smith, John Cordell, Chris Franklin, Chris Nyman, Gayna Williams, Lisa Sanford, Shawna Swanson, Jennifer Shetterly, Shawn Murphy and many others on the Internet Explorer 4.0 and 5.0 development teams. Without the major impact these individuals had, the Explorer Bar concept would never have been realized.

References

Abrahms, D. (1997), Human Factors of Personal Web Information Spaces, Master's thesis, Department of Computer Science, University of Toronto. http://www.dgp.toronto.edu/~abrahms.

Berkun, S. (1996), "Sitemaps in Internet Explorer 4.0", Microsoft Interactive Developer Magazine. http://www.microsoft.com/Mind/1196/preview1196.htm.

Egan, D. E., Remde, J. R., Gomez, L. M., Landauer, T. K., Eberhardt, J. & Lochbaum, C. C. (1989), "Formative Design-Evaluation of SuperBook", *ACM Transactions on Office Information Systems* 7(1), 30–57.

Pitkow, J. (1996), "GVU's 5th WWW User survey". http://www.cc.gatech.edu/gvu/user_surveys/survey-04-1996.

Tauscher, L. (1996), Evaluating History Mechanisms: An Empirical Study of Reuse Patterns in World Wide Web Navigation, Master's thesis, Department of Computer Science, University of Calgary, Alberta, Canada. http://www.cpsc.ucalgary.ca/grouplab/papers/.

Human–Computer Interaction — INTERACT '99
M. Angela Sasse and Chris Johnson (Editors)
Published by IOS Press, © IFIP TC.13, 1999

The Contribution of Thumbnail Image, Mouse-over Text and Spatial Location Memory to Web Page Retrieval in 3D

Mary P. Czerwinski, Maarten van Dantzich, George Robertson & Hunter Hoffman

Microsoft Research, One Microsoft Way, Redmond, WA 98052, USA.

{marycz,ggr,maartenv,a-hunhof}@microsoft.com

Abstract: We present an empirical evaluation of the contribution of pictorial image and spatial location information on the retrieval of previously stored Web pages. Subjects were given 100 snapshots of Web pages that they stored in spatial locations on an inclined plane in a desktop 3D environment (Data Mountain). We had them return and try to retrieve their pages again, using a variety of retrieval cues. Even though users had not seen their Web page layout for several months, their retrieval times were not significantly slower. In addition, on half of the trials, stored pages were not presented as thumbnail images of the Web pages but as blank icons. Taking the pictorial thumbnail images away initially led to a significant drop in subjects' ability to find the pages, although within a short period of time subjects were able to find the pages equally fast without the thumbnail information. These results indicate that the use of 3D visualization techniques such as those described in this paper can lead to improved user memory for where favourite or frequently used information is stored in an electronic environment.

Keywords: 3D information visualization, information retrieval, thumbnail images, spatial location memory.

1 Introduction

In a recent paper we described a desktop 3D environment for document management (Robertson et al., 1998), and reported that users retrieved documents reliably faster in this environment than with a traditional Web browser's bookmarking mechanism. Since our novel environment (which we call the Data Mountain) had a number of new features that might benefit the user, this paper attempts to tease apart the relative contributions of these features. In particular, we wanted to determine whether retrieval time is helped primarily by users' spatial memory for the location of a document or by the ability to do a visual match using thumbnail miniatures. We also wanted to determine if spatial memory is retained after a long period of time.

1.1 Spatial Cognition

There has been much research investigating the role of spatial memory on our ability to navigate and retrieve information in virtual environments (Darken, 1993; Darken & Sibert, 1996; Jones, 1986; Ruddle et al., 1997; Waller et al., 1998). Darken & Sibert (1996) empirically validated several principles that designers can follow if they strive to design easily navigable

worlds that promote the acquisition of a mental map of the space. These include the use of directional landmarks, gridlines, paths, boundaries and maps to help the user navigate more efficiently to targets. In addition, they recommend combining sensory modalities, like adding 3D sound cues to visual worlds, to aid the navigator. Interestingly, Darken & Sibert (1996) observed that if the space is not divided using these simple, organizing principles, then users will impose their own, conceptual organization upon the space. While we will not explore navigation in head-mounted 3D in this paper, we have leveraged several of the design principles espoused by Darken & Sibert (1996). For instance, we have included left-right and front-back spatialized audio as indicative of where information is in the 3D space. We have also included the use of passive landmarks and allowed users the ability to build a personal organization of their information over time.

Research on navigation has also shown that subjects build up spatial representations of environments by interacting with those environments over time (Montello & Pick, 1993; Franklin et al., 1992; Ruddle et al., 1997). In the study presented in this paper, we brought back a group of subjects to re-experience their spatial layout of Web pages that they themselves manually arranged in a 3D environment approximately 6 months earlier. These subjects had seen their layouts one additional time prior to this return visit. They returned 6 weeks after their first visit to retrieve their Web pages in a pilot study. There was no significant change in their speed at retrieving Web pages at that time, compared to the session in which the subjects created their layouts. In this study (their 3rd visit to our laboratory), an additional 4 months had gone by since the subjects had last seen their stored Web pages in the 3D environment. We were uncertain whether or not subjects would remember much about their layouts after such an extended period of absence. However, it was our hypothesis that the benefits of the 3D environment (3D perceptual cues and spatial arrangements) would enable subjects to either find their targets just as quickly as when they originally stored them, or at the very least quickly re-learn their layouts and find pages increasingly quickly over trials in the return session.

1.2   Textual Titles

In addition to spatial layouts in 3D, our subjects were provided with the title of a Web page whenever they moved their cursor over one. The work of Jones & Dumais (1986) has shown that the power of semantic labels as cues during retrieval is very strong, but document retrieval can benefit to some degree from the addition of spatial location knowledge. In their study, a condition that included both a semantic label and a specific spatial location for a document was superior to conditions that simply included the label only or the spatial location only. Therefore, we attached the text titles to the pages stored in our environment, and used 3D spatial locations to help users create an organization that made sense to them.

1.3   Clustering in Memory and Retrieval

According to the memory literature, people have a natural inclination to cluster items in memory when allowed to do so, and the amount of organization created (with or without experimenter-supplied category structure) strongly influences how easily the information is later remembered. Bousfield (1953) used a 60-item list comprised of 15 words from four distinct categories: animals, personal names, professions and vegetables. Although presented with these list items in a randomized order, subjects had a strong tendency to recall the items and write them down by category (e.g. owl, hawk, sparrow, carrots, cucumbers broccoli), evidence of what Tulving (1962) calls 'subjective organization' (as opposed to organization imposed by the experimenter or Web

browser). The Data Mountain facilitates a computer user's natural tendency to cluster information into meaningful, informal chunks (Miller, 1956) by making it easy for people to represent their Web pages in clusters on the mountain's surface. According to Mandler:

> "memory and organization are not only correlated, but organization is a necessary condition for memory ... all organizations are mnemonic devices" (Mandler, 1967, p.328-9).

We hypothesized that the clustered Web page layouts built by users would provide a strong mnemonic aid that might hold over long periods of absence from the user interface.

Bower et al. (1969) showed how such organization can improve the storage of information into long term memory. Words were presented in a hierarchy that was organized in a meaningful way for one group, or randomly for a second group. Subjects were given four trials to learn all the words in the hierarchy. On the fourth trial, subjects who studied the meaningful hierarchy performed with 100% accuracy, while those in the random condition only reached 62% recall accuracy on the fourth trial.

The memory literature is informative about what sorts of Web page representations are likely to lend themselves to this powerful mnemonic of clustering and which ones will not. Gollin & Sharps (1988) gave participants items derived from four categories (animals, medical things, vehicles, and kitchen things) with 10 items per category. For one group of subjects, the stimuli were photographs of the items (e.g. a photo of a lion). Another group got printed names of the items presented verbally only (e.g. LION). The category superiority effect was only found for the VERBAL items. Thus, the text titles and spatial segregation of clusters we used may prove essential for exploiting the organizational structure of items in memory during retrieval in 3D environments.

On the other hand, retrieval cues must be easily associated with the information being sought in a personal information space. The greater the number of features (cues) provided to a user during search that might benefit activation in memory for where that information is stored, the higher the probability of recall (Underwood & Schulz, 1960). Classical mnemonic research has documented that mental cues in the form of visual images are an excellent way to enhance memory for items. As a result, classical mnemonic procedures emphasize using vivid visual images to enhance memorability of information

(Patten, 1990). To increase ease of retrieval, the Data Mountain includes the thumbnail images of Web pages, in addition to the spatial and textual cues mentioned above. Unfortunately, little is known about the contribution of pictorial images during the storage and retrieval of Web pages. For instance, do pictorial cues provide better cues than either semantic labels or knowledge of the target page's spatial location? How do the various cues combine during the retrieval process?

In this study, we used a desktop 3D application to help tease apart what it is that subjects actually do remember about the spatial location of Web documents, as well as the contributions of Web page titles and their pictorial images (thumbnails) on the retrieval of those pages. It was our hypothesis that the Web page title, its unique spatial location on a user's desktop, and its pictorial thumbnail image would combine to form a powerful retrieval cue that would aid users trying to return to a Web site after a long period of time has passed since their first visit.

2   The Desktop 3D Application

The desktop 3D environment used in this study is referred to as the Data Mountain, and has been described in detail elsewhere (Robertson et al., 1998), so only a short overview of the environment will be provided here. Currently the Data Mountain is being used as a 3D alternative to a Web browser's favourites or bookmark mechanism.

The Data Mountain uses a planar surface (a plane tilted at 65 degrees; see Figure 1), on which documents are dragged. A document being dragged remains visible so that the user is always aware of the surrounding pages. The user can place her Web pages (or documents) anywhere on the mountain. In practice, the user creates meaning by organizing the space in which she lays out these documents. In our study, there were many ways to organize the Web pages in the space. Each user was allowed to freely choose a method and alter it at any point throughout the study. It is our belief that the manual layout of Web pages in 3D space is a strong determinant of spatial location memory during storage.

The Data Mountain allows users to quickly see which Web pages have been stored in a particular cluster via inspection of each Web page's thumbnail, and its title in 'mouse-over' text. A user need simply rest the mouse over a Web page and the mouse-over text is popped up immediately. Note that mouse-over text has some similarity to hover tool-tips (where causing the mouse to hover over an object for some period of time brings up a tool-tip), except that in our

case the appearance delay is zero. In addition, a yellow halo surrounds the Web page and the title so that it is clear to which page the title text belongs.

Figure 1: Data mountain with 100 user-organized Web pages.

There are a number of 3D depth cues designed to facilitate spatial cognition. The most obvious are the perspective view, accompanying size differences, and occlusion, particularly when pages are being moved. Simple, circular landmarks on the surface of the Data Mountain also offer obvious cues, which may or may not be utilized during page placement as well as retrieval. Less obvious, but also quite important, are the shadows cast by the Web pages, and the spatialized audio cues that provide the user with right-left, front-back differential audio feedback as Web pages are moved in the space.

Previous research (Robertson et al., 1998) showed that the Data Mountain was a significant improvement in design over the standard, hierarchical tree mechanisms used to store Web pages today (e.g. Microsoft's Internet Explorer 4.0). However, in that study users stored and retrieved 100 Web pages in a same-day session. It was not clear whether the observed advantage for the Data Mountain environment would hold over a long period of absence. In addition, it was not clear from the earlier research which features were contributing to superior performance in the Data Mountain. To explore the contribution in performance from the thumbnail images, we did not show the thumbnails for half of the retrieval trials. Subjects were only shown a white placeholder outlined in black where each thumbnail would have occurred on these trials, as shown in Figure 2. If the thumbnail image was one of the stronger contributors to performance when subjects retrieved Web pages, we would hypothesize that performance would be especially bad on these trials after 6 months. However, if subjects could leverage their spatial location memory for Web pages, perhaps performance would be no slower in this condition.

Figure 2: Same data mountain without thumbnails.

3   User Study

3.1   Subjects

Nine subjects, all of whom participated in a previous study investigating the Data Mountain, returned after approximately 6 months. All subjects had created a layout of 100 Web pages during a storage phase in the first session, and then retrieved each of those pages in the same session.

In order to qualify for participation in the initial study, all users had to successfully answer a series of screening questions pertaining to Web browser and Internet knowledge. Subject ages ranged from 18 through 50 years old, and all had normal or corrected-to-normal vision. There were 5 females in the return sample.

3.2   Stimuli and Equipment

The study was run on high-end Pentium machines (P6–300s), with 128MB of memory, and a 17-inch display. The machines had either an Intergraph Intense 3D Pro 1000 or 2200 graphics accelerator card and ran WindowsNT4. One hundred Web pages were used in this study; fifty pages were selected randomly from PC Magazine's list of top Web sites and fifty pages selected randomly from the Yahoo! database. Figure 1 shows an example of a subject's Data Mountain layout that was stored and reused for this study. Each subject was provided with the layout created in a session 6 months prior to the current session. For the trials in which the Web page thumbnails were turned off, a simple outline of a white placeholder image was viewable by the subject.

3.3   Procedure

Subjects were briefly welcomed back to the lab and informed that they would be seeing their old Data Mountains, and would be asked to find the same 100 Web pages they stored previously. Subjects were also told that, on half of the trials, the thumbnail images would be missing from their view of the Data Mountain. Once subjects indicated that they understood the instructions, the study was started. Subjects were allowed 5 minutes to review their Data Mountain before starting the retrieval trials.

During the test session, participants were shown one of four different retrieval cues and asked to find the related page. The four retrieval cueing conditions were: the title of the page, a one or two sentence summary of the page's content, a thumbnail image of the page, and all three cues simultaneously (called the 'All' cue). Participants saw 25 trials of each cueing condition, for a total of 100 retrievals. All pages presented for retrieval were seen in the first visit's storage phase and thus present in the environment. The Web pages to be stored and the subsequent retrieval cues were presented in a random order for each participant. Figure 1 shows an example of each of the four styles of retrieval cues. If a participant could not find the target page within two minutes, a 'time-out' was enacted and the participant was instructed to proceed to the next retrieval task. A Web page retrieval was defined as bringing a page forward to a close-up position by clicking on it. Users were not explicitly discouraged from producing incorrect retrievals.

This version of the study was run in blocks of 10 trials, with the display alternating between having a thumbnails 'on' (Figure 1) and a thumbnails 'off' (Figure 2) view of the subject's organization. The study always started with the thumbnails turned on for each subject, as a way of allowing them to familiarize themselves with their layouts over the first 10 trials.

Four main dependent variables were used in this study:

1. Web page retrieval time;

2. the number of incorrect pages selected prior to finding the correct page;

3. the number of trials for which the participant failed to retrieve the correct page within the two-minute deadline; and

4. the participants' subjective ratings of the software.

These dependent measures are assumed to be powerful indicators of subjects' ability to locate items

Title	Title, Summary & Thumbnail	Summary	Thumbnail
Bezerk — The Free On-line Entertainment Network	Bezerk — The Free On-line Entertainment Network. The new, FREE premier on-line entertainment network features YOU DON'T KNOW JACK the netshow, the on-line version of the irreverent quiz show party game CD-ROM	The new, FREE premier on-line entertainment network features YOU DON'T KNOW JACK the netshow, the on-line version of the irreverent quiz show party game CD-ROM	

Table 1: Examples of the four cueing conditions used in the study.

in space. If subjects know where their Web pages are, even with the thumbnails turned off, retrieval performance should be efficient. These dependent measures will be compared to the same performance measures collected in the initial session, when subjects were first introduced to the Data Mountain.

4 Results

4.1 Reaction Times — Memory Retention after Absence

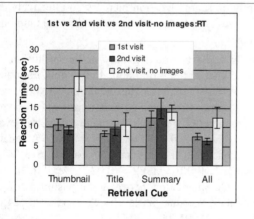

Figure 3: Average retrieval times to find 100 pages.

We analysed retrieval time performance comparing Web page retrieval time after a short break vs. after approximately 4 months delay (thumbnail-visible trials only). We found no reliable difference between performance immediately after storing the 100 Web pages compared to having a 4 month interval of not interacting with the layout on the Data Mountain. This is shown in Figure 3. A 2×4 (length of delay $\times$ retrieval cue condition)

ANOVA with repeated measures showed no significant main effect of delay on reaction time, $F(1,8) < 1$, NS. The main effect of retrieval cue condition was highly significant, $F(3,24) = 11.92, p < 0.001$, MSE $= 12.11$. No significant interaction between length of delay and retrieval cue type was found, $F(3,24) = 1.72, p > 0.10$, NS.

4.2 Number of Incorrect Retrievals

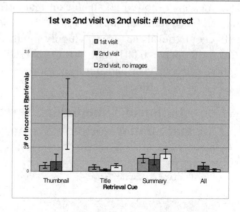

Figure 4: Average number of incorrect pages retrieved before finding the correct page for the first and second visit.

There was no reliable difference in the number of incorrect Web pages visited prior to finding the right page when comparing the two retrieval sessions (thumbnail-visible trials only). This is shown in Figure 4. A 2×4 (length of delay $\times$ Retrieval Cue Condition) ANOVA with repeated measures showed no reliable main effect of delay on number of incorrect pages retrieved, $F(1,8) < 1$, NS. A reliable main effect of retrieval cue condition was found, $F(3,24) = 4.27, p < 0.05$, MSE $= 0.04$, and no interaction between length of delay and retrieval cue type was evident, $F(3,24) < 1$, NS.

4.3   Failed Trials

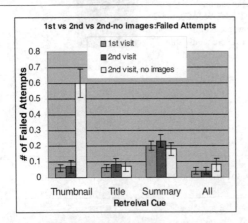

Figure 5: Average number of trials on which a Web page could not be found for first and second visit.

We observed no reliable difference between the number of trials in which the target Web page could not be found between the immediate and delayed retrieval sessions (thumbnail-visible trials only). This is shown in Figure 5. A 2×4 (length of delay between study and test $\times$ retrieval cue condition) ANOVA with repeated measures showed no significant main effect of delay on failed retrieval rates, $F(1,8) < 1$, NS. The main effect of retrieval cue type was highly significant, $F(3,24) = 10.34, p < 0.001$, MSE = 0.11. No reliable interaction between visit and retrieval cue type was found, $F(3,24) < 1$, NS.

4.4   Contribution of Thumbnails, Text Title and Spatial Location Memory

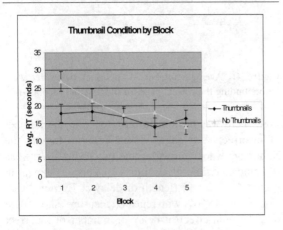

Figure 6: Average retrieval time by thumbnail condition and trial block (1 block = 10 trials).

In the next set of analyses, we examined the contribution of the thumbnail image to the speed and success of finding the target Web page. Only the 6 month delayed retrieval condition included trials when the thumbnails were turned off. We observed an initial significant slowdown in retrieval times when the thumbnail images were not available for inspection. However, this difference went away quickly after the first 2 blocks of the session (see Figure 6). Also, it is clear from looking at Figures 3–5 that the significant drop in performance was due to the thumbnail cueing condition only. Looking only at the results of the 6 month delayed retrieval phase, a 2×4 (thumbnail visible vs. thumbnail not visible $\times$ retrieval cue condition) ANOVA with repeated measures showed that removing the thumbnail images led to significantly longer reaction times, $F(1,8) = 10.97, p < 0.01$, MSE = 42.69. A significant effect of retrieval cue type was evident, $F(3,24) = 6.42, p < 0.002$, MSE = 30.77, and a significant interaction between visibility of the thumbnail and retrieval cue type was found, $F(3,24) = 6.03, p < 0.003$, MSE = 33.68. A separate repeated measures ANOVA examining block (5) $\times$ thumbnail condition (2) showed that there was a significant effect of block on retrieval times, $F(4,32) = 3.8, p = 0.013$, and no other effects were significant. In other words, thumbnail images were more important for speedy retrieval in the first few blocks, but over time subjects learned to rely on spatial location memory so effectively that there was no difference between seeing the thumbnail or not.

In addition, looking only at the results of the second visit, a 2×4 (thumbnail visible vs. thumbnail not visible $\times$ retrieval cue condition) ANOVA with repeated measures showed that removing thumbnail images led to significantly more failed retrievals, $F(1,8) = 12.42, p = 0.008$, MSE = 0.02. A reliable effect of retrieval cue type was found, $F(3,24) = 15.40, p < 0.001$, MSE = 0.02. And there was a reliable interaction between the visibility of the thumbnail and the retrieval cue type, $F(3,24) = 30.36, p < 0.001$, MSE = 0.33.

Finally, looking only at the results of the second visit, a 2×4 (thumbnail-visible vs. thumbnail-not-visible $\times$ retrieval cue condition) ANOVA with repeated measures showed that removing thumbnail images led to a marginally significant increase in number of incorrect pages retrieved, $F(1,8) = 4.35, p = 0.07$, MSE = 0.32. Retrieval cue type had no reliable effect on incorrect retrieval rates, $F(3,24) = 2.04, p = 0.14$, MSE = 0.75. A marginally significant interaction between visibility of the thumbnail and retrieval cue type was found, $F(3, 24) = 2.50, p = 0.08$, MSE $= 0.43$.

4.5 Subjective Ratings

After retrieving all 100 Web pages, subjects filled out a subjective questionnaire in each session. Figure 2 shows subjects' subjective ratings for their first and second retrieval sessions in this study. In general, the ratings were very favourable of the 3D environment. In two cases, subjects were reliably more positive after the 6 month delayed session. Specifically, subjects rated the software as feeling more familiar in the second session, and they also felt that the spatial layout of their Web pages aided their performance 6 months later more than in the initial session. All significant differences were determined by a paired t-test, one-tailed, $\alpha = 0.05$. (We used a one-tailed test because we were looking for improvements of subjects' ratings over time.)

In addition, we had subjects rank the relative effectiveness of four of the features in the Data Mountain that we hypothesized might benefit retrieval of the Web pages. A rank of 1 meant that a feature was considered the best for retrieval, 4 was the worst ranking. On average, subjects ranked the thumbnail images as the most helpful (avg. = 1.8), followed closely by the mouse-over text (avg. = 2.0) and the spatial location of the Web page on the Data Mountain (avg.rank = 2.2). The spatialized audio feedback was consistently ranked the least helpful cue (avg.rank = 4.0). These differences were significant as determined by a Kruskall-Wallis non-parametric test, $\chi^2(3) = 24.02, p < 0.001$.

Questionnaire Item (Scale: 1 = Disagree, 5 = Agree)	1st Session	2nd Session
I like the software I used today.	3.87	3.8
The software was easy to use.	4.1	4.2
The software feels familiar.	3.4	**4.1
It was easy to find the page I was looking for with the software.	3.67	3.56
Laying items out spatially helped me find them later.	3.56	**4.2

Table 2: Average satisfaction ratings for 2 retrieval sessions, on scale 1 (worst) to 5 (best). (** indicate significant differences between the 2 sessions).

We asked subjects to tell us how they found Web pages when the thumbnails were turned off in a multiple-choice format (guessed the location, knew the relative location or knew the exact location). Of the nine subjects, only 2 said that they simply guessed where the Web page was. The remaining 7 subjects said that they remembered the general vicinity of the Web page. We often observed subjects honing in on the cluster of Web pages they knew to contain the target page, after which they would use the mouse-over text to find the specific target page.

5 Conclusion

We developed a 3D environment for storing favourite Web pages, called the Data Mountain. Previous studies had shown the benefits of using the Data Mountain for retrieving stored Web pages over traditional, hierarchical tree user interfaces. However, it was unclear from those studies what particular features of the 3D environment were benefiting performance. This study explored the contribution of the thumbnail images, spatial location, and mouse-over text on the Data Mountain. With the thumbnail images viewable, subjects were no slower after an absence of approximately 4 months in retrieving Web pages previously stored. When the thumbnail images were turned off, performance was disrupted, but only initially and only for the thumbnail retrieval cueing condition. After 2 blocks of trials, subjects were just as fast at retrieving their Web pages with absolutely no pictorial cues. This is quite interesting, given that subjects often chose the thumbnail image as their preferred cue. Of course having the thumbnail images turned off when the thumbnail cue was presented was an extremely difficult trial type, and accounted for the majority of the disruption in subjects' retrieval performance in the no thumbnail condition. Although subjects preferred to use the thumbnail image during retrieval, they could perform just as well using the mousing-over text title and the spatial location of the page. We think that this is an important finding for the design of 3D environments, especially for instances in which no visual features are available to distinguish one item from another. For example, if a subject is looking through a variety of electronic documents that are primarily text, there will be little distinguishing visual detail in a thumbnail or iconic representation. Our findings suggest that, by allowing the subject to manually lay out their data in 3D space, and by providing a title on mouse-over, subjects will be able to remember where they have stored their non-pictorial information quite well. Especially if one considers the fact that our subjects had not seen their 3D layouts for a 4-month period, the present results indicate that this combination of pictorial image, spatial location and mouse-over text title can be quite effective. We encourage designers to consider these issues when designing information spaces.

Future work will explore these design issues in larger, 3D information visualizations. We were surprised to see how robust subjects' memory for their layouts was, and we intend to continue to examine how this spatial memory holds in new designs where the information spaces scale up to 100s and 1000s of Web pages or documents. In addition, we would like to explore subjects' spatial memories with and without the benefit of mousing-over text titles, in order to better isolate just how much each of those particular cues are contributing to retrieval performance in new designs. Finally, the thumbnails used in this study were snapshots of Web pages. Future research will explore whether it is possible to design more effective 'smart icons' as one means of improving ease of memory retrieval in the Data Mountain.

Acknowledgements

We would like to thank Sue Dumais for her feedback on the study, Scott Tiernan for help with the statistical analysis of this study, and the user interface research group at Microsoft for their work on the Data Mountain visualization.

References

Bousfield, W. A. (1953), "The Occurrence of Clustering in the Recall of Randomly Arranged Associates", *Journal of General Psychology* **49**, 229–40.

Bower, G. H., Clark, M. C., Lesgold, A. M. & Winzenz, D. (1969), "Hierarchical Retrieval Schemes in Recall of Categorical Word lists", *Journal of Verbal Learning and Verbal Behaviour* **8**, 323–43.

Darken, R. P. & Sibert, J. L. (1996), Wayfinding Strategies and Behaviours in Large Virtual Worlds, *in* G. van der Veer & B. Nardi (eds.), *Proceedings of CHI'96: Human Factors in Computing Systems*, ACM Press, pp.142–50.

Darken, R. P. and. Sibert, J. L. (1993), A Toolset for Navigation in Virtual Environments, *in* S. Ashlund, K. Mullet, A. Henderson, E. Hollnagel & T. White (eds.), *Proceedings of INTERCHI'93*, ACM Press/IOS Press, pp.157–65.

Franklin, N., Tversky, B. & Coon, V. (1992), "Switching Points of View in Spatial Mental Models", *Memory and Cognition* **20**, 507–18.

Gollin, E. S. & Sharps, M. J. (1988), "Facilitation of Free Recall by Categorical Blocking Depends Stimulus Type", *Memory and Cognition* **16**, 539–44.

Jones, C. B. (1986), *Systematic Software Development Using VDM*, Prentice–Hall International.

Jones, W. & Dumais, S. (1986), "The Spatial Metaphor for User Interfaces: Experimental Tests of Reference by Location versus Name", *ACM Transactions on Office Information Systems* **4**(1), 42–63.

Mandler, G. (1967), Organization and Memory, *in* K. W. Spence & J. T. Spence (eds.), *The Psychology of Learning and Motivation*, Vol. 1, Academic Press, pp.327–72.

Miller, G. A. (1956), "The Magical Number Seven, Plus or Minus Two: Some Limits on our Capacity for Processing Information", *Psychological Review* **63**, 81–97.

Montello, D. R. & Pick, H. L. (1993), "Integrating Knowledge of Vertically-Alligned Large-Scale Spaces", *Environment and Behavior* **25**, 457–84.

Patten, B. M. (1990), "The History of Memory Arts", *Neurology* **40**, 346–52.

Robertson, G., Czerwinski, M., Larson, K., Robbins, D., Thiel, D. & van Dantzich, M. (1998), Data Mountain: Using Spatial Memory for Document Management,, *in Proceedings of the ACM Symposium on User Interface Software and Technology, UIST'98*, ACM Press.

Ruddle, R. A., Payne, S. J. & Jones, D. M. (1997), "Navigating Buildings in Desk-top Virtual Environments: Experimental Investigations using Extended Navigational Experience", *Experimental Psychology* **3**, 143–157.

Tulving, E. (1962), "Subjective Organization in Free Recall of Unrelated Words", *Psychological Review* **69**, 344–54.

Underwood, B. J. & Schulz, R. W. (1960), *Meaningfulness and Verbal Learning*, Lippincott.

Waller, D., Hunt, E. & Knapp, D. (1998), "The Transfer of Spatial Knowledge in Virtual Environment Training", *Presence* **7**, 129–44.

Human–Computer Interaction — INTERACT '99
M. Angela Sasse and Chris Johnson (Editors)
Published by IOS Press, © IFIP TC.13, 1999

Spatial Data Management Systems: Mapping Semantic Distance

T. Cribbin & S.J. Westerman

Psychology Institute, Aston University, Birmingham, UK.

{t.cribbin,s.j.westerman}@aston.ac.uk

Abstract: This study examined the extent to which the semantic proximities identified by automatic text analysis routines match human cognitive models of document collections. Experiment 1 tested the reliability of human judgements of document similarity and compared these ratings with commonly used automatic text analysis algorithms. Analyses showed relatively poor inter-rater reliability but moderate levels of shared variance between human and computer solutions. However, this depended to some extent, on the document set used and the expertise of the human raters. In Experiment 2 participants were asked to identify and describe semantic dimensions appearing within 2D plots of computer generated information spaces. Qualitative analysis found generally poor inter-rater agreement. Again this tended to vary between document sets.

Keywords: automatic text analysis, information retrieval, individual differences, database.

1 Introduction

1.1 Background

Recent advances in computing have led to an information explosion. Through networking technologies, most notably the Internet, vast information resources are now available to an ever increasing user population. Indeed, many people are finding that their work is becoming more knowledge oriented requiring them to access electronic information quickly and effectively.

Computer algorithms that are able to retrieve documents by simple query matching have been in use for some time. For example, search engines, such as Yahoo! or HotBot, that employ this method are widely used on the Internet.

The user inputs one, or more, words that relate to information required and, following a search, the computer presents a list of documents that contain some, or all, or the search terms. The advantage of such a simple approach to information retrieval is speed. Thousands, or often millions, of documents can be scanned within just a few seconds. The penalty for this speed, however, is poor accuracy. Although the computer simply matches terms, the users and designers of information systems are likely to define the information required with respect to broader concepts or themes. This leads to problems of 'synonymy' and 'polysemy'. There are usually many words and phrases that can be used to describe

a particular concept. Users are unlikely to be able, or bothered, to input exhaustive lists of synonyms, and different users may employ different terms to describe the same concept.

This difficulty of terminology results in the search engine only retrieving a small proportion of relevant documents. The converse problem, 'polysemy', refers to the fact that a single word often possesses several context-dependent meanings. Take, for example, the following phrases — "Computer memory has never been cheaper" and "Today's storms were the worst in living memory". If 'memory' was the search term, both phrases would cause a 'hit' from the search engine although they refer to very different subjects. As a consequence, relevant documents may be only a small proportion of thousands of retrieved items, with the only criterion to help the user identify relevant documents (without reading each document) being a ranking, based on the frequency of term hits. What is needed is a way of placing documents within a context that is both natural and logical to the user.

1.2 Spatial Data Management Systems

One possible means of achieving this is through the use of Spatial Data Management Systems (SDMSs). SDMSs enable users to access electronically stored information through the implementation of Graphical User Interfaces (GUIs) that exploit real-world navigational skills. Such systems represent documents spatially, in either two or three dimensions,

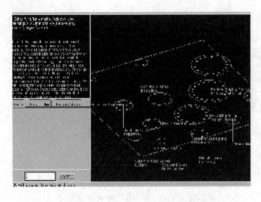

(a) JAIR space (Mark Foltz, MIT AI Labs).   (b) PathFinder Network (Chaomei Chen, Brunel University).

Figure 1: Example screenshots of SDMSs.

in a configuration that describes the underlying semantic relationships between the documents. The assumption is that users will find searching more intuitive as similar documents tend to cluster together. Figure 1 shows example screen shots from two SDMSs that are currently under development.

The authors of this paper are currently engaged in an EPSRC funded research project investigating SDMS usability issues. Later stages of the project will be concerned particularly with examining the cognitive demands associated with the navigation and interpretation of two- vs. three-dimensional information spaces. However, at the present time we are investigating cognitive issues relating to the assessment of document similarities.

1.3   The Creation of a Semantic Space

One of the main difficulties with SDMSs is that the semantic content of each document must be assessed in relation to other documents in the corpus (set of documents), in order that each can be positioned within a spatial setting.

Although in some instances it may be possible to use human judges to index documents (e.g. if the document set is small and unchanging), given the huge amount of information now available within the Internet and other electronic information resources, the advantages of using computer algorithms to map semantic relationships within textual databases are clear and significant. Moreover, in contrast to traditional database media, digital information is becoming more diverse and unstructured and this, in itself, is presenting new challenges to designers of information retrieval systems.

The task facing the programmer who wishes to implement an effective automatic text analysis (ATA) algorithm is a complex one, particularly when the content of the corpus contains casual language or poor spelling. Obviously, computers have no innate linguistic ability, and yet the algorithm must be both sensitive and tolerant to the subtlety and diversity encountered in modern language.

One technique is to parse the contents of electronic documents, using grammatical rules to assess the meaning of sentences. For example, knowledge bases such as WordNet (Kominek & Kazman, 1997; Smeaton & Quigley, 1996) store concept information in the form of 'is-a' hierarchical relationships between words. However, such databases must be constantly updated and may never be complete.

An approach that deals more easily with rapidly changing knowledge domains is the vector space model (VSM). Although computationally more expensive in general operation, as a real-time system it offers far greater flexibility. Traditionally, VSM applications have used individual words as terms. Analysis begins with routines that parse the target corpus for unique terms. This forms a list of words (target vocabulary) where each is a component in a vector assigned to each individual document (see Figure 2). The computer then proceeds to count the frequency with which each term occurs in each document, and to assign the value to the corresponding vector cell. Each vector component (term count) can be thought of as a dimension within a t-dimensional vector space where t is the number of unique terms occurring within the document corpus.

The resulting vectors are then compared, in a pairwise fashion, by measuring their similarity (or dissimilarity). There are a number of different algorithms that can be used to this. Some can be referred to as 'extrinsic' (Korfhage, 1995) as the similarity measure is effectively an angle within vector space and is dependent on the location of the origin. In contrast, Minkowski-based metrics reflect distance (dissimilarity) between points in multidimensional space and can be thought of as 'intrinsic' or absolute, being independent of the origin. Extrinsic measures are thus more flexible and allow operations like removing the centroid (origin) which can be helpful in the pursuit of removing least variant or 'stop' terms (e.g. 'and', 'into'). Those used in this study are described below in Figure 3, where i and j refer to the two document vectors being compared. Similarity (dissimilarity) refers to the resulting coefficient indicating the degree of semantic relatedness found between documents i and j.

	Doc_1	Doc_2	Doc_3	...	Doc_n
$Term_1$	1	2	0		0
$Term_2$	0	1	3		2
$Term_3$	0	0	1		1
$\vdots$					
$Term_t$	1	0	0		1

Figure 2: Term by Document matrix.

These algorithms are used to generate an $n \times n$ matrix, that describes the similarity (dissimilarity) of each possible pair of documents (see Figure 4). This matrix is transformed, using Multidimensional Scaling (MDS), into spatial co-ordinates. MDS provides an optimal spatial solution, by preserving, as far as possible, the original inter-item distances. An SDMS can be used to represent the resulting document co-ordinates. The MDS process is not a perfect one. A certain degree of 'stress' (or error variance) usually remains within a solution. From a scaling point of view, a three-dimensional, virtual reality enabled interface has the potential to retain more of the original variance than a two-dimensional representation.

The basic word frequency approach tends to be insensitive to the relationships between words and their prefixed or suffixed variants. Variant spellings (e.g. 'behavior' and 'behaviour') also suffer in this respect. van Rijsbergen (1979) details a 3-point plan which involves stripping prefixes and suffixes out of the text, using look-up tables before it is analysed. 'Stop' words are also removed in the same way. This is a cumbersome approach and still does not tackle the problem of variant spelling. A more

recent technique, pioneered by (Damashek, 1995), goes some way towards addressing these problems. Instead of words, the n-Gram approach uses character strings of fixed length (n) as component terms. These strings can contain whole words or parts of one or more words. For this reason, analysis using n-Grams has the advantage of being more tolerant of mis- or variant spellings as well as being more sensitive to the relationships between words and their prefixed and suffixed variants.

Dice:
$$\text{Similarity} = \frac{2\sum_{k=1}^{t} \text{term}_{ik}\, \text{term}_{jk}}{\sum_{k=1}^{t} \text{term}_{ik} + \sum_{k=1}^{t} \text{term}_{jk}}$$

Cosine:
$$\text{Similarity} = \frac{\sum_{k=1}^{t} \text{term}_{ik}\, \text{term}_{jk}}{\sqrt{\sum_{k=1}^{t} \text{term}_{ik}^2 + \sum_{k=1}^{t} \text{term}_{jk}^2}}$$

Overlap:
$$\text{Similarity} = \frac{\sum_{k=1}^{t} \text{term}_{ik}\, \text{term}_{jk}}{\min(\sum_{k=1}^{t} \text{term}_{ik}, \sum_{k=1}^{t} \text{term}_{jk})}$$

Asymmetric:
$$\text{Similarity} = \frac{\sum_{k=1}^{t} \min(\text{term}_{ik}, \text{term}_{jk})}{\sum_{k=1}^{t} \text{term}_{ik}}$$

Minkowski:
$$\text{Dissimilarity} = \sqrt[r]{\sum_{k=1}^{t} (\text{term}_{ik} - \text{term}_{jk})^r}$$

Figure 3: Similarity/dissimilarity algorithms — see (Rorvig, 1998).

	Doc_1	Doc_2	Doc_3	...	Doc_n
Doc_1	1.0	0.5	0.3		0.4
Doc_2	0.5	1.0	0.2		0.2
Doc_3	0.3	0.2	1.0		0.6
$\vdots$					
Doc_n	0.4	0.2	0.6		1.0

Figure 4: Example of matrix used for MDS.

1.4 Study Aims

So far, in this paper, SDMSs have been identified as a possible means of improving access to large textual databases. Further, techniques for automatically analysing text, so that semantic content can be mapped to spatial position within an SDMS, have been described. However, an important area for investigation concerns how such representations of information relate to human cognitive models. If the nature of the semantic relationships expressed by the computer model differ from that of the user then information retrieval performance may be hindered rather than enhanced. In the remainder of this paper we report two experiments that directly address this issue.

2   Experiment One

The purpose of this experiment was to establish:

1. The degree of human rater agreement as to the similarity of documents contained within corpora (inter-rater reliability). It is not clear the extent to which different individuals are able to agree on the concepts described by document sets. If agreement is low it could be predicted that a single ATA would be inadequate to represent the range of user cognitive models.

2. The extent to which human rater agreement is influenced by expertise. It was predicted that the agreement between expert participants would be greater than that between non-experts.

3. The degree of agreement between human ratings and various ATA metrics across a range of corpora. The assumption is that it is beneficial to have a good match.

4. Whether a single ATA algorithm (see Figure 3) is consistently closer to human ratings across different corpora.

In order to examine these issues two small documents sets, each comprising eight abstracts from psychology journal papers, were prepared. Participants were required to rate the similarity/dissimilarity of all possible pairs of documents within each corpus. The task was presented in a context-free manner (i.e. participants were not instructed to rate pairs according to any particular criteria). These were compared with a variety of ATA solutions for the same information.

2.1   Method

2.1.1   Participants

Two groups were sampled, psychology experts and non-experts. Experts were drawn from the psychology teaching staff and post-graduate psychology research students of Aston University. Non-experts were 2nd year undergraduate psychology students. 12 experts and 24 non-experts took part with equal numbers from each group being assigned to each of two document sets. All participants were paid.

2.1.2   Procedure

Document sets comprised psychological abstracts drawn from the social-science section of the BIDS on-line database using simple search queries. Set one comprised abstracts retrieved using the query 'Schizophrenia'. Set two resulted from the query 'Working+Memory'. Eight documents were selected for each set from the chronologically most recent 32 retrieved items.

Human judgements were collected using purpose-written software. Participants were presented, in a random sequence, with all possible pairings of documents in each set. They were required to indicate, using a visual analogue scale, the degree of similarity they perceived for each pairing. Participants also completed a 20 item multiple choice test, presented prior to the rating task. Two sets of questions were formulated, one for each document set. These included items relating to a general knowledge of the subject area, as well as more specific questions relating to the abstracts contained in the corpora. The time taken for the whole procedure varied (being self-paced), but most people completed within 40 minutes.

Another computer program, that incorporated all of the ATA algorithms described above (see Figure 3), was used to analyse each document set. Due to their greater flexibility (Damashek, 1995; Gustavsson, 1996) *n*-Grams, rather than whole words, were chosen as the term type for input into the algorithms. The program built a target vocabulary by moving a window 5-characters in width across the whole document corpus, with each unique 5-gram being stored as a separate element of a the first dimension of a two-dimensional array (terms by documents). The corpus was then rescanned one document at a time and 5-gram frequencies stored in their respective elements. Finally, inter-document similarities were computed using each algorithm.

2.2   Results

The test scores of experts and non-experts were compared for both document sets. Although there was a tendency for psychology experts to score more highly, this difference was not significant, $t(34) = 0.81$. Consequently, additional high and low test scoring groups were created using a median split, and these were included in subsequent analyses.

Inter-rater reliability was computed as the mean inter-rater correlation between participant rating sets (vectors comprising ratings for 28 unique document pairs). Tables 1 & 2 summarize the results for both document sets. It is interesting to note the difference in reliability between the two document sets, with inter-rater agreement being higher for Document Set 1. Also of note are the group effects within document sets. As expected psychology experts showed a higher level of agreement than non-experts and the ratings of 'high test score' participants were more similar than those of 'low test score' participants. While these differences were not significant for Document Set 1, within Document Set 2 both high scorers on the test, $t(70) = 1.95, p < 0.05$, and psychology experts, $t(79) = 1.89, p < 0.05$, showed a significantly higher level of agreement.

	Non-experts	Experts	Low test score group	High test score group	Overall
Mean	0.32	0.39	0.32	0.37	0.34
Std Dev.	0.16	0.19	0.15	0.16	0.16
Min	0.00	0.02	0.01	-0.01	-0.01
Max	0.66	0.73	0.60	0.73	0.73
Valid N	66	15	21	55	153

Table 1: Inter-rater reliability for Document Set 1 ('Schizophrenia').

	Non-experts	Experts	Low test score group	High test score group	Overall
Mean	0.12	0.23	0.10	0.18	0.14
Std Dev.	0.20	0.18	0.18	0.17	0.20
Min	-0.34	0.03	-0.32	-0.11	-0.34
Max	0.63	0.59	0.48	0.52	0.63
Valid N	66	15	36	36	153

Table 2: Inter-rater reliability for Document Set 2 ('Working+Memory').

Participant ratings were correlated individually with the computer generated ATA ratings. Participant ratings were also averaged for each expertise group and these mean ratings were correlated with a range of different ATA metrics. The resultant coefficients (Tables 3 & 4) show several interesting patterns. First, it is clear that when using mean participant ratings, human–computer agreement was highest when extrinsic (angular) measures of similarity were applied. These metrics are quite similar in terms of the arithmetic involved, particularly cosine and dice, and so it is unsurprising that all yielded similar coefficients. Minkowski ratings were inferior in terms of human equivalency, although these ratings were still significantly correlated with mean human judgements, with the exception of non-expert participants rating Document Set 2. Overall, Dice and Cosine shared the most variance with human ratings. Also of

note, the mean of coefficients computed for individual participant rating sets was considerably lower than those coefficients computed from the mean human ratings. This possibly results from the considerable variation between participant rating sets.

Also of interest was the effect of topic familiarity on Participant-ATA agreement. No significant differences, for any of the metrics, were found between the 'expertise' groups in this respect. However, promising correlations (given $n = 18$) were found between Participant-ATA correlations and test scores. Participants obtaining higher scores tended to provide ratings that matched those of the ATA algorithms more closely, with this trend being consistent across both document sets. Coefficients ranged from weak ($r = 0.19$, n.s.) to modest ($r = 0.44, p < 0.05$) with most falling somewhere between 0.30 and 0.40.

As can be seen in Tables 3 & 4, there were clear differences between document sets in terms of human-ATA shared variance. Significant differences were found between sets for all metrics used ($p < 0.05$).

	Non-expert A	Expert A	Non-expert B	Expert B
Cosine	0.43	0.44	**0.72	**0.61
Dice	0.45	0.47	**0.75	**0.62
Overlap	0.40	0.43	**0.68	**0.55
Asymmetric	0.41	0.48	**0.67	**0.61
Minkowski	0.36	0.37	**0.55	**0.47

$n = 28, *p < 0.05, **p < 0.01$
Note: A = mean correlation between participant ratings and ATA; B = correlation between mean participant ratings and ATA.

Table 3: Human–computer agreement, Document Set 1 ('Schizophrenia').

	Non-expert A	Expert A	Non-expert B	Expert B
Cosine	0.20	0.24	*0.43	**0.46
Dice	0.20	0.21	*0.43	*0.41
Overlap	0.15	0.23	0.32	*0.41
Asymmetric	0.20	0.27	**0.45	**0.50
Minkowski	0.13	0.24	0.21	*0.39

$n = 28, *p < 0.05, **p < 0.01$
Note: A = mean correlation between participant ratings and ATA; B = correlation between mean participant ratings and ATA.

Table 4: Human–Computer agreement, Document Set 2 ('Working+Memory').

2.3   Discussion

It is apparent, from these experimental results, that inter-rater reliability is dependent on the corpus under consideration, but that it is, at best, modest. The highest inter-rater reliability was found for experts assessing Document Set 1. It may be that, for this experiment, reliability was influenced by the 'context free' nature of the task, and that if participants were involved in a more specific database search then inter-individual agreement with respect to document similarity would be greater.

It should also be noted, the experimental design was such, that participants' knowledge of corpus increased with successive pairwise ratings of documents. Consequently it seems reasonable to assume that criteria on which ratings were based were refined. As pairs of documents were presented for rating in a random order, this would impose a general degree of 'noise' across the resulting rating set. This, however, may not be an unrealistic reflection of inter-individual variation, in that this process (the gradual acquisition of knowledge relating to a corpus) would also be expected when searching an unknown database for information.

One of the principle aims of this study was to establish the degree of shared variance between computer generated similarity ratings and those made by human raters. Results for two small document sets show moderate to good agreement between human and computer ratings with most correlations falling within the range +0.4 to +0.7. Highest levels of shared variance in all conditions resulted from extrinsic measures, in particular Dice and Cosine. It is possible that the Minkowski metric was disadvantaged by the fact that vector lengths are not standardized in this algorithm, thus there is no control over document length variability.

There was no consistent effect of expertise on shared variance (human-ATA) for either document set. This was surprising given the significant differences found between the groups in terms of inter-rater reliability. Slightly stronger effects were found with respect to subject knowledge test score but this only came close to significance with the Document Set 2 data. Significant differences in participant-ATA coefficients between document sets appeared consistently across all metrics, although with only two sets for comparison the reasons for this are uncertain, and further research is required to address this issue.

Interestingly, shared human-ATA variance was considerably greater when correlations were calculated on the basis of mean participant ratings, as opposed to taking the mean correlations between individual participant ratings and each ATA algorithm. Given the low inter-rater reliability this suggests that while there are broad individual differences in the way people judge the content similarity of documents, the ATA algorithm is representative of general human opinion rather than a particular style or strategy.

3   Experiment Two

In the previous experiment it was apparent that agreement between individuals as to the similarity of documents in a corpus was relatively poor. Similarly, although ATA algorithms were able to achieve a good approximation of human ratings, the correlations with human raters was only moderate. This raises the question as to whether automatically generated semantic dimensions identified will be interpretable to human users of resulting SDMSs. In order to investigate this issue, Experiment 2 required participants to identify dimensions within computer-generated spatial solutions of the same two document sets.

3.1   Method

For each of the document sets, used in the previous experiment, the ATA assessment of document similarity (based on the cosine algorithm) was used in conjunction with MDS to generate two sets of three-dimensional coordinates. From these, two paper and pencil forms were developed. Form 1 used data computed from Document Set 1 with Form 2 using data from Document Set 2. Each form consisted of three document maps showing the spatially represented document sets from different perspectives (XY, ZX, YZ). Documents were represented on the maps (see Figure 5) using numbered points. The full text of the document sets were included with each form for reference.

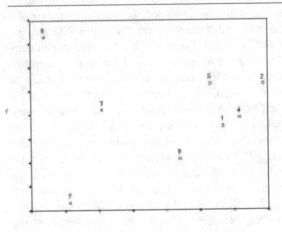

Figure 5: Document map.

Participants were required to study each document map and, having referred to the texts, identify one or more semantic dimensions. Participants marked a dimension by drawing a line across the map. The only constraint being that the line had to pass through a centre point marked on the map. This was to simplify the subsequent coding process. For each dimension drawn, participants were required to give a brief description. Descriptions could be either bi-polar (e.g. about anxiety — about depression) or uni-polar (e.g. degree of reference to the articulatory loop). After each description participants also expressed a rating of confidence in their decision using a five point scale.

Six copies of each form were distributed. Of these, five sets of Form 1 ('Schizophrenia') and three sets of Form 2 ('Working+Memory') were returned. This eventual sample comprised five female and three male participants. All conformed to the 'expert' criteria used in Experiment 1. None of the participants had seen their assigned document set prior carrying out the task. All participants were paid.

3.2 Results and Discussion

Discussions with participants who returned forms revealed that all found the task to be extremely difficult. Nevertheless, all returning participants managed to identify at least one dimension for each document map. Coding of responses was achieved by separating each map into 8 sectors split at equal (45 degree) intervals (see Figure 6). As dimension lines were all drawn through a centre point, this meant each identified dimension could be placed into one of four orientation categories (1, 5; 2, 6; 3, 7; 4, 8), based on the sectors associated with the end points of the line. In instances where a line straddled two categories (e.g. was vertical or horizontal) the description was placed into both categories.

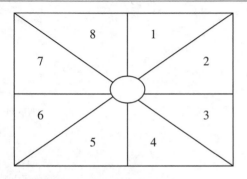

Figure 6: Coding scheme for Experiment 2.

When all dimension descriptions were combined into orientation categories it was clear how little

agreement there was between participants. Agreement was more common amongst Form 1 ('Schizophrenia') participants. Two or more similar dimension descriptions were found in four out of the twelve cells (4 orientation categories × 3 document maps). Only one such case was found for document set two ('Working+Memory'). The poorer inter-rater reliability found in Experiment 1 for this Document Set may indicate that it was harder to rate, and the results of this experiment suggest that concepts also were more difficult to identify. This may be because the set was more homogeneous in content. As with Experiment One, further research on a broader range of document sets would be useful.

4   Overall Conclusions

It would seem that agreement between raters of document similarity is relatively poor. However, this is dependent, to some extent, on the contents of the corpus be assessed, and the expertise of the raters. Given this, it is surprising that computer algorithms for ATA performed comparatively well, with correlations with mean human ratings generally stronger than between individuals. We take this to reflect the fact that computer algorithms provide a good approximation of the average human rating.

Interestingly, when asked to identify dimensions that had been generated in this way, people had great difficulty. This may be due to the amount of information loss that occurs within the MDS process. Again this appeared dependent on the contents of the corpus. Nevertheless, these results strongly suggests that SDMSs should incorporate techniques for identifying and labelling semantic dimensions, and further research might usefully address this issue.

Acknowledgements

Figure 1a provided by Mark Foltz, MIT AI Labs. Figure 1b provided by Chaomei Chen, Department of Information Systems and Computing, Brunel University, UK. This figure can be found at http://www.brunel.ac.uk/~cssrccc2/.

References

Damashek, M. (1995), "Gauging Similarity with n-Grams: Language-independent Categorization of Text", *Science* **267**(5199), 843–8.

Gustavsson, J. (1996), "Text Categorisation using Aquaintance", http://www.student.nada.kth.se/ f92-jgu/c-uppsats/Cupps.e.html.

Kominek, J. & Kazman, R. (1997), Accessing Multimedia Through Concept Clustering, *in* S. Pemberton (ed.), *Proceedings of CHI'97: Human Factors in Computing Systems*, ACM Press, pp.19–26.

Korfhage, R. (1995), "Some Thoughts on Similarity Measures", *SIGIR Forum* **29**(1), 8.

Rorvig, M. (1998), "Images of Similarity: a Visual Exploration of Optimal Similarity Metrics and Scaling Propertties of the TREC Topic-Document Sets". Submitted for review by Journal of the American Society for Information Science.

Smeaton, A. & Quigley, I. (1996), Experiments on using Semantic Distances Between Words in Image Caption Retrieval, *in* H.-P. Frei, D. Harman, P. Schauble & R. Wilkinson (eds.), *SIGIR'96 Proceedings of the Nineteenth Annual International ACM SIGIR Conference on Research and Development in Information Retrieval*, ACM Press, pp.174–80.

van Rijsbergen, C. (1979), *Information Retrieval*, Butterworth–Heinemann.

Human–Computer Interaction — INTERACT '99
M. Angela Sasse and Chris Johnson (Editors)
Published by IOS Press, © IFIP TC.13, 1999

Do Thematic Maps Improve Information Retrieval?

Kasper Hornbæk & Erik Frøkjær

Department of Computing, Universitetsparken 1, DK-2100 Copenhagen Ø,
Denmark.
{kash,erikf}@diku.dk

Abstract: Thematic maps in the context of information retrieval are tools that graphically present documents and characterising terms. We investigated the usefulness of thematic maps in a laboratory experiment comparing a thematic map with a command language interface. Six subjects solved eight search tasks producing ten hours of logged and tape-recorded data. The experiment revealed no improvement in the quality of the documents retrieved when using a thematic map. A majority of the subjects considered the thematic map pleasant to use and thought that useful information was found on the map. However, searching took longer time using the thematic map compared with the boolean interface. Several subjects occasionally misinterpreted the structure and content of the map. The common expectation that thematic maps improve information retrieval lacks empirical underpinning and is in the present study only weakly confirmed.

Keywords: user study, information visualization, information retrieval, interaction, thematic map.

1 Introduction

This paper describes an exploratory investigation comparing a visual information retrieval interface (VIRI) and a command language interface. The background for this study is an appreciation of the importance of user interfaces in information retrieval (IR), the growing interest in VIRIs, and the few empirical studies of such interfaces.

The user interface of an IR system is of crucial importance to the interaction between user and system, and to the information retrieved. Different interfaces to the same search engine may lead the user to dissimilar results, and alter the search process. Special support of information searchers beyond traditional command language interfaces may increase searchers' performance and satisfaction by supporting formulation of queries and browsing of documents (Shneiderman, 1998; Hearst, 1999), and influence the number of queries formulated and the search strategies and tactics employed (Hertzum & Frøkjær, 1996).

In the 1990s there has been a continually growing interest in visual user interfaces to IR systems. VIRIs graphically display queries, documents, or meta information. Such interfaces have been expected to support formulation of queries, to facilitate browsing of document collections, and to support assessment of the relevance of documents. The usefulness of

VIRIs supposedly is rooted in the characteristics of the human visual system, in the popularity and efficiency of graphical user interfaces generally, and in the concentration of information displayed in a VIRI.

Even though more than 20 interfaces satisfying the above definition of VIRI have been described in the literature — cf. Shneiderman (1998), Hearst (1999) — few studies provide any empirical consolidation of the claims on the usefulness of visual interfaces. We expect that empirical investigations of the usefulness of VIRIs will raise new research questions and point to promising ways of improving VIRIs.

The remainder of the paper is structured as follows. We first delineate the work done on VIRIs and the underlying hypotheses about the advantage of VIRIs. The next two sections present the method used in our empirical investigation and the results of this investigation. The results are discussed and a conclusion is drawn.

2 Thematic Map Interfaces

Hearst (1999), Shneiderman (1998), and Gershon et al. (1998) describe VIRIs and the underlying assumptions. This paper focuses on a subset of VIRIs called thematic map interfaces. The term thematic map designates an information retrieval interface that depicts themes in a document collection on a two or three dimensional map, showing documents and characterising terms in an analogy to a geographical map.

The literature proposes numerous hypothesis about the general advantages of VIRIs and the more specific benefits of thematic map interfaces. VIRIs are claimed to improve the quality of the search, to improve the search process, and to improve the subjective satisfaction with the information retrieval system. Especially, in virtue of the overview produced by a thematic map, the quality of open-ended or explorative information retrieval tasks is believed to be supported by VIRIs (Chalmers & Chitson, 1992). It is also commonly assumed that searchers will perform faster because they rely on their perceptual rather than their cognitive capabilities (Korfhage, 1991). With respect to the search process, it has been argued that VIRIs will support users in their initial orientation in a system and in their endeavour to express their information needs (Shneiderman, 1998). The graphical arrangement of documents and terms on a map is expected to support decision on whether or not a document is relevant. Thematic maps are also thought to inspire the user in finding documents that would otherwise have been unnoticed (Lin, 1997). VIRIs are also conjectured to increase subjective satisfaction. These claims will form the hypotheses of the empirical investigation described in Sections 3 and 4.

2.1 Previous Work

Thematic map interfaces were first introduced to IR by Xia Lin — cf. Lin (1997). Lin used an algorithm devised by Kohonen to construct a two dimensional representation of document collections. The technique was demonstrated using two collections, one indexed by 140 titles, one by 660 titles, keywords, and abstracts. Through an iterative procedure, the Kohonen algorithm organizes documents using similarities in the words occurring in the documents. Major themes in the collection are extracted and the documents grouped according to those themes. Lin's thematic map interface shows documents and terms in distinct areas, where each area is characterised by the term occurring most frequently in the documents in that area. Consequently, the map is thought to convey information about salient terms and the overall structure of the document collection. In a recent experiment, Chen et al. (1998) created a thematic map interface to 110,000 Web pages. Furthermore, Chen and his colleagues added some interactivity to the Kohonen map by making it possible to click on an area of the map and get a new thematic map, showing themes only from the Web pages in that area.

Another group of thematic map interfaces is based on multidimensional scaling (MDS), a family of statistical projection techniques that maps documents into low dimensional space (Chalmers & Chitson, 1992; Wise et al., 1995). In the BEAD system documents are distributed in a three dimensional space using physical modelling of documents (Chalmers & Chitson, 1992). So-called forces between documents are calculated using keywords in the documents thus grouping documents according to themes. Wise et al. (1995) also uses multidimensional scaling to create a topological map of themes in a large document collection (>20,000 documents). The map shows themes in the corpus, with related themes adjacent. The system described in Wise et al. (1995) also shows the strength of the different themes in the collection as the height of the topological structures representing themes.

2.2 Empirical Investigations

Few empirical investigations of VIRIs have been published and only a couple treat thematic maps. Lin investigated how 68 users solved simple search tasks on different kinds of paper-based thematic maps — cf. Lin (1997). With respect to search time Lin concluded that the Kohonen-map was as good as a humanly constructed map for locating titles and significantly better than a random arrangement of documents.

Chen et al. (1998) made a comparison of a thematic map with browsing the hierarchical structure of the Internet search site Yahoo. 31 subjects tried to locate a Web page which contained "something of interest to you" (Chen et al., 1998, p.587). First the subjects tried to retrieve an interesting page using either the thematic map or the hierarchical structure. Afterwards subjects were to repeat the search task using the other interface. Chen et al. found that subjects were able to browse a thematic map and locate relevant information. However, searching in the map after a page already found was inefficient. Chen et al. also found that subjects seemed to like the graphical aspects of the map and thought that browsing using a map was a convenient way of searching for information. However, some subjects had difficulties in understanding the map and the words on the map.

As a consequence of the meagre empirical understanding of thematic map interfaces, the hypotheses mentioned above are largely untested. In a recent review, Gershon et al. (1998) point out that we need to make information visualization systems that are easy to use. Further, Gershon et al. argue that we should design human- and usage-centred information visualizations. This challenge is being faced here, based on the assumption that empirical knowledge about the use of VIRIs is necessary for designing useful visual interfaces.

3 Experimental Method

In order to study differences in the interaction process between a non-graphical information retrieval interface and a VIRI, a command language and a thematic map interface were constructed. The command language interface allowed subjects to formulate queries using boolean logic, to scan the result of a query, and to inspect full-text. In the following this interface is called the boolean interface. The thematic map was constructed using multidimensional scaling. In addition to the thematic map the VIRI had exactly the same functionality as the boolean interface. Therefore, observed differences in searching behaviour and in the search results between the two interfaces are attributable to the presence or absence of the thematic map.

The experiment was conducted employing a within-group design with interface type as the independent variable. Six subjects participated in the experiment solving eight tasks each, four task with each interface. The order of tasks as well as the order in which the subjects experienced the two interfaces were alternated, minimising learning effects. The hypotheses for the experiment were taken from the literature, outlined in Section 2. Tasks were given to the subjects on separate sheets concisely describing the search task. Four of the experimental tasks explicitly described the documents that were to be found and what would count as a satisfactory answer, for example "Find the paper by Rudolf Darken on wayfinding in virtual worlds." The remaining four tasks were aimed at a broader group of documents and could be answered in more diverse ways, e.g. "Imagine that you are to give a talk on the use of computers in education. What is available on that topic?" The experiment was conducted in a dedicated lab with subjects who were master thesis students in computer science. All subjects had self-acclaimed knowledge about human–computer interaction, the subject area of the document collection used, and all had experience in using boolean logic in IR systems.

During the experiment, queries, inspection of full-text, and interaction with the map were logged. The subjects were encouraged to think aloud while searching. The think aloud utterances were recorded on tape. Before solving the search tasks, the subjects were interviewed concerning their personal and educational background and search experience. A short post-search interview about the satisfaction with and usefulness of the two interfaces was also conducted.

3.1 Boolean Interface

The boolean interface is shown in Figure 1. The user may formulate queries using search terms in combination with the boolean operators AND, OR, and NOT. The documents retrieved in response to a query are shown in an unranked list. The full-text of documents can be displayed by double clicking on the titles/authors of the retrieved documents. The full-text is automatically formatted using information about document structure; the appearance of the documents may therefore be different from the original article or conference paper. Full-text is presented within one second.

The experimental interfaces give access to 436 documents from conferences and journals on human–computer interaction. The documents were taken from HCILIB, an experimental IR system developed at University of Copenhagen (Perstrup et al., 1997). The documents accessible through the thematic map and boolean interface were indexed using full-text where non-content bearing words (stop-words) had been removed and the terms stemmed — see Salton & McGill (1983) for a description of these standard information retrieval techniques.

Figure 1: The boolean interface used in the experiment. In the edit box in the upper part of the screen search terms and boolean operators may be entered. Below the edit box are shown the stemmed terms used in the search. On the lower part of the screen are shown the author and title of the retrieved documents in an unranked list. If one clicks on one of the titles the full-text is shown.

3.2 Thematic Map Interface

The thematic map was constructed using multidimensional scaling (MDS) (Borg & Groenen, 1997). The MDS algorithm constructs a two dimensional arrangement of documents using a measure of similarity between documents. Document similarity was calculated from counts of words in the documents, using the cosine similarity measure (Salton & McGill, 1983). The MDS algorithm calculates the two dimensional arrangement through minimising the difference between the original inter-document similarity and the distances between documents in the two dimensional arrangement. The resulting thematic map is shown in Figure 2.

Terms describing themes were placed on the thematic map together with the documents. The terms on the map were selected by first calculating the discrimination value (Salton & McGill, 1983) for all terms and then placing the 20 terms with the largest discrimination value on the map. Intuitively, a term having a high discrimination value occurs frequently in some documents and rarely in others, for example 'evaluation' in this document collection. Such terms is here used for describing documents in which they frequently occur. The position on the map of the individual terms were found by calculating the 'mass' midpoint of the square of the number of occurrences of the term in all documents. The most frequent stem of a term was used as the actual text displayed on the screen.

The thematic map offers several ways of interacting with the VIRI that link the thematic map, the document list, and the query text. All documents on the map retrieved by a query are coloured yellow. Likewise, all terms on the map occurring in a query are coloured yellow. If the user selects one or more documents on the list of retrieved documents, the position of those documents are displayed on the map by a different mark than other documents. If the mouse is moved over a document on the map, the title and author of the document is shown in a pop-up box. It is also possible to right click with the mouse on a document on the map to see the full-text of documents.

If the user wants to enlarge a portion of the map it is possible to zoom. Zooming is smooth and is accomplished by holding down the left mouse button. It is always possible to zoom out to see the entire document collection. There is constantly about 20 terms on the visible portion of the map. When a user zooms on the map more terms with a decreasing discrimination value become visible. The thematic map described here employs a wider range of interaction techniques than maps described in the literature. A wider range of interaction techniques was suggested by Chen et al. (1998) as a way to improve thematic maps.

4 Results

In analysing the behaviour of the subjects the data logs were integrated with the verbal protocol. The statistical analysis was done using analysis of variance (ANOVA) and t-tests after removal of persistent differences between subjects and between different search tasks — cf. Hertzum & Frøkjær (1996). The quantitative analysis focused on confirming the qualitative results and describing search behaviour on the thematic map.

4.1 Documents Retrieved and Search Time

Table 1 shows the number of documents marked as relevant by the subjects upon using the two interfaces. There is no significant effect of interface type upon the number of documents retrieved ($F(1, 0.07), p > 0.79$). Nor is there any significant difference in the number of documents marked as relevant between the two interfaces ($F(1, 0.36), p > 0.55$). The relevance was judged by the first author. There is no significant difference between interfaces either, if relevance is approximated as documents marked relevant by more than one subject ($F(1, 0.32), p > 0.57$).

The time taken to complete the search tasks is shown in Table 2. Subjects use significantly longer time in the visual information retrieval interface compared with the boolean interface ($t = -2.975, p < 0.01$). There are also large individual differences in task completion time; averaged over the eight tasks the slowest subject took twice the time of the fastest. Within individual tasks solved using the same interface, task completion time differ by a factor of seven.

	Interface type	
	Boolean	Visual
Relevance	(N = 113)	(N = 108)
Relevant	66% (75)	77% (83)
Partial relevant	26% (29)	16% (17)
Non-relevant	8% (9)	7% (8)

Table 1: Documents marked as relevant by the subjects in the two interfaces. Relevance is expressed as one of three levels: relevant; partial relevant, for example documents about multimedia in response to a task on interfaces using sound; and non-relevant, that is documents containing no information relevant to the task.

Notable was the large proportion of time subjects used on scanning full-text. On the average one-third

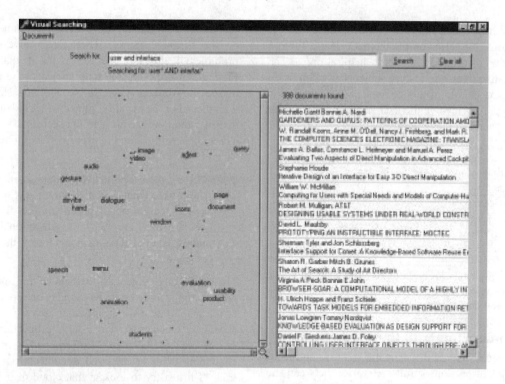

Figure 2: The thematic map interface used in the experiment. The input area in the upper part of the display as well as the list of document titles and authors to the right are identical to the boolean interface. On the map to the left documents are shown as dark and bright dots. The terms on the map are supposed to describe the contents of the documents around them. Documents retrieved by entering the query 'user and interface' are bright (yellow) on the map. The scrollbars next to the map allow navigation when there is zoomed on a region of the map.

of the time used for searching was spend on inspecting full-text, trying to judge relevance of the document or to locate useful search terms.

| Time per task | Interface type | |
	Boolean	Visual
Mean	10.8 (6.2)	14.2 (7.0)
Minimum	1	2
Maximum	22	25

Table 2: Time elapsed searching per task, in minutes. Searching in the visual interface is significantly slower than using the boolean interface. 24 tasks were done in each interface. Standard deviation is given in parenthesis.

4.2 Queries and Terms

The difference in the use of queries in the two interfaces is shown in Table 3. There is no statistically significant difference between the numbers of queries issued in the two interfaces ($F(1, 0.16), p > 0.6$), but there is a tendency towards issuing less complex queries using the thematic map ($t = 1.91, p < 0.07$). The average number of constituents of a query

(counting terms and boolean operators), was 2.8 in the thematic map as against 3.4 in the boolean interface.

| | Interface type | |
| | Boolean | Visual |
No. queries	(N = 105)	(N = 112)
Mean	4.4 (4.0)	4.7 (3.2)
Minimum	1	0
Maximum	17	11
Average number of constituents	3.4	2.8

Table 3: Queries in the boolean and visual interfaces. The table shows the average number of queries and query constituents, i.e. terms and operators, used in solving a task. One search task was solved exclusively using the thematic map, hence zero as the minimum number of queries using the map.

The think aloud protocol has been analysed as to where the inspiration to search terms came from. Inspiration to search terms is divided into four categories: 1) inspiration from the text describing the search task, 2) inspiration from association or ways invisible in the think aloud protocol, 3) inspiration from the titles and full-text of documents, and 4) inspiration from terms on the thematic map. Table 4 shows the distribution of term inspiration. The thematic map seems to inspire subjects as often as do the full-text or title of a document. Such inspiration would typically involve the user seeing a term on the map and then using that term in a query.

Inspiration to terms from:	Interface type	
	Boolean (N = 101)	Visual (N = 91)
Task description	56% (57)	51% (46)
Association	34% (34)	30% (27)
Title/Full-text	10% (10)	9% (8)
Thematic map	–	11% (10)

Table 4: Inspiration to search terms. The table shows the number of search terms unique to each solution of a task divided between different sources of inspiration.

4.3   Interacting with the Thematic Map

The subjects' use of the thematic map, scanning of titles, and inspection of full-text varied between the interfaces. This search behaviour may be described in terms of interaction shifts. An interaction shift is a change from one interaction mode (e.g. formulating queries) to another (e.g. scanning titles), as it can be detected from the log and the verbal protocol. Significantly more interaction shifts happen when using the VIRI than when using the boolean interface ($t = -2.957, p < 0.01$). This is partly because 14 out of 24 tasks in the boolean interface was solved by issuing one or more queries and then inspecting titles and full-text. That way of solving a task involves only one interaction shift, while the average number of shifts in the VIRI were six. The analysis of interaction shifts also show the different use of queries in the two interfaces. With the boolean interface the queries occur in sequences of average length 2.8, while with the visual interface queries are interwoven with browsing on the map and inspection of titles and full-text (the average number of queries without interaction shifts is 1.5).

Browsing on the map was preferred to scanning list of titles/authors. In two out of three searches the interaction with the visual interface started with the formulation of a query; the remaining tasks were begun by browsing the map. In the cases where the interaction with the visual map began with a query the first interaction shift often lead to the map; in 14 out of 24 search tasks the map is thus preferred to scanning the list of titles and authors.

In the 24 tasks solved with the visual interface, subjects directly interacted with the map in 16 tasks.

It is difficult to quantify and evaluate search behaviour on the thematic map. There are, however, four prominent features of the use of the thematic map. First, when browsing the map subjects tend to focus on specific words or areas. In 14 out of 16 tasks solved with the aid of the map, the subjects focused on a word that was thought pertinent to the search task. During a task concerning sound in user interfaces, one subject said:

> "User interfaces using sound ... then there was, what was it I found ... it was called 'audio' and 'speech' on the map, because there are such words there [on the map], I think I'll zoom in and look if there is something."

There were also subjects who assumed that documents relevant to the task should be found in one specific area of the map. Focus on a particular area was observed especially when there was a large proportion of hits in one area of the map. Referring to a small area containing a lot of retrieved documents one subject said, "I'll just try to look at that cloud over here [on the map], to see why they are placed over here".

Second, there were several examples where subjects used the position of a document to judge its relevance, and where subjects used the position of a document on the thematic map to find other relevant documents. Pondering the relevance of a paper called "Relief from the audio interface blues" one subject said: "Well, I would say it [the document] is relevant, because it is next to the other [documents on the map judged relevant]".

Third, in a number of cases the interpretation of the map and of the relation between documents found adjacent on the map was haphazard. One example of such interpretation occurred when one subject focused on the rim of an area containing a lot of retrieved documents. The subject did so searching for documents on practical applications of GOMS. Since GOMS is a theoretical model the subject thought that relevant documents would be on the border of that area.

Forth, several of the subjects lost track of their task and browsed the map in a aimless way. This phenomena was primarily seen in searches for well-specified documents, where some subjects — when they couldn't find the document satisfying the task description — looked several times at the same areas and documents.

4.4   Subjective Satisfaction

Four out of six subjects expressed preference for the thematic map interface over the boolean interface;

they found the graphics pleasing, liked the overview gained from browsing the map, and found inspiration to formulating queries from the terms on the map. The following quotes describe this: "I preferred the graphical, it was more fun in some way. That's probably the best part about it [the thematic map]", and:

> "On the one hand you've got the words on the map and you can see how many documents you've retrieved, so it was faster to get an overview of your search: did you retrieve few or many, how are they placed in relation to each other [on the map], are they close to each other or more scattered."

One subject preferred the boolean system only because the window showing titles and authors was re-sizeable, and one subject found the thematic structure too difficult to understand.

Half of the subjects in the post-search interview expressed difficulties in understanding the map. The relation between terms and documents on the map was thought to be unclear as was the thematic structure of the map. One subject commented:

> "I'm wondering about the categories shown, they are a bit ... some of them are main themes in computer science like 'evaluation' and 'usability' that one can relate to but something like 'hand' ... that can mean anything."

Also several subjects expressed surprise when they inspected documents adjacent on the map and could not tell what the documents had in common. One subject remarked in the post-search interview: "One hopes that when they [the documents] are close they are about the same." Asked if documents adjacent did share a common theme the subject continued: "Perhaps half of the times".

5 Discussion

The hypotheses about VIRIs, outlined in Section 2, are only weakly confirmed in this experiment. Thematic maps used for IR did not improve the quality or number of documents retrieved, nor was searching faster.

However, thematic maps improve certain aspects of IR: users find searching on the map pleasant, prefer browsing to scanning list of titles, and get inspired to search terms from the map. Why, then, are the results of the retrieval process not improved? One explanation might be that users lose focus on the search task, given the number of interaction shifts between the thematic map and issuing queries, and the aimless browsing on the map observed in some search tasks. Both these distractions may also result in a time overhead compared with the boolean interface. Similar problems have been observed in other empirical studies. Hertzum & Frøkjær (1996) found that search time was negatively influenced by the availability of several interaction modes. Chen et al. (1998) reports that some users browsed the thematic map in an aimless way; aimless browsing is also reported in the literature on hypertext usage. These problems might be inherent in the graphical, non-sequential presentation of documents and in the combination of browsing and query use.

One way of improving IR with thematic maps might be to increase the understandability of thematic maps. This study documents that users experience problems with understanding the terms on the map and the relations between documents. The difficulty with understanding terms could be addressed by adding more context to the terms presented on the thematic map, e.g. by using phrases, sentences, or groups of words. The understandability of relations between documents might be improved by introducing explicit connections between documents presented, as in networks showing documents and terms (Fowler et al., 1991). Several subjects wanted the possibility of getting a part of the map presented as a list of document titles/authors. They argued that the manageable, linear structure of a list in certain situations was preferable to the associative structure of the map. Whether or not such changes to thematic maps will improve IR remains to be empirically investigated.

The present experiment supports the integration of browsing using a VIRI and searching using queries. Querying was used with the same frequency with the thematic map and the boolean interface. Some search tasks were successfully solved only using the querying function of the map. Other work comparing searching and browsing has also reached this conclusion (Hertzum & Frøkjær, 1996). It is much too simplistic to assume that IR can be improved using a browse-only thematic map, as in Lin (1997) and Chen et al. (1998).

The generality of the above conclusions may be questioned because of the relatively small number of subjects and the unrealistic experimental situation. Thus, further experiments should include more subjects, investigate support for complex tasks developing over time, and address the use of thematic maps by subjects experienced with such interfaces.

6 Conclusion

Contrary to the expectations raised in the literature, this study did not find any quantitative improvements of information retrieval using a thematic map. However, subjects prefer the thematic map compared with the boolean interface. The thematic map is also extensively used in the information retrieval process, for instance in finding useful search terms. A problem with thematic maps is the distraction caused by unfocused browsing and by shifts between different interaction modes. The thematic map was also misinterpreted with respect to relations between documents, and the significance of terms displayed on the map were not directly understandable.

In brief summary, this study and the few other studies of thematic maps have shown that far more work is needed to really improve information retrieval by thematic maps.

Acknowledgements

We would like to thank the HCILIB-group for granting us access to the documents used in this study. We also acknowledge comments on a earlier version of this paper by Peter Naur, Kristian Bang Pilgaard, and Ketil Perstrup.

References

Borg, I. & Groenen, P. (1997), *Multidimensional Scaling*, Springer-Verlag.

Chalmers, M. & Chitson, P. (1992), BEAD: Explorations in Information Visualization, *in* N. Belkin, P. Ingwersen & A. M. Pejtersen (eds.), *SIGIR'92 Proceedings of the Fifteenth Annual International ACM SIGIR Conference on Research and Development in Information Retrieval*, ACM Press, pp.330–7.

Chen, H., Houston, A. L., Sewell, R. R. & Schatz, B. R. (1998), "Internet Browsing and Searching: User Evaluations of Category Map and Concept Space Techniques", *Journal of the American Society for Information Science* **49**(7), 582–603.

Fowler, R. H., Fowler, W. A. L. & Wilson, B. A. (1991), Integrating Query, Thesaurus and Documents through a Common Visual Representation, *in* A. Bookstein, Y. Chiaramella, G. Salton & V. Raghavan (eds.), *SIGIR'91, Proceedings of the Fourteenth Annual International ACM SIGIR Conference on Research and Development in Information Retrieval*, ACM Press, pp.142–51.

Gershon, N., Eick, S. G. & Card, S. K. (1998), "Information Visualization", *Interactions* **5**(2), 9–15.

Hearst, M. A. (1999), User Interfaces and Visualization, *in* R. Baeze-Yates & B. Ribeiro-Neto (eds.), *Modern Information Retrieval*, Addison–Wesley.

Hertzum, M. & Frøkjær, E. (1996), "Browsing and Querying in Online Documentation: A Study of User Interfaces and the Interaction Process", *ACM Transactions on Computer–Human Interaction* **3**(2), 136–61.

Korfhage, R. R. (1991), To See, or Not to See — Is *That* the Query?, *in* A. Bookstein, Y. Chiaramella, G. Salton & V. Raghavan (eds.), *SIGIR'91, Proceedings of the Fourteenth Annual International ACM SIGIR Conference on Research and Development in Information Retrieval*, ACM Press, pp.134–41.

Lin, X. (1997), "Map Displays for Information Retrieval", *Journal of the American Society for Information Science* **48**(1), 40–54.

Perstrup, K., Frøkjær, E., Konstantinovitz, M., Konstantinivitz, T., Sørensen, F. S. & Varming, J. (1997), A World Wide Web-based HCI-library designed for interaction studies, *in Proceedings of the 3rd ERCIM Workshop on User Interfaces for All*, INRIA Lorraine, pp.137–42.

Salton, G. & McGill, M. J. (1983), *Introduction to Modern Information Retrieval*, McGraw-Hill.

Shneiderman, B. (1998), *Designing the User Interface: Strategies for Effective Human–Computer Interaction*, third edition, Addison–Wesley.

Wise, J. A., Thomas, J. J., Pennock, K., Lantrip, D., Porttier, M., Schur, A. & Crow, V. (1995), Visualizing the Non-visual: Spatial Analysis and Interaction with Information from Text Documents, *in* N. Gershon & S. Eick (eds.), *Proceedings of Information Visualization'95*, IEEE Computer Society Press, pp.51–8.

Human–Computer Interaction — INTERACT '99
M. Angela Sasse and Chris Johnson (Editors)
Published by IOS Press, © IFIP TC.13, 1999

Balancing Generality and Specificity in Document Management Systems

W. Keith Edwards & Anthony LaMarca

Xerox Palo Alto Research Center, Palo Alto, CA 94304, USA.

{kedwards,lamarca}@parc.xerox.com

Abstract: This paper describes an experiment to extend the reach of the document-centric metaphors of computing to new physical and virtual objects in the workplace. By bringing these entities into the sphere of electronic documents, we leverage users' knowledge and expectations about how documents work, and also leverage existing tools and applications that understand and manipulate documents. Being able to use general-purpose tools on semantically-loaded content types can be useful, but there are potential pitfalls with the loss of the functionality provided by special-purpose applications. We investigate a solution to this problem that strikes a balance between generality and specificity by allowing application functionality and user interface components to be associated with the document and used by general-purpose applications that operate on that document.

Keywords: document management, user interface, extensible architectures, placeless documents.

1 Introduction

Much of contemporary computer use is characterized by document-centred tasks: we edit, create, mail, print, and file electronic documents. We commonly see file and folder icons on our desktops, and the Web has brought a document-centred metaphor to network computing tasks. The prevalence of electronic documents on our virtual desktops mirrors the use of physical documents in the workaday world (Adler et al., 1998; Bellotti & Rogers, 1997). The result is that the metaphors of document-centred computing — opening and closing, reading and writing, searching and printing — have become part of the lingua franca of computing.

Our desktop tools are specialized to match our document management tasks and have increased in sophistication to support the various uses to which documents are put. Modern tools support such techniques as indexing, hyperlinking, collaborative document filtering and recommendation (Shardanand & Maes, 1995), organization and browsing of document collections (Lamping et al., 1995), automatic identification of document genre (Kessler et al., 1997), and so on. The diversity of document management tools is indicative of the prevalence of electronic document management in our online work.

But there is still a large portion of our day-to-day work which is not document-centric. We commonly perform system administration tasks such as managing printers or installing software; control processes such as databases or other applications; collaborate with users by initiating on-line conferences or managing work flow tasks; and control external devices such as attached cameras or speakers. While these tasks may use documents — a work flow task is typically focused around some shared set of documents for instance — the commonly used and understood metaphors of document-based computing do not apply to these tasks. In short, while they may *involve* document use, creation, and management, the tasks themselves are not directly *represented as* documents, with the same affordances and utility of existing electronic documents.

At first glance, many of these tasks seem qualitatively different than typical document management: they involve working with processes, users, and devices that have no innate and *a priori* existence as readable and writable content. On closer examination, however, one can see similarities between these currently non-document centred tasks and document management. In particular, many of these tasks involve the creation and manipulation of externally-represented state: system management involves retrieving and updating system status. Work flow involves determining the steps a task has passed through, and updating some external record of the task to move it to new states. Many devices are readable and writable and can both provide and accept what may be thought of as content.

With these similarities in mind, we have begun an investigation into whether a document-centred model could be expanded to include both physical and virtual entities not previously represented as documents. Essentially, the objects at the focus of this work would be reified as documents, allowing the metaphors of document creation and manipulation to be applied to new tasks. And — perhaps more importantly — such an extension of the document metaphor would leverage the wide body of existing applications, tools, and services that already understand how to work with documents.

In such a system, users would 'live' in a document-oriented world and would be able to use familiar tools such as editors, and techniques such as cut and paste or drag and drop, to interact with a much wider range of computational and physical entities than before. In essence, electronic documents become a metaphor for the interactive objects in both the virtual and the physical worlds, rather than simply a metaphor for physical documents.

1.1   Goals

Building a system to support a document-centric view of the world has two major challenges. First we need a document management infrastructure that can seamlessly support the mapping from physical and computational entities to documents in such a way that these new documents appear as first-class peers of their existing cousins. Our investigation is part of a larger project called Placeless Documents (Dourish et al., submitted for publication) which provides this needed functionality; an overview of Placeless Documents is given in Section 3.

Second, we need to understand how the concept of the document as a user interface metaphor be mapped to these other entities. We believe that by creating such a mapping, we can achieve a number of benefits.   There are the obvious benefits of leveraging users' knowledge of document systems in new domains, and leveraging existing document tools to apply them to new types of objects. But beyond these benefits, we believe that two particular effects will come into play in such a system.

The first is *multiplicity*.   Multiplicity is the combinatorial effect which occurs when a document is accessible by any number of tools, users, and protocols. Multiplicity allows users to select their preferred tools for interacting with our new document types, rather than having to rely on customized,

special-purpose tools. It is multiplicity which makes these new entities seem like 'real' documents by allowing users to interact with them using, say, Microsoft Word or the File Manager, like they would any other file on their computer.   Multiplicity also encourages adoption by supporting users' desired tools, rather than forcing them on to new applications.

The second effect is *knitting*.   Knitting is the ability use a document as a representation of a live and up-to-date view of the world. The content for these live documents can come from any number of sources: it can be composed from pieces of traditional static content, formed from query results, or read from on- line devices.   By having live content, knitting allows documents to know the context and history of their use, and respond in appropriate ways to changes in their environment.   Knitting not only supports documents that can provide an instantaneous, updating view of some state, but also supports documents which carry their own behaviours, semantics, and perhaps even interfaces with them. In our discussion of the new document types we have created, we shall see several examples of multiplicity and knitting in action.

1.2   Striking a Balance

There is a delicate balance to be struck in this work. The reason that these computational objects have not been represented as documents is that they often carry with them such a great deal of domain- specific semantics, and the functionality that encodes these semantics, that general-purpose document tools are an inappropriate medium for working with them. Clearly, specialized functionality for a camera would not be accessible through tools like Word or Excel.

To expose this functionality, such computational entities are usually manipulated via special-purpose applications. For example, a cellular telephone may come with a special purpose application to allow the editing of its internal phone book from a desktop computer. This application reflects the functionality supported by the phone, and yet may allow its content — the actual names and numbers in the phone book — to be imported or exported in some common formats. The fact that the content may be imported or exported is an acknowledgment of the 'documentness' of the phone book.

This approach to using specialized applications for accessing and manipulating specialized sorts of data is, of course, very common, and represents one endpoint in the spectrum of possibilities.   At this endpoint, the content is so laden with domain semantics that it is best manipulated via specialized tools rather than general purpose applications. Video games are a prime example: they may contain traditional content in the form of images and sound samples, but without the game specific functions, the experience is quite different.

At the other end of the spectrum we see purely general purpose tools such as word processors, spreadsheets, and Web browsers. These tools, while they may operate on only a small number of types of data, still impose very few restrictions on the content they manipulate — the domain semantics, if any, in the content they manipulate are not reflected in the applications themselves. Although, just as specialized applications may attempt to support general purpose tools through importing and exporting, general purpose applications may attempt to reflect application semantics through the use of extensions such as ActiveX controls, browser plug-ins, or macros carried with the content.

Traditionally, these two endpoints of the spectrum have been the only options available. In our desire to leverage the power of general-purpose tools and take advantage of the combinatorial effects of multiplicity, we wish to strike a new balance. We want to be able to expose content — even semantically-loaded, domain-specific content — as documents. And yet we need to provide ways for documents to carry enough of their application behaviour that they remain useful in this new setting.

2 Related Work

Some work has been done in the past to expose computational, and sometimes physical, objects as documents. On the Unix system, the /proc filesystem (Curry, 1996) is a specific example of making one particular type of entity — a Unix process — appear as a file. These files can be read to determine the state of a process, and written to effect changes in the state of a process. Operating systems such as Mach (Rashid et al., 1989) provide a generalization of this feature by supporting easily-loadable filesystem code that can be used to provide filesystem interfaces for arbitrary entities. As opposed to these example, we have available to us a general framework for easily extending any type of entity into the realm of documents. Further, Placeless documents are more fully realized as first-class documents than the files in such filesystems: they can be freely created, grouped, and renamed. The /proc filesystem in particular imposes sufficient restrictions that process files are noticeably different than 'normal' files in the Unix filesystem.

On the Web, cgi scripts (Gundavaram, 1996) are used to dynamically create Web pages based on some

external state — an online catalog may use a cgi script to create a page with product listings from a database. An essential distinction between such scripts and our work, however, is that Placeless documents are full-fledged documents with their own innate identity. The URLs that refer to cgi scripts, on the other hand, are simply the *names* of documents. The 'documents' that they refer to actually have no inherent identity as documents — they cannot be renamed, foldered, sent to other users, and so on. As opposed to simply providing a naming system which can refer to new types of content, Placeless provides a system in which entirely new first-class documents can be created.

3 Architecture

This section presents an overview of the architecture of our system. We begin with a discussion of the basic facilities of the Placeless architecture, highlighting those features that were necessary to build our document-centric metaphor.

3.1 Overview of Placeless Documents

Traditional document management systems and filesystems present a hierarchical organizational to their users: documents are contained in folders; folders can be nested within other folders. This structure, while easy to understand, is limiting. For example, should an Excel document for a project's budget be contained in the Excel folder, the budget folder, or the project's folder?

The goal of the Placeless Documents project is to build a more flexible system for organizing a document space. In the Placeless model, organization is based on *properties* that convey information about its context of use: the document is a budget; it's shared with my workgroup, and so on.

3.1.1 Active Properties

While many systems support the association of extensible metadata with files and documents, properties in Placeless can be active *entities* that can augment and extend the behaviour of the documents they are attached to. That is, rather than being simple inert tags, extensionally used to *describe already-extant* states of the document, properties can also be live bits of code that can support the *user's desired intentions* about the state of the document.

These active properties can affect the behaviour of the document in multiple ways: they can add new operations to a document as well as govern how a document interacts with other documents and the document management system in which it exists. For example, in Placeless, active properties are used to implement access control, to handle reading and writing of document content from repositories (such properties are called 'bit providers'), and to perform notifications to interested parties.

It is these active properties in the system, particularly the bit providers, which accomplish the 'knitting' together of dynamic information described in the introduction. Since property code can perform arbitrary actions when it is invoked, properties can return arbitrary results based on the context of their use, and the state of the document management system at the time they are invoked. We shall see some examples of these in Section 4.

3.1.2   *Distribution and Compatibility*

Placeless Documents was architected to be a robust distributed system. Our design allows users to access document collections across the network and, more importantly, *serve* document collections where they see fit. So, for example, a user who is often disconnected can run an instance of the Placeless Documents system on a laptop to provide full Placeless functionality, even when disconnected from the rest of the world. Such a user could not, of course, see documents that reside on other, unreachable systems with full consistency.

A final feature of Placeless Documents is to provide compatible interfaces for supporting off-the-shelf applications. The attributes of the Placeless system described above — active properties and robust distribution — enable the construction of novel applications and document services. To be truly useful, however, the system must also work with *existing* document- and file-based applications. To this end, we architected a number of 'shims' which map from existing document- and file-management interfaces and protocols into the concepts provided by Placeless. Examples of such shims might include file system interfaces, HTTP, FTP, IMAP and POP3 protocol interfaces, WebDAV, and so on.

For example, we have built a Network File System (NFS) server layer atop Placeless. This layer lets existing applications, which are only written to understand files, work with live Placeless documents. Existing applications do not have to change to work with Placeless, although there is a loss of power since many of the Placeless concepts do not find an easy expression in a more traditional file system model.

For the purposes of this paper, the Placeless infrastructure can be thought of as a middleware layer, capable of reusing or generating content from varied sources, creating a uniform notion of 'documents' from that content, and then exposing the resulting documents via a multiplicity of interfaces.

As mentioned in the introduction, one of the key benefits of our model is in its multiplicity of access: by exposing arbitrary entities as documents, and then making these documents widely available through arbitrary interfaces, we gain great leverage from existing tools and applications. We shall see some examples of multiplicity in use in the next section.

4   Documents as a Metaphor for the World

Within the context of Placeless, we have built the infrastructure that allows us to experiment with document-centric computing. Our work has followed two main paths. First, we implemented a set of novel document types within the Placeless framework. These new document types reflect objects and tasks commonly used in office work. So far, we have focused on documents as representations for:

- Physical devices.

- People.

- Computational resources, including processes, machines, and the Placeless system itself.

- Abstract tasks and processes such as work flow.

The challenge here was to implement such disparate concepts within a document metaphor — that they would act like documents in all important ways. By leveraging users' knowledge we can build on their *expectations* of document systems, so that our documents will behave in predictable ways. We believed that if we could achieve this goal, then the Placeless infrastructure would allow existing document management tools to be brought to bear on these new document types.

The second path of our research was to use the facilities provided by Placeless to augment and enhance the semantics and behaviours of these new documents in powerful ways. While pre-existing applications can use these documents without understanding their special qualities, we felt that there was great utility to be had by providing a means through which tools *specifically written* for the Placeless environment could interact in a *general way* with these new document types in novel ways. In particular, the manifestation of this idea we have focused on has been to allow documents to provide portions of their own user interface and application behaviour. Through this mechanism, applications which are open to runtime extensibility can essentially be configured by the documents they are working with to have new behaviours and interfaces.

The following sections describe a number of case study experiments we have done.

4.1 Physical Devices as Documents

The first — and perhaps most obvious — extension of the document model was to represent physical devices as documents. In some ways, the mapping of devices to documents has been accomplished before; note the prevalence of live cameras pointed at coffee pots on the Web, for instance.

There is a subtle but important difference between this work and 'Web cams' however. While Web cams provide live content from a device, they are not true first-class documents that support organizing, sharing, annotating and customizing as our Placeless documents do. In addition, Web pages do not offer multiplicity as the content is only available through a limited set of interfaces. A URL pointing to a Web cam could be part of the implementation of a first-class document, but without the rest of the Placeless functionality it is just a pointer to a set of content.

Still, in the tradition of the Web cam, one of the first physical devices we modeled as a document was a camera. This document's bit provider generates a stream of JPEG images, and appears in the filesystem as a JPEG document. The document is not writable.

A more interesting example of a document representing a physical device is our printer document. A printer document is instantiated by creating a new document with the PrinterBitProvider attached to it. This bit provider looks for a property called 'Printer' that designates the name of the printer it represents. Reading from this file generates content representing the current state of the print queue at the moment in time at which it is read. Any content which is written to the document is printed.

Our final device document is the most complicated. We have built an interface to a digital cellular telephone. Our particular telephone (a Nokia 6190 GSM phone) affords two possible document representations. The first is the telephone's role as a carrier of a personalized phone book. The second represents the telephone's role as a sender and receiver of SMS (Short Message Service) messages.

In our system, both of these capacities are represented as documents. Reading from a phonebook document downloads the contents of the phone into the system for viewing and editing. Writing this document updates the stored information on the telephone itself. Since the phonebook content is a true Placeless Document, it can be indexed and edited using existing

tools on the desktop. With this particular device, information can only be read or written if the phone is physically docked with the computer. Therefore, the Placeless system binds the 'readable' or 'writable' attributes of the phonebook document to the phone's connection to the computer.

In its second capacity, the phone can send and receive Short Message Service (SMS) messages. This role is represented as a separate document which, when read, downloads the list of stored messages from the phone and presents them as the document's content. Any text written to this document will be sent via an SMS gateway to the physical phone represented by this document. In the case of this SMS document, messages can be read only when the phone is docked, but messages can be written anytime. So one can message a remote user by opening his or her phone document in Word or other tool, creating some content, and them simply saving the file.

While specialized tools can provide access to all of these features of the phone, multiplicity allows us to leverage existing tools in an extremely powerful way. Both the phonebook and SMS documents can be indexed by existing tools such as AltaVista Personal, edited via existing tools such as MS Word, and grouped and managed in collections just as any other document on the desktop.

4.2 People as Documents

Clearly one of the entities that people most often work with on-line is other people. Placeless has a cryptographically secure notion of a principal, with a one-to-one correspondence to physical users. We have constructed an on-line representation of the users of the system as 'person documents'. These documents are more than simple home pages for users of the system. First, we use the document for a principal as the locus of interaction with that person. All references to a principal are established as references to that principal's document. Second, we use the idea of knitting to build a representation of the state and context of the person in the world at the time the document is viewed.

The person document for an individual is created as a collection of properties that contain personal preferences and settings, and a bit provider which can assemble this information, and other information from the state of the world, into a cohesive form. These documents can be annotated by their owners (or, in some cases, others) with properties for telephone numbers, email addresses, and so forth. These properties are also used by the bit provider in constructing its content when the document is read.

Figure 1 shows an example of a person document. Contact information is retrieved from the properties attached to the document and displayed as HTML.

More interestingly, however, is the 'live' content the bit provider constructs based on the context of the user in the world. The person document for a given user will contact the Placeless Documents system and retrieve a list of all currently open documents the user is working with. These documents are represented as HTML links to the actual documents. Here we see both an example of knitting — the construction of dynamic, live content from multiple sources — and multiplicity — since these documents are available as Web documents, we can access them through a Web browser or other tool which understands HTML.

Figure 1: A people document.

Writing to a person document transmits the written information to the person represented by the document. A property on the document, settable by its owner, denotes the 'preferred' contact method — email, SMS message, etc. The bit provider for the document will consult this property to see how to transmit the information. It may also use the type and size of the information in its process (it probably makes no sense to send a JPEG file over SMS to the user's telephone, for instance). As we shall see in Section 4.5, applications which are aware of Placeless Documents can be written to interact with person documents in a more intelligent way.

4.3   Computation as Documents

A third class of entity we have experimented with is computational processes. To this end we have created document types for two computational processes: the

Java Remote Method Invocation (RMI) registry, and the Placeless kernel itself.

The Java RMI system uses a nameserver, called the registry, on each host on which a remote object runs. The RMI registry document provides a means for determining the objects named in the registry by reading it. Currently the registry document is not writable, although one could imagine a process by which writing to the registry caused new objects to be registered, or changed the state of the registry.

More interesting is the Placeless kernel document. This document represents the instantaneous state of a user's Placeless kernel. When read, the bit provider creates a page that contains information about the type of the kernel on which it is running (the version number, database implementation being used, etc.), and information about kernel status (whether certain internal threads are active, and which documents are currently in the kernel's internal cache). See Figure 2. The kernel document is updated live as the kernel changes states. While the kernel document is not writable, it does use properties as a way to provide mechanisms for controlling it from Placeless-aware applications (see Section 4.5).

Figure 2: A kernel document in a placeless content viewer application.

4.4   Tasks as Documents

The final type of entity we have brought into the document domain is abstract tasks. In particular, we have created a workflow process that is reflected in documents and properties.

In a traditional workflow system, a tool will be used to shepherd some document through a set of required steps (usually approvals by managers) until it reaches a final state. This workflow application understands the semantics of the particular tasks it is administering, perhaps via some rule set that encodes the company's policies. The workflow application provides a centralized point of focus for the process; the documents that are being approved are the things which move through this process under the control of the workflow tool.

We wanted to turn the traditional arrangement on its head. Rather than using a single workflow tool that operates on particular types of form documents, we wanted to be able to use *any* type of document as the object of a workflow. Further, rather than using a specific application that manages a given workflow interaction, we use a document that represents the abstract *process* of a particular workflow situation.

Our primary example of this is a travel approval document, used to obtain management permission to take a trip. Rather than representing a travel approval form or request, this document represents the *abstract process* of travel approvals. Opening the document causes its bit provider to scan the system, retrieving a set of documents flagged via properties as being used in the travel approval process. The bit provider then generates an instantaneous summary of the state of the world from the perspective of the travel approval process — which requests are outstanding, which have been fully approved, which have been denied.

A document is marked as being "part of the travel approval process" by having a specific property attached to it. Thus, any document (not just a particular form) can be the source of a travel request. By attaching the travel approval property to it, it *becomes* a travel request and makes its way through the system. Opening the process document retrieves the complete state of all travel approvals involving the current user; dropping a new document on the process document causes that document to become a travel request, and begins the approval process.

When a document that is involved in the process is viewed by a user who needs to make a decision about that approval, the document can actually communicate its new affordances — acceptance or denial of the travel request — through extensions to its interface. While this process is described more fully in the next section, this ability for documents to carry their own behaviours, and be aware of the context of their use, is one of the key benefits of our system.

The travel approval workflow is an example of knitting: documents remain the focus of activity, but their behaviour is affected by the context of their use, and by the states of other documents in the system.

The travel approval process also introduces an interesting quandary. Specialized forms and applications for managing a particular process exist because they encode the semantics of a particular task. Once we've removed both the forms and the applications, we've entered a world of generality in which we are no longer constrained by the semantics of the tasks at hand. The next section presents some thoughts at a solution to this problem.

4.5 Documents that Carry their Interfaces

In the current world, specialized forms of content are operated on by specialized interfaces. To revisit some of the examples in this paper, the phonebook of my phone can be updated by specialized software that comes with the device. The corporate travel approval process uses a set of forms that represent the steps and signatures required for the process.

These specialized applications exist because the data they operate on are not general-purpose, free-form documents: they have restrictions on them by virtue of the semantics of the applications in which they are used. The applications for these data present specialized interfaces which reflect these restrictions. By moving to the lowest common denominator of the document we gain a certain power (reuse of existing tools, leverage of existing knowledge), but we also lose the application-specific support which makes specific tools valuable. Thus, there is a tension between the desire for generality and the need for application-specific knowledge to be involved in the editing of these documents.

We have investigated a solution to this problem in which we use the property system provided by Placeless to allow documents to carry active behaviour and even portions of their own user interfaces. In essence, 'atoms' of application code are broken out and, rather than existing solely in a centralized application, travel with the documents they are attached to. Obviously, existing tools and systems will have no way to know about Placeless' properties on documents; this facility is useful for applications specifically written for the Placeless setting.

We have established a number of conventions by which Placeless-aware applications can have portions of their behaviour and interfaces dynamically loaded from the documents they are operating on. For this investigation, we have defined three classes of new document behaviours: *actions, views* and *components*.

Actions are simple argumentless commands that documents can be given. The actions are free to do whatever computation and produce whatever side effects they desire, but provide no return result. Actions provide a way for documents to export simple operations. As examples, the Placeless kernel document has an action to flush its internal caches, the people document has an action to bring up a window for composing email to the person, and the camera document has actions to adjust the colour, size and timestamps on the image from the camera.

Views are like actions in that they are simple argumentless commands, but differ in that they return another document as the result of their execution. Views provide an extensible way for documents to point to or themselves produce other documents. As an example, people documents have views that both return the resume and homepage of the person.

The last class of behaviour extension is the *component* which, when evaluated, returns a UI component to help display some aspect of the document's state. Component extensions provide the ability to extend the UI beyond the chosen rendition of the document's content type. The kernel document, for example, has a component extension which returns a progress bar widget which shows how full the system's internal caches are.

Placeless provides a way to programmatically discover and access the extensions that a document is offering. To demonstrate the use of this, we have built a general purpose document viewer/editor which introspects the displayed document and makes the extensions available in a sensible way: Actions are put both in an menu named 'Action' and on a tool bar. Selecting an action causes it to be executed.

View extensions are put in a menu called 'View', and selecting it causes its execution and the resulting document to be viewed. Component extensions are all executed and the resulting widgets are placed in a status bar at the bottom of the viewer. (See Figure 2.) In this way, we have populated a new point in the spectrum between general-purpose and domain-specific applications. Our document viewer is general purpose in that it is free of application specific semantics and can view many different content types, yet it offers some application specific functionality via action, view and component extensions.

5   Conclusions

This work has investigated a model in which the notion of an electronic document is extended to new types of physical and virtual entities. Our system, built atop the Placeless infrastructure, provides a way to represent novel entities as documents. Further, the system can present these documents in such a way that they can be used by existing applications, including tools that read

and write to the filesystem, and that read and write to the Web.

Unlike related work on loadable filesystems, cgi scripts, and the like, Placeless takes a holistic approach to document management: our system is extensible in how it exposes underlying content, and extensible in how it makes this content available to applications. The resulting multiplicity — the ability to make most anything look like a document to any most application — is a key source of power in this system.

Likewise, the ability to dynamically create content which exists nowhere in the physical world and is based on the state of world and the context of the use of the document is of key importance. This ability to take multiple information sources and knit them together based on context is essential in turning isolated sets of documents into a coherent whole.

6   Status and Future Work

While the implementation of the Placeless system is ongoing, the core functionality has been developed to the point that we were able to build all of the document types described here. The core Placeless system is approximately 100,000 lines of Java code. The properties needed to support particular document types, however, are only about 300 lines of code each. We have been encouraged by our experiments in mapping physical and virtual objects into the document space. Our work has validated the usefulness of the facilities provided by Placeless as an infrastructure on which to base this metaphor.

As discussed, one of the problems with representing arbitrary entities as documents — and making them usable via general purpose tools — is that these entities may lose some of the semantics which are the basis of their utility. To this end, we have investigated a set of conventions for allowing documents to carry with them fragments of application behaviour that are made manifest when the document is used by a Placeless-aware application. This solution represents a middle ground between using existing general-purpose document tools (and hence losing all semantics associated with the document), and using specialized applications (and losing the ability to use existing tools on the application content). This approach deserves more work to determine if it is a truly viable solution.

References

Adler, A., Gujar, A., Harrison, B. L., O'Hara, K. & Sellen, A. (1998), A Diary Study of Work Related-Reading: Design Implications for Digital Reading Devices, *in*

C.-M. Karat, A. Lund, J. Coutaz & J. Karat (eds.), *Proceedings of CHI'98: Human Factors in Computing Systems*, ACM Press, pp.241–8.

Bellotti, V. & Rogers, Y. (1997), From Web Press to Web Pressure: Multimedia Representations and Mulyimedia Publishing, *in* S. Pemberton (ed.), *Proceedings of CHI'97: Human Factors in Computing Systems*, ACM Press, pp.279–86.

Curry, D. (1996), *UNIX Systems Programming*, O'Reilly.

Dourish, P., Edwards, K., LaMarca, A., Lamping, J., Petersen, K., Salisbury, M., Terry, D. & Thornton, J. (submitted for publication), "Extending Document Management Systems with Active Properties", ACM Transactions on Office Information Systems.

Gundavaram, S. (1996), *CGI Programming on the World Wide Web*, O'Reilly.

Kessler, B., Nunberg, G. & Schuetze, H. (1997), Automatic Detection of Text Genre, *in Proceedings ACL/EACL*, pp.32–8.

Lamping, J., Rao, R. & Pirolli, P. (1995), A Focus+Context Technique Based on Hyperbolic Geometry for Visualizing Large Hierarchies, *in* I. Katz, R. Mack, L. Marks, M. B. Rosson & J. Nielsen (eds.), *Proceedings of CHI'95: Human Factors in Computing Systems*, ACM Press, pp.401–8.

Rashid, R., Baron, R., Forin, A., Golub, D., Jones, M., Julin, D., Orr, D. & Sanzi, R. (1989), Mach: A Foundation for Open Systems, *in Proceedings of Second Workshop on Workstation Operating Systems (WWOS2)*, IEEE Computer Society Press, pp.109–13.

Shardanand, U. & Maes, P. (1995), Social Information Filtering: Algorithms for Automating Word of Mouth, *in* I. Katz, R. Mack, L. Marks, M. B. Rosson & J. Nielsen (eds.), *Proceedings of CHI'95: Human Factors in Computing Systems*, ACM Press, pp.210–7.

Human–Computer Interaction — INTERACT '99
M. Angela Sasse and Chris Johnson (Editors)
Published by IOS Press, © IFIP TC.13, 1999

The Writing on the Wall

Elizabeth D. Mynatt

Graphics, Visualization and Usability Center, Georgia Institute of Technology, Atlanta, GA 30332–0280, USA.

mynatt@cc.gatech.edu

Abstract: Using two weeks of daily whiteboard snapshots and interviews, we describe patterns of whiteboard use in individual offices. First, we profile four study participants highlighting the different tasks carried out on whiteboards, how physical placement and social factors bias whiteboard use and some of the features people want in next-generation whiteboards. Following these profiles, we detail our observations: how users manage space on the whiteboard, what tasks they use the whiteboard for and how other people influence their whiteboard use. We close by describing what users want in future whiteboard interfaces including how the virtual space should be organized and how the whiteboard should connect with desktop computer tools.

Keywords: ethnography, interaction design, interaction technology, office computing, pen-based input, ubiquitous computing, user studies, work analysis.

1 Introduction

One way to view the proliferation of computerized tools in the office place is to look at the tools that were displaced. The typewriter beget the word processor which beget the desktop computer. The slide rule preceded the hand-held calculator and the personal organizer beget the potpourri of PDAs such as the Pilot. Of course not all of these transitions have been completely successful. For example, many still prefer paper organizers and notebooks to PDAs. If a new technology fails to capture important affordances of existing technology, such as speedy input, then people who rely on, or strongly prefer, those capabilities will resist transitioning. Yet augmenting office tools with computational capabilities holds much promise. Efforts in ubiquitous computing (Weiser, 1991), augmented reality (CACM, 1993, 1993) and tangible media (Ishii & Ulmer, 1996) point to the potential of extending computation into new parts of the physical realm.

At Xerox PARC, we are currently investigating strategies for augmenting the environment of the individual office. By this distinction, we envision the principally private space of an individual employee. Despite experiments with 'hoteling' and other de-personalized environments, the use of personal spaces is still the norm for many cultures. Our goal is to blur the boundaries between the physical and virtual realms by augmenting common office tools with computational capabilities. One design goal underlying this approach is to retain the natural affordances of the existing tool, even if this constraint requires limiting the features or complexity of the augmented tool.

We are currently focusing on extending the common office whiteboard — an ubiquitous writing surface typically hung on many office walls. While envisioning replacing the whiteboard with a touch sensitive surface, 'coloured' stylus makers and video projection, we first wanted to understand the typical uses and affordances of office whiteboards. Although whiteboard and wallboard use has been studied in other settings such as meeting rooms (Kraut et al., 1993; Moran et al., 1996; Streitz et al., 1994; Whittaker et al., 1994), classrooms (Abowd et al., 1996), and production environments (Bellotti, 1997), our preliminary observations indicated that whiteboard use in the office differed from the use of whiteboards in more public spaces. These differences motivated our initial areas of inquiry:

- In contrast to meeting room or production environments, office whiteboards tend to be used for a heterogeneous set of tasks *in parallel*.

- Whiteboard content seems to be grouped in natural clusters or *segments*. These segments may correspond to different tasks, different people, or writing at different points in time.

- Although located in the setting of an individual office, the whiteboard's use spans a *personal to semi-public* spectrum. Moreover, interactions and collaborations with other colleagues affect how individual whiteboards are used.

- Particularly personal whiteboard content seems to be heavily *context-dependent*. Whether it is a seven-digit number, or a list of items, the user must remember why and when it was written. Likewise the content may be incomplete, with just enough information present for the user to remember the missing data.

Commercial augmented whiteboards, such as the SmartBoard are geared to meeting and presentation settings. Since these interfaces do not match the needs for long-term use in the office, this study is aimed at understanding office use and informing the design of a computer-augmented whiteboard for that environment.

In this paper, we report on an initial study of office whiteboard use in an office environment. In the following section, we briefly describe the research plan and methodology for the study. Next we profile four of our observed study participants. These profiles highlight the different tasks carried out on whiteboards, how physical placement and social factors bias whiteboard use, as well as some of the features these people would like to see in next-generation whiteboards. Following these profiles, we then detail the observations organized around themes of how users manage space on the whiteboard, what tasks they use the whiteboard for and how other people influence their whiteboard use. We close this paper by describing what users indicate they want in future whiteboard interfaces including how the virtual space should be organized and how the whiteboard should connect with desktop computer tools.

2 Study Overview

We embarked on this study to gain a better understanding of how people use whiteboards in their individual offices. The study took place in a large research laboratory populated by researchers, managers, administrative assistants and other support personnel. Our overall plan was to collect observations of whiteboard use, informing subsequent interviews.

2.1 Selecting Participants

Since the study was geared toward understanding typical office environments, we sought a diversity of participants. Eighteen participants were selected from a pool of volunteers including people who claimed that their 'whiteboard rarely changes'. The distribution of job classifications for the participants is shown in the following table.

Managers	2
Administrative Assistants	1
Support Personnel	4
Researchers	11

Table 1: Distribution of study participants.

The researchers ranged in seniority from the highest to the lowest ranking, from a visiting researcher to those with 20 years of experience in that laboratory. The support personnel came from four different organizations: computer support, communication, technical writing, and information centre. Six of the participants were women.

2.2 Two Weeks of Snapshots

With the observational data, we wanted to get an indication of the tasks people were using their whiteboards to accomplish, how often the whiteboard changed as well as other patterns of use, such colour selection. To minimize intrusion, we decided against any form of live capture of activities and opted for daily snapshots of the whiteboard surface. Each day we photographed the contents of each whiteboard as well as some of the surrounding context. Some participants had multiple whiteboards in their office and all the boards were photographed. The 640 × 480 resolution of the digital camera was insufficient for simply taking one picture of the entire board so we took multiple overview and detail shots to ensure readability of the material. In the end, we took 660 snapshots during the two-week period.

The snapshots proved to be useful clues in understanding how whiteboard content changes on a day to day basis. Although it was often difficult to completely decipher the tasks behind the content, the snapshots were incredibly useful for grounding subsequent discussions with study participants.

2.3 Questionnaire + Interview

Working from initial observations as well as our speculations about whiteboard use, we created a four page, 22 item questionnaire inquiring about current whiteboard use as well as projected use of a computer-augmented whiteboard. Sample questions are shown in Figure 1. Participants completed the questionnaire during their face-to-face interview and were able to ask clarification questions. Only interviewed participants (9 total plus 1 questionnaire beta tester) completed the questionnaire.

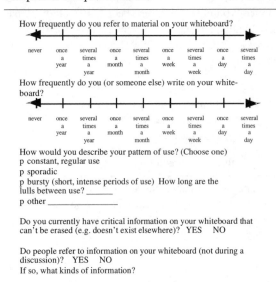

Figure 1: Questionnaire excerpt.

We interviewed half of the study participants following the data collection period. Out of the subject pool, we interviewed one manager, the one administrative assistant, two support personnel (tech writer and communications) and five researchers of varying levels of seniority. One of the interviewed researchers collaborates closely with the interviewed manager and some of the observations stem from that collaboration. The interviewees were chosen based on their diversity in role and in whiteboard use and their availability.

Each interview lasted for approximately one hour. During that time the interviewee would complete the questionnaire, and then we would review their answers while looking at observational data. As we were particularly interested in the design of an 'erase-safe' board where whiteboard content is automatically saved, during the remaining interview time (~20 mins), we would discuss what clusters of content were on the whiteboard at different times, and how they might retrieve a cluster at a later time without naming it a-priori.

3   Four Profiles

In this section, we describe four of the study participants in detail. These profiles highlight the different tasks carried out on whiteboards, how physical placement and social factors bias whiteboard use and some improvements people would like to see

in their whiteboards. Although the participants have agreed to be described in this paper, their names have been changed to ensure confidentiality.

3.1   The TechWriter

Andrew is a contractor hired to write technical documentation for a multi-year, multi-person project. With a inside office (no windows), Andrew has two whiteboards, one located near the door and one located at the far end of the office behind a desk. Project members use the near whiteboard during discussions with Andrew while he uses the second whiteboard as a personal scratch-pad. During our interview, Andrew commented that the whiteboard drawings were catalysts for conversation with team members.

In his role as technical writer, Andrew referred to the board's contents during the writing process. Despite the utility of Andrew's shared board, numerous important discussions would take place in the offices of the individual project members, and more whiteboard drawings would be created. Andrew would then have to capture this material at the end of the discussion. The social influences of who was working for whom made it more likely for Andrew to go to someone else's office than for that person to come to Andrew's office. It was those occasions when Andrew wished that there was some way that his whiteboard could show the contents of another person's board.

In general, Andrew is not an avid whiteboard user; typically other people initiated using the whiteboard in his office. As a personal space, Andrew uses the other board for short to-do lists, reminders and jotting down specific data (he doesn't like using post-its). Although Andrew doesn't like using the whiteboard (or any other tool) for outlining, he does admit to 'doodling' on the board when 'stuck' and 'getting out of the chair' helps break the mental logjam.

3.2   The Communications Director

Diane is the manager of a small communications group. Although she is similar to most whiteboard owners with 'bursty' whiteboard use, she tends to use her whiteboard daily for a variety of tasks. At the top of her whiteboard, she has her yearly production schedule. Schedule changes are indicated in red, letters (A, B, C) denote categories, and line thickness represents committed hours.

Crossed-out items are not erased because she wants to remember that they were originally part of the plan. Although the schedule is technically inaccurate, as some unanticipated items are missing and others have not been rescheduled, the plan is a useful reminder/tool. One indication of its utility is that it has not been erased despite a repeated need for more whiteboard space.

Diane describes the whiteboard, like her desk, as a 'working space' and her computer as a production tool as well as a filing system. The bottom middle of her board is the working area where projects are discussed with other team members over the course of the project (typically ranging from multiple days to weeks). One segment shows a green list of material for a videotape to be made by Diane and the video producer. Later the two of them and the photographer annotate the list in purple with descriptions of how to visualize the material. Another colour (blue) is used to add particularly good visual material to the green list. Later, Diane continues to add more visualization notes in purple.

Diane prefers the large, flexible visual/spatial medium of the whiteboard for brainstorming and outlining tasks. She thinks computerized tools are too rigid in the ways that information can be represented. When needing to capture material on the whiteboard, she will take a photograph instead of trying to translate the material into a text description since "retyping wouldn't maintain the meaning". The photographs can then be distributed amongst team members and referenced as the project progresses.

Diane remarked that she jots something down on the whiteboard when "she needs to get something out of her brain". At the far right is a list of people (initials) who expressed interest in writing a mission statement. Although the list has been there for over two months and the extra space would be useful, she doesn't erase the list because she "knows that one of the volunteers will slip through the cracks". Nevertheless she doesn't capture the material in her computer because it "doesn't seem important enough".

Although her whiteboard is occasionally used as a reference by other team members during projects, Diane would like to see this kind of use increased. Her frustration is that while her board is well placed for supporting discussions as well as her own personal use, to be used daily as a reference however, it needs to be visible from a more public setting. Diane would like to experiment with pointing a video camera at her whiteboard where the image could easily be seen by team members.

3.3 The Researcher

Charles is a visiting researcher whose tasks include computer programming and various forms of writing (e.g. papers, presentations). He is informally working with a number of research groups in the laboratory.

Like most whiteboard users, Charles' whiteboard is typically divided into a number of segments. In the upper left he has a few to-lists: things to do, people to talk to, people to email. Typically, these lists are persistent and are amended often enough to keep them relatively up-to-date. In the upper middle, he has a list of concepts stemming from a current project that he has been working on for multiple days. Other ponderings are in green at the right edge. The bottom area is the area that is most often erased. Currently it has some "muddled modelly thoughts" and some ideas to try to program. The lower right corner can be reached while talking on the phone so it occasionally has notes scrawled along a diagonal line.

Charles curiously answered in the questionnaire that he writes on his whiteboard more often than referring to it. He describes the act of writing as a way to organize his thoughts. Generally a day will pass between using the whiteboard as he needs to "step back and think" before writing again. Sometimes his goal is to write down tasks that need to be done so that he can figure out what to do next. When stressed he'll use the board to structure his pending tasks noting their current status and deadline. By having all of the tasks on the board (including grocery shopping) the board becomes a 'public reassurance' even if he doesn't need to read it. Despite this strategy, Charles is a self-described, 'Mr. triple-booked'. Appointment dates on his board are meaningless and there is little consistency between his board and his diary/notebook.

As another form of thinking, Charles uses the board to work through concepts whether he is programming or writing. As he works and re-works material, he uses the board to "build arguments in his head". He almost never captures material that is on his board — the ideas "flow into other things". Sometimes this thinking process is collaborative as he illustrates points during a discussion with a colleague in his office. When working at his computer, Charles' back is to his whiteboard. He generally doesn't look back to his board, as the board's function as a thinking device has already been accomplished.

Charles prefers using a whiteboard for these 'thinking' tasks to his diary/notebook as there is more space available and it is not in the way on his desk which he admits is just a repository organized with a 'sedimentary' model. Although similar sets of notes can be found in his notebook, the notes on his board are 'more significant' as the notebook contains 'everything'.

3.4 The Manager — A Collaborative Place

Barbara is a senior researcher and manager. Her office is organized so that the whiteboard is close to the door and is surrounded by multiple seating opportunities (couch, chair). At the other end of her office is her desk and computer terminal. As per her design, she uses the whiteboard almost exclusively during discussions with other people. When working by herself, she sits at her desk and uses either paper, email to herself, or a linear text file (searchable via emacs) for notes, outlines, reminders and the like.

Although almost solely used for discussions, Barbara generally uses her whiteboard several times a week depending on the intensity of particular collaborations.

Material remains on the whiteboard until it is translated into an email message or a PowerPoint slide, an event that occurs approximately once a week. During the two weeks of observation, Barbara's board was used to work through a Gantt chart, illustrate multiple organization charts, develop multiple scenarios for business plans, list internal business opportunities, work through resource allocations, sketch a particular scenario in further detail, draw a decision tree, illustrate resource planning with bar charts, illustrate existing business relationships and commitments, work through multiple outlines to "understand how to articulate a concept", compile and renumber lists of action items, sketch ideas for icons and illustrations, and capture specific details (dates, costs). Surprisingly, it was a slow week as Barbara and others were often out of the office!

One of Barbara's close collaborators also participated in the study. Material bounced back and forth between their boards as their discussions ranged between their offices. Although exact consistency wasn't important, both remarked that it would be helpful if they could see each other's board from their office even if simply to jump start the next conversation. By watching material appear on both boards, the power of these simple sketches became more apparent. A crude drawing or short phrase was a sufficient, but necessary tool in discussions of much greater complexity.

4   Observations

4.1 Managing Space

Segments: One of our intuitions about whiteboard use was that people typically create and maintain multiple clusters of content on their whiteboard. Assuming that we would find these clusters (which we did), we wanted to see how the clusters changed over time and how different tasks might be associated with different clusters. We were curious as to whether computers could identify these clusters and perhaps, the corresponding tasks.

We certainly did see clusters (or segments) of whiteboard content. An average of five segments was typical. When queried, participants rarely identified *nested* segments. The only exception was when the entire board was used for an illustration that had multiple parts. Some participants pointed to related segments that were all part of one project or large task. Even then, participants were unsure that when retrieving a segment, whether they would want the one segment or all of the related segments.

We were surprised at the longevity of some segments with continued input. A common example is itemized to-do lists where items are checked off and new items added. But many segments stayed in flux as individuals and then multiple people took turns working with the material.

Off-line computer recognition of segments would be difficult at best especially as the board changed over time. In general, handwriting quality is poor making domain-based recognition difficult. Most people are space scavengers, erasing only the amount needed and leaving traces of out-of-date and now incomplete content behind. Additionally one segment may extend around the board circumventing other material that cannot be erased. Continued input to a segment, by different people at different times with different colours, makes recognition of that complete segment less and less likely. As already shown by previous systems (Moran et al., 1995; Saund & Moran, 1994; Shipman et al., 1995), there is more promise in continuous, real-time recognition of groups of content especially lists. Recognizing more structureless content is likely to be difficult. Nevertheless, with human inspection of whiteboard snapshots, identifying segments was reasonably easy as they still tended to maintain an overall gestalt.

Getting White Space: A common complaint from most whiteboard users is the continual challenge to find usable space amongst content they do not want to erase. We identified two strategies in play. First, there are *clean desk* users who would often erase their entire whiteboard at the beginning or end of the day. As the name implies, these users often had neat offices and clean desks. We interviewed one of these users who reported that she captured and erased her board multiple times a week. In casual conversation with another 'clean desk' user, he described using the board primarily for illustrating points during conversations in his office. He typically would not need these illustrations after the discussion.

Most users are *space scavengers* and these folks came in two flavours. Many had a known *hot spot*, where material changed frequently, that was bordered by longer-lived content. This hot spot is typically used when other people are in the office either for brainstorming with multiple writers or for illustrating points to an office visitor. In any case, content in this area is known to be short-lived. Other users have no obvious hot spot but migrate across the board, erasing where and when possible.

Colour: One question was whether participants had strategies for using colour and if, knowing those strategies, computerized tools could more easily recognize segments and tasks. For the most part colour choice is random and uninformative. A few users did create on-the-fly colour codes when working with more complex material. A larger number of users commented that they would automatically pick up a contrasting colour when writing near, unrelated material. But often, users work with one colour, occasionally locating another marker. Some participants avoided colours that they perceived as harder to erase than others, although hard-to-erase colours varied per user/board.

4.2 Tasks

As already described in the profiles, users undertook a variety of tasks with their whiteboards. In the questionnaire, users were asked to mark tasks that they did on their whiteboard.

Reminders: Whether in the form of a to-do list or simply some notes on the board, a common use of the whiteboard is to remind the user of future tasks. Set up as a catalyst for later doing a task, the reminders free users to spend their cognitive cycles elsewhere. The constant visibility of the whiteboard is important as one user remarked that they put things on their board that they need to feel 'guilty' about doing. Few users put long-term plans or calendars on their whiteboard. More common is a short-term calendar, generally expressed as a reminder with a date and time attached. Competing technologies for reminders are paper, post-its, and PDAs.

Quick Capture: Especially users who disliked post-its and are concerned about more paper disappearing into their desk, the whiteboard is a favoured medium for capturing quick, specific data such as phone numbers. One surprise is the number of URLs given how cumbersome they are to write. Most URLs came from visitors who would write it out during a discussion. The use of the whiteboard as a capture tool also depends on its proximity to the phone. If the whiteboard was in reach, it is used to write down details of phone calls such as prices, names and phone numbers.

GENERAL

8	to-do lists
5	outlining a paper or talk
9	illustrate points in a discussion
7	facilitate discussions in your office (multiple people contributing)
5	short-term calendar (1-week period or less)
2	long-term calendar (multiple weeks or months)
10	organize thoughts

free-form answers: [list code details, class name hierarchies, random doodling, think out problems (algorithms specifically)]

JOT DOWN SPECIFIC DATA

3	URLs
7	phone numbers

free-form answers: [program commands, dates/topics/mtg places, prices, conversions]

Figure 2: Reported whiteboard tasks.

Thinking: All manner of incomplete and seemingly vague content was written as participants used their whiteboard as a scratch surface while pondering concepts much larger than their surface representations. Few illustrations resemble traditional outlines, at best a list was used. Whiteboard content often seems to be the minimal clues needed for the user to remember the surrounding context and details. When material is created by multiple people, more details and labels are apparent but frequent collaborators still utilize an amazingly small set of notations.

The most often cited competition to the whiteboard in this domain is paper. The visibility, size and other factors favouring collaboration boost use of the whiteboard. Paper's strength stemmed from its availability (i.e. no need to erase) and its portability. No one mentioned using computerized tools unless they were able to go directly into a production task such as writing prose or code.

4.3 Frequency of Use

Most whiteboard users described their use as 'bursty' (short intense periods of use with lulls in between). Depending on the circumstances, days to months pass between uses. An open question is if basic support for whiteboard use is improved, such as making it possible to retrieve whiteboard content and thus freeing visual space, how much would whiteboard use increase?

4.4   Other People Matter

Although the office whiteboard is ostensibly a personal tool with the same ownership norms as desktop computers, it is commonly used with other people in the office and, in general, relationships between colleagues bias how and when a particular whiteboard is used.

Sharing   Information: Collaborators   who frequently use whiteboards in their discussions are typically frustrated with the difficulty of sharing information following a discussion. Various strategies for sharing are employed including translating the contents of the board into an email, photographing the board and establishing social conventions so it is permissible to later return to an office to look at the board.

Your Board or Mine: Various social factors determine which boards are used amongst a group of collaborators. As already mentioned, the tech writer as a contractor, often went to the offices of the permanent employees, even if the subsequent whiteboard content was needed by him.   Although these same social patterns may exist in sharing desktop computers, or when working from paper, whiteboard content is much less portable thus hampering the effectiveness of these interactions.

In close collaborations of peers, material flows from individual boards as discussions range between offices. Yet, even amongst a group of collaborators, the board is still *owned* by the office resident as others ask for permission to write, especially if erasing is required.

Multiple Boards: Users with multiple boards tend to treat one board as a collaborative space and one board as a private space with the private board located closer to the individual's workspace (e.g. desk, desktop computer, phone). Although users do not place particularly private content on these boards, they are typically located where they cannot be easily read by an office visitor.

5   Projected Use

Although it can be difficult for users to forecast what they would like in a future tool, we wanted to

stimulate some discussion of desired improvements to whiteboards, as well as ways strategies for likely computer augmentations.   In these discussions, we asked users to imagine a whiteboard with two characteristics: it has a virtual projected space larger than their current whiteboard and that it automatically stores whiteboard segments without requesting a filename.

5.1   Retrieval

Naming a file and deciding on its location is a common, albeit heavyweight task, too heavyweight for informal interaction with a whiteboard. Simply determining a name for content that is loosely associated with any product or deliverable is difficult. We speculate that an augmented whiteboard would automatically save all segments.

With saving as an automatic process that doesn't require explicit attention from the user, the user still needs a means for retrieving saved segments. Users cited time and visual appearance as the two most salient cues for retrieving segments. Although they could not say exactly when they had written something on their board, users often had a good idea for a general range in time (e.g. few days ago, sometime last week, couple months ago). Users asked for the ability to scan thumbnails of whiteboard segments using time as a control. Although they doubted that they would *remember* visual context associated with a segment (e.g. colours, location on board), they believed that they would recognize a segment when presented with a set of choices.

5.2   Managing the Virtual Space

Assuming that the available whiteboard space is larger than what is visible on the wall, users are uncertain as to how that space should be organized. Choosing between a scrollable space, a zoomable space (e.g. Pad++ (Bederson & Hollan, 1994) and a segmented space (e.g. flipcharts), users show a slight preference for a scrollable space. However, users are concerned about losing track of items in the virtual space and prefer a virtual space only three to four times larger than their current whiteboard. In contrast to using a larger than life virtual space, some users want mechanisms for gaining whitespace while maintaining the visibility of other whiteboard content.

5.3   Connection with the Digital World

Many users are frustrated by the lack of connection between their whiteboard and their desktop computer. For example, a commonly requested feature is the ability to move outlines from the whiteboard to a desktop word processor. However, other users note that their free form whiteboard content would be difficult to represent in their desktop software.

5.4 Desired Features

Given the list of features, users chose the following:

5	handwriting recognition
6	to-do list support (check off items, store history, set priorities or dues dates)
6	making lists of action items in a mtg (assign names, due dates)
5	click on a name or phone number to call someone
6	outlining support (create hierarchies, move, copy, promote, demote)
7	drawing support (clean up drawings, alignment)
6	print contents
4	access whiteboard content from Web pages
6	see though overlays
4	filters or magic lenses
2	easily hide personal information
7	transition outlines to a desktop word processor
5	transition schedules to a desktop calendar (or PDA)
6	transition to-do lists to a desktop tool or PDA

Figure 3: Desired whiteboard features.

6 Conclusions

Especially in contrast to computerized devices, whiteboards are an incredibly simple tool to use. More importantly, the tasks connected with whiteboards, whether it is quickly capturing a phone number, facilitating a discussion or pondering a plan of action, or thread of thought, require this simplicity.

Nevertheless current whiteboards have many limitations that could potentially be met with computational support. Namely users are often constrained by the space available, and material once erased cannot be recovered. However typical desktop interfaces for managing multiple 'documents' are not appropriate. As a tool for reminding and reassurance, the visibility of whiteboard content is important even if it has not been 'used' recently. Moreover the overhead of naming, filing, and retrieving whiteboard segments would likely overwhelm the whiteboard's current fast and simple interaction.

Recognizing, and thus supporting, particular whiteboard tasks will be difficult given the context-specific representations of much larger content that is often only in the users' heads. Only two basic tasks, clustering content and writing lists, are consistently performed in any recognizable way. Otherwise the whiteboard is used for multiple purposes in parallel such that a more feature-full interface will be difficult to design.

Complex social relationship underlie how whiteboards are used by groups of people. One challenge for next generation whiteboard designers is to better support these practices.

References

Abowd, G., Atkeson, C., Feinstein, A., Hmelo, C., Kooper, R., Long, S., Sawhney, N. & Tani, M. (1996), Teaching and Learning as Multimedia Authoring: The Classroom 200 Project, *in Proceedings of Multimedia'96*, ACM Press, pp.187–98.

Bederson, B. B. & Hollan, J. D. (1994), Pad++: A Zooming Graphical Interface for Exploring Alternate Interface Physics, *in Proceedings of the ACM Symposium on User Interface Software and Technology, UIST'94*, ACM Press, pp.17–26.

Bellotti, V. (1997), Design for Privacy in Multimedia Computing and Communications Environments, *in* P. Agre & M. Rotenberg (eds.), *Technology and Privacy: The New Landscape*, MIT Press, pp.63–98.

CACM, 1993 (1993), "Special Issue on Augmented Environments", *Communications of the ACM* **36**(7).

Ishii, H. & Ulmer, B. (1996), Tangible Bits: Towards Seamless Interfaces Between People, Bits and Atoms, *in* G. van der Veer & B. Nardi (eds.), *Proceedings of CHI'96: Human Factors in Computing Systems*, ACM Press, pp.234–41.

Kraut, R., Fish, R., Root, R. & Chalfonte, . (1993), Informal Communication in Organizations: Form, Function and Technology, *in* R. Baecker (ed.), *Groupware and Computer-supported Co-operative Work*, Morgan-Kaufmann, pp.287–314.

Moran, T. P., Chiu, P., Harrison, S., Kurtenbach, G., Minneman, S. & van Melle, W. (1996), Evolutionary Engagement in an Ongoing Collaborative Work Process: A Case Study, *in* M. S. Ackerman (ed.), *Proceedings of CSCW'96: Conference on Computer Supported Cooperative Work*, ACM Press, pp.150–9.

Moran, T. P., Chiu, P., van Melle, W. & Kurtenbach, G. (1995), Implicit Structures for Pen-based Systems within a Freeform Interaction Paradigm, *in* I. Katz, R. Mack, L. Marks, M. B. Rosson & J. Nielsen (eds.), *Proceedings of CHI'95: Human Factors in Computing Systems*, ACM Press, pp.487–94.

Saund, E. & Moran, T. P. (1994), A Perceptually-supported Sketch Editor, *in Proceedings of the ACM Symposium on User Interface Software and Technology, UIST'94*, ACM Press, pp.175–84.

Shipman, F. M., Marshall, C. C. & Moran, T. P. (1995), Finding and Using Implicit Structure in Human-organized Spatial Information Layouts, *in* I. Katz, R. Mack, L. Marks, M. B. Rosson & J. Nielsen (eds.), *Proceedings of CHI'95: Human Factors in Computing Systems*, ACM Press, pp.346–53.

Streitz, N., Geißler, J., Haake, J. & Hol, J. (1994), Dolphin: Integrated Meeting Support Across Local and Remote Desktop Environments and Liveboards, *in* R. Furuta & C. Neuwirth (eds.), *Proceedings of CSCW'94: Conference on Computer Supported Cooperative Work*, ACM Press, pp.345–58.

Weiser, M. (1991), "The Computer for the 21st Century", *Scientific American* **265**(3), 94–104.

Whittaker, S., Frohlich, D. & O., D.-J. (1994), Informal Workplace Communication: What is It Like and How Might We Support It, *in* B. Adelson, S. Dumais & J. Olson (eds.), *Proceedings of CHI'94: Human Factors in Computing Systems*, ACM Press, pp.131–7.

Human–Computer Interaction — INTERACT '99
M. Angela Sasse and Chris Johnson (Editors)
Published by IOS Press, © IFIP TC.13, 1999

Facilitating Video Access by Visualizing Automatic Analysis

Andreas Girgensohn, John Boreczky, Lynn Wilcox & Jonathan Foote

FX Palo Alto Laboratory, 3400 Hillview Avenue, Palo Alto, CA 94304, USA.

{andreasg,johnb,wilcox,foote}@pal.xerox.com

Abstract: When reviewing collections of video such as recorded meetings or presentations, users are often interested only in an overview or short segments of these documents. We present techniques that use automatic feature analysis, such as slide detection and applause detection, to help locate the desired video and to navigate to regions of interest within it. We built a Web-based interface that graphically presents information about the contents of each video in a collection such as its keyframes and the distribution of a particular feature over time. A media player is tightly integrated with the Web interface. It supports navigation within a selected file by visualizing confidence scores for the presence of features and by using them as index points. We conducted a user study to refine the usability of these tools.

Keywords: content-based access, video, multimedia, keyframes, speaker identification, automatic analysis, visualization, skimming.

1 Introduction

In recent years, we have seen increasing availability and use of digital video. Inexpensive mass storage and efficient data compression have made it possible to store large amounts of video on-line. The ability to watch any full-length video is useful, but for many applications, a user simply wants to skim through one of more long videos to get the gist of their content. Alternately, a user may want to watch a short segment of a particular video.

If videos are transcribed or otherwise labeled with text, text retrieval techniques can be used to locate passages of interest (Christel et al., 1998; Brown et al., 1995). For the types of video we are interested in (e.g. weekly group meetings), the effort of adding that information is often not acceptable. Instead, we use automatic analysis techniques that identify features in the media such as certain sounds in the audio or certain types of shots in the video. These features support access to video even if no textual information is available.

While much research has been done on the automatic analysis of video content (Arman et al., 1994; Hampapur et al., 1997; Zhang et al., 1993), less attention has been directed at how to make such analysis useful to the user. Ideally, automatic analysis can make multimedia data less opaque by giving the user an indication of the contents (e.g. shot change (Zhang et al., 1993) and face detection

(Wang & Brandstein, 1998)). However, even the most sophisticated analysis will be of little value unless it can be presented in a manner appropriate for the user.

This paper presents techniques and applications for interacting with the results of such analyses to aid content-based location, retrieval, and playback of potentially relevant video data. The details of the analysis techniques used in this paper are discussed in (Foote et al., 1998).

In this paper, we describe interaction techniques for accessing video facilitated by automatic analysis techniques. After describing our video environment, we present the analysis techniques used to automatically create video indices. We then show how this information can augment user interfaces that display available videos and play back selected video files. We conclude with the results of a user study designed to help us refine the useful features of our interfaces, and a discussion of future research.

2 The Problem

At our company, weekly staff meetings and other seminars and presentations are held in a conference room outfitted with several video cameras and microphones. Formal meetings and presentations are videotaped, MPEG-encoded, and made available to the staff via the company intranet. These videos amount to about three hours per week; currently we have more than 120 hours of video in our database.

In such an environment, users often want to retrieve information such as "the name of the executive visiting next week" or "the report Jim gave about a conference in Monterey". Finding the desired few minutes in a one-hour staff meeting can be problematic. If users do not remember at which meeting the desired information was presented, they might have to play through several hours of video to find the desired segment. Other users might have missed a meeting and want to review it without having to spend a whole hour watching the entire video.

We want to help users locate specific video passages quickly and provide them with visual summaries of the videos. We want to accomplish this without manual preparation work such as manual transcription and/or speaker identification. Therefore, we use a number of automatic techniques that provide indices into the video material and interfaces that allow users to browse video using those indices.

3   Automatic Media Analysis Techniques

Useful information may be automatically derived from sources such as audio and video. This information, or meta-data, can be generally described as a time-dependent value or values that are synchronous with the source media. For example, meta-data might come from the output of a face-recognition or speaker-identification algorithm.

Meta-data for video materials can be derived from the analysis of the audio and video streams. For audio, we identify features such as silence, applause, and speaker identity. For video, we find features such as shot boundaries, presentation slides, and close-ups of human faces. These provide several dimensions of data for our browser and player. To detect video features such as presentation slides, we use statistical models applied to discrete cosine transform coefficients that are trained with a set of example slides (Girgensohn & Foote, 1999). In our setting, such models recognize more than 85% of all slides while having less than 10% false positives.

Because automatic techniques do not always work reliably, rather than provide a yes or no answer, it is useful to translate meta-data values into a 'confidence score' for presentation to the user (Foote et al., 1998). For example, rather than having a binary decision for the presence or absence of a feature, we present the user with an interface that shows degree of certainty in decision.

3.1   Using Automatic Analysis

Even the most powerful analysis is useless unless it can be made meaningful to the user. With the analysis techniques described above, the amount of automatically generated meta-data can be overwhelming; it is common to generate multiple data points for each video frame, at a rate of 30 per second. An effective method for presenting confidence scores is a graphical visualization, as in Figure 1, in which the confidence score for a feature over time is depicted by levels of gray. Automatic analysis will never be perfect, and will sometimes yield inaccurate meta-data. Our approach is to acknowledge that the meta-data is inaccurate, but that hiding the errors achieves little. Conversely, presenting it fully as a confidence score lets the user decide what is important. In addition, user-selectable thresholds can take full advantage of all the meta-data.

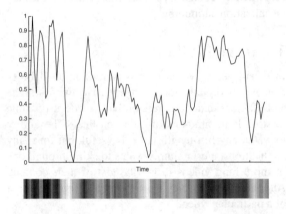

Figure 1: Mapping confidence scores to gray levels.

4   Web-based Video Directory Browser

To provide access to our video collection, we implemented a Web-based browser that presents directory listings of videos (see Figure 2). The directories organize videos by content (e.g. staff meetings or conference reports) and sort them by date within each directory. Clicking on a video opens a viewer to play it. The use of a Web browser and the MPEG file format enables casual access to the video archive for almost all potential users without the need for additional software or plug-ins.

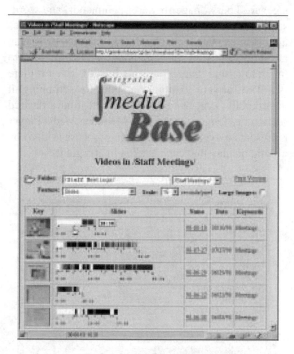

Figure 2: Web-based video directory browser.

4.1 Keyframe Use

We enhance each video directory listing with representative frames to help recognize the desired video, and to provide access points into the video. Well-chosen keyframes can help video selection and make the listing more visually appealing. Because it is both difficult to determine a single frame that best represents the whole video as well as to distinguish videos based on a single keyframe, we provide a number of keyframes. The positions of the keyframes are marked by blue triangles along a mouse-sensitive time scale adjacent to the keyframe (see Figure 3). As the mouse moves over the time scale, the keyframe for the corresponding time is shown and the triangle for that keyframe turns red. This method shows only a single keyframe at a time, preserving screen space while making other frames accessible through simple mouse motion. This interface supports very quick skimming that provides a good impression of the content of the video. Clicking anywhere on the time scale opens the video and starts playback at the corresponding time (by invoking the Metadata Media Player described in the next section). Using multiple keyframes in this way gives users an idea of the context and temporal structure of a video.

We experimented with animating keyframes by constantly rotating through the keyframes sequence associated with a video, but a display with dozens of animated images proved to be very distracting, even

when image changes were synchronized to each other. Access to keyframes via mouse movements gives a better impression of temporal sequence because it is correlated with mouse position.

Moving the mouse changes the time and the keyframe. Triangles mark keyframe positions.

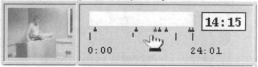

Figure 3: Keyframes attached to time scale.

We automatically determine a number of keyframes relative to the length of the video as discussed in (Girgensohn & Boreczky, 1999). Keyframe extraction is independent of any confidence score computed by other automatic analysis techniques. We found that 25 keyframes per hour of video work well for our default display. These keyframes are not distributed evenly over the length of the video but are concentrated in areas of interest. Our approach differs from other keyframe extraction methods — e.g. (Christel et al., 1998; Zhang et al., 1995) — in that it can determine an arbitrary number of non-evenly spaced keyframes that does not depend on the number of shots in the video.

We determine keyframes for an entire video by clustering video frames using a distance measure based on colour histograms (Zhang et al., 1993). This yields clusters that match human perception of similarity in most cases. In addition, temporal constraints for keyframe distribution and spacing are applied. Our approach produces keyframes that summarize a video and provide entry points to areas of interest. We store the clusters produced by the hierarchical clustering of the video frames so that any number of keyframes can be determined rapidly at presentation time. In this fashion, additional detail can be presented on demand. A static display that shows multiple keyframes for each video is available for printing.

4.2 Feature Display

Different features such as camera changes and slides can be selected from the pull-down menu above the video listing in the Web browser. To show how a feature varies with time, it is represented graphically in the time scale such that the shade of gray indicates the confidence level (see Figure 4). High confidence areas are marked in black while areas of lower confidence fade progressively to white, which indicates minimum confidence. Different features can be selected from a pull-down menu. For example, the display of the confidence for presentation slides provides a quick indication for the meetings with slide presentations as well as entry points to those presentations.

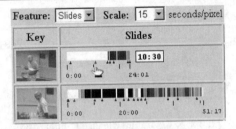

Feature and scale menus affect the confidence score display

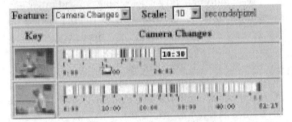

Figure 4: Confidence score display.

The feature time scale can be shown at different resolutions to support zooming in and out (see the 'Scale' menu in Figure 4). Presenting the feature graphically aids users in selecting the appropriate video. For example, if they seek a long presentation from a particular speaker, they can ignore videos containing only short examples of that speaker. When launching the Metadata Media Player for viewing a video, the presented feature is automatically selected in the Metadata Media Player, so that locating high confidence areas is rapid and easy.

5   Metadata Media Player

After finding one or more videos in the directory listing, the user must still investigate the videos to find the relevant one(s). It is not simple to determine whether a long video contains desired information without watching it in its entirety. Standard MPEG players only provide access at the granularity of whole videos. We developed a Metadata Media Player that allows finer-grained access by taking advantage of the meta-data extracted from the video. While there are convenient methods for the graphical browsing of text,

e.g. scroll bars, 'page-forward' commands, and word-search functions, existing video playback interfaces almost universally adopt the 'VCR' metaphor. To scan an entire video, it must be auditioned from start to finish to ensure that no parts are missed. Even if there is a 'fast forward' button or a slider for scrubbing,* it is generally a hit-or-miss operation to find a desired section in a lengthy video. The Metadata Media Player represents a dynamic time-varying process (video) by a static display that can be taken in at a glance.

Figure 5: Metadata Media Player.

Figure 5 shows the player interface. The usual transport controls are placed just below the video window. To the right of the window is a menu that selects which confidence score to display. In our case, features are 'slides', 'camera changes', and 'applause&laughter'. Confidence scores are displayed time-synchronously below the video slider. The confidence score gives valuable cues to interesting regions in the source stream by using the time axis for random-access into the source media stream. For example, from Figure 5 it is obvious that slides were presented in the last third of the meeting but not at the beginning. Selecting a point or region on the time axis starts media playback from the corresponding time. Clicking at the start of the initial dark bar will start playback with the first slide (see Figure 6). Thus time intervals of high potential interest can be visually identified from the confidence display and easily reviewed without a linear search.

---

*Scrubbing is moving the thumb of the time slider slowly so that video images are displayed in sequence.

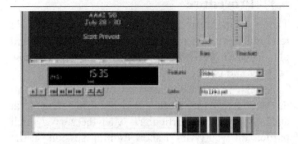

Figure 6: Skipping to the first slide.

Another way to use confidence scores is to threshold them, that is, to find the times when the confidence score is above, below, or crossing a certain threshold value. The threshold control (above the feature menu) determines index points by thresholding the selected confidence score (see Figure 7). Interface buttons change the current playback time to the next (or previous) index point. Unlike many other implementations, the threshold is user-selectable: a high threshold yields fewer index points and thus a coarser time granularity, while a lower threshold allows finer placement. This is helpful for several reasons: in an area of large confidence variation (many index points), the user can select the most significant indication by increasing the threshold. In a region of small confidence scores the user can still find index points within the region by reducing the threshold, though they may be less reliable. At the bottom of Figure 5 the buttons labeled ◀◀ and ▶▶ move the playback point to the previous or next index point, as determined from the threshold. The index points are marked in red at the top of the confidence score display.

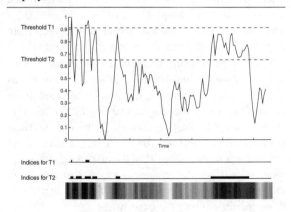

Figure 7: Index points for different thresholds.

6   User Study

An initial version of the video database system was deployed at our company in the spring of 1998.

It consisted of a Web-based directory browser that presented for each video the title, the date, the duration, and a list of keywords. Clicking on the title of a video opened the Microsoft Media Player and started playing the video from the beginning.

In order to investigate the usage of the system, we conducted a survey of 13 employees at our company. Users described how often they used the current system, which features they liked, and which features they thought were missing. The survey pointed out several features that would make the system more useful and increase usage.

The system was modified to include a Java applet to display multiple keyframes for each video and a Metadata Media Player that displayed confidence score information. This modified system was deployed to a small group of video researchers at our company.

Early feedback led us to believe that we had included a useful set of features, but that the interface might be too difficult for novices to use. We decided to conduct a small study to observe user behaviour during a set of typical browsing tasks using our initial design and the modified design.

6.1   Participants

Twelve participants (8 male, 4 female) were used in the study. The participants were a mix of researchers, support staff, and administrative staff with varying degrees of expertise in using video browsing software.

6.2   Materials

We created two versions of each interface. One set consisted of a simple Web-based directory listing that resembled our initial release (see Figure 8) coupled with a simple media player that contained the standard ActiveMovie controls (see Figure 9). The second set consisted of our latest release version of the Web-based directory browser and the Metadata Media Player described earlier in this paper and shown in Figures 2 & 5. All of the applications were instrumented to record the time of every mouse action to the nearest millisecond.

We created six information retrieval tasks, labeled A through F, that were representative of the typical activities of our users. Tasks A, C, and D required finding information that was presented on slides shown during a trip report. The information was shown for 3.3 seconds (D), 10.4 seconds (A), and 324 seconds (C), respectively. Task B required finding information presented for 1.3 seconds in the audio by a specified speaker, but the task description mentioned several visual cues that occurred within 110 seconds before the audio segment. Task E required counting the number of award recipients which were shown in a 5-minute video segment. Task F (which was performed last by participants) required finding the video that contained a particular trip report. This could be verified from information on several slides that were shown for 7 minutes.

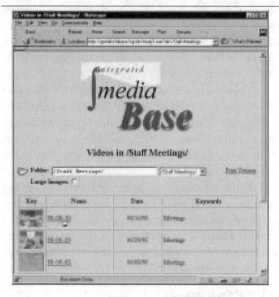

Figure 8: Video directory browser without meta-data.

Figure 9: Simple Media Player.

The six relevant staff meeting videos were presented in the directory browser, and no non-relevant videos were included in the list. Our automatic analysis techniques were applied to the videos to create three feature indices: 1) camera changes, 2) detected slides, and 3) laughter and applause.

6.3   Procedure

The experiment used a between-subjects design. Six randomly chosen participants used the old browser and player, while the other six participants used the new browser and player.

Each participant answered an initial survey to discover familiarity with video browsing in general and our system in particular. After the survey, each participant was given a short training session on the browser and player they would use to complete their tasks. This training took one minute for the old system and three minutes for the new system for most participants. Participants were encouraged to use the system until they felt comfortable with the features.

For each task, participants had to read a description of the information they were looking for, find the relevant video segment, and then write the answer on a sheet of paper. All mouse actions were recorded and time-stamped. The participants were videotaped and an experimenter noted the strategy used to discover the information required for each task. The completion time for each task was measured from the first mouse action to the last significant event (either stopping video playback or closing the browser).

An exit survey was used to assess the difficulty of the task and the usefulness of various features. Participants rated interface features on a 5 point scale.

6.4   Results

Participants used a wide variety of strategies to find the required information in the video documents. This led to a large variation in task completion times. There were no significant differences in performance between the two groups $(F(1, 10) = 1.15, p > 0.3)$. The average time to complete each task ranged from 32 seconds to 148 seconds among the participants.

Participants using the new interface commented that the ability to easily see multiple keyframes was useful. They also gave high scores for the usefulness of the display of the confidence scores for locating video passages. Participants using the old interface commented on the need for better information about the contents of the videos. For the new interface group, there were large differences between participants in the rating of interface features, reflecting the use of those features during the experiment.

6.5   Discussion

Participants using the old interfaces had two possible strategies: scrubbing or playing. Participants scrubbed until they saw an image related to the query and then used a combination of playing, scrubbing, and random positioning near the relevant passage until the desired information was found.

Participants using the new interfaces had a wider range of options. Some participants ignored the new features and followed the strategies mentioned above. Most participants moved the mouse along the time-line for the desired video until a keyframe related to the task was shown and then they clicked to start playback at that point. Participants were often confused by the fact that playback started at the point they clicked on the time-line and not at the time of the currently displayed keyframe. Only one participant selected different indices in the Web-based directory browser, but all of the participants in this group selected different indices in the player to help them find relevant passages. Some participants used the buttons to jump the next or previous index points, but more often they clicked at the start of the high-confidence areas on the time-line.

For both groups of participants, the first action taken after opening the media player was to stop video playback, usually accompanied by a mild exclamation of displeasure. Autoplay is a feature that works well for users who want to watch a full video from the start, but it aggravated users who wanted to browse. Another problem that both groups encountered was the lack of resolution of the slider and time-bar.

Participants using the new interfaces almost always used the indices and other features to help them find the required information quickly and easily. However, the large number of user interface elements occasionally sidetracked the participants, so that their overall task completion times were not significantly faster.

The wide variety of strategies used to complete the given tasks implies that even if we make a simplified interface the default, users should have the ability to activate additional features for specific tasks.

We have made a number of changes to the interfaces based on the results of the user study. The Metadata Media Player no longer starts playing the video upon start-up by default. We plan to study different solutions to the problem of the keyframe image not corresponding with the video playback starting point. The pause button has been eliminated, since it was functionally equivalent to the stop button. We are adding a default index feature that combines the applause and laughter detection feature with slide changes to give a generic 'interesting event' feature. We are also adding a zoom feature that expands a small segment of the video to fill the entire time-line, to facilitate fine positioning.

7 Related Work

Previous related work has been concerned with techniques for presenting and browsing continuous media database query results, and with techniques for presenting confidence values for full-text search. Bronson (1992) describes using time-stamped keyframes and keywords to access portions of a video sequence. Yeung et al. (1995) cluster keyframes to represent of the structure of a video sequence. Arman et al. (1994) use keyframes supplemented with pixels from the video sequence to represent content and motion within a sequence. In these systems, the keyframes are static and represent fixed points within the video sequence.

Wilcox et al. (1994) developed a system for graphically displaying the results of speaker segmentation and classification. The user is presented with the best classification estimate instead of the confidence values of those estimates. Brown et al. (1995) provide a set of confidence values for segments of (text) captions. In that system, a set of confidence values can be selected to start playback of the associated video segment. Confidence values from multiple features are not used. Tonomura et al. (1993) describe an interface that allows users to visualize multiple index features for video clips. Low-level features are displayed, making comparison difficult, but by mapping to a single time-line, correlations become evident. Their interface is intended as a visualization of the video indices, and is used for content analysis more than for browsing and playback. The STREAMS system (Cruz & Hill, 1994) supports the browsing of presentation recorded with several cameras. While it does not use automatic analysis techniques, it presents hand-annotated speaker information in a colour-coded time-line. None of these systems closely integrates automatic analysis with video content browsing and playback. Many of the systems also rely heavily on text extracted from close captions.

The NewsComm system (Roy & Schmandt, 1996) is a hardware device that allows users to navigate stored audio recordings. Automatic analysis is used to generate index points based on speaker changes and speech pauses. Users can skim the audio and skip to the next or previous index point. An early design of this system incorporated a graphical display of the index points available in the audio stream. This display was removed during the design process to simplify the interface, but not directly as a result of user tests.

There are many commercial and research systems used for video database access. The Virage Video Engine (Hampapur et al., 1997) is an example of a typical video indexing and retrieval system. This system provides several different indices, but a limited user interface. Video clips are found by specifying a set of low-level query terms. The meta-data that leads to the retrieval of specific clips is not presented to the user. This supports the goal of reducing the information presented to users, but in our opinion, the presentation of confidence scores derived from the meta-data provides more support for locating a desired clip quickly and easily for some users.

8   Conclusions

As video databases become larger and more common, intelligent video browsers will become critical for navigating, locating and accessing multimedia data. In this paper, we describe an interface that presents results from automatic video analysis and a media player for viewing and skimming a particular video. The browser presents a video directory listing that allow users to find a single video clip from a collection of videos. Keyframes appear in the video directory to distinguish different videos. Different meta-data types can be selected and a confidence-score scale indicate the likelihood and location of meta-data features in the video. Clicking at a point on the confidence scale provides direct playback of the video from the selected point. Both the directory listing and the media player use automatically-generated confidence scores to distinguish videos and to navigate within a single video.

A user study showed that both the dynamic keyframes and the feature scores helped users locate passages of interest. The study also uncovered a number of usability problems that prevented the participants of the study from being more efficient than the members of the control group. We will use the insights gained in the study to improve the user interfaces.

The technique for determining keyframes, the slider interface for changing keyframes, and the display of confidence scores for the presence of features are all innovative elements for facilitating access to video. Use both inside our company and in the user study show that our approach is a promising one. In the future, we plan to address the usability problems uncovered in the study, to introduce new techniques for navigating video, and to conduct a follow-up user study.

References

Arman, F., Depommier, R., A., H. & M.-Y., C. (1994), Content-Based Browsing of Video Sequences, *in* J. J. Garcia-Luna (ed.), *Proceedings of Multimedia'94*, ACM Press, pp.97–103.

Bronson, B. S. (1992), "Method and Apparatus for Indexing and Retrieving Audio-Video Data", US Patent 5,136,655.

Brown, M. G., Foote, J. T., Jones, G. J. F., Spärck Jones, K. & Young, S. J. (1995), Automatic Content-Based Retrieval of Broadcast News, *in* R. Heller (ed.), *Proceedings of Multimedia'95*, ACM Press, pp.35–43.

Christel, M. G., Smith, M. A., Taylor, C. R. & Winkler, D. B. (1998), Evolving Video Skims into Useful Multimedia Abstractions, in Human Factors in Computing Systems, *in* C.-M. Karat, A. Lund, J. Coutaz & J. Karat (eds.), *Proceedings of CHI'98: Human Factors in Computing Systems*, ACM Press, pp.171–8.

Cruz, G. & Hill, R. (1994), Capturing and Playing Multimedia Events with STREAMS, *in* J. J. Garcia-Luna (ed.), *Proceedings of Multimedia'94*, ACM Press, pp.193–200.

Foote, J., Boreczky, J., Girgensohn, A. & Wilcox, L. (1998), An Intelligent Media Browser using Automatic Multimodal Analysis, *in* H. J. Zhang & L. Carr (eds.), *Proceedings of Multimedia'98*, ACM Press, pp.375–80.

Girgensohn, A. & Boreczky, J. (1999), Time-constrained Keyframe Selection Technique, *in* D. C. Martin (ed.), *Proceedings of IEEE Multimedia Systems*, Vol. 1, IEEE Computer Society Press, pp.756–61.

Girgensohn, A. & Foote, J. (1999), Video Classification Using Transform Coefficients, *in International Conference on Acoustics, Speech, and Signal Processing*, Vol. 6, IEEE Publications, pp.3045–8.

Hampapur, A., Gupta, A., Horowitz, B., Shu, C.-F., Fuller, C., Bach, J., Gorkani, M. & Jain, R. (1997), Virage Video Engine, *in* I. K. Sethi & R. C. Jain (eds.), *Storage and Retrieval for Still Image and Video Databases V*, Vol. 3022, SPIE, pp.188–97.

Roy, D. K. & Schmandt, C. (1996), A Hand-Held Interface for Interactive Access to Structured Audio, in Human Factors in Computing Systems, *in* G. van der Veer & B. Nardi (eds.), *Proceedings of CHI'96: Human Factors in Computing Systems*, ACM Press, pp.173–80.

Tonomura, Y., Akutsu, A., Otsuji, K., & Sadakata, T. (1993), VideoMAP and VideoSpaceIcon: Tools for Anatomizing Video Content, *in* S. Ashlund, K. Mullet, A. Henderson, E. Hollnagel & T. White (eds.),

Proceedings of INTERCHI'93, ACM Press/IOS Press, pp.131–41.

Wang, C. & Brandstein, M. S. (1998), A Hybrid Real-time Face Tracking System, *in Proceedings of ICASSP '98*, Vol. VI, IEEE Publications, pp.3737–40.

Wilcox, L., Chen, F. & Balasubramanian, V. (1994), Segmentation of Speech Using Speaker Identification, *in Proceedings of ICASSP '94*, Vol. S1, IEEE Publications, pp.161–4.

Yeung, M. M., Yeo, B. L., Wolf, W. & Liu, B. (1995), Video Browsing using Clustering and Scene Transitions on Compressed Sequences, *in* A. A. Rodriguez & J. Maitan (eds.), *Proceedings of Multimedia Computing and Networking*, Vol. 2417, SPIE, pp.399–413.

Zhang, H. J., Kankanhalli, A. & Smoliar, S. W. (1993), "Automatic Partitioning of Full-motion Video", *Multimedia Systems* **1**(1), 10–28.

Zhang, H. J., Low, C. Y., Smoliar, S. W. & Wu, J. H. (1995), Video Parsing, Retrieval and Browsing: An Integrated and Content-based Solution, *in* R. Heller (ed.), *Proceedings of Multimedia'95*, ACM Press, pp.15–24.

Human–Computer Interaction — INTERACT '99
M. Angela Sasse and Chris Johnson (Editors)
Published by IOS Press, © IFIP TC.13, 1999

Privacy Issues in Ubiquitous Multimedia Environments: Wake Sleeping Dogs, or Let Them Lie?

Anne Adams & M. Angela Sasse

Department of Computer Science, University College London, Gower Street, London WC1E 6BT, UK.

{A.Adams,A.Sasse}@cs.ucl.ac.uk

Abstract: Many users are not aware of the potential privacy implications of ubiquitous multimedia applications. Decision-makers are often reluctant to raise users' awareness, since this may open a '*can of worms*' and deter potential users. We conducted an opportunistic study after video-conferencing developers placed a camera in the common room of their university department, broadcasting the video on the Internet. The email debate following the common room users 'discovery' of the camera's existence was analysed as well as 47 anonymous questionnaire responses. Three distinct types of responses were identified, varying with the *media type* (audio vs. video) transmitted and *scope of distribution* (local vs. global). The groups also differ in their perception of the common room *situation* (public vs. private) and the degree of *control* exerted by observers and those observed. We conclude that privacy implications of ubiquitous multimedia applications must be made explicit. Users who discover privacy implication retrospectively are likely to respond in an emotive manner, reject the technology, and lose trust in those responsible for it.

Keywords: Internet, multimedia applications, privacy, trust, ubiquitous computing, grounded theory

1 Introduction

1.1 Background

With the rapid advance of network and compression technology, ubiquitous multimedia is fast becoming a reality (Crowcroft et al., to appear). Applications of this technology include broadcasting of multimedia data on a global scale (e.g. putting lectures and seminars on the Internet) and continuous recording of such data (e.g. video diaries). Remote access is an inherent feature of ubiquitous multimedia applications: data captured locally by microphones, cameras and sensors can be accessed through the network. Many users will welcome the chance to remotely check their windows at home if a storm breaks while they are at work, or to survey the contents of their fridge before going to the supermarket on their way home. The same users would not, however, allow anybody to view live video from their home, or to monitor their food preferences, since such data are regarded as private. Clearly, the increase in multimedia data, and functionality for accessing and using them, carries risks for users as well as benefits (Bellotti, 1997; Neumann, 1995; Smith, 1993).

Privacy is a basic human requirement. The US supreme court ruled that privacy is a more fundamental right than any of those stated in the Bill of Rights (Schoeman, 1992). Providing adequate protection of people's privacy is complicated by the phenomenon's socio-psychological nature — what is regarded as private varies across individuals, organizations and cultures. This is especially true in ubiquitous multimedia environments, which can involve many individuals, domains and cultures. There is, therefore, an obvious need for a HCI model of salient factors, which allow prediction of perceived privacy invasions. The main problem with establishing such a model in is that privacy factors vary according to users' perceptions, which are manipulated by an array of personal trade-offs (Davies, 1997). It is, therefore, necessary to consider social norms that guide our interactions, and how ubiquitous multimedia environments distort these norms and relevant privacy factors.

1.2 Social Norms

There is evidence that users equate computer-mediated interaction with interaction in the real world. Users' perception of social factors, such as privacy, is, therefore, vital to the successful and effective introduction of technology. Social norms (such as politeness and decency) guide social interactions and determine socially rich responses — irrespective of whether a system was designed to cater for them (Laurel, 1993; Reeves & Nass, 1996). Based on existing knowledge, users construct social representations that allow them to recognize and contextualize social stimuli. These representations originate from social interaction and help us construct an understanding of the social world, enabling interaction between groups sharing the representations (Augoustinos & Walker, 1995). Social situations provide cues that allow people to make assessments of those situations. Harrison & Dourish (1996) argue that it is a *sense of place* that guides social interactions and our perceptions of privacy, rather than the *physical* characteristics of a space. This is because social norms guide our perceptions of spaces allowing us to interpret them as places and adapt our behaviours accordingly. All parties within the same culture understand what is — and is not — acceptable in a given situation (i.e. it is acceptable to stare at a street performer but not at a passer-by). However, our perception of a situation also depends on how we see ourselves in that situation. Goffman (1969) pointed out that, when an individual takes part in an interaction, there is an intentional and unknowing perception of being involved in the situation. The presentation of the *self* within a perceived situation increases the risks attached with potential consequences extending from the personal to the social level. If an individual's perception of a situation turns out to be incorrect *after the event*, there are far-reaching consequences. Previously natural interactions suddenly seem inappropriate, making individuals feel awkward and flustered. The perception of the self and others is also likely to change. Ultimately, how we perceive ourselves depends on assumptions made about a situation that are based on social norms. If these assumptions are vastly inaccurate, there will be far-reaching repercussions.

1.3 Ubiquitous Multimedia Technology

Cowan (1983) argues that invasion of privacy is merely a by-product of the information society. Technology increases potential invasions of privacy because of the perceived *control* of certain applications. Karabenick & Knapp (1988) studied students who failed to identify concepts in a task, and were allowed to seek help from a computer or another person. The

proportion of those seeking help from the computer was significantly greater than those turning to a person. Since a computer does not make psychological judgements about abilities, users' felt in control of the situation and trusted in the technology. Surveillance technology, on the other hand, has been used to curtail our freedom in a way so as to control and manipulate socially unacceptable behaviour. Jeremy Bentham (1832) argued for control by surveillance, in the preface to his *Panopticon*, whereby every person in a building is watched from a central tower. Although people are not watched all the time, they maintain their standards of behaviour for *fear of being watched*. Fear is maintained by examples being made of odd individuals, "*to keep the others on their toes*". The *Panopticon's* modern-day equivalent, closed-circuit television (CCTV), is one of the fastest growing technologies. In the UK, for instance, coverage is such that there will soon be a national CCTV network. Although CCTV provides little or no means of control by those being observed many users accept the potential risks to their privacy (e.g. security staff using CCTV footage for their entertainment or profit) in a trade-off with perceived benefit (e.g. preventing crime). Such trade-offs are usually made within an environment where the perceived individual risks are low (*I am doing nothing wrong, so I am OK*) and/or the perceived benefits (e.g. personal safety) are high. If such a risk assessment (based on social cues) turns out to be inaccurate, the implications for privacy are far-reaching.

People need social cues about the type of situation in which they find themselves (e.g. public/private), and the types of appropriate behaviour with which they should respond (Goffman, 1969). We also use social cues to assess who we are interacting with and how we think others perceive us. Multimedia environments vary in the level of contextual cues provided that enable users to appropriately frame their interactive behaviour (Harrison & Dourish, 1996). Privacy problems often occur when people who *are observed* cannot *see how they are being viewed*, by whom (the information receiver), and for what purpose (Bellotti, 1997; Lee et al., 1997). Users may make assumptions about the information receiver (IR) viewing a picture of a certain size or quality, but technology may allow the receiver to configure and manipulate the image they receive. Interpersonal distance has, in the past, been found to dictate the intensity of a response: faces in a close-up are scrutinised more often than those in the background. Reeves & Nass (1996) argue that, because the size of a face is more than just a representation of an individual, it can influence psychological judgements of a person and thus become an invasive piece of information. Image quality and camera angles may result in a perception of the viewee by the viewer that the viewee regards as inaccurate. Users' assumptions about the IR can similarly be distorted by the technology. A system allowing the viewer to freeze the video (e.g. so that they appear to be avidly watching the screen, when they have actually gone to make themselves a cup of tea) could produce an inaccurate appraisal of their attention within the interaction. Another privacy issue associated with the IR is the viewee's assumption that there is only one viewer, when the information is actually accessible to many others. It has been argued that — if a system is embedded in the organizational culture — social controls will establish a culture of use which will restrict these activities (Dourish, 1993). Relying merely on social controls for safeguarding privacy is dangerous if assumptions based on social cues are distorted by the technology itself. The aim of the study reported here was to identify users' perceptions of ubiquitous multimedia, and its relationship to privacy factors. A specific model of the factors guiding users in their privacy assessments will then be developed.

1.4   Privacy Factors

To define privacy adequately, it is important to identify privacy *boundaries* which, if breached, are likely to cause resentment among users. If such boundaries can be identified and mapped, appropriate organizational behaviour and security mechanisms could be formulated and integrated into organizational policy (Smith, 1993). Previous research has identified three main privacy factors: *information sensitivity, information receiver, and information usage*:

Information Sensitivity: Previous work on users' perception of authentication mechanisms (Adams et al., 1997; Adams & Sasse, to appear) identified the concept of *information sensitivity*: users rate certain types of information as sensitive or private. This perception determines the amount of effort that users are prepared to expend on protecting that information. Discussions of privacy often ignore that the same information may be rated — and therefore treated — differently by different users. Another common misconception is that users make a simple binary *private/not private* distinction: users actually describe information sensitivity as a dimension with varying degrees of sensitivity.

Information Receiver (IR): Users' privacy can be invaded without them being aware of it (Bellotti, 1997). This leads to a further important distinction: whether it is *what is known* about a person that is invasive, or *who knows* it. To date, research on privacy has not clearly identified the role of the IR — who receives information that is rated as sensitive by a user. Users' perception of being *vulnerable to* — and *trusting* — the IR can enable or restrict self-expression and personal development within multimedia communications. Certain technology may apply well in an environment of trust but fail in an atmosphere of distrust (Harrison & Dourish, 1996; Bellotti, 1997).

Information Usage: Information about users can promote concerns about how and for what purposes it is used. (Dix, 1990). At the same time, privacy concerns can be reduced through trust, i.e. in an environment that have an '*acceptable use*' policy for potentially invasive applications and/or data (Bellotti & Sellen, 1993). It has been suggested that a lack of contextual elements in processing and use may be a key factor in potential invasions of privacy (Dix, 1990). These concerns can be addressed by providing users with mechanisms for control and feedback (Bellotti & Sellen, 1993). Such mechanisms, though, do not necessarily cover information which users initially perceived as innocuous but is potentially invasive when viewed out of context.

Finally, it must be identified whether users trade off perceived privacy risks against benefits (see Section 1.3).

2   The Study

2.1   Situation

Two video-conferencing developers (not the authors) placed a small camera in the staff common room of their university department. Their immediate colleagues knew about the camera, but the general staff of the department were not consulted. The camera captured a limited view of the common room, including the entrance, pigeonholes and some of the seating area. The camera view was transmitted over the multi-cast backbone of the Internet* and thus could be viewed potentially by thousands of users

---

*See Macedonia & Brutzman (1994) for an introduction to multi-cast conferencing technology and its applications.

anywhere in the world. The developers placed a notice explaining the purpose of the camera on the common room door. However, most common room users did not read the notice because the door was always open, obscuring the notice.

The purpose of the camera — to contribute to an existing "*Places around the World*" multi-cast session — was also announced in a casual message to a small email list of multi-cast tool developers. A week later, an email message about the availability of images from the common room was sent to a larger multimedia research list, and finally to the departmental mailing list. Three reasons were cited for placing the camera:

1. "We can see from our desks what's going on in the common room, and decide whether to go there."

2. "To stop people taking coffee from other people's pigeonholes" (followed by a ";-)" smilie).

3. "This helps us gain experience with tele-presence."

An email debate ensued, in which several departmental members stated they were unhappy about the camera being in the common room. It was then suggested that the camera would be more beneficial in the photocopier room to check the accessibility of the copier. After a day's debate, the camera was moved to the photocopier room. Placed behind the copier, it transmitted a close-up view (at hip level) of photocopier users. There was a prominent notice on the photocopier room door and an announcement on the multimedia research list. The email debate continued, and further objections were raised, until the camera was finally removed.

The authors decided to seize the opportunity and distributed a 2-page anonymous[†] paper questionnaire, with both closed and open-ended questions[‡] to all departmental members. The questionnaire asked how comfortable respondents were about:

1. Audio and visual transmission.

2. The situation (common vs. photocopier room).

3. For different levels of transmission (department vs. university vs. world).

4. The re-use of the information within a different context.

Grounded theory methods (Strauss & Corbin, 1990) were used to analyse the questionnaire responses and all relevant email messages.

2.2 Results

Pearson's correlation coefficient was used to analyse 47 questionnaire responses. The majority of respondents agreed on two points:

1. They were significantly less comfortable with audio rather than video data being transmitted — both generally and in the specific situation of the common room.

2. They were significantly less comfortable with the re-use of (recorded) video data as opposed to continuous transmission (see Table 1).

	No	Mean	Sig
General	47	3.10	$p < 0.005$
Visual & Audio		4.619	
Specific*	47	3.17	$p < 0.005$
Visual & Audio		4.643	
Specific*	47	3.17	$p < 0.005$
Visual & Reuse		4.24	

Table 1: Significant findings for all respondents (*specific situation of the common room).

In a cluster analysis, 3 groups with significantly different *perception profiles* emerged (see Table 2 and Figure 1).

	Group 1	Group 2	Group 3
Group size	15	14	13
Significance levels			
Visual transmission General / Specific	*0.029	0.655	0.053
General Visual / Audio	*0.005	*0.000	*0.000
Specific Visual / Audio	0.055	*0.000	*0.000
CS / UCL	0.189	*0.047	1.000
CS / World DIS	0.096	*0.028	0.721

Table 2: Clustered groups comfort levels (*$p<0.05$).

Further qualitative analysis provided distinct profiles of each group (see Tables 3 & 4). The qualitative issues were categorized according to the 3 privacy factors previously highlighted (see Section 1.4). A clear difference was identified between respondents in Group 3's perspective of the situation and the other two groups.

[†]We did not ask for information which could potentially be used to identify respondents (e.g. multimedia expertise, gender).
[‡]These sections allowed respondents to 'let off steam' — several pages were filled out by some respondents, providing a rich source of qualitative data.

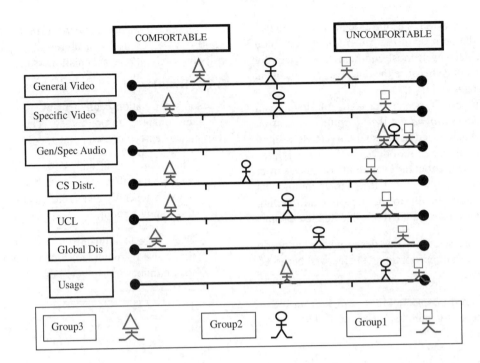

Figure 1: Group profile for relevant privacy issues.

	Group 1	Group 2	Group 3
Information Receiver			
Observed Control	9	5	0
Observer Control	0	0	7
Information Sensitivity			
CR Private Situation	3	4	1
CR Public Situation	0	0	4
Information Usage			
Benefits	0	6	7
Costs	14	8	0

Table 3: Sample of qualitative analysis by groups.

	Group 1 & 2	Group 3
Observed Control	"…how to become one of the peeping toms"	No comments
Observer Control	No comments	"Could also be used as a soap substitute"
Emotive response	"only for nosy computer scientists wishing to assess the usefulness of their technology"	No comments

Table 4: Sample of coded comments.

Since questionnaire responses were collected anonymously, we were not able to identify Group 3 members. However, analysis of the email debate indicates that many of the respondents who placed the camera in the common room (multi-cast tool developers) exhibited Group 3 profiles (discussed in detail in Section 3.2).

The degree of invasiveness of the video was also identified as related to the quality and focus of the picture being transmitted.

3   Discussion

3.1   Privacy Model Validated

One pivotal finding of this study is the impact that users' perception of *information sensitivity* has on their assessment of privacy invasions. All users were significantly less comfortable with *audio* — rather than visual data — being transmitted. Users perceive what they say to be potentially more sensitive than what they do — in general, and in the specific case of this study (where video only was transmitted). All respondents also expressed strong discomfort if the video data transmitted were to be recorded and re-used (*information usage*) out of context (Dix, 1990). This highlights the flexible nature of *information sensitivity* — data initially considered to be non-invasive may be perceived as invasive when used out of context. Contrary to our expectations, the majority of respondents did not perceive the *information receiver* as an important factor effecting *information sensitivity* — except for Group 2, who was significantly more uncomfortable with distribution of the visual data beyond the department. Ultimately, the two groups that did not perceive the *information receiver* as a factor, either perceived the data as highly sensitive and thus invasive regardless of who viewed it (Group 1) or very low in sensitivity and non-invasive whoever saw it (Group 3).

3.2 Individual Differences or Social Norms

The study revealed different perceptions of the *situation* and relevant privacy implications. Although this divide may not represent a split prior to perceived privacy invasions, it could be concluded that the divisions are due to individual differences in privacy needs. There have been arguments presented regarding the individual differences in privacy responses. Underwood & Moore (1981) argued that some peoples' behaviour varies according to the situation, whereas others' does not. Those with a high degree of 'private self-consciousness'[§] carefully monitor their own behaviour (even when not being observed) and show consistent behaviour from situation to situation.

There are arguments, however, that organizational culture and social control can be traded-off against users' individual differences in privacy concerns (Dourish, 1993). Bellotti & Sellen's (1993) research identified that a reduction in users' concern about privacy was related to a general environment of trust, and the development of acceptable practices governing the use of the application. This brings to the forefront issues of trust, legitimate use and confidence in the information receivers. Ultimately trust — or lack of it — in *information receivers* and *information usage* is an important variable amongst all users, which can determine the information sensitivity. Our results show clear divisions in levels of trust in the technology. Whilst Group 3 expressed a high degree of trust (high usage benefits and no cost) in multi-cast conferencing, respondents in Groups 1 and 2 (68% of the respondents) expressed a lack of trust in the system (high usage costs). A key factor for Groups 1 and 2 appears to be the perception of being observed in a *private* situation (the common room) — a violation of a social norm. Group 3 in contrast perceived the common room to be a *public*

situation with reduced social norms on observing people. This finding emphasises the importance of the perceived distinction between private and public, and the expected social norms in each situation, when defining *information sensitivity* (Schoeman, 1992). It could be argued that Group 3's perception of the common room as public is connected to their view of *observing*[¶] rather than *being observed* in this situation (Group 1 & 2's assessment). It is interesting that those who originally placed the camera (technical experts in network multimedia) showed Group 3 profiles in the email discussion. A sense of being in *control* of the technology could therefore be linked to a distorted perception (from the majority) of the situation. These differences in perceptions may have already existed within the department. However, the technology introduction brought these differences to the fore, resulting in tension and an emotive debate which ended with a formal departmental decision to remove the technology. This is a lesson for other organizations: to assess how the relationships between organizational *control* and *trust* will affect users' privacy. Trust is undermined if users are not allowed to judge trade-offs for themselves or feel part of the proposed solution. Guidelines and boundaries (rather than restrictive controls) for use of the technology is required to encourage and nurture trust.

3.3 Technologies Distorting Social Norms

To understand the power of ubiquitous multimedia applications, we must understand the social and psychological factors governing its use. Most people are social creatures who are naturally interested in the world and people around them. The key question is whether that interest is socially acceptable and where the dividing line between benign and intrusive lies. *Being watched* is not a problem *per se* — it depends on our awareness of *how, when and by whom*. The type (e.g. camera angle), quality (e.g. resolution) and continuity (still images or continuous film) of video images can make them more or less invasive. It is not only important to an individual that they are identifiable in certain situations, but also how they are perceived. Film makers have used camera angles (close-ups, long shots) distorted quality (frosted lenses, lighting from below) and film continuity (stills, slow motion) for decades to aid film viewers in a crafted perception (as busy, slovenly, evil or good) of characters (Reeves & Nass, 1996). Thus, the individual's need to control how others

---

[§]This relates to Schoeman's (1992) idea of certain behaviours being mediated by social norms.
[¶]These respondents also frequently used the common room and commented on this factor.

view them cannot be ignored. Several respondents objected to the second situation (in the photocopy room) because the camera showed the hip portion only — producing a potentially comical or embarrassing image. How we are viewed is also dependent on the situation in which we are observed. Harrison & Dourish (1996) pointed out the importance of our perception of *place* in social interactions. We expect different behaviour in private and public situations. In this study we identified a division in the perceptions of the common room situation. An individual's failure to accurately identify a situation as private can have serious consequences. To assess a technology-mediated situation accurately, users require adequate feedback and control mechanisms (Bellotti, 1997). Users' assessment of a situation depends on the degree of *control* they retain over how they are viewed and by whom. Our study highlighted how the observer's control of the technology distorted their perception of the place being observed. To explain this complex phenomenon, consider the analogy of sitting in a café (semi-private) watching people in the street (public) — which is socially acceptable in most cultures. However, someone in the street (public) pulling up a chair and staring in at the diners of the café (semi-private) would be perceived as unacceptable. Relating this analogy to this study, we can understand that the common room users perceived the situation as their café (semi-private) looking out on the street and corridor (public), able to see who can see them. The common room observers, however, were sitting at their desk — equivalent to their café — (private) looking out on the common room (public), seeing people who cannot see them. The issue highlighted by this example is the perceived ownership and control of the 'window'. We know and accept the risk of being watched and scrutinized as we walk in the streets (public). However, in more private situations (e.g. a café or changing room), our acceptance of being watched is reduced. Ultimately, our behaviour is guided by the situation. If we misjudge the situation then we are at more of a risk of socially embarrassing ourselves. Assessing that situation is, therefore, of immense importance in our social interactions. This may help to explain the emotive response that ensued from the camera installation: a perceived privacy invasion. The emotive response was caused by Group 1 & 2's perceived *lack of control* over the situation, whereas Group 3 could not understand what all the fuss was about. Emotive responses are produced as a defence mechanisms to a perceived threat, resulting

from a lack of control over — potentially detrimental — representations of the self (Goffman, 1969; Schoeman, 1992). Once users experience a lack of control and respond emotively, a total rejection of the application and all similar technology is the likely consequence. In this study, those who felt the most discomfort subsequently rejected transmission of any audio and video data under any circumstances.

4   Conclusions

In any social interaction, implicit assumptions are made to ensure the success of the interaction. If those assumptions are incorrect, we are more likely to misjudge a situation and act inappropriately. Multimedia environments have the potential to distort the assumptions that guide our behaviour (Reeves & Nass, 1996). The technology developers' (who placed the camera) surprise at the emotive reactions to the perceived privacy invasion shows they had made inaccurate assumptions and misinterpreted the situation. The key to their perception of the situation as *public* is their familiarity with the technology, and thus their sense of control over it. This is probably why, even though Group 3 used the common room, they still retained an over-riding perception of the situation as an observer — they viewed the situation "through the camera's eyes". The reasons for placing the camera, as detailed by the technology developers' in an email, were primarily those of the observers, and not of those being observed. The 'security' motivation (catch those who take other people's coffee) behind the camera placement, shows how the camera instigators dangerously crossed the line between multi-media environments and CCTV. Crossing this line breaks many implicit assumptions underlying multimedia environments as a tool for increased co-operation, communication and thus freedom of information. Similarly, if CCTV broke the assumptions[||] underlying their successful implementation, they would be in danger of producing an emotive backlash. The camera instigators also stated that the purpose for the technology was to increase tele-presence and allow users to see what was going on in the common room. However, as the Web site was not initially advertised to the whole department, this again decreased a sense of control over the technology for those being observed, and produced an emotive rejection of it beyond the confines of the present situation. This is an important finding for anyone introducing ubiquitous multimedia technology in an organization. Because of the degree

---

[||] If CCTV in a department store is used by management to assess staff performance, or by marketing to profile customers, this would violate passer-by assumptions of both the perceived information receiver (security personnel) and usage (security) factors.

of personal infringement experienced and the resulting emotive response, it is vital that the situation and implicit assumptions are judged accurately prior to installation. Privacy problems need to be addressed before they arise — before users lose trust and become emotive. Once a problem becomes emotive it is far harder to solve. However, this danger arises from the organizational philosophy of '*if it isn't broken, don't fix it*'. When it comes to ubiquitous multimedia technology and privacy — such an approach is likely to lead to rejection of the technology, and loss of trust in the organization that introduced it. Ultimately it is too dangerous to let those sleeping dogs lie.

5   Acknowledgements

We gratefully acknowledge the help of staff in the Department of Computer Science at UCL. Anne Adams is funded by BT/ESRC CASE studentship S00429637018.

References

Adams, A. & Sasse, M. A. (to appear), "The User is not the Enemy", *Communications of the ACM* . Department of Computer Science, University College London RN/97/40.

Adams, A., Sasse, M. A. & Lunt, P. (1997), Making Passwords Secure and Usable, *in* H. Thimbleby, B. O'Conaill & P. Thomas (eds.), *People and Computers XII (Proceedings of HCI'97)*, Springer-Verlag, pp.1–19.

Augoustinos, M. & Walker, I. (1995), *Social Cognition*, Sage Publications.

Bellotti, V. (1997), Design for Privacy in Multimedia Computing and Communications Environments, *in* P. Agre & M. Rotenberg (eds.), *Technology and Privacy: The New Landscape*, MIT Press, pp.63–98.

Bellotti, V. & Sellen, A. (1993), Designing for Privacy in Ubiquitous Computing Environments, *in* G. de Michelis, C. Simone & K. Schmidt (eds.), *Proceedings of ECSCW'93, the 3rd European Conference on Computer-Supported Cooperative Work*, Kluwer, pp.77–92.

Bentham, J. (1832), Panopticon, *in* J. Bentham (ed.), *The Panopticon Writings*, Verson.

Cowan, R. S. (1983), *More Work for Mother: The Ironies of Household Technology from the Open Hearth to the Microwave*, Basic Books.

Crowcroft, J., Handley, M. & Wakeman, I. (to appear), *Internetworking Multimedia*, UCL Press.

Davies, S. (1997), Re-Engineering the Right to Privacy, *in* P. Agre & M. Rotenberg (eds.), *Technology and Privacy: The New Landscape*, MIT Press, pp.143–65.

Dix, A. (1990), Information Processing, Context and Privacy, *in* D. Diaper, D. Gilmore, G. Cockton & B. Shackel (eds.), *Proceedings of INTERACT '90 — Third IFIP Conference on Human–Computer Interaction*, Elsevier Science, pp.15–20.

Dourish, P. (1993), Culture and Control in a MediaSpace, *in* G. de Michelis, C. Simone & K. Schmidt (eds.), *Proceedings of ECSCW'93, the 3rd European Conference on Computer-Supported Cooperative Work*, Kluwer, pp.125–137.

Goffman, E. (1969), *The Presentation of Self in Everyday Life*, Penguin.

Harrison, R. & Dourish, P. (1996), Re-Place-ing Space: The Roles of Place and Space in Collaborative Systems, *in* M. S. Ackerman (ed.), *Proceedings of CSCW'96: Conference on Computer Supported Cooperative Work*, ACM Press, pp.67–76.

Karabenick, S. A. & Knapp, J. R. (1988), "Effects of Computer Privacy on Help-Seeking", *Journal of Applied Social Psychology* **18**(6), 461–72.

Laurel, B. (1993), *Computers as Theatre*, Addison–Wesley.

Lee, A., Girgensohn, A. & Schlueter, K. (1997), NYNEX Portholes: Initial User Reactions and Redesign Implications, *in* S. C. Hayne & W. Prinz (eds.), *Proceedings of International ACM SIGGROUP Conference on Supporting Group Work, GROUP'97*, ACM Press, pp.385–94.

Macedonia, M. R. & Brutzman, D. P. (1994), "MBone Provides Audio and Video Across the Internet", *IEEE Computer* **27**(4), 30–6.

Neumann, P. (1995), *Computer Related Risks*, Addison–Wesley.

Reeves, B. & Nass, C. (1996), *The Media Equation: How People Treat Computers, Television and New Media Like Real People and Places*, Cambridge University Press.

Schoeman, F. D. (1992), *Privacy and Social Freedom*, Cambridge University Press.

Smith, J. (1993), "Privacy Policies and Practices: Inside the Organizational Maze", *Communications of the ACM* **36**(12), 105–22.

Strauss, A. & Corbin, J. (1990), *Basics of Qualitative Research: Grounded Theory Procedures and Techniques*, Sage Publications.

Underwood, B. & Moore, B. S. (1981), "Sources of Behavioural Consistency", *Journal of Personality and Social Psychology* **40**(4), 780–5.

Human–Computer Interaction — INTERACT '99
M. Angela Sasse and Chris Johnson (Editors)
Published by IOS Press, © IFIP TC.13, 1999

Evaluating Gedrics: Usability of a Pen-centric Interface

Jörg Geißler[1], Michele Gauler[2] & Norbert A. Streitz[3]

[1] Plenum Systeme GmbH, Hagenauer Straße 53, 65203 Wiesbaden, Germany.
[2] Johannes Gutenberg University, Institute of Psychology, Staudingerweg 9, 55099 Mainz, Germany.
[3] GMD-IPSI, Dolivostraße 15, 64293 Darmstadt, Germany.
Joerg.Geissler@plenum.de, gaulm000@mail.uni-mainz.de,
Norbert.Streitz@gmd.de

Abstract: Many users of today's pen computers have an ambiguous attitude towards these devices. On the one hand, they like the ease of use, especially in the beginning. On the other hand, after some time, they often feel hampered by the systems since the user interfaces do not reflect the users' individual skills, experiences, and preferences. Pen interfaces treat all users in the same way — like novices. Becoming an expert or 'power' user is quite difficult. In this paper, we report on the *gedric* approach (Geißler, 1995) to this problem and evaluate an application with a so-called *pen-centric user interface* (Geißler, to appear). We will show that such an interface efficiently supports experienced as well as novice users. By having the freedom to choose from two popular interaction styles — menus and gestures — and to mix them arbitrarily, gedrics support a wide range of user preferences and skills. This results not only in efficient individual working styles but also in a high user satisfaction.

Keywords: pen computing, gestures, menu interaction, gedrics, usability, study evaluation.

1 Introduction

A widely used statement in the research field of pen computing (Meyer, 1995) says that the pen is mightier than the mouse. In addition to pointing, people are able to sketch, annotate, gesture, and even write with an electronic stylus as they can do with pen and paper (Wolf et al., 1989). Unfortunately, today's user interfaces for pen computers — so-called pen-based interfaces — only use a fraction of the capability of the pen. A small number of gestures is used for simple editing tasks but most of the interface is still based on traditional concepts like push buttons, pull-down menus or other point-and-click components. Strictly speaking, in these interfaces, the pen primarily simulates the mouse and just offers some neat add-ons in terms of gestures. Pen interfaces seem to ignore that pen interaction primarily is stroke-based, and not tap-based (Geißler, 1995).

In the long term, those 'gesture-enhanced point-and-click interfaces' obstruct users who have become experienced or even experts because there are no short cuts for all the functions that are available. Users are forced to continue working with inappropriate interface components — see also (Grudin, 1989). Current pen interfaces may be attractive for inexperienced users, but they do not support their learning process and finally they still treat skilled users like novices.

Extending the influence of gestures on the overall interface design is not that easy. Most of the time, studies about the usability of pen gestures restricted the number of gestures deliberately to ten or even less (Geißler, to appear). Gestures are only useful if they are easy to remember and this depends on their 'naturalness' or familiarity to users. For this reason, only very specific tasks have been observed. Evaluators admitted that the usability of gestures in other, more complex tasks or even in applications that are completely based on gestures, is not yet clear and require further observations (Wolf, 1992).

An attempt to overcome these shortcomings is a user interface component that combines traditional interface concepts with pen gestures. Therefore, we developed the *gedric* (Geißler, 1995). It is part of a so-called *pen-centric interface* (Geißler, to appear) that also covers aspects like ubiquitous annotations, handling user input tolerantly, and more. Gedrics provide an efficient way of interacting with a pen system while engendering a high level of user satisfaction.

In this paper, we briefly describe the concept of gedrics and present an application that makes use of gedrics. Then, we report on an evaluation of this application as well as its results. After a discussion, we will conclude and provide an outlook onto our future work.

2   Gedrics

A gedric (Geißler, 1995) is a *gesture-driven icon*, i.e. it is an interface component that has an iconic form and on that users draw strokes with a pen. These strokes are interpreted by the gedric and transformed into commands. Gedrics belong to the functional parts of a pen interface, like tool bars or pull-down menus in mouse interfaces.

A gedric bundles many functions of an application in a small display area. Users can access this functionality not only directly by gestures but also in a way similar to pop-up menus: by tapping on them, a menu appears on top of the gedric and users can select one of its items. Each function of the gedric is displayed in the menu next to a visualization of the corresponding gesture. In addition, the shape of a gesture always corresponds to the gedric's image, making the gesture more intuitive to users. The examples mentioned in the following section will show this clearly.

Gedrics enable developers of pen-based software to create complex applications with a simple and clear interface instead of using cluttered tool bars that provide one button for each function. Moreover, several types of users are supported by gedrics. Inexperienced users may first interact via pop-up menus. Later on, they will use gestures as short cuts to application functionality. With gedrics, it is possible to become a 'power user' of a pen application by incremental learning. Most of the time, any user is experienced in a certain subset of the application's functionality and a novice with respect to the rest of the functions. By providing two interactions styles — menu-based interaction as well as gesture interaction — gedrics support those partial experts.

At first glance, gedrics seem to be similar to the concept of pie menus (Kurtenbach & Buxton, 1991; 1993). But in contrast to this interface element, gedrics can provide free-form input shapes as gestures and are not restricted to straight lines (Geißler, to appear). Furthermore, pie-menu gestures are only based on the position of the corresponding menu items whereas

gedric gestures are semantically related to the gedric image. This supports users to remember them.

3   Sample Application

In order to demonstrate the power of gedrics, a sample application has been developed. This application makes use of several gedrics and hereby illustrates the main aspects of the gedric concept. In order to reduce the complexity of the following evaluation, only three stroke-based gedrics with limited functionality were actually used (Figure 1). The full power of the application is described in (Geißler, to appear).

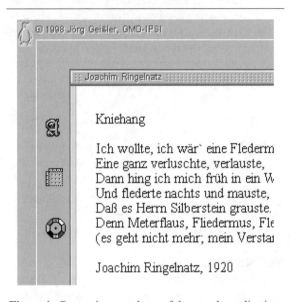

Figure 1: Cropped screen-dump of the sample application.

The purpose of the sample application is to enable users to format an existing text by changing font attributes, like style, size, and colour, as well as aligning passages of the text. This functionality is accessible through the gedrics called TYPOGRAPHER, LAYOUTER, and PAINTER.

First, users select a portion of the text by underlining phrases or by marking lines or paragraphs at their sides. Then, they use the gedric to perform a format operation on that selection. This working style corresponds to traditional direct-manipulation interfaces. However, since each word and even each character shown in the window is a component of the pen-centric interface, i.e. developed in a gesture-sensitive way — similar to gedrics, the application also supports direct content-oriented manipulation of text, e.g. insertion and deletion of phrases. As mentioned above, this functionality was not available in the evaluation.

In the following sections, we describe the three gedrics and the functions used in the evaluation in more detail.

3.1 Font Manipulation: The TYPOGRAPHER

The TYPOGRAPHER controls the font attributes of selected text. Users change those attributes by drawing one of the TYPOGRAPHER'S font-changing strokes on top of it. In the evaluation, only those gestures were available that change the size and the style of the font (Figure 2). Setting the font family by writing the name onto the gedric as well as combinations of strokes were not available. As a reaction to the input strokes, the gedric modifies the selected text accordingly. The icon of the TYPOGRAPHER shows the letter 'A' in an ornate style, indicating the typographic task of the gedric.

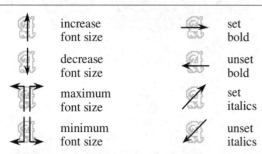

	increase font size		set bold
	decrease font size		unset bold
	maximum font size		set italics
	minimum font size		unset italics

Figure 2: Gestures of the TYPOGRAPHER.

Font Size: The font size is changed by drawing vertical strokes onto the TYPOGRAPHER. Strokes that go straight up increase the font size, those going straight down decrease it. Thus, these pen movements correspond to the application feedback, since it makes the characters larger (pen up) or smaller (pen down).

All in all, the application supports five different font sizes. An additional pair of gestures has been added to increase the efficiency of work: two L-like strokes, directed mainly up or down. As used for other components of the pen-centric interface (Geißler, 1998), these L-like strokes indicate functions that maximize (pen up) or minimize (pen down) an attribute. In this case, they set the maximum and minimum font size that is available for the selected text.

In the evaluation, users were not able to write absolute size values onto the TYPOGRAPHER, which is normally possible.

Font Style: Changing the font style is done by drawing horizontal or diagonal strokes onto the

TYPOGRAPHER. A horizontal stroke from left to right sets the bold attribute, indicating that the modified text will require more horizontal space to the right. The same stroke but with the opposite direction — from right to left — is used for unsetting this attribute. The italics attribute is set by diagonal strokes. A stroke from the lower left to the upper right is used for setting this attribute, indicating that the resulting text will be tilted like the input stroke is. Again, the opposite direction will unset this attribute. Gestures for underlining, for additional styles as well as combinations of strokes were not available in the evaluation.

3.2 Alignment of Lines and Paragraphs: The LAYOUTER

The second gedric used in the sample application is the LAYOUTER. Originally designed for any layout-related task, it is used in this context simply as a tool for aligning text lines and paragraphs. All major alignment operations are supported by the LAYOUTER (Figure 3). Its icon shows a grid with two rulers, one at the top and one at the left.

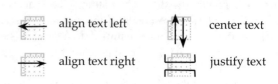

	align text left		center text
	align text right		justify text

Figure 3: Gestures of the LAYOUTER.

The most simple alignment operation is achieved by straight horizontal strokes onto the LAYOUTER. A stroke to the left results in left alignment of the selected text portion, a stroke to the right aligns the text right. Vertical strokes, either straight up or down, let users centre lines or paragraphs. Bracket-like input will justify it. Again, the pen movement corresponds with the following application feedback.

3.3 Colour Settings: The PAINTER

Similar to the LAYOUTER, the functionality of the PAINTER was specified for a broader application scenario and was limited for the evaluation. Normally, any colour-related aspect of the interface is handled by this gedric. With respect to the experimental setup, the PAINTER was used only to colour selected text portions.

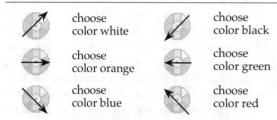

	choose color white		choose color black
	choose color orange		choose color green
	choose color blue		choose color red

Figure 4: Gestures of the PAINTER.

The icon of the PAINTER shows a colour wheel from which users can choose one of six pre-defined colours. This is done by drawing strokes from the middle of the gedric to the direction the colour is available on the colour wheel (Figure 4); e.g. to colour a selection in red, which is available in the upper left corner of the gedric, users draw a diagonal stroke from the lower right to the upper left onto the gedric. Functions for additional colours, for setting the six colours, and for changing the brightness of colours were not available in the evaluation.

4 Experiment

In this section, we describe an experiment we carried out to investigate the usability of the gedric concept.

4.1 Questions and Hypotheses

A usable interface is 'easy to learn', 'efficient to use', 'easy to remember', 'pleasant to use', and has 'few errors' (Nielsen, 1993). An empirical user study should show whether gedrics have these qualities or not.

The two interaction styles: An important attribute of a gedric is that it offers two possible interaction styles. On the one hand, the gedric can be compared with a traditional icon that has a pop-up menu. By tapping on it, the menu opens and a command can be selected (also by tapping on the menu item). On the other hand, the gedric command can be executed by using the corresponding gesture. We assumed that offering these two interaction alternatives for all commands would increase the users satisfaction (Shneiderman, 1998) with the interface. Users are not forced to use gestures if they find them difficult to learn or to perform. We were interested in finding out which interaction style the users would prefer, if they would show interest in using the gestures or if they would stick to the pop-up menus.

Gesture interaction: Using a gesture on a gedric is a short cut for the corresponding command.

It speeds up the interaction with the gedrics because it requires fewer interaction steps. But, of course, for most users, the gesture interaction represents a novel form of interaction and the gestures have to be learned first to have the effect of speeding up. Therefore, we were especially interested in the usability of the gestures in comparison to the usage of the pop-up menus. We supposed that for novices the gesture interaction would be more difficult than using the pop-up menus.

The underlying concepts of gedrics and gestures:
As described above, each gedric is a combination of several carefully designed aspects:

- The chosen icon of a gedric should match with its functionality.

- The commands of each gedric should correspond to its functionality.

- The order of the commands in the pop-up menu and the association of the gestures to the commands should be logical.

For example, the gesture which changes text into italics indicates the sloping position of italics. This logical design should facilitate the interaction with the gedrics and accelerate the learning process.

We supposed that the logical design of the gedrics would especially lead to less confusion between the different gedrics. During gesture interaction, one gesture can release different commands dependent on which gedric it is performed on. For instance, a stroke from the left to the right performed on the TYPOGRAPHER sets the bold font style. The same gesture performed on the LAYOUTER aligns objects to the right. With this gesture on the PAINTER the colour orange is chosen. An elaborated introduction to the logic of the functionality underlying each gedric and the classing of gestures with commands should lead to fewer confusions with respect to the multiple usage of the same gestures.

In contrast to similar implementations, like 'marking menus' (Kurtenbach & Buxton, 1991; 1993), where the direction of the gesture has no logical association with the semantic of the corresponding command, we believe that these underlying concepts of the gedrics and their gestures make it easier to learn the gestures. We supposed that an elaborated introduction into the concepts would increase usability.

4.2   Method

Experimental Design: We used a between-subject design in order to investigate the usability of the two interaction styles and the need of a specific introduction to the gedric concept.

The two independent variables are: *interaction style* with three values and *introduction* with two values. Subjects were assigned randomly to the experimental conditions.

The three values of the *interaction style* variable are a *combined condition*, and two other conditions with only one interaction style serving as control conditions:

- In the *combined condition* (C), the gedrics were presented with their full functionality, i.e. interaction with pop-up menus and via gestures. It was explained that both interaction styles are equivalent and can be used according to personal preferences.

- In the *gesture condition* (G), subjects could only interact with the gedrics by using gestures. The pop-up menus were used only as passive help menus showing the list of commands and their associated gestures.

- In the *menu condition* (M), the gedrics could only be used by opening the pop-up menus and by tapping on the commands in the menus. The gedrics in this condition are equivalent to traditional icons with pop-up menus.

The *introduction* variable had two values:

- Subjects in the *elaborated introduction condition* were introduced to above described underlying concepts of each gedric.

- In the *simple introduction condition* all gedrics, commands, and gestures were explained without reference to underlying concepts.

Subjects had to work on the same task twice resulting in a $3\times2\times2$ experimental design with 'task' as the repeated measurement factor.

Setting: The experiment took place in July and August of 1998 in the AMBIENTE Lab at GMD-IPSI. In this room, so called *roomware* components (Streitz et al., 1998; 1999) can be found. We used one of these components, the DynaWall (Geißler, 1998), consisting of three segments, each realized by an interactive rear-projection whiteboard. A pen was used for interacting with the DynaWall. We used the DynaWall because large interactive displays represent one of the typical touch-sensitive devices. Furthermore, the DynaWall provided us with excellent conditions of observing the users' performance.

The sample application was running on the middle segment while the right segment showed the instructions in parallel. The experimenter was in the room. All actions of the subjects were recorded by a video camera. Figure 5 shows the setup as recorded by the camera.

Figure 5: Still picture from the video recordings showing a subject working with the gedrics at the DynaWall.

Subjects: A total of 54 subjects participated in the experiment, 27 men and 27 women. Their age varied between 17 and 31. Most subjects were students and had basic computer skills, primary in the area of text processing, drawing programs, and e-mail.

Procedure: After filling in a demographic questionnaire, subjects were introduced to the procedure of the experiment and to the software.

Subjects then worked twice on a text-formatting task by using the three gedrics described before. In 40 subtasks, they were asked to reformat a text displayed in a text editing window. Each subtask concerned a part of the text to be formatted using one of the 16 possible gedric operations. The TYPOGRAPHER was used 19 times, the LAYOUTER 11 times and the PAINTER 10 times. The operations were used in no systematic order.

The instructions for the subtasks were given on the right segment of the DynaWall in sentences of the following character: "Please change the colour of the text of the third paragraph to blue". Three to five of such instructions were given per presentation slide.

After each task session, the subjects filled in a questionnaire in which they were asked to assess different aspects of the software. The whole procedure took about one hour, the work on each task took about 15 minutes.

4.2.1 Measures

Performance variables: Several interaction and performance measures were extracted:

- *Confusion of gedrics:* A wrong gedric was activated either by opening the menu or by performing a gesture. We recorded also which of the three gedrics were mixed up.

- *Error:* The number of errors, which were made during the performance of the task. Possible errors were: selecting a wrong menu command, using a wrong gesture, and confusing gedrics.

- *Time on task:* Time on task was recorded by monitoring the start and end of the interaction.

The following variables reflect the learning of the gestures in the interaction conditions G and C:

- Correct gesture without opening the menu: A correct gesture is performed without opening the menu of the gedric first. In this case, the user has learned the gesture and performs it

- Correct gesture after first opening the menu: A correct gesture is performed immediately after opening the menu of the gedric. In this case, the user has not learned the gesture yet.

In condition C, the proportion of the *number of menu commands used* and the *number of gestures used* was recorded.

User Satisfaction: The questionnaire consisted of 18 questions in which the subjects were asked to give their opinion about the task, the gedrics, the menus and the gestures.

The subjects in condition C were asked after both task performances, whether they preferred the gestures or the interaction with the menus.

5   Results

For analysing the data of this experiment, we used an analysis of variance with three factors (one factor being the repeated measurement). We were using levels of significance of 1% or 5%.

5.1   The Two Interaction Styles

In condition C, there was a significant switch from the dominance of *menu commands used* in the first performance of the task to a dominance of *gestures used* in the second ($F(1,18) = 11.911, p < 0.05$). This development is shown in Figure 6.

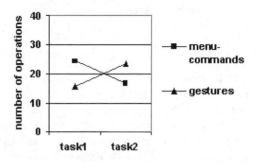

Figure 6: Switch from menu commands to gestures in condition C.

In the questionnaire, the subjects significantly changed their preferences of interaction styles from liking the menu interaction most in the first task to liking the gesture interaction most in the second task ($F(1,18) = 4.571, p < 0.05$).

In comparison to the subjects in condition G, the subjects in condition C using gestures found them significantly more illogical ($F(1,36) = 6.415, p < 0.05$), and highly significant more difficult to remember ($F(1,36) = 7.935, p < 0.01$).

An analysis of the different relations of *used gestures* and *used menu commands* in condition C shows three interaction profiles:

- Subjects who — on the average — performed 0 to 13 of the 40 operations by gestures in both tasks.

- Subjects who used 13 to 26 gestures.

- Subjects who used 26 to 40 gestures.

The 18 subjects of condition C are distributed almost equally over these three groups: six subjects used few gestures, seven subjects used gestures and menu commands equally, and five subjects used more gestures than menu commands.

5.2   Gesture Interaction

The comparison of the three interaction conditions C, G, and M showed no significant differences between the groups concerning *time on task, error, confusion of gedrics*, and *user satisfaction*.

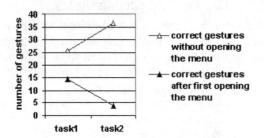

Figure 7: Gestures usage in condition G.

In condition G, the analysis of the performance of gestures shows that the number of *correct gestures without opening the menu* increased highly significant ($F(1,18) = 39.859, p < 0.01$) and the number of *correct gestures after first opening the menu* decreased significantly ($F(1,18) = 43.768, p < 0.01$) in the second performance of the task (Figure 7).

Also in condition C, the number of *correct gestures without opening the menu* increased very significantly ($F(1,18) = 29.638, p < 0.01$) in the second time on the task.

5.3   The Introduction Variable

Subjects in condition G with an *elaborated introduction* performed significantly more *correct gestures without opening the menu* ($F(1,18) = 5.699, p < 0.05$) than subjects in condition G who belonged to the *simple introduction* condition. These subjects performed significantly more *correct gestures after first opening the menu* ($F(1,18) = 5.877, p < 0.05$).

The confusion between the gedrics varied in general over all conditions. Most confusions occurred between the TYPOGRAPHER and LAYOUTER (mean(task1) = 3.43, std(task1) = 3.17 and mean(task2) = 1.89, std(task2) = 2.42). The TYPOGRAPHER and PAINTER as well as the LAYOUTER and PAINTER were hardly mixed up. The influence of the introduction condition was significant on the confusion of the TYPOGRAPHER and LAYOUTER ($F(1,53) = 4.105, p < 0.05$) — an *elaborated introduction* led to fewer confusions. In the questionnaire subjects in the *elaborated introduction* condition judged the gedrics to be easier to differentiate than did the subjects in the *simple interaction* condition ($F(1,54) = 5.142, p < 0.05$).

6   Discussion

6.1   The Two Interaction Styles

It can be seen that the possibility of interacting with the gedrics by using the pop-up menus or the gestures offer a smooth transition from novice to expert performance with the sample application. In addition, it supports personal preferences and individual skills without causing any deficits in usability. On the average, a preference for gesture interaction can be stated, although this interaction style was new to all subjects.

Results show that subjects switched from a dominance of the usage of the pop-up menus in the first task to a dominance of gesture interaction in the second task. Furthermore, they also switched in their preferences from liking the menu interaction most in the first task to liking the gestures most in the second task. The preference of the gestures was stated although in some aspects subjects in condition C perceived the gestures as more difficult than subjects in condition G. This switch in performance and preference is even more interesting under the aspect that subjects were not instructed to use the gestures but did it spontaneously.

The analysis of the performance characteristics shows that there seems to exist personal preferences of using the pop-up menus or the gestures. Not all subjects switch to gestures in the second task and not all operations were performed by gesture. All in all, these personal preferences do not lead to any interaction constraints compared to the other two interaction conditions. The power of the combined interaction should increase by the increase of the number of gedrics and commands.

6.2   Gesture Interaction

Analysing the subjects' performance of gestures and keeping in mind that the gestures were a novel form of interaction for subjects, we found satisfactory results for the usability of gesture interaction with the gedrics.

The three interaction conditions did not show any significant differences in any of the three interaction variables *time on the task, error* or *confusion of gedrics*. The novelty of the gestures and the higher effort of learning the gestures does not seem to affect these aspects of usability. Concerning the *time on the task*, the effects of higher learning effort (for gestures) and higher number of interaction steps (for menu commands) seem to compensate each other. We assume that gesture interaction will become more efficient the more experienced a user is.

The execution of a gesture without the prior opening of the gedrics' menu shows that the respective gesture is performed by rote. In condition G, in the second task on an average 36.33 gestures were executed without opening the menu (std = 7.75). The subjects were able to learn almost all the gestures. Also in condition C, where subjects were not instructed to use the gestures, they showed a highly significant learning effect of the gestures. This is a pleasing result and shows that the gesture interaction is easy to learn in an interaction period of about 30 minutes. Of course, the degree of learnability may change with an increasing number of possible gesture operations.

6.3 The Introduction Variable

The type of introduction (*elaborated* or *simple*) had influences on the learning of the gestures and on the confusion between the gedrics.

In condition G, an *elaborated introduction* was helpful for learning the gestures. Subjects performed significantly more *correct gestures without opening the menu* which indicates that the gesture has been learned. The *confusion of gedrics* over all interaction conditions was reduced by giving subjects an *elaborated introduction*. And subjects in the *elaborated introduction* condition themselves stated the gedrics to be more easy to differentiate than those in the *simple introduction* condition.

The higher number of confusions between the TYPOGRAPHER and the LAYOUTER than between each of them and the PAINTER shows that there is not a clear distinction of the functionality of these two gedrics. If it is not easy to differentiate the gedrics, the number of mistakes increases. These results — the increase of usability caused by the *elaborated introduction* — show that the logical concepts are also evident to the user and not only to the designer of the software.

7 Conclusions and Future Work

In this paper, we introduced a simple application that makes use of gedrics — gesture-sensitive icons as part of a pen-centric interface. We evaluated this application with respect to several usability aspects. It turned out that users like the different interaction styles provided by gedrics very much and that they can work with interfaces like this efficiently, independent from their skills, experiences, and preferences.

The results of this evaluation are the starting point for further experiments. Especially with respect to complexity and scaling to higher numbers of gedrics, the gedric approach has to be observed

in more detail. In our sample application, only three gedrics with a total of 16 functions were available. Although the subjects were able to learn these functions and the corresponding gestures very fast, more gedrics with more functionality for each gedric — as specified in (Geißler, 1995; to appear) — may cause problems. We are currently in the process of setting up an experiment with less variables to examine but with more functionality to be learned by the subjects, because we believe that especially free-form input shapes as gestures offer more possibilities for interaction.

The conceptual clarity in the design of gedrics, i.e. choosing the right set of functions they represent, their appearance as an icon, a good menu design, as well as intuitive gestures that correspond with the functions and the icon, is the most important factor for the usability of gedrics. All in all, the TYPOGRAPHER, the LAYOUTER, and the PAINTER seem to be designed quite well but there is still space for improvements. Especially the distinguishability of gedrics with respect to their task as well as their visual appearance has to be taken into account.

However, the findings we got from our evaluation encourages us to design and implement the basic interaction concept of gedrics — gestures and menus — on a larger scale. Not only icons can be made gesture-sensitive that way but any interface component. At the moment, we are improving a set of gesture-sensitive widgets (Geißler, 1998) and basic data elements like characters and text that react directly on pen input in the same way (Geißler, to appear). This set of components will be an important step from traditional pen-*based* interfaces towards pen-*centric* interfaces. With these interfaces, users always will have the freedom of choosing that mix of interaction styles that is most appropriate for them.

Acknowledgements

At the time the work described in this paper took place, all authors were affiliated to the Integrated Publication and Information Systems Institute (IPSI) of the German National Research Center for Information Technology (GMD).

We would like to thank the members of the AMBIENTE team at GMD-IPSI for making the system development and this evaluation possible. Special thanks go to Torsten Holmer who developed software for recording user actions at the DynaWall.

References

Geißler, J. (1995), Gedrics: The Next Generation of Icons, *in* K. Nordby, P. H. Helmersen, D. J. Gilmore & S. A. Arnessen (eds.), *Human–Computer Interaction — INTERACT '95: Proceedings of the Fifth IFIP Conference on Human–Computer Interaction,* Chapman & Hall, pp.73–8.

Geißler, J. (1998), Shuffle, Throw or Take it! Working Efficiently with an Interactive Wall, *in* C.-M. Karat, A. Lund, J. Coutaz & J. Karat (eds.), *Proceedings of CHI'98: Human Factors in Computing Systems*, ACM Press, pp.265–6.

Geißler, J. (to appear), Design and Implementation of Pen-centric User Interfaces, PhD thesis, Technical University of Darmstadt.

Grudin, J. (1989), "The Case Against User Interface Consistency", *Communications of the ACM* **32**(10), 1164–73.

Kurtenbach, G. & Buxton, W. (1991), Issues in Combining Marking and Direct Manipulation Techniques, *in Proceedings of the ACM Symposium on User Interface Software and Technology, UIST'91,* ACM Press, pp.137–44.

Kurtenbach, G. & Buxton, W. (1993), The Limits of Expert Performance Using Hierarchic Marking Menus, *in* S. Ashlund, K. Mullet, A. Henderson, E. Hollnagel & T. White (eds.), *Proceedings of INTERCHI'93*, ACM Press/IOS Press, pp.482–7.

Meyer, A. (1995), "Pen Computing. A Technology Overview and a Vision", *ACM SIGCHI Bulletin* **27**(3), 46–90.

Nielsen, J. (1993), *Usability Engineering*, Academic Press.

Shneiderman, B. (1998), *Designing the User Interface: Strategies for Effective Human–Computer Interaction,* third edition, Addison–Wesley.

Streitz, N. A., Geißler, J. & Holmer, T. (1998), Roomware for Cooperative Buildings: Integrated Design of Architectural Spaces and Information Spaces, *in* N. A. Streitz, S. Konomi & H.-J. Burkhardt (eds.), *Cooperative Buildings. Integrating Information, Organization, and Architecture,* Vol. 1370 of *Lecture Notes in Computer Science*, Springer-Verlag, pp.4–21.

Streitz, N., Geißler, J., Holmer, T., Konomi, S., Müller-Tomfelde, C., Reischl, W., Rexroth, P., Seitz, P. & Steinmetz, R. (1999), i-LAND: An Interactive Landscape for Creativitiy and Innovation., *in* M. G. Williams, M. W. Altom, K. Ehrlich & W. Newman (eds.), *Proceedings of CHI'99: Human Factors in Computing Systems*, ACM Press.

Wolf, C. G. (1992), "A Comparative Study of Gestural, Keyboard, and Mouse Interfaces", *Behaviour & Information Technology* **11**(1), 13–23.

Wolf, C. G., Rhyne, J. R. & Ellozy, H. A. (1989), The Paper-like Interface, *in* G. Salvendy & M. J. Smith (eds.), *Designing and Using Human–Computer Interfaces and Knowledge-based Systems*, Edward Arnold, pp.494–501.

A Toolkit for Exploring Electro-physiological Human–Computer Interaction

Jennifer Allanson, Tom Rodden & John Mariani

Computing Department, Lancaster University, Lancaster LA1 4YR, UK.
{allanson,tam,jam}@comp.lancs.ac.uk

Abstract: This paper describes a toolkit designed to explore the role of electro-physiological data in future forms of human–computer interaction. The electro-physiological data set considered includes galvanic skin resistance, electrical brain wave activity and electrical signals generated by individual muscles. Clinical biofeedback research indicates that it is possible to gain conscious control over certain electro-physiological signals. This ability could lead to new, hands-free forms of human–computer interaction, which has implications for the future of HCI generally. Of most immediate importance is the potential of hands-free controllers to provide access to computers for those with impaired or limited motor abilities.

Keywords: hands-free control (HFC), physiological signals, disability.

1 Introduction

As computer systems have become increasingly sophisticated we have seen a considerable diversification in the ways in which users interact with computers. The earliest machines provided support for interaction using a series of switches. As machines have matured so have the techniques used to interact with these machines. As the interface has reached out from the machine (Grudin, 1990) a raft of new interaction approaches have emerged. Electric switches gave way to punched cards, these were replaced by teletypes with real time editing facilities and desktop windowing environments eventually replaced these.

Although the ubiquitous arrangement of screen keyboard and mouse is now considered the norm for computer interaction considerable research is still pondering what future forms of interaction may be possible. Perhaps the most notable of these are explorations in virtual reality (Singh et al., 1996) and the development of augmented electronic environments made up of tangible interfaces (Ishii & Ullmer, 1997).

However, while these new advances are tremendously exciting, they are still fundamentally physical interfaces requiring users to manipulate the environment through some form of electro-mechanical device. We wish to complement these explorations of future forms of interaction by considering the development of interfaces that exploit an electro-physiological approach to interaction.

In this paper we describe our initial exploration of the potential of electro-physiological human–computer interaction. This involves detecting electrical information generated by muscles, organs and the human nervous system, and translating these into computer-control parameters.

We explore the potential of electro-physiological data as the means to facilitate hands-free interaction. This is done in the context of existing systems, which incorporate physiological data at the human–computer interface. To support the development of investigative applications we have designed a toolkit to enable the rapid construction of interfaces suitable for hands-free human–computer interaction via electro-physiological signals.

The rest of this paper is structured as follows. In section two we highlight situations where alternative, hands-free interaction methods are desirable. In section three we consider the potential information that can be gained from electro-physiological data. We build upon this in section four where we consider how this data can be exploited in a simple toolkit. Finally, we end in section five with a discussion of our system in use and outline our intentions for further work in this area.

2   Background

Over the past 30 years, people have interacted with computers via mechanical devices external to both themselves and the computer. The most popular input devices — keyboards, mice and trackballs — all require the periodic dedication of one or both hands. Even gesture recognition systems that use video systems or wireless tracking require the user to execute a particular physical maneuver. Whilst this correspondence between physical movement and interaction is fine for many computing applications, there are a number of situations where it would be desirable to interact with computers in a hands-free manner where interaction is not dependent on physical manipulation. These include:

High workload environments: Hands-free interaction is ideal for situations where a user's hands are already occupied by some other task. For example, a surgeon operating on a patient could rotate a computer-generated surgery planning model via some hands-free control device.

Disabled users: Undoubtedly the most important role for hands-free control devices is as a means for disabled users to interact with computers. Existing mechanical control devices are only of use to those with mechanical control. Disabled users require alternative tools which are flexible enough to be tailored to suit their individual needs and abilities.

Mobile computing applications: Away from the desktop, computer users find themselves in situations where is it difficult to find surfaces on which to rest and operate traditional input devices. Hands-free controllers will address some of the issues arising from increasing mobility and decreasing device size.

Each of these different application domains all highlight the need for users to occasionally break free from the limits of physical interaction and indicate their purpose to the computer using other techniques. Explorations in this area have tended to focus on voice recognition as a promising hands-free alternative input mechanism. However, this is not always possible or desirable — consider very quiet or particularly noisy working environments.

We have been exploring the use of electro-physiological data as computer control signals as an alternative technique for computer interaction that breaks free of the limits of physical manipulation as a basis for interaction. The starting point for our exploration is a consideration of the data we can make available to a computer and how. In the following section we briefly review some of the signals that are available to us if we wish to develop interfaces of this form.

3   Electro-physiological Data Available to the Computer

Communication between the brain and the outside world takes place via the body. Electro-chemical signals are sent, via the nervous system to regulate organs and to stimulate muscles into mechanical action. Responses from the environment, in the form of sensory input, are converted into electro-chemical data and sent back to the brain. By placing electronic sensors on the body surface, it is possible to detect some of these electrical messages moving around the body. Furthermore, we can incorporate some of them in our interactions with computers.

For more than 25 years the field of clinical biofeedback has been training individuals to gain conscious control over certain physiological signals. Signals from the brain, muscles, skin, respiratory and cardio-vascular systems are all trained using biofeedback techniques.

Weiner (1948) first defined feedback as "a method of controlling the system by reinserting into it the results of its past performance". Biofeedback involves reinsertion of physiological data into a subject (the 'system') in a way which enables that subject to learn how to control subsequent physiological data output. As human beings, our input mechanisms are our sensory organs. Thus the best ways to reinsert physiological data is by converting it into audio, visual and tactile forms.

If we can use biofeedback techniques to train for control of some suitable subset of electro-physiological signals, we would have the ability to operate electronic devices in a hands-free manner. In the following section we describe three electro-physiological signals, information about where and how they can be detected, and how they can be used as computer-control signals.

3.1   Electroencephalograph

By applying electrodes to the surface of the scalp, it is possible to detect electrical signals emanating from the brain. A trace of raw brain activity is known as the electroencephalograph (EEG). This can be filtered into recognizable components, which can in turn be utilized as computer input in various ways.

Alpha components, for example, are near-sinusoidal waves of between 8 and 13 Hertz (Hz) whose amplitude is measurably reduced when a subject closes his or her eyes. Kirkup et al. (1997) have created an electronic device called MindSwitch, which uses eyes open/closed alpha signals to operate lights and other binary devices.

Beta EEG components (14–30Hz) are known to be present during mental activities requiring focused attention. They are seen to be present in different regions of the brain depending on the nature of the current mental activity. For example, spatial tasks generally produce greater beta activity in the right-hand side of the brain, whereas language-based tasks produce greater activity in the left-hand side. By looking at EEG signals taken from across the brain, it is possible to differentiate between various classes of mental activity. In one study, Keirn et al. (1990) instructed subjects to undertake 5 mental tasks, to see if it was possible to differentiate between right-brain and left-brain tasks. The first 'task' was a baseline measure of EEG, so the subject was told to relax and think of nothing. The other four tasks were:

- A non-trivial multiplication (left-brain).

- Mentally composing a letter to a friend (left-brain).

- Imagining a 3D object in space (right-brain).

- Visualizing numbers being written on a blackboard, and subsequently being rubbed off and overwritten (right-brain).

By analysing the EEG signal patterns from repeated instances of these tasks they were actually able to differentiate between all 5 tasks, with an accuracy of between 82% and 98%. This provided them with the equivalent of 5 recognizable symbols, which they believed could form the basis for a simple control language.

Performing EEG pattern recognition or translating alpha into a switching signal involves no training on the part of the subject. These systems are responding to naturally occurring changes in the EEG. Perhaps more interestingly, clinical research (Lubar, 1997) indicates that it is possible to train the brain to elicit certain specific brain signals.

In clinical settings EEG feedback training is used to increase the level of beta activity and decrease the level of theta (4–7Hz) activity in subjects suffering from attention deficit disorder (ADD). Training involves making brain waves visible to a subject, who attempts to consciously increase or

reduce the amplitude of the signal. The visualization is usually a simple polygraph trace of the electrical signal. The same technique has been used to train disabled users to change the amplitude of an EEG component in order to move a cursor on a computer screen (Kubler et al., 1999; Wolpaw & McFarland, 1994).

3.2 Electromyograph

Another option for electro-physiological interaction is muscle-state information. A muscle can be in one of three states — complete relaxation, partial contraction or complete contraction. A contracting muscle produces a combination of electrical, chemical, structural and thermal changes, that together are known as a muscle action potential or MAP. A series of MAPs makes up the electromyograph (EMG) (Greenfield & Sternbach, 1972).

Each time an action potential passes along the muscle, a small amount of electrical activity spreads from the muscle to the skin. By positioning two electrodes on the skin over the muscle, it is possible to record this activity.

In clinical applications, EMG is used in the retraining of muscle control, lost due to accident or illness. EMG feedback allows the patient to see that there is electrical activity within the muscle even when there is no visible indication of movement. EMG training, like EEG, usually involves using a computer monitor to display the electrical signal as a polygraph wave. Alternatively EMG has been used to control a simple computer game or an electronic remote-controlled car (Bowman, 1997).

EMG has also been investigated as a general-purpose computer input mechanism for individuals with limited motor skills. An EMG feedback device, attached to the face of a 10-year-old boy paralyzed below the neck, enabled him to move objects on a computer screen by tensing certain facial muscles (Lusted & Knapp, 1996). Other work (Rosenberg, 1998, p.170) has looked at EMG as a mechanism for hands-free control of mobile computing devices.

3.3 Galvanic Skin Resistance

A third potential source of control data comes from measuring the changing resistance of the skin. If two electrodes are placed on the skin and a small constant current is passed through them, the skin behaves as a variable resistor. The conducted voltage is referred to as a measure of Galvanic Skin Resistance (GSR).

GSR reflects changes in excitation of sweat glands located in various layers of the skin (Greenfield & Sternbach, 1972). Changes in skin resistance occur in response to stimulation. This can be an internal stimulation, such as a change in physical excitation or arousal, or external, such as sudden loud noises. At least two commercial devices exist which take GSR as their control input. The first, UltraMind, is designed as a recreational relaxation device. It displays changes in GSR as a sequential animation, which changes from a fish, to a mermaid, a girl, an angel and finally a star as the user relaxes and GSR decreases. The second device, MindDrive, has been designed specifically as a computer input device, and comes bundled with interactive games, which respond to changes in GSR.

We mentioned earlier that useful electro-physiological signals are ones that can be brought under conscious control. We have now seen that such signals exist and are easy to access. But exactly how long does it take to train an individual to elicit controllable electro-physiological signals? What factors affect training time? Are there combinations of signals that make more reliable control inputs than any single signal? Does signal reliability deteriorate due to environmental factors? And what other factors impact the reliability of a given signal? Perhaps the most important question is how usable these signals are in real-world computing situations?

In order to answer some of these questions, we considered experimenting with existing biofeedback systems. But their limitation is that they have been designed with specific clinical applications in mind. This means they are 'closed' to development and/or experimentation with different media. To fully explore the potential of training electro-physiological signals and using them as control inputs, we needed to develop a system with:

- The flexibility to exploit as full a range of media components as possible, for training and evaluation purposes.

- The means to quickly create different interfaces to look at various combinations of electro-physiological signals.

To this end, we have built a software toolkit, consisting of a set of interface widgets, which can be combined to create experimental interfaces for electro-physiological human–computer interaction.

4   The Electro-physiological Toolkit

The developed toolkit is built on top of a commercial biofeedback system called the WaveRider. This is a PC-based device with a Windows interface called WaveWare. This includes a dynamic link library (DLL)

for development purposes that provides a means of interaction with the device.

To realize our toolkit we have outlined an initial set of widgets that can act as a means of collecting signals from the hardware and driving applications. We have chosen the Java language for our implementation, with each widget written as a JavaBean.

The use of JavaBeans means electro-physiologically-responsive interfaces can be constructed from the pre-defined widget set, using a standard 'bean builder' tool. As all components comply to the JavaBean standard, the bean builder can introspect each widget. With information about the widget's interface, the builder can be used to set up the subsequent flow of data (Java events) between widgets.

The implemented widgets are independent of the biofeedback hardware. The Java/Native translation layer sitting between the Java widget set and the biofeedback hardware is all that would need to be replaced in order to use our toolkit with another biofeedback hardware device (Figure 1).

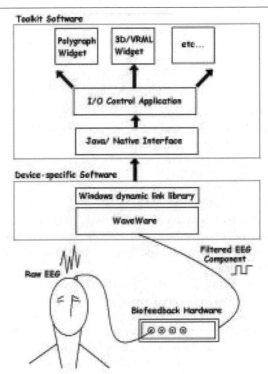

Figure 1: The toolkit software is independent of the biofeedback system used.

Our current widget set consists of the following components that allow both the monitoring and presentation of the input signals and the ability to exploit the signals to cause interaction with other applications.

Polygraph: Existing biofeedback systems most often present physiological signal data as a polygraph trace. This can be a raw (unfiltered) EEG trace, a single filtered EEG component (alpha or beta for example) or any other single data signal (EMG or GSR). The polygraph component expects a single stream of data, whose values signify the changing amplitude of a signal. It uses these to dynamically plot the polygraph itself.

Bargraph: As we have seen, it is sometimes desirable to look at combinations of signals, such as multiple EEG components, or a mixture of EEG and EMG. Any combination of EEG, EMG and GSR signals can be displayed on a bargraph, where the height of each bar corresponds to the amplitude of an individual signal.

Graduated Scale: The graduated scale widget can take a single signal as its input. It acts as an alternative method of representing the amplitude value of a single EEG component or other signal, as a sliding pointer moving along a graduated scale.

Slider: This widget is used as a sliding scale for visually setting data values. For example, if a given signal is being used as a switch, this slider can be used to visually set the amplitude value, above and below which the switch state changes from off to on.

Latching and non-latching switches: The switch takes a single signal as its input. An amplitude value, known as the threshold, is set (using the Slider, above). When the signal amplitude goes above this value, the switch is set. In the latching switch, the amplitude must drop below this value and rise above it once again to un-set the switch. The non-latching switch is set any time we are above the threshold and un-set as soon as we drop below it.

Timer: In clinical EEG feedback training, subjects are encouraged to raise the amplitude of an EEG component for as long a time as possible. In order to emulate this, we have added a timer widget, which takes a notification event as input. This could be notification that a signal amplitude has gone above its threshold. The timer is subsequently stopped by another event, such as the signal amplitude dropping below its threshold.

The timer outputs notification events to indicate when it has been started, and when it has stopped.

Integrity Indicator: In order to maintain system integrity, it is necessary to know if we have a valid input signal from the biofeedback hardware. Commercial systems rely on the user to spot when an electrode has become displaced and a signal lost. This widget periodically checks the integrity of the signal, and outputs a notification event if it detects loss of a valid input.

Alarm: It will sometimes be necessary to notify the user about some state change in the system. The integrity indicator, for example, sensing a change in the signal from a detached electrode, can send its notification event to the alarm. The alarm widget's output event can be used to provide audio or visual alarm event. Depending on the application, if the lack of signal is critical, the alarm can be configured to interrupt the running of the system.

Audio: This widget can be configured to output various types of audio data, from a single tone, to a piece of music or voice clip. We have indicated that the audio widget could be used by the alarm widget, as its sound source. It can also be used to play audio files in response to changing signal amplitudes, and so be used as part of a biofeedback training session.

Video: Similarly, the audio widget can be configured to play video clips in response to changing signal amplitudes.

Animation: This widget can be configured to change the appearance of a 2D animation in response to the changing amplitude of a signal.

Dialogue: The dialogue widget can be used to relay various types of information to the user. It can alternatively display signal amplitudes as numerical values. It can be used to give information or instructions to the user. It can also respond to integrity indicator notification events, and other instances where information about the occurrence of some error is required.

3D Environments: This widget allows the building of simple 3D environments whose objects respond to changes in physiological data. A dialogue widget is used to set up the initial environment, specifying objects in the world and their relation to any given physiological data input. Once the world is launched, it can take a number of electro-physiological signals as input. It produces no output but translates the signal data into movement and changes of appearance of objects within the 3D scene.

I/O: The input/output (I/O) widget is really an application that sits between the biofeedback hardware and the user-interface. When constructing a training or application environment, all widgets used register interest in one or more physiological data signals. The I/O widget processes the data it receives from the biofeedback hardware. It then notifies interested widgets when it receives a signal that they have registered interest in.

This set of feedback widgets all present electro-physiological information to the subject in an audio or visual format. Whilst considering the needs of disabled users, we felt there was a need to think of as broad a range of users as possible. The I/O widget could, therefore have external haptic feedback devices register for physiological data signal information. This would enable biofeedback to take place with blind or deaf/blind users where they receive feedback via a vibrating device, or one that changes temperature. It should also be possible to provide output via an optically isolated, low voltage 'muscle-stimulator' device, similar to the SlenderTone.

5 Using the Toolkit

We have ascertained that the development of conscious electro-physiological signal control takes place though a process of biofeedback training. So training is the first step towards hands-free human–computer interaction via electro-physiological data. We therefore start by using the toolkit to construct an interface suitable for biofeedback training.

Imagine we wanted to train an individual to control the amplitude of a single EEG component, such as beta (frequency 14–30Hz). We have the means to represent beta activity to a trainee in various ways. For example, we could display the subject's beta activity simultaneously as a polygraph, a simple graduated scale, and as the movement of some object in a 3D world. Each of these are widgets within our toolkit with the overall interface composed using a simple bean builder (Figure 2).

In the 3D world, the subject's beta wave amplitude can be associated with the height of a free-moving block. Raising the signal amplitude causes

the block to rise. Decreasing the signal amplitude causes the block to fall. In clinical EEG biofeedback applications, it is often desirable to encourage a subject to maintain amplitude above a certain value or level for a predetermined period of time. To effect this, we can set the target value or level using a *Slider* widget. We could also incorporate a *Timer*, which starts when the signal amplitude is raised above the target level, and stops when the signal falls below it. We can indicate a time we would like the subject to maintain target amplitude for (0.5 seconds, perhaps). If the subject maintains the signal above the target for the pre-specified time, they will be rewarded with an animation — perhaps the block moves onto a stack of other blocks — and they are presented with a new block.

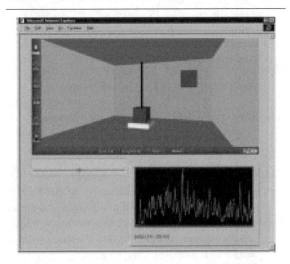

Figure 2: An EEG component being shown simultaneously as a polygraph, a value on a graduated slider, and as an interaction parameter in a 3D environment.

In terms of constructing this from the interface widgets, we exploit the feature of JavaBeans. The *Polygraph, Graduated Scale* and *3D* widgets all register interest via the *I/O* widget, in data coming from the biofeedback hardware about the signal 'beta'. They all also register interest in the *Slider*, which is being used to set the target amplitude for the beta signal-training programme. A *Switch* widget registers interest in both the *Slider* target value and the beta signal. The *Switch* would be set once the beta amplitude goes above the target value. A *Timer* widget registers interest in the *Switch*, so that when the *Switch* is set (amplitude above target) the *Timer* is started. When the *Switch* is un-set (amplitude fallen below the target), the *Timer* is notified, and stops. The 3D widget registers interest in the *Timer*, and if the time returned when the *Timer* stops is equal to or above the value pre-determined with the 3D widget, then the animation is triggered.

6   Future Work

The nature of our work is exploratory in that we are seeking to discover the interaction potential offered by electro-physiological techniques. We plan to use our toolkit to further explore the issues raised in Section 3, and explore the advantages and limits of this approach to interaction. As part of this overall exploration we would like to extend the toolkit to respond to information about blood pressure volume, heart rate and respiration. We envisage the toolkit being used not only for training and control applications, but also for implementing systems that monitor the users' physiological condition. Reasons for doing this include:

Health: Devices monitoring physiological parameters of those with heart disease, dangerous levels of stress, even epileptics, in order to warn them of some impending event.

Safety-critical system operator monitoring: Is the pilot dead? Alternatively is he or she in such a heightened state of anxiety that the system should double check any commands it is given?

Affective computing applications: A field of research concerned with training devices specifically to recognize emotional states by assessing physiological states (Picard, 1995).

Systems evaluation: Measuring stress indicators in order to monitor the effects of new systems on users.

In this paper we have outlined the principles involved in this form of interaction and described a simple toolkit which provides the basis for the further exploration of this form of interaction for these future application domains.

Acknowledgements

Thanks to Simon Lock for comments on early drafts of this paper.

This work is currently being supported by an EPSRC Research Studentship and the Computing Department at Lancaster University.

References

Bowman, T. (1997), "VR Meets Physical Therapy", *Communications of the ACM* **40**(8), 59–60.

Greenfield, N. S. & Sternbach, R. A. (1972), *Handbook of Psychophysiology*, Holt, Rinhart and Winston, Inc.

Grudin, J. (1990), The Computer Reaches Out: The Historical Continuity of Interface Design, *in* J. C. Chew & J. Whiteside (eds.), *Proceedings of CHI'90: Human Factors in Computing Systems*, ACM Press, p.261.

Ishii, H. & Ullmer, B. (1997), Tangible Bits Towards Seamless Interfaces Between People, Bits and Atoms, *in* S. Pemberton (ed.), *Proceedings of CHI'97: Human Factors in Computing Systems*, ACM Press, pp.234–41.

Keirn, Z. A., Aunon & Jorge, I. (1990), "Man-Machine Communications Through Brain-Wave Processing", *IEEE Engineering in Medicine and Biology Magazine* **9**(1), 55–7.

Kirkup, L., Searle, A., Craig, A., McIsaac, P. & Moses, P. (1997), "EEG-based System for Rapid On-Off Switching Without Prior Learning", *Medical and Biological Engineering and Computing* **35**(5), 504–9.

Kubler, A., Kotchoubey, B., Hinterberger, T., Ghanayim, N., Perelmouter, J., Schauer, M., C., F., Taub, E. & Birbaumer, N. (1999), "The Thought Translation Device: A Neurophysiological Approach to Communication in Total Motor Paralysis", *Experimental Brain Research* **124**(2), 223–32.

Lubar, J. F. (1997), "Neocortical Dynamics: Implications for Understanding the Role of Neurofeedback and Related Techniques for the Enhancement of Attention", *Applied Psychophysiology and Biofeedback* **22**(2), 111–26.

Lusted, H. S. & Knapp, B. R. (1996), "Controlling Computers With Neural Signals", *Scientific American* **275**(4), 58–63.

Picard, R. W. (1995), *Affective Computing*, MIT Press.

Rosenberg, R. (1998), Computing Without Mice and Keyboards: Text and Graphic Input Devices for Mobile Computing, PhD thesis, Department of Computer Science, University College London.

Singh, G., Feiner, S. K. & D., T. (1996), "Introduction", *Communications of the ACM* **39**(5), 35–6. Special section: "Virtual Reality: Software and Technology".

Weiner, N. (1948), *The Human Use of Human Beings: Cybernetics and Society*, Houghton, Mifflin and Company.

Wolpaw, J. R. & McFarland, D. J. (1994), "Multichannel EEG-based Brain-computer Communication", *Electroencephalography and Clinical Neurophysiology* **90**(6), 444–9.

Human–Computer Interaction — INTERACT '99
M. Angela Sasse and Chris Johnson (Editors)
Published by IOS Press, © *IFIP TC.13, 1999*

The Perceptual Window: Head Motion as a New Input Stream

François Bérard

CLIPS-IMAG, BP 53, 38041 Grenoble Cedex 9, France.

francois.berard@imag.fr

Abstract: We introduce a novel interaction technique using head motions to control the location of a window viewpoint within its document space. Head motion is acquired by a non-intrusive head-tracker using computer vision. The tracking technique used in the system, namely correlation matching, is described in order to exhibit its strengths and weaknesses in the context of tightly coupled interaction. The output of the tracker is used in both a rate control interaction and a position control interaction. The benefit is demonstrated by two user studies built around two common GUI tasks: navigating in a two-dimensional document space, and moving an object from one place to another in a document. Our system, The Perceptual Window, allows significant improvements in task completion time after a short learning period.

Keywords: input devices, computer vision, head tracking, multiple streams of spatial input, interaction techniques, perceptual user interface, scrolling, drag and drop.

1 Introduction

The idea of using head tracking as an input component for interactive systems has appeared in the literature for some time. Most publications emphasize techniques for head tracking rather than its benefit in human computer interaction (Yang et al., 1998). Toyama (1998) proposes the use of head posture to control the pointer of a GUI but the benefit is not clearly demonstrated. Gaver et al. (1995) presents a promising application of face tracking, the Virtual Window, but the face tracker used in the system can not meet HCI requirements. The work presented here focuses on measuring the benefits of head motion as a general purpose spatial input stream in standard Graphical User Interfaces (GUI).

This paper is organized as follow: the work is motivated with a review of previous results on multiple streams of spatial input. Our face tracker is then presented, followed by a description of the global system. The Perceptual Window uses head motions to set the location of a window viewpoint within its document space. We present the results of two user studies demonstrating that the system is easily accepted by users and significantly improves performance for two common GUI tasks.

2 Motivations

The benefit of using a second stream of input, in addition to the mouse, has long been known (Buxton & Myers, 1986). Continuous and compound tasks are achieved with greater performance when their load is balanced over two hands, rather than with only one hand holding the mouse. The most intuitive source of the improvement is motion efficiency. However, more recent studies have shown that two streams of input can be worse than one if they are not appropriately designed (Kabbash et al., 1994). It seems that the cognitive load has a greater impact on task completion time than the amount of motion involved. Therefore, parallelization of user actions should associate a simple, coarse-grained action with a more complex, accurate one. (Guiard, 1987) presents a model which characterizes the complementary use of two hands to achieve such parallelization. He describes the respective roles of the 'dominant hand' and the 'non-dominant hand'. Guiard's model was successfully applied by Zhai & Selker (1997), in an experiment where the best combination was scrolling with the non-dominant hand and pointing with the dominant hand, compared to other multiple spatial input devices.

In our studies, the head plays the role of the non-dominant hand because we claim that it fulfills its three characteristics:

1. The head defines the frame of reference for the mouse: it sets the viewpoint of the window representing the mouse workspace.

2. Motion sequence is: head first (set the viewpoint), then the mouse (click in the window).

3. The head executes coarse-grained motions (window viewpoint does not have to be set accurately) compared to the mouse.

3 The System

Our system, called 'Perceptual Window', is based on a Computer Vision tracker measuring the head motions involved in the interaction. The system is 'perceptual' in the sense that it reacts directly to user's actions without need for separate physical contact. In this section, we describe the system from the low-level hardware set-up to the high-level interaction control.

3.1 Hardware Setup

The input to the Perceptual Window is provided by a video camera (pan-tilt-zoom SonyEVID31) placed in front of the user's head, on top of the monitor. The camera provides a video stream of images of the user to the frame grabber. The workstation is an Apple Power Macintosh 8600 equipped with a PowerPC 604 processor running at 350MHz and a built-in frame grabber. Note that this setup uses only off-the-shelf hardware, which is not the case for most new input devices.

3.2 Head Tracker

Head motion is detected by tracking a region of the face over time using *correlation matching* (Anandan, 1989). The principles of correlation matching are:

1. Memorize an image of the target at initialization.

2. Search the target in a new image by *correlating* (measuring similarity with) the memorized target image to subparts of the new image. The subpart that *matches* (that most resembles) the target image is selected as the new target location. Details on the matching formula are available in the appendix. In order to keep computation cost low, the search in the new image must be restricted to a small area, centered on the target location in the previous image.

In the context of tightly coupled interaction, correlation matching has two key features making it suitable for our system:

1. The system is fast. In our implementation, the processing of a new image takes less than 16 milliseconds (image size is 384×288 pixels, target image is 32×32 pixels, search area is 60×60 pixels). Adding the time necessary to generate the feedback, our system has a maximum latency of 65 milliseconds (translating to a running frequency above 15Hz). Achieving low latency is critical for the usability of the system.

2. The system is stable: if the target does not move, the output of the tracking remains strictly constant. A magnetic tracker, for example, does not achieve such stability. Stability is equally a requirement for tightly coupled interaction.

None-the-less, we observe three main limitations of correlation based tracking:

1. Tracking fails when the target is too fast. This occurs when the target speed is such that the displacement between two frames is greater than the search area. In the context of this work, this was not a problem because the speed range of face motions are easily bearable by the tracker.

2. Tracking fails if the target undergoes significant rotations or large changes in distance. Such motions induce modifications of the appearance of the target in the image. The new target image fails to match the memorized target image, causing the tracking to fail. The phenomenon is aggravated if the target is chosen on an area of the face having variable depths (such as the nose or the frame of the eyeglasses). In our context, we carefully chose the target on a planar area of the face.

3. Tracking fails if the neighborhood of the target has a similar appearance to the one of the target itself. This occurs for example when choosing a target on a wide non-textured area of the face, such as the forehead.

In our experiment, the most annoying limitations were numbers 2 and 3, as we were forced to manually initialize the tracking to a suitable target. We chose the area between the two tips of the eyebrows because the appearance of this area would not change significantly with head rotations (Limitation 2), and because it is dissimilar enough to any of its neighboring areas (Limitation 3).

Manually initializing the target of the tracking would be a serious limitation for general use of our system. Making the tracking autonomous is one of our research efforts. Encouraging initial results have recently been obtained (Bérard et al., 1997). In our user experiments, the lack of autonomy was not a limitation. The tracking was initialized by an operator only once at the beginning of the experiment. The tracking requires re-initialization only if the user turns his head away from the monitor, which typically did not occur during the experiments.

In order to maximize the resolution of the tracker output, the camera field of view was manually adjusted to maximize target translations corresponding to the widest comfortable head motions. However, there is a trade-off between maximizing the resolution and minimizing the risk that the target leaves of the camera field of view. To get an idea of the resolution achieved, typical target translations remained in a 260×200 pixel rectangle within a 384×288 image (thus about 70% of the maximum in both dimensions).

3.3   Interaction

The tracker outputs the two-dimensional coordinates (x, y) of its target in the image space. When integrated over time, this results in the translation parameters of the target (variation in x and y from some original location). The target being set on the face of the user, the system is informed about face motions. Note that the estimated translation is the translation of the *image* of the target, not of the *target* itself. The benefit is that users do not have to actually translate their face to operate the system, they rather rotate it, which is a much more comfortable motion to execute. The head being rotated, a target set on the face appears to translate in the image.

The head is allotted the task of navigating within the document space. Head motions are used to set the view location of a window showing a subpart of the document (on standard workstations, this task is typically allotted to the mouse and scroll-bars). The interaction is controlled with a *trigger* key. We used either 'tab' or 'space' for the trigger key but modifiers ('shift', 'control' or 'alt') would also be good candidates. The trigger key has two purposes. When the user first depresses it, the *origin* of the translation is set to the user's current head location. Secondly, the system is switched into head control mode: the control occurs only while the trigger key is depressed; it stops immediately when the key is released.

We use this setup to implement two different kind of interactions: one is a rate control interaction, the other one is a position control interaction.

3.3.1   *Rate Control Interaction*

As the head is tilted upward outside of a neutral area, the window content is scrolled down. The more the head is tilted, the faster the scrolling. Upward scrolling is stopped by returning the head inside the neutral area. Tilting the head downward induces a symmetrical behaviour. Rotating the head left or right causes scrolling to the right or to the left, respectively. Scrolling speed is governed by an exponential rather than a linear relationship to this movement, permitting both accurate adjustments and fast scrolling depending on the degree of head rotations. Figure 1 shows the transfer function for upward/downward head rotations. The transfer function for left/right head rotations has exactly the same shape. Diagonal scrolling is achieved by rotating the head both horizontally and vertically. To get a better feeling of the perceptual window behaviour, movies of the running system are available on the Web[*].

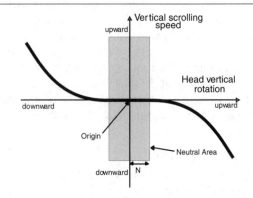

Figure 1: Transfer function for upward / downward head rotations. N is the radius of the neutral area.

Considering that it is possible to initiate and stop the scrolling in two different ways (neutral area and trigger key), we observed the two following behaviours:

1. Novice users sometimes found it difficult to return the head to within the neutral area in order to stop the scrolling. They preferred to press and release the trigger key for this purpose. The radius of the neutral area was set to 0 in order for the scrolling to start as soon as the trigger key was depressed.

2. Some trained users performed a more continuous navigation by maintaining the

[*]http://iihm.imag.fr/demos/pwindow/

trigger key in the depressed position. They used the neutral area to stop the scrolling when needed. In that case, the radius of the neutral area was set to 3% of the processed image height. The trigger key was only used as a higher level start / stop control, at the beginning and the end of the global task.

A usability study has been performed on this interaction (Bérard, 1999). A summary is presented in Section 3 ('Exploratory Experiment').

3.3.2 Position Control Interaction

This interaction is similar to the mouse interaction in the sense that translations performed by the user are directly reflected by the system. User head translations results in the same translation of the window viewpoint in the document. The only processing applied to the tracker output is amplification (multiplication of the translation by a constant).

Amplification is necessary because of the relative low resolution of the tracker (see end of Section 2.2) compared to the mouse resolution. If amplification were not performed, many *repositioning* would be necessary for large viewpoint translations. A repositioning occurs when the head is rotated to its maximum, but a wider translation is necessary. The trigger key is released so that the head is able to return to its neutral posture without changing the window viewpoint. Then, the trigger key is depressed again to apply a further translation in the initial direction. This is similar to a mouse repositioning occurring when the mouse has reached the limit of a comfortable wrist motion (or the limit of the mousepad). The mouse must be raised in order to move it to a new location without sending inputs to the workstation. In our experiments, users almost never had to reposition their head because they were able to go from one border of the document to the opposite with a single head-rotation.

Applying a high *gain* (the amplification factor) to the tracker output has the inconvenience that it increases the minimal step of viewpoint translation. In our experiments, a 1-pixel translation of the head triggers a 31 pixel translation of the document (6.2% of the window height). The movies (see footnote on previous page) provide an appreciation of the system behaviour.

Usability of the perceptual window has been tested against users for two different families of navigational tasks. An initial experiment tested the rate control interaction in an exploratory task (users had to follow a path to the target). In the second experiment, position control interaction was used in a 'drag and drop' task in which the destination of the navigation was made immediately available to the user.

4 Exploratory Experiment

This experiment is reported in another publication (Bérard, 1999), results are summarized in this section for the completeness of the paper.

The experiment task is based on real two-dimensional navigational tasks such as following lines and columns of a large spreadsheet, following the shape of a mechanical part on a high resolution technical sketch, or navigating via a mental representation of a large picture when only a small part of it is visible.

Users were presented a succession of 50 targets. They had to click on a target, follow the line to the next target by scrolling the window, click on the next target and so on (Figure 2). Subjects performed the task once while scrolling the window with the scrollbars and once with the rate control interaction.

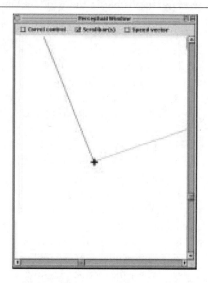

Figure 2: A target along the path.

Head motion interaction significantly out-performed scrollbars by an average improvement of 32% on task completion time.

This experiment showed that subjects were able to use this new modality surprisingly well: in less than a minute, they knew how to use it and could do so with skill. All users preferred head motion over the scrollbars. One user commented that scrolling control with the head was very *natural*: he simply had to orient his head towards what he wanted to see, and it just appeared in the middle of the window.

Rate control interaction is suitable for exploratory navigations because it allows a user to easily set the speed and direction of scrolling (which scrollbars can not do). However, in the case where the user knows where to go at the beginning of the navigation, we found that position control interaction was more appropriate.

5 'Drag and Drop' Experiment

In this experiment, we reproduce the steps necessary to move an object from one location to another in a large document displayed in a smaller window. This is a very common task when editing large texts, pictures or spreadsheets.

5.1 Motivations

Consider the two different situations occurring in standard GUI:

1. Both the object and its destination are visible in the window.

2. The object is visible in the window but not its destination.

In the first case, many applications allow a 'drag and drop' operation: the object is 'caught' by depressing the mouse button and maintaining it depressed while the mouse pointer is on top of the object. The object is then moved to its destination by moving the pointer while still maintaining the button depressed. The object is actually moved when the user releases the button after pointing to the destination.

In the second case, a drag and drop operation becomes difficult because the user has to set the viewpoint to destination while 'holding' the object. The mouse button being depressed, it can not be used to operate the scrollbars or any kind of navigational means requiring button clicks. Most applications offer an alternative: when the pointer holding the object crosses one of the window borders, the content of the window starts to scroll towards the opposite border. This navigational means is very limited in the sense that it does not allow the user to set the scrolling speed. It is very unlikely that the arbitrary scrolling speed suits the needs of the navigation. The scrolling is either too fast (the drop location comes in and out of the window before the user has a chance to stop it) or too slow (the user has to wait a long time before the destination appears in the window). In practice, when the destination is far away from the object, drag and drop is abandoned for a more efficient cut, navigate and paste sequence.

By using the perceptual window the mouse is freed from the navigational task. Therefore, the user can perform a drag and drop operation and leave the navigation to head control. As drag and drop requires less articulatory tasks than the sequence "select, cut, navigate, select destination, paste", we anticipate better performances of the perceptual window compared to standard GUI.

5.2 Task

Users are presented a black square that must be put in a succession of 50 black frames (the *targets*). Only one target is visible at any time. Target locations are randomly distributed within the 1600×2000 pixels document space. Once the black square has been put in a target, the target disappears and the black square is moved at a random position in the window. The next target is created at the same time in the document space.

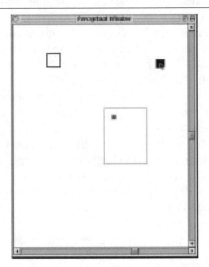

Figure 3: The radar view overlaid on the window. The big frame represents the current position of the window in the document space. The small square represents the target. The frame up-left is the target, the mouse is currently holding the black square.

At any time, only 6.2% of the document space is visible through a 400×500 pixels window. Users set the window viewpoint in the document space by using a *radar view*. The radar view represents a global view of the document space showing the current position of the window and the current target location in this space. When activated, the radar view is overlaid on top of the window: the window surface represents the document space, the current position of the window is represented by a red frame, the current target is represented by a small red square. Figure 3 shows an example of the radar view overlaid on the window. The radar view is activated when the space bar is depressed and remains active as long as the space bar is not released. The space bar is thus used as a trigger for both the radar view and the head control interaction.

Two different conditions were tested in this experiment. In the first condition, called *mouse condition*, the subject is asked to use the mouse and the keyboard to carry out the task. Subjects must select the black square (by clicking on it), depress the 'Command-X' key combination to cut it, call the radar view by maintaining the spacebar depressed, click near the target in the radar view. The window view-point is set to the click location in the radar view, the target is then apparent in the window. Subjects finish the operation by clicking on the target and depressing the 'Command-V' key combination to paste the black square.

In the second condition, called the *head condition*, subjects carry out drag and drop operations by performing the following actions: depress and hold the mouse button on the black square, depress and hold the space bar to start the radar view and start head control interaction, rotate the head to let the window viewpoint include the target, release the space bar, drop the black square in the target.

Nine volunteer subjects performed the experiment twice for the two conditions. Four subjects started with the head condition, the other ones started with the mouse condition. Subjects had a minimal training by performing a test series of 50 targets before each of the two conditions.

5.3 Results

Data were analyzed with a paired samples t-test which revealed a highly significant difference between conditions ($t(8) = 7.24, p = 0.00008$). As shown in Figure 4, head condition outperformed mouse condition by an average improvement of 18% (mouse condition average completion time was 190s vs. 155s for head control, standard errors were respectively 9.10 and 7.42).

Five users expressed their preference for the head condition, the four others preferred the mouse.

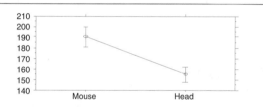

Figure 4: Completion time means (seconds) and standard errors by condition.

5.4 Discussion

As with the exploratory experiment, the most striking results are the generality of the performance improvement and the ease of learning the system. All users where faster with the head condition, in spite of the fact that this was a completely new way for them to interact with a computer.

Post experiment interviews revealed a strong contrast between users that liked the head control and those that did not like it. This second group were impeded by the inability to stabilize the window location when controlling with the head. They incorrectly thought they had been faster with the mouse. The task of navigation did not require to accurately locate the window, navigation could stop as soon as the target entered in the window.

Replacing a cut and paste operation in a large space by a drag and drop improves user performance. The required number of user action is reduced, and furthermore, the operation seems to have a lower cognitive cost. How can a user know, for example, if the object has been cut when it is not visible? It may be cut, or it may be out of the window view. This does not occur with drag and drop as you can see if you are 'holding' the object with the mouse.

6 Conclusion

This paper presents a novel means to provide spatial input to computers using head motions. The interaction is sufficiently natural that users can immediately improve their performances on common GUI tasks. The success of the experiments was due to the adequate allocation of tasks to the new input. Rather than replacing the mouse, head rotations can complement the mouse in a task at which the head naturally excels: setting the point of view.

It is noticeable that the hardware required for this input is already available on many workstations. As video-conferencing promotes the development of video-capable workstations, perceptual interfaces could be integrated as easily as a software component.

Another important point in favor of the acceptance of this kind of interaction is that it *complements* standard interaction rather than *replacing* it. The Perceptual Window features fully functional scrollbars. It simply offers new alternatives to allow a more natural interaction for some particular tasks.

Finally, we think this work opens a new path of possible GUI improvements. An interesting method to explore would be the suppression of the homing for the mouse in text editing tasks: wide cursor motions would be allocated to head motion while fine adjustments would still be accomplished by the cursor keys.

Acknowledgements

The author wish to thank James L. Crowley, Marie-Claude Frasson, and Leon Watts for their contribution to this work.

Appendix

Normalized Cross Correlation (NCC) formula:

Let $I(x,y)$ be the intensity of the pixel at coordinates (x,y) in image I. Let T be the image of the target, having size $n \times m$.

The Normalized Cross Correlation of target image T in image I at location (x,y) is given by:

$$NCC(x,y) = \frac{\sum_{u,v} I(x+u,y+v) T(u,v)}{\sum_{u,v} I^2(x+u,y+v) \sum_{u,v} T^2(u,v)}$$

A publication (Crowley et al., 1995) motivates the use of NCC and documents a fast implementation of a NCC based tracker in the context of finger tracking. The same implementation was used in the Perceptual Window.

References

Anandan, P. (1989), "A Computational Framework and an Algorithm for the Measurement of Visual Motion", *International Journal on Computer Vision* **2**(3), 283–310.

Bérard, F. (1999), A Study on Two-dimensional Scrolling with Head Motion, Technical Report IMAG_CLIPS_IIHM_199901, CLIPS-IMAG. http://iihm.imag.fr/.

Bérard, F., Coutaz, J. & Crowley, J. L. (1997), Robust Computer Vision for Computer Mediated Communication, *in* S. Howard, J. Hammond & G. K. Lindgaard (eds.), *Human–Computer Interaction — INTERACT '97: Proceedings of the Sixth IFIP Conference on Human–Computer Interaction*, Chapman & Hall, pp.581–2.

Buxton, W. & Myers, B. (1986), A Study in Two-Handed Input, *in* M. Mantei & P. Orbeton (eds.), *Proceedings of CHI'86: Human Factors in Computing Systems*, ACM Press, pp.321–6.

Crowley, J. L., Bérard, F. & Coutaz, J. (1995), Finger Tracking as an Input Device for Augmented Reality, *in Proceedings of International Workshop on Automatic Face and Gesture Recognition*.

Gaver, W., Smets, G. & Overbeeke, K. (1995), A Virtual Window on Mediaspace, *in* I. Katz, R. Mack, L. Marks, M. B. Rosson & J. Nielsen (eds.), *Proceedings of CHI'95: Human Factors in Computing Systems*, ACM Press.

Guiard, Y. (1987), "Asymmetric Division of Labor in Human Skilled Bimanual Action: The Kinematic Chain as a Model", *Journal of Motor Behavior* **19**(4), 486–517.

Kabbash, P., Buxton, W. & Sellen, A. (1994), Two-Handed Input in a Compound Task, *in* B. Adelson, S. Dumais & J. Olson (eds.), *Proceedings of CHI'94: Human Factors in Computing Systems*, ACM Press, pp.417–23.

Toyama, K. (1998), "Look, Ma - No Hands!" Hands-free Cursor Control with Real-Time 3D Face Tracking, *in Proceedings of the 1998 Workshop on Perceptual User Interfaces*.

Yang, J., Stiefelhagen, R. & Waibel, A. (1998), Visual Tracking for Multimodal Human–Computer Interaction, *in* C.-M. Karat, A. Lund, J. Coutaz & J. Karat (eds.), *Proceedings of CHI'98: Human Factors in Computing Systems*, ACM Press, pp.140–7.

Zhai, S. Smith, B. A. & Selker, T. (1997), Improving Browsing Performances: A Study of Four Input Devices for Scrolling and Pointing Tasks, *in* S. Howard, J. Hammond & G. K. Lindgaard (eds.), *Human–Computer Interaction — INTERACT '97: Proceedings of the Sixth IFIP Conference on Human–Computer Interaction*, Chapman & Hall, pp.286–93.

Human–Computer Interaction — INTERACT '99
M. Angela Sasse and Chris Johnson (Editors)
Published by IOS Press, © IFIP TC.13, 1999

Designing Awareness with Attention-based Groupware

Roel Vertegaal

Cognitive Ergonomics Department, Twente University, The Netherlands.

roel@acm.org

Abstract: A design rationale for the implementation of awareness features in the attention-based GAZE Groupware System is discussed. Attention-based groupware uses a framework for the design of awareness features based on the capturing, conveyance and rendering of information about human attention. The aim is to integrally provide information about the focus of conversational as well as workspace activities of participants. Our design themes were: implicit capturing of awareness information; scalability of networked awareness information; and representation of awareness information using natural affordances. Eye tracking provides a direct and non-command way of capturing human attention. It allows attentive information to be conveyed separate from the communication signal itself, in a machine-readable format. This eases the integration of Conversational and Workspace Awareness information, and allows network bandwidth consumption of this information to scale linearly with the number of users. Attentional focus also provides an organizational metaphor for the rendering of awareness information. By combining a more strict WYSIWIS general communilaboration tool (a 3D virtual meeting room) with more relaxed-WYSIWIS focused collaboration tools (2D editors), the attention of human participants can be guided and represented from broad to focused activity.

Keywords: CSCW, groupware, video-conferencing, awareness, attention, gaze, eye tracking.

1 Introduction

Groupware systems have long suffered from the lack of an integral paradigm for the provision of awareness information. This has led to a plethora of user interface widgets for awareness support, each using its own metaphoric representation of awareness information (Greenberg, 1996; Gutwin et al., 1996a; Sohlenkamp & Chwelos, 1994). Vertegaal et al. (1997) presented a comprehensive framework for the design of awareness features based on the capturing, conveyance and rendering of information about human attention. In this approach, awareness is defined as *knowledge about the attention of others*. Their model focused on the provision of Micro-level Awareness information, which conveys the attention of users during synchronous distributed communication and collaboration (we will use the term *communilaboration* for the intersection of these two). Micro-level Awareness provides two kinds of information: information about whom participants are communicating with (Conversational Awareness), and about what they are working on (Workspace Awareness). Vertegaal (1999) showed how representations of visual attention in the form of gaze directional cues (relative body positioning;

head orientation; and gaze at the facial region) are the most reliable non-verbal indicators of whom people communicate with (their *dialogic attention*) in multi-party face-to-face situations. More generally, we recognize the potential of human visual attention as a transparent and ubiquitous means for mediating awareness about other participants' attention for:

1. Persons.

2. Objects in a workspace.

3. The relation between these entities.

In this paper, we discuss our design rationale for the implementation of awareness features in the GAZE Groupware System (Vertegaal et al., 1998; Vertegaal, 1999), based on conveying the attention of others. First, we discuss the design constraints of the capturing, conveyance and rendering of human attention. Then, we will briefly discuss our prototype.

2 Design Rationale

Our aim was to design a groupware system with integrated and transparent support for Micro-level awareness features. As a main functional requirement, our system was to provide a seamless integration between Conversational and Workspace Awareness (Buxton, 1992). The use of gaze directional cues in face-to-face conversations provided a paradigm on which such integration could be based. Our design strategy was motivated by the following themes:

Implicit Collection of Awareness Information: Rather than asking users to make explicit verbally or otherwise whom or what they are attending to, a clever monitoring of the spatial properties and timing of normal user behaviour (e.g. their system input) can provide a wealth of implicit information about their activities. We thus took a non-command approach to providing awareness information, as discussed by Nielsen (1993). This should lead to a more transparent and efficient interface, with lower mental load and less interruption of task-oriented activities. In order to accomplish this in a mediated setting one does not necessarily need intelligent systems. All that is required is a paradigm for monitoring input activity of individual users, and presenting this as awareness information to users on the other side of a network.

Scalability of Networked Awareness Information: Since the purpose of groupware systems is to support many users, typically across a computer network, scalability of awareness information should be seen as an essential technical requirement. This is particularly true if one plans to use standard internet connections (Vertegaal & Guest, 1995).

Representing Awareness Information With Natural Affordances: According to (Sohlenkamp & Chwelos, 1994), the design of the '*Look and Feel*' (i.e. the perceived aspects of a user interface) of groupware applications should, where possible, be based on intuitions, knowledge and skills that people have acquired through years of shared work in the real world. Such knowledge may include the current Graphical User Interface (GUI) *Desktop Metaphor*, with its direct manipulation character. Gaze directional cues may provide us with a suitable metaphor for representing Conversational Awareness information. All that is required is an extension of this metaphor to the workspace, providing information about other users' relations to shared objects.

2.1 Implicit Collection of Awareness Information: Measuring Attention

We agree with Dourish & Bellotti (1992) that awareness information should be collected in a passive fashion, rather than being provided explicitly by participants. Nielsen (1993) describes a completely new user interface paradigm based on this principle: *non-command interfaces*. According to Nielsen, non-command interfaces, like face-to-face conversations, rely on a more fuzzy dialogue between users and user interfaces than is the case with current user interface paradigms. In the non-command paradigm, instead of a user issuing commands (by means of a command line syntax or by clicking menus or icons with a mouse), the computer *observes* user activity. The system then tries to make sense of available human input using a set of heuristics or a disambiguation process which could be similar to *grounding* in human dialogue (Clark & Brennan, 1991). Thus, computers would only need to query the user when certain information, required to understand what action should be taken, is deemed missing. We believe non-command interfaces, if applied appropriately, can lead to a more transparent and efficient interface, with lower mental requirements and less interruption of task-oriented activities. By means of anticipation and estimation, non-command input may take us a step further towards the original goal of direct manipulation interfaces: the shifting of user attention from tool to task. In order to accomplish this in a mediated setting, we do not necessarily need intelligent systems. All that is needed is a specification of what individual user activity should be monitored, and how this should be presented as awareness information to users on the other side of a network. Based on our definition of awareness, what we should monitor is the locus and temporal pattern of individual users' attention — see (Vertegaal et al., 1997) for a discussion. Depending on the application, there are a number of ways in which such monitoring might be accomplished:

1. Using Video Cameras: A great benefit of video data for Micro-level Awareness purposes is its real-world and temporal nature. For example, video data may be very useful for conveying the attention span of others by means of their body movements, or real-world objects in the focus of other people's attention. A problem with video is that it can be difficult to achieve a seamless integration of spatial Conversational and Workspace Awareness properties (Buxton, 1992; Okada et al., 1994). If the shared workspace is displayed on computer screens, then depending on the positions of computer screens and the representation of work spaces on those screens, angles of looking or gesturing may easily become incoherent with actual participant attention. The problem of achieving eye-contact using camera/display units is good example of this issue —

see Vertegaal (1998; 1999) for a discussion. Another problem with video input is that the conversion of *generic* video images into a machine-readable format is still problematic. This problem may, for now, inhibit the use of such information by a non-command interface for resolving decisions, e.g. about what awareness information to convey. A third problem with use of video data may be the heavy network bandwidth requirements, which we will discuss later.

2. Using Microphones: According to Vertegaal (1998), speech activity can be an excellent predictor of turn-taking patterns. As such, data from individual users' microphones might be used to gauge Conversational Awareness information. However, microphone data may need disambiguation before being useful as a provider of awareness information, or as input data in a non-command decision process. Too literal an interpretation of such information, for example, when determining whom people are listening to in multi-party communication, may therefore be detrimental to user performance — e.g. see (Buxton et al., 1997) for a discussion of problems with LiveWire voice-activated switching. Again, the temporal properties of audio data seem the most relevant. Microphone input could, for example, be used to monitor user presence or activity. Microphone input seems less appropriate for providing Workspace Awareness information. As for network constraints, audio data requires far less bandwidth than video data. In addition, we believe the availability of speech should be regarded a minimum requirement during synchronous mediated communilaboration anyway (Chapanis, 1975).

3. Using Manual Input Devices: Manual input devices such as the mouse and keyboard are important means for gauging Micro-level Awareness information. In text-based environments, the duration and aim of keyboard input may provide Conversational Awareness information in ways similar to the above use of microphone input. Attention of users could then be represented by, e.g. font size of textual communication. In graphical user interfaces, a representation of the location of pointing devices within a shared workspace may be used to convey Workspace Awareness information. Many current-day groupware systems already provide such *telepointers* as an indication of the locus of participant activity (Gutwin et al., 1996b). Advantages of the use of manual input devices for providing awareness information include: they are low-cost and ubiquitous; they already are the main means of

manipulating objects in shared workspaces; their data is machine-readable and low-bandwidth by nature. A disadvantage of manual pointing devices may be that they often do not return to a zero state. If a participant leaves her mouse pointer at a position within a shared workspace, the telepointer representation may falsely indicate her attention to that part of the workspace. In the future, such problems might be circumvented by basing the decision to represent a telepointer on a fuzzy assessment of data from different input devices. We believe a more important restriction in the use of manual pointing devices is that they typically require an explicit manipulative action. Hence, they seem suitable mostly for gauging action-related awareness information, such as conveying the direct manipulation of shared objects. The use of manual pointing in providing Conversational Awareness information seems limited to manual deixis towards other participants.

4. Using the Real World as an Input Device: A recent development is the use of real-world objects, rather than software objects, as a user interface to software processes — so-called Tangible Media, see (Ishii & Ullmer, 1997). In this approach, the orientation and position of objects in the real world, e.g. on a desk, is gauged by means of sensors or simple image recognition techniques — for example, by recognizing barcode stickers on objects (Underkoffler & Ishii, 1998). Attributes of real objects could thus provide low-bandwidth Workspace Awareness information to participants on the other side of a network, where they could be re-synthesized by projection onto their desk. The biggest advantage of this approach is the richness and transparency of the interface for single users. For now, the biggest drawback is that software manipulation of real-world artifacts is still limited. Thus, the joint manipulation of real objects may be problematic. Although we recognize the potential of this technique, we consider it beyond the scope of this paper. In a related approach, data-suits and other forms of sensor technology may gauge a wide range of parameters of human behaviour in various forms of transparency, such as head or body orientation (Rabb et al., 1979). Eye and head orientation tracking are examples of such technology. These techniques would seem the most relevant in this category for comprehensive gauging of awareness information in general, and Conversational Awareness information in particular.

5. Using Eye and Head Tracking Devices: The orientation of the human eye or head can be gauged by tracking devices. Although at the moment, eye tracking technology is not yet used for generic input purposes, this is changing rapidly (Joch, 1996; Nielsen, 1993). Capturing the actual focus and span of visual attention by means of an eye-tracking system may provide a relatively direct and high-resolution means of capturing information about participants' attention for actions, objects and people alike. Eye input may thus provide an integrated approach for gauging Conversational and Workspace Awareness information. In addition, eye-tracker information is machine-readable, low-bandwidth and non-command by nature (Nielsen, 1993). Many problems with the application of eye-tracking in user interfaces were in fact *due* to inadvertent use of eye fixation information for issuing system commands — the '*Midas Touch*' problem, see (Velichkovsky et al., 1997). A clear disadvantage of eye input is that eye-tracking devices are still rather expensive. However, this seems mostly due to the low production volume. Indeed, low-resolution eye-trackers are already becoming available for less than $1500. Unfortunately, eye-tracking still has an undeserved negative reputation in terms of usability. Archaic requirements such as bulky head attachments or fixation of the user's head need no longer apply. With up to 900 cm^3 of head movement tolerance, the transparent application of desk mounted eye-trackers for desktop computer input purposes has recently become a realistic option (ASL, 1998; LCT, 1997). It is with ranges larger than these that head orientation sensors become a good alternative, at least for gauging Conversational Awareness information (Rabb et al., 1979). The inaccuracy of head orientation information would probably require an alternative source of input for the measurement of Workspace Awareness information.

Next, we will discuss the impact of the selection of input modality on network bandwidth requirements of a groupware system.

2.2 Scalability of Networked Awareness Information

Since the purpose of groupware systems is to support many users, in our case across a computer network, scalability of the network bandwidth consumed by awareness functionality is a technical design constraint that should be taken seriously (Greenhalgh & Benford, 1995; Vertegaal & Guest, 1995). We will limit our discussion to a simple comparison between the impact on network resources of methods of input for Conversational Awareness information. From the above discussion, it becomes apparent that currently, the most integral candidates for gauging

Conversational Awareness information are *1) video cameras and 5) eye or head tracking devices*.

Figure 1: Video tunnel setup. Each participant is represented by a camera/display unit.

2.2.1　System 1: Using Video Cameras

As discussed, Conversational Awareness can effectively be constituted by mediation of information about the relative position, head orientation and gaze of individual users (Vertegaal, 1999). When video cameras are used to capture this information, it is advisory to use a multiple camera setup, such as the one depicted in Figure 1. Each participant has a camera/display setup for each other participant using the system. In between the camera and display of each unit, a half-silvered mirror is placed at an angle of 45 degrees. This *video tunnel* principle allows gaze at the facial region, at least to some extent, to be conveyed (Acker & Levitt, 1987). A good example of a mediated system using such setups is *MAJIC* (Okada et al., 1994). Although there are problems with the consistent preservation of eye contact using such systems (Vertegaal, 1998; 1999), there are also problems with the network load generated by such systems. In normal packet-switched networks (such as the Internet), the video from each camera and audio data from the microphone in the above system would need to be broadcast individually to each other participant in a meeting (rather like in a Cable TV network). *Multi-casting* is a new Internet technique which prevents the inefficient use of the network bandwidth caused by such individual broadcasting techniques (Ericksson, 1994; Vertegaal & Guest, 1995). In Multi-casting, each unique stream of video data is put on the net only once, and is then picked up by the system of each other participant in the meeting (rather like a standard TV broadcast is picked up by the TV antenna of viewers that are tuned in). Thus, using Multi-casting, the total bandwidth consumption for System 1 would be equal to:

$$B = nA + n(n-1)V \qquad (1)$$

In this equation, B is the total amount of bandwidth used, n is the number of participants, A is the amount of bandwidth per audio input, and *V* the amount of bandwidth used per unique video stream. It is clear that System 1 does not scale linearly with the number of participants. With four participants, 12 units of video bandwidth are required. With six participants, this rises to 30 units of video bandwidth.

2.2.2 System 2: Using Eye or Head Tracking Devices

When eye or head tracking devices are used, the manipulation of images of individual users could be used to convey Conversational Awareness information to other participants (Vertegaal, 1999). In such system, pictorial representations of users would be manipulated such that their relative positioning, head orientation and gaze would be preserved (Vertegaal, 1997). This manipulation could occur according the measured locus of visual attention. An example of a system in which head trackers are used to convey head orientation is the *Talking Heads* system by (Negroponte). When motion video would be conveyed using such systems, the total bandwidth consumption *B* in a Multi-cast network equals:

$$B \approx nA + nV \qquad (2)$$

Since video is not used to convey visual attention *itself*, this system scales linearly with the number of participants. When still pictures are used, *V* approaches zero, since all that is conveyed is the coordinates of visual attention of the participants. In that case, the amount of bandwidth needed is no more than would be required by audio only.

2.2.3 Concluding Remarks

Use of video input for conveying Conversational Awareness information simply does not scale well with the number of participants. This, and the fact that the availability of a measure of visual attention should ease the integration of Conversational and Workspace Awareness information, led us to prefer System 2 with eye-tracker input as a basis for our system design. Given the spatial range of available eye-tracking devices, we, for now, limited our design to a desktop computer environment. We decided to initially build an audio-mediated environment in which still images of participants are manipulated in order to visually represent Conversational Awareness information. Empirical evidence shows that still images can successfully convey such information — see (Vertegaal, 1999) for a discussion. Next, we will discuss design issues in the representation of awareness information.

2.3 Representing Awareness: Designing a Virtual Meeting Room

In our discussion of the design of representations for groupware system functionality, we will concentrate on how Micro-level Awareness information could be represented in an audio-visual desktop computer environment. We will focus on the integral and synchronous provision of Conversational and Workspace Awareness information, rather than on the design of the communication and collaboration tools themselves.

This design theme relates to the 'Look and Feel' of awareness functionality, guiding how the perceived aspects of a groupware system awareness interface could be rendered. In doing so, we wanted to make use of existing knowledge and skills of users as much as possible. We therefore chose a metaphoric design approach, in which elements of the interface and their behaviour would be based on real world equivalents as much as possible. We tried to use Gibsonian affordances to render awareness functionality into the user's perception as directly as possible. Thus, we tried to allow users to rely as much possible on knowledge in the system image, rather than on knowledge in their heads. We agree with Sohlenkamp & Chwelos (1994) that a metaphoric design approach should not be followed too rigidly in order to prevent the inadvertent modelling of limitations inherent to the real world. Instead of modelling the real world on a one-to-one basis, we therefore attempted to model the essential bits only. Finding a basis for our representations in the real world included making use of users' knowledge of current Graphical User Interface *Desktop Metaphor* Smith et al. (1982). In the design of their DIVA groupware system functionality, and Sohlenkamp & Chwelos (1994) simply expanded the single-user desktop paradigm to include multiple users, adding the elements *people* and *rooms* to elements already present in the desktop paradigm: *documents, desks* and *pointers* (with the latter becoming telepointers). Thus, they padded an existing computer metaphor with elements borrowed from the real world. In order to achieve a seamless integration of representations for Conversational and Workspace Awareness information (our main functional requirement), different user interface elements should have some form of spatial and temporal relation with each other. We therefore followed an approach similar to Sohlenkamp & Chwelos, building a *virtual meeting room* in which the above user interface elements are jointly represented (Ensor, 1997). However, as we will now discuss, a virtual meeting room alone may not be sufficient for supporting focused collaboration.

2.3.1   General vs. Focused Collaboration

Stefik et al. (1987b) proposed the '*What You See Is What I See*' (WYSIWIS) paradigm as a means of providing a consistent and coordinated display of user interface elements to all participants. In strict WYSIWIS, all participants essentially have exactly the same display containing exactly the same information at exactly the same moment in time. In their Colab environment, Stefik et al. (1987a; 1987b) supported WYSIWIS by maintaining synchronized views, and by offering facilities for telepointing with publicly visible cursors.   This would allow participants to have a common understanding of their virtual world, permitting them to rely on the availability of external context in, for example, deixis. However, Stefik et al. (1987a) also pointed out that a strict application of WYSIWIS throughout user interface elements may be too inflexible. It may, for example, lead to problems in supporting the parallel work on different tasks by subgroups, or the transfer of information between private and public spaces. Instead, they recommended strict WYSIWIS as a foundational abstraction, with a selective easing of compliance (relaxed-WYSIWIS) along four dimensions:

1. *Display space.*   Strict WYSIWIS applies to everything on an individual display; applying it only to a subset of visible objects (e.g. windows and cursors) relaxes this constraint.

2. *Time of display.* Strict WYSIWIS requires that images be synchronized; allowing delays in updating or viewing of images relaxes this constraint.

3. *Subgroup population.* Strict WYSIWIS requires shared viewing to apply to everyone in the full meeting groups; allowing sharing to be limited to subgroups relaxes this constraint.

4. *Congruence of view.* Strict WYSIWIS requires that images be identical; allowing alternative views relaxes this constraint.

As a response to this, Gutwin et al. (1996b) warned that relaxed-WYSIWIS may actually lead to a lack of awareness, since increased individual control reduces the group focus inherent in strict WYSIWIS systems. Thus, there may be a conflict between requirements for general and focused collaboration. We therefore decided to have a more strict environment for general group activities, and a more relaxed environment for focused collaboration activity. The virtual meeting room would provide a place on the display where general group activity is

grounded in a rather strict manner. Within it, only congruence of view would be relaxed, and only in that each participant's viewpoint would be strictly located at the position of his representation.   This way, we ensured effective application of gaze as a metaphor for conveying Conversational Awareness information. Individual viewpoints would otherwise be fixed such that all awareness information would be within field of view of all participants. On the rest of the display, around the virtual meeting room, focused collaboration could take place using task-specific relaxed-WYSIWIS document editors — e.g. those proposed by Gutwin et al. (1996a; Greenberg, 1996). Our WYSIWIS relaxation requirements for focused document editing were based on recommendations made by Baecker et al. (1993), and almost the opposite of those of the virtual meeting room.   Different documents may appear at different locations on displays of individual participants; updating of images may depend on where individuals work within the document; document contents need be displayed only to the subgroup working on them; document contents is typically viewed from the same angle by all participants (e.g. during text editing), but position of individual users within documents (i.e. the part of the document that is displayed) is totally relaxed. However, in order to provide a common glue between document editors (focused collaboration tools) and the virtual meeting room (the general communilaboration tool) we introduced one constraint: there should always be at least one WYSIWIS representation of a telepointer linking the attention of a participant in the meeting room to his attention to sections of document content.

2.3.2   Attentional Focus as an Organizational Metaphor

In a larger perspective, the concept of *attentional focus* can be regarded as an organizational metaphor throughout the design,   gluing   representations of awareness functionality at different levels of refinement together so that they can be recognized as a whole. This becomes apparent when we consider the suggested user interface elements as a way of representing attention of participants. *Rooms* are ways of organizing the presence of people, signalling the general availability of their attention for a common communilaborative goal.   Within rooms, the co-location and orientation of *persons* is a way of organizing the joint attention of sub-groups towards a common communilaborative task (Nakanishi et al., 1996). *Desks* are ways of organizing task-specific objects, providing an overview of their availability for collaborative attention. Within desks, *documents* signal the availability of a task as a focus for collaborative attention. Also within desks, *telepointers* signal the actual focus of collaborative attention towards a certain task. Finally, when documents are opened, relaxed WYSIWIS document editors allow participants to focus their attention according to individual interest. As will be discussed, telepointers link this focus within the document to the focus within in the virtual meeting room — as an example, see the Gestalt view of the SASSE environment (Baecker et al., 1993). Thus, using the above organizational metaphors, the focus of attention of participants may be described and guided from the very general to the very specific.

2.3.3 Visual Representation of Interface Elements

We will now discuss how the above discussed user interface elements could be rendered with visual behaviour. To keep the user interface as simple as possible, we chose to represent only five elements of real meeting rooms: *rooms*, *desks*, *persons*, *documents*, and *pointer light spots*. Other attributes include a stationary pad, exit sign, and a trash can.

Rooms: Rooms contain all the people, desks and documents required for a synchronous distributed communilaboration session. Depending on the environment, rooms could be represented by text windows (e.g. in chat environments), 2D surfaces — e.g. DIVA (Sohlenkamp & Chwelos, 1994), or 3D worlds — e.g. MASSIVE (Greenhalgh & Benford, 1995). As will be discussed later, we wanted to use head orientation as a metaphor for conveying visual attention of participants. If this information was to be used for conveying Conversational Awareness as well as Workspace Awareness, 3D orientation would seem a requirement. We therefore chose a 3D room design, which could function as a container for organizing the attention of participants at the *presence* level. Just like people located in the same real room are able to see and hear each other, so too would people within a our virtual room hear and see each other. As with DIVA (Sohlenkamp & Chwelos, 1994), the entering of a person into a room could establish audio-visual communication links with people already present. We restricted ourselves to using rooms as a means for organizing private meetings only — i.e. a virtual meeting room (Ensor, 1997).

Desks: These containers represent a way of organizing attention of participants towards any

number of collaborative objects. Depending on the environment, a simple representation of a directory structure might be used for grouping shared files. However, we chose the single-user desktop metaphor as a basis, expanding it into a shared surface onto which iconic representations of shared file objects could be placed and organized by position (Smith et al., 1982). However, our representation would function not just as a means for organizing collaborative objects, but also as a means of organizing persons. By placing representations of persons around a 2D desk surface in our 3D meeting room, face-to-face round-table communilaboration could be used as a metaphor for integrating Conversational and Workspace Awareness information.

Persons: A participant is represented by a *persona*: a metaphoric rendering of real participant behaviour (Negroponte). An important functional requirement for personas is that they represent a participant's visual attention (Vertegaal, 1999). Although, depending on the environment, personas may be rendered by a name (chat environments), a 3D model (avatar environments), or a video stream (video-conferencing), this rendering would need to include a visual representation of real participant attention towards other persons. Gaze may be considered an ideal metaphor for this purpose. Real images of participant gaze are the most effective way of conveying this (Vertegaal, 1998; 1999). As discussed, we chose to initially base our design on still images, rather than motion video images. This to circumvent problems of parallax between camera position and participant representation, which, even when video tunnels are used, may impair correct perception of visual-attentive cues (Vertegaal, 1998; 1999). In order to achieve a smooth integration of the persona in the 3D meeting room, we decided against the use of different images for conveying different loci of visual attention (Tanaka et al., 1996). Instead, for each participant, we suspended a single frontal snapshot — made while looking into the camera lens — in the 3D meeting room. 3D orientation of this 2D persona would then metaphorically convey the direction of gaze of that participant, as measured by the eye-tracking device.

Documents: These containers represent a way of organizing attention of participants towards a particular task. In standard desktop environments, document icons typically function as a representation of associated document content (Smith et al., 1982). We took a similar approach. Document icons can be placed on a desk in the virtual meeting room as a means of sharing the associated content. This content can be accessed by opening the document icon (e.g. by double-clicking it), at which moment it is downloaded and displayed in a focused collaboration editor outside the virtual meeting room. Document editors appear only to those participants that opened the document, but the associated document icon on the desk remains visible to all. Documents can be associated with local editors, or editor software could be embedded as part of the document content. In principle, documents can contain any kind of information, as long as an associated editor is available to all parties. As discussed, information display in such editors would typically be based on all participants having the same point of view, but should otherwise follow a relaxed-WYSIWIS paradigm. As discussed, telepointers provide ways of linking the focus of attention of individuals on sections of document content to the document representation in the virtual meeting room.

Telepointer Light Spots: These represent the actual attention of participants for objects in a shared work space. During presentations by an individual in a group meeting, light spots produced by laser pointing devices are now widely used to communicate the exact focus of attention of a presenter. We used these light spots as a metaphor for telepointing, illuminating objects in a shared workspace according to the attention of individual participants. As a source of information about this attention, we could use mouse position or the actual point of gaze as provided by the eye-tracker. With the latter, participants need not take any action other than looking to provide others with Workspace Awareness information. During general communilaboration in the meeting room, when a participant looks at a location on a desk, a light — appearing to be emitted from his persona — illuminates the spot. We thus borrowed a functional metaphor from the helmets used by miners to illuminate their work environment (the *Miner's Helmet* metaphor). The light spot is also associated with the emitting persona by means of colour coding. Multiple light spots of the same colour can be used to represent the same focus of attention at different levels of refinement. During focused collaboration in a document editor, when a collaborator looks at a location within the document content, a light with her colour illuminates the spot. This light spot is visible only to persons working within the document. Therefore, whenever a person looks at document content, the associated document icon in the meeting room should also be illuminated

by a light spot of his colour. This light spot is visible to all. If documents contain multiple sections, multiple light spots of the same colour could indicate in a strict-WYSIWIS fashion which section each collaborator is focusing on (see the Gestalt viewer of the SASSE environment (Baecker et al., 1993) as an example of how this might be accomplished). All light spots generated by a single persona were to remain tightly associated by movement and colour. This way, light spots may provide a kind of attentional glue between focused collaboration and general communilaboration activities.

3   The GAZE Groupware System

Based on the above rationale, we developed a prototype groupware system which provides integral support for Conversational and Workspace Awareness by conveying the participants' visual attention. Instead of using multiple streams of video for this purpose, the GAZE Groupware System (GGS) measures directly where each participant looks by means of an advanced desk-mounted eye-tracking system. The system represents this information metaphorically in a 3D virtual meeting room and within shared documents. The system does this using the Sony Community Place (Sony, 1997) plug-in, which allows interactive 3D scenes to be shared on a Web page using a standard multi-platform browser such as Netscape. In this prototype, we did not yet integrate support for multi-party audio communication. Instead, the GAZE Groupware System can be used in conjunction with any multi-party speech communication facility such as an Internet-based audio conferencing tool, or standard telephony.

3.1   A Session in the GAZE Virtual Meeting Room

The GAZE Groupware System simulates a four-way round-table meeting by placing a 2D image (or persona) of each participant around a desk in a virtual room, at a position that would otherwise be held by that remote participant. Using this technique, each person is presented with a unique view of each remote participant, and that view emanates from a distinct location in space. Each persona rotates around its own x and y axes in 3D space, according to where the corresponding participant looks. Figure 2 shows the system in use in a four-way situation. When Robert looks at Roel, Roel sees Robert's persona turn to face him. When Robert looks at Harro, Roel sees Robert's persona turn towards Harro. This should effectively convey whom each participant is listening or speaking to. When a participant looks at the shared desk, a light spot is projected onto the surface of the desk, in line with her persona's orientation. The colour of this light spot is identical to the colour of her persona. This allows a participant to see exactly where the others are looking within the shared workspace. By direct manipulation, e.g. with their mouse, participants can put document icons, representing shared files, on the desk. Whenever a participant looks at a document icon or within the associated file, her light spot is projected onto that document icon. This allows people to use deictic references for referring to documents (e.g. *"Here, look at these notes"*). Shared documents are opened by double clicking their icon on the desk. When a document is opened, the associated file contents appears in a separate frame of the Web page (see Figure 2). In this frame, an editor associated with the file runs as an applet. When a participant looks within a file, all participants looking inside that file can see a light spot with her colour projected over the contents. This light spot shows exactly what this person is reading. Again, this allows people to use deictic references for referring to objects within files (e.g. *"I cannot figure this out"*). For a more complete and technical description of the GAZE system — see (Vertegaal, 1999).

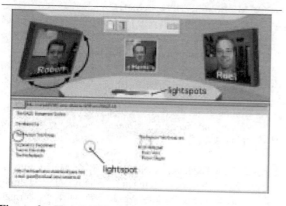

Figure 2: The GAZE virtual meeting room (top) with a shared document editor (bottom).

4 Conclusions

In this paper, we discussed a design rationale for the implementation of awareness features in the attention-based GAZE Groupware System. Attention-based groupware uses a framework for the design of awareness features based on the capturing, conveyance and rendering of information about human attention. Our main functional requirement in the design process was to achieve a seamless integration between Conversational Awareness information ("Whom are participants communicating with?"), and Workspace Awareness information ("What they are working

on?"). Our design themes were: the implicit collection of awareness information; the scalability of networked awareness information; and the representation of awareness information using natural affordances. Eye tracking devices provide a direct and non-command way of capturing multi-modal human attention. Their main advantage is that they allow attentive information to be conveyed separate from the communication signal itself, in a machine-readable format. Not only does this ease the integration of Conversational and Workspace Awareness information, it also allows networked bandwidth consumption of this information to scale linearly with the number of users. We have shown how attentional focus may also provide an elegant organizational metaphor for the rendering of awareness information. By combining a more strict WYSIWIS general communilaboration tool (a 3D virtual meeting room) with more relaxed-WYSIWIS focused collaboration tools (2D WIMP editors), the attention of human participants can be guided and represented from broad to focused activity. Thus, the attention-based groupware paradigm provides an integral approach to the capturing and guidance of human awareness of others.

References

Acker, S. & Levitt, S. (1987), "Designing Videoconference Facilities for Improved Eye Contact", *Journal of Broadcasting & Electronic Media* **31**, 181–91.

ASL (1998), "ASL Eyetracking Systems", http://www.a-s-l.com. Applied Science Laboratories.

Baecker, R. M., Nastos, D., Posner, I. R. & Mawby, K. L. (1993), The User-centred Iterative Design of Collaborative Writing Software, *in* S. Ashlund, K. Mullet, A. Henderson, E. Hollnagel & T. White (eds.), *Proceedings of INTERCHI'93*, ACM Press/IOS Press, pp.399–405.

Buxton, W. A. S. (1992), Telepresence: Integrating Shared Task and Person Spaces, *in Proceedings of Graphics Interface '92*, Morgan-Kaufmann, pp.123–9.

Buxton, W. S., Sellen, A. J. & Sheasby, M. C. (1997), Interfaces for Multi-party Video-conferences, *in* K. E. Finn, A. J. Sellen & S. B. Wilbur (eds.), *Video-mediated Communication*, Lawrence Erlbaum Associates, pp.385–400.

Chapanis, A. (1975), "Interactive Human Communication", *Scientific American* **232**, 36–42.

Clark, H. H. & Brennan, S. E. (1991), Grounding in Communications, *in* L. B. Resnick, J. Levine & S. D. Teasley (eds.), *Perspectives on Socially Shared Cognition*, American Psychology Association, pp.127–49.

Dourish, P. & Bellotti, V. (1992), Awareness and Coordination in Shared Workspaces, *in* J. Turner & R. Kraut (eds.), *Proceedings of CSCW'92: Conference on Computer Supported Cooperative Work*, ACM Press, pp.107–114.

Ensor, J. R. (1997), Virtual Meeting Rooms, *in* K. E. Finn, A. J. Sellen & S. B. Wilbur (eds.), *Video-mediated Communication*, Lawrence Erlbaum Associates, pp.415–34.

Ericksson, H. (1994), "MBONE: The Multicast Backbone", *Communications of the ACM* **37**, 54–60.

Greenberg, S. (1996), A Fisheye Text Editor for Relaxed WYSIWIS Groupware, *in* M. Tauber (ed.), *Companion Proceedings of CHI'96: Human Factors in Computing Systems (CHI'96 Conference Companion)*, ACM Press, pp.212–3.

Greenhalgh, C. & Benford, S. (1995), "MASSIVE: A Collaborative Virtual Environment for Teleconferencing", *ACM Transactions on Computer–Human Interaction* **2**, 239–61.

Gutwin, C., Greenberg, S. & Roseman, M. (1996a), Workspace Awareness Support with Radar Views, *in* M. Tauber (ed.), *Companion Proceedings of CHI'96: Human Factors in Computing Systems (CHI'96 Conference Companion)*, ACM Press, pp.210–1.

Gutwin, C., Roseman, M. & Greenberg, S. (1996b), A Usability Study of Awareness Widgets in a Shared Workspace Groupware System, *in* M. S. Ackerman (ed.), *Proceedings of CSCW'96: Conference on Computer Supported Cooperative Work*, ACM Press, pp.258–68.

Ishii, H. & Ullmer, B. (1997), Tangible Bits Towards Seamless Interfaces Between People, Bits and Atoms, *in* S. Pemberton (ed.), *Proceedings of CHI'97: Human Factors in Computing Systems*, ACM Press, pp.234–41.

Joch, A. (1996), "What Pupils Teach Computers", *BYTE* **21**, 99–100.

LCT (1997), "The Eyegaze Communication System", http://www.lctinc.com. LC Technologies Inc.

Nakanishi, H., Yoshida, C., Nishimura, T. & Ishida, T. (1996), Freewalk: Supporting Casual Meetings in a Network, *in* M. S. Ackerman (ed.), *Proceedings of CSCW'96: Conference on Computer Supported Cooperative Work*, ACM Press, pp.308–14.

Nielsen, J. (1993), "Noncommand User Interfaces", *Communications of the ACM* **36**, 83–99.

Okada, K.-I., Maeda, F., Ichikawaa, Y. & Matsushita, Y. (1994), Multiparty Videoconferencing at Virtual Social Distance: MAJIC Design, *in* R. Furuta & C. Neuwirth (eds.), *Proceedings of CSCW'94: Conference on Computer Supported Cooperative Work*, ACM Press, pp.385–93.

Rabb, F., Blood, E., Steiner, R. & Jones, H. (1979), "Magnetic Position and Orientation Tracking System", *IEEE Transactions on Aerospace and Electronic Systems* **15**, 709–718.

Smith, D. C., Irby, C., Kimball, R., Verplank, B. & Harslem, E. (1982), "Designing the STAR User Interface", *Byte* **7**(4), 242–282. Reprinted in Baecker, R. M. & Buxton, W. A. S. (1987), *Readings in Human–Computer Interaction: A Multidisciplinary Approach*, pp.653–61, Morgan Kaufmann.

Sohlenkamp, M. & Chwelos, G. (1994), Integrating Communication, Cooperation, and Awareness: The DIVA Virtual Office Environment, *in* R. Furuta & C. Neuwirth (eds.), *Proceedings of CSCW'94: Conference on Computer Supported Cooperative Work*, ACM Press, pp.331–43.

Sony (1997), "Sony Community Place", http://vs.spiw.com/vs/.

Stefik, M., Bobrow, D. G., Foster, G., Lanning, S. & Tatar, D. (1987a), "WYSIWIS Revised: Early Experiences with Multiuser Interfaces", *ACM Transactions on Office Information Systems* **5**(2), 147–67.

Stefik, M., Foster, G., Bobrow, D. G., Kahn, K., Lanning, S. & Suchman, L. (1987b), "Beyond the Chalkboard: Computer Support for Collaboration and Problem Solving in Meetings", *Communications of the ACM* **30**(1), 33–47.

Tanaka, S., Okada, K.-I., Kurihara, S. & Matsushita, Y. (1996), Desktopconferencing System Using Multiple Still Pictures: Desktop-MAJIC, *in* M. S. Ackerman (ed.), *Proceedings of CSCW'96: Conference on Computer Supported Cooperative Work*, ACM Press.

Underkoffler, J. & Ishii, H. (1998), Illuminating Light: An Optical Design Tool with a Luminous-Tangible Interface, *in* C.-M. Karat, A. Lund, J. Coutaz & J. Karat (eds.), *Proceedings of CHI'98: Human Factors in Computing Systems*, ACM Press, pp.542–50.

Velichkovsky, B., Sprenger, A. & Unema, P. (1997), Towards Gaze-mediated Interaction: Collecting Solutions of the "Midas Touch Problem", *in* S. Howard, J. Hammond & G. K. Lindgaard (eds.), *Human–Computer Interaction — INTERACT '97: Proceedings of the Sixth IFIP Conference on Human–Computer Interaction*, Chapman & Hall.

Vertegaal, R. (1997), Conversational Awareness in Multiparty VMC, *in Companion Proceedings of CHI'97: Human Factors in Computing Systems (CHI'97 Conference Companion)*, ACM Press, pp.6–7.

Vertegaal, R. (1998), Look Who's Talking to Whom, PhD thesis, Cognitive Ergonomics Department, Twente University, Enschede, The Netherlands.

Vertegaal, R. (1999), The GAZE Groupware System: Mediating Joint Attention in Multiparty Communication and Collaboration, *in* M. G. Williams, M. W. Altom, K. Ehrlich & W. Newman (eds.), *Proceedings of CHI'99: Human Factors in Computing Systems*, ACM Press.

Vertegaal, R. & Guest, S. (1995), "Network Issues in the Growth and Adoption of Networked CSCW Services", *ACM SIGCHI Bulletin* **27**, 63–68.

Vertegaal, R., Velichkovsky, B. & van der Veer, G. C. (1997), "Catching the Eye: Management of Joint Attention in Cooperative Work", *ACM SIGCHI Bulletin* **29**.

Vertegaal, R., Vons, H. & Slagter, R. (1998), Look Who's Talking: The GAZE Groupware System, *in* C.-M. Karat, A. Lund, J. Coutaz & J. Karat (eds.), *Proceedings of CHI'98: Human Factors in Computing Systems*, ACM Press.

Human–Computer Interaction — INTERACT '99
M. Angela Sasse and Chris Johnson (Editors)
Published by IOS Press, © IFIP TC.13, 1999

SeeWeb: Dynamic Improvement of the Accessibility of HTML Documents for Blind Persons

Siwar Farhat & Yacine Bellik

LIMSI-CNRS, BP 133, 91403 Orsay Cedex, France.

farhat.s@decade.fr, bellik@limsi.fr

Abstract: This article deals with blind user access to the Web. We first present the different existing approaches that facilitate Internet access to blind users and the different ergonomic rules that HTML page designers should respect. Then, we present our approach for a dynamic improvement of the accessibility. This approach uses a customization interface that allows the user to choose the modifications to perform on the Web pages and the information to visualize. Our system, called SeeWeb, operates between the user and a traditional navigator (Netscape, Internet Explorer, etc.). It allows the analysis of the HTML document and its content. It also enables to modify the page structure, according to user's preferences and some ergonomic rules. The user interface coupled to a screen reader allows the restitution of information in a more comprehensive way for the blind user. This work has been carried out as a cooperation between LIMSI-CNRS (a research laboratory) and TECHNIBRAILLE (an industrial partner).

Keywords: blind user, non-visual interaction, internet access, Web access, ergonomic rules.

1 Introduction

The World Wide Web (WWW) presents an interesting opportunity for direct access to information by blind users. But the very visual nature of the Web may be considered as a major difficulty for them. This paper deals with the different aspects of Web accessibility by blind users. It presents the solution we adopted in order to improve the access to HTML pages according to users preferences. This work takes part of a project dealing with Internet access.

We first studied the different approaches used to solve Internet access problems. Then we present some studies that concern ergonomic rules in designing accessible HTML pages. After that, we present a method that allows the reorganization of HTML pages according to some ergonomic rules. This method enables the modification of original Web pages and the addition and/or the suppression of information contained within these pages in order to improve the accessibility and to facilitate the navigation for blind users. The modified pages can then be consulted using a screen reader in a more adapted way.

2 Information Access

Electronic documents and the infrastructure being developed in Internet and World Wide Web (Wesley & Millns, 1998) are interesting technologies to increase information access for blind users. Electronic documents can be structured with languages like HTML (Hypertext Markup Language) and XML (Extensible Marking Language). The HTML format is a labelling system that delimits and identifies the different logical and physical components of the document. It uses, very largely, multimedia possibilities offered by nowadays microcomputers. It can hold images, audio and video, animations, etc. This fact can be considered as a navigation problem for blind users. But there exist some access tools for blind users that allow them to access and to read HTML pages (e.g. WebSpeak,[*] Lynx,[†] Smart-Net (Truillet et al., 1997; Vigouroux & Truillet, 1998) and WAB (Perrochon & Kennel, 1995; Kennel et al., 1996)). These tools have some limitations at the access level, as they cannot describe images, tables, frames and Java applets (but some systems such as JAWS[‡] screen reader start to deal with these problems).

---

[*] http://www.prodworks.com/pwwovw.htm
[†] ftp://ftp2.cc.ukans.edu/pub/DosLynx/readme.htm
[‡] http://www.nanopac.com/jaws.htm

An access to these objects by blind users is still a difficult task. In order to make HTML pages more accessible to blind users it is important that HTML page designers consider some ergonomic design rules. Different research groups have examined the problem of Web document accessibility for blind users. Some Web pages design guidelines are under definition. This may help authors of Web pages to make the information more accessible for handicapped people.[§] These design guidelines have been originally provided by the Trace Center at the United States (Arato et al., 1998). Currently, the World Wide Web Consortium (W3C) attempts to provide some detailed directives for Web pages author.[¶] This recent work is being done under the "Web Accessibility Initiative (WAI)" project.[‖]

3 Design Rules for Accessible Web Pages

In this paragraph, we provide the main design rules of accessible HTML pages. These rules are parts of the design guidelines of WAI project and Starling Access Services.[**]

3.1 Links

The problem of links concerns the loss of the semantic context when the text link does not provide the amount of words, necessary for the understanding of the link reference. For example, let us take the following text extracted from the Starling Access Services Web site:

> "Canada is blessed with thousands of freshwater *lakes* and navigable *rivers*. It is no surprise then that boating is a popular recreation. The Ottawa *River* is a prime example of a great recreational waterway. The Ottawa *River* is ideal for power *boats*, sail *boats*, house *boats*, *canoes*, row *boats* and *kayaks*."

This text illustrates the problem of loosing the semantic context. It is very frequent that blind users navigate from link to link, rather than from line to line. In this case only the link text is announced. A blind user having a screen reader would perceived the following words: 'lakes', 'rivers', 'river', 'boats', 'boats', 'canoes', 'boat' and 'kayak'. These links do not contain enough information for the user to take a clear decision and a good choice of the subject. To determine the context of the links, it becomes necessary to read the whole paragraph or phrases.

To explicit context information, the simplest solution would be to attribute more text in the HTML links. The previous text would become:

> "Canada is blessed with thousands of *freshwater lakes* and *navigable rivers*. It is no surprise then that boating is a popular recreation. The *Ottawa River* is a prime example of a great recreational waterway. The Ottawa River is ideal for *power boats*, *sail boats*, *house boats*, *canoes*, *row boats* and *kayaks*".

3.2 Images

We know that the screen readers cannot describe an image if the author of the HTML page did not comment it. Systems that would allow a verbal reproduction of a pixel image do not exist yet. Research works about indexing images is a first step toward this aim, but the results are still rather premature. On the other hand, reconstitution of image in relief is much more costly. Furthermore, its pertinence is not yet proven.

The only solution for the moment, which allows a blind user to perceive images, is that the author of the HTML page provides supplementary textual information that describes the images.

3.3 Tables

For tables, the design rules recommend to provide an equivalent version in text mode. This should help the screen reader program to describe tables clearly.

3.4 Punctuation

It is recommended that a point or any other convenient punctuation should terminate phrases, titles and lists. Considering that voice synthesis of screen readers provide the complete punctuation to the listener, phrases, titles and lists having no punctuation, will be read without interruption. This may confuse the listener and compromise the good understanding of the text.

For seeing users, titles are typographically and spatially separated and so well perceived. Lines or numbers separate list elements. This simplifies the visual reading, but it can be a source of confusion for blind users.

[§] http://trace.wisc.edu/
[¶] http://www.w3.org/WAI/
[‖] http://www.w3.org/TR/WD-WAI-PAGEAUTH/
[**] http://www.starlingweb.com/acc/

4   Contribution of our Work

The rules of Web page design that were described above are important for accessibility by blind users. Unfortunately, these rules are not always respected from the Web authors. To resolve this problem, we have developed a system that dynamically improves accessibility of HTML pages. A customization interface allows the blind user to choose the modifications to perform on the Web pages and information to visualize.

Furthermore, we have carried out a study on the use and the evaluation of design guidelines of HTML pages. We have also taken into account some queries provided by blind users and by some teachers specialized in access at graphical interfaces, particularly those of the "TECHNIBRAILLE" company. This allows us to generate reconstruction rules for HTML pages that were considered by our system to improve the accessibility for the blind persons.

In the following we will present the different approaches allowing access to the Web for the blind persons. Then, we will compare them and discuss their advantages and drawbacks. Finally the conception and the implementation of our system will be described.

5   The State of the Art

This research revealed three main approaches allowing Web access for the blind (Farhat et al., 1998):

- The dedicated approach: consists in the development of browsers specially dedicated to the blind persons. The non-visual interface is designed as ergonomic as possible for blind users.

- The generic approach: is based on the use of screen readers allowing access to a graphical operating system in a generic way. The screen reader is used with a traditional visual navigator, such as Netscape, Internet Explorer or Lynx to allow Web access for blind users.

- The intermediate approach is an extension of the generic approach. It consists in the modification of HTML pages through a proxy server in a way to be more easily readable by a blind user, before sending them to the traditional visual navigator.

6   Comparing the Three Approaches

With the first (dedicated) approach, the dedicated browser is in charge of the downloading of the HTML page, of its interpretation as well as the restitution of the page contents. This allows better access. For instance, multi-modal interaction can be optimally exploited by the system (Bellik, 1995; Vigouroux & Truillet, 1998). This method allows the modification of HTML pages in accordance with some ergonomic rules. Since the navigator takes charge of the interpretation process, the system depends on the HTML syntax. Consequently, it is necessary to update the navigator to each evolution of the HTML norm. Furthermore, this approach requires the direct interpretation of the source code of certain languages such as JavaScript and VBScript as well as Java.

The generic approach which consists of using a general filter (Farhat, 1997), used by screen readers, allows to avoid the problem of interpreting HTML and other languages (JavaScript, VBScript), as this task is done by the visual navigator (Netscape, Internet Explorer). On the other hand, this approach highly depends on the operating system. A screen reader developed in a specific environment cannot be used in other different environments.

For instance, the Windows 3.11 screen readers cannot be used under Windows 95. The program code needs to be rewritten for the new environment. Furthermore, the screen readers that begin to work under Windows 95 cannot identify all the graphical elements of the interface, fact that does not allow the blind user to perceive all the pertinent elements of the Web page. In the other hand, some ergonomic problems may reduce the quality of adaptation. Instead of focusing the blind user to the significant elements of the HTML page, this method provides a large amount of information, which is not necessarily useful for him.

The intermediate approach attempts to resolve the inconvenient of the generic approach. It introduces some static treatments on the original HTML page in order to produce a new page, whose organization and contents are more adapted to a non-visual consultation. But this implies an obligatory passage through the proxy server. For example, if the proxy server is located in the US and the user in France, a transmission of information between France and USA is necessary even if the visited Web site is in France.

7   Description of the Adopted Approach

The adopted approach consists in an improvement of the intermediate approach under two principle points:

- Local spy.

- Dynamic customized adaptation.

7.1 Local Spy

The interpreter of the original Web page and the generator of the new modified page consist in a local application. It takes place between the user and the navigator (Netscape, Internet Explorer, etc.). It allows the analysis of the HTML document and the modification of its contents and of its logical structure according to user preferences. In the opposite of the third approach, we do not use a distant proxy server. This allows us to avoid the unnecessary transfer of information between the navigator client, the proxy server and the visited Web site.

7.2 Dynamic Customized Adaptation

Modifications done by existing systems on HTML pages are static and don't allow the user to choose which information will be presented and how. In contrast to this principle, each modification we do on the HTML document can be enabled or disabled by the user. An interface allowing a customizable adaptation has been developed. The new page generated by the system in this way is more adapted to each blind user.

8 Architecture of the System

Figure 1 presents the general architecture of the system.

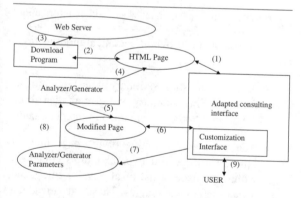

Figure 1: General architecture of the system.

When the user wants to consult an HTML page (1) the system attributes the task of downloading the desired page to the download program (2). The page is then examined by the analyser/generator (4). Thanks to the representation language of the HTML norm, all the syntactic, morphologic and typographic elements of the electronic document are identified (5). The generator will analyse these elements in order to extract the key elements of the page and to modify

them according to the user specified modifications. The process performed by the analyser depends on the parameters of the user customization (8). A new modified page is then generated (5) and provided to the user (6). Using the customization interface (9), the user has the possibility to choose the elements to add and/or suppress and the tags to modify in the Web page. With this choice (7), specific treatments will be executed by the generator (8). This affects instantaneously the reorganization of the document in a dynamic way. It is based on the new parameters introduced by the user. The user can then consult the page adapted to his preference (9) using a screen reader.

9 Modification of HTML Pages

The HTML pages are reorganized on two levels. The first concerns the page contents and the second the interpretation of its elements.

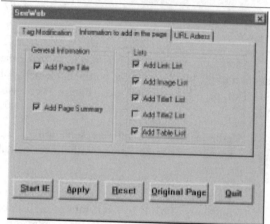

Figure 2: The customization interface: adding information.

The first level (Figure 2) consists of:

- Adding the information necessary for the navigation, such as the list of hypertext links that exist in the current page.

- Adding references of key elements of the page (such as tables) for direct access.

- Adding global information describing the page such as a statistic summary for the different elements contained in the page.

- Adding a key word before images, tables and interaction objects (radio buttons, edit objects, checkboxes, etc.) in order to inform the user of these elements, even if the screen reader does not detect them. Most of the screen readers do not indicate the presence of a link. Therefore, further manipulations are required in order to find the links, according to their associated attributes (blue underlined). This process makes difficult the access and the reading of HTML pages. Adding keywords makes easier the research process of information in HTML pages.

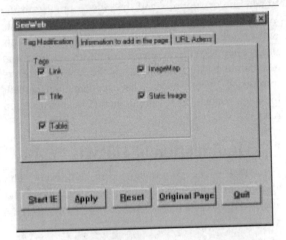

Figure 3: The customization interface: tag modification.

Adding this information is aimed at focusing the attention of the blind user to the pertinent elements of the HTML page. The second level (Figure 3) consists of:

- Modifying the physical representation of the document by interacting with the logical structure.

- Modifying the structure of the active images (containing links) by generating a list of hypertext links. With a Braille display or a speech synthesizer images are not perceived. This shows the importance of reorganizing the HTML source code, especially for describing images.

- Modifying the cell space in tables.

- Modifying the style attributes such as indicating title levels using [T1], [T2], etc.

10 Example of Page Modification

In this paragraph, we provide an example of HTML page reorganization. We suppose that the user made the following choices:

- To modify the hypertext links.

- To modify the images.

- To add a statistical summary.

- To add a list of all hypertext links.

- To add a list of tables.

- To add a list of images.

- To add a list of level1 titles.

Figure 4 shows an example of the resulted modified page.

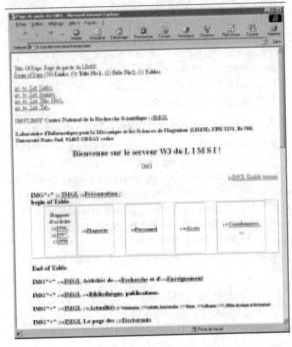

Figure 4: The customization interface: adding information.

In this case, the different document modifications consist of:

- Adding a statistical summary at the beginning of the page. This summary will give an idea about the different objects contained in the document.

- Adding at the beginning of the page internal links to a list of all hypertext links contained within the page, a list of all level 1 titles, and a list of tables and images. These lists are added at the end of the document. Links to the same address are placed on the same line in the lists. The user can activate the links from a list or can go directly to the corresponding position in the document. This allows a blind user to avoid a sequential research, word by word or line by line of hypertext links in the document.

- Inserting before each hypertext link a 'L' indicator in order to inform the user of the existence of this link.

- Inserting before each image an '{IMG <descriptor>}' or '{IMGL <descriptor>}' where <descriptor> is a text provided by the page designer to describe the image. 'IMG' indicates that the image is static (without links) and 'IMGL' indicates that the image contains links.

After this page reorganization, the user obtains a general presentation of the document and using the lists it is possible to directly access the pertinent elements of the page. To provide an easier access, vertical lists (one item per line) are used instead of multiple items placed on the same line.

11 Implementation

To test our approach, we chose to use Internet Explorer provided by Microsoft Corporation to modify, internally, the HTML pages. The user interface will be then the Internet Explorer navigator coupled with any screen reader. Our system takes place between both applications. It allows spying the internal behaviour of Internet Explorer in order to filter the Web page and to modify it before displaying it.

Microsoft offers an ActiveX controller (Roberts, 1998), which allows developers to add Internet navigation possibilities to their applications. As Internet Explorer is developed as an OLE object,[††] it is possible to control it from another program.

Internet Explorer has been chosen because it offers an event interface (Table 1) allowing the possibility to intercept messages, to pilot the navigator and to modify its original behaviour. Table 1 describes some events sent by Internet Explorer to our application.

Before Navigate	Occurs when the WebBrowser control is about to navigate to a new URL
Title Change	Occurs when the title of a document becomes available to change
Download Begin	Occurs when a navigation operation is beginning, shortly after the 'Before Navigate' event
Status Text Change	Occurs when the status bar text has changed
Navigate Complete	Occurs after the browser has successfully navigated to a new URL
Quit	Occurs when the Internet Explorer application is ready to quit

Table 1: Notification messages of Internet Explorer.

As previously indicated, our aim is to modify the physical aspect of original HTML pages. Thanks to

events sent by Internet Explorer, we can determine the URL address provided by the user, and disable the original page display. In order to intercept the display command, we build a new action for the notification message "BeforeNavigate". This message is sent when the user provides an URL address, activates Next or Back button or any other action that activates the navigation. The process consists in disabling the page display, modifying the original page using the user choices and then displaying the new generated page thanks to the 'Navigate' method (Table 2) inside Internet Explorer.

Table 2 lists the methods used to control Internet Explorer from another application.

GoBack	Navigates to the previous item in the history list
GoForward	Navigates to the next item in the history list
GoHome	Navigates to the current configured home or start page
Navigate	Navigates to a resource identified by an URL or file path
GoSearch	Navigates to the current configured search page

Table 2: Internet Explorer methods.

12 Conclusion

Internet access by blind users is a non-trivial problem for the research in Man-Machine communication. The multimedia nature of HTML documents is not the unique difficulty. Java applets, scripts, and the very visual conception of HTML pages are also important problems. To solve these problems the existing approaches provide only partial solutions. The approach we presented here has been adopted because of its two major qualities. The first one is the respect of the blind user's work habits. This aim is reached because our approach uses a usual screen reader associated to a traditional Web browser. The second one is the ability for a blind user to configure by himself the modification process of HTML pages. The customization interface allows a complete personal adaptation. This customization interface has another advantage. It will allow us to make, in the near future, detailed evaluations about different adaptation types without having to change the source code of our system.

[††]http://msdn.microsoft.com/library/periodic/period97/d1/vc0297.htm

References

Arato, A., Graziani, P. & Vaspori, T. (1998), Hybird Book: A New Perspective in Education and Leisure for Blind People, *in Proceedings of INSERM Conference*.

Bellik, Y. (1995), Interfaces Multimodales: Concepts, Modès et Architectures, PhD thesis, Université d'Orsay PARIS XI. Thèse de doctorat en Informatique.

Farhat, S. (1997), Outil d'adaptation d'interfaces graphiques pour les non voyants, PhD thesis, Université d'Orsay PARIS VII. Thèse de doctorat en Informatique.

Farhat, S., Bellik, Y. & Ducros, T. (1998), A Survey of Approaches for Access to the Web by Visually-Disabled, *in* G. Michel, G. Uzan, J. C. Sperandio & D. Burger (eds.), *Proceedings of the International Conference on Complex Systems,Intelligent Systems and Interfaces*.

Kennel, A., Perrochon, L. & Darvishi, A. (1996), "WAB: World Wide Web Access for Blind and Visually Impaired Computer Users", *SIGCAPH Newsletter* pp.10–5.

Perrochon, L. & Kennel, A. (1995), World Wide Web Access for Blind People, *in Proceedings of the IEEE Symposium on Data Highway*.

Roberts, S. (1998), "Keeping an Eye on Your Browser by Monitoring Internet Explorer 4.0 Events", *Microsoft System Journal* .

Truillet, P., Oriola, B. & Vigouroux, N. (1997), Multimodal Presentation as a Solution to Access a Structured Document, *in Proceedings of the 6th World Wide Web Conference*.

Vigouroux, N. & Truillet, P. (1998), A Friendly Document Reader by Use of Multimodality, *in Proceedings of the Csun Conference*.

Wesley, T. & Millns, I. (1998), Secure Delivery for Blind and Partially Sighted People: The SEDODEL Project, *in Proceedings of the INSERM Conference*.

Human–Computer Interaction — INTERACT '99
M. Angela Sasse and Chris Johnson (Editors)
Published by IOS Press, © IFIP TC.13, 1999

A Principled Design Methodology for Auditory Interaction

Evangelos N. Mitsopoulos & Alistair D.N. Edwards

Department of Computer Science, University of York, York YO10 5DD, UK.

enm@cs.york.ac.uk

Abstract: When the visual channel of communication is unavailable, non-visual user interfaces must be developed. The proposed methodology aims at the specification of auditory representations for interactive tasks. It consists of three interrelated specification levels. Information and supported tasks are specified in abstract terms at the conceptual level. The structure of the auditory scene is specified at the structural level in terms of auditory streams. The physical dimensions of sound are defined at the implementation level. The design guidelines have been validated by the experimental evaluation of a list of auditory checkbox widgets.

Keywords: extra-ordinary human–computer interaction, auditory display, auditory widgets, blind user.

1 Introduction

Sight is a very powerful means of communication. It is used in everyday communications through diagrams, pictures, gestures and many other forms; it is also the basis of most human–computer interaction. When that channel of communication is unavailable because the person is blind or the environmental conditions are disabling, then non-visual alternatives must be developed.

Numerous methodologies for the specification of user interfaces exist and whether yet another one has to contribute anything of value is indeed the first question to be asked. For instance, consider (Foley et al., 1990). Their framework essentially consists of a medium-independent level of meaning (divided into conceptual and functional design) and two medium-dependent levels, the syntactic and lexical design. Although their focus is mostly on graphical user interfaces (GUIs), there is no reason, in principle, why their framework could not be applied to the specification of auditory interfaces. In fact, the methodology presented in this paper consists of three levels of specification which are conceptually similar to those of Foley et al. Despite this similarity, the two methodologies have very different specification objectives.

Visual experience accumulated with every-day communications can be invaluable to GUI design because, combined with a set of empirical guidelines on visual design, it provides the basis for designing visual representations. *Assuming* that a suitable visual representation can be designed allows the next step

forward, that is, the specification of that representation in the user interface. The specification must capture the "...2D and 3D layout of a display, as well as any temporal variation in the form of the display" — Foley et al.'s (1990) syntactic design. The specification is also restricted at a lexical level by the available system primitives, such as the display primitives of a graphics subroutine package.

However, designers probably have considerably less experience with auditory information and, most of the time, no auditory representations exist to serve as paradigms. Despite the considerable volume of literature on auditory perception and attention, there are just a few guidelines accessible to the auditory interface designer. Even worse, designers might inadvertently apply visual design guidelines, achieving adverse results because of the inherent differences in sight and hearing.

Hence, in the case of auditory interfaces, it is most important to provide guidelines for the design of auditory representations in the first place. Given these guidelines, one may then proceed to address the issue of interface specification. Auditory design guidelines, derived from theories on auditory perception and attention, are the objective of our methodology. These guidelines are organized in a framework similar to Foley and colleagues' to aid a structured design approach. However, our methodology has to satisfy user constraints (perceptual and attentive) rather than system constraints (imposed by the available hardware and software). In this respect, we believe that it represents a valuable contribution to the field of auditory interfaces and, more generally, to multi-modal interface design.

1.1 Related Work

A significant amount of research effort has been expended in recent years on the problem of how to substitute the visual communication of the GUI so that it can be used by blind people — see, for instance, (Edwards, 1989; Mynatt & Weber, 1994; Weber, 1993). Most approaches are based on translation of the surface visual representation to a non-visual equivalent. The clearest example of translating at the *surface* level is the GUIB project (Weber, 1993). However, as illustrated by (Edwards, 1995), visual representations naïvely translated to an auditory form can become very difficult to use. The weak point of surface transformations is their failure to acknowledge the inherent differences between the perception of auditory and visual information. To design an efficient auditory representation, be it either a transformation of a visual representation or a novel form of information, it is essential to take into account some fundamental principles of auditory perception and attention. This is also the case for transforming visual to haptic representations (Kurze, 1997).

There is a linkage to the proposed methodology and the general notion of auditory earcons. Earcons have been designed not only for widgets such as buttons, menus or progress bars but also to convey navigation cues for hierarchical structures (Brewster, 1998). Our methodology is not confined to the design of auditory widgets, either. It is intended to be applicable to the design of *all* aspects of auditory user interfaces. For instance, it could be used to design an interactive presentation of charts to blind users.

Nevertheless, apart from the relationships between the methodology and earcons, there are some important distinctions, too. Earcons have mostly been designed as 'sonic enhancements' to the visual interaction. This methodology primarily address the issue of substituting the visual presentation with a non-visual one, an issue fundamentally different than enhancing visual interaction. More importantly, the design of the 'soundscape' is theory-driven relying on theories of auditory perception and attention. This contrasts with the design of earcons, which is based on empirical guidelines. The theoretical perspective of the methodology provides the means to systematically drive the designer's intuition, to assess the suitability of the resulting design, and to eliminate a considerable number of inappropriate alternatives prior to any experimental evaluation.

The objective of the research effort discussed herein is to develop a more principled basis for the design of non-visual interfaces. Widgets are used as exemplars since: they are essential components of GUIs; their simplicity lends themselves to a compact specification and they clearly capture interaction issues such as ear-hand coordination and auditory-haptic multi-modal integration. However, they only serve to illustrate the fundamental issues involved in the methodology; we understand them to be suitable exemplars rather than the most important design issue in non-visual interaction. The focus of this paper is on the specification of the auditory part of non-visual widgets and, in particular, the design for interactive tasks where users control the presentation of information depending on the task in hand.

1.2 Auditory Representations

In designing an auditory alternative to a visual representation it is necessary to take into account the inherent differences between auditory and visual information. One of the most important differences is the dynamic character of sound. Visual interfaces are mostly static (although animation is becoming increasingly important). Users can inspect any part of the display at their convenience. A computer-based example is the visual widget in Figure 1.

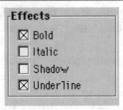

Figure 1: A visual 'widget' with a number of components, including four checkboxes.

It is a property of this representation that the user can view it in at least two ways. It is possible to *glance* at it to quickly perceive patterns. Based on this information, the user can accomplish a number of tasks such as to identify that several checkboxes are checked (but not all of them). However, the user might choose (depending on the task in hand) a different approach to this item, and to *interact* with it — toggling the value of a particular effect or browsing the list of available effects, for instance. All information necessary to the performance of both groups of tasks is accommodated in a single external representation.

This is not the case with auditory displays. Because of the dynamic character of sound and the short-term memory limitations imposed by the serial presentation of auditory information over time, it is difficult to accommodate all tasks into a single representation. Different rates of presentation are required for each group of tasks. Extracting information at a glance should use the fastest possible rate, whereas the rate of interactive tasks must be considerably slower and, most importantly, the user should have control of the information flow.

The distinction between two groups of tasks (the first based on fast rates of presentation and the second involving exploring and interacting with the information at much slower rates) extends to the relevant psychological theories, too. For instance, Auditory Scene Analysis (Bregman, 1990) deals mostly with the organization imposed on the auditory scene by perceptual processes at fast rates of presentation. Cognitive issues, such as selective attention or memory, become more prominent at slower rates of presentation. Issues relevant to fast rates of presentation have been discussed in Mitsopoulos & Edwards (1997; 1998). This paper deals with the design issues of auditory representations for interactive tasks. The methodology as a whole is outlined in Mitsopoulos & Edwards (to appear).

2 Methodology

The design methodology consists of three levels of specification, the conceptual, structural and implementation level. The reasoning for partitioning the specification process in three distinct levels has been discussed in detail in (Mitsopoulos & Edwards, 1998). In the following sections, each level will be illustrated using the example of the checkbox widget in Figure 1.

2.1 Conceptual Level

The set of tasks associated with the widget under design as well as the (abstract) information necessary to perform them is specified at this level. For the checkbox example, these tasks would include: identification of the state of the checkbox column at a glance (whether all or most of the checkboxes are checked or unchecked); browsing of available effects ('Bold', 'Italic', 'Shadow', 'Underline'); identifying and/or toggling of the value of an effect etc. The first task is relevant to fast presentation and has been considered in details in (Mitsopoulos & Edwards, 1998). We will focus our attention on the other two interactive tasks.

The necessary information to perform the related tasks can be defined in terms of abstract dimensions which can be of nominal, ordinal, interval, or ratio type (Zhang, 1996). For example, because the

two states of a checkbox (checked, unchecked) are distinct but not ordered they can be represented by two values along a nominal dimension. When physical dimensions of sound are selected to convey the information specified at the conceptual level, they should be of the same scale as their abstract counterparts so that they convey no more or less information. Timbre is a nominal dimension and it would be appropriate to represent the state of a checkbox. Pitch (on its own) would be a less appropriate dimension since it is ordinal and the user might erroneously deduce that the two states are ordered (for example, low — high).

Use of an interaction device introduces a number of navigation tasks which require additional information. For example, for a user browsing the list of checkboxes using the keyboard cursor keys, it is necessary to provide information about whether either end of the list has been reached. However, the keyboard does not provide this information. The 'missing' information is defined in conceptual terms so that it can be accommodated in the auditory representation. For instance, another abstract dimension would be the position relative to either end of the list, which is ordinal and has three values: first item in the list, last item, elsewhere in the list.

Moreover, ear-hand coordination may pose additional requirements (such as advance auditory feedback) which affect conceptual specification. For example, it is necessary to warn the user in advance when approaching a target such as either end of the list; otherwise, the user is very likely to overrun the ends at fast browsing rates. The information about position would include two more values: next-to-first item and next-to-last item.

Abstract dimensions are the constituents of semantic entities. A checkbox widget is an entity that has three dimensions, two nominal ones representing its *state* and its *label* ('Bold', for instance) and an ordinal one for its *position* in the list.

The fundamental difference between the conceptual and the other levels of specification is that only the former is medium-independent. Because it mediates between the visual and the auditory representation, had it not been medium-independent, it would be possible to erroneously include in the specification of the auditory representation some information necessary to the visual widget only. Another reason is the number of multi-modal issues (missing haptic information and advance feedback) considered and resolved at this level.

2.2 Structural Level

At this level, the structure of the auditory scene is defined in terms of auditory streams. The term stream here implies a series of auditory events with some common physical characteristic. The term 'channel' used in the early literature on auditory attention corresponds to the notion of a stream (Neumann et al., 1986).

One distinction found in the auditory attention literature is that between voluntary and involuntary attention. In general, we are able to control our attention and selectively attend to a particular stream, or divide our attention among a number of streams at will. However, our auditory system can detect changes in sounds, especially when these are sudden ones or when a new sound is introduced. Then, depending on task load, attention can be involuntary drawn by these sounds, even if they have not been attended to previously.

Most of the debate in auditory attention has been focused on voluntary attention issues. There have been a number of theories on voluntary auditory attention — see ten Hoopen (1996) for a review. According to Hawkins & Presson (1986):

> "To a certain point in the information processing sequence it appears that information from several sources ... can be processed in parallel. Beyond this point, however, inputs usually must be processed in series."

Nevertheless, there is no consensus on where this point lies in the information processing — theories of early selection, late selection and multiple loci theories (ten Hoopen, 1996).

It is a common finding that subjects are able to focus their attention on a particular stream of sounds (selective attention tasks) quite effectively. Most of the time, they are able to tune out all the other sounds. They will notice only gross changes in the physical characteristics of the non-attended auditory material, such as changes from male to female voice or from voice to a tone. Subjects are usually unable to report the semantic content of non-attended sounds. The consequence for auditory design is that, if users are attending selectively to a stream of sounds while performing a task, then it is quite likely that they will miss information conveyed in the non-attended streams. In other words, when performing a selective attention task, all the required information should be contained in the stream attended to, otherwise users might fail to integrate information presented in non-attended streams.

Nevertheless, a number of studies have reported that non-attended sounds are processed to some extend. Despite the fact that the so-called breakthrough of the non-attended sound is very limited (as low as 6%), the phenomenon has been used as evidence for late-selection theories. These imply that full semantic processing of all sounds in the auditory scene takes place before one of these sounds is selected for further processing. However, the interpretation of these findings is not unequivocal, since most of these studies have not adequately controlled where subjects had been directing their attention. Early-selection theories could also account for these findings. It might have been the case that subjects were relaxing their attention and sampling the non-attended stream(s) out of curiosity or that some non-attended sounds introduced a change in the auditory scene large enough to trigger involuntary attention. In either case, the breakthrough of the non-attended is very limited and it would not be safe practice for a designer to assume that users will reliably integrate non-attended information.

It is not necessary that users will selectively attend to a stream. They may also divide their attention among a number of streams. In this case, they will be able to integrate information among a number of streams. But then, they are usually subject to 'divided attention costs', that is, liable to more errors and increased reaction times. Moreover, even given considerable practice:

> "... it appears doubtful, practically speaking, that practice under divided attention conditions ... would ever bring performance up to levels achieved under focused [selective] attention conditions." (Hawkins & Presson, 1986).

Consequently, it appears that all information required for performing a task should be bound in a single stream, although a stream may support more than one task. If information for a task is distributed over a number of streams then users would find the task more difficult; designing for selective attention, optimizes performance.

Returning to the checkbox widget example, we have to examine whether the auditory scene complies with the above guideline. It seems reasonable to map each of the three dimensions of a checkbox entity to a distinct stream. This is mostly because we would like the user to be able to attend to any of these independently, but also because the sounds used would be substantially different from each other and hence they would be perceived as distinct streams.

Each stream has to be examined with respect to the tasks associated with it. The stream corresponding to the abstract dimension of position contains all the information required to locate either end of the list. Nevertheless, most tasks rely on information about the state and the label of each checkbox, too. For instance, the task of browsing the labels of the checkboxes would result in the stream with that information becoming the attended one. What would happen if the last checkbox in the list had been reached? From the above discussion it follows that if users were selectively attending to the label stream they would be likely to miss the position information. If they were dividing their attention between the label and position stream, it would take more time to complete the task and they would occasionally overrun the end of the list. Consequently, the abstract dimension of labels must be re-defined at the conceptual level to include the information: first item in the list, last item, elsewhere in the list. Identifying the state of each checkbox is also liable to the same problem. The conceptual level has to be re-specified until the structural level constrains are satisfied.

2.3 Implementation Level

The designer has also to decide on the physical dimensions of sound that will implement the auditory representation. A number of dimensions have been suggested for making a stream easier to attend to. These include pitch, timbre, spatial origin, temporal organization, onset asynchronies, intensity, as well as familiarity with the sound — see for instance (ten Hoopen, 1996; Deutsch, 1996; Bregman, 1990).

It seems that a good design principle is to use a number of physical dimensions to implement an abstract one. This redundancy is necessary to accommodate individual differences and hearing impairments users might have, as well as to make sure that a number of auditory illusions are avoided. For instance, consider the octave illusion (Deutsch, 1986) where frequency and spatial origin cues are opposed to each other. Frequency dominates, giving rise to a number of illusory percepts. However, if the spatial origin information is supported by a number of additional cues such as timbre and onset asynchronies, then the illusion disappears.

The following would be a possible implementation for the checkbox widget. It is *not* intended as an example of an artefact; the aim here is to illustrate the specification process at the implementation level and demonstrate how the abstract specifications derived at the conceptual and structural level are applied to the realization of the auditory widget.

Labels are presented using synthetic speech which is interrupted as soon as the user moves to an adjacent checkbox. The list is portrayed in a horizontal orientation, so that the speech is displaced to the left or right for the first and last checkboxes respectively. Since the other sounds are non-speech ones, labels form a distinct stream easily attended to.

The state of a checkbox is represented by a sampled sound produced by scratching a pen on a paper as if ticking a checkbox. The pitch of the sampled sound is varied to produce a dull or bright sound so that the two states are distinguishable (unchecked or checked respectively). Conforming to the re-definition in the conceptual level imposed by the structural level, the state sound of the first or last checkbox in the list is displaced to the left or right.

Position in the list is represented by a brief tone. For advance feedback, a simultaneous dissonant tone is presented and both tones are displaced to the left or right, appropriately. For the first and last item, the sound is again displaced as above. In this way, five values are created as prescribed in the conceptual level. Importantly, the user can not only discriminate one value from the other but may also identify each value on its own and hence, his or her position in the list at any time. Thus, even if disrupted, the user may resume a task without having to remember the current position in the list. It should be noted that in order to derive a number of absolutely identifiable values it might be necessary to use more than one dimension — yet another reason for redundant dimensions in the implementation. For instance, it is easy to distinguish a large number of pitches from one another but only few people have the ability of absolute pitch.

3 Experimental Evaluation

The aim of the experiment described here was to investigate the validity of a basic guideline of the methodology for the structural level, namely that all information required for performing a task should be in one stream. Numerous psychological experiments have demonstrated that performance deteriorates when attention is divided to more than one stream. However, the stimuli typically used in these experiments are austere and experimental conditions tightly controlled. It might be the case that, in practice, the design guideline in question does not introduce any particular improvements just because there is enough time to switch attention between streams, as in some psychological experiments that failed to show performance deterioration.

Also, most psychological experiments on selective attention have been employing presentation of spoken messages. It is quite likely that non-speech sounds can be semantically processed faster; this would largely eliminate any costs of dividing attention. Consequently, we would like to examine the validity of the guideline proposed in Section 2.2 in a situation more ecologically appropriate to the auditory user interfaces.

3.1 Method

Subjects: Eight subjects, from the academic community of the University of York were recruited. Most subjects were experienced musicians apart from two who were less experienced, though they used to play a musical instrument. The reason for using experienced musicians as subjects is that we expect them to be more practiced in attending to a number of instruments at a time. Consequently, they could be better in divided attention tasks than subjects with no significant experience in music. If musicians' performance in selective attention tasks is found to be superior than in divided attention tasks, then it is quite likely that the difference will be more pronounced for other users and even persist despite any practice given.

Stimuli and Apparatus: Sounds were generated with a SB-AWE64 Gold sound card and then presented over headphones. Subjects had to use the left and right cursor key and space bar of a PC keyboard; there was no visual contact with the computer monitor. Subjects' answers and presented sounds were taped using a Sony DAT recorder.

The experiment was a repeated-measures 2x2 factorial design. The two factors were the condition and the task factor. After having completed a training session, each subject served in all four blocks, the order of which was determined by a balanced Latin square. Each block contained 24 lists of checkboxes randomly generated by the computer. The first four lists in a block were discarded prior to any analysis.

Each condition level was a variation of the checkbox sounds (label, state and position) described in Section 2.3. The only difference between the two conditions was that, in the selective condition, all required information was in the label stream whereas, in the divided condition, information had to be integrated across the label and the position streams.

In more detail, for the selective condition, the position stream was kept to the centre providing no spatial information. The sounds in the label stream were displaced to denote the leftmost and rightmost checkbox in the list. For the divided condition, labels did not provide any spatial information; this had to be extracted from the position stream which was displaced following the same rule as labels in the selective condition. The checkbox stream did not provide any spatial information and was kept the same under both conditions; information contained in this stream was not required by any of the tasks in the experiment.

Sounds departed slightly from those described at the implementation level. Digits (0, 4, ..., 9) were used for labels. Advance feedback was substituted by random variations in the position sounds, to keep the spatial information provided by the label stream in the selective condition *equivalent* to that of the position stream in the divided condition. Position sounds were louder and prolonged to make attending to them as easy as possible. These changes were introduced following a pilot study.

The first task level was the *target* task. For each list, its leftmost or rightmost checkbox was presented at random. Subjects had to move towards the other end of the list, one checkbox at a time, using the cursor keys. They had to press the space bar as soon as they had reached the other end of the list or a target checkbox (labelled '0') had been encountered.

The second task level was the *addition* task which was essentially a target task with the variation that numerical labels had to be summed for each list. At the end of each list, subjects had to say aloud the sum.

Three dependent variables were of interest for each list: the mean key-press rate, the first-key-press time and errors (target and list-end overruns). For time measures the upper and lower quartiles for each subject and each block were discarded to control for outliers.

3.2 First-Key-press Times

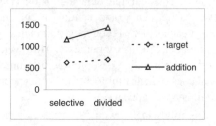

Figure 2: First-key-press reaction times (ms).

For the first checkbox presented in a list subjects had to integrate *two* pieces of information:

- First, whether or not the checkbox was a target. If it was, they had to press the space bar immediately.

- Second, subjects had to work out whether they were at the leftmost or the rightmost checkbox, in order to move towards the other end of the list.

For the selective condition this information was in the label stream; for the divided, in the position stream. For the target task, subjects had to compare the label to the target value (zero). For the addition task, the value of the number had to be identified and remembered for the additions to follow though as yet no mental arithmetic took place. First-key-press mean times are shown in Figure 2. The following results are obtained running the repeated-measures ANOVA test:

Source	F	Sig.
Task	58.088	0.000
Condition	12.110	0.010
Interaction	6.555	0.038

The significant condition main effect reveals that subjects were reacting faster in the selective condition. But this is not necessarily attributed to divided attention costs. An alternative hypothesis might be that extracting spatial information was more difficult from the position stream than the label stream. Since the same mapping rules were used, the problem would not be in interpreting the values but in perceiving the physical dimensions of the position sounds in the first place. However, this is unlikely for a number of reasons. First, the position sounds were designed to be as easy to attend to as possible. Second, during the training session, subjects had to selectively attend to the label stream in the selective condition and to the position stream in the divided condition to extract spatial information only. When asked to compare the difficulty of selectively attending to either stream, most subjects found no difference though a few preferred either the label or the position sounds to convey spatial information. Overall, there was no trend revealing preference of either condition.

The alternative hypothesis is refuted by the significant interaction effect. If spatial information was harder to extract from position sounds then the added amount of difficulty should remain constant for either task since:

1. the processing of digits remains unaffected by the condition factor (they are always on the label stream); and

2. extracting spatial information is the same for both tasks under divided conditions, since the addition task is essentially a target task as far as processing of spatial information is concerned.

A constant level of difficulty implies no interaction between tasks and conditions. Hence, the alternative hypothesis is rejected.

Thus, an examination of the first-key-press reaction time allows us to conclude that differences in performance can be attributed to costs of divided attention rather than the relative difficulty, if any, of extracting spatial information from the position sounds. This would validate our guideline from the designer's point of view *if* significant differences exist in overall performance measured by the mean key-press rate variable.

3.3 Mean Key-press and Error Rates

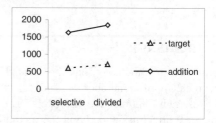

Figure 3: Mean key-press rates (ms/key-press).

Mean performance is a more important factor to the designer. Mean key-press rates are shown in Figure 3. The following results are obtained running a repeated-measures ANOVA test:

Source	F	Sig.
Task	44.768	0.000
Condition	7.391	0.030
Interaction	1.166	0.316

The two main effects (task, condition) are significant. The insignificant interaction cannot be related to absence of divided attention costs. First, while browsing the lists in the divided condition, subjects may be able to successfully accomplish the tasks without having to divide their attention for every checkbox, as long as the end of the list has not been reached. Thus, it is difficult to unequivocally associate results with the underlying psychological processes. Moreover, the variance in key-press rates attributed to the mental arithmetic task would by large enough to absorb any divided attention costs.

The target task is particularly interesting from the designer's point of view, since it is a fundamental constituent for most tasks in the auditory interface. Performance was worse by 20.7% or 115 msecs per key-press in the divided condition. Subjectively, only one subject weakly preferred the divided condition to the selective one, although all subjects performed significantly better in the selective condition. Most subjects felt that the selective condition was easier; two of them believed that it was much easier than the divided condition. Individuals were affected to different extents. For two of them, divided attention costs were less than 10%, for three it ranged between 15% and 20%, for the rest between 25% and 55%.

The results for error rates are not significant in general because four out of eight subjects had almost errorless performance. The trend was a total of 14 errors in the selective condition and 28 in the divided. The addition task errors were significantly more than the target task errors (1.5 vs. 3.75 errors per subject, significant at 5%).

4   Conclusions

The proposed methodology has been applied to the specification of a number of widgets such as checkboxes, radio buttons and listboxes. The basic psychological principles underlying the methodology have been experimentally evaluated. It appears that significant improvements in performance can be gained by applying the methodology in the design of auditory representations. Because of space limitations, a detailed discussion of several issues considered in the methodology has been omitted (such as how involuntary attention can be used appropriately or how the physical dimensions of sound can be manipulated to implement a desirable auditory scene structure). However, we believe that the main issues have been highlighted and validated, proving the methodology to be a valuable tool for auditory interface designers.

Acknowledgements

The work presented in this paper is part of a long-term project sponsored by EPSRC (grant number GR/M12063), which aims to derive a principled design methodology for the specification of multi-modal (auditory and haptic) non-visual interfaces.

References

Bregman, A. (1990), *Auditory Scene Analysis*, MIT Press.

Brewster, S. A. (1998), "The design of sonically-enhanced widgets", *Interacting with Computers* **11**(2), 211–35.

Deutsch, D. (1986), Auditory Pattern Recognition, *in* K. R. Boff, L. Kaufman & J. P. Thomas (eds.), *Handbook of Perception and Human Performance*, Vol. 2, John Wiley & Sons, chapter 32, pp.32.1–32.49.

Deutsch, D. (1996), The Perception of Auditory Patterns, *in* W. Prinz & B. Bridgeman (eds.), *Handbook of Perception and Action*, Vol. 1, Academic Press, pp.253–96.

Edwards, A. (1989), "Soundtrack: An Auditory Interface for Blind Users", *Human–Computer Interaction* **4**(1), 45–66.

Edwards, A. D. N. (1995), Outspoken Software for Blind Users, *in* A. D. N. Edwards (ed.), *Extra-Ordinary Human–Computer Interaction*, Cambridge University Press, pp.59–82.

Foley, J. D., van Dam, A., Feiner, S. K. & Hughes, J. F. (1990), *Computers Graphics: Principles and Practice*, second edition, Addison–Wesley.

Hawkins, H. & Presson, J. (1986), Auditory Information Processing, *in* K. R. Boff, L. Kaufman & J. P. Thomas (eds.), *Handbook of Perception and Human Performance*, Vol. 2, John Wiley & Sons, chapter 26, pp.26.1–26.64.

Kurze, M. (1997), Rendering Graphics for Interactive Haptic Perception, *in* S. Pemberton (ed.), *Proceedings of CHI'97: Human Factors in Computing Systems*, ACM Press, pp.423–30. http://www.acm.org/sigchi/chi97/proceedings/paper/mk.h

Mitsopoulos, E. & Edwards, A. D. N. (1997), Auditory Scene Analysis as the Basis for Designing Auditory Widgets, *in* E. Mynatt & J. A. Ballas (eds.), *Proceedings of the International Conference on Auditory Display (ICAD'97)*, Xerox Corporation, pp.13–8.

Mitsopoulos, E. & Edwards, A. D. N. (1998), A Principled Methodology for the Specification and Design of Non-visual Widgets, *in* S. Brewster & A. D. N. Edwards (eds.), *Proceedings of the International Conference on Auditory Display (ICAD'98)*, The British Computer Society.

Mitsopoulos, E. & Edwards, A. D. N. (to appear), A Methodology for the Specification of Non-visual Widgets, *in Adjunct Conference Proceedings of HCI International '99*.

Mynatt, E. D. & Weber, G. (1994), Nonvisual Presentation of Graphical User Interfaces: Contrasting Two Approaches, *in* B. Adelson, S. Dumais & J. Olson (eds.), *Proceedings of CHI'94: Human Factors in Computing Systems*, ACM Press, pp.166–172.

Neumann, O., van der Heijden, A. H. C. & Allport, D. A. (1986), "Visual Selective Attention: Introductory Remarks", *Psychological Research* **48**(4), 185–8.

ten Hoopen, G. (1996), Auditory Attention, *in* O. Neumann & A. F. Saunders (eds.), *Handbook of Perception and Action*, Vol. 3, Academic Press, pp.79–112.

Weber, G. (1993), Access by Blind and Partially Sighted People to Interaction Objects in MS-Windows, *in* The Swedish Handicapped Institute (ed.), *Proceedings of the 2nd European Conference on the Advancement of Rehabilitation Technology (ECART)*, p.2.2.

Zhang, J. (1996), "A Representational Analysis of Relational Information Displays", *International Journal of Human–Computer Studies* **45**(1), 59–74.

Human–Computer Interaction — INTERACT '99
M. Angela Sasse and Chris Johnson (Editors)
Published by IOS Press, © IFIP TC.13, 1999

A Multimedia Presentation System for the Remediation of Sentence Processing Deficits

Martin A. Beveridge & M. Alison Crerar

School of Computing, Craiglockhart Campus, Napier University, Edinburgh EH14 1DJ, UK.

martin.beveridge@virgin.net, a.crerar@dcs.napier.ac.uk

Abstract: This work builds on an earlier study in which clinical use of software known as Microworld for Aphasia led to significant and durable improvements in the written sentence comprehension of a number of long-term aphasic subjects. This follow-on study was undertaken with two main objectives: a) to re-design the software, making it easier for clinicians to create exercises and review performance data; and b) to explore the contributions of computer and clinician to the previous results. We describe the architecture of the resulting system, Multimedia Microworld, which is novel in its use of a single multimedia grammar and lexicon from which text, speech and graphics are assembled. The system has been evaluated with three aphasic subjects and the results corroborate the earlier findings regarding efficacy. In this recent work, however, we have demonstrated statistically significant improvements using a treatment protocol that could be self-administered, or used with the help of a carer.

Keywords: aphasia, agrammatism, computer, multimedia, language, therapy, rehabilitation.

1 Introduction

So far more effort has been put into the development of augmentative communication devices, or prostheses, to assist those with limited speech output than into exploring the rehabilitation prospects for those with cognitive deficits resulting in impaired comprehension. Our work has focused on stroke victims with sentence comprehension difficulties. We have shown in a previous study using purpose built software known as 'Microworld for Aphasia', that given appropriately targeted treatment, some stroke victims are capable of significant and durable improvements in their language comprehension, even many years post-onset (Crerar & Ellis, 1995; Crerar et al., 1996). Unfortunately, the position in the UK is that only a small amount of language therapy is provided by the National Health Service; this usually happens in the early months following a stroke, after which the client is discharged, often with the prognosis that further improvement is unlikely. The work reported here suggests that for some patients and for some conditions, computer technology may be the key to extending the reach of clinical services.

1.1 Asyntactic Comprehension

For survivors and their carers the commonest long-term effects of brain injury due to a stroke are physical disability and disruption of language skills. Brain injury can disrupt language in many different ways, causing complex patterns of spared and impaired functions. Total loss of language is rare, more commonly a subset of processes is implicated and the severity of impairment varies greatly between functions and between individuals. The generic term for such acquired language disorder is *aphasia* (Ellis & Young, 1988).

Our work has concentrated on *asyntactic comprehension* which is characterized by a preserved knowledge of the meanings of individual words and yet poor ability to interpret sentences. Individuals with asyntactic comprehension are unable to make use of syntactic cues (e.g. word order, function words) to determine the roles played by noun phrases in a sentence, e.g. which is the Agent (i.e. the one doing the action) and which is the Theme (i.e. the one that the action is being done to). They instead have to rely on semantic information to interpret sentences. For example, in a scenario involving a boy, an apple and an eating action, most people will assume that the boy is the one doing the eating (the Agent) and the apple is the thing being eaten (the Theme). This interpretation is arrived at purely by semantic means, namely knowing that apples cannot eat boys but boys can eat apples. However, this natural assumption can be overridden by syntax. In the sentence *the apple is eating the boy*, a normal hearer/reader is forced to the interpretation that the apple is the Agent and the boy is the Theme, whereas an asyntactic comprehender, who does not have access to the syntactic information, will arrive at the opposite (semantically sensible) interpretation. For this reason asyntactic comprehension is best detected by the use of *semantically reversible* sentences such as *the boy chases the dog* where the Agent and Theme can be interchanged equi-plausibly (i.e. neither interpretation is more likely). Unfortunately, for diagnosticians, fully reversible sentences are hard to construct using everyday vocabulary; in most examples one of the scenarios will seem a little more likely than the reverse.

1.2 Microworld for Aphasia

To overcome the difficulty of creating fully reversible sentences, Crerar created a computer-based microworld for assessment and therapy. This consisted of three 'characters' (ball, box and star) which could engage in a limited number of actions and could occupy a limited set of spatial relationships. The assessment software used a sentence-picture matching paradigm in which a target sentence was displayed, such as *the ball gives a box to the star*, and the subject had to select from among four candidate pictures, using a mouse. The treatment software provided two types of task, sentence-building (in which a sentence was constructed, by selecting from among given segments, to describe the presented picture) and picture-building (in which a picture was constructed, by selecting graphical components, to illustrate a presented sentence). A clinical trial involving 14 long-term aphasics demonstrated significant and durable treatment effects after only 6 hours of therapy in each of the functions treated, viz. verbs and locative prepositions (Crerar et al., 1996).

1.3 Multimedia Microworld

The current system, the *Multimedia Microworld* (Beveridge, 1998), is based on the original microworld concept (and uses the same restricted vocabulary) but is a completely new system which addresses several issues raised by the earlier project concerning both the design of the system itself and the subsequent clinical intervention.

The main technical requirement for this system was to devise an architecture that would allow clinicians to easily create sentence sets for assessment/treatment sessions and would provide more flexible data collection and reporting facilities. Furthermore, the system was required to be extensible, allowing the microworld vocabulary and sentence structures to be expanded and new assessment/treatment programs to be written. The resulting architecture is the main topic of this paper and is described in Section 2.

The main clinical aim was to reduce the clinician's role in the remediation process in order to investigate whether beneficial treatment effects could be obtained just using an automated protocol. Positive results would mean that we had the basis for a system that could be used at home to supplement face-to-face therapy and perhaps extend the reach of clinicians to long-term aphasics who would otherwise get no treatment at all. The clinical intervention used and the results obtained are described briefly in Section 3.

2 System Architecture

The overall design of the Multimedia Microworld follows a client-server architecture, as shown in Figure 1.

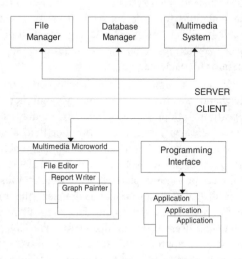

Figure 1: The architecture of the Multimedia Microworld.

The *server* component comprises three modules. The *file manager* provides functions for opening and saving data files containing lists of sentences. The *database manager* provides functions for collecting performance data during execution of an assessment or treatment program as well as handling the storage of that data in a database. The key component of the server side is the *multimedia system* which contains functions to realize text, speech and graphics objects from abstract descriptions. This component is described in more detail in Section 2.1.

The *client* component comprises a user interface, a series of client application programs and a small programming interface. The *user interface*, described in Section 2.2, consists of a general workspace containing various document windows for managing sentence lists and viewing patient performance. The *application programs* implement particular assessment and treatment protocols and can access server components via the *programming interface*: a library of functions described in Section 2.3. The application programs developed for the current clinical intervention are described in Section 2.4.

2.1   Multimedia System

In a summary of state-of-the-art multimedia presentation systems, Maybury (1993) points out that most systems simply build upon single-media components and do not address issues such as "the relationship of textual and graphical generation" (Maybury, 1993) or "the degree of reuse and/or refinement of pre-existing canned media" (Maybury, 1995). Instead, such systems tend to employ different representations for different media (e.g. representing graphical objects as geometric algorithms but text objects as strings) and hence require a separate generator for each medium.

A key design feature of our work, on the other hand, was the use, following Maybury's (1995) suggestion, of pre-stored (canned) media as the input to the generation process, rather than abstract medium-specific representations. This approach has also been used by Kohlert & Olsen (1995) who employed pre-stored pictures (e.g. bitmap files) as the basis for defining visual languages, the major benefit being that the input data was then in a format that users were familiar with. We have also applied this approach to speech synthesis. Pre-recorded samples of words and phrases have been stored as speech objects (e.g. audio files) and then concatenated to generate the speech output, a process referred to as phrase-based concatenative synthesis. One advantage of this method over alternative approaches is that it preserves prosody (intonation, rhythm) within the pre-recorded words and phrases and so produces better quality speech overall (Katz, 1995).

The use of canned media provided two major benefits for the design of the multimedia system. First, the graphical, speech and text representations of a particular vocabulary item could be stored together as properties of a single multimedia object. These multimedia objects could then be combined to form a multimedia *lexicon*, allowing easy editing or extension of the microworld vocabulary. Second, the generation of all three media could be achieved by a common process of assembling (lexical) multimedia objects according to a set of rules, or multimedia *grammar* (which therefore captured the common structure of those media). Hence the process of multimedia generation became simply a generalization of the approach typically employed in text generation systems. The architecture of the multimedia system was therefore based on the consensus architecture for text generation systems described by Reiter (1994) comprising five stages:

1. Creation of a *semantic representation* defining the message to be realized. This entailed a definition of the logical proposition to be realized, e.g. *paint'(ball', box')* (where *paint'*, *ball'* and *box'* denote lexical items), along with some pragmatic information, namely: which element of the semantic description was the focus, and which sentence structure to use for the text/speech media.

2. The creation of a *deep syntactic structure* from the semantic representation. This involved selecting the appropriate multimedia objects from the lexicon and combining them into a single structure reflecting the relations between them. This was achieved via the application of media-independent rules which ensured the underlying coherence and completeness of all the generated media. The resulting structure was therefore simply the projection of lexical properties (which captured the superficial differences between media) via these general principles (which captured their common underlying structure).

3. The creation of a *surface syntactic structure* from the deep structure. This process only applied to text and speech in which the elements had to be mapped into a specific sentence structure (e.g. passive) according to grammar rules. In the case of graphics, the positioning of elements was actually specified in the lexical representations of verbs, and so no further rearrangement was required.

4. A *morphological* stage in which more fine-grained changes were made to the surface structure representation (in the case of text and speech) or deep structure (in the case of graphics). Because these changes were highly dependent on the particular media to be generated, separate processes were required for each medium. In particular, it was at this stage that the prosody of the speech output was defined. Rather than recording just one speech sample for each lexical item, a variety of recordings were made of each item occurring in varying sentence positions (initial, medial, final) and with varying stress (accented, neutral, de-accented). A set of simple heuristics at this stage selected the correct version of each speech sample.

5. Finally, a rendering stage employing media-specific procedures.

The syntactic component of this generation process (creating the deep and surface structures) was formalized as a *unification grammar* (Shieber, 1986). Lexical items were represented as *feature structures* (using the features PICTURE, TEXT and SPEECH to define how items were to be realized in those media) and the creation of deep and surface structures was described in terms of *unifying* those feature structures. This formalism led to a straightforward implementation in the visual object-based programming language Visual Basic by mapping feature structures on to visual objects (forms and controls) and implementing unification in terms of combining the attributes (property lists) of those objects.

2.2   User Interface

The user interface is a Multiple-Document Interface comprising a workspace and three types of documents: sentence lists, graphs and reports. Figure 2 below shows the workspace with an example of each of those document types open.

A *sentence list* document allows the clinician to create a set of sentences (by selecting *semantic representations*: Predicate, Agent, Theme) to be used in an assessment/treatment session and to specify the order in which they are to be presented. The sentence list interface is based on the metaphor of a card file in which each sentence is a card which can be taken out, edited and replaced. New cards can also be inserted at any point in the card file and others removed, and the entire set shuffled to produce a new ordering. Individual sentences may be dragged either

from one position in a list to another, or between lists (assuming multiple sentence list documents are open). The clinician is also able to preview the pictorial and spoken representations of a selected sentence.

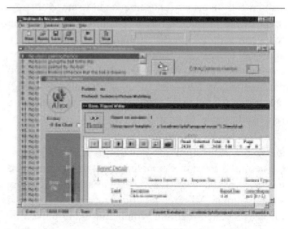

Figure 2: The Multimedia Microworld workspace with sentence list, graph and report documents.

A *report* document provides facilities to review interaction data collected during an assessment or treatment session. The contents of the database are presented hierarchically as a series of folders and sub-folders and for each selected session the generated report shows summary statistics (such as overall score, average response time etc.) along with a detailed breakdown of the patient's interaction with the program.

A *graph* document provides summary score and response time information for selected sessions, broken down by sentence type to allow the clinician to easily compare patients' performances across different structures. Summary statistics can also be overlaid on the generated graphs.

2.3   Programming Interface

The programming interface is a small library of functions allowing client application programs to access server components. There are three main categories of functions: data collection functions, semantic functions, and media realization functions.

The *data collection* functions allow an assessment/treatment program to collect interaction data during the execution of a client program (this data can be later viewed through graphs or reports as described in Section 2.2). It contains functions to specify when a multimedia presentation for a sentence has been generated, the time and type of tasks set for the patient, the patient's responses to those tasks, and whether a patient has finished with the current sentence presentation.

The *semantic* functions are provided for dealing with the semantic representations outlined in Section 2.1. Three high-level functions are provided: one to retrieve the next semantic representation in sequence from the current sentence list, one to create a reverse-role distractor for a semantic representation (e.g. *paint'(box', ball')* from *paint'(ball', box')*), and one to create a random lexical distractor (e.g. *paint'(star', box')* from *paint'(ball', box')*). Two complementary low-level functions are also provided: one to *get* the value of a particular part of a semantic representation and one to *set* its value.

The *media realization* functions are provided to allow the realization of semantic representations in the required media. Separate functions are provided to create a picture, display a textual sentence or play speech output. All three functions return a description of the generated medium which can then be used by the application program to support interaction (e.g. by defining picture hot-spots).

2.4   Assessment/Treatment Programs

The assessment and treatment programs written for the current clinical intervention are described briefly below. These programs were developed using the programming interface functions described above and execute within the Multimedia Microworld workspace. So far three programs have been developed: an Interface Test, a Sentence–Picture Matching Test and a Mapping Therapy treatment program.

The *Interface Test* is used to determine whether or not an individual is able to use the computer interface. The patient must locate an object displayed on the screen, move the mouse cursor to that position and finally click the mouse button whilst remaining over the target object. Twenty items are presented in succession, each one a constant distance but in a random direction from the previous one (thus ensuring that the test is always different but of constant difficulty) and evenly distributed across the screen to test all parts of the patient's visual field.

The *Sentence-Picture Matching Test* is used both to determine the subject's ability to associate the textual representations of lexical items with their pictorial representations (Lexical Test), and to determine the type and severity of any sentence comprehension deficit (Syntax Test). In the *Lexical Test* (see Figure 3), the textual representation of a target lexical item is displayed centred at the bottom of the screen. Pictorial representations of the target and three other items chosen at random from the lexicon are displayed in separate windows, one in

each quadrant of the screen: the task is to select the target picture, using the mouse. In the *Syntax Test* the textual representation of a target sentence is displayed centred at the bottom of the screen and graphical representations of the target and three distractors are displayed in windows arranged as before. The task is again to select the target picture. Two of the sentence types presented in this test were not trained during the subsequent therapy and were included to test for any generalization from the trained structures to these untrained ones. Furthermore only half the verbs in the test were trained. The untrained verbs were included to test for generalization from treated to untreated verbs.

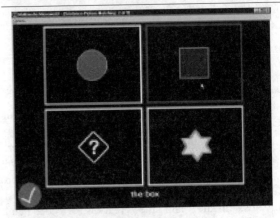

Figure 3: The Multimedia Microworld Lexical Test (target item is the box).

The *Microworld Mapping Therapy* protocol is a novel therapy protocol based on the picture-building task of the Microworld for Aphasia (Crerar et al., 1996) and the Mapping Therapy protocol described in (Schwartz et al., 1994). The aim of the protocol is for the patient to build a pictorial representation of a sentence by selecting picture elements from a palette and assembling them. The picture building process starts with the predicate (verb) of the sentence, then each of its arguments are added in turn to the overall picture. The task is therefore to place the pictorial representations of these arguments in positions in the overall picture appropriate to their roles (i.e. the Agent as the thing doing the action and the Theme as the thing that the action is being done to). This is demonstrated in Figure 4 which shows the picture of the *star* being selected (Figure 4a), and being dropped in its correct position in the picture (Figure 4b). At each stage the sentence is also spoken by the computer, with the current target item stressed and a 250ms pause between sentence segments (e.g. for the presentation in Figure 4a, the speech produced would be "The STAR / is holding / the ball" where upper case indicates stress and slashes indicate pause points). When the patient has finished constructing their picture, the computer constructs the correct picture next to it so that they can be compared. The clinician then reads the target sentence once more, slowly, whilst simultaneously illustrating each segment by pointing to its representation in the correct picture. No other feedback is provided.

3 Clinical Intervention

3.1 Subjects

Three subjects, MS, DR and AM were selected for treatment based on their asyntactic comprehension profile and confirmation that they could use the computer interface. Brief details are given in Table 1. Although this may seem a restrictively small sample, it is consistent with the case-study approach of cognitive neuropsychology where single-case studies are the norm, on the assumption that general conclusions about brain function can be derived from close examination of individual patients (Ellis & Young, 1988).

Subject	Age	Sex	Time post-onset
MS	60	F	3 yrs
DR	47	F	2 yrs 9 mths
AM	69	M	4 yrs 7 mths

Table 1: Subjects' details.

3.2 Materials

The Microworld tests described in Section 2.4 (*Interface Test*, *Lexical Test* and *Syntax Test*) were all administered along with parts of the Philadelphia Comprehension Battery (PCB), a standard language comprehension test (Saffran et al., 1988) which was used to test for generalization of therapy beyond the Microworld environment.

3.3 Procedure

The experimental design for the clinical intervention is summarized in Table 2. The subjects attended for two separate hours per week for nine weeks.

Subjects' baseline performance profiles were tested before therapy using the PCB. Subsequently, they were trained to use the computer mouse (by using the Interface Test as a training exercise). All subjects used their non-dominant hand to operate the mouse since they were all pre-morbidly right-handed and now had right-sided hemiplegia. MS and DR had used computers previously and had no difficulty using the mouse. AM did have some problems with it initially

but these were overcome. Subjects were then trained to associate the textual representations of lexical items with their pictorial representations. This lexical training is particularly necessary for the verb items which have quite abstract pictorial representations. Initially, subjects were trained on these items using more naturalistic hand-drawn pictures before being introduced to the computer graphics by using the Lexical Test as a training program and providing feedback when a wrong selection was made.

Time (hrs)	Activity
2	Language Assessment Battery (Baseline)
1.5	Microworld Training
1.5	Microworld Tests (Baseline)
2	**Microworld Mapping Therapy (Active Sentences)**
1	Generalization Probe
3	**Microworld Mapping Therapy (Passive Sentences)**
1	Generalization Probe
3	**Microworld Mapping Therapy (Object Cleft Sentences)**
1	Microworld Tests (Generalization)
2	Language Assessment Battery (Generalization)

Table 2: The experimental design for the clinical intervention (treatment sessions are emboldened).

After mouse training and lexical training the Microworld Interface Test was administered, to ensure subjects were fully able to use the interface, followed by the Lexical Test and Syntax Test to obtain baseline scores on these tests for each participant.

After the baseline Microworld tests, therapy was then conducted in three phases: 'Active', during which active sentence structures were trained (e.g. *the ball is painting the box*); 'Passive', during which passive sentence structures were trained (e.g. *the box is painted by the ball*); and 'Object Cleft', during which object cleft sentence structures were trained (e.g. *it is the box that the ball is painting*). In treatment sessions, subjects worked through each sentence in turn in a specified order with no sentence repeated. The amount of time taken to complete a treatment session varied from 40 minutes to 1 hour.

Between treatment phases a set of generalization tests (generalization probes) was administered comprising the Microworld Lexical and Syntax Tests and a subset of the PCB. The Lexical Test was used to check that subjects were maintaining their lexical comprehension across therapy phases. The Syntax Test was used to assess each subject's

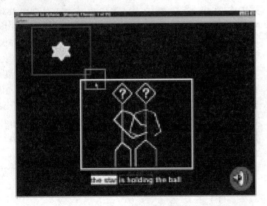

(a) Selecting the agent.

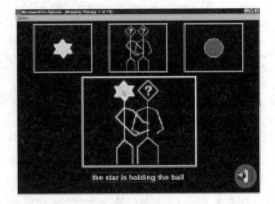

(b) Dropping the agent into the correct place in the picture.

Figure 4: The Multimedia Microworld Mapping therapy protocol.

improvement on the treated sentence structures and treated verbs, as well as to test for any generalization from treated verbs to untreated verbs and from treated structures to as yet untreated structures. The PCB was used to check for generalization of therapy to 'real world' sentences such as *the dog is followed by the hunter*.

Subjects' final performance profiles were assessed at the end of therapy using the Microworld Lexical and Syntax Tests along with the complete PCB.

3.4   Results

This section presents the results of the clinical intervention for the three subjects MS, DR and AM. Since the experimental design involved repeated measures of the same subject group, a two-tailed t-test for pairwise correlated samples was used to analyse group results. When analysing individual results the sample measures were categorical (correct or incorrect responses) rather than scores and so the McNemar test for significance of changes was used instead (Siegel & Castellan, Jr., 1988).

Table 3 shows the scores obtained across all four administrations of the Microworld Syntax Test. The group as a whole showed statistically significant improvement on the Syntax Test from baseline to post-object cleft ($t = 8.08, p < 0.05$) with the mean group score being 17/40 at baseline and 31/40 post-therapy. All three individuals made significant improvements in the Syntax Test comparing their first and last performances: MS ($\chi^2 = 11.13, p < 0.01$), AM ($\chi^2 = 8.45, p < 0.01$), DR ($\chi^2 = 4.76, p < 0.05$).

Subject	Baseline (n=40)	Post-Active (n=40)	Post-Passive (n=40)	Post-Object Cleft (n=40)
MS	18 (45%)	21	34	35 (88%)
DR	18 (45%)	11	24	29 (73%)
AM	15 (38%)	16	20	29 (73%)

Table 3: Scores for all three subjects across all administrations of the Microworld Syntax Test.

Table 4 shows the baseline and post-therapy scores for all subjects on the written and spoken sentence comprehension tests from the PCB.

Subject	Baseline sentence comprehension		Post-therapy sentence comprehension	
	Written (n = 60)	Spoken (n = 60)	Written (n = 60)	Spoken (n = 60)
MS	48	51	58	58
DR	40	48	49	53
AM	43	43	52	46

Table 4: Scores for all three subjects across baseline and post-therapy administrations of sub-tests of the PCB.

The group as whole improved significantly on the written sentence comprehension test ($t = 28, p < 0.01$) indicating that the Microworld therapy had generalized beyond the Microworld environment to a standard paper-based test containing wider vocabulary and different sentence structures. There was also significant group improvement on the spoken presentation of the test ($t = 4.33, p = 0.05$) indicating generalization at the group level from the written to spoken modality.

At the individual level, the overall changes from baseline to post-therapy on the written sentence comprehension test were significant for each of the subjects MS ($\chi^2 = 8.10, p < 0.01$), DR ($\chi^2 = 4.92, p < 0.05$) and AM ($\chi^2 = 3.76, p = 0.05$). None of the subjects individually improved significantly from baseline to post-therapy on the spoken sentence comprehension test, although MS showed near-significant improvement ($\chi^2 = 3.27, p = 0.07$).

The sentence comprehension of all three subjects therefore improved significantly after just 8 hours of therapy using the Multimedia Microworld. This is comparable to the treatment period of the Microworld for Aphasia study (Crerar et al., 1996) and markedly less than for similar paper-based treatments (e.g. the Mapping Therapy of Schwartz et al. (1994) in which subjects attended three sessions per week of between 60 and 90 minutes each for up to 4 months). Furthermore, unlike the Microworld for Aphasia study, this was achieved with minimal input from the clinician. Finally, these results were not due simply to spontaneous improvement since all three subjects were stable across the screening test-to-baseline period and were furthermore long-term aphasics who were unlikely to experience such spontaneous recovery. Neither were the results due to general stimulation, since the improvements were specific to the functions treated, with other aspects of language comprehension tested by the PCB remaining unchanged.

4 Implications

This study adds to the growing body of evidence that some aphasic subjects are capable of significant improvements in their language understanding, even several years post stroke. Unfortunately, one-to-one therapy is costly and time-consuming, so long-term aphasics typically receive no on-going help. The Multimedia Microworld is a step towards offering an alternative.

Preliminary results suggest that we have achieved a therapeutically useful tool, which requires no trained clinical input during use. The restriction of the clinician's role in the therapy protocol to a purely supportive rather than a participative role did not affect the success of the clinical intervention. This opens up the possibility of this system being applicable for home-based self-administration of therapy (with the help of a trained carer). Apart from reducing the

clinician's workload this also empowers the patient (Katz, 1995) who can then take a more active role in their treatment.

Furthermore, the architecture of the Multimedia Microworld means that data files can be exchanged between client and clinician quickly and easily (for example as email attachments). Multimedia presentations are then rendered on the client's machine without the need for tedious downloading of large multimedia files. Given the rapid penetration of PC technology into homes, the 'virtual case load' is a distinct possibility.

References

Beveridge, M. A. (1998), A Multimedia Microworld for the Treatment of Asyntactic Sentence Comprehension, PhD thesis, Napier University, Edinburgh.

Crerar, M. A. & Ellis, A. W. (1995), Computer-based Therapy for Aphasia: Towards Second Generation Clinical Tools, in C. C. & M. D. (eds.), *Treatment of Aphasia: From Theory to Practice*, second edition, Cole and Whurr, pp.223–50.

Crerar, M. A., Ellis, A. W. & Dean, E. C. (1996), "Remediation of Sentence Processing Deficits in Aphasia using a Computer-Based Microworld", *Brain and Language* **52**(1), 229–75.

Ellis, A. W. & Young, A. W. (1988), *Human Cognitive Neuropsychology*, Lawrence Erlbaum Associates.

Katz, R. C. (1995), Aphasia Treatment and Computer Technology, in C. C. & M. D. (eds.), *Treatment of Aphasia: From Theory to Practice*, second edition, Cole and Whurr, pp.253–85.

Kohlert, D. C. & Olsen, Jr., D. R. (1995), Pictures as Input Data, in I. Katz, R. Mack, L. Marks, M. B. Rosson & J. Nielsen (eds.), *Proceedings of CHI'95: Human Factors in Computing Systems*, ACM Press, pp.464–71.

Maybury, M. T. (1993), Introduction, in M. T. Maybury (ed.), *Intelligent Multimedia Interface*, AAAI Press.

Maybury, M. T. (1995), "Research in Multimedia Parsing and Generation", *Artificial Intelligence Review* **9**(2/3), 103–27.

Reiter, E. (1994), Has a Consensus NL Generation Architecture Appeared, and is it Psycholinguistically Plausible?, in *Proceedings of the Seventh International Workshop on Natural Language Generation*, Springer-Verlag, pp.163–70.

Saffran, E. M., Schwartz, M. F., Linebarger, M. C., Martin, N. & Bochetto, P. (1988), Philadelphia Comprehension Battery, Available from E M Saffran,

Department of Neurology, Centre for Cognitive Neuroscience, School of Medicine, Temple University, 3401 N. Broad Street, Philadelphia, PA 19140, USA.

Schwartz, M. F., Saffran, E. M., Fink, R. B., Myers, J. L. & Martin, N. (1994), "Mapping Therapy: a Treatment Programme for Agrammatism", *Aphasiology* **8**(1), 19–54.

Shieber, S. M. (1986), *An Introduction to Unification-Based Approaches to Language*, University of Chicago Press.

Siegel, S. & Castellan, Jr., N. J. (1988), *Nonparametric Statistics for the Behavioural Sciences*, McGraw-Hill.

Human–Computer Interaction — INTERACT '99
M. Angela Sasse and Chris Johnson (Editors)
Published by IOS Press, © IFIP TC.13, 1999

Justice and Design

Penny Duquenoy & Harold Thimbleby

Middlesex University, Bounds Green Road, London N11 2NQ, UK.

{penny2,harold}@mdx.ac.uk

Abstract: Within the field of HCI there are a number of preferred approaches towards design. As within other disciplines, these approaches are often irreconcilable. We explore the possibilities of using ethics as a way to bridge the gap and re-establish the design focus of doing good towards the user. This is the idea of 'justice' to aid improved design. According to Aristotle, justice is classed as a virtue: to do justice is to act for the good, which is what is wanted for good HCI design. John Rawls's (1972) classic "A Theory of Justice", talks about justice as fairness, and it is in this context we apply justice to the area of design. We show some surprising links with HCI practice, and hence suggest some new perspectives on HCI.

Keywords: ethics, justice, veil of ignorance, design

1 Introduction

This paper introduces the concept of justice to the area of design. HCI is concerned with making things better, improving usability and making interactive systems (for one or more people) better.

Aristotle defines justice as doing good for others (Nicomachean Ethics). This is essentially what HCI is: doing good for others through the interactive systems designed and imposed on others' lives and work. Aristotle warns that justice is the only one of the virtues that can be accidental: that is, justice can be achieved unintentionally (unlike integrity, for example). This paper, then, can safely argue HCI is like justice (in ways to be elaborated). However, the fact that this has previously gone unnoticed is not a counter-argument to ours.

Following John Rawls's (1972) idea of justice as fairness, we explore the notion of system design from the point of view of an 'original position' of equality. From this ethical perspective, (the core concept being the 'veil of ignorance') the designer adopts the standpoint of *unspecified* potential users. From an HCI perspective, we see the veil of ignorance as corresponding to the principle that designers should know the user and not design for themselves. Ideally, they should design for people they know they do not know (Thimbleby, 1998b).

Computers are complex systems, and so are humans, the design of complex systems for complex systems can lead to complex design procedures. Where design approaches and methodologies differ

'fairness' in design provides a simple ethical foundation of certain principles, which are commonly understood and promoted within our culture. We begin the paper from this standpoint, examining the concept behind the Rawls Theory of Justice and explaining how the principles of liberty and equality are derived from that concept.

As far as these principles are important to us as members of society, they should be equally important in our work, especially when that work directly relates to, and impacts upon, other members of the society to which we belong. This is of course not a novel ideal within the design arena — e.g. on the subject of Information Systems Design, see (Hirschheim et al., 1995); on social/democratic design context, see (Feng, 1998).

The impact of software on others is recognized by Collins, Miller, Spielman, and Wherry, who not only include the buyers and users of the software, but also recognize "bystanders who fall under the shadow of the behaviour of the software" (Collins et al., 1994, p.81). Their article (based on a case study) used a Rawlsian approach, emphasising responsibilities and obligations during the initial negotiation period of the design proposal. In this paper we are particularly interested in the suitability of Rawls' theory to the field of design, with the emphasis on 'being fair to do good', following Rawls' two principles of liberty and equality, arrived at from the veil of ignorance.

We finally assess the advantages and disadvantages of Rawls' theory as an aid to good design, and offer some practical ideas on implementation.

2   The Rawls Theory of Justice

The Rawls theory of justice emphasises justice as fairness, arriving at two fundamental principles — liberty and equality. This theory is intended for application in a political sphere, and as such addresses social, rather than individual, ethics. The essential idea is of a social contract — the key elements of the Rawls' theory are 'the original position' (the veil of ignorance) and the two principles of liberty and equality.

2.1   The Original Position

Rawls uses this idea to provide a justification for the basic principles, which constitute his theory. The strategy aims to disassociate the individual from preconceptions and prejudices by adopting a starting point (original position) of 'ignorance'. From this position, the individual is free to perceive the world from any potential vantage point — unencumbered by inherited social status. Thus the original position is a device for ensuring an equal starting point, and from this point the individual perceives the world through a veil of ignorance. This gives the basis for entering a fair social contract.

The next stage is to construct the contract in such a way as to ensure a fair outcome. This, according to the Rawls theory, is best achieved by the parties concerned imagining that they could be at any potential 'receiving end' of the contract. So, for example it would be unwise to devise a contract that benefited, say, the homeless, at the expense of the property owner, if you were to become the property owner. As Dworkin (1977, p.181)) says:

> "Men who do not know to which class they belong cannot design institutions, consciously or unconsciously, to favour their own class."

For institutions, read systems: in HCI, designers create systems (for example, software systems or physical devices). These systems become embedded within the users' world, and constrain what those users can and cannot do. They are social institutions, not enforced by law or convention (as Rawls conceives it) but enforced by design. For example, a hardware device (say, a mobile phone or video recorder) is unalterable by the user, an aircraft flight management system is far too complex for a pilot to change (and, yes, there are social conventions that stop pilots tinkering with the aircraft software!) Thus to design

means to create a 'world'. To design a good world is to act justly. Following Rawls, one should design the good world acting under a veil of ignorance. To do otherwise allows the designer to create a special world in which they are treated beneficially, typically at the expense of others.

According to Rawls:

> "The original position is defined in such a way that it is a status quo in which any agreements reached are fair. It is a state of affairs in which the parties are equally represented as moral persons and the outcome is not conditioned by arbitrary contingencies or the relative balance of social forces." (Rawls, 1972, p.120)

2.2   The Two Principles

It is Rawls' argument that a search for basic principles to underpin a social contract, from the perspective of the veil of ignorance, must result in the two principles of *liberty* and *equality*:

- The *principle of liberty* ensures against persecution, discrimination, and political oppression.

- The *principle of equality* allows each person of equal ability and motivation the same chance of success, regardless of social status.

3   The Theory and Design

This theory then, addresses issues of rights and social advantages and disadvantages. These issues are very much incorporated into the design sphere, they are highlighted in today's technological society and are particularly magnified by the Internet. For example, the Internet has raised issues of the right to freedom of expression, and equality of access (in financial terms and in terms of technological capability).

There are inequalities between designers and users, by definition designers will have more knowledge of these systems than most users. Rawls recognizes this natural inequality in a social system, and utilises it within a third principle (the 'difference' principle) which states that inequalities are justified only if they benefit the worst off. Therefore, the inequality in knowledge, which exists between the designer and potential user, can only be justified if the designer uses that knowledge to benefit the user. So, for example, in a design context those who have the advantage of say, expertise and knowledge, should use that to give benefit to the otherwise disadvantaged.

The theory (being a political theory) is specifically a 'group' ethic, to be utilised in the group situation, rather than an individual ethic. Individual ethics are notoriously difficult to apply in group situations. Design is a group situation. Things that are designed are designed (usually) for groups. This applies particularly to technology. In addition, it is usually the case that groups are involved in the design process, and that the resulting artefact will have an impact on groups of people. (The manufacturing and marketing industries are based on these assumptions.)

3.1 Links to HCI Slogans

The idea of beginning from a veil of ignorance is anyway enshrined in conventional good practice: 'know the user' — cf. (Thimbleby, 1990; Landauer, 1995). Rather than merely 'know' one's way into all the other possible roles, one might more easily and reliably carry out some experiments and surveys with other people (although this would require the product or perhaps an earlier version of it, to exist). It is pleasing that accepted design practice is also just (who wants to be called unjust?)

Conventional HCI has a range of slogans. We briefly show that these slogans have Rawlsian counterparts:

Know the user: Under the veil of ignorance, the designer has to anticipate they may be some other person (user) of the system. They cannot do this reliably unless they know what the class of users will be.

Don't design for yourself: Without guidance to the contrary, designers design for themselves. This is, of course, designing a world where there is no veil of ignorance — where you will be yourself.

4 Advantages and Disadvantages

A Rawlsian approach is not an automatic solution to good design. The approach has advantages and disadvantages.

4.1 Advantages

- The theory applies to social groups, and is therefore designed for use by groups. Design is (usually) for groups, by groups and impacting on groups — e.g. Participatory Design, see Kuhn & Muller (1993) for an overview.

- The theory provides worthwhile aims, liberty and equality, with which people can identify.

- The concepts of liberty and equality are well understood in western society, those involved

in design are not required to make great mental 'shifts' to incorporate new concepts.

- The theory calls for a fair and equal impact on society, fitting well with the current trend in Information Technology.

- Equal rights includes minority groups who therefore have a right to be 'designed for'.

4.2 Disadvantages

- The favoured method of manufacture (i.e. mass production) is not geared to minority groups (very often the less advantaged).

- Designing from a veil of ignorance requires designers to 'imagine' all possible users — an unlikely, if not impossible, scenario.

- Is it even desirable to design an artefact for all possible users? A design that is easy to use by everyone may not provide any satisfaction for anyone. Reeves & Nass (1996) suggest that computer systems have personalities, and a 'generic' personality would be disliked by everyone; better, they say, to create a distinctive personality, which is at least liked by *some* users!

- It is arguable whether it is even possible to design an artefact for all possible users. (For example, special efforts will have to be made to design international user interfaces that work in other cultures.)

- The theory is not viable in some areas of design. (For example missile design; you would design a missile very differently if you were to imagine being at the receiving end.)

To summarise, on the advantages side we have some principles that equate to a democratic approach to design, but there are disadvantages in the practical application of the theory. How far should a social contract for design go? Depending on one's politics, one might asseverate Rawls and claim missiles are wrong; or you might say we need missiles, and there are some circumstances where Rawls is inappropriate. (See also Section 5.)

Finally, there are difficulties with taking Rawls too seriously. There are duties of just action to non-contracting parties, such as to the environment. How we design things to take their responsible place in a larger ecosystem beyond other users, say to be recyclable, is beyond the scope of this paper but that is not to imply such issues are optional — see Borenstein

(1998) and IIE (1999). Rawls is but one approach to justice, and (for many moral philosophers) is by no means the last word. It seems likely, then, that the approach will not be sufficient for all purposes in HCI.

5 Practical Applications

The Rawls theory of justice makes a nice match with HCI, but can this insight be used creatively or constructively to actually improve design?

Abstract theories and discussions help to highlight issues, but what of the practical applications? Although the 'ideal' implementation of this theory in design is unlikely, if not impossible, the basic principles could be incorporated within a design policy. A starting point might be a simple check sheet addressing:

- The principle of liberty (does the design "persecute, discriminate, oppress" the user?)

- The principle of equality (does the design address issues of equal access/opportunity/use, or redress inequalities of access/opportunity/use?).

- Have specific user-assumptions been built in?

We now give some more concrete examples.

Returning to the missile example: suppose someone wished to design ballistic missiles. If they design them under a veil of ignorance, then they are supposed to be creating a world in the future where the missiles exist, but where they do not know what roles they will have. Well, they may end up living in the cities targeted by the missiles. Since most designers probably would not wish to live under the threat of being hit by a missile, they should not make them. Of course, in reality, the designers are affiliated to a particular country and they do not consider it *likely* that they would live in their own country's enemy's territories. However, Rawls' conception does not admit 'likely' because it is a possibility the designer should account for it. (The relationship between missile design and HCI is mentioned in Thimbleby (1997).)

It is widely recommended that software writers should include comments in their programs. This advice is often strongly resisted, because when one writes program code, it is obvious what it is supposed to do, and a further explanation seems tedious. Yet in the future, the programmer may be a different person. How would the original programmer like to be the future programmer and not have the privileged insight into how the code is supposed to work? More to the point, in the future the programmer may have forgotten

what was going on — in a sense they will be a different person (their mind will have changed). Thus by acting fairly under the veil of ignorance, a programmer would anticipate that the people reading the code in the future world where it exists might not have the benefit of his or her timely insights. Comments would help!

When a sweet bar has to be divided fairly between two people, a standard approach is for one person (*A*) to divide the bar approximately into two equal halves. The other person (*B*) chooses which ever half they prefer. The intention is that *A* will not cheat, because if *A* does so, then *B* can take the larger piece. This is a good example of creating a world under a veil of ignorance. Person A must create a future world, and there are two possible worlds, "*A* has this piece" and "*A* has the other piece" — the protocol of the sharing ensures that *A* cannot guarantee which of these worlds they will end up in. They are under a veil of ignorance, so they tend to promote equality — by making the pieces as nearly equal as they can, thus whichever world they end up in (owning one piece or the other) they end up as well off.

It would be very interesting to pursue sharing algorithms in the context of CSCW and of sharing resources between users. For more details of sharing algorithms — see Robertson & Webb (1998).

Fair sharing is a nice example of using Rawls to promote justice in a practical way. It should be considered an existence proof that there are (interesting) ways in which Rawls can be used to achieve practical and just ends in design.

Now consider a directly HCI example. A typical designer creates a product, and can be certain that in the new world where that product exists they will still be the designer of that product. They are therefore in a privileged position; they will know how it works, and all of its curious features will be 'obvious'. Now consider a Rawlsian designer. They design a similar system, but being under a veil of ignorance, they do not know whether they will have the designer's insight into that system. Indeed, they may be on the product support team, having to explain the system to irate users. Or they may be the technical authors who have to explain the system in plain English. Or they may be the pilot who has to land their aeroplane in fog.

Finally, consider the 'oracle effect'. (Oracles are standard computing science devices — see, for example, (Thimbleby, 1990). When a user complains that they do not know how to do something, some expert typically condescends to tell them that "it is obvious" — that doing something trivial (like pressing the twiddle key) has the appropriate effect. This is trivial knowledge, but the (ignorant) user had no way of finding the fact out. An oracle was needed. Without an oracle, the system is unusable. With the oracle, the system is trivial. Thus users are often made to feel stupid, because they do not know trivial facts. In a Rawlsian world, designers of systems would have to be more careful, because they have to consider how to design systems where they would not have access to the oracular knowledge. Probably, they would design their systems to be more self-explanatory.

Since programmed systems are intrinsically complex, it is inevitable that the designer (or at least the programmers) have oracles into the system's detailed behaviour. Thus, we see an application of Rawls' 'difference principle'.

6 Meta-HCI

Thus, creating systems for other people to use, which is the concern of HCI, can be conceived as an act of justice. Rawls has a particular conception of justice that makes a fruitful correspondence with HCI practice. Moreover, there are alternative conceptions of justice (for example, utilitarianism): we might suggest that some disagreement in HCI methodologies would be fruitfully related to the great ethical traditions — that is, if after several thousands of years, ethics has not reconciled itself to a single point of view, then HCI is unlikely to reconcile itself to a single view, whether social, computational, psychological, phenomenological, or otherwise. All represent (in ways we do not have space to explore) ethical conceptions, and each suits particular agendas. HCI, then, we can surmise should take a 'meta-ethical' stance:*meta-HCI* is the study of choices in HCI.

What is meta-HCI? Some people in HCI consider that any valid contribution must involve empirical evaluation with users. Not to involve users would seem to them to be anathema to the ideals of HCI. This might be equated with utilitarianism: what is the greatest good for the greatest number — and can it be measured? Or we might view HCI as a creative discipline, where expert designers use their artistic intuitions to create new innovative systems — this might be equated with virtue ethics. Our analogies are not intended to be close, but rather to suggest that doing good (in the ethical sense) is as complex as doing good (in the HCI sense), and that the great traditions of ethics have not reconciled themselves — but instead lead to higher-level, meta, debate. HCI may well be enriched by taking meta-HCI seriously.

7 Summary

The hypothetical model of a social contract brings an explicit ethical focus into our working world. Is such a contract applicable in the area of design? We believe that the notions, arguments and concepts presented by Rawls can be applied to the area of design, and that the resultant outcome is as beneficial to the 'user society' as Rawls implies it would be to the 'political society'. Politics refers to 'rights' — in a design context does the user have rights? If so, according to Rawls' theory, the notion of equal rights comprises not only the right to equal treatment, but also the right to treatment as an equal.

Do designers of things act justly by the Rawls definition? Mostly not. They design things they know they will not use, and even if they did use, they would have oracular knowledge. Designers are *never* in a veil of ignorance. Many programmers build systems that they have no intention of using. If, instead, they worked under the Rawls veil of ignorance, they might try harder — in case they ended up being a user of their system. If they were programming a tax program, they might end up 'born as' accountants, tax-payers, civil servants designing tax law, tax evaders, auditors, managers, as their own colleagues having to maintain their system at a later date, or even as the manual writers — they would have to design their tax program carefully and well from all points of view.

Perverting the course of justice is one of the most serious crimes. Perhaps if HCI was seen as a primarily ethical discipline, pursuing the good, and employing justice, doing HCI diligently would be seen as the serious discipline that it is. To do HCI well is to improve human life.

Acknowledgements

Diane Whitehouse and other members of the IFIP WG 9.2.2 made many valuable suggestions after a presentation of these ideas at Namur, 1999. Nick Merriam suggested some of the algorithmic approaches to justice.

This paper has in part been funded by the EPSRC.

References

Borenstein, N. S. (1998), "Whose Net is it Anyway?", *Communications of the ACM* **41**(4), 19.

Collins, W. R., Miller, K. W., Spielman, B. J. & Wherry, P. (1994), "How Good is Good Enough?", *Communications of the ACM* **37**(1), 81–91.

Dworkin, R. (1977), *Taking Rights Seriously*, Gerald Duckworth.

Feng, P. (1998), Rethinking Technology, Revitalizing Ethics: Overcoming Barriers to Ethical Design, *in Proceedings of EthiComp'98*, Center for the Philosophy of Information and Communication Technology, Department of Philosophy, Erasmus University Rotterdam, pp.201–14.

Hirschheim, R., Klein, H. K. & Lyytinen, K. (1995), *Information Systems Development and Data Modeling:Conceptual and Philosophical Foundations*, Cambridge University Press.

IIE (1999), "IBM Launches PC with Recycled Plastic Parts", *IIE Solutions* **31**(4), 18.

Kuhn, S. & Muller, M. J. (1993), "Participatory Design", *Communications of the ACM* **36**(4), 24–8.

Landauer, T. K. (1995), *The Trouble with Computers: Usefulness, Usability and Productivity*, MIT Press.

Rawls, J. (1972), *A Theory of Justice*, Oxford University Press. Originally published 1971, Harvard University Press.

Reeves, B. & Nass, C. (1996), *The Media Equation: How People Treat Computers, Television and New Media Like Real People and Places*, Cambridge University Press.

Robertson, J. & Webb, W. (1998), *Cake Cutting Algorithms*, A K Peters.

Thimbleby, H. W. (1990), *User Interface Design*, Addison–Wesley.

Thimbleby, H. W. (1997), "Design for a Fax", *Personal Technologies* **1**(2), 101–17.

Thimbleby, H. W. (1998), The Detection and Elimination of Spurious Complexity, *in* R. C. Backhouse (ed.), *Proceedings of Workshop on User Interfaces for Theorem Provers*, Eindhoven University of Technology, pp.15–22. Available as Report 98–08, also http//www.cs.mdx.ac.uk/harold/.

Human–Computer Interaction — INTERACT '99
M. Angela Sasse and Chris Johnson (Editors)
Published by IOS Press, © IFIP TC.13, 1999

An Empirical Study of Auditory Warnings in Aircraft

Charles H. Morris[1] & Ying K. Leung[2]

[1] School of Engineering & Science
[2] School of Information Technology
Swinburne University of Technology, PO Box 218, Hawthorn, Victoria 3122, Australia.
YLeung@swin.edu.au

Abstract: Although voice and non-voice warnings have been used in a variety of applications, research in this domain is still in its infancy. This paper describes a study which investigated the design and use of auditory warnings in aircraft. An experimental study was undertaken to examine the effectiveness of three types of auditory warnings, in terms of reaction time, error and learnability in noisy environments, such as the cockpit of an aircraft. The three types of auditory warnings used were synthetic voice, earcons and hybrid warnings. The hybrid warnings used in the experiment consisted of an earcon followed by a voice message. Results indicated that voice warnings are superior to the other two types tested. A discussion of the results highlights a number of experimental design issues for auditory warnings.

Keywords: auditory display, earcons, hybrid warnings.

1 Introduction

Rapid technological advances in aircraft development during recent decades have contributed to a significant increase in information provided to flight crews at the human–machine interface. As complexity grows and technology provides the capability of presenting large amounts of information to the operator, problems with human performance have emerged (Stokes & Wickens, 1988). In these data-rich environments, information must be transferred accurately and rapidly from the source to the pilot, who subsequently derives meaning from the experience (Hawkins, 1987). Although it is important that pilots be provided with comprehensive and detailed information during flight, consideration needs to be given to how this information should be presented. In this context, auditory displays may provide a powerful link between the human and machine.

The function of an auditory display is to assist the operator to monitor and comprehend whatever it is the sound represents. On the flight deck of an aircraft this usually takes the form of alarms and warnings that are symbolic auditory representations of discrete events. Generally they are associated with urgent situations and are accordingly designed to stand out in the

prevailing acoustic ecology (Kramer, 1994). Aircraft designers have been steadily increasing the use of auditory information systems in aircraft displays over recent years. This has occurred, in part, because of the progressive automation of aircraft systems and the subsequent increase in visual workload (Stokes & Wickens, 1988).

As visual information has increased, some tasks have been assigned to the auditory channel to the extent that auditory clutter now rivals visual clutter (Stokes & Wickens, 1988). In the aviation domain, more resources are being directed towards a greater understanding of such human–machine interface problems, in acknowledgement of the fact that greater than 70% of all aircraft accidents can be traced to human error (International Civil Aviation Organization, 1992; Federal Aviation Administration, 1996). According to Woods (1995), designers tend to be inappropriately confident that an alarm or warning will always function to break the operator away from other ongoing activities in order to attend to the alarmed condition.

Despite extensive research over the last two decades, there still exists considerable dissatisfaction with the design of alarms and warnings (Stanton & Edworthy, 1998). Auditory warnings continue to proliferate throughout the aviation domain, with as many as twenty-five different voice and non-voice auditory warnings being fitted to modern commercial aircraft. On the basis that development and use of auditory warnings has proceeded faster than the accumulation of knowledge regarding their operational impact, further research in this area is warranted.

The main aim of this research is to investigate the design and use of auditory warnings in aircraft. Although a large variety of voice and non-voice warnings are used, research in this domain is still in its infancy. An experimental study was undertaken to examine the effectiveness of three types of auditory warnings, in terms of reaction time, error and their learnability in a noisy environment.

2   Auditory Warnings

The increase in use of auditory warnings on the flight deck has not occurred exclusively due to an increase in visual workload. Although an operator can decode greater amounts of visual information, in specific circumstances auditory warnings have distinct advantages over other modes, even during periods of low activity (Stokes et al., 1990). At present there is no complete theory of human auditory perception; consequently, the design of auditory displays is necessarily experimental, requiring validation through user evaluation (Williams, 1994). However, sufficient previous research does exist that can indicate the general benefits of auditory displays.

Auditory information can be received regardless of head position, where the operator is required to maintain visual contact with other elements of the environment. Response time to an acoustic signal can be shorter than for a visual signal, which enhances the capacity for rapid detection, enabling auditory warnings to play a key role at human–machine interface (Kramer, 1994). If they are loud enough, auditory warnings will attract attention more or less regardless of the task on which the operator may be currently engaged. This is particularly important in high workload environments where the operator may otherwise miss a visual signal (Edworthy, 1994).

In multi-crew situations, auditory warnings are the most effective method for communicating simple messages to more than one operator simultaneously (Edworthy, 1994). When operators are required to perform at night, in bright sunlight or glare, auditory displays can also be valuable, as vision in these environments is likely to be degraded, particularly where CRT visual displays are used (Stokes & Wickens, 1988). Moreover, in military operations,

auditory perception is not affected as much as visual perception during periods of high g-forces or anoxia (Stokes et al., 1990).

Despite these benefits, auditory displays are subject to various limitations and disadvantages, which must be addressed by system designers and operators. According to Kestin et al. (1988), alarm manufacturers design intrusive and aggressive alarms in an attempt to ensure that their equipment is not faulted for failing to alert the operator when necessary.   Flooding an area with a harsh and unpleasant sound may secure a person's attention, but it will also inhibit communication at what may be a critical time (Patterson, 1985).   Thorning & Ablett (1985) have found that alarms that are too loud may startle operators and impede communication between crew members, to the extent that cancelling the alarm takes priority over directing attention to the alarmed condition.   An additional problem of incompatibility may arise when two or more warnings occur simultaneously, as the resultant sound may not convey the meaning of either.   This effect is known as masking and occurs when one component of the sound environment reduces the sensitivity of the ear to another component. (Sanders & McCormick, 1987).

The practical effectiveness of warnings extends beyond the users' ability to simply recognise a voice or abstract auditory display.   The flight deck of a commercial or military aircraft is a cognitively demanding place consisting of a large number of data channels (Woods, 1995).   In an environment where multiple factors are at work, designers must ensure that warnings are incorporated into the system as a whole.

Gaver (1986) has proposed the use of *auditory icons* as an effective method of providing non-voice sound to convey information.   Auditory icons are caricatures of natural sounds that are designed to capture the essential feature of the event that they portray.   The main advantage of this approach is that auditory icons can represent conceptual objects more clearly than other arbitrary sounds that have no analogues in the everyday world.   Although auditory icons were developed to convey information in computer interfaces, research conducted by Leung et al. (1997) has indicated that they have a potential for use as auditory warnings in the aviation domain.

Auditory icons use naturally occurring sounds that represent actions and objects within an interface. However, they encounter a significant disadvantage in situations where a natural sound equivalent does not exist. According to Brewster et al. (1995), in these circumstances *earcons* can be used as another useful method of presenting information through sound.

Earcons are structured sequences of synthetic tones that can be combined to create sound messages that represent parts of an interface. Earcons are composed of motives, which are short sequences of pitches with variable intensity, timbre and register (Blattner et al., 1989). Brewster et al. (1995) argue that investigation into this form of auditory display has shown that earcons are an effective means of communicating complex information in sound. However, because earcons are complex artificial sounds, they may be difficult for the user to associate meanings to them, thus limiting their recognisability. This is especially so when the user has to remember a large set of earcons. Nevertheless, experimental tests with earcons have demonstrated good recall and recognition amongst operators which makes this type of auditory signal potentially promising for continuing research within the flight deck environment (Brewster et al., 1995).

3 The Experiment

Auditory displays represent the most effective means of unburdening the visual channel and subsequently improving human performance on the flight decks of aircraft. However, further investigation is necessary. At present, little is known about the factors that influence error rates or response times when aircrew operate in noisy and distracting environments.

Existing evidence suggests that tones preceding voice messages do not enhance pilot response times or decrease error rates (Simpson & Williams, 1980; Hakkinen & Williges, 1984). However, if a different earcon were to precede each individual voice message, then an improvement in response times and error rates may be observed. Although the mapping between earcons and their interpretation must be learnt, an earcon's ability to communicate complex information may facilitate a faster comprehension of the intended message. Moreover, because they are abstract non-voice sounds, they may have the potential to stand out in the acoustic ecology of the flight deck, reducing the risk of masking which can have an adverse effect on voice messages.

The main purpose of this study was to examine human performance when earcons, voice and hybrid warnings (earcons followed by a voice message), were used as auditory warnings. Human performance was firstly considered in terms of how easily operators learnt the various types of warnings. It was also considered both in terms of how quickly and how accurately operators could respond to various types of

auditory warning when warnings were presented along with other typical flight deck environmental noises.

Accordingly, the first part of this experimental study was designed to measure the relative effort in *learning* various types of auditory warnings. Such a comparison would provide an indication of how suitable these sounds would be for use on the flight deck. It also provided an opportunity to replicate Leung et al. (1997) investigation into how well participants learnt and then recalled voice warnings compared with earcon warnings.

The second part of the experiment examined human performance in terms of the *time* it took participants to respond to the three different types of warnings. Unlike the previous conditions, which examined the effort required during learning, subsequent manipulations introduced typical flight deck environmental sounds that made the detection of auditory warnings more difficult. Because of limited previous research, a prediction of which type of warning would produce the fastest response time could not be made with any degree of certainty. Although earcons are complex warnings that can stand out in the acoustic environment, voice messages are a highly familiar set of stimuli, yet may be subject to possible masking. Moreover, it is possible that hybrid warnings may enjoy an advantage over both voice and earcons, as they stand out acoustically and can be easily comprehended.

The final part of the experiment turned to human performance in terms of *accuracy* in responding to auditory warnings. As with the two previous conditions, earcons, voice and hybrid warnings may each have their own advantages and disadvantages; however, it could not be predicted which warning type would result in fewer errors at the user interface. Because earcons are complex artificial sounds, they may be difficult for the user to associate meanings to them, thus limiting their recognisability, especially when the user has to remember a large set of earcons. Voice warnings have the advantage of familiarity with operators and this may relate to fewer errors in comprehension. Once again, hybrid warnings were included in the comparison as they may enjoy advantages over the other two types.

3.1 Subjects

Twenty-one male and three female students, who were enrolled in tertiary aviation courses at Swinburne University, participated in this experiment. The mean age of the participants was 21.4 years (S.D. = 2.6 years). All participants had some previous flying experience, with flying hours mainly ranging from

100–435 hours. A sole participant had accrued 6,500 hours flying experience; however, the median number of flying hours was 175. The students were divided into three groups of eight participants each. Participants were fluent in the English language and their hearing standard was sufficient to qualify for an Australian Airline Transport Pilots licence.

3.2   Materials

All participants were asked to complete two computer-based exercises.

The first exercise was a sound training session that assisted participants in learning eight auditory warnings. Each group was presented with a set of eight auditory warnings that were solely abstract in nature (earcons) or solely voice in nature or a combination of abstract followed by voice (hybrid warnings). Each series of eight warnings represented threats that may occur in military aircraft environments. Table 1 shows the warnings, which include eight threat warnings that could be generated by an on-board radar warning receiver and one advisory message (chaff) that could be generated by an on-board self-protection counter-measure.

Event	Voice
Ship	Boat
Air Interceptor	Fighter
Anti-aircraft Artillery	Guns
Missile Launch	Launch
Surface to Air Missile	Missile
Search Radar	Search
Unknown Threat	Unknown
Chaff Dispensed	Chaff

Table 1: Voice sets used during the experiment.

Abstract earcon warnings comprised of a synthetic complex sound that varied in both frequency and time domains and had been designed for maximum discriminability as specified by Patterson (1982). The pulses were 100–150ms in duration, with an onset and offset of 20–30ms. Each sound consisted of 5 or more pulses in a distinctive temporal pattern. Spectral components were primarily between 0.5–5.0kHz with 4 or more harmonically-related components and fundamental harmonics in the range of 150–1000Hz. The abstract sounds were randomly assigned to events.

Voice sounds were created synthetically by DECtalk V4.2 (Digital Equipment Corporation), which utilises text-to speech technology. The voice used was the adult male default voice (Paul) at a speech rate of 180 words per minute, with an average pitch 120Hz

and a pitch range of 100Hz. The choice of warnings was determined by interviewing Royal Australian Air Force (RAAF) aircrew. All warnings were stored on the hard disk of a laptop computer.

The second computer based exercise involved participants listening to three and a half minutes of flight deck environmental sounds. These sounds were stored on the hard disk of a laptop computer and consisted of a pre-recorded segment of a busy flight in a two-crew military jet aircraft. The sounds included air noises that can be heard during flight, radio communications to and from the aircraft, and speech communication between the crew members. At approximately 15-second intervals, a series of the recently learnt auditory warnings were presented randomly and concurrently with the prevailing environmental noises.

3.3   Procedure

Each participant completed the experiment separately in a quiet room while being accompanied by the researcher. The experiment began with a sound training session where participants learnt a set of eight auditory warnings. This experiment is a between-subject design and each group of participants was given one of the three types of warnings to learn. All warnings were played over a set of headphones at a moderate volume.

At the commencement of the sound training, participants were asked to imagine that they were the pilot of a sophisticated jet fighter. They were also asked to imagine that this aircraft was equipped with auditory warnings that could alert them to the presence of eight external threats. The eight warnings were *boat, chaff, fighter, guns, launch, missile, search* and *unknown*; these were presented on the computer screen. When the space bar was pressed the first warning sound was played to the participant. This warning represented boat. Participants were asked to listen carefully to the sound and try to remember it. When they were ready they were asked to press the F1 key (which is the specific key for *boat*) on the computer keyboard and the next warning (*fighter*) was played to them. Participants were required to work their way through the sounds in turn, remembering each one and learning which function key applied to which event. The F1 to F8 function keys were used for the eight events as listed in Table 1 respectively, i.e. F1 for *boat*, F2 for *fighter* etc.

After listening to all eight warnings, a test was carried out to assess retention; this was called the *first trial*. The criterion used for assessing retention was that the participant was able to successfully recognise each auditory signal during two consecutive trials and within 15 seconds of it being presented. If they were unable to recall each warning (twice) then participants repeated the sound training exercise. The computer recorded each trial. All participants eventually met the training criterion outlined above. On successful completion of the training session, the total number of trials was recorded. Participants then progressed immediately to the testing phase. To avoid confusion, this second part of the experiment shall be referred to as the *flight test*.

Once again participants were asked to imagine they were the pilot of military aircraft. They were also asked to imagine that they were conducting a flying mission and that over the intercom they would be able to hear other members of the crew talking, in addition to flight noises and general radio conversation. Participants were told that one of their duties during this mission was to respond to all auditory warnings that they may hear. They were told to listen carefully and that speed and accuracy were essential. If they heard a warning, then they must quickly and accurately identify it and press the appropriate function key on the computer keyboard.

Once the participant understood the requirements, the exercise was commenced. A set of eight auditory warnings was played concurrently with the environmental aircraft noise. Warnings were spaced at least 15 seconds apart and presented in random order; each warning was presented twice. The warnings that were presented were the same as in the training session. All warnings were presented at the same volume to prevent loudness being used as a cue in the experiment.

4 Results

The results of the experiment are summarised in Table 2.

A one-way independent groups analysis of variance revealed a significant difference at 95% confidence level in the average number of learning trials required to learn the different sets of warnings, $F(2,21) = 19.80, p < 0.05$. Further analysis revealed that significantly more trials were needed to learn the earcons than either the voice warnings, $t(7.04) = 4.62, p < 0.05$, or the hybrid warnings, $t(7.25) = 4.32, p < 0.05$. There was no significant difference between the voice and hybrid conditions in the average number of trials required to learn these warnings.

A second one-way independent groups analysis of variance also revealed that at 95% confidence level, average reaction times varied significantly according to sound condition, $F(2,21) = 8.44, p <$

0.05. Further analysis revealed that average reaction times were significantly longer both when the earcon condition was compared with the voice condition, $t(8.86) = 3.07, p < 0.05$, and when the hybrid warning condition was compared with the voice condition, $t(14) = 7.08, p < 0.05$. A comparison of average reaction times between the earcon and hybrid warning conditions revealed no significant difference.

A third one-way independent groups analysis of variance also revealed that at 95% confidence level the average number of errors differed significantly between the types of warning, $F(2,21) = 11.24, p < 0.05$. Further analysis showed that that average number of errors was significantly higher in the earcon condition when compared with both the voice condition, $t(14) = 3.37, p < 0.05$ and the hybrid warning condition, $t(8.31) = 3.81, p < 0.05$.

A comparison of the average numbers of errors made in both the voice and hybrid warning groups revealed no significant difference at 95% confidence level.

		n	Mean	S.D.
Learning Trials	Earcons	8	13.00	6.65
	Voice	8	2.12	0.35
	Hybrid warnings	8	2.75	0.89
Reaction Times (s)	Earcons	8	2.88	0.87
	Voice	8	1.87	0.32
	Hybrid warnings	8	2.80	0.19
Errors	Earcons	8	2.37	1.51
	Voice	8	0.37	0.74
	Hybrid warnings	8	0.25	0.46

Table 2: Means and standard deviations for number of learning trials, reaction times and recognition errors for earcon, voice and hybrid warning stimuli.

5 Discussion

5.1 Learnability

As expected, it took significantly longer to learn the eight abstract earcon warnings than to learn the voice or hybrid warnings. This was consistent with Patterson & Milroy's (1980) findings and more recently with Leung et al. (1997) investigation. Despite the potential that earcons may have in the aviation domain, the relationship between the sound and its representation must be learned and, as a consequence, the learning period is likely to be longer. This should not represent a problem to system designers as long as measures are taken to restrict the number of abstract warnings to eight or less. Moreover, aircrew should be provided with adequate opportunities to learn these abstract warnings during training.

In terms of learning, there appears to be no significant advantage in using hybrid warnings in preference to using voice alone. If hybrid warnings do have an advantage over voice (only) or earcon (only) warnings, then it is likely to be derived from other areas of human performance within the flight deck environment.

5.2 Reaction Time

The observation that earcon response times were significantly slower than voice warnings is not consistent with Edworthy's (1994) assertion that well designed non-voice sounds could actually reduce operator reaction times. Although Brewster et al. (1995) have argued that earcons are capable of keeping up with the pace of interaction at the human–machine interface, this study suggests that it may be *voice* warnings and not earcon warnings that have the advantage in terms of response time.

Given other researchers' optimism regarding well-designed abstract sounds, along with their belief that response times *can* be superior to voice warnings, the results of this study may appear puzzling. Due to the complex nature of earcons, it might be argued that once they had been adequately learnt, earcons could be just as effective as words in communicating information. One possible explanation might lie in the fact that participants were required to learn eight abstract warnings; a number that approaches the maximum recommended by Patterson (1982). This in turn may have placed a greater processing burden on participants and consequently inhibited their recall ability.

According to the *levels of processing* theory (Eysenck & Keane, 1995, citing (Craik & Lockhart, 1972)), there are a number of different levels to which a stimulus can be processed, these range from shallow to deep. At the shallow end of the continuum, a stimulus is processed according to its appearance, size and shape. The next level in depth involves a stimulus (e.g. an auditory warning) being processed according to its acoustic qualities. This is followed by the semantic level (the final and the deepest level), where a stimulus is processed according to its meaning.

The level or depth of processing of a stimulus has a substantial effect on its memorability. Deeper levels of learning may produce more elaborative, longer lasting and stronger memory traces than do shallower levels of processing (Eysenck & Keane, 1995; Reber, 1985). Therefore, it is possible that earcons were processed to a shallower depth than was the case with voice messages. Although their acoustic properties were learnt during the sound training, full

semantic processing may not have occurred. On the other hand, the eight words that were used to represent warning signals may have already undergone significant processing, even prior to the experiment commencing. This in turn may have been reflected in response times.

When comparing the response time between hybrid and voice warnings, the experimental results are consistent with Simpson & Williams (1980) and Hakkinen & Williges (1984) observations. Our study confirmed that an abstract warning that precedes a voice message actually increases response times. It might have been expected that owing to the earcon's communicative qualities, comprehension of a hybrid warning may have occurred prior to the voice component of the warning being played. This does not seem to be the case and there may be a number of factors that could explain this occurrence.

It is possible that participants did not act upon a warning until communication of the entire warning had finished. Simpson & Marchionda-Frost (1984), cited in Stokes et al. (1990), have pointed out that a listener typically does not comprehend the meaning of a voice message until transmission is nearly complete. This same rationale may apply to hybrid warnings also.

Alternatively, other cognitive processing strategies might serve as a useful explanation for the observed responses. A basic task of cognition is concept thinking or concept formation; this is where an individual identifies the properties that are common to a class of objects or ideas (e.g. an auditory warning). Clearly, a person's memory system requires a certain economy in the organization of experiences. Humans employ a *cognitive economy* that assists in the amount of time and effort required to process information (Zimbardo, 1992; Eysenck & Keane, 1995).

During the training session when hybrid warnings were presented to participants for learning, it is possible the earcon component of the message was not processed to the same degree as the voice component. Although the meaning of the hybrid warning may have been learnt rapidly, by virtue of its voice content, the earcon may have been subject to cognitive economising. If this were the case, then the earcon segment of hybrid warnings may have become redundant, this in turn might have influenced participant response times.

5.3 Error

The results of the study revealed a significant difference between the number of errors made in the earcon condition compared with the voice condition.

The error rate in the voice condition was low, with an average of only 0.37 errors being recorded for each participant. Considering that participants had demonstrated their ability to accurately recall the set of 8 earcons during the training session, it may appear surprising that the error rate was so high for the earcon condition, at an average of 2.37 errors per participant. In fact, it might have been expected that earcon recognition rates would have been superior to the voice condition; after all, their acoustic character confers distinctiveness to these sounds.

As with reaction times, error rates may have been affected if earcons had not been processed to the same depth as voice warnings during the training session. Such an effect may have been compounded if the environmental noises distracted participants while they attempted to identify the earcons.

A speed-accuracy trade-off may have also influenced these results. When humans are pressured to respond quickly, the chance of making an error increases; this phenomenon is known as the speed-accuracy trade-off (Wickens & Flach, 1988, citing (Pacella, 1974) and (Wickelgren, 1977)). Prior to commencing the flight test, participants were urged to respond as quickly and accurately as possible to the warnings when they were presented. In this context, it is possible that participants sacrificed accuracy for the sake of speed, instead of speed for the sake of accuracy. It is also likely that participants began the flight test in a high state of arousal. Conditions that increase the level of arousal will lead to faster but less accurate responses (Wickens & Flach, 1988, citing (Posner, 1978)).

Presumably a speed-accuracy trade off would have occurred with the voice and hybrid warnings as well as the earcon condition. However, in the voice and hybrid warning conditions, accuracy may not have been such a critical issue, as the voice components would have been processed to a far greater depth than earcons during training. This could explain why the voice condition recorded lower error rates than the earcon condition.

No significant difference in error rates was recorded between hybrid and voice warnings. Given that the earcon component of a hybrid warning was not processed to the same degree as the voice component, the earcon would have been partly or fully redundant during the flight test. If this were the case, then the experiment was effectively measuring error rates between two forms of voice warning; thus the lack of significance in the results is not surprising. It is also possible that the participants who were presented with hybrid warnings employed a speed-accuracy trade off. In this case however, speed may have been sacrificed for the sake of accuracy.

During the analysis of the data and while calculating rates of error, difficulty was experienced in accounting for some unexpected participant responses with all three groups. While this experiment was designed, in part, to examine incorrect responses when an auditory warning was presented, different types of error were observed. During the flight test, some participants responded even though no stimuli had been presented to them at that particular instant. In other examples, participants did not respond in any way, either correctly or incorrectly, when an auditory warning was presented. Although the number of these occurrences was low, it does suggest that some participants heard a warning when none was presented and others heard nothing when they should have. It seems likely that the environmental noises that were played concurrently with the auditory warnings, interfered with the participants ability to accurately complete the exercise.

6 Conclusion

This study was designed to examine human performance in terms of reaction time and the number of errors made at the human–machine interface. Despite a body of research suggesting that well-designed abstract warnings may be superior to voice warnings, this experimental study indicated that it was the *voice* condition that had an advantage. Voice warning error rates were lower and reaction times faster than both earcon warnings and hybrid warnings. It was also confirmed that warnings which contained a voice component could be learnt and retained very much faster than abstract warnings.

Nevertheless, some aspects of the experimental design may have influenced the final outcome. If participants had been asked to learn a smaller number of abstract warnings, then retention and recall may have been more effective. If this were to be the case, conceivably reaction times for abstract warnings may improve and errors decrease.

More research is required in the area of auditory displays in aircraft. It should address issues such as fatigue, vigilance along with variations in the age and hearing capability of operators. The effects of perceived urgency and how operators determine their priorities when confronted with multiple warnings are also worthy of investigation.

Acknowledgements

The authors would like to thank Simon Parker, Russell Martin and Sean Smith of the Auditory Interface Research Group, Air Operations Division, Aeronautical and Maritime Research Laboratories in Melbourne for their assistance in this project.

References

Blattner, M. M., Sumikawa, D. A. & Greenberg, R. M. (1989), "Earcons and Icons: Their Structure and Common Design Principles", *Human–Computer Interaction* 4(1), 11–44.

Brewster, S. A., Wright, P. C. & Edwards, A. D. N. (1995), "Parallel Earcons: Reducing the Length of Audio Messages", *International Journal of Human–Computer Interaction* 43(2), 153–75.

Edworthy, J. (1994), "The Design and Implementation of Non-verbal Auditory Warnings", *Ergonomics* 25(4), 202–10.

Eysenck, M. W. & Keane, M. T. (1995), *Cognitive Psychology: A Student's Handbook*, third edition, Psychology Press.

Federal Aviation Administration (1996), "The Interface Between Flight Crews and Modern Flight Deck Systems", *Flight Safety Digest* 15(9), 5–132.

Gaver, W. W. (1986), "Auditory Icons: Using Sound in Computer Interfaces", *Human–Computer Interaction* 2(1), 167–77.

Hakkinen, M. T. & Williges, B. H. (1984), "Synthesised Warning Messages: Effects of an Alerting Cue in Single and Multiple Function Voice Synthesis Systems", *Human Factors* 26(2), 185–95.

Hawkins, F. H. (1987), *Human Factors in Flight*, Gower Technical Press.

International Civil Aviation Organization (1992), "Operational Implications of Automation in Advanced Technology Flightdecks", Human Factors Digest No.5 (Circular 234-AN/142).

Kestin, I. G., Miller, B. R. & Lockhart, C. H. (1988), "Auditory Alarms During Anaesthesia Monitoring", *Anesthesiology* 64(1), 106–9.

Kramer, G. (1994), An Introduction to Auditory Display, in G. Kramer (ed.), *Auditory Display: Sonification, Audification, and Auditory interfaces*, Addison–Wesley.

Leung, Y., Smith, S., Parker, S. & Martin, R. (1997), Learning and Retention of Auditory Warnings, in J. Ballas (ed.), *Proceedings of the 4th International Conference on Auditory Display*, pp.128–31.

Patterson, R. D. (1982), "Guidelines for Auditory Warning Systems on Civil Aircraft", CAA Paper 82017.

Patterson, R. D. (1985), Auditory Warning Systems for High-Workload Environments, in I. D. Brown, R. Goldsmith, K. Coombes & M. A. Sinclair (eds.), *Proceedings of the Ninth Congress of the International Ergonomics Association*, Taylor & Francis, pp.163–5.

Patterson, R. D. & Milroy, R. (1980), "Auditory Warnings on Civil Aircraft: The Learning and Retention of Warnings", CAA Paper 7D/S/0142.

Reber, S. R. (1985), *Dictionary of Psychology*, Penguin.

Sanders, M. S. & McCormick, E. J. (1987), *Human Factors in Engineering and Design*, McGraw-Hill.

Simpson, C. A. & Williams, D. H. (1980), "Response Time Effects of Alerting Tone and Semantic Context for Synthesised Voice Cockpit Warnings", *Human Factors* 22(3), 319–30.

Simpson, I. & Marchionda-Frost, K. (1984), "Synthesized Speech Rate and Pitch Effect on Intelligibility of Warning Messages for Pilots", *Human Factors* 26(4), 509–17.

Stanton, N. & Edworthy, J. (1998), "Auditory Affordances in the Intensive Treatment Unit", *Applied Ergonomics* 29(5), 389–94.

Stokes, A. F. & Wickens, C. D. (1988), Aviation Displays, in E. L. Wiener & D. C. Nagel (eds.), *Human Factors in Aviation*, Academic Press, pp.387–409.

Stokes, A., Wickens, C. D. & Kite, K. (1990), *Display Technology: Human Factors Concepts*, Society of Automotive Engineers.

Thorning, A. G. & Ablett, R. M. (1985), Auditory Systems in Commercial Transport Aircraft, in I. D. Brown, R. Goldsmith, K. Coombes & M. A. Sinclair (eds.), *Proceedings of the Ninth Congress of the International Ergonomics Association*, Taylor & Francis, pp.163–5.

Wickens, C. D. & Flach, J. M. (1988), Information Processing, in E. L. Wiener & D. C. Nagel (eds.), *Human Factors in Aviation*, Academic Press, pp.111–55.

Williams, S. M. (1994), Perceptual Principles in Sound Grouping, in G. Kramer (ed.), *Auditory Display: Sonificaction, Audification, and Auditory Interfaces*, Addison–Wesley, pp.79–92.

Woods, D. D. (1995), "The Alarm Problem and Directed Attention in Dynamic Fault Management", *Ergonomics* 38(11), 2371–93.

Zimbardo, P. (1992), *Psychology and Life*, Harper Collins.

Coordinating the Interruption of People in Human–Computer Interaction

Daniel C. McFarlane

Naval Research Laboratory, Code 5513, Washington DC 20375, USA.

mcfarlane@acm.org

Abstract: People have cognitive limitations that make them sensitive to interruption. These limitations can cause people to make serious mistakes when they are interrupted. Unfortunately, interruption of people is a side effect of systems that allow users to delegate tasks to active background processes, like intelligent software agents. Delegation carries the costs of supervision, and that often includes being interrupted by subordinates. User interfaces for these kinds of computer systems must be designed to accommodate people's limitations relative to being interrupted. A theory-based taxonomy of human interruption was used to identify the four known methods for deciding when to interrupt people. An experiment was conducted with 36 subjects to compare these four different design approaches within a common context. The results show important differences between the four user interface design solutions to the problem of interrupting people in human–computer interaction (HCI).

Keywords: interruption, human–computer interaction, user interface design guidelines, experiment, mixed-initiative dialogue, intelligent software agents, coordination.

1 Introduction

Advances in computer technologies have increased the practicality of building systems that allow people to perform multiple activities at the same time. However, people's cognitive capabilities have not increased. It is possible that these technological advancements carry unfortunate side effects that conflict with people's unchanging cognitive limitations.

The telephone is a familiar example. This technology allows people to do several things concurrently and is useful for isolated conversations. However, in real work environments it also allows people to have several concurrent dialogues that become intermixed over time. This kind of multitasking is useful and natural, however it also introduces the unfortunate side effect of causing people to be interrupted. Telephone users must accept a certain amount of interruptions as the unavoidable cost of doing several things concurrently. Intelligent software agents cause this same problem. These systems can be assigned to do useful things in the background while their human users work on other tasks. However, whenever an agent must initiate an interaction with its user, it must first interrupt them from whatever else they are doing.

Interruption of people is problematic because people have cognitive limitations that restrict their ability to work during interruptions. For example, an interruption of a commercial airline crew before takeoff contributed to their subsequent crash of the plane. A Northwest Airline crew was preparing to fly out of Detroit. They began their pre-flight checklist, but were interrupted by an air traffic controller with new taxiing instructions and a warning about wind shear. After the crew finished talking to the controller they made the mistake of not resuming their checklist. They took off without checking the status of the airplane's flaps. A flight emergency occurred shortly after takeoff because the flaps were in the wrong position. The crew mistakenly interpreted the problem as wind shear and crashed the plane (NTSB, 1988).

It is essential to discover user interface design solutions that accommodate peoples' limitations and allow them to be interrupted safely.

2 Background

Researchers have observed that interrupting people affects their behaviour. This is the basis of a classic effect from psychology called the Zeigarnik Effect (Van Bergen, 1968). This effect was first identified in 1927 and describes a finding that people have selective memory relative to interruption, i.e. that people are able to recall the details of interrupted tasks better than the details of uninterrupted tasks. Results from many studies of the Zeigarnik Effect have produced somewhat inconsistent results. However, two findings seem universal:

1. interrupting people affects their behaviour; and

2. the interruption of people is a complicated process.

Work has also been done to compare different user interface design approaches for solving the problems associated with interrupting people. It was found that interaction design affects people's ability to successfully resume previously interrupted tasks. Two examples are interaction logic approaches for calculators (Kreifeldt & McCarthy, 1981) and backtracking control for database access (Field, 1987). Other work has been done to begin to identify which aspects of human interruption cause people to make mistakes (Czerwinski et al., 1991; Gillie & Broadbent, 1989; Cellier & Eyrolle, 1992).

A set of new interdisciplinary theory-based tools provides a general definition and taxonomy of human interruption (McFarlane, 1997; McFarlane, 1998). This taxonomy identifies eight major dimensions of the problem of human interruption that are exposed in the current literature. The third factor from the taxonomy, 'Method of Coordination', is a critical aspect of human interruption that has not yet been directly investigated.

The 'Method of Coordination' is the technique used to decide when to interrupt people. The taxonomy identifies the four known ways of coordinating user-interruption:

1. immediate;

2. negotiated;

3. mediated; and

4. scheduled.

No comparison of the relative utility of these four design approaches exists in the current literature. Instead, previous research focuses only on the separate individual solutions without comparing the alternatives.

3   Approach

The approach of this paper is to discover the relative strengths and weaknesses of the four different 'Method of Coordination' solutions. An experiment

was performed that compared all four methods for coordinating user-interruption within a common context.

A fictitious example can illustrate the four user interface design approaches for determining when to interrupt people. Suppose that a person is performing two tasks concurrently: (1) indirectly driving a car by supervising a robotic driver, and (2) conversing with another human passenger in the car. Whenever the robotic driver must initiate an interaction with its human supervisor it must first interrupt them from their conversation. An 'immediate' solution would have the robot interrupt the person at any time in a way that insists that the person immediately stop conversing and interact with the robotic driver. A 'negotiated' solution would have the robot announce its need to interrupt its supervisor, and then support a negotiation with the user. This would give the person control over when to deal with the interruption. A 'mediated' solution would have the robot not directly interrupt its supervisor, but instead contact the person's PDA (personal digital assistant) and request interaction with the person. The PDA would then determine when and how the robot would be allowed to interrupt the person. A 'scheduled' solution would restrict the robot to interrupt its supervisor on a prearranged schedule such as once every 15 minutes.

Driving errors are more serious than conversational errors. Therefore a successful user interface design for a robotic driver would have to ensure people's performance on the supervised driving task regardless of the side effects on other activities. However, there is not enough design knowledge available in the current literature to say which 'Method of Coordination' would be best for this problem, and different people have surprisingly different intuitive answers.

Prior studies have looked at topics related to each of the four 'Methods of Coordination'. One cost that has been identified for the 'immediate' solution is that people experience a troublesome initial decrease in performance called automation deficit when they try to resume interrupted tasks (Ballas et al., 1992). A few authors have investigated ways to help users more easily resume interrupted tasks. For example: awareness of backgrounded tasks can be heightened with sonification; reminders can prepare people to resume interrupted tasks (Davies et al., 1989); and tools can be devised to help people quickly review interrupted tasks when resuming them (Field, 1987).

The 'negotiated' solution is an attempt to exploit people's natural ability to negotiate changes in their activities. Clark (1996) says that in normal human-human language usage people have four possible responses to interruption:

1. take-up with full compliance;

2. take-up with alteration;

3. decline; or

4. withdraw.

Some papers have investigated usefulness of presenting interruption in ways that allow people to ignore them if they choose. Katz (1995) found that there are overhead costs related to negotiating interruptions, and that users sometimes prefer immediate interruption solutions when that overhead cost is not justified.

The 'mediated' solution is an attractive but controversial approach. Delegating the interruption problem to a mediator begets a new task of supervising the mediator (Kirlik, 1993). There are five main approaches for mediation:

1. predict people's interruptibility (Miyata & Norman, 1986);

2. implement intelligent user interfaces for supervision tasks;

3. automatically calculate users' cognitive workload for dynamic task allocation;

4. apply human factors techniques for supervisory control; and

5. use cognitive models to guide interaction.

The 'scheduled' solution is an attempt to give a degree of reliable expectation to a user about when they will be interrupted. In many ways, scheduling times for unexpected activities transforms interruptions into normal planned activities. Time management training has been found to have a positive effect on people's ability to manage interruptions.

These four approaches for determining when to interrupt people have not been compared before. A conservative first question is: "Does it matter which coordination method is chosen as a solution to this user interface design problem?" If this question can be answered that, "Yes, it does matter", then the relative strengths and weaknesses of the different solutions can be compared.

The main hypothesis of this paper is therefore that the particular method for coordinating user-interruption that is implemented in a user interface will affect user's performance on interrupt-laden computer-based multi-tasks.

4 Method

Four different user interfaces were built for a common computer-based multi-task. These four interfaces are representative implementations of the four known solutions for 'Method of Coordination'.

4.1 Subjects

Thirty six subjects were compensated for participating in this experiment (18 males and 18 females). Subjects completed an entrance questionnaire before beginning the experiment, and most reported that they had substantial experience with computer-based tasks. These 36 subjects, however, had highly diverse backgrounds on many other dimensions: age (mean 24.7, min. 18, max. 47), race, years of college education, amount of video game experience, level of typing skill, and self-reported vulnerability to the negative effects of interruption.

4.2 Design

A single-factor, within-subjects, Latin square design was chosen as an appropriate design for this experiment. Six treatments were devised: four experimental and two base case control treatments. Each of the four experimental treatments represented one of the four methods for coordinating interruption identified in the Taxonomy of Human Interruption (McFarlane, 1997; McFarlane, 1998).

Each treatment condition used a different version of a user interface (the independent variable). The computer-based multi-task was not varied between treatment conditions. Subjects' performance (the dependent variable) on the multi-task was observed and recorded under the six treatment conditions.

All subjects received all six treatments. However, each subject was assigned to one of six groups that defined the counterbalanced ordering (digram-balanced) of the presentation of the six treatments. The presentation of each treatment was divided into two contiguous trials to avoid the confounding influences of fatigue and boredom. Male and female subjects were randomly assigned to groups, but with three males and three females in each group.

Each subject performed a total of 24 trials of the computer-based multi-task. Each trial was 4.5 minutes long, and there was a brief rest period with a masked screen between each session. Rest periods were a minimum of 25 seconds each. Therefore the total time for a subject to complete the experimental task was about 2 hours. For all subjects, the first 12 trials were practice (~1 hour) and the following 12 trials were experiment (˜1 hour). Subjects received the same counterbalanced ordering of trials on practice trials as they did on experimental trials.

4.3   Multi-task

An interruption-laden computer-based multi-task was created as an appropriate testbed for this experiment. This multi-task itself represents an important contribution to the study of interruption. It was very carefully contrived to be both well controlled and appropriately complex.

The background literature identifies many subtle sources of possible influence on people's behaviour during interruption. It was judged that a fully realistic multi-task would not allow for the control of irrelevant confounds, and, therefore, would not afford the collection of valid or reliable observations. The use of a realistic multi-task would degrade the internal validity of the experiment and muddle the results. An abstract multi-task had to be found that would isolate just those issues relevant to the hypothesis of this paper.

The interruption of people during human–computer interaction is a high-level interdisciplinary topic. The interdisciplinary background literature also shows that interruption is a complex process that involves many subtle low-level mechanisms of human cognition. These individual mechanisms, however, are not the focus of this experiment. It was judged that a simplistic and antiseptic task, typical of those used in studies about low-level topics of human cognition, would be inappropriate for this experiment. The use of such a simplistic multi-task would not allow the observation of the high-level effects, and would degrade the external validity of the experiment. A reasonably complex experimental multi-task had to be contrived to elicit people's behaviour at an appropriately high level.

It is possible to investigate the process of interruption at the level of user interface design without fully understanding the many subtle low-level cognitive mechanisms involved. In this experiment, the interesting, but irrelevant, smaller effects were ignored and isolated from the high-level effects by imposing pure noise into several aspects of the human–computer interaction. This intentional noise equalizes the many smaller effects across the different treatment conditions, and allows the direct observation of relevant high-level behaviour.

An abstract multi-task was chosen. It is a simplified model of a class of common real world multi-tasks. Examples of people performing multi-tasks from this class are 911 emergency dispatch operators and aviation radar operators. A Naval aviation task, for example, requires an operator to identify and maintain tracks of radar images as they appear and change over time. These identification and tracking subtasks do not occur at conveniently spaced times, but can often overlap. These overlapping subtasks can only be attended to one at a time, but the operator must also maintain a concurrent awareness of all subtasks. The operator must also be available for arbitrary interruptions by their leaders for direct requests of information.

The multi-task is a dual-task (a two-task multi-task) composed of a continuous game task and an intermittent matching task. The game task is modelled after a video game by Nintendo Corporation called 'Fire' that was originally released in 1980 & 1981 as a version of the Nintendo Game & Watch product series. The matching task is modelled after the matching tasks used in experiments of the Stroop Effect. The dual-task is conceptually simple and yet can be very difficult for people to perform. The results of pilot studies confirmed that this dual-task elicits the kind of human errors associated with the interruption phenomenon.

The game task required subjects to control the movement of cartoon style stretcher bearers. The object was to direct the stretcher bearers to catch other game characters as they fell from a building. Each falling character had to be successfully caught and bounced three separate times at three different locations (total time to save each jumper was 16.9 sec.). If a character was missed at any of the three bounce points, then it was lost (see Figure 1).

Figure 1: Game task.

This game task is both continuous and discrete. It is a single continuously running game, however saving each individual jumping character was a completely independent discrete subtask. Errors made while performing one subtask do not automatically cause errors on other subtasks. This subtask composition allowed observations of peoples' behaviours to be easily broken down into discrete units. It was the interactions of several randomly intermixed subtasks that required dynamic problem solving. This arrangement allows the overall complexity of the game task to be conveniently manipulated.

The level of difficulty of the game had to be contrived so that it was complex enough to attack subjects' vulnerability to interruption, but simple enough not to cause subjects to despair of performing well. Through testing with pilot subjects, it was discovered that 59 game subtasks per trial was appropriate.

The second task of this dual-task was the interruption task. This task was an intermittent graphical matching task loosely based on the textual matching tasks reported in investigations of the Stroop effect. The interruption task required subjects to make matching decisions either based on colour or shape. Subjects were presented with a coloured shape at the top of the window, and instructed to choose one of the bottom two coloured shapes according to the matching rule displayed in the centre. The matching rule instructed subjects to either 'Match by shape' or 'Match by colour' (see Figure 2).

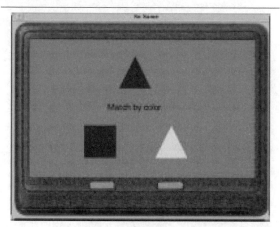

Figure 2: Matching task.

This matching task is conceptually simple, but deceptively difficult to perform. Pilot studies found that people were not able to automate this task through over-learning even after 2.5 hours. Each individual matching task required a short focus of attention. It was discovered through pilot testing that 80 matching tasks per trial were appropriate.

Subtasks were independent. The graphic nature of the matching task corresponded with the graphic nature of the game task. Matching subtasks had to be done one at a time from a first-in-first-out queue, so there were no interruptions of interruptions.

Each of the 864 trials in this experiment (36 subjects × 24 trials each), provided an unpredictable multi-task. The schedules for game and matching subtasks were created with constrained randomization schemes that produced unique (unlearnable) schedules for each trial that were kept constant in the frequency domain.

4.4 Treatments

Subjects performed the multi-task with one-handed keyboard key presses on an isolated group of six keys of a common extended computer keyboard (see Figure 3). The 'Home' and 'End' keys were only used in the 'negotiated' treatment condition.

Figure 3: Keys used for performing the experiment.

Whenever a matching task was in the foreground, it appeared in the same window as the game task and totally obscured the view of the game. The game task continued to run without possibility for pause regardless of whether subjects could see it or not. In all treatments, except 'Negotiated', once the multi-task was switched to the matching task subjects had to perform all queued matching tasks before they could resume the game task in progress. Whenever a user completed the last queued matching task, the multi-task switched back to the game task. The following are descriptions of the six treatment conditions:

Treatment 1: 'Game Only' base case implemented the game task with no matching tasks.

Treatment 2: 'Match Only' base case implemented the matching task with no game task.

Treatment 3: 'Immediate' treatment condition presented matching tasks directly whenever they occurred regardless of the state of the game task.

Treatment 4: 'Negotiated' treatment condition gave subjects control over when they would handle interruptions. When a matching task occurred, its arrival was immediately announced with a flash of a blank matching task for 150ms and then the game task display resumed. Subjects had to decide when to begin the queued matching task. Subjects could use the 'Home' and 'End' keys at any time to bring the queued matching tasks to the foreground or push them to the background.

Treatment 5: 'Mediated' treatment condition dynamically calculated a simple function of subjects' workload that measured how many jumping diplomats were on the screen. Interruptions were automatically held until workload metric was low.

Treatment 6: 'Scheduled' treatment condition held all interruptions and only switched from the game task to the matching task on a prearranged schedule of once every 25 seconds.

4.5 Apparatus

All subjects performed the computer-based dual-task on a laptop computer (166MHz Pentium CPU, Windows95) using the built-in monitor (1024 × 768 pixels, 16 bit colour) and an external extended keyboard. The computer-based dual-task was displayed in a single 640 × 480 pixels window in the top left corner of the screen. The laptop was raised 4.75″ above the tabletop in front of subjects to create a comfortable viewing angle. The experimental software was implemented with double-buffered frame animation running at 20 frames a second.

4.6 Procedure

Subjects participated one at a time and were required to pass a standard test for normal colour vision. They then received written instructions that described the multi-task and all treatment conditions. Subjects were able to refer to these instructions throughout the experiment. Each trial was preceded with an on-screen messages announcing which treatment condition would be next, and reminders to avoid fatigue, and that the game and matching tasks were equally important. Detailed interaction data were unobtrusively recorded by computer throughout the experiment.

5 Results

The hypothesis asserts the existence of a causal relationship between coordination method used and subjects' performance on the multi-task. Six different measures of subjects' performance were chosen as appropriate for testing this hypothesis: 1) number of jumpers saved on the game task ('jumpers saved'); 2) number of switches between game task and matching task in both directions ('task switches'); 3) number of matches done wrong ('matched wrong'); 4) percent of

matches done wrong of those attempted ('% m.wrong of done'); 5) number of matches not done ('matches not done'); and 6) average time from the scheduled onset of each matching task until it was actually completed or the trial timed out ('avg. match age').

Note that three performance measures, task switches, matches not done, and avg. match age, are not 'traditional' experimental dependent variables because their value was not free to vary under subjects' direct control (except in the negotiated condition). These performance measures are appropriate here, however, because these limitations on subjects' performance are directly linked to the application of the different treatments and therefore illustrate how the four treatment conditions differentially affect subjects' behaviour.

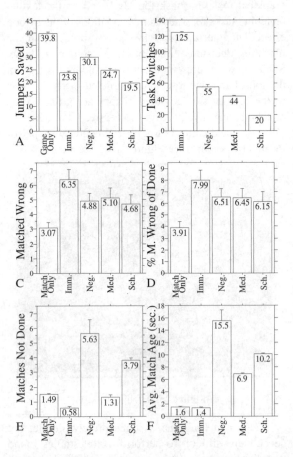

Figure 4: Average scores for 6 performance measures on experimental data. The bar charts show the mean with error bars that depict one standard error. There were 59 jumpers on the game task, and 80 matches on the matching task. Trials lasted 4.5 minutes. The abbreviations are: Imm. (immediate); Neg. (negotiated); Med. (mediated); and Sch. (scheduled).

The data from the practice trials were not included in these analyses. Figure 4 contains bar charts for the six performance measures investigated here. These graphs show the data for 32.4 total hours of human performance on the experimental multi-task (36 subjects × 6 experimental treatments per subject × 2 trials per treatment × 4.5 minutes per trial). Note that these error bars reflect the total variance contained in the data and include some graphical distortion because of the inclusion of outliers.

Since this experiment is the first to compare the four methods for coordinating user interruption, it was important to attempt to maximize the validity of the results. Non-parametric statistical tests were employed. The decision to use non-parametric tests avoids potential confusions about the validity of parametric analyses. For example, it may be argued that the data do not have consistency of variance between conditions, because the different experiment conditions did not give subjects equivalent kinds of control over all kinds of multi-task performance. The non-parametric Friedman two-way analysis of variance by ranks test with correction for ties was selected (denoted by F_r), with its methods for post hoc comparisons. This test is calculated on within-subject ranks, and is useful for analysing within-subjects effects for interval level data. The Friedman test is therefore immune to the biasing influences of abnormal variance or outliers.

5.1 Overall Effects of Interruption

There must be an overall effect of interruption — otherwise a discussion of the differential effects of alternative methods for coordinating interruptions would not make sense. Two base case treatment conditions were included in this experiment so that this assertion could be validated before testing the main hypothesis. Table 1 summarizes the results of the Friedman test to determine whether there are any significant differences between the five relevant conditions for each measure of performance (the four treatment conditions and one base case). For comparison, F_r must be greater than 9.49 for $p < \alpha$ of 0.05.

Performance measure	Base case	F_r	p	$p < \alpha$
jumpers saved	game only	120.410	<0.0001	YES
task switches	[no appropriate base case]			
matched wrong	match only	39.627	<0.0001	YES
% m. wrong of done	match only	32.911	<0.0001	YES
matches not done	match only	65.960	<0.0001	YES
avg. match age	match only	117.956	<0.0001	YES

Table 1: Comparison to base cases.

These results validate the basic assertion that being interrupted affects people's behaviour. The significance of these results permits post hoc analyses. Table 2 summarizes the results of a comparison of individual conditions with the appropriate base cases using the Friedman test's post hoc analysis methods. Each cell reports the results of significance tests with $\alpha = 0.05$. Figure 4 can be used to determine the direction of significant pairs.

Performance measure	Base case	base & Imm.	base & Neg.	base & Med.	base & Sch.
jumpers saved	game only	YES	YES	YES	YES
task switches	[no appropriate base case]				
matched wrong	match only	YES	YES	YES	no
% m. wrong of done	match only	YES	YES	YES	YES
matches not done	match only	YES	no	no	YES
avg. match age	match only	no	YES	YES	YES

Table 2: Post hoc comparison to base cases.

5.2 Effects of Different Interruption Coordination Methods

Do the different methods of coordinating interruption affect people differently? Table 3 summarizes the results of the Friedman test to determine whether there is any significant difference between the four experimental conditions for each measure of performance (base cases are not included). For comparison, F_r must be greater than 7.82 for $p < \alpha$ of 0.05.

Performance measure	F_r	p	$p < \alpha$
jumpers saved	72.263	< 0.0001	YES
task switches	87.000	< 0.0001	YES
matched wrong	17.599	0.0005	YES
% m. wrong of done	10.267	0.0164	YES
matches not done	53.034	< 0.0001	YES
avg. match age	78.100	< 0.0001	YES

Table 3: Analysis of experimental conditions.

The data from all six performance measures support the main hypothesis with statistical significance. It is concluded that the particular method for coordinating interruptions of people implemented in user interfaces affects people's performance. These significant results permit post hoc analyses. Table 4 summarizes the results of pairwise comparisons between the four experimental conditions using the Friedman test's post hoc analysis methods. Each cell reports the results of significance tests with $\alpha = 0.05$. Figure 4 can be used to determine the direction of significant pairs, with two exceptions. The 'Neg.& Sch.' pairs for Figure 4 E & F have significant differences in opposite directions from the graphs. This is possible because the statistics were performed by ranks on a within-subjects effect, but the graphs portray the raw data that includes large individual difference effects (between-subjects) especially for the negotiated interruption solution.

Performance measure	Imm. & Neg.	Imm. & Med.	Imm. & Sch.	Neg. & Med	Neg. & Sch.	Med. & Sch.
jumpers saved	YES	no	YES	YES	YES	YES
task switches	YES	YES	YES	no	YES	YES
matched wrong	YES	YES	YES	no	no	no
% m. wrong of done	no	no	YES	no	no	no
matches not done	YES	no	YES	no	no	YES
avg. match age	YES	YES	YES	no	no	YES

Table 4: Post hoc analysis of main effect.

5.3   Interpretation and Guidelines

Being interrupted affects people. Unfortunately, the above analyses reveal that there is no one 'best' choice of method for coordinating interruptions for all kinds of human performance. There are instead, trade-offs between the four coordination methods and the different kinds of human performance. The following discussion does not include the base cases.

The negotiated coordination method was very successful in several ways. Negotiation resulted in the best performance on the jumpers saved measure, and it produced matched wrong performance as good as any other coordination method, and it produced many fewer total task switches than the immediate interruption solution. There was, however, a large price to pay in the completeness (matches not done) and promptness (avg. match age) of performing the matching subtasks.

The results from the percent matched wrong of done measure confirm that the negotiation solution did not pay a penalty in increased matching errors. The negotiated solution did not have relatively few matching errors simply because subjects performed fewer total matching subtasks on this condition. Subjects sometimes delayed handling interruptions quite long on the negotiated condition compared to other treatment conditions. This was not a classical speed-accuracy tradeoff. Subjects were not taking more time to make careful matching choices in the 'negotiated' condition; they were only taking more time to procrastinate making matching choices.

The immediate coordination method produced nearly opposite performance of the negotiated solution. Immediate resulted in the best performance of any coordination method on the matches not done and avg. match age performance measures. However, these successes were gained at large costs in performance relative to the other coordination solutions on jumpers saved, matched wrong, and task switches performance measures.

The scheduled coordination method resulted in the best performance on task switching measure, but paid a heavy price on all other kinds of performance. The mediated coordination method produced mediocre levels of on all kinds of performance. It was neither the best nor worst for any performance measure.

No single method for coordinating user-interruption is a clear winner. Instead, each solution has its pros and cons relative to the different measures of human performance. These results alone do not have the external validity required for creating formal user interface design guidelines. These results do, however, have some value. They may support the following generalizations:

1. People perform very well when they can negotiate for the onset of interruptions, however giving people this kind of control also means that they may not handle interruptions in a timely way.

2. When people are forced to handle interruptions immediately, they get the interruption tasks done promptly but they make more mistakes and are less effective overall.

The following tentative user interface design guidelines are only informed speculations and ignore concerns about generalizability, however since no guidelines exist they may be somewhat useful:

1. Negotiated solution is best and scheduled solution is worst for accuracy on a continuous task.

2. Scheduled solution is best and immediate solution is worst for causing fewest task switches.

3. Immediate solution is worst for accuracy on an intermittent task.

4. Immediate or mediated solutions are best for completeness on an intermittent task.

5. Immediate solution is best for promptness on an intermittent task.

6 Conclusions

This paper presents the first empirical comparison of all four known approaches to the problem of coordinating user-interruption in HCI. This topic is an important factor for user interface design of systems that must interrupt their users. The results of this experiment suggest that the 'best' solution is strictly relative to the particular kinds of human task performance judged critical to the success of the system.

Acknowledgements

This work was funded by James Ballas at NRL, Michael Shneier at ONR, and John Sibert at George Washington U. Portions of this work were performed as part of a doctoral dissertation at GWU under the direction of John Sibert. Editing performed by: James Ballas, Astrid Schmidt-Nielsen, Susan McFarlane, Derek Brock, and Justin McCune.

References

Ballas, J. A., Heitmeyer, C. L., & Pérez, M. A. (1992), Evaluating Two Aspects of Direct Manipulation in Advanced Cockpits, *in* P. Bauersfeld, J. Bennett & G. Lynch (eds.), *Proceedings of CHI'92: Human Factors in Computing Systems*, ACM Press, pp.127–34.

Cellier, J. M. & Eyrolle, H. (1992), "Interference Between Switched Tasks", *Ergonomics* **35**(1), 25–36.

Clark, H. H. (1996), *Using Language*, Cambridge University Press.

Czerwinski, M. P., Chrisman, S. E., & Rudisill, M. (1991), Interruptions in Multitasking Situations: The Effects of Similarity and Warning, Technical Report JSC-24757, NASA Johnson Space Center, Houston, Texas.

Davies, S. P., Findlay, J. M. & Lambert, A. J. (1989), The Perception and Tracking of State Changes in Complex Systems, *in* G. Salvendy & M. J. Smith (eds.), *Designing and Using Human–Computer Interfaces and Knowledge-based Systems*, Elsevier Science, pp.510–7.

Field, G. E. (1987), "Experimentus Interruptus", *ACM SIGCHI Bulletin* **19**(2), 42–6.

Gillie, T. & Broadbent, D. E. (1989), "What Makes Interruptions Disruptive? A Study of Length, Similarity, and Complexity", *Psychological Research* **50**(4), 243–50.

Katz, R. (1995), "Automatic Versus User-controlled Methods of Briefly Interrupting Telephone Calls", *Human Factors* **37**(2), 321–34.

Kirlik, A. (1993), "Modeling Strategic Behavior in Human-Automation Interaction - Why an Aid Can (and Should) Go Unused", *Human Factors* **35**(2), 221–42.

Kreifeldt, J. G. & McCarthy, M. E. (1981), Interruption as a Test of the User–Computer Interface, *in Proceedings of the 17th Annual Conference on Manual Control*, JPL Publications, pp.655–67.

McFarlane, D. C. (1997), Interruption of People in Human–Computer Interaction: A General Unifying Definition of Human Interruption and Taxonomy, Technical Report NRL/FR/5510-97-9870, US Naval Research Lab, Washington, DC.

McFarlane, D. C. (1998), Interruption of People in Human–Computer Interaction, PhD thesis, George Washington University, USA.

Miyata, Y. & Norman, D. A. (1986), Psychological Issues in Support of Multiple Activities, *in* D. A. Norman & S. W. Draper (eds.), *User Centered Systems Design: New Perspectives on Human–Computer Interaction*, Lawrence Erlbaum Associates, pp.265–84.

NTSB (1988), Aircraft Accident Report, Technical Report NTSB-AAR-88-05, National Transportation Safety Board.

Van Bergen, A. (1968), *Task Interruption*, North-Holland Publishing Company.

Human–Computer Interaction — INTERACT '99
M. Angela Sasse and Chris Johnson (Editors)
Published by IOS Press, © IFIP TC.13, 1999

How Can Groupware Preserve Our Coordination Skills?
Designing for Direct Collaboration

Stéphane Sire, Stéphane Chatty, Hélène Gaspard-Boulinc & François-Régis Colin

Centre d'Etudes de la Navigation Aérienne, 7 Avenue Edouard Belin,
31055 Toulouse Cedex, France.
{sire,chatty,helene,fcolin}@cena.dgac.fr

Abstract: Groupware systems often propose coordination protocols inspired from computer technologies. Such protocols are rigid compared to the subtle coordination hints and to the social rules used by humans. Protocols act as intermediate between users in the same way as command languages once did between users and tasks. We propose to reduce the role of those intermediates in what we call direct collaboration interfaces. We then explore design rules that support direct collaboration: media and activity integration, and interaction styles that support prosody and social hints. We finally describe an application to air traffic control.

Keywords: groupware, collaborative work, interaction style, air traffic control, direct collaboration.

1 Introduction

Although research in the field has been very productive in the last ten years, there are still few applications of groupware systems in domains other than office systems. Among them, air traffic control (ATC) is probably one of the domains that would benefit most from advances in Computer Supported Collaborative Work (CSCW). A candidate application for groupware is the negotiation that occurs when a controller wants to modify the route of an aircraft in a way that affects another controller who works in another room, hundreds of kilometres away. Today's negotiations, carried through a telephone, routinely take half a minute for exchanges that would take less than ten seconds if the controllers were sitting next to each other. It is tempting to believe that adequate groupware support would help sparing those precious twenty seconds, and improve the comfort of negotiations.

However, providing the adequate groupware support is not easy. A classical technique used by engineers consists in analysing telephone conversations between controllers, classifying the different types of exchanges and then proposing a computer equivalent for each of them. Taking advantage of the evolution of ATC systems towards graphical interactive systems (Chatty & Lecoanet,

1996), it is easy to extend data input with collaboration capacities. For instance, a controller who wants to allow an aircraft to climb can input the proposed flight level, then make a dialogue box appear on a colleague's screen, as shown in Figure 1.

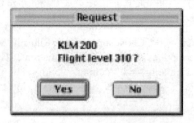

Figure 1: Proposing a new flight level to another controller, a rigid protocol.

Using the computer as an intermediate like this is technically easy, and looks like an efficient reuse of the user previous input actions. But is it efficient for negotiating with other users? This is far from obvious. As far as ATC is concerned, dialogue boxes like the one shown in Figure 1 were not considered as fully satisfactory, because air traffic controllers felt that communications would be too constrained. We consider this as a hint that there are mechanisms in human communication that are not easily captured by computer-mediated interaction.

In this article, we analyse how computer-based coordination protocols come in the way of collaboration and we introduce the notion of direct collaboration, by comparison with direct manipulation. We then propose some rules for designing direct collaboration systems, and we describe metaphors for data exchange that support direct collaboration. Finally, we take as an example the application of direct collaboration techniques to air traffic control.

2 Collaboration with CSCW

Collaboration with CSCW tools requires more than one application program or technology because each one often covers a limited set of requirements. Some of these applications impose coordination protocols on users.

2.1 Classification of Groupware Systems

The Clover model, a functional classification of groupware systems, decomposes collaborative work into three types of activities: *communication, production* and *coordination* (Calvary et al., 1997). Each of these activities is supported by different components of groupware systems. Communication is the activity aimed at exchanging information among persons. Production is the central activity of shared editors, it is composed of all the actions that aim at building a common artifact. Coordination is the activity that deals with resource allocation and dependencies between users' tasks.

Using the Clover model, a distinction between three types of groupware systems appears. Mediaspaces, video and telephone applications are centred around communication, provide little coordination support and have no production component. Shared editors are centred around production, have a strong coordination component, and provide little communication. Finally, a few systems integrate shared data editing and communication channels (Buxton, 1992). Their communication and production components are both strong, while their coordination component is variable. For example, Clearboard merges a video connection and a shared drawing tool by superposing them on the same screen with a transparent overlay technique (Ishii & Kobayashi, 1992).

2.2 Coordination Protocols

When people produce documents or other artifacts in common, they coordinate their actions with each other. They apply coordination *protocols* for that purpose. Anyway, the introduction of groupware systems modifies the nature of these protocols. Most shared editors provide functions that impose new coordination protocols on users. For instance turn-taking is a simple protocol that prevents two persons from modifying the same piece of data at the same time. Unlike their real-world equivalent, when users are next to each other and do not need groupware assistance, these mechanisms are more rigid and more formalized. Sometimes they are even modelled after data consistency algorithms. The resulting protocols are more adapted to computers than to users. Their abstract concepts need to be translated into notions that can be manipulated by users, usually through software layers and user interfaces. This leads to paradoxical situations where users have to coordinate themselves through multiple computer layers, and thus interact with each other by manipulating the concepts of the computer instead of their own human concepts.

A consequence of such designs is to induce extra manipulation costs for users to get access to the protocol management layer. For instance, shared drawing tools allow multiple users to manipulate the same drawing. In order to protect graphical objects from parallel modifications, they provide handles or even a lock button that can be added to an object to gain property rights on it. Similar mechanisms can be found in conferencing systems where floor control policies are used to designate a floor-holder who is allowed to manipulate the shared windows. In the same way, role attribution is another coordination protocol that requires explicit manipulation from users. All these manipulations can distract users from their main goal.

In addition to manipulation costs, designing the computer as an intermediate leads to coordinations that are much poorer than their natural equivalent. Our introductory example from ATC illustrates such losses. As short as they may be, conversations between controllers are negotiations, in which voice intonations or hesitations may be very meaningful. These extra messages convey social meaning, like stress, or availability. They allow controllers to adapt their strategy, for instance by making counter proposals if they think their colleague can manage, or by simplifying his task if they perceive a serious problem, thus improving security. Replacing them with dialogue boxes eliminates that wealth of additional information. One can thus wonder if generalizing the use of computer protocols is always necessary, or if human natural protocols should be used instead when explicit coordination is not needed.

3   Coordination without CSCW

When people do not use groupware tools, they use their own coordination policies based on their social skills. A quick review of these skills suggests new ways for supporting coordination.

3.1   Implicit Coordination Protocols

In the physical world, we also use coordination policies: we take turns when talking and avoid collisions when walking on a crowded pavement. At a more sophisticated level, we use coordination policies that we call social rules, like politeness or honesty. These rules may be very subtle. For instance, politeness often requires innocent lies. A very innocuous example consists in not answering your phone when you are busy talking with someone. At the opposite, efficiency or security sometimes requires impoliteness: when urgent attention is requested, we do not hesitate to break into conversations. Such examples show how hard it is to formalize coordination policies, and what kind of losses formalization can bring. Conversely, it is true that we sometimes refer our actions to explicit protocols that are comparable to computer protocols. But this is limited to specific situations such as testifying in court or signing a contract. In most situations, we use our 'natural' social skills. We call them *implicit protocols*.

Some of those implicit protocols are supported by the communication space. Studies on turn taking in face to face meetings have shown that eye gaze is a clue used to distribute speaking time among participants. In the same way, voice intonation or body movements also contribute to the coordination. This suggests that in real life, *communication cannot be dissociated from coordination*.

3.2   Coordination Objects

When communication is not sufficient to ensure an implicit coordination of people's activities, the set of objects present in the environment can suggest some implicit protocols. Most objects have a social signification and support complex social rules. For instance, you know that you must not search the drawers of your office-mate, except if she or he is out of town and gives you a phone call asking to do so. Like drawers, many objects support social rules, but impose them only up to a point. We call them *coordination objects*.

Unlike their electronic counterparts, such as lock handles, coordination objects are not dedicated only to coordination. They belong to the production space and share the same characteristics as the artifacts produced in common. They can be exchanged between people.

They can also represent abstract notions. For example a key can be seen as an access right. In the same way, a hand set during a phone conversation can be seen as an 'half-communication' which can be given to a third person. Objects and their manipulation are the real world equivalent of the production space in computer applications. This suggests that in the real world *production cannot be dissociated from coordination*.

4   Direct Collaboration

The previous intuitive analysis of coordination suggests that coordination needs not to be explicit to be efficient. It even appears that implicit coordination can be very effective and flexible when adequate support is offered by the communication and production components. This is what we call direct collaboration. *A direct collaboration system is a collaborative system in which coordination between users is supported by communication and production tools, and not by dedicated coordination tools.*

Direct collaboration can be compared with direct manipulation (Shneiderman, 1983). The latter was introduced when most applications provided command languages that users had to master in order to interact with their data. Command languages acted as an intermediate between users and tasks, like coordination protocols do between users. They introduced manipulation costs in the same way. Direct manipulation was introduced as an incentive to eliminate that intermediate. It was associated with requirements such as the continuous presentation of the objects of interest, with immediate feedback for actions.

Direct collaboration suggests that explicit coordination in groupware systems be replaced with adequate communication and production, which would then play the same role as presentation and actions in direct manipulation. In both cases, the computer has to be a medium rather than an intermediate. In direct manipulation, it is a medium between a user and virtual objects. In direct collaboration, it is a medium between users, with virtual objects as part of the medium as physical objects are part of our environment.

Even the limitations of direct collaboration can be compared to those of direct manipulation. In single-user interfaces it is sometimes necessary to constrain the user to a limited choice of actions, because a strict procedure has to be followed. In groupware systems, this corresponds to the situations when rigid protocols are necessary and cannot be ensured through implicit social rules.

5 Design Rules

Direct collaboration appears as a fertile support for analysing groupware. But can direct collaboration systems be really designed, and how? In order to use people's natural skills for implicit coordination, a groupware application should not filter out the clues on which they base that implicit coordination. We have defined three rules that can be applied to design systems featuring a more direct collaboration between people.

5.1 Integrating Communication Media

Communication channels whether natural (e.g. voice) or electronic (e.g. a connection between shared windows or a telepointer connection) are not always easy to access in the interface. When switching a task from foreground to background attention, it is often desirable that media are more integrated so that the groupware system can manage them and avoid extra manipulation costs. For instance such manipulations are required to send a fax during a phone conversation, when a single phone line is available. This implies at least five different steps: decide who will call back, hang up, dial the fax number, send the fax, then make a phone call again. It could be avoided with multiplexed voice and data.

The definition of a session in a groupware system involves the same kind of manipulations. The definition of a session is sometimes required to be able to connect together shared applications. Only then, the documents of interest can be imported into the session, through the selection of the session among the list of available sessions. Another solution would be to start the session directly from the document or to have an icon representing the session and to drop it onto a document to share it.

Natural communication channels, especially when their manipulation cost is negligible according to the task, provide effective coordination support. For example, informal observation of war-game players who have concluded an alliance, but play in different rooms, indicates that a voice link is better than a chat box to communicate information and coordinate actions. Giving a phone call implies a manipulation cost that is negligible for game players. However, in another situation, this would be perceived as a disruption in the task. The prototype described in Section 7 shows how to integrate phone calls with other objects from the production space.

5.2 Integrating Activities

During collaboration, background and foreground activities are run at different paces, and from time to time they are synchronized or interchanged. These synchronizations are natural coordination points, as they integrate threads of activity into one main stream of collaboration. To avoid unintended disruptions of a task, groupware systems can manage pending tasks and let the choice of when to collaborate to the users.

In media-spaces, permanent video links between different places help people to find appropriate times to get each other's attention, and to switch collaboration from a background activity to a foreground activity. When two persons can see they are both present, with the help of a media-space, they can decide to start a desktop video-conference, launching extra applications like a shared drawing tools if necessary. The media-space interface can be used to leave information accessible when a person is not available, like calendar browsing, e-mail, or notes to leave them a message (Tang & Rua, 1994). Likewise, a coordination object can be left on somebody's workspace to remind her or him of doing something with no interruption of the current activity. For example a shared workspace can be associated with each user and receive objects representing pending requests such as a 'phone call' button.

5.3 Production Space as a Medium

The two rules described above have sometimes been addressed by previous literature. They mainly correspond to an improvement of communication channels. But groupware also provides us with another communication channel: the production space, in which digital objects are being exchanged and manipulated. The production space can be used as a channel for conveying social hints in the same way as traditional communication channels. This is possible by introducing interaction styles that support prosody in the same way as voice intonation or gestures accompany oral communications, thus reinforcing coordination hints.

Whether working in a real or digital setting, users fill their environment with the objects they produce or manipulate during their activity: documents, pens, or other artifacts. These objects easily become part of the communication space when they are referred to in a discussion: "Give me this paper, please". They can also become part of the coordination space when one manipulates or displaces them. Seeing what happens and how it is done provides information about how to react: depending on how far and how quietly a document is pushed into your private space, you will stop what you are currently doing or not. As cartoon animation shows: objects and their manipulation can indeed carry a form of prosody, just like voice carries prosody.

In Bentley et al. (1992), the observation of air traffic controllers shows that physical manipulations of paper strips representing aircraft routes convey information to controllers working side by side. Coordination objects, where, when and how they are manipulated and the standard social rules combine to suggest implicit protocols.

6   Object Exchange

To explore how objects from the production space can be integrated into the coordination space, we have developed several experimental prototypes. We designed them so that they convey implicit coordination cues for their users.   We call them *Transfolders*, a contraction of two words: transmission and folder.

6.1   Transfolders

Any graphical object like an icon is a potential coordination object. By moving it in someone's space, it can be used for catching her or his attention. If that space is filled with other objects, representing communication channels for example, they can be used to start communications.   For instance, URL objects could be dropped onto a URL viewer object to open a window showing that URL onto someone else's screen.   Many transmission protocols, like email or remote folders, do not provide any information about the moment at which the document or the message transmitted is accessed. We defined transfolders so that they provide that feedback.

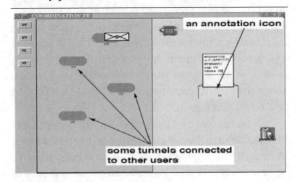

Figure 2:   A shared transfolder for an ATC research prototype.

A *tunnel* is a replicated place in an interface. Each replica is an end of the tunnel and can be located in different users' applications. When a user drags an object onto a tunnel end, that object becomes visible to any user looking at the tunnel end. When a user removes an object from a tunnel end, that object

disappears from every visible end of the tunnel. To enforce that feedback, the object cannot be used as long as it is visible inside a tunnel.   The left part of Figure 2 shows four grey holes which are tunnels connecting a user with four other users so that they can exchange annotations, represented by an envelope icon.

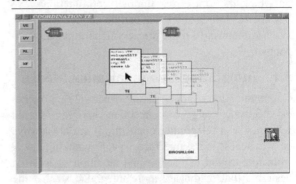

Figure 3:   A transfolder connected to another one, side by side.

A *shared transfolder* is a replicated workspace in an interface. Anyway, by convention it is associated with one user and represents a personal space. Actions occurring inside a shared transfolder are replicated when at least two shared transfolders are connected together. To access a user's shared transfolder, one needs to connect his or her own transfolder with that user's transfolder, as shown on Figure 3. Then they can exchange and manipulate their objects, and disconnect their shared transfolders when terminated (their transfolder then looks like Figure 2, with the tunnels on the left side).   Section 7.2 describes our application of transfolders to ATC. In this prototype, we have not implemented URL and URL viewer objects, but we use a phone object in quite the same way. Dropping an annotation on the phone icon gives a phone call to the owner of the icon.

6.2   Transfolders and Shared Workspaces

Like shared workspaces, shared transfolders are persistent stores for the objects they contain. They can be used either in synchronous (more than one person at a time) or asynchronous mode (different persons at different times). But they differ from shared workspaces on a few points:

- They are limited to a small portion of screen space as they are more oriented towards document exchange than towards in-place edition of shared documents. Thus workspace navigation is reduced to the connection to the transfolder of another user, and not to the synchronization of user's view (to maintain the What You See Is What I See property).

- Access control is made simple as edition of objects occurs in the user's personal space and not inside a shared space. Shared objects are replaced by mobile objects exchanged between users.

- Connections between shared transfolders are 'lateral'. In our prototype, each shared transfolder represents a different place. When connected together, these places are just aligned border to border so that an object can be dragged from one to another.

When accessing a user's shared transfolder is intrusive (for example if the transfolder contains personal annotations), a second public transfolder can be used instead. That public transfolder is visible to everybody and acts as a repository for messages between all the group members. For example in a computer-supported meeting room, Courtyard uses a large display common to all users (Tani et al., 1994). A 'lateral' connection between the border of each user's private display and the main display allow them to exchange objects.

Tunnels are limited to object exchange. They increase the visibility of the transmission in a way similar to the Pick-And-Drop metaphor (Rekimoto, 1997). With the Pick-And-Drop metaphor, the tunnel is replaced by a stylus (a physical device) which holds the data until it is dropped onto a screen sensitive to the stylus.

7 Example Application

As we explained in the introduction of this article, our aim is to improve the collaboration tools used by air traffic controllers. In order to avoid the limitations of the dialogue box shown in Figure 1, we propose tools that improve the temporal efficiency of collaborations without degrading their flexibility and their support for traditional social policies.

We took a two-step approach based on the design rules described in Section 5. The first step was to propose a compromise between an improved efficiency and the preservation of the directness of collaboration. The first prototype described below proposes the integration of a voice link with an ATC workstation. In the second step, we applied the integration of activities rule. This required the definition of new ATC objects that could serve as coordination objects. These objects have been integrated in the workspace of controllers through a transfolder metaphor. Following the third rule, the next step will consist in further developing the role of the computer as a medium by using the manipulation of these objects as a support for implicit coordination.

7.1 Integrating Media: DuoPhone

As explained above, in order to keep the role of phone calls as a support for collaboration, our first step was to add communication capabilities to a prototype ATC workstation. For that purpose we used Grigri, a gesture-based prototype of ATC workstation developed at CENA (Chatty & Lecoanet, 1996) and extended it with our DuoPhone communication software. We called the resulting prototype GriPhone. Figure 4 shows the physical layout of GriPhone.

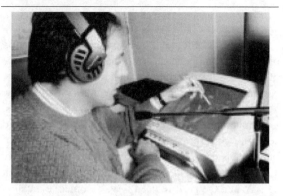

Figure 4: GriPhone: a telephone link controlled through the same interface as the ATC functions.

For our voice channel, we used the ISDN capability of the Sun SPARCstation 10, managed through our dedicated software layer DuoPhone. This allowed us to use a high quality voice link (digital telephone), with no constraints on the computer network. This is also important for backward compatibility with traditional communication channels: with DuoPhone, a controller can call any control room in the world. DuoPhone, developed at CENA in 1994, works as a server. It manages the ISDN link of the workstation, and allows client applications to give, answer, and transfer calls, connect the microphone and loudspeaker of the workstation to the phone link. It also allows them to subscribe to events such as incoming calls or disconnections. DuoPhone also monitors the telephone or any device connected to the same ISDN outlet, so that end users may freely choose between their favorite device: telephone handset or computer microphone and loudspeaker. Finally, DuoPhone allows applications to manipulate the facilities offered by ISDN: caller ID and messages. Therefore, when an application gives a call, it can decide to send a short text message with the call. If the recipient of the call is another computer running

DuoPhone, client applications are informed of the origin of the call and the contents of the message, and thus can decide how to handle or display the call.

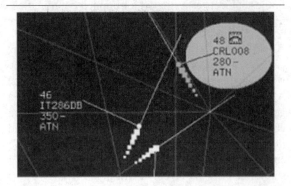

Figure 5: Someone is calling about aircraft CRL008.

Using DuoPhone allowed a seamless integration of voice communications into the main user interface of our ATC workstation. In the case of GriPhone, we just had to enrich the gesture library with a new gesture for giving phone calls. Upon such gestures, GriPhone just needs to decide whom to call, and send the corresponding request. This integration of phone calls into the graphical interface becomes really significant when using the message associated to each call. When the gesture used to give someone a call is drawn on the representation of an aircraft, GriPhone interprets it as a call related to that precise aircraft. It thus passes the ID of the aircraft along with the call. Therefore, the other GriPhone workstation that receives the call knows which aircraft is concerned, and can display it (see Figure 5). As the call is displayed next to the relevant aircraft, controllers can start the phone conversation without using the voice link for locating the aircraft that caused the call.

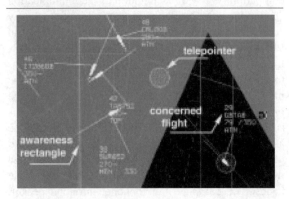

Figure 6: A communication between sectors.

Once voice communications are smoothly integrated into the system and calls are initiated from the display, further uses of the display as a communication channel become natural. We chose two services responding to a request from controllers to improve mutual awareness. The first service is a rectangle that shows what part of the display is seen by the other controller (see Figure 6). This helps controllers to understand what their counterpart knows. The second service is a telepointer, adapted to the use of touch-screens. The telepointer is represented as a coloured disk. Each controller has a different telepointer and can move it on both screens with a finger. With those services, GriPhone becomes a communication channel, through which users can talk and show things to each other. Shared sessions initiated from a phone call do not disrupt controllers from their main activity, which is centred around the radar display.

GriPhone has been informally presented to more than 20 air traffic controllers. As a large majority of them reported us their enthusiasm about the integration of communication media and the comfort it would bring them, we asked an evaluation of a similar prototype to another team. That formal evaluation, not described here, indicates an improvement of 17% in the time taken for a coordination using the phone when the incoming phone call is shown by an icon next to the relevant aircraft instead of not displaying any information about the relevant plane. This evaluation is described in (Karsenty & Pecaut, 1998).

7.2   Coordination Objects for ATC

As mentioned above, we believe that voice communications, because of their flexibility, are important to security and efficiency of communication. However, the number of phone calls is sometimes perceived as too large, and many air traffic controllers ask that routine phone calls be eliminated.

For that purpose, our second step was to define coordination objects. We chose to introduce objects that controllers can exchange through transfolders to integrate theirs activities. In addition to being perceived as a 'physical' support for coordination, such objects also had to be relevant to the task of individual controllers. We analysed the ATC activity from that specific point of view, compared collaborations in different European ATC systems, and identified potential candidate objects at three levels of abstraction:

- Aircraft are the most obvious objects referred to in dialogues. However, controllers mention aircraft or point at their representation, but do not exchange them.

- Flight plans, or more generally contracts with pilots, are more abstract but more pertinent: controllers read them and are notified of changes in the contracts.

- The most pertinent objects are alterations of contracts, such as clearances. Even though these objects have no concrete existence as of today, they are well understood by controllers and essential to their activity.

Most manipulation tasks performed by air traffic controllers can be reinterpreted as manipulation of contract alterations, and collaboration tasks as their exchange:

- Taking notes after giving an instruction to a pilot creates and archives an alteration.

- Preparing an instruction creates a draft alteration.

- Presenting a choice or a proposal to another controller consists in transmitting a draft alteration, that can be confirmed, modified and sent back, or built together.

This suggests some designs for creating, editing and exchanging alterations. For instance, the dialogue box of Figure 1 is a possible design for exchanging a flight level alteration. But applying direct collaboration metaphors we described, alterations can also be made first class visible objects. This is what we did, by giving a representation to contract alterations and using transfolders to exchange them (see Figures 2 & 3).

7.3 Production Space as a Medium

With this design based on transfolders and icons, controllers will be able to choose their coordination styles, and even their degree of synchronization. Dropping an alteration in a remote corner of the working area will probably mean a low need for synchronization, while one dropped next to the phone icon in the transfolder will be interpreted as a request for a phone call. We hope to observe emerging working conventions, which would give us hints that we provided controllers with a new medium they can tailor to their needs.

Bentley & Dourish (1995) discuss the idea of supporting collaboration vs. providing coordination mechanisms embedded in the heart of the system. They propose to provide a medium through different levels of customization. Each level, from parametrization of interface and of deeper system features to attachment of scripts to system events,

allows users to invent new protocols. Our approach is different because, unlike customization, which needs to be expressed in a form understandable by the system, prosody needs not be understood by the system. Prosody just needs to be carried by the system, its interpretation being left to users. Creating that sort of systems requires enriched feedback and a better control of users on actions and their transmission.

8 Conclusion

In this article we have outlined a potential problem of groupware systems that impose rigid coordination protocols on users and prevent them from applying their social skills for implicit coordination. As a consequence the computer is perceived as an intermediate rather than a truly collaborative medium. We introduce the notion of direct collaboration interfaces, focusing the design of interfaces around rules that could lead to a better integration of collaborative activities with other activities. As in the physical world, this integration can be improved by manipulation of adequate coordination objects. Once identified and implemented into the system, these objects can be used to integrate communication channels so that people can start collaborations directly from the relevant objects with a minimum number of manipulations. They can be used to integrate activities so that people can start their collaborations at the best time according to their activities. The manipulation and the circulation of coordination objects can support the exchange of implicit coordination clues, thus increasing the ability of the production space to be a medium. To demonstrate the feasibility of direct collaboration interfaces, we have presented some prototypes and metaphors we are applying to ATC workstations. Beyond ATC, we expect that many other domains will benefit from the same design rules.

Acknowledgements

We would like to thank the persons who have contributed to GriPhone: Patrick Lecoanet, Frédéric Lepied, Jean-Luc Dubocq.

References

Bentley, R. & Dourish, P. (1995), Medium Versus Mechanism: Supporting Collaboration through Customization, *in* H. Marmolin, Y. Sundblad & K. Schmidt (eds.), *Proceedings of ECSCW'95, the 4th European Conference on Computer-Supported Cooperative Work*, Kluwer, pp.143–8.

Bentley, R., Hughes, J., Randall, D., Rodden, T., Sawyer, P., Shapiro, D. & Sommerville, I. (1992), Ethnographically-informed Systems Design for Air Traffic Control, *in* J. Turner & R. Kraut (eds.), *Proceedings of CSCW'92: Conference on Computer Supported Cooperative Work*, ACM Press, pp.123–9.

Buxton, W. A. S. (1992), Telepresence: Integrating Shared Task and Person Spaces, *in Proceedings of Graphics Interface '92*, Morgan-Kaufmann, pp.123–9.

Calvary, G., Coutaz, J. & Nigay, L. (1997), From Single-user Architectural Design to PAC*: A Generic Software Architecture Model for CSCW, *in* S. Pemberton (ed.), *Proceedings of CHI'97: Human Factors in Computing Systems*, ACM Press, pp.242–9.

Chatty, S. & Lecoanet, P. (1996), A Pen-based Workstation for Air Traffic Controllers, *in* G. van der Veer & B. Nardi (eds.), *Proceedings of CHI'96: Human Factors in Computing Systems*, ACM Press, pp.87–94.

Ishii, H. & Kobayashi, M. (1992), Integration of Inter-personal Space and Shared Workspace: Clearboard Design and Experiments, *in* J. Turner & R. Kraut (eds.), *Proceedings of CSCW'92: Conference on Computer Supported Cooperative Work*, ACM Press, pp.32–42.

Karsenty, L. & Pecaut, I. (1998), Évaluation d'un Collecticiel D'aide aux Coordinations dans le Contrôle aérien, Technical Report NR98–798, Centre d'Études de la Navigation Aérienne.

Rekimoto, J. (1997), Pick-And-Drop: A Direct Manipulation Technique for Multiple Computer Environments, *in* D. Fay (ed.), *Proceedings of the ACM Symposium on User Interface Software and Technology, UIST'97*, ACM Press, pp.31–9.

Shneiderman, B. (1983), "Direct Manipulation: A Step beyond Programming Languages", *IEEE Computer* **16**, 57–69.

Tang, J. C. & Rua, M. (1994), Montage: Providing Teleproximity for Distributed Groups, *in* B. Adelson, S. Dumais & J. Olson (eds.), *Proceedings of CHI'94: Human Factors in Computing Systems*, ACM Press, pp.37–43.

Tani, M., Horita, M., Yamaashi, K., Tanikoshi, K. & Futakawa, M. (1994), Courtyard: Integrating Shared Overview on a Large Screen and Per-user Detail on Individual Screens, *in* B. Adelson, S. Dumais & J. Olson (eds.), *Proceedings of CHI'94: Human Factors in Computing Systems*, ACM Press, pp.44–50.

Human–Computer Interaction — INTERACT '99
M. Angela Sasse and Chris Johnson (Editors)
Published by IOS Press, © IFIP TC.13, 1999

Multi-mediating Multi-party Interactions

A.H. Anderson, J. Mullin, E. Katsavras, R. McEwan, E. Grattan, P. Brundell[1] & C. O'Malley[1]

University of Glasgow, Glasgow G12 8QQ, UK.
[1] University of Nottingham, Nottingham NG7 2RD, UK.
anne@mcg.gla.ac.uk

Abstract: Multimedia communications technologies are predicted to have a major impact over the next few years. In a carefully designed experimental study, we explored how users of such systems perform in remote problem solving collaborations supported by video links over high bandwidth networks. We compared the task performances and communications of users to investigate how three-party multi-mediated interactions differ from two-party and how these multi-mediated interactions differ from similar face-to-face interactions. The results were generally very encouraging: tasks were successfully completed equally well in all conditions. More interactive work, that is, more words were needed, to complete the tasks in 3-party interactions, whether face-to-face or mediated. The only feature of our analysis which showed specific difficulties for 3-party mediated interactions was turn taking: more interruptions occur in 3-party mediated interactions.

Keywords: multimedia, video-conferencing, CSCW, communication, high bandwidth networks.

1 Introduction

Multimedia communications technologies are predicted to have a major impact. Two rather different forms of multimedia communications are becoming popular: video-conferencing, traditionally in the form of specialist video meeting rooms designed to support distributed group meetings and desktop video-conferencing tools which allow person-to-person conferencing usually with additional shared software applications.

In many commercial settings, much work which would benefit from this latter form of richer information technology support using shared software applications, involves collaborations among two or more colleagues. Yet we know rather little about the nature of such multi-party interactions or how they are affected by the introduction of support by computers and communications technology.

There are several published studies in the literature which explore the impact of various forms of multimedia computer supported collaborative work (CSCW), for example O'Conaill et al. (1993), Sellen (1995), Olson et al. (1995), Isaacs & Tang (1997).

Such studies have mainly focused on the effects of different forms of communications technologies on groups, such as higher or lower quality video-conference links or differently configured video communications systems.

Few studies have compared the nature of interaction in two party and multi-party interaction, though the work of Clark and his colleagues has indicated that the process of establishing mutual understanding or 'common ground' might be significantly more difficult in three party interactions compared to two, (Schober & Clarkg, 1989; Wilkes-Gibbs & Clark, 1992). There has also been a substantial research tradition in social psychology studying patterns of interaction in small groups, e.g. (Dabbs & Ruback, 1987).

From earlier studies of mediated dyads and small groups (Olson et al., 1995; Doherty-Sneddon et al., 1997) we might expect that mediated interactions even if supported by high quality video conference links, would require lengthier interactions to accomplish collaborative tasks than equivalent face-to-face interactions would. In our study we aim to unpack the relative impacts of the number of collaborators and the use of multimedia technologies.

In the longer term we hope that this research will have relevance to the use of such technologies in real tasks at work or in education. To this end we wished to test the effects of high quality video-conference links delivered over high bandwidth digital networks supporting genuinely remote collaborators. Most previous studies of high quality video links have not had the opportunity to test the effects on users of services delivered over commercially available digital networks.

Despite our interest in real applications, in this study we used a standard collaborative problem-solving task. Although this sacrifices some degree of face validity there are considerable benefits in that we can make careful and controlled comparisons of the effects of our variables of interest. We chose a collaborative problem solving task, The Map Task (Brown et al., 1984) which we have used in earlier studies, e.g. (Anderson et al., 1997; Doherty-Sneddon et al., 1997). This provides an objective measure of task outcome and allows many detailed analyses of the associated dialogues which can be directly compared across a large number of different speakers. The task has also been found to be sensitive to the effects of communicative medium. This kind of multifaceted approach to evaluating the impacts of IT technologies has been advocated by several researchers, e.g. (Monk et al., 1996).

In this paper we will use data on task performance combined with analysis of the communication process to address the following questions:

- How do three party multi-mediated interactions differ from two?

- How do these multi-party multi-mediated interactions differ from similar face-to-face interactions?

2 Method

2.1 Participants

The participants in the study were 148 university students recruited and paid £5 for taking part. For the mediated conditions of the study, participants were recruited at both the Glasgow and Nottingham Universities. For the face-to-face condition all were from Glasgow University.

2.2 Design

Due to the need to configure the computers differently for the video mediated communications (VMC) conditions of the study, participants were assigned on a week by week basis to the 2 party VMC, 3 party VMC or 3 party face-to-face conditions. Each participant took part in two versions of the Map Task. In two party conditions participants swapped between the instruction giver (IG) and the instruction follower (IF)

role, on trials one and two. In three party tasks, two of the participants swapped between instruction giver and instruction follower roles, while one participant remained an instruction giver on both trials.

All participants were unfamiliar to one another before the start of the trials. Forty-six sessions were run in the 2 party VMC condition, 36 sessions in the 3 party VMC condition and 32 sessions in the 3 party face-to-face condition. Subjects were randomly assigned on their first task to the instruction giver or instruction follower roles. All the interactions were tape recorded and subsequently transcribed and checked.

2.3 Task

The task used in this study was the Map Task (Brown et al., 1984). This is a collaborative problem-solving task which elicits spontaneous yet comparable dialogues from different speakers. In this study two different versions of the Map Task were used. Participants each have access to a copy of a schematic map, either on screen or on paper. The maps both/all show a start point and a number of named landmark features. Some of these features are identical on each participant's map, whilst some differ. The number of landmarks and the number of discrepant features are the same in both map tasks. The task is illustrated in Figure 1.

The instructions giver(s) map also shows a route. In three party versions of the task both instruction givers have the identical route but again some of the landmark features differ between their copies of the map. The object of the task is for the instruction giver(s) to communicate how to complete this route to the instruction follower.

2.4 Procedure

Face-to-Face conditions: In the 3 party face-to-face conditions, participants sat at different sides of a table, with low screens placed between them to prevent them from seeing one another's maps, to ensure that communication had to take place verbally as in the VMC conditions. Participants' faces were fully visible to one another and paper maps were used.

Video Mediated Conditions: In the VMC conditions all the participants, who were novices at video-conferencing, were shown how the camera captured and relayed their images and were shown how to use the mouse to draw the route on screen. Participants were reminded that the other (or one of the other) participants was at a remote site (approximately 300 miles away).

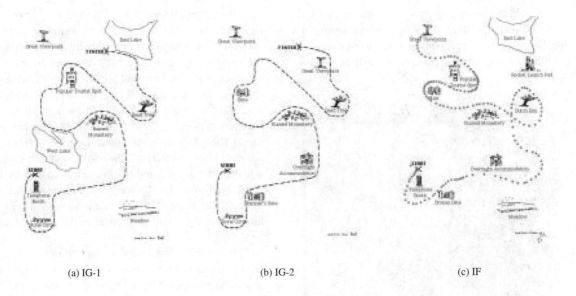

(a) IG-1   (b) IG-2   (c) IF

Figure 1: Examples of Task in 3 Party Conditions: Maps of Instruction Giver 1 (IG-1), Instruction Giver 2 (IG-2) and Instruction Follower (IF).

2.5 Instructions to Subjects

For the video mediated conditions the instructions for the participant who was an instruction giver in Task 1 and an instruction follower in Task 2 were as follows: (additional instructions for the 3 party condition are shown in brackets). Participants who were first instruction followers were given the same instructions in reverse order. Participants in the face-to-face conditions were given the same instructions, omitting mention of the video link:

> "Your map was drawn by an explorer to provide a route to some buried treasure at the finish point. (Your partner also has a map with a route drawn on it. The routes on both your maps are exactly the same. However, the maps were drawn by different explorers thus some of the landmarks may differ.)
>
> Your task is to explain to another person (the third party) as accurately and fast as possible, the route shown on your map.
>
> The other person (third party) has a map similar to yours but with no route drawn on it. Their map was also drawn by a different explorer so some of the landmarks may vary.
>
> Once you have completed this task you will then be given a different map that will

> not have a route drawn on it. (Two other people) Someone will explain the route to you and your task is to draw the route on the map, the same regulations as above apply (i.e. some landmarks may differ). The path does not have to be drawn as a continuous line, a dotted path is equally as good.
>
> These tasks will take place across a video link with all three of you at different sites. If you wish to make eye contact with another person, look directly into the camera."

2.6 Equipment

Each participant in the VMC conditions sat at a Sun Ultra workstation with 21″ colour monitor which displayed an image of the map (160mm × 200mm, 6.3″ × 7.85″) and video window(s) of the other participant(s). At each workstation, a JVC GR-AX60 camcorder was trained on the local participant, sourcing PAL video of 768 × 576 pixels at 25fps. These images were input via SunVideo board to the participant's workstation where the images were processed and sent across a data network to be displayed to the other participant(s).

Sun's rtvc_video_conference software was used to process and send video images across the network to the other workstation(s). The resolution of the video images was reduced to 384 × 288 pixels and the video stream compressed using Sun's CellB compression algorithm.   After transmission the decoded images were displayed on the screen(s) of the other participant(s) in an area of 107mm × 80mm (4.2″ × 3.15″).

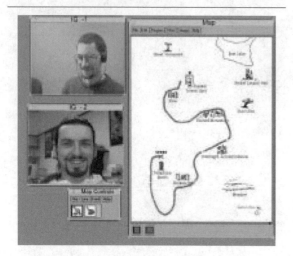

Figure 2: Illustration of the Instruction Follower's screen display in 3 party VMC condition.

In the 2 party VMC condition each participant viewed an image of the other participant. In the 3 party VMC condition the instruction follower viewed images of both instruction givers, while the instruction givers only viewed an image of the instruction follower. An example of the screen layout for the instruction follower in the 3 party condition is shown in Figure 2.

A high bandwidth network — Asynchronous Transfer Mode (ATM) — directly connected the workstations using IP over ATM. Connections between Glasgow and Nottingham were made via the SuperJANET ATM network, within which a PVC of 34Mbps peak rate and 12Mbps bi-directional sustained rate was reserved for the experimental trials. Round trip time on this network was around 14ms. Delivery of video images from the transmitting workstation to the receiving workstation averaged over 24.9fps in every session with very little variability.

Delivery of audio across the network in the 2 party VMC condition was made using 'vat' software (*www-nrg.ee.lbl.gov/vat*). In the three-participant task vat had to be abandoned due to technical problems with multi-cast IP packets on the ATM network switches. Instead, it was decided to adopt 'nevot' (*www.fokus.gmd.de/step/nevot*).   For both vat and nevot, audio format was PCM, 8KHz sampling, 20ms frames. A psychophysics experiment was run in order check that there were no perceptual differences in audio quality between vat and nevot.

We recorded conversational speech and extracted short samples (average length 4sec) from four different speakers, and relayed these through vat and nevot, on the same equipment to be used in the main study. A stimulus tape of 64 pairs of speech samples, with half the pairs being relayed through the same audio tool and half through a different tool was compiled. Six listeners then took part in a small psychophysics study rating the pairs as identical or different. When the subjects chose 'different', they were asked to indicate whether the audio quality was better in the first or second sample. The listeners were unable to reliably discriminate between the two audio tools — producing almost exactly chance responses in the discrimination task.

From this pilot study we felt confident that the audio quality delivered to end users in the main study would be unaffected by the necessity of using different audio tools in the two VMC conditions.

3   Results

3.1   Analysis of Task Performance

To assess how well each task had been completed, the map drawn by the instruction follower was compared to the original being described by the instruction giver(s). For mediated conditions the screen based maps were printed out and enlarged to be the same size as the paper maps used in the face-to-face condition (A3 sized paper: 297mm × 420mm). The area of deviation between the two routes was calculated by overlaying the two copies of the maps on a squared grid and counting the number of square centimetres in the area of difference between the two routes. These deviation scores are used as the performance measure, with high deviation scores indicating less successful performances.

Deviation scores were used to compare performance in the task conditions and submitted to a 2 (Trial 1 vs. Trial 2) × 3 (Condition: 3 Party Face-to-Face, 3 Party VMC, 2 Party VMC) Mixed Analysis of Variance (ANOVA), with Condition as a between subjects variable and Trial as a within subjects repeated measure. This analysis showed only a significant difference in the overall scores for trials one and two, with a significant improvement in scores on the second task. No other significant main effects or interactions were found.

Overall task performance does not differ significantly in two or three party mediated interactions and these do not differ from those achieved in three party face-to-face interactions. Table 1 shows these data, with higher deviation scores indicating *less* accurately completed Maps.

3 Party Face-to-Face	62.9	(MSE=7.1)
3 Party VMC	49.0	(MSE=6.7)
2 Party VMC	60.1	(MSE=6.0)

Table 1: Mean map performance scores (area of deviation from original route in cm. sq.).

3.2 Communication Analyses

To explore the interactions among participants a number of analyses were conducted. First the overall lengths of the dialogues were examined and the number of words spoken in each dialogue was totalled. These data were subjected to a 2 (Trial 1 vs. Trial 2) × 3 (Condition:3 Party Face-to-Face, 3 Party VMC, 2 Party VMC) Mixed ANOVA, with Condition as a between subjects variable and Trial as a within subjects repeated measure.

This analysis showed only a significant main effect of Condition, ($F(2,54) = 3.27, p < 0.05$). Post hoc tests showed that 2 party VMC dialogues were significantly shorter ($ps < 0.01$) than those in either of the 3 party conditions which did not differ. The effect of Trial and the Trial × Condition interaction were not significant ($Fs < 1$). The mean numbers of words spoken are shown in Table 2.

3 Party Face-to-Face	1649.5	(MSE=186.4)
3 Party VMC	1759.5	(MSE=175.7)
2 Party VMC	1199.6	(MSE=155.5)

Table 2: Mean number of words spoken per dialogue by condition.

It seems to take more interactive work to achieve task success in three party interactions but mediation does not seem to have a significant impact.

The possible impacts of the number of participants and the medium of communication was further explored by totalling the number of turns of speaking in each interaction. This analysis showed very similar patterns, with a significant main effect of Condition ($F(2,54) = 3.1, p = 0.05$), and again no significant effect or interaction with Trial ($Fs < 1$). Post hoc tests showed that 2 party VMC dialogues contained significantly fewer turns than 3 party VMC interactions ($p < 0.01$). The difference between 2 party VMC and 3 party face-to-face conditions approached significance ($p = 0.08$). Three-party VMC and face-to-face interactions again did not differ in length. The mean numbers of speaker turns are shown in Table 3.

3 Party Face-to-Face	189.9	(MSE=20.8)
3 Party VMC	224.3	(MSE=15.8)
2 Party VMC	150.7	(MSE=11.9)

Table 3: Mean number of speaker turns per dialogue by condition.

To assess how actively involved all the participants were, in the task in three party interactions, and the possible influence of technological mediation on the way the task talk was distributed among the participants, an ANOVA was conducted on the number of words spoken by each participant (Instructions Givers 1 and 2 and Instruction Follower) in the three party conditions of the experiment.

This 2 (Trial 1 vs. Trial 2) × 3(Role:Instruction Giver 1, Instruction Giver 2, Instruction Follower) × 2(Condition: 3 Party Face-to-Face vs. 3 Party VMC) Mixed ANOVA, with Condition as a between subjects variable, Trial and Role as within subjects repeated measures.

There was a significant main effect of Trial with participants producing more speech during their first trial but there were no significant interactions of map with medium or party. The relative equality of participation of all three participants in the task conditions is illustrated in Table 4.

Instruction Giver 1	519.5	(MSE=53.5)
Instruction Giver 2	577.6	(MSE=48.5)
Instruction Follower	607.2	(MSE=54.3)

Table 4: Mean number of words spoken per dialogue by participant role.

To explore the effects of the number of participants and the medium of communication on how the process of turn taking was managed, the total number of times in each interaction that a speaker was interrupted was calculated. These data were subjected to a 2 (Trial 1 vs. Trial 2) × 3 (Condition:3 Party Face-to-Face, 3 Party VMC, 2 Party VMC) Mixed ANOVA, with Condition as a between subjects variable and Trial as a within subjects repeated measure.

This analysis showed a significant main effect of Condition ($F(2,54) = 16.6, p < 0.001$). Post hoc tests showed that there were significantly more interruptions in 3 party VMC interactions than in either of the other two conditions ($ps < 0.01$) which did not differ. There were no other significant effects. The mean numbers of interruptions in the conditions of the study are shown in Table 5.

3 Party Face-to-Face	27.5	(MSE=5.0)
3 Party VMC	58.0	(MSE=4.7)
2 Party VMC	23.8	(MSE=4.1)

Table 5: Mean number of interruptions per dialogue by condition.

It appears that handling smooth turn taking is considerably more difficult in three party mediated interactions. To check that this finding was not caused by any slight variations in the lengths of the various dialogues, a second analysis was conducted which held the lengths of the dialogues constant and considered the % of turns in each dialogue which contained an interruption. This analysis, of the same design as the previous one, again showed a significant main effect of Condition ($F(2,54) = 21.9, p < 0.001$). Post hoc tests again showed that there was a significantly higher percentage of interrupted turns in 3 party VMC interactions ($ps < 0.01$) than in the other two conditions which did not differ. These data are shown in Table 6.

3 Party Face-to-Face	14.6	(MSE=1.3)
3 Party VMC	25.3	(MSE=1.2)
2 Party VMC	16.4	(MSE=1.0)

Table 6: Mean percentage of interrupted turns per dialogue by condition.

Another feature of turn taking which research has shown can be influenced by the introduction of computer mediation, is the extent to which speakers produce back-channel responses during an interaction. Back-channel responses are those short turns of speech where a speaker says 'mhmm' or some similar sound, where the function is merely to confirm that the speaker is still listening.

The introduction of communications technology has been reported (O'Conaill et al., 1993) to decrease the extent to which such turns are produced as the mediated interactions become more formal. We searched our dialogues for all turns of speech which had been transcribed as back-channels and totalled these by condition. These data were subjected to an ANOVA of the same design as the previous dialogue analyses.

This analysis showed a significant main effect of Condition ($F(2,54) = 3.26, p < 0.05$). No other effects were significant. Post hoc tests on the Condition effect, showed that there were significantly more back-channel responses in 3 party face-to-face interactions than in either of the mediated conditions ($ps < 0.01$) which did not differ. These data are shown in Table 7.

3 Party Face-to-Face	11.8	(MSE=1.8)
3 Party VMC	6.3	(MSE=1.7)
2 Party VMC	6.2	(MSE=1.5)

Table 7: Mean number of back-channels per dialogue by condition.

As in the analysis of interruptions, we checked that this effect was not due to minor variations in the lengths of dialogues by calculating for each dialogue the percentage of turns that consisted of back-channel responses and subjecting these data to an ANOVA. This again showed a significant main effect of Condition ($F2,54 = 5.14, p < 0.01$). No other effects were significant. Post hoc tests showed that there is a significantly higher percentage of back-channel turns in 3 party face-to-face interactions than in either of the mediated conditions ($ps < 0.05$) which do not differ. These data are shown in Table 8.

3 Party Face-to-Face	6.0	(MSE=0.7)
3 Party VMC	2.7	(MSE=0.7)
2 Party VMC	4.2	(MSE=0.6)

Table 8: Mean percentage of back-channel turns per dialogue by condition.

As in other studies, we find that participants are less likely to produce back-channel responses as confirmation of their continued attention in mediated interactions.

Another aspect of interaction, which has previously been reported to show effects of mediation, is the average length of turns of speech (O'Conaill et al., 1993; Sellen, 1995). Longer turns of speech can indicate a less interactive more formal style of communication. To test this in our study we calculated for each interaction the mean length of turns of speech (in words) and subjected these data to an ANOVA of the usual design.

This analysis showed a significant main effect of Condition ($F(2,54) = 4.79, p < 0.02$). No other effects were significant. Post hoc tests showed that the average length of turn was significantly *longer* in 3 party face-to-face interactions than in either of the mediated conditions ($ps < 0.01$) which did not differ. These data are shown in Table 9.

3 Party Face-to-Face	12.1	(MSE=1.1)
3 Party VMC	7.8	(MSE=7.8)
2 Party VMC	8.0	(MSE=0.9)

Table 9: Mean turn length per dialogue by condition.

4   Discussion

In this study we asked how three party mediated interactions differed from those involving only two participants and how these multi-mediated interactions differed from equivalent face-to-face interactions. In terms of task performance the results show that participants can achieve an equally effective outcome in dyads or in groups of three when they use high quality multimedia communications technology. This was achieved using high bandwidth digital technology over a distance of several hundred miles and not a lab based simulation of high quality service. The levels of task performance were as good as those achieved in equivalent co-present face-to-face interactions.

In this study we did not collect data on two party face-to-face interactions. In previous research we have conducted such studies and published data from similar conditions and subject populations (Anderson et al., 1991; Boyle et al., 1994). The performance scores recorded in the present study do not show any detrimental effects of three party mediated interactions. They are at least as good as those we reported in earlier studies of two party face-to-face interactions (mean deviation scores for unfamiliar pairs of 79.3, a higher value and hence a poorer performance, than those reported here).

Unlike studies by Schober & Clarkg (1989), and Wilkes-Gibbs & Clark (1992) which report detrimental effects of being involved in a three party interaction as an overhearer or bystander, our three participants in both face-to-face and video-mediated groups, were all actively and almost equally involved in the task interactions. This led to task outcomes as good as those achieved in two person interactions. The analyses of the dialogues revealed that the interactive effort which participants had to expend to achieve this task success did differ across conditions.

In three party VMC interactions significantly more talk was needed: on average 47% more words and 49% more turns of speaking than in two party VMC interactions. The data clearly indicate however, that it is the complexities of multi-party interaction that seem to produce these lengthier interactions not the addition of technological support. No significant differences were observed in the lengths of three party mediated and face-to-face interactions.

The levels of task performance achieved in the technologically mediated conditions is encouraging for developers and implementers of technologies to support remote collaborative working. Doherty-Sneddon et al. (1997) reported a study using the map task and two person interactions supported by a high quality video link known as 'video tunnels' with life size images which allowed eye-contact between participants. Doherty-Sneddon et al. (1997) found *longer* dialogues were required to achieve the same level of task performance as in face-to-face conditions.

In that paper several possible explanations are offered for this finding. One possibility is that the novelty of the large and life like video tunnel images where the participants could engage in eye contact, elicited much more gazing at the interlocutor than was found in face-to-face interactions. This 'overgazing' may have interfered with speech planning and hence led to longer task dialogues.

The high quality video images used in the present study were considerably smaller than in the Doherty-Sneddon et al. (1997) study and were not configured with mirrors to support eye contact as in the video tunnel apparatus. Although in the present study it was not possible to record and analyse participants' eye gaze, it seems unlikely from the present results that these smaller more conventional video images produced the overgazing and associated interference effects found by Doherty-Sneddon et al. (1997).

Commercial multimedia communication systems generally have to run over digital networks and hence cannot usually support the kind of images relayed in video tunnels. From the results of the present study and that reported by Doherty-Sneddon et al. (1997), this apparent limitation in the quality available to end users, may in fact offer some advantages for remote collaborative working.

We would not claim however that high quality VMC delivers identical communicative experience to taking part in face-to-face interaction. Our participants did seem to communicate somewhat more formally in VMC, producing significantly fewer back-channel responses than in face-to-face interactions. This seemed to be a general effect of mediation as it occurred in both mediated conditions.

The other effect of formality which researchers such as O'Conaill et al. (1993) report for mediated groups, the increase in lengths of turns compared to equivalent face-to-face interactions, was not evident in our data. In contrast the average length of speakers' turns was significantly longer in three party face-to-face interactions. It may be that the highly interactive nature of the Map Task, unlike the formal meetings studied by O'Conaill et al. (1993), protected our participants from this aspect of mediation.

The one feature observed which did characterise multi-party mediated interactions was the way in which turn taking was handled. This difference was not only statistically significant but the number of interruptions in the 3 party VMC condition was more than double that recorded in either of the other conditions. In some of our previous research on lower quality VMC systems we found that a significant rise in the number of interruptions had an associated decline in task outcome, (Anderson et al., 1997). In the present study the difficulty of smoothly managing turn taking does not seem to impact upon overall performance.

From the classic studies of the effects of technologies on communication and collaboration, such as Short & Christie (1976) onwards, researchers have been trying to characterise the features of various technologies and their key impacts on users. In this study we hope we have contributed to this body of knowledge, in particular by testing the extent to which new high bandwidth network technologies can deliver a high quality communicative environment to end users. The results here are broadly encouraging. The challenge for future research is to understand more about the subtle characteristics of multi-party interaction and whether a better understanding of these processes might produce design guidelines for future improvements in communications technologies.

Acknowledgement

This research was supported by a ROPA award from the UK Economic and Social Research Council (R0022250096) to Anderson, Mullin & O'Malley and the authors gratefully acknowledge their support.

References

Anderson, A. H., Bader, M., Bard, E., Boyle, E., Doherty, G., Garrod, S., Isard, S., Kowtko, J., McAllister, J., Sotillo, C., Thompson, H. & Weinart, R. (1991), "The HCRC Map Task Corpus", *Language and Speech* **34**(2), 351–66.

Anderson, A. H., O'Malley, C., Doherty-Sneddon, G., Langton, S., Newlands, A., Mullin, J., Fleming, A. & van der Velden, J. (1997), The Impact of VMC on Collaborative Problem Solving, *in* K. E. Finn, A. J. Sellen & S. B. Wilbur (eds.), *Video-mediated Communication*, Lawrence Erlbaum Associates, pp.133–56.

Boyle, E., Anderson, A. H. & Newlands, A. (1994), "The Effects of Eye Contact on Dialogue and Performance

in a Co-Operative Problem Solving Task", *Language and Speech* **37**(1), 1–20.

Brown, G., Anderson, A. H., Yule, G. & Shillcock, R. (1984), *Teaching Talk*, Cambridge University Press.

Dabbs, J. M. & Ruback, R. B. (1987), "Dimensions of Group Process", *Advances in Experimental Social Psychology* **20**, 123–69.

Doherty-Sneddon, G., Anderson, A. H., O'Malley, C., Langton, S., Garrod, S. & Bruce, V. (1997), "Face-to-Face Interaction and Video Mediated Communication", *Journal of Experimental Psychology:Applied* **3**(2), 105–25.

Isaacs, E. & Tang, J. (1997), Studying Video-based Collaboration in Context: From Small Groups to Large Organisations, *in* K. E. Finn, A. J. Sellen & S. B. Wilbur (eds.), *Video-mediated Communication*, Lawrence Erlbaum Associates, pp.173–98.

Monk, A., McCarthy, J., Watts, L. & Daly-Jones, O. (1996), Measures of Process, *in* M. MacLeod & D. Murray (eds.), *Evaluation for CSCW*, Springer-Verlag, pp.125–40.

O'Conaill, B., Whittaker, S. & Wilbur, S. (1993), "Conversations over Video Conferences.", *Human–Computer Interaction* **8**, 389–428.

Olson, J., Olson, G. & Meader, D. (1995), What Mix of Video and Audio is Useful for Small Groups doing Remote Real Time Design Work, *in* I. Katz, R. Mack, L. Marks, M. B. Rosson & J. Nielsen (eds.), *Proceedings of CHI'95: Human Factors in Computing Systems*, ACM Press, pp.362–8.

Schober, M. & Clarkg, H. H. (1989), "Understanding by Addressees and Overhearers", *Cognitive Psychology* **21**, 211–32.

Sellen, A. (1995), "Remote Conversations: The Effects of Mediating Talk with Technology", *Human–Computer Interaction* **10**(4), 401–44.

Short, J. W. E. & Christie, B. (1976), *The Social Psychology of Telecommunications*, John Wiley & Sons.

Wilkes-Gibbs, D. & Clark, H. H. (1992), "Coordinating Beliefs in Conversation", *Journal of Memory and Language* **31**, 183–94.

Human–Computer Interaction — INTERACT '99
M. Angela Sasse and Chris Johnson (Editors)
Published by IOS Press, © IFIP TC.13, 1999

How Stories Capture Interactions

Manuel Imaz & David Benyon

Napier University, Edinburgh, UK.

imaz@compuserve.com, d.benyon@dcs.napier.ac.uk

Abstract: Stories have an important role in designing HCI systems because they contribute to the representation of contextual information. User Stories are the first artefacts we use in order to describe interactions, but for implementation purposes we need something more formal such as Use Cases. In this sense, Use Cases are similar to user stories but different in that they lose most of the context that user stories maintain. User stories are the bones with which to complete a skeletal script of interactions. At the same time, stories capture much of the intentions of the users, allowing to trace intentions (derived from the context of the activity or workplace) to a set of interactions between actors and system that constitute a set of use cases. The paper proposes an approach to analysing user stories through experientialist concepts of stories, mental spaces, projection and blends in order to be able to establish a more rigorous traceability between user stories (which could be considered as pre-requirements) and semi-formal requirements such as use cases.

Keywords: story, user story, use case, mental space, blend, interaction, script, traceability.

1 Introduction

During the mid-late 1980s and into the 1990s, HCI has witnessed a rise in methods and approaches to design which emphasise the need to see human activities in context. The emphasis is on understanding user actions within this context. For others, the concept of 'context' is a combination of notations which aid envision, design rationale, scenarios and the more formal notations needed to communicate contextual information to designers (Cockton et al., 1996).

A number of techniques have been adopted to facilitate the gathering and representation of contextual information, the most prominent being 'scenarios of use'. Scenarios are narratives describing what people do when engaged in particular activities (Carroll, 1995), although how scenarios are actually used varies widely. Scenarios might be based on in-depth ethnographic studies (Nardi, 1995) or on brief collaborative sessions with managers.

On the other side of the HCI/Software Engineering divide, object-oriented (OO) methods of systems development advocate the adoption of 'Use Cases' (Jacobson, 1995). Jacobson describes how use cases should present a 'black box' view of the system. A use case model defines the system's behaviour and is developed alongside, and orthogonal to, an object model. Jacobson employs a graphical representation showing the interaction between entities outside the system ('actors') and the use cases which are inside the system. When an actor uses the system, the system performs a use case and hence the use cases describe the complete functionality of the system.

Use cases are a more formal representation of interactive situations than scenarios. The question remains, how can we move confidently and consistently between these two representations. Moreover, scenarios are themselves more structured than the original 'user stories' that might be gathered during a work place study or systems analysis. In this paper we describe how such transitions may be accomplished.

Furthermore, we believe that scenarios, user stories and use cases can all be seen as types of stories and that story-telling, as a mental activity, is a constant activity of human beings. We are constantly constructing small spatial stories and projecting them to other stories. The capacity to categorize is tightly associated to small spatial stories in which we partition the world into objects. This partitioning into objects depends on the typical stories in which they appear: we catch a ball, sit on a chair, take a drink from a glass (Turner, 1996). Categorizing is associated to stories as we do not just recognize a collection of particular objects involved in particular events, but also a set of objects that belong to *categories* in events. In their turn events belong to categories as well.

Thus human capacities to categorize, to tell and understand stories and to project from some stories to others, provide the cognitive foundations of requirements capture from informal stages to more formal ones. In this paper we illustrate these ideas. The purpose of this paper is not to provide a critique of experientialism, nor to engage in the debate about task-based, data-centred or object-oriented methods in HCI as these issues have been dealt with elsewhere (Benyon, 1992; Benyon & Imaz, 1999). Instead we want to illustrate how some principles of experiential cognition may be applied to the considered development of user-centred computer systems.

A brief introduction to some key areas of experientialism, or cognitive semantics (Lakoff, 1988) is provided in Section 2. This is followed by a longer discussion of the different roles that stories and use cases have in systems design. Some pragmatic considerations are considered in Section 5.

2   Experientialism, Spaces and Blends

In the early 80s, Lakoff & Johnson (1980) offered a new vision of cognitive processes as the capacity of projecting from a given domain — the well known — to a new domain — the less known. This capacity, of applying partial mappings between domains, is immediately recognized as *metaphor*. What Lakoff & Johnson have shown is that metaphor is not only a literary trope; it is an essential cognitive process. Metaphor is based on another crucial concept, that of projection.

Lakoff (1987) and Johnson (1987) developed their ideas of metaphor into a modern approach to cognition, known as experientialism. One of the main concepts of experientialism is that of image-schema. Image schemas are abstract patterns derived from our bodily experience, and other interactions with the external world. Such patterns are embedded in our everyday interactions and they structure, at the same time, our experience of the world. They are the basis of more abstract conceptualization by means of projections from concrete spaces to more abstract ones.

Consider, for example, the CONTAINER schema — a schema consisting of a boundary distinguishing an interior from an exterior:

"We understand our own bodies as containers — perhaps the most basic things we do are ingest and excrete, take air into our lungs and breathe it out. But

our understanding of our own bodies as containers seems small compared with all the daily experiences we understand in CONTAINER terms." (Lakoff, 1988, p.140).

In software engineering we conceptualize as containers heterogeneous things such as Entities, States, Objects, Processes and so on.

Other image-schemas such as LINK are used for concepts like Relationships, Transitions from one state to another, etc. This is only a minimal list of image-schemas as the basis of a conceptual domain like software engineering.

Continuing this experientialist tradition, (Turner, 1996) has evolved a more radical approach: that of stories, mental spaces, projections and blends. The adjective 'radical' is used to indicate that stories are important in cognitive processes to such a degree that Turner (1996) considers them as fundamental:

"[They] ... make everyday life possible; they are the root of human thought; they are not primarily — or even importantly — entertainment ... We might therefore think that story-telling is a special performance rather than a constant mental activity. But story as a mental activity is essential to human thought." (Turner, 1996, p.12)

A metaphor connects two different mental spaces. When a connection is established between more than two spaces it is termed a blend. Blending receives a partial structure from two or more input spaces, producing a new space that has emergent structure of its own (Fauconnier, 1997). New relationships arise that did not exist in the separate inputs and, taken in the context of background cognitive and cultural models, allows the composite structure projected into the blend to be viewed as part of a larger self-contained structure. The structure in the blend can then be elaborated in terms of its own logic.

Our aim in this paper is to show how stories are the basis, on one hand, for requirements, and on the other, for designing interaction between different agents (users, devices, systems). Notions of image schemata, metaphor and blends all contribute to this conceptualization.

3 Stories

3.1 Stories' Structure

The simplest story structure includes an agent, an action, and an object. In this basic abstract story there is an animate agent that performs a physical action on an object. Moreover, in a general sense, we can consider this basic abstract story to be an *interactional* story: the agent interacts with an object. Conceptualization of reality derives from interactions with objects: interactions are the basis of stories and of the categorization of objects involved in such interactions. What experientialism adds to these stories is the fact that our:

> "understanding of social, mental and abstract domains is formed on our understanding of spatial and bodily stories" (Turner, 1996, p.51).

Where there is a human agent in the story, we can observe additional aspects like intentional acts. If we watch someone sitting down onto a chair, the sitting involves an animate (human) agent's act with *intentionality* and an object; the chair. Prototypical actors are human beings and many animals: they are able of self-moving and capable of sensation. When we observe a small spatial story where an actor — other than ourselves — behaves in certain ways, we immediately project features of animacy, intentionality and agency onto it from stories in which we are the actors.

3.2 User's Stories

Based on this experientialist approach, we can consider requirements as a collection of users' stories. Some authors have proposed that patterns can capture these stories (Beck, 1999). Beck proposes:

> "I want business to feel ownership of and take responsibility for the care and maintenance of 'the requirements' ... I want business to feel free to add new requirements, and add new detail to existing requirements, as development progresses."

Another proponent of patterns (MacBreen, 1999) explains the main difference between a User Story and a Use Case:

> 'A Use Case is very precise and attempts to completely formalise all of the requirements relating to a particular interaction with the system. A User Story gives a specific example of what

the results of the interaction should be. A specific, concrete example, is more accessible than the more abstract formats that are often used for a Use Case.'

He proposes a technique based on a collection of cards on which the stories are captured, each one with its own name.

3.3 Objects as Blends of Stories

In a previous work Imaz (1995) demonstrated that the paradigm shift in software engineering from data-centred to object-oriented methods could be understood by recognizing that objects are based on a new underlying metaphor: OBJECTS ARE PEOPLE. The following step was to think of objects as (conceptual) blends from two or more input spaces (Benyon & Imaz, 1999). Now we can streamline this idea proposing that objects are designed on a blend of stories.

We have said that when we experience a story we project the features of animacy and agency on other actors. In a workplace like a bank we can have different processes represented by stories. One possible story is that of a client going to the bank office to withdraw money from his/her account. It is a typical interaction story in which the client asks the human teller to withdraw an amount of money. Another similar story could be that of printing the account balance.

We can imagine a set of basic stories where the object is the same: in the case above there are two stories about the client account. These basic stories may be in different sequences of stories — corresponding to different activities and actors — and the same object may be manipulated by different actors. If we project all these physical actions on the same object in such a way that the object becomes self-moving or animated, we have a blend from different spaces and at the same time we project the agency (or animacy) from the set of all actors to the same object.

So, we can think of objects as a blend from different basic stories in which the object is the same even if the actors are different and from which we project the features of agency on the blend: on the object itself. We have then a new character, an Object (as in OO terminology), which is a blend from several possible spaces. The projection from the input spaces is selective: we have only selected those stories in which the same workplace object appears (the client account). It is also partial, as we have not included all elements from input stories. The blend develops an emergent structure not provided by the inputs: we can imagine new stories in the blend.

In OO design, the CRC method (collaboration, responsibilities, communication) of using cards in order to collect a set of stories — called a responsibility — for the class under discussion (the agent), is a practical illustration of this concept. Objects are blends from different basic stories.

The richness of features the new blend may have depends on the richness of stories that occur in the workplace. The stories of the blends correspond to operations or methods (in OO terms) of the Object.

3.4   Users' Stories

Beck's proposal about users' stories involves a name describing the story and one or two paragraphs describing the story. The importance of these users' stories is that they capture the intentionality of users and this is essential when trying to understand users' activities and context. Often, the intentionality is richer than the interaction allowed by the system. This usually occurs because when designing the interaction with the system we unconsciously include in the blend the technological constraints or usual interface solutions. In design activities we are unconsciously and continually creating blends.

Goguen (1996) speaks of degrees of formality in requirements information, ranging from informal to semi-formal or formal information. It is useful to capture a degree of informality in such a way that context can be represented in a suitable way. Context maintains its advantages of flexibility and source of new design solutions.

These stories are part of real requirements. Traditional HCI systems design has underestimated the importance of stories, considering them as second hand information, as non-scientific discourse. More recently this trend has been reversed:

> "knowledge, then, is experiences and stories, and intelligence is the apt use of experience and the creation and telling of stories" (Schank, 1990).

Other authors (Turner, 1996) even consider stories as the basis of language:

> "With story, projection, and their powerful combination in parable, we have a cognitive basis from which language can originate" (p168).

Our main source of requirements is then the set of stories from our users. What has been proposed by the OO standard Unified Modelling Language (UML) is to capture such requirements in a special form of stories: use cases. In reality, use cases are prototypical stories, stories that correspond to prototypical situations, in which anybody (any person in a given role, e.g. a category of actors) should act in the same way. Some authors call them scripts or scenarios, but this last word has been maintained in UML to indicate a given flow of events corresponding to a given situation (or condition).

Users' stories are related to a given workplace context and technological set-up. What is important in these stories is the intentionality of the user as such intention gives meaning to a group of otherwise isolated stories. This meaning gives coherence to stories by connecting them to activities and objects. Meaning is never local, it is not a deposit in a concept-container, it is a complex operation of blending, projecting and integrating over multiple spaces (Turner, 1996).

3.5   Use Cases

Cockburn (1997) has found 18 different definitions of use cases. He argues that there are four main issues that can help to define use cases: Purpose, Contents, Plurality and Structure. He proposes the usual definition of use case (shared by Jacobson) as consisting in the following mapping:

> Purpose = requirements
> Contents = consistent prose
> Plurality = multiple scenarios per use case
> Structure = semi-formal

Cockburn points out that:

> "if the purpose of using use cases is to collect user stories, they may be self-contradicting, informal, and have no structure — and still be useful."

However, this contradicts the definition above (which has also been included in UML) in two main aspects; being written in a *consistent prose* and having a *semi-formal* structure.

Use Cases are special cases of user stories. They are generalised stories, not stories corresponding to any individual user but to a category of users. They are useful for understanding the possible interactions between an actor (an occurrence of the category of users) and the system we are about to develop. A Use Case is a set of stories belonging to two different sub-sets: one set is defined by the user viewpoint and the other corresponds to the system viewpoint. As Turner (1996) points out:

> "in imagination, we can construct spaces of what we take to be someone else's

focus and viewpoint. We can, for example, in imagination, take the spatial viewpoint of one of the actors in the story."

The case is that we, as use case designers, take the viewpoint of at least two actors in the story of interaction between the user (or another system) and the system.

Just in the same way that we project the features of agency on an object, we also project on the system the features of agency and treat it as another agent acting on objects. In the Use Case, the objects that both agents (the user and the system) are acting upon are the same. The interface between both agents is a collection of objects that both user and system are sharing, so both sub-sets of stories apply to the same shared objects. The whole story defines a dialogue (conversation) between two actors: user and system.

3.6 Comparing User Stories and Use Cases

We can differentiate use cases from user stories in a number of ways. First, a user story may have many foci and many viewpoints. In general, these stories may be complex as the changing of viewpoint may imply some future consequences of early actions. In a use case, each sub-set of stories of the use case involves only a spatial and temporal viewpoint (that of the user or the system) and the same synchronous focus: an object of the interface. The focus may change, but it does so simultaneously for both agents; for a dialogue to exist, focus should change in a synchronous way for user and system. The list of actions in a use case defines a temporal sequence. Sometimes there is a split of a large main story in a set of subsets corresponding to exceptions, groups of reusable stories and so on.

Second, a user story usually contains intentionality and motives. This intention tells us why the user is doing something, it is the sense of the user action. Use cases, on the other hand, say nothing in relation to intentions (neither the user's nor the systems'). Once the use case concludes, we may be able to infer what was it for. There is no need to wait until the end of the use case, as its name gives us an indication of its goal.

There is a new proposal to capture user goals as *Business Use Cases* (Fowler, to appear):

"With system use cases, you can say that the use cases would include scenarios along the lines of 'define a style', 'change a style', and 'move a style from one document to another'. However, all these scenarios reflect things the user is doing with the system rather than the real goals the user is trying to achieve. The real business use cases might be described with terms like 'ensure consistent formatting for a document' and 'make one document's format the same as another.'"

Third, users' stories may be an individual story standing for a general one. It may contain some design ideas for the designer in addition to desired requirements. The use case is a general, skeletal story: all members of the same category will act the same way. There are no surprises: even exceptions are already included in the stories. These stories tell us how things happen, independently of users' intentions or motives.

4 Example

In order to illustrate how we can better understand users' stories through the concepts of experientialism and in order to illustrate the differences between users' stories and use cases, we provide the following example — taken from Jeffries (1999). It is typical of the sort of requirements that a company may have for a payroll system:

"SPLIT COLA: When the COLA rate changes in the middle of the B/W Pay Period, we will want to pay the 1st week of the pay period at the OLD COLA rate and the 2nd week of the Pay Period at the NEW COLA rate. Should occur automatically based on system design.

For the OT, we will run a m/frame program that will pay or calc the COLA on the 2nd week of OT. The plant currently retransmits the hours data for the 2nd week exclusively so that we can calc COLA. This will come into the Model as a '2144' COLA Gross Pay Adjustment. Create RM Boundary and Place in DE Ent Excess COLA BIN"

4.1 As a User Story

In this example we can see that some issues are general ones (related to the workplace context) and other are specific to certain conceptual spaces.

Workplace context categories: These issues are things such as abbreviations (B/W, meaning *bi-weekly-*, COLA, OT ('overtime'), etc.), local artefacts ('2144', DE Ent Excess COLA BIN, RM Boundary, m/frame program, etc.), and so on.

Conceptual spaces: The main conceptual space is that of paying (payroll) which is a good example of blend. This blend could be considered as a classical business rule with two basic stories: "we want to pay the 1st week of the pay period at the OLD COLA rate" and "the 2nd week of the Pay Period at the NEW COLA". The original blend comes from two spaces: the space of paying and the space of rates, with a generic space of 'paying'.

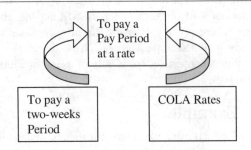

Figure 1:

It is interesting to observe how the split of one of the input spaces determines the split in the second input space:

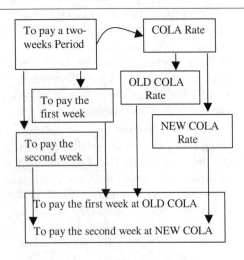

Figure 2:

The user story originates as a blend, which is possible through restructuring old conceptual spaces as a consequence of splitting one of the input spaces.

Viewpoints: In the user story we witness viewpoint changes. In one case, from the space of paying

("we want to pay the 1st week of the pay period at the OLD COLA rate)" to that of business processes ("we will run a m/frame program that will pay or calc the COLA on the 2nd week of OT" or "This will come into the Model as a '2144' COLA Gross Pay Adjustment)". In another to the space of communication (or transmission) between geographical sites ("The plant currently retransmits the hours data for the 2nd week exclusively"). There is also some explicit intentionality ("we will want to pay" or "Should occur automatically based on system design") and other intentions expressed in terms of projections from one space (business process) to other (software applications) in the basic story of "Should occur automatically based on system design". In this last statement, intentionality is expressed as a change of viewpoint. The change of viewpoint can go from a current system ("the plant currently retransmits ...") to a future one ("should occur automatically ...").

4.2   As a Use Case

In the user story above we have a core story that we have to transform into a use case. The central story is the blend that could appear in an already specified main use case: Bi-weekly Payroll.

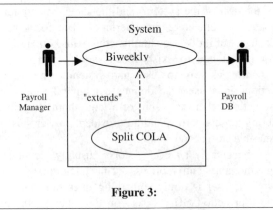

Figure 3:

In the use case Bi-weekly Payroll we will have a story such as:

1. The use case starts when an actor (Payroll Manager) requests to pay employees.

2. The system requests the database to find all employees (or those marked as bi-weekly ones).

3. For each bi-weekly paid employee If there has been a COLA rate change during the period then Split COLA.

And the Split COLA extension will contain the core user story:

If there has been a COLA rate change during the bi-weekly period then Split COLA:

1. Calculate pay of the 1st week of the pay period at the OLD COLA rate.

2. Calculate pay of the 2nd week of the pay period at the NEW COLA rate.

The user story may be a whole use case, a partial use case (a 'uses' or 'extend' use case, as in the present example), or some rules to be applied in a use case (new calculations). So the concept of use case has an integral conceptual entity that users' stories do not.

Another question concerns the convenience of having two types of stories: why not use users' stories directly to implement the system? This returns to an issues raised at the beginning of the paper; the need for a gradual transformation from informal to semi-formal information to get usable models in implementation. We consider that it is quite convenient to use *use cases*, as this intermediate semi-formal information determines a better understanding between the community of users and that of developers. Our experience is that semi-formal notation, when learned by users, pays off the effort of training them in the new diagrams as the communication increases and users may offer new design issues that might otherwise have been overlooked.

5   Pragmatic Considerations

Our purpose is to maintain both informal and semi-formal (or formal) information in modelling HCI systems. Both types of information have their advantages, so it will be helpful to have both types of representations simultaneously. Some authors point out the importance of pre-requirement-specification traceability:

> "that is, traceability that addresses the question: Where do requirements come from?" (Ramesh, 1998, p.40)

In order for this proposal to be useful, we believe that a good solution would be to implement traceability from user stories to use cases. Several solutions could be proposed but the simplest is to create HTML documents in which to include the user stories — as can be seen in Jeffries (1999) — in JPEG or GIF format. These documents would include image maps to link them to other UML documents (glossary for abbreviations; vision for aspects of the new systems to be taken into account; parts of use cases for core user stories and so on) in order to maintain most of the user semi-formal information. This contextual information has the advantage of being source of new design solutions as well as a reference for a contractual basis.

6   Conclusions

In order to develop effective human–computer systems, there is a need to understand and represent contextual information. We propose that including users' stories in the system model instead of maintaining them in secondary (manual) files or even losing them is one contribution to this aim. In order to get traceability between users' stories and use cases we have studied what could be the possible mappings between both types of representations.

The concepts of story, projection, mental (or conceptual) spaces and blends, derived from experientialism, help us to understand the structure of users' stories and where the concepts have originated from. This in turn allows us to develop object definitions based on the shared objects of the different stories, with operations corresponding to the actions. Actors in the users' stories become actors in use cases with the use case description capturing and structuring the partial stories inherent in the full users' stories.

Finally, we propose the usual solution of linking user stories — informal requirements — and use cases — semi-formal requirements — through HTML documents in which user stories could be maintained as JPEG or GIF images and creating on them mappings zones to other UML documents. UML documents may be as varied as *glossary* entries, paragraphs in the *vision* document, parts of — or whole — *use case diagrams* and *use case descriptions*.

As with many other aspects of software engineering and HCI, it is not sufficient to rely on ad hoc methods of systems design. Bringing the concepts of experientialism to bear on why a particular design is appropriate enables a more rational, rigorous and user-centred decision to be taken.

Acknowledgements

Thanks to Kent Beck for facilitating the task of finding User Stories pattern; Ron Jeffries for his Stories cards. and Martin Fowler for sending the revised version of Chapter 3 of Use Case. And thanks for all of them for their comments.

References

Beck, K. (1999). ¡http://c2.com/cgi/wiki?UserStory.

Benyon, D. (1992), "Task Analysis and System Design: The Discipline of Data", *Interacting with Computers* **4**(2), 246–59.

Benyon, D. & Imaz, M. (1999), "Metaphors and Models: Conceptual Foundations of Representations in Interactive Systems Development", *Human–Computer Interaction* **14**, 159–89. Special issue on Representations in Interactive System Development.

Carroll, J. M. (ed.) (1995), *Scenario-Based Design: Envisioning Work and Technology in System Development*, John Wiley & Sons.

Cockburn, A. (1997), "Structuring Use Cases with Goals", *Journal of Object Oriented Programming* . http://members.aol.com/acockburn.

Cockton, G., Clarke, S., Gray, P. & Johnson, C. (1996), Literate Development: Weaving Human Context into Design Specifications, *in* D. R. Benyon & P. Palanque (eds.), *Critical Issues in User Interface Systems Engineering*, Springer-Verlag, pp.227–48.

Fauconnier, G. (1997), *Mappings in Thought and Language*, Cambridge University Press.

Fowler, M. (to appear), *UML Distilled*, revised edition, Addison–Wesley, chapter Last draft of Chapter 3 about Use Case.

Goguen, J. (1996), Formality and Informality in Requirements Engineering, *in Proceedings of Fourth International Conference on Requirements Engineering*, IEEE Computer Society Press, pp.102–8.

Imaz, M. (1995), Object Oriented Methods: An Epistemological Approach, Master's thesis, Open University.

Jacobson, I. (1995), The Use Case Construct in Object-Oriented Software Engineering, *in* Carroll (1995), pp.309–36.

Jeffries, R. (1999). http://www.armaties.com/StoryCards.htm.

Johnson, M. (1987), *The Body in the Mind. The Bodily Basis of Reason and Imagination*, University of Chicago Press.

Lakoff, G. (1987), *Women, Fire and Dangerous Things: What Categories Reveal About the Mind*, University of Chicago Press.

Lakoff, G. (1988), Cognitive Semantics, *in* U. Eco, M. Santambrogio & P. Violi (eds.), *Meaning and Mental Representations*, Indiana University Press.

Lakoff, G. & Johnson, M. (1980), *Metaphors We Live By*, University of Chicago Press.

MacBreen, P. (1999). http://c2.com/cgi/wiki?UserStory.

Nardi, B. (1995), Some Reflections on Scenarios, *in* Carroll (1995), pp.387–99.

Ramesh, B. (1998), "Factors Influencing Requirements Traceability Practice", *Communications of the ACM* **41**(12), 37–44.

Schank, R. (1990), *Tell Me a Story. Narrative and Intelligence*, Northwestern University Press.

Turner, M. (1996), *The Literary Mind*, Oxford University Press.

Human–Computer Interaction — INTERACT '99
M. Angela Sasse and Chris Johnson (Editors)
Published by IOS Press, © IFIP TC.13, 1999

Patterns, Claims and Multimedia

Alistair Sutcliffe & Maia Dimitrova

Centre for Human–Computer Interface Design, City University
Northampton Square, London EC1V 0HB, UK.
A.G.Sutcliffe@city.ac.uk, M.T.Dimitrova@city.ac.uk

Abstract: A framework for pattern-led development of multimedia is proposed. Patterns are expressed within a claims-based schema, so the general pattern is linked to a specific artefact, usage scenario and design rationale. Examples of content script patterns for procedural and causal explanation are given with recommended media combinations. Examples of patterns illustrated from different sources for directing user attention in multimedia and hypermedia presentations are presented. The prospects for pattern-led development are discussed.

Keywords: patterns, claims, multimedia, guidelines, knowledge representation.

1 Introduction

Patterns have become an established part of software engineering practice (Gamma et al., 1995); however, in HCI this approach has received little attention. Patterns have been an implicit part of user interface development toolkits, i.e. dialogue boxes, windows, menu bars, sliders; however few patterns have been specified for more complex UI components. Patterns are apparent in commercial multimedia products (Dimitrova & Sutcliffe, 1999), even though they may not be articulated as such and patterns may encapsulate poor rather than good design practice. For instance, Schaife & Rogers (1996) reported that many tutorial multimedia applications are ineffective in promoting learning and have usability problems. A first step in pattern-led development is to develop a framework that defines what types of pattern may contribute to multimedia development and how the contents of such patterns may be specified.

In our previous work we have proposed guidelines, principles, a method for multimedia design, and an adviser tool based on a survey of the relevant literature and experimental investigations (Sutcliffe & Faraday, 1994; Faraday & Sutcliffe, 1997a; 1997b; 1998). Design guidelines for multimedia have also been proposed by others (Alty, 1997); however, guidelines frequently encounter problems of interpretation that hinder their effective use, hence one motivation for a pattern-led approach is to deliver multimedia guidelines as claims (Carroll & Rosson, 1992) to improve their acceptability.

This paper proposes a framework for multimedia patterns in Section 2, drawn from our previous research, a survey of commercial products (Dimitrova & Sutcliffe, 1999), and the published literature. The framework is illustrated by examples in Section 3, which also elaborate pattern representations as claims. The paper concludes with a brief discussion of future prospects for reuse of multimedia patterns.

2 A Framework for Multimedia Patterns

The framework proposes families of patterns that address different aspects of the design problem. Within each family a schema describes the content and structure of the pattern. The framework follows a set of design issues with pattern families mapped to each stage in the design process (see Figure 1). Design commences with requirements mapped to content/explanation patterns in stage one, then progresses to media combination patterns in the second stage.

The third stage then provides smaller scale design patterns that add features for presentation control, user navigation and dialogue support. The framework is intended to be general so we do not provide domain oriented patterns; although we have proposed a library of domain oriented patterns for a variety of software engineering and information systems problems (Sutcliffe & Carroll, 1998).

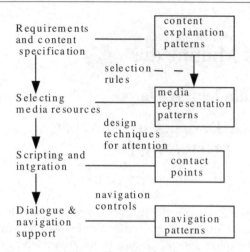

Figure 1: Multimedia design issues and outline process, illustrating the contribution of different families of patterns to each process stage and guidelines used to create pattern variants within a family.

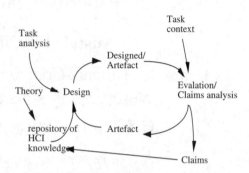

Figure 2: Summary of the task artefact cycle. The cycle is seeded by an artefact designed with previous knowledge and task analysis.

2.1 Claims and Patterns

Patterns in software engineering are normally specified as a set of cooperating objects (Gamma et al., 1995). However, such representations do not provide any additional knowledge to help the designer's interpretation or understanding. Accordingly we have adopted a claims approach (Carroll & Rosson, 1992). Briefly, claims are small chunks of HCI knowledge, expressed in natural language that describe usability arguments for an artefact. Claims have upsides and downsides that present usability arguments as trade-offs in psychologically based design rationale. Claims are generated by basing design on task analysis and influences from theory, then subsequently evaluating the usability of artefacts, and then extracting the claim from the design (see Figure 2).

Claims are situated in a context by a scenario of use, and the artefact that helps designers understand how to apply usability arguments, hence overcoming some of the limitations of expressing patterns as a schema. A knowledge representation schema for claims (Sutcliffe & Carroll, 1998; n.d.), and an example of a claim are illustrated in Figures 3 & 4.

Our previous schema has been extended with a model or specification to represent the pattern. The artefact then becomes an example that instantiates the pattern, while the claim and links to theory provide justification about why a pattern should deliver usability, with supplementary information on dependencies, and design trade-offs.

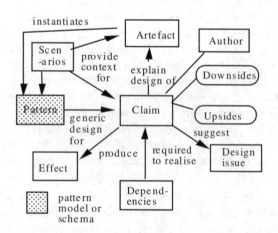

Figure 3: Schema for representing claims related knowledge. The patterns schema is the addition described in this paper.

Claim ID:	Colour-coded Telegraphic Display
Author:	Singley, M. K.; Carroll, J. M.
Artefact:	MoleHill tutor — Goalposter tool
Explanation:	The presentation of individual goals in the window is telegraphic, several words at most. However, the learner can expand any of the telegraphic goals (through a menu selection) to display a fuller explanation of why the goal is worthwhile pursuing or not. Thus the system provides both shorthand feedback on correctness and access to further help.
Upside:	Provides persistent feedback on the correctness of actions as well as access to further information.
Downside:	Learners must learn the display's feature-language and controls.
Scenario:	The learner is trying to create an UpperCaseTextPane, the system infers that the learner is "searching for relevant classes and methods" and posts this phase in the GoalPoster, the learner selects the posted goal to display an expansion of why the goal should be pursued and how it can be advanced, the learner resumes work navigating to the Window class and causing this sub-goal to be posted in the GoalPoster.
Effect:	Improved learning by provision of appropriate feedback.
Dependencies:	Tracking user's progress in learning tasks, known goal structure.
Issues:	What sorts of feedback displays are effective and under what circumstances? Is hue coding effective for indicating the three-way distinction between achieved sub-goals, apparently correct sub-goals, and apparently incorrect sub-goals?
Theory:	Feedback in discovery based learning.

Figure 4: Example of a claim.

3 Multimedia Representation Patterns

In this section two examples of content related patterns are described. Each pattern has a goal and a specification of the expected content. Mapping rules based on our previous research (Sutcliffe & Faraday, 1994; Sutcliffe, 1998) are then applied to create a media script pattern to deliver the content.

The rules (see Table 1) are used in multiple passes, for example when a procedure for explaining a physical task is required; first, realistic image media will be selected, then a series of images and text. The guidelines, which differentiate physical from abstract information, are used first followed by the other guidelines.

3.1 Task-based Explanation

Goal: To explain a task or procedure.

The content is organized to first provide the task goal (purpose), then give details of its procedure, followed by the post conditions (end state) and a summary of the key steps.

Text is used to provide a plan and explain the task goal; then the action steps are explained by speech synchronized with step by step still image illustration, augmented by captions (see Figure 5). This is followed by moving image of the procedure to reinforce the message and integrate the actions, and then bullet points text with a subset of still images summarize the key steps in the procedure.

The rules produce pattern specializations for different information types. For instance, explaining how to carry out a mathematical task (e.g. integration) involves abstract information hence text, mathematical symbols and diagrams would be used. Many tasks are composed of actions that are normally perceived of as a continuous sequence (e.g. skiing), so the pattern advises showing the actions as both discrete steps and a continuous sequence. Using multimedia redundantly and giving slightly different viewpoints on the same material helps to improve learning (Gardiner & Christie, 1987). The resulting pattern owes its heritage not only to the selection rules but also to design principles (Sutcliffe, 1998) and these influences are expressed in the accompanying claim.

Information type	Preferred media selection	Example
Physical	still or moving image	building diagram
Abstract	text or speech	explain sales policy
Descriptive	text or speech	chemical properties
Visio spatial	realistic media — photograph	person's face
Value	text/tables/numeric lists	pressure reading
Relationships (values)	designed images — graphs, charts	histogram of rainfall/month
Discrete Action	still image	make coffee
Continuous Action	moving image — video, animation	manoeuvres while skiing
Events	sound, speech	fire alarm
States	still image, text	photo of weather conditions
Composition	still image, moving image	exploded parts diagram

Table 1: Overview of Media selection preferences and examples, derived from media — information type mapping rules (Sutcliffe, 1998; ISO, 1998).

Claim ID:	Multimedia-Procedural explanation
Artefact:	Maths: The Journey to Swallow Farm (Aircom Education) (see Figure 6)
Pattern	Multimedia procedural explanation (see Figure 5)
Explanation:	The presentation of the procedure starts with the goal and then provides detail of the actions with a summary. A combination of media is used to reinforce different aspects of the content.
Upside:	A clear structure of the content and presentation by a combination of media reinforces the explanation.
Downside:	The presentation may be too complex for experts; too much detail may annoy users.
Scenario:	The procedure for navigating with a compass is explained by text and redundant speech, supported by an animation, giving instructions for each step.
Effect:	Learning is improved by media combination, which reinforces the message.
Dependencies:	Known goal and task structure, animation, text, and speech media resources.
Issues:	How much detail is necessary for learners with different levels of knowledge and abilities?
Theory:	Task knowledge structures, depth of encoding, memorability of static vs. dynamic media (Gardiner & Christie, 1987).

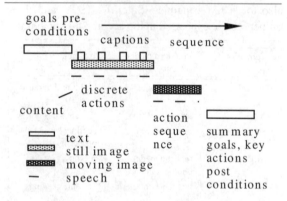

Figure 5: Schema for procedural explanation showing the initial content pattern overlaid with the media presentation pattern.

The claim above draws attention to the design trade-off linked to the issue of user's existing knowledge. While the pattern should have the desired effect for novices, experts may find the repetition annoying. The theory link allows exploration of the underpinning of this pattern in theoretical and experimental evidence drawn from psychology. This evidence was also used to derive the mapping rules (see Table 1), that were applied to the content patterns to produce the media representation patterns.

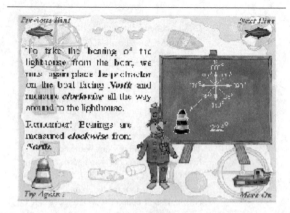

Figure 6: Screen shot from "Maths: The Journey To Swallow Farm" CD-ROM, explaining the procedure of navigating with a compass.

3.2   Causal Explanations

We distinguish causal explanations from procedural, by the goal of causal explanation that emphasizes transfer of knowledge about how and why an event occurs in natural or artificial phenomena.

Goal: To explain why an observed event occurs in either natural or designed systems.

The explanation starts by introducing the domain, important objects and concepts, then the causal model is described using background knowledge to explain why the observed events happen. A summary concludes with key events and their causal explanation. The content pattern and the media selected by application of the mapping rules are illustrated in Figure 7.

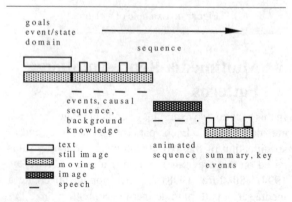

Figure 7: Media representation pattern for causal explanation.

Text introduces the goal of the explanation, i.e. the observed event or state, followed by important objects in the domain illustrated with a diagram. The event sequence of cause and effect is presented by diagrams and speech, using text captions to explain key facts and background knowledge, with animation of the sequence to reinforce the message. The explanation is summarized by returning to the original diagram and text captions for key events. Again the mapping rules indicate specialized patterns for abstract and physical domains, and designed vs. natural domains. Causal explanation for designed systems emphasizes explanation on mechanisms, whereas natural systems focus more on the sequence of events leading to the observed state.

Claim ID:	Multimedia-Causal explanation
Artefact:	Etiology of Cancer (Silverplatter) (see Figure 8)
Pattern	Media representation script for causal explanations (see Figure 7)
Explanation:	The presentation starts with the goal and then describes the causal sequence of the event with a summary. A combination of media is used to reinforce different aspects of content with diagrams showing abstract views linked to realistic images.
Upside:	The media combination of abstract and realistic images provides causal concepts linked to a realistic context to reinforce the explanation.
Downside:	The presentation may be too simple for experts. Insufficient links to background knowledge may frustrate users. Too much detail may overwhelm novices.
Scenario:	The presentation shows how DNA is repaired by a photo-activated enzyme. A beam of light strikes the enzyme causing the repair reaction to start.
Effect:	Learning is improved by media combination which reinforces the message.
Dependencies:	Conceptual diagram, image media, speech explanation.
Issues:	What level of detail is necessary for learners with different levels of knowledge and abilities? How far should the explanation trace backwards into background knowledge?
Theory:	Causal knowledge structures, depth of encoding, memorability of static v. dynamic media (Gardiner & Christie, 1987), linking viewpoints (Rogers & Schaife, 1998).

The claim draws attention to the design issue of user's existing knowledge and the trade-off decision about how much background information to include. For instance, the artefact illustrated in Figure 8 relies on assumed knowledge about biochemistry, function of enzyme in cell biology, etc. The designer has to decide how much to include in any one explanation as well as trying to adapt the presentation to students with different abilities. The theory link points to the claim's origins in psychological evidence used

in the mapping rules and HCI knowledge created by a process of evaluation of educational multimedia (Rogers & Schaife, 1998).

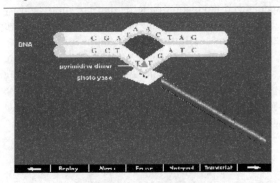

Figure 8: Screen shot and an animation from "Etiology of Cancer" CD-ROM, explaining the repair of DNA.

4 Navigation and Dialogue

This family of patterns addresses lower level design issues of user navigation and control. Navigation and control are interpreted in two ways, first, control of the user's viewing sequence by the designer — in this case the patterns suggest design features to direct the user's attention between media, and secondly, control functionality — in this case the patterns suggest additional functions to facilitate user navigation. Only the former are described in this paper. The patterns are organized in specialization hierarchy, which is divided into two main sub-classes:

- Concurrent source and destination — in this case the origin and destination are either visible within the same presentation, or audio media are played while the image is visible.

- Sequential hypermedia — the origin has an explicit link to the destination, so the pattern advises on hypermedia links.

The patterns have slots, which are instantiated with attention directing effects in the source and destination medium (see Figure 9).

Thus, to link a text to a still image the pattern advises on choice of salience cues in the source medium (e.g. bold, underline, large font, different font, colour), any possible link structures (e.g. arrow, line, spatial juxtapositioning), and a salience cue in the destination medium (e.g. highlight, movement, boundary, colour). Use of the slot structure enables a simple pattern to be specialized for a wide variety of different media and hypermedia combinations. The justification for these patterns is taken partially from a synthesis of design ideas in industrial products and partially from experimental studies on multimedia (Faraday & Sutcliffe, 1997b). In addition to these baseline patterns, we have also developed more specialized navigation patterns that are motivated by goals of achieving specific presentation effects. Two such patterns are illustrated in a claims format.

The pattern originates from Rogers & Schaife (1998) and was used in the media representation pattern for causal explanation. This demonstrates the composability of the framework and how patterns that address different design issues can be aggregated.

Claim ID:	Dynalinking abstract concepts to event sequences
Artefact:	Pondworld (see Figure 10)
Pattern	Media representation script for explaining dynamic behaviour
Explanation:	An animation is displayed showing a sequence of events in the domain. This is linked to a diagram showing the conceptual relationship between objects in the domain.
Upside:	The juxtaposition of realistic details and an abstract representation of the relationships between objects in the image encourage comprehension.
Downside:	Objects in the realistic image may be hard to discriminate, thus hindering understanding of the relationships.
Scenario:	Two interlinked displays are shown; a canonical food web diagram and a concrete animation of it. The learner can 'Turn on' different combinations of feeding relationships in the food web and observe the weeds being eaten by the tadpoles in the adjacent animation.
Effect:	Learning is improved by linking specific elements of the diagram to animated event sequences.
Dependencies:	Media resources- conceptual graphs of relationships, animations and still image of domain.
Issues:	How should the animation be linked to specific elements of the conceptual graph?
Theory:	Dynalinking viewpoints for learning (Rogers & Schaife, 1998).

The pattern advises combination of realistic images with diagrams and text to explain concepts, e.g. a photograph of a pond is linked to a diagram that explains the food chain between plants and animals in the pond. Diagram components cue animations, so the abstract concept is illustrated by playing the appropriate event sequence.

The second pattern comes from our own work on eye-tracking in multimedia presentations where we investigated how dynamically revealing captions on an image direct the user's attention to a sequence of events or objects in an explanation.

Claim ID:	Sequential reveals.
Artefact:	Etiology of Cancer (Silverplatter) (see Figure 8).
Pattern	Media script for controlling the sequence of user's attention on an image by captions.
Explanation:	The image is displayed and captions are revealed successively to point out thematically related events or objects.
Upside:	The user's attention is directed to important information in the appropriate sequence.
Downside:	User's attention may be diverted from other static information. The pace of revealing captions may not match the user's viewing sequence.
Scenario:	Captions are revealed to draw the user's attention first to the DNA, then the enzyme and finally the activation by light energy.
Effect:	Comprehension is improved by drawing the user's attention to key facts in the appropriate message.
Dependencies:	Displays, which enable captions to be used without obscuring the image.
Issues:	How many captions to add and when they should be revealed?
Theory:	Directing user's attention by dynamic presentation effects (Faraday & Sutcliffe, 1997a).

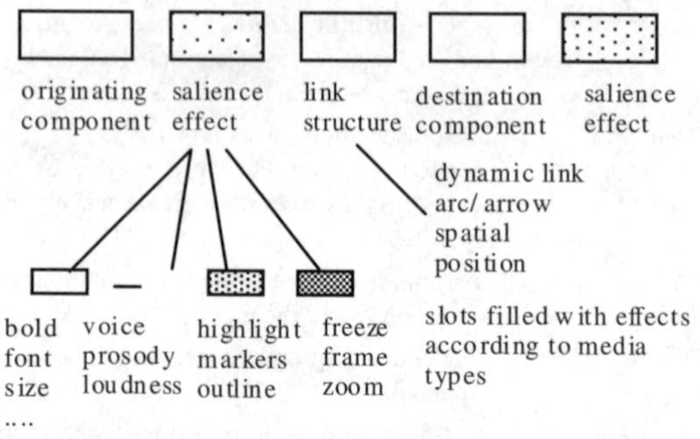

Figure 9: Pattern schema for attention directing links.

Both of these patterns recommend design effects that enhance comprehension by manipulating the user's attention. The claims format provides an aggregation of knowledge to help designers understand and hence effectively reuse the pattern.

5   Conclusions

The main contribution of this work is the framework and schema of multimedia patterns that extends our previous work on the generality of claims for reuse (Sutcliffe & Carroll, 1998). The extended claims schema includes a generalized specification of the designed artefact (the pattern), a specific artefact that illustrates the pattern, complemented by the claims rationale for design trade-offs and the scenario context. This aggregation of knowledge provides designers with comprehensive information pertinent to a class of design problems. However, there are several problems to overcome before this approach can be realized in practice.

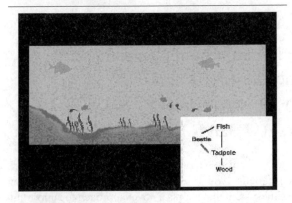

Figure 10: Pondworld artefact; arcs on the diagram trigger an animation that illustrates the concept.

First, a process for generating patterns is necessary. This paper has given some directions, such as applying rules and heuristics to a general schema, thereby populating a pattern family. In previous work a process for claim factoring has started to address this issue (Sutcliffe & Carroll, 1998). However, further research is necessary on the relationship between the scope of a specific artefact and scenario, with a more general pattern. Furthermore, success of pattern-led development always depends on generation of a 'critical mass' library of patterns. The framework and examples we have proposed are a first step in this direction.

References

Alty, J. L. (1997), Multimedia, *in* A. B. Tucker (ed.), *The Computer Science and Engineering Handbook*, CRC Press, pp.1551–70.

Carroll, J. M. & Rosson, M. B. (1992), "Getting Around the Task–Artefact Framework: How to Make Claims and Design by Scenario", *ACM Transactions on Office Information Systems* **10**(2), 181–212.

Dimitrova, M. T. & Sutcliffe, A. G. (1999), Designing Instructional Multimedia Applications: Key Practices and Design Patterns, *in* B. Collins & R. Oliver (eds.), *Proceedings of Ed-Media 1999*, AACE, pp.358–63.

Faraday, P. M. & Sutcliffe, A. G. (1997a), Designing Effective Multimedia Presentations, *in* S. Pemberton (ed.), *Proceedings of CHI'97: Human Factors in Computing Systems*, ACM Press, pp.272–9.

Faraday, P. M. & Sutcliffe, A. G. (1997b), Multimedia: Design for the Moment, *in* J. D. Hollan & J. D. Foley (eds.), *Proceedings of Multimedia'97*, ACM Press, pp.183–93.

Faraday, P. M. & Sutcliffe, A. G. (1998), Providing Advice for Multimedia Designers, *in* C.-M. Karat, A. Lund, J. Coutaz & J. Karat (eds.), *Proceedings of CHI'98: Human Factors in Computing Systems*, ACM Press, pp.124–31.

Gamma, E., Helms, R., Johnson, R. & Vlissides, J. (1995), *Design Patterns: Elements of Reusable Object-Oriented Software*, Addison–Wesley.

Gardiner, M. & Christie, B. (1987), *Applying Cognitive Psychology to User-interface Design*, John Wiley & Sons.

ISO (1998), "Multimedia User Interface Design Software Ergonomic Requirements — Part 1: Introduction and Framework, and Part 3: Media Combination and Selection". ISO 14915.

Rogers, Y. & Schaife, M. (1998), How can Interactive Multimedia Facilitate Learning. In Intelligence and Multimodality in Multimedia Interfaces, *in* J. Lee (ed.), *Research and Applications*, AAAI Press. Issue on CD-ROM.

Schaife, M. & Rogers, Y. (1996), "External Cognition: How do Graphical Representations Work?", *International Journal of Human–Computer Studies* **45**(2), 185–213.

Sutcliffe, A. G. (1998), User-centred Design for Multimedia Applications, *in* B. Furht, T. Ichikawa & A. W. Smeudlers (eds.), *Proceedings of International Conference on Multimedia Computing and Systems (ICMCS'98)*, Vol. 1, IEEE Publications, pp.116–23.

Sutcliffe, A. G. & Carroll, J. M. (1998), Generalising Claims and Reuse of HCI Knowledge, *in* H. Johnson, L. Nigay & C. Roast (eds.), *People and Computers XIII (Proceedings of HCI'98)*, Springer-Verlag, pp.159–76.

Sutcliffe, A. G. & Carroll, J. M. (n.d.), "Designing Claims for Reuse in Interactive Systems Design", *International Journal of Human–Computer Interaction* **50**(3), 213–42.

Sutcliffe, A. G. & Faraday, M. P. (1994), Designing Presentation in Multimedia Interfaces, *in* B. Adelson, S. Dumais & J. Olson (eds.), *Proceedings of CHI'94: Human Factors in Computing Systems*, ACM Press, pp.92–8.

Human–Computer Interaction — INTERACT '99
M. Angela Sasse and Chris Johnson (Editors)
Published by IOS Press, © IFIP TC.13, 1999

Desperado: Three-in-one Indexing for Innovative Design

Thomas C. Ormerod[1], John Mariani[2], Linden J. Ball[3] & Nicki Lambell[3]

[1] Department of Psychology; [2] Department of Computing
Lancaster University, Lancaster LA1 4YF, UK.
[3] Division of Psychology, Derby University DE3 5GX, UK.

{T.Ormerod,J.Mariani}@lancaster.ac.uk, {L.J.Ball,N.Lambell}@derby.ac.uk

Abstract: Despite the potential offered by reuse of information from previous projects in ongoing design work for greater cost-effectiveness and innovation, it is beset by problems, which are not resolved by existing design documentation approaches. We describe Desperado, an indexing system that adopts a novel approach to supporting design reuse. Desperado offers three concurrent facilities — component encoding, rationale capture and guided retrieval — within a single environment. Each facility is supported by a system-initiated search of an object-oriented database of previous design episodes.

Keywords: design rationale, documentation, solution reuse, information retrieval, information indexing, ethnography.

1 Introduction

Expert designers working in commercial environments face a constant dilemma in which they must balance innovation against efficiency. In such an environment, the reuse of previous design work is an attractive proposition. Reuse avoids repetition of design effort, and maintains upward product compatibility and consistency with legal or company standards. Furthermore, with appropriate tools to support the process, reuse might actively enhance innovation. The notion of innovative design reuse sounds at first like an oxymoron. However, providing access to previously considered design options enables the maintenance of innovative ideas over time. When designers know that ideas, if not implemented immediately, may be useful to future projects, they may explore design problems more creatively.

Two types of design reuse information can be identified. The first is product-oriented, focusing upon reuse of solution or component information. The second is process-oriented, focusing upon reuse of ideas, conversations, arguments, decisions and critiques, an orientation associated with 'design rationale'. Design rationale is the documentation of the underlying reasoning behind an artifact design, in which attempts to improve productivity are centred around encouraging a reflective examination of the design process itself. Design rationale might aid understanding amongst stakeholders in the design process and improve the quality of their reasoning. Also it can aid redesign and modification. There is evidence that previous design concepts and prototypes do get reused in many 'routine' design situations (Gero, 1990). However, despite their promise, solution and rationale reuse are limited in application. This is partly because the effort needed to carry them out outweighs the apparent benefits. Often the people who create a design rationale are not motivated because they do not directly benefit from it (Grudin, 1988). There is evidence that designers suffer from 'design rationale fatigue' (Conklin & Begeman, 1988). Existing methods for eliciting design rationales have been shown to be difficult to grasp at first and can cause disruption during the 'construction phase' (Buckingham Shum, 1996). Also, existing solutions can restrict the range of options pursued by designers. Even experts engage in 'satisficing' behaviours, becoming fixated upon single solutions rather than exploring alternatives in order to optimise choices (Ball et al., 1997).

Despite these problems, we believe that there is great potential for effective design reuse. In this paper, we describe an ongoing project to develop Desperado, a computer-based indexing system for supporting the reuse of rationale and solution-based design information. Our approach is to provide a method for capturing solution and rationale information within an information retrieval environment. This contrasts with approaches in which solution reuse, design rationale and information retrieval are separate, either by time or by artifact.

In the next section we report an ethnographic study of documentation and reuse practices in industrial design groups. Then, the features of Desperado are described, a walkthrough of a typical user interaction is outlined.

2 A Study of Reuse Practices

We carried out ethnographic studies of documentation and reuse practices in four industrial, software and aerospace engineering companies. Although design activities differed substantially across companies, our data (videotapes, conversation and meeting transcripts and field notes) reveal consistencies of both problems faced in, and opportunities for, reuse of design information. In this section we focus upon main aspects of the data: existing documentation practices, information retrieval strategies and situated design activities in each company. For a detailed description see (Ball & Ormerod, to appear).

2.1 Existing Documentation Practices

Assessment of existing documentation practices was important for two reasons. First, in designing Desperado we had to ensure that it supports existing documentation requirements, since designers would be unlikely to adopt a new system that did not also deliver existing functionality. Second, we needed to assess the extent to which designers were willing to engage in documentation, and to investigate aspects of existing systems that frustrate documentation behaviours.

Each company had in place a number of information repositories, such as paper-based archives, computer-aided design databases and diary-based file stores. The extent to which each repository was used successfully was extremely variable, though an overall evaluation (not only by ourselves but more importantly by designers and design managers who used the systems) is that they failed to support systematic and optimal reuse practices.

In many instances, documentation was sporadic and unsuccessful. For example, one company had installed a project management system based around a computer-networked diary, which automatically created folders in a project file hierarchy for designers to deposit project-related information. In demonstrating the system to our researcher, the team

manager was unable to find a single folder that had any contents, despite the fact that the system had been running for two years prior to our visit. It became clear, from subsequent conversations with members of the design team that they maintained their own information repositories, only occasionally shifting files to the designated project folders immediately prior to team meetings. In this case, the benefits of central organization of project-related information, although recognised by each member of the design group, were not regarded as sufficient to overcome the additional burdens faced by individual designers in re-assigning their files during an ongoing design process to a central repository.

In all companies information was typically encoded in a piecemeal fashion, with file names specifying either the players, project names, components under design, the date, or some combination of these categories. There was no evidence of encoding by process, criteria or question-based categories. This contrasts with transcripts of conversations and meetings, in which process, criteria and question topics were typically the focus of discussions.

While encoding was piecemeal, it nonetheless was regularly practised. Informal conversations with the designers indicated a frustration with existing systems, and a desire for better documentation technologies. It appears, then, that designers are willing to invest time in encoding for reuse and that they do recognise the benefits of such practices. Thus, an important outcome from the studies was an increased motivation to develop an effective documentation technology.

Observations of documentation problems revealed a need to support the process of encoding in three main ways. First, problems in naming consistency that have been observed elsewhere were apparent in many of our companies. Second, the extent to which documentation took place was variable. In the two companies where extensive documentation was kept reliably, design work was only documented formally at a late stage when a component or design approach had received managerial approval. Records of design alternatives or criteria for rejection and acceptance were rarely recorded. Thus there is a need to provide structure to the documentation process, through some form of concurrent model that steps designers through the documentation process. Third, it was apparent that, despite the willingness of designers to engage in documentation, it was determined in large part by response to organization or managerial demands.

Thus, system design needs to be flexible enough to embody existing organizational practices (e.g. company-specific stages).

2.2   Information Retrieval Strategies

The presence of existing reuse practices is potentially a useful resource for modelling system-initiated retrieval. In particular, we were interested in the knowledge sources and types that designers relied upon to cue reuse.

We encountered many examples of retrieval failure. For example, we observed one designer engaging in a week-long search for a piece of design information. It took him a day to locate the 'owner' of the project to which the information pertained, and a further two days to find that this individual had retired from the company some years previously, taking with him the knowledge of how to retrieve the information sought by the designer (though he was sure that is was held "somewhere in the central files of the group"). We also encountered many examples of successful retrieval. The first, and most common type was for individual designers to recall from memory previous work in which they were involved or components and solution options (and occasionally, critiques) that they had experienced. The second type was essentially managerial, in that design team managers often made suggestions as to the information designers might seek to solve particular problems as well as suggested ways of locating relevant information.

The key point emerging from these observations of reuse is that none of them is based upon retrieval from existing repositories. This negative result must be seen in the light of both the designers' willingness to undertake documentation, and also the failures of existing technologies to facilitate either the encoding or retrieval of documentation. In all the companies, encoding and retrieval of design information were separated by time and device from ongoing design activity. Two important design considerations are: first, that a system to promote reuse needs to make encoding and retrieval contemporaneous, and second, that designers require data-oriented encoding support (e.g. recording of component and project names) to supplement process encoding elicited through design rationale.

2.3   Situated Design Activities

A key issue was to understand the consequences of sub-optimal reuse strategies such as satisficing. The results of our ethnographic research contrast markedly with previous studies of individual and de-contextualized designers (Ball et al., 1997). Almost all team-based episodes reflect a motivated attempt to generate and evaluate multiple solutions options. For example, a major function of review meetings was for the design team to critically appraise alternative design concepts. Experienced designers entered review meetings armed with alternative design options for discussion together with detailed knowledge of their associated costs and benefits. The role played by the team manager was also important, as a safeguard against premature commitment to single solution options. For example, in one session, where a project champion is describing the unsatisfactory aspects of a solution that they are committed to, the team manager interjects "I think the thing to do is look at all the other options". This simple interjection is striking as it is only the third statement that he made in the first 30 minutes or so of the session. Thus, an important outcome is the need for the system to act as a 'surrogate manager', encouraging designers working in individual contexts to consider alternative options.

Another key question concerns the currency of reuse, particularly for rationale-based design information. Our analysis was driven by the goal of identifying the nature and size of a design episode. From inspection of the transcripts, shifts in *question* focus were an apparently natural transition point between episodes. Designers work upon criteria and options in parallel with pursuing a specific question, in what we term a *focus constellation*.

Identification of the focus constellation gives us a framework for choosing between different approaches for capturing design rationale. The two most widely reported of these are Issue Based Information Systems (Conklin & Begeman, 1988) and Questions, Options and Criteria, or QOC (MacLean et al., 1991). While either representation is feasible, the QOC notation was chosen for Desperado for two reasons. First, the QOC notation is consistent with our observation of the focus constellation as defining a design episode. Second, evaluation of options in relation to plausible alternatives is fundamental to QOC, and is especially useful for reuse as it specifies not only the reasoning behind an artifact but also offers a host of plausible alternatives which can be reused, thereby challenging satisficing behaviours. MacLean et al. propose a set of nine heuristics that capture advice on optimal design as practised through concurrent design rationale elicitation. One of our objectives for system design was to implement these heuristics, either implicitly through the processes of encoding and retrieval, or explicitly through system prompts.

3 Desperado: An Overview

Desperado is an environment for component encoding and design rationale elicitation during an ongoing design episode. Design activities are supported by provision of automatically selected episodes or design object names from a database of previous episodes. The basic system structure is shown in Figure 1.

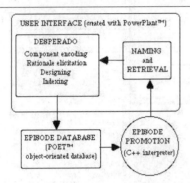

Figure 1: Users encode in Desperado using names retrieved from stored episodes. Episodes that inform design are retrieved concurrently by the promotion interpreter recognizing the state of the current episode.

3.1 The Episode Cycle

We chose the episode as the unit of encoding, defined as pursuing a focus constellation centred around a single design question. Our approach contrasts with reuse systems which take the component as the unit of encoding (Duffy & Duffy, 1996). Sectioning of episode by focus constellation gives a manageable chunk size for indexing reuse information. For example, two weeks of data from the aerospace company gave us 50 episodes that subsequently seeded the database for that company.

Segmenting episodes by focus constellation affords considerable advantages since Desperado can support structured, goal-oriented shifts in activity which we argue are a hallmark of design expertise. Furthermore, it makes explicit the elicitation of design rationale. Pursuit of an episode is the place at which the encoding of component-based and rationale-based information and the retrieval of potentially valuable previous episodes take place. The processes of encoding, design and retrieval are therefore interactive: encoding is supported by using previous episodes to supply terminology for naming, design is supported by prompting through system-initiated retrieval of episodes that are likely to be of value, and retrieval is guided by the current state of information encoded by the designer. The point is for all aspects of reuse, from the designer's perspective, to be singular and seamless.

3.2 Guided Encoding

Encoding is guided by Desperado in three ways. First, it offers a sequenced dialogue, in which design information is elicited in four main phases:

1. data-oriented encoding (e.g. project, user, component information);

2. stage (e.g. requirements vs. conceptual vs. detailed design) and scope (e.g. project-specific, organizational, standards);

3. focus constellation (i.e. QOC information); and

4. location of documentation (e.g. CAD files, requirements specifications).

The value of a procedural dialogue is in providing a seamless environment for solution and rationale encoding during ongoing design and in ensuring that encoding is continuous rather than postponed or only from partial aspects of ongoing work.

Second, Desperado offers a naming window (see Figure 2) in which labels supplied in previous episodes for the current encoding event are promulgated using a prioritising mechanism described below. The user clicks on a relevant label in the naming window which places the label in the current episode event text box, which can subsequently be modified if necessary. The naming window addresses two encoding problems, enhancing naming consistency and reducing data entry requirements.

Third, encoding is managed by system prompts, in which the exploration of one event (e.g. a solution option from a previous project) elicits a prompt to explore related events (e.g. criteria concerning that option, or alternative solution options). In essence, prompts serve as surrogate managers to encourage designers to encode reasons behind choices, a key factor identified in our examination of existing documentation practices.

3.3 Guided Retrieval

Rather than relying solely on user-initiated retrieval, Desperado prompts the user as to when, what, and from where, to retrieve episodes during an ongoing design process. This is done through provision of a retrieval window (see Figure 2), in which episodes that are deemed to be of potential value are promulgated continuously. Episodes are promulgated to a 'retrieval window' and refined continuously during an episode cycle. There are three modes of episode retrieval. First, users can select a re-use class name (e.g. 'the T900 project') from the list of unique names, and view

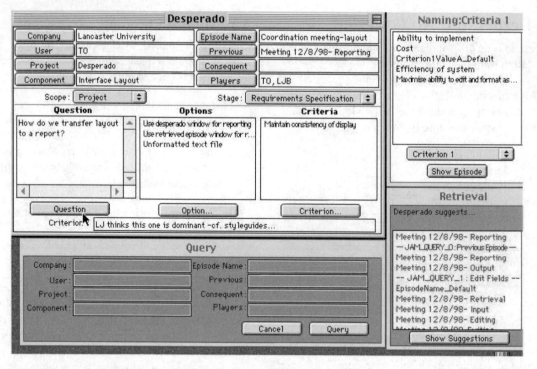

Figure 2: The Desperado window presents the encoding cycle, specifying Company, User, Project, Component, Episode name, Previous episode, Consequents, Players, Scope, Stage and QOC components. The user steps through these with a keystroke command. The Naming window offers a list of event labels from previous episodes that can be selected for and modified in the event text boxes in the Desperado window. The Retrieval window provides a list of system-prompted priority episodes. The user clicks on one for retrieval, and a summary is shown (see Figure 5) along with records of the location of additional documentation (e.g. CAD files). The Query window can be used to search for episodes containing specific terms.

a list of episodes that invoke this name. Second, the user can use Boolean queries to search for episodes. Third, a set of surrogate manager suggestions are made available and continuously updated. In all cases, episodes are prioritised for display so as to maximise their potential *impact*.

The mechanism for promoting previous episodes in the retrieval window and for promoting relevant labels in the naming window are identical. An interpreter (written in CodeWarrior C++) uses prioritization data to rank order previous episodes or event names from within previous episodes. There are five sources of prioritization data: time of episode, defaults ('must see' episodes specified during encoding or querying), key word matches, frequency of retrieval, and weightings derived as a by-product of design rationale elicitation. The interpreter contains an algorithm that evaluates the values of promotion data from each source for each episode. The current algorithm treats data from each source as being of equal value (though see control flexibility, below). However, a re-designed interpreter currently under construction uses a simple learning algorithm to

assess the success of each promotion data source for each user, and increments or decrements its relative value accordingly. Part of maintaining *impact* is to introduce perturbation into prioritization, so that designers do not simply revisit the same set of episodes. Therefore, prioritization data can work in two directions, depending upon the stage of ongoing design. For example, frequency of retrieval data can be used to promote or demote frequently retrieved episodes depending upon whether or not promoted episodes are regularly retrieved, and infrequently retrieved or 'lost' episodes can be promoted after set time periods both within and between projects.

One of the key types of promotion data are user-derived weightings elicited during encoding. This is a novel addition to design rationale methods. Weightings consist of evaluations by users of the extent to which an episode event exemplifies a fixed set of general criteria. The criteria are attributes (e.g. novelty, quality, standard practice), alarms (unexpected problem, pre-technological idea) and dependencies (pre-conditions and implications). Users select general criteria as relevant markers. This does not capture a full rationale for each criterion judgement, but it elicits valuable retrieval cues while minimising the requirement to provide justifications.

As well as being sensitive to the promotion data within previous episodes, the interpreter additionally prioritises previous episodes that are impactful for the current encoding state, as well as the stage and scope of an ongoing episode. For example, different types of reuse information are appropriate in each phase of design. The presentation of questions or criteria-related information in the phase of problem understanding facilitates the orderly decomposition of a complex design problem, whereas the early prompting of option-related information. Thus, Desperado promotes episodes that have heavily weighted questions and criteria early in the design process, and demotes episodes that have only weighted options.

3.4 Control Flexibility

An outcome of our iterative prototyping approach to the development of Desperado has been the finding that system-initiated encoding, retrieval and prompts (e.g. suggestions and warnings regarding un-encoded elements) need to be flexible. For example, the validity of these mechanisms changes depending on whether system use is concurrent during an ongoing design episode or retrospective. Thus, we have added switchability to many aspects of the system. For example, users can choose prioritization to be either entirely system-determined or a user-specified combination of weighting, key-word, date/time, default or simple alphabetical ordering.

4 A Walkthrough of an Episode

We have been using Desperado to document our own project. This has lead us to modify later versions of the system in the light of our own project needs, but has also demonstrated the value of system-initiated retrieval. This walkthrough describes encoding that occurred during a meeting between the first and third authors, who were discussing changes that were needed for the layout of the user interface. Figures 2–5 show some of the episode data that were encoded and retrieved during this meeting. Prior to this meeting, Desperado had been used in a two-hour meeting where all five project members attended, during which 13 episodes were encoded, and then by the first author working on his own on a specification for reporting functions (i.e. a facility for users to collate reports over projects, users, components etc.) in which two episodes were encoded. Immediately prior to the current episode, the first author used the database

to encode an episode pertaining to another research project.

On launching the system, the main encoding window (labelled Desperado) was shown, along with the naming and retrieval windows. The only components of the encoding window that were visible were the data items *company* and *user*, whose text boxes showed the encodings from the previous episode ('Lancaster University' and 'TO'). The naming window showed a list of all the other company names in the database prioritised according to frequency of selection in previous episodes by TO. Since neither needed modification, the user (TO) moved forward (by keystroke selection) and the next items (*project* and *component*) were shown with defaults to TO's previous project ('Reasoning experiment' and 'Timing software'). The naming window showed a list of all the other project names, prioritised by the frequency of TO's involvement. Since the project had changed between episodes, the user selected 'Desperado' (the most highly prioritised label) from the naming window. At this point the *component* text box defaulted to 'Interface layout'. This was not the previous component worked upon by TO in the Desperado project, but was promoted on the strength of other data, namely the frequency with which TO had encoded episodes in the first meeting to do with the interface layout, and the weightings that focus constellations within these episodes received. This was fortuitous, since the component that TO and LJB were engaged with concerned the interface layout.

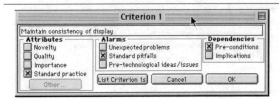

Figure 3: The Criterion capture dialogue. After stating their own episode specific criterion (e.g. by selecting a previous criterion from the Naming window), the user checks those fixed criterion weights that apply.

The episode continued with increasingly sensitive defaults being selected by the system interpreter for event text boxes, and with continual updating of the naming and retrieval windows. At the stage of encoding the focus constellation (effectively the point at which design rationale is elicited), the designers (TO and LJB) specified the question that formed the focus of the episode ("How do we transfer layout to a report?"). A number of options were suggested verbally in rapid succession. An attempt to encode the first of these in Desperado prompted a system message to encourage the user to consider criteria before engaging in further option specification (see Figure 4). The system message can be overridden, or the advice followed, depending upon user needs. The designers switched their attention to considering criteria for selecting between options, and developed two key criteria (flexibility for output for text-editing reports etc., and consistency of display within Desperado). After the options were added, a discussion arose as to which of these criteria was the more important.

To resolve this issue, the designers looked at the retrieval window and saw that the highest promoted episode in the window was one from the first meeting that mentioned 'reports'. On selection of this episode (see Figure 5) and browsing through the additional documentation (whose file location was given on retrieval) they found that a similar discussion had taken place at that meeting, in this case with respect to the consistency or flexibility of formatting within a report itself. Using the retrieved notes the designers were able to see that in this instance having flexible output outweighed the need for display consistency, especially since most users will view reports outside Desperado itself. The episode then continued to completion, which was marked by the recognition that a new question had arisen, necessitating the start of a new episode. By stepping through to the end of the cycle, the episode was stored in the database and its data became available for default and episode promotion for the next episode.

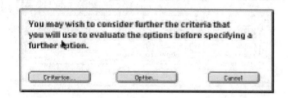

Figure 4: A prompt to encourage the consideration of criteria. The prompt is shown when the user proceeds to state options without encoding any evaluative criteria.

Not all episode encoding cycles work as smoothly or demonstrate so convincingly the added value of the system-initiated retrieval. However, we have engaged in a number of single-session evaluation trials with professional designers at the companies studied in the ethnographic study. In general the system has been favourably received. Though a number of modifications were suggested by each design group we visited, these did not implicate the basic functionality of the episode cycle and the guided encoding and retrieval. Typically they involved things

like replacing a generic 'waterfall' model of design stages with company-specific stages.

Figure 5: Display of a retrieved episode. The user can select buttons to get further detail (e.g. notes, locations of documentation and weighting information).

5   Conclusions

Desperado provides a single environment in which designers encode component-related and design rationale information, whilst making use of system-initiated episode retrieval to guide these encodings and to promote effective exploration of the design space. In developing Desperado, we have endeavoured to minimise the effort required of the designer in encoding and retrieval, whilst recognising that to remove these activities entirely from user control is to hide a crucial aspect of design.

We have carried out single-session evaluations of Desperado with individual designers, and are using the system continuously in our ongoing work. Some measure of the effectiveness of the system is that we captured over 400 episodes in just five weeks of design work on the project. To fully judge the effectiveness of our approach will entail a longitudinal study of Desperado in professional design environments. Before we commit designers to using a new system, we need to validate it in a less commercially sensitive environment. To this end we are currently evaluating the use of the system by postgraduate Engineering students at Lancaster who are using Desperado to document ongoing assignments.

Acknowledgements

This research was supported by an ESRC Cognitive Engineering Programme grant (L127251027). We are grateful to the managers and designers in our end-user companies for their extensive assistance. We also thank Gary Spiers for his assistance with the programming.

References

Ball, L. J. & Ormerod, T. C. (to appear), "Applying Ethnography in the Analysis and Support of Expertise in Engineering Design", *Design Studies* .

Ball, L. J., Evans, J., Dennis, I. & Ormerod, T. C. (1997), "Problem Solving Strategies and Expertise in Engineering Design", *Thinking and Reasoning* **3**, 247–70.

Buckingham Shum, S. (1996), Analyzing the Usability of a Design Rationale Notation, *in* T. P. Moran & J. M. Carroll (eds.), *Design Rationale: Concepts, Techniques and Use*, Lawrence Erlbaum Associates, pp.185–215.

Conklin, E. J. & Begeman, M. L. (1988), "gIBIS, A Hypertext Tool for Exploratory Policy Discussion", *ACM Transactions on Office Information Systems* **6**(4), 303–31.

Duffy, A. H. B. & Duffy, S. M. (1996), "Learning for Design Reuse", *AI-EDAM* **10**, 139–42.

Gero, J. S. (1990), "Design Prototypes: A Knowledge Representation Schema", *AI Magazine* **11**, 26–36.

Grudin, J. (1988), Why CSCW Applications Fail. Problems in the Design and Evaluation of Organizational Interfaces, *in* D. G. Tatar (ed.), *Proceedings of CSCW'88: Conference on Computer Supported Cooperative Work*, ACM Press, pp.85–93.

MacLean, A., Young, R. M., Bellotti, V. M. E. & Moran, T. P. (1991), "Questions, Options and Criteria: Elements of Design Space Analysis", *Human–Computer Interaction* **6**(3-4), 201–50.

Human–Computer Interaction — INTERACT '99
M. Angela Sasse and Chris Johnson (Editors)
Published by IOS Press, © IFIP TC.13, 1999

A Framework for Usability Problem Extraction

Gilbert Cockton & Darryn Lavery

School of Computing, Engineering and Technology, University of Sunderland,
PO Box 299, Sunderland SR6 0YN, UK.

{Gilbert.Cockton,Darryn.Lavery}@sunderland.ac.uk

Abstract: We present a new framework for Structured Usability Problem EXtraction (SUPEX), which structures decision making during problem extraction. It avoids the unreliability and inconsistency associated with direct extraction of problems from raw test data. It does so via flexible phases that ground user difficulties in test data, and then systematically group and generalise difficulties before causal analysis and solution recommendation. The SUPEX framework can be adapted to different evaluation contexts.

Keywords: usability engineering, user testing, research methods.

1 From Data to Problem Sets

Raw data occurs in various forms in usability evaluation: in inspection methods as analysts' predictions; in user testing as tapes, notes and questionnaire data. Usability engineers must form consolidated problem sets from such raw data. In practice, this process tends to be informal.

Informality does have the advantage of efficiency, which may be the overriding concern in industrial settings. However, informality does introduce clear risks of unreliability and inconsistency that are unacceptable in evaluation contexts such as experimental evaluation of interaction devices and techniques or assessment of usability inspection methods, where scientific criteria of reliability and repeatability are more important than efficiency.

In this paper, we present a new framework for Structured Usability Problem EXtraction (SUPEX), which structures decision making during problem extraction. We begin with a review of the problems that SUPEX aims to overcome. We then present SUPEX, its flexibility and further work.

2 Reliability in Evaluation

User testing has been held up as a gold standard (Landauer, 1995), but recent studies indicate major analyst and procedural variations. In one study, four analysts examined the same videos of user tests. They produced distinct problem sets (Jacobsen et al., 1998). Similarly, when four usability labs were asked to test the same product, they produced different problem sets (Rowe et al., 1994). Jacobsen et al.'s study isolates problem extraction as a major cause of analyst variation. In the earlier study differences in test planning and execution would cause further variation. Neither study controlled for usability goals, yet clearly analysts' views of product targets affect problem isolation.

In another study (Lee, 1998), 30 usability reports were analysed using an approximate model of user action. The study found that problems focussed on users' action specification at the expense of their goal formation and action execution. This systematic bias was not created by the products under test: "user testing might be unintentionally ignoring important types of usability problems" (Lee, 1998, p.32).

If there are doubts about the 'gold standard' of user testing, then it is not surprising to find problems with the validation of usability inspection methods. These have been extensively criticised on methodological grounds (Gray & Salzman, 1998). Objections to this critique generally fail to move beyond the apologetic pragma of pioneers of industrial HCI.

Usability inspection methods are validated by matching analysts' predictions to known problems. The two weak links in such studies are:

1. Construction of a set of known problems.

2. Matching analysts' predictions to problems.

Both are unreliable in current studies (Lavery et al., 1997). Known problem sets are too often based on the researchers' experience of a system, e.g. (Nielsen, 1992), rather than systematically derived from test data. Even where user testing has been used as a baseline to compare methods, problem extraction procedures have not been considered as a source of bias (Lee, 1998).

3 The SUPEX Framework

The SUPEX method is derived from an analysis of fundamental concepts in usability evaluation. The structure of SUPEX is derived from logical constraints between these constructs (i.e. difficulties must be established prior to causal analysis, which in turn should precede generation of recommendations).

3.1 Fundamental Concepts

SUPEX is based on analysis of existing published work (Lavery et al., 1997). It is derived from a definition of 'problem', which is "something that causes some difficulty". In everyday use, 'problem' may refer to a cause, a difficulty, or both. For usability problems, we must cover both and pay close attention to the context in which difficulties arise.

In much industrial practice, the goal is to form problem-recommendation pairs, where 'problem' and 'difficulty' are generally synonyms. Yet a difficulty with no cause (as in many empirical tests) cannot be rationally addressed. Nor can a difficulty out of context be reliably analysed. Also, a hypothesized cause with no specific associated difficulties (e.g. as in some heuristics) cannot reliably predict anything.

Problem extraction should separate *difficulty in context, cause* and *recommendation*, and address them in order. Analysis should begin by isolating and relating difficulties. Their context guides subsequent causal analysis. Recommendations would then address causes, rather than superficial user difficulties. Even this simple ordering has more structure than the common practice of forming pairs of problems and recommendations with no explicit causal analysis (Lee, 1998).

3.2 SUPEX Structure

SUPEX maintains a simple focus which reduces cognitive load. Multiple related simultaneous judgements give way to single decisions, i.e.:

1. Isolation — is this a difficult episode with respect to product/evaluation targets?

2. Analysis — at what level of generality (if any) is this an instance of a difficulty?

3. Diagnosis — what (and how plausible/ credible) are the possible causes of difficulty?

4. Treatment — what changes (design, documentation or training) could remove causes?

This compares favourably with existing structured approaches to empirical evaluation, which tend to address the isolation of difficulties, e.g. (Siochi & Ehrich, 1991). Not only does SUPEX extend through causal analysis to recommendation generation, it also introduces a novel approach to isolating difficulties.

SUPEX isolates and analyses *episodes* of interaction before it analyses difficulties. The introduction of episode isolation was a response to our unsatisfactory experiences when grounding problem reports directly in user test data. This approach not only obstructed the generalization and combination of instances of difficulties, but also failed to assess difficulties in the context of eventual outcomes. This led to both over-reporting of problems from which users recovered immediately and effortlessly, and also under-reporting of apparently innocent slips and mistakes that caused major difficulties later.

In summary, approaches that proceed directly to the isolation of difficulties risk both under- and over-reporting by both failing to assess difficulties in context and to consider eventual outcomes. SUPEX combines and generalises over episodes by abstraction, coding and threading. Each contributes to effective and efficient reporting by supporting accurate prioritization and generalization of difficulties in the second stage of SUPEX.

3.3 An Overview of SUPEX

The SUPEX framework identifies four distinct major phases of activity. Sub-stages refine activities within each phase, but many can be fused or eliminated. It is not necessary to complete each phase before undertaking the next. For example, recommendations can be proposed at any point (test users often make them). The major phases are:

1. isolation of relevant episodes;

2. analysis of relevant difficulties;

3. causal analysis; and

4. recommendation generation.

3.3.1   *Isolation of Relevant Episodes*

This is potentially the most complicated and resource intensive phase.   The sub-stages are transcription, segmentation, abstraction, coding, threading and filtering.

This phase aims to produce a set of episodes that fail to meet product or evaluation targets.   Targets are essential when isolating relevant episodes.   They should be established before planning user tests. Targets can be based on performance or preference. They should be grounded in an expected context of use as there can be no universal definition of 'usability problem'.   Thus, inefficient episodes may be difficulties for some contexts, but not for others. Similarly, user satisfaction may be critical in some contexts and not in others.

The first sub-stage is *transcription* of user actions and utterances, and (if present) the observer's utterances.   Transcription is laborious, but greatly simplifies later stages.   Transcription results in complete records of interaction. The second sub-stage *segments* these into coherent episodes.

Episodes are crucial to isolating relevant difficulties in SUPEX. An episode is a contiguous sequence of interaction events that starts and ends on identified boundaries.   Boundaries guide the segmentation of the interaction data (Jordan & Henderson, 1995). The start and end of a test session are fixed boundaries.

SUPEX requires specific criteria that determine the boundaries between episodes.   In our generic research context, we have found that segmentation should begin a new episode when the system is in a stable state after the user pauses or changes focus. This rule recognizes that pauses and utterances are the main observable evidence of user consciousness, but also that an episode also needs to be coherent in system terms.   As system responses determine many user actions and reactions, episodes need to correspond to well-formed units of system activity. Segmentation for HCI research needs to be based on a combination of theories about systems and people. Our segmentation rules for HCI research are discussed further in Section 4.

The segmentation sub-stage produces a sequence of basic episodes.   The *abstraction* sub-stage exposes qualitative differences in user performance. Novice interaction consists of very fine grained episodes, that coarsen as users gain familiarity with the system.   Skilled behaviour creates longer episodes with boundaries corresponding to high-level system capabilities (complete commands) or user tasks.

To expose such qualitative differences in interaction, the abstraction sub-stage overlays basic episodes with hierarchies of planned, skilled or abandoned interaction.   Where users have to plan action execution, episodes fold up to intermediate episodes with syntactic boundaries within command execution. Once users are skilled in command usage, basic episodes fold up immediately to functionally folded episodes.   With skilled task execution, a basic episode spans a whole task, folding up without punctuation by syntactic or semantic system boundaries. Interaction here is transparent.

Abstraction supports powerful visualizations of the rhythm of interaction.   We currently use a spreadsheet to fold episodes.   Figure 1 shows a schematic of folded episodes based on experience with our test corpus (Lavery et al., 1997).

Basic	Intermediate	Functional	Task
Cursor to Edit menu			
Cursor to File menu			
Cursor to Tools			
Pause			
Cursor to Utilities	Select and cancel menu Utilties		Add Lists env
Depress button			
Pause			
Release button			
Pause			
Cursor to Utilities	Select Add from Utilties menu	Add env to Search Path	
Depress button			
Cursor to Add			
Release button			

Figure 1: Schematic of folded episodes.

The transcript is in the leftmost columns (starting at top).   Related information (e.g. user focus) appears next to the transcript in our spreadsheets, but is omitted from the schematic.   In Figure 1, basic episodes are represented by bold rectangles over the transcript (in our spreadsheets they are a separate column). Each rectangle spans steps in the basic episode. Intermediate, functional and task episodes occupy columns to the right of the basic episode column, except where interaction is abandoned at a low level of interaction.   Then cells to the right are greyed out. Large areas of grey clearly expose a user in difficulty (we do not grey out 'intervals' within task execution). Uniform rectangles spanning all four columns of episodes indicate transparent interaction. Where users have developed competence but not fluency, spanning rectangles grow deeper from left to right, revealing a well-formed although halting hierarchy of command elements and task steps.

Abstraction is critical for high quality problem sets, as it separates difficulties according to an approximate model of user interaction, and thus provides direct support for Lee's (1998) approach. Our experience is that only the multiple representations of interaction in abstraction trees allow identification of all user difficulties.

In the next *coding* sub-stage, episodes are grouped by recurring difficulties with specific interaction objects or task steps (e.g. repeated attempts). The evaluation context should determine which forms of coding are used. For method assessment, we again use a comprehensive set of coding dimensions. As well as content coding by system (faulty features) and task focus (tricky steps), we have used *outcome* coding to classify episodes. Example classifications include (no) progress and (no) setback. The evaluation context should determine the choice of such content and outcome codes.

Segmentation, abstraction and coding reduce the fragmentation and over-reporting common in approaches based on dialogue failures (Cockton & Lavery, 1998):

- Segmented episodes within suitable boundaries overcome the tendency to treat all breakdowns as separate problems.

- Abstract episodes rendezvous with Activity Theory as they describe "dynamic movement between levels of activity rather than assuming stasis" (Nardi, 1996, p.10).

- There need be no breakdown in an episode's coherent and focused sequence of interaction.

However, this is not enough to completely eliminate over-reporting and fragmentation. Interaction following a difficult episode can both deteriorate and improve:

- A minor breakdown and successful recovery from it can form a thread that highlights significant dynamics in the interaction.

- Adverse interaction may shape subsequent episodes.

- Inappropriate episode outcomes can cause delayed difficulties, but no obvious immediate need for recovery.

All the above requirements are addressed by the penultimate *threading* sub-stage. A thread is a *sequence of related episodes*. Episodes in a thread need not be contiguous. Threads avoid over-reporting by identifying difficulties from which users recover immediately and effortlessly. In such threads, an episode containing a difficulty is followed by an immediate recovery episode. Threads simplify later analysis of difficulties in context, for example, a thread could relate an episode with poor feedback or poor response times to subsequent exploratory episodes where users attempt to establish what has happened or is happening. Lastly, threads avoid under-reporting by associating minor difficulties with subsequent major negative outcomes. In such threads, an episode containing an inappropriate action is associated with later episodes containing difficulties caused by the earlier action.

The final sub-stage is *filtering*, which is straightforward and reliable when episodes have been systematically segmented, abstracted, coded and threaded. Filtering preserves episodes that do not satisfy product and evaluation targets. Essentially, episodes that aren't disappointing are deleted from further consideration (good coding can make this a trivial task).

Filtering occurs at all levels of abstraction. Abstraction trees can be pruned in any way. For example, only the most abstract episodes may be preserved. Alternatively, pervasive problems with action execution may preserve basic episodes, but not their more abstract spanning episodes.

When all sub-stages are performed rigorously, episode isolation can involve considerable iteration and inter-dependencies. For use of the full version of SUPEX in research contexts, we see this as a strength, since each sub-stage forces reflection on the quality and extensiveness of decisions made in previous sub-stages. Thus, while inefficient, backtracking secures a high quality of analysis.

3.3.2 Analysis of Difficulties

Extensive episode analysis simplifies subsequent phases. The sub-stages for difficulty analysis are *description, collection* and *generalization*.

Many difficulties can be pinpointed in filtered coded episodes. The task at this point is to describe them succinctly. This is easier for *outcome difficulties* that are properties of an episode, for example inefficiency resulting from an inappropriate task method (e.g. delete then add instead of move). For point difficulties that correspond to critical incidents or dialogue failures, succinct descriptions do present a challenge.

Content coding is used to *collect* together instances of similar difficulties with system features or task steps. These are then generalised and given a minimally abstract description (i.e. difficulties are generalised no further than is necessary). Generalization is a challenging and skilled activity, as descriptions must preserve the common relevant context of each instance.

Generalization can be repeated to create a hierarchy of difficulties. It greatly simplifies causal analysis and aids readers of reports, especially where word processor outliners can expand and collapse difficulty hierarchies.

Figure 2 shows difficulty hierarchies for two test participants. The lowest level (specific instances of difficulties in context) is not shown. There are several instances of some difficulties. It is easy to merge difficulties for several users (i.e. 1.1 with 2.1 and 1.2 with 2.2). Also action specification difficulties for S4 (1.3.) never arose for S7 (due to 3 — serious problems with goal formation). The latter two difficulties cannot be merged, but can be generalised into difficulties with re-ordering.

---

1. S4 cannot always operate menus or dragging
    1.1. S4 often selects menu with button 3
        1.1.1. Tries to select menus with button 3
        1.1.2. Surprise at button 1 selecting a menu
    1.2. S4 expects to click menus to activate them
        1.2.1. clicks GlobalVariables once
    1.3. S4 often tries to re-order with button 1
        1.3.1. S4 does not know how to re-order
        1.3.2. Tries dragging with button 1
2. S7 doesn't try to select menus with button 1
    2.1. To select menus S7 tries to use button 3
    2.2. Instead of revealing menus by holding down left button, S7 expects to click on the menu
3. S7 never finds how to re-order by dragging

Figure 2: Difficulty hierarchies.

3.3.3   Formation of Problems

This phase forms a set of problems by adding causal analyses to difficulties. Multiple possible causes are preferable to a single probable cause, since establishing causes beyond reasonable doubt may require formal experiments that cannot be justified within available resources.

The quality of causal analysis is absolutely dependent on the analysts' grasp of relevant theories (cognition, perception, attention, social interaction, motivation) as well as their understanding of the software under test. Usability Engineering is a knowledge-based activity. Possible sources of support here are taxonomies of user error and dialogue failures, e.g. (Booth, 1990), as well as specialised theories of learning, e.g. CE+ (Polson & Lewis, 1990) and cognition. The need for a potentially deep understanding of a system and its application domain

means that collaborative causal analysis by a multi-disciplinary team is generally preferable to analysis by a single usability professional.

3.3.4   Recommendations and Reporting

Generation of recommendations in SUPEX is supported by prior causal analysis. As with causal analysis, collaborative generation of recommendations by a multi-disciplinary team is generally preferable. Further resources can be recruited, such as results of HCI experiments.

3.4   Current status of SUPEX Work

SUPEX has been applied independently in its early form by both authors to one test user's data. A further three user sessions have been successfully segmented by both authors. The second author has refined SUPEX by repeated revision and re-application to this user's and a further user's test data.

Four users' difficulties have been extracted and analysed by the second author using SUPEX in its current form. Merging of users' difficulties has been explored. A further user's session has been successfully segmented and abstracted. Such low numbers are not a problem for qualitative research, which is not based on attainment of some statistical significance. Hundreds of hours have been spent on re-transcription, re-segmentation, re-coding and re-analysing difficulties to conform to evolving versions of SUPEX since July 1997. For example, an early change to our segmentation rules forced us to re-code the transcripts to consider pausing in the user's interaction. Indeed, Jordan & Henderson (1995, p.48) have commented that:

> "... in practice, the transcript emerges as an iteratively modified document that increasingly reflects the categories the analyst has found relevant to his or her analysis."

SUPEX has stabilised recently and can now be more readily applied to further test data. Current work focuses on further application of SUPEX by the authors and a research student, and a survey of operational requirements based on industrial practice.

Space limitations force the credibility and value of the framework as presented here to rest more on the coherence and pertinence of its concepts, rather than on thorough demonstration of effectiveness. Our hope is that SUPEX is sufficiently comprehensive and innovative in its synthesis to warrant the interest of fellow HCI researchers.

4   SUPEX as a Framework

SUPEX specifies a full structure of activities for the most demanding context of evaluation: the preparation of a known problem set for method assessment. Less demanding contexts of evaluation can fuse and eliminate phases and sub-stages. However, removal of all structure greatly increases risks of over-reporting and fragmentation (loss of the 'big picture') in commercial testing.

SUPEX can be adapted to the operational requirements of various contexts of evaluation. This flexibility makes SUPEX a framework rather than a method. Operational requirements require variation points within SUPEX to let it be adapted to available time, skill, collaboration and experience of analysts, required deliverables and purpose. To illustrate the flexibility of SUPEX, its use in three evaluation contexts will now be described.

4.1   Industrial Use

Industrial requirements for SUPEX have been gathered continuously from informal discussions with practitioners and researchers in response to presentations of SUPEX.

Industrial use must start with product and evaluation targets that recognize the contextual nature of 'real' user difficulties. There can be no compromises here as there is no universal definition of a 'usability problem', nor can there be one. What is a problem for one system (e.g. poor task completion times for hotel reservation by a travel agent) is not a problem for all systems (e.g. task completion time for infotainment). Thus the nine criteria for difficulties in (Jacobsen et al., 1998) are not all appropriate for all contexts of computer use.

The main time demands in SUPEX are associated with isolating and organizing difficulties, where the most reliable approaches from interaction analysis (Jordan & Henderson, 1995) demand extensive resources for video analysis, transcription, segmentation and cooperative analysis of episodes. In some contexts, analysts may proceed directly to isolating difficulties. The first phase of SUPEX would thus be omitted. The consequences of reduced resources here depend on the skills of data analyst. Skilled usability practitioners may be able to rapidly isolate the 'critical incidents' in a test session, but novices need structured support.

Omitting the first stage of SUPEX thus carries risks that should be properly assessed. An alternative to completely omitting episode isolation would be to proceed immediately to the final sub-stage of episode filtering. Analysts must rely on experience and vigilance to isolate (threads of) episodes of interaction where product goals are not met. Risks can be reduced further by opportunistically revisiting the sub-stages of abstraction, coding and threading to reduce over- and under-reporting.

When moderate resources are available (perhaps supported by semi-automated transcription tools) all sub-stages of episode isolation may be performed, considerably reducing the risks of inconsistency, inappropriateness or oversight. However, all of the sub-stages can be simplified, for example transcripts can be made from notes rather than video tape. Using a coarser grain of interaction than the keystroke level will reduce the time needed to produce a transcript. Segmentation can be adapted to evaluation procedures, e.g. where evaluators are active during user testing, help and hints can start new episodes, as can dialogues with users.

Where evaluation resources do not allow painstaking and systematic segmentation, video tools can be used to rapidly segment on the basis of analyst experience and intuition. Segmentation need not be at the basic level when resources are limited (or when product/evaluation targets do not require it). Where segments correspond to coarser units of interaction, the analyst effectively combines segmentation with abstraction.

Many evaluation contexts do not have the resources for extensive coding. However, risks accompany its omission, since summative coding exposes problem episodes without objective critical incidents. Our experience is that an exclusive focus on critical incidents can overlook structural user difficulties that are critical for product and evaluation targets. Also, feature and task step coding greatly assist in subsequent difficulty and causal analysis.

In the *episode filtering* sub-stage, the least risky strategy is to exclude smooth episodes rather than to include awkward ones. However, the resulting set of episodes may be too large for efficient processing in industrial contexts, in which filtering should add rather than exclude episodes. Also, if difficulty description and generalization would be too time consuming, they can be omitted. Causal analysis would then operate on episodes.

In many industrial settings, problem extraction becomes a group activity once difficulties have been analysed. Developers are best involved in causal analysis. Marketing staff need to be involved in recommendation generation. In these cases, the last two phases of SUPEX should be performed as group activities. Existing meeting formats can be used.

4.2   General Research Use

For research use, considerable resources must be allocated to episode isolation. However, there are difficulties associated with the segmentation and filtering sub-stages, as the contextual nature of successful interaction limits the value of generic usability criteria (especially where *thresholds* are concerned: when is a user's pause too long?)

Our response is to adopt a theoretical approach to segmentation that can reasonably cover a wide range of usage contexts. We have thus based segmentation for HCI research on key concepts and perspectives from Activity Theory (Nardi, 1996). This guides us to end an episode on evidence of conscious user intent or concentration. Thus a user expressing a conscious goal can mark a boundary between episodes, as can classic usability 'problems' such as abandoning a task, expressing surprise, confusion or dissatisfaction, or seeking help. However, consciousness alone is not adequate as a segmentation criterion.

By definition, interaction requires some change in system state, if only at the keystroke level of interaction (e.g. cursor movement). Episodes organize interaction and this must involve some change of system state. At their end, the system state must be stable, as formalised by Dix: further time intervals with no user input don't alter the state (Dix, 1987, p.219). If the system is not stable at the onset of consciousness, the episode continues until it is. Stability keeps interleaved inputs and outputs together, greatly easing subsequent isolation of user difficulties. Without the stability rule, threads of fine-grained interaction disperse across several episodes. However, we apply similar notions of 'stability' to user consciousness, and thus extend an episode boundary beyond the first onset of consciousness when, for example, a chain of utterances or reactions belong together.

Stability unites both the user's and system's state within a single focus. Episodes can thus vary in the level of activity that they describe, as required by the principles of Activity Theory. This forces analysis to understand both the user (consciousness suggests breakdowns) and the system.

Episode abstraction combines well with this approach to segmentation. Where a task episode is formed from several basic/intermediate/functional episodes, an Activity Theory account would classify episodes as part of an action, consciously punctuated between system level operations. Where task episodes correspond directly to basic episodes, the task is an operation with no evidence of conscious planning (Nardi, 1996).

We feel that the above approach to segmentation is valid for a range of research uses, especially given the complementarity of segmentation and abstraction. However, there are special considerations associated with the assessment of usability inspection methods, which are now given special attention.

4.3   Method Assessment

Predictive methods for usability inspection are assessed by matching analysts' predictions to known problems. As noted above, the two weak links in such studies are:

1. construction of a set of known problems; and

2. matching analysts' predictions to problems.

SUPEX is ideally suited to constructing reliable known problem sets (its fourth stage may be omitted). When coding episodes, we use a superset of established evaluation concerns and segment on the slightest hint of user consciousness. The episode filtering sub-stage can be omitted for method assessment where methods predict success as well as failure. Clearly, it is important to have a measure of correct success prediction, and this is not possible if only problematic episodes are considered.

For reliable matching of analysts' predictions to known problems, the format for problem reporting is crucial. Gray & Salzman (1998) overlooked this in their critique of method assessment research. They argue that *construct validity* problems arise when predictions based on intrinsic properties of a design (as in Heuristic Evaluation) are matched to external user behaviours (from user testing).

It is highly unlikely that Gray & Salzman's construct validity challenges can be fully met until inspection methods are better supported by theory. However, improvements can be made by applying empirical research methods to the matching problem. Better procedures would allow us to determine whether the following describe the same problem:

- The 'Clashes' label does not afford selection.

- User selected 'Tools' menu (not 'Clashes' button).

- Users must know that the 'Clashes' label is selectable.

Different extents of match can be considered when assessing predictive methods (total/partial match on some/all elements).

Empirical research can develop common report formats for usability problems and improve the reliability of method assessment without solving the deeper problems of construct validity. We demonstrated the worth of empirical approaches when grounding an earlier problem format (Lavery et al., 1997) against a transcribed video corpus. Not only was the format inadequate, but so was our problem extraction method (Cockton & Lavery, 1998). This successful invalidation of a carefully derived format showed that empiricism can move beyond discount validation of discount methods. It helped us both improve our report format and led to the development of SUPEX.

Improving problem extraction and reporting will improve assessment of predictive HCI methods. They can profile the types of usability problems that a method predicts to some degree of accuracy, and thus improve on simple percentages that hide the product-critical usability problems that fall within the 30–50% that methods don't predict.

5 Further Work

Existing work has focused on the first two phases of SUPEX, since this has been most important for our research on the assessment of usability inspection methods. We are steadily improving the later stages of SUPEX prior to industrial validation and development of tool support.

5.1 Recommendations and Reports

We are simplifying our previous problem format (Lavery et al., 1997) for use within SUPEX report. It will have three main elements:

1. Generalization(s) of collections of difficulties in context.

2. Alternative causal analyses for appropriate levels of difficulty generalization.

3. Recommendations based on causal analysis for addressing difficulties at appropriate generalizations.

5.2 Method Assessment and the Matching Problem

A research student is using SUPEX to assess the scope and accuracy of Heuristic Evaluation by deriving a problem set from a new test corpus.

5.3 Validation and Tool Support

Comprehensive assessment and development of SUPEX is beyond the resources of a single research group. We therefore intend to collaborate with other HCI research groups in academia and industry.

We will formally survey current industrial approaches to problem extraction and reporting. We will identify requirements for an industrial application and tool support for the SUPEX method. Survey work will be complemented by re-analysis of existing test corpora. This will let us benchmark existing practice and demonstrate over-reporting, under-reporting and fragmentation.

We will develop tool support for SUPEX, with a specific emphasis on complementary support for analytical and empirical evaluation, which are less distinct than many recognize (both depend on folk theory and analyst judgement for causal analysis).

6 Conclusions

For a decade, Usability Engineering have been guided by the pragmatism and politics of the uptake of HCI methods. Best was the enemy of good, and even good was often too much for the development budget (never mind the mind-set). In a world where most user interfaces were poor, introducing any user- centred perspective was progress.

In many software development organizations, HCI methods are now part of best practice. Requirements engineers embrace scenarios and observation of work. In the UK, end-users are seconded to acceptance tests in supermarket chains and government departments (Maguire & Wheeldon, 1998). Such teams eventually look to HCI research to improve on their common sense. HCI research can provide methods for both empirical and analytical evaluation. However, many methods have been progressively 'discounted' to reduce barriers to uptake. The result is that HCI methods may offer little beyond the well-intentioned common sense of the new generation of 'bare foot' usability amateurs.

As uptake of HCI methods improves, we need no longer discount all methods for all practitioners. Thus, researchers now criticise existing approaches to user testing and validating inspection methods.

Better problem extraction procedures improve both empirical *and* analytical evaluation, because better problem sets support method improvement. Usability inspection methods should be further improved by common report formats, allowing more reliable matching, and thus more reliable assessment of method scope and effectiveness.

SUPEX is unique in its synthesis of advanced methods from interaction analysis with existing user testing procedures. It is the only structured framework to offer support from the initial analysis of test data to problem reporting. It is also the only such framework to address the needs of research as well as industry!

SUPEX responds to critiques of method assessment by offering a way forward that does not depend on major theoretical advances in our understanding of human–computer interaction.

Landauer (1995, p.274) has likened good user testing to washing away the dirt from gold nuggets. Much user testing is more akin to picking nuggets out from dirt! We hope that SUPEX will thoroughly wash away the dirt to reveal every nugget.

Acknowledgements

This research was initially funded by UK EPSRC grant no. GR/K82727. Discussions with Nigel Bevan (NPL/Serco), Bronwyn Taylor (IBM), Mary Czerwinski, Ken Dye, Wai On Lee, Dennis Wixon and other Microsoft usability staff have provided valuable insights about industrial practice and needs.

References

Booth, P. A. (1990), "Identifying and Interpreting Design Errors", *International Journal of Human–Computer Interaction* **2**(4), 307–32.

Cockton, G. & Lavery, D. (1998), What's the Problem with Usability Problems?, Technical Report TR-1998-2, Department of Computer Science, University of Glasgow.

Dix, A. J. (1987), The Myth of the Infinitely Fast Machine, in D. Diaper & R. Winder (eds.), *People and Computers III (Proceedings of HCI'87)*, Cambridge University Press, pp.215–28.

Gray, W. D. & Salzman, M. (1998), "Damaged Merchandise? A Review of Experiments that Compare Usabilty Evaluation Methods", *Human–Computer Interaction* **13**(3), 203–61.

Jacobsen, N. E., Hertzum, M. & John, B. E. (1998), The Evaluator Effect in Usability Tests, in C.-M. Karat, A. Lund, B. Bederson, E. Bergman, M. Beaudouin-Lafon, N. Bevan, D. Boehm-Davis, A. Boltman, G. Cockton, A. Druin, S. Dumais, N. Frischberg, J. Jacko, J. Koenemann, C. Lewis, S. Pemberton, A. Sears, K. T. Simsarian, C. Wolf & J. Ziegler (eds.), *Companion Proceedings of CHI'98: Human Factors in Computing Systems (CHI'98 Conference Companion)*, ACM Press, pp.255–6.

Jordan, B. & Henderson, A. (1995), "Interaction Analysis: Foundation and Practice", *Journal of Learning Sciences* **4**(1), 39–103.

Landauer, T. K. (1995), *The Trouble with Computers: Usefulness, Usability and Productivity*, MIT Press.

Lavery, D., Cockton, G. & Atkinson, M. P. (1997), "Comparison of Evaluation Methods using Structured Usability Problem Reports", *Behaviour & Information Technology* **16**(4-5), 246–66.

Lee, W. O. (1998), Analysis of Problems Found in User Testing using an Approximate Model of User Action, in H. Johnson, L. Nigay & C. Roast (eds.), *People and Computers XIII (Proceedings of HCI'98)*, Springer-Verlag, pp.23–36.

Maguire, A. & Wheeldon, K. (1998), Introducing the Benefits and Employment Services Model Office — Testing the End-to-End Processes, in J. May, J. Siddiqi & J. Wilkinson (eds.), *Adjunct Proceedings of HCI'98*, pp.52–53.

Nardi, B. A. (1996), Activity Theory and Human–Computer Interaction, in B. A. Nardi (ed.), *Context and Consciousness: Activity Theory and Human–Computer Interaction*, MIT Press, pp.7–16.

Nielsen, J. (1992), Finding Usability Problems Through Heuristic Evaluation, in P. Bauersfeld, J. Bennett & G. Lynch (eds.), *Proceedings of CHI'92: Human Factors in Computing Systems*, ACM Press, pp.373–80.

Polson, P. G. & Lewis, C. H. (1990), "Theory-based Design for Easily Learned Interfaces", *Human–Computer Interaction* **5**(2), 191–220.

Rowe, A. L., Lowry, T., Halgren, S. L. & Cooke, N. (1994), A Comparison of Usability Evaluations Conducted by Different Teams, in C. Plaisant (ed.), *Companion Proceedings of CHI'94: Human Factors in Computing Systems (CHI'94 Conference Companion)*, ACM Press, pp.109–10.

Siochi, A. C. & Ehrich, R. W. (1991), "Computer Analysis of User Interfaces Based on Repetition in Transcripts of User Sessions", *ACM Transactions on Office Information Systems* **9**(4), 309–35.

Human–Computer Interaction — INTERACT '99
M. Angela Sasse and Chris Johnson (Editors)
Published by IOS Press, © IFIP TC.13, 1999

Classification Space for Augmented Surgery, an Augmented Reality Case Study

Emmanuel Dubois[1,2], Laurence Nigay[1], Jocelyne Troccaz[2], Olivier Chavanon[3] & Lionel Carrat[2]

[1] Laboratoire CLIPS (CLIPS-IMAG), BP 53 38041 Grenoble, France.

[2] Laboratoire TIMC (TIMC-IMAG), Faculté de Médecine, 38700 La Tronche, France.

[3] Cardiac Surgery Department, University Hospital, 38043 Grenoble, France.

{Emmanuel.Dubois,Laurence.Nigay,Jocelyne.Troccaz}@imag.fr

Abstract: One of the recent design goals in Human Computer Interaction has been to extend the sensory-motor capabilities of computer systems to combine the real and the virtual in order to assist the user in his environment. Such systems are called Augmented Reality (AR). Although AR systems are becoming more prevalent we still do not have a clear understanding of this interaction paradigm. In this paper we propose OPAS as a generic framework for classifying existing AR systems. Computer Assisted Medical Interventions (CAMI), for which the added value of AR has been demonstrated by experience, are discussed in light of OPAS. We illustrate OPAS using our system, CASPER (Computer ASsisted PERicardial puncture), a CAMI system which assists in surgical procedures (pericardial punctures).

Keywords: augmented surgery, CAMI, augmented reality, classification space.

1 Introduction

The term 'Augmented Reality' (AR) appears in the literature usually in conjunction with the term 'Virtual Reality' (VR). The difference between AR and VR involves the 'immersiveness' of the system. A VR system strives for a totally immersive virtual environment in which the user is performing his task. In contrast, an AR system combines the real and the virtual in order to assist the user in performing his task in a physical setting.

In recent years, Augmented Reality (AR) has been the subject of growing interest. However, there is currently no consensus either on a precise definition of AR or on a design space (Milgram & Kishino, 1994). Within this context, it is therefore difficult to compare the existing AR systems and explore new designs. In this paper we present a classification space, OP-a-S, to provide a systematic classification process of augmented reality systems.

Our approach draws from the study of Computer Assisted Medical Intervention (CAMI) systems and augmented reality systems. The next section describes CAMI systems and their goals. We then describe the components of our classification space OP-a-S and illustrate it using our system CASPER (Computer ASsisted PERicardial punctures). In the final section, we use the notion of adapters between the real and the virtual to show how OPAS allows us to classify existing AR systems.

2 Computer Assisted Medical Interventions (CAMI)

There are many application domains of Augmented Reality (AR), including construction, architecture (Webster et al., 1996) and surgery (Bainville et al., 1995; Cinquin et al., 1995; Taylor et al., 1992). The variety of application domains makes it difficult to arrive at a consensus definition of AR: i.e. different people, having distinct goals are using the term 'Augmented Reality'. Our application domain is the augmented surgery or CAMI systems. The main objective of CAMI systems is to help a surgeon in defining and executing an optimal surgical strategy based on a variety of multi-modal data inputs. The objectives aim at improving the quality of the interventions by making them easier, more accurate, and more intimately linked to pre-operative simulations where accurate objectives can be defined. In particular, one basic challenge is to guide a surgical tool according to a pre-planned strategy: To do so robots and 3D localizers (mechanical arms or optical sensors) perform real time tracking of surgical tools such as drills (Cinquin et al., 1995).

Augmented reality plays a central role in this domain because the key point of CAMI systems is to 'augment' the physical world of the surgeon (the operating theatre, the patient, the tools etc.), by providing pre-operative information including the pre-planned strategy. Information is transmitted between the real world and the computer world using different means: computer screens, mouse, pedals, tracking mechanisms, robots, etc.

Since 1985, the TIMC laboratory is working on designing, developing and evaluating CAMI systems. Through progress of technology and growing consciousness of the possibilities of real clinical improvements with computers (Taylor et al., 1992), augmented reality systems are now entering many surgical specialties. Such systems can take on the most varied forms (Bainville et al., 1995). Three classes of CAMI systems are identified in (Troccaz et al., 1997):

1. The passive systems allow the surgeon to compare the executed strategy with the planned one.

2. The active systems perform subtasks of the strategy with the help of an autonomous robotic system.

3. The semi-active or synergistic systems materialize the surgical strategy but the surgeon is in charge of its execution. The system and the surgeon are working in a synergistic way.

At Grenoble, three golden rules have guided the CAMI project for about 14 years:

R1 Design systems for which the clinical value is well defined.

R2 Develop generic systems that can be applied to different clinical applications.

R3 Provide effective collaboration between the surgeon and the system through efficient interfaces.

Our approach in designing CAMI systems, based on these three rules, encompasses three domains:

- Medical domain and clinical requirements.

- Safety critical systems.

- Human–Computer Interaction.

In this paper we focus on the interaction between the surgeon and the computer (Rule R3). As pointed out during the CHI'98 panel (Coble, 1998) on HCI in Health Care, user-centred design can play a central role in designing CAMI systems. Indeed CAMI systems are numerous in many different surgical specialties but the most attention has been paid to the technical issues related to image processing, data fusion and surgeon assistance stemming from the clinical specifications of the problem. Very little effort has been applied to modelling the interaction between the surgeon and the system. The design approach of this clinically-oriented CAMI project so far has been technology-driven. Such a technology driven approach also characterizes AR systems in general. As a proof, let us consider the technology driven definition of AR quoted in (Milgram & Kishino, 1994) concerning a session in a conference:

> "a form of virtual reality where the participant's head-mounted display is transparent, allowing a clear view of the real world."

Nevertheless, augmenting the reality of a user may also rely on the use of force or aural feedback, which is not reflected by Milgram's definition. We adopt here a complementary user-centred approach providing a user-centred classification space for augmented reality systems.

3   The OPAS Classification Space

Our classification space, OPAS, is dedicated to interactive systems including AR ones. We first explain the four components of OP-a-S and their relationships. We then consider the target of the tasks supported by the system and the type of augmentation. Finally we demonstrate how to apply OP-a-S using our system CASPER.

3.1   Four Components

We model the interaction between the user and an interactive system by identifying four components: **O**bject, **P**erson, **A**dapter and **S**ystem (OP-a-S).

The computerized component of the system, called System (S), is able to store, retrieve and transform data. The real object (O) including a drill, a pen or a sheet of paper is manipulated by the user or a robot in order to perform the task. The Object component may include human beings provided that they are involved in the process without interacting directly with the system. This is the case of the patient for example in a CAMI system. The person (P) uses the system. The user (P) and the object (O) belong to the real world ('atom world') while the system component (S) belongs to the virtual or synthetic world ('bit world'). In order to establish a bridge between these two worlds, we introduce a fourth component called Adapter (A). Obvious examples of adapters are the mouse, the keyboard and the screen. Examples of adapters in CAMI systems are ultrasonic or electro-magnetic localizers. In Embodied User Interfaces (i.e. the user uses a computational device by physically manipulating the device), adapters are pressure sensors or tilt sensors (Fishkin et al., 1998).

The four components of OPAS are clearly defined above. The main difficulty is to distinguish between adapters (A) and objects (O). For example, in the most common case, a mouse is an adapter because a mouse is dedicated to transforming physical movements of the user to movements in the virtual world displayed on screen. But if the user employs the mouse as a paperweight, the mouse then becomes an object.

3.2 Links between the Components

The interactive system is composed of these four components which are also able to exchange information with each other. Exchange of data is uni-directional and represented on OP-a-S diagrams with an arrow, from the source-component to the destination-component of the system. An example is the flow of data from the surgical tool (O) to a localizer (A) in a CAMI system, where the localizer (A) performs the tracking of the surgical tool (O):

O (Surgical tool) ⟹ **A** (Localizer)

Data Flow

An adapter according to our definition allows flow of data:

- between the adapter and the system component (S, 'bit world'); and

- between the adapter and the user or the object (P or O, 'atom world').

3.3 Target of the Tasks

Because two worlds 'atom' and 'bit' belong to OPAS modelling, it is important to specify if the system's user is performing a task in order to modify the real world or in order to modify the state of information maintained by the computer. One may thus consider P's task in terms of target operations in:

- real world (human–real world interaction); and

- computer (human–computer interaction).

For example in CAMI systems the target is mainly the real world (performance of the medical intervention) and, in clinical information systems the target is the computer (modification of the state of medical records). The two possible targets of the user's task, real world and computer, respectively correspond to the two terms presented in (Milgram & Kishino, 1994): 'Augmented Reality' (AR) and 'Augmented Virtuality' (AV). Reality designates the real world of the user while virtuality corresponds to the virtual world created by the computer. Applying the two concepts to characterize interaction we obtain:

- In AR, interaction with the real world is augmented by the computer.

- In AV, interaction with the computer is augmented by objects and actions in the real world.

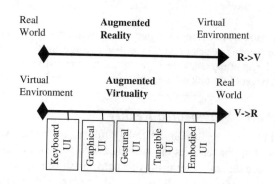

Figure 1: Two parallel continua for characterizing interaction, based on the Reality–Virtuality continuum (Milgram & Kishino, 1994). Along the $V \longrightarrow R$ (Virtuality $\longrightarrow$ Reality) continuum, we position the different interaction paradigms presented in Fishkin et al. (1998).

In Milgram & Kishino (1994) the two concepts AR and AV are presented as belonging to the Reality-Virtuality continuum in order to classify displays. Yet characterizing interaction requires us to distinguish two parallel continua as presented in Figure 1: AR and AV applied to interaction will never meet at a point because the target of the user's task is different. This is because the $R \longrightarrow V$ continuum of Figure 1 is dedicated to human-real world interaction while the $V \longrightarrow R$ continuum characterizes human–computer interaction.

3.4   Type of Augmentation

The augmentation provided by the system can take on a number of different forms. For example, using an AR system (target of the task = real world), the user's action (performance) in the augmented real world and/or the user's perception of the augmented real world can be enhanced. If we refer to the Theory of Action (Norman, 1986), augmentation can be dedicated to the execution phase and/or to the evaluation phase. As shown in Figure 2 the two types of augmentation [execution and evaluation] are applied to the two types of target of the tasks [real world (AR) and computer (AV)]. We illustrate this last point in the next two subsections.

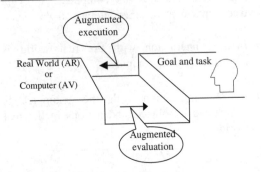

Figure 2: Two types of augmentation: augmented execution and/or augmented evaluation applied to Augmented Reality (Target of the task = Real World) and Augmented Virtuality (Target of the task = Computer).

3.4.1   *Augmented Reality*

For example, the DigitalDesk (Wellner, 1993) is an AR system that enables the user to cut and paste drawings made on real paper using real pens. Such action is not directly possible in the real world: the execution phase is augmented by the computer. Likewise, a system that automatically opens the door when a person wearing an active badge (Want et al., 1992) appears in front of it is also a case of an augmented execution phase: The same task in the real world (open the door) would not be executed the same way.

As opposed to the active badge, the NaviCam system (Rekimoto & Katashi, 1995) is an AR system that augments the evaluation phase. NaviCam displays situation sensitive information by superimposing messages on its video see-through screen. For example one application is the augmented museum: the visitor is looking at a picture while obtaining a textual description of it on screen. Another example of augmented evaluation, which is not visual, is the Audio Aura system. The Audio Aura system (Mynatt et al., 1998) provides information, via background auditory cues, that is tied to the user's physical actions in the workplace. For example, when a visitor discovers an empty office, in Audio Aura he hears auditory cues that convey whether a person has left his office a long time ago or if the visitor has just missed him. Other scenarios presented in (Mynatt et al., 1998), such as hearing a cue that conveys the number of email messages received while entering the coffee room, are not examples of augmented reality but examples of augmented virtuality because the target of the task is the computer. Augmented virtuality is the topic of the next subsection.

AR	Augmented execution	DigitalDesk Active badge: open a door
	Augmented evaluation	NaviCam Augmented museum Audio Aura

3.4.2   *Augmented Virtuality*

Examples of augmented execution in human–computer interaction involve input modalities (Nigay & Coutaz, 1995) based on real objects, such as Fitzmaurice et al. (1995) bricks or Ishii & Ullmer (1997) phicons. Ishii has described this interaction paradigm as the Tangible User Interface. Another example of augmented execution is defined by the more recent approach called Embodied User Interface (Fishkin et al., 1998): the user executes tasks with the computer by physically manipulating the computer.

Examples of augmented evaluation in human–computer interaction refer to more realistic graphics on screen and to output modalities that mimic the real world feedback (visual, audio and tactile feedback).

AV	Augmented execution	Tangible I/O: Brick, Phicons Embodied UI
	Augmented evaluation	Realistic graphics Tactile feedback, etc.

In both cases (AR and AV), a system may augment the execution and the evaluation phases. For example, the DigitalDesk augments the execution phase because of the copy/paste service it supports, and also the evaluation phase by mixing real drawings made on real paper with displayed graphics.

3.5   OPAS Modelling of CASPER

We describe here the OPAS modelling of our CASPER application developed in collaboration with the Grenoble University Hospital. The clinical problem is to remove a build up of fluid (water, blood) in the region around the heart (pericardium), the effect of which is to compress the heart. This procedure is performed through minimal access to the chest.

CASPER (Computer ASsisted PERicardial punctures) allows the pre-operative acquisition and modelling of a 3D stable region in the pericardial effusion from which a target is selected and a safe trajectory is planned. The success of the planned strategy for a surgery is markedly enhanced by on screen guidelines available to the surgeon. Indeed, as shown in Figure 3, CASPER assists the surgeon by providing in real time the position of the puncture needle according to the planned strategy. The user interface of CASPER has been designed by a multidisciplinary team including a surgeon and is fully described in (Chavanon et al., 1997). Figure 3 shows also the components of CASPER in use.

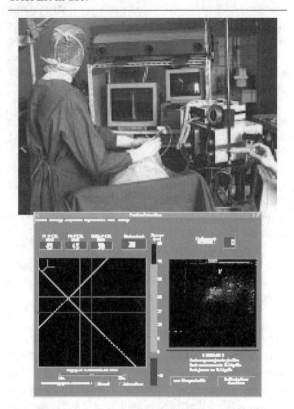

Figure 3: The CASPER application in action.

An OP-a-S description is as follows. The System component (S) transforms the signal from the needle localizer into a graphical representation of the position and the orientation of the needle. In the same window on screen, the current position and orientation of the needle are represented by two mobile crosses, while one stationary cross represents the planned trajectory. When the three crosses are superimposed the executed trajectory corresponds to the planned one. Two adapters (A1, A2) are necessary: The first one (A1) is the screen for displaying guidance to the surgeon, and the second one (A2) is dedicated

to tracking the needle position and orientation. The latter is composed of diodes firmly fixed on the needle and three cameras mounted on a rigid bar. The objects (O) involved in the task are the puncture needle and the patient. Because the surgeon is handling the needle, there is a link from the surgeon (P) to the needle (O) and vice-versa (tactile feedback) (Figure 4). Finally CASPER is a CAMI system and therefore the task's target is the real world (pericardial puncture). In addition CASPER augments the reality of the surgeon by providing pre-operative information during the intervention: CASPER therefore augments the evaluation phase within the surgeon-real world interaction. Indeed the surgeon is still executing the puncture using a needle.

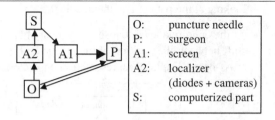

Figure 4: OPAS modelling of CASPER.

So far we have presented and illustrated our OPAS classification space, and by doing so we have defined an Augmented Reality (AR) system as a system that enables the user to perform tasks that have their target in the real world (target of the task = real world). We now focus on the Adapters in AR systems. In particular we study the ergonomic property of continuity in OPAS.

4 Adapter: Boundary between the Real and the Virtual

Adapters are the key component of OP-a-S because they establish a bridge between the real and the virtual world. Adapters determine the type of boundaries between the two worlds that in turn characterize the AR systems.

If we adopt a System-centred view, we distinguish Input Adapters (IA) (inputs to the System component) from Output Adapters (OA) (outputs from the System component):

$$IA \Longrightarrow S \qquad S \Longrightarrow OA$$

For example a keyboard or a pressure sensor are input adapters while a screen, a projector or a head-mounted display (HMD) are output adapters.

In addition matching input/output adapters can provide continuity in task achievement: no shift between the real and the virtual worlds is necessary to perform the task. We identify two concepts that are relevant for continuity: action/perception and cognition. Action/Perception and cognition represent two levels of abstraction. Continuity can be defined at the action/perception level or at the cognitive level:

- No action/perceptual gap between the real and the virtual world.

- No cognitive gap between the real world and the representation defined by the virtual world.

For example in CASPER, the screen is an OA that does not provide continuity:

- At the action/perception level, the surgeon must always shift between looking at the screen and looking at the patient and the needle.

- At the cognitive level, the surgeon must always shift between the position of the needle and the cross-based graphical representation on screen.

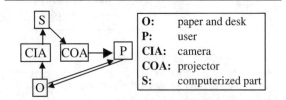

O:	paper and desk
P:	user
CIA:	camera
COA:	projector
S:	computerized part

Figure 5: OPAS modelling of the DigitalDesk.

In this way, OP-a-S shows that at both levels of abstraction, CASPER's screen is a Discontinuous Output Adapter (DOA). Even if we modify CASPER to display the cross-based representation on a see-through HMD, the HMD still does not provide continuity at the cognitive level and is therefore a DOA. Now consider DigitalDesk from an OP-a-S perspective. As opposed to CASPER, the DigitalDesk includes an OA, that is a projector that provides continuity (COA), as modelled in Figure 5. Indeed the DigitalDesk user can draw on real papers on which information can also be displayed via the projector. In addition the Input Adapter in the DigitalDesk is a camera on top of the desk that recognizes the user's gestures: the camera is a Continuous Input Adapter (CIA). Indeed there is continuity both at the action level (actions are performed at the same place on the same object) and at the cognitive level (same actions as in reality). In CASPER the localizer also serves as a Continuous Input Adapter (CIA): no modification of the actions of the surgeon. To conclude the main difference between CASPER and DigitalDesk is that one Output Adapter is continuous (DigitalDesk, Figure 5) while the other one is discontinuous

(CASPER, Adapter A1, Figure 4). Moreover, OP-a-S establishes that CASPER and the DigitalDesk are different not only because of the domain but because of the kind of interaction induced.

5 Conclusion

This paper introduces our interaction-centred approach for classifying Augmented Reality/Virtuality systems. We have presented a conceptual framework, OPAS, in which to place the various aspects of interaction of augmented reality systems as well as augmented virtuality systems. For CAMI systems, OPAS enables us to differentiate between systems that previously all belonged to the passive CAMI systems class (Troccaz et al., 1997). More generally, for augmented reality/virtuality systems, the ability of OPAS to classify existing systems has great promise, especially in light of the rapid technological progress that we are experiencing.

By identifying and organizing the various aspects of interaction, our framework should also help the designer to address the right design questions and to envision future systems. Our goal is to establish a complete interaction-centred design space for AR systems and more specifically CAMI systems. To do so, further work primarily involves linking ergonomic criteria and OPAS modelling in order to identify design principles.

We are currently developing a version of CASPER that represents the trajectory in the form of a cone on a head-mounted display in order to address the discontinuity problem in the current version.

Acknowledgements

This work is supported by the French National Scientific Research Center (CNRS) and by the Grenoble University Hospital. It was influenced by stimulating discussions with our TACIT partners (TMR Research Network). We wish to thank George Serghiou and Leon Watts for reviewing the paper.

References

Bainville, E., Chaffanjon, P. & Cinquin, P. (1995), "Computer Generated Visual Assistance to a Surgical Operation: The Retroperitoneoscopy", *Computers in Biology and Medicine* **25**(2), 165–71.

Chavanon, O., Barbe, C., Troccaz, J., Carrat, L., Ribuot, C. & Blin, D. (1997), Computer Assisted Pericardial Punctures: Animal Feasibility Study, *in* G. Goos, J. Hartmanis & J. van Leeuwen (eds.), *Proceedings of MRCAS'97*, Springer-Verlag, pp.285–91.

Cinquin, P., Bainville, E., Barbe, C., Bittar, E., Bouchard, V., Bricault, I., Champleboux, G., Chenin, M., Chevalier, L., Delnondedieu, Y., Desbat, L., Dessene, V., Hamadeh, A., Henry, D., Laieb, N., Lavallée, S., Lefebvre, J. M., Leitner, F., Menguy, Y., Padieu, F., Péria, O., Poyet, A., Promayon, M., Rouault, S., Sautot, P., Troccaz, J. & Vassal, P. (1995), "Computer Assisted Medical Interventions", *IEEE Engineering in Medicine and Biology* pp.254–63.

Coble, J. (1998), Human–Computer Interaction in Health Care: What Works? What Doesn't?, *in* C.-M. Karat, A. Lund, J. Coutaz & J. Karat (eds.), *Proceedings of CHI'98: Human Factors in Computing Systems*, ACM Press, pp.80–1.

Fishkin, K., Moran, T. & Harrison, B. (1998), Towards Invisible User Interfaces: Embodied User Interfaces, *in* S. Chatty & P. Dewan (eds.), *Proceedings of EHCI'98*, Kluwer, pp.1–18.

Fitzmaurice, G., Ishii, H. & Buxton, W. (1995), Bricks: Laying the Foundations for Graspable User Interfaces, *in* I. Katz, R. Mack, L. Marks, M. B. Rosson & J. Nielsen (eds.), *Proceedings of CHI'95: Human Factors in Computing Systems*, ACM Press, pp.442–9.

Ishii, H. & Ullmer, B. (1997), Tangible Bits Towards Seamless Interfaces Between People, Bits and Atoms, *in* S. Pemberton (ed.), *Proceedings of CHI'97: Human Factors in Computing Systems*, ACM Press, pp.234–41.

Milgram, P. & Kishino, F. (1994), "A Taxonomy of Mixed Reality Visual Displays", *IEICE Transactions on Information Systems* **E77-D**(12), 1321–9.

Mynatt, E., Back, M., Want, R., Baer, M. & Ellis, J. (1998), Designing Audio Aura, *in* C.-M. Karat, A. Lund, J. Coutaz & J. Karat (eds.), *Proceedings of CHI'98: Human Factors in Computing Systems*, ACM Press, pp.566–73.

Nigay, L. & Coutaz, J. (1995), A Generic Platform for Addressing the Multimodal Challenge, *in* I. Katz,

R. Mack, L. Marks, M. B. Rosson & J. Nielsen (eds.), *Proceedings of CHI'95: Human Factors in Computing Systems*, ACM Press, pp.98–105.

Norman, D. A. (1986), Cognitive Engineering, *in* D. A. Norman & S. W. Draper (eds.), *User Centered Systems Design: New Perspectives on Human–Computer Interaction*, Lawrence Erlbaum Associates, pp.31–62.

Rekimoto, J. & Katashi, N. (1995), The World through the Computer: Computer Augmented Interaction with Real World Environments, *in* G. Robinson (ed.), *Proceedings of the ACM Symposium on User Interface Software and Technology, UIST'95*, ACM Press, pp.29–36.

Taylor, R., Paul, H., Cutting, C., Mittlestadt, B., Hanson, W., Kazanzides, P., Musits, B., Kim, Y., Kalvin, A., Haddad, B., Khoramabadi, D. & Larose, D. (1992), "Augmentation of Human Precision in Computer-integrated Surgery", *Innovation and Technology in Biology and Medicine* **13**(4), 450–68. Special Issue on Robotic Surgery.

Troccaz, J., Peshkin, M. & Davies, B. (1997), The Use of Localizers, Robots and Synergistic Devices in CAS, *in* G. Goos, J. Hartmanis & J. van Leeuwen (eds.), *Proceedings of MRCAS'97*, Springer-Verlag, pp.727–36.

Want, R., Hopper, A., Falcao, V. & Gibbons, J. (1992), "The Active Badge Location System", *ACM Transactions on Office Information Systems* **10**(1), 91–102.

Webster, A., Feiner, S., B., M., Massie, W. & Krueger, T. (1996), Augmented Reality in Architectural Construction, Inspection, and Renovation, *in* J. Vanegas & P. Chinowsky (eds.), *Proceedings of Computers in Civil Engineering*, ASCE, pp.913–19.

Wellner, P. (1993), "Interacting with Paper on the DigitalDesk", *Communications of the ACM* **36**(7), 87–96. Special Issue on Computer Augmented Environments.

Human–Computer Interaction — INTERACT '99
M. Angela Sasse and Chris Johnson (Editors)
Published by IOS Press, © IFIP TC.13, 1999

Weak at the Knees? Arthroscopic Surgery Simulation User Requirements, Capturing the Psychological Impact of VR Innovation Through Risk-based Design

John G. Arthur[1], Avril D. McCarthy[2], Henry P. Wynn[1], Peter J. Harley[3] & Chris Baber[4]

[1] The Risk Initiative, Statistics Department, University of Warwick, Coventry CV4 7AL, UK.

[2] Department of Medical Physics and Clinical Engineering, University of Sheffield, Royal Hallamshire Hospital, Sheffield S10 2JF, UK.

[3] School of Mathematics and Statistics, University of Sheffield, Hicks Building, Hounsfield Road, Sheffield S3 7RH, UK.

[4] Industrial Ergonomics Unit, School of Manufacturing and Mechanical Engineering, University of Birmingham, Birmingham B29 2TT, UK.

J.G.Arthur@warwick.ac.uk, hpw@stats.warwick.ac.uk, A.D.McCarthy@sheffield.ac.uk, P.Harley@sheffield.ac.uk, C.Baber@birmingham.ac.uk

Abstract: Reforms of laparoscopic surgery training called for reduction of patient's risks from surgeons in training. In arthroscopy (joint surgery), like all keyhole surgery, training is a mixture of formal courses and practice on patients. Simple arthroscopy simulation models used in courses only cater adequately for an early learning curve. This leaves a gap in patient risk. VR applications are increasing in power to produce complex training devices such as the Sheffield Knee Arthroscopy Training System (SKATS), an advanced knee surgery trainer. Requirements capture for safety critical VR training is more complex than conventional design. This paper discusses SKATS psychological requirements capture process. This exceeds accepted human factors in design and embraces the idea of risk-based innovation. We argue that design aim to reduce risk must utilise operationally defined risk concepts as design inputs. The system is substantially weakened if, due to the primacy of technological and HCI considerations, these are consigned to post design validation.

Keywords: risk, virtual reality, surgery, training.

1 Introduction

1.1 Arthroscopy

Arthroscopy is a form of minimally invasive surgery used for viewing inside joints. The view of the joint is relayed to a video monitor via a rigid endoscope (miniature camera and fibre optics), which is introduced into the joint through a small incision (portal). The reduced degrees of translational freedom imposed by the entry portal mean the surgeon must adapt to moving the body of the arthroscope in the opposite direction (to that anticipated) to where the image is required. Considerable practice is required to achieve the necessary hand–eye coordination for arthroscope navigation. This task is further complicated because, to increase the effective field of view, arthroscopes are constructed with an optical offset (generally 30°). Bringing the tip of an instrument into the field of view of the camera is a skill termed 'triangulation' and it requires considerable practice to perform consistently and quickly. The 3D view of the joint is presented to a standard video monitor via a monocular camera and binocularity (an important depth cue) is lost. Adjusting to the use of other forms of depth cue requires practice. In the UK surgical training using both animals and cadavers is prohibited, thus restricting surgeons to using physical 'black box' type simulators or supervised surgery for training. Arthroscopic surgery is the commonest form of minimal access orthopaedic surgery in the USA and the UK. It is generally a safe form of surgery. However, scuffing of the joint articular surfaces can lead to arthritis in later life and damage to nerves and vascular structures have been reported following arthroscopy. Misplacement of cruciate ligament grafts can be expensive, in terms of patient rehabilitation and revision surgery of failed grafts. The psycho-motor skills required make minimally invasive surgery complex to learn (Dumay & Jense, 1995). Miller (1985) suggested that between 500 – 800 procedures are needed to gain diagnostic proficiency using arthroscopy. Supervised surgery, the traditional method of training, is highly expensive in theatre time and the time of the supervising surgeon. Consequently, many surgeons are trained inadequately and thus place patients at risk of injury (Bamford et al., 1993).

The development of a high fidelity VR simulation has undoubted benefits in this setting. From the initial proposals of VR in surgery e.g. (Satava, 1993), the bulk of virtual reality applications seem to be for minimally invasive surgery such as eye surgery (Sagar et al., 1994), laparoscopy (Ota et al., 1995), arthroscopy (Langrana et al., 1994; Hollands et al., 1995; Ziegler et al., 1995; Mabrey & Merril, 1997).

VR is potentially ideal for simulating dangerous environments or environments in which user cannot be present, it is useful for simulating unusual/rare situations, it offers flexibility with the data or model presented. For example the 3D visualization of complex datasets may enable easier understanding. When used VR should allow the user to interact with and manipulate models in real time and it should allow for 'what if' scenarios to be modelled to enhance learning, that is, simulation. Specifically for arthroscopy VR offers significant flexibility over current physical models for training, e.g. software change of optical offset rather than an actual camera change, left and right joints, varying model complexity. It is potentially less expensive than real arthroscopy instrumentation and physical models.

As an education tool the Sheffield Knee Arthroscopy Training System (SKATS) provides replicable, standardised virtual tasks which generate the potential for objective assessment of performance, self-paced learning, modelling of unusual pathologies — selectable in software, recording and review of practice sessions and recall of 'gold standard' solutions to procedures. For the novice surgeon these benefits in fact could eventually supersede the benefit of training on live patients for navigation, triangulation and some diagnosis tasks by offering an extremely flexible and potentially risk free training environment. There is a totally crucial question however. In the development of such complex devices to be deployed in a high stress environments with high levels of task complexity, precisely what design process should be used?

1.2 Design Process

It has been argued by McCleod (1998) and others that a typical generic cascade design process (i.e. user requirements — detailed specification — high level functionality — detailed functionality — 1st prototype — prototype testing and iteration — user testing) relies on protocol to the detriment of effective user requirements capture.

In the case of SKATS a design team set about an applied problem which was clearly in the domain of a technologically based training system. User requirements were elicited by examination of the physical processes involved in the operation, a review of the current state of the art and interviews with users. Detailed specifications were drawn up incorporating the technical feasibility of the requirements in terms of VR imaging and tracking technologies. A high level functionality was set around the need to create a intuitively believable knee model with physical characteristics which contained the necessary real-time interactive images to allow well-defined procedures to be practised and recorded. The detailed functionality included rules for collision detection and feedback, physical rules for the image boundaries behaviours etc. and game rules for the structure of the control interface functionality.

Tests with the first prototype revealed a need to include accurate force feedback (haptics), a route which had initially been rejected at an early stage in the design. A route which would deeply compromise and complicate the hard won and very sophisticated imaging technology which took great advantage of the absence of the need to interact with any actual real physical structure within the knee.

Computer based products with a long lead time have to remain flexible because technical advances during the project are almost certain (which is particularly the case with VR). This phenomenon could also be said to be true of psychological requirements for SKATS. This is despite a basic level of user feedback during the design cycle just described.

There is a highly concentrated body of work in HCI, for a good general discussion see (Dix et al., 1998). There is also a growing literature which looks at the complex problems of usability and validity of interfaces and 'requirements engineering' (Macaulay, 1996). This sort of work has led to dramatic reconsideration of standard design processes inherited from the physical sciences e.g. (Noyes & Baber, 1999). This has spurred the development of new approaches and a plethora of supporting evaluative tools. 'Usability Engineering' (Nielsen, 1993) has come into focus. Hartson (1998) argues:

> "The central concept of HCI is usability, ease of use plus usefulness. Achieving good usability requires attention to both product and development process, particularly for the user interaction design, which should serve as requirements for the user interface software component."

In the midst of these highly focussed debates there is a need to consider a wider psychology of design. Carroll (1997) states:

> "HCI continues to provide a challenging test domain for applying and developing psychology and social science in the context of technology development and use."

This psychology perhaps is situated in the close relative of usability — functionality.

1.3   Fidelity as a Model for Design

The definition of fidelity varies but a model as follows would find broad agreement:

Physical fidelity: The degree to which a simulation looks like the simulated object and its control inputs have the same behaviour.

Operational fidelity: The degree to which a simulator will actually operate in the same way as the simulated object.

Functional fidelity: The degree to which it is possible to carry out the same tasks in the simulation as in the real object.

Motivational fidelity: The degree to which the simulator is acceptable to users and valued as a source of legitimate and validated training.

SKATS' aim was to have a system which looked and behaved like a real knee under certain conditions (navigation, triangulation, diagnosis) and allowed for the assessment of performance. Essentially they adopted the fidelity models which are technical i.e. physical and operational. In trials of the prototype with users however there was a ground swell of demand for a far higher level of functional and motivational fidelity, these are essentially more psychological in character. Haptic feedback, as the team discovered, was defended from the perspective that 'It just doesn't feel right' and that 'feel' was more than physical.

SKATS was developed working at one or two very legitimate levels of design which were from an engineering requirements perspective and not a psychological requirements. This phenomena has been observed by other people in the HCI field. Stammers (1981) noted that functional fidelity was sufficient if a simulation based trainer was aimed at cognitive aspects of a task. However, if the training was to deal with the 'true' psycho-motor level of the task, then a substantial increase in physical fidelity would be required. This is arguably what happened with SKATS.

The original trainer was for cognitive orientation tasks i.e. navigation, triangulation diagnosis, orientation. Subsequently, surgeons desired a trainer that would have greater psycho-motor fidelity than the prototype; that is, one that would 'feel' like the inside of a knee joint.

The original SKATS, as Figures 1 & 2 show, clearly looks like the real environment and has a set of images and interfaces which behave like a real knee (Figure 2).

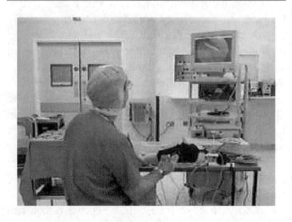

Figure 1:

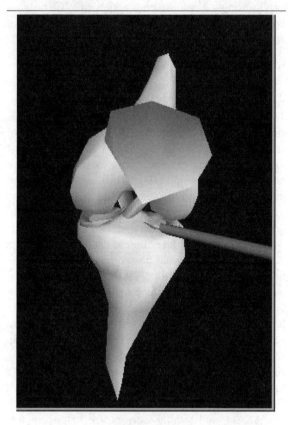

Figure 2:

In the applied setting however it did not seem sufficient. The process they followed was excellent design but it proved to have shortcomings. A more multi-prototypical, multi-iterative design process with a long lead in time for testing and re-definition of user requirements would have foreseen this. This in itself is not a new in HCI design. The adoption of a far more incremental design process is a well rehearsed argument. How to realise this ideal within the working constraints of a fixed design project is however another matter.

We would argue that SKATS suffered from a technological project concept which drove the vast majority of the development work. A useful project concept which could go a long way to realising a multi-iterative design process is that of risk. Some generic design approaches are cognisant of this and may involve risk metrics such as cost benefit filters, risk diagnoses methodologies (Halman & Keizer, 1994) or engineering systems approaches, for example FMEA in reliability. For a summary of techniques to reduce risk in design see (Crossland, R, 1998). What many HCI theorists may be driving at is in essence a strategy which minimises product failure risk. This could be either through low usability, low acceptability or that the device does not have high enough utility — in simple terms does not work well enough.

If the entire life history of a VR simulator for surgery were to be taken into account in its design the necessity to define and control risk in the live setting would be manifest. The control of risk in its design process would be paramount. The control of risk in the training environment would be assumed. End of line (patient) inspection of risks is totally unacceptable.

1.4 VR Design as a 'Risk Solution'

SKATS is a PC based VR system designed to address the risk to patient safety from surgeons in training. There are three interconnected classes of risk:

- Risks to patients in the live setting.

- Risks in the design process.

- Risks in the use of the design (technology transfer).

Risk to patients for our purposes can simply be equated with the likelihood and type of physical harm which can be caused by inexperienced surgeons. This also includes an element of the unknown since symptoms may take 20 years to emerge. Risks in the design process covers a gambit of technical feasibility and reliability of components, sufficient system functionality specification, inevitable design trade-off in the physical build and eventual system technical performance. This too covers an element of the unknown since the system is novel and prototypical. Risk in the use of the design is far more complex. The risk of negative transfer of training is important but there are many others in how the system is actually used and perceived by trainees and trainers, e.g. control of self-directed learning. Also there are functional fidelity issues, is the matching between the generic model knee and the live knee sufficient for safe skill transfer etc. Similarly here there is an element of the unknown, until real data is available one cannot be sure.

These three risk areas, given exclusive focus, would generate significantly different, if overlapping, user requirements. We would argue that a safety critical design approach must identify a design process which mediates all three. Risk in the non-simulated environment is mediated through risk identification and control processes in the deployment of the simulated environment. These are technical, innovation and the psychological (motivational and psycho-motor) impacts of the trainer.

1.5   Reviewing SKATS

The user requirements in SKATS aimed themselves mainly at the technical design, seeing this as a proxy for curing the patient risks. An intuitive, realistic user interface, a (physical) manipulable lower limb and an accurate model of the knee joint and surfaces were designed. SKATS became a complex, dynamic VR model of the knee joint. Its construction had to resolve technical challenges in tracking, imaging and collision detection in VR. The designers felt that these key challenges were being met, the translation of a sophisticated high level specification into high level functionality had been mostly achieved. In prototype testing it became clear that either the user requirements had altered dramatically, which was unlikely, or that they were in fact altered by the presence of the device (early technology transfer). A crucial example of this is that the design of haptic feedback mechanisms, a new technology for this application, is now being developed by the team. It has become clear that, without this, the simulation appears to lack validity to the user groups.

We suggest that this kind of phenomenon is particularly prominent in the design of VR safety critical systems and uncovers a serious flaw in the conventional design process which was used here.

This uncertainty is unacceptable for a risk-based design process. A surer route would have been to adopt an iterative requirements validation procedure with the target users. This procedure would break some overall hypothesis concerning functionality meeting user requirements into lots of smaller hypotheses which could be tested in a sequential fashion. The main reason this was not understood was design aim solidification. High level specifications from an early user group, incorporated with a tacit real user metaphor, were sufficient design criteria. In terms of sequential testing this provided too rigid a set of working hypotheses.

Users were not systematically involved again until the prototype. These still included a sample of highly skilled surgeons acting as a testbed — parallel users. The result was firm and unanimous recommendations for the necessity of haptic feedback mechanisms in the design. In short a costly re-design; innovation.

SKATS discovered that design which is intended to deal with psychological as well as physical aspects of risk needs to measure both.

Risk-based user requirements, particularly for innovations, can be more focussed and comprehensive. This is because they extend not only to device function, as is commonly the case, but to design application — a risk driven functionality. This cannot be achieved if the patient, design and use risks are not articulated as real behaviours.

2   New Design Process

2.1   Risk-based Design

The aim was to reduce the levels of risk in knee surgery, that is to modify the risk behaviour of surgeons. In adopting a generic cascade version of the technical design process the development team encountered major pitfalls. The original level and nature of user requirements capture appeared not to be sufficiently comprehensive or iterative. This led to late, expensive requirements which came from trials with the prototype. The notion of haptic feedback was discarded in the original design but, for motivational fidelity, (Brooks & Arthur, 1997), and the functional — physical fidelity interface reasons, it became clear this was 'essential'. The exact fidelity of the haptics has to be resolved, it ranges from a minor problem of 'cues' to a totally innovative VR technology. In retrospect the importance of operationally defining the risks, in particular the risks these haptics are believed to counteract, has been underestimated by omission from the design process.

SKATS and similar devices are unique in that human factors, VR and safety critical training have to feature in a single product. The end use is not static, for example the use of a machine. Rather, it is sharp (literally) and dynamic. It must interact as safely as possible with things that it may be impossible to capture, for example professional judgement, diverse training schemes, future patient condition and user behaviour.

2.2   Risk Reduced Requirements

The need for risk-based design rests on the highly innovative technology base to the training; the safety critical nature of the domain; the high level of complex human factors and a special, even traditional, work culture. The requirements capture has to make reference to the psychological impacts of the innovation on the user. To this end the user needs to be more intimately involved in a dynamic evolutionary process. In the case of SKATS a continuous user specification process may have highlighted haptics earlier. Classical user involvement at the beginning and end of a closed process is unsuitable. A formal dynamic system of user input to mediate design risk without allowing user involvement that is continuous but incoherent has to be sought.

This risk mediation of the system is not simply through continuous validation processes, as these may achieve little more than a more regular assessment of the same technology focussed parameters. Rather iterative validation should address a known set of measurable risks. These can generate risk-reduced requirements capture particularly if they are predicated by incremental user access to the dynamic prototype development.

Where a product is to be used as part of a safety critical (high risk) procedure, risk itself should be the *main mediator* for the design process because in this setting even discrete failures of design have lasting implications for the unseen end user, the patient. In a risk-based design process functionality is tied to objective risks. Mismatch of requirements and functionality should be avoided. Such mismatches are tempting because the development of HCI and VR technology can become a highly rewarding focus of the design tasks for a technically oriented team. In a technology oriented design process this would be defensible and may progress relatively unchecked. In risk mediated design it would be brought up sharp. Firstly it would introduce new design risks by expanding the remit, these would need to be evaluated. Secondly if it was not able to be mapped to an objective patient or training environment risk, then it would be questioned. This orientation of design does go some way to providing a focus and a rationale for multi-iterative design cycle.

3 Conclusion

The intention of a risk-based design approach is to avoid the size of innovation required for solving the problems. Satchell (1998) suggests that sequential discrete innovation is a key to organizational success. We argue that the complexity of VR design work is so great that an organizational approach is important. For the elements of the design process to work well a clear understanding of the impact of the organizational context into which the system will be placed is essential.

The risks of product failure or product misuse should be articulated as design inputs so that course corrections can be taken rather than abutting a complex organization with a fait accompli. This is a broader definition of user requirements than is commonly found. We argue that a risk-based approach is more holistic in that the risks articulated backwards into the design mean that the interface between the simulation and any further training has to be directly planned to prevent risks i.e. the level to which features of the simulation dictate post training practice should not be a haphazard and emergent feature of a technological product.

Although the issues are complex, a blunt criticism could be that the present preferred user specification system from high level users is a full scale virtual reality simulation of the totality of the arthroscopic environment in the knee joint. This large scale design challenge satisfies the well known penchant which experienced surgeons have for high technology. In reality this is technologically impossible at present. The innovation has to be far smaller and indicate *essential* levels of haptic feedback. Therefore the risks associated with this limitation must be explicit. The first high level specification dictated navigation, triangulation and some diagnosis as the key training outcomes to do this. Changing this so late introduces new risks. It is known that trainee surgeons use physical contact with the structures in the knee as a crude source of orientation and have many more collisions with the probe. Experienced surgeons use the arthroscope carefully as an initial orientation procedure. The former contains a heightened level of risk for the patient. A part task simulator which offers no direct haptic cues is arguably safer for trainee surgeons in the early learning curve, since they will learn via the correct visual and instrument cues.

SKATS' design iterations have left the team under pressure to create state of the art innovation. A route which had been determined in a field which does not always allow coherent validation on the real target user group. A route whose main focus was at risk of becoming the development of HCI and VR technologies. SKATS design procedure is however currently being re-evaluated. Using a risk based design approach the team are re-visiting their requirements in order to break the self stoking demands for increases in high level fidelity. The team has now adopted a research based approach which seeks to mediate their own design-based risks. Their aim is twofold. Firstly the psychology of the users is being evaluated via a combination of prototype use, interview and questionnaire. This will enhance the context of the requirements. Secondly the team aims to draw a very clear line under the user requirements capture process and the functionality identification methodologies which will give the simulator the highest level of validity for the target users. Through these processes it is considered that SKATS will be designed to eradicate some of the risks to patients from surgeons in training. Its original aim.

References

Bamford, D. J., Paul, S. A., Noble, J. & Davies, D. R. (1993), "Avoidable Complications of Arthroscopic Surgery",

Journal of Royal College of Surgeons of Edinburgh **38**, 92–5.

Brooks, P. & Arthur, J. G. (1997), Computer-based Motorcycle Training: The Concept of Motivational Fidelity, *in* D. Harris (ed.), *Engineering Psychology and Cognitive Ergonomics*, Vol. 1, Ashgate, pp.403–10.

Carroll, J. M. (1997), "Human–Computer Interaction: Psychology as a Science of Design", *International Journal of Human–Computer Studies* **46**(4), 501–22.

Crossland, R (1998), "Survey of Current Practice in Managing Design Risk". Published by Design Information Group University of Bristol, EPSRC grant No. GR/L38745.

Dix, A., Finlay, J., Abowd, G. & Beale, R. (1998), *Human–Computer Interaction*, second edition, Prentice–Hall Europe.

Dumay, A. C. M. & Jense, G. J. (1995), "Endoscopic Surgery Simulation in a Virtual Environment", *Computers in Biology and Medicine* **2**(139-48).

Halman, J. I. M. & Keizer, J. A. (1994), "Diagnosing Risks in Product-Innovation Projects", *International Journal of Project Management* **12**(2), 75–80.

Hartson, H. R. (1998), "Human–Computer Interaction: Interdisciplinary Roots and Trends", *Journal of Systems and Software* **43**(2), 103–18.

Hollands, R. J., Trowbridge, E. A., Bickerstaff, D., Edwards, J. B. & Mort, N. (1995), The Particular Problem of Anthroscopic Surgical Simulation — A Preliminary Report, *in* R. A. Earnshaw & J. A. Vince (eds.), *Computer Graphics: Develpments in Virtual Environments*, Academic Press, pp.475–82.

Langrana, N. A., Burdea, G., Lange, K., Gomez, D. & Deshpande, S. (1994), "Dynamic Force Feedback in a Virtual Knee Palpation", *Artificial Intelligence in Medicine* **6**, 321–33.

Mabrey, J. D. & Merril, J. R. (1997), "Development of the Virtual Knee for Orthopaedic Surgical Training and Research", http://mabrey.uthscsa.edu/virtknee.html.

Macaulay, L. A. (1996), *Requirements Engineering*, Springer-Verlag.

McCleod, I. S. (1998), A Case for the Consideration of System Related Cognitive Functions, *in* E. E. Barker, A. Morrison & K. Toth (eds.), *Proceedings of the 5th Annual International Symposium of the International Council of Systems Engineering*, Boeing Company, pp.26–30.

Miller, W. E. (1985), "Learning Arthroscopy", *Southern Medical Journal* **78**(8), 935–40.

Nielsen, J. (1993), *Usability Engineering*, Academic Press.

Noyes, J. & Baber, C. (1999), *Designing Systems*, Springer-Verlag.

Ota, D., Loftin, B., Saito, T., Lea, R. & Keller, J. (1995), "Virtual Reality in Surgical Education", *Computers in Biology and Medicine* **25**(2), 127–37.

Sagar, M. A., Bullivant, D., Mallinson, G. D. & Hunter, P. J. (1994), A Virtual Environment and Model of the Eye for Surgical Simulation, *in Proceedings of SIGGRAPH'94*, ACM Press, pp.205–12.

Satava, R. M. (1993), "Virtual Reality Surgical Simulator: The First Steps", *Journal of Surgical Endoscopy* **7**, 203–5.

Satchell, P. (1998), *Innovation and Automation*, Ashgate, chapter 4.

Stammers, R. D. (1981), "Theory and Practice in the Design of Simulators", *PLET* **18**(2), 67–71.

Ziegler, R., Fischer, G., Muller, W. & Gobel, M. (1995), "Virtual Reality Anthroscopy Training Simulator", *Computers in Biology and Medicine* **25**(2), 193–203.

Human–Computer Interaction — INTERACT '99
M. Angela Sasse and Chris Johnson (Editors)
Published by IOS Press, © IFIP TC.13, 1999

Telemedical Consultation in Primary Care: A Case Study in CSCW Design

Andrew F. Monk[1] & Leon Watts[2]

[1] Department of Psychology, University of York, York YO10 5DD, UK.
[2] Equipe IIHM, Laboratoire CLIPS-IMAG, BP 53, 38041 Grenoble, France.

A.Monk@psych.york.ac.uk, Leon.Watts@imag.fr

Abstract: Telecommunications technologies are beginning to find their way into medical practice, to allow consultation between primary care practitioners, with their patients, and hospital-based medical experts. The purpose of these field studies was to determine how these communications facilities affected consultation. The results were analysed by describing the different activities carried out and then identifying effects of the communications technologies with particular activities. The implications of this analysis for the design of appropriate technologies are expressed as a checklist of issues that can be used to match the available technology with particular situations of use. The analysis is presented as a case study in CSCW design.

Keywords: health care systems, video, telemedicine, teleconsultation, work analysis, Comms Usage Diagram (CUD).

1 Telemedicine

After some early disappointments (Dunn et al., 1977; Moore et al., 1975), and although it retains its detractors (McLaren & Ball, 1995), telemedicine continues to offer great promise for improving the quality of health-care and to reduce its costs. One obstacle to its effective deployment is that many clinicians think of telemedicine as a single entity, a particular treatment like a new drug. In fact, there are many kinds of equipment that may be configured in many different ways to serve many different medical purposes. Wootton (1996), for example, describes five distinct families of telemedical application: education, treatment, radiology, pathology and consulting.

This paper is concerned with telemedicine as the application of a particular kind of telecommunications equipment to the delivery of a consultation, by which we mean a patient consulting with a medical specialist. Ordinarily, the procedure for seeing a consultant in the UK requires:

1. paperwork on the part of the primary care practitioner to refer the patient describing what is wrong;

2. appointment booking and the patient travelling to a centre of expertise such as a hospital; and

3. a consultation with a medical specialist, including a diagnostic procedure, the provision of treatment advice and so on.

The telemedical consultations we observed operated on a different basis. A primary care practitioner and patient, in one location, communicate electronically with a specialist in another. This arrangement removes the necessity for the patient to travel to the consultant and the patient can have a familiar and medically competent advocate. Also, the primary care practitioner and specialist can learn much more from each other than is possible over the limited channel of communication afforded by referral notes.

The study described here was to find out about the work of telemedical consultation from a variety of perspectives, including: hospital specialists, primary care practitioners, attendant nurses, managers, and other medical professionals. The following sections describe:

1. details of where and how this was done;

2. how the accounts given by our informants were analysed using a novel tabular representation, the Comms Usage Diagram (CUD);

3. the findings themselves; and

4. a discussion of how these findings might be used to optimise the design of such facilities and how they relate to previous studies of video communication.

2 Method

Three field studies were carried out in 1996. They consisted of visits to independent telemedical consultation links (hereafter, 'sites'), where consultations were being carried out in the course of day-to-day practice work (see Table 1). Sites A and B had arranged to carry out consultations on a dial-up ad-hoc basis and Site C was by prior arrangement through a booking system. In every instance, the decision to carry out a consultation in this way was taken by the primary care practitioner, having obtained the patient's consent. There were no formal criteria to be met for initiating a telemedical referral but the cases chosen tended to be those where it was not entirely clear whether the patient should be physically referred on for specialist treatment.

Site	Primary location	Specialist location	Informants
A	Peterhead Community Hospital, staffed by nurses and GPs from an attendant practice	Aberdeen Royal Infirmary, Accident and Emergency Department	1 consultant 4 registrars 2 GPs 2 nurses 1 department manager.
B	Minor Treatment Centres of the Riverside Health Authority staffed by Nurse Practitioners.	Belfast Royal Infirmary, Accident and Emergency Department.	1 consultant, 2 nurse practitioners 1 medical director.
C	Six General Practices in North London.	Royal Free Hospital, various locations	2 telemedicine specialists, 1 GP.

Table 1: The three sites visited.

The facilities consisted in each case of an audio-video link from a primary care centre to a specialist location, operating over ISDN2, a standard connection for data transmission compatible with the telephone network. The audio-video link was provided by off-the-shelf products (BT's VC7000 and VC8000 equipment). These products allow one to see as well as to talk to a remote party, using a video monitor with either a conventional telephone

handset or a loudspeaker-microphone combination for 'hands-free' operation. Each study consisted of semi-structured interviews organized around the process of carrying out a consultation (see Appendix 1 of Watts & Monk (1999) for details). Informants (see Table 1) were asked to talk through what happens in a consultation and so describe how they saw their role with respect to the video link, whether or not it had lived up to their expectations and how it had helped and hindered their work. Where possible, interviews were carried out 'in situ' with the telemedical equipment, so combining description of consultation with demonstration. In one case, the interview with a consultant was conducted over the telemedical link. Throughout, informants were encouraged to indicate how they thought their work with the video link might be made easier, drawing on their experience and making reference to specific incidents. Video recordings of the demonstrations and video recordings of several 'live' consultations were also employed.

3 Analysis

It is important to note at this point that this is not a study to evaluate telemedical consultation over an audio-video link. Telemedical consultation using video telephony is not widespread in the UK and these three sites probably represent a large proportion of the sites that could have been visited at the time. There is no claim that the sites have been randomly sampled from, or selected as representative of, some well defined population. It is thus impossible to make generalizable claims about the effectiveness or otherwise of the technology. Rather, we would make a more conservative claim that studying the application of some technology in a real work situation can identify well grounded issues that a designer might consider when thinking about the application of similar technologies to similar work situations. The purpose of this analysis then is to identify these practical issues and clarify their implications for design.

A tabular representation was devised to integrate the information provided from all the many different sources used. 'Comms' is a common abbreviation for communications technologies in engineering. The representation used is described as a Comms Usage Diagram or CUD as it is intended to draw out the way 'comms' are used at various points in a cycle of work and how they affect the participants' ability to carry out that work. The tabular format serves to associate these effects with particular activities in the work as carried out by particular people and so helps to understand more clearly the nature of the effect. An outline of the structure and use of the CUD follows. For a full account see (Watts & Monk, 1998).

3.1 Sequence

The main purpose of a CUD is to associate the merits and demerits of communications technologies with particular activities. The cost of additionally providing an unambiguous explicit coding of the sequential dependencies between activities would be considerable both in terms of the analyst's time and in terms of overloading the representation. Furthermore the opportunistic nature of collaboration suggests that the precise ordering of sub-tasks, at least at some level, has much more to do with descriptive convenience than reflecting the actual organization of work. For these reasons the coding of sequence is minimal. The CUD is simply divided into relatively invariant 'task phases'.

3.2 Primary and Peripheral Participants

Two levels of involvement are coded. The first is in the usual sense, where the parties are directly and explicitly involved in the carrying forward of the exchange. This is referred to as primary participation. Thus, a GP and a consultant might be primary participants in the activity of discussing an X-ray. Additionally we introduce the notion of peripheral participation. Peripheral participants can influence the interaction between the primary participants, or else derive from their indirect involvement in one interaction some influence on their own subsequent activity. For example, because a nurse could overhear the GP discussing the X-ray, he or she may be able to anticipate a request for re-sending the image to the consultant, if the original X-ray was not clear enough. Anticipating this anticipation, the consultant may speak to the GP about the X-ray in a particular way.

3.3 Comms Resources

The CUD specifies which media are used to support which tasks. At each point where activity is represented as occurring between different locations the media through which this activity is carried out are specified in the column headed 'Comms Resources'.

3.4 Effects

In the course of the interviews, and in the small amount of observation that was possible, certain effects of the technology on the work became apparent. The entries in the rightmost column of the CUD record these. The purpose of the CUD is to locate the advantage or disadvantage more precisely within

the work and to find other places in the work that could be affected similarly. In the case of advantages one can then see what steps can be taken to configure the technology or work so that they apply as widely as possible. In the case of disadvantages one can reason about interventions needed to minimise their impact. The effects then should be viewed as potential advantages and disadvantages of using some specific part of the technology for some specific part of the work, rather than 'data' as such.

4 Findings

In this section the 'effects' recorded in the CUDs constructed for the three sites are gathered together under four headings:

1. things to consider about talk;

2. seeing and being seen;

3. looking at things; and

4. extra work.

These categories have very general application and have implications for design outside of the domain of telemedicine. In each case they are listed in a table with the communication resource and activities to which they apply. Individual effects are identified with particular participants in the consultation, along with whether they were seen as an advantage or a disadvantage. By gathering together the effects noted in the three field studies it is possible to describe important characteristics of the work, specifically as they relate to the equipment used. These issues for consideration in design are not intended as an exhaustive account of relevant factors. Resources did not permit extended observation of work practices or even interviews with patients (but see Section 4.2). Nevertheless we believe that the issues identified can inform design and are consistent with many of the findings from other work contexts where video has been used.

4.1 Things to Consider about Talk

Novel technologies can be very seductive. When using video phone technology, roving cameras, etc. it is easy to forget that most of the work involves speaking to one another. Table 2 notes some of the things our informants said about the effects of the communications equipment on their work to do with talk.

Category: the effects of overhearing.
Activities: discussion of history and diagnosis; providing treatment advice.
Comms resource: hands-free audio.

1. + for all: P, GP and C interact simultaneously, improving efficiency of information exchange.

2. + for C: improves diagnosis (talking to P unlikely with phone).

3. + for GP, N and P: P and N have overheard GP and C discussing treatment so there is less to explain to P at the end of the consultation.

4. + for N: enhances awareness of P's needs and adds to expertise.

5. – for all?: rare confidentiality problems.

6. + for P: enhances confidence in diagnosis and treatment.

7. – for (some) GPs: perceived loss of control of treatment.

Category: the effects of degraded sound quality.
Activities: discussion of history and diagnosis; providing treatment advice.
Comms resource: hands-free audio.

8. – for C and GP: hands-free mode audio gives poor quality sound transmission and slows conversation.

Key: + = advantage over alternatives (e.g. telephone or standard referral); – = disadvantage or problem; P = patient; GP = general practitioner; NP = nurse practitioner; C = consultant; N = attendant nurse.

Table 2: Effects having to do with talk. Note that each effect is associated with particular participants at particular parts of the consultation.

The number of people involved in a consultation, and hence who had an interest in hearing and speaking, varied considerably. As well as the primary medic, the hospital specialist and the patient, it is not uncommon for a relative of the patient to be in attendance, along with a nurse and sometimes other medical professionals such as a radiographer or physiotherapist.   Effects 1 to 4 attest to the benefits of overhearing and being able to contribute occasionally to someone else's conversations (Clark, 1996). Those who are not being directly addressed by a speaker can tell what is going on very easily, rather than struggling to infer the progress of the consultation from one half of the conversation. This means that the person using the link does not have to spend time bringing other relevant parties up to date with the suggestions and questions of the remote

person(s). Furthermore, overhearing makes it possible for a previously peripheral participant to join the conversation if they feel they have something relevant to offer. Such interventions are extremely efficient because of their timeliness, benefiting the diagnostic process as a whole.

All three sites valued the hands-free audio facilities, particularly during the part of the consultation where the remote specialist was finding out about the patient's history. The perceived value of this facility was underlined by the fact that it was preferred despite the costs associated with its use. Multi-party sound is hard to achieve and the sound quality was generally very poor, requiring a conscious effort to speak slowly and clearly.   Interrupting someone else's conversation was made difficult because the sound would cut out with simultaneous speech, thus reducing one of the most important benefits of overhearing (see above and Effect 1). Telephone handsets avoid the problem of echo by placing the microphone close to the mouth and away from the earphone. Of course if both ends use the handsets overhearing is impossible. Using hands-free audio in the treatment room and having the consultant use the handset was found to increase sound quality somewhat, though the handset user still heard an echo of their own voice.

Matters of privacy (Effect 5) did not often arise in the sites studied, perhaps because the equipment was typically installed in a treatment room and hence privacy was subject to the usual safeguards.   The context of treatment in a medical centre may thus be seen to have underwritten the patient's confidence on this matter.

4.2   Seeing and Being Seen

Video links are most often arranged to show pictures of a single designated speaker's face. This allows for 'reading between the lines', gauging reaction and so on (Effect 12). However, where there are several people involved, and potentially sensitive matters are at stake, knowledge of who else is around could be greatly informed by a whole-room view.   The systems studied did not offer such a context view. Effective communication depends on judging the common ground one has with the intended recipients of that communication (Clark, 1996; Clark & Brennan, 1991) and 'designing' one's utterances for that audience. Thus, consultation is most effective when questions and advice are tailored for the specific people making up the group. The consultant in the hospital must make assumptions about the knowledge and experience of all the people listening in the treatment room. A view of the whole room would allow the consultant to see who is there and to make appropriate guesses about their backgrounds.

Category: the effects of self-view image.
Activities: setting up for consultation.
Comms resource: video-phone image from local fixed camera.

    9. + for GP and P: mirror-reversed self-view on display makes positioning in front of the camera easy.

Category: the effects of seeing a remote person's face (1).
Activities: initial phase of greeting and establishing context.
Comms resource: video-phone image from local fixed camera.

    10. + for GP and C: recognize one another more easily.

Category: the effects of seeing a remote person's face (2).
Activities: discussion of history and diagnosis; providing treatment advice.
Comms resource: video-phone image from local fixed camera.

    11. + for P: seeing C may add to confidence of P.

    12. + for C: Better determination of the parties emotional state and so on aids diagnosis.

    13. − for (some) GPs: may add to perceived loss of control.

Table 3: Effects having to do with seeing the people's faces. (See Table 2 for key.)

In this connection it is interesting to note Effect 10. Being able to see a face as well as to hear a name stands to be a great help to the consultant in recalling previous dealings with a GP. Something that might be difficult just on the basis of a name and a voice on the end of a telephone (Bruce, 1996).

The patient's confidence in the outcome of the consultation is always an important issue. Although our studies did not directly involve patients, one of the sites examined (Site C) was subject to an independent questionnaire-based study including patient reactions (Harrison et al., 1996). The link was rated highly on all questions by over 40 patient respondents. They felt positive about using the link (95%) and about using it again (80%). Several of our informants asserted that the image of the consultant's face at the other end of the link helped to foster such confidence (Effect 11). It is not possible to determine whether patients' attitudes to their consultation were uniquely determined by this kind of access to the consultant, any more than being

able to talk to the consultant (Effect 6), or indeed a general reaction to receiving high-budget treatment.

4.3 Looking at Things

For all the emphasis placed on speaking and hearing above, the physical and visual examination in medical work is clearly important. Sites B and C used Sharp Viewcams on flying leads as roving cameras, to allow for close-ups of visible trauma or examinations and so on. Site A had a tele-radiology work station that allowed X-rays to be scanned and sent to the remote location. Site B used their roving camera to send images of X-rays to the remote site by focusing on a light box in their treatment room.

Pictures of the 'materials of consultation' are at least as important as pictures of the parties involved, serving in a sense as common property to those on the spot and the remote consultant (Effects 14, 15 and 16). It is important that they are as similar as possible for all concerned otherwise the role of these images as communication aids can be severely compromised (Effects 17 and 23). This can be a subtle matter as the process of turning an image into a form suitable for transmission can transform it in some important ways, such as misrepresenting colours, and may also delay its display to the remote parties. Shared images operate as resources for communication so long as they afford reference that can be resolved easily by both parties. If a GP says 'that red area is rather worrying' and the consultant's screen shows no unambiguously red area, conversational breakdown will ensue. On the other hand, if they can both be confident that they know what the other person is looking at, communications can be very efficient. Effect 18 records that problems may ensue when people assume that a view is shared when it really is not. For example, when the camera operator was positioning the hand-held roving camera for the consultant, it was easy for the camera operator to assume that what could be seen in the ViewCam's display was also what the consultant could see. In fact, the image experienced by the consultant was subject to motion-induced break up and colour inconstancy, as well as a delay. Consequently the consultant's instructions to the camera operator referred to a quite different image to the one they were looking at and so were very difficult to follow.

As noted above, the technologies employed at the sites studied resulted in image transmission which was highly susceptible to break-up with motion. For this reason, the practical advantages of mounting the portable camera on a tripod (Effects 20 and 21 cf. 17, 18 and 19) outweigh the disadvantages (Effect 22).

There was a 'freeze frame' facility that allowed a high quality still image to be transmitted. However, the image sent was not viewable from the local end and so, though the quality of the image received by the consultant might be improved, the problem of discrepancy remained.

Category: shared view of problem (1).
Activities: discussion of X-ray.
Comms resource: tele-radiology equipment.

> 14. + for C and GP: can both see the X-ray though remote (normally only one copy).
> 15. + for GP: learns how do diagnose a new kind of borderline case.

Category: shared view of problem (2).
Activities: diagnosis of skin problem.
Comms resource: hand-held roving camera.

> 16. + for C: consistent viewpoint for inspection and discussion.
> 17. − for C and NP: hard to obtain stable close-up image.
> 18. − for NP: cannot tell (poor) quality of image transmitted to C.
> 19. − for NP: cannot manipulate or palpate P while holding camera.

Category: shared view of problem (3).
Activities: diagnosis of skin problem.
Comms resource: tripod-mounted roving camera.

> 20. + for C: consistent viewpoint for inspection and discussion.
> 21. + for P: knows that C can inspect the problem area.
> 22. − for C: lack of control of scope of image.
> 23. − for GP: cannot see C's image of the problem.

Table 4: Effects having to do with views of the problem. (See Table 2 for key.)

4.4   Extra Work

Any technological innovation is likely to require adjustments to the daily routine. Effects 24 to 26 list the adjustments that resulted in extra work at Site A. In this case, the changes were judged acceptable, given the benefits of the new procedures. This will not always be so. Sometimes the cost of finding the relevant staff and staff time will outweigh the potential benefits. It should be noted that at the two general practitioner sites studied (A&C), some GPs did not use the telemedical link at all, preferring other means

of securing additional advice when 'grey area' cases arose.

Category: extra work.
Activities: preparation prior to consultation.
Comms resource: tele-radiology equipment.

> 24. − for N: switching on and calibrating takes some time each morning.
> 25. − for N: scanning X-ray and informing hospital reception it has been sent is extra work.
> 26. − for GP: delay while C comes to tele-radiology workstation.

Table 5: Effects resulting in extra work. (See Table 2 for key.)

5   Discussion

The three field studies summarised in this article considered the apparently simple and well-specified situation of a primary care practitioner, in the presence of a patient at a general practice, consulting with a specialist in a hospital, over a video telephone. Despite this apparent simplicity, the actual situation at the three sites was found to vary in important ways. The above analysis suggests that subtle differences in the way the equipment was used, for example, choosing between hands-free audio and a handset or mounting the roving camera on a tripod, could have important effects on certain aspects of the work. Similarly, the people present at the treatment room location varied from site to site and this again could have implications for the effectiveness of the equipment for performing certain activities. Note that the analysis suggests that these effects are specific to given participants when performing specific activities. Equipment configured in a particular way may be quite suitable for one activity from one person's viewpoint but may be quite unsuitable for another activity, or indeed from another person's point of view. It is thus very difficult to provide general advice about requirements even within the apparently limited scope of telemedical consultation over a video-phone. Our analysis allows us to draw out issues that one should be sensitive to expressed as practical 'questions to ask' in Table 6. Each question corresponds broadly to one or more of the categories of effects in Tables 2–5. By re-expressing the findings of this case study in this way we can avoid the problem of over-generalization and make them applicable much more generally to CSCW outside of telemedicine.

1. What extra work is required to make the connection and start the session? Can you adjust your procedures to cover this?

2. How easy will it be for the main parties in the work (here patients, GP and consultant) to contribute? Can they overhear what has been said already and so join in easily?

3. Are there likely to be other people present, in your situation, (here relatives and nursing staff)? If so, will they be able to hear and see? Will the a remote party know they are there; do they come and go; are they visible and/or audible?

4. Will it be necessary to share images (here an X-ray, or an image of some part of the patient's anatomy)? If so, can a sufficiently high quality image be transmitted? Will the local and remote images be the same, or suffer a disparity of quality?

Table 6: Questions to ask when considering the use of an audio-video link.

Question 1 asks someone wanting to introduce communication equipment into the work place to think about their particular circumstances of use in terms of the daily routine and the adjustments that will have to be made because of that equipment. Question 2 asks them to think about the issue of sound quality. This will depend on where the equipment is sited and precisely how it is configured. Question 3 asks them to consider the problems of knowing who is at the other end of a communication link so as to be able to word what is said appropriately for the people who will hear. To answer Question 4 requires an understanding of the kinds of images needed to do the work and thus the needs for a shared view of some kind.

Making sure that the equipment is optimally adapted to the work is only the first step in implementing some new technology. This paper has not considered the other main factor contributing to the success or failure of technology, that is the suitability of the new way of working implied by the technology to the organizational context. Such issues surface in Effects 7 and 13 that suggest some doctors are wary of 'loosing control' of treatment. More positively, Effects 4 and 15 point out how the organization may benefit through the primary care practitioner learning new skills. The organizational effectiveness of telemedical consultation requires a global view of the acceptability of new medical practices, including matters of professional competence and legal responsibility. For example, it is interesting to note that Site B was nurse-practitioner lead and the existence of the link was part of the insurance for doctor-independent medical work, a relatively new and controversial matter in the UK. Other aspects of the economic and political context have to be thought through if a change of practice is to be successful. There are a number of human factors techniques for doing this (Blyth & Chudge, 1993; Checkland & Scholes, 1990; Damodaran, 1996; Vidgen, 1997).

Looking outside of the medical arena, this study reinforces many of the conclusions drawn by other investigators. The idea of a video picture as the object of shared work as well as the medium for its execution, and that users may need several views of a remote location, is consistent with the media-space investigations at Rank Xerox' Cambridge Labs. (Gaver et al., 1992; 1993; Nardi et al., 1993; Whittaker, 1995). The idea of using multiple views presents several challenging technical and human factors problems, not the least of which is how to combine or switch between them. Ishii's Clearboard and TeamWorkstation (Ishii et al., 1993) are particularly interesting in this connection as the top half of the body of the other participant is viewed through the work, achieving what Ishii describes as a seamless interface. There are also parallels to be drawn between the importance, noted here, of knowing who can overhear you and systems claiming to provide tele-proximity awareness(Fish et al., 1992; Ronby-Pederson & Sokoler, 1997; Tang & Rua, 1994).

Perhaps what is most notable is that these issues, and many more discussed in the findings section, could be identified in a study of a relatively low budget and 'lo-tech' application. The video-phone technology used can in no way be considered to be state of the art, nor indeed was it marketed as such by its manufacturer. Yet, by looking in detail at the demands of the work performed these issues readily became apparent. We see this as a strong recommendation for the approach taken here. Using the CUD focused the work on understanding how communication technologies interact with real work, making it possible to identify important issues that must be considered in the design of communication technologies for telemedical consultation.

Acknowledgements

This work was supported by the UK's Economic and Social Research Council's 'Cognitive Engineering Programme', grant L127251024. We would like to thank all those who contributed to our field studies but in particular Robert Harrison and Will Clayton for their help and advice.

References

Blyth, A. J. C. & Chudge, J. (1993), "The Role of Interaction Analysis in Requirements Engineering", *IFIP Transactions A — Computer Science and Technology* **30**, 189–205.

Bruce, V. (1996), "The Role of the Face in Communication: Implications for Video-phone Design", *Interacting with Computers* **8**(2), 166–76.

Checkland, P. B. & Scholes, J. (1990), *Soft Systems Methodology in Action*, John Wiley & Sons.

Clark, H. H. (1996), *Using Language*, Cambridge University Press.

Clark, H. H. & Brennan, S. E. (1991), Grounding in Communications, *in* L. B. Resnick, J. Levine & S. D. Teasley (eds.), *Perspectives on Socially Shared Cognition*, American Psychology Association, pp.127–49.

Damodaran, L. (1996), "User Involvement in the Systems Design Process — A Practical Guide for Users", *Behaviour & Information Technology* **15**(6), 363–77.

Dunn, E. V., Conrath, D. W., Bloor, W. G. & Tranquada, B. (1977), "An Evaluation of Four Telemedicine Systems for Primary Care", *Health Services Research* **1**(1), 19–29.

Fish, R. S., Kraut, R. E., Root, R. W. & Rice, R. E. (1992), Evaluating Video as a Technology for Informal Communication, *in* P. Bauersfeld, J. Bennett & G. Lynch (eds.), *Proceedings of CHI'92: Human Factors in Computing Systems*, ACM Press, pp.37–48.

Gaver, W., Sellen, A., Heath, C. & Luff, P. (1993), One is Not Enough: Multiple Views in a Media Space, *in* S. Ashlund, K. Mullet, A. Henderson, E. Hollnagel & T. White (eds.), *Proceedings of INTERCHI'93*, ACM Press/IOS Press, pp.335–41.

Gaver, W. W., Moran, T., MacLean, A., Lövstrand, L., Dourish, P., Carter, K. & Buxton, W. (1992), Realizing a Video Environment: EuroPARC's RAVE System, *in* P. Bauersfeld, J. Bennett & G. Lynch (eds.), *Proceedings of CHI'92: Human Factors in Computing Systems*, ACM Press, pp.27–35.

Harrison, R., Clayton, W. & Wallace, P. (1996), "Can Telemedicine be Used to Improve Communication Between Primary and Secondary Care", *British Medical Journal* **313**(7069), 1378–80.

Ishii, H., Arita, K. & Yagi, T. (1993), Beyond Videophones: Team WorkStation-2 for Narrowband ISDN, *in* G. de Michelis, C. Simone & K. Schmidt (eds.), *Proceedings of ECSCW'93, the 3rd European Conference on Computer-Supported Cooperative Work*, Kluwer, pp.325–41.

McLaren, P. & Ball, C. J. (1995), "Telemedicine — Lessons Remain Unheeded", *British Medical Journal* **310**(6991), 1390–1.

Moore, G. T., Willemain, T. R., Bonanno, A. B., Clark, W. D., Martin, A. R. & Mogielnicki, R. P. (1975), "Comparison of Television and Telephone for Remote Medical Consultation", *The New England Journal of Medicine* **13**(14), 729–32.

Nardi, B. A., Kuchinsky, A., Leichner, R., Whittaker, S. & Sclabassi, R. (1993), Turning Away from Talking Heads: The Use of Video-as-Data in Neurosurgery, *in* S. Ashlund, K. Mullet, A. Henderson, E. Hollnagel & T. White (eds.), *Proceedings of INTERCHI'93*, ACM Press/IOS Press, pp.327–34.

Ronby-Pederson, E. & Sokoler, T. (1997), AROMA: Abstract Representation of Presence Supporting Mutual Awareness, *in* S. Pemberton (ed.), *Proceedings of CHI'97: Human Factors in Computing Systems*, ACM Press, pp.51–8.

Tang, J. C. & Rua, M. (1994), Montage: Providing Teleproximity for Distributed Groups, *in* B. Adelson, S. Dumais & J. Olson (eds.), *Proceedings of CHI'94: Human Factors in Computing Systems*, ACM Press, pp.37–43.

Vidgen, R. (1997), "Stakeholders, Soft Systems and Technology: Separation and Mediation in the Analysis of Information System Requirements", *Information Systems* **7**(1), 21–46.

Watts, L. A. & Monk, A. F. (1998), "Reasoning About Tasks, Activity and Technology to Support Collaboration", *Ergonomics* **41**(11), 1583–606.

Watts, L. A. & Monk, A. F. (1999), "Telemedicine: What Happens in Teleconsultation", *Journal of Technology Assessment in Health* **15**(1), 219–34.

Whittaker, S. (1995), "Rethinking Video as a Technology for Interpersonal Communications: Theory and Design Implications", *International Journal of Human–Computer Studies* **42**(5), 501–29.

Wootton, R. (1996), "Telemedicine: A Cautious Welcome", *British Medical Journal* **313**(7069), 1375–7.

Human–Computer Interaction — INTERACT '99
M. Angela Sasse and Chris Johnson (Editors)
Published by IOS Press, © IFIP TC.13, 1999

An Imprecise Mouse Gesture for the Fast Activation of Controls

Martin S. Dulberg, Robert St Amant & Luke S. Zettlemoyer

Department of Computer Science, North Carolina State University,
EGRC-CSC Box 7534, Raleigh, NC 27695–7534, USA.
{msdulber,stamant,lszettle}@eos.ncsu.edu

Abstract: A common task in graphical user interfaces is selecting or activating a single control from a small group of plausible candidates. This task ordinarily requires the same precise movements as any other; if we could reduce the precision needed, however, we might also reduce the target acquisition and activation time. This paper describes the flick gesture, designed for this purpose. Our experimental results demonstrate that the gesture performs well with regard to speed, accuracy, and variability, compared to conventional gestures in a laboratory setting. We also describe a testbed we have implemented in Microsoft Windows that lets us explore and evaluate the use of such gestures in settings with more ecological validity.

Keywords: direct manipulation, marking menus, intelligent user interfaces, interaction techniques.

1 Introduction

Modern graphical user interfaces (GUIs) rely heavily on precise movements of the mouse. Immediately after Microsoft Word 6.0 starts up on the Macintosh, for example, almost eighty distinct visible targets for the mouse pointer appear. These include menu titles, buttons, palettes of tools, text boxes, pop-up menu indicators, scroll bar gadgets, window decorations, and mouseable documentation. Without our ability to position the pointer precisely, we would find manipulation of such densely clustered objects extremely difficult, no matter how good the overall organization.

Such precision, however, should not always be necessary. In many situations, only one or two controls in the interface have any relevance for an interaction. For example, when the user selects the Print command from a menu, a dialogue box appears that allows the modification of settings and the initiation of the printing action. The OK button must be activated at some point to successfully print — but clicking on the button requires the same effort as changing any one of the less frequently used controls. We propose that in such a situation, when a specific control is inevitably part of a given interactive task, the system can arrange for an imprecise activation gesture, for faster, more streamlined operation.

We have developed a gesture, which we call a *flick*, or flying click, for this purpose. To carry out a

flick gesture, the left mouse button is briefly pressed and held while the mouse is quickly moved a short distance. Releasing the mouse button completes the gesture. (Some users have described this gesture as *dragging toward a target*.)

The flick gesture has a few attractive features. The most obvious advantage is that precise target acquisition, the zeroing-in phase of conventional Fitts' Law tasks, is bypassed. The gesture can thus in theory be faster than clicking directly on a control. Once a control has been activated through a flick, the mouse pointer also remains very close to its previous location, minimizing the repositioning effort needed to resume a previous activity. Flicking is directional, and can be applied, within limits, to any visible target in the interface. Though not intended to replace any existing gestures, flicking is also a useful alternative to keyboard shortcuts, such as pressing the Enter key to indicate confirmation. It does not require the user's hand to leave the mouse. Unlike keystrokes, the flick gesture also has the potential to be applied dynamically to different targets, rather than statically associated with specific commands.

This paper has two general themes. One theme concerns the feasibility of an imprecise gesture: how well does it work? We describe two experiments that explore the potential uses and limitations of the flick gesture. Our first experiment assumed an unambiguous goal of activating a single control, with no other legal actions possible. We compared the flick gesture to two alternatives: the conventional selection of a control with the mouse, and pressing the Enter key. Encouraging results prompted a follow-on experiment, in which we tested whether the system could distinguish between flicks to alternative targets and could differentiate the flicking gesture from other types of high speed mouse movement. In both cases, our expectations were largely met.

The other theme concerns evaluation: can we confidently apply our laboratory results to the real world? We briefly discuss the implications for implementing the flick gesture in a conventional user interface, and describe a general-purpose testbed for incorporating novel gestures into an existing interface and testing their impact.

2   Related Work

Practically speaking, the flick gesture is little more than a shortcut for entering a command. A comparable shortcut, common in conventional GUIs, is the keyboard accelerator. A keyboard accelerator allows the user to execute a command by recalling and executing a particular sequence of keystrokes that are mapped to a particular function. Accelerators suffer from two limitations: they require the user to retain and recall information related to specific commands, and they require the user to drop out of a direct manipulation interaction style in favour of a command/response conversational style. Novice users can find large vocabularies of keystroke accelerators difficult to acquire (Shneiderman, 1998). Further, even when keystrokes have been completely internalized, so that they can be recalled without conscious effort, the cognitive burden of switching between the direct and indirect style of interaction remains (Norman, 1986). The alternative of pop-up menus presents similar difficulties (Norman, 1991). The flick gesture is not subject to these limitations. It is easily learned, and because flick targets are generally visible, it remains within the direct manipulation framework.

Though our presentation of the flick gesture from a precision perspective is novel, the action itself is not. The WebBook (Card et al., 1996) implemented a gesture called a ruffle, similar to the flick, for rifling through a set of Web pages like a book. The use of marking menus, a more extensively examined technique, is also very similar to flicking. Pie menus are circular menus that pop up in the interface directly where the user has either clicked or moused down. The user then moves to the desired wedge of the pie menu and either clicks again or mouses up to activate an item. A drawback of pie menus, despite their speed and accuracy, is their inefficient use of

screen space (Callahan et al., 1998; Hopkins et al., 1988). With marking menus, in contrast, an expert user can quickly perform the same dragging gesture without waiting for the appearance of the pie menu (Kurtenbach & Buxton, 1991). Our work differs from these earlier efforts in the consideration of flicking in a novel context and by a more detailed evaluation in some regards, of the gesture in use (Kurtenbach & Buxton, 1993).

3   Experiments

We conducted two formal experiments to explore the characteristics of the flick gesture, both on a personal computer running Windows 95, using a $17''$ monitor in SVGA (1024×768) mode. Participants used a Dell two-button mouse and standard keyboard. Only right-handed participants were used for the experiment. All participants were un-compensated undergraduate or graduate Computer Science students. The experimental software logged all mouse clicks, mouse up, and mouse down events with the corresponding time and position of the mouse cursor during the event. We also conducted a number of informal observations, as a part of the development described in Section 4.

3.1   Experiment 1

Eighteen participants were presented with a screen (Figure 1) that contained two command buttons, each 20 pixels square, one located in the centre of the screen and one randomly positioned between 20 and 300 pixels away from the centre button. This 'outer' button was repositioned after each trial using polar coordinates to uniformly distribute its position in terms of distance and angle. The experiment consisted of three different tasks, presented to participants in blocks of 50 trials.

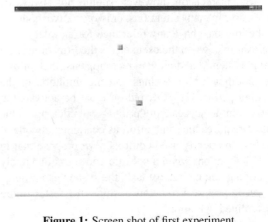

Figure 1: Screen shot of first experiment.

Click: The participant was instructed to click on the outer button, then click on the centre button as quickly as possible.

Enter: The participant was instructed to click on the outer button, then press Enter with the same hand, as quickly as possible to activate the centre button. The Enter gesture was used to determine whether allowing a control to be activated by a shortcut key was as efficient as the flick gesture.

Flick: The participant was instructed to click on the outer button, then perform a flick in the general direction of the centre button.

The order of presentation was varied in all possible permutations across the participants. The participants were given three trials of training with on screen instructions for each condition to practice before the block began. No data was collected during the training. A within-subjects design was used for data analysis.

3.2 Results

Figure 2 shows a comparison of mean duration (task completion time) over the three conditions. Each point in the plot represents the value for one of the 18 participants in each of the conditions. To conserve space we have included the data for all of the conditions on one plot. We used two-tailed t-tests for all the pairwise comparisons discussed here.[*] The bars across the centre of Figures 2 & 3 represent the mean across all three conditions. There was no order effect observed between the three conditions.

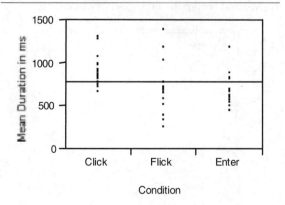

Figure 2: Mean duration by condition.

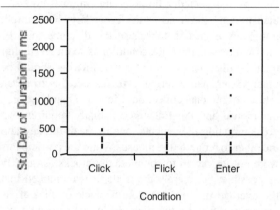

Figure 3: Standard deviation of duration by condition.

Flicking is significantly faster than clicking ($t(34) = 3.053, p = 0.0044$), taking 692ms on average compared to 940ms. The Flick condition is not significantly faster than the Enter condition ($t(34) = 0.294, p = 0.7708$), at 716ms. Note that the spread in the data for each condition in Figure 1, especially for the Flick condition, reflects the expected variability between participants. The lower values, for example, are associated with participants who were on average faster than the others.

Figure 3 shows a comparison of the standard deviation of duration over the three conditions. That is, here each data point measures the variability in duration for a *single* participant (rather than between participants, as in Figure 2.) Flicking shows less variability than clicking, at 227ms vs. 314ms, but the difference is not significant ($t(34) = 1.497, p = 0.1437$). Flicking is however significantly less variable than pressing Enter, at 793ms ($t(34) = -2.112, p = 0.0421$).

We are aware of no work that explains in detail the differences between the Flick and Click conditions at the motor level. Research into the nature of targeting movements does however give insight into our results (MacKenzie, 1992). Such movements do not exactly follow the smooth log curve suggested by the simple form of Fitts' law. Rather, an initial imprecise movement is followed by a few more precise targeting movements that end on the target (Meyer, 1988). This first movement or primary sub-movement may correspond to the flick gesture. The variability in the duration of the flick gesture might be accounted for by neuro-motor noise.

For similar reasons, we found less variability in the Flick condition than in the Enter condition.

---

[*]Note that we are not comparing the three conditions against one another in a single analysis of variance. The relative speed of Click vs. Enter is irrelevant and its inclusion reduces the power of the test; we are interested in how the Flick condition compares with the Click and the Enter conditions independently.

Perhaps unexpectedly, however, flicking was no faster than moving the hand to the Enter key. One might intuitively expect that because the distance that the mouse moves in the Flick condition is so much smaller than the distance to the Enter key, flicking should be much faster than entering. We suspect this to be an artifact of our data collection. Moving a hand between the mouse and the Enter key actually requires two gross targeting movements, one to reach the key and the other to return to the mouse. While the participants were not instructed to complete the blocks as quickly as possible, but merely the trials, it was noticed that the average time to complete a block of flick trials was shorter than for the click blocks. In retrospect, we should have measured the entire end-to-end task time. We would then expect to find the difference between flicking and entering to be much greater.

To summarize, Experiment 1 was a pilot study into the potential effectiveness of the flick gesture. Though the number of trials per participant was relatively small, the results were unambiguous. The flick gesture is 26% faster than the click gesture, with equal variability. It is also at least as fast as the enter gesture, and significantly less variable.

3.3   Experiment 2

Twelve participants were presented with a screen (Figure 4) that had a red circle 20 pixels wide in the centre. They were instructed to move the mouse cursor to the centre circle at which time a green circle, also 20 pixel in diameter would appear somewhere at a fixed distance (400 pixels) from the centre. The participants were told to flick by initiating the mouse down event inside the red circle and complete it by moving the cursor towards the green circle while releasing the mouse button.

Participants were told that they could move as far or as little as they desired towards the circle and that the accuracy and speed with which they performed the gesture was being measured. Once they understood these instructions in both written and verbal form, the gesture was demonstrated for them three times by the same experimenter and they were asked to practice the gesture seven more times. All participants were then asked if they understood the directions or wished to practice any additional trials. All of the participants indicated that they were ready to begin. The participants were then presented with three blocks of 100 trials of the flick task with a one minute rest interval between blocks. This phase recorded information about accuracy and speed.[†]

After completing the three blocks, participants were then asked to complete two blocks of 100 iterations of a task where they were presented with blue circles in an identical fashion and asked to click on the centre blue circle and then click on the outer blue circle. This phase gathered information about the nature of a click so that we could determine if we could easily distinguish between flicks and clicks.

3.4   Results

The median distance travelled during the flick gesture was 48.4 pixels. Figure 5 shows the distribution of flick distances. The median duration of the flick gesture was 284ms. Figure 6 shows the distribution of flick duration. The difference in duration between the two experiments is explained by the fact that the users were not required to click on the centre circle in Experiment 2; duration was measured from mouse down to mouse up events. In the first experiment we included the interval after the centre button was clicked and before the flick gesture was initiated.

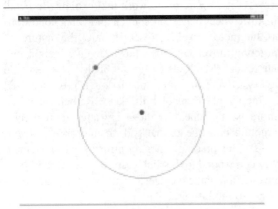

Figure 4: Screen shot of Experiment 2.

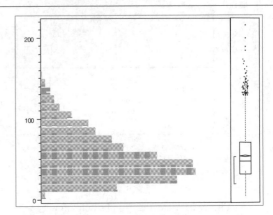

Figure 5: Distribution of flick distance in pixels.

[†]One participant's data was discarded for procedural reasons; the participant told the experimenter, "I wanted to see how I would be penalized if I flicked away from the circle".

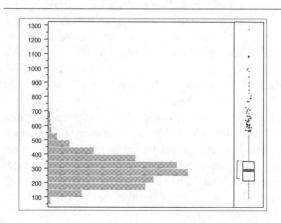

Figure 6: Distribution of flick duration in ms.

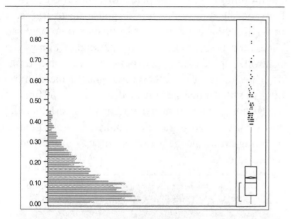

Figure 7: Distribution of flick accuracy in radians.

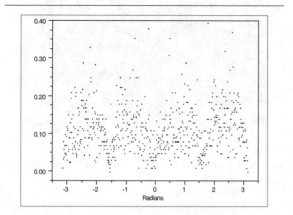

Figure 8: Flick accuracy in radians as a function of the location about a circle.

The accuracy of the flick gesture was computed by measuring the angle between the vector formed by the centres of the circles and the point at which the mouse was released at the end of the flick

gesture. The median difference between the optimal vector, which would point in the same direction as the vector between the circles and the actual flick vector, was 0.10 radians or 5.73 degrees. Figure 7 shows the distribution of flick accuracy. Note that 90% of the flicks lie within 0.27 radians (15.48 degrees) and 97.5% of the flicks lie within 0.41 radians (23.5 degrees). Since the differences were calculated as absolute values they should be doubled to allow for errors in either a positive or negative direction. Finally, the magnitude of errors was not distributed uniformly over the range of $-\pi$ to π radians (-180 to 180 degrees.) The variance in errors for non-vertical and non-horizontal motion is also noticeably greater. We suspect that this pattern is due to inherent behaviour of the human motor system based on Jagacinski and Monk's work (Jagacinski & Monk, 1985). Figure 8 shows that the differences between the optimal vector and the actual vector were found to be smaller in either the horizontal or vertical direction and larger along the diagonals.

It is possible that a user might flick over an area that will actually accept a click. For this reason it is important to be able to distinguish between the two gestures. Based upon the data we collected in the last 2 blocks (a total of 400 clicks per participant) we found that it was relatively easy to disambiguate flicks from clicks by looking at the distance travelled by the mouse between the mouse down and mouse up events. We observe that 90% of the clicks made by the user last no longer than 157ms and cause the mouse pointer to move no more than 3 pixels. For flicking, 90% of the cases last longer than 163ms and are associated with mouse movements of more than 21 pixels. We can set one user-modifiable threshold for flicking based on the distance between a mouse down/mouse up combination. One possible source of bias is the possibility that the distance of the flick gesture might have been skewed by the requirement that we placed on the participants to start the flick inside the centre circle and finish outside. This will not increase the difficulty of distinguishing flicks from clicks, though, since more than 75% of the flicks were longer than the diameter of the centre circle.

3.5 Summary

We have demonstrated that where precision is not required the flick gesture is 26% faster than the conventional click gesture (692ms vs. 940ms) on a button. While the flick gesture is comparable in duration to the enter gesture, the flick gesture is superior to the enter gesture in terms of the time required for the user to 'recycle' or get ready for the next task.

Results for the second experiment indicate that about eight targets can be presented to the user if they are spaced at 45 degree intervals from the user's current mouse position. Our findings on flick accuracy suggest that the most frequently used targets should be placed on the midpoints of the left and right edges of the interface, followed by the midpoints of the top and bottom edges. Less frequently used controls should be placed along the diagonals (in the corners). This would result in the best frequency of selection to accuracy ratio. This is a very different strategy than what is currently taken in the placement of items in a linear menu where items are generally placed from top to bottom in reverse order of frequency to minimize the serial order effect of selection (Norman, 1991).

Users found the flick gesture potentially useful. There was some difficulty training participants to perform the flick without giving explicit examples, since it is a relatively novel gesture. Most participants in the first experiment did not distinguish between the instructions 'click then drag' and 'drag'. In the second experiment the users did not suffer from confusion because the click was not required. Surprisingly over 3300 trials, the 11 participants made just 4 errors while flicking. An error was considered to be any mouse events other than a mouse down inside the red (centre) circle followed by a mouse up outside of the red circle. This indicates that the flick gesture is an easily learned skill that maps well to previous knowledge of graphical user interfaces, and suggests that there should be little difficulty, from the user's perspective, in adding the flick to the conventional set of gestures.

4   Real-world Integration

Graphical user interfaces conventionally use an object-oriented, event-driven model in which a dispatcher directs events to objects in order to be processed. Objects in the interface are treated as hierarchical groups of geometrical containers: windows contain buttons, for example, because the button occupies a region in the window's interior (Olsen, 1998). Gestures are dispatched in either top-down or bottom up fashion to the appropriate container object. The flick gesture breaks this convention, however; the gesture may occur over an object that can in principle interpret the event but is not the intended target (the target may be a control in an entirely unrelated application.)

We can address this problem in two ways. First, we ensure that the system can reliably distinguish between flicking and simple clicking, dragging for selection, mousing down on a button but then cancelling by moving away before a mouse up, and so forth. The solution we describe above is a reasonable first step. Second, we dissociate the processing of the flick gesture from a given application, and give the responsibility to the operating system.

Our implementation is based on VisMap (Zettlemoyer et al., 1999; Zettlemoyer & St. Amant, 1999), a visual manipulation system that allows an application to control the Windows user interface at the event level. Flick is implemented as a VisMap controller that monitors the event queue for candidate sequences of events. Sequences are disambiguated from clicks and drag-and-drop gestures by two user-setable parameters. The radius parameter controls the minimum number of pixels that must be travelled between the mouse down and mouse up to trigger a flick, allowing the controller to differentiate between clicks and flicks. The velocity parameter allows the controller to disambiguate between flick and drag-drop gestures. The velocity is equal to the number of pixels that must be travelled in the last 110ms of the gesture. Our informal findings suggest that the end of a drag-drop gesture requires a more precise targeting effort, hence a slower velocity at the end of the gesture.

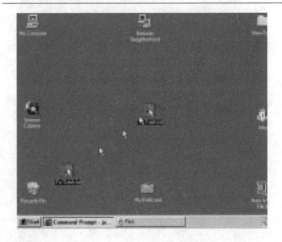

Figure 9: A flick gesture being performed with the VisMap flick controller (graphical annotations added).

An informal usability test was conducted on the VisMap controller. Six participants were introduced to the flick gesture and allowed to become familiar with the gesture over a five minute period. During this training period they were asked to flick towards various icons to change the focus of the icons on the desktop. Figure 9 shows the arrangement of the icons on the desktop. The participants were then asked to perform a variety of tasks such as flicking to give an icon focus or flicking a file on the desktop to a specific target as shown in Figure 9. None of the participants had any trouble executing the tasks. Five of the six participants also indicated that they found the flick gesture to be useful and would use it if it were available in the operating system.

5 Discussion

Our current work involves testing the flick gesture in different contexts of varying artificiality. The flick controller, for example, allows the experimenter to specify one of three actions when a flick is received:

Interpolate To: where the mouse cursor is slowly moved in a straight line to the target of the Flick.

Click On: where the mouse cursor jumps to the target of the Flick.

No Effect: where the target is activated by the Flick but the cursor remains under the user's control.

Currently the experimenter is required to enter the coordinates of the flick enabled controls in the flick controller. We allow a maximum of eight flick enabled areas. With these factors under our control, we can test a wide variety of possible scenarios.

As our initial observations of users suggests, our implementation will allow us to test the integration of flick into real work environments. The simplest case is the most obvious: if the interface presents a modal dialogue window containing information for the user to confirm, a flick gesture can substitute for clicking OK or pressing the Enter key. An extension of this approach could establish a convention that flicking to the lower right portion of the screen always signifies a confirmation, whenever the context is appropriate. A flick to the lower left signifies a cancellation. These are arbitrary choices that will require practical experience to validate.

More generally, we propose that any row or column of icons alongside the general workspace of an application might provide targets for a flick gesture. This requires some analysis into geometrical relationships between the selectable controls and the majority of user activities. Some of the necessary design guidelines are already available, however, in the results we have presented. For an accuracy of 90% in targeting with the flick gesture, for example, we must position the controls at least 0.54 radians (30 degrees) apart, as measured from the origin of the gesture.

For conventional interfaces, adoption of the flick gesture could lead to some interesting possibilities

for more efficient and less distracting interactions by the user. We envision an alternative to the message box that would provide the user with a faster, less intrusive alternative to the current style. Message boxes often interrupt the users work-flow and require them to either accept, cancel, or request help from the system at some critical juncture of a task. The standard commands, OK, CANCEL and HELP, could be mapped to flick gestures to the left, right and bottom respectively. As long as the standard commands are presented in a clear and consistent manner the user should have no trouble dispatching the message in a clear and efficient manner. Novice users could be presented with a set of tool tips presented in the correct orientation to provide them with an appropriate mapping of flick direction to command location. In addition to potentially increasing accuracy by giving the user a close target to aim at when performing the flick, displaying tool tips in this fashion would mimic some of the advantages of pie menus or marking menus. The message could be displayed as a transparent or semi-transparent window so that the user doesn't become disoriented in the workspace.

The flick could also be useful in an intelligent user interface, one that anticipates user selection of specific commands. In most such arrangements, the system takes one of two paths: it generates actions autonomously, providing choices of results to the user — e.g. Letizia (Lieberman, 1995) — or it provides the user with a special command that carries out whatever action the interface predicts is appropriate —e.g. Eager (Cypher, 1993). With the flick we have another choice that lies between these: the interface can highlight a specific control and allow the user to flick in an appropriate direction. If several commands have a reasonable probability of being the most appropriate choice, the interface can highlight all of them, provided they are sufficiently separated spatially, for the user's gesture. The flick gesture offers a partial solution to at least one of the usability problems for anticipatory interfaces. For example, if the occurrence of a selection, cut command, and mouse down action in a word processor is highly predictive of a paste command immediately to follow, then the standard alternatives for an intelligent user interface are to execute the paste autonomously or tell the user that a paste may be appropriate. Flicking supports a better possibility: the interface can pop up a small window containing the text 'Paste', near the Edit menu for the user to flick towards.

Acknowledgements

The authors wish to thank James Lester, David McAllister and Eric Wiebe for their invaluable suggestions and inspirations. We are also grateful to our participants for graciously giving of their time.

References

Callahan, J., Hopkins, D., Weiser, M. & Shneiderman, B. (1998), An Empirical Comparison of Pie vs. Linear Menus, *in* C.-M. Karat, A. Lund, J. Coutaz & J. Karat (eds.), *Proceedings of CHI'98: Human Factors in Computing Systems*, ACM Press, pp.95–100.

Card, S. K., Robertson, G. G. & York, W. (1996), The WebBook and the Web Forager: An Information Workspace for the World Wide Web, *in* G. van der Veer & B. Nardi (eds.), *Proceedings of CHI'96: Human Factors in Computing Systems*, ACM Press, pp.111–7.

Cypher, A. (ed.) (1993), *Watch What I Do: Programming by Demonstration*, MIT Press.

Hopkins, D., Callahan, J. & Weiser, M. (1988), Pies: Implementation, Evaluation and Application of Circular Menus, HCIL Technical Report 88-11, University of Maryland.

Jagacinski, R. J. & Monk, D. L. (1985), "Fitts' Law in Two Dimensions with Hand and Head Movements", *Journal of Motor Behavior* **17**(1), 77–95.

Kurtenbach, G. & Buxton, W. (1991), Issues in Combining Marking and Direct Manipulation Techniques, *in Proceedings of the ACM Symposium on User Interface Software and Technology, UIST'91*, ACM Press, pp.137–44.

Kurtenbach, G. & Buxton, W. (1993), The Limits of Expert Performance Using Hierarchic Marking Menus, *in*

S. Ashlund, K. Mullet, A. Henderson, E. Hollnagel & T. White (eds.), *Proceedings of INTERCHI'93*, ACM Press/IOS Press, pp.482–7.

Lieberman, H. (1995), Letizia: An Agent That Assists Web Browsing, *in* G. Weiss & S. Sen (eds.), *Proceedings of the International Joint Conference on Artificial Intelligence*, Springer-Verlag.

MacKenzie, I. A. (1992), Movement Time Prediction in Human Computer Interfaces, *in* N. Jaffe (ed.), *Proceedings of Graphics Interface '92*, Canadian Information Processing Society, pp.483–93.

Meyer, B. (1988), *Object Oriented Software Construction*, Prentice–Hall.

Norman, D. A. (1986), Cognitive Engineering, *in* D. A. Norman & S. W. Draper (eds.), *User Centered Systems Design: New Perspectives on Human–Computer Interaction*, Lawrence Erlbaum Associates, pp.31–62.

Norman, K. (1991), *The Psychology of Menu Selection*, Ablex.

Olsen, D. (1998), *Developing User Interfaces*, Morgan-Kaufmann.

Shneiderman, B. (1998), *Designing the User Interface: Strategies for Effective Human–Computer Interaction*, third edition, Addison–Wesley.

Zettlemoyer, L. & St. Amant, R. (1999), A Visual Medium for Programmatic Control of Interactive Applications, *in* M. G. Williams, M. W. Altom, K. Ehrlich & W. Newman (eds.), *Proceedings of CHI'99: Human Factors in Computing Systems*, ACM Press, pp.199–206.

Zettlemoyer, L., St. Amant, R. & Dulberg, M. (1999), IBOTS: Agent Control Through the User Interface, *in Proceedings of the Fifth International Conference on Intelligent User Interfaces*, ACM Press, pp.31–7.

Human–Computer Interaction — INTERACT '99
M. Angela Sasse and Chris Johnson (Editors)
Published by IOS Press, © IFIP TC.13, 1999

What You Feel Must Be What You See: Adding Tactile Feedback to the Trackpoint

Christopher S. Campbell, Shumin Zhai, Kim W. May & Paul P. Maglio

IBM Almaden Research Center, 650 Harry Road, San Jose, California, USA.

{ccampbel,zhai,kim,pmaglio}@almaden.ibm.com

Abstract: The present study makes two contributions to the literature on tactile feedback. First, it investigates the effect of tactile feedback in isometric rate control devices. The use of tactile feedback in this type of device has not been systematically investigated. An isometric joystick, such as the IBM Trackpoint™ in-keyboard pointing device does not perceptibly move and is operated by force. Can tactile information delivered to the user's fingertip through such a device provide a feeling of texture? Second, it investigates the interplay of tactile and visual information. We hypothesized that tactile displays are often ineffective because they are not synchronized with visual information. We developed a simple isometric tactile device, Tractile, based on the Trackpoint pointing device, which can vibrate its tip under program control. We conducted an experimental study using this device. Under various visual and tactile feedback conditions, experimental participants performed a tunnel steering task that resembles menu navigation and other real tasks. We found that tactile feedback did in fact give users a feeling of texture, and can speed up steering performance when the texture presented visually matches the texture presented tactilely.

Keywords: tactile feedback, isometric joystick, touch, feel, multi-modal interface, computer input device.

1 Introduction

In the real world, people are adapted to make optimal use of multiple sources of information (Massaro, 1998). However, most human–computer interfaces provide users but a single channel of information, namely visual. Recently, together with auditory interfaces (Gaver, 1997), tactile and force feedback interfaces for mainstream computing applications have begun to emerge, making it at last practical to construct multi-modal human computer interfaces.

"Computing with feeling" has a long research history. Atkinson et al. (1977) described one early effort in this field. Force-coupled master-slave robots for tele-operation, which feed back the force at a remote robot arm (slave) to the master controller arm in a control room, has an even longer history in hazardous material handling. Brooks, Jr. et al. (1990) applied such an approach to 'visual reality', in which the remote site was a data field in a 3D computer visual display rather than a hazardous environment in the physical world. Recently, force feedback or tactile devices have begun to become commercially available, such as the Phantom (SensAble Technologies Inc.) and the MouseCAT (Haptic Technologies), in addition to the more ubiquitous force feedback joysticks for computer games. More recently, Immersion Corp announced the FEELit mouse.

Two factors motivated our current study. One is that despite various engineering efforts, empirical evidence on the usefulness of tactile information for computer applications is scarce and unconvincing — see Shimoga (1993), for a review. Balakrishnan et al. (1994) showed users' performance improve in a virtual carving task that mimics physical actions in real work but this rarely occurs in ordinary human–computer interaction. Engel et al. (1994) showed that contextually appropriate force feedback delivered through a track-ball can speed cursor pointing tasks. Akamatsu (1992) showed that shape-tracing speed decreases when appropriate feedback is provided to the fingertip, and that eye movements (fixations) decrease when such haptic feedback is provided. Payette et al. (1996) showed that operators subject to extreme conditions in zero gravity could achieve better performance with force feedback devices than with free moving devices (both in speed and error rate).

We believe that one of the key reasons for the lack of empirical evidence on the utility of tactile feedback is because the interaction between tactile and visual modes is often overlooked. To make the most of multiple information sources, it is reasonable to assume that the tactile feedback should provide information that is consistent with the visual information displayed. Conflicting or unrelated information should hinder performance whereas consonant information should facilitate performance.

The striking effect of combining information from different modalities is a familiar experience. For instance, flight simulators that add three-dimensional motion of the cockpit to what is presented visually give users a far more realistic experience. An amusement park theatre that shakes the viewer's seat when the visually presented images shake give a different experience than either visual or physical shaking alone.

The second factor that motivated the current study is that it was unknown if tactile information can be presented through an isometric device, such as the IBM Trackpoint™ in-keyboard pointing device used in many notebook computers. Such a device is most compact and well suited for mobile computing but it does not perceptibly move. Can tactile information be presented effectively at all in such a case?

In summary, our goal is to understand whether tactile information can be presented through an isometric device, whether it enhances user's performance when interacting with computers, and how such an effect relates to visual information. To investigate this, we first developed a simple, compact tactile device based on the Trackpoint isometric joystick.

2   Tractile Device

We recently developed the Tractile device, which is a tactilely enhanced Trackpoint (Rutledge & Selker, 1990). The design goal was to provide tactile vibration with a very compact size and power consumption suitable for laptop computers. An actuator on this modified Trackpoint includes a cylindrical coil that — when carrying a current — produces a magnetic field to drive a ferromagnetic slug upward toward the actuator tip, providing tactile feedback to the user (see Figure 1). As shown in the figure, a plastic cap is attached to the post of the pointing device. This cap is rounded to fit inside a cylinder relatively the same size as the ferromagnetic slug, which is housed inside the cylinder. The coil wrapped around the bottom of the sensor has a resistance of 70ohms. The ferromagnetic slug is inserted into the cylinder with the correct polarity. A rubber cap is attached to the top of the cylinder to retain the ferromagnetic slug. The coil is excited by external electronics to apply a 10ms pulse at 5volts/100ma. Thus, a magnetic field repels

the slug from the coil in an upward motion, striking the underside of the top rubber cap, which is what the user feels as tactile feedback. The maximum pulse rate without significant loss of amplitude is 30Hz, which might be lower than the ideal frequency for a fine texture display, but is acceptable for the task in this experiment.

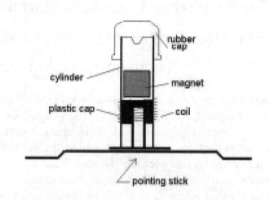

Figure 1: Schematic of the Tractile device.

While the cursor control on the screen is communicated through the PS/2 port as usual, the pulsing of the Tractile is controlled through the computer's serial port. Using the serial connection, a program can control the tactile feedback presented to the user, both when to pulse and how often. The entire Tractile device can be fit into the IBM Thinkpad notebook computers, presenting the same appearance as an unmodified Trackpoint.

3   Method

We selected a task that is common in today's computer applications: steering a cursor through a tunnel. This is an elemental task that is similar to highlighting a line of text or selecting an item from nested menus, such as traversing the path Start — Program — Accessories — Notepad in Windows or similar GUI operating systems. Recent studies by Accot & Zhai (1997; 1999) showed that such tasks can be reliably modelled by the steering law, similar to the way pointing tasks can be modelled by Fitts' law. In the present experiment, we asked participants to steer a cursor though tunnels that were filled with small bumps (Figures 2–5). The experiment was aimed at determining whether tactile information can facilitate users' steering performance under various visual conditions. That is, if what appears to be a bumpy texture on the screen *feels* bumpy to the user when the mouse pointer is moved over it, can the user more quickly or more easily steer the pointer? To make the task sensitive to performance differences, we choose circular shaped tunnels because they are more difficult to navigate (Accot & Zhai, 1997; 1999).

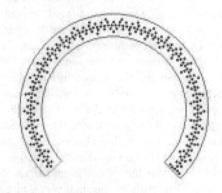

Figure 2: Visual + Tactile and Visual Only.

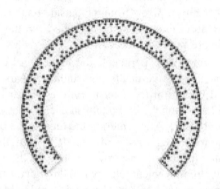

Figure 3: Unconcerted Visual + Tactile stimulus.

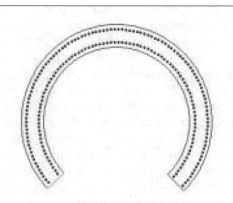

Figure 4: Botts stimulus.

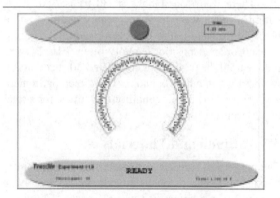

Figure 5: Screen shot of experimental set up.

3.1 Participants

Sixteen experienced computer users were recruited from the staff of our research lab (5 females, 11 males). Four had little or no experience using the Trackpoint (never or only used a Trackpoint a few times) whereas the remaining twelve had moderate to high experience (used the Trackpoint regularly). None of the participant had prior experience with this type of tactile device. All participants had normal or corrected vision.

3.2 Design

Participants were presented with four within-subject conditions: Visual + Tactile, Visual Only, Botts dots, and Unconcerted Visual + Tactile. In the Visual + Tactile condition, participants both saw and felt a bumpy texture inside the tunnel. In the Visual Only condition, the texture was merely seen and not felt. For the Botts condition, two rows of bumps lined the inside of the tunnel 5 pixels from the upper and lower borders.* These bumps could be both seen and felt. Finally, for the Unconcerted Visual + Tactile condition, bumps that could be seen became denser toward the tunnel borders whereas bumps that could be felt became denser toward the centre — the tactile bumps and the visual bumps did not occur in concert. In other words, seeing a bump at a certain location did not necessarily mean feeling a bump at that same location.

Two performance measures were collected, reaction time and accuracy. Reaction time was measured as the time (in milliseconds) starting when the pointer entered the tunnel through the left-end until the pointer exited the tunnel thought the right-end. Accuracy was measured as the number of times the pointer was steered out-of-bounds.

---

*The Botts condition is named after 'Botts dots', small, raised ceramic lane dividers common on California freeways. When an automobile crosses from one lane to the other, a sudden bumpiness is felt as the tires roll over the 'dots'. This bumpiness is particularly startling if the lane-change maneuver was unintentional.

There were four blocks of 30 trials. All trials within a block were from the same condition. The blocks were balanced so that each condition occurred in each ordered position equally often. Trials were redone until the participant completed 30 successfully (without going out of bounds). Thus, each participant was exposed to all four conditions 30 times, for a total of 120 trials.

3.3   Stimuli and Materials

The participant's task was to steer the mouse pointer through a circular tunnel as quickly and accurately as possible. The pointer used was the normal Windows arrow pointer. The visual bumps appeared as small (4x4 pixel) half-spheres protruding out of the surface of the tunnel. A light reflectance point in the upper left corner of each bump created a three-dimensional effect. Many participants reported that the bumps gave a good illusion of 3D texture. Tactile bumps felt like a ticking or snapping sensation in the tip of the Trackpoint device. Pulsing the Trackpoint only occurred when the mouse pointer was in motion and only when it passed over a bump point.

For the Visual + Tactile condition, bump points were seen as bumps on the screen. However, for the Unconcerted Visual + Tactile condition, bump points were not seen. A bump point is a 4x4 pixel area (the same size as a visual bump). When the pointer enters this area from any direction a single pulse is sent to the Trackpoint. When the pointer then leaves the bump area another single pulse is sent. Thus, each bump point feels like the pointer hits the raised bump and then falls from the top of the bump back to the surface. The pulse strength was strong enough so that participants could feel single pulses, although feeling single pulses becomes more difficult when the pulse frequency increases (due to moving the pointer more quickly over the bumpy texture). With faster movements, we noticed that the synchronization of seeing the pointer pass over a bump and the time that bump was felt began to deteriorate. To remedy this, the Trackpoint driver's sampling rate was increased from the default 40Hz to 200Hz. This adjustment was highly effective at maintaining the visual-tactile information synchronization even at a fast rate of movement.

The tunnel that participants had to steer the pointer through was a semi-circle covering 270 degrees of arc, starting at 240 degrees and moving clockwise to 330 degrees. In essence, the tunnel appeared as a large upside-down horseshoe. The radius of the tunnel from the centre to the outside boundary was 150 pixels and the width from outside to inside boundaries was 35 pixels.

For the visual only conditions, the texture visually appeared as very dense bumps in the centre of the tunnel, becoming less dense towards the outer and inner boundaries (see Figure 2). No tactile information was provided in this condition. For the Visual + Tactile condition, the texture was the same as in Figure 2 but the user also felt the texture through the tactile feedback. In other words, what was felt was what was seen. The frequency of the bumps indicated how closely the steering was on track: the more frequent the user felt the bumps, the closer to the centre the user was steering. In the Unconcerted Visual + Tactile condition, what was felt was different from what was seen: the texture visually appeared very dense at the boundaries of the tunnel and became less dense toward the centre (see Figure 3), opposite to how the tactile information was displayed. For the Botts condition, there were no graded levels of texture but a solid line of bumps 5 pixels from the outside boundary and another solid line of bumps 5 pixels from the inside (see Figure 4).

During the experiment, the tunnel was centred horizontally and vertically with indicator bars at the top and bottom of the screen. Before the participant entered the tunnel, the bottom indicator showed the word, 'Ready'. After entering the tunnel, the bottom indicator showed the word, 'GO!!!' and the top indicator displayed an arrow pointing in the correct direction of movement (clockwise) through the tunnel. If the participant went out-of-bounds, a red light would flash but if the participant went completely through without going out-of-bounds, a green light would flash on the top indicator. The total time steering through the tunnel was displayed on the top indicator after every trial. Finally, the trial number (out of 30 trials for the block) was displayed at the far right on the bottom indicator. Figure 5 shows a sample screen.

All participants were run on the same IBM Thinkpad 760E, which has an SVGA display 1024 pixels wide by 768 pixels high. The special Trackpoint was mounted on a plastic surface and placed next to the computer within comfortable reaching distance of the participant. A custom computer program administered the entire experiment, including instructions, practice and experimental trials, and saving the results to disk.

3.4   Procedure

Each participant sat in an isolated room with only the Thinkpad 760E and the tactile Trackpoint prototype placed on the desk. Participants were given both written or oral instructions to steer the pointer through the tunnel from left to right clockwise as quickly and accurately as possible. Additionally, participants were told that on some trials they would receive tactile feedback through the Trackpoint and on other trials they would only see the texture in the tunnel. Finally, the indicator bars were explained, including the reaction time information given in the top display. Participants were encouraged to check their time on every trial and try to improve. After the instructions, two practice trials of each condition were administered and then, if there were no questions the participants began the experiment.

During the experiment, participants steered the pointer through each tunnel entering on the left and exiting on the right. After successfully steering through the tunnel, a green light and the reaction time were given on the top indicator and the bottom indicator displayed the word, 'Done'. The experimental program then reset the trial and the bottom indicator displayed the word 'Ready'. During the experiment, there was no indication that a different block was starting other than the reset of the trial number display to 1. Participants were allowed to take a break between any trials for as long as they liked but no formal break was given. Each participant took approximately 25 minutes to complete all 120 trials.

After completing the experiment participants were debriefed and ask about their impressions of the Tractile device and the experiment. Participants were also asked to reflect on the usefulness of tactile feedback for pointer control. Finally, participants were reimbursed for their time with a $5 cafeteria voucher.

4 Results

Task completion time and error rate were calculated for each participant. We discuss these results in turn.

4.1 Task Completion Time

Mean trial completion time was 4.7 seconds (s) for the Visual + Tactile condition, 5.2s for Visual Only, 5.5s for Botts, and 5.2s for Unconcerted Visual + Tactile (see Figure 6). Since the completion time data were skewed, as they usually are for reaction time data, a logarithmic transformation was taken for statistical variance analysis. A repeated measures ANOVA showed that the feedback condition had a significant effect on trial completion time ($F(3,45) = 5.22, p < 0.005$). Pairwise t-tests showed that the mean trial completion time under the Visual + Tactile condition was significantly shorter ($p < 0.01$) than each of the other three conditions, Visual Only, Botts, and Unconcerted Visual + Tactile. The difference among the latter three conditions was not significant.

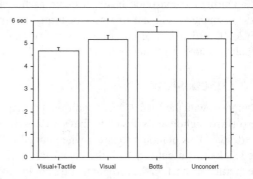

Figure 6: Mean completion time.

During the course of the experiment, participants made small but significant ($F(2,30) = 4.02, p < 0.05$) progress in completion time. The mean completion time of the first ten trials (Block 1) was 5.3s. The mean completion time of the last ten trials (Block 3) was 5.1s. However, practice did not affect the difference between feedback conditions, as the interaction term, Condition X Block, was not significant ($F(6,90) = 0.89$).

4.2 Error Rate

Given the difficulty of the steering task, participants often steered out of the boundaries of the tunnel. In that case, an error was registered but the participant had to re-start the trial until successfully steered out of the end of the tunnel. The mean number of errors was 0.53 for Visual + Tactile, 0.54 for Visual Only, 0.36 for Botts and 0.60 for Unconcerted Visual + Tactile (see Figure 7). A repeated measures ANOVA showed that condition had a significant effect on number of errors ($F(3,45) = 2.87, p < 0.05$). Pairwise t-tests showed that participants made significantly fewer ($p < 0.05$) errors under the Botts condition than under each of the other three conditions. Differences among Visual + Tactile, Visual Only, and Unconcerted Visual + Tactile were not significant.

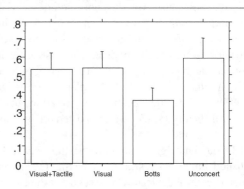

Figure 7: Mean number of errors made.

During the course of the experiment, participants did not make significant progress in terms of errors ($F(2,30) = 0.16$). The interaction term Condition X Block was not significant either ($F(6,90) = 0.8$).

5 Discussion

Compared with the Visual Only condition, participants performed significantly faster in the Visual + Tactile condition. This demonstrates that when added tactile feedback was in concert with the visual information, the tactile feedback in the form of texture could indeed help user's steering performance. Note that this time advantage was gained without significant change in the number of errors made.

In contrast, participants made no performance improvement — either in terms of completion time or in terms of error — from the Visual Only to the Unconcerted Visual + Tactile condition. In the latter case, although both visual and tactile information were present, and the participants could conceivably utilize both sources of information, the incompatible mapping between the two modalities apparently prevented participants from taking advantage of the additional tactile information. This confirmed one of the main hypotheses of this study: Tactile information can effectively aid user's performance only if it is presented in concert with visual information. In other words: *What you feel must be what you see.*

In the Botts condition, both visual information and tactile information were presented in concert. As shown, this had an effect on accuracy. The bumps near the boundary served as a warning that the pointer was heading out of the tunnel. Thus, we see significantly fewer errors made in this case. Note that the reduced error rate was at the expense of a small but insignificant increase in completion time (see Figures 6 & 7). The Botts dots might have encouraged some participants try to stay within the boundary of the dots, making the tunnel effectively narrower. Because we did not include a visual only Botts condition, we do not know if or how much tactile information contributed to the results. According to the Accot & Zhai (1997) steering law study, human steering time linearly increases as the width of tunnel decreases. We plan to investigate the effect of tactile feedback in relation to the steering difficulty (tunnel width and length) in future work.

To our knowledge, the current study is the first published empirical research on tactile feedback in isometric control devices. The Trackpoint device does not perceptibly move. In daily life, we can only feel texture if we move a finger across a surface — cf.

(Loomis & Lederman, 1986). In the case of isometric device, there is no physical, kinesthetic motion of the user's hands, only the visual motion of cursor movement on the screen. Nevertheless, our results show that tactile feedback suggesting texture is still effective. Future work will explore if the influence of tactile information can be enhanced with kinesthetic hand motion.

This study has many practical implications. First, it shows that an effective tactile input device can be made in an isometric form, which is well suited for mobile and many other computing applications. Second, it illustrates that we cannot expect user performance improvement by simply adding a tactile device to today's computer systems without modifying the visual GUI interfaces. Because today's GUI is not designed with tactile feedback in mind, it may be difficult to fit tactile feedback to current visual interfaces. Third, the study also suggests that some common human computer interaction tasks can benefit from tactile feedback. For example, hierarchical menu navigation is often slow and error prone, particularly with the long and narrow menu items (see Figure 8). According to the results of this study, the user may accomplish such a task more quickly if the words in the menu item can be felt. Furthermore, the results also suggests the benefit can only be achieved if the words are visually raised (e.g. as in Figure 9) so that the look and feel of the words are consistent. When the goal is to reduce error and 'safe guard' the user by facilitating path through a sequence of menu items, our results suggest that placing 'Botts dots', both visually and tactilely, inside the boundary of the menu items can be useful. Feeling raised text may facilitate other tasks, such as selecting a block of text in a word-processing application.

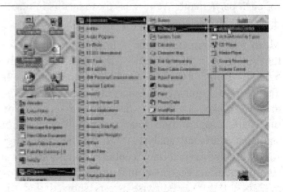

Figure 8: Nested long menu items.

We studied one example of multi-modal interfaces. By combining multiple sources of information, multi-modal interfaces can:

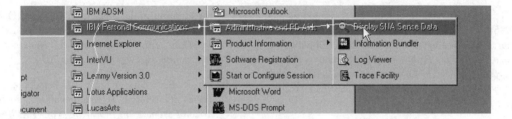

Figure 9: Mockup of menu items with raised 3D-looking text.

- increase realism;

- provide a feeling of immersion;

- facilitate reliable or robust performance;

- reduce fatigue; and

- add redundant information to provide assistance for users with special needs.

One important conclusion of this study is that information presented by multi-modal interfaces ought to work to together to give users a coherent impression of the world.

6   Conclusion

Based on the results of our study, we can make the following conclusions. First, tactile feedback can improve users' performance, either in reducing error rate or in increasing steering speed. Second, the effect of the tactile feedback depends on how the tactile feedback is presented in relation to the visual feedback. Tactile feedback helps only if it is presented in concert with visual information. If the tactile and visual information are at odds, the information can not be effectively used. Third, tactile feedback in the form of texture can be effectively used in isometric control devices — even without the user having to move a finger across a surface.

Acknowledgements

We thank Ted Selker for encouragement and thoughtful discussions on this topic. We also thank the reviewers, whose careful comments helped us improve the paper.

References

Accot, J. & Zhai, S. (1997), Beyond Fitts' Law: Models for Trajectory-based HCI Tasks, *in* S. Pemberton (ed.), *Proceedings of CHI'97: Human Factors in Computing Systems*, ACM Press, pp.295–302.

Accot, J. & Zhai, S. (1999), Performance Evaluation of Input Devices in Trajectory-based Tasks: An Application of Steering Law, *in* M. G. Williams, M. W. Altom, K. Ehrlich & W. Newman (eds.), *Proceedings of CHI'99: Human Factors in Computing Systems*, ACM Press, pp.466–472.

Akamatsu, M. (1992), "The Influence of Combined Visual and Tactile Information on Finger and Eye Movements During Shape Tracing", *Ergonomics* **35**(5/6), 646–60.

Atkinson, W. D., Bond, K. E., Tribble III, G. L. & Wilson, K. R. (1977), "Computing with Feeling", *Computer Graphics* **2**(2), 97–103.

Balakrishnan, R., Ware, C. & Smith, T. (1994), Virtual Hand Tool with Force Feedback, *in* C. Plaisant (ed.), *Companion Proceedings of CHI'94: Human Factors in Computing Systems (CHI'94 Conference Companion)*, ACM Press, pp.83–4.

Brooks, Jr., F. P., Ouh-Yong, M., Batter, J. J. & Kilpatric, P. J. (1990), "Project GROPE — Haptic Display for Scientific Visualization", *Computer Graphics* **24**(4), 177–85.

Engel, F. L., Goossens, P. & Haakma, R. (1994), "Improved Efficiency through I- and E-Feedback: A Trackball with Contetual Force Feedback", *International Journal of Human–Computer Interaction* **41**(6), 949–74.

Gaver, W. (1997), Auditory Interfaces, *in* M. Helander, T. K. Landauer & P. Prabhu (eds.), *Handbook of Human–Computer Interaction*, second edition, Elsevier Science, pp.1003–41.

Loomis, J. M. & Lederman, S. J. (1986), Tactual Perception, *in* K. R. Boff, L. Kaufman & J. P. Thomas (eds.), *Handbook of Perception and Performance: Volume II, Cognitive Processes and Performance*, John Wiley & Sons.

Massaro, D. W. (1998), *Perceiving Talking Faces*, MIT Press.

Payette, J., Hayward, V., Ramstein, C. & Bergeron, D. (1996), Evaluation of a Force-Feedback (Haptic) Computer Pointing Device in Zero Gravity, *in Proceedings of the Fifth Annual Symposium on Haptic Interfaces for Virtual Environments and Teleoperated Systems*, Vol. DSC-58, pp.547–53. ASME Dynamic Systems and Control Division.

Rutledge, J. & Selker, T. (1990), Force to Motion Functions for Pointing, *in* D. Diaper, D. Gilmore, G. Cockton & B. Shackel (eds.), *Proceedings of INTERACT '90 — Third IFIP Conference on Human–Computer Interaction*, Elsevier Science, pp.701–5.

Shimoga, K. B. (1993), A Survey of Perceptual Feedback Issues in Dexterous Telemanipulation: Part II. Finger Touch Feedback, *in Proceedings of VRAIS '93*, IEEE Publications, pp.271–9.

Human–Computer Interaction — INTERACT '99
M. Angela Sasse and Chris Johnson (Editors)
Published by IOS Press, © IFIP TC.13, 1999

Effects of Orientation Disparity Between Haptic and Graphic Displays of Objects in Virtual Environments

Yanqing Wang & Christine L. MacKenzie

School of Kinesiology, Simon Fraser University, Burnaby, BC V5A 1S6, Canada.

{wangy,cmackenz}@move.kines.sfu.ca

Abstract: Spatial disparity between a physical object and its visual presentation is very common in virtual environments. An experiment was conducted to systematically investigate the effects of orientation disparity between haptic and graphic displays of objects on human performance in a virtual environment. It was found that human performance was optimum with no orientation disparity. Orientation disparity had significant effects on the object orientation component, but did not appear to affect the object transportation component of human movements. It appeared that, when the orientation disparity was present, the orientation speed relied more on the haptic display of objects while the orientation accuracy depended more on the graphic display of objects. Implications for human–computer interface design were also discussed.

Keywords: human performance, virtual reality, object manipulation, object transportation, object orientation, object docking, 3D graphics, user interface, haptic feedback, visual feedback, visual dominance.

1 Introduction

Objects in the real world are a unitary whole, that is, haptic and graphic displays are spatially consistent. Haptic displays are perceived by the hand in the control space, and include the physical characteristics (e.g. shape and size) of an object. Graphic displays of an object are perceived by the eyes. For object manipulation in the real world, what you see is generally consistent with what you feel. Humans perform daily activities in an environment where haptic and graphic displays of objects are completely superimposed.

However, this is hardly the case in human–computer interaction (HCI). In a typical human–computer interaction setup, the control space of the hand is separate from the display space of the objects, where what a user feels with her hand is not the same with what she sees with her eyes. For example, in a desktop HCI situation, the movement of a mouse on a horizontal plane is transformed to the movement of a cursor on a vertical screen. A cursor is a visual presentation of the mouse, but with different shape, size, location and orientation from the mouse. The mouse and the cursor are not spatially superimposed. In other words, haptic display of a mouse is different

from its graphic display, a graphic cursor (Graham & MacKenzie, 1996).

We use the term disparity in this study to refer to the spatial difference between haptic and graphic displays of objects. Disparity between haptic and graphic displays is an important feature that distinguishes most virtual environments from real world environments. In human–computer interaction applications, the graphic object being manipulated by a physical controller rarely has the same characteristics (e.g. shape, size, location and orientation) as the controller (Wang & MacKenzie, 1999; Wang et al., 1998; Ware, 1990; 1998; Zhai & Milgram, 1997). Disparity between haptic and graphic displays can have significant effects on human performance in virtual environments. The purpose of this experiment is to investigate how the disparity between haptic and graphic displays affects human object manipulation in virtual environments, and to provide further insight into HCI design.

1.1 Previous Research

Effects of disparity between haptic and graphic displays have been rarely studied. An experiment was conducted by Wang & MacKenzie (1999) to investigate the effects of relative size among the controller, cursor and target on docking tasks in virtual environments. The difference between the controller and cursor sizes indicated the effects of size disparity between haptic and graphic displays. They found that human performance was better when the controller and cursor had the same size, that is, when the haptic and graphic displays were superimposed.

Graham & MacKenzie (1996) conducted experiments to examine human pointing performance under different relationships between the display space and control space. They found that users generally achieved better performance when the display space and control space were superimposed than other conditions. Their results can be related to the effects of transportation disparity between haptic and graphic displays of objects since only object transportation was required in their experiments. Ware (1990; 1998) noticed that object transportation and orientation in virtual environments were much slower than in the real world. He suggested that it could be the object orientation components that slowed down the object manipulation process in virtual environments.

We are unaware of research in the literature that systematically studied the effects of orientation disparity between haptic and graphic displays on object manipulation in virtual environments. This disparity may play an important role in human performance and is the focus of this study.

1.2 Research Hypotheses

An experiment was conducted to investigate the effects of orientation disparity between object haptic and graphic displays on object transportation and orientation in virtual environments. Two research hypotheses were proposed:

1. It was predicted that human performance would be optimum under the no orientation disparity condition, when the haptic and graphic displays were superimposed. When no disparity was presented, humans could take advantage of easily transferring their object manipulation skills from the real world into the virtual world. This hypothesis was suggested by the converging evidence from previous research (Graham & MacKenzie, 1996; Wang & MacKenzie, 1999; Wang et al., 1998).

2. Another hypothesis was that the orientation disparity between haptic and graphic displays of an object would not only affect the orientation process but also the transportation process. Previous research showed that object transportation and orientation processes

interacted with each other, suggesting an interdependent structure (Wang et al., 1998). Even though orientation disparity can be considered as an input to the object orientation process, it may still affect the output of the object transportation process. At the same time, it was expected that the disparity would affect the orientation process more than the transportation process.

2 Method

2.1 Subjects

Eight university students volunteered to participate in this experiment. Each subject was paid $20 for a two-hour session. All subjects were right-handed, and had normal or corrected-to-normal vision. Informed consent was provided before the experimental session.

2.2 Experimental Apparatus

This experiment was conducted in the Virtual Hand Laboratory at Simon Fraser University. The experimental setup is shown in Figures 1a & b. A Silicon Graphics Indigo RGB monitor was set upside down on the top of a cart. A mirror was placed parallel to the monitor screen and the table surface. A stereoscopic, head-coupled graphical display was presented on the screen and was reflected by the mirror. The image was perceived by the subject as if it was below the mirror, on the table surface. The subject was wearing CrystalEYES Goggles to obtain a stereoscopic view. Three infrared markers (IREDs) were fixed to the side frame of the goggles and their positions were monitored with an OPTOTRAK motion analysis system (Northern Digital, Inc.) with 0.2mm accuracy to provide a head-coupled view in a 3D space. The subject held a wooden cube (30mm) on the table surface. Three IREDs were placed on the top of the wooden cube, driving a six degree-of-freedom (DOF) wire-frame graphic cube with 1 frame lag. The target was a wire-frame graphic cube that appeared on the table surface to the subject. The graphic six DOF cube and the target cube had the same size as the wooden cube, 30mm. The stereoscopic, head-coupled, graphic display was updated at 60Hz with 1 frame lag of OPTOTRAK coordinates. Data from the OPTOTRAK were sampled and recorded at 60Hz by a Silicon Graphics Indigo Extreme computer workstation. A thin physical L-frame (not shown in the figure) was used to locate the starting position of the wooden cube, at the beginning of each trial. The experiment was conducted in a semi-dark room. The subject saw the target cube and the six DOF cube presented on the mirror, but was unable to see the physical controller

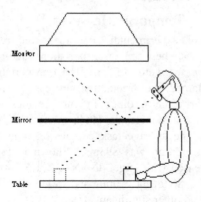

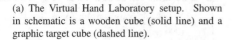

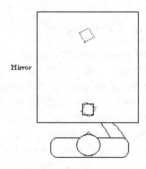

(a) The Virtual Hand Laboratory setup. Shown in schematic is a wooden cube (solid line) and a graphic target cube (dashed line).

(b) Top view of the experiment setup. Two graphic cubes (dashed line) were perceived during the experiment. The graphic cube further away from the subject was the target cube. The graphic cube closer to the subject was the graphic display of the wooden cube (solid line) where there were 30 degrees of orientation disparity between them. Subject could feel the wooden cube in hand, but could not see the wooden cube.

Figure 1: The experimental set up.

cube and the hand. The wooden cube was referred as the physical object, the six degree-of-freedom graphic cube as the graphic object, and the target cube as the graphic target. The task was to match either the physical object or the graphic object to the graphic target as fast and accurately as possible.

2.3   Experimental Design

The centre of the graphic object was always superimposed with the physical object (Figure 1b). In one experimental condition, the graphic object was oriented 30 degrees clockwise from the physical object around their common centre (vertical axis), therefore generating the orientation disparity between haptic display and graphic display. In another condition, the graphic object and physical object were totally aligned, with no orientation disparity.

The graphic target was located at either 100mm or 200mm away from the starting position of the physical object. In the no disparity condition, the graphic target was oriented 30 degrees clockwise; in the disparity condition, the target was oriented 60 degrees clockwise. This target angle arrangement guaranteed that the physical object was always oriented 30 degrees to match the target orientation regardless of disparity or no disparity condition so that the results in different disparity were comparable.

Subjects were asked to perform two kind of tasks: physical match and graphic match. Physical match was to match the physical object to the location and orientation of the graphic target according to the haptic information felt with the hand. Graphic match was to match the graphic object to the graphic target based on what they saw with their eyes. In all conditions, subjects saw the graphic object and graphic target; they did not see the physical object or the hand. In summary, this was a balanced experimental design with repeated measures on eight subjects: 2 task conditions × 2 disparity conditions × 2 distances.

Dependent variables were derived from OPTOTRAK 3D position data collected from two IREDs on the top of the physical object (wooden cube). Data from the IRED on the top centre of the physical object were used for object transportation measures, and two IREDs on the top of the physical object were used to calculate the angular value for object orientation measures. Dependent variables included four temporal measures and four spatial error measures. The temporal measures were: task completion time (CT), object transportation time (TT), object orientation time (OT), ratio (R) between orientation time (OT) and transportation time (TT).

The spatial error measures included: constant distance error (CED), variable distance error (VED), constant angle error (CEA), and variable angle error (VEA).

2.4   Experimental Procedure

In each experimental session, individual eye positions were calibrated relative to the IREDs on the goggles to provide a customized stereoscopic, head-coupled view. The table surface was calibrated and the relative orientation between the physical object and the graphic object was determined. A subject was comfortably seated at a table, with forearm at approximately the same height as the table surface. The subject held the physical object with the right hand, with the thumb and index finger in pad opposition on the centre of opposing cube faces which were parallel to the frontal plane of the body. The subject was instructed to match either the physical object or the graphic object to the location and angle of the graphic target as fast and accurately as possible. To start a trial, subjects placed the physical cube at a start position on the table surface. A graphic target appeared at one of two distances and two angles. The subject made either physical match or graphic match as quickly and accurately as possible. When the subject was satisfied with the match, he/she held the controller still and said 'OK' to end that trial. Trials were blocked by task and disparity conditions. The target location and angles were randomly generated. At the beginning of each block of trials, subjects were given 20 trials for practice.

2.5   Data Analysis

Data were filtered with a 7Hz low-pass second-order bi-directional Butterworth digital filter to remove digital sampling artifacts, vibrations of the markers, and tremor from the hand movement. Original IRED 3D position data were interpolated and filtered once only, and then were used for the following data manipulation including angular data generation. A computer program determining the start and end of a pointing movement was used separately for the transportation and orientation processes, based on criterion velocities. The start and end of each process were then confirmed by visually inspecting a graph of the velocity profile. A trial was rejected if the program failed to find a start and end or there was disagreement between experimenter's visual inspection and computer's results. For dependent measures, ANOVAs were performed on the balanced design of 2 task conditions × 2 disparity conditions × 2 distances with repeated measures on all three factors.

3   Results

3.1   Temporal Measures

In all experimental conditions, the relative time courses between transportation and orientation processes were similar. The transportation process contained the orientation process. These results confirm the findings in our previous experiments (Wang & MacKenzie, 1999; Wang et al., 1998).

The average task completion time (CT) across all condition was 893ms. Shown in Figure 2, CT increased with target distance, $F(1,7) = 659.78, p < 0.001$, 807ms at 100mm and 980ms at 200mm. There was no other significant effect.

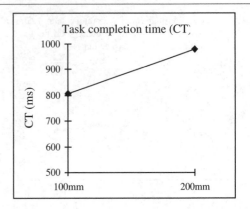

Figure 2: Task completion time.

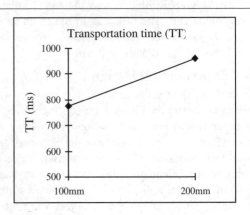

Figure 3: Object transportation time.

The transportation time (TT) had an average value of 868ms, taking up 97.2% of the task completion time (CT). Statistics of TT were similar to those of CT. TT increased from 776ms at 100mm to 959ms at 200mm, $F(1,7) = 617.13, p < 0.001$, as shown in Figure 3. No other significant effects were found. Disparity between haptic and visual information in orientation did not appear to have effects on TT. It appeared that once visual information was presented, the subject

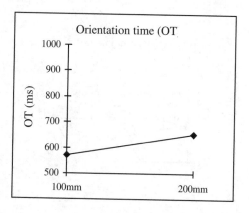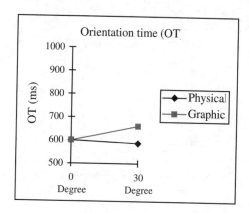

Figure 4: Object orientation time.

could easily transport either the physical or the graphic object to the target location.

The orientation time (OT) was 612ms on average, 70.4% of the task completion time (CT). Distance had a significant effect also on OT, $F(1,7) = 56.91, p < 0.001$. OT was 572ms at 100mm and increased to 651ms at 200mm (Figure 4a). There was a significant interaction between orientation disparity and tasks using haptic information and visual information, $F(1,7) = 13.95, p < 0.005$. As shown in Figure 4b, OT of 661ms was longest when the task was to match the graphic object to the target when there was disparity between the haptic and graphic displays. In contrast, for the other three conditions, OT values were very close, around 600ms. When there was no disparity, it took 601ms to match the physical object to the target, and 598ms to match the graphic object to the target. Those values were close to 586ms where there was disparity, but the task was to match the physical object to the target. Thus, subjects took extra time to orient the graphic object if there was disparity between haptic and visual information. It also suggested that the subjects could successfully disregard the discrepant visual information to achieve a fast orientation of physical object. It is interesting to note that the orientation disparity between haptic and graphic displays only affected the orientation process, OT, but not the transportation process, TT.

The ratio (R) of OT against TT, shown in Figures 5a & b, is indicative of the structure of object transportation and orientation. R represents the proportional time of simultaneous control of the orientation and transportation processes. R reduced significantly with increases in target distance ($F(1,7) = 39.14, p < 0.001$), 0.78 at 100mm and

0.70 at 200mm (Figure 5a). There was a significant interaction between disparity and task conditions, $F(1,7) = 7.97, p < 0.026$, as shown in Figure 5b. When the disparity was presented, R was 0.80 for graphic to graphic match, and was 0.69 for physical to graphic match.

In case of no disparity, R was 0.73 for graphic to graphic match and 0.74 for physical to graphic match. The subjects took less time to integrate the orientation process into the transportation process when they were asked to use the haptic information than the visual information.

3.2 Spatial Error Measures

The average constant distance error (CED) was very small, 0.13mm, and was not significantly different from 0. The average constant angle error (CEA) was 0.96 degree, not significantly different from specified target angles. This result reflects that system errors of the Virtual Hand setup used for this experiment were minimal and did not cause significant performance bias.

Task conditions had main effects on the variable distance error (VED), $F(1,7) = 6.34, p < 0.040$. As shown in Figure 6, VED was 1.5mm for graphic to graphic match, increasing to 2.5mm for physical to graphic match. This result showed that subjects achieved better accuracy in object transportation by using visual information than by using haptic information. The disparity between haptic and graphic displays had no significant effects on VED. Similar to the TT measure, the orientation disparity between haptic and graphic displays did not affect the spatial error of the transportation process. This might be due to the fact that the centre of the physical object was required to be superimposed with that of the

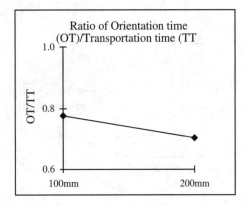 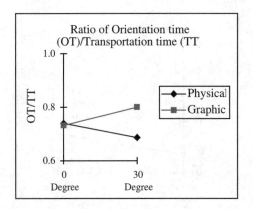

Figure 5: Ratio of orientation time against transportation time.

graphic object, regardless of whether or not there was orientation disparity.

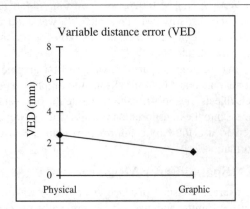

Figure 6: Variable distance errors.

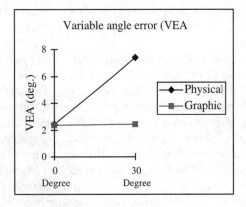

Figure 7: Variable angle errors.

The variable angle error (VEA) was 3.7 degrees on average. There was a significant two-way interaction between disparity and task conditions, $F(1,7) = 21.22, p < 0.003$. As shown in Figure 7, the greatest VEA of 7.4 degrees occurred for physical to graphic match when there was disparity. For the other three conditions, VEAs were similar: with no disparity, 2.5 degrees for physical to graphic match and 2.3 degrees for graphic to graphic match; with orientation disparity, VEA was 2.4 degrees for graphic to graphic match. Patterns of VEA data in Figure 7, are opposite to those of OT data in Figure 4b. It should also be noted that distance had no significant effect on VEA.

4   Discussion

Results from this experiment supported our first hypothesis: human performance was better when there was no spatial orientation disparity between haptic and graphic displays of objects. With no disparity, there was no difference in object manipulation between subject using haptic information and using visual information about objects. It is not clear, in the case of no disparity, which information was actually used for the subject to perform the task. Based on the theory of visual dominance (Posner et al., 1976), visual information may be the primary source guiding object manipulation. We suggest that both haptic and graphic displays played a role in object manipulation (Wang & MacKenzie, 1999), and therefore it was the consistency between haptic and graphic displays that resulted in optimum human performance.

Haptic and graphic displays are superimposed in the real world. Thus, 'natural' object manipulation in the real world generally yields optimum performance, compared with that in the virtual environment. This suggests advantages of an augmented environment which has graphic displays superimposed on physical objects.

Our second hypothesis about human performance under conditions of orientation disparity between haptic and graphic displays was not supported. The disparity only affected the orientation process, but not the transportation process. If the disparity is considered as an input for the orientation process, it only influences the output of the orientation process. In other words, the transportation process appears to be independent of the orientation disparity between haptic and graphic displays. This result was not predicted by our hypothesis. However, the result supported the hypothesis that the orientation disparity would affect the transportation and orientation differently. The orientation disparity between haptic and graphic displays only affected the orientation process of object manipulation.

Object transportation and orientation had a parallel, interdependent structure, consistent with previous experiments (Wang & MacKenzie, 1999; Wang et al., 1998). Specifically, the time course of transportation contained that of orientation. The change in target distances affected both TT and OT. The ratio between OT and TT suggested that haptic information might be very important to integrate the orientation process with the transportation process. This experiment showed that certain factors (e.g. orientation disparity) only affected one component of object manipulation processes while other factors (e.g. target distance) affected both processes. To identify those factors may provide further insight into the underlying mechanisms for object manipulation in virtual environments.

The above findings provide important implications for HCI design. If interaction tasks involve only object transportation, the graphic object can be designed with arbitrary orientation in relation to the controller. In current 2D graphic user interfaces, for example, the graphic arrow cursor usually has a fixed orientation of 45 degrees, regardless of mouse orientation. This orientation design has no effect on human performance since the cursor is only required to do translation movements. However, if tasks require object rotation such as multidimensional manipulation in virtual environments, then the orientation of a 3D cursor relative to the controller will be critical. Our evidence indicates that user's performance will be better if the orientation of the cursor is properly aligned with that of the controller.

The orientation time was shorter for physical to graphic matches than for graphic to graphic matches when the disparity was present. This indicates that the subject was able to make use of haptic information to facilitate object orientation speed. The evidence supports our suggestions that the subject may use both visual and haptic information to perform manipulation, that is, visual dominance does not mean that visual information totally overwrites the haptic information presented to the subject. The extra orientation time for graphic to graphic matches when there was disparity could be because the visual feedback process was somehow interrupted by the disparity between haptic and graphic displays.

Spatial errors measures, however, demonstrated quite a different picture from the temporal measures in terms of the disparity effect. The variable angle error was much smaller for graphic to graphic match than that for physical to graphic match. This indicates that spatial accuracy of object orientation is generally determined by the visual information regardless of the haptic information. When subjects were asked only to use the haptic information and discard the visual information, significant spatial uncertainty occurred. The increase in orientation errors for physical to graphic matches may be attributed to the interference from the inconsistent visual information. Altogether, the results suggest that haptic information and visual information may affect different aspects of orientation process. Haptic information may be more related to manipulation speed while visual information more related to manipulation accuracy. Accordingly, in virtual environment design, consideration should be given to the realism of haptic display when fast manipulation is required such as gaming; in contrast, if accuracy is the main concern, the quality of graphic display should be emphasized.

5   Conclusions

We conclude:

1. Humans can achieve optimum manipulation performance when haptic and graphic displays of objects are superimposed.

2. Disparity in orientation between haptic and graphic displays of objects appears to have no significant effects on object transportation processes.

3. Disparity in orientation between haptic and graphic displays of objects significantly affects the object orientation process, increasing the orientation time for graphic to graphic matches and the spatial errors for physical to graphic matches.

4. It appears that speed of object manipulation relies more on the haptic information while accuracy of object orientation depends more on visual information.

Acknowledgements

We would like to thank Valerie A Summers for her help in software design for the Virtual Hand Laboratory.

References

Graham, E. D. & MacKenzie, C. L. (1996), Physical Versus Virtual Pointing, *in* G. van der Veer & B. Nardi (eds.), *Proceedings of CHI'96: Human Factors in Computing Systems*, ACM Press, pp.292–9.

Posner, M. I., Nissen, M. J. & Klein, R. (1976), "Visual Dominance: An Information-processing Account of its Origins and Significance", *Psychological Review* **83**, 157–71.

Wang, Y. & MacKenzie, C. L. (1999), Object Manipulation in Virtual Environments: Relative Size Matters, *in* M. G. Williams, M. W. Altom, K. Ehrlich & W. Newman (eds.), *Proceedings of CHI'99: Human Factors in Computing Systems*, ACM Press, pp.48–55.

Wang, Y., MacKenzie, C. L., Summers, V. & Booth, K. S. (1998), The Structure of Object Transportation and Orientation in Human–Computer Interaction, *in* C.-M. Karat, A. Lund, J. Coutaz & J. Karat (eds.), *Proceedings of CHI'98: Human Factors in Computing Systems*, ACM Press, pp.312–9.

Ware, C. (1990), "Using Hand Position for Virtual Object Placement", *The Visual Computer* **6**, 245–53.

Ware, C. (1998), Real Handles, Virtual Images, *in* C.-M. Karat, A. Lund, B. Bederson, E. Bergman, M. Beaudouin-Lafon, N. Bevan, D. Boehm-Davis, A. Boltman, G. Cockton, A. Druin, S. Dumais, N. Frischberg, J. Jacko, J. Koenemann, C. Lewis, S. Pemberton, A. Sears, K. T. Simsarian, C. Wolf & J. Ziegler (eds.), *Companion Proceedings of CHI'98: Human Factors in Computing Systems (CHI'98 Conference Companion)*, ACM Press, pp.235–6.

Zhai, S. & Milgram, P. (1997), "Anisotropic Human Performance in Six Degree-of-Freedom Tracking: An Evaluation of Three-Dimensional Display and Control Interfaces", *IEEE Transactions in Systems, Man and Cybernetics — Part A: Systems and Humans* **27**(4), 518–28.

Human–Computer Interaction — INTERACT '99
M. Angela Sasse and Chris Johnson (Editors)
Published by IOS Press, © IFIP TC.13, 1999

Successful Case Study and Partial Validation of MUSE, a Structured Method for Usability Engineering

James Middlemass, Adam Stork & John Long

Ergonomics & HCI Unit, University College London, 26 Bedford Way,
London WC1H AP, UK.

J.Middlemass@ucl.ac.uk, A.Stork@ucl.ac.uk

Abstract: The practices of HCI research are the acquisition and validation of HCI knowledge to support design practice (Long, 1996). Validation of HCI knowledge requires its conceptualization, operationalization, test, and generalization. This paper reports a partial validation using a case-study, which operationalizes MUSE (a previously conceptualized method), on the basis of a set of user requirements. The case-study is successful; the artefact specification being tested against the user requirements, demonstrating the applicability of MUSE to requirements of the type described. To illustrate generalization, the case study is compared to an earlier one, and the user requirements assessed against the dimensions of complexity, definition, and observability.

Keywords: human–computer interaction, human factors, structured methods, software engineering.

1 Introduction

The need for more effective human–computer interactions and research to support their design has been argued by Long (1996). He suggests the practices of HCI research are the acquisition and validation of HCI knowledge to support design practice. Validation of such knowledge by HCI research is specified as 'the conceptualization, operationalization, test, and generalization of its HCI knowledge', where the four constituents are defined as follows. 'Conceptualization involves specified, and so explicit, representation. Operationalization involves the mapping of concepts onto observables and ultimately metrics. Test involves the evaluation of the assertions implicated in the concepts operationalized. Last, generalization involves the abstraction and generification of the outcomes of the tests.' This paper reports a partial validation of such knowledge in the form of a design method. In so doing, this paper provides an illustration of how HCI knowledge validation can be performed using case-studies.

According to these definitions of validation, the MUSE method (Lim & Long, 1994) is conceptualized as HCI knowledge by virtue of its explicit specification as a set of procedures and representations intended to support design; the method is operationalized when it is applied to a set of requirements to produce an artefact specification. The present case study demonstrates correct operationalization of the method by showing that the principal features explicit in the method's conceptualization are evident in its application. Testing involves evaluation of the 'assertion implicated in the concepts' that the method relates a set of requirements to an artefact specification, which satisfies the requirements. Generalization would involve abstraction and generification of the outcomes of a number of such tests, and would demonstrate that the design knowledge was 'fit-for-[general-] design-purpose'.

Stork et al. (1995), based on earlier work by Lim et al. (1990), propose that case-studies of methods can be considered 'successful' or 'unsuccessful'. Successful case-studies demonstrate that a method is applicable to a type of user requirements (and so contribute to the validation of the method) by producing interaction artefacts that satisfy the requirements. Unsuccessful case-studies demonstrate that a method is not applicable to a type of user requirements by producing interaction artefacts that fail to satisfy the requirements. Stork et al. suggest that to enable reasoning about the implications of successful and unsuccessful case-studies, the type of requirements should be characterized in terms of how well-defined, complex, and observable are the user requirements. Thus, unsuccessful case studies can provide input to the development of further versions of a method by indicating that the applicability of the method in its present state does not extend to requirements of a certain type.

Stork et al. describe a successful case-study application of MUSE, a structured Method for Usability Engineering (Lim & Long, 1994), to a set of domestic energy management user requirements to produce an interaction artefact. These user requirements are well-defined, simple, and observable. Stork et al. claim that the case-study is successful because the interaction artefact fulfils the user requirements, and MUSE was applied in the development of that artefact. Thus, the successful case-study demonstrates that MUSE is capable of producing artefacts that satisfy well-defined, simple, and observable user requirements. This paper also describes a successful case-study application of MUSE, but to a different set of user requirements — those for recreational facilities booking, which are considered to be less well-defined and more complex than the domestic energy management user requirements of Stork et al., but equally observable.

2   Overview of MUSE

(The superscript numbers in the text refer to the 'features of a MUSE application', described in the following section, and are intended to illustrate the derivation of the features)

MUSE is a structured analysis and design method for human factors engineers. The method is configurable for use with software engineering structured methods. The product of MUSE is the specification of an interaction artefact, the software engineering method producing a specification of an implementable artefact, incorporating the interaction artefact.

MUSE approaches design in a 'top-down' manner[2] based on information derived 'bottom-up'. MUSE involves specification of design products as defined by the method, employing a specific notation[7]; design progresses from the specification of general features of the tasks to be performed by the user, derived from analysis of the user requirements and from existing systems, to the specification of the details of the interaction artefact[1]. The application of MUSE is considered to be an iterative process, both overall and internally, supporting the production of the best 'first-attempt' artefact following the initial complete application.

Figure 1 shows a schematic diagram of the MUSE method together with an (unspecified) software engineering method. There follows an outline of the

three phases of the method and a description of its main products, each of which is accompanied by a supporting table recording the design rationale[6].

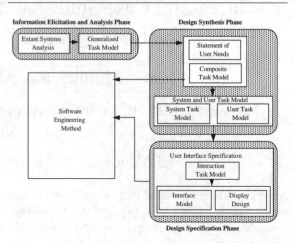

Figure 1: Schematic representation of the MUSE method.

The first phase is that of Information Elicitation and Analysis which involves identification of features of extant systems that are problematic for users and so are to be excluded from the target system, and desirable features that are to be included[4,5]. The phase also involves the creation of a general model of the target artefact following the users' requirements.

The second phase, Design Synthesis, establishes the human factors perspective on the design[4], the semantics of the application domain[3], and a conceptual design of the target artefact. The conceptual design is checked with that of the software engineering method[4], to ensure that a correct implementation is possible. Allocation of function between the user(s) and computer(s) is performed towards the end of this phase.

The final phase is that of Design Specification in which the conceptual design is decomposed to a detailed device-specific implementable specification of the interaction artefact.

3   Features of a MUSE Application

The following features were identified by Stork et al. (1995); all of these features should be evident in a correct operationalization of MUSE, as they are explicit in its conceptualization. The presence of each feature will be indicated, where it occurs in the description of the case study, by use of superscript numbers:

1. The artefact is considered completely and appropriately at all levels of design, from conceptual to detailed.

2. The artefact is consistent across all levels of design (including the user requirements).

3. Domain knowledge is assessed and applied to the artefact at appropriate levels of design.

4. Human factors knowledge (as well as software engineering knowledge) is assessed and applied to the artefact at appropriate levels of design.

5. Desirable qualities of extant systems are assessed and integrated into the artefact at appropriate levels of design.

6. The design rationale implicated in the previous three concerns is made explicit with respect to the artefact.

7. The above concerns are addressed by MUSE products, with appropriate scope and notation, using MUSE procedures.

4   User Requirements

The user requirements resulted from the observation by two sports players, using the sports centre of University College London ('A' and 'J'), that the booking system for recreational facilities (squash and pool) was less than satisfactory. The sports centre had installed a computerized recreational facilities booking system (RFBS) with a single 'terminal' (a small liquid crystal display and keyboard), located in the same building as the sports facilities. Both players were dissatisfied by the booking of the recreational facilities, even when they were available. This dissatisfaction was associated with the user interface and the functionality of the system, and its location in a different building, at some distance from where the two players worked; ideally, the players would have preferred to make bookings without leaving their desks. The sports centre had some rules concerning the booking of the recreational facilities, which were considered acceptable by the two players: only members may make a booking, and members must not book more than seven days in advance, must pay the appropriate booking fee at the time of booking, must book sessions in units of one hour, and must not change a booking.

The sports centre recognized that the computerized booking system raised difficulties for users generally, since it replaced the system by another (which in turn was replaced by a manual system using a reservation book). However, since the replacements were located in the same place as the original computer terminal, the two players remained dissatisfied.

A requirement for an example application of MUSE for dissemination purposes[*] led to the application of MUSE to the user requirements of 'A' and 'J' for a bespoke artefact to address the above dissatisfaction. An assumed appropriate cost for a new recreational facilities booking system was considered to be £10,000. The users were expected to be the two players who expressed the dissatisfaction, 'A' and 'J'; both of whom were regular users of Apple Macintosh computers.

5   Application of MUSE to the User Requirements

The features of a MUSE application(above) embodied in the case history are highlighted by placing the number of the feature in superscript at the end of the sentence containing the feature.

5.1   Information Elicitation and Analysis Phase

A list of extant systems which promised to inform subsequent design was produced. The list included the existing computerized booking system and several related systems, such as 'client' software for remote access across computer networks, on-line diary systems, multiple-selection configuration screens of applications software, and tele-shopping systems[5]. Three extant systems were selected for analysis, sufficient to inform the first iteration of MUSE[5]:

1. The existing system was selected to examine the extant tasks of booking squash and pool facilities. Analysis identified user problems resulting from design features of the system. Such features were to be excluded from the target artefact[4,5].

2. A related system, an Apple Macintosh-based network terminal emulator, Telnet 2.5, was selected to examine the tasks of accessing remote computers across networks[3,4,5].

---

[*]The ESSI (1995) project at University College London required an example application of MUSE to support the teaching of MUSE to the industrial partners on the project.

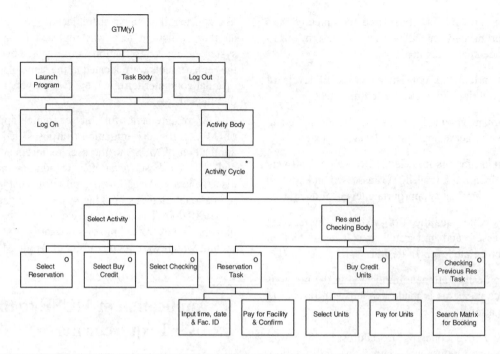

Name	Description	Observation	Design Implication	Speculation
Input time & Facility ID	Users select the day and time of recreation, and what facility they want to book	The user would be best supported by having all of this information on screen simultaneously		
Pay for Facility and confirm	The user finalizes the booking			There will also be an option not to book
Activity cycle	The iteration has been changed from that shown in CS TD(ext)	The user is not required to re-enter the facility and date if they want to change the time		

Figure 2: RFBS: Generalized Task Model of target artefact structured diagram and extract from supporting table.

3. A related system, an Apple Macintosh-based network information retrieval program, TurboGopher, was selected to analyse tasks involving partially-automated host selection and control. It does not require users to select the host or enter details of their user identifier(ID) and password, features of Telnet found problematic by some users[3,5].

Appropriate human factors techniques (observational studies, task analysis, etc.) were applied to construct MUSE extant Task Descriptions containing structured diagrams and supporting tables[6,7]. These analyses identified information likely to inform later design and support novel design speculations[1,4,5].

The high-level tasks represented in these MUSE products were based on different systems combined into a Generalized Task Model of existing systems[5,6,7].

The user requirements form the basis of a Generalized Task Model of the target artefact shown in Figure 2[2,7]. Comparison with the Generalized Task Model of existing systems shows that the high level structure of the task remains the same, but the lower level activity has been modified consistent with the user requirements[2,5]. The purchase of credit units has been included in the target artefact, as suggested by analysis of the existing system[5].

5.2   Design Synthesis Phase

The first activity of the Design Synthesis Phase summarizes the information from the extant systems analysis to produce a human factors perspective on the user requirements[4,5,6]. The statement exposes both specific design issues arising from analysis of the existing system, and general issues arising from the application of human factors knowledge[6].

A further product generated at this time is the Domain of Design Discourse description[1,7], which summarizes the information collected during the analysis of existing systems, concerning relationships between entities in the task domain[3]. It is shown in Figure 3, with the table detailing the nature of the relationships assumed between domain entities[6]. The description records such details as the fact that the system should restrict access to 'legal' users (i.e. those who have a valid identity), and that these users will demand rights to a particular facility at a particular time[3,6]. These rights are transferred by allocation of a specific 'slot', on a 'first come first served' basis (i.e. there are no users who receive preferential treatment) in return for a payment of 'rent'[3]. Notice that the Domain of Design Discourse description is only concerned with details of the task domain and does not specify device-specific details, such as how payment for the use of the facility is to be made[3].

The Composite Task Model Stage produces a conceptual design for the target artefact based on the associated artefact Generalized Task Model and the Generalized Task Model derived from information elicited concerning existing systems[1,2,5,7], for example, once a user has opted to make a booking[6], they check their free time (an off-line task, i.e. one not supported by the target artefact) and their funds are checked (an on-line task, i.e. one supported by the target artefact). If they have insufficient funds, they are notified, and prevented from booking facilities for which they cannot pay[3]. If their funds are sufficient, they enter details of the facility, day, and time that they wish to book[3]. They then have the opportunity to confirm or cancel the booking (in accordance with the Statement of User Needs)[2,4,5]. As the Composite Task Model is device independent (and error free), no assumption shave yet been made concerning the details of implementation[1].

Production of the System Task Model involves further decomposition of the Composite Task Model's on-line tasks to specify the structure of the dialogue between the user and the computer by attribution of actions to the computer ('C') or to the user ('H')[1,2,4,7]. Figure 4 shows an extract from the System Task Model structured diagram, the decomposition of the 'make reservation' body of the Composite Task Model.

Additionally, a User Task Model of the target artefact is produced, containing details of off-line tasks[1,7]. In this case, the off-line tasks involve the user comparing their existing plans for the period available for booking to establish suitable times for recreation[1]. It was considered that these plans were likely either to be represented mentally or in a diary. The supporting table for the User Task Model records that the representation of the booking period in the target system should be compatible with the user's representations in order to provide the most effective support for the booking task[4,6,7]. Human factors guidelines inform this design feature[4,6].

5.3   Design Specification Phase

The first activity of the Design Specification Phase involves producing an Interaction Task Model of the target artefact, based on the System Task Model[2,7].

The Interaction Task Model is a device dependent, but error-free, model of the interaction[1]. It shows user actions required to progress the task as well as the interaction, and indicates where screens are to be consumed and new screens are to be presented[1,2]. In accordance with the Statement of User Needs, the Interaction Task Model conforms to the conventions of the Apple Macintosh system[2,4]. References to specific details of the Macintosh User Interface Guidelines (Apple Computer Inc, 1985)) are recorded in the supporting table[2,4]. If insufficient funds are available, the user is notified[3]. In line with Macintosh conventions, notification is by a modal dialogue, with the user clicking an 'OK' button to continue the dialogue[4]. If sufficient funds are available, no acknowledgement is required, and the user selects the booking details before clicking an 'OK' button to indicate that they have finished making selections[3,4]. The Interaction Task Model and the Domain of Design Discourse description are used to inform the design of Pictorial Screen Layouts, which show the layout of interface objects on the screens comprising the user interface[1,2,3,7]. An example Pictorial Screen Layout is shown in Figure 5; the screen illustrated corresponds to the 'make booking' part of the Interaction Task Model[2,6]. Although 'payment checking' is allocated to the computer, a human factors guideline suggests that the amount of credit should be visible to the user (Smith & Mosier (1986); 6.3/16: Displaying Data to be Changed)[4]. In line with the guideline listed in the Statement of User Needs (Smith & Mosier (1986); 4.4/1: Guidance Information Always Available), on-screen instructions are specified to provide the user with additional support for the task[4].

The behaviours of the objects included in the screens are described using a set of Interface Model products[1,2,7]. The radio buttons are used to select

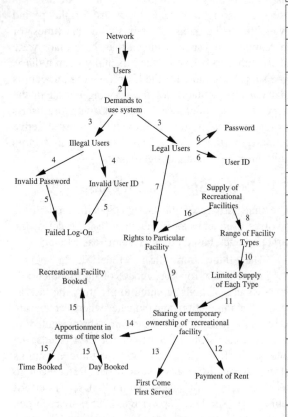

Node	Description	Number	Relation
Network		1	has a number of
Demands to use system		2	from
Demands to use system	Demands for booking the facilities may come from legal or illegal users	3	there are 2 types of user
Illegal Users	May be legal users who do not identify themselves correctly, or hackers	4	are identified by
Failed log-on	There are two conditions that should lead to a failed log-on	5	leads to
Legal users	Legal users will have a valid identity	6	have a
Legal users	Legal users are entitled to demand rights to facilities	7	demand
Supply of Recreational facilities	There are Squash Courts and Pool Tables	8	there are a
Rights to particular facility		9	given by the process of
Range of Facility types	There is a finite quantity of each facility	10	with a
Limited Supply of Each Type	The supply of facilities is limited by the opening hours of the sports centre	11	requires
Sharing or Temporary Ownership of Recreational Facility	Customers require the exclusive use of the facilty for some period	12	temporary ownership requires
Sharing or Temporary Ownership of Recreational Facility		13	on the basis of
Sharing or Temporary Ownership of Recreational Facility		14	organized by
Apportionment in terms of time slot	Customers will book the facility for a definite period of time	15	booking has attributes of
Supply of Recreational Facilities	The availability of rights to a facility is determined by the supply of those facilities	16	provides

Figure 3: RFBS: Domain of Design Discourse description.

the facility, day, and time desired by the user. Following MacIntosh conventions, selection of one radio button de-highlights other members of the same group, and those unavailable for selection remain dimmed[4]. Hence, until a button from the 'facility' group has been selected, the 'day' buttons remain dimmed, and until a 'day' button has been selected, the 'time' buttons remain dimmed. Days or times which are already booked or unavailable, are indicated by the corresponding button remaining dimmed[2]. The objects comprising the user interface are further described in the Dictionary of Screen Objects[1,7].

The specification of the User Interface for the case-study artefact is completed by a Dialogue and Error Message Table, which lists all the error messages that could be presented during the interaction, and a Dialogue and-Inter-Task Screen Actuation Description which details the points in the interaction at which screens are consumed and the conditions that trigger the presentation of an error message[1,2,7].

Taken together, the products of the Design Specification phase constitute the specification of the RFBS interaction artefact.

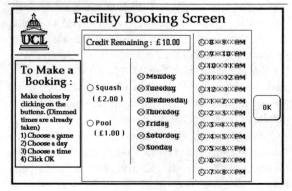

Figure 5: RFBS: Pictorial screen layout of booking screen.

6   Assessment of the Artefact

Assessment of the artefact was conducted by asking the target users ('A' and 'J') whether the artefact

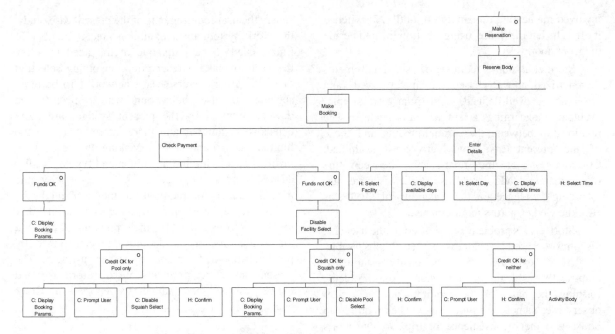

Figure 4: RFBS: Extract from System Task Model structured diagram.

corresponded to the requirements that they had expressed. Both were surprised by some aspects of the design. In addition, some (detailed) aspects did not meet their (detailed) requirements. However, the users agreed that the artefact satisfied their requirements as they had been originally, and generally, expressed (as stated at the beginning of this paper). Thus, the application of MUSE was considered to be successful in this respect.

Further assessment of the artefact was obtained by means of an expert walkthrough, conducted by an experienced human factors engineer. The conclusions of the report are that overall the artefact successfully addresses the user requirements, is easy to use, and easy to learn. However, some reservations were expressed concerning incompatibility between the instructions given to the user and the apparent representation of the task domain at the start of the booking transaction. Before a facility has been selected, all 'day' and 'time' buttons are dimmed (to indicate that they cannot be selected at that stage of the interaction). The on-screen instructions state that 'dimmed times are already taken', and it was considered that a naïve user may conclude that there are no available slots and attempt to terminate the booking at that stage. A further reservation concerned incompatibility between booking pool facilities by the hour and the conventional process for establishing rights to a pool table, which is on a 'payment per game' basis. Finally, it was felt that when a user cancels a potential booking they may expect to be returned to the booking screen, rather than to the main menu, since such a return would be more consistent with the notion of 'quitting' an operation, rather than cancelling it. These reservations violate none of the necessary features for a MUSE application indicated above. They may merely indicate that more than one artefact is able to satisfy the same set of user requirements; that experts differ in their designs; and that empirical assessment and asking users may be needed to decide between such differences. Thus, the application of MUSE was again considered to be successful in that the RFBS was considered to fulfil the user requirements.

7 Comparison with the Requirements of Stork et al. (1995)

The user requirements from Stork et al. involve the specification of a bespoke artefact to solve the following problem (at a reasonable cost for the benefits): 'A's domestic routine occasionally requires him to remain at home to work in the mornings, after the central heating normally switches off. On these days, he finds it difficult to estimate when he will leave, which can result in him being too cold, if he is at home for longer than expected. The specified artefact involved the heating remaining on, until 'A' switched it off as he left the house, using a button located beside the front door.

Stork et al. addressed a set of user requirements (summarized above), based on an 'observed (and observable), well-defined, and relatively simple' problem, concerning a single individual.   The relationship between these requirements and those of the present case study are now examined. Consideration of the relationship between the requirements of additional case studies is necessary to provide evidence for the generality of MUSE, as HCI knowledge, across requirements.

Stork et al.'s problem experienced by the user (i.e. discomfort caused by coldness) was easily observable, in that its existence could be easily established empirically.   In the present study, the problems forming the basis of the requirements were also observable, namely the iterative searches required to book, and the inconvenience of trips to the sports hall. Compared to those of Stork et al., the user requirements here are equally observable, because the problems are also equally easy to establish empirically.

The user requirements of Stork et al. may be considered well-defined from a human factors point of view. The user population (consisting of one person) was known (and available), the problem to be solved concerned a specific usage scenario, redesign of the entire system was excluded and circumstances, other than those expressed in the requirements, could be assumed not to occur.   Thus, the constraints applicable to the target system are well known. In the present case-study, although the rules applicable to bookings are defined and the user population and task of the user are known, the exact circumstances of use are not known to the same extent. Further, some of the constraints imposed on the target system by the particular circumstances of use (e.g. other tasks to be performed concurrently) may remain unknown.   The present set of requirements are therefore assumed to be less well-defined than those of Stork et al.

The problem described in Stork et al. was characterized as relatively simple. Satisfaction of the user requirements resulted in the target work system exhibiting a number of behaviours likely to result in the required level of effectiveness. The device had to maintain heating for 'A', whilst he was in the house, and when 'A' left the house, it would switch the heating off without requiring 'A' to spend long interacting with the device (or learning to interact with the device).   By comparison, to

satisfy the user requirements of the present case-study, the work system must exhibit a greater number of (interrelated) behaviours due to the need to allow the user to make a reservation, involving selection of multiple parameters over a network. To be more specific, the user behaviours with respect to the device, required by the present system, are more extensive in number and more interrelated than the limited behaviours of 'A'. Making the reservation involves specifying the day, time, and type of facility desired, and making payment.   Additionally, the mental behaviours required of the user might be claimed to be more complex, as the user's availability to play is constrained by their previous plans, and the availability of the facilities is constrained by previous bookings made by other users.   The present set of requirements are therefore assumed to be less simple than those reported in Stork et al.

8   Discussion

At the beginning of the paper, it was claimed that the relationship between the present case-study's requirements and those of Stork et al. (1995) is that the present requirements are more complex, less well-defined, but equally observable. The basis of this claim has been set out in the previous section.

It has been shown that the artefact was developed by the application of MUSE to the user requirements, and that the artefact satisfied the user requirements; therefore it can be claimed that MUSE is applicable to the kind of requirements used as the basis of the present case study, as well as the type of requirements used by Stork et al. (1995). The present case-study has therefore made some contribution to the validation of the discipline knowledge comprising the method by increasing the known generality of MUSE with respect to user requirements.

As noted above, the user requirements were characterized   according   to   their   observability, complexity, and definition. Comparison of the case studies using the three dimensions shows that MUSE as HCI knowledge is general at least across the two types of requirements. Further case studies are now required to verify that the present set of dimensions are related to attributes of requirements that significantly affect the application of structured methods and possibly to establish additional dimensions for the characterization of user requirements. The objective would be to support additional generalization of the outcomes of the case-studies and completion of the validation of MUSE to demonstrate known 'fitness-for-[general-] design-purpose'.

Acknowledgements

This research was partially supported by the European System and Software Initiative as part of application experiment 10290 (Benefits of Integrating Usability and Software Engineering Methods).

References

Apple Computer Inc (1985), "Inside Macintosh. Volume 1", Addison–Wesley.

Lim, K. Y. & Long, J. B. (1994), *The MUSE Method for Usability Engineering*, Cambridge Series on Human–Computer Interaction, Cambridge University Press.

Lim, K. Y., Long, J. B. & Silcock, N. (1990), Requirements, Research and Strategy for Integrating Human Factors with Structured Analysis and Design Methods: The Case of the Jackson System Development Method, *in* E. J. Lovesey (ed.), *Contemporary Ergonomics: Proceedings of the Ergonomics Society's 1990 Conference*, Taylor & Francis, pp.32–38.

Long, J. B. (1996), "Specifying Relations Between Research and the Design of Human–Computer Interactions", *International Journal of Human–Computer Studies* **44**, 875–920.

Smith, S. L. & Mosier, J. N. (1986), Guidelines for Designing User Interface Software, Technical Report MTR-10090, EDS-TR-86-278, The Mitre Corporation.

Stork, A., Middlemass, J. & Long, J. B. (1995), Applying a Structured Method for Usability Engineering to Domestic Energy Management User Requirements: A Successful Case-Study, *in* M. A. R. Kirby, A. J. Dix & J. E. Finlay (eds.), *People and Computers X (Proceedings of HCI'95)*, Cambridge University Press, pp.367–85.

Human–Computer Interaction — INTERACT '99
M. Angela Sasse and Chris Johnson (Editors)
Published by IOS Press, © IFIP TC.13, 1999

Embedding Ergonomic Rules as Generic Requirements in a Formal Development Process of Interactive Software

Philippe Palanque, Christelle Farenc & Rémi Bastide

LIHS, University Toulouse 1, Place Anatole France, 31042 Toulouse Cedex, France.

{farenc,palanque,bastide}@univ-tlse1.fr

Abstract: This paper presents a formal framework for the development of interactive software that bridges the gap between ergonomic knowledge and software design. It builds upon previous work on formal notations and proposes an integrated development process from requirements to model-based execution. It also embeds ergonomic knowledge in requirements, and proposes a way to formally represent them and to prove their fulfilment over a detailed formal specification of the interactive software.

Keywords: formal notations, development process, ergonomic rules , model-based systems.

1 Introduction

The usability and reliability requirements in the design of Interactive Systems are usually investigated in separate and limited ways. There is a lack of structured methods and related tools that can drive the work of designers and developers to take into account these two requirements in a complementary way. We believe that formal specification techniques can help to take into account the reliability requirement, while task modelling and ergonomic rules are a concrete way to cope with usability.

For several years we have been working on the building and the use of formal specification techniques for the design and the implementation of interactive applications (Bastide & Palanque, 1990). A formal specification technique called ICO (Palanque & Bastide, 1995) is now available and we are now focusing on the case tool supporting it (Bastide & Palanque, 1995b). This work is directly dealing with the reliability requirement, which cannot be met, as far as interactive systems are concerned, without the mathematical tools underlying formal specification techniques.

It is now widely agreed that usability is also a key issues in the design of interactive systems. One of the tools for meeting usability requirement is to take into account users' activities while designing the system. Task modelling (through task analysis) is a way to represent these activities and we have

shown in previous work that activity can be captured using formal notations. This can be done with formal specification techniques or by translating task models built using dedicated notations such as the User Action Notation (Hartson & Hix, 1989) to formal notations (Palanque et al., 1995).

Using formal notations for task modelling provides a number of benefits that are otherwise very hard to reach. For instance, we have shown in (Palanque et al., 1997) the possibility to assess complexity and performance of a given system with respect to its potential use (described in the task models).

The benefits increase significantly when formal notations are used for modelling both the activity and the system. In this case the gap between task models and system models can be bridged and properties (such as compatibility and conformance) between the two kind of models can be proven. Compatibility (i.e. the set of actions represented in the task model is included in the set of actions offered by the system model) deals with *what* a system offers to the user. Conformance (i.e. the temporal relationship between the actions described in the task model is compatible with the temporal evolution described in the system model) deals with *how* this is offered to the user.

Another way for increasing the usability of interactive software is the use of Human Factors knowledge expressed in terms of ergonomic rules. Ergonomic rules come from a number of different sources: recommendation papers (Smith, 1988), design standards (Organization, 1992), style guides which are specific to a particular environment (Corporation, 1993), design guides (Scapin, 1986; Vanderdonckt, 1994) and algorithms for ergonomic design (Bodart & Vanderdonckt, 1994).

An ergonomic rule can be considered as a principle that has to be taken into account for the building or the evaluation of user interfaces (UI) in order to respect cognitive and sensory-motor capabilities of users. These principles can have a general scope, or can be tailored to a specific 'context of use' dependent on tasks, user models, user environment, location, organizational aspects, etc.

Most of times, ergonomic rules are used during the evaluation phase of the development process of interactive application. Sometimes, however, they are used in the design phase, either implicitly as in most of the User Interface Development Environments (UIDE) or explicitly in research tools such as TRIDENT (Bodart et al., 1994).

However, during the design phase, ergonomic rules are often taken into account only implicitly (i.e. hidden in a supporting tool) or as generic guidelines and thus do not receive the same treatment as other requirements of the application. This specific use of ergonomic rules make cumbersome both design and validation phase when requirements are to be studied.

In this paper we focus on bridging the gap between ergonomic rules and the actual design of interactive systems. Section 2 proposes a design process that integrates the various components introduced above in order to take into account both usability and reliability requirements. Section 3 shows how to represent explicitly ergonomic rules as requirements by means of a temporal logic. The claim here is not to represent them exhaustively but to show that some of them can be represented this way, and that this representation can then be exploited afterwards in the design process. Section 4 exemplifies the design process presented in Section 2 on a case study. The last section shows how the ergonomic rules represented as requirements are used in the validation phase.

2   Development Process

Early software development models (including waterfall and V models) focussed mainly on the identification and the clear separation of the various phases of the development of software systems. However, the way they represent the process (i.e. in a linear and mainly one-way structure) is very limited and not able to deal with prototyping issues. Boehm (1988) introduced the spiral development model to deal explicitly with prototyping and iteration. Prototyping is an essential issue in the development of interactive systems and thus this model has been widely adopted.

However, this model is incomplete with respect to the various models that have to be built during the development of an interactive system. For instance, it does not refer to task modelling and usability evaluation, that are now recognized as critical for the design of usable interactive systems. Research has been also conducted in this field, and the star model (Hartson & Hix, 1989) explicitly introduces task analysis and usability evaluation as phases of the development process. However, most of the phases are generally conducted without computer support for representing and analysing the produced models. This is not critical when dealing with 'classical' interactive systems, but each manual operation may be source of a fatal error when safety critical systems are concerned.

The development process of a software system is highly iterative (as for the spiral model) and presents various phases (definition of informal requirements, specification, design, coding, user testing) that require human creativity and intervention. An important aspect is that each phase produces several models corresponding to the top-down process of taking into account information in a stepwise refinement manner. When dealing with interactive systems it is now widely accepted that user information has to be taken into account and that this must be done through task analysis and task modelling. In this way, user goals have to be analysed as part of the specification phase, while task analysis is conducted during the design phase.

Concerning the integration of formal methods, we argue that, although the phases involving creativity remains unchanged, the use of formal methods provides benefits in the design process.

If formal methods are used during the design process, the coding phase can be at least partly automated for instance by means of code generation. This automation can also be done by the interpretation at run-time of the models built in the earlier phases, following a model-based approach (Wilson et al., 1993; Szekely et al., 1993). We have previously investigated the pros and cons of these two approaches in (Bastide & Palanque, 1995a).

The advantage of using formal notations to support the design is the potential for mathematical verification they provide. A formal model (whether it describes a task or a system) may be automatically checked for several important properties such as deadlock freedom or termination. If, at a given stage, the model fails to comply with such properties, it has to be reworked and corrected until the problem is solved. This process is illustrated in Figure 1.

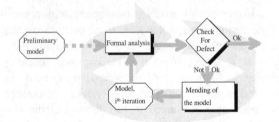

Figure 1: Design process of the various models within a phase using formal notations.

In order to cope with all the issues and thus deal both with safety and usability requirements that are crucial for safety critical interactive applications we propose an iterative development process based on formal notations.

2.1   A New Development Process

The solution we propose to this end relies on four principles:

1. We propose a formal notation that spans both system modelling and task modelling. This brings to task modelling the advantages of formal approaches, the most important of which are conciseness, consistency and lack of ambiguity. This also makes task models amenable to mathematical verification.

2. The fact that both task and system models are constructed within the same formal framework enables us to consistently merge task and system models. This, in turn, allows checking that task and system models comply with each other, and moreover enables us to perform quantitative analysis on the task/system merger in order to check whether the models comply with pre-planned objectives in terms of complexity and timing.

3. We represent requirements using a dedicated formal notation different from the one used for task and system modelling. This allows taking advantage of each notation and, as we provide bridges between them, it is possible to check their mutual conformity. In order to take full advantage of the benefits of the use of formal specification techniques, it is necessary to follow a rigorous development process rooted on mathematically founded notations. Temporal logics belong to the category of

declarative languages. This class of languages provides abstract specifications, as they are adequate for describing 'what' a system does. This is significantly different from procedural languages such as process algebra (Hoare, 1985) or Petri nets (Murata, 1989) that cannot describe 'what' a system does without describing at the same time 'how' this is done. This is a reason why we have decided to use two different formalisms for the modelling of single system: a temporal logic for the description of the properties of the system and a dialect of Petri nets for the description of its behaviour.

4. We propose a development process supporting the use of formal notations for requirements, task and system modelling. This process (see Figure 2) instantiates the development process described in Figure 1 as a sub-process to support formal modelling and extends it to explicitly represent cross verification between the three models.

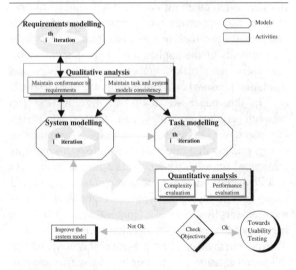

Figure 2: The design life cycle using both tasks and system models.

The development process in Figure 2 might start by some initial requirements description, by some rough model of the system (which may originate from the existing situation, e.g. analysis of the paper documents in an information system analysis) or with an initial task model. The initial model is then submitted to the formal sub-life-cycle of Figure 1. The aim of the formal analysis is to check whether the model is 'defect free' or not. This 'defect free' characteristic varies according to the model under consideration. For instance, in the system model it means absence of deadlocks, in the task model it means termination and in the requirement model it means the absence of conflicts.

A higher-level design loop is then initiated, where (for each iteration) task models are built in accordance with the current system model and both the complexity and the performance of these models is quantitatively analysed. The system designers propose modifications in the system models, in order to allow simpler and more efficient task models to be built.

Formal analysis that looks for defects aims at checking whether designers build the *system right*, qualitative analysis aims at checking whether they build the *right system* i.e. a system corresponding to users' needs as expressed in both task and requirements models. In our development process, qualitative analysis aims at checking that the system model is conformant to both task model and requirement model. So, each time a new system model is produced, the qualitative analysis checks whether or not this model still meets the requirements and is still consistent with the task model. If not, one or several models are modified and the verification process is carried out again.

This design loop may be undertaken successfully only if the analysis of the task models yields precise and quantitative results, that may be checked against pre-planned objectives. We have devised a set of metrics that can be applied to Petri net models. Those metrics are based on well established Petri net analysis techniques (e.g. the checking of place and transition invariants), but also on weightings applied to the various components of the net (places, transitions, arcs, inscriptions, functions), that will allow us to quantitatively assess the complexity of the analysed tasks (Palanque et al., 1997).

3   Ergonomic Rules as Requirements

Not all the ergonomic rules can be taken into account as generic requirements; Some are too specific or too close to some kind of interaction technique (Farenc et al., 1996).

For these reasons we have only selected some ergonomic rules that are both generic to interaction techniques and application domains. However, we are currently investigating most of the documents gathering ergonomic rules in order to classify them, to select the ones that can represented as generic requirements and to formally describe them.

We have selected rules belonging to two different classes: dynamic behaviour and interface objects behaviour.

Dynamic Behaviour

Rule 1: Any command must have a visible result.

Rule 2: When the result of a process activated by a command is displayed in more than 2 seconds and less than 6 seconds the mouse pointer must become a waiting pointer (hourglass, clock).

Rule 3: When the result of a process activated by a command is displayed in more than 6 seconds a progress indicator box must be displayed.

Rule 4: When a command might lead to loss or modification of data or to a long process a message box requiring confirmation of the command must be displayed (warning message).

Interface Objects Behaviour

Rule 5: Any user action on an Interactive Object must be graphically displayed.

Rule 6: Any message box must remain displayed until an explicit user action.

Rule 7: Action or warning message box display must be associated with a sound feedback.

3.1   Formal Description of Ergonomic Rules

In order to represent ergonomic rules in a precise and non-ambiguous way we have decided to use a specific temporal logic called ACTL. Temporal logics (Emerson & Srinivasan, 1988) allow for the description of qualitative temporal aspects of systems. In order to describe these temporal aspects, specific temporal operators have been added with respect to other modal logics. While modal logics permit the description of properties over a given state, temporal logics aims at describing them over an execution path, i.e. a set of states. For this purpose linear time temporal logics propose basically four operators: always (G), eventually (F), next (X) and until (U). Branching time temporal logics allow describing and reasoning about non-deterministic systems amongst which interactive systems belongs to (Dix, 1990). Non determinism is thus dealt with by means of representation of several alternative futures in the evolution of a system. For this propose, ACTL (that belongs to the category of branching time temporal logics) provides two other operators:

$\forall$ for all the possible paths
$\exists$ there exist at least one possible path

One of the problem in using 'classical' temporal logics is the difficulty to relate the properties described in terms of states with the behaviour the system described in terms of actions (that cause state changes). Several logics have been built in order to allow describing properties both in terms of states and in terms of actions. ACTL (DeNicola & Vaanrager, 1990) is one of these, chosen for its expressiveness and its potential for automated model checking (DeNicola et al., 1993).

The use of a formal notation for representing ergonomic rules presents a double advantage:

- First, it is possible to describe in a concise and non-ambiguous way ergonomic knowledge and thus making both its use and understanding easier,

- Second, it is possible to use verification tools for checking whether or not a given system is conformant with a set of selected rules. Some tools (Löwgren & Nordqvist., 1992; Kolski & Millot., 1991) used ergonomic rules in order to verify this conformance, but this verification is realized too late, i.e. during the evaluation phase of the development process when the interface presentation is developed. The use of ergonomic rules as requirements provides a verification before the development of the interface presentation and consequently minimize the number of iteration in the development process.

For instance, using ACTL, Rule 1 can be formally expressed as follows:

Let Commands be the set of commands that an application can perform, CVisible the set of system commands with a visible result, and UCommands the set of command that can be initiated by the user, such that CVisible $\subseteq$ Commands:

$$\forall c \in \text{UCommands}, \exists c' \in \text{CVisible},$$
$$\forall G[\text{execute}(c)](\forall X < \text{execute}(c') > \text{true})$$

This can be read as follows:

For all the possible futures ($\forall$ operator), it is always true (G operator) that if the user command c is executed, then for all the possible futures ($\forall$ operator) in the next state (X operator) a system command c' (with visible result) is executed.

4 Case Study: The ATM

This section's aim is to demonstrate how to model a software prototype of an Automated Teller Machine (ATM), using the Interactive Cooperative Objects (ICO) formalism. The ATM offers a keyboard for entering the pin number and devices for entering the card, getting the card back and getting the cash. The ATM allows the user to change the amount selected if it is greater than the one allowed by its credit card. The entering of the pin number (number of trials allowed) is not described as it do not add to the specification.

4.1 Modelling the ATM

The ATM is modelled as an ICO class, featuring attributes, services, a formal behavioural specification (the Object Control Structure, or ObCS) and a complete presentation part. The description of the class, specifying the first three components, may be seen in Figure 3. In this software prototype, the interface consists of user interface widgets such as push buttons, whereas the final system would use specialized physical devices.

According to the Arch architecture, the dialogue is modelled by a high level Petri net (HLPN). The main difference with basic Petri nets is that this formalism allows coping with data structure and data values in the models (as for example the precondition in transition T7). In this kind of Petri nets, tokens are references to other objects of the system. This formalism provides a concise, yet formal and complete specification for the control structure of the application as each feature is formally described in the mathematical foundation of Petri nets. The modelling power of the formalism allows describing a lot of constraints, otherwise hard to describe in natural language.

Class ATM
Attributes
   a, b: Real;
   c: Card;
   r: {CANCEL, RETRY};
Methods
   Ok <a, b: real>: Boolean;
   Avail <c: Card>: Real;
Visible commands
   DisplayCardIn, DisplayPin, DisplayAmount,
   DisplayCashCardAvail, DialogWindow,
   DisplayCardRemoved, DisplayCashRemoved
Sound commands
   Alert
Services
   InsertCard <c: Card>;
   Select <a: Real>;
   GetCash; GetCard;
  ObCS (see Figure 4)
Presentation

Activation function

Widget	User's actions	Service
Pushbutton InsertCard	Click	InsertCard
Pushbutton '£20'	Click	Select
Pushbutton '£40'	Click	Select
...	...	Select
Pushbutton '£160'	Click	Select
Pushbutton Cash	Click	GetCash
Pushbutton Card	Click	GetCard
Pushbutton Cancel	Click	User Cancel
Pushbutton Retry	Click	User Retry

Rendering

ObCS's transitions	Method
InsertCard	DisplayCardIn
Enter Pin	DisplayPin
Select	DisplayAmount
T4	DisplayCashCardAvail
T5	DialogWindowAlert
T8	DisplayCardRemoved
T9	DisplayCashRemoved
Others	No specific Rendering

Layout: Main and Dialog Windows

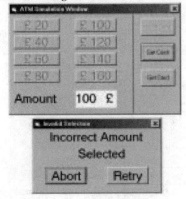

end

Figure 3: The ICO class ATM.

A transition of a HLPN may occur if each of its input places holds at least one token, so that each variable labelling an input arc may be bound to an object. When a transition occurs, the objects bound to input variables are removed from the input places and their values are processed by the transition's action that may also generate or delete objects. The new or modified objects are finally set into the output places, according to the variables labelling the arcs and thus fully stating the flow of references of objects in the net.

Behaviour of the System

The current state of the ObCS of the ATM (Figure 4) is fully determined by the distribution and the value of tokens (black dots in the places) in the various places of the net. The current marking corresponds

to the presentation in Figure 3, where card, pin number and amount have been entered. The amount entered is 100£. According to the current state in the ObCS, only transitions T8 and T9 are available. This is rendered in the user interface by showing the corresponding buttons (this is stated in the activation function Figure 3) are available. This shows how it is possible to describe with the ICO formalism multi-threaded dialogues. Indeed, if those two services have required several actions from the user, the user would have been able to handle them concurrently. As the transition T4 deposits one token in both places P7 and P8 this describes a production of parallelism in the model.

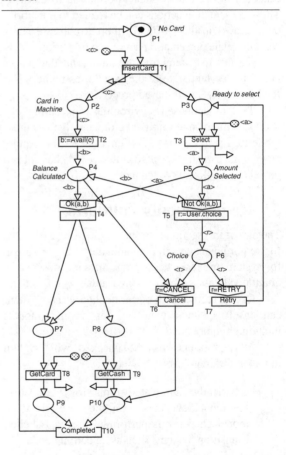

Figure 4: ObCS of the ATM Class.

At the opposite the transition T10 (that is enabled only when the user performs both GetCash and GetCard services) describes a reduction of parallelism in the model. This is usually called a synchronization (of several flows of control).

When the transition T10 is fired, the system comes back into its initial state i.e. one basic token in the *No Card* place and no token in all the other places of the model.

Link with the Presentation Part of the UI

The activation function is used for presenting, at each state of the interaction, the legal actions to the user. Thus, the active or inactive state of the widgets is fully determined by the possible occurrence of the transitions they relate to in the ObCS. The fact that a transition appears in the activation function (i.e. is triggered by the action of the user on a widget) is graphically represented in the formalism using greyed out circle with broken arrows above the transition (see for instance T9).

The rendering function determines, when a transition is fired, if some presentation action must be executed in order to present information to the user. Those presentation actions can be related to transitions or to places in the ObCS. In the current case study we only relate presentation actions to transitions i.e. to user actions. In general they are often related to places i.e. to the current state of the system, as rendering is fundamentally a state-based process.

The model-based environment executing the ICOs specification at runtime automatically does these rendering activities. This environment is under development and the algorithms used have been presented in (Bastide & Palanque, 1995b).

5   Requirements Validation

The aim of this section is to show how the use of ACTL for requirement description and the ICO formalism for system and tasks description makes it possible to qualitatively assess that they are mutually conformant.

Of course, the result of this qualitative assessment can result in modifying one or several models including requirements.

ACTL formulas can be checked with system model at different levels:

- Classically, automated tools for verification are model checkers. In the case of ACTL model checking is performed over a Labelled Transition Systems such as an automaton.

- Over the ICO specification by checking rendering and activation functions.

For space reasons we focus on the principles and thus only present here the validation of two requirements over the specification presented in the previous section.

Rule 1 (see Section 3) can be easily proven over the structure of the ICO specification. Indeed, there is always a rendering performed by the system, as for each possible user action of the ObCS, there is

a presentation function executed before and after the action occurs.

Rule 7 is also easy to prove, as each transition that opens a dialogue window (in this case only transition T5) is associated to the method Alert in the rendering function.

Model checking techniques are usually exploited in order to prove generic behavioural properties related to liveness and safety. For the case study presented here one such property could be re-initializability. Using model checking, ACTL properties are proven over a labelled transition system (LTS). The marking graph of the ObCS of Figure 4 is an LTS and, even without the help of an automated verification tool, its shape clearly shows the re-initializability of the ATM. Indeed, whatever the state the system is in, it always exist an execution path that leads to the initial state. For less trivial system tool support is usually mandatory.

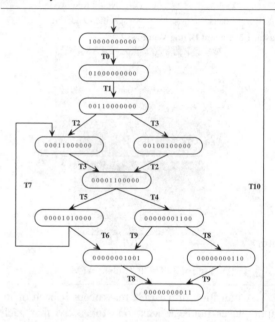

Figure 5: The set of possible states corresponding to the ObCS in Figure 4.

6   Conclusions

This paper has presented a formal framework for the design of interactive software. Its aim is to integrate knowledge in the HCI field usually treated in an independent way. For instance, we propose a way to bridge the gap between ergonomic knowledge and software design through formal notation and verification techniques. The framework we propose requires tool support in order to ensure efficiency. The PetShop (Petri nets Workshop) environment is currently under development. This workshop provides tools for the editing of the various graphical models (tasks and systems) and for the temporal logics specifications (ergonomic rules and generic requirements). Besides, tools for computer supported verification (both qualitative and quantitative) and for the run time execution of models are key parts of the environment.

Acknowledgement

The work is mainly funded by the Esprit project MEFISTO 24963 on Modelling Evaluating and Formalizing Interactive Systems using Tasks and Objects.

References

Bastide, R. & Palanque, P. (1990), Petri Net with Objects for the Design, Validation and Prototyping of User-driven Interfaces, *in* D. Diaper, D. Gilmore, G. Cockton & B. Shackel (eds.), *Proceedings of INTERACT '90 — Third IFIP Conference on Human–Computer Interaction*, Elsevier Science, pp.625–631.

Bastide, R. & Palanque, P. (1995a), Implementation Techniques for Petri Net Based Specifications of Human Computer Dialogues, *in* G. de Michelis & M. Diaz (eds.), *2nd Workshop on Computer Aided Design of User Interfaces, CADUI'96*, Presses Universitaires de Namur, pp.285–302.

Bastide, R. & Palanque, P. (1995b), A Petri Net Based Environment for the Design of Event-driven Interfaces, *in* J. Vanderdonckt (ed.), *16th International Conference on Applications and Theory of Petri Nets, ICATPN'95*, Vol. 935 of *Lecture Notes in Computer Science*, Springer-Verlag, pp.66–83.

Bodart, F. & Vanderdonckt, J. (1994), On the Problem of Selecting Interaction Objects, *in* G. Cockton, S. Draper & G. Wier (eds.), *People and Computers IX (Proceedings of HCI'94)*, Cambridge University Press, pp.163–78.

Bodart, F., Hennebert, A.-M., Leheureux, J.-M., Provot, I. & J., V. (1994), A Model-based Approach to Presentation: A Continuum from Task Analysis to Prototype, *in* F. Paternò (ed.), *Proceedings of 1st Eurographics Workshop on Design, Specification and Verification of Interactive Systems (DSV-IS'94)*, Springer-Verlag, pp.77–94.

Boehm, B. W. (1988), "The Spiral Model of Software Development and Enhancement", *IEEE Computer* **21**(5), 61–72.

Corporation, I. (1993), Common User Access Guidelines, Object-Oriented Interface Design, Technical Report SC34-4399, IBM Corporation.

DeNicola, R. & Vaanrager, F. W. (1990), Action Versus State Based Logics for Transition Systems, *in* I. Guessarian (ed.), *Ecole de Printemps on Semantics of Concurrency*, Vol. 469 of *Lecture Notes in Computer Science*, Springer-Verlag, pp.407–19.

DeNicola, R., Fantechi, A., Gnesi, S. & Ristori, G. (1993), "An Action Based Framework for Verifying Logical and Behavioural Properties of Concurrent Systems", *Computer Networks and ISDN Systems* **25**(7), 761–778.

Dix, A. J. (1990), Non Determinism as a Paradigm for Understanding the User Interface, *in* M. D. Harrison & H. W. Thimbleby (eds.), *Formal Methods in Human–Computer Interaction*, Cambridge Series on Human–Computer Interaction, Cambridge University Press, chapter 4, pp.97–127.

Emerson, E. A. & Srinivasan, J. (1988), Branching Time Temporal Logic, *in* G. Goos & J. Hartmanis (eds.), *Linear Time, Branching Time and Partial Order in Logics and Models for Concurrency*, Vol. 354 of *Lecture Notes in Computer Science*, Springer-Verlag, pp.123–72.

Farenc, C., Liberati, V. & Barthet, M.-F. (1996), Automatic Ergonomic Evaluation: What Are the Limits, *in* J. Vanderdonckt (ed.), *Proceedings of 2nd International Workshop on Computer Aided Design of User Interfaces*, Presses Universitaire de Namur, pp.159–70.

Hartson, R. & Hix, D. (1989), "Human-Computer Interface Developement: Concepts and Systems for Its Management", *ACM Computing Surveys* **21**(1), 5–92.

Hoare, C. A. R. (1985), *Communicating Sequential Processes*, Prentice–Hall International.

Kolski, C. & Millot., P. (1991), "A Rule-based Approach to the Ergonomic Static Evaluation of Man–Machine Graphic Interface in Industrial Processes", *International Journal of Man–Machine Studies* **35**(5), 657–74.

Löwgren, J. & Nordqvist., T. (1992), Knowledge-Based Evaluation As Design Support for Graphical User Interfaces, *in* P. Bauersfeld, J. Bennett & G. Lynch (eds.), *Proceedings of CHI'92: Human Factors in Computing Systems*, ACM Press, pp.181–88.

Murata, T. (1989), "Petri Nets: Properties, Analysis and Applications", *Proceedings of the IEEE* **77**(4), 541–80.

Organization, I. S. (1992), "ISO/WD 9241: Ergonomic Requirements for Office Work With Visual Displays Units".

Palanque, P. & Bastide, R. (1995), "Synergistic Modelling of Tasks, Users and Systems Using Formal Specification Techniques", *Interacting with Computers* **9**(2), 129–53.

Palanque, P., Bastide, R. & Paternò, F. (1997), Formal Specification As a Tool for the Objective Assessment of Safety Critical Interactive Systems, *in* S. Howard, J. Hammond & G. K. Lindgaard (eds.), *Human–Computer Interaction — INTERACT '97: Proceedings of the Sixth IFIP Conference on Human–Computer Interaction*, Chapman & Hall, pp.323–30.

Palanque, P., Bastide, R. & Sengès, V. (1995), Validating Interactive System Design Through the Verification of Formal Task and System Models, *in* L. J. Bass & C. Unger (eds.), *6th IFIP Conference on Engineering for Human–Computer Interaction, EHCI'95*, Chapman & Hall, pp.14–18.

Scapin, D. (1986), Guide Ergonomique De Conception Des Interfaces Homme–Ordinateur, Technical Report INRIA 77, INRIA Le Chesnay.

Smith, S. L. (1988), Standards Versus Guidelines for Designing User Interface Software, *in* M. Helander (ed.), *Handbook of Human–Computer Interaction*, North-Holland, pp.877–89.

Szekely, P., Luo, P. & Neches, R. (1993), Beyond Interface Builders: Model-based Interface Tools, *in* S. Ashlund, K. Mullet, A. Henderson, E. Hollnagel & T. White (eds.), *Proceedings of INTERCHI'93*, ACM Press/IOS Press, pp.383–90.

Vanderdonckt, J. (1994), *Guide Ergonomique Des Interfaces Homme–Machine*, Presses Universitaires de Namur.

Wilson, S., Johnson, P., Kelly, C., Cunningham, J. & Markopoulos, P. (1993), Beyond Hacking: A Model-based Approach to User Interface Design, *in* J. Alty, D. Diaper & S. Guest (eds.), *People and Computers VIII (Proceedings of HCI'93)*, Cambridge University Press, pp.217–31.

Human–Computer Interaction — INTERACT '99
M. Angela Sasse and Chris Johnson (Editors)
Published by IOS Press, © IFIP TC.13, 1999

The Principle of Rationality and Models of Highly Interactive Systems

Richard Butterworth & Ann Blandford

School of Computing Science, Middlesex University, Bounds Green Road, London N11 2NQ, UK.

r.j.butterworth@mdx.ac.uk

Abstract: One approach to reasoning about interactive behaviour is to assume that users of computer systems are rational, and that the behaviour of an interactive system results from the rational behaviour of the users together with the implemented behaviour of the devices that make up the total system. These assumptions can be expressed as a coherent set of principles. This approach enables an analyst to identify likely sources of user error as well as predicting (error-free) behaviour patterns. This, in turn, can be used as a basis for identifying requirements on device designs. We present principles, based on those originally proposed by Newell, that can be used as a basis for reasoning about interactive behaviour. In particular, we accommodate the role of devices as resources that support memory and reasoning, active devices, and multi-agent systems in which one user may be interacting with multiple devices and other users.

Keywords: rationality, cognitive modelling, PUM, interactive system modelling.

1 Introduction

The behaviour of a computer user is influenced by a broad range of factors, including their goals, their knowledge of the devices they are working with, the behaviour of those devices, distractions in the environment, the number of tasks they are working on at the time, etc. For the purposes of predictive evaluation (i.e. reasoning rigorously about likely user behaviours with a proposed computer system design) it is necessary to make some simplifying assumptions and to describe the interactive system at an appropriate level of detail.

Newell (1990) identifies levels of structure from the neural through to social and evolutionary. Between these levels are the one's best suited to reasoning about human–computer interaction: the levels of simple operations, rational behaviour and social interaction.

An example of work at the level of simple operations is to be found in the GOMS tradition (Card et al., 1983; Gray et al., 1993; John & Kieras, 1996), including EPIC (Kieras et al., 1997). At this level, the analyst is expected to produce a task description that will enable a simulation model to 'execute the task correctly and reasonably efficiently' (Kieras et al., 1997). This approach involves detailed specification of user actions and mental operations, and results in simulation models that can be used for predicting, for example, task performance times. At the other end of this spectrum there is work, notably in Computer Supported Collaborative Working, which focuses on the role of context and awareness of other users, and can be seen as working at the level of social interaction.

The model we propose is an 'engineering model', in the sense that it encapsulates core theory in a way that is simple and robust enough to be used in design contexts. This paper primarily reports how very general, almost philosophical, principles can be restated in a way that is relevant to reasoning about interactive systems. Related work (Good & Blandford, to appear) describes how models and approaches based around those principles can be successfully and usefully integrated into real-world design processes.

Our work is based in the tradition of Programmable User Modelling (PUM) (Young et al., 1989; Blandford & Young, 1995; 1996). The purpose of a PUM is to make predictions about user behaviour at the interface and to force software designers into at least thinking about, and hopefully being explicit about, what cognitive demands a proposed interface makes of a user. Early PUM work revolved around the philosophy of 'weak mini-planning', using simple means-ends planning algorithms to work out how to use interface models, on the basis that if a weak planner can sort out an interface then a user will probably be able to do so as well. Subsequent work (Blandford & Duke, 1997; Blandford et al., 1997; Butterworth et al., 1998a) has developed user-centred models of a range of interactive systems.

If a model is to have good scope (i.e. be applicable to a broad range of devices and contexts) and explanatory power, it needs to capture many important properties of interactive behaviour. The main properties we are concerned with are:

- users exhibit simple planning behaviour; for example, a user wishing to send an electronic mail message to a colleague may plan to open their electronic address book to find the address, which in turn necessitates them launching the email application (if it is not already running);

- much behaviour with graphical user interfaces is 'display-driven' or exploratory — cf. Cognitive Walkthrough (Wharton et al., 1994);

- the device is a resource (Fields et al., 1996) that supports or directs the user's behaviour and provides a record of the current system state, supplementing or replacing the user's memory (Payne, 1991);

- the user's knowledge comes from somewhere — whether that is from prior experience, from the display, from their knowledge of the effects of actions (e.g. 'copy' in a word processor places a copy of the currently selected text in a hidden buffer), or through a process of inference from other knowledge; that knowledge is not necessarily correct;

- a user may be working with multiple devices and other users in a dynamic, or active, environment;

- these different types of behaviour are tightly interleaved within any particular interaction episode.

In this paper, we use the term 'system' to refer to the total interactive system, and the term 'device' to refer to computer system components. For simplicity, we consider just one user, and refer to the remainder of the interactive system as a 'device'.

2 Rationality

There is a large body of work, most of it within a philosophical tradition, on rationality. For example, Pollock states that:

> "...a rational agent has beliefs reflecting the state of its environment, and it likes or dislikes its situation. When it finds the world not entirely to its liking, it tries to change that. Its cognitive architecture is the mechanism whereby it chooses courses of action aimed at making the world more to its liking." (Pollock, 1993)

Most of this work is expressed in terms that make it difficult to use as a starting point for reasoning about interactivity and the design of devices. However, it gives a clear basis for understanding rationality.

Newell (1981) proposes 'principles of rationality' as the behaviour laws for 'knowledge level systems'. These principles have formed the basis for much work in cognitive science. For example Soar, Newell's (1990) candidate for a unified theory of cognition, is an approximation of a knowledge level system.

Newell's *'principle of rationality'* asserts that:

> "If an agent has knowledge that one of its actions will lead to one of its goals then the agent will select that action." (Newell, 1981, p.8)

There is a collection of actions that can legally update the state of the system. Actions typically update both the device and belief state. The 'legal' behaviour of the system is any sequence of these actions. Effectively such a legal behaviour simply describes the system performing actions in a random order. 'Rationality' forms a constraint on 'legality'; there are legal behaviours that are not rational, but an illegal behaviour cannot occur. So a rational behaviour is a sequence of actions such that certain actions only occur when it is rational for them to be invoked by the user.

However the device may have behaviour that is independent of the user, so we make no assertion that device invoked actions occur rationally. Hence we divide the set of actions into two (possibly overlapping) sub-sets of actions: user actions and device actions. More specifically a rational behaviour is a sequence of actions such that the user actions only occur when it is rational for them to be invoked by the user.

Newell proposes two auxiliary principles that refine behaviour predictions. The principle of 'equipotence of acceptable actions' asserts that, for given knowledge, if actions A_1 and A_2 both lead to goal G then both actions are selected. Rather than determining a unique possible behaviour, as would generally be the case for simulation models, this principle clarifies the fact that there are alternative, equally rational and reasonable, possible behaviours.

The principle of *preference of joint goal satisfaction* asserts that for given knowledge, if goal G_1 has the set of selected actions $\{A_{1,i}\}$ and goal G_2 has the set of selected actions $\{A_{2,j}\}$ then the effective set of selected actions is the intersection of $\{A_{1,i}\}$ and $\{A_{2,j}\}$. That is: the space of possible behaviours is constrained such that actions that achieve more than one goal are selected in preference to actions that achieve only one.

Newell has a stated aim of developing a deterministic model; our aim is somewhat different: to investigate properties of interactive behaviours and to relate those to device design.

We are now in a position to lay out a set of principles that form a coherent basis for reasoning about rational interactive behaviour. Here our aim is to state principles precisely, and to illustrate how they can be used in reasoning; formal models that express some of these ideas in mathematical notation can be found in (Blandford et al., 1997; Butterworth et al., 1998b).

3 Introduction to Example

To illustrate the approach, we exemplify each style of interaction with tasks taken from the domain of Web usage. More details of the design of Web browsers can be found elsewhere — e.g. (Dix & Mancini, 1998). The features we assume for the Web browser are that the user can navigate from page to page by selecting labelled links and can retrace steps through pages that are in the 'history' list by using the 'Bwd' (or 'Backwards') button.

The device maintains a 'history' list of pages visited that the user can access by pulling down a 'Go' menu. Pages are listed by title. The user can jump to pages previously visited by pulling down the 'Go' menu and selecting the page by title. This history list is a stack such that when the user jumps to a new page it is added to the stack immediately above the current page, and any pages later in the list are lost.

The user can also store a set of 'bookmarks', again labelled with the title of the page pointed to. Accessing a bookmark (also via a pull-down menu) enables the user to jump directly to the selected page.

The tasks selected to illustrate the application of the rationality principles make use of only these

features rather than the full functionality of a typical Web browser.

4 Rational Planned Behaviour

As part of the user's cognitive state there are a set of goals which describe states of the world that the user finds desirable.

Planned behaviour describes how the user moves the goals toward their current state by identifying intermediate goals and aiming to achieve those (through means-ends reasoning).

Assume that a user knows of an action that will take them to a goal state but that a precondition to that action is not currently satisfied (either it is not possible to perform that action in the current state, or the action will not achieve the intended effect from the current state; for example, pressing the delete key will only delete a particular word if that word is highlighted or the cursor is located just after it). The user will then adopt a goal to get to a state such that the action can be performed and plan to invoke the action when they get there.

Planned behaviour is cognitively expensive to the user; the user needs to expend effort making the plan and remembering it. The plan is formed in the user's head and needs to be kept there until it has been executed. Furthermore the user also needs to be able to distinguish between states and judge how close they are to the goal.

Planned behaviour is described and illustrated in detail by (Blandford & Young, 1996). In particular, two principles that describe planning behaviour can be stated:

Selection by purpose: If there is a goal G and if there is a known operation O whose user-purpose matches G and whose filters are satisfied, then the user will choose O — or one such operation if there are several possibilities. This principle summarises both Newell's principle of rationality and that of equipotence of acceptable actions.

Precondition sub-goaling: If the user has chosen an operation O, and if it has precondition(s) P that are not satisfied then they set up the subgoal(s) to achieve P.

In addition, we might state selection heuristics for choosing between alternative possible operations (analogous to Newell's principle of *preference of joint goal satisfaction*). For the purposes of the example below, we can identify an intuitively appealing heuristic:

Preference for immediately doable operations:

> Where there are multiple possible operations that lead to a goal, the user will prefer one that can be applied immediately.

4.1 Example

Consider a user with reasonable knowledge of the Web, attempting to discover menu design heuristics. This user knows that there is a useful jump off a page on the BCS site, but how to get there? They know that Fred Blogg's site has a link to the BCS site and that they have a link to Fred's site in their set of bookmarks. A precondition of this is that the user has a Web browser running. The user builds a plan 'backwards' from the goal; assuming that a Web browser is already running, they can start to 'unwind' the plan they have made (of invoking the bookmark for Fred, then linking to the BCS site).

Stating this in terms of the principles: the user knows that one way to view a page is to follow a link that is known to lead to it, for which the precondition is that the starting page is displayed; having this page displayed is adopted as a goal; ways of achieving this (sub)goal are identified and one operation is selected; the user knows of an immediately doable operation that will achieve this goal, namely selecting Fred's bookmark, so they do it. The outstanding operation can then be immediately applied.

Because Web browsers typically assume that users behave reactively they do not tend to support planned behaviour very well. In fact, as has been argued elsewhere (Butterworth et al., to appear), the history mechanism offered by most Web browsers is rather antithetical to planned behaviour; unless the user is concentrating and has a very good memory of past actions its behaviour can be rather unpredictable. Although the behaviour of the history mechanism is deterministic, it is only predictable *from the user's point of view* if the user understands it, which many users do not, and if the user can remember how they have navigated to the current page.

For example, consider a user who has a fairly specific goal which they are using a Web browser to satisfy; they want to find information about heuristics for designing a menu structure. They are at a page which discusses colour schemes for menus. While this is all very interesting, they first want to learn about menu structuring before getting involved in such aesthetic issues. Therefore, the user moves off to other pages, intending to return to the menu colour guide later using the 'Bwd' button. Unfortunately the stack structure of the history list means that the menu colour page can easily be erased from the history list (Dix &

Mancini, 1998); to make matters worse, the browser does not make the contents of the history list readily visible (it is buried in a menu). Consequently, the user may not only lose the ability to perform a plan, due to the perceived unpredictability of the browser, but will also not be aware that they have lost the ability because the state of the browser is concealed.

4.2 Design Guidelines

An understanding of mini-planning and precondition subgoaling can be used to identify some general guidelines for designing interfaces that support this kind of behaviour. The device needs to make it clear to the user where they are in relation to where they want to be, so the current device state needs to be clear and comprehensible to the user. More subtly we need to consider the actions that the user can perform; in order to make successful plans the user needs to have fairly correct a priori knowledge of the effect of actions. This motivates arguments about interface consistency: similar actions should do similar things.

5 Rational Reactive Behaviour

It has long been recognized — e.g. (Suchman, 1987; Payne, 1991) — that planning is only a small part of the story about interactive behaviour. We use the term 'reactive' to refer to behaviour characterised by the user identifying an immediately doable action and doing it. In a goal-oriented context, rational reactive behaviour describes how the user moves the state of the world towards the current goal state.

In any system state various possible actions present themselves to the user; if the device is well designed, the user will be aware of a set of possible 'next-states'. The rational user will judge which of these next-states are closer to the goal than the current state and will invoke an appropriate action to take them closer to the goal.

Reactive rationality is very simple and requires very little effort on the part of the user; it is very 'here and now'. The user simply observes where they are now, decides where they can go next, decides which of those next-states will take them closest to their goal and moves accordingly. However the user needs to have beliefs about the effects that user actions will have. We place no requirement that these beliefs be correct. Rationality describes how a user behaves with particular knowledge; a user can still behave rationally based on incorrect knowledge.

Cognitive Walkthrough (Wharton et al., 1994) is a usability evaluation technique that is particularly tailored to the assessment of interfaces that are designed to be used in a 'rational reactive' (or 'exploratory') way.

For rational reactive behaviour we can state one simple principle:

Display-based selection: If there is a goal G and if there is an operation O that corresponds to an immediately doable action displayed at the interface, and that is likely to bring the state closer to G, then the user will choose O — or one such operation if there are several possibilities.

5.1 Example

Again, we use the example of Web browsing to illustrate behaviour. The user is (still) seeking information about the design of menu systems. Note that the goal is expressed in terms of a desired belief state; the user wants their beliefs to be in such a state that they (believe that) they understand how to design a good menu structure. In order to get their beliefs into such a state it is likely that they will have to get the device into a series of several different states; there is no 'right' answer to designing menus, so it is unlikely that the user will be able to satisfy their goal by getting to just one page. The user will have to browse several pages, refining their knowledge about menu design until it is such that they think they can attempt to design a menu system.

The browser presents the user with many 'hints' about possible next-states, including highlighted tags on the displayed pages, the buttons along the top of the browser and the browser's menu system.

Many of these hints about the next-states are of no relevance to the user goal and will therefore not be selected. The user will select an operation that they believe will take them closer to their goal. If there are links marked 'HCI design guidelines' or similar then they will be selected. If no such links are available then the user may know that they have some likely jump off points in their bookmarks, so they will trawl through there; this involves a little planning: to pull down the menu of bookmarks.

5.2 Design Guidelines

We can make general statements about how a user interface should support a user who is interacting reactively. For example, the tools that the user is offered to change the state of the device (menus, icons, buttons etc.) should all be clearly labelled so that the user can make a fairly accurate guess about what the next-state of the device will be having invoked that action, without actually having to invoke the action.

Furthermore all the possible next-states should be visible from the interface; there should be no hidden actions.

Such interface design heuristics typically come under the heading of 'predictability'.

Design guidelines for a browsing system which supports exploratory behaviour would assert obvious things such as tags being a fairly accurate approximation of the pages that they lead to.

In addition we could make recommendations regarding the design of the bookmarking system. Most implementations simply present the title of the bookmarked page. The title of a page may give little or no indication of its content. If the user could annotate their bookmarks then they could give themselves much more helpful next-state hints.

6 Mixed Behaviour

These two rational behaviours are complementary; a typical interaction will consist of a mix of planned and reactive behaviour. The user may initially plan parts of the interaction that they know about and then reactively move towards a state such that they can put a plan into action; conversely, they may form a plan that can be immediately executed, but that will only get them part-way towards the goal, and then behave reactively. A user may also interact reactively to recover from errors or to overcome difficulties caused when a plan does not have the effect that was expected of it.

It is simple to combine reactive and planned behaviour into our system model; the user reactively moves towards the set of goal states that are generated by planning behaviour. The effect of planning is not only to generate new goals that are closer to the current state, but is also to increase the number of goals that the user can aim at when interacting reactively. So we have a trade-off; the user expends cognitive effort in making plans, but the cost of that effort is balanced against reduced effort needed to interact reactively.

6.1 Example

An example we gave earlier described a plan for getting to the BCS page. Suppose, instead, that the user's goal is to view the British HCI group page, and that they know that the British HCI group page is likely to be linked to the BCS page. The user is likely to form a plan to get to the BCS page, as described above, then reactively navigate to the HCI Group page, based on their knowledge about the relationship between the two organizations. In mixed behaviour the user forms plans, executing the plans when possible and behaving reactively when they cannot.

7   Communication Goals

As well as knowledge of preconditions that a user may have to inform planning, users often know that there are things they have to communicate to a device — or to another user (Blandford & Young, 1998). For example, the user of an Automatic Teller Machine (ATM) is likely to know that they are going to have to specify how much money they wish to withdraw; through the interaction with the ATM they are likely to be alert for situations where they can communicate this information. Without prior experience of interacting with a particular device, the user is going to not know precisely when the opportunity will arise; if the user is expecting to communicate multiple items of information, there may not be a natural order for those items, though in many cases the order will be dictated by the device design. This knowledge; that achievement of a goal will entail communication of data leads us to propose a further principle.

Communication goals: If a user knows that achievement of a goal necessitates imparting data values (to a device or another user) then the user will adopt the communication of that information as a goal.

7.1   Example

There are some Web-based resources that can only be retrieved by subscribers, who are required to use password identification. A user who has subscribed to such a service will adopt the goal of supplying the password as a subgoal of retrieving a resource. Until the user is familiar with the action sequence needed to retrieve the resource, they will not know exactly when they are required to enter the password, and it is the responsibility of the interface designer to make it clear what information is needed, and when.

7.2   Design Guidelines

Users may reasonably be expecting to enter particular information in the course of an interaction. It should be clear to users how to get a device into a state where that information can be entered; in cases where the user may expect to enter multiple data items, there should be no room for confusion over which to enter at a particular time.

8   Interactive Goal Acquisition

The discussion so far has centred around passive devices — that is, ones that only change state in direct response to user actions. The approach is readily extended to account for active devices and multi-agent systems that involve other users too. We restrict the discussion to simple systems in which actions are treated as being discrete, and do not consider parallel activity by multiple agents. Such a system can be viewed as comprising a particular user (whose behaviour we describe in terms of rationality) and that user's 'environment'. With these simplifying assumptions, we can draw on Pollock's definition of rationality, as stated above, and say that there are events that occur in the environment that cause the user to adopt new goals. For example, an air traffic controller who is responsible for a particular sector of air space will have a persistent goal of ensuring that all aircraft within that sector are in a safe state; as soon as they become aware of any problem, they will adopt a goal of restoring the state to being safe. Note here that we are distinguishing between two types of goals: traditional goals, or goals of achievement, that can (at least as a first approximation) be forgotten about once they are satisfied; and persistent goals, or maintenance goals, that the user is continually monitoring to check that they remain satisfied. In these terms, we can restate Pollock's definition of rationality as a principle.

Goals of maintenance: If the user has a goal of maintaining some aspect of the state then whenever the state violates that goal the user adopts a goal to restore the state.

8.1   Example

Although it is a passive system (under most circumstances!), Web navigation provides some examples of interactive goal acquisition. One such example is that of dynamic information on the display (e.g. links that move or flash), which can attract the user's attention and cause the user to adopt the goal of finding out 'what this is about'. The user can be characterised as having a general maintenance goal of acquiring new, interesting information and being entertained. Such a goal is difficult to state rigorously, but is clearly significant in people's interactions with information systems.

We can identify further examples in a closely related domain: that of receiving and reading electronic mail (email). Many devices that provide email facilities offer the user the option of being notified when new messages arrive. A user who is engaged in some completely unrelated task is alerted to the fact that new mail has arrived, and can choose whether or not to shift their attention to that mail. The user may have any one of several maintenance goals relating to email; for example, they may have a goal of having no unread email, of being seen to respond to all email messages promptly, or simply of not having a distracting little icon (that informs them of the arrival of new mail) flashing in the corner of the screen. Any of these maintenance goals will result in the user adopting the goal of having read the incoming mail. This goal will be added to the set of outstanding goals; it might be addressed immediately, or might be delayed until various other goals have been achieved.

8.2 Design Guidelines

In this section, we have discussed the fact that goals of maintenance can 'trigger' achievement goals. As illustrated in the email example, the goals of maintenance can take different forms for different users; if users were able to specify their particular maintenance goals to a device, then that device could be better tailored to support the user in maintaining those goals. In particular, the device could be set up to alert the user in an appropriate way to any violations of his personal maintenance goals.

More generally, the role of the environment in causing the user to adopt new goals should be recognized. While this may sometimes be exploited (e.g. for advertising purposes), it can also be used to improve user effectiveness.

9 Discussion

Starting from very simple and general ideas about rationality, we have identified and stated various principles that apply to any rational agent. Making the assumption that users of computer systems can usefully be regarded as being rational, we have identified ways in which such users can interact with computer systems, and have illustrated the approach with examples taken from the use of a Web browser. From this discussion, we have extracted some general design principles that can be applied to the design of interfaces that are intended to support users in their rational behaviour.

In this paper we have tried to achieve an appropriate balance between discursive description and the level of rigour that is a necessary precursor to mathematical modelling. In general, descriptive approaches run the risk of lacking rigour: it is too easy to 'cheat' by engaging in 'mental hand-waving' that allows the analyst to overlook important but subtle points about the interactive behaviour and the design of devices. Conversely, formal mathematical modelling runs the risk of losing touch with reality and abstracting away from essential points. However, such mathematical models can be used to reason rigorously about interactive system properties; one of our aims in stating a set of principles of rationality is to provide a foundation for the mathematical modelling

of interactive systems that is grounded in established cognitive science theory.

Once we embed the rationality principles in abstract mathematical models, we lose the need to fully determine behaviour. Rather than having to produce simulation models that generate a single rational behaviour — or perhaps a very small space of possible behaviours (Blandford & Young, 1995) — it becomes possible to reason about properties of the set of all possible behaviours. For example, it is possible to establish whether all possible behaviours are 'safe', or whether there are errors that users can rationally make in certain circumstances.

A corollary to this is that the assumptions made about rational user behaviour are all 'essential' assumptions; it is not necessary to make additional implementational assumptions simply to get a model running. By focusing on these essential assumptions, we are in a better position to reason about device design and the way that influences rational user behaviour.

We have shown elsewhere (Blandford et al., 1997; Butterworth et al., 1998a; to appear) how mathematical models based around the principles described here can be used to reason about and predict the behaviour of abstract interactive system models. However we need to ground our work further by demonstrating that:

1. the predictions made by the abstract models reflect empirical data, and;

2. the models can be usefully integrated into real interactive system design practice.

Work on demonstrating point 1 is underway, and we have results which positively demonstrate point 2: in the case study reported by (Good & Blandford, to appear) knowledge requirements and the consequences of rationality were successfully incorporated into the safety case for a real, engineered system.

Acknowledgements

We are grateful to Richard Young, Jason Good and David Duke for helpful discussions. This work is funded by EPSRC, grant number GR/L00391. See http://www.cs.mdx.ac.uk/puma/.

References

Blandford, A. & Duke, D. (1997), "Integrating User and System Concerns in the Design of Interactive Systems", *International Journal of Human–Computer Studies* **46**(5), 653–79.

Blandford, A. & Young, R. M. (1995), Separating User and Device Descriptions for Modelling Interactive Problem Solving, *in* K. Nordby, P. H. Helmersen, D. J. Gilmore & S. A. Arnessen (eds.), *Human–Computer Interaction — INTERACT '95: Proceedings of the Fifth IFIP Conference on Human–Computer Interaction*, Chapman & Hall, pp.91–6.

Blandford, A. & Young, R. M. (1996), "Specifying User Knowledge for the Design of Interactive Systems", *Software Engineering Journal* **11**(6), 323–33.

Blandford, A. & Young, R. M. (1998), The Role of Communication Goals in Interaction, *in* J. May, J. Siddiqi & J. Wilkinson (eds.), *Adjunct Proceedings of HCI'98*, pp.14–5.

Blandford, A., Butterworth, R. & Good, J. (1997), Users as Rational Interacting Agents: Formalising Assumptions About Cognition and Interaction, *in* M. Harrison & J. Torres (eds.), *Design, Specification and Verification of Interactive Systems'97*, Springer-Verlag, pp.43–60.

Butterworth, R., Blandford, A. & Duke, D. (1998a), The Role of Formal Proof in Modelling Interactive Systems, *in* P. Markopoulos & P. Johnson (eds.), *Design, Specification and Verification of Interactive Systems'98*, Springer-Verlag, pp.87–101.

Butterworth, R., Blandford, A. & Duke, D. (to appear), Using Formal Models to Explore Display Based Usability Issues, To appear in forthcoming JVLC special issue on 'Formal methods for Visual Interaction'.

Butterworth, R., Blandford, A., Duke, D. & Young, R. M. (1998b), Formal User Models and Methods for Reasoning about Interactive Behaviour, *in* J. Siddiqi & C. Roast (eds.), *Formal Aspects of the Human–Computer Interaction*, Sheffield Hallam University, pp.176–91. ISBN 0 86339 794 8.

Card, S. K., Moran, T. P. & Newell, A. (1983), *The Psychology of Human–Computer Interaction*, Lawrence Erlbaum Associates.

Dix, A. & Mancini, R. (1998), Specifying History and Back Tracking Mechanisms, *in Formal Methods in Human–Computer Interaction*, Formal Approaches to Computing and Information Technology, Springer-Verlag, chapter 1, pp.1–23.

Fields, B., Wright, P. & Harrison, M. (1996), Designing Human System Interaction using the Resource Model, *in* L. Yong, L. Herman, Y. Leung & J. Moyes (eds.), *Proceedings of the APCHI'96 Conference*, pp.181–91.

Good, J. & Blandford, A. (to appear), Incoprporating Human Factors Concerns into the Design and Safety Engineering of Complex Control Systems, Accepted for publication in People in Control '99. PUMA working paper WP22. See http://www.cs.mdx.ac.uk/puma/.

Gray, W. D., John, B. E. & Atwood, M. E. (1993), "Project Ernestine: Validating a GOMS Analysis for Predicting and Explaining Real-world Task Performance", *Human–Computer Interaction* **8**(4), 237–309.

John, B. & Kieras, D. (1996), "Using GOMS for User Interface Design and Evaluation: Which Technique?", *ACM Transactions on Computer–Human Interaction* **3**(4), 287–319.

Kieras, D., Wood, S. & Meyer, D. (1997), "Predictive Engineering Models Based on the EPIC Architecture for a Multi-modal High-performance Human–Computer Interaction Task", *ACM Transactions on Computer–Human Interaction* **4**(3), 230–75.

Newell, A. (1981), "The Knowledge Level", *AI Magazine* **18**, 1–20.

Newell, A. (1990), *Unified Theories of Cognition*, Harvard University Press.

Payne, S. J. (1991), "Display-based Action at the User Interface", *International Journal of Man–Machine Studies* **35**, 275–89.

Pollock, J. (1993), "The Phylogeny of Rationality", *Cognitive Science* **17**, 563–88.

Suchman, L. A. (1987), *Plans and Situated Actions — The Problem of Human–Machine Communication*, Cambridge University Press.

Wharton, C., Rieman, J., Lewis, C. & Polson, P. (1994), The Cognitive Walkthrough Method: A Practitioners Guide, *in* J. Nielsen & R. L. Mack (eds.), *Usability Inspection Methods*, John Wiley & Sons, pp.105–140.

Young, R. M., Green, T. & Simon, T. (1989), Programmable User Models for Predictive Evaluation of Interface Design, *in* K. Bice & C. H. Lewis (eds.), *Proceedings of CHI'89: Human Factors in Computing Systems*, ACM Press, pp.15–9.

Human–Computer Interaction — INTERACT '99
M. Angela Sasse and Chris Johnson (Editors)
Published by IOS Press, © IFIP TC.13, 1999

Case-based Reasoning Systems for Knowledge Mediation

A.D. Griffiths, M.D. Harrison & A.M. Dearden

Human–Computer Interaction Group, Department of Computer Science,
University of York, Heslington, York YO10 5DD, UK.
{Tony.Griffiths,Michael.Harrison}@cs.york.ac.uk

Abstract: A knowledge mediation system eases the transfer of knowledge between two communities of practice. We describe one such system, based upon case-based reasoning, which reuses cases representing previous instances of mediation between two different communities. The system's specific purpose is to support management processes to plan the maintenance and operation of a utility distribution network, by mediating knowledge from the conceptual world of engineers in the business. This paper focuses on two particular issues. The first is the means by which a case is represented so that it characterises an instance of translation between the two conceptual worlds and the second concerns the mechanisms in the system for adapting the previous case to the current problem.

Keywords: knowledge mediation, case-based reasoning, communities of practice.

1 Introduction

Recent literature in Computer Supported Cooperative Work has drawn attention to problems that arise in the interface between so-called communities of practice (Wenger, 1998). In order to carry out their work efficiently, communities of practice typically make use of a specialised vocabulary, which eases communication about the work that has to be carried out. In addition, repetition and the internalization of particular forms of work mean that their activity may be based substantially on implicit and tacit knowledge. However, specialised vocabularies are not necessarily understood by adjacent communities and differences in language and knowledge mean that the *boundary objects* (Star, 1995) which provide potential interfaces between the two communities can be interpreted quite differently from the two perspectives. A process of *knowledge mediation* is therefore needed when knowledge and information is moved between the two communities to provide the *translations* and *transformations* that will allow the communication to be assimilated by the receiving party.

This paper is concerned with the proposal that software systems, if correctly designed, can make a contribution to *improved* knowledge mediation between different communities of practice. We describe a specific development, which is designed to mediate knowledge between two such communities in

response to the need for detailed and rapid interactions between the two groups of workers.

Although the system has not been completed we have prototyped parts of it. These parts will be described in the current paper, along with the relevant design issues. In a future paper we shall describe the evaluation of the system. The development is intended to explore generic issues of technology and knowledge mediation. Its *specific purpose*, however, is to support business planning carried out by company managers. We have taken, as a case study, the task of business planning undertaken by Northern Electric Distribution Limited (NEDL or 'the business'). NEDL is an asset management company within the recently privatised Northern Electric group. NEDL owns and operates a large network distributing electricity to consumers in the Northern Electric area. 'Business planning' in this context means deciding how money will be spent on maintaining and operating the distribution network. This is a difficult task; one engineer told us that the situation of the business is characterised by "...increasing expectations, falling revenue and an ageing system". Pressure is placed on the business by the scrutiny of an external regulator appointed by the government. The regulator has power to penalise the company if very high standards of reliability are not met while at the same time cutting the charges, which may be made by the business for the transport of the utility. The business must consider all its activities carefully!

Business planning is an uncertain process. However, some of the uncertainty *currently* associated with the process could be resolved by information which is already 'known' or recorded within the organization, but requires substantial transformation or interpretation to answer business planning questions in forms that are posed by business managers. In particular, the engineering teams who make up the majority of the headquarters' staff of the business are routinely involved in creating or accessing a number of rich sources of information. These include the current maintenance policy of the business, the asset registry, including information about the age and condition profile of the components of the distribution network, and fault records detailing the incidence of failures in different parts of the network. All of this information is potentially very relevant to issues arising in business planning, but is not accessible directly by the business planners. It is only currently accessible through interaction and negotiation with the engineering personnel since the knowledge, tacit or otherwise, held by the engineers about the existence, location and structure of this information and about how its representations should be interpreted, is not necessarily shared by the business planners.

The motivating concept behind our 'knowledge mediation tool' is therefore to *increase the value of information sources already available* within the business by decreasing the cost of exploiting this information within the community of practice of the business managers. We argue that technology supporting knowledge mediation between the conceptual world of the business planners and the conceptual world of the engineering teams might decrease the cost to the business planners of accessing some of this information, reducing *some* of the uncertainty about future outcomes associated with business planning through the provision of extra information. In addition, by reducing the cost to the business managers of obtaining information in relevant forms, the scope of the analytical investigations that might be carried out in the course of business planning is broadened.

The remainder of the paper discusses the design of a prototype 'knowledge mediation' system, designed in response to these issues. Section 2 outlines the system and explains the role played by Case Based Reasoning. Section 3 describes the notation used to describe cases so that they are instances of translation between conceptual worlds. Section 4 describes the means by which the system supports the adaptation of a retrieved case to the current problem.

2   A 'Knowledge Mediation System'

The designated role of our prototype system is to facilitate knowledge mediation so that information, which previously was only accessible to the business managers by interaction with the engineering community, is made available at a decreased cost. Fortunately, most of this information is stored in the form of relational databases on electronic media. Other relevant knowledge, which is currently only represented on paper, could also be coerced into this form. The knowledge mediation system will stand as a proxy for the engineers who currently access these information sources, allowing the business managers greater independent access to the information. To achieve this, the system must do two things:

- It must provide a user interface where the business manager may express requirements for business planning information and be presented with this information appropriately aggregated in an accessible form.

- It must encode the engineer's knowledge of the databases and provide the processes, which will translate and transform the information into forms that are digestible by the business manager.

In our system, the former is provided by a spread-sheet style interface where the business manager can create schematic representations of the required information, while the latter is provided by the knowledge-based technology of *case-based reasoning*. These two aspects of the system are explored in the following sub-sections.

2.1   User Interface to the Knowledge Mediation System

Figure 1 illustrates the requirements for the user interface to the knowledge mediation system. The business manager must be given the means to translate requirements for information arising during the business planning process into some kind of formal representation of those requirements. For this purpose, we are developing a graphical representation for the conceptual structure of tables. We assume that the idiom and usage of the spreadsheet package are familiar to business managers (a legitimate part of the business planning domain) and in this way we have attempted to minimise the additional skills that must be assimilated by the user of the knowledge mediation system. Associated with the table representation are a set of 'intuitive' table manipulation operations by which requirements for information can be expressed. These operations are:

1. Specifying a *type* which indicates *what kind of object* is described by each row of the table. In general, the types in the script language must be recognizable categories of object from the point of view of the business manager. Types playing a prominent role in our prototype system include assets of the business, sub-types of *asset* such as network *components* or operational *locations*, or associated entities such as fault incidents or maintenance tasks. In addition, the user may specify combinations of types in a single table.

2. Adding *data requirements* to the table. These indicate what is wished to be known about the entities which are represented by the records (rows) of the table. They are *properties* of the different types of object known to the system and are shown in the graphical representation as additional columns added to the table representation. In Figure 1, the 'Age of Component' has been chosen as a data requirement.

3. Adding *conditions* to the table. These determine the choice of rows (records) that are to be included in the table. The table represented in Figure 1 will contain only components of a certain subtype ('switches').

4. *Aggregating* tables. The user can specify aggregations of tables in order to create a digestible summary of information, for example summing items of expenditure according to geographical location or using budget headings showing the type of expenditure.

Figure 2 illustrates the requirements for the internal processing functions to be provided by the knowledge mediation system. The schematic representation of 'information required' must be translated into an executable database query in order to populate the business model created by the business manager. Many different kinds of knowledge are needed to carry out this translation and to transform the retrieved data into the form required by the user. The following kinds of knowledge, needed to use a database system and presumably part of the tacit knowledge of the engineering community, can be differentiated:

Schematic Knowledge: knowledge about what different kinds of information are available and where this information can be accessed; detailed knowledge about the way in which the represented information has been organized. In the case of relational databases, this includes knowledge of the way in which the information is divided up into relations and the names of the attributes defining each relation.

Procedural Knowledge: procedural knowledge and skills necessary for accessing the information. In the case of relational databases, this includes knowledge of the SQL query language through which the databases are accessed.

Usage Knowledge: knowledge about the way that the database has been populated in practice; knowledge about the completeness of different representations of information and about the reliability of any information recorded.

Interpretative Knowledge: domain knowledge about the 'meaning' of any represented information, and particularly knowledge about how this can be translated into knowledge at the 'business level'.

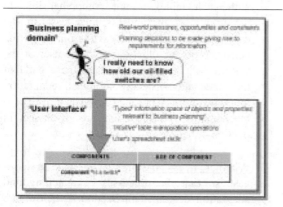

Figure 1: The user interface to the knowledge mediation system.

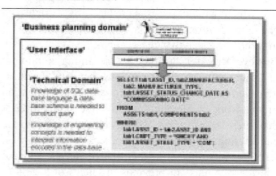

Figure 2: The user interface to the knowledge mediation system.

We have chosen to take a 'case-based' approach to the representation and manipulation of this knowledge. This choice is explained in more detail in the next sub-section.

2.2   Case-based Reasoning in the Knowledge Mediation System

Case-based reasoning (CBR) systems (Dearden & Harrison, 1997) are knowledge-based systems which use a memory of relevant 'past' cases to interpret or solve a new problem situation:

> "Rather than creating a solution from scratch, a reasoner using case-based reasoning recalls cases similar to its current problem situation and solves or interprets a problem by reasoning with past solutions and interpretations." (Rissland et al., 1989)

Case-based reasoning offers a number of advantages for building software systems in large and complex domains such as the one we have described. In particular, the knowledge content of the system can be built up incrementally, as the system is used. This may be achieved by simply adding new cases to the case memory as they are created in the course of problem solving. As a result of this process, the knowledge of the system will be most comprehensive in precisely those areas where the system finds most use.

In order for case-based reasoning to be used successfully, there must be a stable correspondence between problem situations and solutions to those situations. A solution, which is a sufficient response to a particular situation on one day, must suffice again on a different day if the same problem recurs. In addition, it must be possible to identify when a new problem situation is different but *analogous*, or sufficiently *similar*, to a previously occurring problem for which a solution is known. In a rich and changing environment such as business planning, it may not be clear that these conditions can be met. However, we felt justified in assuming a number of characteristics of interactions between business managers and engineers, after a careful investigation of the work environment. The first assumption is that there is sufficient stability about work in the engineering domain. The sources of information will remain sufficiently static that it makes sense to consider the reuse of previous instances of access to these information sources. The second assumption is that, although business-planning scenarios might vary widely and appear to be unique to the current situation,

the procedures by which these scenarios are analysed may have a significant degree of commonality. With these assumptions it makes sense to explore the role of an Interactive Case Memory (a form of CBR system where precedent cases are retrieved and re-used in cooperation with a user of the software system) as a basic technology for the Knowledge Mediation System.

The case-based knowledge mediation tool will therefore provide a record of previous examples of business planning episodes where the 'engineering community' provided information in response to requests by the business managers. This memory will be in the form of sets of tables of information of the kind manipulated in the user interface of the knowledge mediation system along with the executable database queries necessary to populate the tables. The interface provides access to these previous episodes in terms that are meaningful to business managers and supports *adaptation* of the 'nearest' example so that it can be used to inform the scenario currently being evaluated.

Several research issues are important here not only to the CBR community but also from a human computer interaction point of view:

1. How to represent the cases in a way that supports the demanding requirements just stated. The 'script language' that we have developed for this purpose is described in Section 3, below.

2. How to re-use knowledge represented in this language in the context of a new business planning situation. One particular problem is that some of the information represented in our cases, i.e. the database queries associated with each table, is not comprehensible to the user. If the most similar case in the case memory is only a *partial* match to the current problem situation, then the user of the system will be unable to adapt these parts of the case and, instead, automated adaptation must be carried out by the system. These mechanisms of adaptation are discussed in Section 4, below.

3. Whether it is possible to populate a case-base so that the processes of matching and adaptation described in Section 4, below, are feasible. These issues will be considered as part of the future evaluation of our prototype system.

3 Representation of Mediated Knowledge

We have developed a 'script language' to represent *instances of translation* between the conceptual world of the business manager and the conceptual world of the engineering teams. In terms of knowledge mediation, three main requirements have applied to the development of this language:

1. Each case contains a table or set of tables representing the information required by the business manager and its desired presentation.

2. Each case must include, in addition, the executable database queries that are needed to populate the table specified by the business manager.

3. Each case must be represented in a way which facilitates the adaptation of retrieved cases to meet the needs of a new problem situation.

Existing notations for representing tables, relations and database queries are insufficient for a number of reasons. With respect to requirements (1) and (2) above, the script language plays a *mediating* role in bridging two different levels of representation. One is the *conceptual* structure of the table, as presented to the business manager in the user interface of the system, and the second is the *implementational* structure of the table, where the table structure is described by database invocations which must be provided by the engineering community of practice. At the first level, the elements of the table structure, specifically the *conditions* and the *data requirements*, are recognizable concepts in the business-planning domain and are named in terms chosen by the business manager. At the second level, these 'user level' concepts must be implemented in terms of the actual values and parameters which are recorded in the mediated information sources. This dual structure is not reflected in current table representation languages, which maintain only a single level of representation.

With respect to requirement (3), adaptation of existing table representations is difficult because conventional table description languages fail to express any *rationale*. For example, these languages will list the selection criteria which must be satisfied by any record that is to be included in the table, but do not show *why* each condition has been included or differentiate the roles played by the different conditions. In addition, there may be dependencies between conditions, which mean that it does not make sense to delete one of the conditions without deleting a number of them. Again, these dependencies are not normally represented. Without the explicit representation of the conceptual structure of the table, adaptation of existing table representations by any means, whether manual or algorithmic, is difficult.

Our approach, therefore, has been to develop a representation language which provides a restricted but sufficient sub-set of the manipulations possible in existing table manipulation languages. This language describes the table both at the conceptual (user) level and the implementational (internal) level. It also organizes table descriptions into meaningful chunks, where elements of the implementation level, which share in translating a user-level concept, are grouped together in a single syntactic unit.

Each table is represented in the script language by a sentence of the following form:

```
TABLE(NAME(TABLE_NAME),
      OF(TYPE),
      CUSTOMISERS(CUSTOMISERS),
      PRESENT(PRESENTATION))
```

TABLE_NAME simply names this table for reference by other table descriptions. The *TYPE*, `CUSTOMISERS` and `PRESENT` keywords are interpreted *cumulatively* to reconstruct the represented table.

Firstly, the *TYPE* expression records the type assigned to the table by the system user (see Section 2.1). In particular, the script language is designed to represent *combinations* of types. For example, each row of a table might contain *asset* characteristics along with details of a *maintenance task* associated with that asset.

Secondly, the `CUSTOMISERS` clause modifies the 'base-table' defined by the *TYPE* expression. A 'customiser' is either an additional data requirement or a condition added to the definition of the table.

Thirdly, the *PRESENTATION* of a table provides the rest of the information needed to display the table. This includes; the name given to each of the columns of the table; the order in which the columns of the table will be presented to the user; the aggregation of the rows of the table. An 'aggregation attribute' associated with each column of the table specifies the aggregation of the table. An aggregation attribute is either the name of an aggregation operator (COUNT, SUM, MIN, MAX, etc.) or the term NONE which indicates that the column is an aggregating column.

The script language representation of the problem-solving episode in Figure 1 is shown below:

```
TABLE(
    NAME(''Age of switches''),
    OF( tp( components, [])),
    CUSTOMISERS(
```

```
      DEF( cond, ''is a switch'', components,
         CMPT_TYPE = ''SWCH'', []),
      DEF( data, ''Age of Asset'', assets,
         ASSET_STAGE_TYPE = COM,
         global::  CURRENT_DATE ---
              ASSET_STATUS_CHANGE_DATE),
   PRESENT( [
         (''ASSET #'', NONE, ASST_ID),
         (''COMPONENT DESCRIPTION'', NONE),
         (''AGE OF COMPONENT'', NONE)]))
```

This example illustrates the mediating role played by the script language. A condition such as "*is a switch*" is a concept from the business planning domain and is displayed and manipulated in the user interface of the system. The script sentence shown above links this concept to its translation in the language of the database schema: CMPT_TYPE = ''SWCH''. Similarly, the data requirement "*Age of Asset*" is associated with the condition and formula which translate this element of the 'conceptual structure' of the table into a piece of executable database query. 'Real world' translations may obviously be much more complex.

The similarity between representations of conditions and data requirements is deliberate, since we found that, although the distinction between the two is meaningful at the user level, in practice the two may require both a logical condition and a number of additional columns to be added to the database query. We asked an informant to demonstrate how items of plant, which had been replaced during the course of a recent asset replacement programme, could be identified in the asset database. In the course of this, the informant proceeded to translate the 'commissioning date' of a piece of plant (the date on which the asset entered service). The informant indicated the database attribute which recorded this information but simultaneously added the condition: ASSET_STAGE_TYPE = COM to the selection criteria in the query.

4   Re-using Mediated Knowledge

Case-based Reasoning systems are based around a characteristic series of processing steps e.g. (Aamodt & Plaza, 1994), where, following the presentation of a description of the current problem situation, stored cases which are potentially relevant to the new problem are *retrieved* from the case memory. These are inspected to determine which are most *similar* to the current situation; the selected cases are *adapted* to create solutions for the current situation and so on. Many variants of each of these steps have been explored according to the representational form given to the stored cases. Our task was to develop a case-based reasoning cycle, which could exploit

cases encoded in the script language described in the previous section.

4.1   Retrieval of Stored Cases

Methods for the efficient retrieval of cases in a structured representation such as ours have been discussed in (Plaza et al., 1996;   Tammer et al., 1996). In these methods, an incomplete fragment of case is presented to the case memory, which returns the most similar, complete, stored case. This style of operation fits the requirements of knowledge mediation, since cases expressed in the script language of Section 3 combine information from both the business planning viewpoint (the 'conceptual' structure) and the engineering viewpoint (the 'implementational' structure). However, the business planner using the system is only required to describe the information required on the 'conceptual' level, i.e. from the business planning point of view; the role of the case memory system is to provide relevant complete cases from which the missing 'implementational' level can be inferred.

The partial case representation, which will act as a query to the case memory system, is created through the interactions described in Section 2.1. These operations create a graphical 'table schema' representing the information required by the user (Figure 1) and an *internal* representation of the same information in a sentence of the script language. Section 3 emphasised how the script language associates the 'name' of each element of a table specification with its 'translation'. However, only the name of the element is provided by the user when a query is being created. These 'names' are chosen by the user from a list presented by the knowledge mediation system of elements which have already been defined in the cases held in the case memory. If the user believes that the concept being introduced into the query is genuinely new, then a new 'name' may be added. In either case, the system places a special 'null' term into the script language term to mark the location of the missing translation. Thus the user only provides those parts of the case representation corresponding to the conceptual structure of the table. Cases are retrieved by matching this partial case fragment to the more complete cases stored in the case memory.

The case memory and its associated retrieval mechanisms are currently being implemented.

4.2   Structure Matching and Adaptation

The knowledge mediation system must now compute a single representation in the script language which combines all the relevant information from the script representing the user's query and from the scripts retrieved as cases from the case memory. We call the process that carries out this transfer of knowledge 'structure matching and adaptation'. This process is based on algorithms described in (Jantke, 1993; Plaza, 1995) for transfer of knowledge between structured case representations. Taking a similar approach, our process proceeds in two steps:

Structure matching: Taking the 'query' script with each of the retrieved cases in turn, the system calculates the 'intersection' of the two representations by 'matching' one representation onto the other. This results in a new sentence in the script language that represents precisely what the two scripts 'have in common' (i.e. their *similarity*). The process also generates two series of operators, which specify a series of transformations by which the two original scripts could be recovered from their intersection. These two series of operators thereby encode the *differences* between the query and the retrieved case.

Adaptation: The two initial scripts are set on one side, and the adaptation process takes as input their intersection and the two operator traces. The adaptation process traverses these two lists in turn, using a set of heuristics to decide whether the operation to recover the query script or the retrieved script should be used. The result is a hybrid of the query and the retrieved case. In particular, the adaptation process is required to replace any 'null' terms representing missing translations of user concepts in the query script with translations of those concepts derived from the retrieved cases. However, our implementation in fact does more than just filling in missing translations — elements of the retrieved case representing the *context of use* of the translated concept, such as other elements which refer to that element or the associated aggregations, may also be transferred to the query script.

We have developed a set of heuristics for structure matching and adaptation in the script language described in Section 3, and have implemented a 'structure matching and adaptation engine' based on these heuristics.

4.3 Manual Refinement of Cases

The automatic process, described above, for the adaptation of retrieved cases, is an *heuristic* one, as in fact are all case-based reasoning processes. A necessary final step therefore is that the user of the

system must ensure that the information that has been retrieved by the knowledge mediation system through the execution of the computed script is in fact the information that was expected. We envisage that the use of the knowledge mediation system is an iterative and interactive process. The knowledge mediation system must support at least three further interactions:

Validation of the results of knowledge mediation: In case there is any doubt about the information that has been presented by the knowledge mediation system, the user must be able to inspect the formulae into which each of the elements in his query has been translated. Here, there are issues about how to support the comprehension of user as the 'knowledge mediation threshold' is crossed, which we hope to explore in the remainder of the project.

Iterative refinement of the user's query: Even where there is no doubt about the translation of the user's query, we would expect the user of an interactive system such as this to refine the concept of what information is required iteratively through interaction with the data that is available. The structure matching and adaptation process uses the same representational space for the inputs and outputs of case-based reasoning. It is therefore straightforward to use the same facilities of the user interface as have been used to create the initial representation of the requirement for information to refine the user's query.

Incremental addition of mediation knowledge: A final possibility is that the system contains no suitable precedent for the translation of the user's requirement for information into an executable database query. In this case, the knowledge mediation system must provide facilities for a suitable translation to be provided by the engineering community of practice and this translation to be added to the case memory. In this way the knowledge base of the system is incrementally extended and future breakdowns can be avoided.

5 Conclusions

It has been argued for a number of years that knowledge-based systems should be designed to empower users to carry out their tasks (Woods et al., 1994; Fischer et al., 1991). This suggestion may be contrasted with the 'expert system' philosophy of knowledge-based systems which attempts to solve problems *on behalf of* rather than *in cooperation with* the user. Our version of a 'knowledge mediation system' has aimed from the start to support the task of business planning rather than to automate or constrain it. Our approach to this has been two-fold. On the one hand, we began our development by using methods of enquiry developed for general "non knowledge-based" software development, for example scenarios-based methods (Carroll, 1995) and contextual enquiry (Beyer & Holtzblatt, 1998). Through these methods we sought an understanding of the work to be supported so that we could envisage the ways in which the technology might impact the work system. On the other hand, we argue that our knowledge mediation tool has the potential to empower users. The recall of previous instances and comprehension of their connection with the current problem instance in terms that are relevant to the business manager provides access to detailed knowledge about the current state of the business so that it can be directed to supporting decision making. The algorithms that support the reuse of these previous instances and their matching to the current problem provide an appropriate level of control of the information that is relevant to the current problem.

The main issues in implementing case-based reasoning processes as part of our prototype knowledge mediation tool have been to do with developing a suitable representation for the storage of cases in the case memory, and to find appropriate algorithms for the retrieval and re-use of these representations. In particular we have focussed on the script language, although we have also attempted to outline the ways in which stored cases are exploited by re-use. The main requirement on the script language is to be able to associate concepts which are meaningful to the business managers using the knowledge mediation system with the translation of those concepts into database invocations and formulae which will construct the required information from the available data sources. This requires structuring the language so that each syntactic element of the language corresponds to a meaningful conceptual element of the query. The SQL database language does not have this property; if an arbitrary sequence of tokens is deleted from an SQL query, the resulting string will almost certainly not be a well-formed query. Our script language is designed so that removing any of the constituent elements of a script will result in a new script which still has a valid interpretation, and in addition the chunk that has been removed is a separable and independent piece of knowledge.

Future evaluation of the system in the context of use should address a number of issues associated with knowledge based tools of this kind, for example:

1. Problems of 'false certainty' associated with automatic translation.

2. Problems of breakdowns where the system is not providing the appropriate level of knowledge.

We have created a proxy for the engineer, but still need to enlist the engineer to fill in gaps in the knowledge of the system.

Acknowledgements

We acknowledge with gratitude the support of Northern Electric Distribution Ltd and the UK Engineering and Physical Sciences Research Council (Grant GR/K84752).

References

Aamodt, A. & Plaza, E. (1994), "Case-based Reasoning: Foundational Issues, Methodological Variations, and System Approaches", *Artificial Intelligence Communications* **7**(1), 39–59.

Beyer, H. & Holtzblatt, K. (1998), *Contextual Design: Defining Customer-centered Systems*, Morgan-Kaufmann.

Carroll, J. M. (ed.) (1995), *Scenario-Based Design: Envisioning Work and Technology in System Development*, John Wiley & Sons.

Dearden, A. M. & Harrison, M. D. (1997), "A Software Engineering Model for Case Memory Systems", *The Computer Journal* **40**(4), 167–82.

Fischer, G., Lemke, A. C., Mastaglio, T. & Morch, A. I. (1991), "The Role of Critiquing in Cooperative Problem Solving", *ACM Transactions on Office Information Systems* **9**(3), 123–51.

Jantke, K. P. (1993), Nonstandard Concepts of Similarity in Case-Based Reasoning, *in* H.-H. Bock, W. Lenski & M. M. Richter (eds.), *Information Systems and Data Analysis, Proc. 17th Annual Conference of the Gesellschaft für Klassification*, Springer-Verlag, pp.28–43.

Plaza, E. (1995), Cases as Terms: A Feature Term Approach to the Structured Representation of Cases, *in* M. Veloso & A. Aamodt (eds.), *Case-based Reasoning Research and Development, Proceedings of ICCBR '95*, Vol. 1010 of *Lecture Notes in Artifical Intelligence*, Springer-Verlag, pp.265–76.

Plaza, E., Lòpez de Màntaras, R. & Armengol, E. (1996), On the Importance of Similitude: An Entropy-based Assessment, *in* I. Smith & B. Faltings (eds.), *Advances in Case-based Reasoning, Proceedings of EWCBR-96*, Vol. 1168 of *Lecture Notes in Artifical Intelligence*, Springer-Verlag, pp.324–38.

Rissland, E. L., Kolodner, T. & Waltz, D. (1989), Case-based Reasoning from DARPA: Machine Learning Program Plan, *in* K. Hammond (ed.), *Proceedings of the DARPA Case-Based Reasoning Workshop*, Morgan-Kaufmann, pp.1–13.

Star, S. L. (1995), The Politics of Formal Representations: Wizards, Gurus and Organizational Complexity, *in* S. L. Star (ed.), *Ecologies of Knowledge, Work and Politics in Science and Technology*, SUNY Press, pp.88–118.

Tammer, E.-C., Matuschek, D., Jantke, K. P. & Steinhöfel, K. (1996), Learning Case Classification for Improving Case-based Reasoning, *in* W. Dilger, M. Schlosser, J. Zeidler & A. Ittner (eds.), *Proceedings of Fachgruppentreffen Maschinelles Lernen der GI Fachgruppe 1.1.3*, Universität Chemnitz-Zwickau. Chemnitzer Informatik-Bericht CSR-96-06, ISSN 0947-5125.

Wenger, E. (1998), *Communities of Practice: Learning, Meaning and Identity*, Cambridge University Press.

Woods, D. D., Johannesen, L. J., Cook, R. I. & Sarter, N. B. (1994), Behind Human Error: Cognitive Systems, Computers and Hindsight, Technical Report 94-101, CSERIAC SOAR.

Human–Computer Interaction — INTERACT '99
M. Angela Sasse and Chris Johnson (Editors)
Published by IOS Press, © IFIP TC.13, 1999

Model-aided Remote Usability Evaluation

Fabio Paternò & Giulio Ballardin

CNUCE-CNR, Via S. Maria 36, Pisa, Italy.

{f.paterno,g.ballardin}@cnuce.cnr.it

Abstract: In this paper we present a method for providing remote usability evaluation with the support of powerful task models able to describe concurrent and interactive activities. The method is tool-supported and it is able to analyse the logs of user actions performed during work sessions by using information contained in such task models. The overall goal is to provide useful information to usability evaluators with limited effort.

Keywords: usability engineering, remote evaluation, task models, tool-supported evaluation, formal methods.

1 Introduction

Usability engineering (Nielsen, 1993) concerns the development of systematic methods to support usability evaluation. Various types of approaches have been proposed for this purpose.

Model-based approaches to usability evaluation use some models, usually task or user models, to support this evaluation. They often aim (John & Kieras, 1996) to produce *quantitative predictions* of how well users will be able to perform tasks with a proposed design. Usually the designer starts with an initial task analysis and a proposed first interface design. The designer should then use an engineering model (like GOMS) to find the usability problems of the interface. While model-based evaluation is useful to highlight relevant aspects in the evaluation, it can be limiting to not consider empirical information because the possible predictions in some cases can be denied by the real user behaviour. Thus, it is important to find methods that allow designers to apply meaningful models to some empirical information. An attempt in this direction is USAGE (Byrne et al., 1994) that provides a tool supporting a method where the user actions required to execute an application action in UIDE are analysed by the NGOMSL approach. However this information is still limited with respect to that contained in the logs of the user actions performed during work sessions by users.

In *empirical testing* the behaviour of real users is considered. It can be very expensive and it can have some limitations too. It requires long observations of users' behaviour. Often these observations are supported by video that can be annotated by some tool. Even observing video describing user behaviour,

either in work places or in usability laboratory, can take a lot of time to designers (a complete analysis can take more than five times the duration of the video) and some relevant aspects can still be missed.

In *inspection-based techniques* to usability evaluation designers analyse a user interface or its description. Several of these techniques, such as heuristic evaluation, cognitive walkthrough, and software guidelines, have been found useful but limited because dependent on the ability of the evaluator or requiring multiple evaluators, or missing some relevant problems (Jeffries et al., 1991).

In order to overcome some of the limitations considered we developed a method (Lecerof & Paternò, 1998) based on the possibility to use task models for analysing empirical data. We present in this paper an extension of this method (RemUSINE, **Rem**ote **US**er **IN**terface **E**valuator) to exploit its possibilities for supporting remote evaluation. The new method is more efficient and provides a richer set of results such as results related to a group of users sessions rather than just one.

2 The RemUSINE Approach for Remote Evaluation

In the last years there has been an increasing interest in remote usability evaluation (Hartson et al., 1996). It has been defined as usability evaluation where evaluators are separated in time and/or space from users.

This approach has been introduced for many reasons:

- The increasing availability and improvement of network connections.

- The cost and the rigidity of traditional laboratory-based usability evaluation.

- The need to decrease costs of usability evaluation to make it more affordable.

There are various approaches to remote usability evaluation. One interesting approach is automated data collection for remote evaluation, where tools are used to collect and return a journal or log of data containing indication of the interactions performed by the user. These data are analysed later on, for example using pattern recognition techniques, however usually the results obtained are rather limited for the evaluation of an interactive application.

We think that task models can provide additional support for analysing such data. However to this end it is necessary that task models are powerful, non-prescriptive, and flexible. This means they should be able to describe concurrent activities that can interrupt each other dynamically. To support this analysis, task models should be refined to indicate precisely how tasks should be performed following the design of the application considered.

If we consider current approaches, briefly summarised in the introduction, we can notice a lack of methods that are able:

- To support the evaluation of many users without requiring a heavy involvement of designers.

- To support the evaluation gathering information on the users' behaviour at their work place without using expensive equipment.

- To apply powerful and flexible task models in the evaluation of logs of user events, thus linking model-based and empirical evaluations. Current automatic tools, such as ErgoLight, that support usability evaluation by task models, use simple notations to specify such models, thus still requiring a strong effort from the evaluator.

These three relevant results are obtained by our RemUSINE method following an approach that is summarised in Figure 1 where ovals represent data files and rectangles programs.

We have multiple instances of one application that can be used by many users located in different places. Then we have the RemUSINE tool with the following input:

- *The log files with the user interactions*, by the support of a logging tool it is possible to automatically generate a file storing all the events performed by a user during a work session. One or more of these files have an additional use that is the creation of the log-task table.

- *The log-task association table*; the purpose of this table is to create an association between the physical events, that can be generated by the user while interacting with the application considered, and the basic interaction tasks (the tasks that cannot be further decomposed in the task model and require only one action to be performed). This association is a key point in our method because through it we can use the task model to analyse the user behaviour.

- *The task model*, it is specified using the ConcurTaskTrees notation (Paternò, 1999) by using an editor publicly available at http://giove.cnuce.cnr.it/ctte.html.

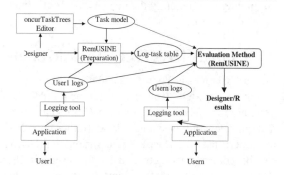

Figure 1: The architecture of our approach.

In our method we can distinguish three phases:

- *The preparation part*, that is mainly the development of the task model and the association between physical user-generated events, extracted by log files, and the basic interaction tasks of the task model;

- *The execution of the evaluation tool*, during which the tool first processes the related precondition for each task (if any) from the temporal relationships defined in the task model, and then, using also this information, it elaborates its results: the errors performed, task patterns, duration of the performance of the tasks and so on;

- *The analysis of the results of the tool*, in this phase the designer can provide suggestions to improve the user interface by using the information generated by the RemUSINE tool.

The user interactions are captured by logging tools that are able to get this information without disturbing users during their work. These logs are useful to identify user errors such as attempts to activate an interaction that was not allowed because some precondition was not satisfied or selections of elements of the user interface that were not selectable. An action is an error if it is not useful to support the current task.

One problem is how to identify automatically the tasks that the user intends to perform. To this end the knowledge of the user actions can be useful because, for example, if the user tries to print a file and s/he does not specify the name of the file to print, it is possible to understand what the current user intention is (printing a file) by detecting the related action, for example the selection of a Print button. Besides, a similar precondition error highlights that there is a problem with the user interface, as it probably does not highlight sufficiently the need to specify the name of the file to print.

3   ConcurTaskTrees Task Models

ConcurTaskTrees is a powerful and flexible notation to specify task models. It aims to overcome limitations of previous approaches such as GOMS (Card et al., 1983) that considers only sequential tasks (rather unrealistic in modern user interfaces where various interactions can be concurrently activated by the user) or UAN (Hartson & Gray, 1992), which made an important contribution by providing concurrent operators, but it entails specifying a lot of details (such as highlighting buttons when the cursor is over them). Such details expressed in UAN textual syntax and its lack of tool support, make the specifications difficult to interpret, especially in real, large-size case studies.

ConcurTaskTrees is powerful and flexible because it allows designers to specify concurrent tasks, tasks that dynamically disable other tasks, iterative and recursive tasks and so on.

By using different icons it is possible to indicate the allocation of the performance of the task (to the user or application, or to their interaction).

In Figure 2 you can find an example of ConcurTaskTrees specification. It concerns a museum application. The related user interface is shown in Figure 3. In this specification we did not consider user tasks (tasks associated with internal cognitive actions

such as recognizing a visual element in the interface or deciding how to carry out a set of tasks) because we want to focus on interaction tasks that can be associated with the user actions stored in the log files and application tasks that are tightly related to them.

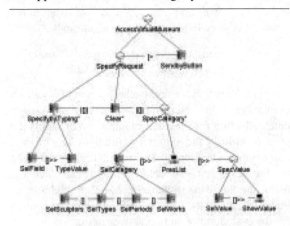

Figure 2: An example task model.

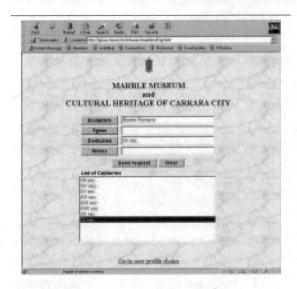

Figure 3: The user interface considered.

At the first level there is a distinction between the part to specify the request (*SpecifyRequest* task) and that for sending the request (*SendbyButton* task) that can disable ([> operator) the first one. *SpecifyRequest* has iterative children tasks (iterative tasks are indicated by the * symbol) as they can be performed multiple times. These tasks support specifying and clearing the request and they are concurrent communicating tasks (indicated by the |[]| operator) disabled by the sending the request (*SendbyButton* task).

More specifically, specifying a request can be performed either by mouse selection (*SpecCategory* task) or by typing (*SpecifybyTyping* task). They are communicating because a specification done in one way can override a specification done in the other way beforehand and vice versa. The specification by mouse requires first to select a category (*SelCategory* task), next the application presents the list of related values (*PresList* task) and then the user can select a value (*SelValue* task) and the application shows it in the related field (*ShowValue* task). These are sequential activities with information passing ([] >> operator). Selecting a category is decomposed into the choice ([] operator) among different tasks, each one associated with a specific category of request (by sculptor, by type of work, by historical period, by work name).

Once the list of values is presented the user can activate another request for another field by selecting another category. Specifying by typing requires first to select the field of interest (*SelField* task) and next to type the value (*TypeValue* task).

The cloud icon is used to indicate abstract tasks, i.e. tasks that have subtasks whose performance is allocated differently (either user, application, or interaction tasks).

It is important to remember that for the RemUSINE analysis it is required that the task model is refined so as each possible user action, supported by the user interface considered, can be associated with one interaction basic task (that are leaves in the task tree).

4 The Preparation Part

There are various tools available to collect automatically data on the user-generated events during an interactive session, for example, JavaStar (http://www.sun.com/suntest/JavaStar/JavaStar.html) or QCReplay (http://www.centerline.com/productline/qcreplay/qcreplay.html).

They are able to provide files that contain indication of the events occurred and when they occurred. The events considered are mouse click, text input, mouse movements, and similar. When interaction techniques such as menu, pull-down menu are selected they are able also to indicate what menu element was selected. The resulting files are editable text files.

Similarly, using the ConcurTaskTrees editor it is possible to save the task model specification in a file for further modifications and analysis.

In RemUSINE there is a part of the tool that is dedicated to the preparation part whose main purpose is to create the association between logs of user events and the basic tasks in the task model. Association that

will be used to analyse the user interactions with the support of the task model.

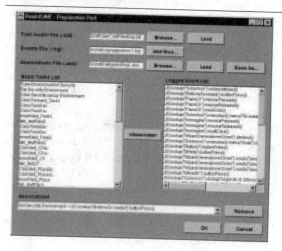

Figure 4: The tool supporting the preparation phase.

In the preparation part (as you can see in Figure 4) the evaluator can load one log file and one file with the task model. The lists of elements contained in the two files appear in two different, parallel columns. In the task-related part only the basic interaction tasks appear, as they are the only elements that can be associated with logged events. While in the list of basic tasks each of them is indicated only once, the number of times that one specific event can appear on the related list depends on the session considered and the number of times the user performed it during such a session. The application designer then has to select one physical event on one side and the corresponding basic task on the other side, and then add it to the table containing all the associations by means of the related button. Once a basic task has been associated with the related event it will disappear from the list of tasks that thus indicates only tasks that still need to be associated with the related event by the designer. The associations performed can be displayed by the *Associations* pull-down menu. In case of mistakes the designer can remove elements from this list by the *Remove* button. The associations can be saved in a file and loaded later on for further expansions or for the evaluation phase.

This association can be made only once to evaluate as many user application sessions as desired because it contains the information required by the evaluation tool. Indeed, each session is associated with one event trace whose elements belong to the set of input events supported by the user interface in question. Thus, once the association has been created, only the log file to be analysed needs to be changed in order to evaluate each session.

5 The RemUSINE Elaboration

In the evaluation phase the RemUSINE tool scans the elements of the log considered. For each element it identifies the corresponding basic task by the log-task association table. It has to check whether such a task exists, if not it means that the user performed an error of the type selection of an item that was not selectable. If it exists then it has to check whether it could be performed when it occurred. This is obtained by checking whether the task had preconditions (tasks that have to be performed before the one considered) and, in the event they exist, if they were satisfied. If yes then the task can be considered executed correctly otherwise a precondition error is annotated giving an indication of what precondition was not satisfied. Then the next user action in the log file is considered and the same elaboration is applied.

When a task is performed correctly the internal data structure of the tool are updated to maintain updated the context that will be used in the evaluation of the next user actions.

An example of task with precondition in Figure 2 is the task related to typing a value in one field of the request form. If the user has not selected such a field this task cannot be performed and this has a consequence also on higher level tasks such as formulating the request because they too cannot be performed correctly.

In the tool we have incorporated the implementation of an algorithm that takes a ConcurTaskTrees specification and it is able to provide the preconditions for all the tasks at all the levels. Such preconditions indicate the tasks that have to be performed in order to complete the accomplishment of the task considered.

The method for finding the preconditions and creating the precondition table searches through a pre-order traversal of the task tree. For every non-optional task we check if its *left brother is an enabling task* (a task on the left of the >> operator). If so we know that the left brother is the precondition of the current task and add this (the task and its precondition) to the result.

If the current task is a high level task then the left enabling brother is a precondition also for the children of such a task that are available at the beginning of its performance. These children are those which are on the left of the leftmost enabling operator. An example is the case of *SpecValue* in Figure 2 with the left enabling brother *PresList*. We will first put *PresList* as the precondition of *SpecValue*. Then we find also that *PresList* is a precondition for *SelValue*. If there is

no enabling operator it means that all the children are available at the beginning.

In any case when we consider a non-basic task (a task that is not a leaf in the task tree) we have to search for its preconditions which are among its children. While searching the method collects the results. For example, if we apply the method to the example in Figure 2 we will find that *SendbyButton* is precondition of *AccessVirtualMuseum* because only when this task terminates the parent task will be considered completed as the brother task (*SpecifyRequest*) has iterative children that never terminate unless they are interrupted by the disabling task. At the next levels of the task tree we can find that *SpecifybyTyping* has *TypeValue* as precondition which has *SelField* as precondition. The algorithm can continue similarly until the entire tree has been considered.

Another element that we have to take into account is that sometimes the performance of one task has the effect of undo the effects of another task thus making unverified a precondition that beforehand was true. For example we can have a deselect task that makes false a precondition requiring a certain selection. The tool considers this possibility too when it keeps updated the state of the task model for evaluation purposes.

6 A Small Example of Log Analysis

We can consider a small example of log taken using JavaStar applied to the museum application in Figure 3 to better understand how our method works once it has calculated the preconditions for all the tasks. In the log we have removed the information useless for our tool. We consider seven events in the log file:

```
1.  JS.applet(''Insertions'',0).
      member(''NewPanelSfondo2'').
      multiClick(124,93,16,1);
```

The tool detects that the user has selected an area that does not correspond at any interaction technique, it provides the position where it occurred, in this case it corresponds at the name of the town. Probably the user thought it was selectable and tried to receive some information about it,

```
2.  JS.delay(7310);
```

Between each couple of actions an indication providing the time passed among their occurrence is provided in millisecond. We will not report the other occurrences of similar actions.

```
3.  JS.applet(''Insertions'',0).
       button(''Sculptors'').
       typeString(''Bodin'');
```

In this case the user started to type the name of a sculptor (*TypeValue* task in Figure 2) without selecting first the related field, our tool detects a precondition error

```
4.  JS.applet(''Insertions'',0).
       member(''java.awt.TextField'',0).
       multiClick(0,8,16,1);
```

The user has probably understood now the type of error performed and s/he has now correctly selected a field (*SelField* task) that can receive text input

```
5.  JS.applet(''Insertions'',0).
       member(''java.awt.TextField'',0).
       typeString(''Bodini Floriano'',0,0);
```

The user has now provided correctly the name of a sculptor ("Bodini Floriano"), performing the *TypeValue* task

```
6.  JS.applet(''Insertions'',0).
       button(''Periods'').buttonPress();
```

Now the user has selected the button corresponding at the request to show the list of historical periods considered (*SelPeriods* task)

```
7.  JS.applet(''Insertions'',0).
       member(''NewPanelSfondo2'').
       member(''java.awt.List'',2).
       select(4,''XVIII sec.'');
```

Finally the user has selected the historical period of interest (*SelValue* task) from the list dynamically shown by the application.

7 The Results Provided

Our method can provide a wide variety of results that can be useful for the evaluator. They can be related to both single sessions and groups of sessions. It is possible to obtain some general information on the user sessions (such as duration, number of tasks failed and completed, number of errors, number of scrollbar or windows moved, see Figure 5), more detailed information for the tasks considered, and some graphical representations of such results. When tasks are counted we consider all the tasks in the ConcurTaskTrees specification both basic tasks and higher levels tasks.

The more detailed information about the tasks include:

- The display of the accomplished tasks and how many times they are performed. The frequency of the tasks can be useful when deciding the layout of the interface. For example, it is often preferable to highlight the interaction techniques associated with frequent tasks.

- The display of the tasks the user tried to perform but failed because their preconditions were not satisfied, and how many times each task failed.

- The display of the tasks the user never tried to perform, this information can be useful to identify parts of the user interface that are either useless or difficult to achieve for the users; this result is more difficult to obtain with other approaches based on observations.

- Display of all the errors divided into precondition errors and others.

- The display of the task patterns found (specific sequences of tasks) among the accomplished tasks (see Figure 6). The presentation shows first the frequency and next the pattern, and orders them by frequency. Patterns are useful to identify sequence of tasks frequently performed by users. This information can be useful to try to improve the design so as to speed-up the performances of such tasks.

- The display of the entire result from the evaluation in temporal order. It is also possible to save this result in a file and load it at a later time.

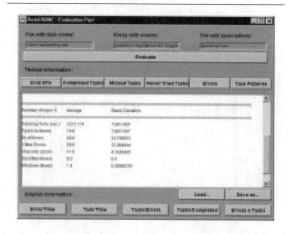

Figure 5: An example of general information.

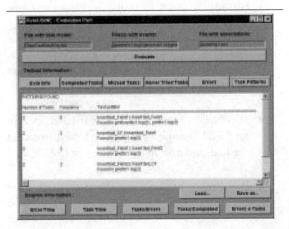

Figure 6: An example of task patterns detected.

The different graphs, showing the data from the evaluation in different manners, are:

- The *Tasks/Time* chart graph with the tasks on the x-scale and how long they took to perform on the y-scale (see Figure 7). For each task the related bar chart highlights the fastest, the slowest and the average performance in the group of sessions considered.

- The *Errors/Time* graph with the number of errors on the y-scale and the time on the x-scale.

- The *Tasks/Errors* chart graph containing the number of precondition errors associated with each task.

- The *Tasks/Completed* chart graph containing the number of times the tasks were performed.

- The *Errors & Tasks* pie chart containing the different types of errors and their percentage, and another containing the number of tasks accomplished, missed and never attempted.

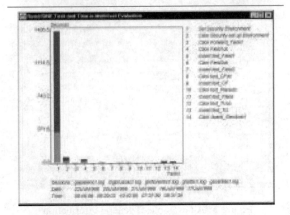

Figure 7: A diagram indicating task performances.

It is possible to provide all this information related to a single user session or to groups of user sessions. The utility to apply the tool to groups of sessions is that in this way it is possible to immediately identify if in any session there was some abnormal behaviour. For example, a task that was performed in a long time just because the user was interrupted by external factors during its accomplishment. For example, in Figure 7 evaluators can notice that the first task has a particular long performance. Then they can interactively select the task and receive information on each session concerning that task (Figure 8). In this case they can see that there is only one session during which the task required a particularly long time of performance thus indicating that there were problems only for one user and not for the others.

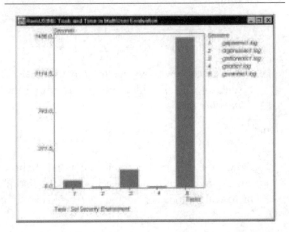

Figure 8: Representation of time performance of a selected task for each session.

8   How to Interpret the Results

The method proposed has been applied to three case studies. The first concerned the evaluation of an application for making cinema reservations. The evaluation was performed by considering eighteen computer science students.

We then applied the method in a large software company developing an application for supporting management of tax declarations and their transmission to the national centre after performing some controls. The third case study considered is a hypermedia museum application. They are all Java applications, even if the RemUSINE method can be applied to applications written in other languages.

The case studies performed showed that it is possible to find various causes for the errors detected. Possible examples are:

- *The task model supported by the user interface imposes temporal constraints too rigid for the conceptual task model of the user*; for example if a movie database application allows only to select a cinema and next the movies projected in the selected cinema, it can be too limiting for users who may want to select first the list of movies available and then ask where they are projected. This can happen, for example, when people first decide a time when to go to the cinema and thus they want to see what movies are available at that time and only after that where a specific movie is projected.

- *The user interface does not provide enough guidance on how a task should be performed*; for example the user can try to send a request to an application without having specified enough fields in the request form because the user interface does not highlight sufficiently what the mandatory fields are.

- *A label is not sufficiently explicative*; for example in some user interfaces there are buttons with a More Info label but it is not clear what the topic related to the more info is.

The reasons for the errors do not say explicitly how to improve the interface. However, they show that improvements must be made and indicate which part of the design of the user interface should be improved. The performed improvements must then be decided by the designer, helped by these results.

These errors may be found by observing users. However, our tool-supported method can guarantee a more reliable and precise detection of these errors, especially if the application is complex or things happen fast, and these errors are detected automatically without having an observer spending time on analysing user interactions.

In our experience our method has showed to be particularly suitable for applications that can be used in centres located in various remote sites because it does not require movements of users or evaluators and at the same time allows an evaluation that takes into account the real behaviour of users in their work place.

9 Evaluation of RemUSINE

One reasonable question is whether the benefits of our new approach justify the extra time and effort involved.

The additional effort required only regards the design of the task model for the application considered

and to make the log-task table (all the other tables in the preparation part are automatically completed).

We think that the task model is a useful exercise for user interface designers to develop an understanding of the application considered and it should be done even if our approach for user interface evaluation was not used. Indeed, at this time the most common use of task models is in the design phase (Wilson et al., 1993) and not in the evaluation phase. It is used to discuss design solutions among the different people involved (designers, developers, managers, end users and so on). Furthermore, the task model can also be useful to support the software development phase.

The mapping between user actions in the log file and tasks should be done only once for an application and then it is valid for analysing all the user tests of that application. Thus it is a limited additional effort.

On the other hand, it is possible to achieve more reliable evaluations of the application as no action to be analysed is omitted because we can automatically detect their occurrence. This is not possible with other approaches. For example, in one case study we noticed that video-based observations were not able to detect some users' clicks.

Additional results such as tasks never tried are provided. When our approach gives similar results to those obtained by observing users, it has some advantages because in our case we can run various user tests in parallel in the users' workplaces without having to move them to a usability lab or to move observers to their workplaces. Then we can let the automatic tool evaluate the results, whereas in the other case we need an observer to sequentially follow each user and analyse his/her behaviour manually. This implies great effort in terms of time from both the user and the observer and lower reliability of the results, especially when user interactions evolve rapidly. If multiple observers are used then there is the problem of consistency among the results of their observations.

One potential concern with our method is that the evaluators could be missing some information that would only be gained by actually observing users and hearing their comments. We thus propose its use complemented with user interviews to gather direct comments. The questions would be limited to the part of the interface that our tool indicates the user found difficult to use.

Overall, we believe that our approach is worth using especially if the application considered has many dynamic dialogues and a substantial complexity. It complements and strongly reduces the need for evaluation done by observing and interviewing users that can be limited to an additional analysis of the parts of the user interface that our method finds problematic.

10   Conclusions

In this paper we have presented a new method for supporting remote usability evaluation. It is based on a model-aided analysis of the log of user events. The purpose of the analysis is to give evaluators a lot of information useful for identifying problematic parts of the user interface and possible suggestions to improve it. Consequently the effort required to the evaluators decreases so as the overall costs of the evaluation phase especially when many users sessions are considered.

References

Byrne, M., Wood, S., Noi Sukaviriya, P., Foley, J. & Kieras, D. (1994), Automating Interface Evaluation, *in* B. Adelson, S. Dumais & J. Olson (eds.), *Proceedings of CHI'94: Human Factors in Computing Systems*, ACM Press, pp.232–7.

Card, S. K., Moran, T. P. & Newell, A. (1983), *The Psychology of Human–Computer Interaction*, Lawrence Erlbaum Associates.

Hartson, H. R. & Gray, P. D. (1992), "Temporal Aspects of Tasks in the User Action Notation", *Human–Computer Interaction* **7**, 1–45.

Hartson, R., Castillo, J., Kelso, J., Kamler, J. & Neale, W. (1996), Remote Evaluation: The Network as an Extension of the Usability Laboratory, *in* G. van der Veer & B. Nardi (eds.), *Proceedings of CHI'96: Human Factors in Computing Systems*, ACM Press, pp.228–35.

Jeffries, R., Miller, J. R., Wharton, C. & Uyeda, K. M. (1991), User Interface Evaluation in the Real World: A Comparison of Four Techniques, *in* S. P. Robertson, G. M. Olson & J. S. Olson (eds.), *Proceedings of CHI'91: Human Factors in Computing Systems (Reaching through Technology)*, ACM Press, pp.119–24.

John, B. & Kieras, D. (1996), "Using GOMS for User Interface Design and Evaluation: Which Technique?", *ACM Transactions on Computer–Human Interaction* **3**(4), 287–319.

Lecerof, A. & Paternò, F. (1998), "Automatic Support for Usability Evaluation", *IEEE Transactions on Software Engineering* **24**(10), 863–88.

Nielsen, J. (1993), *Usability Engineering*, Academic Press.

Paternò, F. (1999), *Model-Based Design and Evaluation of Interactive Applications*, Springer-Verlag.

Wilson, S., Johnson, P., Kelly, C., Cunningham, J. & Markopoulos, P. (1993), Beyond Hacking: A Model-based Approach to User Interface Design, *in* J. Alty, D. Diaper & S. Guest (eds.), *People and Computers VIII (Proceedings of HCI'93)*, Cambridge University Press, pp.217–31.

Human–Computer Interaction — INTERACT '99
M. Angela Sasse and Chris Johnson (Editors)
Published by IOS Press, © IFIP TC.13, 1999

Remote Usability Testing of a Web Site Information Architecture: "Testing for a Dollar a Day"[†]

Klaus Kaasgaard, Thomas Myhlendorph, Thomas Snitker & Hans-Erik Sørensen[1]

Kommunedata, Lautrupparken 40, 2750 Ballerup, Denmark.
[1] Department of Computer Science, University of Århus,
Ny Munkegade 535.217, 8000 Århus C, Denmark.
{kka,thm,tsn}@kmd.dk, hes@daimi.au.dk

Abstract: With the advance of new Internet technologies usability specialists face shortcomings in their traditional methods, specifically in connection with defining and involving representatives for different user groups and testing in as natural a working environment as possible. Usability specialists need to look for alternative ways of dealing with complexities arising from heterogeneous user groups and heterogeneous use settings. This paper explores the potential of utilizing the network itself in testing a Web site information architecture by using a remote testing technique. Following a presentation and discussion of a case-story, the paper concludes that the main problem of remote testing is analysing data. Research is needed in order to develop, test and refine methods to support this process. The paper discusses a method — use case signature — in which data is represented so as to reveal the most typical configurations of use in connection with a particular task.

Keywords: remote usability testing, heterogeneous use, use case signature, user-centred design, information architecture design.

1 Introduction

With the advance of new Internet technologies and with an increasing number of potential users, software firms face new challenges in connection with developing products. A corner stone in developing software products is to carefully identify and define the specific needs and characteristics of a user population as well as characteristics of the use situation(s). This central task has become more difficult to carry out for usability specialists when evaluating Internet sites and applications addressing a very large and heterogeneous group of users. In many companies performing usability tests, approximately 5 users have been considered a reasonable number of test users to evaluate an application (representing a maximum cost-benefit ratio, see Nielsen (1994)). As a result of the heterogeneous user group we must now consider how to involve more users in the evaluations without having the amount of needed resources explode.

But just as the use of Internet applications present usability specialists with new challenges, the Internet also provides opportunities in collecting usability data. In this paper we discuss the use of a remote testing technique as an important element in a user-centred approach to Web design and as a cost-effective method for collecting use data. We suggest that when used in connection with other user-centred design techniques it offers easy access to vast amounts of use data and provides a way to address problems that might otherwise have been overlooked as a consequence of heterogeneous use. The most insistent problem with the suggested remote testing techniques concerns data analysis. We suggest a simple way to represent data graphically, thus supporting the process of analysis.

1.1 What Is Remote Usability Testing?

In general terms remote usability testing can be defined as usability evaluation:

[†]The subtitle is a paraphrase of a paper by Morten Kyng (1988a; 1988b) in which he coined the phrase "designing for a dollar a day" in connection with a discussion of the use of mock-ups in cooperative design processes.

"wherein the evaluator, performing observation and analysis, is separated in space and/or time from the user" (Hartson et al., 1996, p.228).

Remote usability testing can be carried out in a variety of ways each of which have different advantages and disadvantages. Examples of remote usability techniques are: remote questionnaire or survey, collaborative remote evaluation, video-conferencing-supported evaluation, instrumented/automated data collection for remote evaluation (Fuller & de Graff, 1996; Hilbert & Redmiles, 1998a) and the user-reported critical incident method (Hartson & Castillo, 1998). All of these methods adhere to the definition of remote testing since the network is used as an extension of the usability lab (Hartson et al., 1996).

All these techniques can be classified according to what kind of feedback is gathered: direct feedback or indirect feedback (Hilbert & Redmiles, 1998b).

Direct feedback is gathered directly from users subjective reports. The key advantage of this kind of feedback is its ability to capture the users needs, desires, thoughts and subjective experiences. A problem with direct feedback is that it can be problematic to contextualize the feedback in regards to what the user have done previously.

In contrast, indirect feedback is gathered by observing the user interacting with the application. The observer can both be persons or a computer collecting data. The reason for using indirect feedback is its ability to capture 'objective' information about the behaviour of user and application. The limitations of this kind of feedback is its lack of ability to capture the users thoughts and other subjective experiences.

2 The Case of KMD-Portal

Of 275 Danish municipalities only about half have their own Web sites and only about 10% have sites at a high level of ambition incorporating discrete applications. But as Danes rush to the Internet, so does the demand for more Web service from the public sector. To reduce the need for maintenance and to provide a skeleton for discrete Web applications, that enables citizens to retrieve all kinds of public information, the construction of a Web portal to the public sector began at Kommunedata.* The portal integrates public information from several sources because citizens do not really bother whether the information source is local, regional or national, as long as they get valid information quickly and

with minimal effort. Today the portal encompasses information from all levels of administration, from a municipal kindergarten to the office of the Prime Minister, including the cooperation of the National Association of Local Authorities and the Danish State Information Service. This huge body of information raised the question whether any given user would be able to find relevant information, and how the information should be organized to support information retrieval by any Danish citizen.

Since the target group of the portal is very wide and heterogeneous, the designers should consider users with all sorts of experience with the domain of public administration, for instance persons buying their first house with little idea of the real-estate legislation or the specific regulations concerning their neighbourhood etc., or persons with a vaguely defined wish to apply for a grant for some purpose. This implies that the structure and the terms of the portal must be directed at novices as well as persons with a clear picture of what they want, and of what this service is called at the city hall and maybe even which office handles it. Also, the portal addresses users with very different demographic profiles. In short, we not only faced the problem of understanding the users' mental model (Norman, 1986) but rather several user models of public information retrieval. These user models should be seen in relation to the design model initially implemented in the system as well as the official structure and semantics of Danish municipals. Our goal was to design the information architecture to fit all the user groups/use situations as a boundary object (Star & Griesemer, 1989). This means that the information architecture should be:

"both plastic enough to adapt to local needs and constraints of the several parties employing them, yet robust enough to maintain a common identity across sites" (Star & Griesemer, 1989, p.393).

The portal encompasses four navigational structures for more than 1,000 public information items (see Figure 1).

The structure is a hierarchy shown as a tree of folders containing sub-folders and documents containing the information. This entrance to the portal supports 'the clicking user' — the one who moves around via the hypertext-links that she or he sees. Other entrances support search ('type the subject here and hit the go-button'), organization, displaying the

---

*Kommunedata is the largest supplier of software for the public sector in Denmark. The name is often abbreviated KMD.

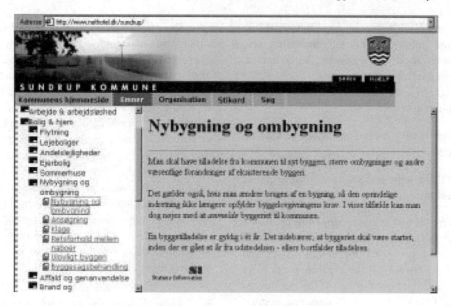

Figure 1: An example from KMD-Portal.

full administrative structure to the benefit of users familiar with that, and an index with an alphabetical list of selected key-words to choose from. As we wanted to learn from the users how well the information was structured only the first-mentioned entrance was available in the prototype, forcing users to relate to the information architecture itself.

3 Field Work and Card Sorting

We applied various methods to reach our goal of producing a flexible information architecture. We started out by conducting field studies in three municipalities with different demographic conditions (respectively metropolitan, urban province, and rural). In order to explore the physical surroundings built and designed to facilitate contact between citizens and the municipality we went to city hall, to the municipal information booth on the city hall square, to a public library, and to the place where telephone calls to the municipality are distributed to the appropriate administrators. We interviewed the employees on the nature of the inquiries:

- How well do citizens articulate their claims?

- What are the most common questions and requests?

- Are the citizens aware of the organizational structure of the municipality?

Also, we collected artefacts to be used in forthcoming workshops and 'recruited' citizens to join the workshops.

Following the field work, workshops were held in the three municipalities. Citizens organized information items (tasks, requests, problems etc.) by placing Post-Its on posters and consequently organizing them according to their own sense of how things were related. The information items were gathered from the citizens own personal experience from interacting with public authorities on different occasions. The workshops gave us concrete ideas to work with and we found typical ways of structuring information between citizens from the three municipals. Knowledge gained in this process was fed directly into the design.

4 Remote Usability Technique

At this point we began to test and evaluate the information architecture that had been produced. Considering the heterogeneity of user profiles and use situations we decided to use the net itself as an extension of the usability lab.

Our intention was to combine automated data collection with some of the principles of the user-reported critical incident method (Hartson & Castillo, 1998). This way we hoped to support both direct feedback from users based on their subjective reports and indirect feedback by capturing detailed 'objective' information about sequences of interaction between user and system. In themselves both techniques pose problems, but by combining the two sorts of feed-back, the intention was to connect specific instances of interaction with subjective reports, thus enabling us to make not only temporal inferences but also causal inferences about user–system interaction in connection with specific tasks.

Accordingly, in the remote usability test we collected data in two ways:

1. We automatically logged the users actions on the Web site.

2. We had them write a diary upon completion of each session.

The actions were logged in connection with the user's carrying out specific tasks[†]which were sent to them once a week for a period of one month. Over that month we had each of the 24 participating users carry out 15 tasks resulting in a maximum of 360 sequences of interaction. One of the authors designed a small software tool to log the users actions on the Web site. The result of each sequence of interaction was a list of nodes that the user had clicked in order to carry out the task.

An often used component of log-data is time-stamps which is used for calculating user motivation and other calculations of time spent working on a task/project. Fuller & de Graff (1996) addressed some technical problems concerning the credibility of time-stamps in server log files, but a more fundamental problem concerns the reliability of them. In our case we had no control of the environment that people were in when they were carrying out the tasks. This way we have no way of knowing when they were distracted or doing other things not related to carrying out the task in spite of the fact that 'the clock is ticking'. Thus, we decided against using time-stamps as a measure of Web site usability. Instead, we prioritised qualitative comments from users during and after the process. In the diary, which was made available directly from the Web site, the users were encouraged to write down first impressions, perception of problems, reflections, thoughts and suggestions in relation to the structure and semantics of the information architecture. In this sense the diary was different from a remote user survey, in that we did not ask people to answer specific questions, but rather to formulate, in their own words, how they experienced interacting with the Web site. This was a very valuable contribution to the sequences of interaction produced from log data. It was problematic, though, that it was obviously difficult for the users to abstract from the concrete graphical design of the Web site and focus exclusively on the information architecture.

The largest problem we faced had to do with structuring and analysing the data we received, particularly in connection with the automated log-data. The software returned the addresses of user movement, thus providing us with several pages of Web site addresses to be deciphered, understood, analysed and interpreted. While data collection had proved fairly cost-effective, the process of analysing data consumed most of the man hours spent on our remote testing technique. This is not unusual when working with qualitative data, but it seems to us that the analysis of the log data could be supported more efficiently methodologically and perhaps technically. Therefore, we generated a way to represent data in a more supportive way hoping to make the process of analysis more effective.

5   Use Case Signatures: A Graphical Representation of Data

In order to support the process of analysing data from our remote tests we used a simple graphical representation of data inspired by the use of narrative methods in qualitative research. The aim of introducing this method is to keep expenses down by providing analysts with an easy-to-apply tool for analysing data and to provide a tool for representing data in a systematic and illustrative way. One of the authors has worked on projects in the health care sector in which a narrative method was used to support the analysis and presentation of qualitative data (Elsass et al., 1994; Elsass, 1997). The intention of using a narrative method in these projects was to prioritise the phenomenological aspects of actors' experience as opposed to the more formal efficacy studies focusing on measuring an effect of a specific therapeutic intervention and to support the analysis and presentation of qualitative data. Once data are scored, they can be represented graphically in a so called narrative signature. A narrative signature consists of lines drawn between categories identified in the text reflecting not only what the narrator talks about but the structure of the story.

A narrative signature, made out of several narratives, gives the analyst an opportunity to "see at a glimpse" what is typical and what is atypical about the actors' narratives and to compare narrative signatures between several groups distinguished either by certain categories (such as gender or occupation) or distinguished through a cluster analysis.

[†]The tasks were represented as small scenarios (Bødker, 1999).

In the context of the present case-study we are inspired by the narrative method only as far as to a graphical representation of narratives told by actors.

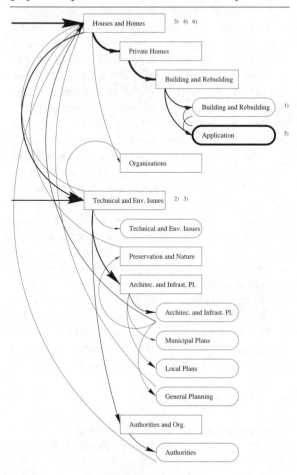

1. "I need a phone number to a person at the local authorities who I can get specific information from."

2. "It should be possible to find the answer under "Technical and Environmental Issues" since it is common known that this is where you get a building license."

3. "My opinion is that it would be most logical that the information about getting a building license would be to find under "Technical and Environmental Issues" or alternatively under "Houses and Homes"."

4. "First I looked under "Houses and Homes" but I did not think there were any logical links."

5. "I was a little surprised that I could not fill out and send the application right away."

6. "I searched under "Houses and Homes" but I did not find anything that sounded usable."

Figure 2: A use case signature including user comments representing 16 users working on a task concerning identifying necessary public information (the judicial frame, application forms, etc.) about rebuilding a private house.

We conceive each sequence of interaction produced in remote testing as a narrative (a user story) in that they are complete stories with a beginning, a plot (a task and a goal) and an end. It is possible then to represent the way that each user "tells his story", i.e. how each user solves the task at hand in the context of the information architecture. We call this graphical representation a use case signature (see Figure 2), thus referring to the signature as a model of interactions between the system and external actors related to a particular goal. The intention of the graphical representation is to focus attention on the typical problem solving strategies as opposed to individual ones and, thus, highlight how users navigate in the information structure and whether the 'system image' reflects the user model (Norman, 1986). The signature, then, reflects both how the users goal might be delivered or might fail.

The nodes of the structure (the folders) are represented as boxes and the documents containing actual information are represented as rounded boxes. From the diary we have comments about the structure and semantics of the information architecture. We collected these comments and placed references to them at the relevant folder or document. The navigation of the users is represented as arrows showing the direction of the navigation. The width of the arrow represent the number of times this movement took place, i.e. the number of users selecting this particular folder or document from a particular position. The head of the arrow is placed at the middle of the left side of the box representing the folder or document where the movement was directed towards. The start of the arrow is placed either at the bottom of the box or in the left corners. If the movement is down the structure, the start of the arrow is placed at the bottom and if the movement is towards another part of the structure, the start is placed in the left corners. Finally, we have marked the information that is supposed to be the goal of the search. In the example in Figure 2, there is only one document containing the relevant information, the document marked with a thicker box width (the one labelled "Application").

Let us take a closer look at the use case signature in Figure 2 and see what conclusions we can draw from it. One can see that approximately half the users in the test started by going to the folder "Technical and Environmental Issues". Most of them continue down the hierarchy to "Architectural and Infrastructural Planning". Here they can not find anything that can help them so they either look around 'in the dark' or go to "Houses and Homes". Some of the users who chose to start in "Houses and Homes" could not find anything in that category that could help them in their search so they moved to "Technical and Environmental Issues". Those who found out that they had to move to "Private Homes" also found the next step easy — the folder "Building and rebuilding". Then it became difficult again. Half of these people chose the document "Building and rebuilding" and the other half chose "Application" but none of them were satisfied with the information they got according to their diaries. For example, one of them expressed the need for a telephone number and went searching in other documents for this.

The analysis suggests several things concerning the information architecture. First of all, one could assume that the reason why so many users chose "Technical and Environmental Issues" is that these words remind them of the official name of the department in most Danish municipalities covering issues such as the one requested. In this particular case it suggests having relevant information (including the application form) placed in both folders ("Houses and Homes" and "Technical and Environmental Issues" instead of only "Houses and Homes") as is the case now. The most logical place following the use case signature would be in the folder "Architectural and Infrastructural Planning". Generally, reflections such as this sharpened our awareness of the official structure and semantics in Danish municipalities, which we thought the citizens were mostly unfamiliar with.

All in all, the use case signature shows potential semantic or structural problems in relation to the information architecture by focusing our attention on the typical as opposed to the individual sequences of interaction. It provides a tool for structuring and analysing data and can be automated as far as to drawing the signature from data input.

6   Increasing Our Knowledge

Although the use case signatures revealed problems with the information architecture, there were still aspects of how people used the information architecture that we did not feel we knew enough about. For example in Figure 2 there are no comments about why people used the architecture as they did beneath the folder named "Technical and Environmental Issues".

To make design suggestions based on the use case signatures alone would be a hazardous task since it would necessarily involve a lot of assumptions and presuppositions based on our own experiences and not on the users' experiences.

By automating the data collection completely we could not ask questions about topics that needed

further illumination. To fully use the potential of the collected data we felt that more communication and cooperation with the involved users was needed.

To support this communication and cooperation, we ended the entire process with a workshop with 6 users who had been actively engaged in the process from the start. In this workshop users could elaborate on some of the problems and solutions they had reported in the diary. At the end of the day, the users had not only given us answers to our questions but also contributed with design suggestions that were implemented in the final product.

The fact that the users came up with usable design suggestions may not be surprising. The users hands-on experience with a prototype continually for four weeks encouraged user involvement that goes beyond the detached reflection that is required by textual systems descriptions and supported the users understanding of the future system in a more immediate way. Notions of immediacy and practical experience are also stressed by researchers and practitioners within the Participatory Design approach. For example, Kyng (1988a; 1988b) and Ehn & Kyng (1991) note that hands-on experience in familiar situations is necessary to support reflection and design by users as well as designers in a cooperative design process.

7   Conclusion

In this paper we have discussed the relevance of using a remote usability testing technique in designing a coherent Web site information architecture. It is our experience that remote usability testing can be used as a serious usability test technique and even as a cooperative design technique, since users seem to be able to enter into constructive discussion about such questions. In our case, they not only reported problems; they suggested solutions.

While data collection was very cheap it became clear to us that in order for the technique to be usable in 'real life' usability work, the process of analysis should be supported. We suggest use case signatures as a way to represent use data and support analysis. This implies that it is possible to include a larger number of test users which is needed when addressing heterogeneous user groups. To reduce time even more it would be desirable to automate the process of drawing the use case signatures on the basis of log file data. It should be possible to develop such a program, but it has not been pursued in this project.

Besides problems with analysing huge amounts of data, the technique has obvious limitations that must be confronted. While minimal interaction between user and evaluator is considered by some to be desirable, we missed the closer relationship and the communication characterizing a usability test in a lab or in the field. The diary was a valuable contribution to the log data and helped us gather more useful data than we could have hoped to obtain by automated data collection alone. Still, the diary is a poor substitution for face-to-face communication.

It is our experience that the lesser the direct, subjective feed-back, the harder it is to make causal inferences about usability problems. Therefore, it is extremely important that users are encouraged to give subjective feed-back — not just about perceived problems but generally about the background for their choices and actions and about their wants and needs concerning the application and use-situation(s) in question. It would therefore be desirable if subjective feedback could be further supported technically and/or organizationally, e.g. by giving users the possibility to comment continually and without leaving an application. The backside of this is that it is hard to say in what ways and to what degree such a functionality influences on the use of the system in question. Therefore, it is our experience that remote testing data (whether direct or indirect) should be supplemented with face-to-face cooperative activities.

The last thing that we wish to point out regards the context of use. It is of particular importance that usability specialists can use remote testing techniques to facilitate the collection of use data collected from day-to-day use-situations in which tasks are carried out in their natural context. While the test users in our case worked from wherever and whenever they felt comfortable, the context of use is only partly 'natural' and realistic since we created the tasks to be carried out on the Web site. In order for our remote usability testing techniques to prove their worth as more than just a cheap technique addressing a potentially large and heterogeneous group of users, we must consider how the technique can be applied to support continual evaluation of Web sites and applications in their natural context(s) of use.

Acknowledgements

The work on which this paper is based was carried out as part of the BIDI project (Usability Work in Danish Industry). BIDI is sponsored by the Danish Center for IT Research through grant no 23. We wish to thank Susanne Bødker, Wendy Mackay, Olav Bertelsen, José C Castillo and the 3 anonymous reviewers for valuable comments on earlier drafts of this paper.

References

Bødker, S. (1999), Scenarios in User-centred Design — Setting the Stage for Reflection and Action, *in* R. H. Sprague, Jr. (ed.), *Proceedings of the 32nd HICSS'99*, IEEE Computer Society Press. Published as CD-ROM.

Ehn, P. & Kyng, M. (1991), Cardboard Computers: Mocking-it-up or Hands-on the Future, *in* J. Greenbaum & M. Kyng (eds.), *Design at Work: Co-operative Design of Computer Systems*, Lawrence Erlbaum Associates, pp.169–96.

Elsass, P. (1997), *Treating Victims of Torture and Violence. Theoretical, Cross-cultural and Clinical Implications*, New York University Press, New York.

Elsass, P., Rosenbaum, B., Kaasgaard, K. & Lauritsen, P. (1994), "Klientoplevelsen af Psykoterapi", *Agrippa — Psykiatriske Tekster* **15**(3-4), 145–69. (The Clients' Experience of Psychotherapy).

Fuller, R. & de Graff, J. J. (1996), Measuring User Motivation from Server Log Files, *in Proceedings of Designing for the Web: Empirical Studies*, Microsoft. http://www.microsoft.com/usability/webconf/fuller/fuller.htm.

Hartson, H. R. & Castillo, J. C. (1998), Remote Evaluation for Post-deployment Usability Improvement, *in* T. Catarci, M. F. Costabile, G. Santucci & L. Tarantino (eds.), *Proceedings of the Conference on Advanced Visual Interface (AVI'98)*, ACM Press, pp.22–9.

Hartson, R., Castillo, J., Kelso, J., Kamler, J. & Neale, W. (1996), Remote Evaluation: The Network as an Extension of the Usability Laboratory, *in* G. van der Veer & B. Nardi (eds.), *Proceedings of CHI'96: Human Factors in Computing Systems*, ACM Press, pp.228–35.

Hilbert, D. M. & Redmiles, D. F. (1998a), An Approach to Large-scale Collection of Application Usage over the Internet, *in* K. Torii (ed.), *Proceedings of the the 20th International Conference on Software Engineering*, IEEE Computer Society Press.

Hilbert, D. M. & Redmiles, D. F. (1998b), Separating the Wheat from the Chaff in Internet-mediated User Feedback, *in* M. Divitini, B. A. Farshchian & T. Tuikka (eds.), *Proceedings of the Workshop on Internet-based Groupware for User Participation in Product Development*. http://www.idi.ntnu.no/~igroup/proceedings/.

Kyng, M. (1988a), "Designing for a Dollar a Day", *Office, Technology and People* **4**(2), 157–70.

Kyng, M. (1988b), Designing for a Dollar a Day, *in* D. G. Tatar (ed.), *Proceedings of CSCW'88: Conference on Computer Supported Cooperative Work*, ACM Press, pp.178–88.

Nielsen, J. (1994), Guerrilla HCI: Using Discount Usability Engineering to Penetrate the Intimidation Barrier, *in* R. G. Bias & D. J. Mayhew (eds.), *Cost-Justifying Usability*, Academic Press, chapter 11.

Norman, D. A. (1986), Cognitive Engineering, *in* D. A. Norman & S. W. Draper (eds.), *User Centered Systems Design: New Perspectives on Human–Computer Interaction*, Lawrence Erlbaum Associates, pp.31–62.

Star, S. L. & Griesemer, J. R. (1989), "Institutional Ecology, 'Translations' and Boundary Objects: Amateurs and Professionals in Berkeley's Museum of Vertebrate Zoology", *Social Studies of Science* **19**, 387–420.

Human–Computer Interaction — INTERACT '99
M. Angela Sasse and Chris Johnson (Editors)
Published by IOS Press, © IFIP TC.13, 1999

On Not Being There: Watching Intranet Tele-presentations

Ben Anderson

ACR, BT Laboratories, Ipswich, Suffolk IP5 3RE, UK.

ben.anderson@bt.com

Abstract: This paper describes preliminary results from an experimental trial of Intranet tele-presentations — the provision of broadcast television quality corporate audio/video communications to the desktop via an IP based intranet. It reports empirical data on usage patterns of specific events such as seminars, lectures and internal briefings. The paper uses this data to examine patterns of use, to explain users' reported experiences and to illustrate the ways in which people use the apparently 'suboptimal' features of tele-presentation systems to their own advantage. The implications for the design of tele-presentation systems are discussed.

Keywords: video, tele-presentation, usage patterns, intranet.

1 Introduction

Following the success of the Internet multi-cast backbone (MBone) experiments in demonstrating the potential for audio/video tele-presentation over IP networks (Macedonia & Brutzman, 1994), there has been a growing interest in providing such services to the desktops of an organization's workforce via corporate intranets. Proponents of these services focus on the scope for low-cost, convenient, live and 'on-demand' access to corporate briefings, events, seminars and educational resources.

In this context a number of large organizations who currently use internal satellite or cable TV channels for these purposes are considering or trialing a switch to internet protocol (IP) based solutions. Here employees view 'broadcasts' not in specially equipped rooms but on standard PCs at their desks or, in some cases, on the move. To date, these kinds of systems have received less attention in the literature than have studies exploring the use of high bandwidth audio/video to support group working (Finn et al., 1997).

In order to improve our understanding of how tele-presentation services might be engineered, supported and used we have conducted a number of experimental trials of network and end-user client technologies that provide broadcast TV quality audio and video to the desktop PC. In doing so the historically problematic issues of bandwidth constraints and network performance have largely been eliminated as factors affecting the user's perception of the utility of the services.

2 Related Work

Whilst there has been significant work devoted to understanding the place of multimedia telecommunication in closely collaborative situations (Finn et al., 1997), there has been less effort devoted to studying its use in tele-presentation.

In a comparative study of remote and face-to-face presentations, Isaacs et al. (1995) found that distributed presentations could effectively convey information to large groups who might not otherwise have attended. Their recommendations for improving the design focus very firmly on improving audience feedback through video or audio channels and on the use of a combined co-present/remote audience to improve the presenter's experience. In such an event they suggest that careful thought needs to be given to integrating the two audiences to prevent the remote ones from feeling less involved. The system used in their study, Forum, leads them to conclude that:

> "A distributed environment can provide adequate support for asking and answering questions, but it is not ideal for encouraging active audience participation or providing fine-grained feedback from the audience." (Isaacs et al., 1994, p.361)

but that:

> "With improved technology and designs, audience interaction will become easier and more natural ..." (Isaacs et al., 1994, p.361)

In an earlier study of this same system, Isaacs et al. (1994) note that many people made use of their remoteness to engage in activities such as reading email or talking to visitors which would have been considered rude in a co-present audience.

In a more technologically oriented report on their own experiences Gemmell & Bell (1997) note that providing back-channels (i.e. channels from the remote audience to the presenter) is not only technically difficult but may not be important for very large audiences, a figure they suggest to be 50 or more. In addition they note that some presenters may find the lack of back-channels an improvement.

The study reported in this paper was intended to further explore the significance of back-channels and context specific social pressures in affecting audience participation and behaviour during tele-presentations.

3   Study Details

This study took as its starting point Isaacs et al. (1994) recommendation for a mixed co-present and remote audience. It concentrated on tele-presentations which were made to a local audience but which were also viewed by remote audiences both at their desks and in groups at public PCs. The presentations themselves were part of a wider experimental trial of broadband multi-cast services which included replay of recorded lectures and continuous TV channels.

3.1   Intranet-TV Infrastructure

The experiments were run over BT Laboratories' 'Futures Testbed' IP multi-cast network. This network uses IP over ATM to provide high bandwidth connectivity (10Mb/s standard, 100Mb/s common) to desktop PCs. It is therefore a production network seeing 'real use' as well as a testbed for experimentation with high bandwidth services.

The trials discussed in this paper used a commercial implementation of the MPEG and H.261 encoding standards specifically engineered to send and receive real time data over IP multi-cast networks using the Internet Engineering Task Force's (IETF) RTP transport protocol. Whilst IP multi-cast can in principle enable any participant to send data streams to any other, this implementation followed the 'TV broadcast' metaphor by physically separating the source of the media streams (*server*) from the viewer (*client*).

The server required a high end Win95/NT PC and could encode audio and video from a capture card as well as an on-screen window. It was therefore possible to send audio/video of a presenter as well as their slides if using a PC-based presentation tool. In general

the server used hardware assisted MPEG encoding for the audio and video but uses H.261 for the presenter's slides.

For the purposes of these trials, a number of lecture/seminar rooms were equipped with servers. Each server was then the dedicated source for a particular 'channel'. Channels were announced and managed using a modified World Wide Web server to which clients periodically connect in order to refresh their channel listings. Events were also announced via a trial mailing list.

Reception and viewing of the streams required only a software client and a moderately fast PC to produce a full screen frame rate of up to 25 frames per second together with TV quality audio. As mentioned above the software model assumed that there need be little or no audience participation and so did not allow remote participants to send audio or video.

3.2   Usage Contexts

The existence of the trial was announced to the Advanced Research Group at BT Laboratories — a population of some 300 professional research scientists. The trial users self-selected by joining an email list and installing the multi-cast client. The total number of people who used the services during the trial was 51 and they represented a variety of organizational positions from research managers to intern students.

A range of live events was multi-cast during the trial including internal research briefings, personnel briefings and lectures. In each case it was possible for users to attend these events either physically or remotely using the system. The coverage of these events was announced by email to the entire ART department.

In addition a number of 'public PCs' were set up within a number of work and 'social' spaces. These PCs were configured to receive particular events and provided the opportunity to explore users' behaviour when watching remotely in a group.

3.3   Data Capture Methods

In order to gain a rich picture of user behaviour and attitudes towards the trial services, three data collection techniques were employed.

3.3.1   Network Activity

Network activity was captured using a modified version of the MBone audio tool VAT (McCanne & Jacobson, 1996). As a reference implementation of the RTP protocol VAT can be used to monitor RTP traffic on a particular channel being multi-cast by the commercial client/server solution used in the trial. The

RTP protocol contains a control component (RTCP) which circulates information on client activity to all other clients (and the server) that are 'tuned in' to that multi-cast channel. VAT can therefore be modified to output detailed network related data and, as a side effect, certain kinds of user behaviour because RTCP passes information about clients joining and leaving particular channels. Thus data such as the identity and number of clients active every t seconds can be logged and user behaviour can be inferred.

3.3.2 Observations

In order to provide a baseline for comparisons human activity at both the 'public PC' and audiences physically present at briefings was captured using standard behavioural observation techniques. The activity of each participant was logged on a time-line and notes made on the extent of side conversations and any other potentially relevant activities.

3.3.3 Interviews

A random selection of the users logged during network data capture was invited to take part in a semi-structured interview.

The results from these interviews captured views of not only the specific events or services for which behavioural data was captured, but also various other seminars and lectures which were multi-cast during the trial period.

Initially twenty users were selected but only eleven interviews were completed. As a result the data are used to try to make sense of the activity captured by the network data logging rather than as a source of statistically valid inferences.

4 Analysis of Results

The three methods described above generated a wealth of usage and experiential data which is reported in a more complete form elsewhere (Anderson, 1999). The analysis presented here uses selected elements of this to illustrate a number of themes that have become apparent from the data as a whole.

4.1 Reasons for Use

A general picture emerged of users who had initially used the system out of curiosity, had continued to access it fairly frequently for a week or two, and now used it more selectively to access briefings, seminars and lectures. The limited availability of such material was a key reason for declining usage, but also nearly half of those interviewed said that they rarely used the system at the time of interview because they had only ever wanted to assess it as a technology. This underlines the need to adopt lengthy time-scales in

assessing the usage levels of novel facilities in a user population of this nature.

The interviews suggested a clear and consistent preference for business-related material. Lectures and seminars were most often cited as the most useful material (7 of 11), with internal briefings and BT Vision (BT's internal TV channel) the only other content rated as 'most useful'. The interviews also suggested that the availability of this informative content was the main determinant of access patterns, although some did occasionally access the continuously available news and music channels.

Only two of the interviewees reported regular and frequent use of the latter and they tended to use it as entertainment during tea breaks and lunch times. Most users denied using it as 'background', and those who did use it in this way said that they did so occasionally and for short periods, often in order to demonstrate the technology to visitors.

This self-reported view is supported by the network activity data. As an example, Figure 1 shows the number of clients accessing a continuous music channel during a two-week period in which a departmental briefing was also multi-cast. Clearly the general usage of the permanently available MTV channel is relatively low but continuous compared to usage of the briefing which is, as would be expected, both much briefer and much higher.

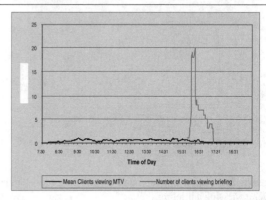

Figure 1: Mean number of clients viewing MTV at particular times of the day (over 14 days) compared with the number watching a briefing on one afternoon in the same period.

The interviews suggested that people who used the system to 'attend' live events such as briefings would have, or might have attended *some* of the events in person had the tele-presentation system not been available. As might be expected users offered, in decreasing order of importance, convenience, time-saving, selectivity (the ability to sample an event to determine its relevance), multitasking and monitoring (only attending to relevant parts) as reasons for using the system.

4.2   Social Rules in Tele-presentations

Our observations of audiences that are physically co-present with the presenter suggests that in these instances, and in the organizational context concerned, people rarely leave before the presenter has finished. If they do so they make use of 'natural pauses' such as breaks between presenters or the opening up of the presentation to audience questions. This is not to say, of course, that all those present are fully attentive. Audience members doodle or give their attention to papers they have brought with them whilst peripherally monitoring the presentation. In addition whilst members do indulge in short whispered asides or brief conversations these rarely continue for long. Thus the cultural rules of what it is polite and impolite to do as an audience member of a presentation tend to keep people there, and keep them quiet.

In the case of the remote audiences however this is not the case. Figures 2 & 3 shows not only the number of people (at the public PC) and number of clients viewing a briefing remotely but also the churn rate — the number of people leaving or joining each group.

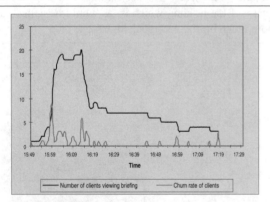

Figure 2: Comparison of number and churn of remote clients viewing a briefing.

The strong relationship between churn and the number of viewers/clients for either group is to be expected. However the data also demonstrates that their apparent relative stability at various times is a false representation (Anderson, 1999). In reality, the membership of the groups is continually changing.

Remote audience members repeatedly left and re-joined the group and this was particularly true of the group gathered around a public PC. Individuals left the group if the content appeared uninteresting and continued with background tasks whilst monitoring the event. Audience members had conversations about

the briefing presentations and frequently brought drinks or food to consume whilst watching. None of these activities were thought to be 'rude' by the other members of the watching group nor, of course, by the presenters who couldn't know what any of the remote audience were doing. Thus we can confirm the finding that remote audiences did not appear to find themselves subject to the same social pressures as those who were physically present (Isaacs et al., 1994).

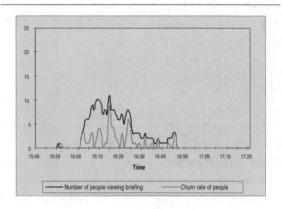

Figure 3: Comparison of number and churn of remote clients viewing a briefing at a public PC.

Discussions with participants in these studies suggest that this has both advantages and disadvantages. When the lack of social pressure does allow people to 'switch off' they can miss presentations that they may have found interesting had they actually stayed and listened as would have been the case if they had been there in person and not felt able to leave. Conversely the ability to leave a dull or irrelevant presentation was seen as an advantage. The ability to hold side conversations when viewing remotely together was thought of as both good and bad in that it can be stimulating but also distracting and noisy for those who are trying to attend to the briefing.

4.3   Selectivity and Serendipity

The ability to be selective in what to view combined with the social mores discussed above provided two advantages.

Firstly the system makes it possible to peripherally monitor an ongoing event whilst the user proceeds with background work or other tasks. Not only is this made clear by the interviews but also by the observational studies of the usage of the 'public PC'. In the latter case a number of people whose desks were close to the group watching the event remotely were monitoring the content, speaker and local audience reaction whilst working at their desks. In a number of cases they came back to watch the event for a short period of time when something 'of interest' seemed to be happening.

This 'TV' as 'Radio' highlights a major difference between attending the briefing in person and watching it using the system — people can peripherally monitor the media streams whilst continuing with their work, dealing with calls, whilst having conversations about the briefing presentations or whilst enjoying a coffee break. As discussed in Section 4.2 none of these activities were deemed to be rude by other members of the watching group.

Secondly, users reported that they viewed some events that they would *not* have gone to in person. In these instances the ability to leave an event unobserved enabled them to sample technical seminars in areas outside their usual field. Interviewees said they would not have attended these events in person because they felt the probability of finding the content relevant to them was not high enough to justify devoting a whole hour to it. However they were prepared to invest 10 minutes via the system to find out if it was worth attending any further.

4.4 Watching Together vs. Watching Alone

The data also suggest differences between watching remotely together and watching remotely alone. For example Figure 4 shows that in general people appeared to watch at the public PC for less time in total than did people apparently watching alone.* Whilst not represented above, the data show that almost 50% of people watched the presentation at the public PC for less than four minutes in total. In conjunction with churn data, which indicate people repeatedly joining and leaving the group, the public PC is dominated by users who briefly stop to watch as they pass by, together with a small group who watched for some time.

It is possible that their mutual awareness then caused a crowd to congregate independently of the actual content of the broadcast. As people noticed the crowd, they joined it and either continued to watch or, after some time, left the group to return to their previous activities.

In contrast, the desktop users have no notion of crowd — they have no idea who else is watching and as a result appear to attend to the briefing in a very different way. Since there is no interference from crowd-forming effects, it may be that the pattern of activity more accurately mirrors the different presentation stages of the event — numbers of active

clients drop each time the two main speakers finish at around 16:19 and 16:45 respectively (see Figure 2). The remaining clients then stay active until the briefing ends although a few continue beyond this suggesting that they are not being attended to at all.

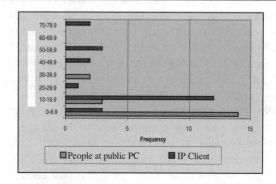

Figure 4: Frequency of total time clients and people at public PC were 'watching'.

5 Conclusions

This paper has described a number of themes emerging from some preliminary studies of Intranet tele-presentations.

Given that the trial is very much at early stages in terms of service maturity and content provision we would expect to find that usage was dominated by the novelty effect of the technology. We would expect this to be compounded by the fact that the user population is by nature professionally interested in the technology rather than what the technology is conveying. Whilst the interview data confirm that this is indeed the case, we have started to see a maturity in usage with users switching from initial 'channel-hopping' to more focused use when a briefing or particular lecture is being multi-cast. It remains for future studies to capture network activity data over a significant time-frame in order to provide more extensive data on these patterns.

It seems that some people use the system as 'radio'. They will peripherally monitor an event, briefing or lecture until something relevant or interesting appears at which point they will switch attention back to it. Although this has advantages for the listener, the subtle difference of this method of participation should not be overlooked because it may imply that a presentation devised for and given to a live co-present audience will not have the same effect on a remote partially attentive participant. It is currently unclear what these differences are and how

---

*Noting that this data cannot determine whether an IP client's user was actually watching at any point.

remote 'tele-presenters' can tailor their presentations to suit these situations other than addressing obvious problems such as not walking out of camera shot. A systematic set of comparative studies would be necessary to explore these issues.

The ways in which remote attendees behave causes us to doubt that true 'tele-presence' would be *necessarily* attractive to members of remote audiences. To be 'tele-present' would expose the remote participants to the social mores of the physical event. This in turn may remove the very reasons for watching remotely by preventing the kinds of behaviour patterns observed in this trial.

This point has implications for the design of tele-presentation systems because although it is well known that the physical presence or visual availability of even a small audience is crucial to an effective presentation this does not necessarily apply to all or any of the remote attendees. On the other hand there are likely to be cases where the remote attendees want to be visible not only to the presenter but also to the audience to show that they *are* watching and are attending. In what contexts this is so is unclear but it appears that tele-presentation systems will need to be far more flexible than is currently the case because some remote attendees will want to be seen and some won't at different times and in different situations.

Rather than *tele-presence*, it may therefore be more fruitful to explore support for graded *semi-presence* so that users may choose to remain anonymous, to be seen to be present or somewhere between the two. It may also be that control of degrees of presence is better placed under user control because their need or wish to be present is likely to be highly context sensitive and thus impossible to predict.

This view is consistent with the findings from recent studies of the long-term use of multimedia telecommunications services as part of an office media space (Dourish et al., 1996). In contrast to the commonly voiced assumption that 'as good as being there' technologies should be the optimal design goal, Dourish et al. illustrate the importance of new interaction practices that the technological make-up of the media space enables. Thus sets of practices tailored to the nature of the medium evolve over time as people come to see and use the new interaction possibilities that the system provides.

This kind of adaptation of unintentional[†] technological features by users to their own advantage is known to be crucial to understanding the usage patterns of information and communication technologies (Robinson, 1993).

If this concept were applied to technologies for tele-presentation it would predict that audiences would use the lack of back channels to their own advantage in exactly the ways reported in this paper. Thus an apparently 'non-optimal' system might provide a better experience to one which enables audience and presenter to interact as if they were co-present. It also leads to the suggestion that remote and co-present audiences might be better viewed as distinct entities with different goals and needs.

To conclude, the studies reported in this paper confirm the utility of tele-presentation system to reach audiences who might not otherwise have attended (Isaacs et al., 1994; 1995). Given that serendipitous relationships between subject areas are a known source of innovation (Brown, 1997) this phenomenon is of particular significance in research and development activities.

The studies also provide some evidence for Gemmel & Bell's contention that back-channels to enable audience participation may not be desired by the remote audience in some contexts.

Finally the studies suggest that a conceptualization of tele-presentation systems purely in terms of improving the remote audience's perception of being 'tele-present' over-simplifies the way in which remote audiences use tele-presentation systems so that the advantages of being *semi-present* are masked.

Acknowledgements

Celia Miller conducted and analysed the results from the interviews as well as providing many useful comments on early drafts of this paper. Uma Kulkarni and Margarida Correira created and supported the Intranet Tele-presentations trial. BT's Advanced Research and Technology Department provided the setting, the infrastructure, the content and the users.

References

Anderson, B. (1999), As We May Watch: Preliminary Studies of Intranet Telepresentations, *in* L. Elstrom (ed.), *Proceedings of HFT 1999*, TeleDanmark, pp.133–41.

Brown, J. S. (1997), Rethinking Innovation in a Changing World, *in* J. Seeley Brown (ed.), *Seeing Differently: Insights on Innovation*, Harvard Business School Publishing, pp.5–12.

Dourish, P., Adler, A., Bellotti, V. & Henderson, A. (1996), "Your Place or Mine?   Learning from Long-term

---

[†] In the sense that they were not explicitly 'designed in'.

Use of Audio–Video Communication", *Computer Supported Cooperative Work* **5**(1), 33–62.

Finn, K. E., Sellen, A. J. & Wilbur, S. B. (eds.) (1997), *Video-mediated Communication*, Lawrence Erlbaum Associates.

Gemmell, D. J. & Bell, C. G. (1997), "Non-collaborative Telepresentations Come of Age", *Communications of the ACM* **40**(4), 79–89.

Isaacs, E. A., Morris, T. & Rodriguez, T. K. (1994), A Forum for Supporting Interactive Presentations to Distributed Audiences, *in* R. Furuta & C. Neuwirth (eds.), *Proceedings of CSCW'94: Conference on Computer Supported Cooperative Work*, ACM Press, pp.405–16.

Isaacs, E. A., Morris, T., Rodriguez, T. K. & Tang, J. C. (1995), A Comparison of Face-To-Face and Distributed Presentations, *in* I. Katz, R. Mack, L. Marks, M. B. Rosson & J. Nielsen (eds.), *Proceedings of CHI'95: Human Factors in Computing Systems*, ACM Press, pp.354–61.

Macedonia, M. R. & Brutzman, D. P. (1994), "MBone Provides Audio and Video Across the Internet", *IEEE Computer* **27**(4), 30–6.

McCanne, S. & Jacobson, V. (1996), "vat — LBNL Audio Conferencing Tool". http://www-nrg.ee.lbl.gov/vat/.

Robinson, M. (1993), Designing for Unanticipated Use, *in* G. de Michelis, C. Simone & K. Schmidt (eds.), *Proceedings of ECSCW'93, the 3rd European Conference on Computer-Supported Cooperative Work*, Kluwer, pp.187–202.

Human–Computer Interaction — INTERACT '99
M. Angela Sasse and Chris Johnson (Editors)
Published by IOS Press, © IFIP TC.13, 1999

Being in Public and Reciprocity:
Design for Portholes and User Preference

Andreas Girgensohn[1], Alison Lee[2] & Thea Turner[3]

[1] FX Palo Alto Laboratory, Palo Alto, CA 94304, USA.
[2] IBM Research, Hawthorne, NY 10532, USA.
[3] Motorola, Schaumburg, IL 60196, USA.

andreasg@pal.xerox.com, alisonl@us.ibm.com, thea@acm.org

Abstract: We found that Portholes users want to know about being in public, who can see them (audience) and who is looking at them (lookback). We developed one 2D and two 3D theatre layouts of the display and different amounts of audience information to address these concerns. Different layout sections display core and non-core team members and lookback information. A survey of and a preferences experiment with 28 first-time users revealed two key results. First, there was a strong preference against the use of blue rectangles for audience information but preferences varied on the amount of detail. Second, layout preferences matter but were varied.

Keywords: audience, awareness, cluster, lookback, place, portholes, preference, public, reciprocity, usability, unfolding, video, visualization, World Wide Web.

1 Introduction

As we become better connected by communication networks, geographically-distributed individuals and groups are using mediated communication technologies (e.g. video-conferencing) to support work collaborations. Group and collaboration *awareness* tools (Cool et al., 1992; Narine et al., 1997; Tang & Rua, 1994) have been proposed for enabling non-co-located people to be aware of their coworkers and of the potential for collaboration. They largely use video images as the information kernel for awareness. *Portholes* is one flavour of such a tool that provides an integrative view of one's community through a matrix of still video images. These images are snapped periodically (e.g. every 5 minutes) and updated automatically. As a result, users can get a background and peripheral sense of co-workers and their activities.

Over a three year period, we developed, and deployed a Web-based version of this tool within NYNEX (Lee et al., 1997). The objective was to explore how it improves communication and facilitates a shared understanding among distributed development groups. We chose this tool because of the positive experiences at Xerox with using Polyscope and Portholes (Borning & Travers, 1991; Dourish

& Bly, 1992). However, despite our efforts to involve users throughout and to make it accessible and useful, it was difficult to gain adoption by all users or to recruit new groups. In discussions with people ambivalent about this tool, we found at least two design limitations:

- Sense of being in public — cues about being in public that help users frame their behaviour.

- Reciprocity — information about who can see a user and who is currently looking at the user.

The next section elaborates on the two limitations. The third section proposes a redesign of the Portholes display to include critical information along with the rationale. The fourth and fifth sections describe a preference experiment and results exploring users' initial impressions which have been so critical in influencing their adoption of the tool. The last section discusses the implications of this study on not only Portholes but other communication tools.

2 Portholes Limitations

2.1 Sense of Being in Public

In an effort to lower the barriers to communication and collaboration posed by physical distance, awareness tools have created new channels of access to distant co-workers. However, these channels have brought many formerly private and public situations found in a person's office into a new unitary public setting (Meyrowitz, 1985). This blurring of public and private situations changes their structure and reveals information once exchanged only among people under each other's direct observation. That is, Portholes users have gained a 'sidestage' view into their co-workers' offices. Meyrowitz (1985) suggests that when new electronic media widens the on-stage (public) region onto the backstage (private) region, a new 'middle region' is formed which leads to new social behaviours.

While the effect of Portholes has been to make offices more public, many who used it are uncertain whether this places them in a public forum. The image matrix display did not clarify their concerns (e.g. Figure 1). If anything, some drew an incorrect association between the layout and a security-monitor setup. This resulted in negative impressions that amplified rather than clarified their concerns about surveillance and privacy.

Such uneasiness supports Meyrowitz' argument that electronic media has "undermined the traditional relationship between physical setting and social situation". People no longer seem to 'know their place' because "they no longer have a place in the traditional sense of a set of behaviours matched to physical locations and the audiences found in them". Similarly, Portholes users do not know that they are in a public place and feel disembodied from the context of interaction (Bellotti & Sellen, 1993; Harrison & Dourish, 1996). They are at a loss about what the interactional setting is. Such uncertainties highlight the need to make the situation, being in public, more explicit in a social interface.

2.2 Reciprocity

Users are also uneasy about the absence of information reminding them that they are in public. In the physical world, we have access to cues that other people are around when we are out in public (Bellotti & Sellen, 1993; Goffman, 1959). These cues let us regulate our behaviour accordingly. However, Portholes designs focus on making users aware of their coworkers and opportunities for collaboration but not on the reciprocal information about when and which of these people are seeing the user.

Reciprocity describes the situation where all communications are two way. If you are able to see or hear others, they can see or hear you, at the same time. It is an essential element of communication, allowing

users to monitor behaviour and to control how others perceive them (Cool et al., 1992; Tang & Rua, 1994).

Our Portholes provided reciprocity information in the form of two lists. As we began to show the system to more people, we were told that they wanted to know "the people who can view their images". In fact, they really wanted see the information not in a list but in the main display. This was contrary to most Portholes systems which used the display to present images for a user's personal work-group.

As we expanded our user base, we heard objections along the lines of "I want to know who is looking at me". We initially misunderstood these comments and thought that they simply did not know about the second list; the people who selected the user's image in their own Portholes display. In actual fact, they wanted to know who was looking at them NOW! In effect, as an electronic analogue of looking in through co-worker's offices, it has lost an important but subtle reciprocity property; letting the observed know who is looking in.

This feedback highlights the need to prominently display two pieces of reciprocity information:

- Audience — people who can see a user's image.

- Lookback — people looking at a user's image.

3   New Portholes Design

Harrison & Dourish (1996) suggested that a meaningful location can be useful to frame behaviour. They argued that the notion of a place is in fact based on a cultural and social understanding of the behaviour and actions appropriate to the space. This idea that 'we act in a place' is not unlike Goffman's (1959) view that a setting and an audience shape people's behaviour in public situations. However, this should not be confused with the notion that the physical setting is a large determinant of behaviour (Meyrowitz, 1985). It is the social information (i.e. being in public, audience, lookback) that can be perceived within the setting, its access and its flow within the setting that determines the nature of the interaction.

Building on the notion of a place to frame behaviour (Harrison & Dourish, 1996) and in particular the theatre (Goffman, 1959), our screen layout recreates a theatre setting. This setting is a metaphor for a public forum and conveys a sense of being in public. People are familiar with it and what it represents. Also, this setting provides a context for the situation and the placement of certain social information. The theatre's various regions contain the audience and look-back reciprocity cues that other people are present and looking in. The combination of the theatre setting and reciprocity cues addresses the two primary user concerns. They remind users that they are in a public setting with an attendant audience and this helps them frame their behaviour accordingly (Goffman, 1959). This design blueprint was used to construct several designs that differ in two characteristics:

- Screen layout of the various regions of a theatre.

- Detail of the audience information.

Figure 1: Traditional design with pictures for non-core team at the bottom (541×525).

3.1 Screen Layout

Each user has a customized Portholes display containing a 3D presentation that places the user on stage and looking out to an audience encompassing all the Portholes users that can view the user's image (see Figures 2 & 3). The theatre metaphor makes it explicit that use of Portholes positions them in a public forum; albeit to their co-workers only. Furthermore, their view is from the stage looking out at their audience and this allows them to see how public the distribution of their images is (e.g. size of their audience) and to whom they are being distributed to.

The images in the front and back rows reflect different *audience* reciprocity information (see Figures 2 & 3). The images in the front rows include the people in a user's core work-group (i.e. images appearing in the traditional image matrix). The images in the back rows are the remaining people in a user's formal work-group (i.e. people whom the user does not consider to be in her core work-group — non-core team members). These non-core team members have access to a user's image just as the user has access to their images by virtue of being in the same formal work-group. Hence, images in the front and back rows provide the complete audience for a user's own image.

Figure 2: Theatre design with orchestra for reciprocity and blue rectangles for non-core team (601×496)

Figure 3: Theatre design with side rows for reciprocity and named rectangles for non-core team (727×447).

We explored two configurations of the theatre layout for presenting the *lookback* reciprocity information; one with images placed in an orchestra pit and the other with angled images at the sides (see Figures 2 & 3). These images represent the people in the user's work-group that are currently running Portholes and thus, looking in on the user. The first layout, Theatre/Orchestra, localizes the images in one place — orchestra pit — to allow an efficient visual scan of the lookback information (see Figure 2). The second layout, Theatre/Side, positions the images at the sides to differentiate lookback information from audience information (see Figure 3). More importantly, the images are angled and not face-on and positioned at the periphery to reflect the fact that this lookback reciprocity is not a two-way exchange.

3.2 Secondary Audience Information

An important goal of the redesign was to provide users with information about their complete audience. However, the addition of many images can be distracting. Hence, we explored the notion of providing pictures for core team members and using one of four alternatives for representing non-core team members: None, Size, Names, and Pictures. Each successive option presents additional information.

The first option excludes the display of one's non-core team members (None). The second option presents the size of one's non-core team (Size) using a collection of blue rectangles to represent occupied theatre seats. In keeping with the graphical and theatrical metaphor, the occupied blue seats provide a gestalt of the non-core team member size (see Figure 2). The third option adds name labels to the blue seats (see Figure 3) to allow the user to find out who is seated in the back rows. The fourth alternative uses pictures to provide views into non-core team member's offices (Pictures).

4 Preference Experiment

A preference experiment was conducted to see which of the different screen layouts and audience options a first-time user would like. The reason to examine people's first-time preferences is because our experiences with recruiting users have shown that their initial perceptions and reactions play a critical role in the impressions they formulate and their willingness to use the technology (Lee et al., 1997). Thus, our redesign is an effort to make Portholes not only useful and usable but also more acceptable to first-time prospects (Lee et al., 1997). The first evaluation of the design is to examine its effectiveness in guiding new users to formulate appropriate impressions and expectations about Portholes and thus to improve its uptake. If people use it, then it would be appropriate to conduct a longitudinal study of its impact.

4.1 Evaluators

28 evaluators (14 males and 14 females) were recruited through an electronic call for volunteers. All evaluators worked at NYNEX S&T and willingly volunteered for the experiment. None of them used Portholes but a few heard about it from their colleagues. Some of them worked together on past projects and others were unknown to each other. This is not unlike the situation of how work-groups are assembled at NYNEX and elsewhere. It is also not unlike the context in which we intended NYNEX Portholes to be used (i.e. among people who knew each other and those who did not). As compensation

for their time and feedback, each evaluator was rewarded with a Swiss chocolate bar.

4.2 Layout and Audience Effects

There are two principal effects examined in the experiment through the different design options: layout and audience.

Three different layout options for organizing the information differently in the Portholes display were compared: Portholes, Theatre/Orchestra, and Theatre/Side (Figures 1–3). The Portholes layout displays images in a two-dimensional grid, with sections designated as core team members, lookback and non-core team members. Its layout is simpler, but is ambiguous about the issue of being in public. It was included to see if evaluators would prefer it over the theatre designs. This layout is essentially the same as the one used in NYNEX Portholes, except that the non-core team member information was added at the bottom of the layout; differentiated from the other quarter-size, lookback images by having the same background colour as the images for the user's core group members.

The two theatre designs were described in the previous section. They use perspective cues to create a 3D appearance and place the lookback images in different locations. The theatre setting conveys a sense of being in public and on-stage. The Theatre/Orchestra is in between the other two layouts; it is visually simpler than Theatre/Side but more three-dimensional than Portholes.

Four different audience options were shown for presenting people who were not explicitly selected by the user (non-core team members). These four options correspond to the four audience options presented earlier: None, Size, Names, Pictures.

4.3 Materials

Nine co-workers (5 males and 4 females) permitted us to use their pictures as part of the collection of video images used to assemble the various screen designs used in the experiment. We took colour JPEG pictures (160×120 pixels) just like Portholes would take them. Also, we took a colour picture of each evaluator in the same fashion at the beginning of the experiment. The evaluator's picture appears among the images of co-workers who were part of the evaluator's core team. From past experiences, we learned that including the individual's own picture into the Portholes display subtly affected the individual's perception of the tool; from one of looking in at others to one of being among the group of people who can view as well as be viewed. We wanted the evaluators to experience a group awareness tool as an insider and not as an outsider.

The ten pictures were used to assemble the twelve different screen designs (3 layout and 4 audience conditions). Evaluators were told which co-workers filled the role of core team and non-core team members. They were told that all co-workers had access to Portholes. The various options for the display of the information about the non-core team members were introduced to the evaluators. Evaluators were shown the three layouts and where the information about core and non-core team members and lookback would appear in each of the layouts.

4.4 Procedure

In the first part of the experiment, 72 pairs of designs were shown to the evaluators. An initial warmup block of comparisons was presented, in which all twelve designs were displayed as six pairs. Then evaluators saw each design eleven more times over 66 paired comparisons, once with each other design. To avoid biases, each design was shown five times on one side and six times on the other. Also, each design appeared only once within every blocked sequence of six comparisons.

Each design pair was shown at the same time. A button, labelled 'I like this better', appeared below each design. Clicking on a button recorded the choice. Then the next design pair was presented.

At the conclusion of the paired comparison phase, evaluators were given a three-part survey. Parts 1 and 2 will not be discussed here. Part 3 assessed the importance of a set of eighteen design requirements.

5   Preference Results

The data from the warm-up block was discarded. Preference scores were calculated for each evaluator by totalling the number of times a design, layout option, or audience option was preferred, normalized to a range between 0 and 1. As well, the 'dissimilarities' between evaluators and designs were described as the rank of the design preferences for each evaluator, based on the number of times a design was chosen. In a few cases, an evaluator did not exhibit a clear preference for one design over the other or was inconsistent. These ties were resolved based on the choice made by the evaluator in the direct comparison between the two designs.

Most evaluators exhibited a strong internal consistency in their preferences. An interaction between Audience and Layout was seen in three evaluators.

5.1   Audience

Preferences were significantly influenced by the audience information ($F(3,81) = 11.59, p < 0.05$). However, it was not the case that preferences increased as the amount of information provided about the audience increased (see Figure 4). Evaluators overwhelmingly disliked the use of blue rectangles to represent seats occupied by non-core team members. The sum of these images and those of the core team members represents one's audience size. The survey results underscored the undesirability of the use of blue images to indicate audience size (26% preferred the use of blue images while 67% preferred the use of a number — see Q3 and Q14 in Table 1). Evaluators preferred Names over None, but were mixed as to the desirability of Pictures over Names or None.

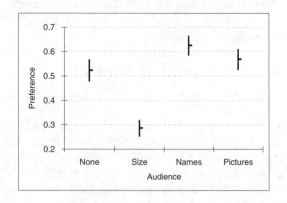

Figure 4: Audience preferences.

5.2   Layout

Personal preferences were expected to surface in the reactions of the evaluators to the three layouts. Patterns of preference were varied, resulting in a statistically insignificant effect of Layout ($F(2,54) = 0.906$). We used multidimensional weighted unfolding (MDU) (Shepard, 1972) to analyse the underlying structure in the individual preferences.

Unfolding was originally suggested by Coombs (1950) for a single dimension and has since been extended to multiple dimensions. Unfolding assumes that stimuli are aligned along one or several dimensions and that individuals observe the experimental conditions from their own perspectives. It places objects, conditions and evaluators, in a spatial model in such a way that the significant features of the data about these objects are revealed in the geometrical relations among the objects.

Item	Requirement	Important or Nice to Have (%)
Q1	See my non-core team members along with my core team members at all times.	61
Q2	Assess how many people on my non-core team.	68
Q3	See a set of blue images for my non-core team members instead of a number for size of non-core team.	26
Q4	See the names of my non-core team members at all times.	71
Q5	See the pictures of my non-core team members at all times.	46
Q6	See not only the blue images but also the names of my non-core team members at all times.	64
Q7	See not only the names but also the pictures of my non-core team members at all times.	57
Q8	See my own image in the layout.	64
Q9	Control whether I see my own image.	89
Q10	Control the placement of my image.	75
Q11	Control the placement of core and non-core team member images in the layout.	86
Q12	Control the placement of images of team members looking back right now.	89
Q13	Assess how many people can potentially see my image.	71
Q14	See a number for how many people can potentially see my image.	67
Q15	See team members looking back right now at all times.	86
Q16	Look in one place to see the team members looking back right now.	89
Q17	Display information about team members looking back right now separately.	54
Q18	Display a marker on the images of the team members looking back right now instead of duplicate images.	68

Table 1: Results of requirements survey.

The MDU analysis was performed using ALSCAL (SPSS 6.1.4 for Windows) which yielded a RSQ of 0.870 — the amount of variance in the data accounted for by their distances. The inputs to the analysis were the positions of the layout and audience conditions and the 'dissimilarities' between evaluators and designs. The screen layout conditions were positioned on the grid based on our assessment of the dissimilarity among the conditions. The Portholes condition is more dissimilar than the Theatre/Side because of the 3D nature of the design while the Theatre/Orchestra was placed between them because of its hybrid 2D/3D

design. The placement of the audience conditions made use of the observation that Size was the least preferred condition and thus placed at one endpoint. The other three conditions were then placed in the order of increasing information value with the Pictures condition being placed at the other endpoint.

Using the positions produced by the unfolding analysis, we performed a hierarchical cluster analysis using the Ward method. This produced four distinct clusters. An examination of the results from both analyses (see Figure 5) showed that people did differentiate the layouts. As expected from unfolding theory, the cluster analysis revealed that there was not one single preferred view but rather four.

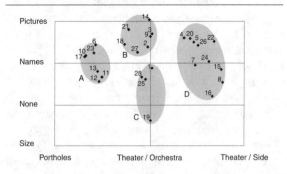

Figure 5: 2-Dimensional Unfolding of Preferences

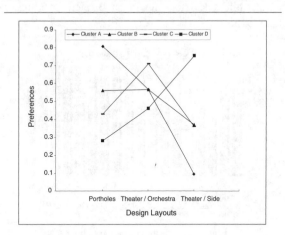

Figure 6: Preferences grouped by clusters.

Figure 6 shows the average layout preferences for each of the clusters. Individuals in Clusters A and D clearly prefer Portholes and Theatre/Side, respectively. However, the placement of Clusters B and C near the centre of the Layout dimension (see Figure 5) does not necessarily imply a preference for Theatre/Orchestra; they include people who based their preference more strongly on the audience conditions (see Evaluators 14 and 19 as extreme examples of this). Overall, individuals in Clusters B and C have similar preferences for layout and could be combined if Evaluator 19 was treated as an outlier.

5.3 Requirements Survey

Participants rated the importance of 18 design requirements for a Portholes display (see Table 1). The five-point rating scale was 1 for No Way, 2 for Should Not Have, 3 for Don't Care / Either Way, 4 for Nice to Have and 5 for Important to Have.

The requirement Q3 to use blue rectangles to complete the audience size information, was the only one generally rejected by evaluators, rated a 1 or a 2 by eighteen out of twenty-eight people. This corroborates the objective preference selection for the audience Size option, reported earlier (see Figure 4).

The universally agreed upon requirement was Q16; to be able to "look in one place to see the team members looking back right now", rated 'Important to Have' by twenty-three evaluators. Interestingly enough, this includes all individuals in Cluster D — Theatre/Side — whose most preferred design required the user to look to the right and to the left to see who was looking back (see Figure 7). Almost as highly rated was requirement Q15 to "see team members looking back right now at all times". Evaluators in Cluster C rated both of these requirements significantly below Clusters A and D. Meanwhile, evaluators in Cluster B rated Q16 higher than Q15.

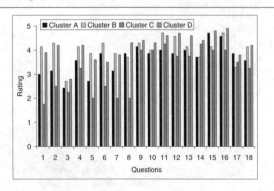

Figure 7: Average ratings by cluster.

Three questions addressed the issue of the non-core team member images: Q1 (show the images), Q5 (show as pictures), and Q7 (show with names and pictures). Clusters B and D evaluators wanted to see as much as possible (average preference = 3.95 and 3.77, respectively) while Cluster A evaluators were indifferent. Individuals in Cluster C did not want to see any of the information (average = 1.92).

The user's own image has been a concern to some Portholes users in the past. This issue was explored with three questions: Q8 (in own display), Q14 (on

other's display), and Q13 (how many can see own image). Except for Q8 for Cluster C, these were rated nice to have by all evaluators. The people in Cluster D (Theatre/Side preference) were more concerned about their image and who saw it than the people in the other three clusters. Looking at the survey data as a whole, most requirements were regarded as positive additions to Portholes by people in Clusters A, B, and D. Evaluators in Cluster C did not want to see much information in their display or for that matter, use an awareness tool.

6 Summary and Discussion

The results reveal four different clusters of preferences regarding the layout and audience options to use; representing differences in importance of the information to different groups of people. Clusters A and D clearly prefer Portholes and Theatre/Side, respectively. However, Clusters B and C based their preference strongly on the audience conditions; it was not necessarily the case that they preferred Theatre/Orchestra. Clusters B and D wanted to see as much information as possible.

Evaluators indicated a strong universal dislike for the use of blue rectangles to represent occupied seats for non-core team members; with no information being more preferred. Our intuition is that people reacted strongly to the choice of representation rather than usability concerns; they viewed the blue images as nameless, faceless individuals. This result supports the argument for paying attention to how people relate to technologies (Reeves & Nass, 1996). This speculation could be validated in a preference study using a number in place of blue rectangles.

The preference and survey results show that there is no universal agreement on the choice of the layout and the level of detail for audience information. Evaluators want to see at least the names of the non-core team members. A large percentage ($\geq 75\%$) want to control the placement of the information. Evaluators differed also on which layout is preferred. This suggests that all three layouts should be provided as user-selectable options.

Finally, among long-term users of Portholes, we have found that the needs for Portholes change (Lee et al., 1997). That is, the customizations for new users differ from those who use it for a long time. This evolution can be, in part, attributed to the emergence of the new 'middle region' behaviour formed in response to the effect of using Portholes over time (Meyrowitz, 1985). See Harrison & Dourish (1996) for similar observations associated with long-term use of a media space. It would be useful to examine the structure of the users' preferences and its evolution over time.

7 Conclusions

This paper argues for the importance of the social interface and its design. From a narrower perspective, it provides an understanding of these issues for Portholes and group awareness tools. It illustrates two pieces of information needed in such a social interface and how it appears in the user interface: sense of being in public and reciprocity. The design uses a theatre setting to provide a familiar behavioural context and uses different sections to present a user's community, their audience, and who is looking in on the user. We argue that without this information and a way to present and access it, users do not 'know their place'.

From a broader perspective, the paper provokes thinking about what the social information is in other computer-mediated communication tools and how to bring forth this information in the user interface to elicit the desired impressions and reactions. Concerns for surveillance and privacy are not unique to Portholes. Even technologies like television and radio have wrought changes in social behaviours, roles, order, and situations. In grounding the discussion with Portholes, we try to relate the studies of face-to-face and mediated interactions, to make the concepts of 'sense of place', social information, and social interface more concrete and applicable to the design of computer-mediated tools and to show that its design can be fraught with issues that we are just beginning to understand (Dourish & Bly, 1992; Goffman, 1959; Meyrowitz, 1985; Reeves & Nass, 1996).

Acknowledgements

Debbie Lawrence and Jim Kondziela provided valuable suggestions in the design of the experiment. Mike Atwood and John Thomas have supported the Portholes research throughout. This research was performed at NYNEX Science & Technology which is now part of Bell Atlantic.

References

Bellotti, V. & Sellen, A. (1993), Designing for Privacy in Ubiquitous Computing Environments, *in* G. de Michelis, C. Simone & K. Schmidt (eds.), *Proceedings of ECSCW'93, the 3rd European Conference on Computer-Supported Cooperative Work*, Kluwer, pp.77–92.

Borning, A. & Travers, M. (1991), Two Approaches to Casual Interaction over Computer and Video Networks, *in* S. P. Robertson, G. M. Olson & J. S. Olson (eds.), *Proceedings of CHI'91: Human Factors in Computing Systems (Reaching through Technology)*, ACM Press, pp.13–9.

Cool, C., Fish, R. S., Kraut, R. E. & Lowery, C. M. (1992), Iterative Design of Video Communication Systems, *in* J. Turner & R. Kraut (eds.), *Proceedings of CSCW'92: Conference on Computer Supported Cooperative Work*, ACM Press, pp.25–32.

Coombs, C. H. (1950), "Psychological Scaling Without a Unit of Measurement", *Psychological Review* **57**, 145–58.

Dourish, P. & Bly, S. (1992), Portholes: Supporting Awareness in Distributed Work Groups, *in* P. Bauersfeld, J. Bennett & G. Lynch (eds.), *Proceedings of CHI'92: Human Factors in Computing Systems*, ACM Press, pp.541–7.

Goffman, E. (1959), *The Presentation of Self in Everyday Life*, Doubleday.

Harrison, R. & Dourish, P. (1996), Re-Place-ing Space: The Roles of Place and Space in Collaborative Systems, *in* M. S. Ackerman (ed.), *Proceedings of CSCW'96: Conference on Computer Supported Cooperative Work*, ACM Press, pp.67–76.

Lee, A., Girgensohn, A. & Schlueter, K. (1997), NYNEX Portholes: Initial User Reactions and Redesign Implications, *in* S. C. Hayne & W. Prinz (eds.), *Proceedings of International ACM SIGGROUP Conference on Supporting Group Work, GROUP'97*, ACM Press, pp.385–94.

Meyrowitz, J. (1985), *No Sense of Place: The Impact of Electronic Media on Social Behavior*, Oxford University Press.

Narine, T., Leganchuk, A., Mantei, M. & Buxton, W. (1997), Collaboration Awareness and its Use to Consolidate a Disperse Group, *in* S. Howard, J. Hammond & G. K. Lindgaard (eds.), *Human–Computer Interaction — INTERACT '97: Proceedings of the Sixth IFIP Conference on Human–Computer Interaction*, Chapman & Hall, pp.397–404.

Reeves, B. & Nass, C. (1996), *The Media Equation: How People Treat Computers, Television and New Media Like Real People and Places*, Cambridge University Press.

Shepard, R. N. (1972), Introduction, *in* R. N. Shepard, A. K. Romney & S. B. Nerlove (eds.), *Multi-dimensional Scaling:Theory and Applications in the Behavioral Science*, Vol. 1, Seminar Press, pp.1–20.

Tang, J. C. & Rua, M. (1994), Montage: Providing Teleproximity for Distributed Groups, *in* B. Adelson, S. Dumais & J. Olson (eds.), *Proceedings of CHI'94: Human Factors in Computing Systems*, ACM Press, pp.37–43.

Human–Computer Interaction — INTERACT '99
M. Angela Sasse and Chris Johnson (Editors)
Published by IOS Press, © IFIP TC.13, 1999

Illustrative Browsing: A New Method of Browsing in Long On-line Texts

Stefan Schlechtweg & Thomas Strothotte

Department of Simulation and Graphics, University of Magdeburg,
Universitätsplatz 2, D-39106 Magdeburg, Germany.
{stefans,tstr}@isg.cs.uni-magdeburg.de

Abstract: We have developed a new method, called *illustrative browsing*, for users to get an overview of long on-line texts. When users begin their work, we assume the text to contain no illustrations, but that structured geometric models are available for the domain of the text. Users first select such a model; a collection of tools we have implemented, called the TEXTILLUSTRATOR, then couple the text and the geometric model with one another. This enables users to interact with the text to obtain automatically graphical illustrations. Interaction on the image can also be performed in order to browse in the text. An advanced feature enables the use of the automatically generated images individually as bookmarks. Finally, the users can tune the generated images and embed them in the text for the purpose of illustration.

Keywords: interactive system design, interaction design, multimedia systems, information visualization, browsing, illustrating texts.

1 Introduction

In the 1980s, the hypertext revolution led to the practice of breaking up long text passages, commonplace in print materials, into small segments richly connected by links. This propagated up to the World Wide Web (WWW), where style guides often recommend that documents shall not fill more than one page. Consequently, most tools for navigation in hyperdocuments work well for such short texts, while at the same time there is significant room for improvement in methods and tools to support the handling of long texts.

However, as with every pendulum which has swung far off into one direction, it is coming back. Long texts, namely those spreading over anywhere from at least several pages to dozens or hundreds of pages, are beginning to be used more and more even on-line. One important reason for this situation is that many long reports are written for print media (like annual reports, theses, etc.), and are deposited basically *as is* on the WWW without taking into consideration that completely different demands are made on the different kinds of media.

One of the problems with long texts is that users find it difficult to get an overview of the topics covered. Different navigation and interaction methods have been developed to aid the user in this process. However, the methods of using a combination of scrolling, sectioning, and keyword search are outdated and lack both effectiveness and aesthetic appeal, particularly when compared to interaction methods with graphics. Moreover, methods of automatically decomposing long documents into smaller ones (e.g. LATEX2HTML) often make navigation even worse rather than better, because they tend to cut off conceptual links between sections of text due to restructuring the document into separate pages for the WWW.

In this paper we present a new method, called *illustrative browsing*, for browsing through long texts and show how it can be applied, using medical texts as an example. The paper is organized as follows. Related work and an analysis of the background is presented in Section 2. The principles underlying our new method of working with long on-line texts are given in Section 3. These principles have been implemented in a system called the TEXTILLUSTRATOR. User interaction with the system as well as advanced uses of the method and features of the system are outlined in Section 4. We conclude the paper by pointing out interesting future improvements.

2 Background

2.1 Browsing through Texts, Short and Long

While addressing the issue of navigation in large information spaces, several methods have emerged which are also suited for the purpose of browsing through long texts. The INFORMATION MURAL, as presented in (Jerding & Stasko, 1998), is a two-dimensional, reduced representation of an entire information space and fits completely within a display window or screen. It creates a miniature version of the information space using virtual attributes (colour, etc.) to display its properties. It may be used as an overview of the structure of the observed information space and as a navigation tool.

To display long unstructured texts in a manner which resembles a stack of pages, the DOCUMENT LENS approach (Robertson & Mackinlay, 1993) provides an innovative interface. Here, the pages are displayed as if the user looked at them through a magnifying glass. The currently selected page is shown in every detail, whereas adjacent pages are reduced in their size and perspectively warped. Also the WEBBOOK approach (Card et al., 1996) provides an interesting interface for handling long texts.

The methods mentioned above concentrate on the inherent properties of the text and do not make use of any related information and of any possibilities which emerge from including knowledge about the contents of the text into the interface. The method we propose for enhancing browsing through long texts is based on the interactive illustration of an otherwiese long, unillustrated text. This raises the general issue of the interaction between texts and images, both in traditional print media and in multimedia systems. We shall therefore discuss these in turn.

2.2 Traditional Print Media: Atlases vs. Textbooks

Two fundamental forms of information presentation can be distinguished in traditional print media. On the one end of the spectrum, we have *atlases* whose primary focus is on graphics which illustrate the subject matter at hand in a very detailed way. The understanding of the subject is supported by labels and figure captions, and somewhat more rarely by additional texts and tables; thus text plays only a marginal role in such books. The attached labels have to be mentally integrated and — much more important — sorted out by the viewer to get the information he or she wants. Even more crucial for getting a complete impression of the subject matter is that one specific topic is dealt with in several images to convey the three-dimensionality from different viewpoints.

On the other end of the spectrum, we have *textbooks* which focus primarily on a verbal description of the subject matter at hand. For example, in medical books, structure and functionality of the body parts and organs are described with an almost uniform terminology. The images used here accompany and illustrate the text and are thus less detailed than in atlases. The labelling of the text-book images is sparser than in atlases; in most cases only labels with a reference in the text are shown. Since images in textbooks concentrate on specific aspects, the number of images needed to illustrate a subject to a certain degree of completeness is rather high. This means that also here images may be spread over several pages aggravating problems associated with the mental integration of all information. A new problem arises here since the reader needs to combine both types of information, texts and graphics.

Both types of books, atlases and textbooks, have in common a high navigational effort to integrate textual and graphical information and to build up a mental model of the described contents. Flipping through pages as well as the use of different books at once is a standard — cumbersome and tiring — procedure for a student when learning anatomy.

2.3 Coupling Text and Graphics in Interactive Systems

Multimedia systems try to overcome some of the problems, especially those associated with the three-dimensional nature of the underlying geometric knowledge. They offer navigation facilities for 3D models by directly using them as source for the image generation and by offering the user possibilities to interact with the model and thus change the viewpoint to whatever position he or she needs. Furthermore, text and graphics are directly linked to each other. Thus a user may request an image for a specific part of the text or an explanation of a specific part of the image by activating the link. However, practically all systems commercially available or reported on in the literature so far use predefined images or animations and the user generally has no possibility to request a *customised* illustration which exactly fits his or her intentions or reading history.

For interactive illustration systems, which often try to resemble the traditionally known media, we can also identify two major groups of systems. We will call systems which focus mainly on the graphics (and thus are similar to atlases) *graphics-driven*, and those which concentrate primarily on textual information (like textbooks) *text-driven*.

2.3.1   Graphics-driven Systems

Graphics-driven systems are widely used nowadays. Here a user interacts mainly with the graphical visualization to explore the information space. By interacting with the image, further data can be obtained, like object names, relationships, or additional facts. Texts are only used in small quantities and displayed as labels, figure captions or tables close to the image or in a separate window. As an example, this can be seen in "Sobotta. Atlas of Human Anatomy. CD-ROM edition". Here the very detailed images take almost the complete screen space. Picking an object in the image leads to the appearance or highlighting of a label or an entry in a supplimentary table. Hence the image is in the centre of interest and is used to obtain any information needed.

Graphics-driven systems can rely on a close connection between the textual information and the parts of the graphics they describe. Thus it is not astonishing that for this type of system a tight coupling between graphics and text is established where the graphical model plays the central role. The ZOOMILLUSTRATOR by Preim et al. (1997) is an excellent example for this. Here, short texts are used to label an image which in turn is generated from a 3D model. The user selects the parts he or she wants to be labelled and the ZOOMILLUSTRATOR generates and displays the labels. Interaction with the labels yields a more or less detailed description. The size and placement of the labels is hereby controlled by a fisheye zoom algorithm (Furnas, 1986). An advantage is that because of this rigid link, search operations in the information space are kept to a minimum. However, the biggest drawback is that this strategy can not be used for long texts where more than one paragraph apply to one part in the image. Also, to change the texts here means to change the model as a whole.

Not only textual labels but all kinds of information can be attached to a graphical model in the system VOXELMAN. Here, voxel models serve as a basis for the graphics generation and to each voxel pointers into different information spaces are attached (Höhne et al., 1994). All information spaces are linked to each other and form a kind of a semantic network so that a wide variety of information can be explored and displayed on the user's demand. This approach is promising since it enables to combine many different types of data, though it is cumbersome to use for long texts. Furthermore, the information space is built on (artificial) physical parts of the model (the voxels) instead of logical parts (organs, body parts) and is thus very expensive to create.

2.3.2   Text-driven Systems

Text-driven systems, by contrast, are still rather underestimated as to their usefulness in learning environments. An example for such a system is the "Microsoft Encarta Encyclopaedia". Here the main information source are textual descriptions of things, events, persons, etc. Those texts are connected with predefined images, sounds, or video clips. As the user scrolls through the text, this related information is displayed depending on the topic currently shown in the text. If the topic changes (for instance, if the next entry starts), the image (or whatever is currently displayed) also changes. Hence all information presented to the user is kept consistent.

A major problem when relying on textual information in on-line systems is the amount of text being displayed. Due to screen space limitations only a very small part can be shown at any one point in time. As a metaphor for flipping pages, scrolling through the text by using scrollbars and other interaction facilities is not very well suited. Reading long texts on a computer screen differs from reading text on paper in many respects. Experiments like the one done by O'Hara & Sellen (1997) show that the standard interaction facilities offered so far do not help to concentrate on the task at hand but distract the user by drawing his or her attention to the interaction which has to be performed.

When building a text-driven illustration system, we consider the following points as being important:

Provide integration of text and images: Textual and graphical information are to be incorporated in a way to make the relationship between them immediately clear to the user.

Facilitate interaction: Interaction facilities with the illustration should at least support change of viewpoint and zooming.

Provide multiple access to information: Access to information should not be restricted to one particular interaction method; instead, many possible ways should be offered to get a specific piece of information.

Provide flexible levels of detail: The amount of information (especially textual information) provided to the user should be controllable by the user, though in certain situations the system itself may decide that more or less detailed information will be presented.

Our goal has been to design a system which enables users to browse through long texts to get an overview and to find quickly sections of interest and interrelations between them. In particular, we emphasise the coupling of text and custom generated images, as well as providing access to the text also through the images.

3 System Architecture

The TEXTILLUSTRATOR is the system which was designed and implemented to meet the above requirements. Techniques for interacting with the displayed text, adding annotations and changing the level of detail the text is displayed with help the user to navigate within the textual domain. On the graphical side we use rendered 3D images with standard interaction facilities like rotation, translation and zoom. A new quality, however, comes into play when providing interaction facilities which use both text and graphics together to help the user navigate through the integrated information space.

The basis for our system architecture are two models: a specially prepared text to display and interact with the textual information, and a 3D geometry model for the graphics (see Figure 1).

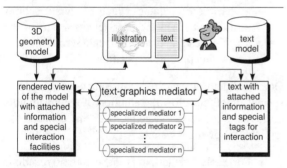

Figure 1: Architecture of the TEXTILLUSTRATOR.

If we use the system to create illustrations for a given (long) text based on the user's interaction, a loose coupling between the parts of the information space is necessary so that user interaction may create new connections between the models, remove such connections, or even change the models themselves. Thus, we build on a special entity which connects the given models with each other. This is not a simple connection between parts of the involved models, but more a 'mediator' which acts as a 'broker' between text and graphics and which translates interactions on one representation to changes in the visualization or even the structure of the other model(s). For the case of having a text and an illustration, our system architecture can be seen in Figure 1.

3.1 The Text Model

Since the text is the main information source, it plays a central role in the system. Before it can be used, it has to be prepared for the special requirements by paying attention to the following:

- Every text has an inherent structure based on sections and paragraphs which should be visible and can be used as a navigation aid.

- Text formatting is important for the recognition of structures in the text and logical structures of the subject matter at hand.

- Parts of the text which refer directly to parts of the image should be used for interaction.

For including structural as well as additional information directly into the text, mark-up languages like SGML are particularly well suited. From our SGML file we create an internal representation which we call a *tagged text*. This representation is based on the ASCII values of the text and contains for each character:

- formatting instructions (boldface, italic, etc.);

- type tags which hold information of the text structure (headings, paragraph text, etc.); and

- an array of tags which themselves can hold arbitrary references. Those 'slots' are filled later during the user's interaction with the text.

While parsing the SGML file, formatting instructions lead directly to the desired appearance of the displayed text, all other mark-ups are converted into tags which are assigned appropriately (see Figure 2). These tags include, for instance:

- references (links) with their destination;

- object names (for accessing the objects in the graphics);

- associations between text parts; and

- values which are assigned and changed based on the user's interaction, as, for instance, an importance value which will change each time the characters this value belongs to is involved in an interaction process.

In medicine and anatomy, the area of application we are dealing with in particular, the text itself can be prepared semi-automatically without using sophisticated linguistic methods. Due to the almost standardised terminology in this area (i.e. Latin names of all objects), a keyword search procedure can create many of the mark-ups we need. However, user interaction may be needed to prepare the text to a degree of completeness which is required by the application. We have also successfully applied the text preparation process for texts from other domains, like operation manuals, and for architectural texts describing ancient buildings.

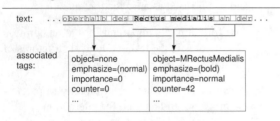

Figure 2: General concept of the tagged text.

3.2   The Graphical Model

The illustrations are generated from a 3D geometry model which the user must obtain. To fully qualify models stemming from an arbitrary modelling system for the use with the TEXTILLUSTRATOR, at least unique identifiers for any model part have to be present. Those IDs should be based on logical rather than physical portions of the model. As a further preparation step, the user may need to structure the model if this has not been done in the original modelling system. This means grouping the model parts which belong to a certain organ or organ system and further grouping the organs to body parts, and so on. As a result, we get a hierarchically structured model where all parts need to possess a unique identifying name, so also the groups created in this step get such an ID. Optionally, we may now add further information to the model which is needed by the rendering system to display the image. Here especially colours and surface textures are included if this has not already been done in the geometric modelling process.

3.3   Coupling of Graphics and Text

For coupling graphical and textual information in an interactive system based on the models described above, the following considerations are made:

- Connections between text and graphics have to be bi-directional so that interaction on either one trigger actions on the other side.

- Text and graphics should be loosely coupled so that new interaction facilities can easily be added and existing ones can be enabled/disabled.

- Standard interaction facilities on the text as well as on the graphics are to be supported to provide a familiar environment to the user.

The text-graphics mediator (recall Figure 1) as implemented in the TEXTILLUSTRATOR fulfils these requirements. It builds the connection between the text and the view which displays the model. Before the application is opened, all tags in the tagged text which contain a reference to a part of the model are linked with this model part. This is realised by a translation table which automatically assigns an identification key in the model to all keywords found in the text (e.g. the Latin name). After having established this connection, a set of specialised mediators is registered with the general text-graphics mediator. Each of them is responsible for a specific interaction task. Some mediators are always present and provide a set of basic interaction facilities. These are:

- a 'picking mediator' which supports selections based on picking actions in the text;

- a 'scrolling mediator' which triggers reactions based on a change of the visible text portion, i.e. when the user scrolls through the text; and

- a 'selection mediator' which triggers reactions on the text when the user selects a part in the graphics leading to an automated scrolling of the text to an appropriate position.

Other mediators can be implemented easily and special functions allow the addition of new mediators during runtime of the system. With this concept, we gain the following advantages:

- For each interaction event, different reactions can be implemented and used, even different reactions for one particular event are possible.

- New interaction facilities can be added easily.

- A specific interaction scenario can be put together by selecting an appropriate set of mediators.

- Text and graphics remain relatively independent from each other, i.e. they do not form a single monolythical model (loose coupling).

Using this connection between graphics and text enables the user to browse through a long text while being supported by customised illustrations generated on-the-fly. Objects mentioned in the currently visible text portion or objects being explicitly selected are automatically highlighted in the image (see Figure 3). The changes in the graphical representation when interacting with the text help to get an overview of the text — the user sees in the image what the currently displayed text portion is about. Furthermore, picking an object in the graphics brings up the text which is most closely connected to this object. This feature prevents browsing through the whole text when searching for specific information. Further, more elaborate methods can also be implemented.

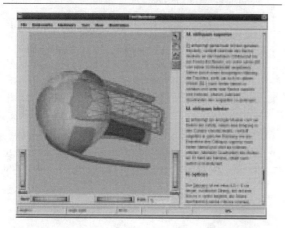

Figure 3: Objects corresponding to the technical terms in the text are highlighted in the illustration.

4 User Interaction and Advanced Browsing Facilities

The text-graphics mediator ensures interaction with both types of media involved. The requirements for interactive systems pointed out above include also interactive techniques which are restricted to only one type of information. So on the graphical side, standard interaction techniques like scaling or rotating the model are implemented to ensure that the user may look at the model from different viewpoints. This enables the user to build up a mental impression of the three-dimensional objects and replaces the need to show multiple illustrations on different places.

Interaction with the text includes scrolling through the text to reach all parts of the long text. As pointed out by O'Hara & Sellen (1997), it is of utmost importance to support reading on-line with additional possibilities for interaction. To explore the structure of a text, a reader may consult the table of contents. This is often not available for short texts (up to 20 pages in a book) so section and paragraph headings play this role. Using the section headings as table of contents and 'hiding' the actual text until the user explicitly selects the heading is one way to implement

the 'table of contents' metaphor which is being used in the TEXTILLUSTRATOR. This technique is known from so called *folding editors* for programming and reduces the amount of data being shown to the user and helps to concentrate on a specific part of the information space.

So far, we have seen our method applied to interactive exploration of the information space which is defined by the text model and the graphical model. When interacting with the graphics and even more with the text, a user leaves behind a trace of what he or she has been most interested in. This is also the case when surfing the WWW and used there by some companies to build a user profile and create special offers for this particular user. In our case such a trace is built up and used to provide the user with a customised illustration which he or she can print out to use it for learning at home or in presentations or reports.

Our informal tests with subjects have shown that users will want to save information about the results of their interactive sessions. This is so that they can get an even better overview the next time they open the document, to help jog their memory about the text contents, to find specific parts of the text again, and to better explain the contents to others. Two features which we designed and implemented are steps for facilitating these processes: illustrative bookmarks, and embedded illustrations.

4.1 Illustrative Bookmarks

A user may wish to store a pointer to a particular location within a text, a range or even a collection of places or ranges. Bookmarks, as provided by hypertext systems, identify these locations by simple textual descriptions which are often not meaningful enough when combining graphical and textual information — see also (Abrams et al., 1998).

The TEXTILLUSTRATOR offers users the possibility to use the described functionality to create individual frames which can be saved as bookmarks. As an example, the user has highlighted a portion of text within the document and asked for an illustration. Using a menu entry "File → Save as Bookmark", a pictorial representation of a pointer to this text portion is stored in the user's file system. The icon for the bookmark is created by building a thumbnail-sized image of the larger TEXTILLUSTRATOR output image.

Since this image represents the user's interaction history and state by colour coding the parts which are described in the currently visible text portion or which are currently selected, it is particularly suited as an indication of the system's state at this point in time. Clicking on such a bookmark from the file system results in the image being loaded in full size, and the associated text portions being highlighted.

4.2   Embedded Illustrations

The illustrations created by the TEXTILLUSTRATOR are useful not only for interactive navigational purposes, but also for illustrating the text itself. This can be used within the on-line document as well as for a printout of the text. The TEXTILLUSTRATOR provides sophisticated support for this process of embedding illustrations in documents.

The main problem here is that automatically generated illustrations usually cannot adequately pay tribute to a user's reasons for wanting to include an illustration at a particular location. Such reasons may be to highlight an aspect of the text which the user considers particularly important for his or her own purposes; however, the author of the text may in fact have had something else in mind and not considered the same point to be of particular relevance.

Information about what a user considers important can be obtained from tags associated with objects in the text which are used to store importance values. These values are updated each time the user interacts with this particular object. If, for example, the user directly selects 'optic nerve' in a medical text to explore its position in the graphics he or she shows a very high interest in this nerve and thus the importance value stored with it is increased. If the optic nerve is selected directly in the graphics, we also increase the importance value. If, however, the optic nerve comes into the visible portion of the text by scrolling through the text, this may be by accident or on purpose when the user's interest is in a topic connected with the optic nerve. Here, the interest in this particular object is not that strong and the importance value is only slightly increased. So each user action leads to a change of the importance values. We then create an image which reflects the user's interest by drawing the parts differently, according to their importance.

For this purpose we developed a set of special rendering tools which focus on non-photorealistic rendering. A detailed description can be found in (Schlechtweg et al., 1998). These rendering tools consist mainly of a core render engine and highly parametrizable visualization modules. With these tools we are now in a position to translate the importance values into a certain kind of visualization.

To do so, we use a lookup table to determine the visualization to be used depending on those normalised importance values which have been normalised to fall in a range between 0 and 1. For an interval of values, a specific visualization (or drawing)

style is applied to the object falling in this interval. In this way we achieve different styles for differently important objects. For those objects falling in the same range, the parameterization of our visualization modules comes into play. Based on the distance of the object's importance values to the interval bounds we adjust the drawing parameters to differentiate objects in one visualization style from each other. A typical set-up for the lookup table is as follows:

importance	visualization
0.9 ... 1.0	shaded image with enhanced edges
0.7 ... 0.9	shaded image
0.5 ... 0.7	contour drawing with added details as line drawing
0.3 ... 0.5	contour drawing
0.0 ... 0.3	coloured silhouette of the object

The user may change this set-up to adapt the visualization to his or her demands. Figure 4 shows an example of a customised, non-photorealistic image created by the system which is ready to be embedded in the text.

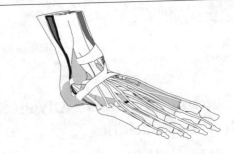

Figure 4: Non-photorealistic illustration created by the TEXTILLUSTRATOR.

The page layout is composed from the text and the rendered image where the image takes a prominent position on the page and the text floats around the illustration with the part referring to the image close to it. This page can then be printed and used for documentation or learning off-line.

Putting it all together, the interaction facilities offered in the TEXTILLUSTRATOR bear a high potential for combining textual and graphical information in an interactive system, where the focus is on long explanatory texts. Interaction via the combination of graphics and text are very well suited to explore the contents of a given text or model and ease the understanding of the structure. Additional techniques help to embed those new features in an environment with which the user is already familiar. Even more, by collecting data during the interaction process it is possible to create meaningful printed illustrations for further off-line use.

In this paper we have presented a new method, called *illustrative browsing*, for supporting users in exploring long on-line text. We have devised and implemented new interaction techniques based on the contents of long texts displayed on a computer screen and linked to a graphical image. The illustration and the text are kept in unison with one another so that both can be used together to explore an information space.

This work has a variety of implications. The geometric models used for our application are assumed to be well structured into objects and sub-objects; however, commercially available geometric models still tend to be entirely unstructured and do not contain any identifiers for the objects nor any additional information. We hope that applications like the one we present will motivate those building and possibly selling geometric models to provide more than just the raw geometry.

Our work assumes that the user has found a geometric model which is appropriate for the text he or she wishes to illustrate. It would be interesting to develop a softbot to find such geometric models from a database, since many researchers and even companies place their models at the disposal of others on the network.

More work can also be done on improving the quality of the illustrations being produced by the TEXTILLUSTRATOR. In particular, the reading history could be encoded in a more sophisticated way than it is being now done, and a wider range of graphical techniques could be explored for producing the custonised illustrations for the text. Also, the understanding of the subject and especially of the changes in the illustration caused by the user interacting with the system can be supported by the automated generation of figure captions as reported in (Preim et al., 1998). However, before going the next step towards the automatic generation of illustrations, a detailed evaluation of the techniques presented here is necessary and will be carried out.

Acknowledgements

The ideas reported on in this paper emerged from discussions with other members of the Graphics and Interactive Systems Laboratory at the University of Magdeburg. Special thanks to Andreas Raab for his contributions in this regard. Thanks also to Sylvia Zabel for proofreading the final version of the paper.

References

Abrams, D., Baecker, R. & Chignell, M. (1998), Information Archiving with Bookmarks: Personal Web Space Construction and Organization, *in* C.-M. Karat, A. Lund, J. Coutaz & J. Karat (eds.), *Proceedings of CHI'98: Human Factors in Computing Systems*, ACM Press, pp.41–8.

Card, S. K., Robertson, G. G. & York, W. (1996), The WebBook and the Web Forager: An Information Workspace for the World Wide Web, *in* G. van der Veer & B. Nardi (eds.), *Proceedings of CHI'96: Human Factors in Computing Systems*, ACM Press, pp.111–7.

Furnas, G. W. (1986), Generalized Fisheye Views, *in* M. Mantei & P. Orbeton (eds.), *Proceedings of CHI'86: Human Factors in Computing Systems*, ACM Press, pp.16–23.

Höhne, K.-H., Pommert, A., Riemer, M., Schiemann, T., Schubert, R. & Tiede, U. (1994), Medical Volume Visualization Based on "Intelligent Volumes", *in* L. Rosenblum, R. A. Earnshaw, J. Encarnacao, H. Hagen, A. Kaufman, S. Klimenko, G. Nielson, F. Post & D. Thalmann (eds.), *Scientific Visualization. Advances and Challanges*, Academic Press, London, chapter 2, pp.21–35.

Jerding, D. F. & Stasko, J. T. (1998), "The Information Mural: A Technique for Displaying and Navigating Large Information Spaces", *IEEE Computer Graphics and Applications* **4**(3), 257–71.

O'Hara, K. & Sellen, A. (1997), A Comparison of Reading Paper and On-Line Documents, *in* S. Pemberton (ed.), *Proceedings of CHI'97: Human Factors in Computing Systems*, ACM Press, pp.335–42.

Preim, B., Michel, R., Hartmann, K. & Strothotte, T. (1998), Figure Captions in Visual Interfaces, *in* T. Catarci, M. F. Costabile, G. Santucci & L. Tarantino (eds.), *Proceedings of the Conference on Advanced Visual Interface (AVI'98)*, ACM Press, pp.235–46.

Preim, B., Raab, A. & Strothotte, T. (1997), Coherent Zooming of Illustrations with 3D-Graphics and Text, *in* W. Davis, M. Mantei & V. Klassen (eds.), *Proceedings of Graphics Interface '97*, Canadian Human–Computer Communications Society, pp.105–13.

Robertson, G. G. & Mackinlay, J. D. (1993), The Document Lens, *in Proceedings of the ACM Symposium on User Interface Software and Technology, UIST'93*, ACM Press, pp.101–8.

Schlechtweg, S., Schönwälder, B., Schumann, L. & Strothotte, T. (1998), Surfaces to Lines: Rendering Rich Line Drawings, *in* V. Skala (ed.), *Proceedings of WSCG'98*, University of West Bohemia Press, Plzen, pp.354–61.

Human–Computer Interaction — INTERACT '99
M. Angela Sasse and Chris Johnson (Editors)
Published by IOS Press, © IFIP TC.13, 1999

Choice and Comparison Where the User Wants Them:
Subjunctive Interfaces for Computer-supported Exploration

Aran Lunzer

Meme Media Laboratory, Hokkaido University, Sapporo 060-8628, Japan.

aran@meme.hokudai.ac.jp

Abstract: There are many kinds of computer system that are intended to support users in performing an exploration among a range of possible results. However, such tools often allow only narrow progress through the result space, forcing users to trade off the breadth of search they would like to pursue against the time and effort required. The aim of the 'subjunctive interface' concept is to make broader searches more manageable, by letting users propose multiple alternative values for each parameter where normally only a single value can be supplied, and by supporting the viewing and comparison of the various resulting outcomes.

This paper clarifies the motivation and principles underlying the subjunctive interface concept, describes implementation work that illustrates the approach, and outlines directions for further pursuit of this research.

Keywords: user interface, interaction style, interaction techniques, cognitive dimensions, subjunctive interface, parameter exploration, medical image segmentation.

1 Introduction

How pleasing it is that flight enquiries, like many other services, are now available through the World Wide Web. How depressing that the enquiry procedure is just as constrained as it ever was at the travel agency: typically, information about available seats is only revealed for a single fully specified journey at a time — in particular, with precise dates for departure and return. So if one wishes to compare, for example, the available schedules and fares for a two- or three-week trip to Scotland starting during any weekend in August, one has to submit a laborious sequence of individual queries and to make a separate record of the most interesting-looking items returned in each case — maybe putting up with an occasional response of the form 'Nothing available. Please try again.'

Should the system be more helpful? It is entirely within the scope of modern database technology to deal with much richer query specification, but this seems to be overridden by an imperative to keep the interface simple. Maybe the system should at least avoid producing the 'nothing available' response, by attempting to find a result that *almost* matches the query — but what compromises are to be assumed acceptable? Some travellers may want to try other dates; some might be insistent on keeping the separation of outbound and return date constant; some

might be restricted, as suggested above, to travelling at the weekend. There may be desires regarding airline, route, flight duration and, naturally, cost. The complexity of attempting to cater for compromises may be just as much a factor in the decision to support only fully-specified queries as is the need for efficiency in handling the enormous transaction traffic. Furthermore, this is a domain in which one cannot generally extrapolate among results: even if some special-deal fare is sold out on one day it may be available on the day before or after, or there may be similar or better deals to other nearby cities. An exhaustive (and tedious) search of the full range of results of interest is therefore the only way to discover all the possibilities.

In the *cognitive dimensions* framework being developed by Thomas Green and others to express the usability or otherwise of interactive computer systems — e.g. see (Green & Blackwell, 1998; Green & Petre, 1996) — all interaction is characterised as the building or modification of an information structure. Flight enquiry fits into their broad category of *exploratory design*, involving a mixture of adding to and modifying the structure that is being built (in this case, a query that produces acceptable results), and with the crucial property that the user does not know in advance which combination of these activities will result in a desirable end state. Other activities in this category would include simulation-based exploration of real-world entities ranging from astrophysics to home decoration, and the design of purely computer-generated artifacts such as Web pages and animations. In all cases it is the presence of complexity at some level — whether in the processing that generates results from parameter settings, or in the synergistic effects of numerous simple elements — that makes it hard for the user to predict the result that will emerge from a given specification.

Cognitive dimensions that are relevant to exploration include *visibility*, which concerns the ability to obtain a view of some desired information, *juxtaposability*, being the ability to place different items side by side (helpful in making comparisons), *viscosity*, which expresses cost of changing something that has already been specified, and *premature commitment*, which captures the concept of users being forced to make decisions before sufficient information is available. Some difficulties in using exploration-support systems can be described as follows:

- systems in which results are only available one at a time in response to a precise specification have poor *visibility* — it takes a lot of separate attempts to work through a range of alternatives;

- some systems have high *viscosity* insofar as moving on from one request to another involves numerous fiddly actions;

- poor *juxtaposability* arises where the handling of one request causes its results to replace the previous ones, making comparison difficult;

- the above combine to engender a feeling of *premature commitment* in making choices, since a user feels pressured to use the first reasonable result rather than keep trying alternatives.

1.1 Improved Support for Static Data

For exploration among collections of data that can be held entirely within a local computer and processed quickly enough to produce highly dynamic visualizations, a number of techniques have been developed to assist the user. A well known exemplar is the *dynamic query* approach — e.g. (Ahlberg & Wistrand, 1995). These tools keep *visibility* high by being able to map the entire data set into a single

visualization with interactive zooming; *viscosity* low by mapping parameters to sliders and filtering the display in real time (less than 100ms) as the sliders are manipulated; *juxtaposability* is improved by the ability to move rapidly back and forth between settings; thus also reducing *premature commitment* insofar as every setting is easily reversible. The key is that you can summarise the items in the collection and work with them at an overview level, requesting detailed views just for those that look particularly interesting.

Arising from these ideas, one approach to improving exploratory tasks is to generate in advance a set of data items representing the range of results that are of interest. For example, if a suitable subset of the worldwide flight database could be downloaded to one's own computer it would become straightforward to use dynamic-query facilities to explore the available options. The challenge then becomes that of defining and collating this 'suitable' set of results, especially where — as in explorations based on simulation or design — the results don't actually exist until they are specifically requested. Existing approaches range from explicit user-defined result ranges, as in the author's earlier work on *result-space reconnaissance* (Lunzer, 1996), to automated sampling such as in Design Galleries (Marks et al., 1997) or even randomised adjustment as in Mutator (Todd & Latham, 1992).

1.2 When Static Sampling is Not Enough

Transforming an exploratory design task into the post-processing of a set of sample results is not always satisfactory. Not only are the non-sampled results sidelined, but it remains difficult to steer the search towards regions that are interesting — analogous to the difference between visualization of the end results of a simulation, as opposed to *computational steering* that allows an experimenter to direct progress on-the-fly.

So how might one reconcile the goal of working with multiple alternative results at the same time — to support overviews, comparisons and dynamic filtering — with the goal of interactively steering the specification of these results? This is the question that led to the proposal for *subjunctive interfaces*, as first described in (Lunzer, 1998).* The following section outlines how the approach is intended to improve exploration support; subsequent sections discuss an implemented example, the principles of what is being proposed, and plans for further work.

---

*The subjunctive mood deals with acts or states not as facts but as possibilities — how things might be, considered in contrast with how they currently are. The term *subjunctive interface* was chosen in appreciation of Douglas R. Hofstadter's idea of the *Subjunc-TV*, a magical television that would be able to show alternative versions of a given broadcast corresponding to different circumstances chosen by the viewer — for example, showing how a football match would have played out if the weather had been fine instead of wet.

2   Broadening One's Outlook

This section gives examples of how the subjunctive interface concept can alleviate a user's dissatisfaction with only being able to pursue a single, narrow path of interaction within a rich result space governed by parameter settings.

2.1   Pursuing Provisional Choices

During parameter-based exploration, a user may often be asked to specify a single value for some parameter for which he or she does not (yet) have a clear preference. For example, the flight-enquiry interface mentioned above can only handle queries based on precise dates for departure and return, whereas the customer in our scenario has a range of alternative dates in mind.   To meet the constraints of the underlying computer system while also satisfying the user's wish to explore a range of alternative values, a 'subjunctive' approach would involve the creation of separate processing 'realities' in which the different values could be handled — one reality for each alternative that the user wants to try. With each reality maintaining its own thread of control, the handling of the multiple queries could appear to the user to be simultaneous, so the various results that could normally only be obtained through a series of separate interactions would become available at the same time. The issue that then arises is how to provide an interface that supports the examination, comparison, filtering and so on of these multiple results.

Figure 1 shows a working model built as a canonical example of subjunctive-interface principles. It simulates the launch and flight of un-powered projectiles under the influence of gravity and air resistance. Launch energy is fixed, but the projectile weight, the turret angle and headwind speed can be adjusted. If the user is interested in comparing flight paths that correspond to these settings — for example, to find a weight of projectile that can travel far under a range of wind conditions — an interface that supports just a single set of parameter values at a time is painfully restrictive. The user might set one value for weight, then vary the wind speed to generate various results, then change the weight and vary the wind speed again, trying to remember the previous results to compare them with the new ones. In Figure 1 we see that the user has specified two separate settings for wind-speed, and three separate values for projectile weight. In this case it is simple to overlay the alternative realities to support overview and comparison of the different parameter settings and the different flight paths that result.

In general, where a computer-based exploration would normally demand a single value — a date for a flight, an additional criterion to refine a query, a yes/no decision on forcing a page-break before some part of a document — our aim is to free the user to supply multiple alternatives if that will help the pursuit of the task. In cognitive dimension terms such support contributes to *provisionality,* i.e. reduced commitment to actions, and thus directly counteracts premature commitment.

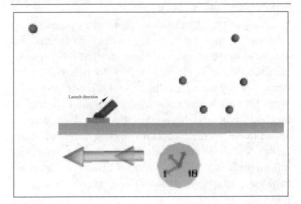

Figure 1: A snapshot of a simple subjunctive interface built using the locally developed 'IntelligentBox' 3D construction environment (Okada & Tanaka, 1995).   Here a user is exploring two different speeds of headwind (set using the large arrow at bottom left) and three values of weight (set using the dial) on the trajectory of a launched ball. The widget states corresponding to these different settings are overlaid using semi-transparent rendering.   The six resulting parameter combinations lead to independent but synchronised launches; this image shows the six balls that emerged simultaneously a short time ago, all following different trajectories.

2.2   Steering Multiple Alternatives

Although the 'dynamic query' tools make parameter adjustment cheap and its feedback instantaneous, the user is still only steering a single path through the result space. A subjunctive-style interface supporting multiple alternative settings can multiply the rate of examining alternative result-space regions.

For example, in the flight-booking scenario one may decide to switch from an originally specified destination (say, city x) to a nearby alternative city y, or to try flying into x but home from y. A user who has already specified a range of alternative dates is now likely to want to re-submit all those queries with the new itineraries. In a standard interface the re-specification of all the queries with the new routes would be almost unthinkable. But if the realities created to handle the various dates are linked so that they share all attributes apart from the date, a change to an independent parameter such as the destination can be reflected automatically in all the alternative cases.

The projectiles model exhibits this form of parameter sharing. For example, of the six realities shown in the picture, three are using one value of wind-speed while three are using the other. If the user decides to reduce the higher of the wind settings, all three realities using that setting will automatically change. Such sharing can be said to improve the system's rating on the *visibility* scale.

2.3 Adjustment From a Distance

One of the frustrations that can arise during parameter-based exploration is being unable to see the effect of some setting at the time when it is being made. For example, a flight-enquiry interface may have one 'screen' on which the user specifies dates and the route, which then disappears during query processing and is replaced by the result display. To try other settings the user must abandon the result display and return to the setting screen. This kind of *viscosity* is side-stepped by interfaces such as the dynamic query tools, by casting the exploration into the form of a single view manipulated using controls that fit alongside it. For the more general case, a subjunctive-interface approach should let users work on one view while being able to see simultaneously what would be appearing if the viewpoint were somewhere else instead — e.g. by use of multiple windows connected to linked realities.

Since many explorations are driven not just on the basis of a mapping from parameter state to results, but by the history or path of interactions, a subjunctive approach that allows a user to revisit a decision early in the history will require a mechanism for re-playing all user interactions that may have a new effect under the new setting.

2.4 Combining Partial Results

Rather than regarding the various realities as separate entities illuminating alternative possibilities, in some cases having the various different solutions available simultaneously can help the user to pull complementary parts of those solutions together into one result that could not otherwise have been generated.

An example of this form of result combination appears in the following section, which describes recent implementation work on applying subjunctive techniques to enhance an existing tool.

3 Application Example

The system currently being used as a test platform for implementing subjunctive interface ideas is 3DVIEWNIX, a portable Unix-based medical-image processing tool.[†]

Work to date has focussed on the support for image segmentation — i.e. the division of a multi-dimensional scene into distinct regions of interest to a doctor, such as individual bones or organs. The segmentation support in the current release of 3DVIEWNIX (1.2) includes a simple form of *live wire* boundary-detection tool that must be 'trained' to detect the kind of edge that is of interest.[‡] Since only one instance of training can be in force at a time, with this tool there is currently poor support for tracing accurately and reproducibly any boundary that has different features in different regions — such as that highlighted in Figure 2. We realised that if 3DVIEWNIX were extended to support multiple 'subjunctive' states we could let the user handle a range of alternative training settings simultaneously, and hence overcome this restriction.

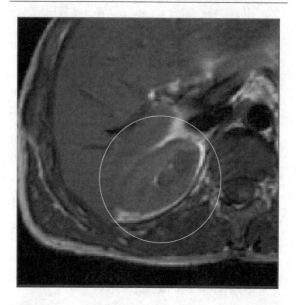

Figure 2: An example of a boundary with different characteristics in different regions. Within the white circle on this MRI image of a horizontal slice through a person's abdomen is the outline of a kidney. However, the nature of the boundary on the left (where it abuts the liver) is rather different from that of the rest of the organ. This presents a problem to some kinds of image-segmentation support tools.

[†]3DVIEWNIX has been developed over several years by the Medical Image Processing Group of the Department of Radiology at the University of Pennsylvania, Pittsburgh. The system and its source code can be purchased from MIPG for research use.

[‡]The 'live wire' technique has been developed principally at Brigham Young University; for an overview see (Mortensen & Barrett, 1998).

3.1   Implemented Subjunctive Features

To date, the following operations have been implemented for the 3DVIEWNIX segmentation tools:

Reality cloning: Creation of a new reality based on a copy of the current application state. The user's actions are directed to the new reality, leaving the previous reality as a snapshot that can be returned to at any time. As well as allowing the realities to be developed further in parallel, this operation can also be used simply as a way of freezing the current state for later use. This would be useful, for example, in an application in which the user finds some result that might be satisfactory, wants to explore further in case a still better result can be found, but also wants to keep tabs on this state in case it turns out to have been the best available.

Event echoing: Enabling/disabling the broadcast of interface events (at the level of mouse movements and clicks) to all currently active realities. If a user has set up a number of realities with different parameters, this facility allows the same operations to be carried out simultaneously on all of them. Alternatively, if the difference between the realities is in the currently selected meaning of mouse input (for example, one is supporting live-wire while another is performing manual tracing), event echoing allows the user to observe the different effects of these various operations. Given appropriate provision to mix the realities' result displays, the different results can be watched simultaneously.

Event echoing can be enabled and disabled at any time, for example to make adjustments to just one reality in the midst of a broadcast operation. However, in the current implementation it is the user's responsibility to ensure that each reality is in an appropriate state to receive the broadcast events.

Primary reality switching: Moving the application on to the next/previous reality, replacing the current operation context, including the display. During the use of event-echoing, operations to copy the results from one reality through to others use the 'primary reality' as the source.

3.2   Usage Scenario

Figure 3 shows the behaviour of the 'live wire' algorithm when trained for the liver/kidney boundary as found in the displayed slice. Although it follows the edge well in the trained region (and would also work for such an edge found in other slices within this study), it is not useful for the remainder of the kidney boundary. Normally the boundary would have to be guided manually around any untrained segments; although this would not be especially laborious for this simple shape, an undesirable side-effect is the risk of inconsistent edge paths being plotted for different slices and different studies, making comparisons difficult.

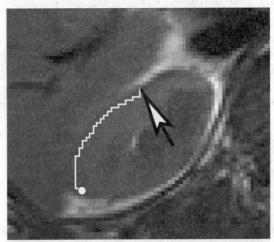

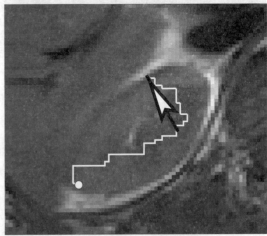

Figure 3: A segmentation in progress using the 'live wire' tool, after training it to follow the liver/kidney boundary. The user clicks somewhere on the desired boundary to establish a start point (here highlighted with a white blob). Thereafter, a live wire is continuously plotted linking the start point to the pointer's current position (shown by the arrow); clicking the mouse again captures the displayed wire and establishes a new start point. The wire follows the trained boundary well (upper image), but when the mouse is outside the region of good fit for the current training (lower image) the algorithm may be attracted to paths other than the intended one.

With the subjunctive interface features an alternative approach is available: the definition of multiple training settings to handle various parts of the boundary, by cloning the application state and training each one using a different edge section. In this case just one further definition suffices; Figure 4 shows an instant during outlining using 'event echoing' to join two application states.

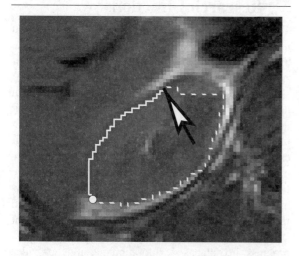

Figure 4: A subjunctive display. Here a second 'reality' has been added with different training, and both are performing the live-wire operation in parallel by means of event-echoing. The wire contributed by the secondary reality is displayed as a dashed line, its attraction to the bright edge of the kidney being so strong that it almost spans the whole path from the present mouse position back to the start point. By assembling the path using selected contributions from the different realities, an entire outline can be built quickly.

3.3 Experiences

These initial experiences of implementing and experimenting with subjunctive interface features for 3DVIEWNIX have been rewarding. At this stage of still learning how the segmentation activity is steered by the environment's parameter settings, and thus how best the addition of multiple realities might be of benefit, simply the facility of storing and recalling a snapshot of the entire set of parameters while experimenting with alternative values provides considerable relief. Merging the interactive responses of multiple realities has also proved to be practicable, and appears to resolve some of the difficulties of using the original system.

With the guidance of our medical-faculty colleagues we aim to refine the subjunctive facilities, for example to decide on how to handle gracefully any divergence between the states of realities that are being driven simultaneously. We aim to

produce demonstrations of how these new facilities enable novel interaction techniques with benefits over existing medical image handling procedures, both in the area of segmentation and in other operational aspects in which exploration appears to be needlessly difficult.

4 Principles and Related Work

4.1 What is a Subjunctive Interface?

Starting from observation of difficulties commonly encountered in the use of computer systems for exploratory tasks, this work aims to improve support for these tasks. In particular, it was noticed that facilities now commonly available for exploration of static data — overview, juxtaposition, reversible interaction — are not yet supported for exploration involving dynamically generated results (although Truvé (n.d.) provided a wake-up call and a useful example). A 'subjunctive' interface is simply one that attempts to provide these facilities, by supporting the modelling, comparison and adjustment of numerous alternative states simultaneously.

4.2 An Extension, Not a New Tool

Support for simultaneous exploration of multiple results could be provided using novel kinds of interface that re-cast the task into a form that particularly suits this kind of interaction — much as *dynamic query* tools re-cast parameter-based data filtering into a combination of sliders and a single two-dimensional view. However, given an existing tool that supports some exploratory task, there are various incentives to providing the additional support as an extension to the existing interface components — i.e. for provisional settings to be specified using the same widgets as usual, and for the different results of provisional choices to be displayed using the same output devices.

One benefit is the ability to stick with an interface has been optimised to suit the task in question, and that is familiar to existing users of the system. Learning to use new exploration mechanisms should be less of a burden if they are based on the existing controls than if based on new exploration-specific tools and abstractions.

Given that a system designer cannot predict all the kinds of exploration a user may wish to do, it is desirable to let the standard facilities constitute a framework within which a user constructs the facilities needed for each occasion of exploration — in line with the *visual formalisms* approach proposed by Nardi & Zarmer (1993). Facilities for *programming by demonstration* — e.g. (Myers, 1998) — likewise seek to integrate the definition of occasion-specific facilities with the normal use of the system, aiming to minimise any self-conscious switch between 'use' and 'programming'. Perhaps our ideal should be to engender in users the feeling that it's acceptable to make tentative rather than firm decisions on any setting in the interface.

4.3   Interface Challenges

Particular challenges arise in helping the user to view and work with the various alternative results, and to understand their relationship to the controlling parameters. The projectiles model provides help in isolating individual cases temporarily to clarify which tentative parameter settings belong with which results: while the user is adjusting any parameter value the interface temporarily dims out all objects in realities other than those being fed by that value. Similarly, if any ball is probed with the mouse, all widgets other than those involved in its creation are faded away so the user can see which settings gave rise to a particular flight path.

A similar need can arise in Computer-Supported Collaborative Work, when collaborative tools have to handle alternative versions of some information to reflect choices or enhancements made by separate users. The work on conflict display and resolution in the Timewarp collaborative toolkit (Edwards & Mynatt, 1997) provides excellent guidance on the interface and system-level handling of such presentation issues.

In some domains, alternative results cannot be merged just by overlaying them — for example, textual lists that would become unreadable, or images that would become a jumble. Various policies could be pursued — for example, one might merge salient aspects of the results into a single list or image, as shown in the 3DVIEWNIX example above, or one could show the various results in separate regions of the display. A disadvantage of the latter approach is that the user has to pay attention to multiple items rather than having the results all placed at a single focus of attention, but in some cases this could be compensated by mechanisms for increasing the salience of results identified as being of particular importance.

4.4   Processing Model

Underlying the subjunctive display one needs a system model that can represent and process the alternative results. A simplistic method would be to replicate the entire underlying environment, again mirroring CSCW mechanisms in which different users each run their own copy of the software connected only by update propagation. However, one can envisage considerably more efficient approaches based on the techniques being developed to support multiple versions of system state for provision of rich undo/redo facilities — e.g. (Abowd & Dix, 1992; Berlage, 1994) — or Atwood et al.'s (1996) powerful support for history reversion and rewriting as offered by 'time travel' facilities in visual programming environments.

5   Research Directions

The subjunctive interface concept is still young, but it is hoped that the ideas described so far will motivate the enhancement of various kinds of exploration-support system.

For each such branch of investigation, empirical testing will provide the litmus test as to whether the additional complexity is providing any benefit in the ability of users to find good results for their explorations. As part of this evaluation there will be much to learn about how the addition of subjunctive facilities changes the paths that users normally follow in their explorations among dynamically constructed results. There seem to be few existing studies of such paths, although Lee's (1998) account of users' progress in database exploration sessions provides welcome insight, especially as his work bridges the domains of static data in databases and the dynamic construction of views derived from the data.

Another field that awaits experimentation is support for parameters whose values occupy a continuous range, rather than a few discrete alternatives. Typically a user working with such a parameter would choose discrete values to represent what are felt to be salient regions within its range, then as long as there are no strong discontinuities in parameter effect between these values the results may be interpreted with the help of interpolation. Where discontinuities do exist, a subjunctive-interface approach that allows detailed sampling and simultaneous consideration of the parameter's effects may be useful in highlighting the nature of the affected operational regions.

As shown by the work by Ahlberg & Truvé (1995) and Tweedie (1997) on 'design spaces' for input devices and interactive visualizations respectively, the development of a design space describing subjunctive behaviour in general will be a major undertaking. However, even at this early, implementation-biased stage of exploring the concept we can benefit from these classifications in considering how it may eventually be generalised. A long-term goal would be a stage where subjunctive interaction mechanisms can be built into frameworks for application construction so that, like the windowing facilities that effectively come 'for free' for applications built with today's interface toolkits, implementors will only need to supply minimal details to be able to offer subjunctive facilities within their applications.

6 Conclusions

This paper has reported progress on the characterization of *subjunctive interface* features in terms of the *cognitive dimensions* framework, and has introduced recent implementation work that is starting to illustrate benefits derived from this interface approach.

Although simple in concept, the idea of giving exploratory interfaces 'subjunctive' behaviour — representing simultaneously what would happen under the influence of a variety of choices — appears to give rise to a complex yet potentially rewarding area of interaction research. In the many domains of computer-supported human activity in which the computer can only act as a tool steered by the user to illuminate interesting results, this new form of support brings the hope of greater confidence in that steering and in the quality of the results that are found.

Acknowledgements

The author is currently a research assistant funded under a donation by Hitachi Software; parts of this work were undertaken during a previous term at the same laboratory as a European Union postdoctoral research fellow. I am very grateful to the staff, students and visiting researchers for providing a supportive atmosphere, and especially to Professor Yuzuru Tanaka, laboratory director, and to Matthew Chalmers for discussions and encouragement. The medical image used here is a sample from the PACS Web site of the University Hospital of Geneva.

References

Abowd, G. D. & Dix, A. J. (1992), "Giving Undo Attention", *Interacting with Computers* **4**(3), 317–42.

Ahlberg, C. & Truvé, S. (1995), Exploring Terra Incognita in the Design Space of Query Devices, *in Proceedings of Engineering for Human-Computer Interaction (EHCI '95)*, IFIP Transactions Series, Chapman & Hall.

Ahlberg, C. & Wistrand, E. (1995), IVEE: An Information Visualization and Exploration Environment, *in* N. Gershon & S. Eick (eds.), *Proceedings of Information Visualization'95*, IEEE Computer Society Press, pp.66–73.

Atwood, Jr., J. W., Burnett, M. M., Walpole, R. A., Wilcox, E. M. & Yang, S. (1996), Steering Programs via Time Travel, *in Proceedings of IEEE Symposium on Visual Languages (VL'96)*, pp.4–11.

Berlage, T. (1994), "A Selective Undo Mechanism for Graphical User Interfaces Based on Command Objects", *ACM Transactions on Computer–Human Interaction* **1**(3), 269–94.

Edwards, W. K. & Mynatt, E. D. (1997), Timewarp: Techniques for Autonomous Collaboration, *in* S. Pemberton (ed.), *Proceedings of CHI'97: Human Factors in Computing Systems*, ACM Press, pp.218–25.

Green, T. R. G. & Blackwell, A. F. (1998), "Cognitive Dimensions of Information Artefacts: a tutorial", http://www.ndirect.co.uk/~thomas.green/.

Green, T. R. G. & Petre, M. (1996), "Usability Analysis of Visual Programming Environments: A 'Cognitive Dimensions' Framework", *Journal of Visual Languages and Computing* **7**(2), 131–74.

Lee, J. P. (1998), A Systems and Process Model for Data Exploration, PhD thesis, Computer Science Department, University of Massachusetts, Lowell, USA.

Lunzer, A. (1996), Reconnaissance: A Widely Applicable Approach Encouraging Well-informed Choices in Computer-based Tasks, PhD thesis, Department of Computing Science, University of Glasgow. TR–1996-4.

Lunzer, A. (1998), Towards the Subjunctive Interface: General Support for Parameter Exploration by Overlaying Alternative Application States, *in Proceedings of IEEE Visualization 1998: Late Breaking Hot Topics*, pp.45–48.

Marks, J., Andalman, B., Beardsley, P. A., Freeman, W., Gibson, S., Hodgins, J., Kang, T., Mirtich, B., Pfister, H., Ruml, W., Ryall, K., Seims, J. & Shieber, S. (1997), Design Galleries: A General Approach to Setting Parameters for Computer Graphics and Animation, *in* T. Whitted (ed.), *Proceedings of SIGGRAPH'97*, ACM Press, pp.389–400.

Mortensen, E. N. & Barrett, W. A. (1998), "Interactive Segmentation with Intelligent Scissors", *Graphical Models and Image Processing* **60**, 349–84.

Myers, B. A. (1998), Scripting Graphical Applications by Demonstration, *in* C.-M. Karat, A. Lund, J. Coutaz & J. Karat (eds.), *Proceedings of CHI'98: Human Factors in Computing Systems*, ACM Press, pp.534–41.

Nardi, B. A. & Zarmer, C. L. (1993), "Beyond Models and Metaphors: Visual Formalisms in User Interface Design", *Journal of Visual Languages and Computing* **4**, 5–33.

Okada, Y. & Tanaka, Y. (1995), IntelligentBox: A Constructive Visual Software Development System for Interactive 3D Graphics Applications, *in Proceedings of IEEE Computer Animation 1995*, pp.114–25.

Todd, S. & Latham, W. (1992), *Evolutionary Art and Computers*, Academic Press.

Truvé, S. (n.d.), Dynamic What-If Analysis: Exploring Computational Dependencies with Slidercells and Micrographs, *in CHICompanion1995*, pp.280–1.

Tweedie, L. (1997), Characterizing Interactive Externalizations, *in* S. Pemberton (ed.), *Proceedings of CHI'97: Human Factors in Computing Systems*, ACM Press, pp.375–82.

Human–Computer Interaction — INTERACT '99
M. Angela Sasse and Chris Johnson (Editors)
Published by IOS Press, © IFIP TC.13, 1999

Design and Evaluation of Phrasier, an Interactive System for Linking Documents Using Keyphrases

Steve Jones

Department of Computer Science, University of Waikato, Private Bag 3105, Hamilton, New Zealand.

stevej@cs.waikato.ac.nz

Abstract: When documents are collected together from diverse sources they are unlikely to contain useful hypertext links to support browsing amongst them. Manual, or semi-automated link creation is often infeasibly time-consuming for large document collections. We present Phrasier, an interactive system which automatically introduces links to related material into documents as the user browses and queries a digital library collection. Suitable links are identified using keyphrases that are identified within document text and support both topic-based and inter-document navigation. Previews of link destinations are provided to reduce unproductive link traversals, and important segments of document text are identified and highlighted to support skimming of viewed documents. Evaluation has shown that Phrasier's keyphrase-based linking mechanism produces sparse hypertexts, although similar documents tend to have short paths between them. A study using human assessors in a simulated document retrieval task indicated that the generated links are perceived to be useful and relevant.

Keywords: browsing interface, dynamic hypertext generation, keyphrase extraction, evaluation.

1 Introduction

Users of interfaces to normative information retrieval systems (such as Web search engines, digital libraries and on-line library catalogues) often face a range of difficulties. These include the need to specify potentially complex information requirements using a few keywords or terms, to do so within the constraints of a query language, and with little indication about the range of valid query terms. For some of these systems — the Web, for example — retrieved documents contain explicit links that support browsing between related elements of the information space. For others, such as digital libraries, the content of the space is drawn from a variety of sources, and there are no explicit links to support browsing activities.

Our motivating examples for the work presented here are reference collections from the New Zealand Digital Library (NZDL), http://www.nzdl.org (Witten et al., 1998; 1999b). One collection, the Computer Science Technical Reports (CSTR) contains more than 40,000 technical research reports from hundreds of publicly-accessible repositories around the world. Another is a mirror of the Human–Computer Interaction (HCI) Bibliography, http://www.hcibib.org

(Perlman, 1991). Although these collections and most of the others in the library contain no embedded links we wish to link documents to support user browsing. Manual creation and maintenance of links within the collections is precluded by the enormous amount of time and effort that would be required — there are several gigabytes of text.

One solution is to identify appropriate links between documents using an automated computational process. This is often done by using information retrieval (Salton, 1989) statistical measures to compute (prior to browsing) semantic similarity values for all pairs of documents — links are created between documents with a similarity above a certain threshold. This is a computationally intensive process that must be repeated each time the collection is updated. Many of the NZDL collections are updated every few days, and such an approach is not suitable.

Our solution is to generate links interactively as the user browses, and to provide interaction techniques which allow fluid transitions by the user between querying and browsing tasks. Browsing is supported by emphasis of key segments of viewed documents which act as link anchors, provision of lists of related documents and suggestions of related query terms.

In this paper we describe Phrasier, an interactive system that incorporates these facilities. The paper is organized as follows. In the next section we give an overview of the facilities provided by Phrasier, its use of automatically identified keyphrases and its user interface. This is followed by a report on evaluation of the hypertexts generated by Phrasier which addresses coverage, soundness and user perceptions. We then present conclusions and discuss directions for future work.

2   Phrasier

Phrasier blends querying and browsing (Golovchinsky, 1997) to support navigation between related documents in a digital library document collection. Its main features are:

- Automatic identification and user-controlled variable highlighting of key words and phrases within a viewed document.

- Generation of ranked lists of links to other documents in the collection that are related to the viewed document.

- Generation of links from identified keyphrases to related documents.

- Provision of previews of the content of link destinations.

Highlighting of identified keyphrases supports skimming (Masson, 1982) — quickly scanning through a document to get a sense of it. This is helpful in information exploration tasks to allow users to rapidly ascertain whether or not a document is useful, and which segments of it are important. Although this technique has been used in other systems such as the XLibris active reading machine (Schilit et al., 1998), Phrasier's interactive control of variable highlighting is novel.

Often users will find a useful document and require others that are similar. Generation of links to other documents, ranked by similarity, supports navigation to such documents. Other systems such as The InfoFinder Agent (Krulwich & Burkey, 1997) use keyphrases to induce user interests during a retrieval session and suggest related material. Phrasier differs from this system in that it makes the attributes that determine related documents (the keyphrases) explicit and interactive.

Links based on keyphrases support topic-based navigation. This allows users to utilise particular concepts that occur within a document as the path to

other documents. In PHIND (Nevill-Manning et al., 1997) keyphrases provide a table of contents-like overview of the topics within a document collection. Phrasier offers a similar facility, but shows phrases that relate to a particular document.

Previews of the content of destination documents allow users to briefly evaluate links without the cost of navigation along them.

The Phrasier user interface can be seen in Figure 1. There are three panes: to the left is the document pane where viewed documents are displayed and edited, in the middle is a list of keyphrases identified within the viewed document, and to the right is a list of similar documents.

The documents that are viewed in Phrasier can be loaded from a user's filestore, retrieved from the document collection of a digital library, or entered using Phrasier's text editor. Links are created from the viewed document to others in a digital library collection. Phrasier currently works with two collections of the New Zealand Digital Library: the CSTR collection and a mirror of the HCI Bibliography — a bibliographic database of more than 15,000 HCI related publications.

A keyphrase-based retrieval engine underpins Phrasier, retrieving and ranking lists of documents to form the links within documents. Rather than using the full-text of documents like many retrieval systems — such as MG (Witten et al., 1994) — this performs retrieval, similarity measurements and link creation based on keyphrases within documents.

Some documents (such as conference papers) often contain keywords and phrases provided by their author. Others are allocated keywords and phrases when they are catalogued. However, in many cases there are no keywords or phrases associated with a document. For example, fewer than a third of the items in the HCI Bibliography have associated keywords or phrases.

The Kea system (Frank et al., to appear) has been used to automatically extract document keyphrases for use in Phrasier. Kea uses a machine learning approach, building a model of distinguishing characteristics of keyphrases from a training set of documents for which keyphrases exist (such as those specified by authors). Different models can be built by providing different training sets, and models exist (among others) for World Wide Web pages, computer science technical reports, bibliographic databases and newsgroup postings. For document collections which contain no suitable training material, an existing model which most closely matches the characteristics of the documents can be used.

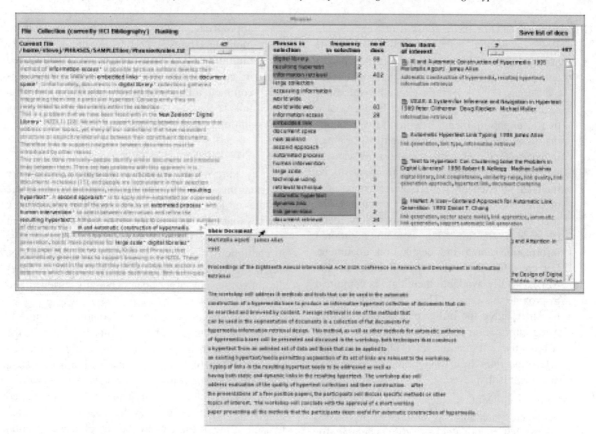

Figure 1: The Phrasier user interface. In the document pane (to the left) each keyphrase acts as a link anchor. A gloss is displayed when an anchor is selected. The middle pane shows the keyphrases that have been identified within the text. To the right is a ranked list of documents retrieved using the selected keyphrases as a query.

During the keyphrase extraction process, Kea produces a list of phrases from each document, ordered on the likelihood of them being keyphrases of the document. These keyphrases can be used to augment available keyphrases (such as those specified by the author), or as surrogates where none exist. For our keyphrase-based retrieval engine, we build keyphrase indexes from Kea's output. These hold frequencies of keyphrases within documents, the keyphrases that are allocated to a particular document, and the documents to which a particular keyphrase is allocated.

2.1 Linking Documents

The *document pane* enables users to enter the text of a document that they are authoring, to load a previously created document from disk, or to load a document from the library collection. As a user enters text, or it is read from a file, a background process identifies keyphrases from the collection that occur within the text. To do this the input is tokenized to find candidate phrases. This entails determining

word boundaries and building sequences of adjacent words up to the length of the longest phrase in the keyphrase index. Heuristics identify components of the text which can not occur within keyphrases, such as sentence boundaries, which leads to immediate rejection of some candidates.

Remaining candidates are passed to a query process of the retrieval engine, which responds as to whether they occur as keyphrases within the collection. Only direct matches are considered at present, although an obvious extension might be to introduce synonym identification. If a match occurs, the phrase is highlighted within the text and the retrieval engine identifies related documents within the collection, ranking them and returning pointers to them to Phrasier. A link anchor is then inserted into the text for the keyphrase, pointing to the set of related documents. Insertion of links in real-time, as the user types, allows related material to be uncovered as part of the writing process rather than a separate and distinct querying activity.

Glosses: Each anchor has a *gloss* (Zellweger et al., 1998) associated with it. Glosses provide an indication of the nature of the destination content, the need for which has been discussed by Furnas (1997) (referred to as residues or scents). In Phrasier this takes the form of a two-level pop-up menu. The first level contains the titles of the target documents, presented in an ordered list with the most relevant at the top. The number of destinations to be included for each anchor defaults to a maximum of five, but can be specified by the user. The user can choose to pop up a secondary menu for each destination. This contains additional information about the destination document. For the HCI Bibliography collection of the NZDL, readily available meta-data is combined to provide this detail. The glosses allow users to partly judge the utility of link destinations, using information derived from the destinations without the cost of a link traversal. When a user selects an item from the menu the associated document is displayed.

In other collections, such as the CSTR where documents are sourced in Postscript format, no explicit meta-data is readily available for inclusion in a gloss. However, text mining techniques — e.g. (Witten et al., 1999a) — show promise for automated extraction of 'interesting' components from text documents. Many of these components such as: authors' names, dates, sources and URLs would be suitable for inclusion in glosses.

Link highlighting: The user can also toggle whether link anchors are displayed or not. Further, key phrase anchors can be displayed in a range of grey levels. The grey levels correspond to a measure of importance of a phrase within the document text. A slider control allows the user to manipulate the contrast between key phrase anchors and the text of the document to emphasise or hide phrases. At one extreme the anchors are indistinguishable from the rest of the document text, at the other only anchor text is visible. The link anchors can be used as 'skimming' aids, to enable readers to rapidly consider key topics in the documents.

Multiple anchors, multiple destinations: The document pane enables the author or reader to move beyond the 'one anchor, one target' model commonly used in linked structures such as the Web, by providing multiple targets where

appropriate. It also supports 'multiple anchors, multiple targets'. Using a keyboard modifier multiple key phrase anchors can be selected in the document pane, and once selection is complete a list combining destinations for each link is formed and displayed in the document summary pane (see Section 2.2).

2.2   Summary Overviews

As key phrases are identified in the text they are inserted into the *key phrases pane* (shown in the middle of Figure 1). This contains a list of key phrases that have been identified within the document pane. Phrases in the list can be selected individually, in contiguous blocks, or in multiple disjoint blocks. Selections behave as they do in the document pane- the most relevant target documents are retrieved and displayed.

The *document summary pane* (shown in Figure 1) displays a ranked list of documents from within the collection which are related to sets of user selected key phrases. When bibliographic information is available, some items (such as title, author, year, and keywords) are displayed in the summary pane. This is augmented by display of the key phrases that have been allocated to each of the documents by the key phrase extraction process. Currently displayed summary information can be saved to disk for later consideration. The text of a document can be retrieved and viewed by selection of its anchor in this pane.

2.3   Implementation

The interface of Phrasier is implemented in Tcl/Tk (Welch, 1997) and runs on systems with standard Tcl/Tk installations. The retrieval engine is implemented in Perl (Wall et al., 1996). The client-server architecture renders the interface more portable, data is centralised and servers can be tailored to the requirements of particular collections. The drawback is that this approach incurs the costs of transferring data over the network.

3   Evaluation

Our first step in evaluation has been to evaluate the hypertexts created by Phrasier. Although Phrasier dynamically generates links at browse time, for the purposes of evaluation we have built pre-computed hypertexts using Phrasier's linking mechanism.

3.1   Coverage of Generated Hypertexts

One way to characterise a hypertext generated by Phrasier is the degree of *coverage* (Blustein et al., 1997). This indicates the fraction of document pairs that have paths between them. If there was a path between all pairs of nodes in the hypertext coverage would be 100%. We can consider coverage at a variety of levels of out-degree (the maximum number of links allowed from each node). For coverage analysis we drew ten sets of 100, 500 and 1,000 randomly selected documents from the HCI Bibliography collection. Links from each document were generated at out-degrees from one to ten using similarity measures provided by the retrieval engine. This is a common approach in automated hypertext construction (Agosti et al., 1997; Allan, 1997; Bernstein, 1990). The most similar returned document was selected at out-degree one, the next most similar at out-degree 2 and so on. Table 1 shows the mean coverage achieved across the document sets at each out-degree.

Out Degree	Mean percent coverage over 10 sets of 100, 500 and 1000 documents.					
	100		500		1000	
	Mean	SD	Mean	SD	Mean	SD
1	0.94	0.19	0.28	0.03	0.16	0.01
2	2.47	0.96	1.20	0.29	0.86	0.016
3	4.57	1.92	5.50	2.81	7.69	3.27
4	7.23	2.71	16.60	5.52	24.76	4.21
5	9.61	3.41	28.64	4.29	35.57	4.14
6	12.60	5.50	34.12	3.86	41.39	3.78
7	16.07	7.65	37.81	3.44	45.90	3.43
8	19.00	9.22	40.55	3.47	48.99	4.18
9	20.81	9.06	43.31	3.50	51.41	4.17
10	22.94	9.03	44.83	3.61	53.33	3.83

Table 1: Mean coverage at out-degree 1 to 10 for randomly selected sets of 100, 500 and 1000 documents from the HCI bibliography collection.

With one link from each document only a small fraction of document pairs are connected — fewer than 1% for each size of hypertext. Coverage increases with out-degree as we might expect, up to approximately 23%, 45% and 53% for hypertexts of size 100, 500 and 1000 documents respectively with out-degree 10. Coverage decreases with hypertext size at out-degrees of 1 and 2, but increases for larger out-degrees.

In a comparable study Blustein et al. (1997) report coverage for a document collection of 1608 document of similar length those in our evaluation. They deployed a range of full-text similarity measurement techniques to which the similarity measurement of Phrasier is similar except for the use of keyphrases rather than the full-text of documents. They achieved coverage in the range 0.17% to 0.18% for outdegree 1. For the maximum out-degree of 5 that they tested they achieved coverage in the range 81.24% to 88.72%. At each out-degree from 1 to 5 Phrasier produces sparser hypertexts than they achieved — comparatively fewer documents are accessible from any given document.

3.2 Soundness of Generated Hypertexts

Of course, even if all other documents were accessible from a given document, 100% coverage would likely overwhelm the user with decisions about which links to follow. The goal is therefore to provide the most effective number of links from each document which provide the shortest possible paths to the most strongly related documents. This is reflected in the degree of *soundness* of the hypertext — how well the distance between nodes reflects their similarity. Soundness can be expressed as the correlation between the path length between pairs of documents and their similarity (as determined by the phrase-based similarity measure).

The coefficient of correlation (Pearson) between path length (for document pairs with a path between them) and semantic similarity measure is shown in Table 2. Larger magnitudes of coefficients indicate a strong relationship between path length and document similarity. We expect values that are less than zero because high similarity should be reflected by small path lengths. For all out-degrees in the range 1 to 10, and for each size of hypertext we observe a significant correlation, although it generally weak. There is a tendency for correlation to become weaker as the number of links from each document increases. This is to be expected because the most sound link is always selected at out-degree 1, and at out-degree 10 several poorly related documents are likely to be included. The strength of correlation tends to decrease with the size of hypertext and rapidly diminishes for 1000 documents with out-degrees of more than 2.

Blustein et al. (1997) report strong correlations with magnitude greater than 0.7 for out-degree of 1 and weaker correlations with magnitude in the range 0.0265 to 0.2122 for out-degree of 5. The soundness of Phrasier's links is comparatively worse than achieved by the full-text techniques that they used for link generation.

3.3 Human Assessment of Links

Although coverage and soundness characterise the hypertext as a whole, they indicate little about the utility of the links provided from each document. A study was carried out in which the quality of generated links was determined by human assessors. The links generated by Phrasier (using a phrase-based similarity measure) and those generated using a full-text measure were evaluated.

Out Degree	Mean coefficient of correlation between similarity and path length over 10 sets of 100, 500 and 1000 documents.					
	100		500		1000	
	Mean	SD	Mean	SD	Mean	SD
1	-0.4351	0.0871	-0.4971	0.0428	-0.5041	0.0222
2	-0.5210	0.0282	-0.4846	0.0378	-0.4622	0.0354
3	-0.5351	0.0458	-0.3761	0.0700	-0.2673	0.0734
4	-0.5036	0.0607	-0.2591	0.0602	-0.1604	0.0381
5	-0.5030	0.0691	-0.1989	0.0390	-0.1177	0.0342
6	-0.4746	0.0779	-0.2030	0.0309	-0.1319	0.0334
7	-0.4730	0.0673	-0.2047	0.0310	-0.1347	0.0573
8	-0.4609	0.0900	-0.2134	0.0336	-0.1378	0.0468
9	-0.4648	0.0735	-0.2089	0.0404	-0.1491	0.0476
10	-0.4562	0.0796	-0.2174	0.0426	-0.1534	0.0492

Table 2: Mean coefficients of correlation at out-degree 1 to 10 for randomly selected sets of 100, 500 and 1000 documents from the HCI bibliography collection.

Six volunteer subjects each provided two HCI-related research papers that they had recently authored. For each paper, the reference list was removed and the text submitted to Phrasier, which returned and stored links to the ten most similar documents within the HCI Bibliography collection. The full-text of each paper (without the reference list) was also submitted to the HCI Bibliography collection of the NZDL proper, and the first ten documents in the ranked result list were stored.

For each paper the two lists were combined into a composite list (with duplicates removed) which was then presented to the paper's author. The author scored the relevance of each document in the list to their original paper on a scale of 1 (irrelevant) to 7 (highly relevant). Each subject then viewed the full top ten list generated by both of the systems and scored them as a whole on the same relevance scale. We considered only the first ten returned documents because transaction log analysis of digital libraries and WWW-based search engines shows that users rarely look beyond the first few returned documents (Jones et al., 1998; Spink et al., 1998).

Overall, analysis of collated results revealed no significant difference between the performance of keyphrase or full-text retrieval mechanisms as scored by human assessors, or in the number of identifiably relevant documents that were returned. We considered the references from the source papers that occurred within the document collection to be relevant result documents. Recall of these relevant documents is almost identical (approximately 25%) with out-degree of 10 for both the full text system and Phrasier.

The scores allocated to individual documents in the composite list were collated back into the top ten lists from which they originated. A mean score for each system-paper combination was calculated. The mean document relevance for Phrasier was 4.13 ($s.d. = 1.67$) and for the full text system 3.33 ($s.d. = 1.22$). On average, links created by Phrasier were found to be slightly more relevant than irrelevant, and slightly better than those returned by a full text search. However, this is not a significant difference (Friedman two-way analysis of variance by rank, $p = 0.05$). There was a high degree of variation in subject responses. Some found the links to be highly relevant, others almost completely irrelevant. We believe this to be the case because although all papers mentioned HCI topics, the primary focus of several papers was not HCI and so did not overlap well with the content of the HCI Bibliography.

The same observations hold when subjects' relevance scores assigned to each top ten list as a whole were considered (mean of 4.67, $s.d. = 1.83$ for Phrasier and 3.75, $s.d. = 1.66$ for the full text system).

There is only one measure by which the methods vary significantly — the mean relevance scores assigned to links in each of the first ten locations in each list. These are significantly higher (Friedman two-way analysis of variance by ranks, $p = 0.05$) for the phrase-based methods than for the full-text method. Figure 2 shows the mean scores assigned to the two systems. Perceived relevance tended to decrease from the beginning to the end of the top ten list for all methods, so it appears that they are effectively ranked in relevance order.

Overall we see little difference in the performance of the two methods, either in recall of identifiably relevant documents or perceived relevance of returned documents. This indicates that Phrasier's phrase-based linking technique produces links of a comparable quality to that of a standard full text retrieval system.

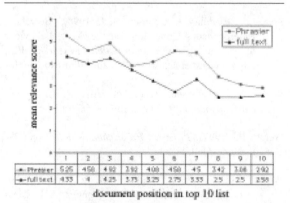

Figure 2: Comparison of mean relevance score (across subjects) allocated to each position in the list of ten generated links.

4   Conclusions

The aim of Phrasier is to support effective interactive exploration of a document collection. To this end it utilises a range of interaction techniques such as link anchor glosses, multi-headed links, and variable emphasis of important segments of text which act as link anchors. A primary consideration is the quality of the links generated through a novel phrase-based similarity measure. Although there is room for improvement the results of our evaluations are encouraging — similar documents tend to be linked with short paths between them, and users perceive the links as appropriate. The approach merits further investigation.

We observed three factors that impact upon the quality of the generated hypertext: the number of documents, the set of documents used and the number of links allowed from each document. Tables 1 & 2 indicate substantial variations across randomly selected document sets, and between different document set sizes. Awareness of the effect of the size and characteristics of a document set is important in evaluation of automatically generated hypertexts. It is clearly important to undertake multiple trials across multiple set sizes.

The number of links allowed from each document is one determining factor in the coverage and

soundness of a generated hypertext. This knowledge can be exploited within an information exploration interface. Putting out-degree under users' control allows them to manage the trade-off between coverage and soundness interactively, as they see fit. Indeed, we support this in Phrasier.

5   Future Work

The results of the evaluations described above indicate that our technique shows promise, particularly in the case of the user assessments. However, it is clear that further work is required to improve the soundness of the generated links. This is somewhat dependent on the effectiveness of the automated keyphrase extraction process. Refinement of this system is ongoing and we believe that the keyphrases produced will improve in their ability to characterise and differentiate between documents.

We are currently investigating how the phrase-based similarity measurement can be optimised to improve retrieval of relevant documents in Phrasier, and most appropriately manage the coverage/soundness trade-off.

When we are satisfied with the quality of the links provided by Phrasier we will undertake usability evaluation of the Phrasier interface. In particular we will investigate two novel aspects, evaluating the utility of multi-level glosses as previews of link destinations, and evaluating the utility of variable level highlighting for document skimming. A paper-based evaluation of variable keyphrase highlighting is currently in progress.

Acknowledgements

Thanks to Carl Gutwin, who collaborated on the initial design of Phrasier; Gene Golovchinsky and Gordon Paynter for useful discussions about this work; and Mark Staveley for administering the user study and undertaking initial data analysis.

References

Agosti, M., Crestani, F. & Melucci, M. (1997), "On the use of information retrieval techniques for the automatic construction of hypertext", *Information Processing and Management* **33**(2), 133–44.

Allan, J. (1997), "Building Hypertext Using Information Retrieval", *Information Processing and Management* **33**(2), 145–59.

Bernstein, M. (1990), An Apprentice that Discovers Hypertext Links, *in* A. Rizk, N. Streitz & J. André (eds.), *Proceedings of the European Conference on*

Hypertext (ECHT'90), Cambridge University Press, pp.212–33.

Blustein, J., Webber, R. E. & Tague-Sutcliffe, J. (1997), "Methods for Evaluating the Quality of Hypertext Links", *Information Processing and Management* **33**(2), 255–71.

Frank, E., Paynter, G. W., Witten, I. H., Gutwin, C. & Nevill-Manning, C. G. (to appear), Domain-specific Keyphrase Extraction, *in Proceedings of the Sixteenth International Joint Conference on Artificial Intelligence*, Morgan-Kaufmann.

Furnas, G. W. (1997), Effective View Navigation, *in* S. Pemberton (ed.), *Proceedings of CHI'97: Human Factors in Computing Systems*, ACM Press, pp.367–74.

Golovchinsky, G. (1997), What the Query Told the Link: The Integration of Hypertext and Information Retrieval, *in* M. Bernstein, L. Carr & K. Østerbye (eds.), *Proceedings of Hypertext'97*, ACM Press, pp.67–74.

Jones, S., Cunningham, S. J. & McNab, R. J. (1998), An Analysis of Usage of a Digital Library., *in* C. Nikolaou & C. Stephanidis (eds.), *Proceedings of Second European Conference on Digital Libraries (ECDL'98)*, Springer-Verlag, pp.261–77.

Krulwich, B. & Burkey, C. (1997), "The InfoFinder Agent: Learning User Interests Through Heuristic Phrase Extraction.", *IEEE Expert* **12**(5), 22–7.

Masson, M. E. J. (1982), "Cognitive Processes in Skimming Stories", *Journal of Experimental Psychology: Learning, Memory and Cognition* **8**(5), 400–17.

Nevill-Manning, C. G., Witten, I. H. & Paynter, G. W. (1997), Browsing in Digital Libraries: A Phrase-Based Approach, *in* R. B. Allen & E. Rasmussen (eds.), *In Proceedings of ACM Digital Libraries '97*, ACM Press, pp.230–6.

Perlman, G. (1991), "The HCI Bibliography project", *ACM SIGCHI Bulletin* **23**(3), 15–20.

Salton, G. (1989), *Automatic Text Processing: The Transformation, Analysis and Retrieval of Information by Computer*, Addison–Wesley.

Schilit, B. N., Price, M. N. & Golovchinsky, G. (1998), Digital Library Information Appliances, *in* I. Witten, R. Akscyn & F. M. Shipman (eds.), *Proceedings of ACM Digital Libraries '98*, ACM Press, pp.217–26.

Spink, A., Bateman, J. & Jansen, B. J. (1998), "Searching Heterogeneous Collections on the Web: Behaviour of Excite Users", *Information Research* **4**(2). http://www.shef.ac.uk/ is/publications/infres/ircont.html.

Wall, L., Christiansen, T. & Schwartz, R. L. (1996), *Programming Perl*, second edition, O'Reilly.

Welch, B. (1997), *Practical Programming in Tcl and Tk*, Prentice–Hall.

Witten, I. H., Bray, Z., Mahoui, M. & Teahan, W. J. (1999a), Text Mining: A New Frontier for Lossless Compression, *in* J. Storer & M. Cohn (eds.), *Proceedings of Data Compression Conference*, IEEE Publications, pp.198–207.

Witten, I. H., McNab, R., Jones, S. & Cunningham, S. J. (1999b), "Managing Multiple Collection, Multiple Languages, and Multiple Media in a Distributed Digital Library", *IEEE Computer* **32**(2), 74–9.

Witten, I. H., Moffat, A. & Bell, T. C. (1994), *Managing Gigabytes: Compressing and Indexing Documents and Images*, Van Nostrand Reinhold.

Witten, I. H., Nevill-Manning, C., McNab, R. & Cunningham, S. J. (1998), "A Public Library Based on Full-text Retrieval", *Communications of the ACM* **41**(4), 71–5.

Zellweger, P. T., Chang, B. & Mackinlay, J. D. (1998), Fluid Links for Informed and Incremental Link Transitions, *in* K. Grønbæk, E. Mylonas & F. M. Shipman (eds.), *Proceedings of Hypertext'98*, ACM Press, pp.50–7.

OTree: A Tree Visualization using Scaling and Omission

Karlis Kaugars

Western Michigan University, Department of Computer Science, Kalamazoo, MI 49008, USA.

kkaugars@cs.wmich.edu

Abstract: Trees are a nearly ubiquitous information structure, used in applications including source code display, document categorization and directory browsing. We describe a mechanism to manage the exponential growth of tree displays utilizing both scaling and omission which allows the display of large trees in an intuitive and familiar form. A description of the mechanism used for omission is given along with display variations which may prove useful when including the OTree display in applications.

Keywords: tree display, information visualization, fisheye view, focus + context technique.

1 Introduction

Hierarchical structures are nearly ubiquitous, appearing in such diverse information sources as tables of contents, organizational structures, internet addresses, directory structures, and source code. Since they are so common, displays of hierarchical structure are present in a wide variety of applications including knowledge representation (Reinfelds, 1991), hypertext systems (Feiner, 1988), and document category hierarchies (Hearst & Karadi, 1997).

One feature which contributes to the popularity of hierarchical information structures is the exponential growth behaviour of the structure. Given a branching factor of b, the depth of a balanced tree containing n nodes is $log_b n$. Unfortunately, the very same feature makes presentation of large trees very difficult as drawings of even moderate trees such as those containing fewer than 50 nodes can easily grow beyond available display space, not to mention the cognitive capacity of the user.

The display of hierarchical structures by nature has two contradictory goals: provide contextual orientation within the structure and show the contents of the nodes. Given a large tree, the number of nodes to display to the user precludes including every node at full scale, but diagrammatic overviews of the entire structure preclude the display of node details. We must therefore seek to find an appropriate balance between context and detail and we attempt to do so by providing a new display technique for large trees.

Our display allows the user or system to select areas of the tree to display at full scale and includes as much context as possible by utilizing scaling and priority-based pruning.

1.1 Related Work

Many interactive systems use tree diagrams to display hierarchical information structures. Most of these systems use conventional tree diagram representations, which lay out nodes on a two dimensional plane as attractively as possible (Wetherell & Shannon, 1979; Reingold & Tilford, 1981; DiBattista et al., 1999). All of these methods include every node in the display, and as the number of nodes increases so must the amount of display space. Most systems based on diagrams use scrolling or some type of panning and zooming technology to expand the drawing surface beyond available display space, but as the size of the drawing increases, so must the distance between nodes (especially at the root of the tree) and therefore the user cannot see sibling relationships of the tree.

Some of the difficulties with planar drawings can be overcome by using three dimensional layouts of hierarchical structure. The most well-known of these three dimensional tree layouts is the Cone Tree (Robertson et al., 1991; Hearst & Karadi, 1997) which positions nodes in three dimensions by adopting the layout formalism that all subtrees are laid out as a cone with the parent node at the apex of a cone and all children at the base of the cone. As demonstrated by Koike & Yoshihara (1993), this approach does not eliminate the exponential growth problem, but only postpones it.

Tree Maps (Johnson & Shneiderman, 1991) produce space-efficient diagrams of hierarchical structure by allocating the entire display area to nodes, recursively dividing the available space among children based on the properties of the node. The space allocated to each node is outlined or filled according to the properties of the node and this technique can be used to efficiently search for property patterns between nodes. The technique tends to obscure hierarchical structure and by virtue of at a minimum displaying all leaf nodes of the tree may exhaust the available display space.

Distorting views of trees such as the hyperbolic displays of Lamping & Rao (1994; Lamping et al., 1995), fractal displays of Koike & Yoshihara (1993) and the fisheye views of Furnas (1986) utilize the idea that while a user of a hierarchical display may be interested in overall structure, the user is in reality focusing on a small portion of the tree. Hyperbolic trees perform initial tree layout on the hyperbolic plane which is mapped to the unit circle for display to the user. The focus node is placed at the centre of the display and is shown at full scale, and nodes are shown at progressively reduced size as distance from the node of interest increases. While elegantly supporting focused views of tree diagrams, the method does not allow the user to simultaneously view multiple nodes at full scale.

Pruning the set of nodes to display was first proposed by Furnas during development of Fisheye Views (Furnas, 1986). He proposed that every node x be assigned a Degree of Interest (*DOI*) based on the user's current focus on y and an A Priori Importance (*API*) using the formula:

$$DOI_{fisheye}(x|.=y) = API(x) - D(x,y)$$

where D represents the distance between x and y. Applied to tree displays, the *API* of node x is negative distance to the root and D is the path distance between two nodes. Furnas proposes the use of a threshold value for *DOI* to determine which nodes should be displayed to the user. This approach can potentially select only the nodes of interest to the user, but may equally well not utilize the available display space when the threshold is set to include too few nodes or may overrun the available display space when the threshold is set too high.

Our approach to the display of hierarchical structures accepts that we will eventually have to prune the number of nodes displayed to the user, but does not prune unless absolutely necessary. It utilizes available

display space to present the user with as much of the tree as possible, attempting to scale nodes to fit the available space and thereby preserving as much of the contextual structure as possible.

2   OTree Views

The OTree visualization uses three views of trees selected depending on the available display space. Small trees are rendered with all nodes fully visible, larger trees are rendered using a focus + context technique which scales non-focus nodes and very large trees use a combination of scaling and omission to render focus areas of the tree. One of the three methods is chosen at run time after initial tree layout based on the size of the unscaled layout and the available display area.

The same layout algorithm is used regardless of the selected view with nodes positioned during a postorder traversal. For nodes without children, the initial position is set based on the position of the left neighbour of the node, and nodes without left neighbours are positioned at the x coordinate origin. For a node with children, the position is calculated so that the node is centred above the children. If this position overlaps left neighbour nodes, the node is positioned to the right of the left neighbour and the descendants of the node are shifted so that a parent node always remains centred above the children.

This layout suffers from the common problem of tree diagrams in that it grows exponentially with depth. For trees which fit entirely within the available display space, this does not cause difficulty but even moderate trees can easily exceed the available display space. As only one example, a four-level complete binary tree with three-character labels will exceed a 500 pixel display. Figure 1 shows the outline structure of this paper presented without scaling.

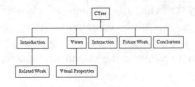

Figure 1: Unscaled tree diagram.

Given the difficulties of displaying hierarchical structure, it is not unreasonable to switch to alternate visualization techniques such as hyperbolic displays (Lamping et al., 1995) or TreeMaps (Johnson & Shneiderman, 1991). There are, however, usability advantages to using a layout method which most users find intuitive if not familiar. We therefore overcome the disadvantages of the layout by utilizing scaling and omission to render the trees within the available display space.

Since most trees will not fit within the available display area, we provide a preliminary fall-back display which attempts to scale nodes so that they all fit within the available space. Nodes which have been marked as important by the user or system are left unscaled, but all other nodes are scaled to fit the available display space. Figure 2 shows a directory tree scaled to fit the available space with the 'Papers' subtree selected to show all nodes.

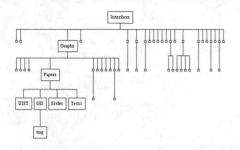

Figure 2: Scaled view of a directory tree.

When a tree is sufficiently large, any uniform scaling will result in nodes and in extreme situations entire regions of the tree which must map to areas sufficiently small to be of no practical use — if individual nodes fall below the size of approximately four by four pixels, they become essentially unselectable and while they still may provide structural information they can serve no useful interactive purpose. Uniform scaling of even larger trees can result in situations where nodes map to areas of less than a single pixel, obliterating structural information as well.

We avoid excessive reduction by limiting the smallest size at which a node may display. If the tree is sufficiently large, we switch to a second fall-back position, an omissive display. In this display, each node is assigned a negative priority equal to the path distance between the node and the nearest selected node. The assignment is illustrated in Figure 3. This assignment with a single selected node gives equal weight to siblings and parents and with a single selected nodes is in effect a simplified form of the Fisheye formula with all $API(x) \equiv 0$.

Each selected node is still displayed at full size, and all non-selected nodes are scaled to a user-defined minimum size. Layout proceeds by successively removing the lowest priority nodes in the tree until

a display is generated which fits the available area. Since this process may remove an excessive number of nodes, we then proceed to restore as many sibling sets at possible while still remaining within the available space. In order to guarantee a consistent tree presentation, we set two limits on node removal:

1. All selected nodes (those with priority 0) along with all nodes of priority -1 are always visible on the display. This forces the display to always be maintained in a state where the user can still navigate the tree.

2. If a node is visible, all of the ancestors of the node are visible. This maintains the connection between a selected node and the root of the tree.

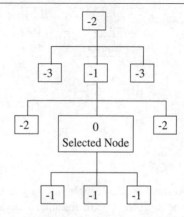

Figure 3: Node priorities based on the selected node.

Hidden subtrees are indicated on the display by small triangles drawn immediately below the last visible ancestor. Drawing these triangles considerably eases user navigation through the tree, allowing differentiation between leaf nodes and nodes which have non-visible children.

Figure 4 illustrates successive selection on a large tree — in this case a directory tree containing 675 nodes. The initial image shows the directory tree with no selected nodes. The next image shows three hidden directories opened. This is followed by successive selections of larger portions of the 'Classes' subtree. As nodes are added to the subtree, less room is available for the display of hidden directory subtrees and these subtrees are collapsed so that more display area is available for the selected nodes. As illustrated by the final display of the sequence, selecting nodes at a depth greater than the collapsed subtrees does not impact the collapsed subtrees.

Although the primary concern with this type of representation is width, deep hierarchies can overrun the available height as well as width. As with width, we use a two-fall-back strategy to handle display, but

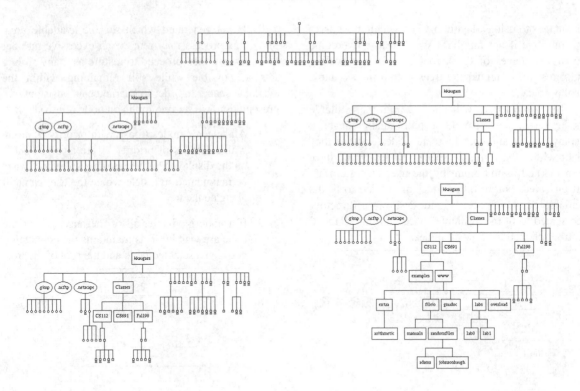

Figure 4: A sequence of selections in a directory tree.

since the vertical space occupied by any level of the tree must be able to contain the tallest node on the level, instead of manipulating the nodes we manipulate the space allocated to links.

Through trial and error, we have found that a gap of approximately 1.5 times the node height produces an aesthetically pleasing display. If the depth is such that it would exceed the available height, we uniformly reduce the inter-level spacing to accommodate the additional height. If the space available for links is reduced below 0.75 times the node height, we switch strategies and move to an edge-scrolled display.

Any display supporting more than a single focus node can exceed the available display area by user action. The OTree display is no different, and if the user selects too many nodes for simultaneous viewing, the display can still overrun the available space. In these instances we resort to active edge scrolling by pointer movement to allow interactive panning of the display.

For the displays used to illustrate this work, we have chosen to draw the trees using a vertical orientation and brushed link drawings. There is no reason the drawings could not be oriented horizontally or individual straight line segments could not be used for rendering the edges.

2.1   Visual Properties

The hidden node displays can change radically as the result of node selection or deselection — selection can remove a substantial amount of display space forcing subtrees to collapse into single nodes. Deselection can allow entire subtrees to open. A sudden transformation of the display can cause unnecessary user confusion, and we believe that the use of interactive animation is essential for successful use of this display method.

We implement animation by pre-calculating each node's final position and size after each selection or deselection event. If a node will be hidden after transformation, the target position is set to be the centre of the triangle representing the hidden subtree and the size is set to be zero. Similarly, a node just becoming visible is set to originate at the triangle's centre point and start with size zero. For each node, we calculate size and positional delta values so that it will move to the final display position within a two-second animation interval.

The diagrams do not use colour or node shape to display information about the properties of nodes. We can use both colour and node shape to indicate any property of nodes which can appropriately map to these display dimensions. As one example, we could colour the nodes of a directory browser by mapping the total size of the directory tree to colour using a standard red to violet mapping.

There are several other simple mappings of properties which could be easily included in the display: continuing with the same example, We could further use the node shape to indicate the disk or disk partition on which a node resides, thereby encoding an additional property in the display. Any other limited node property may be encoded using shape — in Figure 4 we have used oval nodes for hidden directories and rectangular nodes for all other nodes.

3 Interaction

Our current implementation supports node selection and deselection using mouse clicks. When a node is selected, it automatically selects all ancestors, which allows the user to easily read the path from the selected node to the root. Maintaining visual consistency in this type of interaction requires more than a simple binary selection status per node. If two selected nodes share common ancestors, deselecting either node will cause part of the path to the root to become unselected.

We circumvent this difficulty by following the UNIX file system model. Each node stores selection as a positive integer which is incremented each time a node is selected and decremented each time a node is deselected. The node is visually deselected only when the selection level is equal to zero. This type of automatic selection is not implicit in the diagram design, and for applications where the path to the root of the tree is not important, nodes may be selected singly.

We also support simple keyboard-based navigation by allowing the user to move the last selected node: the left arrow moves the selection to the left sibling of a node, the right arrow to the right sibling of a node, the up arrow moves the selection to the parent and the down arrow moves the selection to the first child node. This type of navigation allows the user to efficiently select nodes without having to move the pointer.

Since nodes can appear on the display in scaled form, the node label is not necessarily directly visible. We therefore also support a tool-tips style interaction with the tree: moving the pointer over a node with no further interaction causes a pop-up to appear which lists the node label. This further simplifies browsing by allowing the user to scan a series of nodes without changing the form of the display.

Alternate interactions with the display are possible depending on the demands of the application. For example, if the primary task for the user is to choose among a set of alternatives while descending the tree, we could initially select the root and all of the children of the root. When the user selects one of the children for further examination, we can select all of the children of that nodes and so on.

4 Future Work

There are many large hierarchical information space to which a OTree display might be applied, including a full-featured directory browser and document category visualization. Our current implementation supports the visualization of a variety of labelled trees but is essentially a stand-alone application and has not been integrated into a full-featured application.

There are a number of base applications where we would like to deploy and evaluate the OTree display technique. First among these would be a directory browser targeted towards large system administrators. This type of application offers several intriguing possibilities including the need to fully utilize all of the available display dimensions to display information about the nodes of the tree.

The directory browsing application offers another intriguing avenue of future work: the display of large node structures. The current system is limited to the display of text labels — we would like to provide the capability to interactively zoom in on the contents of a node to any desired level of detail and thereby combine focus + context views of trees with semantic zooming to provide a more usable interface.

Another intriguing possibility for future development which would involve using substantially larger node structures might be the display of World Wide Web navigation history. Nodes could include thumbnail images of recently visited pages in the display. Since Web browsing is not limited to hierarchical structure, but can form an arbitrary directed graph, this avenue of development would also allow the extension of the technique to graph drawings.

5 Conclusion

The present work has presented a visual display method for tree diagrams which allows the user to interactively specify areas of interest and uses scaling combined with omission to manage the exponential growth of the diagram.

We have presented several possible interaction strategies along with an animation strategy for changing the views. We have described techniques for mapping node properties to the display and described several enhancements and proposed applications which could serve as an evaluation platform for the technique.

References

DiBattista, G., Eades, P., Tamassia, R. & Tollis, I. G. (1999), *Graph Drawing: Algorithms for the Visualization of Graphs*, Prentice–Hall.

Feiner, S. (1988), Seeing the Forest for the Trees: Hierarchical Display of Hypertext Structure, *in Proceedings of the Conference on Office Information Systems*, ACM Press, pp.205–12.

Furnas, G. W. (1986), Generalized Fisheye Views, *in* M. Mantei & P. Orbeton (eds.), *Proceedings of CHI'86: Human Factors in Computing Systems*, ACM Press, pp.16–23.

Hearst, M. A. & Karadi, C. (1997), Cat-a-Cone: An Interactive Interface for Specifying Searches and Viewing Retrieval Results using a Large Category Hierarchy, *in SIGIR'97 Proceedings of the Twentieth Annual International ACM SIGIR Conference on Research and Development in Information Retrieval*, ACM Press, pp.246–255.

Johnson, B. & Shneiderman, B. (1991), Tree-Maps: A Space-Filling Approach to the Visualization of Hierarchical Information Structures, *in Visualization'91*, IEEE Computer Society Press, pp.284–91.

Koike, H. & Yoshihara, H. (1993), Fractal Approaches for Visualizing Huge Hierarchies, *in Proceedings of the 1993 IEEE Symposium on Visual Languages*, IEEE Computer Society Press, pp.55–60.

Lamping, J. & Rao, R. (1994), Laying Out and Visualizing Large Trees using a Hyperbolic Space, *in Proceedings of the ACM Symposium on User Interface Software and Technology, UIST'94*, ACM Press, pp.13–4.

Lamping, J., Rao, R. & Pirolli, P. (1995), A Focus+Context Technique Based on Hyperbolic Geometry for Visualizing Large Hierarchies, *in* I. Katz, R. Mack, L. Marks, M. B. Rosson & J. Nielsen (eds.), *Proceedings of CHI'95: Human Factors in Computing Systems*, ACM Press, pp.401–8.

Reinfelds, J. (1991), Layered Trees as Data Structures for Knowledge Representation, *in Proceedings of the First Estonian Conference on Graph Theory*, Tartu University, Estonia, pp.135–44.

Reingold, E. M. & Tilford, J. S. (1981), "Tidier Drawings of Trees", *IEEE Transactions on Software Engineering* **7**(2), 223–8.

Robertson, G. G., Mackinlay, J. D. & Card, S. K. (1991), Cone Trees: Animated 3D Visualizations of Hierarchical Information, *in* S. P. Robertson, G. M. Olson & J. S. Olson (eds.), *Proceedings of CHI'91: Human Factors in Computing Systems (Reaching through Technology)*, ACM Press, pp.189–94.

Wetherell, C. & Shannon, A. (1979), "Tidy Drawings of Trees", *IEEE Transactions on Software Engineering* **5**(5), 514–20.

Human–Computer Interaction — INTERACT '99
M. Angela Sasse and Chris Johnson (Editors)
Published by IOS Press, © IFIP TC.13, 1999

Improving Functional Programming Environments

Jon Whittle

Recom Technologies, NASA Ames Research Center, Moffet Field, m/s 269-2, CA 94040, USA.

jonathw@ptolemy.arc.nasa.gov

Abstract: This paper presents a novel program editor, *CYNTHIA*, for the functional programming language ML. Motivated by the current lack of good programming environments for functional programming, *CYNTHIA* incorporates *programming by analogy*, whereby users write programs by applying abstract transformations to existing programs, and sophisticated correctness-checking techniques such as checking for semantic errors, e.g. non-termination. *CYNTHIA* has been used in two introductory courses in ML and the results of these evaluations are presented here. It was found that students using *CYNTHIA* committed fewer errors than students using a compiler/text editor approach. In addition, errors that were made could be corrected more easily.

Keywords: functional programming, editors, evaluation.

1 Introduction

This paper investigates what kinds of programming environments could most benefit novice functional programmers, in particular the language ML (Paulson, 1991). Students are being held back by the primitiveness of current environments which inadequately relay errors. Little attention has been given to developing user-oriented functional programming (FP) editors, a notable exception being MLWorks (Harlequin, 1996). Superior environments would free the novice from trivial debugging tasks allowing them to proceed to more difficult problems.

Most students write programs in a text editor and then compile the file. Current compilers for ML — e.g. SML of New Jersey (SML-NJ) — give only crude error information and only deal with complete definitions. We propose a more incremental approach whereby the users' programs are checked for errors *as* they are written and errors are flagged to the user immediately. These ideas are captured in the notion of *programming by analogy* — whereby the user transforms existing function definitions using a sequence of abstract editing commands. These commands are mostly correctness-preserving and in the case that errors are introduced, the errors can be highlighted easily to the user rather than providing cryptic messages.

We also investigate ways in which students can be prevented from making errors in the first place. Traditional syntax-directed editors prevent the user from writing syntactically incorrect programs by forcing the user to build programs from pre-defined templates. We extend this approach by defining a set of editing commands that generalize the template approach and are oriented towards FP, and by providing semantic guarantees such as termination checking.

The result of this research is *CYNTHIA*, an editor for (a subset of) ML. It has been used extensively in two introductory courses on ML, the results of which are presented in this paper. We do not attempt to describe functional programming here but refer the unfamiliar reader to (Bird & Wadler, 1988). The syntax of ML is best illustrated by example. The following program is a piece of ML code to calculate the length of a list:

```
fun length nil = 0
|    length (h::t) = 1 + length t;
```

where `nil` denotes the empty list and `::` is the *cons* operator for constructing lists. As ML is functional, it makes extensive use of recursion rather than loops. Every object in ML belongs to a type such as list, integer or tree. ML uses *type inference* to infer types at compile time. An ML compiler would deduce that `length` has type `'a list -> int`. `int` is the type of integers. `'a list` is a *polymorphic* list — i.e. the type of elements of the list is unspecified.

C*YNTHIA* is concerned only with a purely functional subset of ML. This is on the grounds that purely functional definitions are easier to analyse.

2   Overview of C*YNTHIA*

C*YNTHIA* provides a small, compact set of commands supporting a sufficiently large subset of the ML language for novice programming. This has been possible partly because of the careful design of the commands and partly because of the uniformity of the functional style.

C*YNTHIA* provides stronger guarantees of correctness than any existing ML environment, namely:

Syntactic correctness: It is impossible to introduce syntax errors into a program.

Type correctness: Strongly-typed languages, such as ML, present particular problems for the novice. Although type inference frees the user from writing type declarations, the complexity of the type inference algorithm means that compilers often report type errors in the wrong place. (Whittle, 1999) measures the type errors encountered by a group of 14 ML students using the SML-NJ compiler. Over a two hour period, 193 type errors were found, compared with 114 other semantic errors and 70 syntax errors. The dominance of type errors suggests that types cause particular problems.

C*YNTHIA* overcomes this by forcing the user to give a type declaration. This makes the student more aware of types and makes type error feedback more meaningful. Since declarations are edited incrementally, the user never needs to write down an entire declaration so there is little extra burden. Type errors in C*YNTHIA* are highlighted to the user in a different colour.

Well-definedness: (Whittle, 1999) also showed students have difficulty when using pattern matching (of which ML makes extensive use). Students tend to understand simple patterns but not complex patterns, especially if defined over non-standard data types. To define a function via pattern matching, each expression of the relevant data type must match exactly one pattern. Otherwise, run-time errors can occur — for example, if a call of f nil is made and there is no case for the nil pattern. Observations of students showed that they had

a good deal of difficulty in formulating well-defined patterns (i.e. those that exhaustively cover the data type and do not contain redundant cases). All patterns in C*YNTHIA* are well-defined by construction. The only way to write patterns is to use the command MAKE PATTERN which replaces a variable by a number of patterns — one for each constructor of the data type.

Termination: All programs in C*YNTHIA* are checked to be terminating. Termination checking is an undecidable problem so C*YNTHIA* restricts the user to a decidable subset of terminating programs — the set of Walther Recursive programs (McAllester & Arkoudas, 1996). This set contains a wide variety of recursive programs sufficient for use in real programming situations, such as multiple recursions, nested recursions, recursion with accumulators, etc.

The underlying framework of C*YNTHIA* is perhaps its most novel feature. It is based on a proof representation of each ML program which is a neat way to structure the editor and provide correctness guarantees — see (Whittle, 1999) for details.

2.1   An Example

The following example is a typical task which might be given to students in the first half of a course on functional programming. The student is asked to write a number of table-accessing functions. Each of these functions has a very similar structure. It is natural, therefore, to use C*YNTHIA* as a way of transforming one function definition into another:

newtable a new table containing no entries.

addentry k v d returns a new table which is the same as table d except that the value entered for the key k is v; this value replaces any entry that might be there for k.

findentry k d given a table d and key k, returns the value entered in d against k. Raises an exception if there is no such entry.

hasentry k d checks if the table d contains an entry for key k.

Assume that the student implements the table as a polymorphic list where the odd elements are the keys and the even elements are the values.[*] Consider defining hasentry. The student must firstly decide upon a starting definition. Since the tables will be

---

[*]This assumes that the keys and values are of the same type but one could imagine a novice making this sort of assumption.

represented by lists, the student chooses `length`. The student renames `length` by selecting one occurrence of `length` and invoking the command RENAME. This gives:

```
'a list -> int
fun hasentry nil = 0
|   hasentry (h::t) = 1 + hasentry t;
```

This updates all occurrences of `length`, not just the highlighted one. Next, the student changes the output type of the definition using the command CHANGE TYPE applied at the point indicated by a box (a box will always denote where a command is to be applied):

```
'a list -> bool
fun hasentry nil = 0
|   hasentry (h::t) = 1 + hasentry t;
```

The definition is now ill-typed (the underlined expressions are ill-typed with respect to the type declaration and are highlighted in *CYNTHIA*). *CYNTHIA* highlights all type inconsistencies in this way. The highlighting serves as a warning to the user but the errors need not be corrected immediately. To access the keys, the program will need to recurse in two steps. To achieve this, the student invokes MAKE PATTERN at the boxed point. This command will replace `t` with two cases — when `t` is empty and non-empty:

```
'a list -> bool
fun hasentry nil = 0
|   hasentry (h::nil) = 1 + hasentry nil
|   hasentry (h::h1::t) = 1 + hasentry t;
```

In the third clause, a new variable, `h1`, has been introduced. In addition, a recursive call using this new variable — namely, `hasentry (h1::t)`, has been made available which can be introduced into the program if required. The system knows that any definition involving this new recursive call will terminate. The definition is still missing a parameter for the key to search for. This can be introduced using the command ADD CURRIED ARGUMENT, which adds a parameter *throughout* the definition:

```
'a -> 'a list -> bool
fun hasentry k nil = 0
|   hasentry k (h::nil) = 1 + hasentry k nil
|   hasentry k (h::h1::t) = 1 + hasentry k t;
```

The user gives a name and type for the new argument and the type declaration is updated automatically. Finally, the user needs to change the output in each case. This can be done using the commands CHANGE TERM and ADD CONSTRUCT(IF THEN ELSE), giving:[†]

```
'a -> 'a list -> bool
fun hasentry k nil = false
|   hasentry k (h::nil) = raise excep
|   hasentry k (h::h1::t) =
            if k=h then true
            else hasentry k t;
```

`excep` is a previously defined exception. The above constitutes a reasonable definition of `hasentry`. The student now proceeds to define `findentry` and notices the similarity between the two definitions. To correctly define `findentry`, the user need only invoke RENAME, CHANGE TYPE and CHANGE TERM twice, to give:

```
'a -> 'a list -> 'a
fun findentry k nil = raise excep
|   findentry k (h::nil) = raise excep
|   findentry k (h::h1::t) =
            if k=h then h1
            else findentry k t;
```

To construct `addentry` is almost as easy. The user needs to invoke ADD CURRIED ARGUMENT, CHANGE TYPE and CHANGE TERM:

```
'a -> 'a -> 'a list -> 'a list
fun addentry k v nil = k::v::nil
|   addentry k v (h::nil) = raise excep
|   addentry k v (h::h1::t) =
            if k=h then k::v::t
            else h::h1::addentry k v t;
```

3   Evaluation of *CYNTHIA*

This section reports on empirical studies undertaken with two groups of students (SG1 and SG2) at Napier University, Scotland, to assess if *CYNTHIA* provides a better environment for FP. The following methods of data collection were employed.

Logging interaction (both SG1 and SG2). The students' sessions with *CYNTHIA* were recorded as they worked.

A 'crossover' experiment (SG1). In a two hour session, students were given a set of six functions to write. SG1 was split into two groups, X and Y. X attempted part A of the test with *CYNTHIA* and part B without. Y attempted part A without and part B with *CYNTHIA*. Both A and B contained tasks of similar difficulty. Hence, each student attempted similar problems both with and without *CYNTHIA*. This meant that individual students' performance could be compared.

Students were observed during their tutorial sessions interacting with and without *CYNTHIA*.

Assessment on the course was by examination and also practical coursework. The subjects in the first evaluation were 40 postgraduates following a one-year Software Technology course. *CYNTHIA*

[†]Strictly, the second argument should now have type `''a list`. `''a` is a polymorphic type over which equality may be defined. *CYNTHIA* does not yet make any distinction between `'a` and `''a`. This is a minor oversight that should be corrected soon.

was introduced in the second week of the course. The students were told that C*YNTHIA* was the result of a research project. C*YNTHIA* was only mentioned in passing in lectures. The subjects in the second evaluation were 29 students in year 4 of an undergraduate course in Computer Science. C*YNTHIA* was one of the main teaching tools in this course. The students were not told that C*YNTHIA* was part of a research project. C*YNTHIA* was introduced more fully in the lectures, although details of editing commands and functionality were only taught in the tutorials.

Most of the evaluation of C*YNTHIA* was informal. Splitting the students into a control and experimental group was not possible. Given that the students were being assessed on their work, giving C*YNTHIA* to only one half of the students would have been unethical. Dividing the students fairly into a control and experimental group was impossible. Randomization would mean that in a given tutorial some students would be using C*YNTHIA* and some would not. This is clearly unacceptable. Since students are all following the same course, they would communicate with each other between tutorial sessions, and there would be no way to stop the control group using C*YNTHIA* outside the tutorials. The different aspects of C*YNTHIA* tend to interact with each other. Therefore, it would have been difficult to isolate any effects of an experiment, even given perfect conditions.

The following sections describe which research questions were asked and how they were answered. The evaluation presented here is only an initial one and further work is needed. In particular, there are interesting issues that have not yet been fully explored, such as whether analogy is a good approach to programming, whether type error highlighting helps learning, etc.

3.1   Research Questions

3.1.1   How Does the Quantity of Errors Made Using C*YNTHIA* Compare to Text Editors?

For both SG1 and SG2, C*YNTHIA* will be compared to a traditional text editor. From the logs of C*YNTHIA*-interaction, a count of the errors was made. For SG1, a count was made of errors made during the crossover experiment. The crossover experiment took place over one hour of intense programming. SG2 errors were counted over 8 weeks during which C*YNTHIA* was used regularly by a large number of students for two hours each week (although less intensely). A classification of all errors made was developed:

Algorithmic errors: suggest a major algorithmic flaw in the program, such as giving the wrong condition in a conditional statement. C*YNTHIA* was not primarily designed to help with this kind of error, so I do not include a count of these (they were roughly the same).

Semantic errors: are split into four categories. Local semantic errors arise in response to a misunderstanding of part of ML's semantics such as trying to define the invalid type int string. Global semantic errors are where the error is dependent on some other part of the definition — e.g. the use of an unbound variable. Although type errors could be seen as global semantic errors, they are given a separate category for emphasis. The same is true of pattern errors (i.e. patterns are overlapping or non-exhaustive).

Syntax errors: include clerical errors where, for example, the student clearly mistyped a name or missed off a bracket. General Syntax errors suggest a cause more than mere carelessness: examples are using a syntax that ML does not support such as return 0.

Usability errors: include incorrect usage errors where the student could not work the system properly. An example is not being able to find the right editing command in C*YNTHIA*. Usability errors also include judgement errors: where the system feedback was misunderstood by the student causing him/her to make an incorrect change to the program.

The errors were counted manually from the logs obtained during the experiment.

	C	NC
Local Semantic	20	33
Global Semantic	14	21
Patterns	0	6
Type Errors	20	36
General Syntax	0	8
Clerical	9	40
Incorrect Usage	53	0
Judgement	50	53
Total	166	197

The table above gives the error count for the SG1 crossover experiment for both C*YNTHIA* (C) and non-C*YNTHIA* (NC) users. The quantative results presented are not meant to be definitive but merely to suggest trends.

The difference in the total error count is not as high as expected. However, the kinds of errors committed are *different* for C*Y*NTHIA and non-C*Y*NTHIA users.

Syntax errors were almost eliminated when using C*Y*NTHIA. In particular, the number of clerical errors has reduced by 78% for SG1.

The number of *semantic errors* was also less for C*Y*NTHIA-users. Note particularly that the number of type errors made using C*Y*NTHIA was just over half that for non-C*Y*NTHIA users. This is as expected. Both the number of local and global semantic errors are fewer with C*Y*NTHIA than without. Again, this is as expected. Editing commands introduce semantically valid expressions so there is less scope for making errors.

For SG1, C*Y*NTHIA seems to score pretty badly on *usability errors*. In particular, 53 Incorrect Usage errors were introduced that could not occur without C*Y*NTHIA (because they are C*Y*NTHIA-specific errors). This is a disappointingly large figure. It suggests first that C*Y*NTHIA's interface is difficult to use and second that students do not read documentation — for most of the errors they committed could have been avoided if they had read the documentation.

Surprisingly, there is no real difference in the numbers of judgement errors. Anecdotal evidence suggests that students using a text editor spend much more time trying to locate errors than C*Y*NTHIA users. The judgement errors were meant to measure this sort of thing, but the results do not back up the informal observations. Closer inspection explains why this is the case. When an editing command is applied, a dialogue box appears for the user to type in the parameters to the command. 35 out of the 50 C*Y*NTHIA judgement errors were caused because C*Y*NTHIA did not adequately explain exactly which parameters were expected. Hence, students would type in the wrong parameters and not understand why they got an error message. This was easily corrected before the second evaluation.

Evaluation 1 showed that there were generally fewer errors when using C*Y*NTHIA but that there were problems with the usability of the system. We expected that most of the judgement errors and many of the incorrect usage errors could be eradicated by making changes to the system and by encouraging students to read documentation. To test out this claim, two changes were made to C*Y*NTHIA before the second evaluation. It was assumed in the first evaluation that the editing commands were simple enough for their functionality to be obvious. Hence,

the only documentation was a short tutorial and a Web page describing each command in detail. For the second evaluation, the documentation of C*Y*NTHIA was more closely integrated into the Napier course notes — each time a new concept was introduced, the corresponding editing command was introduced also and the student was taken through a couple of examples which specifically used C*Y*NTHIA. The other main change was to give keywords in the dialogue boxes that explained specifically which parameters were expected.

In Evaluation 2, C*Y*NTHIA was introduced as one of the main teaching tools. This was meant to give us an opportunity to assess C*Y*NTHIA's usefulness in a teaching environment. It did mean, though, that for SG2 there was no control group. The error counts for SG1 were made during a timed session. For SG2, all errors over the entire course were collected. The table gives the error count for Evaluation 2 (C1 = number of errors, C2 = % relative to experiment 1, C3 = % error rate). To enable a tentative comparison with SG1, the second column of the table gives the increase from experiment 1 to experiment 2 expressed as a percentage of experiment 2 over experiment 1. It gives a very cautious estimate of the change in relative importance of each kind of error. All things being equal, we would expect each error class to increase by the same amount. The third column gives another way of comparing the different error categories — it gives a measure of the number of errors made *per edit*, again expressed as a percentage.

	C1	C2	C3
Local Semantic	39	195	1.19
Global Semantic	41	293	1.26
Patterns	0	0	0
Type Errors	59	295	1.8
General Syntax	0	0	0
Clerical	32	356	0.98
Incorrect Usage	74	140	2.3
Judgement	27	54	0.8
Total	323	175	
Total no. Edits	3266	690	

The total number of edits increased roughly seven-fold. However, most error categories increased by much less. This suggests (as expected) that as users became more familiar with how C*Y*NTHIA worked, they committed fewer and fewer errors. Incorrect Usage errors increased much less than Semantic and Syntax errors.

This is evidence that the improved documentation in the second evaluation meant that students were more comfortable with using the system. Judgement errors are the only error that have reduced in absolute terms. This is due to the improved dialogue boxes. In the first experiment, J3 accounted for 70% of the total Judgement Errors. In the second experiment, it is only 16%. It seems then that Evaluation 2 provides evidence that the initial usability problems were teething problems that could be filtered out. Hence, the saving in other errors is not offset by a gain in usability errors.

3.1.2   How Does CʸNTHIA's Error Feedback Compare to the Compiler's?

Evidence from observations of students seems to suggest very positively that CʸNTHIA does better than a compiler-only approach. Trival errors (e.g. clerical errors) have generally been filtered out so students are less infuriated and so try to work out the problem rather than hacking at their code. In stark contrast to users of the SML-NJ compiler, students were noticed paying attention to error feedback and trying to work through the problem. They did not always succeed, of course, but undoubtedly learnt something along the way. Another point is that it is much easier in CʸNTHIA to distinguish what *kind* of error is occurring. This is because the error feedback is different for different categories of errors. One of the problems with ML syntax is that its succinctness means that syntax errors can often have knock-on effects meaning that they show up as type errors during compilation. This happens less in CʸNTHIA. The divide between errors is more clear-cut. Type errors are always shown by pink highlighting. Global semantic errors are shown by green highlighting, and syntax errors can only occur in dialogue boxes.

Since students are editing smaller chunks of program at a single time, the range over which the error could have occurred is far less. With a text editor, students write an entire function before attempting compilation. With CʸNTHIA, however, each sub-expression is checked for errors immediately. In addition, the user knows that some parts of the program are guaranteed correct — for example, any patterns will have been built up using MAKE PATTERN and therefore must be well-defined.

When dealing with type errors, students in SG1 immediately noticed, thanks to CʸNTHIA's highlighting, that there was a problem and knew which part of the program to change. They did not always know the correct changes to make, however. Students might notice something was wrong but, unable to correct it, go off and edit another part of the program before coming back to it. Students might ignore the highlighting but would have to address it sooner or later. With SML-NJ, students regularly do not know which part of the program is wrong. They make a half-hearted guess and then re-compile the program, only to find more error messages. This process can go on for some time. In CʸNTHIA, students can just change the pink expression and see what happens rather than having to re-compile everything.

3.1.3   How Does Programming by Analogy Compare to Writing a Program from Scratch?

Was the structure of the commands well-understood, was their function clear? Green & Petre (1996) define 'cognitive dimension', a broad-brush evaluation technique for interactive systems. They describe thirteen high-level criteria for discussing the design of a system. The idea is that they will form a common point of discourse for evaluating interactive systems. A few of these criteria are used to answer this question.

Abstraction Gradient: Each editing command is essentially an abstraction, grouping together common sequences of editing operations. But are they at the right level of abstraction? The natural question to ask is if the students using CʸNTHIA could understand the editing commands. Does the abstract nature of the editing commands benefit them in the long run?

The original aim when designing the editing commands was to make the set as small as possible whilst keeping the meaning of the commands transparent to a new user. The former goal was certainly achieved — with as few as 11 commands, a wide variety of programs can be produced. However, the high number of Incorrect Usage errors show that the commands caused some confusion. As already mentioned, this is partly due to practical issues such as documentation. In addition, the abstractness of the editing commands seemed difficult to learn. Some commands are based on functional programming concepts — for example ADD ARGUMENT, MAKE PATTERN, CHANGE TYPE — and if the student has not got to grips with functional programming, s/he is likely to be baffled by the command. There is a chicken and egg situation here — learning the commands is easier if functional programming is understood, but use of the commands can help the understanding of functional concepts.

Premature   Commitment: This   dimension concerns the extent to which the user is forced to make a decision before the information is available. In CʸNTHIA, this manifests itself as the degree to which the order of application of the editing commands matters. One of the main criticisms of the *recursion editor* (Bundy et al., 1991), which is also a transformation-based editor, is that the order of commands is critical to success and so the user must think about the order before delving into the programming task. To what extent is this also true of *CYNTHIA*?

For the most part, the order of editing commands in *CYNTHIA* is irrelevant. If the user applies an incorrect edit, and only realizes this much later, it is easy to undo the edit by applying a short sequence of recovery commands. This contrasts starkly with the recursion editor, where the user can easily get stuck down an incorrect route from which the only way to recover is to re-start from the beginning.

There are a few examples, however, where *CYNTHIA* requires some form of premature commitment. In all of these cases, premature commitment merely makes life easier — it does not prevent the user from doing something. An example is where it is useful to decide upon the patterns that define a function initially, but where it can be awkward to revise this choice. Suppose the user is writing a function, app, to append two lists together and pattern matches on the second argument:

```
fun app l nil = l
|    app l (x::xs) = x :: app l xs;
```

It is at this point that the user realizes s/he should pattern match on the first argument instead. Ideally, there would be a command to transfer the patterns from the second to the first argument. Currently, however, the user must remove pattern matching from the second argument and re-introduce it into the first argument. Hence, although the user can achieve the desired goal, s/he needs to go a long way round to get there. Commands such as one that transfers patterns from one argument to another would be of great use.

Progressive Evaluation: Progressive evaluation means that programs can be evaluated by the user at frequent intervals during their development, not just once the program is completely finished. *CYNTHIA* improves on ML compilers in a significant way here. Although any program must be finished before it is executed (for it still must be accepted by the compiler), the user gets constant feedback about semantic errors during the programming process. This is achieved by the use of the highlighting mechanism for pointing out type errors, etc. The key point is that *CYNTHIA*'s feedback merely notifies the user of a problem, it does not enforce them to change it immediately.

4   Conclusion

This paper has examined the shortcomings of current editors for functional programming languages, in particular ML. *CYNTHIA* is an editor which attempts to overcome some of these problems. First, *CYNTHIA* provides editing commands for allowing old programs to be transformed into new ones. Second, *CYNTHIA* provides correctness checks not found in any other comparable editor. Two trials were conducted to see what effect the use of *CYNTHIA* has in teaching functional programming. These suggest that students generally make fewer errors when using *CYNTHIA* than when using a traditional text editor and that *CYNTHIA*'s highlighting of errors makes the location of type errors easier.

Acknowledgements

The author would like to thank Alan Bundy, Helen Lowe, Richard Boulton and Andrew Cumming. This work was carried out in the Division of Informatics, University of Edinburgh, Scotland under an EPSRC scholarship.

References

Bird, R. S. & Wadler, P. (1988), *Introduction to Functional Programming*, Prentice–Hall.

Bundy, A., Grosse, G. & Brna, P. (1991), "A Recursive Techniques Editor for Prolog", *Instructional Science* 20(2/3), 135–72.

Green, T. R. G. & Petre, M. (1996), "Usability Analysis of Visual Programming Environments: A 'Cognitive Dimensions' Framework", *Journal of Visual Languages and Computing* 7(2), 131–74.

Harlequin (1996), *MLWorks*, Harlequin, Inc.

McAllester, D. & Arkoudas, K. (1996), Walther Recursion, *in* M. A. McRobbie & J. K. Slaney (eds.), *Proceedings of the 13th International Conference on Automated Deduction (CADE13)*, Vol. 1104 of *Lecture Notes in Artifical Intelligence*, Springer-Verlag, pp.643–57.

Paulson, L. C. (1991), *ML for the Working Programmer*, Cambridge University Press.

Whittle, J. N. D. (1999), The Use of Proofs-as-Programs to Build an Analogy-based Functional Program Editor, PhD thesis, Division of Informatics, University of Edinburgh.

Human–Computer Interaction — INTERACT '99
M. Angela Sasse and Chris Johnson (Editors)
Published by IOS Press, © IFIP TC.13, 1999

Incremental Control of a Children's Computing Environment

Robert Sheehan

Department of Computer Science, University of Auckland, Auckland, New Zealand.

r.sheehan@cs.auckland.ac.nz

Abstract: Gaining control of a computer environment, or micro-world, requires programming. This means coming to terms with a variety of abstract ideas before interesting projects can be undertaken. Operations and data which are explicitly represented can help the users of a programming environment understand these abstractions. This paper describes the implementation of a new graphical programming-by-demonstration environment for children which moves gradually from a direct manipulation interface to a complete and powerful programming system by carefully designed steps. The direct manipulation of on-screen objects is visibly recorded as an editable sequence of control icons which can be extracted into named procedures and loops are automatically inferred.

Keywords: children and computers, programming-by-demonstration, Logo.

1 Introduction

Children have been programming computers since at least the 1960s. However the abstractions required by traditional imperative programming such as variables, control structures and the development of procedures, make learning how to program very difficult, especially for young children. From the 1960s on Seymour Papert made great advances with Logo (Papert, 1980), in particular the concretization of turtle geometry. More recently David Smith and Allen Cypher have sparked the imaginations of children, their parents and their teachers, with the KidSim/Stagecast programming environment (Smith et al., 1994). These are superb environments and offer great possibilities for children to control computers and gain understanding of programming abstractions. As with all sophisticated tools these environments require careful supervision and facilitation by experienced adults or peers in order to bring about their promise. In far too many homes and schools children have been exposed to these tools and quickly been bored with them. Many people feel they "have done Logo" when in fact they have just learnt a few of the commands and haven't had an expert show them how to go about implementing a project of personal value. Similarly, recent results (Rader et al., 1997) show that without explicit instruction many of the more interesting features of KidSim/Stagecast are

not understood, and therefore not used, by children, severely limiting the possible tasks they can perform.

If we look at programs for children which are not quite so open ended and powerful as Logo or KidSim/Stagecast, we see creativity environments with which children are happy playing and developing ideas, without the need for the careful supervision of a mentor to guide them. The obvious examples are painting or writing programs such as Brøderbund's KidPix and Creative Writer. There are at least two reasons why children seem to be able to use these programs happily, without careful assistance. First, children already know how to draw or how to write before being exposed to these programs. Second, the environments provided are directly explorable. That is, using direct manipulation techniques the children can find entertaining, amusing effects, which they understand and can put to immediate use. Logo and KidSim/StageCast are almost directly explorable in that children can type different sequences of commands and observe their behaviour or select areas of the screen and then demonstrate changes. However, in Logo the requirement of typing is a hurdle for younger children, not just for the need to read and locate letters on the keyboard but also the need to know the commands which can be typed. (There is an iconic form of Logo which bears similarity to some of the work described in this paper and doesn't require the typing of commands but is otherwise very different from this work.) In KidSim/Stagecast children have to enter a programming mode which is different from the program run mode.

If we can start with a directly explorable environment and gradually introduce more power and abstraction through a series of incremental steps it should be possible to provide an environment with the enjoyment and play-ability of KidPix and the power and sophistication of Logo. The need for explicit instruction will never disappear completely but careful design can make each step towards programming easier. The hope is that the role of the teacher or peer can become one of encouragement and facilitation rather than being largely instructional.

2   ICE

The environment is known as ICE, for Incremental Computing Environment. The incremental property is built into the design. A novice user can start playing immediately; turtles can be dragged around the screen leaving lines behind and control buttons can be clicked with the only required knowledge being how to drag objects and click buttons. But that is only the start. The system can also be controlled in a variety of other ways with links between the simple direct manipulation methods of control and the more abstract stored program methods. In this way the system can be seen as a progressive series of environments:

- a novel painting environment;

- a remote control environment;

- a macro programming environment;

- a programming-by-demonstration environment; and

- ultimately a general purpose programming environment.

It doesn't matter whether a child goes through the progression sequentially. The intention is to allow as much freedom as possible, while still providing hints to lead the child to understand another approach and concept.

2.1   As a Novel Painting Environment

When a child first starts using ICE it looks and behaves like a painting application. The difference is that instead of a palette of pens and drawing tools there is a turtle in the middle of the screen. By moving the turtle, trails of paint of different widths and colours can be left behind. This sounds just like Logo, however the difference is in the way the turtle can be controlled.

The turtle is directly manipulable. The child can select the turtle and then drag the mouse pointer. (Some versions of Logo allow direct manipulation of the turtle's position and heading, but movements do not leave lines on the screen and act only as absolute and not relative state changes.) During the drag a dashed straight line extends from the turtle to the current position of the mouse pointer. The turtle turns to face in the direction of the mouse pointer during the drag. When the drag action is terminated the turtle then walks along the dashed line leaving a solid line behind. This dashed line in other words indicates the path the turtle will follow when the mouse button is released. This makes the turtle appear like a straight-line tool. However dragging from the turtle and leaving the line behind are separate actions. This is significant as will be explained shortly. Figure 1 shows a line being dragged from the turtle.

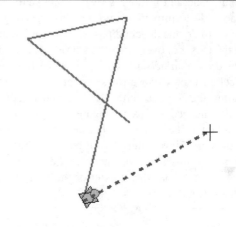

Figure 1:

2.1.1   Comparison with Logo

When a child (or an adult for that matter) is first introduced to the Logo programming environment it is common to draw a square. A series of moves followed by right angle turns is executed. The next challenge is to draw a triangle. It is not surprising that people find this difficult (Abelson & di Sessa, 1980). The trouble is that the turtle turns through the exterior angle of the triangle and people commonly turn the turtle through $60°$ rather than through $120°$. This is a wonderful teaching point if there is a teacher or peer at hand to explain what has happened but otherwise can be a source of frustration. With ICE the user can drag the turtle to its required destination and the correct angle is then visible for inspection in the history list (see later).

As stated previously, separating the action of dragging the turtle from the result of the turtle moving along the line is important. By postponing the turtle's movement until the child releases the mouse button we are making our first step in conveying the concept of delayed execution, which is one of the first concepts we have to assimilate to become programmers. Interactive programming languages, such as Logo, force this understanding because a syntactically correct instruction has to be typed before the command is executed. This advantage is weakened by the requirement of correct syntax. It is impossible to give an incorrect instruction to the turtle in ICE.

Children quickly learn that the turtle responds to a command from them. In practice they have no added difficulty drawing lines with this delayed action. Animating the turtle moving along the line adds to the feeling of having given the turtle a command and is entertaining.

A drag from within the body of the turtle usually conveys two commands to the turtle — a turn command and a move forward command. It is also possible to turn the turtle without changing its position. To do this the child pushes the mouse button when the cursor is over the turtle's head. The head is indicated by a circle outlined in red. The following drag action makes two arrows appear on the screen indicating the original turtle heading and the one it is being changed to, as in Figure 2. The arrows were found to be necessary because children were frequently grabbing the turtle by its head and dragging. The result of this is a turn rather than a move. The arrows indicate both the amount of the turn and the fact that it is just a turn.

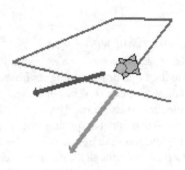

Figure 2:

There is no similar simple method to send a move forward command to the turtle by dragging it. The design could have been that all drags outside the head of the turtle move the turtle forwards or backwards in the direction it is currently facing, thus requiring two explicit actions from the child in order to move the

turtle to a particular point. The principle of making common actions simple to perform meant that this was rejected.

Holding the shift key down during the drag does actually move the turtle without rotating it, but this is an advanced feature, which must be learnt later.

2.2   As a Remote Control Environment

Even at this stage the child can deal easily with the concept of state. The turtle state has several properties including position and heading and those associated with the pen — width, colour and whether it is up or down. These properties can be accessed by right-clicking on the turtle, which brings up the turtle's control panel.

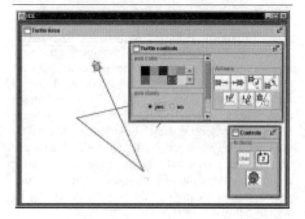

Figure 3:

The turtle control panel, shown in Figure 3, includes an area with action buttons to remotely control the turtle and an area with properties that can be changed directly. This panel takes the place of the palette of drawing tools in a painting application. Clicking on the action buttons is the second way of sending commands to the turtle. This introduces the concept of control without direct manipulation. The commands correspond to the traditional turtle graphics commands: forward, back, right, left, pen up, pen down and hide or show turtle. Having icons on the buttons means there is no need for typing or memorising command names. This is not a claim that the icons are intuitive in the sense of not having to be learned, but they are easy to remember once a child has been shown what they do. Younger children do tend to choose the wrong button to turn left or right if the turtle is facing in the direction opposite to that shown on the buttons, but this is immediately recognized and is easily corrected. The reason the icons don't change to correspond to the current direction of the turtle and thereby reduce the chance of mistakes is that the same icon will be used within programs and there will be no connection between the stored action and the turtle heading at that time.

One reason for the property list area in the control panel is so that state changes can be observed. The pen up command for instance makes no immediate change to the picture in the Turtle Area window but the radio button indicating pen down will change.

Using the control panel gives us a different way of controlling the turtle. In particular it gives finer control. It is very difficult to draw a perfect square by directly manipulating the turtle. Whereas by repeating the following sequence four times: forward, right, right, right (each right turn is 30° by default), we get a perfect square. The concept being developed here is one of discrete actions corresponding to commands.

Sometimes the default values for parameters of actions, such as the distance to move forward, are not suitable. There is an advanced technique to remedy this. By right-clicking on the action buttons the child is presented with two ways of changing the parameter information. The child can type a parameter or directly manipulate a control in the parameter entry box to indicate the parameter value.

2.3 As an Editable Macro Programming Environment

In the description so far we have what looks like a novel painting program without a lot of the extras which come in such programs designed for children. And children can and do use ICE this way. The next stage is to show the children that their actions can be recorded and played back at a later time.

ICE maintains a history list of recent actions, shown in Figure 4. Every manipulation of the turtle is recorded here, including button clicks on the control panel action buttons and property list. Drag operations on the turtle are recorded as two actions: a turn to the left or the right of so many degrees, and then a move forward of so many steps. When this history list is shown it provides a third way to control the turtle. The actions are recorded using the same icons as shown in the control panel. Clicking on any action button in the history list re-executes that action, adding a new copy of it to the end of the list. In this way a child can drag the turtle a particular distance and then can get the turtle to move exactly that distance again by clicking on the button representing the move in the history list. This makes it easy to draw perfect squares of any size for example.

Imperative programming requires a formal description of a sequence of events. This formal description is usually perceptually distant from the events it represents. Even in this system there is a large

gap between dragging the turtle and the representation of the drag as two iconic buttons in the history list. However this distance is minimised because the buttons are the same in looks and behaviour as those in the control panel, and the child has been using those buttons frequently.

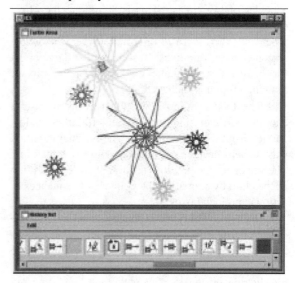

Figure 4:

The history list is not just a list of previously executed actions. If a child repeats the same sequence of actions, e.g. moving forward followed by a right turn followed by moving forward followed by a right turn, a loop recognizer spots this and represents the actions in a loop box.

A loop box is a recessed box surrounding one copy of the list of repeated actions preceded by a loop icon button, inside which is a count showing how many times the actions have been repeated. See Figure 4 for an example of a loop box. Each time the actions are repeated the loop count increases. The loop icon button can itself be clicked on and the entire loop box gets re-executed — possibly causing the creation of a higher level loop box.

This simple process can be used to construct complex drawings with a very small number of user actions. The loop recognizer automatically collapses repetition into loops and works recursively, possibly creating a loop that matches a previous loop thus creating a new loop containing a loop.

It is very common for children to keep clicking on loop buttons because of the large visual changes produced for little effort. The easiest way to get this effect is to draw a few lines, possibly changing colours as you go. Then click on all of the actions in the history list one after another until the loop box is produced. Then go back to the front of the loop box and click on the loop icon button. This causes the entire loop to be carried out again giving rise to a copy of the loop. The loop recognizer turns these two adjacent loop boxes into the contents of a higher order loop box. Continuing in this way children frequently end up with loops repeating the original instructions a power of two times. This is similar to the effect common in early Logo programming where children type `forward 10000` in order to see the whole screen covered with lines. It is this type of large effect for small effort that helps explain the popularity of drawing programs such as KidPix.

The loop recognizer would probably be useful enough as a tool simply for its entertainment value. But it wasn't designed for that. The original intention was to help develop an understanding of repetition. The concept of repetition is brought to the attention of the child by animating the collapse of sequences of actions into loop boxes.

With the ability to produce a whole sequence of actions by clicking on one button, the system is introducing the concept of stored programs to the child. The automatic repetition of commands caused by clicking on the loop icon button shows that not only have the previous commands been remembered but that they can be played out again at a later time.

The history list also demonstrates that state changes from the turtle control panel which don't have iconic buttons representing them, e.g. changing the pen colour, are also represented in the history list by a button. The concept here is that all commands no matter how different they look or are produced are similar in some ways. Hidden state changes like variable assignments are just as important as actions that move the turtle.

Actions in the history list can also be edited. If an action is deleted or added, the drawing is automatically altered to match the current history of instructions. This introduces the concept of debugging.

At this level the system can be thought of as allowing the child to record one (possibly large) sequence of instructions with a loop recognizer to simplify and add structure to the history list. But because the child has been able to click on a loop icon button and see an entire sequence of commands performed it is only a small step to extract any sequence of commands into a named procedure.

2.4 As a Programming by Demonstration Environment

The next level makes it possible to extract from within the history list a group of instructions that can be turned into a single action or procedure.

By selecting a contiguous group of action buttons from the history list they are stored in their own window and the child can re-execute the sequence with a single click. The list can also be edited. More than this, the sequence can be named, either automatically with a reduced icon of the drawing it produces, or by the child. This new command is then added to the turtle's control panel and can be invoked in the same way as a built-in command. Having a command call commands introduces the concept of proceduralization.

Since the new command may be constructed entirely by turning and dragging the turtle, ICE can also be seen as a simple programming-by-demonstration system (Cypher, 1993). It is different from a traditional programming-by-demonstration system because the list of commands is explicitly developed and can be edited at any stage during its development. Some programming-by-demonstration systems can show the user the source code generated by the user's actions and some do require editing but there tends to be a perceptual gap between the actions and the source code. In ICE the same icons used to convey the original commands represent the source code thus reducing the perceived gap between user actions and recorded program.

The programming concepts currently exhibited by ICE include:

- Delayed execution.
- Sequence of commands.
- Repetition of commands.
- Parameters.
- Stored programs.
- Editing/debugging existing programs.
- Control structures — proceduralization.

2.5 As a General Purpose Programming Environment

The original version of ICE is not a general-purpose programming environment. But many of the features necessary for this are being designed. The next stage of implementation of ICE includes branching control structures, parameters for stored procedures, and variables.

There will be a direct manipulation method of extracting parameters from procedures. Variables themselves will then be introduced by highlighting their similarities to parameters. Conditional statements can be inferred under certain circumstances associated with the selection of variables or commands that produce values.

The underlying idea of ICE is that the system can be used by a child at a very simple level and the system design provides hints to gradually lead the child to more sophisticated and general ways of producing the same result. Eventually leading the child to do things which are otherwise impossible. It is not expected that very young children will be able to use procedures with parameters and variables, but they can control the turtle and store their drawings as sequences of actions.

One very important part of ICE, which is still being designed, is the incremental help system. It is impossible to depend solely on the built-in design hints in ICE to lead most children to an understanding of the abstractions needed to become programmers. The help system will include a structured series of exercises and game-like challenges which will reveal the possibilities of using the system.

References

Abelson, H. & di Sessa, A. (1980), *Turtle Geometry*, MIT Press.

Cypher, A. (ed.) (1993), *Watch What I Do: Programming by Demonstration*, MIT Press.

Papert, S. (1980), *Mindstorms. Children, Computers, and Powerful Ideas*, Basic Books.

Rader, C., Brand, C. & Lewis, C. (1997), Degrees of Comprehension: Children's Understanding of a Visual Programming Environment, *in* S. Pemberton (ed.), *Proceedings of CHI'97: Human Factors in Computing Systems*, ACM Press, pp.351–8.

Smith, D. C., Cypher, A. & Spohrer, J. (1994), "KidSim: Programming Agents Without a Programming Language", *Communications of the ACM* **37**(7), 54–68.

Human–Computer Interaction — INTERACT '99
M. Angela Sasse and Chris Johnson (Editors)
Published by IOS Press, © IFIP TC.13, 1999

A Brick Construction Game Model for Creating Graphical User Interfaces: The Ubit Toolkit

Eric Lecolinet

Ecole Nationale Supérieure des Télécommunications & CNRS URA 820
Department INFRES, 46 rue Barrault, 75013 Paris, France.

elc@enst.fr

Abstract: This paper presents 'Ubit', a new graphical toolkit that is based on the 'brick construction game' model. This approach makes it possible to create sophisticated application-specific components by combining simple 'basic bricks'. All bricks can be shared in order to simplify GUI control and to reduce memory cost. This model supports the the concept of ubiquitous GUI components that are inherently able to display several representations of their content on the screen. At last, Ubit provides a simple and flexible C++ API that makes it possible to specify GUIs in a pseudo-declarative style.

Keywords: user interface software, graphical toolkits, declarative GUI language, brick object model, hyperdocument, interaction control, ubiquitous components, multiple views.

1 Introduction

It is a well known fact that user interfaces are not only hard to design but are also hard to implement (Myers, 1995). As a consequence, most people prefer using tools (such as interactive interface builders or other kinds of user interface management systems) rather than programming directly with a GUI toolkit. Thus, in recent years, attention has rather been focused on tools than on the principles of GUI toolkit design. We believe we now need to reconsider the underlying ideas that are at the basis of the implementation of graphical user interfaces. There are several reasons for that:

1. UIMS are very useful tools for creating 'static' GUIs that are mainly made of forms, menus and dialogue boxes. But they generally provide rather limited help for creating application-specific components that evolve dynamically at run time (for instance a graph editor where nodes are application-specific objects that can change dynamically).

2. New interaction and visualization concepts such as zoomable interfaces, magic lenses and other information visualization techniques are now coming to maturity. But such techniques are generally out of the scope of current tools.

Moreover, most tools do not even fully support the implementation of classical but highly interactive GUIs that make an extensive use of direct manipulation techniques.

It may seem reasonable to think that the implementation of sophisticated GUIs will always require a certain amount of textual programming at the toolkit level — although some interesting research has been performed on interactive model-based UIMS able to produce advanced GUIs (Szekely et al., 1993). Most tools just do not provide the appropriate level of abstraction for dealing with loops, dynamic creation and deletion of objects, highly interactive behaviours, etc. Textual programming may just be more appropriate in such cases.

Unfortunately, programming at the toolkit level is often quite a difficult task that is reserved to experienced programmers. GUI toolkits are generally quite complex and hard to use. As a result, GUI source code tends to be verbose and cumbersome. Besides, creating application-specific components may be a non trivial task as toolkit design often makes it difficult to deeply customize the set of standard components.

This paper presents a new GUI toolkit, called **Ubit** (for 'Ubiquitous Brick Interaction Toolkit') that is based on the 'brick construction game' model. In this model, GUI objects are simple **basic bricks** that can easily be combined together. This model makes it possible to create highly customized components in a simple way by combining (or deriving) these bricks. Besides, it also improves GUI source code legibility and simplifies GUI control. Ubit provides a flexible C++ API that supports a generic *adding mechanism*. This feature favours code compactness and makes GUI source code resemble mark-up language text. The brick model also simplifies GUI control thanks to a generalized *sharing mechanism*. This design feature ensure the implicit control of multiple views coherency. Ubit also supports the new concept of **ubiquitous** GUI components: in this model any user interface object is inherently able to manage an arbitrary number of synchronized representations of its data on the screen.

The next sections will describe and compare classical toolkit architectures, introduce the conceptual principles of Ubit model and describe its properties. The last sections will then detail some implementation aspects and present the current status of the system and future work.

2   GUI Architectures

Many graphical toolkits consist in a set of 'fat objects' that implement quite a large variety of functions. As a consequence, GUI objects are often hard to learn and to use because they handle so many different different aspects. Moreover, objects attributes often inadequately fit the real needs of a given application. Paradoxically, most objects attributes are useless for most applications, while GUI objects often lack 'this specific feature' that would be useful for a given application. For instance, the push button widget of the Motif 1.2 toolkit has more than 60 different 'resources', most of them being rarely used. However, in its standard version, this object can *either* display a character string *or* a pixmap image, but can not display both simultaneously.

This points highlights an important conception problem: there is no possible 'best choice' in defining object properties while conceiving a GUI toolkit because applications are simultaneously so similar and so different. They are similar because they use standardized GUI components that should remain similar from one application to another in order to preserve a consistent look and feel. But application are also very different because they deal with specific domains and thus require customized representations and interaction styles. Trying to anticipate all possible GUI component uses is an impossible task. As a consequence, we believe GUI objects should be dynamically adaptable instead of providing a static set

of predefined features that can not fit all application needs. Besides, for the sake of simplicity and memory efficiency, standard objects should not systematically provide a large number of generally useless features. This last point should not be neglected as applications may require quite a large number of GUI components.

The 'fat object' architecture also tends in multiplying similar object classes. For instance, the Java AWT toolkit introduces two different push button classes (depending on whether buttons are located inside or outside menus), while the Motif toolkit even defines six different classes (including 'widget' and 'gadget' variants). This problem clearly shows the limitations of such architectures: fat objects are so complex that they are difficult to derive or to combine together in order to fit application needs. Thus, many objects variants must be provided in order to compensate for the lack of flexibility of standard components.

This lack of generic design leads to many ambiguities and increases the toolkit complexity. Besides, it makes iterative development quite laborious as small UI design refinements may lead to heavy programming changes. Some of these aspects have already been addressed in previous research. MVC based (or derived) systems, such as the Java Swing toolkit (Fowler, 1999) provide more flexible object sets that are easier to customize and to extend. However, these systems generally lead to an increased level of complexity as they require extended knowledge about various components architecture and how they should precisely interact.

3   The 'Ubit' Brick Model

The Ubit toolkit proposes a new approach that is based on the concept of **generic basic bricks**. Basic bricks are specialized C++ objects that only implement and control one specific functionality. These bricks can easily be combined together through a standard and dynamical *adding mechanism*. The model is recursive so that composite objects resulting from brick combinations are brick themselves that can be further combined with other bricks.

Brick combination is always performed in a standardized way through a generic interface: the **Box** object. The Box brick acts as a general container that can contain any possible brick combination, including other boxes. The idea of using container objects is not new: this principle was for instance used by most X-Window (or derived) toolkits (e.g. Motif, Athena, OpenLook, InterViews, Tcl/Tk, Java AWT, etc.). With such systems, GUIs are made by creating instance trees where container objects are able to layout and display their children in an appropriate way. Containers and interactors are generally not dealt with in an homogeneous way: most toolkits do not allow interactive components (such as buttons, text fields, lists, etc.) to contain other interactor objects. However, certain systems offer extended containment capabilities (for instance: Gtk (Mattis, 1999), Fresco (Linton et al., 1994), Self/Morphic (Maloney & Smith, 1995). Applications constructed with Morphic are composite 'morphs' whose submorphs can handle user input events. The Fresco toolkit is based on an advanced composition mechanism that allows the mixture of user interface components and structured graphics objects. Fresco objects derive from a primitive type called 'glyph'. While UI components are organized in a strict hierarchy, primitive glyphs may be shared. Fresco thus supports the redisplay of a direct acyclic graph (DAG) of objects. At last, object composition is also related to the field of Visual Programming (Glinert, 1986). Some VP systems include a special-purpose toolkit layer based on a component combination metaphor (Esteban et al., 1995).

The **Ubit** toolkit is based on a drastic generalization of the containment principle. In this model, a Box is not seen as a window object that can display child widgets, but rather as a generic interface that let other bricks cooperate. By opposition with classical systems boxes do not have graphical properties of their own. Instead, it will be up to the programmer to add all the necessary 'ingredients' to boxes in order to obtain the appropriate effect. A Box brick basically is a 'pure container' which role is to contain children of various types. Depending on their respective classes, these children will dynamically change the appearance and the behaviour of their Box parent. This design principle is related to the Design Pattern concepts of 'Container' and 'Decorator' objects.

Character strings, images, pixmaps, decorations, borders and graphical symbols are first class objects (called **Item** bricks) that can be Box children. A Box can thus contain any combination of Items, manage their layout and display them on the screen. This makes it possible to produce a wide range of customized components by combining a limited set of basic objects (Figure 1). For instance, a push button or any other interactor could contain an arbitrary combination of pixmap images, character strings and various symbols (such as arrows, checking indicators and other special marks). Decorations (the borders, shadows, etc.) could also be dynamically specified in

the same way. This may be seen as an elegant solution to the 'no possible best choice' dilemma that was presented in the previous section, as object attributes are actually chosen by toolkit users, not by toolkit designers.

This flexibility is a direct consequence of the reification of all GUI objects. For instance, the Box container does not need to know how to display any specific child: this service is always provided by the child itself, even if it is a low-level GUI object. Besides, the layout capabilities of the Box container also depends on a separate 'Layout' brick that can be dynamically changed. As said before, a Box is indeed a pure container whose appearance and behaviour depends on more specialized bricks.

The same principle applies for specifying graphical properties such as background and foreground colours, character fonts, background tiling and so on. Graphical properties are not predefined Box attributes. Instead the toolkit provides an extensible set of **Property** bricks that can be dynamically added to Box interactors in the same way as other components.

3.1   Ubit Metaclasses

Box children can derive from five distinctive metaclasses: other Boxes, viewable Items, graphical Properties, Callback bricks and State objects. **Callback** bricks specify that a given call-back function or object method will be invoked when a certain condition is verified on the containing Box (typically, when a certain event occurs on this Box, although more sophisticated conditions may also be specified). **State** bricks makes it possible to change to the graphical state of the Box or to modify its behaviour. Quite an important point is that *child order* matters when meaningful. A Box child list could for instance contain a callback (brick), a pixmap image, a red colour (brick), a first character string, a bold font, a blue colour, a second string and an arrow Symbol. As a result, the containing box would display all viewable elements in sequence, the two strings being drawn by using different colours and fonts (Figure 1a). This box would be sensitive and a given function would be called according to the callback brick specification.

The combination of object reification, list ordering and extended composition capabilities make it possible to create multi-font and multicolour text in an easy way. Besides, it also allows for mixing up text and other GUI components and make them appear in a sequence. This ability of sequencing text, images and interactors and parameterizing their graphical attributes is somewhat similar to the capabilities of

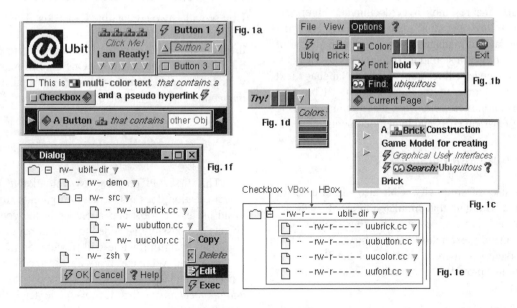

Figure 1: GUI object composition.

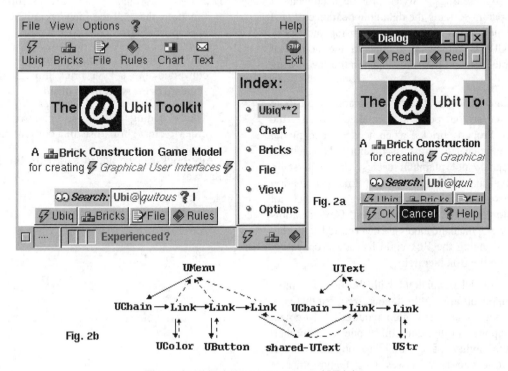

Figure 2: Ubiquitous components and ULinks.

hypertextual languages. This feature makes it easy to create GUIs that resemble hyperdocuments (Figure 2a) and that follow the same logic (especially for what concerns lay out management and the propagation of graphical properties among components). Besides, GUI source code will resemble mark-up language text as will be shown in the next section. Ubit thus proposes an unified framework that attempts to bring together classical GUIs and hyperdocuments.

3.2   Styles and Gadgets

For the sake of simplicity, Ubit also offers a set of predefined **Gadgets** that simulate the usual 'widgets' or 'controls' that can be found in other toolkits (e.g. buttons, menus, text fields, dialogue boxes, etc.). Most Ubit gadgets are mere derivations of the Box brick. They are just provided for convenience and mostly act as 'shortcuts'.

Default Gadget appearance is determined by **Style** bricks. By construction, each Gadget class is associated to (at least) one Style object. A Style object can be seen as a collection of default Properties. Style and customized specifications are cascaded so that Box Property children can override default Style settings. Styles provide a convenient way for parameterizing the default appearance of GUI components. This ability of configuring the 'look' of the GUI is somewhat similar to the notion of 'pluggable look and feel' developed in the Java Swing toolkit.

Gadget instances do not store graphical attribute in a static way but point to specialized objects (the Style and Property bricks) when needed. This model is very efficient in terms of memory management as objects do not maintain useless data and share most physical resources. Moreover, this specification mechanism works in a dynamical way and does not require to create new objects classes. Colours, fonts and other graphical attributes are determined at display time by scanning the Box child list and propagating them along the Box hierarchy.

This model is coherent with the fact that most GUI components are highly standardized, but that very specific objects are also often required. Moreover, such components often quite differ one from another. Thus, the ability of customizing objects without having to create new classes is a feature that is especially well suited for GUI design. This point was formerly addressed in some research systems through the concept of prototype-instance object systems such as Amulet (Myers et al., 1997).

4   The Pseudo-declarative API

Ubit provides two compatible C++ APIs. The first one is a classical object-oriented API: object are created by invoking the 'new' primitive and are added to parents by using their 'add' method. One could for instance write the following source code to create a push button that contains a pixmap and a character string:

```
UButton * b = new UButton();
UPix * p = new UPix("my_image.xpm");
UStr * s = new UStr("Click Me!");
b->add(p);
b->add(s);
```

This first API presents two remarkable points: object creation does not depend on parents (this will avoid useless a priori dependencies in the code) and objects can possibly be added to *several* parents. This important design principle will be detailed in section 5. The second API makes it possible to specify GUIs in a **pseudo-declarative** style. It is based on a generic *adding mechanism* that favours code legibility and compactness:

```
ubutton(upix("my_image.xpm") +
  "Click Me!");
```

This simplified API only makes use of standard C++ features:

1. `ubutton()` and `upix()` are just intermediate functions that call the 'new' primitive with the appropriate class.

2. The "Click Me!" character string is implicitly converted into a UStr brick through the C++ standard conversion mechanism.

3. The '+' adding operator has been overloaded in order to create brick lists in a convenient way.

Any brick can be added to a Box Gadget in a similar way:

```
utext(
  ucallback(foo, UState::action)
  + upix("ubit.xpm")
  + UColor::red
  + "Click Me!"
  + UFont::bold + UColor::blue
  + "I am Ready!"
  + ubutton(
      USymbol::down
    + umenu(
        ucheckbox("Mode")
        + ubutton("Do it")
        + utext("Ubit...")
      )
    )
)
```

Property and Item bricks can either be constants or variables in which case they can be dynamically modified. The containing box will be automatically updated when one of its children is modified:

```
UColor & col = ucolor(UColor::red);
UStr & str = ustr("Click Me!");
ubutton(col + str);
then:
col.set(UColor::blue);
str.set("I am Ready!");
```

This programming style roughly resemble Lisp programming or special-purpose specification languages such as Forms VBT (Avrahami et al., 1989). It is also conceptually similar to mark-up languages (Boxes could be seen as tags whose behaviour and appearance is specified by Property bricks).

4.1 Conditional Specifications

Property and Item bricks can also be specified in a **conditional** way. These bricks will only be active (or visible) when a given condition is verified. For instance the following code specifies that the background colour and the character font will change (respectively) when the mouse enters this text area and when it is pressed:

```
utext(
   ufont(UFont::bold,UState::entered)
   + ubgcolor(UColor::red,
              UState::pressed)
   + "Click Me!"
)
```

Conditions may also depends on timer values or on the State value of another gadget. This makes it possible to program animations or to enforce simple coherency constraints among several GUI objects:

```
UButton *close = null;
udialog(
   .......
   + ubutton(&close, "Close")
   + ushow(false,
           close->when(UState::pressed)
   )
)
```

The 'ushow' Property will close its dialogue parent when the 'close' button is pressed. This example also shows how brick pointers can be initialized by giving them as the first argument of uxxx() functions.

4.2 Customization and Ghost Gadgets

Application-dependent components may be created by adding Decoration or Layout bricks or by including Gadgets Boxes into other Gadgets Boxes. Standard Decoration bricks provide various kinds of borders, shadows, etc. for customizing Box objects. New Decoration bricks can easily be derived from standard ones (the corresponding code being quite simple and limited in size). Decoration bricks may be active and dynamically change according to the current Box State. They may also be specified in a conditional way.

Layout bricks makes it possible to display Box children vertically, horizontally, in a flow or in a table.

The 'flow' mode mimics HTML standard layout. Text can be warped and can be combined with other GUI components (Figure 1c).

The gadget composition mechanism is especially powerful because it has been designed in a way that gives the illusion of perfect inclusion. For instance, Figure 1d shows a button that contains four sub-buttons. Clicking on each subpart will provoke different actions (such as invoking a call back function or opening a pop-up menu). The last button has no visible border and only displays a down arrow. This is not a specific 'ArrowButton' object but a standard button that contains a single arrow Symbol brick (a predefined brick that could easily be subclassed for other purposes).

This visual effect is made possible by using the **Ghost** feature. Ghosts are invisible gadget boxes whose children remain visible. They do not interfere with the propagation of graphical Properties: ghost children are drawn accordingly to the graphical attributes of ghost parents. Ghost Gadgets are not specific new classes. They are just standard Gadgets whose Style specification mechanism has been inactivated (by adding a Ghost State brick) but still behave in the expected way (a ghost button can be clicked, a ghost checkbox can be set, etc.). So, ghosts are not mere sensitive areas but actually act as invisible versions of standard interactors. It should be noted that the same result could be achieved by directly adding the appropriate bricks to an empty Box brick. The Ghost feature produces the same effect, but rather works in a 'subtractive' way. Both techniques are equivalent and can be used according to programmers preferences.

Figure 1f shows a file manager example that is entirely made of standard components. Each directory line is an horizontal box that contains a mixture of items and gadgets (Figure 1e). This GUI component could (almost) be entirely written in pseudo-declarative style. The +/- indicator is a Ghost Checkbox that contains two conditional pixmaps that depends on its on/off state (the '+' pixmap appears when the checkbox is in the 'off' state while the '-' pixmap appears in the opposite case). Clicking on this checkbox will also open (or close) a vertical box that contains the directory subfiles (each subfile line being made in the same way). This basic behaviour is also specified in a declarative way by linking a box 'ushow' brick to the checkbox on/off State. Just one call-back function is needed for searching directory subfiles in the file system.

5   Brick Sharing and Ubiquitous Components

An important consequence of the brick model is that it implicitly transfers GUI control from gadgets to Property and Item bricks. In classical architectures, UI objects store and control the values of their own attributes. Heterogeneous architectures based on the MVC model improve this basic architecture by clearly separating GUIs components into 'model' and 'rendering' objects. Among other characteristics, this makes it possible to create multiple-view GUIs in a simplified way. Besides, some systems also introduce the notion of object groups that makes it possible to handle a collection of primitive objects in a more abstract way (Ousterhout, 1994).

Both aspects are handled in a different way in Ubit interfaces. First, all Primitive and Item bricks can be shared (i.e. have multiple gadget parents). As these bricks control the GUI appearance, they implicitly act as groups. So, changing the current value of a String brick would automatically update all the gadgets that contain this string. This mechanism is completely generic and does not make assumptions on object precise types.

This feature is somewhat similar to the active value mechanism that can be found in certain systems. For instance the UStr and UInt bricks can also be seen as generic data types for representing character strings and integer values. Such objects are not necessarily related to graphical aspects and can be used by non GUI application parts for notification purpose. Similarly, Box objects can be seen as generic data containers.

Data sharing optimizes memory cost and simplifies the synchronization of multiple views. This feature can also be used for parameterizing graphical interfaces. Because graphical properties are reified, Colors, Fonts and Decorations can be shared by an arbitrary number of Box gadgets. Thus, modifying a simple Property brick will automatically update all related UI components. Moreover, common graphical properties such as Fonts and Colors are automatically propagated along the GUI DAG (Ubit interfaces having a DAG structure rather than a tree structure). The combination of both features offers quite a powerful way for controlling GUI aspect.

5.1   Implicit Behaviours

This data sharing principle also applies to all other bricks, including Gadget Boxes. Gadgets are said to be shared when they have multiple parents. Two different cases must be distinguished depending on whether the shared Gadget is a Box or a Window subclass.

A Window is a Box subclass that owns a physical window on the screen. The Window class is the base class for making Menus, Dialog boxes and the main window of the application.

Childhood relationships do not denote physical inclusion when the shared child is a Window subclass but lead to various implicit behaviours that depends on parent/child combinations. So, a Menu parent will for instance automatically open this Menu when it is activated in an appropriate way. The activation condition and the child behaviour depend on context. A Menu Gadget will behave as a pull-down menu if its parent is a Button that is located inside a Menu Bar. But it will behave as a contextual pop-up menu if its parent is an isolated Button. It will only be opened by pressing on the right button of the mouse if its parent is a Label or a Text field. At last, some parent/child combinations will not perform any implicit behaviours. Similar rules applies for Dialog boxes (except that parents must be clicked instead of being pushed).

Implicit behaviours work in a dynamical way. The same Window child may behave in different ways depending on which parent was actually activated. So, the same Menu could either behave as a pop-up or as a pull-down menu depending on activation context.

Implicit behaviours make it possible to encode menu systems and dialogue boxes in a quasi-procedural style, all basic behaviours being automatically deduced from structural relationships among components. Besides, by opposition to most other toolkits, there is no need to use different specific kinds of button or menu classes as instances combinations automatically lead to the appropriate behaviour.

5.2   Ubiquitous Gadgets

The second case concerns childhood relationships when the shared child is not a Window subclass. This case is quite different as this type of parent/child combination do imply physical inclusion of children into parents. Child Gadgets are then *visually replicated* into all parents. However, data is not duplicated, only physical representations are. A single gadget can thus have **ubiquitous** representations of the screen. Moreover, this mechanism is able to virtually replicate an entire instance subtree (all subtree gadgets being then implicitly ubiquitous).

This feature is quite useful when implementing multiple views. It could for instance be used to display a set of checkboxes or composite text (including complex combination of items or other gadgets as in

Figure 2a) in different parts of the GUI. All views would be automatically updated and data would alway be displayed in a consistent way.

The ubiquity mechanism ensures logical coherency but does not impose all views to be strictly identical. As seen before, the Ubit toolkit works in a totally dynamical way. Thus, different graphical properties can simultaneously apply on a shared component, depending on which component parent these properties where added to (each view will recursively use the properties specified by its corresponding parent). This feature can for instance be used to display the same view at different scales, with another layout or with different colours, etc.

This feature could be extended to the case of distributed interfaces, so that ubiquitous gadgets could be represented on several screens. This could be done in a simple way in the case of X-Window applications by using the standard networking capabilities of the X protocol. A single program could then display identical windows on several remote machines in a transparent way (the code being almost identical when displaying GUIs on one or several machines).

6 Implementation

6.1 Box Anatomy and Visual Polymorphism

All gadgets derive from, and are very similar to, the Box brick (or to the Window brick for menus and dialogues). Boxes are conceptually divided into three separate (but logically related) parts: the Style, the Renderer and the State/Behaviour part.

Styles are interchangeable parts that specify all possible default properties (such as colours, fonts, borders, shadows, etc.) that a given gadget class may need for being drawn in all possible states (i.e. when this gadget is pressed, activated, disabled, etc.). Styles are defined in a hierarchical way by further customizing of the Default Style object, so that most data is actually shared between style instances. This feature simplifies Style customizing (for instance for implementing application-defined or native 'look-and-feels'). It also improves data management and makes it possible to optimize certain drawing routines.

Styles can be inactivated, as in the case of Ghost objects. They also allow for *visual polymorphism* as several Styles can be associated to the same gadget class. The appropriate style is then dynamically chosen by the gadget instance depending on its structural context. For instance Button gadgets use different visual Styles whether they are located inside or outside menus.

Behaviours are also defined in a generic way. Typical GUI behaviours are virtually designed at the Box brick level. In most Box subclasses (i.e. the Gadgets) just declare which specific behaviours they will require. This is done by changing the Box State characteristics. Box State can also be changed dynamically by adding appropriate State bricks. So, all gadgets are for instance virtually able to deal with text, can be activated and can have an 'on/off' state.

These design principles simplifies the toolkit architecture and improves memory management efficiency. First, code duplication is avoided as object features are never implemented twice. Moreover, the system does not require programmers to learn a large number of complex object classes that may differ in a subtle way.

6.2 Ubiquitous Objects

Brick sharing and ubiquity are tightly related to the way objects are internally stored. Box objects maintain three different lists: the parent, behaviour and child lists. The behaviour list includes the Callback and State bricks that are relative to this Box while the child list contains its Property, Item and (child) Box bricks. The bricks are indirectly chained through intermediate objects called ULinks. Each list consists in a chain of ULink objects that both point to their corresponding brick and to the next ULink in the list (Figure 2b). This design allows for object sharing as a single brick may belong to several Box child lists.

ULink objects do not only point to brick objects. They can also contain specific data that is used in combination with the brick instance they point to. There are several ULink subclasses that correspond to the main brick metaclasses (Property, Item, Box, Callback and State). This feature is at the base of ubiquitous gadgets: Box sizes and coordinates are not stored in Box instances but in their corresponding links. Thus, Gadget Boxes that have multiple parents can deal with separate coordinate systems. This mechanism is quite general and is transparent to the user. Link handling routines are part of their counterpart brick classes so that correspondence between link and brick objects is performed in an implicit way.

7 Current Status and Future Work

The current version of the Ubit system has been implemented on the top of the X-Window system. It has been tested on several UNIX/Linux operating systems and is freely available, at the time of writing, at URL: http://www.enst.fr/~elc/ubit. A MS-Windows version of the system is currently under development.

Future work will first focus on Information Visualization. We plan adding standard IV capabilities (such as zooming interfaces and miscellaneous focus+context techniques) in the toolkit design. We also plan to adapt the XXL builder (a visual programming tool that was based on textual + visual equivalence and sketch drawing (Lecolinet, 1996; 1998)) to the Ubit toolkit.

Acknowledgements

We would like to thank J-D. Fekete, L. Robert, D. Verna, S. Pook and the anonymous reviewers for useful comments.

References

Avrahami, G., Brooks, K. & Brown, M. (1989), "A Two-view Approach to ConstructingUser Interfaces", *Computer Graphics* **23**(3).

Esteban, O., Chatty, S. & P., P. (1995), Whizz'ed: A Visual Programming Environment for Building Highly Interactive Software, in K. Nordby, P. H. Helmersen, D. J. Gilmore & S. A. Arnessen (eds.), *Human–Computer Interaction — INTERACT '95: Proceedings of the Fifth IFIP Conference on Human–Computer Interaction*, Chapman & Hall, pp.121–7.

Fowler, A. (1999), "A Swing Architecture Overview", http://www.javasoft.com/products/jfc/tsc.

Glinert, E. P. (1986), Towards "Second Generation" Interactive, Graphical Programming Environments, *in IEEE Workshop on Visual Languages*, IEEE Publications, pp.61–70.

Lecolinet, E. (1996), XXL: A Dual Approach for Building User Interfaces, *in Proceedings of the ACM Symposium on User Interface Software and Technology, UIST'96*, ACM Press, pp.99–108.

Lecolinet, E. (1998), Designing GUIs by Sketch Drawing and Visual Programming, in T. Catarci, M. F. Costabile, G. Santucci & L. Tarantino (eds.), *Proceedings of the Conference on Advanced Visual Interface (AVI'98)*, ACM Press, pp.274–6.

Linton, M., Tang, S. & Churchill, S. (1994), "Redisplay in Fresco", *The X Resource* **9**, 63–69.

Maloney, J. H. & Smith, R. B. (1995), Directness and Liveness in the Morphic User Interface Construction Environment, *in* G. Robinson (ed.), *Proceedings of the ACM Symposium on User Interface Software and Technology, UIST'95*, ACM Press, pp.21–8.

Mattis, P. (1999), "The GIMP Toolkit", http://www.gtk.org/docs/gtk.html.

Myers, B. A. (1995), "User Interface Software Tools", *ACM Transactions on Computer–Human Interaction* **2**(1), 64–103.

Myers, B. A., McDaniel, R. G., Miller, R. C., Ferrency, A. S., Faulring, A., Kyle, B. D., Mickish, A., Klimovitski, A. & Doane, P. (1997), "The Amulet Environment: New Models for Effective User Interface Software Development", *IEEE Transactions on Software Engineering* **23**(6), 347–65.

Ousterhout, J. K. (1994), *Tcl and the Tk Toolkit*, Addison–Wesley.

Szekely, P., Luo, P. & Neches, R. (1993), Beyond Interface Builders: Model-based Interface Tools, in S. Ashlund, K. Mullet, A. Henderson, E. Hollnagel & T. White (eds.), *Proceedings of INTERCHI'93*, ACM Press/IOS Press, pp.383–90.

GUITESTER2: An Automatic Consistency Evaluation Tool for Graphical User Interfaces

Hidehiko Okada, Shin'ichi Fukuzumi & Toshiyuki Asahi

Human Media Research Laboratories, NEC Corporation,

8916–47 Takayama-cho, Ikoma, Nara 630–0101, Japan.

{h-okada,fukuzumi,asahi}@hml.cl.nec.co.jp

Abstract: Computer tools for usability evaluation are useful for quantitative usability measurement. We propose methods for automatically evaluating the consistency of GUI widget properties. These methods detect inconsistent widgets by judging widgets which have minor property values as inconsistent with widgets which have major ones, as human evaluators do. We also propose a method for recording widget property values. This method records the data by using GUI application executables, not GUI resource files — the data is recorded by the cycle of 1) detecting widgets on the current screen, 2) recording their property values, and 3) activating one of the widgets to have the application pop-up/close its windows. We developed a computer tool, GUITESTER2, that can implement the proposed methods. The tool could detect inconsistencies in labelling terminology, button locations etc. for seven existing GUI applications, which confirmed the effectiveness of the tool.

Keywords: GUIs, usability, consistency, evaluation, tools.

1 Introduction

The iterative design of user interfaces is effective for developing usable products (Nielsen, 1993). Iterative design is the cycle of designing, prototyping, evaluating and modifying/redesigning user interfaces. We have been researching usability evaluation methods and developing computer tools for such methods.

One of the important research subjects in this field is the method for quantitative usability measurement. Existing evaluation methods (the thinking-aloud (Lewis, 1982), the heuristic evaluation (Nielsen, 1994), etc.) can be used for finding usability problems, but the methods don't cover the measurement. Our goal is to achieve usability benchmarking for GUI applications (Figure 1). The usability benchmarking will enable us to:

1. quantitatively compare usability among applications; and

2. set quantitative usability goals for application development.

To achieve the goal, we must:

1. define usability attributes;

2. develop appropriate evaluation methods for each of the attributes; and

3. develop a method for calculating benchmark scores.

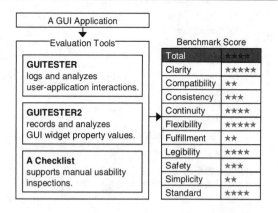

Figure 1: Our concept of usability benchmarking.

We previously defined ten usability attributes based on an analysis of existing user interface design guidelines and the usability problems found in our usability tests (Okada & Asahi, 1998). The three evaluation tools in Figure 1 are for evaluating the ten usability attributes. GUITESTER is for evaluating some aspects of clarity, continuity, safety, and simplicity by logging and analysing user-computer interactions (Okada & Asahi, 1999). GUITESTER2, which is proposed in this paper, is for evaluating some aspects of consistency, legibility, and standard. The checklist is mainly for evaluating compatibility, flexibility, and fulfilment (attributes that require manual inspections).

Consistency is known as an important usability attribute. For example, consistency is included in the ten recommended usability heuristics developed by Nielsen — users should not have to wonder whether different words, situations, or actions mean the same thing (Nielsen, 1994). Mahajan & Shneiderman (1996) reported in their experiment that inconsistent interface terminology slowed user performance by 10–25%.

Screen		
	1. Abbreviations	
a	2. Character typefaces (fonts, font sizes, bolding, underlining, etc.)	
	3. Colour meanings	
a	4. Combination of widgets on each window	
	5. Direction (of items, axes for numerical values, etc.)	
	6. Format of Graphs	
	7. Functional areas in windows	
	8. Grammatical rules for text notations (capitalization, etc.)	
	9. Guidance and messages	
	10. Icons and symbols	
b	11. Terminology in widget labels	
c	12. Terminology in window titles and widget labels	
	13. Order (of items, widgets, etc.)	
d	14. Widget colouration	
e	15. Widget locations	
	16. Widget shapes	
d	17. Widget sizes	
d	18. Window margins/margins between widgets	
User Operation		
d	19. Assignment of keys for accessing functions/widgets	
	20. Operation methods	
	21. Operation orders	
System Response		
d	22. Usage of message windows (critical, warning, information, etc.)	
System State		
f	23. Methods for indicating selected options/currently-focused widgets	
d	24. Rules for controlling user operations (widget disabling/hiding)	

Table 1: The GUI design properties for consistency (the marks *a–f* show classification of methods).

In this paper, we propose methods for automatically evaluating the consistency of GUI widget properties such as labelling terminology, locations, sizes etc. We also propose a method for recording widget property values that are required to evaluate consistency. We developed a computer tool that can implement the proposed methods. The tool, GUITESTER2, records GUI property value data, evaluates consistency for each property, and visualizes the evaluation result.

2   GUI Properties to be Evaluated for Consistency

To evaluate the consistency of a GUI, GUI properties that should be consistent throughout the interface must be specified. For a full list of such properties, we analysed existing GUI design guidelines — including the NASA User-Interface Guidelines (NASA, 1996) — and the results of usability evaluations we conducted, and extracted the properties. For example, the guide to "maintain consistency in labelling terminology", which is included in the NASA guidelines, indicates labelling terminology is one of the properties to be evaluated for consistency. The 24 properties shown in Table 1 were extracted with the analysis.

3   Methods for Automatic Consistency Evaluation

We propose automatic consistency evaluation methods for the 11 properties marked *a–f* in Table 1. We selected these properties because:

1. we thought consistency evaluation of the selected properties can be automated; and

2. the evaluation data (values for the selected properties of a GUI) can be automatically recorded with the recording method we will describe.

Evaluators manually inspect GUIs to evaluate the non-marked properties in Table 1. We developed six methods for evaluating the consistency of the 11 properties. Properties marked with the same character (*a–f*) can be evaluated with the same method. Here we describe methods for the following five properties:

1. terminology in widget labels;

2. terminology in window titles and widget labels;

3. widget locations;

4. widget sizes; and

5. key assignments.

3.1 Terminology in Widget Labels

The terminology should be consistent in widget labels. A typical example of inconsistency is the usage of misleading synonyms in button labels (e.g. 'Close' and 'Exit').

Mahajan & Shneiderman (1996) proposed a good method for evaluating this kind of consistency. Synonym sets (called terminology baskets in their paper) are predefined by human evaluators. The method detects labels that appear in the same basket. We utilize their idea of the baskets. Figure 2 shows our method. This method is different from Mahajan & Shneiderman's because we include word judgement. Words are judged based on the number of their instances — for each set of synonyms, the word that is used the most is judged as the basis for consistency, and other words are judged as inconsistent with the basis.

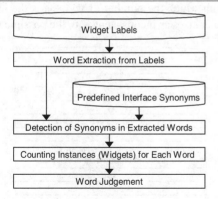

Figure 2: Our method for consistency evaluation of terminology in widget labels.

3.2 Terminology in Window Titles and Widget Labels

The terminology should be consistent in the widget labels and in the titles of windows that are opened by activating the widgets. An example of misleading inconsistency is as follows: a 'search for mail' window is opened when a user selects 'retrieve' in the 'mail' menu.

To evaluate this kind of consistency, the words used in the widget labels and in the window titles must be compared. we propose the method shown in Figure 3. Words used in a window title are extracted and compared with the labels of widgets that are activated to open the window. If all extracted words from a window title are included in the widget labels,

the title is judged as consistent, and if not, the title is judged as inconsistent.

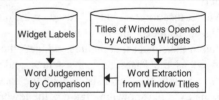

Figure 3: Our method for consistency evaluation of terminology in window titles and widget labels.

3.3 Widget Locations

If widgets with the same label are allocated on multiple windows, the locations of the widgets should be consistent throughout the windows. A typical example is the locations of 'OK' buttons.

To evaluate the location consistency, the locations of the widgets on each window are compared with each other. The comparison must consider window size variations; it is not appropriate to compare the exact coordinate values of the widgets because window sizes are usually different from each other. Therefore, our method normalizes the coordinate value by the window size (Figure 4).

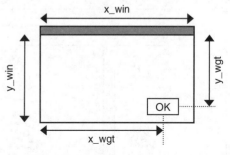

Normalized coordinate values

$x\_wgt^* = x\_wgt / x\_win \quad (0 < x\_wgt^* < 1)$

$y\_wgt^* = y\_wgt / y\_win \quad (0 < y\_wgt^* < 1)$

Figure 4: Normalization of widget location coordinate values.

Figure 5 shows our method for evaluating the consistency of widget locations. The method detects widget clusters by applying a clustering algorithm to the normalized coordinate values of widgets. The clustering is based on the Euclid distance between each pair of the widget locations on the normalized $[0, 1] \times [0, 1]$ plane. For the clustering algorithm, we utilize a hierarchical clustering algorithm (Romesburg, 1989) because of its simplicity and ease of programming. An example of widget location clusters is shown in Figure 6. In this example, widget locations are clustered into three clusters — the lower right, the upper right, and the lower left.

Widget locations are judged based on the number of widgets included in the same cluster — the locations in the cluster that includes widgets the most are judged as the bases for consistency, and other locations are judged as inconsistent with the bases.

In the example shown in Figure 6, the lower right cluster has the most widgets. This means that most of the widgets are located on the lower right area of the windows. Therefore, the locations in the lower right cluster are judged as consistent, and the other locations are judged as inconsistent.

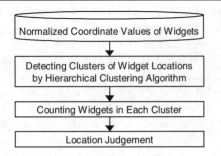

Figure 5: Our method for consistency evaluation of widget locations.

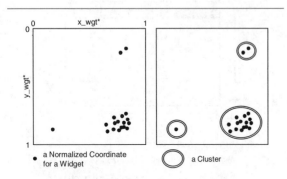

Figure 6: Example of widget location clusters.

3.4   Widget Sizes

Widgets of the same type should have the same size. An example is the height of the buttons. Although some variations in button width may be acceptable because the width depends on the length of a widget label, it is better to reduce the variations. The size of text fields is another similar example.

To evaluate the size consistency, widget sizes are compared with each other. If there are some size variations, an evaluator will judge the major size as the basis for consistency, and the minor size as inconsistent with the basis. The major (minor) size

means that the number of widgets with the size is large (small). A question arises here: if the number of widgets with the same size is not the largest but almost equal to the largest one, what is the appropriate judgement for the size? For example, consider three groups (G1, G2 and G3) of widgets with the same size (S1, S2, and S3 for each group), and the numbers of widgets included in each group are 50,48 and 2. In this case, it is not appropriate to judge size S2 as inconsistent with size S1 — an evaluator will judge both S1 and S2 as possible bases for consistency, and S3 as inconsistent with S1 and S2.

From this consideration, it can be said that sizes must be clustered based on the numbers of widgets detecting relatively major sizes. Figure 7 shows our method. We utilize the hierarchical clustering algorithm (Romesburg, 1989) for the clustering. Sizes with similar numbers of widgets are clustered into the same cluster. In the example described above, S1 and S2 are clustered into the same cluster. Relatively major sizes, i.e. sizes within the cluster C*, are judged as possible bases for consistency, where C* includes the size with which the number of widgets is the largest. The other sizes as inconsistent with the possible bases.

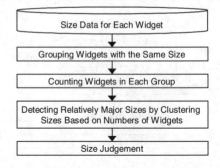

Figure 7: Our method for consistency evaluation of widget sizes.

3.5   Assignment of Keys for Accessing Functions/Widgets

GUI designers can assign keys to widgets for users to activate the widgets by pressing keys rather than pointing and clicking with a mouse. An example is a shortcut key, also referred to as an accelerator key (Microsoft, 1997). It makes a GUI application easier to use by consistently assigning shortcut keys with existing applications that users are familiar with (e.g. CTRL+C for the 'Copy' menu item). This is because the users can activate the same widget with the same key when they use the applications.

Another example is an access key, also referred to as a mnemonic (Microsoft, 1997). For example, users can activate an 'OK' button on a window by pressing ALT+O if the keys are assigned to the 'OK' button. The difference between shortcut keys and access keys is that shortcut keys activate widgets that are displayed and not displayed in the current screen, whereas access keys only activate widgets that are displayed. The same access key should be assigned to widgets with the same labels (e.g. 'OK' buttons on multiple windows) for users to activate the widgets with the same key.

Here we focus on the consistency of access keys within an application. Keys assigned to widgets with the same label are compared to evaluate the consistency of access key assignment. An evaluator will judge major keys as possible bases for consistency and minor keys as inconsistent with the bases. Since this rule is the same as the one for the widget sizes, the method shown in Figure 7 can be applied to the evaluation of access keys. Widgets with the same access key are grouped, and the number of widgets is counted for each group. Access keys with similar numbers of widgets are clustered into the same cluster. Relatively major keys are judged as possible bases for consistency, and other keys as inconsistent with the bases.

3.6 Other Properties

The following four properties, marked *d* in Table 1, can also be evaluated by the same method as for widget sizes — widget colouration, window margins/margins between widgets, usage of message windows, and rules for controlling user operations. This is because the judgement rule for each of the four properties is the same as the one for the widget sizes. We developed another method for character typefaces and widget combination (*a* in Table 1). This method includes vector comparison, because the values of the two properties can be described as vectors. We developed another method for selection indication methods (*f* in Table 1). This method is heuristic-based. In the six methods, the basic rule for the judgement is the same — major values are possible bases for consistency and minor values are inconsistent with the bases.

4   Methods for Recording Widget Property Values

GUI property value data is required for a computer tool to automatically evaluate the consistency described above. The data includes widget labels, window titles, widget location coordinate values on windows (more specifically, the coordinate values for the upper left and the lower right vertices of widgets for the

calculation of the centre coordinate and the size), access keys, etc.

We propose a method for automatically recording the required data. As the data source, the method uses application executables of which the GUI is to be evaluated, not GUI resource files. The most important idea of the method is the utilization of the OffScreen model (Kochanek, 1994), which is technology developed for GUI screen readers. The screen readers enable blind or visually impaired users to use GUI applications. For example, the screen readers read out widget labels displayed on the current screen and indicate the locations of widgets by sounds. To achieve these functions, an OffScreen model manager detects windows and widgets displayed on the current screen, and acquires property values such as labels and location coordinate values of the windows and widgets. The OffScreen model is a database of the property values for the current screen. The data required for consistency evaluation can be obtained by recording property values detected by the OffScreen model manager. To record data of all windows and widgets of a GUI, the windows and widgets must be displayed at least once during a recording session. This can be achieved by automatically activating each detected widget and having the application pop-up/close its windows. Figure 8 shows our method for the data recording.

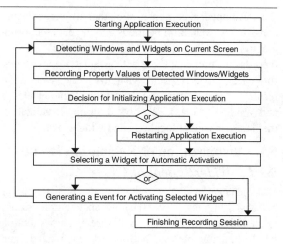

Figure 8: Our method for recording widget property values.

Application Execution (Re)starting: The application is (re) started by referring to the file name of the application program. The file name is pre-registered by an evaluator.

Window/Widget Detection: Windows and widgets displayed on the current screen are detected.

Property Value Recording: Property values for the detected windows and widgets are recorded. The values are recorded only for the windows/widgets that are not yet recorded (those detected for the first time).

Initialization Decision and Widget Selection: If there is a widget on the current screen that is not yet activated, the widget is selected for the automatic activation. Otherwise, the application execution is restarted because there is no widget on the current screen that may have the application pop-up new windows/widgets. After the application is restarted, a widget is selected that is already recorded but not yet activated. If no such widget exists, the recording session is finished.

Event Generation: A mouse-clicking event is generated that activates the selected widget.

Since our method does not require GUI source programs, the method can be applied independently of programming languages. In addition, the method does not require an evaluator's scripting of operation procedures for the automation of widget activation. The method, therefore, can also be applied to the automated testing of GUI application executions.

5 GUITESTER2

We developed a computer tool that implements the consistency evaluation methods and the data recording method described above. The tool, GUITESTER2, records GUI property value data, evaluates consistency for each property, and visualizes the evaluation result. The tool runs on Microsoft Windows95/98 and WindowsNT 4.0. We now describe visualization methods for widget locations and widget sizes.

5.1 Visualization of Evaluation Results

5.1.1 Widget Locations

GUITESTER2 evaluates the location consistency for buttons. Figures 9 & 10 show an example result. Each column in the list in Figure 9 shows button labels, the numbers of buttons for each label, and consistency judgement results. For example, the first row shows that there are 33 'OK' buttons in the evaluated application, and that the locations of the 'OK' buttons are judged as inconsistent.

Figure 10 shows the locations of the 33 'OK' buttons on the normalized plane and judgement results for the locations. Each column in the list of Figure 10 shows the titles of windows on which the 'OK' buttons are allocated and the judgement results. For example,

the first row in the list shows that the location of the 'OK' button on the 'Address' window is not consistent. The graph in Figure 10 shows the locations of the 33 'OK' buttons on the normalized plane and the judgement result for each location. In this example, there are two distinct clusters of locations. The locations in the lower left cluster are judged as the bases and the locations in the upper right cluster are judged as inconsistent with the bases, because the lower left cluster is the major cluster in this example. By clicking a window title in the list, the mark in the graph is highlighted. The image of the window clicked in the list can be displayed (window images are captured and recorded in the data recording session).

Since inconsistent locations are visually indicated by '×', an evaluator can easily find them.

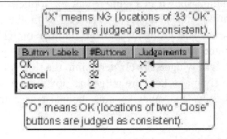

Figure 9: Location evaluation result for each button label.

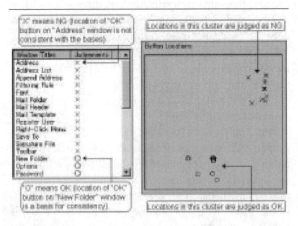

Figure 10: Location evaluation result for buttons with the same label.

5.1.2 Widget Sizes

GUITESTER2 evaluates size consistency for buttons, text fields, listboxes etc. Widths and heights are independently evaluated. Figures 11 & 12 show an example for button heights.

Each column in the list in Figure 11 shows the values of heights, the numbers of buttons with the same size, and the judgement results. There are ten distinct heights ranging from 18 to 45 dots. The first row in the list shows that there are 29 buttons with the height of 23 dots and the height is judged as inconsistent. The two bottom rows show that the two heights, 32 dots and 34 dots, are judged as the possible bases. Note that the height of 34 dots is judged as one of the possible bases, although the number of widgets for the height is not the largest — both of the two heights are judged as relatively major ones based on the clustering result.

When a value in the list is clicked, widgets that have the height of the value are listed. Figure 12 shows an example of the widget list. Each column of the list shows widget labels and titles of windows on which the widgets are allocated.

Since inconsistent sizes are visually indicated by the symbol '×', a human evaluator can easily find them.

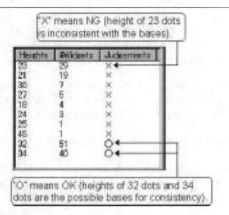

Figure 11: Size evaluation result for button heights.

Widget Labels	Window Titles
Cancel	Right-Click Menu
Cancel	Save To
Cancel	Toolbar
Close	Appended File
Close	Search Mail
Delete	Right-Click Menu
Delete	Toolbar
OK	Address
OK	Mail Folder
OK	Mail Header

Widgets with the same height are listed.

Figure 12: Widgets with the same height.

5.2 Examples of Evaluation Results

We experimentally used GUITESTER2 to evaluate the consistency of seven GUI applications. The applications are three email applications, a Web browser, a text editor, an image processor and a document viewer. For one of the email applications, 22 inconsistencies were detected. For example, the locations of 'OK' buttons and button heights

were inconsistent. Figures 10 & 11 show the inconsistencies. Therefore, it was confirmed that GUITESTER2 can evaluate consistency in GUI widget properties.

5.3 Comparison with Related Work

A set of consistency evaluation tools was previously developed (Mahajan & Shneiderman, 1996). We compare the data recording method and the consistency evaluation methods of GUITESTER2 with those of previous tools.

5.3.1 Data Recording Method

The sources of GUI property value data for GUITESTER2 are application executables. Those for previous tools were GUI resource files — GUI property values are extracted and recorded by analysing the resource files based on string matching.

An advantage of the previous method is that it can record property values that cannot be currently recorded with our method. For example, the values of widget colours cannot be recorded by our method. This is because our OffScreen model manager cannot detect colour values.

An advantage of our method is that it can be applied independently of programming languages. Since the formats of GUI resource files are different among various languages, resource file analysers must be designed and developed for each language in the previous method.

Another advantage of our method is that it can record GUI property data required to evaluate inter-application consistency. To evaluate the consistency of a GUI application with existing applications including ones developed by others, The GUI data of all of the applications are required. Since the GUI resource files of applications developed by others are not usually available, their method cannot be used to evaluate inter-application consistency. Our method can record data for any GUI application executable on an evaluator's PC.

5.3.2 Consistency Evaluation Method

With GUITESTER2, an evaluator can easily find inconsistent widgets because the tool automatically judges widgets as the bases for consistency or inconsistent with the bases and displays the judgement results with distinct symbols '○' (OK) and '×' (NG). Previous tools do not implement such automatic judgement except for the evaluation of terminology. For example, the previous tool for the evaluation of locations (or sizes) generates tables of coordinate values (or width and height values) for buttons on each window, but does not compare the values. An evaluator must manually compare the values and find inconsistent ones from the table. Manual comparisons are more difficult as the number of buttons increase.

6   Conclusion and Future Work

In this paper, we have proposed methods for automatically evaluating the consistency of GUI widget properties and for recording widget property values.   Our tool GUITESTER2 can be applied independently of programming languages because it records the GUI property value data by using GUI application executables. An evaluator can easily find inconsistent widgets by using the tool because the tool:

1. automatically judges widgets as the bases for consistency or inconsistent with the bases; and

2. displays the detected inconsistent widgets with the distinct symbols.

The tool could detect inconsistencies for seven existing GUI applications, which confirmed the effectiveness of the tool.   The evaluator should, however, consider whether the detected inconsistencies are really usability problems that require design modifications.   This is because consistency is merely one of the ten usability attributes (see Table 1) and there may be some trade-offs in the attributes.   Some inconsistencies may be acceptable for making the GUI usable from the viewpoints of the other attributes (e.g. continuity, safety).

To further evaluate the effectiveness, we will compare consistency evaluation results of the tool with results of the heuristic evaluation method (Nielsen, 1994).   We will report this comparison at the conference.   We will also provide the tool for some in-house GUI developers for field evaluation.

We plan to develop evaluation methods for legibility and standard in future research.   These methods will be implemented by GUITESTER2. A method for calculating benchmark scores is also necessary to achieve our goal of usability benchmarking.

References

Kochanek, D. (1994), Designing an Off-screen Model for a GUI, *in* W. Zagler, G. Busby & R. Wagner (eds.), *Computers for Handicapped Persons*, Vol. 860 of *Lecture Notes in Computer Science*, Springer-Verlag, pp.89–95.

Lewis, C. (1982), Using the 'Thinking-aloud' Method in Cognitive Interface Design, Technical Report RC9265, IBM T. J. Watson Research Center.

Mahajan, R. & Shneiderman, B. (1996), Visual and Textual Consistency Checking Tools for Graphical User Interfaces, Technical Report CS-TR-3639, HCIL, University of Maryland. ftp://ftp.cs.umd.edu/pub/hcil/Reports-Abstracts-Bibliography/96-08html/96-08.htm.

Microsoft (1997), "Fundamentals of Designing User Interaction — Input Basics", http://www.microsoft.com/win32dev/uiguide/uigui043.htm. The Windows Interface Guidelines for Software Design.

NASA (1996), "User-Interface Guidelines", http://groucho.gsfc.nasa.gov/Code_520/Code_522/Documents/UG_96/newfrontmatter.html.

Nielsen, J. (1993), *Usability Engineering*, Academic Press.

Nielsen, J. (1994), Heuristic Evaluation, *in* J. Nielsen & R. L. Mack (eds.), *Usability Inspection Methods*, John Wiley & Sons, pp.25–62.

Okada, H. & Asahi, T. (1998), Developing a Usability Map for Graphical User Interfaces, *in Proceedings of the 56th IPSJ Semi-annual Conference*, Vol. 4, pp.78–9. in Japanese.

Okada, H. & Asahi, T. (1999), "GUITESTER: A Log-based Usability Testing Tool for Graphical User Interfaces", *IEICE Transactions on Information and Systems* **E82-D**(6), 1030–41.

Romesburg, H. C. (1989), *Cluster Analysis for Researchers*, Robert E. Krieger Publishing.

Human–Computer Interaction — INTERACT '99
M. Angela Sasse and Chris Johnson (Editors)
Published by IOS Press, © IFIP TC.13, 1999

Towards a Better Understanding of Usability Problems with Virtual Environments

Kulwinder Kaur Deol, Alistair G. Sutcliffe & Neil A.M. Maiden

Centre for HCI Design, City University, Northampton Square,
London EC1V 0HB, UK.

{K.Kaur,A.G.Sutcliffe,N.A.M.Maiden}@city.ac.uk

Abstract: Virtual environments (VEs) offer new challenges to human–computer interface design. In particular, they have been found to be difficult to design and use. A better understanding of their usability issues is needed. This paper reports the results of theoretical work and empirical studies aimed at identifying what usability problems users can encounter when interacting with VEs. Potential usability problems were proposed from models of VE interaction. Empirical studies were then used to test and refine the identified problem set. Results comparing observed with proposed problems indicated that the proposed problems had good coverage, but there were areas where actual difficulties were duplicated. More generally, the results provide important knowledge about likely usability problems with VEs and highlight the more significant issues. Further work involves development of the theories to address usability problems through design and evaluation guidance.

Keywords: virtual environments, usability problems, interaction modelling.

1 Introduction

Virtual environments offer new possibilities and challenges to human–computer interface design. However, major usability problems have been found with current VEs, which result in user frustration and low system acceptability (Miller, 1994; Kaur et al., 1996). Potential usability problems need to be identified and guidance defined to avoid or alleviate the problems. The current literature provides fragmentary knowledge about potential problems. User studies of VEs — e.g. (Mercurio & Erickson, 1990; Wanger et al., 1992) — have tended to evaluate the applicability of VEs or the most appropriate device for a particular application, or, have evaluated the effectiveness of various depth cues, rather than focus on overall usability. However, a few usability problems have been uncovered.

Maintaining spatial orientation can be difficult (McGovern, 1993) leading to disorientation and users losing their whereabouts (Miller, 1994). Perceptual problems have been found, such as difficulties distinguishing objects, and difficulties in size and depth perception (Rolland et al., 1995), for example not perceiving negative obstacles such as ditches (McGovern, 1993). Specific technical problems, such as slow display update rates, can result in usability issues, as well as health problems such as motion sickness (Oman, 1993). Navigation and way-finding problems include difficulty estimating direction of travel, difficulty finding places and finding the quickest paths to places, and difficulty relocating places recently visited (Darken & Sibert, 1996; Ruddle et al., 1998).

Many of these problems are not typical of those found with more conventional interfaces, such as direct manipulation. For example, Springett (1996) reports common problems found with the MacDraw interface, including misleading action cues (e.g. menus not making clear the resulting direction of arrow lines), missing or ambiguous feedback (e.g. inadequate feedback on object selection), and hidden functionality (e.g. the implicit setting of defaults on line styles). VE users face some new problems because of the added spatial dimension, which can place more demand on perception, orientation and object manipulation. Only a small part of the VE is typically available through the interface (whereas direct manipulation interfaces aim to continually present objects of interest), therefore movement through the interface and the locating of objects is a major area of potential difficulty. Finally, novel and more complex interface technology is used which can result in additional difficulties.

Therefore, an understanding of the specific usability issues in VEs is required. Towards this aim, potential usability problems with VEs were proposed through the use of interaction modelling. Studies were then carried out to evaluate the proposed problem set.

2   Theoretical Research

To inform usability issues, models of user interaction behaviour in VEs were developed from Norman's (1988) basic plan-based model of action. This theory represents interaction in cycles of seven stages: form goal, form action intention, specify action sequence, execute, perceive feedback, interpret and evaluate implications for goals. It was elaborated by adding stages to describe exploratory and reactive behaviours, which are important aspects of VE interaction. Tasks in VEs are often loosely structured with more emphasis on exploration (Johnson, 1998) and opportunistic action. VEs are often active, with objects operating independently of the user (Bryson, 1995) and providing events and more complex behaviours for the user to respond to. The theory approximates interaction behaviour into 21 stages divided into three inter-connected models which describe the major modes of behaviour:

Task action model: Describing behaviour in planning and carrying out specific actions as part of user's task or current goal/intention. This model was taken from Norman's with the addition of stages for VE actions, such as the need to approach and orient as required to action objects.

Explore navigate model: Describing opportunistic and less goal-directed behaviour when the user explores and navigates through the environment. The user may have a target in mind or observed features may arouse interest.

System initiative model: Describing reactive behaviour to system prompts and events, and to the system taking interaction control from the user (for example taking the user on a pre-set tour of the environment). This model covers user behaviour in interpreting, monitoring and then responding to system events and controls.

For example, Figure 1 gives the exploratory model.

Since little previous work on understanding VE interaction existed, the models aimed to capture the typical flow of interaction for the more basic type of VE, that is single-user systems generally modelled on real world phenomena. The models were evaluated in studies of user interaction, where observed behaviour was compared with that predicted. Video analysis and 'think-aloud' verbal protocols were used for data on physical and mental behaviour respectively. The study results indicated that the models summarise interactive behaviour through the modes and stages of interaction, providing good coverage and general predictivity. Detailed findings were used to refine the models, to improve predictions of the interaction flow from stage to stage (Kaur et al., to appear).

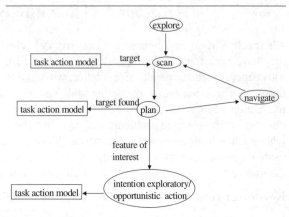

Figure 1: Explore navigate model. The user establishes an intention to explore. They scan the environment and plan how to continue. They may find a feature of interest and decide to carry out an exploratory or opportunistic action on it. Or, they may explore further by navigating and re-scanning. If they are searching for a target object, they navigate in a suitable direction until the target is found.

Using the breakdown of interactive behaviour provided by the models, resources for successful interaction during each stage were proposed. The resources were seen to be distributed between the VE and the user, through a set of desirable properties of a VE design and relevant elements of user knowledge. Design properties identified included requirements for information about the user's task, spatial layout of the VE, the viewpoint and user representation, environment objects, system initiative behaviour, and user actions and action feedback. For example, required information about objects included their identity, covered by the property *identifiable object*. Existing HCI guidance was applied where possible, such as guidance on supporting exploratory behaviour and the planning and executing of actions. Relevant areas of user knowledge included remembered information from previous experiences with a VE, known information about the application domain and task, general real world knowledge and knowledge of standards and commonalities between different VE interfaces.

A set of potential usability problems were then identified through systematic reasoning about:

1. required processing during each stage and the possible breakdowns during this processing; and

2. required information during each stage and the resulting effects of the information being missing or inadequate.

Usability problems could have one or more causes, which were identified through systematic reasoning about design properties and user knowledge relevant to each problem situation and required to avoid the problem. Correspondence rules were used to record the causal relationships between missing required resources and potential usability problems. Seventy-five usability problems in total were defined. Figure 2 gives an overview of the main theoretical components. This paper focuses on the proposed usability problems, but details of other components can be found in Kaur (1998).

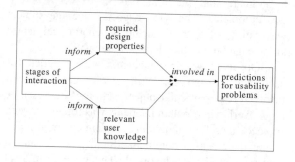

Figure 2: Overview of the components of the theory.

Use of the models of interaction meant that the identified problem set could cover a broad range of interaction issues, including planning and task execution; exploration, navigation and way-finding; action identification and execution; object approach and inspection; and event interpretation and response. Table 1 lists some of the potential problems identified for each interaction stage.

For example, in the evaluation of a virtual submarine (Kaur et al., 1996), submariners noted problems identifying some pieces of equipment due to poor object representations. The following correspondence rule, from the 'scan' stage in explore navigate mode, summarises this difficulty and its cause (required design property *identifiable objects* not supported and no relevant user knowledge):

IF (NOT design property(*distinguishable objects*))
OR (NOT(user knowledge(*identification information for objects*)) AND
  NOT design property(*identifiable objects*))
THEN predicted problem= (difficulty determining what objects are in immediate vicinity);
If objects in view are difficult to distinguish
Or there is not available information about the identity of objects from the user or the design,
Then the user is likely to have difficulties determining what objects are in their immediate vicinity.

Further examples for the problems in Table 1 are given later in the paper.

The problem set was evaluated through qualitative studies, where usability problems encountered were compared with those proposed in the theory.

3   Study Method

The test application was a virtual business-park, which was a commercially developed application used by The Rural Wales Development Board for marketing of business units to potential leaseholders. It was a desktop application consisting of two worlds — an external view of the business-park and an inside view of a unit in the park. Navigation through the worlds was unconstrained, with walking-through most walls allowed. Information about features in the unit was available by mouse clicking on related objects, such as windows and lighting. The application was run on a PC with a 21-inch monitor; a joystick was used for navigation and a standard 2D mouse for interacting with objects.

Eighteen subjects (11 male and 7 female), aged between 21 and 51 years, participated in the study. The subjects were staff and students at the School of Informatics, City University. Subjects were given the goal of gathering information about the architecture and basic services of the site represented in the VE. A range of nine tasks tested various interaction scenarios such as exploration, target searches, actions and object investigation. For example, subjects were given 10 minutes for free exploration, and were asked to find and investigate a water tank object, open a loading bay and compare three toilets in the unit. Subjects were provided with basic interaction notes, such as how to use the joystick. They were asked to provide a concurrent, 'think-aloud' verbal protocol and their interaction sessions were video-recorded. When subjects completed the tasks to their satisfaction, which typically took 45 minutes, they took part in a de-briefing session with the experimenter to clarify any points not covered in their verbal protocol.

Data on usability problem incidents was gathered from subjects' verbal protocols and from observation of video footage. Usability problems were defined as critical incidents or breakdowns in interaction, which interfered with the user's ability to efficiently and effectively complete interaction tasks — from definition by Karat et al. (1992). For example, this would include not being able to understand the current situation, wanting to do something but being unable or not knowing how, and making slips.

Task action	Potential Problem
establish goals	difficulty establishing clear goal
intention task action	difficulty establishing clear intention to act
consider objects	difficulty determining environment components involved in action
approach/ orient	difficulty determining current self position and orientation
	difficulty determining self parts involved in posture/orientation change
	difficulty determining whether further interaction possible
deduce sequence	difficulty determining parts involved in an action
	difficulty determining how to execute action
execute	difficulty executing action efficiently and effectively
	problems trying to execute action which does not exist
feedback	difficulty finding feedback not in immediate view
	difficulty assessing success of action
inspect	difficulty investigating target object
evaluate	difficulty assessing implications of action for goals and intentions
	difficulty assessing implications of system behaviour for goals and intentions

Explore Navigate	Potential Problem
explore	difficulty deciding areas of interest
scan	difficulty determining what objects are in immediate vicinity
	difficulty determining whether target is in immediate vicinity
plan	difficulty determining most suitable route to destination
navigate	difficulty determining current self position and orientation
	difficulty executing navigation effectively and efficiently
	difficulty assessing progress in navigation
intention explore action	difficulty detecting what actions are available with the objects of interest

System Initiative	Potential Problem
event	difficulty interpreting the event
acknowledge control	difficulty realizing commencement of system control
monitor control	difficulty distinguishing system behaviour
intention control action	difficulty determining whether/ what user control can be exercised
end control	difficulty realizing end of system control
plan	difficulty deciding appropriate response to system activity
intention reactive action	difficulty detecting what actions are available on the event objects

Table 1: Some of the potential problems identified for each interaction stage.

An expert in the theory had analysed the test application for the presence of the design properties predicted in the theory, and estimates had been made on average user knowledge. For example, the property *declared system control commencement/termination* was judged to be unsupported for an automatic guided tour of the park, since no information was available to indicate that the tour had started or when it was complete. The knowledge the average subject was estimated to have included general real world knowledge but no knowledge of the test VE.

Observed problem incidents were detailed for each subject and for each environment element involved (e.g. particular object, action of interest). A large overlap in problem incidents was found between subjects, therefore, individual incidents were grouped where there was a common difficulty and common environment element involved. This resulted in a set of observed difficulties and the occurrence of each difficulty was counted across subjects.

Observed difficulties were then matched with potential problems in the theory, using a scheme based on matching the difficulty, context and cause of problems — following advice of Lavery et al. (1997). These three aspects were captured in the correspondence rules as the proposed problem, stage of interaction and missing resource (design property and/or user knowledge) respectively. The matching process involved comparing observed difficulties, for each environment element, with each of the proposed problems. Where the difficulties appeared to match, the context of the observed difficulty was checked against the relevant stage of interaction and, if matching, the cause was checked against those predicted in the relevant correspondence rule. For example, the observed difficulty 'clicking instead of dragging the drawing board handle' (with the drawing board object), was matched to the theory problem *difficulty determining how to execute action* since the difficulties matched, the contexts were both deducing then executing an action sequence, and the cause was the lack of an information resource for an action procedure.

The matching of problems was validated through cross-matching by two observers. Each observer allocated matching proposed problems for each observed difficulty found with one of the elements in the VE. An inter-observer agreement of 80% of the observed incidents was reached. Resulting differences were discussed and reconciled.

The data on observed incidents and the matches with proposed problems was entered into a database, which was queried to test the hypothesis that:

> Significantly more observed difficulties will be predicted in the theory than non-predicted (i.e. matched to at least one proposed problem).

4   Results

The results provided substantial data on usability problems, with users on average encountering 141 problem incidents, about 3 incidents (avg.) per minute of interaction. Table 2 summarises the most common types of observed problems, which were associated with navigation and orientation, object understanding and interaction, and system behaviour.

The activity of navigation had the most associated incidents, but the most common single problem was not being able to recognize available actions in the environment (Problem P9, Table 2). For example there were problems identifying active parts of the drawing board (Figure 3), which could only be tilted using a small obscure handle at the side, but users expected to move the board itself. There were problems bumping too close to surfaces so that they filled the view (nose against the wall), such as the windows, (P3, Figure 4). Navigating tight areas of the environment was found to be difficult, such as corridors and doorways (P2, Figure 5). Users tried to go into areas they did not know were unavailable, such as through the door shown in Figure 6 (P6). Some objects were difficult to identity or recognize, such as the water tank shown in Figure 7 (P11). Finally, maintaining suitable view angles was difficult, for example view angles were sometimes too low and tilted inappropriately for exploring areas, such as toilets (P15, Figure 8).

Figure 3: Difficulties identifying hot-spots on the drawing board.

Figure 4: Problems bumping too close to surfaces, e.g. this is the rather homogeneous view after bumping into the windows.

Figure 5: Problems navigating corridors and doorways.

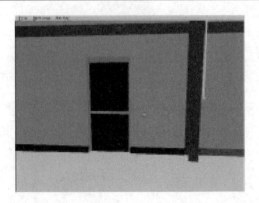

Figure 6: Problems trying to go through unavailable doors.

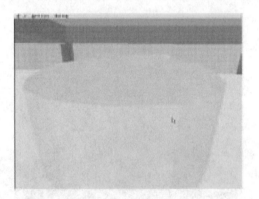

Figure 7: Difficulties identifying the water tank because of lack of detail.

Figure 8: Difficulties maintaining appropriate view angles for exploring the toilets.

Observed problem	Total
P1 Falling through walls accidentally	192
P2 Difficulty navigating tight areas, such as corridors	116
P3 Bumping into walls and other objects (nose against wall)	77
P4 Disoriented and lost (usually after bumping into walls or falling through walls)	57
P5 Difficulty finding or guessing location of target objects	55
P6 Trying to go into unavailable areas	**40**
P7 Difficulty steering smoothly in the intended direction	40
P8 Difficulty following intended paths because of obstacles and clutter	**22**
TOTAL Navigation	599
P9 Trying to interact with non-active parts of VE	359
P10 Using the wrong action sequence, such as dragging instead of clicking the mouse	59
TOTAL Action	418
P11 Not sure of the identity or role of object or area of VE	173
P12 Not noticing an object when it is in view and is the target being searched for	31
TOTAL Object	204
P13 Difficulty approaching objects correctly, such as doors	93
P14 Difficulty getting the intended view angle	50
P15 At an unsuitable viewing angle, such as being upside-down, for an extended period	**37**
TOTAL Orientation	180
P16 Trying to navigate during an automated drive-through	32
P17 Wrongly think controlling the movement during the automated drive-through	32
P18 Not noticing an event that occurs in the vicinity, such as a ringing telephone	22
TOTAL System behaviour	86
P19 Other objects being accidentally activated during mouse drag operations	*58*
P20 Trying to interact with an object, but mouse-clicks not being registered	*50*
P21 Confusion when faced with wrongly rendered graphics	*29*
TOTAL Technological	137

Table 2: The most common observed problems (that occurred more than 20 times). Those in italics were caused by technical problems and those in bold were not predicted in the theory.

The results provided some support for the proposed problem set. Since there were a large number of observed difficulties associated with many different environment elements, only the difficulties related to the main elements, such as navigation and the task-related objects, were analysed and matched against the theory. There were 351 different observed difficulties with these elements. Of these, 80% (282 of the 351) matched with one or more of the proposed problems (significant at $p < 0.01$, binomial distribution). For example, the observed difficulty 'looking for the loading bay but not noticing it when in view' (P12, Table 2) matched to *difficulty determining whether target is in immediate vicinity* (see Table 1). Therefore, the experimental hypothesis was not refuted, since a significant number of observed difficulties were matched to at least one proposed problem.

However, 40% of the observed difficulties investigated (114 of the 282) were matched to more than one of the proposed problems (9% matched to more than two). For example, the observed difficulty 'trying to flush the lavatory, when this action was not available' (P9, Table 2) was matched to two problems: difficulty determining whether further interaction possible and problems trying to execute action which does not exist. The remaining 69 observed problems were unpredicted and were categorized according to the general difficulty involved. Three of these categories were reasonably common (i.e. they accounted for more than 20 problem incidents), and these are summarised below and highlighted in Table 2:

6 Trying to go into unavailable areas
8 Difficulty following intended paths
15 At an unsuitable viewing angle

Of the 75 proposed problems, 20 could not be tested because they were not within the scope of problems possible in this study. For example, user representation problems, such as *difficulty determining self parts involved in posture/orientation change*, were not possible because only a very simple user representation (mouse-pointer) was available in the test application. Of the remaining 55 proposed problems, 44 were observed and 11 problems, for various stages of interaction, were not observed. For example, the theory problem *difficulty interpreting the event* was matched with the observed difficulty 'not sure how and why the speech text appeared'; but the problems *difficulty finding feedback not in immediate view* and *difficulty assessing implications of system behaviour for goals and intentions* were possible yet such difficulties were not found.

The matching of proposed with observed problems was investigated further. Pairs of proposed problems were sometimes matched to the same observed difficulties more than once, indicating that they may be related or may be duplicating actual difficulties. There were 12 pairs that were matched together at least five times. Some of the pairs of problems were from

the same stage of interaction where there were unclear boundaries between predicted problem areas. For example, problems executing navigation and assessing progress in navigation were often matched together (*difficulty executing navigation effectively and efficiently* and *difficulty assessing progress in navigation* respectively). Other problem pairs were from different stages in the models that shared certain interaction issues and where activity could not be reliably categorized as either one of the stages. For example, there were similar problems determining the current view position/orientation (*difficulty determining current self position and orientation*), during both the object 'approach/orient' and 'navigation' stages. The following sections discuss implications of these results for the theory and for research on VE usability.

5 Implications for Theory

The results indicate that the usability problem part of the theory has some descriptive and predictive power. It was able to describe actual usability problems that were observed within a predicted interaction context, that is most problems were found at the predicted stage and were caused by predicted required resources being missing. Its level of completeness was good since only a few additional areas of difficulty were identified.

However, detailed results indicate refinements required to the problem set. In particular, there were unpredicted issues, proposed problems that were not found, and those that were not investigated in this study. Furthermore, the problem set appeared to duplicate actual difficulties, since observed problems could sometimes match to more than one proposed problem and there were pairs of proposed problems that appeared to be closely related. Although, such mismatch issues are common when abstracting problems (Springett, 1996; Lavery et al., 1997), these situations may indicate possible simplifications to the problem set. Conversely, double classification of problems can be a useful feature in providing alternative interpretations, especially where there is limited interaction data, and in providing a specific problem list for each stage.

Other limitations in the theory included its level of precision since the correspondence rules could only predict a set of problems to be likely, rather than whether or not a specific problem would occur in any given situation. There appeared to be gaps of interpretation between the theory and the real world problem of VE usability. Its level of complexity was an issue because not all predicted problems could be tested in one study and the duplications in the problem set made the theory difficult to verify. These limitations reflect general difficulties with HCI theory in making precise predictions, identifying all independent variables, and judging levels of complexity to address a significant set of interaction issues without over-simplifying the problem space.

We are encouraged by the results and have refined the set of proposed problems by removing problems where duplications were judged to be unnecessary, and including additional problems for uncovered issues. For example, the problem *difficulty determining parts involved in an action*, has been removed because it was found to be covered by the problem *difficulty determining how to execute action*, and a new problem added for *difficulties determining available navigation pathways* (see P6, Table 2).

Having gained initial support for our ability to predict usability problems, continuing work involves using our theoretical research to improve interaction, by avoiding the problems. The design properties in the theory have been evaluated in studies where interaction success was found to significantly improve with implementation of relevant properties. For example, implementation of the design property *declared available actions*, such as through the use of highlighting to indicate actions, was found to address problems of being unable to find active parts of the environment (P9 in Table 2). Future work includes targeted studies to evaluate weak and untested areas, and testing the proposed problems with a wider range of VEs to assess their generality.

6   Wider Implications

The approach we adopted demonstrates an effective use of interaction modelling, where the process of user interaction and required resources are described to both identify and situate usability issues. Our theory covered a relatively broad set of interaction stages. Narrower focused theories predict more detailed usability issues, but they sacrifice breadth for depth. For example, LICAI (Kitajima & Polson, 1996) can give detailed advice for the design of command labels, but it has little to offer on icons, objects or interactive metaphors. However, the results found that certain activities, such as navigation, had a large and varied associated set of problems. With such common or critical behaviours, the models may need to be elaborated in depth. For example, Jul & Furnas (1997) outline navigation subtasks such as locomotion, steering, decision-making about where to go, and map building.

The results are important in providing improved knowledge about likely usability problems with VEs.

A more broad and comprehensive set of problems have been identified, which are based on a theoretical model of interaction. The more significant issues have been highlighted, such as those related to object interactions and navigation. Some of the problems, such as disorientation and inaccurate steering, have been found in other studies of VEs — e.g. (McGovern, 1993; Miller, 1994). Few perceptual or motion sickness problems occurred, although these have been commonly reported (Rolland et al., 1995; Miller, 1994; McGovern, 1993; Oman, 1993), perhaps because no head-mounted display was used in this application and objects generally rested on a ground or vertical plane. Many of the problems identified have previously received little attention in the VE literature, including the most common problem of not being able to identify available object interactions. Other problem areas uncovered were approaching objects, maintaining required view angles, identifying and understanding the role of objects and realizing system controls were taking place. Further navigation problems were also identified, such as realizing that collisions have occurred and identifying available navigation pathways. More recent work supports some of the common problems found, such as the difficulties that can occur with collisions and knowing what objects can be acted on and how (COVEN, 1997).

Understanding the types of problems that can be encountered in VE interaction is key to evaluating and improving usability. Presently there is a lack of design and evaluation guidance specifically for VEs, but the work reported here can provide a theoretical basis for such guidance. For example, the models of interaction and correspondence rules can be used in developing walkthrough evaluation methods and question checklists, which highlight potential usability difficulties during each stage of interaction. For example, at the 'scan' stage in the explore navigate model the question checklist could include: when scanning the VE, can the users distinguish and recognize many/few/none of the objects?

Our overall goal is to address problems of interface design for VEs, through design guidance and evaluation methods based on human–computer interaction theories. This paper reports important work in understanding one aspect of this area: the usability problems encountered when interacting with a VE.

Acknowledgements

We thank VE Solutions and The Rural Wales Development Board for loan of the test application, and the Engineering & Physical Sciences Research Council for funding.

References

Bryson, S. (1995), Approaches to the Successful Design and Implementation of VR Applications, *in* R. A. Earnshaw, J. A. Vince & H. Jones (eds.), *Virtual Reality Applications*, Academic Press.

COVEN (1997), D3.3: Usage Evaluation of the Initial Applications, Technical Report AC040, University of Nottingham. COVEN (Collaborative VEs) ACTS Project N.

Darken, R. P. & Sibert, J. L. (1996), Wayfinding Strategies and Behaviours in Large Virtual Worlds, *in* G. van der Veer & B. Nardi (eds.), *Proceedings of CHI'96: Human Factors in Computing Systems*, ACM Press, pp.142–50.

Johnson, C. (1998), On the Problems of Validating Desktop VR, *in* H. Johnson, L. Nigay & C. Roast (eds.), *People and Computers XIII (Proceedings of HCI'98)*, Springer-Verlag, pp.327–38.

Jul, S. & Furnas, G. W. (1997), "Navigation in Electronic Worlds: A CHI'97 Workshop", *ACM SIGCHI Bulletin* **29**(4), 44–9.

Karat, C., Campbell, R. & Fiegel, T. (1992), Comparison of Empirical Testing and Walkthrough Methods in User Interface Evaluation, *in* P. Bauersfeld, J. Bennett & G. Lynch (eds.), *Proceedings of CHI'92: Human Factors in Computing Systems*, ACM Press, pp.397–404.

Kaur, K. (1998), Designing Virtual Environments for Usability, PhD thesis, Centre for Human–Computer Interface Design, City University, London.

Kaur, K., Maiden, N. & Sutcliffe, A. (1996), Design Practice and Usability Problems with Virtual Environments, *in* J. Briet, S. Wawrzinek, A. Rossler & M. Wapler (eds.), *Virtual Reality World '96 Conference*, IDG Conferences & Seminars.

Kaur, K., Maiden, N. & Sutcliffe, A. (to appear), "Interacting with Virtual Environments: An Evaluation of a Model of Interaction", *Interacting with Computers* . Accepted for publication in Interacting with Computers: VR special issue.

Kitajima, M. & Polson, P. G. (1996), A Comprehension-based Model of Exploration, *in* G. van der Veer & B. Nardi (eds.), *Proceedings of CHI'96: Human Factors in Computing Systems*, ACM Press, pp.324–31. http://www.acm.org/sigchi/chi96/proceedings/paper/kitajima/mk_txt.htm.

Lavery, D., Cockton, G. & Atkinson, M. P. (1997), "Comparison of Evaluation Methods using Structured Usability Problem Reports", *Behaviour & Information Technology* **16**(4-5), 246–66.

McGovern, D. E. (1993), Experience and Results in Teleoperation of Land Vehicles, *in* S. R. Ellis, M. Kaiser & A. J. Grunwald. (eds.), *Pictorial Communication in Virtual and Real Environments*, Taylor & Francis.

Mercurio, P. J. & Erickson, T. D. (1990), Interactive Scientific Visualisation: An Assessment of a Virtual Reality System, *in* D. Diaper, D. Gilmore, G. Cockton & B. Shackel (eds.), *Proceedings of INTERACT '90 — Third IFIP Conference on Human–Computer Interaction*, Elsevier Science, pp.741–5.

Miller, L. D. (1994), A Usability Evaluation of the Rolls-Royce Virtual Reality for Aero Engine Maintenance System, Master's thesis, University College London.

Norman, D. A. (1988), *The Psychology of Everyday Things*, Basic Books.

Oman, C. M. (1993), Sensory Conflict in Motion Sickness: An Observer Theory approach, *in* S. R. Ellis, M. Kaiser & A. J. Grunwald (eds.), *Pictorial Communication in Virtual and Real Environments*, Taylor & Francis.

Rolland, J. P., Gibson, W. & Ariely, D. (1995), "Towards Quantifying Depth and Size Perception in Virtual Environments", *Presence: Teleoperators and Virtual Environments* **4**(1), 24–49.

Ruddle, R. A., Payne, S. J. & Jones, D. M. (1998), "Navigating Large-scale Desk-top Virtual Buildings: Effects of Orientation Aids and Familiarity", *Presence: Teleoperators and Virtual Environments* **7**(2), 179–92.

Springett, M. (1996), User Modelling for Evaluation of Direct Manipulation Interfaces, PhD thesis, Centre for Human–Computer Interface Design, City University, London.

Wanger, L. R., Ferwerda, J. A. & Greenberg, D. P. (1992), "Perceiving Spatial Relationships in Computer-generated Images", *IEEE Computer Graphics and Applications* **12**(3), 45–58.

Human–Computer Interaction — INTERACT '99
M. Angela Sasse and Chris Johnson (Editors)
Published by IOS Press, © IFIP TC.13, 1999

Controlling a Single 3D Object: Viewpoint Metaphors, Speed and Subjective Satisfaction

Timo Partala

University of Tampere, Department of Computer Science, PO Box 607, FIN-33101 Tampere, Finland.

tpa@cs.uta.fi

Abstract: This paper presents the results of an empirical study concerning the controlling of a single three-dimensional (3D) object on a desktop computer screen. The subjects used three different interfaces for controlling the 3D object: the virtual trackball, a keyboard interface and an experimental virtual rectangle interface. Each of the three interfaces was tested using two viewpoint metaphors: the world-in-hand metaphor and the eyeball-in-hand metaphor. The results indicate that the virtual trackball and the virtual rectangle were the fastest interfaces with no significant difference, while the users subjectively preferred the virtual rectangle interface. The use of the world-in-hand metaphor results in faster task times and increased subjective satisfaction. There were two object controlling styles, as the virtual trackball interface was used: controlling the object on just one axis at a time and controlling on many axes simultaneously. Using the virtual rectangle interface the users also had two distinct object controlling styles: the feature-based style and the area-based style.

Keywords: 3D interaction, 3D rotation, viewpoint metaphor, virtual rectangle.

1 Introduction

The use of three-dimensional graphics in computer programs has increased rapidly in the past few years, as the three-dimensional visualization of real and fictional objects and environments is becoming more and more popular. Nevertheless, the latest research efforts have concentrated mostly on the construction of new input devices, for instance different types of 3D mice and joysticks. Most of the users still use two-dimensional (2D) input devices such as the mouse, because its relative cost compared to 3D devices is much lower. In this paper, a new interface for 3D rotation using 2D input devices is presented and a comparison to previous work is given. In addition, two problems are studied. First, will the users rotate on one axis at a time even though the interface allows rotation on multiple axes at a time? Second, if the interface allows, do the users manipulate the object by trying to drag distinguishable features of the object? At the end of the paper I will discuss the potential implications of my experiment on the design of new interaction methods for 3D objects.

In this paper, the object of study is interaction with a single 3D object, as opposed to moving in whole virtual worlds. In addition to the methods for moving in three dimensions (x, y and z), the sizing of objects is also excluded.

It is important to study single object 3D rotation for many reasons. First, the user's cognitive load can be minimized. In virtual worlds there are many objects that could get the user's attention. In the single object case it can be assumed that the user's attention is focused on the object. Therefore, the results concerning the user's cognitive processes are likely to be more fundamental and more easily explicable. Second, there are many applications that involve interacting with just one 3D object as opposed to whole virtual worlds, for example some computer-aided design applications (e.g. design of furniture) and many applications related to scientific visualization (e.g. visualizing some part of the human body). Third, the users often break down complex three-dimensional tasks into two subtasks even in the real world: translating to the location in a 3D world and matching orientations with an object (Hinckley et al., 1994). In this paper, only the latter has been studied.

There are three main factors that are studied in this paper: viewpoint metaphors, speed and subjective satisfaction. The users' average times for completing tasks are calculated for each experimental interface. The users carried out the experiments using two different viewpoint metaphors. In addition, the users' subjective satisfaction with the different interfaces is found out using post-hoc commentary.

This paper is structured as follows. First, the most important concepts concerning viewpoint metaphors and 3D interaction styles are clarified by citing previous work. Second, the interfaces used in the experiments are described, followed by an explanation of the method and the tasks. Finally, the results are presented and the most important findings as well as their implications for future work are discussed.

2 Viewpoint Metaphors

Viewpoint metaphors are different ways of representing movement in 3D environments. There are two metaphors that seem to be suitable for controlling a single object: the eyeball-in-hand metaphor and the world-in-hand metaphor. Of the widely used metaphors, the flying vehicle control metaphor has been omitted, because it works best in whole virtual worlds.

The viewpoint metaphor is called the eyeball-in-hand metaphor, if the user can manipulate the viewpoint as if it was held in his or her hand, as the mouse is moved. Eyeball-in-hand is an object-centric metaphor. In the single object case, the users must imagine a sphere around the object, where the viewpoint can be moved. This is the major deficiency of the eyeball-in-hand metaphor: if the users cannot imagine the invisible sphere, they will easily think that the object moves in the wrong (opposite) direction. In short, in the eyeball-in-hand metaphor, the user imagines moving him/herself around the object.

The past research on eyeball-in-hand is twofold. Badler et al. (1986) found that the users have to consciously calculate the activity as they are using this interaction metaphor, which makes the interaction unnatural. However, Brooks (1988) found the metaphor to be somewhat useful. He identified some problems with disorientation and added a plan view of the scene to prevent the problem.

The world-in-hand metaphor (or scene-in-hand, environment-in-hand) connects the user's navigation movements directly to the object or environment to be moved. The world-in-hand is an egocentric metaphor. The user can imagine that the object is in his/her hand, as the mouse is used. Ware & Osborne (1990) found the metaphor to be useful in a single object case (a cube), but not very good in navigating in virtual environments. Six of their seven subjects reported that the world-in-hand metaphor was the best alternative in rotating the cube. The other alternatives were eyeball-in-hand and flying vehicle control. In this paper I report a similar study with a larger number of subjects comparing only eyeball-in-hand and world-in-hand.

I have compared the eyeball-in-hand metaphor and world-in-hand metaphor using many experimental interfaces. Especially at the level of single axes, the directions are not self-evident; many 3D flight simulators use the 'up' direction for ducking and 'down' for gaining altitude. Similarly, rotations may be understood differently, especially when the world-in-hand metaphor is used. For example, when rotating a 3D object using the keyboard, one subject would press 'right' as he/she wanted the top of the object to rotate right and the other would press 'right' as he/she wanted the bottom of the object to go right.

3 Previous Research on 3D Interfaces

The research on interfaces for 3D rotation has not been very extensive. Especially in the last few years the research has concerned mostly the construction of new input devices with additional degrees of freedom. However, it was known early that most people have difficulties with most coupled axes including the x–z and y–z coupled axes (Chen et al., 1988). In fact, all the coupled axes — except for the familiar x–y coupled axis — mostly were rejected by the users.

Chen et al. (1988) have conducted an experiment, which had some elements similar to those of the experiment described in this paper. They compared four distinct interfaces for 3D rotation. The first had three sliders — one for each axis: x, y and z. In the second there were three overlapping sliders: a horizontal slider for x, a vertical slider for y and a circular slider for z. The third interface had continuous movement for x and y (just like the mouse usually has). To control the z-axis, the user had to go outside a circle that had been drawn around the object. The last interface was a virtual sphere that simulates the controls of a physical 3D trackball. Horizontal and vertical movement at the centre of the circle moves the object in x and y dimensions, and movement along (or outside) the edge of the object rotates the object in z-axis.

The results indicate that the simplest interfaces (1 and 2) were the fastest for simple tasks, whereas more complex interfaces (3 and 4) were the fastest for complex tasks. In all, the virtual sphere was the fastest interface. In accuracy, the slider-based interfaces were the most accurate for simple tasks, whereas there were no significant differences between interfaces for complex tasks. The authors suggest that the virtual sphere is the one to choose, if the tasks are not extremely simple.

Another important interface for 3D rotation is the Arcball interface (Shoemake, 1992). The Arcball is like the virtual sphere, but its underlying mathematical quaternion implementation is more sophisticated. In practice, the Arcball is assumed to be better, because it doesn't suffer from some technical problems such as gimbal lock and noisy data.

Though the Arcball seems to be an improvement on the virtual sphere, it has turned out that the two interfaces have no significant differences in task times or accuracy (Hinckley et al., 1997). Nevertheless, the Arcball was rated better in subjective satisfaction. That experiment — like the experiment described in this paper — used a within-subjects design with varied task order.

It seems that the number of empirical experiments in this field is not very large. This paper contributes by describing an experiment that has some common elements with previous research, but also a new experimental interface included.

4   The 3D Object: A Talking Head

The three-dimensional object that has been used in the experiment is a 3D model of the human head (Figure 1). The head was chosen because the results of this experiment will be used to build an intuitive interface for speech therapists to control the 3D talking head that gives examples of correct articulation in our forthcoming speech therapy tutor. In fact, the human head is a good model for experiments concerning 3D rotation in general, because people often have to watch other people's heads and are familiar with it in its various different orientations. In some tasks, the head was examined from below and the throat was represented by a black hole. When asked, the subjects reported no difficulties recognizing that this was the orientation from below the head.

5   The Experimental Interfaces

The interfaces allowed continuous rotation on the x-axis, the y-axis and the z-axis and the test tasks involved rotation to many different orientations. The head was displayed to the user in a window, and the user could directly manipulate the head object, no interface components like sliders or edit boxes being needed. The interface was embedded in the object so that the interface was invisible and the user only saw the object.

The first interface was a virtual trackball. As the user pressed down the mouse button and moved the mouse, the head started rotating based on the initial mouse button location and subsequent mouse movement. In theory, it would have been possible to carry out complete tasks without releasing the mouse button (with fairly complex mouse movements), but few subjects detected this. In fact, most of the subjects made several presses and releases per each task. The z-axis rotations were achieved via a twisting motion similar to the fourth interface of Chen et al. (1988).

Figure 1: A 3D model of the human head.

In the second interface, the head was controlled using the keyboard. There were six keys, two for each axis. The keys were chosen so that the user could move the x and y axis with the right hand (j, i, k and l) and the z-axis with the left hand (d and f). As the user pressed a key down, the head started moving on one of the three axes at constant speed and stopped as the user released the key.

5.1   The Virtual Rectangle

The third interface was a novel experimental interface: a virtual rectangle. It was controlled by the mouse and allowed moving on one axis at a time only. Its most important component is the rectangle, which is situated inside the 3D object (Figure 2). Inside this rectangle, the object can be rotated along the two axes that appear to the user to be the (nearest to) horizontal and vertical axes in the specific orientation. The circular rotations on z can be found outside the rectangle. For example, using world-in-hand, if the user starts dragging, as the cursor is on the top of the head (in the starting head orientation like in Figure 2) and starts dragging right, the head rotates clockwise on the z-axis. Similarly, the user can grasp the ear and move the mouse up or down rotating the head (on the *z*-axis). If the user grasps the right ear and moves left, the head moves on the *x*-axis, just like it would have behaved if grasped inside the rectangle (e.g. at the nose).

In the orientation pictured in Figure 2, *x* is the horizontal direction and *y* is the vertical direction. In the middle rectangle the head can be controlled along the *x*-axis and the *y*-axis. The sectors on the left and on the right move the head on the *x*-axis (mouse moved left or right) and on the *z*-axis (mouse moved up or down), and the upper and lower sectors move the head on the *y*-axis (mouse moved up or down) and on the *z*-axis (mouse moved left or right). Using the world-in-hand metaphor, for example, grasping on the nose and moving the mouse up rises the nose (and the jaw). However, using eyeball-in-hand the movement is exactly the opposite (the head nods), because the user must imagine moving him/herself around the object.

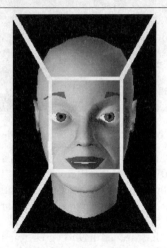

Figure 2: The virtual rectangle.

The background for this interface lies in feature-based theories of visual cognition. In feature analysis theory the human visual perception consists of features Anderson (1995). It is assumed that users first notice the features and try to rotate the head by starting dragging on one of the features most of the time. The head has many features, of which the eyes, the nose and the mouth are inside the rectangle, whereas the ears, the chin and the top of the head are on the outside (in the front view).

Another theory that is consistent with this notion is the recognition-by-components theory by Biederman (1987). According to it, humans perceive images by segmenting the image into arrangements of simple geometric components such as blocks, cylinders, wedges and cones. I consider this theory especially compatible with the perception of 3D

images, since 3D objects consist to a great extent of Biederman's components.

Connecting the theory of feature-based visual cognition to an interface that only allows controlling the object one axis at a time originates in the notion that coupled axes are difficult (Chen et al., 1988). There would have been a possibility to use the *x*–*y* coupled axis inside the virtual rectangle, but since diagonal mouse movement is not supported outside the rectangle (the object only rotates on one axis at a time), I chose not to allow it inside the rectangle, either, for the sake of consistency.

Another important aspect in the design of the image was the user's interaction with real physical objects. In many interfaces the rotations on the *z*-axis can be carried out by dragging the mouse completely outside the object. However, as the users interact with real world objects, they identify features that they want to twist. For example, if a user would like to rotate a physical model of the human head using only hands he/she would probably grasp the ear and pull down. Taking real objects as a basis means that if the interface is successful, it may have applications in virtual reality.

Using the head in the experiments has some disadvantages, too. Some people might be reluctant to grasp the features, just because the object is a head and it is not the most natural object to be turned. However, in the experiments it seemed that the test subjects understood the experimental nature of the test. In addition, they were so busy carrying out the exercises that they did not have much time to think about the naturalness of controlling a head.

To summarize, it is assumed that the users first perceive certain features or components of 3D objects and want to rotate the objects by grasping the features. Because coupled axes in general are difficult, movement is allowed on one axis at a time only. Thus, the virtual rectangle interface tries to be fairly realistic, maybe a little simplistic due to the one-axis-at-a-time rotation technique.

5.2 3D Rotations

In this study, a comparison of an interface, which only allows rotation on one axis (*x*, *y* or *z*) at a time (the virtual rectangle) and an interface, which can control all three rotational degrees of freedom simultaneously (the virtual trackball) is given.

This means that the virtual trackball interface used in this experiment often has a shorter minimal trajectory. For example, a compound rotation of 90 degrees along *x* and 90 degrees along *y* can be modelled as a shorter single rotation on an oblique axis in the virtual trackball interface (Zhai & Milgram, 1998), but in the virtual rectangle and the keyboard the shortest trajectory that the interface allows is 180 degrees (90+90).

However, it is not clear that the users are able to take advantage of this feature. In this paper, this issue is studied by comparing the task times for the virtual trackball and the virtual rectangle. Also studied was the extent to which the users use the coupled axes in the virtual trackball interface.

6   The Experiment

6.1   Subjects

Twelve subjects were tested, consisting of students and faculty of the University of Tampere. There were 10 males and 2 females. The subjects carried out the exercises in varied order. The three tasks can be carried out in six combinatoric sequences. Each of these sequences was carried out by one subject first trying a given interface using world-in-hand and after that the same interface using eyeball-in-hand. Another subject carried out the same combination trying eyeball-in-hand first and world-in-hand after that. Thus, the order of the tasks was varied in regard to all research variables.

The test subjects tried all the interfaces successively in one session, which lasted about 45 minutes. There was a short break between each interface. During this break, the user's subjective opinions about the current interface were asked.

A within-subjects design was used. An analysis of the learning effects indicated that the subjects used most time trying the first task, about 70% more than on other similar tasks. In the tasks from two to twelve, there were no recognizable learning effects. The first task learning effect was quite similar for each interface and viewpoint metaphor.

6.2   Apparatus

The experiment was run entirely on a Pentium Pro 200MHz personal computer, running the Windows NT Workstation operating system. The system was fast enough to display all the rotations of the head in real time.

6.3   Tasks

Using each different interface the subjects were asked to perform a series of rotation tasks. The subjects were shown by the organizer a picture (on paper) of the head in a certain orientation, to which they tried to turn the head on the screen. The picture was available during the experiments so that they could take another look if they wanted to. When the head on the screen

was close enough to the orientation in the picture, the organizer showed the subject a new task. In general, an aberration up to 10 degrees on any single axis or on all of them was still acceptable.

The three interfaces were tested using both world-in-hand and eyeball-in-hand and the subjects carried out twelve matching tasks for each task and metaphor. Thus, one subject carried out a total of 72 matching tasks.

However, only the 24 basic orientations were used in the tasks of this experiment. Examples of the used basic orientations are presented in Figure 3. These orientations include the six basic views (the front view, two side views, the rear view, the upper view and the bottom view). For each of these views, the object can be rotated (on z-axis) to four different orientations, for example the nose pointing up, down, left and right (the upper view, on the right in Figure 3).

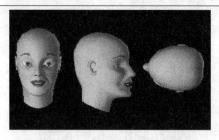

Figure 3: Examples of basic orientations.

While the users tried each of the six interfaces, they carried out twelve different tasks. There were three tasks that were simple 90 degree rotations on one axis (x, y or z). There were three tasks that required a 180 degree rotation on one axis (x, y, or z). There were three tasks that needed a 90 degree rotation on one axis and a 90 degree rotation on another axis. These tasks were chosen so that they could not be completed simply by rotating 90 degrees on the third axis (using the keyboard and the virtual rectangle). Finally, there were three tasks that needed a 180 degree rotation on one axis and a 90 degree rotation on another axis. For example, in Figure 3 the transition from the orientation on the left to the orientation in the middle is a simple 90 degree rotation. The transition from the orientation in the middle to the orientation on the right is a task that needs a 180 degrees + 90 degrees rotation.

These are the shortest possible routes to the destination using the virtual rectangle and the keyboard interfaces, which only allow rotation on one axis at a time. Using the virtual trackball interface, it was possible to use shorter trajectories by moving on oblique axes.

The subjects practiced with each different interface and viewpoint metaphor for at least 30 seconds or until s/he knew how to control all three dimensions using a given interface.

The experiment described in this paper produced results in regard to many different experimental variables. Task times were measured in each of the experiments. In the results, task times are presented as average times for each interface. In addition the users' subjective satisfaction about each interface and viewpoint metaphor was asked. Finally, the controlling styles of the users were analysed by watching the video recording of the experiments afterwards.

7 Results

7.1 Task times

Based on the experiments, six average task times were calculated. The virtual trackball, the keyboard interface and the virtual rectangle model were investigated using both the world-in-hand metaphor and the eyeball-in-hand metaphor. The average task times are presented in Figure 4.

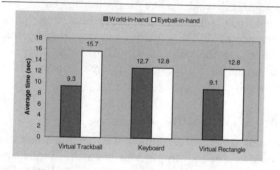

Figure 4: Average task times for the experimental interfaces and viewpoint metaphors.

The world-in-hand metaphor was statistically significantly faster than the eyeball-in-hand metaphor for the virtual trackball ($t = 5.86, d.f. = 11, p < 0.001$) and the virtual rectangle ($t = 2.59, d.f. = 11, p < 0.05$), but there were no significant differences in task times for the keyboard interface. The fastest interfaces were the virtual rectangle and the virtual trackball with average task times of about 9 seconds using the world-in-hand metaphor. The difference between these two interfaces was not statistically significant.

7.2 Subjective Satisfaction

The users' subjective satisfaction with the different interfaces and viewpoint metaphors was found out using post-hoc comments. After trying out each interface with both of the viewpoint metaphors, the users commented about the viewpoint metaphor. After the users had tried all the interfaces, they ranked the interfaces. They had an opportunity to retry the interfaces without any haste. Six subjects revisited the interfaces, while six subjects had earlier formed clear opinions. A summary of the users' subjective opinions is presented in Table 1.

	Virtual trackball	Key-board	Virtual rectangle	Don't know
Number of votes	4	1	7	0

Table 1: The users' subjective opinions about the best interface.

The subjective opinions about the best viewpoint metaphor were almost unanimous. As the mouse-based interfaces — the virtual trackball and the virtual rectangle — were evaluated, 11 subjects ranked the world-in-hand metaphor better than the eyeball-in-hand metaphor in all three interfaces, while one subject though that the eyeball-in-hand metaphor was just as good as the world-in-hand metaphor (in all interfaces).

The users' subjective opinions about the best interface were not unanimous. The most popular interface was the virtual rectangle interface with seven votes, followed by the virtual trackball with four votes and keys with one vote. The most common argument for the virtual rectangle was its robustness and simplicity.

The virtual trackball was supported, because it was fast and supported rotation on several axes at a time. Some subjects stated that this might be the best interface (of these three), but it needs more practice. The keyboard was supported, because the keyboard can be controlled by fingertips, there is no need for moving the whole hand like in the mouse interfaces.

As the object was controlled using the keyboard, the results about the viewpoint metaphors were not as obvious. On the x-axis and the y-axis, 11 subjects still supported world-in-hand, and one subject thought that the two metaphors are about as good. However, on the z-axis the votes divided into two groups. Some subjects wanted the top of the object to rotate right (clockwise), as they pressed the right key, whereas some wanted the bottom of the object to rotate right (counter-clockwise).

	Top of the object	Bottom of the object	Don't know
Persons	5	5	2

Table 2: The starting points for controlling the z-axis using the right key on the keyboard.

Table 2 presents the results of the opinions about rotating the z-axis using the keyboard. The column headers indicate where the subjects want to start rotating the object on the z-axis. Table 2 indicates that five users wanted to start rotating the object from the top, whereas five users wanted to start rotating from the bottom. Two of the users did not have a clear opinion, even after they had retried the interfaces.

7.3 Virtual Trackball Controlling Styles

In the *virtual trackball* interface, a closer analysis of the video material revealed that users manipulated the 3D object in two distinct ways:

- A group of 8 subjects typically broke down the complex tasks so that they moved the object one axis at a time. They moved the mouse up and down or left and right at the centre of the sphere to rotate the object on the x and y axes. The rotation on the z-axis was found outside the object with a roundish motion or by performing a series of short twitches over the object but outside the lines of the x and y axes.

- Four subjects typically managed to get to the desired orientation by holding down the mouse button and making rapid circular movements. Thus they were moving the object on more than just one axis at a time.

The latter controlling style was faster in general, but it sometimes caused some whimsical movements and orientations, which were not even close to the desired orientation. However, this controlling style captures the idea of a virtual trackball better.

7.4 Features

One of the guiding design principles of the *virtual rectangle* interface was the fact that it enabled feature-based manipulation of the object. For example, the user might think that s/he will grasp the nose of the head and then rotate the head to the desired direction. It was assumed that users would use this interface in this manner.

However, in this experiment it turned out that only 47 % of the controlling movements expressed an effort to grasp a feature to move the head (based on the test arranger's very careful interpretation of the video material). If the cursor did not land on a feature, as the dragging begun, or if the movement was so fast that it was not likely to be deliberate, the action was judged not to be feature-based. However, individual differences were large and two different controlling styles could be found:

- Feature-based controlling involved grasping the features of the object. Five subjects belonged to this group. They typically grasped the features in 50–70% of all the mouse clicks.

- The advocates of area-based controlling did not intend to grasp the features but to identify the areas of the interface where the different rotations could be accomplished. They controlled the x-axis and the y-axis by clicking inside the rectangle, but they did not try to grasp the features, they just clicked somewhere inside the area. They typically controlled the z-axis by clicking completely outside the object. Six subjects belonged to this group. Typically 70–90% of their clicks did not land on a feature.

In addition to these two groups, there was one subject that controlled the x and y axes using the feature-based controlling, but performed the rotations on the z-axis by clicking completely outside the object.

The users' comments support this dichotomy. The users that supported the feature-based style commented typically like "I grasped the ear". The users that supported the area-based style often commented that they carried out the drags by first identifying the different virtual rectangle interface areas and then clicking on an area to carry out a rotation.

8   Discussion

In this paper, an experiment was described that has some connections to previous research. The results largely confirm the results by (Chen et al., 1988). The virtual rectangle interface of this paper seems to be an improvement on Chen's third interface, which had a circle outside the object for z-axis rotations. This is because in Chen's experiments the virtual trackball was the fastest interface, whereas in the experiments reported in this paper the virtual trackball and the virtual rectangle did not have significant difference in task times. This experiment also supports Badler et al.'s (1986) notion that using the eyeball-in-hand metaphor users have to consciously calculate the activity. This phenomenon was frequently reported by the users, often even without asking.

This experiment also confirms the results by Ware & Osborne (1990), which indicate that the world-in-hand metaphor is the best in the single object case. This argument was almost unanimously supported by the users of this experiment and the task times were shorter for world-in-hand.

The virtual rectangle interface proved to be as fast as the virtual trackball interface. A previous study by

Hinckley et al. (1997) found no significant differences in task times between the state-of-the-art 2D interface, the Arcball, and the virtual trackball. However, Arcball was rated better than virtual trackball in subjective satisfaction. In this study, the virtual rectangle was similarly preferred over the virtual trackball and there was no significant difference in task times. This suggests that the differences in the usability of the interfaces are subtle and the virtual rectangle is a noteworthy alternative to existing techniques.

This study indicates that there are some cognitive factors, which influence the development of 3D interaction methods. The *cursor-based* manipulation of 3D objects works well and using a cursor the keyboard *z*-axis effect described earlier can be avoided. In designing cursor-based interfaces, this study encourages to support the human feature-based cognition, because many users want to grab the features of the object.

In interface and input device design the keyboard *z*-axis effect has to be noticed. If the input device is linked directly to the object, this effect may occur. The keyboard *z*-axis effect can be avoided for example by introducing a twistable knob for *z*-axis. However, it is not clear that introducing better 3D input devices will completely solve the 3D rotation problem. The possible 3D software components like the virtual rectangle have to be also studied, especially in interfaces which involve multiple 3D tasks such as rotating and sizing the objects and moving in virtual worlds.

In this study, the majority of the users did not manipulate the object by grasping on its features. Nevertheless, the virtual rectangle interface — which was based on feature-based theories of human cognition — did well on both objective and subjective measures. In the future, as virtual reality becomes more popular, the feature-based manipulation of objects seems justified at least in simulations that try to be realistic, because people manipulate objects considerably based on features in real life.

Acknowledgements

This research was supported by Tampere Graduate School in Information Science and Engineering. I would like to thank Kari-Jouko Räihä for guidance, Janne Kulju, Päivi Majaranta and Roope Raisamo for technical help and all the test subjects for participation.

References

Anderson, J. R. (1995), *Cognitive Psychology and its Implications*, Freeman.

Badler, N. I., Manoochehri, K. H. & Baraff, D. (1986), Multi-Dimensional Input Techniques and Articulated Figure Positioning by Multiple Constraints, *in* F. Crow & S. M. Bizar (eds.), *Proceedings of the 1986 Workshop in Interactive 3D Graphics*, pp.151–69.

Biederman, I. (1987), "Recognition-by-Components: A Theory of Human Image Understanding", *Psychological Review* **94**(2), 115–47.

Brooks, F. P. (1988), Grasping Reality Through Illusion: Interactive Graphics Serving Science, *in* E. Soloway, D. Frye & S. B. Sheppard (eds.), *Proceedings of CHI'88: Human Factors in Computing Systems*, ACM Press, pp.1–11.

Chen, M., Mountford, J. & Sellen, A. (1988), A Study in Interactive 3D Rotation Using 2D Control Devices, *in* J. Dill (ed.), *Proceedings of SIGGRAPH'88*, *Computer Graphics* **22**(4), ACM Press, pp.121–9.

Hinckley, K., Pausch, R., Goble, J. C. & Kassell, N. F. (1994), A Survey of Design Issues in Spatial Input, *in Proceedings of the ACM Symposium on User Interface Software and Technology, UIST'94*, ACM Press, pp.213–22.

Hinckley, K., Tullio, J., Pausch, R., Proffitt, D. & Kassell, N. (1997), Usability Analysis of 3D Rotation Techniques, *in* D. Fay (ed.), *Proceedings of the ACM Symposium on User Interface Software and Technology, UIST'97*, ACM Press, pp.1–10.

Shoemake, K. (1992), "ARCBALL: A User Interface for Specifying Three-dimensional Orientation Using a Mouse", *Graphics Interface* pp.151–6.

Ware, C. & Osborne, S. (1990), "Exploration and Virtual Camera Control in Virtual Three Dimensional Environments", *Computer Graphics* **24**(2), 121–9.

Zhai, S. & Milgram, P. (1998), Quantifying Coordination in Multiple DOF Movement and Its Application to Evaluating 6 DOF Input Devices, *in* C.-M. Karat, A. Lund, J. Coutaz & J. Karat (eds.), *Proceedings of CHI'98: Human Factors in Computing Systems*, ACM Press, pp.320–7.

Human–Computer Interaction — INTERACT '99
M. Angela Sasse and Chris Johnson (Editors)
Published by IOS Press, © IFIP TC.13, 1999

Wayfinding/Navigation within a QTVR Virtual Environment: Preliminary Results

Brian E. Norris, Da'oud Z. Rashid & B.L. William Wong

Department of Information Science, University of Otago, PO Box 56, Dunedin, New Zealand.

BNorris@infoscience.otago.ac.nz

Abstract: This paper reports on an investigation into wayfinding principles, and their effectiveness within a virtual environment. To investigate these principles, a virtual environment of an actual museum was created using QuickTime Virtual Reality. Wayfinding principles used in the real world were identified and used to design the interaction of the virtual environment. The initial findings of this study suggests that real-world navigation principles, such as the use of map and landmark principles, can significantly help navigation within this virtual environment. However, navigation difficulties were discovered through an Activity Theory-based Cognitive Task Analysis.

Keywords: wayfinding, navigation, QTVR, virtual environments, activity theory.

1 Introduction

Research into wayfinding in virtual worlds has been concerned with how people interact with the environment, rather than why. Experiments have concentrated on gathering empirical data on wayfinding paths, time to completion, and the number of errors for each Participant (Darken & Sibert, 1995; Navigation et al., 1995; Elvins et al., 1998; Plante et al., 1998). Though these studies have been important in identifying wayfinding principles, they provide little information about how to improve the user interface to virtual worlds. They also do not give an understanding of why people adopt certain wayfinding principles or strategies over others, or what causes people to change their strategy. This study attempts to address the following two questions:

1. Can wayfinding principles used in the real world translate to QTVR (QuickTime Virtual Reality) virtual environments?

2. What difficulties do users have in navigating and searching for objects in QTVR virtual environments, and what strategies do they use to overcome these difficulties?

The purpose of this study is to firstly identify whether 'traditional' wayfinding principles used in the

'real world' could be as effective within a virtual environment such as a QuickTime Virtual Reality (QTVR) environment. Secondly, this study tries to identify the difficulties that users might have with the QTVR environment, and whether these difficulties are influenced by the wayfinding principles that are being tested. A combination of Activity Theory and Cognitive Task Analysis was used to answer these questions. Cognitive Task Analysis was used to elicit the type of information required for study, and Activity Theory was then used to place it in a meaningful context. Wayfinding performance was also measured to provide further insights to the questions. In building the virtual environment for the study, concepts from spatial knowledge theory and environmental design methodology were employed to guide the design of the virtual environment.

The interaction design for the virtual environment is based on spatial knowledge theory (Thorndyke & Goldin (1983) cited by Darken (1995)) and environmental design methodology (Lynch, 1960). Finding new principles that are unique to Virtual Environments is outside the scope of this study. Rather, the aim of the study is to determine whether spatial knowledge theory and environmental design principles are useful for designing QTVR virtual environments.

2   Spatial Knowledge

Lynch (1960) describes spatial knowledge as:

> "...the generalised mental picture of the exterior physical world that is held by the individual."

This 'environmental image' is the 'strategic link' in the process of wayfinding. As this mental picture improves or becomes more detailed, wayfinding performance generally improves. This environmental image consists of three specific types of information (Darken, 1995):

Landmark knowledge: Information about the visual details of specific locations in the environment. This represents notable perceptual features of an environment, such as a unique building, that is stored in a person's memory.

Procedural knowledge: Information about a sequence of actions required to follow a particular route. Procedural knowledge is built by connecting isolated bits of landmark knowledge into larger, more complex structures.

Survey knowledge: Configurable or topological information. Object locations and inter-object distances are encoded in terms of a global, fixed, map-like frame of reference.

Wayfinding in general requires the navigator to visualise the space as a whole. This topological knowledge or spatial knowledge as described above is significantly different from procedural knowledge which is defined as the sequence of actions required to follow a particular route. The route may make use of landmark knowledge which is static information about the visual details of a specific location.

3   Environmental Design

Based on what is known about spatial knowledge theory and its application in wayfinding tasks, environmental designers have developed a design methodology focused on environmental organization and map use. City planners and engineers have long since used spatial knowledge in designing cities that are easy to navigate and to find your way around. Lynch (1960) describes five elements of the contents of city images, which also seem to reappear in many types of environmental images. These elements are:

Paths: Channels of movement. They include streets, walkways, canals, transit lines, and railroads. Paths are predominantly in the eye of the beholder.

Edges: Linear elements not used or considered as paths. They are boundaries or linear breaks between two regions. They include shores, railroad cuts, edges of developed walls, etc.

Districts: Medium to large sections of the city. The observer mentally enters 'inside of' the district. They are recognized as having some common identifying characteristics.

Nodes: Strategic spots into which an observer can enter the city. They are typically linked to travel and are usually transportation breaks, crossings or convergence of paths.

Landmarks: Another type of point reference but the observer does not enter them. They are usually a rather simply defined physical object, building, sign, store, or mountain. They are frequently used clues of identity and are increasingly relied upon as a journey becomes more familiar. A landmark should stand out from its surroundings and have direction information as well.

Landmarks, nodes, and districts divide the city into *places*, which are connected by paths and bounded by edges.

4   Activity Theory

The previous sections highlight the wayfinding principles that are used in the real world. However, these principles do not indicate what difficulties people have in navigating and searching within virtual environments, nor the strategies that they use to overcome these difficulties.

Activity Theory (AT) is a framework designed to facilitate understanding of purposeful human activity. The framework is grounded in Russian socio-psychology of the 1920s. Although it was traditionally applied in the area of child psychology and development, AT has recently gained popularity in the realm of Human–Computer Interaction Nardi (1996).

Activity Theory states that breakdowns occur when the outcome of a Participant's action does not match his or her expected outcome. Once this happens, the Participant 'unrolls' their mental representation of the action. The action is no longer an automatic succession of steps, requiring little or no conscious thought. Instead, the Participant now consciously thinks about each step to determine what caused the unexpected results. During this stage, the Participant will also look for alternative strategies for the successful completion of the action. Once a successful strategy is found, and practiced enough, it 'rolls up' back into subconscious thought.

5   Wayfinding Tasks

Wayfinding can be thought of as three mutually exclusive, yet usually successive, tasks. They are:

Naïve search: Any searching task in which the Participant has no prior knowledge of the whereabouts of the target in question. A Naïve search implies that an exhaustive search must be performed.

Primed search: Any searching task in which the Participant knows the location of the target. The search is non-exhaustive.

Exploration: Any wayfinding task in which there is no target. (Darken & Sibert, 1996)

The tasks can be successive in the sense that a Participant will switch between tasks as conditions change. For example, if a Participant knows roughly where the target is located, they may initially use a primed search strategy to get to the approximate location. Next, they use a naïve search strategy to find the target. Darken & Sibert (1996) state that although naïve searches are rare in the real world, they are common in first time explorers of the virtual environment.

6   The Virtual Environment

Virtual Reality describes a range of experiences that enable a person to interact with and explore a spatial environment through the use of a computer. These virtual environments are usually renderings of simple or complex computer models and offer us the opportunity to:

> "be in worlds that only exist in our imaginations." (Biocca & Levy, 1995, p.vii)

Until recently, most VR applications required specialised hardware or accessories, such as high-end graphics workstations, stereo displays, or 3D goggles or gloves. Research using these 3D Head Mounted Displays (HMD) over the last decade has found that the spatial knowledge and environmental design principles that influence wayfinding in the real world can be effectively translated into these rendered HMD environments (Navigation et al., 1995; Darken & Sibert, 1996).

This specialised hardware has now given way to the desktop VR systems due to their cost and availability. The two main VR technologies that run off a desktop or window system are Virtual Reality Modelling Language (VRML) and QuickTime Virtual Reality (QTVR). These technologies allow the VR experience to be created and viewed using software.

VRML came about from the explosion of interest in the internet or World Wide Web (WWW). It is "a language for describing multi-participant interactive simulations — virtual worlds networked via the global Internet and hyper-linked with the World Wide Web." (Bell et al., 1995). VRML environments are non photo-realistic graphical interpretations of worlds created and limited only by the authors mind.

Apple's QuickTime VR allows Macintosh and Windows users to experience kinds of spatial interactions using only a personal computer. Furthermore, through an innovative use of 360 degree panoramic photography, QuickTime VR enables these interactions to use real-world representations, as well as computer simulations. The technology works by electronically stitching a series of photos (or rendered images) together. The photos are taken by pivoting the camera in regular steps (along the horizon) from a fixed point, in order to create a 360-degree panoramic view. The viewer sees only a part of the image at a time, but can use the mouse cursor to 'turn' and look up and down. The overall effect is much like standing at a fixed point in a room, turning your head from side to side, looking up and down, and turning your body around to explore your environment.

These QTVR nodes can be linked together by hotspots to create a scene or multi-node environment. QTVR includes:

> "continuous camera panning and zooming, jumping to selected points and object rotation using frame indexing." (Chen, 1995)

Currently QTVR uses cylindrical environment maps or panoramic images to accomplish camera rotation. QTVR includes an interactive environment, which uses a software based real-time image-processing engine for navigating in space and an authoring environment for the creation of the QTVR movies.

6.1   Designing the QTVR Virtual Environment

Most research into navigational aids for virtual environments have all dealt with VRML based environments (Darken & Sibert, 1995). These environments have the users point of perspective continuously changing. QTVR on the other hand has the point of perspective constant at all times.

The purpose of this research is to determine whether the wayfinding principles identified previously are affected by this apparent lack of continuous change and photo-realistic representation.

Of particular relevance to the study is Lynch's (1960) description of nodes. QTVR allows movement between panoramic images by embedding 'hotspots' in the image. As a user moves the mouse cursor over a hotspot, the mouse cursor changes; indicating the possibility of movement to another 'node'. If the user presses the mouse button, they will find themselves at a new node. Lynch's (1960) identification and definition of nodes further justifies QTVR's close approximation to real-world spatial environments.

As QTVR is a node based representation of a larger environment, 'jumps', or transitions, between nodes could sometimes become disorienting. A solution was devised using concept of display overlap (Woods, 1984; Wickens, 1993). Display overlap (and subsequently, visual momentum) can be achieved by integrating data across successive glances This was achieved this by adjusting the size and location of each hotspot to match (albeit, as a smaller version) exactly what the user would see upon entering the next node. In this way, before pressing the mouse button over a hotspot, the user's attention would be in the region of the screen that matched what they would see at the next node. In addition, adjusting the starting angles, both horizontally and vertically, from node to node, helped to better support this overlap.

7   Methodology

In order to explore the significance of the spatial knowledge and environmental design principles in wayfinding in virtual worlds, four variations of a virtual environment, a virtual museum, were constructed. A 2 × 2 (map vs. landmark) factorial experimental design was adopted to evaluate the effect of different wayfinding principles on wayfinding performance.

The four treatments were:

Control: No wayfinding assistance.

Map: The use of Map principles.

Landmark: The use of Landmark elements.

Map and Landmark: The use of both Map principles and Landmark elements.

In the Landmark treatment, we embedded textual labels or 'signs' within the environment, to indicate various areas. The labels identified the contents of the area and, hence, enhanced landmark knowledge. For example, the link to the Egyptian section had the words 'Ancient Egypt' written above it. When creating the labels, MacMinner (1996) list several important things to consider. These are:

1. Use a visual guidance system to ensure successful use of the space by the user.

2. Use architectural elements and interior treatments whenever possible.

3. Signs should be placed at decision making areas.

4. Choose appropriate signs for the main group of users.

5. Graphics should be legible, direct to the point, and visible from a reasonable distance.

6. Graphics should be designed and placed consistently throughout the space.

7. Avoid creating visual clutter.

8. Choose visual guidance and orientation devices which are compatible with and are part of your design concept.

Similarly, we supported map principles by providing a map (on the left side of the screen) showing the general layout of the virtual room. The map also identified where the participant was in the room, by showing a red circle (corresponding to the position of the current node) on the map. Darken's (1995) guidelines, with respect to maps, include the following:

1. Show all organizational elements (paths, landmarks, districts, etc.).

2. Always show the observers position. The final treatment, Map and Landmark, made use of both the Map principles and the Landmark principles.

7.1   Apparatus

Photographs were taken of a local museum and used to make 27 QTVR panoramic nodes. These nodes were linked to each other by hotspots. The nodes were then incorporated into one QuickTime VR movie with the use of QuickTime Virtual Reality Authoring Suite (QTVRAS) (Apple Computer Inc, 1997). This VR movie became the control treatment. The map and landmark principles, as discussed earlier, were added to this movie to make the other three treatments. An example of the map condition is shown in Figure 1.

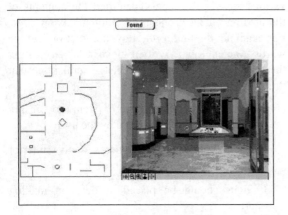

Figure 1: Map condition interface.

The four treatments were implemented on Macintosh PowerPC desktop computers of identical configuration. The testing environment was created in Hypercard 2.4.1 (Apple Computer Inc, 1998), an interactive multimedia authoring tool. All movement and interaction with the virtual world was achieved through the use of the mouse.

7.2 Procedure

67 university students attending a course in Human Factors in Information Science participated in this study. The study was conducted in two phases. The first phase was an experiment to assess the effectiveness of the various wayfinding principles. The second phase was a cognitive task analysis to identify the difficulties participants encountered while navigating the virtual environment.

In the experiment phase, the participants were asked to do a naïve search for four objects within the virtual environment. Participants were given a picture of each target object and were instructed to find it and then to return to the start point before being given a picture of the next object to find.

The Hypercard system recorded various measures as the participants tried to find the target objects. These measures were:

- Errors made in identifying the target object.

- Errors made in identifying the start point.

- Incomplete search for the object.

- Incomplete search for the start point.

- Time taken to find the object.

- Time taken to find the start point.

After the Participant had found all four objects they were asked to fill out a user satisfaction questionnaire and also to sketch a map of the environment, showing the location of the targets and their rough proximity to each other. Participants were given up to 15 minutes to find the object and to return to the start point. If a Participant got past this time limit, they would receive help to find their way. An incomplete result would then be recorded. They would then proceed with the rest of the experiment. The experiment could be terminated at any time at the Participants' request.

In the second phase, a Cognitive Task Analysis (CTA) was conducted. The Critical Decision Method (Klein, 1993), a retrospective verbal protocol technique that used critical decision points as points for further probing, was the technique used. During the CTA, participants were first asked to identify situations in which they had experienced difficulty using the interface to the virtual environment. The researchers then probed each Participant about the difficulties they had identified. In addition, several computers displaying the virtual environment were made available to those participants who wanted to re-familiarise themselves with the system.

Next, the Participants were asked to identify what they were doing (or trying to do) just before experiencing the difficulty, and what they did just after. The researchers then probed the Participants further to clarify their ideas and ensuring that Participants' responses were specific enough to be of use in subsequent analysis. For example, "I was trying to find the object" (the broad purpose of the task) is less useful than the response "I was trying to find the hotspot for the next node".

After this was completed, participants engaged in a fifteen-minute, general discussion about their experiences in the environment. The discussion was recorded.

The data gathered during the CTA was then analysed within the framework of Activity Theory (Kuutti, 1996). The 'difficulties' identified during the CTA correspond to AT's 'Breakdowns' (Winograd & Flores (1986) cited by Bødker (1996)). Similarly, taken together the 'before' and 'after' form AT's concept of a 'focus shift'.

8 Results

For this report, only the significant numerical results from the system and the significant results acquired from the Activity Theory analysis will be discussed.

Eight sets of results of the original 67 were excluded from the analysis due to computer crashes and Participants familiarity with the actual museum. Hence, only 59 sets of results were used in the subsequent analysis. The distribution of Participants across conditions is as follows:

Control: 24 Participants.

Map: 8 Participants.

Landmark: 11 Participants.

Map and Landmark: 16 Participants.

The empirical results from the first phase were analysed with SPSS 6.1.1 (SPSS 1995), a statistical analysis package. A series of T-Tests were performed on the data collected from the experiment. Based on a significance of $p < 0.05$, Table 1 shows any significant difference between the means of the control and other conditions.

Variables	Control vs. Map	Control vs. Landmark	Control vs. Map/ Landmark
Overall Time	No	Yes	No
Time for finding the object	No	Yes	No
Time to get back to the starting point	Yes	No	No
Overall Errors	No	No	No
Errors in finding the object	No	No	No
Errors in getting back to the start point	No	No	No
Total Incompletes	No	Yes	No
Incompletes in finding the object	No	Yes	No
Incompletes in getting back to the start point	No	No	No

Table 1: T-Test results (p¡0.05).

The data collected from the second phase was analysed using Activity Theory, as stated earlier. Breakdowns and Focus Shifts were extracted from the before and after data that was gathered for the participants' experiences. The subjects' notes were gathered and collated on the basis of similar experiences. These experiences were identified as breakdowns according to Activity Theory. Once these main breakdowns were identified, the subject's actions before and after this breakdown identified the subsequent focus shift from what actions the subject expected to work, to what actions they used to overcome the breakdown. These breakdowns and the percentage of Participants who had the breakdown are shown in Figure 2.

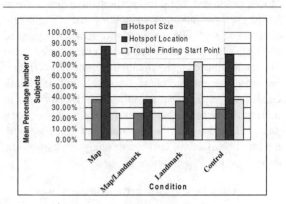

Figure 2: Significant CTA breakdowns.

9   Discussion

The first major finding that the analysis identified was the effectiveness of the map principles. This was shown in Table 1. There was a significant difference ($p = 0.013$) between the mean time to get back to the start point after finding the target object of the control and map conditions.

Common sense tells us that this would be the case as the participants could use the map as an additional navigational aid. The statistical analysis from SPSS give indications that map principles can effectively help wayfinding back to a point within a QTVR virtual environment, but it does not give any indication of the difficulties that the subjects faced with the use of, or lack of, map principles.

Activity Theory, on the other hand, shows us that participants had problems with finding their way back to the start point after finding one of the objects. As Figure 2 shows, only 25% of participants using maps had this breakdown, whereas 73% of participants from the landmark condition and 38% from the control condition had this breakdown. One participant wrote:

> "I was able to use the map to assess where I was when I needed to return to the starting location."

Another participant stated that they:

> "... can't recognize it by sight 100%, have to refer to the map to make sure you are actually at the right place."

This notion of not being able to identify their position, due to the fact that the museum cases all looked the same, was expressed by several participants.

Landmark principles were shown to enhance wayfinding performance. The data from phase one

(Table 1) showed that those participants whose virtual world used the landmark principles had a significant difference ($p = 0.005$) between means when compared to the control condition for the average time. Also the results showed a significant difference ($p = 0.003$) between the means of the control and landmark conditions for the average number of Incompletes in finding the target object. Preliminary analysis of the data collected from phase two has not come up with a related breakdown, but further analysis is still to be done. One participant wrote in phase two:

> "When looking for certain items I was able to use the signs that were situated up by the ceiling."

These results indicate that landmark principles are effective wayfinding principles when looking for a target object.

One issue that was not picked up by phase one experimentation was the difficulty subjects had when dealing with the hotspots that were used to navigate from node to node within the virtual environment. It appears that most participants, no matter which condition they were using, had a behaviour breakdown with the hotspots. Figure 2 shows that these breakdowns could be separated into two different issues, the first being the location of the hotspot and the second being the size and shape of the hotspot. Participants were recorded as saying:

> "...I was in an area and wanted to move into a section I could see but there was no hotspot to go there."

and

> "The hotspots were all different sizes and shapes, which made it difficult to find them."

The subsequent focus shift had the participants either just moving the mouse till they found the hotspot, or the participants would use the hotspot finder. This breakdown was not anticipated, it was due to design oversights of the researcher. The nodes were not placed in uniform distances from each other, which caused the hotspots to vary in size and shape. The issue of hotspots can easily be rectified by either having all hotspots visible (Plante et al., 1998), or by uniformly laying out the nodes so all links (hotspots) are in areas where participants logically would move. This would mean the jumps would be all the same distance, therefore the size and shape of the hotspots would be uniform.

Other noted difficulties identified through Activity Theory were the window or movie size, and the fact that the map did not show the subjects orientation. Participants were recorded expressing these difficulties:

> "...window size of the experiments were too small. I walked passed objects due to size of window."

and

> "...I still don't know which directions will be turned on the map when I turned left/right. It is confusing..."

Re-orienting the map as the user pans left or right, and increasing the window or movie size with an increase in processor speed and memory, can eliminate these breakdowns with the environment.

10   Conclusion

Preliminary findings have indicated that the use of map principles enhance wayfinding when the participant has to get back to a place they have been, whereas landmark principles enhance finding new areas or places. These findings identify which wayfinding principles should be used and when.

The expected outcomes of a particular action are based on a participant's experience. In those cases where participants are unfamiliar with virtual worlds (as was the case with our study), yet familiar with computers, their experiences in wayfinding will be based solely on their experiences with the real world. This means that when a breakdown occurs, it occurs because interaction during a wayfinding task in the virtual world fails to conform to the participant's mental representation (based on years of experience) of interaction during a wayfinding task in the real world. This study has identified several design issues that have been found to cause difficulties in wayfinding within a QTVR virtual environment. These are hotspot identification, size of window or movie, and map orientation. These difficulties can all be rectified with a greater attention to applying real world navigation principles to the design.

The preliminary results have showed that wayfinding principles used in the real world can be effectively applied into the virtual environment. Other issues of the virtual environment design have also been identified as influencing this translation. Further analysis on the data from phases one and two is ongoing and will be reported in future papers.

References

Apple Computer Inc (1997), "QuickTime VR Authoring Suite".

Apple Computer Inc (1998), "HyperCard 2.4.1".

Bell, G., Parisi, A. & Pesce, M. (1995), "The Virtual Reality Modeling Language; Version 1.0". http://www.vrml.org/VRML1.0/.

Biocca, F. & Levy, M. (1995), *Communication in the Age of Virtual Reality*, Lawrence Erlbaum Associates.

Bødker, S. (1996), Applying Activity Theory to Video Analysis: How to Make Sense of Video Data in Human–Computer Interaction, *in* B. A. Nardi (ed.), *Context and Consciousness: Activity Theory and Human–Computer Interaction*, MIT Press, pp.147–74.

Chen, S. (1995), QuickTime VR — An Image Approach to Virtual Environment Navigation, *in* R. Cook (ed.), *Proceedings of SIGGRAPH'95 22nd Annual Conference on Computer Graphics and Interactive Techniques*, ACM Press, pp.29–38.

Darken, R. P. (1995), Wayfinding in Large-Scale Virtual World, *in* I. Katz, R. Mack & L. Marks (eds.), *Companion Proceedings of CHI'95: Human Factors in Computing Systems (CHI'95 Conference Companion)*, ACM Press, pp.45–6.

Darken, R. P. & Sibert, J. L. (1995), "Navigating Large Virtual Worlds.", *International Journal of Human–Computer Interaction* **8**(1), 49–72.

Darken, R. P. & Sibert, J. L. (1996), Wayfinding Strategies and Behaviours in Large Virtual Worlds, *in* G. van der Veer & B. Nardi (eds.), *Proceedings of CHI'96: Human Factors in Computing Systems*, ACM Press, pp.142–50.

Elvins, T., Nadeau, D., Schul, R. & Kirsh, D. (1998), Worldlets: 3D Thumbnail for 3D Browsing, *in* C.-M. Karat, A. Lund, J. Coutaz & J. Karat (eds.), *Proceedings of CHI'98: Human Factors in Computing Systems*, ACM Press, pp.163–70.

Klein, G. (1993), *Naturalistic Decision Making: Implications for Design*, Klein Associates Inc.

Kuutti, K. (1996), Activity Theory as a Potential Framework for Human-Computer Interaction Research, *in* B. A. Nardi (ed.), *Context and Consciousness: Activity Theory and Human–Computer Interaction*, MIT Press, pp.17–44.

Lynch, K. (1960), *The Image of a City*, MIT Press.

MacMinner, S. (1996), "Wayfinding: Human Perspectives and Orientation in the Built Environment.". http://www.uni.edu/casestudy/456/sharon.htm.

Nardi, B. A. (1996), Activity Theory and Human–Computer Interaction, *in* B. A. Nardi (ed.), *Context and Consciousness: Activity Theory and Human–Computer Interaction*, MIT Press, pp.7–16.

Navigation, in Virtual Reality: Finding the Proper Tools, W. & to Enhance Navigation Awareness, C. (1995). http://www.hitl.washington.edu/publications/satalich.

Plante, A., Tanaka, S. & Iwadate, Y. (1998), Designing Effective Navigation for Photo-realistic VR Environments, *in* P. Calder & B. Thomas (eds.), *Proceedings of OzCHI'98 The Eighth Australian Conference on Computer–Human Interaction*, IEEE Computer Society Press, pp.4–5.

Thorndyke, P. W. & Goldin, S. E. (1983), *Spatial Learning and Reasoning Skill. Spatial Orientation: Theory, Research, and Application*, Plenum Press.

Wickens, C. D. (1993), "Cognitive Factors in Display Design", *Journal of the Washington Academy of Sciences* **83**(4), 179–201.

Winograd, T. & Flores, F. (1986), *Understanding Computers and Cognition: A New Foundation for Design*, Addison–Wesley.

Woods, D. D. (1984), "Visual Momentum: A Concept to Improve the Cognitive Coupling of Person and Computer", *International Journal of Man–Machine Studies* **21**(3), 229–44.

Human–Computer Interaction — INTERACT '99
M. Angela Sasse and Chris Johnson (Editors)
Published by IOS Press, © IFIP TC.13, 1999

Sequential Display: An Effective Alternative to Conventional Animation

Mireille Bétrancourt

INRIA Grenoble, 655 Avenue de l'Europe, F-38330 Montbonnot, France.

Mireille.Betrancourt@inria.fr

Abstract: Advanced graphical visualizations, such as virtual reality and animation, are at the forefront of technological development in Human–Computer interfaces. Despite a general belief among multimedia designers, there is little evidence for the claim that animation improves users' cognitive processing. One reason why animation has not met designers' expectations is that animation is usually not used in situations that take advantage of the specific features of animation, i.e. its dynamicity. In this paper, we report the main results of six experiments involving simple animations designed to guide users in their processing of complex graphics. The device, called sequential display, consisted in successively displaying portions of the diagram where the portions were either meaningfully clustered or random. Results showed that the simple animation device of sequential display can guide users in their cognitive processing of the graphic.

Keywords: dynamic interface, cognitive processes, experimental data.

1 Introduction

Under the assumption that "a diagram is worth thousand words", educational and technical materials make extensive use of graphics and diagrams. This has increased with the growing development of computerized and multimedia documents, that provide not only static but also animated graphics (Baek & Layne, 1991). However, the advances in the technology of producing attractive graphics often seem to drive and outstrip the development of tools and devices rather than cognitive principles derived from research on their utility. Graphics are not always effective, or put differently, not all graphics are effective in all situations. The early research comparing learning with graphics to learning with text alone is instructive. It gave mixed results, often in spite of enthusiasm for the pictorial devices (Mandl & Levin, 1989). Moreover, much of the early research used global comparisons between media and did not address the subtler questions of what accounts for facilitation when it occurred. As research progressed, the types of situations, graphics, tasks, and learners for which graphics are effective have become clearer (Peek, 1993).

One of the newer, attractive graphic devices is animation. To date, current uses of animation in interfaces are still limited to few functions, such as improving the information content of icons (typically, the percent-done process indicator) or more generally to provide information about what is going on (Baecker & Small, 1990). Animation as a learning tool presents special challenges for education and interface design because of evidence that people often have difficulties in accurately perceiving and conceiving real-life animations (Kaiser et al., 1992). One critical issue is to define whether the material to be learned would benefit from animation. Insofar as the essential feature of animations is to change over time, (Rieber & Kini, 1991) suggested that using animation is relevant when the learning material entails visualization of motion, trajectory or change over time.

It is often believed that a diagram is processed immediately, as a whole. However, most diagrams require cognitively demanding processing of the details and relationships between elements in order to reveal the entire meaning. This processing is sequential, as revealed by research on eye movements (Hegarty & Just, 1993). Diagrams, though designed sequentially, are usually not available to users until they are complete. As a consequence, in contrast to text, the order in which diagrams are designed is not provided to readers. Readers have to discover the order in which the information is best processed. In the case of complex illustrations, users may not know the best order to process graphics, and may be disoriented using a complex graphic display. This may partly account for the observation that users do not always take advantage of illustration in comprehending text. In many instructional documents, readers are provided with auxiliary text and / or legends which guide them in the processing of the diagram (Hegarty & Just, 1993; Mayer, 1989).

As animations, like language, change over time, simple animations may be used to guide users to an effective order of processing graphic information. Here we investigate the efficiency of a simple animated device, called sequential display, in facilitating comprehension of graphics. In a sequential display, subgroups of items are displayed one after another. The subgroups are either meaningful ordered or not. A similar display was used by Wright et al. (1990). Participants read a text illustrated with a complex diagram that appeared either gradually or all at once depending on the condition. When the diagram appeared gradually, building up with the text, participants took less time to study the document, for equivalent performance to comprehension post-test. However, this advantage disappeared if the observation of the diagram was up to the readers.

2 Synopsis of Experimental Work on the Effect of Sequential Display

2.1 Hypotheses

In this paper, we report the main results of six experiments that were designed to assess the effect of sequential display on users' cognitive processes. More details can be found on experiment 2 in Bétrancourt et al. (1996).

First we assume that temporal clustering, like spatial clustering, facilitates the memorization of a spatial configuration for two reasons. First, the sequential clustering conveyed a meaningful organization that may improve memory for the configuration, as it was observed for the spatial grouping of words according to semantic categories (Bower & Clark-Meyers, 1980). Moreover, the sequential display was expected to guide users in their processing of the diagram as an accompanying text does (Hegarty & Just, 1993). Practically speaking, the temporal clustering refers to a display where the elements of the configuration appeared gradually by clusters, while the elements within a given cluster appeared simultaneously on the screen.

The second hypothesis is inspired from the cognitive postulate according to which mental representations include information about the context in which they had been encoded. That information is used afterwards to retrieve and process the memory content. This hypothesis thus entails that the organization of the representation in memory is affected by the sequence of presentation of the spatial configuration. As a direct consequence, we expect that the order in which information appears will act as a 'recall guide' (Taylor & Tversky, 1992), like the order in which information is mentioned in a text. In other words, participants should recall the items in the order in which they appeared in the sequential display. A further consequence is that users should be better at performing tasks that involve reasoning on the organization provided in the sequential display.

As this paper aims to propose a synopsis of the research we carried out on sequential display, all six experiments will be presented conjointly in the following.

2.2 Method

Participants: Participants were students, either French graduate (respectively 25 in experiment 1, and 40 in experiments 2 and 3) or American undergraduate students (respectively 53, 48 and 59 in experiments 4, 5 and 6).

Material: Various kinds of material were used: network of circles (experiment 1), library map (experiments 2, 4 and 5, see Figure 1), map of a town (experiment 2), biological control system (experiment 3) and map of a fictitious island (experiment 6).

Materials were displayed on computer screen. In sequential conditions, configurations were automatically displayed to insure equal amount of study time across conditions. Clusters previously displayed remained on the screen when a new cluster was added. Graphic devices (such as bold lines or shading) helped users distinguishing between old and new clusters.

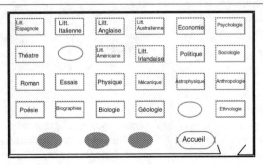

Figure 1: Library map used in Experiment 2.

Conditions: According to the experiment, the sequential display conditions involved various criteria of clustering and ordering. In all six experiments, sequential conditions were compared to static display (control group) where the material was displayed still on the screen.

In experiments 1 (network) and 2 (town and library maps), sequential conditions were designed from the description strategies that were found in the literature as spontaneously used by people to describe spatial configurations. Some conditions involved temporal clustering, in which the elements of the configuration appeared gradually by clusters of 4 to 6 items. The other sequential conditions involved the display of elements one by one, either following the occidental reading order (from left to right and top to bottom) or the connectivity between elements (route condition, in experiment 1 only).

In experiments 4 (library 24) and 5 (library 36), two sequential conditions were used, where the elements of the configuration were temporally clustered either meaningfully or randomly. As the material was the map of a library, elements (domain names) were clustered by academic categories (like Humanities, Medical Sciences, etc.) in the meaningful condition.

Finally, experiments 3 (system) and 6 (geographic map) involved sequential displays using meaningful clustering, but according to different criteria. In experiment 3 (Figure 2), elements in the biological control system (i.e. organs) were clustered either by information flow or by function. In experiment 6, elements in the geographic map (i.e. towns) were clustered either by size or by era (the era in which the town had been established)

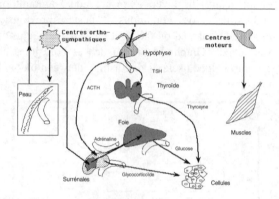

Figure 2: Temperature control system diagram used as material in experiment 3. Additional written explanations were provided in the actual material, identical across conditions.

Procedure: In all experiments, display conditions were groups of different participants (between-subjects factor). According to the experiment, participants were asked to perform three kinds of tasks.

In all six experiments, participants were asked to reproduce the configuration (on paper) from memory. This task was used as memory test for the study phase: participants were asked to recall the configuration again, either until their recall were completed, or a limited number of times (experiments 4,5 and 6).

In some experiments, we used tasks that required the processing of the representation in memory, such as part recognition in experiments 1 (network) and 2 (town and library maps), statement verification and inference solving in experiments 3 (system) and 6 (geographic map).

In experiments 1 (network), 2 (town and library maps), 3 (system) and 6 (geographic map), participants were also asked to describe the configuration in written mode.

Table 1 displays the method used in each experiment (material, display conditions, tasks) and the main results regarding memory performance and the organization of the mental representation.

3   Synthesis of Results

Memory performance was assessed through the number of elements that were recalled in each trial, and the number of trial. Three measures were analysed as indicator of the organization of the mental representation: order in which elements were recalled and, as the case may be, described; clustering of elements of the configuration in recall; and performance to the task requiring the processing of the representation.

From a statistical point of view, we computed analyses of variance (ANOVA) to compare quantitative performance across display conditions. Recall order was analysed using rank correlation coefficients (such as Kendall's or Spearman's). Clustering was obtained from hierarchical analysis on the ranks in recall across participants, which means that elements that were recalled successively by most participants were clustered together. Results were considered as statistically significant when the risk level obtained from the statistical analysis was less than 5% (or $p < .05$).

3.1   Memory Performance

None of the six experiments provided results to support the hypothesis that a sequential display facilitates memory of a spatial configuration compared

	Material	Conditions	Tasks	Memory performance	Organization of the representation
Exp. 1	network of circles	5 conditions: static square clustering, cross clustering route linear horizontal	free recall parts recognition description of the picture, in immediate and delayed testing	free recall and description: static condition > sequential conditions	participants in the sequential conditions recalled the circles in the order they were displayed (100% of subjects for free recall, 85% for the description) participants in the sequential conditions recognized faster parts that were temporally clustered over other parts.
Exp. 2	map of a library and map of a town	4 conditions: static display functional clustering spatial clustering linear horizontal	free recall parts recognition description of the picture, in immediate and delayed testing	free recall: better performance in the static condition over the linear condition ($p < 0.05$). interaction between materials and conditions ($p < 0.05$): the best performance was observed in the functional condition for the library map, while the spatial clustering lead to the best performance for the town.	39%, of participants recalled the elements of the map in the order, and 54%, in the clustering in which they were displayed (in average in the free recall and in the description); these figures varied greatly as a function of the display condition and of the material participants in the sequential conditions recognized faster parts that were temporally clustered over other parts.
Exp. 3	explanatory material of the temperature control system in human body (diagram and written commentaries)	3 conditions: static display functional clustering, according to the function the organs serve process clustering, according to the information flow in the system.	free recall statements verification and inferences making, focusing either on the processes or the functions description of the system from memory	Overall, participants in the static condition recalled more items of the diagram than participants in sequential conditions, but differences were not significant.	recall order: participants in the process condition recalled items of the diagram in the order they were displayed, whereas participants in the function condition did not. recall clustering: participants in both sequential conditions clustered the items the way they were displayed participants in the process condition were better at solving process inferences over participants in other conditions, but participants in the process condition were not better at solving function inferences.
Exp. 4	map of a twenty-shelve library	3 conditions: static display functional temporal clustering: shelves were clustered by academic categories (such as Humanities, Medical Sciences, ...) random temporal clustering	free recall of the names in the shelves, regardless of their location; located recall: recall of the shelves in the correct location. Recall limited to 4 trials.	Participants in the function conditions recalled more items (across trials) than participants in the static and random conditions; the difference between function and random conditions was significant ($p < 0.05$)	recall order: participants in the function condition recalled the shelves in the order in which they were displayed, whereas participants in the static and random conditions did not. clustering: participants in the function condition, and to a smaller extent, participants in the static condition, clustered the shelves according to a functional criteria (i.e. by academic categories).
Exp. 5	a thirty-six shelve library map	3 conditions, as in Exp. 4	free and located recall, as in Exp. 4	Same results as in Exp. 4	Since most participants did not produce a complete recall, statistical analyses of ordering and clustering could not apply.
Exp. 6	map of a fictitious island displaying 9 towns; each town was characterized with its size and with the era in which it had been established	3 conditions static temporal clustering by size temporal clustering by era	recall of the map (one single trial); verification test: stating whether two towns were identical in size (size focus) or in era (era focus) description of the map, that should include all information	no effect of the display condition on the number of items recall overall; significant interaction between information types and display conditions ($p < 0.0001$): participants in the size condition recalled size information more accurately, and conversely,): participants in the era condition recalled era information more accurately.	verification test: participants in the size condition were significantly faster at comparing towns along size, whereas participants in the era condition were significantly faster at comparing towns along era; interaction was significant for time ($p > 0.0001$) and accuracy ($p < 0.01$); clustering: participants in the sequential condition clustered items the way they were displayed, both in recall and description tasks.

Table 1: Synopsis of the six experiments on sequential display: method (material, conditions and tasks) and results, categorized as memory performance or as indicators of the organization of the mental representation.

to static display. In experiments 2 (town and library map), 4 (library 24) and 5 (library 36), sequential conditions with meaningful clustering induced systematically better performance than static condition, but the difference did not reach the level of significance.

However, results of experiments 4 (library 24) and 5 (library 36) showed that meaningful temporal clustering produced faster memorization of the configuration than random temporal clustering, with a statistically significant difference in both experiments.

3.2 Order and Clustering in Recall

Findings of all six experiments provided evidence that users recalled the items of the configuration in the order, and to a greater extent in the clustering in which they were displayed. However, in experiment 2 (town and library map), participants in the spatial condition used rarely the spatial clustering to describe the library, whereas they used it extensively to describe the town. Conversely, participants in the function condition used the functional clustering to describe the library, but not to describe the town. In experiment 3 (system), the function clustering is used to describe, but not to draw the system. Experiments 4 (library 24) and 5 (library 36) showed that participants that studied meaningful temporal clustering used that clustering to recall the configuration, whereas participants in the random condition did not.

Therefore, these results support the claim that users use the display order and clustering as a recall guide (Taylor & Tversky, 1992), provided that these order and clustering are relevant to users in the context of the task.

3.3 Performance in Subsequent Tasks

In experiments 1 (network) and 2 (town and library map), participants in the sequential conditions recognized parts of the configuration that were temporally clustered in the display faster than other parts. Moreover, in experiment 3 (system), participants in the process condition were better at solving procedural inferences over other inferences. These results support the hypothesis that elements are organized in the mental representation the way they were organized in the sequential display. Experiment 6 (geographic map) provided the stronger evidence for this claim, since identical symmetric results were found in both sequential conditions: participants in the size condition were better at reasoning on the size dimension, whereas participants in the era condition were better at reasoning on the era dimension, both in the recall task and in the statements verification test.

4 Discussion

On the basis of the literature, we expected that the sequential display would improve memory compared to static display. Yet, in all six experiments, participants in sequential conditions did better but not significantly better than participants in the static conditions. Two explanations may account for this results. First, participants were undergraduate or graduate students. Thus, they should have been able to use effective memory strategies, such as organizing the configuration into meaningful components. A second and more critical issue is that the sequential display as investigated here did not allow users to control the succession of frames, for methodological reasons (identical study time across conditions). It happens that interactivity is a key factor in the effectiveness of animation in learning (Rieber, 1990; Gonzales, 1996; Palmiter & Elkerton, 1993).

At this point, we propose that sequential display affects the organization of information in the mental representation more than the global memory performance, as evidenced from the results summarized in Section 3.3. These findings support the hypothesis that sequential display emphasizes a given organization over others in the mental model. Therefore, users will be better at performing tasks that are consistent with the organization conveyed through sequential display. These results are consistent with the cognitive point of view that all information in the encoding situation is stored in the mental representation and can be used as a cue for retrieving and processing the stored information.

5 Conclusion: How to Use Sequential Display?

This research provides evidence for the claim that a simple animation, as sequential display, affects users' mental representation and their aptitude to perform subsequent tasks. Based on these results, we assume that sequential displays are particularly effective to facilitate users' understanding of the functioning of dynamic systems. Indeed, sequential display can provide temporal information that conceptually maps the actual process in the system. Moreover, in contrast to conventional animation that is continuous, sequential display provides a series of discontinuous frames, thus enabling users to better distinguish steps in the functioning of the system (Palmiter & Elkerton, 1993).

From an applied perspective, sequential display is a promising tools in interface design and a good alternative to conventional animation. Nevertheless, interface designers must pay careful attention to the tasks that users have to perform from the computerized instruction, in order to propose the most suitable display. As Scaife & Rogers (1996) emphasized, since most real situations are manifolds, one solution is to provide users with alternative presentations, including dynamic and static diagrams, that users could shift according to their knowledge level of the domain and the requirements of the task.

Acknowledgements

I am grateful to Andre Bisseret and Barbara Tversky for their precious collaboration to this research. Thanks to Anne Pellegrin for her helpful comments on this paper.

References

Baecker, R. & Small, I. (1990), Animation at the Interface, *in* B. Laurel (ed.), *The Art of Human–Computer Interface Design*, Addison–Wesley, pp.251–67.

Baek, Y. K. & Layne, B. H. (1991), "Colour Graphics and Animation in a Computer-assisted Learning Tutorial Lesson", *Journal of Computer-based Instruction* **15**(4), 131–135.

Bétrancourt, M., Bisseret, A. & Faure, A. (1996), Effect of the Sequential Display of Pictures on the User's Mental Representation: An Experimental Study, *in Proceedings of the First Interdisciplinary Workshop on Using Complex Information Systems (UCIS'96)*, pp.61–6.

Bower, G. H. & Clark-Meyers, G. (1980), "Memory for Scripts with Organized vs. Randomized Presentations", *British Journal of Psychology* **71**, 369–77.

Gonzales, C. (1996), Does Animation in User Interfaces Improve Decision Making?, *in* G. van der Veer & B. Nardi (eds.), *Proceedings of CHI'96: Human Factors in Computing Systems*, ACM Press, pp.27–34.

Hegarty, M. & Just, M. A. (1993), "Constructing Mental Models of Machines from Text and Diagrams", *Journal of Memory and Language* **32**, 717–42.

Kaiser, M. K., Proffitt, D. R., Whelan, S. M. & Hecht, H. (1992), "Influence of Animation on Dynamical Judgments", *Journal of Experimental Psychology: Human Perception and Performance* **18**(3), 669–90.

Mandl, H. & Levin, R. (1989), "Knowledge Acquisition from Text and Pictures", *Advances in Psychology* **58**.

Mayer, R. E. (1989), "Models for understanding", *Review of Educational Research* **59**(1), 43–64.

Palmiter, S. & Elkerton, J. (1993), "Animated Demonstrations for Learning Procedural Computer-based Tasks", *Human–Computer Interaction* **8**(3), 193–216.

Peek, J. (1993), "Increasing Picture Effects in Learning from Illustrated Text", *Learning and Instruction* **3**(3), 227–38.

Rieber, L. P. (1990), "Using Computer Animated Graphics in Science Instruction with Children", *Journal of Educational Psychology* **82**(1), 135–140.

Rieber, L. P. & Kini, A. S. (1991), "Theoretical Foundations of Instructional", *Journal of Computer-based Instructions* **18**(3), 83–8.

Scaife, M. & Rogers, Y. (1996), "External Cognition: How do Graphical Representations Work?", *International Journal of Human–Computer Studies* **45**(2), 185–213.

Taylor, H. A. & Tversky, B. (1992), "Descriptions and Depictions of Environments", *Memory and Cognition* **20**(5), 483–496.

Wright, P., Hull, A. & Black, D. (1990), "Integrating Diagrams and Text", *The Technical Writing Teacher* **XVII**, 244–54.

Human–Computer Interaction — INTERACT '99
M. Angela Sasse and Chris Johnson (Editors)
Published by IOS Press, © IFIP TC.13, 1999

The Usability of a Computer-based Work System

Kurt Dauer Keller

Department of Communication, Aalborg University, Langagervej 8,
DK-9220 Aalborg, Denmark.

keller@hum.auc.dk

Abstract: Experiences with application development for computer-supported cooperative work (CSCW) indicate that a better understanding of sociocultural aspects of work organization, especially concerning the usability of computer-based work systems, is needed. This paper reports on a case study concerning the development and use of a work system for CSCW. The case study reflects a view of CSCW which is based on phenomenology and the social psychology of work. This approach proposes an analytical framework for the study and discussion of computer-based work systems' usability. Previously presented elsewhere, the framework is only briefly outlined here. The case study indicates that the serious problems in a 'state of the art' case of work organizational system development might be better understood and handled with this approach.

Keywords: CSCW, application development, work organization, work context, usability, virtual artifact.

1 Introduction

Lotus Notes is a well known platform for the implementation of computer-based information and communication systems in work settings within and across organizations. Undoubtedly, Notes also stands for a major commercial breakthrough for the very idea of computer supported cooperative work. However, serious studies of the work organizational usability and utility of the system have been scarce. Surely, one of them is Orlikowski's (1992) study of the introduction and initial use of the Notes system as a platform for application development in a large US department of an international advisory company. This study took place in the early days of the Notes system, when it had just been launched by Lotus. Her investigation clearly illuminated the lack of consideration of the users' needs and the organizational setting in which the system was applied. Later on, Lotus has emphasized, even in their sales campaign, that successful application development with Notes requires a professional expertise in organization analysis and development. It can also be remarked that the British section of the company investigated by Orlikowski — it has become common knowledge (Baecker, 1993; Tilley, 1993) that the company in question is Price Waterhouse — appeared much more reflective and careful as to 'social issues' when the head of the computer science

department presented their plans and experience with the introduction of Notes (Tilley, 1993).

I am going to discuss the case of a rather ambitious Notes application in a Danish credit institution which I shall call 'The Bank'. Developed by an advisory company which is an approved 'Lotus business partner', this application includes about 50 forms (app. 20,000 lines of code) and 2,000 variables on top of the Lotus Notes system. This case is particularly interesting to R&D on the usability of computer-based work systems because a department at The Bank was going to lean on the application as a basis of their work organization and thus use it fairly intensively in their daily work.

I took up this case as an opportunity to study the every day accomplishment of computer-supported work when it (apparently) is developed according to 'the state of the art'. I also wanted to discuss this case in the perspective of a usability oriented approach which is based on phenomenology. This approach was presented in more detail previously (Keller, 1994; 1997a). Another case study concerning 'flight disposition work' (i.e. monitoring and re-planning of ongoing aircraft traffic) has been discussed (Keller, 1997b), and a third case study concerning a large production plant is ongoing (Keller et al., to appear).

Studies of the consequences of a careful and considerate design and introduction of Notes applications (Gallivan et al., 1993; Orlikowski, 1996) have pointed to the still predominant weight of background factors, like organizational changes which were not anticipated, but emergent or opportunistic, and the importance of the existing culture of collaboration for the outcome of the changes. What seems to be missing in reflected discussions of computer interface usability (Hix & Hartson, 1993; Winograd, 1996) as well as in attempts to combine ethnographic studies with constructive design consideration (Bell & Johnson, 1996; Blomberg et al., 1997; Hughes et al., 1992; Plowman et al., 1995; Simonsen & Kensing, 1997) is a tight conceptual coherence between the theme and the context. By 'the theme' I mean the eventually very specific questions of the usability of different socio-technical designs, and by 'the context' is meant the topics of everyday experience and practice which embed the usability matters and involve a complete life-world of pre-structured horizons and implicit backgrounds.

My empirical study at The Bank took place through 9 months, starting 2 months after the new application had been taken into daily use. The investigation consisted in ethnographic observations of work practices, semi-structured interviews and document analysis. About 40 hours of ethnographic observation took place. The interviews comprised one or two individual sessions of 1–2 hours duration with each of the 11 members of the department, with the computer department of The Bank, and with the systems developer from the advisory company who had been most involved in the application development for The Bank. The document analysis included various paper material with information about The Bank, the tasks and work organization of the department, facts concerning the education and work experience of the members of the department, and the Lotus Notes application.

In the following section, the Notes application in The Bank is presented and criticized. The problems which this case study points to are taken up at a theoretical level in Section 3. In line with studies of the informality of organizational learning (Argyris, 1992; Cohen & Sproull, 1996) and explorations concerning the ambiguity of organization culture (Alvesson, 1993; Pondy et al., 1988) the very usage of computer-based information and communication systems is regarded in a sociocultural perspective. This allows an enhanced discussion of the computer system's appearance (to its users) as a more or less appropriate artifact in the different perspectives of the work environment. Finally, it is outlined how the application of this theoretical and methodological framework might be helpful in the reported case of The Bank.

2 The Application in the Bank

The Bank is a credit institution for local governments and for semi-municipal institutions which are economically guaranteed by these governments. In collaboration with The Bank's computer department the department of lending and foreign funding (in the following just called 'the department') hired the Lotus business partner to design and implement a Notes application for their internal completing, handling and communication of lending documents.

Within the last decade The Bank has been subject to radical changes in the financial market and this has entailed a more dynamic view of task and work organization, in particular in the department. The Notes application which we are going to look upon is an important aspect of this process.

The primary reasons for choosing Notes as the computer platform for a new information and communication system in The Bank were of a strategic kind (to approach 'the paper-less office') as well as directed to more immediate goals: first to formalize some simple work routines concerning the wording in standard letters and documents, and secondly to ensure the smooth portability of data between the document handling system and a word processor together with a spreadsheet system with which the users would feel comfortable. So, partly the choice of Notes has to do with the fact that the users were already familiar with Lotus' word processing and spreadsheet systems.

The application includes a database of customer addresses together with two different kinds of document databases: one which has a standard bond document for each type of bonds, and one which has templates for documents that are used in each of the three phases of lending: offer of loan, granting and settlement.

As to *the actual use of the application*, in general, the staff at the department is quite satisfied with the application. It helps them getting trivial and tedious matters right in their production of letters and bonds, and saves time for more creative tasks. Management is also content because the application has implied a rationalization that made it possible to take up new major tasks without hiring more people. Of course, there is much more to the questions of socioeconomic utility and sociocultural usability than the users' expression of some satisfaction. In fact the members of the department have experienced many serious restrictions and problems through the process of system development and introduction as well as in the implemented system.

Largely, the utility domain of the application is restricted to rendering some trivial — in particular: standard — patterns of certain documents (existing types of bonds and letters for trivial cases of loan offer and granting) and to preserve as well as mediate the worked up documents through the process of cooperative work in the department. However, this does not encompass a number of useful operations which members of the department had expected to be automated, in particular the production of statistics. The application does not support the production of non-standard cases of document production: especially compound documents, but also various simple ones. Neither does it limit the paper files which are dealt with throughout the execution of the loan cases: the actual files of the loans are not implemented in the system. What is more, it does not seem to have reduced very remarkably the face-to-face or in-house telephone communication on trivial, task-directed issues.

As regards *the development process*, the main points of criticism are the following: The estimated time of development was a half year, but the actual process took three times as long. The department has had to make an unforeseen renewal of its hardware (PC's and network) in order to optimize the application. Apparently, the available release 3 of the Notes system did not prove to be ripe for an application of this size, so after seven months the application was in urgent need to be transported to the new release 4. The design of the document bases now seems inappropriate, and an architectural re-coding of the application is foreseen. Very predictable needs of maintenance are not fulfilled in a flexible way: The Bank is not able to develop on its own the templates for new types of bonds which are appearing regularly. Finally, it is now expected that the life time of this Notes application will only be a few years because even the architectural re-coding won't satisfy the anticipated needs.

To the department in The Bank it is clear that the advisory company which implemented the Notes application was unable to overview the development project. This is not denied by the advisory company's system developer, but rather excused as a general condition when new tools and tasks are taken up. At the same time, responsible people in The Bank admit that they were unable to see through the opportunities that the Notes system might offer to match the particular work organizational needs in The Bank (of course, that is why they hired the advisory company in the first place). Undoubtedly, the mutual understanding which was attained through the prototyping approach in this case of integrated organization and system development was insufficient to provide a solid foundation and a clear orientation through the process. A significant problem (often seen in practice) was that system prototypes were used for heuristic, incremental system development, not for (the more appropriate) clarification and specification of requirements. In general, we find in this case the lack of a cross-discipline approach (including a basis in human science) which would allow the users and developers to share sociocultural perspectives on work organization, including notions of socio-technical systems.

3   Defining the Usability of a Computer-based Work System

Traditional notions of 'usability' (Hollnagel, 1997; Lim & Long, 1994; Nielsen, 1993; Preece et al., 1993) may be criticized for lacking attention to three crucial matters: the difference between utility and usability, the application domain (e.g. amusement or work), and the computer system's actual appearance to the users. On the basis of phenomenology, social science offers a way to understanding the experience of work systems in use. The theoretical approach which I shall only outline very briefly here concentrates on computer-based work systems. This approach involves concepts of 'work contexts' and of what we call 'the virtual artifact' to emphasize a focus on user's actual experience (rather than the widespread normative models of user's views, goals, problem-solving, etc.).

3.1   The Artifact as a Figure on a Socio-cultural Background

The virtual artifact is the actual appearance of a computer system to its users. The virtual artifact may be very different from the nominal, designed functionality of the computer system (unless the user is regarding it like a systems designer). Only existing for users, the virtual artifact does not at all have to be any kind of a system or model.

When a computer-based system is designed for purposes of supporting human work performance, the virtual artifact must be regarded as a topic of utility and usability. Usability should be distinguished as an analytical topic besides utility. Though both are defining aspects of the practical application of computer-based systems for the support of human work, usability is a sociocultural and psychosocial phenomenon, utility is socioeconomic and socio-technical. Usability may be explored and conceived as a question of latitude and strains in the three dimensions of psychosocial work environment: control, qualifications and social identity.

This has comprehensive implications: We do not regard 'usability' as simply a matter of systems and designs, but find it in contexts, that is to say where some specific foreground (an immediate use situation) is structured in a perspective with a comprehensive background of psychosocial and sociocultural meaning. The actual application of a computer system in human work processes has to be structured in perspectives of sociocultural experience and practice. Thus, the desired usability of a socio-technical design is altogether in a sound work environment, i.e. a contextual interplay of sociocultural rules and resources, which can just as well be judged as a reasonable interplay of psychosocial demands and motives. Therefore, the socio-technical design must be structured and maintained by an understanding of its (contextual) use, which is to a large extent identical by the designer and by the user. This shared understanding is mainly attained implicitly due to their common sociocultural background which allows the dynamic structuring of experience and praxis as the contexts of their explicit communication. This point has been further elaborated elsewhere (Keller, 1994; 1997a), so for now I shall only indicate its conceptual and methodological significance.

On a phenomenological foundation 'context' may be regarded as the background in a figure-background structure, i.e. a perspective, with some 'theme' as the foreground or figure. The context is all the surrounding conditions that goes into the structuring of the subject in focus (the theme). Comprising social identities as well as social fields, this perspective understanding does not imply any conflict between discussing 'situations' and 'contexts' in the same vein as talking about 'rules' and 'general resources'. On the contrary, a figure-background perspective is precisely the structuring relationship between the specific issues at some thematic centre and the general issues closer to a corresponding horizon.

3.2 How Work Environment Corresponds with Design Metaphors

In functional views of work organizational structures we are only able to ensure usability by design in so far as we can make appropriate 'translations' both ways between designed utility and intended

usability. Usability is attained as an approximation to the following: a maximum of human control, a balance of qualifications with demands, and an adequate confirmation of social identity (Keller, 1994). These objectives as to the human experience of work performance can be translated into requirements concerning the design of a work system to be implemented as a computer-based application.

For that purpose we may apply design metaphors which are corresponding to the three dimensions of work environment, control, qualifications and social identity. Respectively these design metaphors are 'a model', 'a tool' and 'a media', each of which has to be guiding for the analysis, design and evaluation of any computer function with which the users are supposed to directly interact. So, there are three perspectives in which to carefully scrutinize a computer-based system for appropriate correspondence between utility and usability regards, in order to design it as a virtual artifact to support human work performance.

In the perspective of *a model*, the virtual artifact (and thus, implicitly the designed work system) allows for transparency (in the sense of looking into something). The users are in control in as much as they know 'the inside' of the computer system, i.e. the architecture and functionality at a level of semantic specification corresponding with the task of the work domain.

In the perspective of *a tool*, the virtual artifact (and thus, implicitly the designed work system) allows for a different sense of transparency: looking through something (not really noticing it). A tool lets the users' qualifications correspond with the demands of the task through a kind of 'prolongation' of the user qualifications. As competent users of a tool, we are able to forget about the tool and focus our attention on the accomplishment of the task.

In the perspective of *a media*, the virtual artifact (and thus, implicitly the designed work system) allows for flexibility. First and foremost, this implies that the computer system does not in fact stand in the way for the users' mutual interaction and communication of intentions, interpretations and motives. The computer-based system should be distinguished by flexible adjustment to human initiative and creativity.

The correspondences between work environmental dimensions and socio-technical metaphors (control ↔ model, qualifications ↔ tool, social identity ↔ media) enable the qualitative analysis and discussion of usability as the better and worse work conditions with differing designs are being determined. In this way, 'usability' is not reduced to questions of design but associated with the

Strains on control	Strains on qualifications	Strains on social identity
obscure functions	training is lacking	lack of 'system ownership'
difficult to remember functions	socio-technical imagination is lacking	positioning conflicts and polarization
distrust of functionality	uncertain responsibilities	lack of collective self-reflection
uncertainty about implications	demanding for some people	labile professional situation
	possible product deterioration	

Table 1: Straining aspects of the work environment.

sociocultural background through the explication of the psychosocial work environment.

4   The Work Environment of the Application in the Bank

The investigation of the usability of the Notes-based work system in The Bank did elucidate a number of straining aspects of the work environment which seemed to emerge or become more salient with this application. To get a very good understanding of how these strains relate to the organizational setting as well as to the new computer system's design and appearance we should look upon the work environment before, during, and after the introduction of the new work system. For now, however, we shall just illuminate how the usability of the computer-based work system is structured in the three perspectives of its psychosocial and sociocultural context. The usability is going to be illuminated as an interplay of foreground structuring and background structuring which encompasses rather profound strains in the psychosocial and sociocultural work context. Of course, it is not supposed that all strains stem from the utility-oriented, socio-technical design of the work system. On the contrary, the virtual artifact is always structured by the context of application as well as by actual design. Furthermore, the virtual artifact can only make up a foreground of the work environment, not all of it. Our objective is an (by no means exhaustive) identification and description of work strains which we could remedy by better systems design, better experience explication and practice negotiation, or both. Some of these strains are listed in Table 1.

4.1   The Control–Model Perspective

Control of the work processes and situations is a recurrent theme for the members of the department. Very often the daily work is marked by hectic activity because tight deadlines have to be respected as well as the intense competition.

In the perspective of control an artifact must appear as *a model*. In our case, the application has

much of this quality because it is in fact designed to preserve existing objects and routines, but now including a number of automated functions to facilitate the production of simple letters and documents and limit the number of errors to be detected and corrected during this production. However, problems do occur by the interpretation of the application as a model. Strains in the control perspective include obscurities in the 'functional architecture' of the application. Users have found it difficult to distinguish between input fields for information to be further processed and input fields for information to be presented in the same way in the final document, e.g. a date (in numbers) to be calculated upon and a date (in text) to be written in a letter, respectively. Some users also have difficulties in remembering specific functions in the application. Fairly often, they have to ask others or look it up how to execute these functions.

Large problems with the functionality of the application during the introduction phase have made a significant impression on the users. At least for some time, this seems to imply less user confidence in the system, and in many cases also less self-confidence by the use of the application. Furthermore, most of the users were very uncertain about the intentions and implications of integrating the application in the department. For a time, this has limited their motivation to be involved with the new work system, and again this may turn into lasting criticism and reservations.

4.2   The Qualifications–Tool Perspective

Concerning *qualifications* it should be noted that most of the employed in the department are upgraded office workers, now taking on fairly high responsibilities in their job. They are specialized through courses and training in various fields of lending and foreign funding. Equally important, they are qualified in the 'intensive' direction of a 'kernel labour force' with such social and personal qualifications as flexibility and loyalty.

In the perspective of qualifications an artifact must appear as *a tool*. In our case, the application has tool qualities as regards some simple work functions like production of a standard bond document. It is not designed as a tool in support of major tasks like offering combined loans and making arrangements of alternative offerings to the customers. Competent users have questioned whether the application is quite 'neutral' to the performance of such tasks (which it does not support) or restricts and strains this work performance. Furthermore, it might seem to be the case that the first phase of the lending cases, the offering of a loan to the customer, has become slightly more cumbersome in some situations.

Concerning the strains on qualifications it can be remarked that the users have not had an organized course in the use of the application, only some exercises to help them 'getting going'. Undoubtedly, a few of them can do very well with that, but probably most of the users would have benefited greatly from well-organized introductory and follow-up courses. In consequence, the users are also missing the socio-technical imagination which would be grounded in a close knowledge of the application as well as the organizational setting, and which would make them able to participate in concretizing new and better work systems for themselves.

It appears to be a recurrent and somewhat frustrating topic in the department to negotiate the distinction between 'minor difficulties' and 'major complications', i.e. user problems which require learning and user problems which should be solved through technical assistance, respectively. Getting the necessary support to fulfill new tasks may require that new routines are developed and negotiated. On the other hand, 'super users' feel that they are being abused when they have to help a person with the same procedure more than once or twice.

Traditional work functions have been influenced by the reorganization, in some ways with far-reaching consequences. As could be expected, this goes for the workers, senior employees in particular, who are uncomfortable with computer technology. Though familiar with all the usual tasks, they may suddenly find themselves in a very demanding situation. Another aspect of the reorganization which provokes and strains the feeling of professional competence is the deterioration or elimination of procedures, such as proof reading, which used to ensure the blameless quality of the work product.

4.3 The Social Identity–Media Perspective

Social identity is manifested as a specific cultural climate of responsiveness and confirmation of positions and relations within the department and through interactions with other departments in The Bank. It is also manifested in the communication with customers and business connections: as a mutual trust and understanding (sometimes to be re-established) of 'the rules of the game'. It is a general aspect of this social identity that it very dynamically combines unassisted work and close collaboration. While a rather clear distribution of tasks exists, the work performance is often marked by a common responsibility (in extension of formalized routines) to ensure the correct wording and handling of documents.

Regarded as a virtual artifact which is focused in the perspective of social identity the Notes application must be scrutinized as *a media*. Then, the application first and foremost appears to us as a device which should promote the smooth communication between the front office and the back office, and not obstruct the interaction between its users. Because, as mentioned, the application has not influenced the document handling routines in the department so very deeply, and because the users work in offices door by door so they can very easily communicate face-to-face (if they do not choose to use the phone), the 'media issue' has not grown into a big one. Most of the users are now accustomed to mediate and receive the simple electronic documents that are carried by the Notes application. On the other hand, the application has hardly been of any help as to the clarification — or enrichment in other ways — of the interaction between the users.

Concerning the strains on social identity it can be pointed out that the users do not show the same feeling of responsibility for the functioning of the application as they do for the functioning of the surrounding social system of work procedures. Thus, it is a source of recurrent frustration that essential parts of the unforeseen situations and difficulties which emerge with the work performance make them feel more helpless and dependent on social support than they are used to.

Friction occurs as to the social positioning which follows with the distribution of new tasks. In certain regards, traditional positions in the department have laid barriers for the appreciation of new opportunities of work organization. For instance, a trainee who played an important role in the introduction of the application was not always respected for her knowledge. Apparently, other employees could not believe that she could be so sure (or tell them that much) about how they were going to do an important part of their job from now on. In general, in our case the question of being skilled with and adaptive to the new application does not seem to become a subject of common explication, but rather a growing frontier of social positioning with its own victories and defeats. Of course, there are real and considerable differences in the members' experience, abilities, and openness to professional challenges. But the low level of collective self-reflection implies that many cultural, social and psychological resources within the community of the department remain passive or implicit. Not much organizational learning is taking place because there isn't much initiative to explicate social relations and discuss social conflicts.

The Bank's principle of job-security together with the department members' positive attitude to technological development make up a fine basis for discussing problems and handling conflicts concerning social identity. Still, the way in which people are professionally situated within the department has become more labile within the last decade. It is no longer evident what kinds of tasks, work conditions and promotion one can look forward to get. Several members of the department think that this process was reinforced by the introduction of the new work system. Consequently, some members indicate that the employees now feel less attached to The Bank than they used to do. Obviously, a straight continuation of this development implies a gradual decomposition of the 'kernel labour force', and thus a decline of the loyalty and commitment which has been built up over long time and make up a background for the very efficient work performance in the department today.

4.4   Conclusion

Through social psychology on a phenomenological foundation a usability-centred approach to the analysis and development of computer-based work organization has been outlined very briefly. By the example of a case study it was indicated in which way this approach enhances our ability to analyse and discuss sociocultural aspects of actual and potential work organization as a basis for the development of computer-supported cooperative work.

The case study clearly shows that the cultivation of common perspectives for the researcher and the participants is not predominantly a question about sharing 'figures' like systems and formal specifications. More importantly, the backgrounds out of which the figures are structured must be shared for common perspectives to be established. To some extent, this structuring of sociocultural perspectives happens implicitly through the user-designer collaboration, like in any other human interaction. But in communication

about intended development of work organization the explication of experience and practice stands out as a principle of systematic R&D which is no less important for analysis and design than formalization.

Defining usability through the three perspectives of work environment is not just a way of categorizing the different sociocultural and psychosocial aspects which make up the context of a work system in use. It is an opportunity for more thorough analysis and discussion of the way in which a computer system actually appears to its users as 'an artifact for this work', embedded in the particular work context. On the one hand this conceptualization of usability allows us to understand with much more accuracy and detail the 'immediate' (unreflected) appearance of a computer-based artifact to its everyday users. On the other hand this understanding is related to the 'remote' psychosocial and sociocultural structures which make up implicit background conditions of the work processes, and which would also have to be reflected and explicated by the users themselves in order to realize their importance as 'all too obvious' and 'all-pervading' circumstances.

Analysing usability as the proposed three-dimensional topic concerning a virtual artifact in a work environment enhances our understanding of technology in use and of work-based technological requirements. While traditional notions of usability are restricted to the foreground aspect of work environment, that is to say the 'control ↔ model' perspective which has perhaps been sufficient for simple computer-based services, walk-up-and-use situations, and the like, the suggested analytical framework implies specific perspectives for studying the background aspects of a virtual artifact's usability in its work environment as well. To appreciate the important issues of pre-given sociocultural meaning, horizons of experience and practice, etc. which may be illuminated in the 'qualifications ↔ tool' perspective and the 'social identity ↔ media' perspective opens the way for studying the users situation more seriously, and thus for more solid organizational system development. Through the case study we have looked upon the structuring of topics such as commitment, community, communicative attitude, professional stance, etc. which belong to the background of the work environment. We have seen that this structuring contributes a lot to determine how a computer-based work system might appear to its users as an artifact with a particular usability.

References

Alvesson, M. (1993), *Cultural Perspectives on Organizations*, Cambridge University Press.

Argyris, C. (1992), *On Organizational Learning*, Blackwell.

Baecker, R. (ed.) (1993), *Readings in Groupware and Computer-supported Cooperative Work: Assisting Human–Human Collaboration*, Morgan-Kaufmann.

Bell, D. & Johnson, P. (1996), A Contingency Model for Groupware Design, *in* M. Shapiro, D. andTauber & R. Traunmüller (eds.), *The Design of Computer-supported Cooperative Work and Groupware Systems*, Elsevier Science.

Blomberg, J., Suchman, L. & Trigg, R. (1997), Back to Work: Renewing old Agendas for Cooperative Design, *in* M. Kyng & L. Mathiassen (eds.), *Computers and Design in Context*, MIT Press.

Cohen, M. D. & Sproull, L. S. (1996), *Organizational Learning*, Sage Publications.

Gallivan, M., Goh, C. H., Hitt, L. M. & Wyner, G. (1993), Incident Tracking at InfoCorp: Case Study of a Pilot Notes Implementation, Technical Report 3590-93, Sloan School of Management, MIT, Cambridge, Massachusetts.

Hix, D. & Hartson, H. R. (1993), *Developing User Interfaces: Ensuring Usability through Product and Process*, John Wiley & Sons.

Hollnagel, E. (1997), Cognitive Ergonomics and the Reliability of Man–Machine Interaction, *in* D. Brune et al.(eds.), *The Workplace*, Vol. 1, CIS and Scandinavian Science Publishers.

Hughes, J. A., Randall, D. & Shapiro, D. (1992), Faltering from Ethnography to Design, *in* J. Turner & R. Kraut (eds.), *Proceedings of CSCW'92: Conference on Computer Supported Cooperative Work*, ACM Press, pp.115–22.

Keller, K. (1994), "Conditions for Computer-Supported Cooperative Work", *Technology Studies* **1**(2), 242–69.

Keller, K. D. (1997a), Understanding of Work and Explanation of Systems, *in* G. C. Bowker, S. L. Star, W. Turner & L. Gasser (eds.), *Social Science, Technical Systems and Cooperative Work*, Lawrence Erlbaum Associates.

Keller, K. D. (1997b), Usability in the Perspective of Work Environment, *in* M. J. Smith et al.(eds.), *Design of Computing Systems: Social and Ergonomic Considerations*, Elsevier Science.

Keller, K. D., Kirk, K. & Malmborg, L. (to appear), "Competence in Computer-supported Work".

Lim, K. Y. & Long, J. B. (1994), *The MUSE Method for Usability Engineering*, Cambridge Series on Human–Computer Interaction, Cambridge University Press.

Nielsen, J. (1993), *Usability Engineering*, Academic Press.

Orlikowski, W. J. (1992), Learning from Notes: Organizational Issues in Groupware Implementation, *in* J. Turner & R. Kraut (eds.), *Proceedings of CSCW'92: Conference on Computer Supported Cooperative Work*, ACM Press, pp.362–9.

Orlikowski, W. J. (1996), Evolving with Notes: Organizational Change Around Groupware Technology, *in* C. Ciborra (ed.), *Groupware and Teamwork. Invisible Aid or Technical Hindrance?*, John Wiley & Sons.

Plowman, L., Rogers, Y. & Ramage, M. (1995), What are Workplace Studies for?, *in* H. Marmolin, Y. Sundblad & K. Schmidt (eds.), *Proceedings of ECSCW'95, the 4th European Conference on Computer-Supported Cooperative Work*, Kluwer, pp.309–24.

Pondy, L. R. et al.(eds.) (1988), *Managing Ambiguity and Change*, John Wiley & Sons.

Preece, J., Benyon, D., Davies, G., Keller, L. & Rogers, Y. (1993), *A Guide to Usability: Human Factors in Computing*, Addison–Wesley.

Simonsen, J. & Kensing, F. (1997), "Using Ethnography in Contextual Design", *Communications of the ACM* **40**(7), 82–8.

Tilley, R. (1993), Groupware Implementation Strategies, *in Groupware 1993 Europe Conference Proceedings*, Morgan-Kaufmann, pp.67–75.

Winograd, T. (ed.) (1996), *Bringing Design to Software*, Addison–Wesley.

Human–Computer Interaction — INTERACT '99
M. Angela Sasse and Chris Johnson (Editors)
Published by IOS Press, © IFIP TC.13, 1999

New Technology and Work Practice: Modelling Change with Cognitive Work Analysis

Peter J. Benda & Penelope M. Sanderson

Swinburne Computer–Human Interaction Laboratory, School of Information Technology, Swinburne University of Technology, PO Box 218, Hawthorn, Victoria 3122, Australia.

benda@it.swin.edu.au, psanderson@swin.edu.au

Abstract: In this paper, the authors examine an approach to describing and predictively modelling the impact of technological change on work practice. Taking Cognitive Work Analysis as a point of departure, an approach is discussed within which one can analyse work domains and work activities and then use these analyses as a 'field' upon which to trace the impact of new technology. Preliminary sets of notational extensions are introduced to Cognitive Work Analysis. A case study of the introduction of an electronic anaesthesia record is then examined. Associated changes to work structures and activities are interpreted and represented using the extended framework. Finally, implications and future directions of the work are discussed.

Keywords: cognitive engineering, technological change, work, ecological approach, qualitative research, organizational change.

1 Predicting Impact of Technological Change

The aim of our research is to develop a predictive model of when, why, and how the introduction of a new technology changes the nature of work (Benda & Sanderson, 1998). Our research question can be broken down into two components:

- What changes does a new technology cause at the level of local work practice? How do these changes translate into structural and functional changes which emerge at an organizational or systemic level?

- Does Cognitive Work Analysis (CWA) (Vicente, 1999; Rasmussen et al., 1994) provide a useful framework for describing and predicting the impact technological change? If so, how must the CWA framework be extended to achieve this? If not, where is the framework inadequate? Can the framework be modified to overcome the inadequacy or should an entirely different approach be used?

We hope to develop conceptual tools that will provide practical help to personnel responsible for introducing new technologies into organizations. Ideally, we would like to help such personnel predict design requirements, organizational changes needed, new training regimes, and the possible procurement of further supporting technologies. Our research therefore echoes the purpose of some CSCW research by aiming:

> "to *understand* work for the purposes of design, and? to *design* systems for the purposes of work." (Fitzpatrick, 1998)

2 Cognitive Work Analysis and Technological Change

2.1 Cognitive Work Analysis

Cognitive Work Analysis (CWA) is a systems-based approach to the analysis, design, and evaluation of complex sociotechnical systems. It has emerged as an important conceptual and methodological tool in the multi-disciplinary, systems-oriented approach to human interaction with complex technologies that is known as cognitive engineering (Rasmussen et al., 1994; Sanderson, 1998; Vicente, 1999).

CWA is most appropriate for the analysis of complex real-time mission-critical work environments, such as power plant control rooms, aircraft cockpits, emergency response centres, and (as in this paper) critical care environments in hospitals. CWA is a form of analysis that is neither normative nor descriptive but instead might be called 'formative' (Sanderson, 1998). It is formative because it points to the constraints and possibilities for action in a work domain that help to *form* or shape the behaviour seen. It is also formative because it suggests the *form* of an interface that will shape human knowledge and activity most effectively.

CWA provides tools for modelling the many different factors that will have a bearing on whether humans can be effective actors within complex systems. These factors can be modelled at six levels of analysis (see Table 1), each of which involves a distinct class of modelling technique and a distinct set of outputs — the table combines levels from Rasmussen et al. (1994; Vicente, 1999). There is insufficient space to discuss these modelling techniques in detail. However, two main points should be emphasised. First, to perform a useful analysis of work it is not necessary to model at all six levels. Second, when considering the impact of technological change on work, each level of CWA modelling is probably uniquely suited to tease out a certain kind of impact (see rightmost column of Table 1).

In this paper we will present an analysis that uses just the first two levels of modelling: Work Domain Analysis (WDA) and Activity Analysis in Work Domain terms (AA/WD).

2.2 Showing Impact of Change with WDA

WDA usually describes a work domain with five different descriptive languages. Going from the highest to lowest level of 'abstraction', they include descriptions of the following:

1. The *functional purpose* of the work domain.

2. The *priorities or values* the work domain must promote or preserve.

3. The *functions* that must be carried out to achieve the functional purpose.

4. The *physical functionality* that is needed for the system to function towards its purposes.

5. The *physical objects and devices* that provide the physical functionality.

Rasmussen et al. (1994, Ch.7) used WDA to describe how changes at the physical or technological level of the system could have a profound effect on higher level purposes, values, and functioning of the system. Benda & Sanderson (1998) extended Rasmussen et al.'s approach from a narrative description to a formal notational extension to WDA that shows different kinds of changes to a work domain that can result from a technological change. However, the Benda and Sanderson paper simply showed *what* the changes to the work domain were, not *how* the change had taken place or *why*.

We are exploring whether CWA can provide an effective basis not only for describing the impact of technological changes in a complex work environment, but also for explaining and predicting such changes. In the remainder of the paper we give a flavour of the approach we are taking and the issues we are facing.

3 Case Study: Anaesthesia

3.1 The Diatek Arkive System

We use a case study to show how WDA and AA/WD can be used to describe the impact of technology. The case study describes the unsuccessful implementation of an automated anaesthesia record keeping system — the Diatek Arkive 'Organizer' system — into the operating rooms of a major university medical centre in the USA in the late 1980s and early 1990s (Block et al., 1998). The individual Arkive units had the following design features:

- High-resolution touch-screen display.

- Array of multi-function modules for interfacing multiple monitors.

- Dot-matrix printer on the back of the cart for the production of anaesthetic records.

- A set of fixed keys and an on-screen keyboard for data entry.

- Possibility of voice entry of drug information and commentary.

The Block et al. (1998) paper describes in great detail the many technical, social, and organizational impacts of the Arkive units, and the adjustments made to accommodate the new system. We have been able to show that each impact described by Block et al., and each change occasioned, can be related to a particular level of analysis in CWA. There is not room to show the full analysis here. Instead we work through a small handful of examples using just two levels of analysis in CWA.

Levels of Analysis	Modelling Technique	Event Dependence	Form of Output	Kind of Changes Most Readily Representable at This Level
Work Domain Analysis	Abstraction Hierarchy	No	Relations between purposes, functions and objects	Changes to the functional structure of the work domain
Activity Analysis in Work Domain Terms	Temporal constraint model, workflow (general)	Yes	Coordination of workflow from constraint-based perspectives	Changes to logical, procedural, temporal and spatial coordination of workflow
Control Task Analysis	Decision Ladders	Yes	Inputs and outputs for effective control	Changes to information gathering and action specification
Mental Strategies	Strategies analysis	Yes	Actor's methods and/or procedures	Changes to strategies possible
Social / Organizational Strategies	Role analysis	Not necessarily	Allocation of function, job descriptions	Changes to allocation of function and job descriptions
Cognitive Resouces Analysis	Skills-Rule-Knowledge Taxonomy	Not necessarily	Actors' aptitudes and training	Changes in eductional level and job training needs

Table 1: Levels of Cognitive Work Analysis and representation of change.

3.2   CWA-based Notation for Change

A notation must meet certain criteria if it is to be an effective instrument for description and analysis. A notation should be applicable over many domains and should show good reliability across codings and coders. The terms in the notation should be mutually exclusive and, for all practical purposes, exhaustive. The notation we are developing for describing and predicting the impact of technological change has the following elements: (Full validation is not complete.)

- Analytic artefacts produced by the modelling techniques used within CWA (see Table 1).

- A coding scheme for describing impacts and changes brought about after a technological change.

Figure 1 shows the latter. For easy superimposition on CWA models, the codes are represented by icons.

3.3   Building CWA Models of Change

In this section we use the Diatek Arkive example to illustrate how Work Domain Analysis (WDA) and Activity Analysis (AA/WD) in Work Domain terms can be used to describe the impact of technological change. These are only two of the six modelling techniques we have outlined in Table 1. However we gain a considerable amount of descriptive power with just WDA and AA/WD.

WDA is a way of modelling the purposes, priorities, functions and devices in a work domain that is *independent* of any events or activities (see

Figure 1) WDA can be extended to show the impact of technological change on the structure of a work domain (Benda & Sanderson, 1998). The text entries in Figure 1 are a description of the anaesthesia system (technology and practitioners) and of the hospital administration at the five levels of abstraction described earlier.   The details of the WDA are generated from our observational studies of hospital operating suites in the USA and Australia (Seagull & Sanderson, 1998; Watson & Sanderson, 1998). The impact of technological change is superimposed on the WDA as a 'trickle up' effect from the level of physical forms and configuration to the functions, priorities, and purposes of the system. The actual nature of the 'trickle up' effect is indicated by icons representing our initial change symbology, which is provided in full in Figure 1. We have taken the impacts from the Block et al. (1998) article and reinterpreted them in the context of this WDA. Figure 1 provides two examples of the impact of the Arkive machine. The examples are by no means exhaustive and not every aspect of each example is shown. Further details will be given in the next section of the paper.

AA/WD models activity that takes place in a work domain and is therefore an event-*dependent* technique (see Figure 2). AA/WD can show the impact of technological change on logical and temporal constraints in workflow and workplace coordination. The AA/WD in Figure 2 has been developed from the description in Block et al. (1998) and fleshed out with our knowledge of procedures in US hospital operating suites. The figure provides three examples of the impact of the Arkive machine, which have been taken directly from the Block et al. (1998) article. The impact of technological change is shown by comparing constraints on the anaesthetist's coordination with other entities in the work domain under two conditions:

- without the Arkive machine; and

- with the Arkive machine.

The change symbology indicates where some key differences lie.

The examples in each case have been generated to show the workings of the modelling technique in question. However, the last example in each case links the two modelling techniques. The examples are summarised below.

3.4 Impact of Arkive per WDA

3.4.1 *Predicted Benefit to Hospital Administration*

The first impact to be illustrated is one hoped for by hospital administration, but which never eventuated because the Arkive technology was not fully implemented (Block et al., 1998, p.93ff). It was hoped that by connecting the Diatek Arkive Network with the Hospital Administration Network (see nodes 1 and 2 of Stream A on Figure 1), electronic data from anaesthesia cases could enhance the ability to track the delivery of anaesthesia services (link to node 3). This would afford the hospital the ability to use anaesthesia data for scheduling, long-range planning, and purchasing, amongst other functions (see links to nodes 4, 5, and 6). For reasons of clarity, we have not shown the complex effect of the changes to these functions on priorities and values, but we have indicated the hoped for positive impact on the functional purposes of the hospital (links to nodes 7 and 8). In reality, the fact that the link between the two networks was never completed is indicated by a zap mark in the line connecting nodes 1and 2. The fact that the hoped for benefits never eventuated is indicated by the fact that the path is rendered with a dotted line.

3.4.2 *Actual Effect on Ability to Meet Legal Recording Requirements.*

The Arkive produced a printed record (see nodes 1 and 2 of Stream B on Figure 1). An initial concern was whether this printout would be acceptable as a legal document. If not, anaesthetists would be unlikely to use the Arkive as intended (Block et al., 1998). Within the hospital administration subdomain, procedural constraints were loosened (see link to node 3) so that the printed record could let the hospital interface with regulatory bodies, so preserving the

hospital's priority of legal accountability (link to node 4). The new means provided by the Arkive for the anaesthesia system to meet legal requirements was therefore made equivalent with the means used by the hospital administration (link between nodes 4 and 5).

At the same time, however, forces were at work within the anaesthesia system to compromise the legal status of the Arkive printout, some of which will be illustrated further in the AA/WD that follows. When an anaesthesia resident was attending a case, the supervising faculty member's signature was also needed for the patient to be billed by accounting, and for the record to be considered authoritative by medical records. Signing requires a physical printout, and a printout with complete anaesthesia information could only be produced at the end of the case (Block et al., 1998). There were now more instances where the record was not co-signed by the faculty supervisor. The anaesthesia system column of Figure 1 indicates a tighter constraint on when the faculty supervisor can co- sign the physical record (link from node 1 to node 6) which introduces a constraint into the anaesthesia system's ability to complete the record (link to node 7). This produces a conflict with the priority of meeting legal requirements (link to node 5) that is shared with the hospital administration, as well as a conflict with the accounting department's billing function (link to node 8).

Therefore, on the one hand the Arkive machine broadened the means by which the hospital could maintain legal accountability for the conduct of anaesthesia, but on the other hand the Arkive machine made it more difficult to produce records with the supervising faculty member's signature, which was legally required.

3.5 Impact of Arkive per AA/WD

Figure 2 shows an Activity Analysis in Work Domain terms (AA/WD) focussing on the coordination between the Arkive machine, the anaesthetist, the surgeon, and personnel from hospital administration. The tracks in Figure 2 have ordinal-scale rather than interval-scale properties. Only the constraints on the sequencing of activities are shown. Points that line up vertically are not necessarily simultaneous: temporal coordination is instead shown by dotted connections between stakeholder tracks. Where sequential constraints do not exist, activities are marked as optional, or constraints governing the universe of options at that point are shown. Figure 2 therefore does not show actual activity sequences, but instead *describes the constraints under which a wide variety of actual activity sequences might be generated.* In accordance

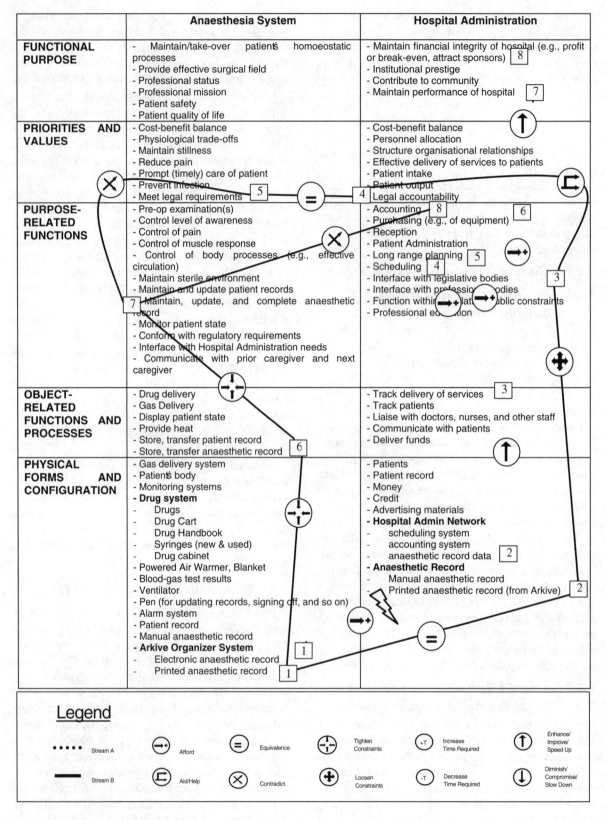

Figure 1: Tracing changes in work domain analysis for the electronic anaesthesia record case study.

with the 'formative' nature of CWA (Sanderson, 1998; Vicente, 1999), the AA/WD is therefore a generative model rather than a descriptive model of activity.

The AA/WD focusses not just on the individual case (a single operation) but on two cases. An important factor in performing an AA/WD is choosing the grain of analysis that will most effectively reveal changes to coordinative structures that might be caused by technological change. An anaesthetist will typically provide anaesthesia for a series of cases in rapid succession within the one operating suite (an anaesthesia 'list'). Therefore we need to examine the impact of the Arkive between cases as well as within cases — this will include system startup, transition, and shutdown. As a result, Figure 2 shows two cases so that such coordination can be represented. Finally, in Figure 2 we show two tracks for the anaesthetist. The upper track shows the anaesthetist coordinating with the Arkive whereas the lower track shows the anaesthetist producing a manual anaesthesia record only.

3.5.1 Actual Lengthening of Preoperative Patient Preparation Time.

It is clear from comparing the two anaesthetist tracks in Figure 2 that with the Arkive machine there are more activities for the anaesthetist to perform while preparing the patient for surgery, and tighter constraints on the sequencing of those activities. The Arkive may need to be configured for the kind of anaesthesia to be performed. Patient data will definitely need to be entered. Hardware and software preconditions for successful recording will need to be checked. Because these activities cannot be timeshared with other activities, the time to prepare the patient for surgery will lengthen.

3.5.2 Actual Constraints on When Anaesthesia Record Can be Signed.

Figure 2 shows that with the Arkive machine there is a strong constraint on when the anaesthesia record can be signed: it can be signed only after a complete record has been printed out which can only happen after the case is completed. With a manual record, however, the paper form is continuously present. The anaesthesia resident and supervising faculty member can, in principle, sign the form at any point.

3.5.3 Actual Effect on Ability to Meet Legal Recording Requirements.

Figure 2 provides an event-dependent representation of the situation when the faculty supervisor is unavailable to co-sign the anaesthesia record. When the anaesthesia resident uses the Arkive machine, there

is a narrower time window in which the supervisor's signature might be obtained than when a manual record is being produced. When a manual record is being used, there is a greater time window for collecting the signature; moreover, the time window opens when the faculty supervisor is most likely to be on hand anyway. In both cases, if the supervisor does not sign it may be hours or days before the omission is discovered (shown in Figure 2 by no temporal coordinations between anaesthesia or surgical tracks and the hospital administration track after the record is transferred. Block et al. (1998) report that once the omission was discovered, hospital administration personnel generally took an average of 30 minutes to locate the faculty supervisor for his or her signature.

4 Relating CWA Modelling Techniques

The immediately preceding example illustrates how the WDA and the AA/WD are linked. In the AA/WD, the fact that the Arkive narrows a time window for coordination increases the likelihood that an activity will not be completed. The AA/WD therefore shows the coordinative mechanisms that explain why fewer Arkive records are signed than manual records. Echoing this in the WDA, the Arkive introduces a constraint in completing a function, which contradicts the hospital's accounting processes and legal priorities. Therefore we have the start of a notation for describing and explaining the impact of technological change on organizations.

A broader CWA-based analysis would use control task analysis (see Table 1) to identify the inputs and outputs needed for functions to be carried out, and to show how new technology might affect these processes. For example, identifying the need for a faculty supervisor signature on anaesthesia records for billing to take place might alert the analyst to conditions that could compromise the collection of that signature. In addition, a broader CWA-based analysis would more fully specify the functions and role allocations (see Table 1) of the various stakeholders in different parts of the hospital who must coordinate. This would make it easier to assess the effects of technological change on them. For example, if administrative personnel must chase up a faculty supervisor signature, how much will this necessarily disrupt the administrator's own functions and ability to coordinate further within the hospital?

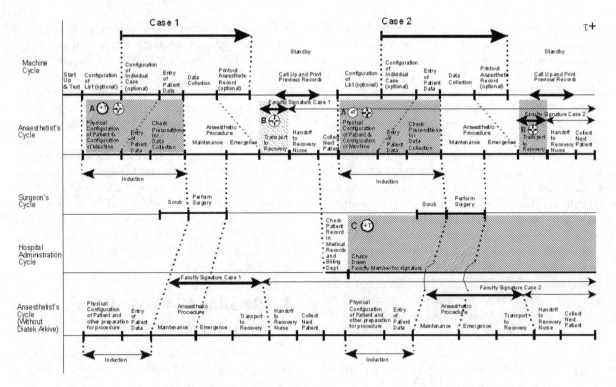

Figure 2: Activity analysis in WorkDomain Terms (AA/WD).

5   Implications for Prediction

How might the CWA-based representational system developed in this paper help analysts predict the impact of technological change? What are the lessons emerging as we develop our analytic framework and notation?

- Particular attention must be paid in understanding what prediction, reliability, and validity mean for CWA, and formative models in general. For instance, it may be more reasonable to think of prediction to indicate that a range of activities may be no longer afforded in a given work domain. Following on with this interpretation, in the Diatek Arkive case it may have been reasonably possible to predict the temporal coordination difficulties as the degrees of freedom for action became narrower with respect to the 'temporal window of activity'. The notions of prediction, reliability, and validity within CWA need to be further explored.

- A WDA that explicitly connects items between levels will show the relations that already exist in the work domain. The analyst can then run a 'what if' procedure, based on the introduction of a new technology. Which

existing relations (shown by links) might be improved, compromised or altered? Where might new relations emerge? In other words, the WDA can provide a structured framework for surveying many possible impacts. Currently, Skilton and colleagues are working on the Work Domain Analysis Workbench (Skilton et al., 1998), a software tool which may provide the necessary support for analysis of technological impacts.

- It will probably help to work on successive cases in a given domain (such as anaesthesia). This would allow generalised templates to be developed that could be adjusted to accommodate particular cases. In this way, a complete CWA would not have to be developed *ab initio* for each new case study.

- In the Block et al. (1998) case and in our current work with university timetabling, it is clear that the exact impact of technological change depends a lot on the priorities and values of individual stakeholders. If resentment of technological change turns into resistance (active or passive) the strength of its impact depends upon whether the stakeholder's resistance jeopardises their ability to function in other ways, and upon personality and interpersonal factors. These will require great care to model.

Finally, these modelling tools must be further developed and used in an empirical setting. A field study examining the impact of technological change at a university's timetabling office is currently being pursued.

Acknowledgements

The authors acknowledge the access and technical background provided by anaesthesia and perioperative staff at Carle Foundation Hospital, Urbana, IL, USA, and at Royal Children's Hospital, Melbourne, Australia. Special thanks are due to Dr.F.E. Block for providing further information about his study of the Diatek Arkive system at Ohio State University hospital.

References

Benda, P. J. & Sanderson, P. M. (1998), Towards a Dynamical Model of Adaptation to Technological Change, *in* P. Calder & B. Thomas (eds.), *Proceedings of OzCHI'98 The Eighth Australian Conference on Computer–Human Interaction*, IEEE Computer Society Press, pp.244–51.

Block, F. E., Reynolds, K. M. & McDonald, J. S. (1998), "The Diatek Arkive 'Organizer' Patient Information Management System: Experience at a University Hospital", *Journal of Clinical Monitoring and Computing* **14**, 89–94.

Fitzpatrick, G. A. (1998), The Locales Framework: Understanding and Designing for Cooperative Work, PhD thesis, University of Queensland.

Rasmussen, J., Pejtersen, A. M. & Goodstein, L. P. (1994), *Cognitive Systems Engineering*, John Wiley & Sons.

Sanderson, P. M. (1998), Cognitive Work Analysis and the Analysis, Design, and Evaluation of Human–Computer Interactive Systems, *in* P. Calder & B. Thomas (eds.), *Proceedings of OzCHI'98 The Eighth Australian Conference on Computer–Human Interaction*, IEEE Computer Society Press, pp.220–27.

Seagull, F. J. & Sanderson, P. M. (1998), Anesthesia Alarms in Surgical Context, *in Proceedings of the Human Factors and Ergonomics Society's 42nd Annual Meeting*, pp.1048–52.

Skilton, W., Cameron, S. & Sanderson, P. M. (1998), Suporting Cognitive Work Analysis with the Work Domain Analysis Workbench, *in* P. Calder & B. Thomas (eds.), *Proceedings of OzCHI'98 The Eighth Australian Conference on Computer–Human Interaction*, IEEE Computer Society Press, pp.260–7.

Vicente, K. J. (1999), *Cognitive Work Analysis: Towards Safe, Productive, and Healthy Computer-based Work*, Lawrence Erlbaum Associates.

Watson, M. & Sanderson, P. M. (1998), Work Domain Analysis for the Evaluation of Human Interaction with Anaesthesis Alarm Systems, *in* P. Calder & B. Thomas (eds.), *Proceedings of OzCHI'98 The Eighth Australian Conference on Computer–Human Interaction*, IEEE Computer Society Press, pp.228–35.

Human–Computer Interaction — INTERACT '99
M. Angela Sasse and Chris Johnson (Editors)
Published by IOS Press, © IFIP TC.13, 1999

Using Contextual Information Effectively in Design

Steven Clarke[1] & Gilbert Cockton[2]

[1] 37 Caird Drive, Partick, Glasgow G11 5DX, UK.
[2] University of Sunderland, PO Box 299, Sunderland SR6 0YN, UK.

steven_clarke@hotmail.com, Gilbert.Cockton@sunderland.ac.uk

Abstract: We describe the evolution of a tool that supports management of the collection and use of contextual information during and after design. The tool supports explicit links between documents on the context of use and design specifications. These direct links remove the need for intervening constructs such as consolidated context models, requirements documents or user–system task models, although all can still be accommodated. We argue that explicit direct use of contextual documents supports more effective use of contextual research, resulting in a product that can demonstrably fit its expected context of use. Experiences with the tool are presented, along with rationales for its evolving and outstanding requirements.

Keywords: UI design environments, software engineering, contextual Design, design rationale.

1 Introduction

To truly understand customer requirements and needs, designers must understand the context in which customers work. Contextual data collection techniques have been developed to gain understanding of both the implicit and explicit aspects of work. Such techniques collect data while potential users carry out their normal work.

Most techniques typically collect large amounts of data. Many contextual factors can affect how users will interact with a product. These can range from the straightforward, such as lighting and noise, to the intangible, such as organizational culture and policies. The major problem is to *ground* an appropriate design in all relevant data. The challenge is to identify relevant data and to use it effectively.

The relationships between contextual research and design decisions are still not fully understood. The most comprehensive current method, Contextual Design (Beyer & Holtzblatt, 1998) provides consolidation and integration techniques for moving from contextual research to design decisions. However, its *Visioning* and *User Environment Design* rely extensively on the design team's memory for *effective and efficient use* of contextual research. They also restrain the strategies that designers may use to ground a design in its context.

We have adopted a very simple approach to improving our understanding of the relationship between context and design. Our approach contrasts with the desires of some researchers for a single overarching integrated model of context (or even more boldly, a single integrated model of context *and the technology*). We endorse consolidation as practised within Contextual Design. Each facet of context should speak for itself in its own voice rather than be attenuated and anonymised in one vast chorus. The comfort offered by a single bounded model that integrates everything is illusory.

A single integrated model would not result in a better understanding of expected contexts of use. Rather, it would *systematically damage separate understandings* of stakeholder capabilities and values, physical space, cognitive activity, organizational structure, work structures and artefact affordances that come from separate models.

Secondly, such a model would be *highly inefficient*, as it would require constant updating as a result of both changes to the actual context as well as shifts in knowledge and scope of the relevant expected context of use.

We have therefore developed a design philosophy that integrates contextual data *via the design*. This is key to our *Grounded Design* approach, requiring:

- Explicit representations of aspects of the expected context of use (e.g. edited video, scenarios, work models of Contextual Design).

- Explicit representations of facets of a design (e.g. screen mock-ups, storyboards, functional models, dialogue models, system-task models).

- Explicit links between aspects of the expected context of use and facets of the design.

The creation and management of all these links and representations will clearly place a burden on designers. We have addressed this via a tool-based approach. We built on Literate Specification (Johnson, 1996), which associates formal specifications with Design Rationales, which in turn was inspired by Literate Programming (Knuth, 1984), which interweaves program code and its refinement.

We developed Literate Specification into *Literate Development*, which potentially inter-links *all* development documents — for more details see (Cockton, 1998). This can increase the traceability of contextual data, and thereby make that data more effective. Links can represent a range of relationships, yielding a clear picture of how contextual data has influenced design. Although there are superficial similarities to hypertext requirements tracing tools — e.g. (Kaindl, 1996) — Literate Development is *not* a requirements tracing approach. Links in Literate Development are currently unrestrained. Some can be based on argumentation, others on trivial imports of objects from the context into a design.

The key point is that we were motivated by uncertainty. We thus adopted a very simple approach, without the constraints of requirements specification or unproven meta-models of context and technology. We see exploration via direct linking tools as a route to a better understanding of the role (if any) of composite models in mediation between context research and design. We thus report experiences with a tool and the insights that its use provided. We offer no definitive position on the relationship between context and design, only some requirements for tools to build an objective corpus of realistic grounded designs.

2 Initial Explorations

We gave initial priority to viable research methods, and later sought access to less controllable industrial development projects. The latter proved to be difficult — there were no locally available design groups and re-organization lost one European prospect. We finally gained access to a US industrial setting, but had to focus on one part of the Literate Development problem — see (Clarke, 1997).

We began with an in-house development project where we tried to track how contextual data influenced

design decisions, and thus expose tool requirements. We used Contextual Design (then *Contextual Inquiry*) techniques to develop a program to track applications for a MSc course at the University of Glasgow. Over a period of six months we collected contextual data from various stakeholders and used this to design and build a new administrative support tool. By designing the application ourselves, we could control the recording of contextual data and the specification and evolution of the proposed design.

We wrote linking notes on context and design documents. The difficulties we experienced were used to form an initial set of requirements for a Literate Development Tool, for example:

- Tools should support multiple views of the design and its context of use.

- Relationships between documents should be separated from the documents themselves.

The second requirement arose because, while building the MSc application system, relationship details were distributed across different documents. We had no central representation, so while it was easier to see the relationships for a particular document by simply reading its set of annotated relationships, it was much harder to examine the bigger picture of how all the relationships combined.

2.1 Literate Development Version 1

The first version of the tool was built using Smalltalk and VisualWorks 1.0. Initial versions were used simply as a means to explore the potential benefits of recording the use of contextual data, and to note any issues that arose. We supported the notations that we generally used, i.e. scenarios, a contextual checklist (Clarke, 1997), UAN (Hartson et al., 1990), NUF (Cockton et al., 1996)), and QOC (MacLean et al., 1991). We abandoned Contextual Inquiry work models, as this method was still maturing. We thus added data from such original models to the contextual checklist.

Each adopted notation has a specific role in design. UAN describes interaction sequences. NUF describes conceptual (or application) models. These express concepts that users should understand to be competent with a system. For example, a NUF model for a word processor could describe objects such as documents, paragraphs and words. Both UAN and NUF are used prior to implementation, but specify different views of a system.

Scenarios and checklists capture aspects of the envisaged context of use. We used *envisionment* scenarios to embed design features into narratives of existing work.   Along with QOC, these scenarios partially integrate technology into context. Like the contextual checklist, scenarios preserved some data from earlier Contextual Inquiry work models.

QOC records questions faced by designers and associates them with alternative options and the criteria used to choose the adopted option. It thus bridges between typically unstructured insights about context (criteria) and broad design policies (options).

Each notation can be inter-linked in different ways, e.g. an option in a QOC diagram can be linked to an interaction sequence in UAN. Also, its criteria may be linked to contextual data. However, QOC alone cannot link recorded context to a fully specified design. QOC options constrain or direct design, but do not describe it in the same detail as UAN and NUF. Not all QOC criteria are contextual, nor do (or need) they combine to cover all aspects of recorded context.   Recent analysis has revealed that many links between context and design need not involve intermediate design rationales (Cockton, 1998).

The Literate Development tool (LD) thus let designs be embedded in envisionment scenarios, described using UAN and NUF specifications and rationalised using QOC rationales.   All can be grounded into a contextual checklist (an organizer for raw contextual data, an alternative/complement to the affinity diagrams used in Contextual Design). For the remainder of the paper, we refer to all these specifications, rationales, scenarios and data as development *documents*.

Figure 1 shows LD's main window.   New documents are named and added to the 'From' and 'To' lists at the top.   The names of the currently selected components in each selected document are shown in the text boxes below the two upper lists. Links are always formed between these current components (for example, a piece of contextual data or an option in a QOC rationale). On selecting the Relationship option (Create menu), the relationship is named and given explanatory text. The name of the relationship then appears in the 'Links' list (main window, bottom left). The explanatory text for the current link is displayed.

Each relationship thus has a name, a source (component in 'From' document), destination (component in 'To' document) and some explanatory text. By using free text, we could explore the nature of links without formal constraints. The link in Figure 1 relates a design decision about functionality (in NUF) to its rationale (in QOC), which in turn could be linked to a scenario or some contextual data.

The relationship editor became LD's main window. To preserve the ability to view relationships for a single document, we provided a filtering feature (Show menu) that only listed links involving the currently selected 'From' document. Note that the only way to see all relationships at a glance is to scan the link list. A graph showing the overall link structure could have been more useful, but we delayed development of visualizations until after the initial case studies. This turned out to be wise, since we uncovered a significant requirement for linking that would have invalidated a simple graph visualization.

Each document is edited and prepared for linking within a separate window. For example, Figure 2 shows a QOC rationale.   At the top, from left to right, three separate list boxes list individual questions and their associated options and criteria. Up to four selections in any order will create a relationship, for example, from a question in the QOC rationale to, say, an item of contextual information. If no current selection is valid, the four selections comprise two documents in the 'From' and 'To' lists and a component each in the QOC and checklist documents. The relationship would then be created (Create menu) and completed by adding a name and explanatory text. This task implementation is admittedly somewhat complex, but this was our first exploratory prototype. We would only use it ourselves to explore further requirements.

3   Improving LD Version 1

We evaluated LD formatively (to identify potential improvements) and summatively (to identify real benefits of use). We used LD ourselves, since it was at an early stage of development.

In one study, we 'retrofitted' the documents and relationships we had used in the MSc applications project, simply to test out how easily relationships could be created. In a second study, we reconstructed our own experiences in designing the tool and recorded these using LD (Figure 1 shows a link from this study). In the third exercise, we reverse engineered an existing system from research papers — see (Gould et al., 1987). Figure 2 shows a QOC from this study. Using LD highlighted several novel issues, which are now discussed.

3.1   What to Link To?

LD initially only allowed links between individual document components — for example, between one option in a QOC rationale and one item in the contextual checklist.   It became clear during the first case study that it would be more useful to

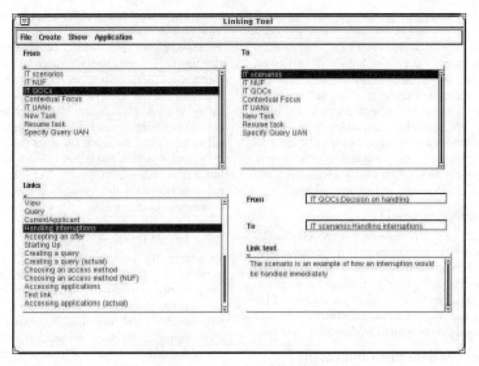

Figure 1: LD's Relationship Editor.

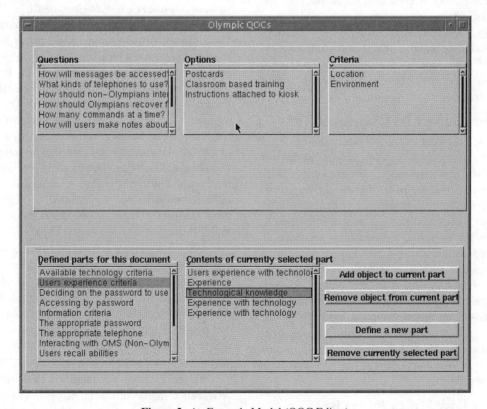

Figure 2: An Example Model (QOC Editor).

link between homogeneous groups of, say, QOC options, NUF objects, UAN table cells or items of context. For example, contextual factors often combine to have a pervasive influence on design. In an organization, staff turnover and attitudes to (and experience with) computers may combine to influence system design and training provision. Initially in LD, multiple relationships were needed to model relationships between factor groups. This was ineffective and time consuming. Supporting relationships between collections of elements would more accurately represent actual relationships.

3.2   What's Not Used?

During each study, relationships were continually formed between documents.   As relationships increased, it was hard to track which contextual information had been used. A simple means was needed to identify data that hadn't yet influenced the design, so that we could assess whether this data should be used or was actually irrelevant.

3.3   Are Relationships Duplicated?

While assessing the number of relationships we were adding between documents, we became concerned with duplicates. As a result of the link list and free text representations, it was too easy to add a new relationship that was identical to an existing one. This leads to inaccurate understandings of the influence on a design of some aspects of contextual data. It also increases the maintenance burden, and introduces risks of inconsistency.

3.4   What Impact Do Changes Have?

During   development,   our   understanding   and knowledge of the context of use changed, as did our design for the new application. When changes were made to documents, we had to assess the impact of a change on related documents. For example, after a change to a context document, it was important to be able to not only find relationships immediately involving contextual data but also important paths of relationships through various models. For example, if item of context A is related to QOC option B which in turn is related to NUF object C, then A (the item of context) has an indirect relationship with C (the NUF object). To assess the impact of a change to A, we needed to be able to find all of the relationships in which contextual component A was involved, both directly and indirectly.

3.5   How Easy Must Linking Be?

His PhD research sufficiently motivated the first author to add relationships to LD. Clearly, industrial practitioners would have different motivations. Work with Design Rationale (DR) — e.g. (Shum et al., 1993) — indicates that its successful use needs careful planning and management, otherwise DRs become burdensome. LD's advantages relative to DR were not clear cut, but DR research exposed problems that we had to address. LD can save effort over DR. *Adopted* design options and contextual criteria are expressed in other documents, reducing DR costs (and vagueness) by replacing option and criteria details with links to full details. Also, LD supports decisions needing no rationale beyond a link between context and design documents (Cockton, 1998).

3.6   LD Version 2

To address the grouping problem (3.1 above), we decided to implement the notion of a 'bag' of components. Documents can have many bags. Each bag contains document components (e.g. UAN cells, NUF objects, QOC questions, options or criteria). Bags cannot contain components from more than one document.   Figure 3 contrasts relationships between individual components (Figure 3a) with ones between bags (Figure 3b).   Boxes containing circles represent context documents. Boxes containing squares represent design documents.   Figure 3a shows relationships between individual components. Lines drawn between circles and squares represent a relationship between individual entities in the different models.   Between the two leftmost boxes are four lines, representing four different relationships.   In Figure 3b, a grouping construct is used. The rectangle represents a 'bag'.   Lines from circles or squares (representing individual components in the context or design documents) indicate that a component is contained within a bag. There is only one line between the bags.   Thus, this makes it clearer that the four different relationships represented in Figure 3a are more accurately seen as one relationship involving multiple document components (Figure 3b).

We implemented a 'bag' in LD as a simple list box. Users select components and add them one by one to bag). Had we developed a link visualization in LD version 1, we would have had to radically revise this to have bags rather than document components as end points of arcs in the graph. Given this, we further delayed visualization development until evaluation of version 2 by user testing. This again proved to be wise.

Figure 2 shows the modified QOC editor (bags were called 'parts' in Clarke & Cockton (1998). The pane at the bottom of the window is used to create and maintain bags. This pane did not exist in LD version 1. Each document editor now has an identical

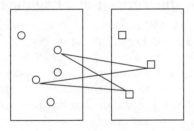

(a) Linking between atomic entities.

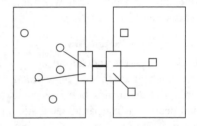

(b) Linking between groups of entities.

Figure 3: Relating between individual entities and collections of entities.

bag manager pane. The list box on the left contains named bags, while the right list shows components in the currently selected bag. The four buttons at the extreme right edit bag contents and the bag list.

Relationships in LD version 2 are created between selected bags in two document editors (the two currently selected bags are now displayed in the relationship editor). For relationships between individual components, these must first be put in bags. This is a significant capability that supports far more complex relationships than we had originally envisaged. Other tools could benefit from such an approach — e.g. Vista (Brown et al., 1998).

Further modifications to LD addressed unused context (3.2 above) and potentially duplicated links (3.3 above). Simple features were added to list all elements of context with no role in any relationship and the ability to look for possible duplicate links.

To address change updates (3.4 above) we added the feature that created a separate window that presented all paths that traverse from a component.

We did not address the potential problem of high link costs (3.5 above), since we did not have full access to a real development project where realistic effort limits could be established. We have however identified ways to ease creation. LD's multi-step relationship creation could be replaced by 'drag and drop' of bags between documents. Automated creation of some relationships and re-use of others is also possible. Developers could define a common set of context relationships for re-use in similar projects. They would only have to address novel relationships.

4 Evaluating LD Version 2.0

After improving LD on the basis of our own experience, we were keen to see how other developers would use it. Lack of access to cooperative

development teams forced us to perform three laboratory based evaluations (Clarke, 1997)). In the last, we recreated a typical design situation (react to a change in the context). Its results follow.

As changes in an expected context of use occur (or are anticipated), a maintenance team must plan a response. We hypothesized that this would be eased if the maintenance team had access to the contextual information that had influenced the design, together with indications of how it had been used.

Five participants were recruited. Each had at least one year's software design experience and exposure to HCI practices. Four were PhD students in a department of Computing Science and one was a software engineer working in industry.

We presented each participant with LD version 2, preloaded with design and context for a hypothetical system. Participants were shown how to use LD and were then told of a particular change to the context: users' experience and attitudes to technology had improved. Participants were to use LD to form a design response to accommodate the context change.

We were particularly interested in what participants would do when planning how to react to the change in context. We wanted to see if they would use links to help identify the impact of the change to context and if so, how easy participants felt it was to work with the relationships.

Each participant carried out the exercise individually, with the first author providing technical assistance in using the tool. Participants were encouraged to think-aloud as they carried out the exercise and to provide feedback on LD. A brief discussion followed each exercise. A log of all actions within LD by the participant was recorded. The main aim of the evaluation was to elicit feedback from participants about using relationships. Several interesting issues arose, which are now summarised — for more details, see (Clarke, 1997).

4.1   Inspecting Relationships

Grounded Design is readily understood as a design philosophy. Each participant understood the concept of explicit relationships between contextual information and design. Most participants attempted to use the relationships to understand how the design had been influenced by contextual data. Indeed, none assumed anything about how the context had been used. Some formed expectations, but used the relationships to test them. Relationships' names and explanatory text guided comprehension. Mostly, participants successfully determined how the design had been influenced by contextual information. Difficulties only arose when participants struggled to understand explanatory text. However, all participants bar the last created more new relationships, rather than studying existing relationships and changing them. This 'quick fix' approach would cause later maintainance problems. Future work should promote editing existing relationships over creating new ones, if that is more appropriate. Detection of duplicate links may have to be more system-driven (see Figure 2 link text).

4.2   Representations

All participants suggested that the representation of relationships could be improved They expected to be able to access relationships from each document, rather than from a separate central area. Furthermore, the bag construct as implemented complicated interpretation of relationships. This was in part due to poor naming ('part' rather than 'bag'), but the concept does require more motivation. While the naïve 1:1 view of Grounded Design is easy to appreciate, the actual m: n links that are really needed are more subtle. Indeed, one has to build such links oneself before the concept can be readily assimilated.

4.3   Using Relationships

Despite knowingly poor representations, participants could articulate benefits for Grounded Design. Explicit links were seen to be worthwhile. Two participants said that the relationships could be useful in maintaining a system, although one participant suggested that creating the links would be annoying, adding to the workload and hence perhaps demotivating designers. However, the real constraints of industrial practice have yet to be established. The cost of adding links may be less than the cost of searching for elusive data or arguing endlessly later about the grounding of a design!

4.4   Interpreting and Exposing Context

By making context explicit, participants were encouraged to think about the potential relevance of different contextual elements. Participants discussed what each element of context meant. Some found names in the contextual checklist ambiguous, and used idiosyncratic definitions. In a group situation, it is likely that discussion would develop consensus. However, the usability and learnability of individual documents and editors is clearly a key success factor.

4.5   Summary

The evaluations suggested that explicit relationships between context and design are worthwhile, but that representations needed improvement. Participants could use relationships to understand how the design had developed from the contextual data. Thus the relationships provided useful 'foot prints' of steps from contextual research to a design (and steps could be automatically combined into paths). Participants tended to associate relationships with documents, rather than separate, as was originally implemented. Here again, it would have been premature to design a link visualization without this knowledge.

It became clear that a composite link visualization needs to support a range of activities beyond design review and audits. Activities such as building comprehension, navigating the document space and revising links all place separate demands on a visualization. We feel vindicated in our minimalist approach to prototyping, which exposed many novel requirements without the expense of producing a 'professional' tool with impressive visualizations.

5   Conclusions and Further Work

Managing and using contextual information in design is difficult. One promising improvement is to support explicit relationships between context and design. By so doing, developers can more accurately determine how the design has been influenced by the context. Developers can use this information to improve a system's fit to its expected context of use.

Due to the potentially large number of relationships involved we argue that a computer-based tool is necessary to support the efficient creation and maintenance of relationships. We described such a tool and demonstrated its use, both by ourselves in informal case studies, and by others in a hypothetical design scenario. We have shown, through the evaluation, that explicit relationships between context and design offer certain advantages:

- Relationships are 'foot prints' of grounding steps, which compose into paths and promote understanding of how context has been used.

- Links let the full impact of a change to context be assessed. Explicit 'paths' ease assessment of direct and indirect relationships from the recorded context to design.

Developers can exploit these benefits to improve fit to context, as long as they respond responsibly and imaginatively to the information presented.

Access to (and representation of) bags requires more work. This should benefit developers of tools that support explicit links between development models — e.g. (Brown et al., 1998). We have experimented with paper prototypes of network visualizations of inter-model links, using line-width to indicate link density (Cockton, 1998).

Links need to be separate yet integrated within design and context models. Separation allows global assessment of the *groundedness* of a design (once the 'bag' metaphor is improved!) Integration allows local exploration of detailed design decisions, emphasising navigation rather than visualization.

The research reported here has allowed co-development of a design philosophy, *Grounded Design*, and an engineering approach, *Literate Development*. This co-development has tied the design philosophy to real case studies and the engineering approach has gained an underlying theoretical motivation. The approach continues to be productive, and has readily absorbed parallel work on usability engineering, offering further opportunities to directly ground designs in evaluations as well as contextual research (and evaluation plans in the latter). We feel we are on the brink of a new paradigm in HCI that effectively integrates the activities of contextual research, grounded design and usability evaluation.

References

Beyer, H. & Holtzblatt, K. (1998), *Contextual Design: Defining Customer-centered Systems*, Morgan-Kaufmann.

Brown, J., Graham, T. C. N. & Wright, T. (1998), The Vista Enviroment for the Co-evolutionary Design of User Interfaces, *in* C.-M. Karat, A. Lund, J. Coutaz & J. Karat (eds.), *Proceedings of CHI'98: Human Factors in Computing Systems*, ACM Press, pp.376–83.

Clarke, S. (1997), Encourage the Effective use of Contextual Information in Design, PhD thesis, Department of Computer Science, University of Glasgow.

Clarke, S. & Cockton, G. (1998), Linking Between Multiple Points in Design Documents, *in* C.-M. Karat, A. Lund, J. Coutaz & J. Karat (eds.), *Proceedings of CHI'98: Human Factors in Computing Systems*, ACM Press, pp.223–4.

Cockton, G. (1998), Let's Get It All Together: Literate Development and the Integration of HCI Research, *in* J. Konstan & J. Siegel (eds.), *Proceedings of CHI'98 Basic Research Symposium*. http://osiris.sund.ac.uk/ cs0gco/brs_full.htm.

Cockton, G., Clarke, S., Gray, P. & Johnson, C. (1996), Literate Development: Weaving Human Context into Design Specifications, *in* D. R. Benyon & P. Palanque (eds.), *Critical Issues in User Interface Systems Engineering*, Springer-Verlag, pp.227–48.

Gould, J. D., Boies, S. J., Levy, S., Richards, J. T. & Schoonard, J. (1987), "The 1984 Olympic Message System: A Test of Behavioral Principles of System Design", *Communications of the ACM* **30**(9), 758–69.

Hartson, H., Siochi, A. & Hix, D. (1990), "The UAN: A User-oriented Representation for Direct Manipulation Interface Designs", *ACM Transactions on Office Information Systems* **8**(3), 181–203.

Johnson, C. (1996), "Literate Specification: Using Design Rationale to Support Formal Methods in the Development of Human–Computer Interfaces", *Human–Computer Interaction* **11**(4), 291–320.

Kaindl, H. (1996), "Using Hypertext for Semiformal Representation in Requirements Engineering Practice", *The New Review of Hypermedia and Multimedia* **2**, 149–73.

Knuth, D. E. (1984), "Literate Programming", *The Computer Journal* **27**(2), 97–111.

MacLean, A., Young, R. M., Bellotti, V. M. E. & Moran, T. P. (1991), "Questions, Options and Criteria: Elements of Design Space Analysis", *Human–Computer Interaction* **6**(3-4), 201–50.

Shum, S., MacLean, A., Forder, J. & Hammond, N. (1993), Summarising the Evolution of Design Concepts Within a Design Framework, *in* S. Ashlund, K. Mullet, A. Henderson, E. Hollnagel & T. White (eds.), *Adjunct Proceedings of INTERCHI'93*, ACM Press/IOS Press, pp.43–4.

Human–Computer Interaction — INTERACT '99
M. Angela Sasse and Chris Johnson (Editors)
Published by IOS Press, © IFIP TC.13, 1999

Supporting Interaction Strategies Through the Externalization of Strategy Concepts

Aston Cockayne, Peter C. Wright & Bob Fields

HCI Group, Department of Computer Science, University of York, York YO10 5DD, UK.

peter.wright@cs.york.ac.uk

Abstract: Recent studies have argued that direct manipulation interfaces do not always promote the most effective problem solving. The paper reports on an experiment that demonstrates how changing the external representation of a problem affects the interaction strategies that users adopt. We show that by consideration of the strategic concepts that underlie a problem, it is possible to externalize key features that afford the use of the most effective strategy. This leads to deeper learning and more effective problem solutions as assessed by the transfer of knowledge to new problems.

Keywords: external representation, problem solving, interaction strategy, direct manipulation.

1 Introduction

It is well known in problem solving research that the way in which a problem is represented can affect the ease with which a solution can be found. In Newell & Simon's (1972) seminal work on problem solving, this point was well made with a number of striking examples. More recently, Norman (1988) has argued that a successful solution to a problem requires the user to have an appropriate conceptual model of the underlying processes of that problem and that certain interface features might more readily afford the appropriate conceptual model. Norman's concern was for how the elements of the problem were externally represented, making the user's cognitive task more perceptual and less demanding. Newell & Simon's primary concern was with the mental representation of a problem. Both strands of research highlight the often subtle and complex relationship between externalized aspects of a problem and the user's representations of a means of solution (Lave, 1988).

Scaife & Rogers (1996) also argue that the way in which information is externally represented materially affects the ease with which users can solve problems. They use the term *computational off-loading* to refer to the way in which computations carried out by the user can be transformed into simpler cognitive tasks by judicious choice of external representation. Similarly, Zhang & Norman (1994) show how different externalizations of problem solving rules lead to different performance levels.

From an HCI perspective, recent papers by Golightly & Gilmore (1997) and Svendsen (1991), have reported that in some problem solving interfaces, design factors such as the directness of manipulation can encourage sub-optimal solution strategies. While these authors have highlighted the context-sensitive nature of observed interaction strategies they have not directly considered the role that interface representations have on such strategies.

In this paper we take as our starting point the work of Golightly & Gilmore but explore the affect that different interface representations can have on the development of user strategies. We then draw some conclusions about the process by which interfaces can be designed to support different interaction strategies.

2 The Study of Golightly & Gilmore

In the study of Golightly & Gilmore (1997), participants were asked to solve a computerised version of the 8-*puzzle*. In its standard form, the 8-puzzle comprises a square board of 9 spaces occupied by eight tiles numbered 1–8. At the start of puzzle solving the tiles can be in any of the nine positions on the board. The goal of the puzzle is to re-organize the tiles so that the numbers 1–8 are positioned consecutively, in a clockwise sequence around the outside of the board leaving the blank space in the centre (see Figure 1a goal state). In Golightly & Gilmore's study, two versions of the puzzle were used. In one version (the DM version), interaction occurred by clicking directly on the tiles of the puzzle (see Figure 1a). In the other version (the IM version), the users were required to click on a separate array of buttons (Figure 1b). In both cases only clicks on the buttons representing tiles adjacent to the space had an effect. A static diagram showing the required arrangement of pieces for the goal state was also provided in both conditions (the right hand 'Goal' square of Figures 1a & b).

The result obtained was that users of the IM interface required fewer moves to solve the problem than users of the DM interface. Furthermore, an analysis of the standard deviation of time taken for moves and a qualitative analysis of move patterns suggested that members of the IM group were following a different strategy from their DM counterparts. The IM users tended to plan ahead based on the current problem state, while the DM group acted in a short-term, opportunistic, 'trial and error' fashion within the confines of a fairly rigid structure of high level goals.

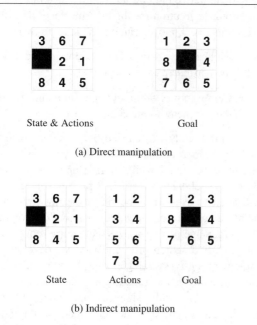

(a) Direct manipulation

(b) Indirect manipulation

Figure 1: Different interfaces for the 8 puzzle.

In Golightly & Gilmore's study, DM users tended to try to solve the 8-puzzle by a placement strategy. The placement strategy decomposes the problem into the sub-goals of getting the top row in place, then

one side, followed by the last corner. This strategy can lead subjects into difficulty since how to move the pieces to achieve the sub-goals is not clear. Indeed, Golightly & Gilmore report that within each of these sub-goals move choices were based on trial and error. An additional problem with the strategy is that once sub-goals have been achieved (such as a correct placement of the top row), these sometimes have to be undone when movements become more constrained. In contrast, Golightly & Gilmore report that the IM users' strategy was more plan-based and attempted to get the tiles in the right order before getting them in the correct place. Both for the IM and DM cases, Golightly &Gilmore's description of the strategy is rather vague, but the point remains, that large differences were observed and these did not always accord with the injunction that DM is better.

Golightly & Gilmore's findings raise the question as to what role the interface design decisions play in shaping the interaction strategies or styles that users adopt and by what means this shaping occurs. What is clear for the Golightly & Gilmore study is that it is not simply a matter of what information is available since both of the interfaces present exactly the same information. What is different is the physical location of the information in each interface. Consequently, Golightly & Gilmore's own explanation for the observed strategic differences is that when the point of action is separated from the point of consequence (as in the indirect interface), the user is forced to bridge the gap by constructing a more sophisticated cognitive representation of the problem state. This encourages a more plan-based style of interaction. Indirect manipulation, is not causing better understanding of the puzzle, it is forcing it.

In this paper we ask whether there aren't more fundamental factors which shape a user's choice of interaction strategy in this kind of problem domain. This raises the question of how we might support users in developing more effective strategies.

3   Strategies for Solving the 8-Puzzle

The traditional 8-puzzle interface used by Golightly & Gilmore has perceptual features and physical constraints that suggest a placement strategy. The square shape of the puzzle groups tiles into rows and columns and the empty space is perceptual marked only by the tiles adjacent to it. It might be argued that such a problem representation suggests or affords a strategy which decomposes the problem into sub-goals of rows and columns like the placement strategy described by Golightly & Gilmore. But there are alternative ways of representing the problem which lead to different solution strategies. One such concept we have developed views the 8- puzzle as a rotatable ring of pieces around a central space as in Figure 2. This conception suggests a strategy we refer to as the *ring ordering* strategy.

The ring ordering strategy works by getting pieces in the outer ring of the puzzle in order first and then rotating them into place. Pieces are put in order by moving them to the central space and rotating the outer ring until the tile in the centre space can be inserted in sequence (e.g. 2 between 1 and 3). Unlike the placement strategy, in the ring order strategy placement of tiles in sequence is monotonic. That is to say, once a sub-goal such as placing 2 between 1 and 3 has been achieved it does not need to be undone when movements become more constrained. Also unlike the placement strategy where the means of achieving sub-goals is unclear, the only sub-strategy needed in ring ordering is for centring pieces and rotating the ring until the tile is vertically or horizontally aligned with the central space.

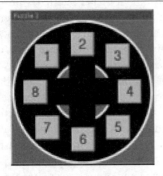

Figure 2: The roundabout interface.

The essential representational concept for the ring order strategy is the idea of tiles forming a moving ring around a fixed central space. We have externalized these concepts in an interface design we refer to as the roundabout interface (Figure 2). In contrast to the traditional layout (Figure 3), the central space is segregated visually by fixed features and the outer spaces are formed into a ring to afford continuous circular movement and to de-emphasise the row and column groupings central to the placement strategy.

4   A Pilot Study

Before we describe the main experiment of this paper, we report a pilot study carried out to explore measures of performance and strategy for the 8-puzzle.

4.1   Measures of Performance and Strategy

In the study of Golightly & Gilmore (1997) performance is assessed by measuring the number of moves and the time taken to complete a game. Time per move and move-time standard deviation is also measured. (In this paper we will not consider move-time standard deviation but see Cockayne (1998) for an analysis showing results consistent with the results presented in this paper). These measures can be used to calculate how much thinking time users take.

Figure 3: The standard interface.

Golightly & Gilmore identified users' strategies by subjective observation. In this paper we introduce a more quantitative method for identifying strategies. In any 8-puzzle solution for the two interfaces described in Figures 2 & 3, moves can be divided into two types:

- Ring moves — in which a tile is moved around the perimeter.

- Centre moves — in which a tile is moved from the perimeter to the centre or vice versa.

A pilot study was carried out — documented in the longer report on this study (Cockayne, 1998) — to determine the relationship of ring and centre moves to strategy choice. Trained 8-puzzle solvers were instructed to use either the ring ordering strategy or the placement strategy to solve a number of problems. The percentage of ring moves and centre moves were noted. An AI search program was also developed to implement the two strategies and the number of ring and centre moves recorded in a similar way.

The pilot study showed that when the ring ordering strategy is used the percentage of ring moves is reliably higher than when the placement strategy is used. Repeated trials in the pilot study allowed us to define criterion percentage of ring moves. A ring move percentage of over 66% indicates that a ring ordering strategy is being used. A ring move percentage of lower than 66% indicates the use of a placement strategy.

5 The Experiment

In this experiment we compare performance on the two interfaces presented in Figures 2 & 3. We argue that the differing interface representations afford different problem solving strategies. In particular, we argue that the standard 8-puzzle affords a placement strategy while the roundabout interface affords a ring ordering strategy. We hypothesize that users are more likely to develop a ring order strategy when using the roundabout interface. We will also explore whether this strategy leads to more effective problem solving.

5.1 Design and Procedure

A within subjects design was used (see Table 1). Subjects were MSc students at York University. Subjects were unfamiliar with the eight puzzle. Some recognized the puzzle in its traditional form but reported that they did not know how to solve it. Group A (comprising 9 users) solved 4 puzzles using the standard interface, and then went on to solve 4 puzzles using the roundabout interface. Group B (comprising 9 users) solved 4 puzzles using the roundabout interface first and then went on to standard interface. The starting states of the games for each group and for each interface in each group were the same. But within in each set of 4 problems the order of problems was varied. After both groups had solved 4 problems with each interface, they answered a questionnaire asking them to describe any strategies they had used.

Group A	4 × standard interface	4 × roundabout interface
Group B	4 × roundabout interface	4 × standard interface

Table 1: Experimental design.

5.2 Results

The percentage of ring moves for each problem type solved is presented in Table 2. Within-subjects ANOVA shows that overall there was a significant difference between the standard and roundabout interface ($F = 7.28, df = (17, 1), p \leq 0.05$) and this was more significant when only the first set of problems were compared using a between subjects ANOVA ($F = 17.54, df = (8, 1), p \leq 0.01$).

The 66% criterion identified in the pilot study can be used to determine the kind of strategy subjects were using to solve the various versions of the 8-puzzle. This reveals that users of the standard interface do not adopt the ring strategy unless the have had prior exposure to the roundabout interface.

In contrast, the roundabout interface affords a ring strategy irrespective of previous experience.

	First set	Second set
Group A stnd → rnd	61%	68%
Group B rnd → stnd	72%	70%

Table 2: Percentage of ring moves for each problem type solved by the two groups.

The graphs in Figures 4a & b illustrate the influence of individual problems on users' strategies. Figure 4a represents ring move percentage averages for group A for each game in the order the experiment was carried out. Figure 4b is the same for group B. The thick horizontal line represents the strategy criterion indicating use of the placement strategy for scores below the line and the ring ordering strategy for scores above the line.

The data suggest that subjects presented with the standard interface first (group A), start with the placement strategy and appear to move towards the ring strategy as their experience grows. However, they do not exceed the criterion until they are given the roundabout interface. In contrast, for group B who start with the roundabout interface, the percentage of ring moves is higher than the criterion on the very first puzzle. While there is a dip when the users move to the traditional interface, the percentage of ring moves is always above 70%.

The results suggest that not only does the roundabout interface afford a ring ordering strategy but that knowledge of this strategy can be transferred to the standard interface.

One possible weakness of the above interpretation is that improvements in the percentage of ring moves might reflect some other unidentified strategy or perhaps some non-specific improvement in performance. A questionnaire was completed by subjects to discover whether users were aware of using a particular strategy for solving the problems. Subjects were asked a general question about whether they had a strategy for solving each version of the puzzle. They were also asked specific questions to identify whether they were using the ring ordering strategy or the placement strategy. The results are presented in Table 3 and are consistent with interpretation based on the percentage of ring moves described above.

The results show how the roundabout interface supports the development of a ring strategy. Next, we determine whether the ring strategy leads to an improved performance in terms of the number of

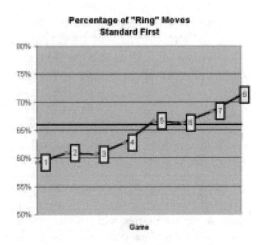

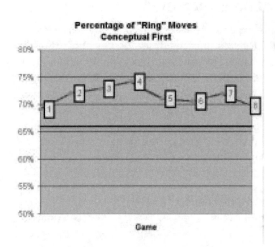

(a) Learning strategy over time. Group A, 1–4: Standard Interface 5–8: Roundabout Interface.

(b) Learning strategy over time. Group B, 1–4: Roundabout Interface 5–8: Standard Interface.

Figure 4:

moves taken to complete a puzzle, the time take to make a move and the overall time to complete a puzzle.

Questionnaire Section	Group A Standard First	Group B Roundabout First
I had a strategy for the square standard puzzle.	44%	78%
I had a strategy for the roundabout puzzle.	89%	78%
Ring ordering reported for standard puzzle.	22%	78%
Ring ordering reported for roundabout puzzle.	56%	78%

Table 3: Summary of questionnaire results.

Average number of moves per game, average total time per game and average time per move was measured in order to judge overall efficiency of problem solving for each version of the puzzle. It should be expected that average move times will be higher for the roundabout interface because it is supposed to be encouraging thoughtful problem solving. The corollary of these higher move times should be fewer moves per game. The test of overall efficacy will be, if the first two expectations are confirmed, whether the roundabout interface puzzles can be solved in the same (or indeed less) time as the standard interface puzzles.

The results for all games did indeed show a higher time per move for the roundabout interface. Subjects using this interface took an average time of 1.80 seconds per move. Subjects using the standard interface took an average of 1.48 seconds per move. ANOVA shows that this difference is statistically significant ($F = 16.85, df = (17, 1), p \leq 0.001$). The figures for average number of moves per game again confirm expectations. Users of the roundabout interface made an average of 88 moves per game whilst those using the standard interface made an average of 125 moves per game. ANOVA shows that this difference is also significant ($F = 6.68, df = (17, 1), p \leq 0.05$). So the longer move times with the roundabout interface are paying off with more direct solutions. Comparing the average times per game, the results show an average time of 158 seconds for the roundabout interface and 185 seconds for the standard interface. It appears that not only is the roundabout interface more efficient in moves but it is faster too. But ANOVA shows that this difference is not significant ($F = 1.07, df = (17, 1), p = 0.25$). However, what is clear is that the roundabout interface is not slower than the standard interface. This suggests that more efficient problem solving in terms of moves can be achieved without a loss of speed.

5.3   Discussion

Some recent work in the area of distributed cognition has argued that the kind of information that is externalized in an interface can effect the kind of strategy that a user adopts. Fields et al. (1997) for example, argue that changes in the externalized resources for action can impede certain kinds of interaction strategy. But they did not test this hypothesis empirically.

Golightly & Gilmore (1997), observed differences in the strategies for solving different versions of the 8-puzzle, but they manipulated the directness of manipulation rather than the quality or nature of the information presented. Their finding that indirect manipulation leads to a more effective planning strategy has been supported elsewhere (Svendsen, 1991; Golightly et al., 1996). The interpretation of these findings is that indirectness forces users to adapt internalised planning strategies as a consequence of the difficulty of making moves. An explanation that does not particularly commend indirect manipulation as an interaction style.

In this study we chose to seek a more supportive means of encouraging effective interaction strategies. We identified a very effective strategy similar to that alluded to in Golightly & Gilmore as planning. This we referred to as the ring strategy. By analysing the ring strategy we were able to identify several key concepts that could be externalized in an interface by careful design of the spatial features associated with the puzzle board.

Our hypothesis was that the features such as an isolated central square, and a circular arrangement of perimeter spaces would support user in discovering the ring strategy. On the other hand, the traditional board with its square layout supported users in discovering the less effective placement strategy associated with the indirect manipulation users in the Golightly & Gilmore study.

The experimental results support this hypothesis, showing a higher prevalence of ring ordering when using the roundabout interface. But what was surprising about the results was the degree of transfer of strategic knowledge gained on the roundabout problems to the solution of the traditional problems solved second. This suggests that while the perceptual features of the roundabout interface support the development of ring ordering, once internalised, ring ordering can be deployed in the absence of the external cues that support it. It would appear that the roundabout interface is fostering a deeper understanding of the underlying problem structure than the traditional interface.

6 Conclusions

One explanation of the fewer moves seen with the roundabout interface may be that the interface is fostering S-mode learning. S-mode learning, (Hayes & Broadbent, 1988) is characterised by insightful solutions to problems and an overall understanding of problem structure. It contrasts with U-mode learning which is characterised by trial and error and an inability to articulate overall problem solving strategy.

Previous studies of direct and indirect manipulation such as Golightly & Gilmore (1997) and Svendsen (1991) have shown that S-mode learning is fostered by indirect manipulation interfaces. The unfortunate problem with this research is that, although the conclusions of it are almost certainly correct, indirect manipulation always leads to slower (even if better) solutions. The results of this experiment suggest that the careful design of the external representation of the problem interface can foster S-mode learning whilst still implementing direct manipulation.

The distributed cognition literature (Zhang & Norman, 1994; Hutchins, 1995; Scaife & Rogers, 1996; Fields et al., 1997) has demonstrated how differences in the externalization of information resources can materially affect ease of use and ease of learning. At times it has been harder to see how to relate these findings to design decisions. By using the notion of interaction strategy and analysing strategies for their underlying concepts, this paper has shown how it is possible to design an interface to support effective interaction.

References

Cockayne, A. (1998), Implenting the Concept of Straegy in Human–Computer Interface Design: Resolving The Dilema of Manipulation Speed Verses Learning Quality, Master's thesis, Computer Science Department, University of York.

Fields, B., Wright, P. C. & Harrison, M. D. (1997), Objectives Strategies Resources as Design Drivers, *in* S. Howard, J. Hammond & G. K. Lindgaard (eds.), *Human–Computer Interaction — INTERACT '97: Proceedings of the Sixth IFIP Conference on Human–Computer Interaction*, Chapman & Hall, pp.164–71.

Golightly, D. & Gilmore, D. J. (1997), Breaking the Rules of Direct Manipulation, *in* S. Howard, J. Hammond & G. K. Lindgaard (eds.), *Human–Computer Interaction — INTERACT '97: Proceedings of the Sixth IFIP Conference on Human–Computer Interaction*, Chapman & Hall, pp.156–63.

Golightly, D., Gilmore, D. J. & Churchill, E. F. (1996), Puzzling Interfaces: the Relationship Between Manipulation and Problem Solving, *in* A. Blandford (ed.), *Adjunct Proceedings of HCI'96*.

Hayes, N. A. & Broadbent, D. E. (1988), "Two Models of Learning for Interface Tasks", *Cognition* **22**, 249–75.

Hutchins, E. (1995), "How a Cockpit Remembers its Speeds", *Cognitive Science* **19**, 265–88.

Lave, J. (1988), *Cognition in Practice: Mind Mathematics and Culture in Everyday Life*, Cambridge University Press.

Newell, A. & Simon, H. A. (1972), *Human Problem Solving*, Prentice–Hall.

Norman, D. A. (1988), *The Psychology of Everyday Things*, Basic Books.

Scaife, M. & Rogers, Y. (1996), "External Cognition: How do Graphical Representations Work?", *International Journal of Human–Computer Studies* **45**(2), 185–213.

Svendsen, G. B. (1991), "The Influence of Interface Style on Problem Solving", *International Journal of Man–Machine Studies* **35**(3), 379–97.

Zhang, J. & Norman, D. A. (1994), "Representations in Distribution Cognitive Tasks", *Cognitive Science* **18**, 87–122.

Human–Computer Interaction — INTERACT '99
M. Angela Sasse and Chris Johnson (Editors)
Published by IOS Press, © IFIP TC.13, 1999

Redundancy Effects in Instructional Multimedia Systems

Frank Vetere & Steve Howard

Swinburne Computer–Human Interaction Laboratory (SCHIL), School of Information Technology, Swinburne University of Technology, PO Box 218, Hawthorn, Victoria 3122, Australia.

{fvetere,showard}@swin.edu.au

Abstract: Redundancy is used when, for example, the same information is presented in both textual and graphical forms. Multimedia designers often employ redundancy to assist users in their interaction with multimedia systems. However, Cognitive Load Theory suggests that information with redundant material negatively impact our interaction with multimedia systems. It has been found that this phenomenon, known as the redundancy effect, is more prominent as learners' level of expertise increases. This paper addresses the tension between multimedia designers and Cognitive Load Theory. We conducted an experiment that aimed to replicate and extend earlier work that investigated the redundancy effect. Contrary to previous findings, our results showed no interaction between the level of redundancy in the instructional material and the level of expertise. Our results also showed little support for a redundancy effect that hinders performance. However, this experiment found some benefit in using between-channel redundancy (i.e. redundant material that exploits different sensory channels), but the benefit was observable only in certain tasks. These results should be seen as a caution against the simplistic views of redundancy currently provided in multimedia design guidelines.

Keywords: multimedia, redundancy, cognitive load theory, learning, instructional systems

1 The Supporters

Designing with the intentional use of redundant elements has been investigated in a number of design activities. These include the development of instructional material, e.g. (Najjar, 1996), the production of television and film, e.g. (Basil, 1994), and the design of the human–computer interface, e.g. (Edwards, 1992). Multimedia designers employ redundancy to assist users in their interaction with multimedia systems. Redundancy is used when, for example, the same information is presented in both textual and graphical forms, or as sound and text. In this context, redundancy is a neutral description of the information. It does not connote either positive or negative effects.

Many Human–Computer Interaction (HCI) researchers propose guidelines and design rules that recommend systems be engineered with redundancy in mind. For example, Vossen et al. (1997), in the 'Design Guide for Multimedia' produced by the European INUSE project, state that: "...the parallel presentation of the same information by means of different media supports and increases the information

perception" (p.16). One of Alty's (1996) design guidelines for multimedia systems is the 'Principle of Apparent Redundancy' in which he states "Human beings prefer redundancy of information" (p.48). In providing guidelines for multimedia interface design, Sutcliffe & Faraday (1993) lists general heuristics about media combination. One of these heuristics, "present the same material on two channels if available" (p.108), clearly advocates the use of redundancy.

Although the above design principles share much in their view of redundancy it is not always clear what redundancy actually means. Concerns are being expressed, e.g. (Johnson & Nemetz, 1998), but much of the literature is anecdotal, and typically, no formal theoretical justification is given for the advice contained in the guidelines.

In an attempt to disambiguate the concept, we will adopt a framework which distinguishes between 'within-channel' and 'between-channel' redundancy (Vetere, 1997). Within-channel redundancy occurs when a mix of related information pertaining to the same sensory channel is presented together, for example a mix of text and pictures from within the visual channel, e.g. (Sweller & Chandler, 1994). Between-channel redundancy refers to the mix of redundant elements drawn from different sensory channels, for example visual and auditory forms of the same information, e.g. (Mousavi et al., 1995). These types of redundancy are not intended to be exhaustive and can be combined in various ways. Consequently it is possible to have a design containing both within-channel and between-channel redundancy.

It is very likely that the type of redundancy being designed will contribute to the impact on the user–system interaction, and yet few researchers in the design literature draw these distinctions. We will build on this distinction below.

2   The Detractors

Whilst the HCI literature cited above redundancy as positively affecting people interacting with multimedia applications, the work of Sweller and colleagues suggests that redundancy may have negative impacts on user–system interaction. This work is interesting not just because the results are counter to much of the design literature, but also because it rests on an explicit psychological foundation called 'Cognitive Load Theory' (CLT).

Cognitive Load Theory (Sweller, 1994) adopts a limited-capacity information processing approach to learning. It assumes that information in long-term memory is stored as schemata and learning occurs through schema acquisition and automation. The greatest impediment to learning is the cognitive load on a limited working memory. Therefore, according to CLT, the primary task in designing for effective learning must be to minimise cognitive load on working memory.

The total cognitive load associated with learning depends, in part, on the information that needs to be learnt. CLT identifies two types of cognitive load associated with the information source; intrinsic and extraneous. The intrinsic cognitive load is due solely to the intrinsic nature (complexity) of the content, which cannot be modified by instructional design. The extraneous cognitive load is due to the presentation format and design of the instructional materials. It is possible, therefore, to manipulate this presentation format in order to minimise extraneous cognitive load on working memory thereby facilitating schema acquisition.

Cognitive Load Theory has been used to develop several instructional design heuristics. One of these is the 'redundancy effect'. The redundancy effect occurs when an information source, which

is self-contained and intelligible in its own right, is added to or integrated with another (redundant) information source. According to CLT, this combined presentation will increase cognitive load and harm performance. Eliminating redundant material results in better performance than when redundant material is included (Kalyuga et al., 1998; Sweller & Chandler, 1994; Yeung et al., 1997)

The redundancy effect has been explored with various combinations of information sources. These include: redundant text added to diagrams (Bobis et al., 1993; Kalyuga et al., 1998); redundant text added to text (Yeung et al., 1997); redundant paper-based software manual (with text and graphics) added to comprehensive computer based instructions (Cerpa et al., 1996); redundant computer based instructions added to comprehensive paper-based instructional manual (Chandler & Sweller, 1996; Sweller & Chandler, 1994). The results of each of these investigations suggest that the inclusion of the redundant material reduces performance due to the increase in cognitive load on working memory.

One study that has investigated the redundancy effect directly is Kalyuga et al. (1998). Three groups of first year electrical trade apprentices were instructed in the operation and function of an electric circuit. This instructional material was presented in three different formats; separate-text-and-diagram, integrated-text-and-diagram and diagram-only. The subjects were then given a questionnaire gauging the difficulty of the task, and then a series of tests measuring the subjects' understanding of the instructional material. After several months, the subjects were given intensive training in electric circuits in order to increase their level of expertise. The subjects then repeated the earlier instruction procedure (presented in three formats) and were tested again.

The results of the experiment showed that as the level of expertise increases, subjects perform better without redundant text. That is, when there is sufficient levels of user expertise, textual material is rendered redundant and instructions in the diagram-only format gives better performance.

The work reported in Kalyuga et al. (1998) is important because it investigated redundancy directly, its conclusions were contrary to the guidelines and heuristics advocated by the HCI literature and the result is a direct consequence of a psychological theory of learning. In addition, the study supports an understanding of redundancy that is not solely a property of the instructional material but one that also depends on user characteristics, in particular levels of domain expertise. It gives empirical support to the notion that the redundancy of an interface element is an emergent feature of the interaction between a human and the task artefact.

3 Experiment

Our experiment aimed to extend the work of Kalyuga et al. (1998). By replicating the experiment we hoped to observe the redundancy effect, measure variations due varying expertise and consequently help to establish clear principles for redundancy design in multimedia learning environments.

In this study we defined four types of formats with varying degrees of redundancy: diagram-only (DO), diagram-text (DT), diagram-speech (DS) and diagram-text-speech (DTS). According to the framework described previously, DO is non-redundant, DT has within-channel redundancy, DS has between-channel redundancy, and DTS has both within and between channel redundancy.

Every attempt was made to remain consistent with the original experiment, it was however extended in significant ways:

- The original experiment used paper-based instructions in the first stages and then moved to computer-based instructions in the later stages with expert users. We used only computer-based instruction. This was important for experimental consistency and is in line with aims to investigate redundancy in multimedia systems.

- The original study employed three presentation formats. The separate-text-and-diagram format was used to test the split attention effect (another CLT effect). Since we were only interested in investigating the redundancy effect, the separate-text-and-diagram format was not used. This study used four instructional formats instead of three.

- This study was conducted over a 90 minute session rather than over several months.

- The subjects in the original study did not use materials with varying of redundancy during training. In this study, participants remained in their experimental groups (DO, DT, DS, DTS) throughout the three phases (initial instruction, training, final instruction) of the experiment. We adopted this change because there was no reason to assume that redundancy would not affect interaction during training.

- Verbal protocols were collected during the interaction between the subjects and the materials by video taping each session. This was not done in the original experiment. This 'process' data allowed us to gain insight into the psychological processes involved in interacting with redundant interfaces.

- The original software was updated and modified to reflect these changes.

These changes do not alter the aims of the original study and should not in any way undermine those aims. The intent has been to strengthen the experimental design in order to obtain robust and reliable results.

3.1 Procedure

Forty subjects participated in this study. The participants were either first (90%) or second (10%) year TAFE (Technical and Further Education) students, enrolled in courses with major studies in electronics or electric circuits. Most of the participants aspired to be technical officers or to progress to a university degree. None were familiar with the particular circuits used in the experiment.

Participants were randomly allocated to one of four instructional format groups: diagram-only (DO), diagram-text (DT), diagram-speech (DS) and diagram-text-speech (DTS). Each group had ten participants and each participant remained in their format group throughout the experiment. All of the instructional and test material was computer based. All scores were electronically recorded. Each session was video taped and participants were encouraged to 'talk aloud'. The sessions lasted no more than 90 minutes and subjects were paid $10 for their participation.

All the instructional material concerned the operation and function of circuits that were based on the Starter circuit. The Starter circuit contained stop and start push buttons and a coil that triggered a switch that created a holding circuit for the current. The circuits were identical in all four experimental groups except for the inclusion or absence of explanatory text and speech. Although the materials were modest in size and complexity, they were representative of circuits used by our subject population during learning activities.

The instructional material used before and after training was presented in one of four formats. The DT format contained a static diagrammatic presentation with descriptive text (see Figure 1). The text was integrated with the diagram in a meaningful way and so avoided possible detrimental split-attention effects

(Sweller & Chandler, 1994). The DO format was identical to the DT format except for the absence of explanatory text. The DS format introduced speech and animation to the DO presentation. The number of explanatory phrases in DT was used to create a series of animations. The animation was a visual representation of the textual description. The animation was accompanied by speech that corresponded exactly to the text in the DT format. The DTS format was identical to the DS with the inclusion of the text. This text was identical to that used in the DT format and the position of the text, with respect to the diagram, was also identical to that in the DT format.

All subjects were given a brief introduction explaining the structure of the study. The study was composed of three stages: initial instruction, training, and final instruction. The initial instruction on the starter circuit (Figure 1) was presented in one of the four format types. After the instruction, subjects were asked to subjectively rate the mental effort associated with learning the instructional material by selecting a rating on a Likert-type scale from 1 (extremely easy) to 7 (extremely difficult). Subjects then began a test phase by completing a fault-finding test and a multiple-choice test. A faulty starter circuit was displayed. The fault-finding task involved clicking on the faulty elements within the one minute time limit. Subjects were told that a fault could be any one of an incorrectly labelled element, an incorrectly positioned element, a switch not in a initial state, or an incorrect connection between elements. Subjects were given one mark for every correct selection. Subjects were warned that marks would be deducted if they selected a non-faulty element or connection. The faulty diagram had five faults and three selectable non-faults. The time remaining on the task was displayed on the screen.

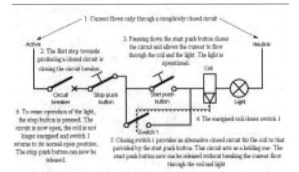

Figure 1: The Starter circuit used in the initial instruction (before training). The textual descriptions were only available for the DT and DTS presentations.

A series of four multiple-choice questions followed the fault-finding task. Subjects were given 30 seconds to select the correct answer for each question. The time remaining was displayed. The questions were presented one at a time and the answers to previous questions were displayed on the screen. Each correct answer was worth one mark.

Once the testing of the initial instruction was completed, the training stage commenced. This training aimed to build domain specific schema in the operation and function of three different circuits, the Bell & Light, the Motor and the Fan circuit. Each was an extension of the Starter circuit introduced in the initial stage. The format of these circuits was the same as that of the initial instructional stage. After each training circuit, subjects were required to complete a series of short exercises about the structure and operation of the circuit. There were no scores given for these exercises and no time limits. Subjects were given hints if they made more than two errors on a particular task.

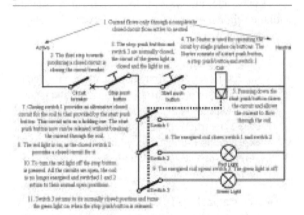

Figure 2: The Red/Green circuit used in the final instruction (after training). The textual descriptions were only available for the DT and DTS presentations.

The third stage of the experiment was very similar to the first. Instruction on the Red/Green circuit (Figure 2) was presented in one of four format types. Participants remained in the same group as the first and second stage. After the instruction, participants gave a subjective rating of difficulty and then completed the fault-finding and multiple-choice tasks. These tasks had the same structure as those during the initial phase. In the final phase the fault finding task had six faults and three selectable non-faults and the multiple-choice task had five questions.

We collected instruction times, test scores, response times on test questions, and subjective ratings of mental effort. Test scores and ratings of mental effort were used to derive cognitive efficiency (Paas

& Merrienboer, 1993). Cognitive efficiency — also known as 'relative condition efficiency' (Paas & Merrienboer, 1993) and 'instructional efficiency' (Kalyuga et al., 1998) — is a metric that combines measures of mental workload and task performance. The method uses a Cartesian plane with standardised performance scores (P) and standardised ratings of mental effort (R) as the axes. The line $P = R$ indicates zero efficiency. A point on this line (cognitive efficiency = 0) suggests a test score is exactly what might be expected given the mental effort invested by a subject. Points above this line (cognitive efficiency > 0) indicate high efficiency (i.e. good performance with little mental effort) and points below this (cognitive efficiency < 0) line indicate a low efficiency (i.e. poor performance with high mental effort). Cognitive efficiency is measured by the perpendicular distance from the score on the Cartesian plane to the line $P = R$ and is given by $E = (P - R)/\sqrt{2}$. Paas & Merriënboer argue that efficiency can help to maximise performance for complex tasks that are constrained by limited cognitive capacity, but also warn that it is only an approximation because it assumes a linear relationship between mental effort and performance.

In addition we conducted an analysis of the video data (principally the verbal protocols) with a view to better understanding the role of redundancy during the interaction. Only the subjective ratings, the test scores and efficiency measures are reported in this paper.

4 Results and Discussion

The initial (before training) and final (after training) means and standard deviations on each format for the five dependant variables (subjective rating, score on fault finding questions, efficiency of fault-finding task, score on multiple-choice questions, and efficiency of multiple-choice task) are shown in Table 1.

A series of 4 (instructional format) by 2 repeated measures (initial and final) ANOVAs were applied to the five variables. The results of this analysis are displayed in Table 2. These results show significant main effects for format on fault finding scores, $F(3, 36) = 2.994$ and for cognitive efficiency on the fault-finding task, $F(3, 36) = 3.413$. They also show significant main effects for training on both multiple choice scores $F(1, 36) = 4.249$ and on fault finding scores $F(1, 36) = 36.88$. There were no significant interaction effects for any of the dependant variables.

Newman-Keuls post-hoc tests were performed on the significant main format and training effects. Analysis of the training effects showed that both multiple-choice scores and fault-finding scores were significantly greater after training than before training, and that the subjective rating of difficulty was significantly less after training. Clearly the training was effective in improving test scores and in reducing the mental effort associated with learning the instructional material. The training did not improve the cognitive efficiency of either the multiple-choice task or the fault-finding tasks. This suggests that even though subjects achieved better scores, the training had no significant effect on the efficiency of the mental effort invested by the subject when completing the tasks.

Analysis of the format effects with Newman-Keuls tests showed that subjects learning with a DT format scored significantly less on the fault finding question than did the subjects learning with a DS format. There was no significant difference with any of the other format combinations. The cognitive efficiency on the fault-finding task was significantly less on the DT format than on the DS format and the DTS format. Even though the difference in efficiency between DT and DO was not significant ($p = 0.053$), the trend suggests that completing the fault-finding task with a DT format was less cognitively efficient (i.e. greater mental effort resulted in less performance effectiveness) than the other formats. So for the fault-finding task, the format with between-channel redundancy (DS) outperformed the format with within-channel redundancy (DT) on both test scores and cognitive efficiency. The least efficient format was the within-channel redundant format (DT).

There were no significant format effects on the multiple-choice task. So, the type of redundancy in the instructional material had no effect on the test scores or on the cognitive efficiency in completing the multiple-choice questions. This suggests the effect of redundancy is task dependent. The two tasks, fault-finding and multiple-choice can be characterised as either visual or verbal (Paivio, 1991). The fault-finding task, a visual activity, showed format effects for both test scores and efficiency. The multiple-choice task, a verbal activity, showed no format effect at all.

There were no significant interaction effects between format and training for any of the test scores or cognitive efficiencies. It is primarily these interaction effects which most concerns the relationship between redundancy and expertise. This result indicates that the effect of training is the same on all formats and the effect of format is independent of training, and therefore expertise (as it was defined in the original study). This is a surprising contradiction to Kalyuga's original results.

			DO		DT		DS		DTS		Total	
			mean	s.d	mean	s.d	mean	s.d	mean	s.d	mean	s.d
rating of difficulty (1–7)		initial	3.7	1.3	3.7	0.8	2.9	1.5	2.9	1.2	3.3	1.2
		final	2.6	1.0	3.4	0.7	2.9	1.2	2.5	0.7	2.9	1.0
		total	3.2	1.2	3.6	0.8	2.9	1.3	2.7	1.0	3.1	1.1
fault finding	score (%)	initial	55	32	40	11	63	30	53	17	53	25
		final	81	16	68	16	85	19	83	15	79	17
		total	68	28	54	20	74	27	68	22	66	25
	efficiency	initial	-0.16	1.28	-0.59	0.46	0.52	1.23	0.23	0.92	0	1.07
		final	0.25	1.14	-0.87	0.75	0.21	1.51	0.40	0.71	0	1.16
		total	0.05	1.20	-0.73	0.62	0.37	1.35	0.32	0.81	0	1.11
multiple choice	score (%)	initial	68	21	63	32	75	31	70	31	69	28
		final	74	23	82	20	74	28	86	21	79	23
		total	71	22	72	28	75	29	78	27	74	26
	efficiency	initial	-0.26	0.88	-0.39	0.86	0.39	1.46	0.26	0.96	0	1.08
		final	0.03	1.12	-0.32	0.83	-0.19	1.45	0.48	0.67	0	1.06
		total	-0.11	0.99	-0.35	0.82	0.10	1.44	0.37	0.81	0	1.06

Table 1: The initial (before training) and final (after training) means and standard deviations on each format. These measures are given for subjective rating of difficulty (1 – extremely easy … 7 – extremely difficult), and for test scores and cognitive efficiencies on fault-finding tasks and multiple choice tasks.

Dependant variable	main format effect		main training effect		interaction between format and training
	F statistic	post hoc multiple comparisons	F statistic	post hoc multiple comparisons	F statistic
rating of difficulty	$F(3,36) = 0.164$	not significant	$F(1,36) = 5.080$	INITIAL≫FINAL	$F(3,36) = 1.359$
score on fault-finding test	$F(3,36) = 2.994$	DT≪DS	$F(1,36) = 36.879$	INITIAL≪FINAL	$F(3,36) = 0.125$
cognitive efficiency on fault finding task	$F(3,36) = 3.413$	DT≪DS DT≪DTS	$F(1,36) < 0.001$	not significant	$F(3,36) = 0.839$
score on multiple choice test	$F(3,36) = 0.879$	not significant	$F(1,36) = 4.249$	INITIAL≪FINAL	$F(3,36) = 0.874$
cognitive efficiency on multiple choice task	$F(3,36) = 1.297$	not significant	$F(1,36) < 0.001$	not significant	$F(3,36) = 0.983$

Table 2: Results of repeated measures ANOVA for the five dependant variables showing the F statistic and post hoc multiple comparisons using Newman-Keuls test for the significant main effects. The 0.05 level of significance is used throughout. The symbol '≪' indicates 'significantly less than' and the symbol '≫' indicates 'significantly greater than'.

There may be several reasons for this inconsistency. It could be argued that the subjects did not achieve a sufficient level of expertise for the instructional materials to be rendered redundant. This is unlikely given the significant improvement in performance gained as a consequence of the training. However, this line of argument does allude to a problem in the experimental design. It is not clear what exactly is 'sufficient training' and how to know when it has been achieved. The redundancy effect:

> "hinges on the distinction between sources of information that are intelligible in isolation and those that are not"

(Kalyuga et al., 1998, p.2).

The mechanism for achieving this state of 'intelligible-in-isolation' is the training. Yet there is no method for determining when this state has been reached.

The inconsistent results may be attributable to the small differences in experimental procedures. The two experiments used participants from similar backgrounds (first year apprentices compared with TAFE students) and almost identical materials. The original study was conducted over several months while participants were attending their first year trade course, whereas this study was completed within

90 minutes. It is possible that the original results were a methodological artefact.

5 Conclusion

The results of this experiment did not support the finding by Kalyuga et al. (1998) that instructional material with redundant information becomes less effective as expertise increases. We found no interaction between redundancy of format and level of training. Nonetheless, one should not discount the importance of human knowledge and prior experience. We agree that:

> "The decisions concerning the intelligibility of modules of information cannot be made without reference to the learners from whom the information is intended." (Kalyuga et al., 1998, p.14).

However, it is likely that the training provided in this experiment is not a sufficient mechanism for discerning the intelligibility of information modules and for controlling expertise. This then would be a methodological artefact affecting both experiments.

This investigation found little evidence in support of the redundancy effect. The only indication of the redundancy effect was the higher cognitive efficiency of the fault-finding task with the DO format over the DT format (though not significant at $p = 0.053$). The redundant formats (DT, DS, DTS) were no different to the non-redundant format (DO) on other measures of mental workload or test scores.

The results also suggest that effects of redundancy have a task dependency. Significant effects for test scores and cognitive efficiency were found only for the fault-finding task. This important result warrants further investigation in order to establish the nature of this relationship.

A better understanding of redundancy may be achieved with a dichotomy of between-channel redundancy and within-channel redundancy. Under this framework, the between-channel redundancy (DS) achieves significantly better performance on all fault-finding measures (scores and efficiency) than within-channel redundancy (DT). In addition, a format that exploits both redundancies (DTS) gives better performance than a format with within-channel redundancy only (DO). Yet this format (DTS) is no better or worse than a non-redundant format (DO). This result has important implications for multimedia designers.

Redundancy cannot be used to wallpaper over the cracks of unusable software. The addition of complex speech, animation or text to mono-media may do nothing to improve the learnability of material. The addition of some redundancies (e.g. within-channel DT) may even reduce performance and decrease the efficiency of mental workload. Design guidelines suggesting that users prefer redundancy of information should be used with great care.

Clearly further work needs to be done. Better measures of intelligibility are needed, the relationship between task and redundancy needs to be investigated, and a better framework for discussing redundancy needs to be established. This will help to inform designers about the use of redundancy in multimedia software.

Acknowledgements

We wish to acknowledge the support and cooperation of Slava Kalyuga and the assistance provided by John Fabre.

References

Alty, J. L. (1996), "Multimedia Interface Design", OzCHI 96: Tutorial Notes.

Basil, M. D. (1994), "Multiple Resource Theory I: Application to Television Viewing", *Communication Research* **21**(2), 177–207.

Bobis, J., Sweller, J. & Cooper, M. (1993), "Cognitive Load Effects in a Primary-School Geometry Task", *Learning and Instruction* **3**, 1–21.

Cerpa, N., Chandler, P. & Sweller, J. (1996), "Some Conditions under which Integrated Computer-Based Training Software can Facilitate Learning", *Journal of Educational Computing Research* **15**(4), 345–67.

Chandler, P. & Sweller, J. (1996), "Cognitive Load while Learning to use a Computer Program", *Applied Cognitive Psychology* **10**, 151–70.

Edwards, A. D. N. (1992), Redundancy and Adaptability, *in* A. D. N. Edwards & S. Holland (eds.), *Multimedia Interface Design in Education*, Springer-Verlag, pp.145–55.

Johnson, P. & Nemetz, F. (1998), Towards Principles for the Design and Evaluation of Multimedia Systems, *in* H. Johnson, L. Nigay & C. Roast (eds.), *People and Computers XIII (Proceedings of HCI'98)*, Springer-Verlag, pp.255–71.

Kalyuga, S., Chandler, P. & Sweller, J. (1998), "Levels of Expertise and Instructional Design", *Human Factors* **40**(1), 1–17.

Mousavi, S. Y., Low, R. & Sweller, J. (1995), "Reducing Cognitive Load by Mixing Auditory and Visual Presentation Modes", *Journal of Educational Psychology* **87**(2), 319–34.

Najjar, L. J. (1996), "Multimedia Information and Learning", *Journal of Educational Multimedia and Hypermedia* **5**(2), 129–50.

Paas, F. G. . C. & Merrienboer, J. J. G. V. (1993), "The Efficiency of Instructional Conditions: An Approach to Combine Mental Effort and Performance Measures", *Human Factors* **34**(4), 737–43.

Paivio, A. (1991), "Dual Coding Theory: Retrospect and Current Status", *Canadian Journal of Psychology* **45**(3), 255–87.

Sutcliffe, A. & Faraday, P. (1993), Designing Multimedia Interfaces, *in* L. J. Bass, J. Gornostaev & C. Unger (eds.), *Proceedings of EWHCI'93: The East–West International Conference on Human–Computer Interaction*, Springer-Verlag, pp.105–14.

Sweller, J. (1994), "Cognitive Load Theory, Learning Difficulty, and Instructional Design", *Learning and Cognition* **4**, 295–312.

Sweller, J. & Chandler, P. (1994), "Why Some Material is difficult to learn", *Cognition and Instruction* **12**(3), 185–233.

Vetere, F. (1997), Redundancy in Multimedia Systems, *in* S. Howard, J. Hammond & G. K. Lindgaard (eds.), *Human–Computer Interaction — INTERACT '97: Proceedings of the Sixth IFIP Conference on Human–Computer Interaction*, Chapman & Hall, pp.648–50.

Vossen, P., Maguire, M. & Heim (1997), *Design Guide for Multimedia*, second edition, NPL Usability Services.

Yeung, A. S., Jin, P. & Sweller, J. (1997), "Cognitive Load and Learner Expertise: Split Attention and Redundancy Effects in Reading with Explanatory Notes", *Contemporary Educational Psychology* **23**, 1–21.

Human–Computer Interaction — INTERACT '99
M. Angela Sasse and Chris Johnson (Editors)
Published by IOS Press, © IFIP TC.13, 1999

Modelling the Learner in a World Wide Web Guided Discovery Hypertext Learning Environment

K.W. Pang[1] & E.A. Edmonds[2]

[1] Application and Technical Consultancy, Enterprise Solutions, ICL Microsoft Solution Centre, Manchester M22 0NE, UK.

[2] LUTCHI Research Centre, Department of Computer Science, Loughborough University, Loughborough LE11 3TU, UK.

kingsley.pang@icl.com, E.A.Edmonds@lboro.ac.uk

Abstract: Weaknesses have been identified in current World Wide Web (WWW) learning systems such as the lack of conceptual support for learning from hypertext, navigational disorientation and cognitive overload. This paper suggests that a system based on a knowledge-based component utilizing a user model similar to the overlay model is able to carry out adaptivity according to a specific Guided Discovery approach.

Keywords: user modelling, guided discovery learning, adaptivity, knowledge-based systems, individualized feedback, online testing, Java, electronic logic.

1 Introduction

This research centres on learning using the guided discovery educational paradigm to construct a hypertext-based environment on the Internet. The aim is to provide a single user system to teach over the World Wide Web (WWW). The subject domain selected was electronic logic, although the results are applicable to other subject areas.

Weaknesses have been identified in current systems that purport to provide distance learning (Pang & Edmonds, 1997). These are the lack of support for cognitive engagement with the material, disorientation when navigating across the knowledge domain and the lack of individualization both in the material and in system support.

The aim is to provide individualistic support that is adaptive to the learner's current state of knowledge. It is suggested that using the Internet for learning purposes is viably different from other uses of this medium. The efficacy of hypertext Web pages to promote learning have yet to be proven. Educational environments that are reactive to individual user needs remain largely unexplored in the context of research on the Internet and education. The difficulty is in producing a system that will be able to adapt sufficiently to providing guidance and effective learning from a distance.

The need is for a system that will permit learner-led exploration but utilizing a knowledge base to control the discovery process. It is proposed that there is a requirement for a system using a tutoring module to carry out decreasing intervention to provide control of both the navigation of the information space and sequencing of the material.

Related to this are issues of the use of hypertext and implications for learning, the use of the WWW as more than just a medium for material delivery and the implementation of Guided Discovery principles in a computerised environment.

The guiding process is the ability to direct the learner (Mosston & Ashworth, 1990), during the exploratory process, when using a hypertext environment on the Internet. The underlying premise is that there needs to be a combination of other components into the learning environment in order to provide different types of overt and covert guidance (Pang, 1998).

It remains difficult in hypertext to know exactly what the user is doing all the time therefore it is hard to evaluate the user's cognitive status. Questions can centre on:

1. whether the learner understands the text that they have read;

2. if the visited nodes have been selected for sensible reasons; and

3. if the navigational behaviour is haphazard and inefficient.

Quantitative analysis of user log files of a hyper-document, carried out by Taylor & Self (1990), revealed a lack of rationality in the users' actions, making it very difficult to predict their behaviour or the reasons for this. Typically there are episodes of unanalysable activity, separated by long gaps, with no user actions. It was difficult to ascertain what had been learnt or the reasons for particular learner actions. Thus the:

> "automatic monitoring of individual actions seems a dubious proposition" (Taylor & Self, 1990).

The users did not adopt a particular strategy, instead following particular goals that they had determined as important at particular moments in the exploration. Hence adapting instruction to an individual's preferred learning strategy is highly problematic.

2   The Student Model

An Intelligent Tutoring System (ITS) diagnoses a student's current knowledge of the subject matter in order to individualise the instruction according to perceived needs. The student model refers to the dynamic representations of the emerging knowledge and skills of the student. No intelligent instruction can take place without an understanding of the student. The student model is an explicit representation of the student's skill and should include aspects of the student's behaviour and knowledge which may offset performance and learning.

The input to the student model is via interaction with the system; the output is dependent on how the student model is used. Common uses for the student model may take the form of automatic advice, generating new problems and changing material to overcome misconceptions. A student model is usually composed of three types of information: the type of domain knowledge (declarative, procedural or causal), bandwidth (amount and type of student input) and differences that the learner has in terms of missing conceptions and misconceptions.

The student model establishes the framework for identifying the student's misconceptions and sub-optimal performance. The structure of the student model can be derived from:

1. the problem-solving behaviour of the student;

2. direct questions asked of the student;

3. historical data (based on assumptions of the student's own assessment of skill level, novice to expert); and

4. the difficulty level of the content domain (Barr & Feigenbaum, 1982).

The simplest kind of student model is represented as a subset of the expert model at particular intermediate stages of the learning process. This overlay model (Goldstein, 1982) shows which pieces of knowledge are believed to have been acquired and verified by the student. A more formative student model provides explicit representations of the student's incorrect version of the target knowledge for remediation purposes. This is the 'buggy approach' (Burton, 1982).

In the 'buggy' model the ITS compares the student's actual performance to the user model to determine if the student has mastered the content domain. Advancement through the curriculum is dependent upon the system's assessment of the student's progress level. The student model contains a database of student misconceptions and missing conceptions. This database is known as the 'bug library'. A missing conception is an item of knowledge that the expert has but the student does not. Bugs are identified from the literature, observation of student behaviour and learning theory of the content domain (Van Lehn, 1988).

With student models there is a tacit assumption that tutoring based on fine-grained student models will be more effective than using course-grained models. Fine grain models are more powerful in that they have more detailed information about the cognitive processes of the learner. A lack of research in this area has led to an absence of clear-cut guidelines about when fine grain models are appropriate. Another difficulty is the 'intractable problem' encountered in student modelling, that of building valid models of the students cognitive processes (Self, 1990). A comprehensive overview of user modelling is given by Van Lehn (1988) and McCalla (1992).

The lack of established research on student modelling in an educational hypertext environment only compounds the problem when applying this to the WWW. WWW users are learning by reading as opposed to learning by doing, where it is possible to monitor the learners' problem-solving activities. Users will most likely adopt opportunistic planning styles with no structured planning beforehand. Instead they tailor actions using a step-by step approach to the situation. This is because by definition it is relatively easy to explore and recover in a hypertext environment.

Overlay models have been criticised for encouraging the view that the student is a 'subset' of the expert. This criticism is not so clear-cut. The subset view originates from confusion in the characteristics of the overlay model. The generative ability dimension of an intelligent tutoring system is often confused with the cognitive scope dimension. The presupposition is that a higher generative ability user model leads to increased cognitive engagement, an overlay model is not generative hence less cognitive engagement. The suggestion in the learning environment by Pang (1998) is that a system that uses an overlay model can still incorporate information about the cognitive growth of the student, and it can still have deep conceptual scope. When it becomes apparent that there are two dimensions that are different then it becomes possible to have overlay models that incorporate overlay bugs (mistakes which the user makes), strategies and other types of user behaviour. Therefore overlay models can possess a detailed understanding of the student, hence its use in the system in this project.

3 Different Requirements of the WWW for User Modelling

In WWW-based learning systems, attempting to maintain an individual user model and also observing and diagnosing the learner's knowledge state is extremely complex (Weber & Specht, 1997). Only a few systems have been built that provide simplistic forms of individualised sequencing and adaptive hypertext guidance.

In terms of student modelling in WWW-based tutoring systems the difficulties of user modelling are exacerbated. The learning system has to play the role of the teacher to a large degree. In a distance learning situation no teacher is directly available during learning who can carry out the task of adapting the number and nature of new concepts presented to the learner's current state of knowledge (Weber & Specht, 1997). WWW browsers only annotate visited links but are not able to provide any guidance as to

which pages are the most useful to be selected next. In this situation an individual learner model can provide the information that can be used by the learning system to adapt the presentation of the pages to the particular user.

A user model in a hypertext learning environment is given less emphasis than in a traditional ITS. There is less of a need to constrict the learner during the exploratory process, with a shifting of emphasis on student-directed and guided learning. But this is counterbalanced by a requirement for greater support when learning from hypertext WWW systems. Individualizing information and link-anchors (adaptive presentation) or providing the user with navigational support (adaptive navigation) is based on information kept in a user-model. This is the system's representation of the user's preferences, knowledge, beliefs, or information seeking goals. An example is the ISIS-Tutor, a hypertext-based system for teaching aspects of programming language (Brusilovsky & Pesin, 1995). The system was able to provide adaptive navigational support based on whether a particular student had selected a node which was already learned, ready to be learned, or not learned at all.

Different techniques have been used to acquire information about the user (Kobsa et al., 1994). These include stereotypes of learners selected by the system and user-supplied preferences at run time. Other methods have been an analysis of user actions and plan recognition or inference. Navigation between pages, methods of selecting the page, or explicit selection of tasks (Hook et al., 1995) have been used by the system in order to build a student model for carrying out inferencing of the user's intentions. The effectiveness of some of these techniques remains controversial (Kay, 1994). Others researchers find commonality with this viewpoint, advocating a 'glass box' approach, in that a user model should be inspectable by users and should work under their control (Hook et al., 1995).

A simple type of user model similar to the overlay model may be sufficient to represent all the necessary knowledge for individualised sequencing and adaptive guidance in the hypertext. Adaptive sequencing and guidance are possible ways to control the navigational process in a WWW hypertext system for learning (Eklund et al., 1997). The simplest form that the overlay model takes is as an information base containing information about whether an item has been learnt. Examples of such systems are ITEM-IP and HyperTutor (Brusilovsky, 1995).

4   Constructing the User Model for Knowledge-based Guided Discovery Support

It is suggested in this paper that providing support based on decreasing intervention, different levels of guidance and predominately learner-controlled navigational selections, using an overlay-type model, will result in measurable gains in learning and satisfaction.

In the system design for this experiment, in terms of obtaining evidence from the Web pages with which to generate the student model, this is partly done implicitly by monitoring the student's problem solving behaviour. This also has the additional, and often underestimated, benefit of making the learner active in the discovery process by taking online testing as shown in Figure 1, and also through the selection of links embedded in the Web pages. In the work by Pang (1998), the guided discovery learning environment on the WWW is designed to monitor the user's interaction and use them as a measure of what the student is believed to have learnt. These will provide detailed records of the learner's level of domain understanding and navigational behaviour. As the learner selects the answers, these are stored in individual records which the knowledge-based module uses to determine conceptual weaknesses in the individual learner to provide effective remediation.

The student or learner model consists only of the nodes that the user has visited. The user's interactions are compared to an expert model of the domain. The system adapts the guidance accordingly, by making specific links available, providing instructional cues at key points in the interaction to direct the student to nodes that have been overlooked or have been accessed in an incorrect sequence, and different types of advice according to different levels of guidance. This is primarily a qualitative approach to modelling the learner to provide individualised instruction and support.

The user model is very much along the lines of an overlay model, but it is proposed that it is powerful enough in terms of providing a level of detail that can provide adaptivity (Pang, 1998).

From the literature, there is the tacit assumption that tutoring based on fine-grained student models will be more effective than tutoring based on course-grained models. Fine-grained student models describe cognitive processes at a higher level of detail, course-grained do not do this. But this assumption needs further investigation to determine whether it is worth the effort. The suggestion in this paper is that there

may be less of a requirement for sophisticated user modelling approaches for this experimental system for exploring guided discovery principles. There are compromises made when using an overlay model but it is proposed that this approach to user modelling is sufficient for providing limited adaptivity.

Employing this approach to user modelling can allow an investigation into specific factors that would affect learning such as:

1. the lack of individualization of domain material for learning; and

2. disorientation when navigating across the information space.

Past research has advocated the structuring of hypertext and system control over the learning process as possible solutions but the use of knowledge-based approaches has generally drawn mixed conclusions with no established guidelines for the design of such systems.

5   The User Model as Part of an Integrated Guided Discovery Learning Environment

A major hypothesis in this paper is that the use of a guided discovery approach will allow a high degree of learner freedom and decreased levels of system intervention. This can be characterised as a shift from a traditional strong reliance on user modelling or AI techniques, to one based on some of the components of a 'minimalist' Intelligent Tutoring system.

Figure 2 provides a screen shot of the guided discovery system with full control by the system. Navigational options are adapted during the learning process, with varying levels of system guidance such as advice displayed in the Advice frame, system control over the navigation buttons and the switching on and off of hypertext links (Brusilovsky, 1995) in relation to the student's progress through the domain material.

Although the components resemble an Intelligent Tutoring System there are many differences. There is less of a reliance on a user model driven approach, with the learner being allowed to explore parts of the hypertext space before system intervention. The learner is given control with the option of ignoring system advice; and the inclusion of online testing with immediate scoring allows the learner to carry out self-assessment concerning knowledge progression.

The guidance component operates at the navigational level to maintain educationally effective

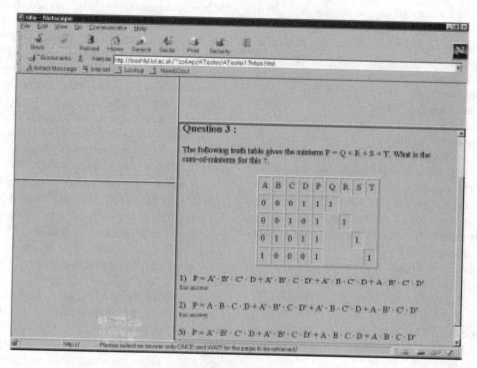

Figure 1: Online testing.

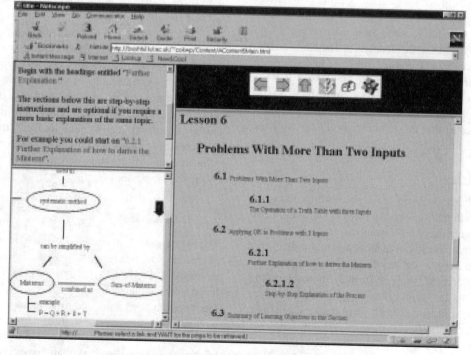

Figure 2: Full navigational control by Expert module.

navigational behaviour and also at the discovery step level, to lead the learner through a sequence of steps to bridge the cognitive gap for understanding a particular concept. The instructional module matches the expert records with those of the learner (recorded as an overlay student model). The expert system module determines the Web page to be selected (this maybe accompanied by advice rather than just the retrieval of the node chosen by the learner). System feedback is displayed in the interface, both with messaging within the browser and also with overt messaging in the form of advice. This is further controlled by modifying the function of the navigational buttons. Online testing (Figure 1) and analysis of the links selected provide information used to determine the current knowledge level of the learner.

This structure allows the system designer to examine each part of a possible learning environment, which is adaptive to the learner and usable for the WWW. These characteristics are reflective of the interpretation of a guided discovery pedagogical approach proposed for learning using a WWW hypertext environment.

Knowledge-based techniques were used in the design of the expert system module to determine the advice to be presented and to exert system control over the learner's navigation. Providing navigational support will help to alleviate the cognitive overload problem caused by learners not knowing where they are, where they have come from and where to go next; again assisting the learner in focusing on the knowledge domain (Conklin, 1987). This was not a strong use of artificial intelligence.

Instead the adaptivity focused on using a system resembling sets of rules (similar to production rules). It was suggested that this could be used to provide the level of individualistic tuition required.

6   Results

Although there has been research into the design of hypertext systems for learning these systems continue to be experimental, lack quantitative data and rely on less formal investigative techniques to collect this data. The results collected from this experiment have been derived from a formal approach using statistical data for gauging learning outcome and user satisfaction; with further analysis of responses using a semi-structured interview.

Three Web-based learning environments were developed, each containing the same subject material but differentiating in the functionality and support that they would provide to the learner during the learning process. The experiment compared a Guided

discovery condition, a Map-only condition and an Unguided condition. The Guided Discovery condition and map only condition required the addition of a cognitive tool, the Concept map. The Guided Discovery condition also provided system-led advice based on navigational and online testing analysis. The unguided condition neither had a map or provided system advice. Subjects were subdivided according to learning styles, with measures for learning outcome and user satisfaction to determine the effect of learning style on level of system guidance received.

A sample of 84 university students were divided into three groups of 28 subjects according to levels of support given by the knowledge-based component.

The results indicate that providing guidance will result in a significant increase in level of learning. Guided discovery condition subjects, regardless of learning styles, experienced levels of satisfaction comparable to those in the other conditions. Those who received the highest degree of navigational support scored a statistically significant score.

The effect of providing individualistic guidance (the Guided discovery condition) was to increase the learning outcome scores to a higher level than the map-only condition and unguided condition. Although having a concept map facility did seem to increase the mean score of the learning outcome and could therefore said to have some effect on learning, this was not at a significant level.

The findings demonstrate that learning can be improved by using a guided discovery framework for constructing a WWW hypertext environment. The effect of providing individualistic guidance, using a combination of structured discovery steps with varying levels of questioning, and navigational guidance carried out by the tutoring module was to increase the learning outcome scores to a higher level than the experimental conditions which did not employ the module.

7   Conclusion

The provision of a knowledge-based component to determine when to provide guided advice has helped to support the learner in bridging any conceptual leaps in the understanding of the material whilst also reducing the navigation and disorientation problem of navigating in the hypertext information space. The learner has been able to focus on learning the attributes of the concepts, rather than devoting cognitive resources in keeping track of nodes previously visited, current position and where next to go in the information space. The use of different levels of intervention by the system ensures that the learner is given the correct level of information at the correct time related to the sequence of the domain material. It has been suggested that a knowledge-based component utilizing a user model based on an overlay approach can individualise the feedback given by the system and can result in an increased learning gain in a WWW exploratory learning environment.

The strength of hypertext is in the ability of the user to browse the information space but hypertext for learning is filled with many unresolved issues. The application of hypertext to the WWW for distance learning brings further complications. In terms of WWW-specific issues there are those related to distance learning; but with the addition of user modelling, adaptive instruction, Web page design, temporal latency, open-corpus of educational material, vast information repositories and haphazard interactivity using continually changing Web technologies. Therefore there remains a distinct paucity of principles for designing a WWW-based environment for supporting learning. Some of these problems such as user modelling and adaptive instruction remain problematic for CAI generally rather than just the WWW and learning.

This research has demonstrated that constraining the information space by using system-led guidance can lead to gains in learning without necessarily sacrificing gains in satisfaction. Shaping learning by using guidance cues controlled by a knowledge-based component may prevent the learner from following disordered tangents in the path through the material, reducing non-optimal navigational behaviour and the resolution of misconceptions (Pang, 1998). The first author is currently investigating how this system can be integrated into a total distance learning scenario to create a bespoke application which can be marketed directly to educational institutions. This is envisioned to incorporate the use of Microsoft Active Server Pages, Microsoft Internet Information Server and Microsoft SQL Server to be integrated with principles derived from the guided discovery learning environment. The construction of a WWW system for providing guidance during learning is therefore a non-trivial, complex task.

References

Barr, A. & Feigenbaum, E. A. (1982), *The Handbook of Artificial Intelligence*, Vol. 2, Kaufmann.

Brusilovsky, P. (1995), Intelligent Tutoring Systems for World-Wide Web, *in* R. Holzapfel (ed.), *Poster Proceedings of Third International WWW Conference*, Elsevier Science, pp.42–45.

Brusilovsky, P. & Pesin, L. (1995), Visual Annotation of Links in Adaptive Hypermedia, *in* I. Katz, R. Mack & L. Marks (eds.), *Companion Proceedings of CHI'95: Human Factors in Computing Systems (CHI'95 Conference Companion)*, ACM Press, pp.222–3.

Burton, R. (1982), Diagnosing Bugs in a Simple Procedural Skill, *in* D. Sleeman & J. S. Brown (eds.), *Intelligent Tutoring Systems*, Academic Press, pp.157–83.

Conklin, J. (1987), "An Introduction and Survey", *IEEE Computer* **20**(9), 17–41.

Eklund, J., Brusilovsky, P. & Schwarz, E. (1997), Adaptive Textbooks on the WWW, *in* P. Ashman, R. Thistewaite, R. Debreceny & A. Ellis (eds.), *Proceedings of AUSWEB97, The Third Australian Conference on the World Wide Web*, Southern Cross University Press, pp.186–92.

Goldstein, I. P. (1982), The Genetic Graph: A Representation for the Evolution of Procedural Knowledge, *in* D. Sleeman & J. S. Brown (eds.), *Intelligent Tutoring Systems*, Academic Press, pp.51–77.

Hook, K., Karlgren, J. & Waern, A. (1995), A Glass Box Intelligent Help Interface, *in First Workshop on Intelligent Multimodal Interfaces*.

Kay, J. (1994), Lies, Damn Lies, and Stereotypes: Pragmatic Approximations of Users, *in* B. Goodman, A. Kobsa & D. Litman (eds.), *UM1994, 4th International Conference on User Modelling*, The MITRE Corporation, pp.175–84.

Kobsa, A., Müller, D. & Nill, A. (1994), KN-AHS: An Adaptive Hypertext Client of the User Modelling System BGP-MS, *in* B. Goodman & A. Kobsa (eds.), *Proceedings of the Fourth International Conference on User Modelling*, The MITRE Corporation, pp.99–105.

McCalla, G. I. (1992), The Central Importance of Student Modelling to Intelligent Tutoring, *in* E. Costa (ed.), *New Directions for Intelligent Tutoring Systems*, Vol. 91 of *NATO ASI Series F*, Springer-Verlag, pp.107–131.

Mosston, M. & Ashworth, S. (1990), *The Spectrum of Teaching Styles: From Command To Discovery*, Longman Scientific and Technical.

Pang, K. W. (1998), The Guiding Process in Discovery Hypertext Learning Environments for the Internet, PhD thesis, LUTCHI Research Centre, Department of Computer Studies, Loughborough University, UK.

Pang, K. W. & Edmonds, E. A. (1997), Designing Learning Environments Using Java: New Functionality, *in* R. Coyne, M. Ramscar, J. Lee & K. Zreik (eds.),

Proceedings of the Sixth International EuropIA Conference EuropIA1997, Europia Productions, pp.93–107.

Self, J. (1990), Bypassing the Intractable Problem of Student Modelling, *in Intelligent Tutoring Systems: At the Crossroads of Artificial Intelligence and Education*, Ablex, pp.107–23.

Taylor, C. & Self, J. (1990), "Monitoring Hypertext Users", *Interacting with Computers* **2**(3), 297–312.

Van Lehn, K. (1988), Student Modelling, *in* M. Polson & J. Richardson (eds.), *Foundations of Intelligent Tutoring Systems*, Lawrence Erlbaum Associates, pp.55–78.

Weber, G. & Specht, M. (1997), User Modelling and Adaptive Navigation Support in WWW-based Tutoring Systems, *in* A. Jameson, C. Paris & C. Tasso (eds.), *Proceedings of User Modeling '97*, Springer-Verlag, pp.289–300.

Human–Computer Interaction — INTERACT '99
M. Angela Sasse and Chris Johnson (Editors)
Published by IOS Press, © IFIP TC.13, 1999

Towards a Methodology Employing Critical Parameters to Deliver Performance Improvements in Interactive Systems

William Newman & Alex Taylor

Xerox Research Centre Europe, 61 Regent Street, Cambridge CB2 1AB, UK.
{wnewman,ataylor}@xrce.xerox.com

Abstract: In the design of interactive systems, overall performance issues tend to receive less attention than provision of functionality. As a result, systems may not always offer performance improvements to their users. In this paper we present some proposals for methods based on the use of application-specific critical parameters, i.e. performance parameters that measure how well the system serves its purpose. We argue that these parameters can provide a basis for dealing with performance issues in design. To construct this basis, there is a need to focus on identifying parameters through field studies, and on constructing models for use in making performance predictions. We provide a number of examples of critical parameters, and discuss problems we have encountered in identifying them and in model construction. We summarise the results of a study of designers working with critical parameters. A final section of the paper discusses the feasibility of introducing critical parameters to HCI design practice.

Keywords: performance metrics, critical parameters, methodology, interactive system design.

1 Introduction

How can interactive systems be designed to deliver real performance improvements to their users? What new methods might help designers achieve this? The research we describe in this paper has been motivated by our perception that performance improvement is one of the most challenging issues facing Human Computer Interaction (HCI). This issue is certain to grow in importance as businesses make increasing demands for measurable returns on their investments in technology. The performance of interactive systems has been on the HCI agenda ever since Card et al. (1983) began their pioneering work two decades ago. It has come to be a cornerstone in the argument for paying attention to HCI in system design.

In these circumstances, we would expect the delivery of performance improvements to the user to figure strongly in present-day HCI design methods, but this is not what we find. Instead there is a lack of attention to performance improvement, noted by a number of writers. Landauer, for example, suggests that progress in most computer applications has been based on responding to market forces rather than on designing to meet productivity targets (Landauer, 1995). In a commentary on HCI, Gibbs remarks on the lack of published papers offering evidence

of improved performance in proposed new systems (Gibbs, 1997). The relatively low priority given to performance issues in the packaged software industry has also been noted, for example in (Lammers, 1986; Cusumano & Selby, 1995).

Studies of designers at work likewise give the impression that performance issues rarely receive attention during design. For example, Herbsleb & Kuwana (1993) conducted a study of 38 design meetings and noted the types of questions that arose. There were so few performance-related questions that they did not merit treatment as a question type (J D Herbsleb, personal communication). In our own study of thirty designers' published accounts of their design projects, we found that performance criteria were rarely mentioned, and that opportunities to quantify performance, e.g. by setting targets or through user testing, were taken only rarely. When attention was paid to performance, the focus was rarely on the design as a whole, and almost always on a poorly performing component of the design: an error-prone selection technique, an easily forgotten command or a slow form of feedback, for example (Newman & Taylor, 1997).

Many proposals have been made for improvements to standard HCI practice, but only a very few attempts have been made to help designers deal with issues of performance. Lim & Long's (1994) MUSE method, for example, includes performance specification within its scope, but its focus is primarily on a comprehensive method for the analysis and specification of functional requirements. One major set of contributions has been the development of the GOMS cognitive modelling technique and its variants (Kieras, 1997), which have proved their effectiveness but are still not widely used by practitioners. The cognitive walkthrough method has also demonstrated its usefulness in achieving designs supporting exploratory learning (Polson & Lewis, 1990); however, it is primarily a fault-detection method rather than a means of achieving learning-rate targets.

Despite this rather gloomy picture, we are encouraged by evidence that designers of interactive systems will pay attention to performance targets, if these are clearly stated and achievable. MacLean et al. (1991) demonstrated this in a study where they asked a pair of designers to design a 'fast ATM' capable of speeding up cash withdrawals. Unlike the teams studied by Herbsleb & Kuwana, the two designers made frequent reference to performance criteria in the course of design. They appeared to have little difficulty in treating these criteria along with the rest of their concerns.

In this paper we describe an exploration of the use of *critical parameters* to define performance targets. This approach is attractive because it permits existing HCI design methods to be retained while introducing performance targets as additional design criteria, rather as MacLean et al. did in their study. We identify two main areas where research is needed, parameter identification and model building, and we summarise our progress in these two areas. We comment on the results of a study of designers working with critical parameters, and conclude with a discussion of some of the principal questions raised.

2   Use of Critical Parameters in Design

Critical parameters are widely used in design as a basis for setting performance requirements. In general terms, they are the "established parameters by which designers measure whether an artefact or system serves its purpose, and compare one design with another" — a definition we have proposed in an earlier paper (Newman, 1997). We went on to argue that the use of critical parameters would be beneficial to the design of interactive systems, because more attention would then be paid to performance

enhancement and less to functional differentiation of products, which we claim is of less value to the user.

The use of critical parameters in interactive system design is attractive because it permits performance targets to be defined at the outset, before commitments have been made to solution strategies. Likewise when usability testing is done these targets can influence the choice of tasks to be performed, instead of vice versa. Altogether, use of critical parameters appears to improve the likelihood that overall performance will be taken into account during design.

We have taken the concept of critical parameters as a representation of system performance, and have begun to develop methods for identifying these parameters and for using them in design. In doing this, we have extended and strengthened our original view of critical parameters in several ways.

2.1   Critical Parameters: A Definition

We define a critical parameter as a metric for an aspect of the system's performance that is:

- *Critical* to the success of the system in serving its purpose.

- *Persistent* across successive systems for this purpose, and therefore valid as a basis for measuring performance improvements.

- *Manipulable* by designers, who can design so as to achieve specific performance targets.

We have thus taken our original definition and added two properties that are essential to the purpose that we see these parameters serving. Performance parameters that are *persistent* not only allow measurement of improvements; they avoid the need to identify design criteria afresh every time a system is developed. Instead the same parameter can be applied as before, setting an appropriate new value as the target.

Parameters that are *manipulable* by designers can influence design decisions directly, during design iteration, rather than after a prototype has been built, tested and found wanting. Techniques such as GOMS can be used to simulate usage and make predictions of performance. Of course these techniques can be applied to any design target, such as the time taken to type a command or resize a window. If the target is critical to the design's overall success, however, performance predictions will enable the designer to manipulate the overall outcome.

2.2 An Example: Reviewer Assignment Time

In the organization of academic conferences, a central responsibility of the programme chair is the distribution of papers to reviewers. The assignment process needs to be completed with the minimum of delay, but is inherently labour-intensive. It involves identifying, for each paper, a set of candidate reviewers who are expert in the necessary areas, and who have not already been assigned their full quota of papers to review. The chair then checks each candidate for possible conflicts of interest, and on this basis selects the requisite number of reviewers, making sure that each reviewer receives roughly the same number of papers. This process is repeated many times during the assignment process — if 400 papers are submitted to the conference and each requires five reviewers, 2,000 selections must be made. The process can therefore involve several days of a highly qualified academic chair's time, an expensive commodity.

An important parameter of this process is the *reviewer assignment time*: the time taken to assign a reviewer to a paper and to record the assignment. Other stages in the process are also time-critical, such as placing hardcopy papers in envelopes and mailing them to reviewers, but these do not depend solely on the programme chair. Assignment time is not only *critical* to completing the entire distribution process; it is *persistent* from one year's conference to the next, and it is *manipulable* through the design of assignment-handling procedures, whether paper- or computer-based. Hence reviewer assignment time can be regarded as a critical parameter in designing ways to support the assignment process. So too can error rate in recording assignments — see (Dix et al., 1998) for an interesting study of reliability in paper reviewing processes. For the sake of this example we will focus on reviewer assignment time.

With this parameter in mind, various support systems can be envisaged and evaluated. An entirely paper-based system could be used, involving a printed master list of reviewers from which selections could be made on a basis of matching reviewers' interests to author-supplied keywords. Records of assignments could be kept manually for each paper and each reviewer. It takes only a cursory analysis to discover that, for a large conference, reviewer assignment time is likely to be very long if accurate matching is to be achieved. A semi-automated system, using a matching program to generate lists of candidate reviewers, could speed up the process, but reviewer assignment time is likely to remain high if the remaining steps are performed on paper.

A more efficient solution is therefore to implement a user interface of the kind shown in Figure 1, presenting the programme chair with a rank-ordered list of candidates generated by the matching program. The names in the list are checked for conflict, and the requisite number are selected and entered in a database, from which mailing labels can be generated later. This solution can be evaluated, for example with the aid of GOMS analysis, to arrive at an estimate of reviewer assignment time. It is feasible to work towards a specific target, such as 30 seconds to assign a set of 5 reviewers, by tuning the user interface and the underlying matching software.

Paper no. 1035
Telemedicine on the World Wide Web
Jane Smith
Health Sciences Dept, Tower Hamlets Univ., London

Candidate reviewers: **5 assigned**

[]	0.85	Peter Smith Tower Hamlets Consultants
[√]	0.81	Doreen Handscombe EE Dept, Driftwood College
[√]	0.72	Terry Johnson Tarragon Inc.
[]	0.71	Patricia Markham CS Dept., Tower Hamlets University
[√]	0.66	James Fallowfield MediOnLine plc
[√]	0.55	Charles Farmer Medical Research Horizons
[√]	0.54	Karl Haflinger Univ. Medical Centre, Kaiserslautern
[]	...	

                                                            ASSIGN

Figure 1: An hypothetical user interface to a reviewer selection system, geared towards reducing reviewer assignment time. Candidate reviewers are displayed in rank matching order. The programme chair selects those that do not appear to present a conflict of interest, and clicks on **ASSIGN** to store these assignments in a database.

---

3 The Methodology of Critical Parameters

Readers who find nothing very remarkable about the foregoing example of critical parameter usage are largely right. The route taken towards the design shown in Figure 1 involves no more than standard HCI principles and evaluation techniques, such as are found in Preece et al. (1994). The significant difference is that a critical parameter is identified at the outset and is used to guide the iteration. Also, alternative designs can be compared for performance without building a working prototype, by using an analytical model.

The two essential activities, identification of critical parameters and construction of models, are what we believe are missing from current practice. They form the basis of the new methods that we propose should be incorporated into HCI methodology. In the remainder of this section we explain our proposals in further detail. The paper then goes on to discuss practical aspects of parameter identification, model building and application of critical parameters.

3.1   Where Critical Parameters are Found

Critical parameters are widely used in established engineering disciplines. They are fundamental, for example, to the ability of aeronautical engineers to design aircraft like the Boeing 777 that can be fully tested on the drawing board. In every discipline in which they are found, critical parameters are treated in much the same basic fashion. We have been able to learn how to introduce critical parameters to HCI by studying accounts of how they have arisen and how they are now used in other disciplines (Vincenti, 1990). In this sense the methods we are proposing for use in HCI are tried and tested, but need to be adapted and integrated into general HCI design practice.

The biggest challenge in adapting critical parameters to HCI is to apply them in a wide range of computer-supported domains. Critical parameters are intrinsically *application specific*. A parameter identified as critical to one application, such as the support of the conference review process, is unlikely to be relevant to another, such as the support of radiologists. Our primary focus is on applying critical parameters in just such knowledge-intensive professional work settings as these, because we believe it is here that the most important and persistent performance challenges lie.

Our choice of professional work as a focus may seem unwise, because professionals have considerable autonomy and individual skill, allowing them to organize their work in a wide variety of ways. Nevertheless we believe there are grounds, both theoretical and empirical, for the existence of critical parameters in much knowledge-intensive professional work. Theoretical grounds lie in the role of *norms* in enabling people to plan their work in the context of deadlines, quality requirements, prior experience and division of labour. Empirical grounds can be found in the results of ethnographic studies of professional work, which provide evidence of people's performance goals and their strategies for achieving them (Orr, 1996; Harper, 1998). We have gained further encouragement from the results of our own

studies of professionals at work, some of which we outline later in this paper.

3.2   The Elements of Critical Parameter Usage

Experience from the engineering world suggests there are three essential components to critical parameter use:

- *Identification* of parameters in the chosen application domain.

- *Model-building* to support predictions of performance.

- *Application* of the parameters in design, as targets during both design iteration and prototype testing.

The methodology of critical parameters is fundamentally iterative, not just when they are used in design, but in all three of these respects. Thus a number of iterations may be required to identify a critical parameter successfully, as Vincenti has described in his account of research into aircraft flying qualities (Vincenti, 1990). Iteration is also intrinsic to the process of developing successively better models to support performance predictions, a process familiar to most engineering researchers. We have begun to gain experience in iterative parameter identification and model-building, and to understand the close relationship between these two discovery processes.

4   Parameter Identification

In our 1997 paper, we suggested that the identification of critical parameters may prove time-consuming (Newman, 1997). Our recent experiences suggest, however, that parameter identification can sometimes be quite quick and straightforward: the parameters become obvious once the application domain has been identified. For example, we have recently begun to investigate the problem of designing tools to support foreign-language translators. Here a critical parameter, familiar to every professional translator, is the number of words translated per hour.

4.1   Model Building

Once a parameter has been found that appears to be critical and persistent, the next question is whether it is manipulable by designers. In other words, can a model be constructed by which performance can be predicted during design iteration? This involves gaining an adequate understanding of the structure of the activity to be supported, as it is performed in the 'real world'. We have applied relatively standard task analysis methods here, relying primarily on data gathered from field studies. The principal challenge is to develop a model that encompasses the work as a whole, rather than selected tasks. In simple cases, such as reviewer assignment, this is quite easy. In other cases we have been unable to develop an encompassing model, and have had to redefine the scope of the parameter itself. The next section provides examples of this.

To illustrate how models can be constructed iteratively to support critical-parameter based design in complex domains, we will use the well-known example of call handling by Toll and Assistance Operators (TAOs), as described by Gray et al. (1993) in connection with their Project Ernestine research. Here the main critical parameters are well established as a set of times for handling roughly 20 different types of calls to the operator, including credit-card calls and collect calls. Various models of TAO call handling have been used in the design of workstations since the 1950s. More recently, Gray et al. developed a comprehensive CPM-GOMS model that they used with success to predict the performance of a new workstation design. The model offered a basis for extension, by those conversant with CPM-GOMS methods, in order to predict the performance of alternative workstation designs. For example, it allowed investigation of pre-recorded voice prompts and of voice recognition applied to caller utterances.

4.2   Setting the Scope of the Search

Parameters that seem obvious as measures of the performance of work do not always turn out to be critical, persistent and manipulable. A fresh search for parameters must then get under way; typically this involves ethnographic field study methods. We have conducted our studies by starting with the obvious parameter, and then either broadening or narrowing the domain of search. The two directions of study are best explained through examples. Our first example covers a successful attempt of ours to identify a critical parameter for the support of General Practice consultations; our second takes as its starting point the observed needs of researchers in libraries.

In the UK the work of the GP revolves around his or her consultations with patients. During the consultation the GP must obtain the history of the patient's problem, conduct any examinations necessary, make a diagnosis, decide on a course of treatment, issue a prescription and instruct the patient on how to manage the problem. All of this must be compressed into a period of 5 to 10 minutes. Since the 1980s there has been increased use by GPs of desktop computers, primarily to maintain patients' notes online and to issue prescriptions. The UK National Health Service has defined outline requirements for these computers, and subsidises the purchase by GPs of accredited computers.

An obvious critical parameter in supporting this work is overall consultation time, and any technology that could reduce this time while maintaining quality of service would be a clear design success. This is an intractable problem, however, not least because patients' perception of service quality is strongly and positively correlated with duration of the consultation. To find a more tractable performance measure we conducted field studies in two GP health centres. We videotaped over 60 consultations and interviewed four GPs, and then analysed the videotapes. After one or two false starts, we were able to identify a quite unexpected problem with tasks involving notes and prescriptions: if these tasks took longer than about 10 seconds to perform, the patient was likely to interrupt — to pick up the 'free turn' in the conversation created by the GP's silence. The interruption could lead to spending up to half a minute on a topic of little importance to GP or patient. On this basis we believe that a critical, persistent and manipulable performance parameter for GP support is the *proportion of accesses to patient documentation that can be completed within 10 seconds*. We believe that a system designed to perform well in these terms would assist the GP in managing consultations within the overall time constraints.

A major barrier to rapid identification of critical parameters lies, we believe, with correctly delineating the application domain. We learned this when we investigated one of the parameters we had previously thought to be critical, the time taken by a library researcher to copy a verbatim passage from a paper source document (Newman, 1997). As O'Hara et al. (1998) have since pointed out, this kind of verbatim copying needs to be treated in the context of the use to which the verbatim material is put, e.g. entry in a notebook, storage in a database or pasting directly into a document. The use of a new technology for copying, such as the overhead camera proposed by Newman (1997), cannot be evaluated purely in terms of its copying speed. Instead the application domain needs to be widened, possibly to include the authoring activity for which the verbatim material is needed. We are currently engaged in investigating possible critical parameters in this wider domain of document authoring.

5   Application of Critical Parameters during Design

Research effort thus invested in identifying critical parameters and constructing models can pay off only if these parameters and models are useful in design. We have gained a limited amount of experience in the use of critical parameters, partly through applying them in our own design projects, partly through conducting experiments with design teams, and partly through the study of others' attempts to design with or without the help of critical parameters. We report here briefly on our experiments and retrospective studies.

5.1   A Design Experiment

We conducted a series of five design exercises, each involving a team of two designers. Three of the five teams included human factors experts, and all of them had experience in designing interactive systems. We gave each team the same design problem, in which the requirements included some performance targets defined in terms of critical parameters. To save them from having to design from scratch, we presented them with an outline description of an existing design. We asked them to critique this design in terms of the requirements, and then to proceed to redesign the system to overcome any identified shortcomings.

We expected the inclusion of performance targets to assist the design teams in making real improvements. Instead, however, the teams appeared to gain little benefit from the parameters, in some cases ignoring them entirely, in other cases commenting on the need for a working prototype in order to test performance. Almost without exception, they devoted the design session to discussions of functionality, either of the existing or of the new design. One of the five teams did take up the challenge presented by the performance targets, and engaged in a rough GOMS-style analysis of the existing design. From this exercise we learned that it may not be realistic to expect designers to construct their own predictive models. We should perhaps have provided our design teams with a usable, tailorable analytical model to help them address performance targets.

In our studies of designers' past experience with critical parameters, we have identified a similar but more basic problem: designers need to be made aware of the parameters' existence, and constantly reminded of them. If they are not, they appear likely to resort to designing purely in terms of functional components. In a follow-up study of the review process, undertaken after identifying reviewer assignment time as the critical parameter, we gathered the data from which Figure 2 is constructed. It shows fluctuations in assignment time for a particular computer conference over a five-year period. A sharp increase occurred when new Web-based supporting technologies were introduced without taking assignment time into consideration.

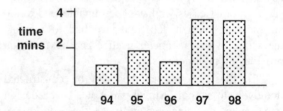

Figure 2: Variation in reviewer assignment time in five successive conferences. After the 1997 conference, a set of Web-based tools were used. Data supplied by programme chairs through personal communication.

A well documented example of the need to maintain awareness of critical parameters is found in Project Ernestine. The new workstation whose performance was modelled by Gray et al., when compared with the workstation it was to replace, turned out to cause an increase in call-handling time. This was confirmed both by the CPM-GOMS model and by a four-month field trial. How could this have happened in the context of known critical parameters? Few details of the new workstation's design are available, but it appears that its performance was evaluated by means of usability tests in which users performed a series of timed tasks (Newman, 1998). Each of these tasks formed part of a call, but no tests of complete call-handling were conducted. Thus the usability tests did not measure the workstation's performance in terms of the critical parameter. The design team was led to believe that performance had been improved, when it had not.

6   Discussion

The concept of using critical parameters in HCI design raises a number of questions. Foremost among these are:

1. How widespread are critical parameters in the domains where interactive systems are used?

2. How persistent can we expect performance parameters to be in the face of rapid technological change?

3. Is performance, in terms of critical parameters, really manipulable by means of analytical models?

4. Can methods based on critical parameters be assimilated into HCI design practice?

The first question basically asks whether critical parameters perhaps exist in so few domains that the proposed new methods will rarely be used. We cannot offer hard evidence that critical parameters are ubiquitous; we can however report that, during just over a year spent searching for them, we have uncovered three sets of parameters and are hard on the heels of a fourth. We still rely to a large extent on arguments given earlier, concerning people's ability to plan their work and consistently achieve targets for completion times and reliability. If these people work to targets, it should be possible to identify related targets for the design of supporting systems.

At the same time, we recognise there are domains of work where people find targets difficult to set, and where we will probably find critical parameters elusive. Our own field of work, research, is one such domain. Indeed any work relying heavily on information search and retrieval is known to be unpredictable and hard to plan. This is one reason why the well-known critical parameters of information retrieval technology, precision and recall, have persisted in use for so long: it is very hard to identify metrics for the work in which these technologies are used. Pirolli and others have made significant progress in this direction in their work on models of retrieval cost structures (Pirolli & Card, 1995).

The second question concerns the persistence of critical parameters. Is there a real danger that parameters will turn out to be no longer critical after a system has been designed and introduced to the workplace? This could mean that effort spent on achieving performance targets is wasted. We accept that there are examples of performance measures becoming obsolete in the face of computerization, e.g. in the printing industry since the move to computer-based typesetting. However, these radical changes to the structure of work are usually followed by many years of incremental, measurable improvements.

We confess to being somewhat worried by Question 3, concerning the feasibility of building models that give accurate predictions of performance. We do not have sufficient experience to answer this question. We do believe, however, that the discovery of persistent critical parameters will encourage researchers to develop models and tools for performance prediction. As designers attempt to meet performance targets, and fail through a lack of analytical techniques, they will start to make demands on the research community.

As regards the last question, we have been concerned from the outset to propose methods that are easy for designers to incorporate in their current design practice. Designers will pay attention to performance issues if they are given clear and achievable targets, as MacLean et al. discovered. We have focused on finding ways to identify parameters that are sufficiently clear and achievable to deserve designers' attention. We have looked for ways to relieve the design team of the burden of identifying performance targets. We also hope we have reduced the need to factor usability testing into the design schedule.

7   Conclusion

We have devoted this paper primarily to discussing what critical parameters might mean for HCI design practitioners. We conclude by pointing out that there are implications for two other communities: researchers and users.

Use of critical parameters promises to introduce a new role for HCI researchers — parameter identification — and to raise the importance of a current role, the construction of models. These roles could provide opportunities to make even stronger contributions to design practice than at present. The contributions could take the form of enhanced models for predicting performance in terms of critical parameters; they might also include newly identified parameters. In this way the partnership between researchers, system designers and HCI practitioners could be further strengthened and enriched.

We hope that critical parameters also offer something new for users. At present, users can have little influence on the directions taken by software product suppliers, except when they switch allegiance en masse from one supplier to another. Critical parameters could provide users with a basis for demanding specific improvements in performance. This would have the beneficial effect of making suppliers more accountable for the performance of their systems, and ultimately might lead to competition on the basis of performance rather than just functionality.

Acknowledgements

We are grateful to our Xerox colleagues for providing constant feedback and encouragement as this work proceeded, and especially to Hervé Gallaire for initially engaging us in discussing the role of critical parameters. We would like also to thank the conference programme chairs who provided the data for Figure 2. Finally, we wish to acknowledge the many insights we have gained from Walter Vincenti, first from reading his remarkable book, and subsequently from a series of all-too-infrequent discussions.

References

Card, S. K., Moran, T. P. & Newell, A. (1983), *The Psychology of Human–Computer Interaction*, Lawrence Erlbaum Associates.

Cusumano, M. A. & Selby, R. W. (1995), *Microsoft Secrets: How the Worlds' Most Powerful Software Company Creates Technology, Shapes Markets, and Manages People*, Harper Collins.

Dix, A., Ramduny, D. & Wilkinson, J. (1998), "Interaction in the Large", *Interacting with Computers* **11**(1), 9–32.

Gibbs, W. W. (1997), "Taking Computers to Task", *Scientific American* **277**(1), 64–71.

Gray, W. D., John, B. E. & Atwood, M. E. (1993), "Project Ernestine: Validating a GOMS Analysis for Predicting and Explaining Real-world Task Performance", *Human–Computer Interaction* **8**(4), 237–309.

Harper, R. H. R. (1998), *Inside the IMF: An Ethnography of Documents, Technology and Organisational Action*, Academic Press.

Herbsleb, J. D. & Kuwana, E. (1993), Preserving Knowledge in Design Projects: What Designers Need to Know, *in* S. Ashlund, K. Mullet, A. Henderson, E. Hollnagel & T. White (eds.), *Proceedings of INTERCHI'93*, ACM Press/IOS Press, pp.7–14.

Kieras, D. E. (1997), A Guide to GOMS Model Usability Evaluation using NGOMSL, *in* M. Helander, T. K. Landauer & P. Prabhu (eds.), *Handbook of Human–Computer Interaction*, second edition, Elsevier Science, pp.733–66.

Lammers, S. M. (1986), *Programmers at Work*, Microsoft Press.

Landauer, T. K. (1995), *The Trouble with Computers: Usefulness, Usability and Productivity*, MIT Press.

Lim, K. Y. & Long, J. B. (1994), *The MUSE Method for Usability Engineering*, Cambridge Series on Human–Computer Interaction, Cambridge University Press.

MacLean, A., Young, R. M., Bellotti, V. M. E. & Moran, T. P. (1991), "Questions, Options and Criteria: Elements of Design Space Analysis", *Human–Computer Interaction* **6**(3-4), 201–50.

Newman, W. M. (1997), Better or Just Different? On the Benefits of Designing Interactive Systems in Terms of Critical Parameters, *in* G. C. van der Veer, A. Henderson & S. Coles (eds.), *Proceedings of the Symposium on Designing Interactive Systems: Processes, Practices, Methods and Techniques (DIS'97)*, ACM Press, pp.239–45.

Newman, W. M. (1998), "On Simulation, Measurement and Piecewise Usability Evaluation", *Human–Computer Interaction* **13**(3), 316–23.

Newman, W. M. & Taylor, A. S. (1997), Critical Parameters in Interactive System Design: Pointers from a Literature-Based Study of Representations of Performance, Technical Report EPC-1999-101, Xerox Research Centre Europe.

O'Hara, K., Smith, F., Newman, W. M. & Sellen, A. J. (1998), Student Readers' Use of Library Documents: Implications for Library Technologies, *in* C.-M. Karat, A. Lund, J. Coutaz & J. Karat (eds.), *Proceedings of CHI'98: Human Factors in Computing Systems*, ACM Press, pp.233–40.

Orr, J. (1996), *Talking About Machines: An Ethnography of a Modern Job*, Cornell University Press.

Pirolli, P. & Card, S. K. (1995), Information Foraging in Information Access Environments, *in* I. Katz, R. Mack, L. Marks, M. B. Rosson & J. Nielsen (eds.), *Proceedings of CHI'95: Human Factors in Computing Systems*, ACM Press, pp.51–8.

Polson, P. G. & Lewis, C. H. (1990), "Theory-based Design for Easily Learned Interfaces", *Human–Computer Interaction* **5**(2), 191–220.

Preece, J., Rogers, Y., Sharp, H., Benyon, D., Holland, S. & Carey, T. (1994), *Human–Computer Interaction*, Addison–Wesley.

Vincenti, W. G. (1990), *What Engineers Know and How They Know It: Analytical Studies from Aeronautical History*, Johns Hopkins University Press.

Human–Computer Interaction — INTERACT '99
M. Angela Sasse and Chris Johnson (Editors)
Published by IOS Press, © IFIP TC.13, 1999

Breaking Down Usability

Martijn van Welie, Gerrit C. van der Veer & Anton Eliëns

Faculty of Computer Science, Vrije Universiteit Amsterdam,
de Boelelaan 1081a, 1081 HV Amsterdam, The Netherlands.
{martijn,gerrit,eliens}@cs.vu.nl

Abstract: Good usability of a system is the main goal of interface designers. Determining the usability is usually done afterwards by performing usability tests with users or by going through checklists. On the other hand, design guidelines and design heuristics give the designer assistance in improving the usability while designing. In practice the available checklists, tests, guidelines, etc. differ in terms of structure, content and terminology and the suggestion is given that one list is more useful than another. This paper breaks down the concept of usability into a layered model that allows comparisons of the available lists and provides better understanding of them. The model also gives a framework for evaluation by showing which usability aspects can be tested empirically and what can be formally checked by analysing designs during the design process itself.

Keywords: usability, evaluation.

1 Introduction

The term usability is used to denote that a design is 'good' from a HCI point of view (Hartson, 1998). Does a design provide the right functionality in the right way and does it satisfy everyone's needs? A designer or a design team can use guidelines, heuristics or rules as aids in the design process to ensure good usability. On the other hand designers should evaluate their design with users in practice to see if the usability is at the desired or required level. For the evaluation with users checklists or sets of ergonomic criteria and heuristics exist. The problem of all these lists, rules and criteria is that it is unclear how they are related (if at all) and *why* one list may be more useful than others. To understand the various checklists and the relationships between them, the concept of usability needs to be broken down in a way that allows comparisons from both theoretical and practical viewpoints. In Section 2, a general background of usability and related knowledge domains are described. In Sections 3 and 4, the most well known definitions of usability are discussed together with some common principles and rules. We then propose a layered model of usability which is described in Section 5. Section 6 will then discuss the usability evaluation process in the light of our model. In Section 7, we provide a discussion about the consequences for task modelling and dialogue modelling.

2 Knowledge Domains

There are many design methods and techniques which all have the goal of designing a usable system. In iterative design methods the main technique is constant evaluation with users. Other methods take a more structured approach and start with task analysis thereby trying to improve the usability of the initial designs and hopefully to have less iterations than iterative prototyping techniques. This shows two viewpoints on usability in the design process:

1. improving usability by evaluation with users; and

2. improving usability already *during* design by applying all available relevant knowledge.

Each of the viewpoints is important and an ideal design process uses both viewpoints effectively. UI design is a process that involves knowledge input from several domains. Each of the knowledge domains is necessarily needed but the actual influence may change per project. The knowledge domains are the primary source of information for improving usability and at the same time also a source when evaluating usability and searching for *causes* of sub-optimal usability.

2.1 Knowledge about Humans

The systems we design are being used by humans so we need to know the abilities and limitations of humans. Especially cognitive and perceptual abilities are relevant to design. Humans have serious limitations when it comes to information processing and other tasks such as decision making, searching and scanning (Shneiderman, 1998). The fields of cognitive psychology and ergonomics give a theoretical and practical background on these matters. Research in those fields has given useful knowledge that can be used in practice, for instance knowledge about short and long term memory can directly be used to improve learnability of systems. In the past, methods such as GOMS (Card et al., 1983) and CCT (Kieras & Polson, 1985) have tried to incorporate cognitive aspects to predict the influence of changes to dialogue aspects of a design. Another important aspect of knowledge about humans is the social and organizational viewpoint. Users perform their tasks in a larger context where they have a social and organizational position that is important to them. In this context they may have to work together or are part of a team. Contextual aspects about users have a less direct impact on the design process and are strongly related to the position of a new system in the organization where it is going to be used. Generally speaking, usability problems are caused by a mismatch between the users' abilities and the required abilities that the system enforces on the users.

2.2 Knowledge about Design

Every designer acquires skills and experiences during projects and that knowledge helps the designer in later projects. This *design knowledge* comes from both practical experience and from literature. Currently the amount of design knowledge available in literature is rather limited which makes the personal experience of the designer an important factor for the usability of the design. Basically the only concrete design knowledge that can be used during design is embedded into *guidelines*. Several guidelines exist but there is no agreement on the form guidelines should have. Some guidelines such as the Macintosh (Apple Computer Inc, 1992) or MS-Windows (Microsoft, 1995) guidelines mainly describe a platform *style* and hardly contain concrete guidelines. The underlying assumption that applications that have been designed according to the guidelines have good usability remains unjustified. Other guidelines such as Smith & Mosier's (1986) focus on narrow scoped list

of guidelines dealing with detailed design choices and consequently they are quickly outdated by new developments of technology. Despite the differences in guidelines they certainly embody design knowledge and every designer should know them. However, there may be several reasons why the guidelines are not followed during the design process. Even if a designer *tries* to use the guidelines there are still many problems *applying* them. In Dix et al. (1998) a number of problems with guidelines are discussed such as when to apply a guideline or choose one out of contradicting guidelines. Also the effectiveness of guidelines is under discussion and research has shown that not all guidelines are as practical as desired (Scapin & Bastien, 1997). Some older guidelines were designed for designing character based applications and it is not clear in how far they apply to e.g. WIMP interfaces or Virtual Reality interfaces. Another way of capturing design knowledge is in *design* patterns (Bayle, 1998). Such patterns describe generalized problems and proven solutions that can be immediately used in practice. Research on design patterns has just started and no concrete results are available yet.

Guidelines deal with both structural (the dialogue) and presentational aspects of a design. For example, guidelines on colour use and button sizes refer to the presentation and guidelines on feedback and menu structure deal with dialogue. Usually no explicit distinction between dialogue and presentation is made, although both have a distinguishable impact on usability. Since guidelines often go into depths on describing a platform's style, mainly presentational aspects are covered and there is little guidance for structural aspects. Because design patterns work from a problem to a solution it is more likely to find guidance on structural aspects emphasized in design patterns.

2.3 Knowledge about the Task World

Besides the design knowledge needed for a good design, every project also needs the right information about the specific design case for basing the design on. Both knowledge about humans and knowledge about design is domain-independent but the task world knowledge is different for every design project. Task analysis should provide the information for the requirements of the system both in the functional sense but also in the ergonomic and cognitive sense. The functional side of a task analysis can be transferred quite directly to the design but the ergonomic and cognitive side is very hard to transfer into design. First of all because it is not clear what the relevant information is; what needs to be known in the task model in order to contribute to a more usable design? Secondly, because cognitive aspects are difficult to translate into concrete design decisions. One of the weak points in task analysis research is that it is difficult to justify how task analysis helps to design more *usable* systems as far as this is not directly based on functional requirements of the systems. An answer to this question may be given if it can be defined which properties of a design make the design usable. It can then be seen which information the task model ideally needs to contain.

3 Definitions of Usability

There is not one agreed upon definition of usability and usability certainly cannot be expressed in one objective measure. Several authors have proposed definitions and categorizations of usability and there seems to be at least some consensus on the concept of usability and they mostly differ on more detailed levels.

ISO 9241–11	Shneiderman	Nielsen
Efficiency	Speed of performance	Efficiency
	Time to learn	Learnability
Effectiveness	Retention over time	Memorability
	Rate of errors by users	Errors/Safety
Satisfaction	Subjective satisfaction	Satisfaction

Table 1: Usability as in ISO 9241–11, B. Shneiderman and J. Nielsen

In the ISO 9241–11 standard (Bevan, 1994), a rather abstract definition is given in terms of efficiency, effectiveness and satisfaction. 'Efficiency' is defined as the *resources expended in relation to the accuracy and completeness with which users achieve goals* and 'effectiveness' as the *accuracy and completeness with which users achieve specified tasks*. 'Satisfaction' is a subjective measure and concerns the *comfort and acceptability of use by end users*. This definition approaches usability from a theoretical viewpoint and may not be very practical. Nielsen (1993) has a slightly different definition that is specified in elements that are more specific. Nielsen only regards expert users when talking about efficiency although learnability is also directly related to efficiency. Memorability mainly relates to casual users and errors deal with those errors not covered by efficiency, which have more catastrophic results. A similar definition is given by Shneiderman (1998). Sheiderman does not call his definition a definition of usability but he calls it *"five measurable human factors central to evaluation of human factors goals"*. As can be seen from Table 1, Shneiderman's definition is essentially identical to Nielsen's definition and only differs in terminology.

Table 2 shows the usability factors as described by Dix et al. (1998). This categorization looks rather different from the ISO and Nielsen definitions. Dix et al. define three main groups; learnability, flexibility and robustness suggesting that those concepts are on the same abstraction level. The groups are specified further by factors that *influence* the concept they belong to. For instance, consistency influences learnability positively when a design is consistent within the application and between applications on the same platform. Learnability is subdivided into aspects that are mostly of cognitive nature thereby giving more grip on the important cognitive skills of users in relation to learnability. Robustness corresponds more or less to effectiveness. In flexibility also some lower level concepts such as multi-threading are mentioned but most aspects are mainly related to efficiency.

Learnability	Flexibility	Robustness
Predictability	Dialogue initiative	Observability
Synthesizability	Multi-Threading	Recoverability
Familiarity	Task Migratability	Responsiveness
Generalizability	Substitutivity	Task conformance
Consistency	Customizability	

Table 2: Usability categorization by Dix et al.

When comparing these categorizations and definitions it is remarkable that Nielsen and the ISO standard give a concise outline of the term usability while Dix et al. focus more on the concrete elements that influence usability. From a practical viewpoint, Dix et al.'s categorization gives the designer concrete measures for improving the usability of a design. On the other hand, it is odd that Nielsen's notions of efficiency or error rate can not be found in Dix et al.'s categorization, as they are clear indicators of usability. The most interesting aspect of Dix et al.'s categorization is that it raises the question what the *causes* for sub-optimal usability might be and how it might be improved.

4 Principles and Rules

In addition to definitions of usability, there are also several lists of design principles, heuristics or criteria. Nielsen gives a set of *heuristics* to follow that should have a positive effect on his categories. These heuristics are kind of general guidelines that should be followed, for example: 'forgive the user' or 'give feedback'. Shneiderman (1998) gives similar heuristics in his *8 golden rules* for design:

1. Strive for consistency.

2. Enable frequent users to use shortcuts.

3. Offer informative feedback.

4. Design dialogues to yield closure.

5. Offer error prevention and simple error handling.

6. Permit easy reversal of actions.

7. Support internal locus of control.

8. Reduce short-term memory load.

From both Dix et al.'s categorization and Nielsen's heuristics it is shown that the root factors that influence usability need to be found in the cognitive and perceptual abilities of users such as long and short-term memory, problem solving, decision making, searching and scanning (Shneiderman, 1998). On the other hand, knowledge about the specific design project expressed in task models is important, especially concerning effectiveness. A similar list is given by the ISO 9241–10 ISOvdt1996 standard and is called a set of *dialogue principles*, see Table 3.

Dialogue Principles
Suitability for the task
Self-descriptiveness
Controllability
Conformity with user expectations
Error tolerance
Suitability for individualization
Suitability for learning

Table 3: ISO9241–10 Dialogue Principles.

Another interesting list is the list of ergonomic criteria developed by Scapin & Bastien (1997), see Table 4. Scapin & Bastien's list of ergonomic criteria mentions 'grouping and distinguishing items'. Grouping is concerned with the *"visual organization of information items in relation to one another"* and is therefore concerned with presentational aspects. Most other lists mention structural aspects rather than presentational aspects.

Usually there is no explicit distinction between dialogue and presentation level aspects and only the design as a whole is considered. It is useful to realize that measures have both dialogue and presentation aspects. However, often a clear distinction cannot be made. Mullet & Sano (1995) show the importance of presentational aspects and their effect on usability. In addition, they also provide techniques for improving presentational aspects such as grouping, grids etc.

1 Guidance
1.1 Prompting
1.2 Grouping and distinguishing items
1.2.1 Grouping by location
1.2.2 Grouping by format
1.3 Immediate feedback
1.4 Legibility
2 Workload
2.1 Brevity
2.1.1 Conciseness
2.1.2 Minimal actions
2.2 Information density
3 Explicit control
3.1 Explicit user actions
3.2 User control
4. Adaptability
4.1 Flexibility
4.2 Users' experience
5 Error management
5.1 Error protection
5.2 Quality of error messages
5.3 Error correction
6 Consistency
7 Significance of codes
8 Compatibility

Table 4: Ergonomic Criteria by Scapin & Bastien.

5   A Layered Model

All the different definitions and principles make usability a confusing concept when actually designing a new system. Usually authors spent a lot effort trying to find out what is the 'best' set of principles or to define a "complete set of heuristics". Although these 'aids' are useful it remains unclear how they are related and how to judge when an 'aid' is useful to improve usability. Figure 1 shows a layered model of usability that helps understanding the various aids. On the highest level, the ISO definition of usability is given split up in three aspects: efficiency, effectiveness and satisfaction. This level is a rather abstract way of looking at usability and is not directly applicable in practice. However it does give three solid pillars for looking at usability that are based on a well-formed theory (Bevan, 1994). The next level contains a number of *usage indicators* which are indicators of the usability level that can actually be observed in practice when users are at work. Each of these indicators contributes to the abstract aspects of the higher level. For instance, a low error-rate contributes to a better effectiveness and good performance speed indicates good efficiency.

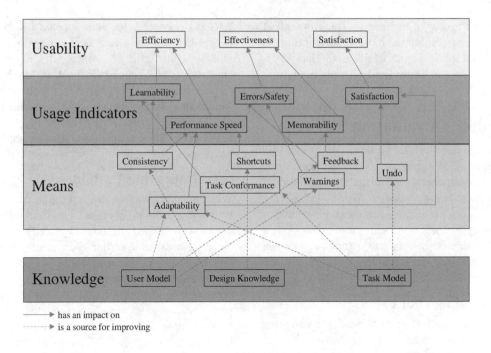

Figure 1: Layered model of usability.

One level lower is the level of *means*. Means cannot be observed in user tests and are not goals by themselves whereas indicators are observable goals. The means are used in 'heuristics' for improving one or more of the usage indicators and are consequently not *goals* by themselves. For instance, consistency may have a positive effect on learnability and warnings may reduce errors. On the other hand, there may be good reasons for not complying completely with a consistent platform style. Each means can have a positive or negative effect on some of the indicators. The means need to be "used with care" and a designer should take care not to apply them automatically. The best usability results from an optimal use of the means where each means is at a certain 'level', somewhere between 'none' and 'completely/everywhere/all the time'. It is up to the designer to find those optimal levels for each means. In order to do that the designer has to use the three knowledge domains (humans, design, and task) to determine the appropriate levels. For example, when design knowledge is consulted by using *guidelines*, it is clear that the guidelines should embody the knowledge of *how* changes in use of the means affect the usage indicators.

The means of Figure 1 are examples of means and usage indicators and the given set is certainly not complete. The different lists and heuristics all give suggestions for useful means. More research is needed to determine which means are most effective for improving usability.

5.1 Comparing Definitions

When comparing the definitions of Section 3 using our layered model it is clear that some definitions are on one level and that others have aspects from more than one level. For instance the dialogue principles of the ISO 9241–10 standard mention "suitability for learning" (which is learnability) and "error tolerance" which are both usage indicators, but it also mentions "suitability for individualization" (=adaptability) which is a means. Looking at the usability categorization of Dix et al. it shows that mainly means are summed up and the categories are a mixture of means and indicators; learnability is an indicator and flexibility and robustness are means. Scapin & Bastien's list of ergonomic criteria is essentially a list of means grouped together. Shneiderman's golden rules say to strive for "a certain level" for each of the eight specific means he considers the most important.

When means and indicators are mixed in one list the semantics of the list are ambiguous which causes confusion and makes it more difficult to apply them for actual design decisions. Additionally, it is good to realize that none of the list can be regarded as being complete. Each of the lists has at least one element not mentioned by any of the others. Therefore, all of the lists can be useful but the most important thing is to realize what the semantics of a list is. That way it is clear how a list can be used and what the limitations are.

6 Usability Evaluation

Evaluation of usability can be done *afterwards* and *during* design. The usefulness of all the guidelines, heuristics and other aids is related to the kind of evaluation that is being conducted. Using our model, it is clear that when evaluating with users, evaluation is being done by looking at the *usage indicators*. When evaluating during design, the usage indicators do not provide any data and one has to look at the *means* and make an estimate on their impact.

6.1 Evaluating with Users

Evaluating with users is good method for obtaining data about the actual usage. Using scenarios and other techniques, data about the number of errors or speed of performance can be obtained which should provide a good indication of the usability of the product. However, when usability is not up to par it is important to find out *why* the level of usability is unsatisfactory. In that case, the usage indicators do not help much. One solution is looking at how the *means* were used in the design and another way is by consulting the knowledge from the user and task model.

6.2 Evaluating during Design

Evaluation during the design process is more problematic than evaluating with users. The usage indicators cannot be evaluated directly and therefore do not provide any hard data. What can be done is looking at the *means* that influence the usage indicators. Using walkthroughs and scenarios each of the means can be evaluated by looking at the way they are present in the design and by estimating the positive or negative impact on the usage indicators. For instance, it can be checked if a design is consistent with a platform's style guideline or if in sufficient warnings are given.

Another way of ensuring usability during the design process is by using formal design models. Many models and techniques exist for describing designs using formal notations. State charts, GOMS, ConcurTaskTree's (Palanque & Paternò, 1997) and similar notations are being used to describe designs. These kinds of notations are usually strong in describing structural aspects of a design (the dialogue structure) and very weak at describing presentational aspects. Payne & Green (1989) say, *"as far as*

TAG is concerned, the screen could be turned off". In relation to the means of our model, this is already a big limitation since a lot of means such consistency, warnings or feedback are strongly related to presentational aspects. Another factor is that most formal models are usually built with the viewpoint of describing 'correct' use of the application and therefore do not describe error handling or issuing of warnings.

6.3 Improving Usability

When an evaluation shows that the usability needs to be improved the problem is to find out *which* means need to be changed and *how* they need to be changed. As was mentioned earlier each means may have a positive effect on one usage indicator while having a negative effect on another. In some cases it may be obvious how to improve usability but in cases where problems are of a more structural kind it may not be so simple to solve. In that case, the designer has to take a step back and look at the knowledge domains again. The knowledge domains are the only sources for judging why and how a means is to be changed. For instance, when the task conformance is seen as a problem the task model can give the designer information about what is wrong with the task conformance. Similarly, the user model may give information about the memory limitations which may require the design to have more or better feedback of user actions. Unfortunately the knowledge domains are not always available or written down in a way that makes it easy to use them in practice. Task models may not contain the right information or the available guidelines do not say anything about a particular problem.

7 Discussion

Our layered model of usability gives a somewhat broader perspective on usability and how to achieve good usability in practice. However, it also shows that there is a dependency on the knowledge available. From a theoretical point of view, it is easy to talk about task models but if the task modelling methods available do not produce the task models with the needed information, the task model is not helping to improve usability. Literature on task modelling still has not convincingly shown how the task models contribute to usability other than improving task conformance. The same goes for user models and design knowledge. There are many design guidelines but it is difficult to separate style definitions with real guidelines and the guidelines themselves are defined rather informally. Design guidelines should tell the designer how the means are used most effectively but currently the guidelines are not in such an explicit form. It seems likely that not every means is equally important and that means could be organized into lists ranked by impact under certain constraints.

Beside knowledge aspects, research is still weak on ways for ensuring usability *during* the design process. After all, it is better to do it 'right' the first time than having to rely on iterative prototyping with user testing. What is needed is a way to use models for usability evaluation that really give a reasonable indication of usability level. However, most modelling techniques only allow some performance evaluation such as by looking at interaction path lengths. Modelling techniques also need to be able to address issues such as task conformance, warnings, undo and feedback. Although it may be very useful to use those techniques for other purposes, if the set of concepts in modelling techniques is not expanded beyond states and state-changes, those modelling techniques cannot be used to ensure usability during design. The next section will discuss some directions for task and dialogue modelling improvements.

7.1 Addressing Task Models

Task modelling research has a strong background in cognitive psychology and the focus was on how users perform their work and think about their work from the viewpoint of looking at one user. The strongest link was the fact that if you know more about the user and his work you can build a more usable system. In practice, most modelling methods such as HTA did not model much more than a task hierarchy. Using the task hierarchy only helps to establish *task conformance* and does not help to improve other means such as adaptability or error prevention. However, when the task model is taken as model describing the users, their work, the objects they use and the organization they are part of, it is possible to capture information that can actually *help* to improve usability. The task model should be able to *answer* questions about the task world related to effective use of means. Table 5 shows some question for a task model in relation to a means. As can be observed from Table 5, a task model needs to contain more than a simple task hierarchy. Task analysis methods such as GTA (van der Veer et al., 1996; van Welie et al., 1998) look at much more aspects of the task world such as roles, agents, objects, event and their relationships.

Besides these concepts, the right information about the concepts needs to be captured. For instance, when a designer wants to know what the critical tasks

are, the task model must be able make a distinction between critical and non-critical tasks, for instance by means of task typing. When the questions from Table 5 need to be answered, all of these aspects and probably even more need to be added. We intend to use the means to check whether our task analysis method GTA (van der Veer et al., 1996) contains the necessary information and indeed add missing aspects.

Means	Question for task model
Warnings	What are the critical tasks?
	How frequent are those tasks performed?
	Always performed by the same user?
Adaptability	Which types of users are there?
	Which roles do they have?
	Which tasks belong to which role?
Undo	Which tasks should be undoable?
	Which tasks have undoable side effects?
Error prevention	What errors are expected?
	What are the consequences for users?
	How can prevention be effective?

Table 5: Questions for task models.

7.2 Addressing Dialogue Modelling

Dialogue modelling and especially *formal* dialogue modelling (Palanque & Paternò, 1997) is gaining interest in HCI research. One problem of most formal methods such as described in (Palanque & Paternò, 1997; Payne & Green, 1989) is that they are designed to describe the *behaviour* of interface and not to enable usability evaluation. Some methods can be used to do verification of systems but this is limited to properties such as state-reachability, deadlocks and interaction path lengths. Although interaction paths can say something about the speed of performance, it is impossible to make predictions about other usability aspects. In the same way as for task models, the means can be used to determine some requirements for dialogue models that enable usability evaluation. A dialogue model also needs to be built using the right concepts and they should be verifiable in some respect.

Looking at Table 6 is it clear that a dialogue model needs to be more than a state-based description. A dialogue model must be able to identify system feedback as either a warning or state feedback and must also contain more detailed information about the functionality as in how far it can be undone or not. In fact there are techniques that partially address these aspects; UAN (Hix & Hartson, 1993) deals with explicitly with feedback and TAG (Payne & Green, 1989) allowed analysis of consistency by identifying similar task–action decompositions. When such additions are done, a dialogue can be evaluated by looking at how well constraints are satisfied, e.g. "Does the user get a warning before executing a function that is undoable?" or "Given a starting point what is the average number of steps needed to perform this task?"

Means	Questions
Warnings	When are warnings given?
Speed of performance	How many steps needed for accomplishing a task?
Undo	Which functions are undoable?
Feedback	When and how is feedback given?
Consistency	What are similar task–action decompositions?

Table 6: Questions for dialogue evaluation.

8   Conclusions

This paper has discussed several definitions of the concept usability along with heuristics and other guidelines. The proposed layered model of usability gives a division into usage indicators and means that affect them. The model gives a view on usability that can be used in both a practical and a theoretical way. Using this model, the definitions of usability were discussed again and it was shown that some definitions and guidelines are actually a mix of usage indicators and means. In addition, usability evaluation was discussed in the context of our layered model, focusing on usability evaluation during and after the design process. Although the model incorporates several knowledge domains as sources for improving usability, it has been argued that the knowledge domains are in practice hard to use or may not contain the appropriate information.

References

Apple Computer Inc (1992), *Macintosh Human Interface Guidelines*, Addison–Wesley.

Bayle, E. (1998), "Putting it All Together: Towards a Pattern Language for Interaction Design", *ACM SIGCHI Bulletin* **30**(1), 17–24.

Bevan, N. (1994), Ergonomic Requirements for Office Work With VDTs, Technical Report 9241-11, ISO.

Card, S. K., Moran, T. P. & Newell, A. (1983), *The Psychology of Human–Computer Interaction*, Lawrence Erlbaum Associates.

Dix, A., Finlay, J., Abowd, G. & Beale, R. (1998), *Human–Computer Interaction*, second edition, Prentice–Hall Europe.

Hartson, H. R. (1998), "Human–Computer Interaction: Interdisciplinary Roots and Trends", *Journal of Systems and Software* **43**(2), 103–18.

Hix, D. & Hartson, H. R. (1993), *Developing User Interfaces: Ensuring Usability through Product and Process*, John Wiley & Sons.

Kieras, D. E. & Polson, P. G. (1985), "An Approach to the Formal Analysis of User Complexity", *International Journal of Man–Machine Studies* **22**(4), 365–94.

Microsoft (1995), *The Windows Interface Guidelines for Software Design*, Microsoft Press.

Mullet, K. & Sano, D. K. (1995), *Designing Visual Interfaces: Communication Oriented Techniques*, SunSoft Press (Prentice-Hall).

Nielsen, J. (1993), *Usability Engineering*, Academic Press.

Palanque, P. & Paternò, P. (1997), *Formal Methods in Human–Computer Interaction*, Springer-Verlag.

Payne, S. J. & Green, T. R. G. (1989), Task–Action Grammar: The Model and its Developments, *in* D. Diaper (ed.), *Task Analysis for Human–Computer Interaction*, Ellis Horwood.

Scapin, D. L. & Bastien, J. M. C. (1997), "Ergonomic Criteria for Evaluating the Ergonomic Quality of Interactive Systems", *Behaviour & Information Technology* **16**(4-5), 220–31.

Shneiderman, B. (1998), *Designing the User Interface: Strategies for Effective Human–Computer Interaction*, third edition, Addison–Wesley.

Smith, S. L. & Mosier, J. N. (1986), Guidelines for Designing User Interface Software, Technical Report MTR-10090, EDS-TR-86-278, The Mitre Corporation.

van der Veer, G. C., Lenting, B. F. & Bergevoet, B. A. J. (1996), "GTA: Groupware Task Analysis — Modeling Complexity", *Acta Psychologica* **91**(3), 297–322.

van Welie, M., van der Veer, G. C. & Eliëns, A. (1998), An Ontology for Task World Models, *in* P. Markopoulos & P. Johnson (eds.), *Design, Specification and Verification of Interactive Systems'98*, Springer-Verlag, pp.57–70.

Human–Computer Interaction — INTERACT '99
M. Angela Sasse and Chris Johnson (Editors)
Published by IOS Press, © IFIP TC.13, 1999

Comparing Usability Evaluation Principles with Heuristics: Problem Instances vs. Problem Types

Iain W. Connell & Nicholas V. Hammond

Department of Psychology, University of York, York YO10 5DD, UK.

{iwc100,nvh1}@york.ac.uk

Abstract: This paper reports the results of two studies which compared Nielsen's heuristics for user interface evaluation with an expanded set of evaluation principles based on the literature. The aim was to discover if both experienced and novice evaluators could identify more usability problems using the principles than with the heuristics alone. Experienced subjects did find more high severity problems; however, novices proved unable to do this at any severity level. Further analysis puts into question Nielsen's claim that the cumulative number of new usability problems found by non-novice evaluators tails off relatively quickly, such that most problems with an interface might be found by only five evaluators. The pattern of the current findings was different in that the number of new problems did not converge in the manner claimed. This is attributed to the differences in the method of early problem identification, rather than categorization, used.

Keywords: usability evaluation, heuristic evaluation, evaluation principles, problem categorization.

1 Introduction

This paper reports the results of two studies which compared Nielsen's heuristics for user interface evaluation (Molich & Nielsen, 1990; Nielsen, 1993) with an expanded set of evaluation principles based on the literature. The aim was to discover if both experienced and novice evaluators could identify more usability problems using the principles than with the heuristics alone. The rationale was that Nielsen's heuristics seemed to be both very general in content and somewhat limited in scope, appearing to rely on evaluator expertise over content. A set of expanded and more closely focused principles might enable experienced evaluators to uncover a wider and more directed set of usability problems. It was thought that this might also be true for novices, if sufficient guidance was provided.

Further analysis of the data from these studies puts into question Nielsen & Molich's (1990) claim that the cumulative number of new usability problems found in a heuristic evaluation tails off relatively quickly, to a point of 'diminishing returns' where the cost of bringing in additional evaluators is not justified by the decreasing number of new problems discovered. This will be attributed to the differences in the method of early problem identification, rather than categorization, used.

1.1 Principles vs. Heuristics

Nielsen and Molich's ten usability heuristics (Molich & Nielsen, 1990; Nielsen, 1993) represent a collection of 'rules of thumb' to be used by evaluators in predicting the likely problems that will arise during interface use. Heuristic evaluation (Nielsen & Molich, 1990; Nielsen, 1993; 1994) is one form of inspection method, constituting part of what Nielsen has dubbed 'discount usability engineering' (Nielsen, 1989). Though the heuristics remain a 'candidate set' (Nielsen, 1994a, p.155), the claim is that the discount approach enables identification of most of the problems which are found by more expensive methods (Nielsen, 1989).

Heuristic evaluation has been compared with other inspection methods such as cognitive walkthrough. For example, Sears (1997) has shown that a combination of these two methods produced results superior to either method alone. However, Sears's and others' primary focus has been on the details of the methods involved. The focus of interest in the current studies was on the content of the materials, the method — derived from Nielsen's descriptions of heuristic evaluation — being held the same. As Gray & Salzman (1998) point out, comparisons between usability evaluation methods are liable to fall down on considerations of effect construct validity if conclusions relating to whole methods are derived from a single dependent measure. The aim here was to show that one set of evaluation materials might elicit more usability problems than another, any differences in the method of use of such materials being left to future investigations.

The same set of heuristics was used in both studies. These were taken in full from Molich & Nielsen (1990), with the addition of 'Help and Documentation' (Nielsen, 1993, p.20). Their titles were as follows:

1. **Simple and Natural Dialogue.**

2. **Speak the User's Language.**

3. **Minimize the User's Memory Load.**

4. **Be Consistent.**

5. **Provide Feedback.**

6. **Provide Clearly Marked Exits.**

7. **Provide Shortcuts.**

8. **Provide Good Error Messages.**

9. **Error Prevention.**

10. **Help and Documentation.**

The principles set was similar to but wider in scope than those developed by Bastien & Scapin — most recently reported in (Bastien et al., 1999). The format was adapted from Smith (1986) and Marshall et al. (1987), the content from Marshall et al. (1987) plus many other sources (not cited here for reasons of space). The first study made use of a summary version, the second a fully worked version plus an extracted summary. The contents of the full version* were as follows:

Requirements   and   Functionality Principles
Requirements Match
Functional Utility

User–System Principles
Navigational Effort
Memory Load
Error Management
Feedback
Location and Navigation
Choice Availability
User Match

User Principles
Modifiability
Flexibility
Accuracy of Content
Salience

Comparative Principles
Consistency

System Performance Principles
Manipulability
Responsiveness

Perceptual and Motor Principles
Visio-perceptual Load
Audio-perceptual Load
Motor Load
Perceptual Clarity
Perceptual Contrast

User Support Principles
General Help
Context-Sensitive Help

1.2   Cumulative Problem Counts

Nielsen's observation that "...heuristic evaluation seems to work best with three to five evaluators" (Nielsen, 1994, p.35) relates to the finding that on average around 75% of the aggregated problems in each of six previous studies could be accounted for by only 5 evaluators (Nielsen, 1994, p.33). These findings have been replicated by Virzi (1992).

The data from the current studies did not seem to support this view. A large proportion of the problems found in each study proved to have been identified only once, with only a small amount of overlap between individual subject accounts. Such a wide problem distribution seemed unlikely to produce results in line with Nielsen's prediction. To test this proposition, cumulative problem counts (additive totals of unique problems found by successive evaluators, discounting repetitions) were performed on the data from both studies. Plotting these curves enabled assessment of the number of subjects which had been required to identify 75% of the problems found by each subject group.

---

*Available on request from the first author.

2   Procedure

In both studies subjects acted as evaluators. Subjects used either Nielsen's ten heuristics or the principles set. Both experiments also had a control condition, in which subjects were provided with no specific guidance or evaluation materials. In the first experiment, both novices (Psychology and other undergraduates, N=24) and experienced evaluators (York HCI Group researchers, N=15) took part; in the second, only novices (Psychology undergraduates, N=23). Most subjects either were paid at hourly rates or received subject credit.

In both experiments subjects were introduced to the evaluation material prior to starting the session and were instructed to refer to the material as needed. After each session subjects were instructed to look again at the material and to add any additional comments. The dependent measure in both experiments was the number of problems which were reported by subjects. The source of this measure was the individual subject protocols which resulted from each session. However, the method of recording problems was different for each experiment.

2.1   Experiment 1

The first experiment was a 2 (group) × 3 (condition) between-subjects design. Subject groups consisted of novices (8 per condition) and experienced subjects (5 per condition); the three conditions were Control, Heuristic and Principle. Group status was assessed by a questionnaire, administered before the start of the session. Subjects were also briefed as to the likely users of the software (here, the general public).

The software under evaluation was a cut down simulation of an existing art gallery hypermedia browser. The on-screen material allowed access to paintings by two artists, plus other related information.

In this experiment Heuristic and Principle condition subjects were presented with the evaluation material at the start of each session. The version of the principles set used was a three-page summary of the then 26 principles.

The procedure for both subject groups was first to answer a non-trivial question relating to one of the paintings, and then to explore until all the on-screen material had been encountered. This was intended to resemble Nielsen's recommendation for heuristic evaluation, namely that evaluators should first run through the whole of an interface in relatively brief fashion, and then proceed in more detail (Nielsen, 1994, p.29).

In this experiment, the experimenter sat with each subject and wrote down her or his comments while she

or he 'thought aloud'. Care was taken not to prime or direct the subject, but unclear or incomplete comments were more fully elicited. The experimenter's account was then read back to the subject and any required changes made. Any duplication in the subject's account, that is, where the same issue had been raised in more than one way, was then agreed with the subject. The subject was then asked to rate each resulting issue in terms of its severity, from 1 (trivial, might be ignored) to 7 (serious, must be addressed).

2.2   Experiment 2

The second experiment was a 3 condition between-subjects design, in two sessions. Only one subject group, novices (different from those in experiment 1), was involved; the three conditions were Control (N=7), Heuristic (N=8) and Principle (N=8). Novice status was assessed by the same questionnaire as used in experiment 1, this time administered by e-mail prior to the first session. Subjects were briefed as to the likely users of the software (here, psychology students).

The software under evaluation was the PsyCLE interactive teaching material for psychology students (Hammond & McKendree, 1998). Session 1 material concerned Piaget's developmental theories, session 2 concerned attribution theory.

In this experiment subjects were sent the evaluation material a few days before the start of the first session. Principle condition subjects received the now 31-page full version of the principles set plus an eight-page summary. During the session these subjects were instructed to use the summary set and to refer to the full version as necessary.

In this experiment subjects participated in an initial training session and an experimental session. The procedure in both sessions was the same: first, to run through the whole on-screen material relatively briefly, and then to work through the material in detail. In the first, training, session subjects were given a set of questions based on the content of the material. The first session was designed to introduce subjects to the evaluation materials and procedure (though Control subjects did not need such full exposure, this aspect of the experiment was held the same); the second session again was intended to resemble Nielsen's (1994) recommendation for heuristic evaluation.

In this experiment subjects entered their reactions directly into a prepared spreadsheet, without experimenter intervention. They were again asked to rate the severity of each issue raised, from 1 (trivial) to 7 (serious), and to add any remedies or comments.

In this case any apparent duplication in each subject's problem accounts could not be assessed until completion. This was later done by the experimenter, using the subjects' written descriptions.

3   Results

Quantitative analysis was performed on all data from experiment 1, but only on data from the second (experimental) session of experiment 2.

The outcome from the experimental sessions were individual subject protocols. In experiment 1 these had been written down by the experimenter and agreed with each subject; in experiment 2 they were the subjects' own written accounts, with only minor editing for spelling or grammar. From these protocols were derived the individual problem counts which were to be used in comparison of the evaluation materials (Section 3.1). This first, 'within subjects', stage of the problem reduction process involved the removal of any duplication in individual accounts, so that each subject's problem set incorporated only one instance of each problem (see Figure 1).

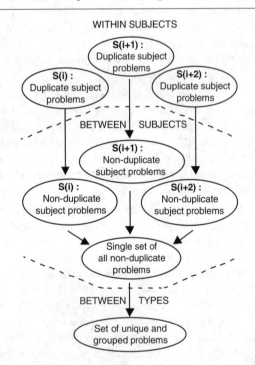

Figure 1: The problem reduction process: from problems separately identified by subjects S(i), S(i+1), S(i+2) ... to a single set of unique, grouped problems.

The second, 'between subjects', stage of the reduction process investigated the manner in which individual problem sets overlapped with those of other subjects. This involved identification of any issues which had been uncovered by more than one subject (i.e. repeating instances of the same problem from the emerging complete set) in each experiment. The result was a single set of non-duplicate problems from which unique problems could be isolated (Figure 1). This set was later used to create the cumulative problem counts described in Section 3.2.

3.1   Principles vs. Heuristics

3.1.1   Experiment 1

A two-way between-subject ANOVA of the complete problem count data from this experiment (Table 1) showed a significant main effect of group (novices vs. experienced, $F(1,33) = 71.42, p < 0.001$). Separate t-tests within condition showed increasingly significant differences between groups. Thus significantly more usability problems (mean ratio 2.84) were uncovered by the experienced subjects than by the novices, in all three conditions.

Control		Heuristic		Principle	
Novice	Exp.	Novice	Exp.	Novice	Exp.
6.38	13.00	6.00	20.20	7.63	23.60

Table 1: Experiment 1. Mean problem counts per subject, all data. (Exp. = experienced.)

There was also a main effect of condition for the novice and experienced groups $(F(2,33) = 5.60, p < 0.01)$. Separate one-way ANOVAs showed no main effect of condition for novices $(F(2,21) = 0.67, p = 0.52)$, but a marginally significant effect for experienced subjects $(F(2,12) = 3.82, p = 0.052)$. Thus for novices the difference between conditions had little effect on the numbers of problems identified, while the results suggest that experienced subjects detected fewer problems in the Control condition than in either of the other two conditions.

However, when high severity problems (rated by subjects as 5 to 7 inclusive on a 1 to 7 scale) alone were analysed, a different view emerged (Table 2).

Control		Heuristic		Principle	
Novice	Exp.	Novice	Exp.	Novice	Exp.
2.50	5.00	2.13	5.60	3.13	12.80

Table 2: Experiment 1. Mean problem counts per subject, high severity data. (Exp. = experienced.)

A two-way between-subject ANOVA of high severity problems alone revealed a further significant main effect of group $(F(1,33) = 31.67, p < 0.001)$. There was again a main effect of condition $(F(2,33) = 8.94, p < 0.01)$ (and no group $\times$ condition interaction). Separate one-way ANOVAs showed a main effect of condition for experienced subjects $(F(2,12) = 6.50, p < 0.05)$, but not for novices $(F(2,21) = 0.49, p = 0.62)$. Separate t-tests for experienced subjects showed significant differences between Principle and Heuristic ($p < 0.05$) and between Principle and Control ($p < 0.01$), but not between Heuristic and Control conditions. Thus experienced subjects proved able to uncover significantly more high severity problems using the principles than the heuristics (and the Control), while novices remained unable to do so.

Similar analyses on the low severity (rated 1 to 3 inclusive) problems alone (Table 3) showed the expected main effect of group $(F(1,33) = 29.32, p < 0.001)$, but not of condition $(F(2,33) = 1.49, p = 0.24)$. No further analysis is presented.

Control		Heuristic		Principle	
Novice	Exp.	Novice	Exp.	Novice	Exp.
2.63	6.60	2.63	11.40	3.13	7.80

Table 3: Experiment 1. Mean problem counts per subject, low severity data. (Exp. = experienced.)

3.1.2 Experiment 2

A one-way between-subject ANOVA of the complete problem count data from session 2 of experiment 2 (Table 4) showed no significant main effect of condition $(F(2,22) = 0.78, p = 0.47)$. Thus in the second experiment the differences between the heuristics and the full principles set proved insufficient to enable new novices to uncover significantly more problems than they did using the heuristics (or indeed the Control materials) alone.

Control	Heuristic	Principle
8.71	11.13	9.00

Table 4: Experiment 2 (session 2). Mean problem counts per novice subject, all data.

Nor was the picture any better for high severity problems (data not illustrated for reasons of space). Taking problems rated 5 to 7 alone, a one-way between-subject ANOVA again showed no significant main effect of condition $(F(2,22) = 0.42, p = 0.27)$. This was also true of the low severity (rated 1 to 3) problems $(F(2,22) = 0.12, p = 0.89)$.

Thus, even with initial training, these novices remained unable to uncover any more problems at any severity level than they did using the heuristics.

3.2 Cumulative Problem Counts

Cumulative problem counts were generated for each experiment. The source was the single set of non-duplicating unique problems created out of the combined sets from all subjects (Figure 1).

Mean cumulative counts of new (non-repeating) problems were computed by generating 100 permutations of the subject orders — adapting the method used by Virzi (1992). This produced the curves shown in Figure 2. These show the mean proportions of the total numbers of unique problems found by subjects in (a) experiment 1 (by group) and (b) experiment 2 session 2 (all subjects), respectively. It will be seen that in both cases the number of subjects required to uncover 75% of the total number of problems found by the group concerned was larger than the 5 predicted by Nielsen and others, namely 10 experienced and 16 novice (experiment 1) and 15 novice (experiment 2). It is clear that the curves do not converge in the manner proposed, and that additional subjects would have generated a large number of further new problems.

To assess the manner in which combined subject sets had been reduced down to the single set of unique problems used to create the above curves (the 'between subjects' stage of Figure 1), random samples of around 30 problems from the combined set from experiment 1 were presented to two independent raters (rater 1 had been a subject in this experiment, rater 2 had not). The raters were asked to assess if one or more problems in each sample were the 'same as' (and *not* 'different examples of the same type of thing as') other problems in the same sample. The resulting matchings were compared with those originally generated by the experimenter. These show good correlations (inter-rater reliability) between the experimenter and each of the two raters, the mean value for Cohen's κ being 0.66 (see Table 5).

	Rater 1	Rater 2	Mean
Experimenter	0.67	0.65	0.66

Table 5: Experiment 1. Mean inter-rater reliability data (Cohen's κ) for the 'between subjects' stage of the problem reduction process.

If the curves in Figure 2 were the result of a low probability of each problem being found by any one subject alone, it follows that a problem count which resulted in a lower number of unique problems would be more likely to produce curves of the form claimed. Put simply, lowering the number of sole problems that there are to be identified increases the chances that any one evaluator will uncover a problem

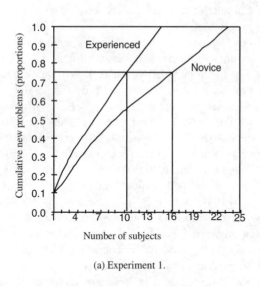

(a) Experiment 1.

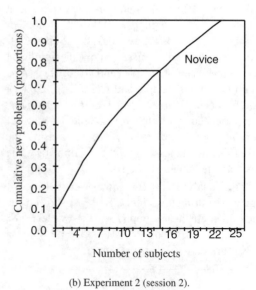

(b) Experiment 2 (session 2).

Figure 2: Proportions of cumulative new problems (mean permuted scores).

already found by someone else — adapting Lewis (1994). To test this hypothesis, new cumulative counts were generated, this time using only the respective problem categories derived from the two versions of the principles set. (The full 23-category set, as used in Experiment 2, is listed in Section 1.1; however, not all of the categories from each set were represented in each group's problems). The resulting curves are shown in Figure 3.

It is clear that counting by problem *type* rather than problem *instance* has enabled the numbers of subjects required to uncover 75% of the totals found to be considerably reduced from those in Figure 2. In particular, that for experienced subjects is now in line with Nielsen's prediction of 5 evaluators or less.

4 Conclusions from Results

1. Experienced subjects in experiment 1 identified significantly more usability problems than did novices, in all three conditions.

2. The expanded set of evaluation principles used in experiment 1 elicited from experienced subjects significantly more high severity problems than did Nielsen's heuristics alone.

3. Nielsen's heuristics did not elicit significantly more usability problems than did a control condition without such guidance. This was so

for both experienced and novice subjects and for high severity problems, in both experiments (session 2 of experiment 2).

4. In neither experiment were novice subjects able to make use of the principles set to elicit a significantly higher number of usability problems than they did using Nielsen's heuristics.

5. In both experiments, cumulative counts of unique problems revealed patterns different to that claimed by Nielsen and others, in that convergence did not occur as early as predicted. This was so for both experienced and novice subjects.

6. The reliability of the method by which combined subject problem sets had been reduced to the single set of unique problems from each experiment was assessed using two independent raters. Good inter-rater reliability was obtained between the two raters and the experimenter, for experiment 1.

7. It was shown that cumulative problem curves of the form predicted by Nielsen and others could indeed be generated using categories derived from the principles set.

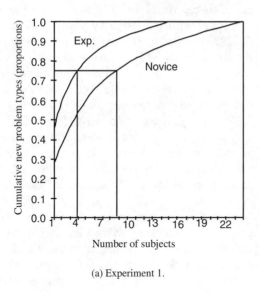

(a) Experiment 1.

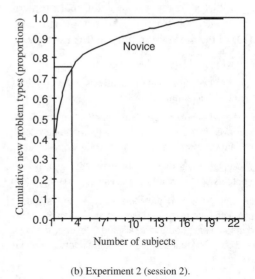

(b) Experiment 2 (session 2).

Figure 3: Proportions of cumulative problem categories (mean permuted scores). (Exp. = experienced.)

5 Discussion

5.1 Principles vs. Heuristics

The only significant difference between principles and heuristics that could be generated proved to be for high severity problems (in experiment 1, by experienced subjects using a three-page version of the principles). This is believed to be encouraging, for it is the more serious issues that one would wish any improved materials to reveal. It is expected (but nevertheless remains to be demonstrated) that the full version of the principles used in experiment 2 would show at least the same results for experienced subjects.

However, in both experiments novices proved signally resistant to such guidance, even (in experiment 2) after an initial training session. It remains to be seen, then, how much training *would* be required to succeed with novice evaluators; there is likely to be a trade-off between the amount of material which unmotivated novices could be expected to assimilate, even when paid, and any benefits which might ensue. So far, this aim — of showing that even non-specialists can make more profitable use of fully worked principles than a set of brief heuristics — has proved elusive.

It also remains to be shown that these results hold when severity is assessed by raters not exposed to the evaluation materials (in case the relative size of the principles set encouraged assignment of greater severity to problems associated with it). Further, and not least, the findings based on the evaluative criteria used here need to be validated against alternative principles sets such as those of Bastien & Scapin.

5.2 Cumulative Problem Counts

We believe that the discrepancy between the original cumulative curves here generated (Figure 2) and those predicted by Nielsen and others reflects differences in the process of problem reduction. We suspect that other researchers have allowed implicit categorizations to influence the first, 'within subjects' stage of this process (Figure 1). In contrast, we would categorize only at the later ('between subjects' and 'between types') stages, when grounds for problem grouping have been demonstrated. Our view is that early categorization tends to drive the whole reduction process, such that problem *instances* become conflated with problem *types* (John & Mashyna, 1997, p.1019).

In further support for this view, we present below an extract from a set of problem descriptions arising from two 'think-aloud' user tests reported by Nielsen (1994b). Using the definition of a usability problem there presented, namely:

> "Simply stated, a usability problem is any aspect of a user interface that is expected to cause users problems with respect to some salient usability measure (e.g. learnability, performance, error rate, subjective satisfaction) and that can be attributed to a *single* design aspect, …"
> (Nielsen, 1994b, p.388, our italics)

we suggest that as many as two additional problems could be generated from the first four (in order presented) of the nine descriptions in this example.

Source: Nielsen (1994b, pp.394–5)

[In the first of two 'think-aloud' user tests, nine problems were found with a commercial word processor.]

Problem 1.   The arrow keys had no effect in this word processor even though they were present on the keyboard. This problem was corrected in version 5 of the application.

This is acceptable as a single problem (or 'design aspect'), but we note its several possible consequences.

Problem 2.   Users had problems learning the standard cut/copy/paste commands.   First, the commands only worked if something had been selected. Second, the copy command gave no feedback, leading some users to wonder if it had any effect.

Two separate problem can be detected, one to do with the need for prior selection (a global issue with several likely ramifications, hence a good candidate for *later* categorization), the other concerned with lack of feedback (perhaps also a global issue here).

Problem 3.   Because this version of the program only supported one open document at a time, it was not possible to open a new document before the previous document had been closed. Closing a document is a very indirect action if one has the goal of opening a document, so many users tried the open command first. Upon seeing it was grayed out in the menu, they often realized that it was disabled for some reason. [Goes on to suggest a remedy involving a dialogue box].

We note conflation of problem description with inferred cause(s). But given a need for more precise quantification ('many', 'often') this is acceptable as a single problem.

Problem 4.   Due to yet another underlying functionality limitation, the word processor could not support undo for the global replacement operation. The interface correctly informed users about the limitation but did so using such scary language that several users did not dare use this feature at all.

Two problems can be detected here, the first concerning the lack of global replacement undo, the second the style of error message (also likely to occur elsewhere).

Continuing in like manner, one further problem might be added to this first list of 9, totalling 3 (33.3%). To the second list of 14 problems (not reproduced here), a further 4 (28.6%) may be added in similar fashion. Thus out of the total of 23 problems reported by Nielsen, an additional 7 problems (30.4%) might be generated.

This can be shown[†] to reduce the probability of each problem being found by a single subject from the 29% reported by Nielsen (Nielsen, 1994b, p.390) to approximately 22%. On a consideration of sample size as discussed in Lewis (1994), this would have the effect[‡] of increasing the number of subjects needed to uncover 75% of the new problem total from the 4 reported by Nielsen (1994b, p.390) to 5 or 6.

It appears, then, that the identification of usability problems by inspection may be a more lengthy and expensive process than has been portrayed.   The proposition arising from the current studies is that up to twice as many experienced evaluators than has been predicted may be necessary to uncover the same proportion of problems with an interface as has been claimed. However, whether *all* of such increases in evaluator numbers can be attributed to the differences in the problem reduction method above described, or to other contributing factors, remains very much in question.

As to those other factors, it is significant that both systems evaluated in the current studies could be described as 'open-ended' rather than 'closed', that is, entailing less goal-directed activity than many others. It may be that the combination of this type of system with the relatively unconstrained evaluation procedures used was responsible for the large number of issues reported (and for the apparent failure of Nielsen's heuristics to elicit more problems than the control). But we have shown how easily an implicit conflation of issues with types, sufficient in the example examined to add up to 30% to the problem total, might creep into the problem identification process.

5.3   Predicted vs. Observed Problems

Finally, a significant omission from many studies in this domain is an attempt to compare the results of an analytic process such as heuristic evaluation with those of an empirical study of the same system in actual use. As Gray & Salzman (1998) point out, problem count is only one possible measure of the quality of a usability evaluation method; moreover, studies which rely solely on predictive data have little to offer on the efficacy of such methods in the world of real users and real user environments. One detailed comparison of predicted and observed data (which also offers a full description of the problem reduction method used) is John & Mashyna's (1997) case study of a cognitive walkthrough.   However,

---

[†] An increase of x over y unique problems represents a decrease in the probability of one problem being found by one subject of $1/(1+(x/y))$ of the original value. In this case, the decrease equates to $1/(1+(7/23)) = 0.77$ of the original value, that is, from 29% to 22%.

[‡] Determined by plotting a new cumulative curve based on the decreased probability value of 22%, using the function $y = 1 - (1-p)^x$, where p is the probability of a single subject finding one unique problem and x is the number of subjects (Lewis, 1994).

the very low predictive power which that account represents — just 2 out of 37 observed problems were unambiguously anticipated — suggests that the effectiveness of analytic inspection methods remains to demonstrated, as much for cognitive walkthrough as for the methods reported in less rigorous studies.

5.4 Concluding Remarks

If our view is justified, the use of problem count as dependent measure in studies in this domain appears to be suspect. We argue that in future reports an account of the problem reduction process such as we have presented should accompany considerations of other factors, such as differences in evaluator task (e.g. goal-driven, step-by-step, exploratory), system type (e.g. open-ended vs. closed) or, indeed, evaluation method itself. This would seem to be a necessary starting point for further progress in this domain.

Acknowledgements

Many thanks to Andrew Monk, Sara Morutto, Philip Quinlan, Andrew Sears and Peter Wright, plus the reviewers of this paper, for comments and suggestions.

References

Bastien, J. M. C., Scapin, D. L. & Leulier, C. (1999), "The Ergonomic Criteria and the ISO/DIS 9241-10 Dialogue Principles: A Pilot Comparison in an Evaluation Task", *Interacting with Computers* **11**(3), 299–322.

Gray, W. D. & Salzman, M. (1998), "Damaged Merchandise? A Review of Experiments that Compare Usabilty Evaluation Methods", *Human–Computer Interaction* **13**(3), 203–61.

Hammond, N. & McKendree, J. (1998), *Interactive Psychology: The PsyCLE Workbook*, Blackwell.

John, B. E. & Mashyna, M. M. (1997), "Evaluating a Multimedia Authoring Tool", *Journal of the American Society for Information Science* **48**(11), 1004–22.

Lewis, J. R. (1994), "Sample Sizes for Usability Studies: Additional Considerations.", *Human Factors* **36**(2), 368–78.

Marshall, C., Nelson, C. & Gardiner, M. M. (1987), Design Guidelines, *in* M. M. Gardiner & B. Christie (eds.), *Applying Cognitive Psychology to User Interface Design*, John Wiley & Sons, pp.221–78.

Molich, R. & Nielsen, J. (1990), "Improving a Human-Computer Dialog", *Communications of the ACM* **33**(3), 338–48.

Nielsen, J. (1989), Usability Engineering at a Discount, *in* G. Salvendy & M. J. Smith (eds.), *Designing and Using Human–Computer Interfaces and Knowledge-Based Systems*, Elsevier Science, pp.394–401.

Nielsen, J. (1993), *Usability Engineering*, Academic Press.

Nielsen, J. (1994a), Enhancing the Power of Usability Heuristics, *in* B. Adelson, S. Dumais & J. Olson (eds.), *Proceedings of CHI'94: Human Factors in Computing Systems*, ACM Press, pp.152–8.

Nielsen, J. (1994b), "Estimating the Number of Subjects Needed for a Thinking Aloud Test", *International Journal of Human–Computer Studies* **41**, 385–97.

Nielsen, J. (1994c), Heuristic Evaluation, *in* J. Nielsen & R. L. Mack (eds.), *Usability Inspection Methods*, John Wiley & Sons, pp.25–62.

Nielsen, J. & Molich, R. (1990), Heuristic Evaluation of User Interfaces, *in* J. C. Chew & J. Whiteside (eds.), *Proceedings of CHI'90: Human Factors in Computing Systems*, ACM Press, pp.249–256.

Sears, A. (1997), "Heuristic Walkthroughs: Finding the Problems without the Noise.", *International Journal of Human–Computer Interaction* **9**(3), 213–34.

Smith, S. L. (1986), "Standards Versus Guidelines for Designing User Interface Software", *Behaviour & Information Technology* **5**(1), 47–61.

Virzi, R. A. (1992), "Refining the Test Phase of Usability Evaluation: How Many Subjects is Enough", *Human Factors* **34**(4), 457–68.

Human–Computer Interaction — INTERACT '99
M. Angela Sasse and Chris Johnson (Editors)
Published by IOS Press, © IFIP TC.13, 1999

Designing for Shared Interfaces with Diverse User Groups

Lynne Dunckley[1], Andy Smith[2] & David Howard[3]

[1] The Open University, Walton Hall, Milton Keynes MK7 6AA, UK.
[2] University of Luton, Park Square, Luton LU1 3JU, UK.
[3] Rank Group Holidays, The Rank Group Plc, 6 Connaught Place,
London W2 2EZ, UK.

l.dunckley@open.ac.uk, andy.smith@luton.ac.uk

Abstract: This paper describes an experimental application of a method for shared interface design for different cultural groups based on the LUCID method. The method is applied to a multimedia computer assisted learning application and evaluated for different user groups, who are categorized using objective factors of gender, ethnicity and special learning needs. The results of the usability evaluation of the prototype interfaces are analysed to distinguish those design factors that are appropriate for global and local interfaces. The method is shown to be able to identify the optimum global interface and also those design factors that should be used to develop localized variations for different user groups.

Keywords: LUCID, international cultural issues, users with special needs, special needs, multimedia.

1 Introduction

The development of shared interfaces, which involve users drawn from different cultural and geographical domains present interface designers with new dilemmas and trade-offs. Cultural differences have significance not only for detailed software design but also for the process of design. Firstly there is the choice of overall strategy, to develop an international culturally free interface, or to provide a number of localized versions.

Day (1998) describes three levels of specialization:

- *Globalization*, applying an allegedly cultureless standard.

- *Internationalization*, designing base structures with the intent of later customization.

- *Localization*, developing specific interfaces to meet a particular market.

Whichever strategy is adopted, effective design will involve recognizing the cultural elements in a given application. This cultural diversity makes it even more unrealistic for designers to rely on intuition or personal experience of interface design. However designing multiple interfaces for different user groups adds significantly to the cost of development.

The Logical User Centred Interface Design (LUCID) has been validated for the development of mono-cultural systems (Smith & Dunckley, 1996; Smith et al., 1997). LUCID aims to provide a user- centred environment through which not only is usability enhanced but, with respect to identified criteria is actually maximized. The LUCID method involves building a set of variant interfaces according to an experimental design strategy based upon orthogonal arrays developed by Taguchi (1986) within the domain of production and manufacturing. The selection of key design factors is crucial to the LUCID method. It is only intended to investigate factors which influence the performance measure and to set levels which are realistic design options. The desire is to find the design that is as robust as possible in terms of noise effects from the environment.

This paper describes investigations into the way the LUCID method is applied to solve the problems of shared global interfaces, as defined by Day (1998), in particular the way in which the method can be implemented to investigate the acceptability of interfaces to users from different cultures, skills and backgrounds. The effectiveness of the LUCID method rests upon the selection of key design factors and levels. It has been found that integration of a variant of contextual enquiry with participative designer sessions provides the rich source of evidence that is needed when cultural variables are involved (Smith & Dunckley, 1999).

The adaptation of the LUCID method for shared interfaces, requires the identification of user factors (user attributes) as well as key design factors (Smith et al., 1997). In preliminary research we have classified these user attributes into the following types:

- *Objective factors*, e.g. gender, age, ethnic background, mother-tongue which can be objectively identified for each user and used to select different user groups.

- *Subjective factors*, which cannot be directly measured or identified such as cognitive style.

This paper describes an experimental application of a small scale pilot study using the outlined method which was proposed but not previously implemented and tested (Smith & Dunckley, 1998). The focus of this study was on using objective cultural factors as user factors for a multimedia application.

2 Cross-cultural Issues

2.1 Cultural Factors

Hofstede's work is particularly relevant because of its focus on human interaction where cultural differences clearly matter. He carried out a study of 116,000 IBM employees distributed through 72 countries using 20 languages in 1968 and 1972. The study was based on a rigorous research design and systematic data collection (Hofstede et al., 1993). He conceptualized culture as 'programming of the mind', meaning that certain reactions were more likely in certain cultures than in other ones, as a result of differences between basic values of the members of different cultures. Hofstede proposed that cultures could be defined through four dimensions:

- *Power distance*, the degree of dependence between boss and subordinate.

- *Collectivism-individualism*, integration into cohesive groups vs. being expected to look after him/her self.

- *Femininity-masculinity*, the extent to which gender roles are distinct or overlap.

- *Uncertainty avoidance*, the extent to which members feel threatened by uncertain or unknown situations.

Hofstede illustrated the implications of these results in terms of organizational design, so that French managers think of their ideal organization as a 'pyramid of people', Germans as a 'well-oiled machine' and the British as a 'village market'. Hofstede recognized that his study was developed from a Western perspective and the underlying philosophy was "to try to find out if they were like us". However, replication studies of Hofstede's work over a period of time have largely confirmed his results (Sondergaard, 1994).

2.2 Multi-cultural Systems

Collectivists, as defined by Hofstede, are seen as considering the impact of their actions on their in-group to be important and therefore perform better as part of a group. The impact of national culture has been reported for international interfaces (Merritt & Helmreich, 1996) where behaviour on aviation flight decks was influenced by many factors including national culture. It was found that Asian pilots' attitudes were closer to other Asian workers than to their US counterparts and that national culture and organizational distinctions took precedence over gender. Cross-cultural effects have been postulated to be particularly relevant to GSS. The GSS concept was developed in the USA and it has been suspected that USA cultural norms were so influential that the applications of this genre would need significant adaptation for different cultures. Watson (1993; Watson et al., 1994) considered the implications of different cultures and social forces on GSS design, since GSS provided meeting designers with a means of amplifying and dampening these social forces to improve the effectiveness of meetings.

2.3 Multi-cultural Interface Design

In terms of practical advice for interface design the following list (Del Galdo, 1990) gives interface factors which are affected by culture, language and local conventions:

- Character sets and collating sequences.

- Format conventions for numbers, dates, time, currency.

- Layout conventions, e.g. for addresses and telephone numbers.

- Icons, symbols and colours; screen text.

- Menu accelerators, e.g. using initial letter of verbs.

In addition cultural problems of interface design (Fernandes, 1995) are categorized as:

- Language.

- Visual communication.

- Appropriateness of design features.

- Taste.

3 Shared Interface Design

3.1 The Application of LUCID

Taguchi (1986) provides a mechanism to investigate both design and external noise factors through two different orthogonal arrays. These are then combined together in one experimental design. Previous published work on LUCID has focused only on the design factors and used evaluation based on seeking representative users, using repetition and randomized designs to minimize the effect of noise.

Orthogonal arrays are a set of tables devised by Taguchi and are used to determine the minimum number of experiments (in our case prototype interfaces) and their input conditions. Figure 1 illustrates the simplest orthogonal array, the L_4 array which would deal with up to three factors. An L_8 array can deal with seven factors or four factors and three interactions.

Column	$L_4(2^3)$		
Condition	1	2	3
1	1	1	1
2	1	2	2
3	2	1	2
4	2	2	1

Figure 1: Orthogonal Array — L_4

The orthogonal arrays are independent: every column covers one factor and has the same number of occurrences of each level as every other column. This ensures that any differences in the results are only due to the change of factors. Orthogonal arrays are balanced because there are always an equal number of occurrences of each level in every column. In some situations factors in the design may influence each other and may not be independent. The Taguchi method will allow the design study to investigate both the input factors and any suspected interactions between the factors. In the inner design factor array each row represents the specification of a different prototype interface, in terms of the settings or levels of the design factors. The number of columns dictates the

number of single design factors or interactions which can be investigated.

The implementation described here expands the experimental design to include noise factors in a systematic manner, so that optimum designs, which are the least sensitive to the noise factors, can then be found. Taguchi classes noise factors as those over which the designer has no control. We have recognized this concept's potential to deal with user factors (Smith & Dunckley, 1998). To incorporate environmental noise factors, such as user differences, into the design they are identified in a similar manner to those used for design factors.

Figure 2 illustrates two orthogonal designs, which could be used. Each row in the inner design array, corresponds to the interface specification, giving the settings of each design factor. The outer array is used to investigate the sensitivity of the design to user (noise) factors. This requires focusing on potential user factors and the subsequent selection of levels. In many cases the choice of user factor will dictate the levels (e.g. gender gives two levels — male and female; locus of control, set at internal and external). Most other factors will require setting a range for each level. In the study, specific objective user characteristics were targeted, an outer array selected and the users found to fit that array. This experimental study focused on the stages of an overall method concerned with design and evaluation.

3.2 Experimental Design

The experimental application involved a multi-media interface front-end for a Computer-Aided Learning application. The application was to develop interfaces for coursework assessment based on a question and answer framework. The software used was Multimedia Toolbook 3.0, which would be used by lecturers, as course developers, and students as end-user learners. The multimedia design space provided developers with a very large choice of widgets, styles and visual presentation options. For example, the software offered four different styles of buttons. The interface factors used were identified through:

- Interviews, with experienced users (lecturers) and designers.

- Observation, of users (students) actually operating existing interfaces.

A number of candidate factors were proposed initially. The number of design factors investigated dictated the size of the array used and the number of variant interfaces, which needed to be built. Factors which could be rejected on the basis of previous

								Outer user array			
								Condition		$L_4(2^3)$	
						Factor		1	2	3	4
						X		1	1	2	2
						Y		1	2	1	2
						Z		1	2	2	1

Inner interface design array

Cond.	A	B	C	D	E	F	G	R_1	R_2	R_3	R_4
			Factor			$L_8(2^7)$		Repetitions			
1	1	1	1	1	1	1	1	111	122	212	221
2	1	1	1	2	2	2	2	111	122	212	221
3	1	2	2	1	1	2	2	111	122	212	221
4	1	2	2	2	2	1	1	111	122	212	221
5	2	1	2	1	2	1	2	111	122	212	221
6	2	1	2	2	1	2	1	111	122	212	221
7	2	2	1	1	2	2	1	111	122	212	221
8	2	2	1	2	1	1	2	111	122	212	221

Figure 2: Example inner and outer orthogonal arrays.

experience and clear application of heuristics, were eliminated. From an initial set of candidate factors a smaller number were considered to be crucial in terms of the performance of the interface. In this case seven factors were identified as important for usability. Each of the factors was associated with two levels or settings as shown in Table 1.

The video factor was concerned with whether to show the video sequences within an in-screen window or to use a separate full-screen. The size and position of the in-screen video was kept constant, to the right of the question text. When full-screen video was used, a clear method was provided for the user to flip between the video and the question text screen, through large navigational buttons. There was particular concern that during assessments students could accidentally leave the system without having saved the answers to the coursework so 'Warning prompts' was included as a factor, with two levels 'on' and 'off'. There had also been disagreement in the design team about the display of status details. Some users thought the amount of information required (current question number, total questions answered, number completed, test time remaining) was distracting and so this factor was set at two levels: either always displayed or hidden and revealed by a user controlled button.

Other design factors were kept constant through the set of interfaces. For example a pushbutton style was used for all buttons. Colours cause problems across cultures and also for users with disabilities. A standard colour set, which aimed to be as neutral and restful as possible was used. Guidelines recommended

by a special educational needs expert were adopted throughout, for example blue was used as the hot word colour and a large font was used (Arial, 14pt, left justified) throughout all interfaces. The system would be used by students from a wide range of cultures and about 10% of students suffered from dyslexia. For this simulated application, which focused on the development of the method using objective user factors, the environmental noise factors and levels are shown in the outer array of Table 1.

Inner Array		
Design Factor	Level 1	Level 2
A Navigation	Dispersed	Horizontal
B Vocal hotwords	On	Off
C Video animation screen	In-Screen	Full Screen
D Status details	Hidden	Displayed
E Warning prompts	On	Off
F Item selection 1	Combo boxes	3D Check boxes
G Item selection 2	Sliders	3D Check boxes
Outer Array		
User Factor	Level 1	Level 2
X Ethnicity	English	Afro-Caribbean /African
Y Dyslexia	High	Non-dyslexic
Z Gender	Female	Male

Table 1: Inner and outer array factors.

Since three user factors at two levels were considered an L_4 outer array was used in conjunction with an L_8 array for the internal design factors. An L_4 array requires four experiments. Therefore each trial of the L_8 must be repeated four times for each of the possible four noise combinations. The outer array, with four combinations of noise for the three noise factors, tests each of the 8 trial interfaces four times. The experimental design with the inner and outer array is that shown previously in Figure 1. The user testing then involved a combined inner and outer array.

The end-users were also asked to identify performance measures for the target interface. The lecturers focused on usability in terms of performance and reliability. The usability metrics agreed were:

- *Total time to complete the task*, as a measure of overall performance.

- *Number of key presses/mouse clicks*, as a measure of effort.

In addition a user satisfaction survey was carried out.

The task scenario allowed a wide range of question styles to be included in the tasks, e.g. multiple choice, true-false, ranking and 'drag & drop'. A dummy interface had been created with examples of the interface objects and a sample exercise was completed by all users as standard initial training. All the target users tested all eight interfaces so a randomized testing design was used to counteract any learning effect. Also the task questions were randomized so that each category of question only appeared once in every interface type and users experienced new but equivalent question sets with different interfaces. The language used throughout was English and all users were competent at English and were IT literate. For each interface there were 4 user results or 4 observations of the performance measure. These observations were first used to calculate the overall performance and the predicted optimum 'global' design.

3.3 Analysis

Table 2 gives the results using Total Task Time (TT) metric with a 'smaller the better' criterion. The preferred levels for the optimum global interface, calculated using the standard method (Taguchi, 1986) is also given in Table 2. The results obtained from the usability tests were analysed by ANOVA and also using Taguchi's pooling method for the least significant factors. The ANOVA method suggested that only design factors E and G are statistically significant which could be expected since in this experiment a large noise factor was deliberately introduced giving a large error term. When Taguchi's method of using average results for each factor and pooling the least significant factors, then design factors A, D, E and G were significant.

In order to investigate the interfaces from the users' view point the arrays were inverted and the noise array analysed using Taguchi's modification of ANOVA which gives the percentage contribution of each design factor, to identify the users favoured on average, by the interface design. In terms of the TT metric alone the favoured user type was 'English, non-dyslexic, females'. In summary, the dyslexic users had more difficulty with the interfaces than the non-dyslexic users and there was also an advantage for 'English' users over Afro-Caribbean users. However the female users achieved greater performance results. Table 3 gives the percentage contribution of the different user factors.

User Factor	Favoured Level	Percentage Contribution
Ethnicity	English	22.4
Dyslexia	Non- dyslexic	35.5
Gender	female	42.1

Table 3: Percentage contribution of the user factors.

The results of one of the disadvantaged user types 'African/Afro-Caribbean, dyslexic, females' were included in the outer array, so it was possible to look at these users' results in detail to find out which factors / levels favoured these users and could be used as the basis for a localized design. Table 4 gives the results of this user type compared to those of the average for all user groups (Table 2). Comparing the results, it can be seen that the contribution of some factors and their preferred settings have changed. *Combo boxes* (Factor F) and *Status details* (Factor D) are now more important. *Vocal Hot Words* (Factor B) were a disadvantage to these users, presumably with the written word being better for communication and the sound of the words being less helpful to users who were 'African/Afro-Caribbean'. *Combo boxes* (Factor F) were more of a problem for these users than *Sliders* (Factor G) so that the preference for *Check Boxes* is much less marked. Thus our original global interface should be modified to be localized, by focusing further development on these factors.

By analysing the data for each interface separately over the four user types within the outer array the average performances can be determined. The L_4 array includes half of the 8 possible factorial combinations so that it is possible to predict the performance of the other four user groups not included in the array to give the results of all the 8 interface designs for each user group. Thus the optimum global interface can be checked across all the user groups and percentage contributions calculated.

	Design factor	Optimum level	F Ratio $F_{crit}(1,23) = 2.94$	F Ratio Pooled $F_{crit}(1,3) = 5.53$	% contribution all user groups
A	Navigation	Horizontal	2.793	27.74	23.36
B	Vocal hot-words	On	0.190	–	1.59
C	Video animation screen	In-screen	0.022	–	0.18
D	Status details	Displayed	1.146	11.38	9.58
E	Warning prompts	Off	4.072	40.45	34.07
F	Item selection 1	Combo boxes	0.090	-	0.75
G	Item selection 2	3D Check boxes	3.640	36.16	30.46

Table 2: Analysis of usability results for TT metric — overall results of all user groups.

	Design factor	Optimum level	% contribution disadvantaged user group
A	Navigation	Horizontal	27.17
B	Vocal hot-words	Off	2.67
C	Video animation screen	Full-screen	6.12
D	Status details	Displayed	24.88
E	Warning prompts	Off	12.11
F	Item selection 1	3D Check boxes	26.59
G	Item selection 2	3D Check boxes	0.47

Table 4: Results of disadvantaged user type using TT metric.

Factors represented by columns A, E and G stand out strongly as factors showing variation in performance between levels. Factors B, C and F have little impact on overall target performance. However Factor F (*Check Boxes / Combo Boxes*) is also important in terms of variability. The averaged results over all users showed a preference for *Combo Boxes* rather than *Check Boxes*. However this was not true for all user groups.

Status details (Factor D) on screen gave performance advantages although the user satisfaction survey indicated users actually preferred them to be hidden. Heuristic guidelines would also recommend on screen display. Analysis for factor G showed *3D Check Boxes* were strongly preferred to *Sliders* which gave poor performance and satisfaction ratings but which are often found in multi-media interfaces.

The next stage of the LUCID method would involve a more detailed analysis of the usability results and confirmatory tests would be carried out on the predicted optimum interface. For example although on the performance measures the *Vocal hot-words* were accepted, the user satisfaction results showed user preference for this facility across all user groups was low. Although the average percentage contribution of the video factor was very small, the user satisfaction study indicated that all users preferred the clarity

of the full-screen video but they also preferred the video being on the same screen as the question posed. This factor would clearly need further refinement even through it made a small contribution.

4   Conclusions

The experimental study of the LUCID method extended to shared interfaces has shown that the method is practicable, using objective user factors to set up the outer noise array and gives clear information to designers for both globalization and localization. The analysis of the results show that a number of the factors are statistically significant in terms of performance even when a noisy user array is used. The analysis of the results from the combined inner and outer arrays give important results and show which factors to develop for both global and local versions of the interface. The method highlights where users from different cultures can be placed at a disadvantage by some designs. The users most disadvantaged would in this study appear to be 'dyslexic, African/Afro-Caribbean, males'. It was important to make the designers aware that the interface design could be biased against these user groups as the target system would be used for student assessment

The results for the outer array in terms of the importance of contribution of the different user factors, are consistent with related experimental results. Leventhal et al. (1996) for example report a low cost approach to evaluate interfaces for users from different genders and cultures by recording their preferences, based on ranking scales. The study showed that gender had a stronger effect than nationality in a study of a group of 105 subjects, 54 American and the rest from 35 other nationalities.

In terms of future work, related studies are currently being carried out to investigate the benefits of using subjective cultural factors, which represent Hofstede's programming of the mind, within the outer arrays instead of the objective factors. Also the statistical analysis of the combined inner and outer arrays needs further development. Taguchi's method only focuses on achieving the most stable design, equivalent to our global design, whereas we are interested in optimum localized designs as well.

Recognizing the optimum design factors for the set of localized interfaces, leads to questions of implementation. The use of an internationalized architecture with locale components as described by Hall & Hudson (1997) has the potential to provide an effective and efficient means of linking localized components into the same core.

We know that we cannot eliminate human variation in the users of our information systems and that diversity in global terms is important but methods like LUCID can reduce the sensitivity of the interface to user variations and help to pinpoint the design factors which are important for localization.

References

Day, D. L. (1998), "Shared Values and Shared Interfaces: The Role of Culture in the Globalisation of Human–Computer Systems", *Interacting with Computers* **9**(3), 269–74.

Del Galdo, E. M. (1990), Internationalisation and Translation: Some Guidelines for the Design of Human–Computer Interfaces, *in* J. Nielsen (ed.), *Designing User Interfaces for International Use*, Elsevier Science, pp.1–10.

Fernandes, T. (1995), *Global Interface Design*, Academic Press.

Hall, P. A. V. & Hudson, R. (1997), *Software without Frontiers*, John Wiley & Sons.

Hofstede, G., Bond, M. H. & Luk, C. L. (1993), "Individual Perceptions of Organizational Cultures - A Methodological Treatise on Levels of Analysis", *Organization Studies* **14**(4), 483–503.

Leventhal, L., Teasley, B., Blementhal, B., Instone, K., Stone, D. & Donskoy, M. V. (1996), "Assessing User Interfaces for Diverse User Groups — Evaluation Strategies and Defining Characteristics", *Behaviour & Information Technology* **15**(3), 127–37.

Merritt, A. C. & Helmreich, R. L. (1996), "Human Factors on the Flight Deck: The Influence of National Culture", *Journal of Cross-Cultural Psychology* **27**(1), 5–24.

Smith, A. & Dunckley, L. (1996), Towards the Total Quality Interface, *in* A. Sasse, R. J. Cunningham & R. Winder (eds.), *People and Computers XI (Proceedings of HCI'96)*, Springer-Verlag, pp.3–17.

Smith, A. & Dunckley, L. (1998), "Using the LUCID Method to Optimize the Acceptability of Shared Interfaces", *Interacting with Computers* **9**(3), 335–44.

Smith, A. & Dunckley, L. (1999), Importance of Collaborative Design in Computer Interface Design, *in* M. A. Hanson, E. J. Lovesey & S. A. Robertson (eds.), *Contemporary Ergonomics '99*, Taylor & Francis, pp.494–8.

Smith, A., Dunckley, L., Burkhardt, D., Murkett, A., Eason, K. & Church, J. (1997), Developing the Optimum Help System using the LUCID Method, *in* S. Howard, J. Hammond & G. K. Lindgaard (eds.), *Human–Computer Interaction — INTERACT '97: Proceedings of the Sixth IFIP Conference on Human–Computer Interaction*, Chapman & Hall, pp.307–14.

Sondergaard, M. (1994), "Hofstede Consequences — A Study of Reviews, Citations and Replications", *Organization Studies* **15**(3), 447–56.

Taguchi, G. (1986), *Introduction to Quality Engineering*, Asian Productivity Organisation.

Watson, R. T. (1993), "Yin And Yang: Social Forces, and Meeting Design", *IFIP Transactions A — Computer Science And Technology* **31**, 197–13.

Watson, R. T., Ho, T. H. & Raman, K. S. (1994), "Culture: A Fourth Dimension of Group Support Systems", *Communications of the ACM* **37**(10), 44–55.

Human–Computer Interaction — INTERACT '99
M. Angela Sasse and Chris Johnson (Editors)
Published by IOS Press, © IFIP TC.13, 1999

Blacksburg Nostalgia: A Community History Archive

John M. Carroll, Mary Beth Rosson, Christina Van Metre, Rekha-Rukmini Kengeri, John Kelso & Mridu Darshani

Computer Science Department & Center for Human–Computer Interaction,
Virginia Tech, Blacksburg, VA 24061–0106, USA.
{carroll,rosson}@cs.vt.edu

Abstract: We describe a case study of community computing: The development of an archive called "Blacksburg Nostalgia". We worked with a senior citizens to create a Web forum for publishing and discussing informal stories about local history. We describe the origins of our project and the design of the system; we analyze an example story and its annotations, as well as usage logs and a recent user survey.

Keywords: public access, community networks, senior citizens, Web forums.

1 Introduction

Community computing is computing support for a particular kind of organization, namely, for the villages, towns, and neighborhoods in which people reside. This is a distinctive context for computing: Users and developers often are the same people; functions and services tend to pertain to non-professional aspects of life such as managing music selection for the church choir, or discussing re-zoning proposals; pockets of development activity occur here and there throughout the community with little overall coordination.

Community computing initiatives incorporate many motivations. For example, building local network infrastructure and expertise, and establishing presence in the Internet is seen as a means to stimulate or attract economic development. Rural areas see networks as a means of virtually relocating nearer to population and commercial centers. Schools, libraries, and local governments regard placing their information on-line as part of their public responsibility. Communitarian idealism and social activism are also major motivations — e.g. (Schuler, 1996). Community computing seeks to enhance access to and participation in community life at a time in history when traditional communities appear to be eroding (Bellah et al., 1985; Putnam, 1996).

Community computing raises many research questions. For example, what sorts of applications are particularly suitable for local communities? Applications that depend upon or develop local information or other resources, or that integrate face-to-face interaction with other channels seem plausible candidates. How can community computing projects be appropriately and effectively developed; how can they be sustained? It seems likely that community computing will require intensified forms of participatory analysis and design, and that sustaining community systems and applications will require new economic models in local government and volunteer organizations. And finally, how can community computing efforts supplement (or even co-exist with) the overwhelming vision of global computing embodied by the World Wide Web?

Our community computing research is carried out in the context of the Blacksburg Electronic Village (BEV), an advanced community network in Southwestern Virginia. A small, part-time group supports a top-level information framework, but generally after one or two links, the information and services in the BEV belong to the town, to various community groups, and businesses, and to individuals. In a prior paper (Carroll & Rosson, 1996), we described three patterns of "grassroots technology development" in the BEV: some groups are managing their own communication and activities through the BEV, and serving as models for others; other groups have made entrepreneurial use of the BEV, reaching out to and inspiring the larger community through advertising and recruiting; still other groups have extended the BEV itself, creating new on-line services and applications, and new activities for the community.

In this paper, we describe an example of the third of these patterns, a community history archive initiated by the Blacksburg Seniors. We first describe the origins of our design collaboration with the seniors group, and the vision that guided the project. We then describe the Blacksburg Nostalgia system with respect to its use, implementation and administration, and design rationale. We present an example story and its annotations to illustrate the kind of informal history material we wanted to capture, archive, and make accessible. We profile the use of the system through analysis of usage logs and user surveys. Finally, we describe our plans for continuing development and analysis of Blacksburg Nostalgia as a community history archive.

2   Origins of Nostalgia

In the Fall of 1995, a friend of one of us (Kelso) decided to move to Blacksburg for her retirement. She was curious about senior's activities that would be available to her. We had heard of the BEV seniors email list; it was well-known as one of the high-activity regions in the BEV. Kelso subscribed to the list to learn more about the group's programs and concerns. One thread that emerged in these email interactions consisted of recollections and discussions about what Blacksburg was like in the 1950s and 1960s. This thread seemed to generate a relatively large amount of the email traffic.

At about the same time (Winter 1995–96), we were planning modifications to our Web StoryBase (Rosson et al., 1996) — a Web archive of stories about personal Internet experiences with annotations. In this context the idea occurred that a very similar kind of tool could support the seniors in gathering, organizing and publishing their recollections.   In May, we met with Keith Furr, who had started the 'nostalgia' thread on the Senior's email list, and who seemed to be a leader in the seniors group. There were several further planning discussions with Furr and with Connie Anderson, another leader in the Seniors group with special interests in email and the BEV.

Late in May, we — along with Anderson and Furr — presented the proposal for a "NostalgiaBase", as it was called then, to an open meeting of seniors. The seniors were generally receptive to the idea. Their chief concerns pertained to privacy and spamming: in our Web StoryBase, stories can be contributed, viewed, and annotated by any Internet user. Some of the seniors did not want their contributions to

be accessible publicly; some did not want their contributions to be freely annotated; some, indeed, wanted all access to the Nostalgia materials to be limited to members of the BEV seniors email list. However, others specifically wanted more visibility for the project, suggesting, for example, that this could be a way of reaching 'lost Hokies' (i.e. former residents of Blacksburg and/or alumni of Virginia Tech).

There was consensus to go ahead with the project; we decided to limit access to Nostalgia, at least for the start, realizing that it would be easy to open access up at a later point, but more difficult to close it down. We decided to do this, however, merely by keeping a low profile for the project. The project was not announced to the larger BEV community at its inception; it was only announced on the seniors' email list, the list on which it had its origins. In point of fact, *anyone* in the BEV community and indeed the Internet community has always been able to contribute stories to Blacksburg Nostalgia. We did this to avoid the distractions of authentication dialogues. The forum is moderated by a system administrator to control content.

There was particular enthusiasm for posting old photographs of Blacksburg on the Web page as a means of evoking stories; this was seen as a specially attractive affordance of the Web over email. The project concept was differentiated from an official history project sponsored by the Town of Blacksburg, as indicated in this excerpt from the seniors' email newsletter:

> "We will be emphasizing contributions of individuals built around their memories and interviews of a number of individuals, not currently in the group. It appears that we will be able to use old photos. This will not be a formal history. The Town already has a group working on that but this will be much more personal and I believe much more friendly to those accessing it. The persons there today seemed very pleased with the concept."

We have pursued the Nostalgia project as action research: We are investigating the possibility and consequences of a community history archive by helping to develop an instance of such a system.

3   Community Memory

As illustrated in Figure 1, the Nostalgia Web site is headed by an old black and white photograph of downtown Blacksburg (clicking on the photograph

Figure 1: Homepage of Blacksburg Nostalgia.

displays a full-sized image). There is a brief introduction, including a 'Compose Your Story' link (to contribute a story by means of a Web form) and a 'Hear From You' link (to send email comments to the developers). Beyond this is the default view of the index of submitted stories, a reverse-chronological enumeration of stories submitted. The index items consist of a story's title, which is the link to its content (and annotations if any), keywords suggested by the author when the story was originally submitted (e.g. weather, stores, downtown, roads, unusual incidents), its author's name, an email link to the author, the story's date of submission, and a summary of its annotation status (total number of annotations made and the date of the most recent annotation).

3.1 Using Nostalgia

Any Internet user can access the Blacksburg Nostalgia at http://miso.cs.vt.edu/nostalgia. The brief introduction encourages visitors to browse the stories, to comment on stories already there, and to contribute

stories of their own. Selecting a story title in the index displays a new Web page with the story title, author, and content, followed by its annotations (if any) in chronological order. Annotations do not have titles, but are date and time stamped. Both stories and annotations have email links to their authors to facilitate one-on-one follow up interactions between Nostalgia authors and visitors to the site. At the end of each story listing is a link to 'add an annotation to this story' (and of course a 'go back' link).

If the user selects 'add annotation' the current story page is redisplayed along with a form for entering an annotation. Thus the most recent annotation is displayed immediately above the form, setting the context in which the new annotation will be published. The annotation author is prompted for the text of the annotation, as well as for his or her name and email address. Selecting the 'submit annotation' button adds the annotation immediately; reloading the story's page will display the updated listing. The annotation also generates two email notifications: one is sent to the system administrators, who periodically review stories and annotations to ensure that they are consistent with community standards and with the content concept of the Nostalgia project. The second notification is sent to the original author of the story.

Visitors to the Nostalgia site can also add a new story; 'compose your story' links appear at the beginning and the end of the story listing. The story composition page includes another black and white photograph of old Blacksburg (even older than the one on the homepage). The title of this page is "Tell us YOUR story …" and it includes a blatantly motivational header: "We appreciate your contributions to the Blacksburg Nostalgia project. Your contribution now will help to preserve your memories for others to enjoy and elaborate — years from now, your loved ones and friends will be able to return to this base of stories and revisit Blacksburg as you and your friends knew it!" Below this material, a form is displayed with prompts for story title, story text, author's name and email, and suggested keywords.

Authors are given an opportunity to preview their formatted stories and annotations (Hypertext Markup Language, HTML, tags are processed if included), and to make editing changes before they submit the story to the database. They are sent a confirmation email message when the contribution is submitted.

3.2   System Details

The Blacksburg Nostalgia system was made available the last week of May 1996. It consists of a set of Practical Extraction and Report Language (PERL) programs and a small database. The PERL programs are Common Gateway Interface (CGI) scripts, called by our Web server as a response to a user filling in a form and pressing a 'Submit' button. The input to the programs is the data that the user has entered on the Web page. The program updates the story database accordingly, then creates appropriate HTML code which is sent back to the user's browser.

The CGI scripts used by Nostalgia are actually part of a larger framework designed to handle multiple story databases of this type. The first version of the program was written in 1994 as part of the Web StoryBase project (Rosson et al., 1996). When the Nostalgia application was created, we generalized the PERL programs so that they could support both applications simultaneously-each application maintains its own index and story database, but contributions are managed by the same scripts. The PERL programs know which database to access by parsing the Universal Resource Locator (URL) that

caused the program to be run. An advantage of this is that creation of new storybases and implementation of generic changes to the framework are simplified; we can easily create additional databases and make program changes that are automatically seen in all applications.

The database itself is a directory of files. Each story and its annotations is stored in a separate file, whose name is a 5-digit number. The story index file stores data about each story, such as keywords, title, author, submittal time, number of annotations; this file is the source of the story index displayed on the first page (see Figure 1). A new story generates a new story file, and a new line in the index file. An annotation to a story appends text to the story's file, and updates the relevant descriptive data in the index file.

All contributions to the Nostalgia story set are reviewed by a system administrator, simply by visiting the Web page and reading through the new material. If an inappropriate story is contributed, the administrator just deletes the relevant line in the story index; if an inappropriate annotation is submitted, the story file itself must be edited. As it turns out, only one contribution has been deleted since the onset of the project, a file whose text consisted almost entirely of "blah blah blah". This relatively benign intrusion stands in marked contrast to analogous contributions removed from the more generic Web StoryBase, where almost as many stories have been removed as have been posted, and where the unwanted stories are sometimes quite offensive (Rosson et al., 1996). We attribute the relative 'well-behavedness' of our Nostalgia contributors to its very evident community project character, and to its smaller and presumably more homogeneous user population (about 100 people).

3.3   Community Archives

Part of our interest in the Nostalgia project was that it was an opportunity to continue our exploration of support for community archives. We had developed two previous Web forum systems, the Web StoryBase (Rosson et al., 1996) and the Blacksburg Electronic Village HistoryBase (Carroll et al., 1995). This set of systems comprises a design space with respect to the issues of:

1. User interface and data presentation.

2. Forum management, including moderation and user authentication.

3. Evoked content, for example, the intimacy and formality of contributions, and the extent and nature of annotation.

As mentioned earlier, the Web StoryBase is a threaded forum of stories about Internet experiences, a shared archive for the vast and fragmented 'community' of the World Wide Web. Initially, the StoryBase had a user interface much like Nostalgia's (as noted earlier the former was the direct model for the latter). As the StoryBase grew, however, an alternate view of the stories was provided, one partitioned by categories. So for example, visitors can now choose to browse only the stories whose main content has been categorized as 'Cyber-relationships' or 'Web Culture'. At this point this additional level of complexity is unnecessary for Nostalgia, although as the number of stories grow we may implement similar distinctions.

Also as mentioned earlier, the target community for the Web StoryBase was the Internet. As is typical practice in Internet communities, we allowed Web StoryBase contributors to remain anonymous: Many have provided a handle in lieu of their real names; many have not provided email addresses. We controlled content by manually pruning inappropriate stories. In the StoryBase project, we found that people were quite willing to share their stories, even some that were very personal. There was an enormous range in the intimacy and formality of the stories contributed: some pertained to the usability of Web software, many described particular Web sites, but some disclosed rather personal experiences (e.g. "I found my love on the Web").

The concept for the BEV HistoryBase was to provide a community archive to document the development of the Blacksburg Electronic Village, a means for the entire BEV community to participate in the construction of the history of the BEV. Thus, we wanted to create a document archive for the BEV management group and other 'official' views of history, but also to give prominence to the information and perspectives of any other member of the community. We imagined that this would yield a vivid and pluralistic view of what it is like to create a community network, and perhaps provide a useful episodic model for those contemplating community network projects.

The HistoryBase interface is organized around a time-line: documents submitted to the HistoryBase are characterized by a fairly elaborate keyword scheme, and by the date ranges to which they pertain, as well as by the date/time of their submission. The main database view is organized by quarters. For example, selecting the second quarter of 1995 displays link to 69 documents; one is a CNN video clip describing how Blacksburg residents can shop online at a local grocery store. This document was submitted to the HistoryBase on April 16, 1996 (submit date), but was created by CNN on May 27, 1995 (the document date). The clip is classified as 'Media coverage: TV'.

We wanted the HistoryBase to be largely self-maintaining and owned by the BEV community; we did not want to overtly moderate it. We implemented password security, using the BEV name server. Thus, *only* people with BEV accounts could make contributions to the HistoryBase. Our goal was that this community archive should incorporate all and only the documents, opinions and accounts of the BEV community. Contributors could not be anonymous. This approach, however, depended on all members of the BEV community having their network accounts through a single service provider, namely Virginia Tech. In 1996, the BEV decentralized the management of user accounts, members without formal ties to Virginia Tech were asked to obtain their networking through commercial service providers.

Unfortunately, this turn of events *excluded* much of the BEV community from actively participating in the HistoryBase project. The overwhelming preponderance of documents in the HistoryBase have been contributed by the BEV management team. Also, and perhaps as a consequence, there has been relatively little annotation of contributions to the HistoryBase.

Blacksburg Nostalgia is anchored in the content, the concerns, and the Blacksburg seniors community and the largely co-extensive BEV seniors community — like the HistoryBase, or at least our initial vision of the HistoryBase. But the Nostalgia project was directed exclusively at personal and informal information, and did not require contributors to go through an authentication process — like the Web StoryBase. We wanted to create an informal archive, perhaps even conversational in nature.

4   Example Story

Our overall objective for Blacksburg Nostalgia was to create an accessible forum for community discussion of local history. An example of this is a story entitled "Nostalgic Musings" and its annotations, shown in Figure 2.

The story itself is implicitly a continuation of a broader discussion. For example, the author begins by saying that other people's contributions helped bring to mind additional memories. He goes on to address one of these with some details about a meat market. He then turns to his memories of big snow storms from 30 years ago, referring to specific places in Blacksburg and depths of snow, particular winter

TITLE: Nostalgic Musings

Author: Keith Furr
Email: furry1@vt.edu

The responses of other's email reminded me of a few additional things. Yes, the dirty meat market was where many of us bought meat. It was in a building not much better than the fruit stands you see beside rural roads and it sure wouldn't pass state health standards now for cleanliness. However the meat was inexpensive and very good. I believe it cost something less than a dollar a pound for T-bone steaks.

The big snow in 1965–6 (I think) piled up drifts such as I have never seen before or since. We had just had Elizabeth & Julie and lived about a mile out on Glade Road in a small house. The drift in our driveway was over eight feet deep and the road into Prices Fork Road was impassable. The County had plowed the latter road so some friends of ours (Webb and Sara Richardson) offered to bring some milk and other groceries to the intersection of Glade and Prices Fork Road. I hiked out but with the deep snow it was hard going. Just behind where Krogers is now, the drifts were over 20 feet deep. I sat down and rested on the top of a telephone pole there! In a similar snow, five years earlier, 1959–60, the men who lived on the road got together and dug a tunnel through a drift at that same location.

That same winter it seemed to snow every Wednesday and Friday starting in Late January and continuing until March. From 1960 until 1966, if my memory serves me correctly, the weather seemed to be much colder in the winter than it was for many years afterwards with the summers being very dry. Lawns were typically brown by July and August. Since then until recently, it seems to me that we have had more moderate weather for the most part except for, I believe 1979, when we had an extreme cold spell during Christmas break when it got to 12 below zero and stayed below zero for about a week. Pipes burst in 68 buildings on campus and many persons who left for the break came home to find a lot of water damage. There were additional cold snaps later on when it got to -18 in Blacksburg and -26 up at Mountain Lake. I hope our current weather trend is not a sign of returning to the 'good old days'.

By the way, in the context of computer interests, I remember Tech's first official computer. It was an IBM 1620 and it had an amazing 32kb of memory. It was located in a wooden building located where Derring is now. This was an immense improvement over the one I had access to at Duke. It had 2km of memory on a rotating magnetic drum. We had to use either of two languages on punched cards, SOAP or Bell. Anyone else remember those two primitive computing languages?

Annotation by: David Mize
Email: dave.mize@tcr.com
Date: Fri Jul 26 23:34:28 1996

I remember being 8 or 9 years old during the heavy snow storm in the early 60's. I was able to walk up a snow drift to the porch roof of our farmhouse. My grandfather pushed out the back door, then went around front and spent two days digging a funnel to the front door.

Annotation by: Elaine Hunter
Email: Hunter_Lane@hq.navsea.navy.mil
Date: Sat Feb 08 22:35:35 1997

I was a student at Tech that winter, and yes, I was female. We girls were not allowed to wear slacks to class, nor were we allowed to wear them to the dining hall. The small group of us who did not live in Hillcrest were taking our meals in the main dining hall. As the temperature dropped to 15 below, we were finally permitted to wear slacks to meals as long as we kept long coats on and buttoned until we were seated at the table! I guess they were afraid the guys would discover that our legs went all the way up. But it was a fine group of men who went to Tech. They always allowed us at the front of the very long line. Jim Sheeler was among them. Where are the rest now?

Annotation by: Barbara Harrell Holdren
Email: BarbH1193@AOL.com
Date: Thu Jun 12 21:12:35 1997

I grew up in Blacksburg where my father was a professor in the Accounting Department for 40 years. When I read your comment about the first official computer, I remembered something he wrote in his autobiography (he realized he was dying and wrote 75 pages on a yellow legal pad). He mentioned the IBM 650 and the fact that in 1957 and again in 1959, IBM sent him to Endicott, NY to train in data processing. For a while he used this information as part of the 'Auditing' course in accounting, and then in 1963–1964 it became a course. I remember visiting the building where the computer filled a good-sized room — I think it may have been in Burrus Hall or a nearby building. Pamplin Hall wasn't there then. Was this the same computer you're remembering?

Annotation by: Ted Shelton
Email: tcsiii@bev.net
Date: Mon Sep 08 01:40:49 1997

Speaking of wooden buildings in the area where Derring is now located: there was a building that contained a firing range. I remember sighting-in my first rifle, a Marlin 22, there. And I remember being taken on a tour of the computer room in a wooden building back in that same area/era. I think it was much later when the computer was moved to Burruss. I remember when 460 all the way thru blacksburg was 2 lanes, with that marvelous 3-lane section south of town going up the hill where the Forest Service is now located. Anybody remember the old Navy barracks at the Tech Airport?

Annotation by: David Moser
Email: dmoser@mail.telis.org
Date: Tue Sep 09 23:50:57 1997

During the 50's that firing range was made available to Boy Scout Troop 56 when my father was scoutmaster. Many of us scouts earned our marksmanship merit badge there. There was nothing unusual about 11–13 year olds carrying rifles WAY back then!

Annotation by: Shannon Bennett
Email: shbennet@vt.edu
Date: Tue Oct 14 22:31:13 1997

I've been in Blacksburg for only three years now, so I don't really have any true stories. However, I am interested in you who do remember Blacksburg in the pre-suburban era to please e-mail me with your opinions of Blacksburg today and how it needs to change to become a more prosperous place.

Annotation by: Wendell Hensley
Email: wendelltsi@aol.com
Date: Sat Nov 08 10:07:06 1997

Yes, Ted Shelton, I remember the Navy barracks at Tech airport, as well as the "Sandy Airfield" next to it (basically the site of the now present main runway) where we used to play cowboys and indians in the 1940's. There was an accessible steam tunnel under this desert-looking area where we little kids could stand and walk through, scaring ourselves in the damp darkness complete with creepy things.

Figure 2: "Nostalgic Musings" and its annotations.

activities (sitting on top of a telephone pole, tunneling in snow drifts), and specific events (pipes bursting in Virginia Tech buildings). Finally, the story turns to memories of the origins of computing at Virginia Tech-again apparently continuing an earlier discussion thread. It recalls the model number of the University's first computer, the location of the old wooden building it was housed in, and its memory capacities and programming languages.

This is a very informal story; the kind of thing you might expect to hear around someone's electronic kitchen table. It casually visits several topics-starting with "yes, I remember the dirty meat market" and ending with "does anyone else remember the SOAP or Bell programming languages?" It vividly sketches an assortment of images. The annotations it evoked are an interesting set; they continue to spin out the historical themes in similar style.

The first annotation points back to the snowstorm theme, offering another recollection of people tunneling through drifts (in this case to get out of their houses). The second (seemingly from a 'lost Hokie') paints a few images of wintertime life for female undergraduates at Virginia Tech during those cold winters in the 1960s. The next pushes the 'first computer' memories back to the 1950s. barracks located at the Tech Airport.

The fourth annotation continues the topic of wooden buildings, but remembers one with a firing range. It also points to the immediately preceding annotation, agreeing that the University's early computer was moved to Burruss Hall. It concludes with a new topic of wooden buildings, asking about a Navy barracks located at the Tech Airport.

The fifth annotation responds to the fourth, introducing the fact that the firing range was made available to a local Boy Scout Troop. The sixth annotation is a meta-comment by a relative new-comer to Blacksburg, thanking the authors for their contributions and asking about the future of the town. The seventh annotation skips back to the Navy barracks subtopic, recalling games of Cowboys and Indians from the 1940s played near there, and an underground steam tunnel that was accessible.

This story has had a fairly rich lifecycle. It was contributed on June 25, 1996, and annotated over a period of 16 months (through November 1997).

5 Taking Stock

In the following we characterize more generally how Nostalgia has been used, the sorts of stories and annotations contributed, and the user population who have contributed stories and annotations.

Month	Accesses	Month	Accesses
May 96	121	Jul 97	273
Jun 96	163	Aug 97	290
Jul 96	682	Sep 97	404
Aug 96	751	Oct 97	284
Sep 96	277	Nov 97	498
Oct 96	296	Dec 97	326
Nov 96	419	Jan 98	336
Dec 96	27	Feb 98	305
Jan 97	249	Mar 98	371
Feb 97	411	Apr 98	393
Mar 97	235	May 98	334
Apr 97	282	Jun 98	303
May 97	281	Jul 98	280
Jun 97	230	Aug 98	288

Table 1: Accesses per month over 28 months.

5.1 Accesses and Posts

The Blacksburg Nostalgia site currently includes the story index page and sixteen stories. Accesses to these pages over a 28-month period beginning in May 96 are summarized in Table 1 (note however that that the 'May' data reflect just the first three days of activity!). During this period there were over 9100 accesses (average accesses per month was 325; median was 293). As the table indicates, use accelerated rapidly during the summer of 1996; in July and August alone there were almost 1500 accesses. We do not know how large the user community was at this point, but we do know that the site was initially advertised only to the BEV seniors, a group of about 100 persons. After the initial flurry of activity (and except for the unaccountable drop in Dec 96) access seems to have leveled off at about 300 per month.

Table 2 summarizes the pattern of story and annotation postings across the same 28 months. Sixteen stories were posted; they received a total of 43 annotations. This pattern mirrors the access data, documenting an early flow of stories and annotations in summer 1996, followed by a more quiescent period. However, there appears to be a modest upward trend in mid to late 1997. We attribute this activity to two factors: during the summer of 1997, the site was 'opened' to the general public via links publicized on other BEV pages; also, students working on a class project contacted some of the seniors in Fall 1997, perhaps reminding them of the site. An examination of the authors of the stories and annotations contributed in the final few months suggests that the site is now used by a broader community-former residents of Blacksburg (the 'lost Hokies') as well as current residents who are not part of the BEV seniors group (VT students).

Accesses to individual stories range from 68 (Story 14) to 484 (Story 3). As one would expect, stories contributed during the first few months (11 of the 14 were submitted by the end of July 1996) have been accessed more frequently than the five contributed after July 1997. The only story that stands out as an 'attractor' is Story 3, entitled "Where was this picture taken?" We suspect that the mention of a picture, presumably an old Blacksburg photo, is especially intriguing to visitors.

Month	Stories	Anns.	Month	Stories	Anns.
May 96	2	4	Jul 97	1	1
Jun 96	8	8	Aug 97	0	1
Jul 96	1	8	Sep 97	0	3
Aug 96	0	1	Oct 97	1	1
Sep 96	0	0	Nov 97	1	5
Oct 96	0	0	Dec 97	0	1
Nov 96	0	0	Jan 98	0	2
Dec 96	0	0	Feb 98	0	1
Jan 97	0	1	Mar 98	0	0
Feb 97	0	0	Apr 98	2	0
Mar 97	0	0	May 98	0	3
Apr 97	0	1	Jun 98	0	0
May 97	0	0	Jul 98	0	1
Jun 97	0	1	Aug 98	0	0

Table 2: Pattern of story and annotation postings over 28 months.

5.2   Story and Annotation Content

In addition to examining the site usage logs, we carried out an informal analysis of the stories that were shared. For each story,* we attempted to identify the main focus of the contribution; in some cases we coded several distinct points for a single story. As Table 3 indicates, the most common story theme was a discussion of a place or places. These stories often named a colourful store or restaurant that no longer exists (e.g. the "Dirty Meat" market). Another common story topic was a memorable event of some sort (e.g. a particularly severe snowstorm). Discussions of people (e.g. the owner of a business and his wife) or of interesting objects (e.g. VT's first computer) generally occurred in concert with memories of places or events. Finally, some stories did not refer to a specific event or experience, but rather tried to convey what life was like at a certain time (e.g. what it was like to be a teenager in Blacksburg in the 1960's); these we have classified under Ambience.

Ten stories provoked annotations by users, with a range of one to nine. The most common role of an annotation was to add detail to the story (or in some cases to an annotation that included a new topic). 34 of the 43 annotations served this role of adding detail; six annotations conveyed a reaction of some sort, generally an appreciation of a specific detail or of the overall contribution. Several others were simply part of a dialogue, for example answering or clarifying a specific question.

The use of annotations to provide further detail is just the sort of use that we had hoped to observe in the Nostalgia Web site — essentially threaded discussions, but with the implicit goal of creating an extended description of specific shared places, events, or perspectives. The fact that many of these details were contributed by former residents is at once a demonstration of the outreach provided by the Web, and of the implicit local community that still exists beyond the physical boundaries of Blacksburg.

Story Theme	Frequency
Memorable Places	12
Specific Events	6
General Ambience	6
Interactions with People	3
Interesting Objects	2

Table 3: Stories grouped into major themes (some appear in more than one category).

5.3   User Population

The Nostalgia content was submitted by 30 distinct contributors; about one-half (17) made a single annotation. The 16 stories were written by 11 different individuals. We classified the contributors (based on email addresses, personal knowledge and comments made in their stories) into three groups: BEV seniors (11), 'lost Hokies' (12), and others (most of these appear to be VT faculty, staff, or students; 7).

As we expected, the core population of authors are members of the BEV seniors group: one senior submitted four stories, and another contributed two. The seniors often also annotated each others' stories; as one reads through the full set, there is very much a sense that these are community members who are longtime friends and are collaborating to produce rich descriptions of the 'old days' in Blacksburg. In several cases it appears that an older couple who share an account have jointly authored a story or annotation. During the first few weeks when stories and annotations were being produced rapidly (22 in

---

*Two of the contributions did not concern Blacksburg nostalgia. Both offered a commentary on Blacksburg and its future.

less than 30 days), the annotations often had a conversational character, beginning with a personal salutation (e.g. "Earl, do I remember correctly, ..."), and a similarly personal response as few minutes later (e.g. "Yes, Connie, there was a Kroger where Tech Bookstore is now located and ..."). This sort of back-and-forth conversation is similar to what one would expect in an email exchange among friends .

However, in the second half of the 26-month period the contributing users are a less homogeneous group. The seniors are still contributing on occasion, but there is now clear evidence of 'lost Hokies' — just the community that the seniors had hoped to reach with a broadly accessible Web forum. For example, story 11 contains a wealth of details about life as a child and teenager during the 60's and 70's: memories of the main highways surrounding town, open land being converted into apartment buildings, development fiascos resulting in legal suits, a high school friend who died in an auto accident, what the 'in' things were for high school students at that time. Its author was a former resident of Blacksburg, now a father in Colorado. Also common are annotations from these former residents, some simply appreciative of the good memories being shared (in one case from an adopted child seeking background and history concerning her birth father), others contributing their own details, or seeking information about their pasts.

5.4 Surveys and Workshops

In October 1997 and March 1998, we surveyed the Blacksburg Seniors by e-mail regarding their knowledge about, use of, and reactions to, Blacksburg Nostalgia. In the October survey, we contacted people who had contributed stories or annotations. For the March survey we used the Seniors mailing list. Both surveys attracted a half dozen respondents. Also in October and March we visited a meeting of the Blacksburg Seniors to discuss the Nostalgia project; each meeting was attended by 35–40 seniors.

Based on these sources, it appears that most seniors learned of Blacksburg Nostalgia through the seniors email list, though a significant minority discovered it while browsing the BEV Web pages. In one case, a former resident who stays in touch with Blacksburg by browsing local Web pages, alerted other members of his family — current residents — about the existence of Nostalgia; two of those family members subsequently contributed. Of those who had visited the Nostalgia site, about half had done so 10 or more times, and half had done so 4 or fewer times.

User comments were positive. Many comments emphasized that it is fun to reminisce: "It is so much fun to be with people and recollect old times." Some users indicated that Nostalgia confirmed specific memories they had; others said it confirmed that their memories were still accurate (i.e. "My memory is pretty good."). A few comments suggested that Nostalgia could be a community information resource: "It provides a source of information of a historical nature and may be valuable to those doing historical research."

Some users felt that the simple sequential organization of the stories and the lack of embellishment in the presentation were strengths of the design. However, others suggested the inclusion of more photographs and the provision of a guest-book as improvements. The inclusion of a topic list of place names, events, etc. that might also help trigger memories was also suggested. Several users expressed the hope that more seniors would contribute stories. One suggested that the project be incorporated into the Town of Blacksburg's Bicentennial commemoration.

5.5 Enhancements and Plans

In response to our user surveys and workshops, we designed and implemented two enhancements to Nostalgia, a guest-book and a photo-gallery. The guest-book permits visitors to record their comments and contact information in a Web form, and browse the entries made by other guests. This may make 'mere' browsing more active and rewarding by providing those who do not contribute a story or annotation a way to express overall impressions. It also may support broader social interests by providing an address book of pointers to persons interested in Blacksburg history (for example, as mentioned earlier, potentially re-acquainting 'lost Hokies'). However, these possible advantages entail increased complexity in the overall Nostalgia site. We are in effect incorporating a parallel forum into our system, which could be confusing to some users.

There has been always great enthusiasm among the seniors for old photographs. The two photographs we had originally incorporated into the Nostalgia pages to create atmosphere attracted considerable interest and discussion. This interest motivated us and a local collector of old photographs to create a page specifically for photographs. Users can browse the photo-gallery page and, from there, contribute a story pointing to a particular photo. They can also contribute their own photographs to the photo-gallery. We will investigate whether providing the photo-gallery triggers any change in the rate or content of new contributions. The photograph collector we are working with is interested in seeing whether the

Nostalgia user community can help him clarify the dates, locations, and identities of people pictured in the photographs.

Our plan is to assimilate, refine, and assess these enhancements through the next 12–18 months. But we also are planning further enhancements in the longer term. One idea we have considered is posting a series of town maps, describing the development of the downtown area, particularly over the past half-century. This might be presented as a series of overlays, or as an animation emphasizing the process of change. We think this might also be an effective stimulus for evoking recollections.

Another idea we have discussed is that of adding a time-line view. A graphical time-line of the history of the Blacksburg Electronic Village project served as the main homepage design element and navigational widget for the BEV HistoryBase (Carroll et al., 1995), and, as far as we could tell, was an effective interface. For Blacksburg Nostalgia, a time-line view might particularly help with evoking temporally-related sequences of recollections. For example, it might trigger memories of incidents that occurred between other incidents previously recalled and described, and already positioned on the time-line.

Finally, we want to broaden the focus of our work to incorporate community groups other than the seniors. We see local history as not merely the concern of the elderly, but rather as a *link* joining the past, present, and future.

6   Community Computing

We are interested in community computing as a distinct and potentially significant 'alternative' paradigm for computing systems and applications. Our primary concerns in this project are not global and general, but local and specific; we are creating an archive for about 100 senior citizens. Beyond the specific concerns and activities of this group, we are concerned with increasing local *social capital* — the trust, social interactions, and norms of mutual reciprocity throughout a community (Coleman, 1990). The general lessons that could emerge from this work would be models for strengthening local human communities through computer-mediated communication.

This may seem quixotic. To some extent, the overall thrust of our project conflicts with an overwhelming theme in the modern age: the global village. McLuhan (1964) early vision of a global village hinged on television, a flexible and engaging medium, available at the user's discretion,

and comfortably cool and predictable compared to the prospect of other people sitting in your living room. Television is very likely the principal factor in the *decline* of social capital and civic engagement in American society (Putnam, 1996). The full social significance of various paradigms for 'virtual communities' supported by the Internet is a current question (Rheingold, 1993; Turkle, 1995). But there are many prima facie similarities between virtual communities and television.

Moreover, even if our Nostalgia project were to 'succeed', it turns out that we have selected a somewhat special generational stratum of collaborators. Our users are members of what Putnam (1996) calls the 'civic' generation, people born between 1910 and 1940, and culminating in the cohort born in 1925–1930. This group of Americans is more likely to trust one another, to participate in civic organizations, and to vote than people born before or since. Managing to engage members of this group in community-oriented endeavors may not really mean all that much

Also, commercial and government economic interests are heavily distracted by a global vision of the impact of networking on human activities. Recently we participated in a special issue of *IEEE Technology and Society* on networking in schools, and were the only authors to address management and use of local community resources (Carroll & Rosson, 1998). Is the internet *only* for global communities and generic information systems?

We are focusing on specific projects to illuminate and articulate the general issues. Our current projects involve the seniors, the county schools, the regional library, and the town government. This work provides wonderful opportunity and obvious need for developing a more longterm view of participatory design, and approaches to leveraging various types of local activity to create critical mass.

One of our objectives in this project is to increase community participation in the Blacksburg Electronic Village and, more generally, social capital in the Blacksburg community, by strengthening interest and participation in community history. An interesting indicator of some grassroots success in this is that the BEV itself adopted an old photograph of the Lyric Theater (a community landmark) as its Web page logo about a year after the initiation of the Nostalgia project. Neither we nor the seniors group explicitly requested this change, but local history is now, literally, on the front page of the BEV.

Acknowledgments

We thank Dave Messner who implemented the first version of the story archive program, and Keith Furr and Connie Anderson who provided the initial goals for the project and who helped us work with the larger BEV seniors group, and Joe Reiss, who helped with visual design of the Nostalgia welcome page.

References

Bellah, R., Madsen, R., Sullivan, W., Swindler, A. & Tipton, S. (1985), *Habits of the Heart: Individualism and Commitment in American Life*, University of California Press.

Carroll, J. M. & Rosson, M. B. (1996), "Developing the Blacksburg Electronic Village", *Communications of the ACM* **39**(12), 69–74.

Carroll, J. M. & Rosson, M. B. (1998), "The Neighborhood School in the Global Village", *IEEE Technology and Society* **17**(4), 4–9, 44.

Carroll, J. M., Rosson, M. B., Cohill, A. M. & Schorger, J. (1995), Building a History of the Blacksburg Electronic Village, *in* G. Olson & S. Schuon (eds.), *Proceedings of the Symposium on Designing Interactive Systems: Processes, Practices, Methods and Techniques (DIS'95)*, ACM Press, pp.1–5.

Coleman, J. S. (1990), *The Foundations of Social Theory*, Harvard University Press.

McLuhan, M. (1964), *Understanding Media: The Extensions of Man*, McGraw-Hill.

Putnam, R. D. (1996), "The Strange Disappearence of Civic America", *The American Prospect* **24**, 34–49. winter.

Rheingold, H. (1993), *The Virtual Community: Homesteading on the Electronic Frontier*, Addison–Wesley.

Rosson, M. B., Carroll, J. M. & Messner, D. (1996), A Web StoryBase, *in* A. Sasse, R. J. Cunningham & R. Winder (eds.), *People and Computers XI (Proceedings of HCI'96)*, Springer-Verlag, pp.396–82.

Schuler, D. (1996), *New Community Networks: Wired for Change*, Addison–Wesley.

Turkle, S. (1995), *Life on the Screen: Identity in the Age of the Internet*, Simon and Schuster.

Human–Computer Interaction — INTERACT '99
M. Angela Sasse and Chris Johnson (Editors)
Published by IOS Press, © IFIP TC.13, 1999

Investigation into the Effect of Language on Performance in a Multimedia Food Studies Application

Trevor Barker, Sara Jones, Carol Britton & David Messer

University of Hertfordshire, College Lane, Hatfield, Hertfordshire, UK.

T.1.Barker@herts.ac.uk

Abstract: An investigation into how performance in a multimedia learning application was related to the level of language support available is reported. Teachers from a College of Further Education, National Vocation Qualification (NVQ) level 2 catering students and Higher National Diploma (HND) catering management students took part. After a language and subject pre-test, participants were randomly assigned to presentations of a multimedia catering course having either full, or no additional language support available. Immediately after completion, a post-test and two weeks later a re-test were taken.

No significant difference between staff or HND users with different levels of language support was found. Significant differences were found for the NVQ users with different language support. The results of this study are discussed in relation to language skills and the potential for the individual configuration of multimedia.

Keywords: multimedia, pedagogy, language skills, multi-modal interface design.

1 Introduction

Blank & Solomon (1969) identified deficiencies in language skills in children and suggested that language deficiencies in children related to the lack of a system of symbolic thinking. It is likely that such serious deficiencies in language skills identified early in life would be carried on throughout the education process into adult life, and have a negative influence at each stage of development. Deficiencies in language skills might therefore lead to a poor educational experience and poor achievement in general.

This is especially true for students entering further education for several reasons. There is evidence that many learners have severe linguistic deficiencies when they enter college (Barnsley, 1996). In many cases their first language is different from the language in which their selected course is delivered. Specialised vocabulary used in some courses may be a problem for many learners with technical and foreign terms and non-standard usage of words being common. There may also be problems of linguistic style, for example, the use of passive rather than active sentences and the use of past tense in technical writing.

It is sometimes assumed that using multimedia in learning with its use of image, video and animation, will compensate for deficiencies in learners language

skills. Petre (1995), however, challenges this view and stresses the importance of text and spoken language in multimedia presentations. This leads to a high requirement for reading and listening skills in the learner. The multi-modal nature of the user interface places additional emphasis on the use of language in multimedia delivered learning. Complex written and spoken instructions are often involved in multimedia learning applications. McAteer & Shaw (1995) recommend that authors pay particular attention to the use of language in multimedia applications and provide support when communication is in the form of written text in the application. Barron & Atkins (1994) have found that listening skills are also important in multimedia learning applications. Poor use of language in the computer interface may also lead to usability problems in applications. Molich & Nielsen (1990) stress the need for clear simple language in the design of computer interfaces.

The objective of the project reported here was to investigate the effect of language on performance in a multimedia learning application. The study was based on food studies courses taking place in a college of Further Education. Catering courses had been identified by language experts in the college as posing special language problems. There were many technical and foreign terms in regular usage and there was a high scientific component in some areas of food studies, for example, food hygiene and nutrition.

A network-delivered computer application was developed to deliver a course based on the food commodities. Teachers from a College of Further Education, National Vocation Qualification (NVQ) level 2 catering students and Higher National Diploma (HND) catering management students followed a multimedia delivered learning application that provided different levels of language support. The aim of the investigation was to relate performance on pre-tests, post tests and re-tests to the levels of language support provided by the application.

2   Development of the Software

Three pieces of software were developed for this investigation:

1. A computer based tool to facilitate the creation of language differentiated materials (Language level tool).

2. A language testing tool to assess students' language skills.

3. A catering commodities multimedia application able to provide differential language support for learners.

2.1   Language Level Tool

A computer program was developed to determine the language levels of texts and narratives used in the course. This application was designed to measure the Adult Literacy and Basic Skills Unit (ALBSU) SMOG levels (Vaughn, 1995). SMOG levels are used as a standard within many Further Education (FE) colleges to classify learners' reading, writing and listening skills. The SMOG level is calculated from the length of sentences and the number of syllables in words used in a text.

The language level tool was used to analyse sections of text and narrative used in the courses and to calculate the SMOG level of the language used. In this way it was possible to prepare text and narrative at a range of levels.

2.2   Language Testing Tool

The language test was based on a simple listening and gapping test as described by Vaughn (1995). The application tested simple listening and reading skills in the catering subject area.

The test developed followed closely existing language assessment and screening tests used routinely in the college based on the ALBSU SMOG test (Vaughn, 1995).

2.3   Multimedia Application

The application was developed by a team of language, subject and computer specialists, using iterative prototyping and user centred methods. A description of the multimedia development process employed in the creation of the materials is given by Barker and colleagues (Barker et al., 1997).

The programme covered aspects of catering practical and theoretical work, including food science, food composition, food hygiene, storage, handling, nutrition, cookery and other related areas. The domain was selected to be relevant to as wide a range of students as possible. Catering specialists created a full specification for the application, which included text and narrative. After measuring the SMOG level of the language used, in the initial text and narrative, the application was differentiated to provide extra language support in the following ways:

1. Alternative words were provided. Instead of a long difficult word, shorter, simpler words were used.

2. Sentences were made shorter. Long sentences were cut up and presented as several smaller ones.

The effect was to create two versions of the text and narrative for the application, a high level version at ALBSU SMOG level 18 and a lower level version at level 14. These were used to create a prototype of the application differentiated at two language levels. Two pathways were provided through the prototype, a high level language route, set at SMOG level 18 and a lower level language route, set at SMOG level 14. The subject content covered in each pathway was identical.

In addition to reducing the SMOG level, additional language support was provided for the lower level pathway in the prototype by the following measures:

3. Sentences were made active rather than passive in the presentation with additional language support.

4. Additional hyper-linked glossaries and explanations were given where the language might be difficult, for example words like vitamin and protein were explained more in the extra support presentation

5. Additional images and videos were available in the extra supported presentation.

Only redundant information was provided by these additional measures to ensure information provided in both paths was identical.

The prototype was designed so that presentation could be varied within the application according to the values of variables held in individual configuration files for each user:

- Language level = 0 — High level presentation, (SMOG level 18) with no extra language support

- Language level = 1 — Low level presentation, (SMOG level 14) with extra language support provided

Sound presentation was configurable within the application in a range of ways to allow flexible use. For this investigation, sound was set on, repeatable and interruptible.

3   Method

Three groups of participants were involved in this experiment. Two groups of students, one following a Higher National Diploma (HND) and the other following a National Vocational Qualification (NVQ) level 2 in catering. A third group of non-catering lecturing staff also took part.

HND and NVQ students, despite their academic separation, follow a similar core course in food commodities as part of their normal curriculum. Differences in their academic levels however meant that these groups had different language support requirements.

The staff group had no vocational or subject experience of catering, yet would be expected to possess good language skills.

Table 1 shows characteristics of the participants involved in the trial. The language score for each group is also shown in the table.

Group	N	Mean Age	Age Range	Mean % Language Test Score
NVQ	32	17.9	16–23	60
HND	32	19.3	17–35	81
Staff	20	29.3	23–47	93

Table 1: Language scores and groups of participants in the study.

Each group was divided randomly into two equal parts. This enabled participants in each group to be assigned to either of the presentation regimes as follows:

- Presentation a) without additional language support (none).

- Presentation b) with additional language support (full).

Details of sub-groupings and the language support presentations given are displayed in Table 2.

Sub-Group	Additional Language Support	N	Mean Age	Age Range	Mean Language test score
NVQ a	None	16	18.3	16–23	62%
NVQ b	Full	16	17.4	16–22	57%
HND a	None	16	19.0	17–25	81%
HND b	Full	16	19.5	17–22	80%
Staff a	None	10	29.2	23–47	94%
Staff b	Full	10	29.8	23–45	92%

Table 2: Additional language support, age and language test scores.

An analysis of variance was performed on the language test scores for all groups. There were significant differences ($p < 0.01$) between the NVQ (a and b) groups and all other groups. There was no significant difference between the NVQ a and NVQ b group ($p > 0.05$).

4   Implementation

Participants were given a brief introductory talk prior to first use of the system. Immediately after induction, participants were administered the multimedia language test, followed immediately by the multimedia pre-test of 30 multiple choice questions.

Participants followed the course over a period of one week in open access computer areas. Students were supervised at all times by tutors who could provide additional help related to using the application rather than subject information.

Once the course had been completed, a multimedia post-test and user-evaluation was taken by all participants.

The user evaluation tool consisted of a set of 30 questions delivered on the computer in multimedia format. It measured how interesting the course material was, any areas of difficulty within the course and users' computer experience and familiarity with the use of multimedia hardware.

Two weeks later a supervised re-test was taken in multimedia format, delivered on a computer. The pre-test, post-test and re-test were in the same format and covered the same subject areas. Questions for these were selected randomly from a bank. A subject expert who assessed the tests during the software development process rated them to be of equal difficulty.

All results were saved securely and anonymously on a computer network. An extensive data log file was created for each subject throughout the course. This held information about navigation and time spent in each section of the course.

In summary, the implementation had the following stages:

- Initial language assessment test presentation.
- Initial subject pre-test presentation.
- User configuration file created.
- Course followed with prescribed language support.
- Post-test presentation.
- Evaluation of the application by users.
- Re-test presentation two weeks after finishing the course.
- Data collected and analysed.

5   Results

In this section, results obtained in the investigation and their statistical analysis is presented. Table 3 presents the pre-test, post-test and re-test scores for groups following the commodities multimedia course. Results of the user evaluation questionnaire are also presented.

Group	N	Pre-test	Post-test	Re-test	Evaluation
Possible Score		(30)	(30)	(30)	(5)
NVQ a	16	11.13	14.44	12.50	3.25
NVQ b	16	12.13	18.56	14.38	3.68
HND a	16	15.81	21.44	18.25	3.32
HND b	16	16.06	19.94	17.69	3.10
Staff a	10	14.50	20.30	17.10	3.20
Staff b	10	16.60	22.60	18.50	3.10

Table 3: Mean Pre-test, post-test and re-test and user evaluation scores for participants following the catering commodities multimedia course.

The greatest difference in the means seen in Table 3 was between the NVQ a and NVQ b groups post test. The NVQ group with additional language support performed on average better than the NVQ group without the benefit of additional support.

5.1   Tests of Assumptions

The statistical methods used in the data analysis assume that the observed covariance matrices of the dependent variables are equal across groups.

Box's Test of Equality of Covariance Matrices was employed to test the null hypothesis that they were equal.

The observed value of $p > 0.05(0.85)$ compels us to accept the null hypothesis.

Mauchly's test was employed to test the sphericity of the data within groups which is also assumed within the methods used. The observed value of $p > 0.05(0.98)$ compels us to accept the null hypothesis and assume sphericity of data.

5.2   Analysis of Variance (ANOVA)

The means of the TRIALS variable (pre-test score, re-test score and post-test score) were subjected to an repeated measures ANOVA to test for the significance of any differences between them. Table 4 below shows the results of this analysis.

Table 4 shows a significant difference between the means of the TRIALS variable ($p < 0.001$). There were significant differences between the mean scores obtained in pre-test, post-test and re-test. Between subject effects were also investigated and results of this analysis are presented in Table 5.

Table 5 shows significant between subject effects for the GROUP and LANGUAGE LEVEL variables.

6   Discussion

The results are taken to indicate that there were significant differences between the performance of individual groups on pre-test, re-test and post-tests under conditions of different language support. Differences in pre-test scores between the NVQ and HND / staff groups ($p < 0.05$) were likely to be due to different abilities, experience and prior knowledge between the groups. In fact HND and staff groups performed better on average in all tests than NVQ groups. This was significant ($p < 0.05$) in all cases except for the staff a group in the pre-test. Staff groups performed no differently from HND groups on average in all tests under both language conditions.

A significant difference was found in the re-test results between NVQ groups under the two conditions ($p < 0.05$). The NVQ group receiving additional support and lower level language presentation performed significantly better on the re-test than the NVQ group at the higher language level with no support. The provision of additional language support therefore, was most effective for NVQ learners who scored lowest of all groups on the language test.

Source	Type III Sum of Squares	df	Mean	F	Sig.
7TRIALS	1087.727	2	543.864	74.74	0.000
TRIALS x GROUP	10.452	4	2.613	0.359	0.837
TRIALS x LANGUAGE LEVEL	32.177	2	16.088	2.211	0.113
TRIALS x GROUP x LANGUAGE LEVEL	14.818	4	3.704	0.729	0.729
Error (TRIALS)	1135.175	156			

Table 4: Tests of within subject effects. Results of repeated measures ANOVA performed on data from Table 3.

Source	Type III Sum of Squares	df	Mean	F	Sig.
Intercept	67519.376	1	67519.3	3010.4	0.000
GROUP	1135.176	2	567.588	25.306	0.000
LANGUAGE LEVEL	158.167	1	158.167	7.052	0.010
GROUP x LANGUAGE LEVEL	38.347	2	19.173	0.855	0.429
Error	1749.438	78	22.429		

Table 5: Tests of between subject effects. Results of repeated measures ANOVA performed on data from Table 3.

Differences in post-test scores between the two NVQ groups therefore, were ascribable to the additional language support provided within the application. Somewhat paradoxically it was not possible to detect differences between HND and staff groups with and without additional language support, even though additional content in the form of images and video were provided with the language support. This may have been due to ceiling effects on performance.

There are implications of these results for the configuration of multimedia learning materials. When learners have high level language skills, the provision of additional language support is not likely to be effective in improving performance on a multimedia course. When learners have language deficiencies, then it is of benefit to learners to provide additional support and to present language at the appropriate level.

All participants undertook an evaluation of the package in the form of a multimedia presented questionnaire. Table 4 shows that groups with the supported presentation on average scored the package higher than those with the unsupported presentation. This difference was greatest between the NVQ groups, those with additional support scoring it higher than those without the benefit of this. This difference however was not significant ($p > 0.05$). Although there was also no significant difference between the evaluation scores ($p > 0.05$), HND and staff groups with additional language support evaluated the application lower than those without additional support. The slightly lower evaluation scores for the higher level groups following the lower level language pathway providing additional support suggests that this may cause some level of de-motivation of learners with good language skills, though there was no statistical support for this idea.

Failure to find significant differences in the perceived quality of the application in three diverse groups of learners suggests that the provision of differential language support in an application is an important way to tailor it to a specific group of users. In this way learners with poor language skills are likely to benefit from the additional language help available and perform better. Learners with good language skills, who were shown not to benefit from additional language support, may prefer a language presentation at their ability level.

The use of sound has been shown to add to a learning presentation, not only in terms of content and information presentation effects, but it may add audio cues and interest to the application as with music and sound effects, (McAteer & Shaw, 1995). The use of sound has been suggested to offer benefits when language skills are poor. Barton & Dwyer (1987) report that subjects with high verbal skills do not benefit from the addition of audio information in learning applications. They do suggest however, that subjects with lower verbal skills might benefit from textual / audio redundancy in learning. Kenworth (1993) supports this view, suggesting that poor readers benefit from hearing text presented.

Meskill (1996), suggests that the control of the rate of language presentation in multimedia applications allows the retention of language chunks in short term memory. This could in itself be important in improvement in performance in learning when listening skills are limiting. Meskill emphasized the potential of multimedia in language learning and sees listening as a skill integral to overall communicative competence.

Coordinated visual, aural and textual information employed in multimedia can provide clues to the meaning of the written and aural text according to Meskill. The results of the investigation reported here indicate that the presentation of information at the appropriate language level assists in this process.

The investigation showed that performance in a multimedia learning application is improved for learners when it is presented at the most appropriate language level. It is also suggested that failure to do this will result in less than optimum performance, either by de-motivating learners with good language skills or by setting the language level too high to be understood. The individual configuration of multimedia presentations is an important area for future research.

References

Barker, T., Jones, S., Britton, C. & Messer, D. (1997), Creating Multimedia Learning Applications in a Further Education Enviroment, Technical Report 271, Division of Computer Science, University of Hertfordshire.

Barnsley, M. (1996), Language Screening Test Results, Technical Report 1996/05, Waltham Forest College, London.

Barron, A. & Atkins, D. (1994), "Audio Instuction in Multimedia Education: Is Textual Redundancy Important?", *Journal of Educational Multimedia and Hypermedia* **3**(3/4), 295–306.

Barton, E. A. & Dwyer, F. M. (1987), "The Effect of Audio Redundancy on the Students' Ability to Profit from Printed-Verbal Visualized Instruction", *International Journal of Instructional Media* **14**(1), 93–8.

Blank, M. & Solomon, F. (1969), *How Shall the Disadvantaged be Taught? Language in Education*, Open University.

Kenworth, N. W. (1993), "When Johnny Can't Read: Multimedia Design Strategies to Accomodate Poor Readers", *Journal of Instructional Delivery Systems* **7**(1), 27–30.

McAteer, E. & Shaw, R. (1995), The Design of Multimedia Learning Programs. Establishing Multimedia Authoring Skills in Higher Education, Technical Report, University of Glasgow. EMASHE Group publication.

Meskill, C. (1996), "Listning Skills Development Through Multimedia", *Journal of Educational Multimedia and Hypermedia* **5**(2), 179–201.

Molich, R. & Nielsen, J. (1990), "Improving a Human-Computer Dialog", *Communications of the ACM* **33**(3), 338–48.

Petre, M. (1995), "Why Looking isn't Always Seeing. Readership Skills and Graphical Programming", *Communications of the ACM* **38**(6), 33–44.

Vaughn, J. (1995), Assessing Reading: Using Cloze Procedure to Assess Reading Skills, Technical Report, Adult Literacy & Basic Skills Unit, London.

Human–Computer Interaction — INTERACT '99
M. Angela Sasse and Chris Johnson (Editors)
Published by IOS Press, © IFIP TC.13, 1999

Examining Users' Repertoire of Internet Applications

Jon Rimmer[1], Ian Wakeman[1], Louise Sheeran[2] & M. Angela Sasse[2]

[1] School of Cognitive and Computing Sciences, University of Sussex, Falmer, Brighton BN1 9QH, UK.
[2] Department of Computer Science, UCL, Gower Street, London WC1E 6BT, UK.

jonr@cogs.susx.ac.uk

Abstract: The language within user interfaces should match the language of the user. However, there has been very little work on how to capture this language and in particular, the lexicon of the user. In this paper we describe how the tools from discourse analysis can be used to capture these lexicons, and show how they vary according to the function of the text. We conducted semi-structured interviews and questionnaires to collect texts for analysis. Analysis showed a variety of repertoires used to describe typical network applications, such as email and Web use. We present these repertoires and describe how they can be used in the design of the user interface.

Keywords: discourse analysis, repertoire, conceptual design, internet interfaces, email, World Wide Web.

1 Introduction

According to New Media, Inc there will be one billion Internet users by the year 2001 (Emerge Incorporated, 1998). With this influx of new users of varying experience, and the majority of use being associated with email and Web applications, it is important that these applications are well designed to be highly usable. Since networks are prone to breakdowns in interesting ways, applications should also educate users to employ appropriate recovery strategies. This can only be done by communicating a pertinent model of the network to the user through the interface, training, and help facilities. For this education to be effective we must use the language of the users.

This requirement is emphasized in heuristic evaluation. This evaluation technique is the most popular of the usability inspection methods, carried out as a systematic inspection of a user interface design. The goal of heuristic evaluation is to find the usability problems in the design so that they can be attended to as part of an iterative design process. (Nielsen, 1994). The second of Nielsen's 10 Heuristics is:

Match between system and the real world: The system should speak the users' language, with words, phrases and concepts familiar to the user, rather than system- oriented terms. Follow real-world conventions, making information appear in a natural and logical order.

However, there has been very little work on how to discover exactly what this language is. Most designers guess what language is appropriate, and then adjust the language (if at all) when evaluating and testing against users. In this paper we describe a methodology and theoretical framework for capturing and analysing and creating lexicons of actual user language about specific applications.

Some studies of discourse have been carried out in the field of Human Computer Interaction, but most concentrate on how language is used to get tasks done in order to understand communication patterns, rather than the actual content itself. Good examples of such work are those carried out by Clark & Shaefer (1989), and McCarthy et al. (1991). However, the closest related work to this study is in the field of mental model elicitation. Norman (1986) explains how the designer has a working model of the system she has designed, and that the user learns to use it through interaction (and possibly instruction too), forming a working model of that system. Problems are likely to occur when the working model is inappropriate increasing the probability that the error rate is high and recovery rate poor. These mental models are internalized cognitive representations and therefore not directly observable. They are inferred from a range of observable behaviours displayed by the user. A description of users' models will be a researcher's externalized conceptualization of user's internalized models (Sasse, 1997). Over the last decade there have been numerous studies and books published in the field of cognitive science that have examined for the existence of mental models and how they can be used, adapted and influenced. Sasse (1997) carried out an extensive review of this work and was critical of over reliance on performance data as an indication of models. The few studies that have analysed verbal protocols offer no clear description of how models are inferred from them or give any indication as to how transcripts were analysed.

This paper deliberately does not define what mental models are in the context of network applications, as we are interested in the examination of users' language using the method of discourse analysis proposed by Potter & Wetherell (1987). We shall explain our methodology through example, which we feel can be put to use in many other contexts. Having carried out this study, we firmly believe that the process of conceptual design would benefit greatly from use of discourse analysis, and this will become apparent throughout the paper.

A definition of discourse has been debated by psychologists, linguists and researchers from other disciplines. Potter & Wetherell (1987) discuss the broad term 'text', which can cover anything that is put into words, and as such becomes discourse. Discourse analysis is concerned with the content of the text, its subject matter and with its social rather than linguistic organization (Edwards & Potter, 1992). This paper takes the position that discourse analysis treats the social world as a system of 'texts' that can be systematically 'read' by the researcher whether it be talk or writing. In fact it is believed that it can be taken even further, to analyse the 'design language' of any artefact or interface. For example, Bannister (1994) carried out discourse analysis on a children's toothpaste packaging which had both words and pictures, as well as shape and form.

Design language denotes the visual and functional language of communication with people who use an artefact. Design language is like a natural language, both in its communicative function and in its structure as an evolving system of elements and of relationships among those elements (Winograd, 1996). Design language is the basis for how we create and interact with things in the world (Rheinfrank & Evenson, 1996).

Language, both natural and design, only works because people share a 'complex symbolic representational system' which is inevitably involved in our thinking and reasoning as well as our communication with others. The interpretative repertoire is basically "a lexicon or register of terms and metaphors drawn upon to characterize and evaluate actions, events, and other phenomena. A repertoire is constituted through a limited range of terms used in a particular stylistic and grammatical constructions. Often a repertoire will be organized around specific metaphors and figures of speech", (Potter & Wetherell, 1987).

We are using the tools of discourse analysis to expose the interpretative repertoires found when people discuss network applications. By building lexicons from the interpretative repertoires people employ within their natural language, we are offering the raw material from which the design language of the interface can be built.

One of the benefits of the discourse approach to categorization is that it has directed attention away from the cognitive processes assumed to be operating under people's skulls and on towards the detail of how categories are actually used. It is not surprising that categories are so important, because they are the nouns from which we construct versions of the collectives in which we live (Potter & Wetherell, 1987). In this study, we have aimed not to hypothesize about cognitive processes, but instead to create a concrete resource from users' texts for use within the design process of interactive network applications.

In the next section we present our methodology and then our results. These describe various repertoires used to explain networked applications. We discuss how these results can be used in the design process and conclude with future directions for this methodology.

2 Methodology

2.1 Considerations

For this particular study, we chose not to look at the repertoires of very inexperienced computer users after examining the results of our pilot study in which we have talked to participants who had little or no knowledge of email and the Web (many of whom refused to even guess a response to the scenarios). Many of the new users of the Internet will already have some degree of computer literacy even if based on knowledge gained through cultural experiences of media, interaction with similar devices/existing interfaces, communications with friends and colleagues, education, and training.

2.2　Participants

The data for this study was collected from texts elicited from 32 participants, and consisted of 19 semi-structured interviews which were then transcribed, and 13 written responses to an informal questionnaire asking the same scenario questions. The people who participated in this study were system administrators for two organizations, postgraduate students, administrative office assistants, medical doctors, as well as Internet Service Provider HelpDesk staff. Experience of email use ranged from 3 months to 8 years and Web usage from 2 weeks to 6 years — see Table 1.

Participant	Age	Internet usage Hours/ week	Email Experience Years or (months)	Web Experience Years or (months)
1	22	1.5	2	2 (weeks!)
2	53	10	6	6
3	38	12	6	3
4	27	2	7	3
5	31	1	8	2
6	53	1	2	1
7	29	5	2	2
8	26	0.5	3	2
9	49	3	1.5	1.5
10	22	1	9 (months)	9 (months)
11	18	2	8 (months)	8 (months)
12	27	10	2	2
13	24	2	10 (months)	10 (months)
14	34	10	1	1
15	45	1	1	1
16	24	1	3	0.5
17	21	2	1.5	1.5
18	38	2	1.5	1.5
19	25	2	2	2
20	23	5	5	4
21	32	5	0.5	0.5
22	30	4	1.5	1
23	28	1	3	3
24	25	1	4	4
25	45	2	5	3
26	22	10	3	3
27	24	5	4	5
28	25	10	6	6
29	36	5	3 (months)	3 (months)
30	30	8	3	2
31	29	10	2	4
32	32	7	3	3

Table 1: A summary of the study participants' details.

2.3　Design

Two scenarios were devised to elicit a user's description of how email and looking at a Web page works. These were then posed to the participants either verbally (semi-structured interviews), or in writing (simple informal questionnaire). The semi-structured interviews were based on the techniques described by Draper & Stribley (1991) who claim that this method of information elicitation has become one of the most important in social science. It allows discussion on the topic in whichever way seems natural and relevant to the interviewee, allowing exploration of the response by the interviewer. This method is far less limiting than the qualitative questionnaire, but more time consuming in that each individual interview has to be transcribed. A questionnaire has the advantage that it can be given to several people to complete at any one time and is returned as a ready made transcript, but misses out on the possible richness of exploratory follow up questions.

2.4　Scenarios

The scenarios were devised in an attempt to elicit a full response to the workings of email and Web use. The content of each scenario posed had to ensure that country boundaries were crossed rather than, for example, sending a person a message who may be on the same network/intranet.

Email: I want to send an email to my friend in Jamaica; what do you think happens to the message when I have composed my email and press the send button?

Web: I want to look at a Web site based in Alaska that has details on grizzly bears. What do you think happens after I have entered the site's address; from the moment I press return, to when I receive the Web pages on my screen?

The questionnaire had an additional question asking the participant to describe a search engine:

Search Engine: What is a search engine and how does it work?

2.5　Analysis

Two people working independently carried out separate analysis on the same data. Each person went over the transcripts several times using the technique of discourse analysis based on the methods suggested by Wetherell & Potter (1988).

The texts for this study were quite concise from the outset; three specific questions were being asked, which inevitably produced answers relating to those questions. The process of coding the text was, therefore, more straightforward than many other studies of discourse. The first stage of coding, consists of each analyst identifying 'rough repertoires'. This can only be achieved by reading and analysing the text several times. In doing so, one can begin identifying patterns and organizations of words and highlight the metaphors employed. This enables the analyst to gradually build them up into more concrete themes that can be categorized, noting clusters of words that were associated with each repertoire. Finally the two analysts went over the transcriptions together in order to compare findings and check similarity. These were discussed and pooled together, producing a listing of the word clustering within the passages and noting the commonalities and exceptions.

3 Results

The repertoires were very distinct, and there were particular words that would almost always appear in a particular repertoire e.g. *Server* in the Computer Based repertoire. Below is a summary of the results showing the words listed in the Lexicon Used — see Table 2. We do not want to claim that these lexicons are complete since in many ways this is chasing a moving target. However, they are exhaustive based on our texts. The words are listed in order of frequency of use.

Unfortunately, the word *message* was used in the email scenario. This may have influenced users. However, *message* was rarely used within telephony-based repertoires, and was found in instances of computer-based repertoire in both Web and email scenarios, so we are reasonably confident that *message* is part of the computer-based repertoire.

In order to further explain the method of analysis and demonstrate results, we shall provide examples of each repertoire in use. In the following examples, repertoire words are highlighted in **bold**, whilst exceptions are *italicized*.

The computer-based repertoire is characterized by descriptions of 'networks' of 'servers' which 'route' 'messages' 'hop' by 'hop'. Sometimes, the description is enhanced by breaking the message into 'packets' or 'chunks'.

Computer Based Repertoire, P32: "My machine sends a **request** to my **server** which sends it to the **server** where the site is stored (unless the pages are in some sort of **cache** somewhere on **route** or on my computer's **hard disk**) and eventually **components** of the page get sent to my machine after it requests them."

In a telephony repertoire, the emphasis is on the telephone line and the attached visible modem, and the communication of information is via one phone call after another. The focus is often on the physical wires connecting the computers, and computers are often referred to as 'centres' or 'exchanges'.

Telephony Based Repertoire, P6: "I should know this but I am aware that I don't really. When I press the send button it then goes to my local **centre** from which I have my email address, so it is a **local call, 'phone call** to my **centre** where *messages* are collected up and then **transmitted** to the foreign country wherever it is on there, across the **telephone cables, wires**. Via the **telephone**, put it that way ..."

In the next example, the user is attempting to justify the time taken by email delivery. Whilst computers and telephone connections are fast, the postal system is slow, so they fall back on a postal repertoire. The mail is 'collected' and 'forwarded'. It is noticeable that the agent doing the work is not identified, possibly since identifying the agent as a computer would cause a contradiction between fast computers and slow delivery.

Postal Repertoire (as description), P20: "I guess it first goes to some place where all the **'outgoing' mails** are **collected**, and then the **address** will be considered and **forwarded** to the appropriate place — some are instantaneous, some are not."

When the user is describing a process which they believe requires intelligence, the explanation is characterized by reference to some unidentified 'it', which performs the actions. This is particularly pronounced when used to describe the functioning of the Web and search engines.

Agent Repertoire, P10: "I think your **computer is searching** for the site first. I don't know why it doesn't come up straight away — it depends on **their connections** and **their modems**. When you press return, **it** searches for it, when **it** finds it, you can see it on your screen."

The specialist repertoires from electronics and computer networks are employed when the user can describe the underlying physical processes of the communication system. The emphasis is on using jargon from a particular technical field, most of which would be unknown to non-specialists. Obviously most users would not be able to employ these repertoires.

Use of Repertoire	Repertoires Identified	Lexicon Used
Description	Computer Based	message, packets, address, file, routes, server, databases, connection[†], connect[†], tags, matches, header, links, chunks, downloaded, request, trawls, packages, reassemble, access, cache, ping, zipped, cables[†].
Description	Telephony Based	telephone line, dials up, modem, connection[†], connect[†], 'phone, directory, yellow pages, telephone socket, 'phone call, exchange, call, centre, transmission, switching telephone conversation, busy, connection, cables[†].
Description	Agent	emphasis on the word 'it', searching, look up, finds, guide.
Description/Analogy	Postal	postal system, post office, letter, forwarded, mails, pigeonhole, collected.
Analogy	Transport	traffic, road, travel, aeroplane, scenic route, rush hour.
Analogy	Library	bookmarked, guide, subject index, library, catalogue.
Description	Electronic	electronics, modem, modulate, demodulate, digital, analogue, signal, on-off.
Description	Computer Network	Domain Name System (DNS), Network Interface Card (NIC), Point to Point Protocol (PPP), Internet Protocol (IP), bandwidth, routing table, buffer, port, protocols, packets, labels, hops, reassembled, dial-up.

Table 2: Identified repertoires and associated Lexicons. [†] Denote instances where a word can be seen as common to both the Telephony and Computer Based Repertoires.

Electronics Repertoire, P2: "It is converted into **electronic pulses** in your software and it goes into your **modem** which converts it into — **modem** being **modulator**, **demodulator**, so it is **modulated** by **modem** and it goes down as a series of **digital**... sensitive to an **analogue signal** which can be **transmitted** down the **telephone line** ..."

Computer Network Repertoire, P4: "The physical **IP address** of the **server** which will deal with the email **request**. So you get your **ISP**, wherever it is in London say, so you will get your **message**, it will be all the **internet packets** will then, all the **packets** with the **message** will be **labelled** with a **destination address** looked at from the **domain name server**. Then they will all be sent to the router on the **ISP's network**. That **router** will then have a huge great big **routing table** and it will look at the **IP address** of the destinations of all these **packets** which your **email address** has been split up into and will work out the next **router** which has the least number of **hops**."

The analogy repertoires are employed to enhance explanations given in a primary description repertoire. The repertoire changes are flagged by use of words such as '*like*'.

Transport Repertoire, P17: "When you press send, it goes off to our **server**, which is called the **SMTP server**, and it looks for a **route** to Jamaica across the servers on the way. It's a bit *like* **catching a plane** and having to keep changing at every county. So it **hops**. And then it sits on her friend's **server** until she switches on her machine and she presses check mail."

Library Repertoire, P21: "A **guide** to help get you to a range of sites, using limited information (i.e. you don't need a particular address). *Like* a **subject index** in a **library** computer system."

Postal Repertoire (as analogy), P9: "You type your **message**, goes to the **outbox**, when ready press **send/receive**. It's a bit *like* the **postal system**. So it goes to a **server**, the **post office**, and your **letter** may **bounce** around **servers** until the person **logs on** in Jamaica and gets it. It would probably take six hours to arrive, depending on how much **traffic** is on the servers."

Below is an example of repertoires being used for different purposes. The user begins by using computer repertoire ('hops', 'computer'). But when trying to explain how the message will sometimes take a long time, the user brings in a transport metaphor, implying that the message goes down many diversions from the direct path. From this point, the repertoire becomes much less computer based, with generic terms such as 'pass' rather than 'send', 'jump' rather than 'hop', 'pick up' rather than 'download' and 'system' rather than 'network', until the transport reference is returned to explicitly for use as an analogy.

P18 "Depending on the systems, number of **hops** — it doesn't go direct from our computer to their computer either, it tends to go the **scenic route**. We may not know who's this is, but we know who will, so we'll pass it to them, and they'll pass it on. I've seen it go 1 or 2, or 5 or 6 **jumps**. I've seen taken, within the XYZ system, I've sent an email to a customer and they've **picked it up** straight away. Anything from a couple of minutes to half and hour to an hour. It depends on how busy the **system** is. Friday afternoons are really bad. People **on-line**, people using the **system**. Another analogy: It's *like* the **roads**. If you go on the **M25**, it's lovely, unless you go on a Friday afternoon in **rush hour** then it's going to be really busy. The standard one is, when America comes **on-line**, because it's so big with the **Internet**, it slows the whole **system** down. But within Britain … Monday morning when everybody comes in to check their email. And Friday afternoon, people are **sending** their email before they go home."

When repertoire are used inappropriately, the user becomes confused in their explanation. In this example, user P6 attempts to transfer the telephony based repertoire used to describe email (above) to describing the Web, and becomes tied up in moving from multiple phone calls lasting finite time to a near-instantaneous connection.

> **P6** "Now you would get that, I know you would get it fairly instantly … I don't understand the fact why that is so direct, but it is. Is it not dependent on **radio**, I mean on **telephone** … It doesn't go to my **local**, it goes direct I understand — I actually don't know."

4 Discussion

Analysis of the text was surprisingly straight-forward due to the conciseness of the initial questions. The high degree of consistency between the analysts' interpretations made it easy to analyse and to agree on the themes of each repertoire identified. Within the descriptions of the email scenario, the user was more likely to use a Telephony Based Repertoire ('phone line'), whereas within the Web scenario the user is more likely to adopt an Agent Repertoire (searching and retrieving) or a Computer Repertoire (packets and servers). We can hypothesize that this may be because email is a person to person(s) behaviour, and such behaviour translates well to a telephone description.

> **P23** "Telephone lines able to reach out across the world to individual users"

It is also possible that home email users who would have a context of 'dialling-up' to send and receive messages offered these descriptions. What is interesting, however, is that the Telephony Based Repertoire used to describe email was not carried over to describe Web usage (apart from the confused example above).

From a pure psychology perspective, it can be argued that the questions in themselves could possibly prime the user repertoires. However, we believe that whilst not all texts are equal in value, they are all valuable in revealing repertoire at work. A more influential factor in priming repertoire may in fact be context. For example, does being confronted by an application's interface change the repertoire compared to when the user is sitting comfortably in an armchair? We have not explored this issue in this study, and hope to explore this in future work.

Repertoires are not static. People continually re-invent the language they use, drawing upon examples of use in conversation, from the media, and from the applications and tools they use. For example, it was very noticeable that the staff from the Internet Service Provider HelpDesk employed a very pronounced procedural stereotype of the email scenario, presumably echoing the lengthy training they would have completed before dealing with customers. The design language of Outlook Express with 'Outboxes' and 'send/receive' labels on its buttons is very apparent in the example below.

> **P10** "When you click on **send** it gets placed in the **outbox**, and the next time you **connect** to the **server** and you press send/receive, it goes to the **server**. If you're **sending** it to Jamaica then it'll go and sit on his **server** until he presses **send/receive**."

The lexicon produced from capturing and analysing the repertoires can be used to inform the design process. Designers can ensure that the lexicon used within the application are from real repertoires, and are thus understandable to the user. Designers can avoid using specialist repertoire when designing for general use. The designers can also ensure that they are using language from a single and appropriate repertoire, and are not confusing users by intermingling repertoires. However, this is a resource for designers; they can still use words from outside the lexicon to describe new features, since the designers' work is part of the evolution of repertoires.

Discourse analysis not only reveals the lexicon of the words and phrase; it can also provide a description of the common metaphors and analogies within and across repertoires. These metaphors and analogies can then be used to inform the conceptual design process, ensuring that the concepts in the interface are rooted in the language of the user.

Interfaces affect the evolution of repertoire as well. Through careful engineering of the interface, designers can affect the repertoire that users will describe their actions. For example, this has obvious implications for ensuring that HelpDesk staff can provide understandable help to users, and in aiding the education of users as to how their applications function.

5   Conclusions and Future Work

We have presented a methodology for capture and analysis of texts. In particular, the analysis techniques can be applied to any text, such as books, manuals, email or even existing computer applications. When designing an application for use within specific contexts, these techniques offer ways to capture application and context specific repertoire, which can then be used to increase understanding of the application and ensure consistent and appropriate language use within the interface.

Users have a range of interpretative repertoire, which are separate and distinct in their usage. We have demonstrated that for texts from a range of individuals describing networked applications, descriptive repertoire can be classified as Telephony Based, Computer Based, Agent Based, or Postal. These are supplemented by a number of analogy repertoires. We have identified Postal, Transport and Library from our texts, and acknowledge that there may indeed be many more. We have also shown the existence of expert repertoire, associated with specialist electronics and computer networks knowledge.

We plan to use this methodology to build further lexicons for networked applications and demonstrate its use in the conceptual design of real applications. We shall also be exploring the variability of repertoire across conditions such as location, network breakdown, and user goals. As well as this, we aim to look at potential differences that could be associated with context — do such repertoires change when describing an application during use? Does a repertoire change depending on the perceived background of the listener by the speaker (expert and novice for example)? Finally, a more detailed analysis needs to be carried out looking at the 'design language' of interfaces.

Acknowledgements

EMMANATE is funded by EPSRC under the Information Technology and Computer Science Programme.

References

Bannister, P. (1994), Discourse Analysis, *in* P. Bannister, E. Burman, I. Parker, M. Taylor & C. Tindall (eds.), *Qualitative Methods in Psychology: A Research Guide*, Open University, pp.108–20.

Clark, H. H. & Shaefer, E. F. (1989), "Contributing to Discourse", *Cognitive Science* **13**(2), 259–94.

Draper, S. W. & Stribley, K. M. (1991), "Practical methods for measuring the performance of Human–Computer Interfaces", Handout from the JCI Summer School.

Edwards, D. & Potter, J. (1992), *Discursive Psychology*, Sage Publications.

Emerge Incorporated (1998), "Market Research Study". http://www.emergeinc.com/statistics.html.

McCarthy, J. C., Miles, V. C. & Monk, A. F. (1991), An Experimental Study of Common Ground in Text-Based Communication, *in* S. P. Robertson, G. M. Olson & J. S. Olson (eds.), *Proceedings of CHI'91: Human Factors in Computing Systems (Reaching through Technology)*, ACM Press, pp.209–15.

Nielsen, J. (1994), Heuristic Evaluation, *in* J. Nielsen & R. L. Mack (eds.), *Usability Inspection Methods*, John Wiley & Sons, pp.25–62.

Norman, D. A. (1986), Cognitive Engineering, *in* D. A. Norman & S. W. Draper (eds.), *User Centered Systems Design: New Perspectives on Human–Computer Interaction*, Lawrence Erlbaum Associates, pp.31–62.

Potter, J. & Wetherell, M. (1987), *Discourse Analysis and Social Psychology: Beyond Attitudes and Behaviour*, Sage Publications.

Rheinfrank, J. & Evenson, S. (1996), Design Languages, *in* Winograd (1996), pp.63–80.

Sasse, M. A. (1997), Eliciting and Describing Users Models of Computer Systems, PhD thesis, School of Computer Science, University of Birmingham.

Wetherell, M. & Potter, J. (1988), Discourse Analysis and the Identification of Interpretative Repertoires, *in* C. Antaki (ed.), *Analysing Everyday Explanation: A Casebook of Methods*, Sage Publications, pp.168–83.

Winograd, T. (ed.) (1996), *Bringing Design to Software*, Addison–Wesley.

Part Three

Doctoral Consortium

Human–Computer Interaction — INTERACT '99
M. Angela Sasse and Chris Johnson (Editors)
Published by IOS Press, © IFIP TC.13, 1999

Automated Generation of Presentations through a Search-based Software Visualization System

Rogelio Adobbati

Computer Science Department, Information Sciences Institute, University of Southern California, 4676 Admiralty Way, Marina del Rey, CA 90292–6695, USA.

rogelio@isi.edu

Abstract: This paper describes work on PESCE (Presentation Engine for Software Comprehension and Explanation), a system that addresses the problem of automatically generating visual explanations of software.

Keywords: software visualization, intelligent user interfaces.

1 Introduction

It has been shown that complex information can be more clearly conveyed by combining text and graphics to form visual representations that place selected, diverse images into the narrative context of a coherent argument (Tufte, 1997). Two tasks must be performed to generate visual representations: select what information to show (*content selection*), and how to show it (*presentation generation*). The work presented here focuses on presentation generation.

2 The Problem

I am investigating how to automatically generate visual explanations about abstract information, in particular, information about software systems. In the domain of software visualization, dynamically generated presentations are highly desirable due to the dynamic nature of software, and to the different characteristics of users trying to perform software understanding (Knuth, 1963). Moreover, the software visualization problem proves very challenging in view of several particular issues, like the multiple levels of abstraction that can be applied to visualize software artifacts, the need to tailor the information to different user levels of expertise and different tasks, the limited amount of graphical resources available at any given time, and the fact that the mechanisms for conceptual comprehension of graphical depictions are not well understood (Adobbati et al., 1998).

3 Related Work

Various visualization systems have been developed that automatically generate visual presentations. Some of them deal with the visualization of mainly quantitative information in the form of tables, graphs, etc. — e.g. SAGE (Roth & Mattis, 1991). These visualization systems do not provide the adequate techniques to represent abstract relationships between concepts, a mandatory feature in software visualization. Other systems generate planned multi-modal presentations from some underlying representation — e.g. WIP (Andre et al., 1993), COMET (Feiner & McKeown, 1991). These systems have been successfully used to explain how to use certain technical devices, but they do not provide the necessary visualization primitives needed to generate useful software explanations. IMPROVISE (Zhou & Feiner, 1997) might provide some of that functionality, but it is not clear if it would be sufficient for the task at hand.

Software visualization tools provide functionality for program understanding and debugging — e.g. GROOVE (Jerding et al., 1997). Nonetheless, the presentations generated are usually designed towards program debugging and algorithm animation at the source-code level. Their focus has not been to visualize the components of a software system at different levels of abstraction.

4   Approach

The PESCE system (Presentation Engine for Software Comprehension and Explanation) addresses the above mentioned issues. PESCE is part of MediaDoc (Erdem et al., 1998), a Web-based software engineering tool being developed at ISI that uses textual and graphical presentations for software explanation. PESCE's approach is an extension of the work of Mackinlay (1991), and consists of automatically searching a space of possible designs to visualize input information produced by some content selection module. My premise is that:

> "explicit knowledge about the design of visual explanations, in the form of constraints and visualization methods, can be used by a general presentation engine to automatically generate coherent visual presentations about complex software systems."

5   Architecture of PESCE

The main components of PESCE are a *repository of visualization rules* for software objects and relationships, a *presentation engine* that uses those rules to generate visual directives to show information about a software system, and a *diagram generator* that realizes those directives.

Visual rules are used by the presentation engine to generate graphical representations of an object or relationship. Each rule has 3 main components: the software object/relationship type it realizes, the visualization method to be called to display that object/relationship, and a set of spatial, temporal, and style constraints for the method. There is usually more than one possible method for a given type of object/relationship; a default order of preference is assigned to each method. The content selection module can pass an alternative order of preference to PESCE, according to the presentation's goals and user preferences. In addition, global constraints related to the presentation intended style and the user's physical characteristics are also passed as parameters for the visualization. Constraints are assigned an importance value to indicate if they are mandatory for the corresponding method.

The presentation engine is the most critical component in PESCE. This module receives, from a content selection module, information about software objects and relationships in a well structured, SGML-like format. After building a linked structure representing that information, the presentation engine searches each element in the structure as follows:

a visual method for the object/relationship type is retrieved from the rule repository to generate the right visual representation for each object and relationship, checking that no constraints are violated, and backtracking if necessary. However, an exhaustive search of all possible visualization methods for every object and relationship to be visualized might lead to exponential explosion. PESCE reduces the search using heuristics (more densely connected objects, which are usually the more constraining ones, are searched first), and minimizing backtracking (non-mandatory constraints are relaxed if possible).

After all the elements have been associated with visualization methods without conflicting constraints, the resulting list of visual directives (in an SGML-like language called MAP — Markup language for Authoring Presentations) is sent to a Diagram Generator for graphical display. The Diagram Generator is a Java applet that represents objects and relationships through an animated graphical layout.

6   Conclusions

Several examples of visual presentations of software have been tested in PESCE. The work to date suggests that, with the current small set of rules, PESCE can achieve clear, coherent presentations for a reasonable number of objects (less than 20) and relationships between them (less than 10). I am currently working on a larger and more general set of visual rules, and on testing the system for usability and scalability. Since PESCE presentations are Web-based, I expect to be able to conduct experiments over a wider range of users without much difficulty. Furthermore, I intend to explore the hypothesis that PESCE's extensible input language and general visual rule format are applicable beyond the software visualization domain. In particular, PESCE is currently being applied to the domain of disaster relief plans, where it may provide an automated alternative to interactively generated plan visualizations — e.g. (Hoebel et al., 1998).

Acknowledgements

I would like to thank my advisor, Dr W. Lewis Johnson, and Dr Stacy Marsella, for their continued guidance and support. This research is sponsored by DARPA under DARPA order number D880.

References

Adobbati, R., Johnson, W. L. & Marsella, S. (1998), Software Understanding Through Automated Visual Presentations, *in Proceedings of California Software Symposium 1998*, pp.31–7.

Andre, E., Finkler, W., Graf, W., Rist, T., Schauder, A., & Wahlster, W. (1993), WIP: The Automatic Synthesis of Multimodal Presentations, *in* M. T. Maybury (ed.), *Intelligent Multimedia Interface*, AAAI Press, pp.75–93.

Erdem, A., Johnson, W. L. & Marsella, S. (1998), Task Oriented Software Understanding, *in Proceedings of ASE'98*, pp.230–9.

Feiner, S. & McKeown, K. (1991), "Automating the Generation of Coordinated Multimedia Explanations", *IEEE Computer* **24**(10), 33–41.

Hoebel, L., Lorensen, W. & Martin, K. (1998), "Integrating Graphics and Abstract Data to Visualize Temporal Constraints", *ACM SIGART Bulletin* **9**(3/4), 18–23.

Jerding, D., Stasko, J. & Ball, T. (1997), Visualizing Interactions in Program Executions, *in Proceedings of ICSE-97*, pp.360–70.

Knuth, D. (1963), "Computer Drawn Flowcharts", *Communications of the ACM* **6**(9), 555–63.

Mackinlay, J. (1991), Search Architectures for the Automatic Design of Graphical Presentations, *in* J. Sullivan & S. Tyler (eds.), *Intelligent User Interfaces*, ACM Press, pp.281–92.

Roth, S. F. & Mattis, J. (1991), Automating the Presentation of Information, *in Proceedings of the IEEE Conference on AI Applications*, pp.90–7.

Tufte, E. R. (1997), *Visual Explanations*, Graphics Press.

Zhou, M. X. & Feiner, S. K. (1997), The Representation and Usage of a Visual Lexicon for Automated Graphics Generation, *in Proceedings of IJCAI '97*.

Human–Computer Interaction — INTERACT '99
M. Angela Sasse and Chris Johnson (Editors)
Published by IOS Press, © IFIP TC.13, 1999

User-centred Relevance Research: Developing a Better Understanding of Searchers' Ultimate Use Requirements

Theresa K.D. Anderson

Department of Information Studies, University of Technology, Sydney,
PO Box 123, NSW 2007, Australia.

theresa.anderson@uts.edu.au

Abstract: This thesis takes an ethnographic approach to the study of information retrieval. It explores the information choices of academic researchers using networked information systems. Researchers perform real searches in a formal usability laboratory. These observations are integrated with user interviews and evaluations of retrieved information at various stages of their research. The study focuses on ultimate use requirements rather than specific search requests and retrieval techniques. This blending of approaches from information retrieval and usability research tries to more fully capture the context of relevance judgements during users' research activities.

Keywords: information retrieval, ethnography, usability testing.

1 Introduction

Understanding what relevance means for users in specific contexts and how they judge the relevance of information sources is fundamental to the design of all information retrieval systems (Schamber et al., 1990). The user's judgement of relevance is dynamic and multidimensional. It is a complex mental activity involving quality judgements of relationships between information and a user's information need (Barry & Schamber, 1998; Mizzaro, 1997). For the user, relevance is intimately related to processes and criteria used to evaluate references obtained in an information retrieval situation (Park, 1994). Meanings of 'relevance' change as a result of encounters with people, things and ideas (Cool, 1993).

This thesis focuses on the interactive construction of meaning attributed to a search topic during information retrieval. It applies usability testing methods to observe the dynamism of relevance assessments made by researchers.

2 Studying Search Behaviour

The selection of 'relevant' information is influenced by interactions during the retrieval process as well as the broader search process. Topic matching is useful for identifying documents held within a retrieval system. However, seeking out the human meaning of 'topical relevance' requires a better understanding

of the learning associated with a user's relevance assessments. This thesis aims to explore these user constructs in the context of individual information seeking experiences.

2.1 Research Questions

Search topics are related to a user's broader research problem to investigate:

- What influences a user's selection of 'relevant' documents?

- Are patterns of topic-related priorities evident?

- How, if at all, do the priorities change? Why?

2.2 Participants and the Context of Study

Academic researchers at the University of Technology, Sydney (UTS) who are experienced database users are participating in this study. A series of search sessions using bibliographic databases accessible through the university network are being observed. Researchers conduct the exact searches they would have done in their own offices, but in a formal usability laboratory where search sessions and 'think aloud' discussions are recorded. This 'real-life' context is needed to better understand *how* these users negotiate with networked information resources that succeed in providing potentially useful — and relevant — information for the researchers' purposes.

2.3 Method

This research uses an ethnographic approach to explore the phenomena influencing a user's relevance assessments. Developing an understanding of changing relevance priorities involves:

- Detailed descriptions of each academic's approach to information evaluation.

- Direct observation throughout their research.

- Observation of personalised information seeking sequences within each academic's framework of evaluation and use.

Searches are observed throughout the academics' research projects in a large industry-standard usability laboratory at the UTS School of Computing Sciences. Each session consists of:

- Semi-structured interview prior to the session.

- Search session conducted in the laboratory.

- Post-search interview.

- Discussions about retrieved sources.

Search sessions are video-taped and logged using a software package known as DRUM — diagnostic recorder for usability measurement (Bevan & Macleod, 1994). Interviews are audio-taped.

Requests made to an information system are related to what users are ultimately looking for during their research and the way they search. All changes in search queries and evaluation criteria are recorded and explored. During the search session, for instance, users are encouraged to discuss thoughts, reactions and actions in a modified 'think aloud' protocol (Nielsen, 1993). Discussion about retrieved items helps identify how well the information satisfied a user's requirements and how that information might affect their research progress.

3 Concluding Remarks

In this research, relevance assessment is related to contextual factors of information seeking in electronic environments. Information retrieval involves more than interaction with a database during a series of searches. Search behaviour is part of the overall research practice of users (Kuhlthau, 1993). They are involved in processes of interpretation and definition as they move toward a better understanding of the problem at hand.

This exploration of system-searcher interaction attempts to take this broader context into account by:

- observing not one but a series of searches conducted by users during their research;

- asking questions and engaging in conversation with users about information retrieval practices, decisions and reactions during searching;

- conducting interviews before and after each computer session to learn more about users' search experiences, expectations and attitudes;

- reviewing with users the material collected as a result of search sessions to learn how retrieved information relates [or fails to relate] to their research goals and how they evaluate information for their own purposes; and

- developing ethnographic 'stories' to encapsulate each user's retrieval experiences.

Preliminary findings using this approach suggest that studies of user-centred relevance addressing evaluation criteria only after a particular information retrieval system has been selected can not adequately address the concept. Many decisions about 'relevance' are made even before the search begins. To explore relevance within the broader context of information retrieval, the searcher's full experience must be recorded and evaluated. Recognising the significance of context also suggests the importance of situating individual information retrieval experiences within the larger information search process. This broader context will be more fully examined during the next stages of the research.

References

Barry, C. L. & Schamber, L. (1998), "User-Defined Relevance Criteria: An Exploratory Study", *Journal of the American Society for Information Science* **45**(3), 149–59.

Bevan, N. & Macleod, M. (1994), "Usability Measurement in Context", *Behaviour & Information Technology* **13**(1-2), 132–45.

Cool, C. (1993), Information Retrieval as Symbolic Interaction: Examples from Humanities Scholars, *in* S. Bonzi (ed.), *Proceedings of the 56th Annual Meeting of the American Society for Information Science (ASIS'93)*, Vol. 30, American Society for Information Science, pp.274–7.

Kuhlthau, C. C. (1993), *Seeking Meaning: A Process Approach to Library and Information Services*, Ablex.

Mizzaro, S. (1997), "Relevance: The Whole History", *Journal of the American Society for Information Science* **48**(9), 810–32.

Nielsen, J. (1993), *Usability Engineering*, Academic Press.

Park, T. K. (1994), "Toward a Theory of User-Based Relevance: A Call for a New Paradigm of Inquiry", *Journal of the American Society for Information Science* **45**(3), 135–41.

Schamber, L., Eisenberg, M. B. & Nilan, M. S. (1990), "A Re-examination of Relevance: Toward a Dynamic, Situational Definition", *Information Processing and Management* **26**(6), 755–76.

Human–Computer Interaction — INTERACT '99
M. Angela Sasse and Chris Johnson (Editors)
Published by IOS Press, © IFIP TC.13, 1999

On Human Error and Accident Causation

Daniela Busse

Glasgow University, 17 Lilybank Gardens, Glasgow G12 8RZ, UK.

bussed@dcs.gla.ac.uk

Abstract: Major accidents, such as Piper Alpha or Three Mile Island, are often mediated by what is termed 'human error'. The analysis of these errors is crucial for assisting future accident prevention and error recovery. Operators' tasks in safety critical systems increasingly shift towards control, with cognitive rather than manual load predominating. A similar trend is noticeable in the form of operator error. These 'cognitive errors' demand a suitable taxonomy and method of analysis in order to be understood and explained thoroughly. An error analysis technique that is rooted in cognitive theory allows the analyst to gain an understanding of the cognitive processes underlying the error. We argue that the use of a cognitive architecture as a structural framework for expressing the cognitive processing underlying operator error will lead beyond an observational approach to error modelling. Further contributing factors to human error in accident causation are also discussed.

Keywords: human error, cognitive modelling, accident analysis, total system analysis.

1 Introduction

Human error plays a major role in the occurrence of accidents in safety critical systems such as in aviation, railway systems, or nuclear power plants (Reason, 1990). Identifying hazardous human involvement in accidents does not, however, imply the identification of the actual 'cause' of the accident. The design of technology, task procedures, or organizational issues may not be well suited to human action and cognitive processing and thus present an 'unkind' work environment which precipitates the occurrence of human error. The understanding of error causes, principles and effects is thus essential to further our understanding of major accidents. Insights into the causes and course of accidents will help us to avoid similar events and situations in the future, and to be prepared for their occurrence (e.g. through error-tolerant design, emergency based training, or organizational change). For this goal it is necessary to perform an accident analysis which recognizes the complexity of the accidents' causality.

Human error makes up a substantial portion of the contributing factors. Their identification is commonly guided by human error taxonomies. These are based primarily on generic theories of human cognition — such as Reason's (1990) taxonomy. Even those taxonomies that

adhere more closely to cognitive theory in their explanation of human fallibility are pitched at too high a level to track the underlying cognitive processing.

Examination of this processing could provide leads to the causes and 'inner workings' of the error mechanisms. We have, therefore, developed a framework to model the cognition that underlies human error. This enables analysts to benefit from error taxonomies' abstracting and simplifying effect on the wealth of error data, as well as from the more refined, structured, and detailed information gained by systematic cognitive modelling.

The possible mappings from category to underlying mechanisms can be examined by reasoning about the underlying processing. This also adds to the modelling process documentation, i.e. the degree to which the technique lends itself to auditable review.

Our approach suggests utilising the cognitive vocabulary that an information processing model offers to express error specifications. However, current cognitive modelling techniques typically focus on expert, error-free behaviour. Such assumptions are built into the technique, hindering its adaptation to the real-life behaviour of users and operators. Similar observations hold for current cognitive simulation architectures.

2   Cognitive Modelling

The first goal of this work was to demonstrate the use of a cognitive architecture as a framework for expressing error classes using a cognitive vocabulary.

This was demonstrated by the cognitive modelling of human error in aviation, such as pilot error in a helicopter accident (Busse & Johnson, 1998).

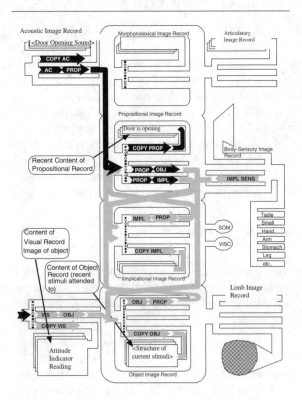

Figure 1: information overload modelled in ICS.

We utilised the Interacting Cognitive Subsystems (ICS) architecture (Barnard & May, 1993). Figure 1 briefly illustrates how a vague classification of pilot error as 'Information Overload' can translate into an ICS model detailing the cognitive resources in demand at different stages of the pilot's cognition and behaviour. The cognitive details of 'overload' can be captured diagrammatically to a greater precision than a single taxonomic label allows, and provide a basis for reasoning about the cognitive precursors of Human Error.

3   Beyond Individuals' Cognition

Reason (1990) maintains that active failure is usually associated with the performance of 'front-line' operators (such as pilots). Latent failure, however, is most often generated by those at the 'blunt end' of the system (e.g. designers, high-level decision-makers, managers) and may lie dormant for a long time. So far we have concentrated on 'human error' leading to active failure. The analysis of these is most likely to benefit from cognitive modelling techniques. Latent failures are best analysed in 'total system' approaches which go beyond an individual's cognition and also take organizational aspects into account.

A case study in an Intensive Care Unit is, therefore, being conducted. This draws on system approaches such as Reason's accident causation model as well as established workplace analysis methodologies (Bogner, 1994).

The investigation will place special emphasis on the identification of latent failures, as well as the cognitive analysis of active failures of staff at the 'sharp end' of the clinical system (i.e. nurses and doctors). By doing this, we will test the transferability of accident analysis concepts and methods from aviation to the medical field. Insights into the complexity of accident causation, and the role of human and organizational error are hypothesized also to benefit medical accident analysis.

References

Barnard, P. J. & May, J. (1993), Cognitive Modelling for User Requirements, *in* P. F. Byerley & P. J. B. J. May (eds.), *Computers, Communication and Usability: Design Issues, Research and Methods for Integrated Services*, Elsevier Science, pp.101–145.

Bogner, M. S. (1994), *Human Error In Medicine*, Lawrence Erlbaum Associates.

Busse, D. K. & Johnson, C. W. (1998), Using a Cognitive Theoretical Framework to Support Accident Analysis, *in* L. D. Pinnel (ed.), *The Proceedings of the Second Workshop on Human Error, Safety, and Systems Development*, Safeware Engineering Corporation, pp.36–44.

Reason, J. (1990), *Human Error*, Cambridge University Press.

Human–Computer Interaction — INTERACT '99
M. Angela Sasse and Chris Johnson (Editors)
Published by IOS Press, © IFIP TC.13, 1999

An Investigation of the Capability of Task Analysis Techniques in Support of the Design and Development of Web-based Interactive Systems

Yousef H. Daabaj & J.R.G. Wood

Department of Computer & Mathematical Science, The University of Salford, The Crescent, Salford, Manchester M5 4WT, UK.

Y.H.Daabaj@cms.salford.ac.uk, J.R.G.Wood@cms.salford.ac.uk

Abstract: The aim of this research is to examine whether the output of Task Analysis (TA) can support and contribute directly each activity of the design life cycle of Interactive MultiMedia (IMM) systems. In this project the application of a variety of TA techniques has been used to assess the adequacy of a proposed design for a 'World Wide Web (WWW)' Site/System within an IMM context, domain and environment which will help research students conduct their doctoral program as carried out at Salford University, Manchester. The results of the application for TA techniques and their input into the design activities have been analysed and compared both to each other and to a defined schema (criteria). The findings have shown that TA techniques have a number of weaknesses in the contributions that they make and therefore questions of how the techniques can be improved to increase their capability are considered.

Keywords: human–computer interaction, task analysis, design process, interactive multimedia, requirements analysis, World Wide Web.

1 Background and Motivation

In recent years software systems have evolved to include IMM technology in which information is communicated to users in several media types including video, audio, pictures, and animation, in addition to text and graphics. While some of the current guidelines of analysis can be extended to the design of IMM systems, they do not contribute directly into the design activities and so address the specific needs, characteristics and features of IMM systems. Key elements of IMM system design should later emerge from early analysis rather than be shaped to fit the results of user testing (Powell et al., 1998).

Although the use of TA techniques in design has been investigated and supported by many authors and researchers, for example (Mantei & Teory, 1988; Johnson et al., 1989; Lansdale & Ormerod, 1994). There is still debate as to whether TA techniques are an appropriate tool for design (Benyon, 1992; Diaper & Addison, 1992). Benyon, for example, has argued that TA should play only a limited role in the design process, since TA details embody facets of the current system and therefore restrict the originality of the new design. Concern about this fact has been also expressed by other researchers in the field (Sutcliffe, 1989; Anderson et al., 1990). However, the advent of larger and more complex IMM systems has resulted in the need to reconsider the ways in which requirements are captured, analysed, formalized, modelled, represented and communicated pertaining to those systems. The problems of current software design methods highlight the importance of the Requirements Analysis (RA) phase in system development, and draw out the importance of integrating TA techniques with other methods in order to design usable IMM systems. The strong desire of users to interact with the WWW using IMM technology presents novel problems for TA techniques and means that the new information and communications involve the automation of conceptual skills rather than the perceptual motor skills required of previous generations of technology and task complexity (Wilson et al., 1988). The complexity of IMM systems is typically associated with the many constraints which have to be accounted for in the RA stage and the techniques that are used within this stage.

It is therefore essential that such task information is accurate and comprehensive as a basis for design decisions.

2   The Aim

There are many serious criticism in the literature concerning the different aspects and issues of TAs. Such criticism constitutes a problem for the application of TA for IMM design specifications and features. The consideration of TA provided here is based on an extensive literature review of those TA techniques that could be utilized in both Web Site and IMM development. Based on this survey, the objective of the research was to examine the issue of whether TA techniques are capable, usable, and strong enough to support and contribute directly to the analysis and design of IMM systems. It is the aim of this research to examine and discuss forms of TA which have been developed in the specific context of knowledge intensive tasks in Human–Computer Interaction (HCI), and to suggest ways in which such techniques may develop in the future. The concern here is with the use and application of TA techniques to support the development of IMM systems and with whether such techniques are capable of capturing the multimedia specific features and characteristics of interactive systems.

3   The Approach

The nature of TA is such that it was felt to be most appropriate to study it in an applied context in order to allow a realistic examination of the methods. The context in which the selected TA methods were carried out, was at the University of Salford, where PhD research students follow steps and procedures to conduct their doctoral research. The problem situation was selected in order to provide appropriate contexts and applications for the analysis methods where adequate access (i.e. easy access to the real users – PhD research students) could be granted. The relevant information required by TA techniques was collected through a series of structured interviews, written materials and focus group discussions with PhD research students at the University of Salford. A total of four case studies were carried out in the context of this research to demonstrate and examine the extent to which the capability of the techniques was achieved. The case studies were based upon the TA methods to find out how research students conduct their doctoral program, and what sort of problems they faced thereby enabling them to perform and conduct their research effectively. It was agreed that the application of

the final analysis is going to be used to design a 'Publishing WWW' Web site within an IMM context and environment which will help research students in conducting their research and thus avoid the current research difficulties.

Having established the importance of analysing the information that should be contributed and supported by TA for each design activity, a defined schema (criteria) which TA techniques should ideally meet was outlined theoretically, and empirically tested. The products of the TA techniques that have been applied within the application area, were compared and analysed under the following four main matrixes:

1. The Scope 'generality' of the Analysis.

2. Representation Form and Support.

3. The Contributions that are required from TA Techniques in the Design Activities of IMM Systems (*What, Where & How*)

4. Core Criteria Matrix for TA Products and Applications.

Each Matrix represented issues, specific and desirable features for IMM approaches and where TA techniques should cover and represent these features in their outputs.

4   Summary

The design of IMM systems is fundamentally context-dependent, in that the details of the situation are critical, and these details interact in ways that cannot be known in advance. Arguments such as these have led us to conclude that the development of successful IMM software application must be predicated on an iterative design process driven by early and continued feedback from TA. The results of the analysis have provided a framework to structure information about a task (including a task description and interpretations of the task description) rather than a tool which gives information that leads directly to design decisions. It has been found that, the TA products have several flaws when applied to the analysis of a problem situation within an IMM environment, domain and context, and TA techniques must therefore be extended to accommodate such new and interactive requirements.

The products of TA techniques, irrespective of their origins and values, can be criticized as follows:

1. They do not provide a direct input into design activities, rather they provide information (i.e. limited to task descriptions) that needs to be

interpreted by a human factors specialist into useful design information.

2. The analysis does not present a formalized means of documenting the assumptions underlying the analysis.

3. They do not provide an approach/tool for deriving design information from an analyst that can be readily adopted by ergonomists and other system designers.

There is a need therefore to develop software tools to support specific TA applications, and the validity of such techniques can only be achieved if the process of analysis is highly proceduralized and constrained. IMM systems design requires techniques and tools to support the development process. These techniques, should have sufficient, extensive and expressive power to capture the nature, the specific features and characteristics of the new domain and to contribute effectively and directly into the design activities of IMM. These techniques are required to produce a logical description of the whole target system and therefore they should consider early design issues, concepts and requirements. There is a need to extend the scope of current TA techniques and to improve their capability, through possessing and utilizing knowledge and understanding about:

1. the general characteristics of the target users;

2. the potential frequency of use and perceived benefits;

3. the context of the interaction and interactivity (style and level);

4. the context of the stored information (content, type, etc.);

5. the delivery environment and constraints;

6. the corresponding limitations that should be placed on multimedia output;

7. the representation of all the requirement information in a form that is communicable and understandable by all stakeholders; and

8. to contribute directly to each activity within the design process.

References

Anderson, R., Carroll, J. & Scapin, D. (1990), Task Analysis: The Oft Missing Step in the Development of Computer-Human Interfaces; Its Desirable Nature, Value and Role, *in* D. Diaper, D. Gilmore, G. Cockton & B. Shackel (eds.), *Proceedings of INTERACT '90 — Third IFIP Conference on Human–Computer Interaction*, Elsevier Science, pp.1051–4.

Benyon, D. (1992), "The Role of Task Analysis in Systems Design", *Interacting with Computers* **4**(1), 102–123.

Diaper, D. & Addison, M. (1992), "Task Analysis and Systems Analysis for Software Engineering", *Interacting with Computers* **4**(1), 124–39.

Johnson, G. I., Clegg, C. W. & Ravden, S. J. (1989), "Towards a Practical Method of User Interface Evaluation", *Applied Ergonomics* **20**(4), 255–260.

Lansdale, M. W. & Ormerod, T. C. (1994), *Understanding Interfaces: A Handbook of Human–Computer Interaction*, Academic Press.

Mantei, M. M. & Teory, T. J. (1988), "Cost/Benefit Analysis For Incorporating Human Factors in the Software Life Cycle", *Communications of the ACM* **31**(4), 428–349.

Powell, T. A., Jones, D. L. & Cutts, D. C. (1998), *Web Site Engineering: Beyond Web Page Design*, Prentice–Hall.

Sutcliffe, A. (1989), "Task Analysis, System Analysis and Design: Symbiosis or Synthesis", *Interacting with Computers* **1**, 6–12.

Wilson, M. D., Barnard, P. J. & Green, T. R. G. (1988), Knowledge-Based Ask Analysis for Human-Computer Systems, *in Working With Computers: Theory Versus Outcome*.

Human–Computer Interaction — INTERACT '99
M. Angela Sasse and Chris Johnson (Editors)
Published by IOS Press, © IFIP TC.13, 1999

An Investigation Into The Effects of Delays in Visual Feedback on Real-time System Users

Philip N. Day

Image Systems Engineering Laboratory, Department of Computing and Electrical Engineering, Heriot-Watt University, Riccarton, Edinburgh EH14 4AS, UK.

P.N.Day@bigfoot.com

Abstract: The project focuses on the effects of visual delay on human controllers of remote artefacts. A review of the current literature has been carried out. A pilot experiment with thirty participants has been completed. The experiment consisted of a remotely controlled, wheeled vehicle being driven along a track towards a target. The vehicle had a video camera mounted on it from which images were sent to a personal computer, delays were introduced and the delayed images were then displayed on the computer monitor. It was discovered that both reaction times and targeting errors increased with the visual delay to a threshold. Further work is discussed and outlined.

Keywords: cognitive effects, delayed feedback, real-time systems, tele-operations, remotely-operated vehicles.

1 Introduction

This research began as a dissertation for the author's MSc in Human-Computer Interaction at Heriot-Watt University (Day, 1998) and is now being continued as a PhD project. This PhD commenced in October 1998 and is supervised by Dr Patrik O'Brian Holt (ph@cee.hw.ac.uk).

The general effects of visual delays on real-time system users are relatively well documented. In particular, visual delays are known to be detrimental to the performance of the users (Smith, 1962; Smith & Smith, 1987). General effects of feedback delay include over-compensation, lack of trust in the feedback (Boyle et al., 1995) and confusion and disorientation (Liu et al., 1993; Smith, 1962; Smith & Smith, 1987). However, what is not well understood are the specific ways in which performance is impaired, and the reasons for this decrease in performance in terms of the underlying cognitive mechanisms being affected by delays.

The purpose of this research is to begin to investigate the confusion that visual delays introduce in users, with an attempt to reproduce this confusion in a controlled environment in order to facilitate further work in this area. Of particular interest in this investigation is the behaviour of the users and the difficulty experienced. This research has implications for the control of remotely operated vehicles in addition to the use of computers with transmission delays (such as across the Internet).

2 Pilot Work

Thirty participants were recruited for the experiments, which consisted of each participant driving a remotely controlled vehicle along a marked track towards a target. On reaching the target, participants aimed the vehicle such that it's central marker hit as close to the centre of the target as possible. Measurements that were made during the experiment included reaction times (RTs), i.e. the time taken to drive the vehicle from the beginning to the end of the track, and targeting errors. The error included not only the distance from the centre of the target that the vehicle hit but also the direction of error (left or right of target).

The reaction times are summarised in Table 1 and Figure 1. Analysis of the variance (using single factor ANOVAs between the 4 delay settings) showed the RTs to be statistically significant (F: 18.88, F crit: 2.43, P-value: < 0.001). The differences in RTs for each delay setting and the control setting (by comparing mean RT for each delay setting with the control using a 2-tail paired 2 sample t-test) was found to be statistically significant $(P(T \leq t) < 0.001$ for all 4 delays with respect to control, i.e. no delay).

Delay	Ctrl	A (0s)	B (2s)	C (4s)	D (6s)
Mean (s)	9.56	65.66	78.06	89.17	89.53
SD	4.87	29.59	52.41	47.63	53.53

Table 1: Summary of reaction times.

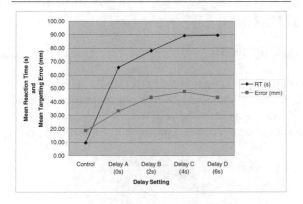

Figure 1: Mean reaction times and errors.

The targeting errors are summarised in Table 2 and Figure 1. Analysis of the variance (using single factor ANOVAs between the 4 delay settings) showed the differences in errors to be statistically significant (F: 3.94, F crit: 2.43, P-value: < 0.01). The difference between errors for each delay setting and the control setting (using a 2-tail paired 2 sample t-test) was found to be statistically significant $(P(T \leq t) < 0.01$ for all 4 delays with respect to control, i.e. no delay).

Delay	Ctrl	A (0s)	B (2s)	C (4s)	D (6s)
Mean (s)	18.53	33.23	43.29	47.49	43.20
SD	15.40	27.52	31.71	46.40	31.83

Table 2: Summary of targeting errors.

3 Discussion and Future Work

Reaction times and errors were both found to increase to a threshold, with RTs increasing linearly. This behaviour will be modelled. Further refinement is needed to ascertain whether the linearity and threshold values are specific to the task being carried out. The manipulation of video delay presents significant technical problems that are currently being addressed.

The next set of experiments will investigate the linear effect on users' performance operating under delays between 0–1 seconds, with other experiments investigating the behaviour of users operating under longer delays around a possible threshold value (3–7 seconds). Tasks will consist of controlling a remote artefact mounted on a test track (with a digital camera being mounted above the vehicle) to avoid additional errors in position.

References

Boyle, B. S., McMaster, R. S. & Nixon, J. (1995), Teleoperation of an Underwater Robotic Repair System Using Graphical Simulation, *in IEE Computing and Control Division Colloquium on Control of Remotely Operated Systems: Teleassistance and Telepresence*, Vol. 101, IEE, pp.2/1–2/4.

Day, P. N. (1998), MSc Dissertation. An Investigation into the Effects of Delays in Visual Feedback on Real-time Users, Master's thesis, Department of Computing and Electronic Engineering, Heriot Watt University.

Liu, A., Tharp, G., French, L., Lai, S. & Stark, L. (1993), "Some of What One Needs to Know About Using Head-mounted Displays to Improve Teleoperator Performance", *IEEE Transactions on Robotics and Automation* **9**(5), 607–23.

Smith, K. U. (1962), *Delayed Sensory Feedback and Behaviour*, Saunders.

Smith, T. J. & Smith, K. U. (1987), Feedback-control Mechanisms of Human Behaviour, *in* S. G. (ed.), *Handbook of Human Factors*, John Wiley & Sons, pp.251–93.

Human–Computer Interaction — INTERACT '99
M. Angela Sasse and Chris Johnson (Editors)
Published by IOS Press, © IFIP TC.13, 1999

Towards a Pattern Language for Instructional Multimedia Interface Design

Maia Dimitrova

Centre for Human–Computer Interface Design, City University, Northampton Square, London EC1V 0HB, UK.

M.T.Dimitrova@city.ac.uk

Abstract: Due to its multidisciplinary nature, the design of instructional multimedia is a complex process. The current design approach is primarily ad hoc, lacking understanding of the cognition of multimedia presentations. There is a clear need for better design support to ensure system's usability. The research work revealed aims to develop a pattern language, comprised of reusable solutions to common design problems, in an attempt to deal with design complexity.

Keywords: multimedia, user interface, design patterns.

1 Introduction

1.1 Research Rationale

The interface design of instructional multimedia (IMM) applications is an intersection of different scientific fields, including pedagogy, cognitive psychology, computer science, and media arts. The effective design of IMM, therefore, is a complex process that needs to take into consideration a number of interdependent factors. The main factors include the learner's needs (Soloway, 1998), their predetermined learning style, and individual approach to learning (Wild & Quinn, 1998), the characteristics of the content, and the learning tasks to be performed (Najjar, 1997), which have to be represented in a variety of media optimising the learner's cognitive processes (Faraday & Sutcliffe, 1997).

There is a need of a way of dealing with the complexity of the design, and reducing the time and effort, without compromising on the software quality. One way of achieving that is to reuse design knowledge by closely examining successful applications to identify recurring solutions to common design problems. These can be encapsulated in design patterns. A design pattern describes the core of a solution to a particular problem in an abstract way, which when used in a given situation can generate effective design. Design patterns are then integrated into a pattern language. Patterns have been successfully used in architecture (Alexander et al.,

1977), and in software engineering, predominantly in the object-oriented software design community (Gamma et al., 1995).

1.2 Research Objectives

The primary aim of the PhD research is to study the process of designing the user interface of multimedia applications, and to develop a coherent pattern language for the design of such interfaces. In order to fulfil these goals, the following research objectives have been set up:

1. To investigate into the existing practices of designing multimedia, in order to identify the approaches adopted to the design, and the major problems designers encounter. A study of the current design practice has been conducted, and a resume of its findings is presented in Section 2.

2. To develop a coherent conceptual framework of the proposed pattern language. A working version of the framework is discussed in Section 3.

3. To study a range of quality multimedia applications, and to extract a library of design patterns. This process is reviewed in Section 4.

4. To develop a systematic method for applying the pattern language to the interface design process.

5. To evaluate the effectiveness of the pattern language.

2 Design Practice Study

Eight IMM designers participated in semi-structured interviews, which provided information about the processes involved in the design, the factors contributing to the main design decisions, and the major design problems encountered. Because of the complex requirements of the design process, specialists with diverse backgrounds were involved, some of who lacked formal training in HCI or cognitive psychology, as well as did not share common perspective on usability. Although some learner characteristics were considered in the presentation design, that was not done in a systematic way. From the study, it became apparent that the selection of appropriate media resources included predominantly high-level and non-scientifically-based factors, such as client preferences and limited memory space. The study also revealed that designers lacked deep understanding of users' cognitive processes, and the effect of multimedia presentations on the learner's attention and comprehension of information. Although available, usability guidelines and principles were not actively used, mainly because designers considered them too general, or inadequate.

The results indicate that a more cognitive approach to the design of multimedia is required. However, generic design guidelines often fail to provide adequate design support. Therefore, there is a clear need to support the process of multimedia presentation design in a new way. Support for multidisciplinary teams is also needed to give designers a common basis for making design decisions. Reusing previous design knowledge has potential for overcoming these problems. The proposed design patterns will encapsulate the core of the solution to particular design problems, presented in an abstract form suitable for reuse in analogous situations.

3 Conceptual Framework of the Pattern Language

In building the pattern language, the first task was to establish the different levels of abstraction of patterns. To date the following three levels have been identified:

Level 1: Content Structure Patterns
Deal with how the content is organized into information nodes, and how they are grouped semantically. These patterns also reveal what navigation strategies can best support the user in building a cognitive map of the information space. Some example patterns are *Linear Structure, Hierarchical Structure*, and *Concept Map Structure*.

Level 2: Content Presentation Patterns
Describe how to effectively represent generic information nodes. They contain prescriptions of how most effectively to represent the real world artefact or situation, in a way that facilitates users in distributing their cognitive resources between the different external and internal representations, allowing them to construct a mental model of the real world. An example pattern is *How-It-Works Mechanism*.

Level 3: Media Integration Patterns
Each information node can be represented by one or more media resources. These patterns are concerned with how to establish contact points between visual and verbal media to enable the user to build a single mental representation of the information presented, e.g. *Diagram with Textual Explanation, Diagram with Speech Explanation*.

4 The Process of Extracting Design Patterns

The process involves examining multimedia products to identify commonalities in the content structure, how different media resources are used to represent information, and how visual balance and temporal synchronisation of media are achieved. The design solutions are then abstracted from their implementation aspects. Good design patterns should encapsulate design expertise that promotes usability and effectiveness of the presentation. Due to the ad-hoc design approach currently adopted in industrial projects, as discussed in Section 2, the patterns need to be enhanced with theoretical findings regarding effective multimedia design. Results from empirical studies of multimedia attention and comprehension are being used to support the design solutions.

5 Conclusions and Future Work

The research work proposes a way of supporting the multimedia interface design process by using design patterns, which encapsulate effective design rationale. Design reuse could potentially speed up the design process, provide professionals with a common lingua franca for communication, ensure interface usability, and pass design expertise to novice designers, so they can produce effective designs faster.

The development of the pattern framework will continue. More multimedia software will be studied and new patterns will be added to the language.

A method for applying the pattern language in a way that fits in the design process will be developed. The effect of the language on the design process will be studied in a case study with professional designers. Finally, the effect of the pattern language on users' comprehension of information will be evaluated.

References

Alexander, C., Ishikawa, S., Silverstein, M., Jacobson, M., Fiksdahl-King, I. & Angel, S. (1977), *A Pattern Language*, Oxford University Press.

Faraday, P. & Sutcliffe, A. (1997), Multimedia: Design for the Moment, *in* J. D. Hollan & J. D. Foley (eds.), *Proceedings of Multimedia'97*, ACM Press, pp.183–92.

Gamma, E., Helms, R., Johnson, R. & Vlissides, J. (1995), *Design Patterns: Elements of Reusable Object-Oriented Software*, Addison–Wesley.

Najjar, L. J. (1997), A Framework for Learning from Media: The Effects of Materials, Tasks, and Tests on Performance, Technical Report GIT-GVU-97-21, Georgia Institute of Technology.

Soloway, E. (1998), The Need: Moving Beyond Ease of Use to Supporting Learning, *in* C.-M. Karat & J. Karat (eds.), *Proceedings of CHI '98 Learner Centered Design Workshop*, ACM Press. http://janice.eecs.umich.edu/chi/LCD-soloway.html.

Wild, M. & Quinn, C. (1998), "Implications of Educational Theory for the Design of Instructional Multimedia", *British Journal of Educational Technology* **29**(1), 78–82.

Human–Computer Interaction — INTERACT '99
M. Angela Sasse and Chris Johnson (Editors)
Published by IOS Press, © IFIP TC.13, 1999

Computing for the Disabled using a New Brain Body Interface

Eamon P. Doherty

School of Computing, Engineering and Technology, University of Sunderland,
PO Box 299, Sunderland SR6 0YN, UK.

cs0edo@isis.sunderland.ac.uk

Abstract: A longitudinal study of traumatically brain injured and comatose participants has already established that they can learn to use a mental interface device use a range of simple applications. Work to date is briefly summarised, and plans for future work are presented.

Keywords: usability engineering, mental interface, cyberlink brain body interface, cerebral palsy.

1 Background

The PhD research reported here is part of the Distance Learning programme at the University of Sunderland. The practical work is begin carried out in New Jersey USA. The PhD candidate has just completed his first year review and is currently finalising plans for the next phase of study.

The PhD research is organized as a longitudinal study involving disabled participants in group homes, nursing homes and private residences. Several pilot experiments have been designed. Where initial results are promising, a pilot is continued and becomes a longitudinal experimental. Two have significant results (Doherty et al., to appear; Doherty et al., n.d.).

2 Cyberlink Technology

The PhD research is investigating the potential of a brain-body interface device as assistive technology for disabled individuals with major motor impairment due to conditions such as cerebral palsy or traumatic brain injury. The device is called a Cyberlink. It combines eye movement, facial muscle, and brain wave bio-potentials ('electric signals') detected at the forehead, to generate computer inputs that can be used for a variety of tasks. The forehead was chosen as the place to collect signals because it is rich in bio-potentials. Three plastic sensors in a head-band detect these signals which are then sent to a Cyberlink interface box, and then to the serial port of the computer. The signals are amplified, digitized, and are translated by a patented decoding algorithm into multiple command signals, allowing hands-free control of the computer (Junker, 1995).

The Cyberlink was chosen after initial experiments with, and analysis of, a range of devices (i.e. mouse, children's giant track ball, eye tracking, voice input, galvanic skin response and touch pad). None were suitable for the study participants. The Cyberlink is the only device that appears to be usable by people with severe physical impairment.

Three different types of control signal are used by the Cyberlink Interface. ElectroOcularGraphic or EOG signals arise from eye motion and are the lowest frequency signals collected.. The second type of signal is called the ElectroEncephlaGraphic or EEG signal. This is subdivided this into ten component frequency bands called 'brainfingers'. These frequencies reflect internal mental/brainwave activity as well as subtle facial muscle activity. A wide range of facial muscles affects these frequency bands. Users typically learn control of these signals through subtle tensing and relaxing of various muscles including forehead, eye, and jaw muscles.

The third type of control signal is called the ElectroMyoGraphic or EMG signal. The EMG signal primarily reflects facial muscle activity. It is typically used for discrete on/off control of program commands (Junker, 1995).

The Cyberlink digital signal processor to produce ten 'brainfingers' mixes these three signals. These respond to changes in the underlying electrical signals and are used to control the cursor and selection functions. A Cybertrainer suite of applications is provided with the Cyberlink.. It includes games such as ping-pong and maze programmes, as well as a typing program.

3   Experimental Design

The Cyberlink Brain Body Interface poses a serious challenge when designing formal experiments. The device's relationship to existing taxonomies of input devices is unclear, as is the relationship of its design parameters (various settings for bias and sensitivity). to different impairments. Little is also known about the links between injury, disability and the ability to control EEG, EMG and EOG signals. In addition, the participants and their care environments rule out controlled studies.

A 'Naturalistic Design' using inductive design has thus been chosen as the initial research approach. Participants use Cybertrainer program in their care or home environments.. The time, date, scores, activities, and any other pertinent data are recorded. Data analysis has revealed a range of device and contextual factors that are relevant to the successful use of the Cyberlink. Data is shared with the participants, guardians, and care-givers at the institutions in order to improve the researcher's understanding of the wide range of relevant individual differences and variations in care regime.

Six longitudinal experiments have been completed and two more are in progress. These include using the Cyberlink to navigate a maze, independent use with games, communication and environmental control software, and use of the Cyberlink with PC desktop software. Initial results have been promising, the most notable being the upgrade of the diagnosis of one participant from coma to traumatic brain stem injury as a result of data collected during the study. In this experiment, three controls were introduced to demonstrate that typing and maze navigation were intentional (Doherty et al., n.d.). The range of tasks performed with a Cyberlink is more extensive than those reported in other studies with brain-body interfaces (Craig et al., 1997; Kalcher et al., 1994).

4   Further Work

The successful extension of several initial pilot studies into longitudinal experiments has confirmed the value of the Cyberlink as an assistive technology. The next phase of work will apply a range of HCI research methods to the development of the Cyberlink and associated programmes:

- Firstly, a programme of contextual enquiry will develop initial understandings of participants and care regimes. The design of future studies will be based on priorities established in collaboration with care-givers and guardians.

- Secondly, a configuration program will be developed to make it easier for care-givers and guardians to configure the Cyberlink.

- Thirdly, a series of experiments will be designed to explore ways to accelerate learning with the Cyberlink device.

Other studies may be added in response to issues arising from the contextual enquiry.

References

Craig, A., Kirkup, L., McIsaac, P. & Searle, A. (1997), The Mind as a Reliable Switch: Challenges of Rapidly Controlling Devices Without Prior Learning, *in* S. Howard, J. Hammond & G. K. Lindgaard (eds.), *Human–Computer Interaction — INTERACT '97: Proceedings of the Sixth IFIP Conference on Human–Computer Interaction*, Chapman & Hall.

Doherty, E., Bloor, C. & Cockton, G. (to appear), "The 'Cyberlink' Brain Body Interface as an Assistive Technology for Traumatically Brain Injured Persons: Results of a Longitudinal Study", *CyberPsychology and Behavior* .

Doherty, E., Cockton, G. & Bloor, C. (n.d.), Independent Use of the 'Cyberlink' Brain Body Interface as a Vehicle of Recreation and Communication for Disabled Persons.

Junker, A. (1995), "US Patent Number 5,474,082".

Kalcher, J., Flotzinger, D., Gölly, S., Neuper, G. & Pfurtscheler, G. (1994), Brain–Computer Interface, *in Proceedings 4th International Conference, ICCHP 94*, pp.171–6.

Development of a Predictive Model of User Satisfaction with Packaged Software

Cecilia M. Finnerty

Department of Computing and Information Systems, London Guildhall University, London EC3N 2EY, UK.

Cecilia@compuserve.com

Abstract: Much of the literature on the subject of the Human–Computer Interface (HCI) investigates the factors influencing satisfaction (or usability) with regard to software that is developed in-house. User involvement in the development process has been shown to have a major influence on user acceptance of the end result. However, many small companies do not carry out in-house development of software. They still have the problem of how to ensure that the software chosen for a particular task is fully accepted by the users. The work described below suggests that user involvement in the selection process of purchased software, as well as ease of use and perceived usefulness, is a key factor in ensuring satisfaction with the software purchased. A model has been developed based on findings from the literature and the satisfaction with software already in use in a company. This model has now to be tested.

Keywords: user involvement, COTS, user satisfaction, SUMI.

1 Background

Having worked for some years in the IT industry and being involved in the introduction of different software packages, I was puzzled by the way some seemed to be more readily accepted than others despite the fact that they all met the requirements specification to pretty much the same degree. The question was raised whether, given that in an open plan office it is almost impossible to provide temperature and lighting to suit everyone, it is possible to ensure satisfaction with software packages which are to be used by more than one person. The aim of the study has been to develop a predictive model of user satisfaction with commercial off-the-shelf software (COTS).

2 The Approach

2.1 Selection of Questionnaire

The first problem was to decide how to measure satisfaction. I felt that use of a questionnaire with follow-up interview would be the best approach. Various questionnaires have already been developed and tested in the area of HCI. Of these, both the Questionnaire for User Interaction Satisfaction (QUIS, University of Maryland, 1989) and the Software Usability Measurement Inventory (SUMI, Human Factors Research Group, University of Cork, 1993) seemed good candidates. However, whilst they both measure satisfaction, QUIS seems to be biased towards measuring satisfaction with the interface, whereas SUMI is slanted towards measuring satisfaction with the software as a whole. Added to this was the fact that SUMI was developed and tested in Europe which was where I was working plus the 'professional' version came with the statistical analysis tool which had been used by the developers. SUMI was the questionnaire selected.

There are 5 sections to SUMI each consisting of 10 questions. Each section measures an area which contributes to overall satisfaction. The 5 areas are: Efficiency (software imposes no extra mental workload to achieve the goal); Affect (how the user feels as a result of using the software); Helpfulness (helpfulness of messages etc.); Control (software responds in a normal and consistent manner); and Learnability (easy to follow, instructive). The results of the SUMI analysis show each of these scales plus a global scale which indicates overall level of satisfaction.

2.2　Determining the Factors

The second problem, as became evident from the various papers that I read, was that the number of factors which could potentially affect satisfaction with software was rather large. To carry out a full investigation into each and to measure their importance relative to each other would not really be feasible, especially given the low size of user population I have to work with. It seemed preferable to concentrate on those factors which were common across a variety of papers. In addition to this, the aim of creating a predictive model is to create something which is useful to people who are tasked with introducing software into the workplace. This means that it should be simple, although with sufficient testable dimensions to allow steps to be taken to improve the chances of acceptance should this be shown to be necessary.

Existing predictive models were also considered. Of these, three in particular were compared and contrasted. They are all based on the Theory of Reasoned Action (TRA) (Fishbein & Ajzen, 1975; Ajzen & Fishbein, 1980) and are: the Technology Acceptance Model (TAM) (Davis et al., 1989; Davis & Venkatesh, 1996); the Theory of Planned Behaviour (TPB) (Ajzen, 1985); and the Decomposed Theory of Planned Behaviour (DTPB) (Taylor & Todd, 1995). A model to Explain the Role of User Participation in Information System Use (Hartwick & Barki, 1994) and the Attributional Model of Resistance to IT (AMRIT) (Martinko et al., 1996) were also considered amongst others.

From the literature and each of the above models, several hypotheses were derived. It was felt that these hypotheses could initially be tested by use of the SUMI questionnaire and interview. The factors measured by SUMI itself fall broadly into two areas — Usefulness (the Efficiency and Control scales) and Ease of Use (the Helpfulness and Learnability scales). The Affect scale, showing how people feel about using the software, could perhaps also be used as an indicator of how likely they are to use it of their own choice. Usefulness and Ease of Use are key factors in each of the above models based on TRA. Other factors which are common in the literature are the influence of peers and of superiors. Different personality characteristics are often mentioned but they are many and varied and it was difficult to find a single definition of different attributes. Different organizational characteristics are also cited and these were considered.

3　Derivation of the Model

The SUMI questionnaire was used to assess the level of satisfaction with different packages currently in use. The aim was to get a mix of work-group types and different interfaces. Three packages were selected. All three were multiuser and so people were dependent on input from others. One was based on the mini system, was character based and used across several sites; one was PC based, multiuser over a LAN on one site, the software being run from PCs running MS Windows (graphical interface); one was PC based, multi-user over a LAN, used at several sites, the software being run on PCs using DOS (character based). In addition to these, SUMI questionnaires were administered to users of a word-processing package. The Windows version of the package was just being introduced and questionnaires were given to users of the original DOS version and to those of the more recent Windows version. The package was loaded on individual PCs and people used it independently of each other. I had been involved in the selection and introduction of all of the packages and, therefore, had both the records and the memory of the method employed in their selection. There is an advantage in being able to use this historical information as the situations were not contrived and occurred as a natural result of the context in which the software was to be used.

The results of SUMI gave scores above the norm for both versions of the word-processing package and for the software based on the mini system. However, the other two packages were both below the norm on all the scales. The Helpfulness and Learnability scales were slightly better than the others but were still below the norm. The results were followed up with informal interviews.

There was evidence that perceived usefulness and ease of use both played a part in the feeling of satisfaction and that both of these were influenced by the attitude both of management and of others in the work-groups. However, from the interviews and indeed general conversations, it seemed that there was another key factor which influenced satisfaction. This was the users' perception of involvement in the selection of the software. Being questioned as to what was required of the software at the analysis stage was not perceived as involvement. Where the feeling that the software had been selected by others was greater, so was the antipathy towards it. Users of the package that scored well, said that they felt they had been fully involved in the selection process.

The need for user involvement in the development of software has long been recognised.

Participative Design (PD), Joint Application Development (JAD) and the Dynamic Systems Design Methodology (DSDM) all place the user in a key role in the process of iterative development. The aim is to give the user a sense of ownership and thence a stake in the success of the system. However, when a company is purchasing a COTS system, the involvement of the hands-on user tends to be at the requirements gathering stage. From the results of the SUMI and the interviews, it was posited that involvement at the actual selection stage would influence the feeling of satisfaction. A model has been developed to show this. It is based on TAM but adds the Subjective Norm and Perceived Involvement to Ease of Use and Usefulness. The two packages which scored badly on SUMI are currently being replaced. A questionnaire to help predict the probable voluntary use of the software (taken from that used by Davis in the development of TAM) has been devised. The intention is to use this before the introduction of the software and SUMI after the introduction to test the model. Questionnaires have also been distributed to an external organization.

References

Ajzen, I. (1985), From Intentions to Actions: A Theory of Planned Behaviour, *in* J. Kuhl & J. Beckmann (eds.), *From Cognition to Behavior*, Springer–Verlag, pp.11–39.

Ajzen, I. & Fishbein, M. (1980), *Understanding Attitudes and Predicting Social Behaviour*, Prentice–Hall.

Davis, F. D. & Venkatesh, V. (1996), "A Critical Assessment of Potential Measurement Biases in the Technology Acceptance Model", *International Journal of Human–Computer Studies* **45**, 19–45.

Davis, F. D., Bagozzi, R. P. & Warshaw, P. R. (1989), "User Acceptance of Computer Technology: A Comparison of Two Theoretical Models", *Management Science* **35**(8), 982–1000.

Fishbein, M. & Ajzen, I. (1975), *Belief, Attitude, Intention and Behavior: An Introduction to Theory and Research*, Addison–Wesley.

Hartwick, J. & Barki, H. (1994), "Explaining the Role of User Participation in Information", *Management Science* **40**(4), 440–64.

Martinko, M. J., Henry, J. W. & Zmud, R. W. (1996), "An Attributional Explanation of Individual Resistance to the Introduction of Information Technologies in the Workplace", *Behaviour & Information Technology* **15**(5), 313–30.

Taylor, S. A. & Todd, P. A. (1995), "Understanding Information Technology Usage: A Test of Competing Models", *Info Systems Research* **6**(2), 144–76.

Human–Computer Interaction — INTERACT '99
M. Angela Sasse and Chris Johnson (Editors)
Published by IOS Press, © IFIP TC.13, 1999

Communication and Collaboration in Virtual Places

Marianne Georgsen

Department of Communication, Aalborg University, Langagervej 8,
9220 Aalborg Ø, Denmark.

marianne@hum.auc.dk

Abstract: This paper presents a PhD project within the field of computer mediated communication and collaboration. The core interest of the project is the importance of the mediation of communication in relation to collaboration. A specific interest is paid to the role of communication in relation to creating and maintaining a virtual space. Empirical work has been carried out, and development of methods for qualitative analysis of video data is also a part of the project.

Keywords: computer mediated communication, collaboration, virtual spaces, video observation and analysis.

1 Background

The area of computer mediated communication and collaboration is one of rapid development and growth. Processes of interpersonal communication and interaction are mediated by computer based tools such as desktop video-conferencing, chat, computer conferencing systems and media spaces in various configurations.

The point of departure for this project is the change in the nature of social interaction, communication and collaboration brought about by the mediation by computers. A central claim is that these new forms of interaction can't be fully understood and explained in the frame of more familiar forms such as face-to-face communication and meetings. Among others, important reasons why computer mediated communication differ from conventional interaction are: distribution of the communicators in time and place, limitations in or complete lack of immediate feedback and limitations in the communication modes available. This imposes upon the interaction fundamentally different conditions than those found in synchronous, interpersonal face-to-face communication and interaction. Similarly, the physical distribution results in loss of a common frame of reference for the participants and in reduced or altogether missing possibilities of relating to the surroundings of one's conversational and/or work partner. Thus referring to artefacts in the physical room becomes difficult, just as gesturing and gazing loose their impact as communicational means. Besides developing an understanding of the communicative acts and their conditions in virtual environments, there is a need to develop an understanding of how virtual rooms are constructed (in a non-technical sense) and how a feeling of presence and co-presence can be acquired and maintained across temporal and geographical gaps.

2 The Aim of the Project

In order to obtain an understanding of mediated communication and collaboration, communicative as well as sociological and psychological aspects of human interaction need to be studied. This project, however, takes the point of departure that the communicative possibilities in a situation are especially determining factors when it comes to constructing rooms or environments for collaboration and interaction.

The overall objective of this PhD project is to develop a theoretical framework for computer mediated communication and collaboration. Such a framework serves the purpose of clarifying in which ways communication and collaboration can be supported by computer based tools. In order to understand this the relation between the task to be performed and the communicative possibilities of the tool needs to be investigated. Thus, a closer definition of the concept of collaboration is needed, including a disintegration of the concept.

A specific interest is taken into understanding how construction of a virtual (work-)room takes place. At this stage in the project it is assumed that the process of creating a virtual place for collaboration takes place in an interaction between the participants. As the virtual place is a non-physical phenomenon, and therefore exists in the heads of the participants (supported by surrounding artefacts and actions in connection with interaction in the virtual place), the participants' use of language becomes vital in understanding how such a common place is constructed and maintained throughout the interaction.

On a more pragmatic level the aim of the investigation is to help produce guidelines for mediated communication, and for conducting meetings and collaborative work sessions in virtual environments.

3 Data

The empirical part of the project consists of a number of meetings in a network of researchers, distributed across Europe (in six different countries). In the meetings, communication and interaction is based on a CSCW-tool called MERCI. This toolset consists of a video-tool, an audio-tool, a shared whiteboard, a session directory-tool and a text-editor. The meetings, which took place within the frame of the MANICORAL project, were attended by a varying number of people (3–10) at a varying number of geographical sites (2–5).

The meetings were all recorded on video; whenever possible, parallel recordings were made, so that each meeting was recorded at all participation sites. In addition to the video recording, observation, note-taking and interviews have been carried out in order to capture the meetings and the way in which the participants experienced them.

4 Methodological Background

Looking at communication, a number of different approaches to understanding and analyses are offered. In this project, concepts developed within the framework of conversational analysis have been chosen as the starting point. In conversational analysis (CA), focus is on both content and form, a very useful combination when focus is on the role

of communication as an instrument for construction virtual places/work-rooms.

A well-known practitioner of CA is Herbert Clark from the Department of Psychology, Stanford University. In his book 'Using Language' (Clark, 1996) a number of concepts of communication are introduced, namely grounding, closure, temporal grain and visual access. Although developed for the area of face-to-face communication, these concepts have proven themselves to be operational also in relation to computer mediated communication. However, some translation work might be needed in order to use the concepts on computer mediated communication. Clark sees common ground as a prerequisite for successful communication and collaboration, temporal grain and visual access as means towards obtaining common ground, and joint closure as the evidence that the performed action has succeeded.

Another central methodological approach to data analysis in this project is video analysis. As a large part of the empirical studies of computer mediated communication have been videotaped at several sites, a considerable number of videotapes has been produced. It would be almost impossible to make analyses of all the tapes — not to mention the relevance of this — whereas a selection in the material is needed. In order to perform this, and subsequently carry out analyses of the selected material, a method developed at Institute for Research on Learning in California will be used as inspiration. The method is known as VIA (Video Interaction Analysis) and has been described by Jordan & Henderson (1995). Further development of the Jordan and Henderson approach is part of the project, as this method will be adjusted to fit into a combination with CA. Where VIA concentrates on contents, interaction, use and importance of artefacts, etc., CA is informative in relation to the structure of the interaction and thus also the possibilities and limitations of the situation.

References

Clark, H. H. (1996), *Using Language*, Cambridge University Press.

Jordan, B. & Henderson, A. (1995), "Interaction Analysis: Foundation and Practice", *Journal of Learning Sciences* **4**(1), 39–103.

Human–Computer Interaction — INTERACT '99
M. Angela Sasse and Chris Johnson (Editors)
Published by IOS Press, © IFIP TC.13, 1999

Incorporating Usability in the Software Design Process

M.J. Mahemoff

Department of Computer Science and Software Engineering, The University of Melbourne, Parkville, Victoria 3052, Australia.

moke@cs.mu.oz.au

Abstract: Usability evaluation, while necessary, is not a sufficient means of incorporating human factors into the software engineering process. More attention needs to be focused on the goal of designing with usability in mind. Principles and guidelines have been unsatisfactory in practice. Design patterns complement principles by helping developers appreciate how typical problems may be solved in accordance to the principles. This research aims to capture generic activities which users typically perform with software (e.g. undo), and document the software design patterns which emerge when these activities are supported.

Keywords: design patterns, generic tasks, user-centred design.

1 Introduction

At present, the typical software engineering process does not adequately consider the needs of users. Human factors are often considered only after implementation, when repair is often impractical (Lim & Long, 1994). While evaluation is certainly necessary, the above observations suggest that effort and quality would be better optimised if usability was considered before evaluation. Design evaluation, via heuristics or cognitive walkthroughs, is not sufficient because it still presumes effective re-design. Simply being able to identify defects does not mean that solutions can be found (Karat & Dayton, 1995). The construction of design artefacts, rather than their evaluation, should be the foremost consideration.

2 Benefits of Design Patterns

One way to improve the design process is with principles and guidelines. However, these documents leave too much room for interpretation (Chapanis & Budurka, 1990); for example, it is easy to state that software features should be 'intuitive', but it is much more difficult to determine what this means in a real-life project. To help provide more concrete guidance to developers, I have been investigating an approach which complements high-level principles, based on design patterns. The concept, originally developed by architects and more recently popularised by software engineers, considers problems which often confront developers.

A pattern takes a particular context, analyses the forces involved, and suggests a solution which successfully resolves those forces. Since they are based on underlying principles, patterns can help designers understand how to derive solutions which obey those principles, and may therefore be seen as complementing design principles. Evolutionary development, an important goal in human–computer interaction, was one of the original goals for architectural design patterns (Alexander et al., 1977), and is reflected in the generative nature of pattern languages. Because a user-centred design process requires input from a diverse group of people, it is also helpful that patterns provide a vocabulary which can be shared among the development team.

3 Constructing Usability-oriented Design Patterns

The intention of this work is to identify the common activities which are performed, and to document practical ways in which software can effectively support these activities. This involves not only identifying the user-interface issues arising from each activity, but also functionality and implications for software design. It may seem surprising to relate software design to usability, since the same user-interface can be constructed with radically different underlying designs. However, some software designs facilitate usability and usability-related changes more than others. For example, architectures which separate the user-interface from the core functionality support usability by isolating those components which interact with the user. Furthermore, there is often a conflict between usability and other software attributes, such as portability and complexity. By capturing those design patterns which help to resolve these conflicts, developers will be more inclined to produce usable systems.

To achieve this goal, generic activities must be discovered, overriding principles must be prepared to ensure that patterns are coherent with one another, and patterns which support the activities should be documented.

3.1 Discovery of Generic Activities

There are many activities which occur across different systems, such as the ability to summarise a document, undo an action, or copy an object. In order to extract usability-oriented design patterns, it is necessary to obtain a set of generic activities. Our primary source of data is a group of requirements specification documents. These specifications are taken from student projects with industrial clients, and represent a cross-section of applications. We are extracting typical activities with the aim of producing a set of generic tasks.

3.2 Construction of Design Principles

A pattern language is a group of patterns which work together harmoniously. In a practical sense, this means that a design constructed using several patterns in the language can be easily modified using another pattern in the language, without disrupting the general style. It should be possible to add a 'Search' function without altering the overall look-and-feel of the interface. Additionally, the change to the underlying design should be straightforward — each pattern should embody the general architecture and interaction mechanisms inherent in the language as a whole.

To achieve this level of coherence, a set of principles for the language is being developed. These are a summary of high-level principles (e.g. the need to consider a variety of interaction styles), desirable properties (e.g. 'Robustness'), and process-oriented principles (e.g. iterative lifecycle). In addition, an overall architectural pattern must be chosen to address

static and dynamic design issues such as constructing the user interface and synchronising between user-interface and core functionality. The Model-View-Controller (MVC) architecture (Krasner & Pope, 1988) is one architectural pattern under consideration, chosen for its simplicity and widespread familiarity.

3.3 From Activities to Patterns

The activities themselves will not all map directly into patterns. Instead, the group of generic tasks as a whole will be used to capture and document patterns of software features which support these tasks. For instance, one activity users sometimes perform is comparing one document with another. The user-interface for displaying a comparison should reuse the user-interface for the individual document. A pattern language can make this possible by ensuring that the document view is designed in such a way that it can be reused by the comparison view (as well as other views described in the pattern language). Even if the designer cannot initially foresee the usefulness of comparing documents, the design will allow it to be added as smoothly as possible, later on. To obtain the patterns, I am constructing some of my own software, as well as observing successful pre-existing designs.

References

Alexander, C., Ishikawa, S., Silverstein, M., Jacobson, M., Fiksdahl-King, I. & Angel, S. (1977), *A Pattern Language*, Oxford University Press.

Chapanis, A. & Budurka, W. J. (1990), "Specifying Human-Computer Interface Requirements", *Behaviour & Information Technology* **9**(6), 476–92.

Karat, J. & Dayton, T. (1995), Practical Education for Improving Software Usability, *in* I. Katz, R. Mack, L. Marks, M. B. Rosson & J. Nielsen (eds.), *Proceedings of CHI'95: Human Factors in Computing Systems*, ACM Press, pp.162–9.

Krasner, G. E. & Pope, S. T. (1988), "A Cookbook for Using the Model-View-Controller User Interface Paradigm in Smalltalk-80", *Journal of Object Oriented Programming* **1**(3), 26–49.

Lim, K. Y. & Long, J. B. (1994), *The MUSE Method for Usability Engineering*, Cambridge Series on Human–Computer Interaction, Cambridge University Press.

Human–Computer Interaction — INTERACT '99
M. Angela Sasse and Chris Johnson (Editors)
Published by IOS Press, © IFIP TC.13, 1999

Evaluating Navigation: Are We There Yet?

Rod McCall

School of Computing, Napier University, 219 Colinton Road, Edinburgh, UK.
rmccall@dcs.napier.ac.uk

1 Introduction

The increasing size and complexity of electronic information spaces has led to increased problems for the user. One major problem is that of users becoming disorientated within an environment, a typical example being within hypermedia systems. The research presented here is concerned with creating a set of guidelines which can be used by designers during the design and evaluation of a system. These guidelines aim to inform design by providing not only a method of evaluation but also extensive supporting documentation to alert designers to navigational issues.

The brief outline of research presented here takes the view that the user is situated within the electronic environment. In essence they are a traveller in information space making use of other cues, users and agents within the environment (Benyon & Höök, 1997). This marks a departure from the traditional view of interaction, which sees the user as being out with the information space.

2 First Year

The aim of the research is to develop a method of evaluating navigation (called The Navigational Instrument). The navigational instrument builds on the basic ideas of navigation *exploration*: where the user has no specific goal, *wayfinding*: (Downs & Stea, 1973) where they have a specific goal and *object identification* (Benyon & Höök, 1997). The navigational instrument draws on various spheres including psychology, architecture, human–computer interaction, urban planning, navigation, semiotics and graphical design. The aim being that by examining the various types of navigation in different spaces ideas can in theory be transferred to aid in designing electronic spaces. Typical examples include the use of consistency and inconsistency from the built environment, different evaluation methods and finally the use of signs within real world spaces to support the navigational process.

One of the principal changes from some existing usability methods is that the navigational instrument supports *exploration, wayfinding* and *object identification*. Exploration is comparable to a task less form of interaction and is therefore difficult to evaluate in many methods. The main reason for this is that urban planning often encourages the idea of incidental activity, whereby people engage in side tasks not directly related to what they are intending to carry out, or they carry out these tasks to supplement their knowledge of the environment.

In addition to the various phases of navigation there is also a need to support the different methods and types of acquiring knowledge within an environment. This falls into three categories *landmark* (navigating by using distinct objects), *route* (a procedural description of how to get from point a to b) and *survey* (a general overview map of the environment). In order to support this and different user types the navigational instrument evaluates the provision of signs, object and agents which aid in the provision of route as well as survey knowledge.

Following this extensive review a number of areas were considered relevant to navigation. From these areas a set of prototype guidelines (called the navigational instrument) were drawn up. The guidelines contained twelve main areas, which included several aspects such as signs, auditory cues and navigation within and between objects. One of the critical points of this checklist was that it adopted a qualitative style of evaluation. However in doing so a number of problems regarding the applicability, interpretation of questions and results arose.

The set of guidelines were then used for evaluating a number of environments (at present 2D only). The purpose of these evaluations was to validate the content and methodology of the navigational instrument. The initial studies involved a Web site,

3COM PalmPilots and Microsoft Word. From this a number of issues were raised. These included the actual content of the navigational instrument, results obtained and the usability of the method. This resulted in a number of small changes to the sections, headings and structure of the navigational instrument. It also became apparent that some issues such as interpreting results and documentation could be overcome by creating a software version. From this an early version was developed in June 1997. In addition to the basic question set the software (ENISpace) also includes examples, references and other features to aid in the evaluation process. ENISpace was demonstrated at the I3 annual conference where delegates were asked to make comments on the system.

Following on from this a more thorough review of the method was carried out. This took the form of evaluating a system called CO-NEXUS which was developed to allow people with learning difficulties to develop internet skills. The test plan consisted of carrying out user trials with the actual users of CO-NEXUS. In addition the system was also evaluated using Cognitive Walkthrough, Heuristic evaluation, the navigational instrument and users were also asked to complete a short questionnaire. Further to this several other evaluators were asked to evaluate CO-NEXUS using heuristic evaluation and cognitive walkthrough. The aim of these evaluations was identify areas of overlap the between methods, problems with the questions in the checklist and other problems which may arise. From this large evaluation a number of problem areas were identified.

A further review was conducted and the navigational instrument was reduced to four key areas (conceptual structure & dynamics, signs, users in the space, navigational methods and aids). The signs sections was refined and focussed on more specific issues. Also an another prototype software version was demonstrated at HCI98. The new software version aimed to take in to account the changes and also problems with the previous software version. It also adhered more closely to the design guidelines within the navigational instrument in particular the use of signs and districts.

3 Future Directions

At the time of writing (January 1999) only the signs section within the navigational instrument had been reviewed. However over the remaining period of time the entire instrument (paper and software versions) will be restructured. In addition it is intended to extend the instrument to cover 3D environments. During the development of both the 2D and 3D systems, a number of environments are scheduled to be evaluated and tested.

4 Anticipated Results

It is anticipated that the navigational instrument will be useful in highlighting relevant issues both during the design and evaluation stages of a project. In addition through the software version, system designers will be able to not only highlight problem areas but will also be given some examples of best practice. Therefore allowing suggestions for improvement.

Acknowledgements

The funding for my PhD is provided by a Napier University Studentship. Acknowledgements are also due to Prof. David Benyon, Dr Alan J Munro and the other members of the I3 PERSONA (25637) project, the funders I3NET, and the members of the CO-NEXUS project.

References

Benyon, D. & Höök, K. (1997), Navigation in Information Spaces: Supporting the Individual, *in* S. Howard, J. Hammond & G. K. Lindgaard (eds.), *Human–Computer Interaction — INTERACT '97: Proceedings of the Sixth IFIP Conference on Human–Computer Interaction*, Chapman & Hall, pp.39–45.

Downs, R. & Stea, D. (1973), *Image and the Environment*, Adeline Press.

Human–Computer Interaction — INTERACT '99
M. Angela Sasse and Chris Johnson (Editors)
Published by IOS Press, © IFIP TC.13, 1999

If Only Design Sophistication Meant Fault and Fool Proof, Easy to Use Systems

Doreen Ng

School of Computing Science, Middlesex University, Bounds Green Road, London N11 2NQ, UK.

D.Ng@mdx.ac.uk

Abstract: The advent of modern day market economy products and systems bring about design sophistication, which is supposed to make life easy for users. But this proved otherwise and the possible solution lies in the design engineering process which could be extended.

Keywords: design, system complexity characteristics, usability.

1 Introduction

Designers aspire to design new products that differentiate in terms of being useful, advanced and futuristic which can be equated as having design sophistication. The result is products that are too complex to use (that is, one that looks nice, feels good but not very practical!) (Sparke, 1998). Users only want to use products that help them accomplish the tasks they set out to do. More often than not, a larger part of the complexity of the products end up not being used at all because users find them too 'technical' or complicated to understand. This only serves to frustrate the modern day users more than to facilitate.

2 The Issues on Hand

Modern day market economy products, as observed by Shanks (1967), have a natural life cycle: novelty, acceptance, familiarity, obsolescence (whether it is due to technical or market factors). This strongly indicated that the distractions of commercial means (like product marketability, profit, competitive selling) partly contribute to the illusion of having to produce products with design sophistication (Christensen, 1997).

One generally popular marketing idea, which is still a product's main selling point is a product which is designed to be fool-proof. This meant that the design is supposed to be sophisticated enough for even a 'fool' who has no prior knowledge about it to be able to use it with ease. Unfortunately, the contrary is true for many products due to the increased complexity designed into the product or system.

To compound the problems on hand, due to commercial reasons, products are frequently designed and put on production lines under strict time limits. Besides, a list of problems emerge when one uses everyday products like the calculators, cameras, domestic telephone with fax and answer-phone features, microwave ovens, video cassette recorder or the HyperCard (Apple's multimedia system) showing that the products have not been explicitly or implicitly tested or both (Thimbleby, 1991; 1997; 1998b; 1998a).

Known problems or some of the shortcomings of the products are documented and accepted (without much choice) by users. This documentation may or may not recommend work around methods or just appear as an acknowledgement that it is there in the first place.

3 Bridging the Gap

The choice of method used in the design engineering process has been largely dependent on an organization's directives, its practice and needs, the type of systems to be built and what the management supports. According to Yourdon (1986), "All systems have some functional and some data and some time-dependent behaviour" and that very often, "one dimension of the system dominates the other two". The traditional system complexity characteristics used to be the main determinant factor for the choice of design engineering process.

With the advent of modern day market economy products and systems, the traditional system complexity characteristics guidelines could no longer be applied as it is not robust enough (Bødker, 1998). The emergent trend indicates that real-time (or time-dependent) behaviour with process controls that would perhaps have complex databases (or information) or function or both, is the 'commonly' accepted and expected package. Designers and product experts consider that anything less than this would not produce sophisticated products and systems.

It is essential to bridge the gap between designers and users who are sitting at both ends of a pole and reduce the chasm that threatens to push them further apart.

4   Methodology

It is necessary to investigate, re-examine and extend the context of specifications led design, its notational representations and techniques applied with relevance to the emergent multi-system complexity characteristics. This should provide the platform on which to derive the important properties required for formulating or extending notational representations and techniques. Variances, implications and the effects of these properties will also be analysed.

The scope of work includes current ongoing critical surveys of a sampling of (modern day consumer mass market) products or systems using a diagrammatic representation (state machines) technique, a natural language goal-based (Cognitive walkthrough) method and a cross-sectional study. The study evaluates the design techniques used and the resultant design by a sample group of designers who are given a sample design task (which include elements of multi-system complexity characteristics). A set of questionnaires-responses from the same group of designers will be used to identify their experiences. The collective information gathered will then be collated statistically for subsequent analysis and conclusion. Experience and information generated from the work done will provide the basis on which to identify, describe and model the 'good and bad' usability of the design interface of design sophistication in products or systems.

We will determine and highlight the design issues encountered and the resultant effects of design sophistication.

After the formulation of 'what is good' modelling theories of the design interfaces and usability of multi-system complexity characteristics (which spells design sophistication), a post test survey will be conducted.

5   Aim of Research

It is envisaged that the scope of this work will culminate in a prototype and the development of a framework of formal notational representations for a more effective, accurate and efficient design process.

Acknowledgement

This work is supported by a postgraduate studentship from the School of Computing Science, Middlesex University.

References

Bødker, S. (1998), "Understanding Representation in Design", *Human–Computer Interaction* **13**, 107–25.

Christensen, C. (1997), "Patterns in the Evolution of Product Competition", *European Management Journal* **15**(2), 117–27.

Shanks, M. (1967), *The Innovators: The Economics of Technology*, Penguin.

Sparke, P. A. (1998), *A Century of Design (Design Pioneers of the 20th Century)*, Reed Consumer Books Limited.

Thimbleby, H. (1991), *User Interface Design*, Frontier Series, ACM Press.

Thimbleby, H. (1998a), "Specification-led Design for Interface Simulation, Collecting Use-data, Interactive Help, Writing Manuals, Analysis, Comparing Alternative Designs, etc.". http//www.cs.mdx.ac.uk/harold/.

Thimbleby, H. W. (1997), "Design for a Fax", *Personal Technologies* **1**(2), 101–17.

Thimbleby, H. W. (1998b), The Detection and Elimination of Spurious Complexity, *in* R. C. Backhouse (ed.), *Proceedings of Workshop on User Interfaces for Theorem Provers*, Eindhoven University of Technology, pp.15–22. Available as Report 98–08, also http//www.cs.mdx.ac.uk/harold/.

Yourdon, E. (1986), *Managing the Structured Techniques, Strategies for Software Development in the 1990's*, Yourdon Press (Prentice–Hall).

Human–Computer Interaction — INTERACT '99
M. Angela Sasse and Chris Johnson (Editors)
Published by IOS Press, © IFIP TC.13, 1999

A Bridge Too Far: Can UML Finally Help Bridge the Gap?

Nuno Jardim Nunes

University of Madeira, Campus Universitário da Penteada 9000, Funchal, Portugal.

dnnunes@uma.pt

Abstract: This paper discusses the role of the Unified Modelling Language in helping to bridge the gap between current HCI practice and object-oriented software engineering practice.

Keywords: UML, software engineering, task analysis, user interface design, user-centred process.

1 Introduction

Object-oriented analysis and design methods have recently come to the forefront as the dominant system development paradigm. The recent adoption, by the OMG (Object Management Group), of UML (Unified Modelling Language) confirms its role as the standard notation and semantics for object-oriented software engineering (OOSE). Several efforts from the human–computer interaction (HCI) community reflect the importance of object models to help bridge the gap between current HCI and OOSE practices. Several CHI workshops discussed the role of object models and task/process analysis in user interface design (UID). The outcome was a collection of contributions discussing how experienced designers use the results of work/task analysis to produce UIDs (Dayton et al., 1998), a general framework for object modelling in UID (van Harmelen et al., 1997), and a set of UML extensions to support task modelling (Artim et al., 1998). All this work stresses the importance and the opportunity of integrating HCI practice in SE.

2 The UML Standard

UML is a language for visualizing, specifying, constructing and documenting the artifacts of a software-intensive system. In order to understand the issues involved in bringing HCI and OOSE practices together, we need to consider UML in a process context. For its close relation to UML, we will use the Rational Unified Process (RUP) (Kruchten, 1998) as a reference OOSE process. RUP is an iterative, OO, model based, architecture centric, use case driven process. RUP's 4 iterative phases encompass several process work-flows. From this reference we built a

new proposal for a user centred OOSE process (see Figure 1). That process introduces several specialized UC work-flows. Our goal is not to discuss process-centric issues, but to build a framework to enable a clearer identification of HCI intervention in the mainstream OO paradigm.

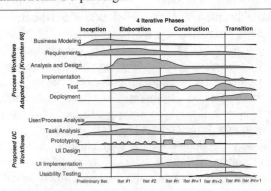

Figure 1: User-centred OOSE process.

3 Research Framework

Using the proposal in Figure 1, we present and discuss HCI contributions to OOSE. We try to focus on selected contributions that can be used later on to extend UML to close the gap with HCI.

3.1 Inception Phase

According to RUP, the inception phase establishes the business case for the system and defines the project scope, using the *business modelling* and *requirements* work-flows. In this phase, the proposed UC OOSE process introduces the *user/process analysis* and the *task analysis* work-flows. There is strong consensus about incorporating task analysis in UML. Use cases lack support for some general task analysis features, particularly, decomposability and task frequency. An UML compliant extension for task analysis (Artim et al., 1998) was already proposed to solve this problem. However, this extension does not use the standard extension mechanisms of UML, so, it requires agreement from OMG. User and process analysis, as some form of aggregation of task analysis, depend on the same integration facility.

3.2 Elaboration Phase

The goals of the elaboration phase are to analyse the problem domain and establish a sound architectural foundation. Here RUP highlights the *requirements, analysis* and *design* work-flows. The proposals for the UC OOSE process are *task analysis* (medium and fine-grained) supporting UID and *prototyping* work-flows. Again, adequate UID support depends on the ability of UML to integrate task analysis. At the design level several approaches describe mappings between tasks and objects (Tarby & Barthet, 1996; Dayton et al., 1998). The translation process depends on the ability of the object modelling language to accommodate additional task information (containment relations, pre- and post-conditions). Such extensions are already proposed in (Kovacevic, 1998).

3.3 Construction and Transition Phases

These two phases accomplish the iterative and incremental development of the solution and the deployment of the software to the end users. Here the highlighted work-flows are *implementation* and *testing*. Dominant work-flows, introduced from UC OOSE, are *Prototyping, UI implementation* and *usability testing*. At the implementation level the fundamental issues are tool support and traceability between conceptual models and the implementation model. Tool support for task analysis is recognized to be insufficient. One approach, described in (Lu et al., 1998), is to transform task analysis models into UML interaction models and vice versa. This pragmatic approach enables the integration of specialized task modelling tools to industrial strength tools. Another interesting proposal is to model views as objects (Roberts et al., 1998) combining and relating them to the analysis model. The drawback is that there is no UML notation to express connection from views.

4 Research Status

I'm concentrating my efforts on the UC OOSE proposal and on the selection process of HCI

contributions. I believe the framework could benefit from close scrutiny from expert designers, already attempting to introduce HCI practice in commercial and industrial OOSE. At the moment, my primary concern is to ensure traceability on the proposed UML extension process. I'm committed to use UML's built-in mechanisms (stereotypes, tagged values and constraints) to extend the language in a controlled and semantically consistent way. The importance of assuring this extensibility process is to facilitate inter-operability between CASE tools.

References

Artim, J., van Harmelen, M., Butler, K., Gulliksen, J., Henderson, A., Kovacevic, S., Lu, S., Overmyer, S., Reaux, R., Roberts, D., Tarby, J. & Linden, K. (1998), "Incorporating Work, Process and Task Analysis into Commercial and Industrial Object-oriented Systems Development", *ACM SIGCHI Bulletin* **30**(4), 198.

Dayton, T., McFarland, A. & Kramer, J. (1998), Bridging User Needs to Object-oriented GUI Prototypes via Task Object Design, *in* L. Wood (ed.), *User Interface Design*, CRC Press.

Kovacevic, S. (1998), UML and User Interface Modelling, *in* P. Muller & J. Bézivin (eds.), *Proceedings of the UML'98 Workshop*, pp.235–44.

Kruchten, P. (1998), *The Rational Unified Process*, Object Technology Series, Addison–Wesley.

Lu, S., Paris, C. & Vander Linden, K. (1998), Towards Automatic Construction of Task Models from Object-oriented Diagrams, *in* S. Chatty & P. Dewan (eds.), *Proceedings of the IFIP Working Conference on Engineering for Human–Computer Interaction 1998*, Kluwer.

Roberts, D., Berry, D., Isensee, S. & Mullaly, J. (1998), *Designing for the User with OVID*, MacMillan.

Tarby, J. & Barthet, M. (1996), The Diane+ Method, *in* J. Vanderdonckt (ed.), *Proceedings of 2nd International Workshop on Computer-aided Design of User Interfaces (CADUI'96)*, Presses Universitaires de Namur, pp.95–119.

van Harmelen, M., Artim, J., Butler, K., Henderson, A., Roberts, D., Rosson, M. B., Tarby, J. & Wilson, S. (1997), "Object Models in User Interface Design", *ACM SIGCHI Bulletin* **29**(4), 55–62.

SPEL — System for Phonic Early Learning

Linda Snape

Department of Computing, University of Central Lancashire, Preston PR1 2HE, UK.

L.C.Snape1@uclan.ac.uk

Abstract: System for Phonic Early Learning (SPEL) is an intelligent tutoring system that has been designed to tutor phonic awareness in children aged 4–7 years. Intelligent tutoring systems comprise four basic components: a used interface; a subject knowledge-base; an expert system; and a user model. The individual tutoring mechanism of the system will be evaluated in primary schools following usability and functionality testing of individual components.

Keywords: intelligent tutoring system, user interface, expert system, user model, phonics, primary education.

1 Background

In a government attempt to raise national standards in core subject areas (namely English and Mathematics), from September 1998 all primary schools in Great Britain have been required to:

- Introduce baseline assessment schemes for core subjects.

- Set and periodically measure improvement targets for core subjects.

- Spend at least one hour a day on literacy (an initiative widely known as 'the literacy hour').

In an age where teachers are already stretched to the limit, the prospect of assessing, monitoring and one-to-one tutoring presents a somewhat daunting if not impossible task. Teachers are therefore looking more and more towards computers to ease the burden of the increasing responsibility being placed upon them.

Until recently, most tutoring systems have been aimed at the area of Mathematics, where problems have exact and predictable solutions. However, a few large tutoring systems, which claim to successfully tutor students in *all* curriculum subjects have recently appeared on the market. An NCET[*] evaluation of these systems concluded that they were more effective

for Mathematics than for English, and in particular appear to be ineffective for Key Stage 1 English.[†] Development of a system that will tutor children in Key Stage 1 English is therefore not only innovative, but will also fill a large hole that is appearing in classroom resources.

Many modern educational computer applications still attempt to teach by presenting information in the form of interactive text books and picture slide shows. While this technique may be successful for a few students, it generally frustrates and disillusions the majority of students by presenting too much information at the wrong level. In order to tutor on an individual level, teachers need knowledge of the subject, knowledge of how to teach the subject and knowledge of the student. In computer terms, one can only begin to model this kind of complex and intangible skill in the form of knowledge bases.

2 System Overview

The project is the development of a prototype intelligent tutoring system that will tutor children aged 5–7 years in the area of phonics[‡] (part of the National Curriculum requirements for English Key Stage 1). The system comprises the user interface, a subject knowledge base, an expert system and a user model.

---

[*]The National Council for Educational Technology.

[†]The Integrated Learning Systems Evaluation Project, Phase 2, 1996, NCET.

[‡]Phonics is one of the skills required by young children learning to read and write. It is the technique of attaching written symbols to spoken sounds.

2.1 User Interface

One of the most interesting features of this project is the design of an interface suitable for very young children.

Teaching literacy to children who are too young to read has previously been impossible for systems using traditional text based interfaces. Multimedia technology, however, is now enabling system developers to consider exciting and innovative subject areas such as literacy by using the same visual and auditory techniques that are employed in the classroom. One subject area that relies heavily on audio and visual teaching techniques is that of phonics. It would be possible to develop a teaching aid for phonics without speech analysis; but, using speech recognition as part of the interface for this system would be highly desirable.

An investigation by the author into the area of speech recognition (Snape et al., 1997) concluded that because speech is a much more natural interface, user expectations of system performance is increased and so is the frustration that users feel at subsequent system failure. These problems are magnified in systems used by young children. Careful design of speech interfaces, however, can minimise the current limitations of speech technology. Investigation into the use of speech as part of the interface to this system will continue.

2.2 Subject Knowledge Base

The subject domain to this system comprises a set of tasks suggested by subject experts. These tasks will be used by the expert system to teach concepts in phonics.

2.3 Expert System

In a tutoring system the expert component would be expected to present the correct amount of relevant information and tasks at the correct level for each user, and to constantly diagnose errors and suggest remedial activity. Expert interviews have been used to construct a rule base for this system, and will continue throughout the project.

2.4 User Model

In order to tutor effectively, both teachers and tutoring systems must also have access to historical information on the strengths and weaknesses of the child. Teachers may also tailor activities according to the personal preferences of the child, how the child approaches problems and even to how the child is motivated. This type of information is widely known in the area of artificial intelligence as the user model. In this system, the information held in the user model will be used by the expert system to assist in problem diagnosis and decision making.

3 Progress

Successful development of each component depends in varying degrees on the information which must be acquired from primary school teaching experts and translated into information to be held by the computer. Two primary schools within the Lancashire area have been working on the project for the past twelve months and Salford City Council Executives have recently offered the services of their teachers and children to be used in the more extensive evaluation necessary in the future.

Development of systems in new and innovative areas is best carried out by building prototypes and testing and evaluating them on real users. This type of iterative design technique will minimise the inherent problems of incomplete requirements specifications through the process of feedback and refinement of the system. In order to eliminate technical integration risks, a small prototype system was developed early in the project, simulating the interaction between the main system components.

Following the successful prototype of the basic system architecture, each component has been developed in isolation in order to eliminate problems within specific domain areas. The primary objective up to now has been to develop the system activities and the interface. The usability and functionality of the interface will be evaluated over the next twelve months. After the development and integration of the other components, there will be a further evaluation of the complete system.

References

Snape, L., Casey, C., MacFarlane, S. & Robertson, I. (1997), Using Speech in Multimedia Applications', *in Proceedings of TCD Conference on Multimedia*, Vol. 7(7) of *Teaching Company Directorate Seminar Proceedings*, TCD, pp.50–60. ISBN 1 901255 08 5.

Human–Computer Interaction — INTERACT '99
M. Angela Sasse and Chris Johnson (Editors)
Published by IOS Press, © IFIP TC.13, 1999

Computer Supported Knowledge Management

Ulrika Snis

Department of Economy and Computer Science, University of Trollhättan/Uddevalla, Östergatan 18, Box 795, S-451 26 Uddevalla, Sweden.

Ulrika.Snis@udd.htu.se

Abstract: The overall knowledge management problem seems to concern communication, coordination and distribution of knowledge between individuals and groups that are dispersed in time and space. Especially the field of CSCW pays attention to specific work domains, where the actual knowledge of work exists. This perspective calls to understand work practices with consequent implications for computer support. Drawing from a number of field studies I want to investigate the general hypothesis of how to support knowledge management with computers. I want to find a discussion about what important aspects in knowledge management activities exist and which technologies can be used. Are there any implementations from which we can learn? The over all study may end in providing recommendations for computer support when managing knowledge.

Keywords: knowledge management, knowledge technology, field studies, interaction modes.

1 Introduction

The concept of knowledge management is considered as the key strategic process in much knowledge intensive companies of today (Spender, 1998). According to Alavi (1998) knowledge management aims at identifying the corporate knowledge in collective memories and facilitating communication and coordination between people that actually create it and people who really need it. Linking the gaps between creating and using knowledge is a central issue in knowledge management (Wathne et al., 1996).

However, in order to become knowledge, some information needs to be interpreted and applied in a specific situation by a human and then also be conceptualised to a certain level of abstraction. This interplay between abstraction and concretion is a true property of knowledge creation process. Nonaka & Takeuchi (1995) are addressing the key issue of interaction in this process. They identify four modes of interaction, which include socialisation, combination, externalisation and internalisation. In respect to this framework my interest has been to analyse the combination process, in which individuals combine and exchange knowledge by interacting with mediated mechanisms such as documents, meetings, telephone conversations, or computerised communication networks. Another interest is now also to analyse the socialisation process. All these

motives put forward the efforts of looking for design of computer supported knowledge management inspired by interaction technologies (van Heijst et al., 1998).

2 Research Approach

During the last couple of years I have been involved in field studies aiming at supporting different kinds of knowledge management processes. (Snis, 1997; Snis & Johansson, 1997).

The main methods that I have applied are inspired by ethnography. Semi-structured interviews, direct observations, meeting participation, and social networking have been applied. By 'walking and talking' through the organizational processes, in which the study takes place, I have gained a rich picture of the work and the different conceptions of the involved actors. This approach has been extremely important when investigating settings where knowledge and knowledge management have a tight coupling to both cooperative work and computer support.

3 Discussing the Results

The empirical data in my licentiate thesis was based on a field study in a very specific and complex problem domain. At Volvo Aero Corporation in Sweden I investigated the management and coordination of knowledge in a manufacturing process called thermal spraying. The point of departure was from the organizational part to investigate the main factors that affected the quality of the product as well as the process. My approach was to explore the human knowledge and expertise that were hidden among the involved actors and in what way computers could support this knowledge. My main conclusion was that there was a totally different view on what knowledge to consider in such solutions. Thereby I proposed the organization to establish a computer support for the network of experts upon which to interact, negotiate and exchange experiences.

My current studies at Novo Nordsk in Denmark reveal some other interesting results. The Health Care Quality Support Group is dealing with the overall problem of providing and developing knowledge about 'good manufacturing practice'. Their knowledge management process is mainly supporting activities dealing with explicit knowledge. However, there exist implicit knowledge as well, but this is not yet further investigated. One main conclusion from this study is the extremely important use of a mediated application system when managing explicit knowledge (according to Nonaka this is called 'combination'). The explicit knowledge embedded in this system is the operational procedures represented as formal documents. An example of such a system is their Web-based tool, which seems to be the very 'lifeline' throughout the organizational work-flow. What I can learn specifically from this study is also that computer support for knowledge management should only formalise knowledge, which is participatory negotiated and accepted. This facilitates also that knowledge can be transferable and distributed electronically among dispersed co-workers, adaptable and tailor-made to the requirements of different users, and applicable directly to practitioners as well as management staff. Once more, this is considered only for the explicit knowledge found in this study (e.g. used as procedures of know-how in work practice).

In order to find out which further technologies that can be used I want to discuss what important

aspects exist in knowledge management. New Web-based knowledge charting tools are advancing. Are there any implementations from which we can learn? The over all study may end up in providing recommendations for computer supported knowledge management.

References

Alavi, M. (1998), "Knowledge Management and Knowledge Management Systems", *in Proceedings of International Conference on Information Systems, ICIS'98.* http://www. rhsmith.umd.edu/is/malavi/icis-98-KMS/.

Nonaka, I. & Takeuchi, H. (1995), *"The Knowledge-creating Company — How Japanese Companies Create the Dynamics of Innovation"*, Oxford University Press.

Snis, U. (1997), Kunskapsutveckling med stöd av expertsystem,, PhD thesis, Göteborgs Universitet,Sweden.

Snis, U. & Johansson, A. (1997), Collaborative Work in Complex Problem Domains — A Case Study in Thermal Spraying, *in* K. Brna & E. Monteiro (eds.), *Proceedings of IRIS 20, Informations Systems Research Seminar in Scandinavia*, Vol. 1, pp.393–405.

Spender, J. C. (1998), The Dunamics of Individual and Organizational Knowledge, *in* C. Eden & J. C. Spender (eds.), *Managerial and Organizational Cognitiion: Theory, Methods and Research*, Sage Publications, pp.13–39.

van Heijst, G., van der Spek, R. & Kruizinga, E. (1998), The Lessons Learned Processes, *in* U. M. Borghoff & R. Pareschi (eds.), *Information Technology for Knowledge Management*, Springer-Verlag, pp.20–34.

Wathne, K., Roos, J. & von Krogh, G. (1996), Towards a Theory of Knowledge Transfer in a Cooperative Context, *in* G. von Krogh & J. Roos (eds.), *Managing Knowledge — Perspectives on Cooperation and Competition*, Sage Publications, pp.55–81.

Human–Computer Interaction — INTERACT '99
M. Angela Sasse and Chris Johnson (Editors)
Published by IOS Press, © IFIP TC.13, 1999

Supporting Visual Query Expression in a Content-Based Image Retrieval Environment

Colin C. Venters

University of Northumbria at Newcastle, Department of Information & Library Management, Newcastle Upon Tyne NE1 8ST, UK.

colin.venters@unn.ac.uk

Abstract: A research project on user interfaces to visual information retrieval (VIR) systems is presented. The purpose of the study is to investigate user interfaces for visual query systems (VQS), in order to define a user interface module that supports non-lexical visual query expression (VQE). The emphasis is on an extension of the query by pictorial example (QPE) paradigm to improve the quality of human–computer interaction (HCI) in a VIR environment. The study is segmented by image type, user group and use function. The study will demonstrate what type of VIR user interface is most suitable for the retrieval of images by shape-similarity and provide the means to understand how well the VIR module supports the activity of VQE. The novelty of the investigation will be the definition of a visual query user interface module, and the establishment of a schema of user interface requirements.

Keywords: content-based image retrieval, digital image, evaluation, query by pictorial example, user interface, visual information retrieval, visual query.

1 Project Background

Rapid advances in technology have resulted in a number of computer-based applications and systems that produce images. Despite these technological advances in image data capture and storage, the expertise and techniques for effective image retrieval have not kept pace with the technology of image production (Mostafa & Dillon, 1996). However, the developing technology of content-based image retrieval (CBIR) is creating new opportunities to enhance access to digitally stored images. At its simplest level, this process involves a direct matching operation between a query image and a database of stored images. Feature characteristics of the query image can then be specified and weighted against each other e.g. colour, shape and texture. While a considerable amount of research in this field has been directed at advancing the underlying retrieval mechanism of CBIR, few studies have focused on the user interface. The majority of CBIR systems currently restrict end users to a QPE interface to facilitate human–computer interaction. By this method, users can progressively refine the search to one or two relevant visual surrogates (Gecsei & Martin, 1989).

Whether this type of user interface is suitable for supporting HCI in the retrieval process is unknown, as evidence to date is contradictory (Batley, 1989; Mostafa & Dillon, 1996).

Gupta & Jain (1997) note that while most current VIR systems are limited in the query types they can handle, they propose that query specification should be extended through a range of different tools: query canvas, containment queries, semantic queries, object-related queries, spatio-temporal queries. However, it is currently unclear whether these interface features match the activities and tasks of end users as no evaluations have been reported. Supporting visual query expression in a visual query system is a non-trivial problem. The more complex the query i.e. the shape and structure, the more difficult it is for the end user to express and produce a meaningful visual example. The literature suggests that there is no clear understanding of the VIR user interface, both in terms of user design requirements and their usability. The purpose of the study is to investigate user interfaces for a visual query system in order to define a user interface module that supports non-lexical, visual query expression. The emphasis is on an extension of the query by pictorial example paradigm to improve the quality of human–computer interaction in a VIR environment. The novelty of the investigation will be the definition of a visual query (VQ) user interface module, and the establishment of a schema of VQ user interface requirements.

2 Research to Date

The project is segmented by image type, user group, and use function. The image type consists of a set of abstract geometric device marks supplied by the UK Trademark Registry. The dataset comprises ten thousand, two-dimensional, bi-level shapes, stored as files in the Xionics SMP format using CCITT Group 4 Fax compression. A randomly selected set of 250 images was selected to use in the user requirements engineering process. The sample population in the study was purposefully selected to produce a group who shared similar task orientation, motivation, systems expertise and domain knowledge (Ford, 1975, p.238). Dependent variables were determined by the user group, all are intermediaries performing a search for an external body with predefined boundaries. Independent variables were categorized from a phenomenological perspective, the users deciding on their own level of ability, which was determined by means of a questionnaire. Three user groups were selected to assist in the user requirements engineering process: patent information network (PIN) libraries, patent services, and trademark agents. The rationale for targeting these specific groups was based on the premise that their primary business function involves the effective identification of similar images from the dataset, and shared similar task orientation and motivation. The use function was restricted to the retrieval of images by shape similarity. The ARTISAN (Eakins, 1996) shape retrieval system was used to demonstrate the novelty of CBIR technology to the end user population. ARTISAN is a similar-shape retrieval system. The system performs automatic shape analysis, and provides both example-based similarity retrieval and partial shape matching facilities. Twenty three semi-structured interviews were conducted between August and September 1997 with individuals from the three selected groups. The aim of the interviews was to explore the user requirements for a VQS supporting the retrieval of non-lexical image. A number of key areas and issues were explored within the topics of system input, system output, and user interface issues.

The data collected from the interviews was analysed using a constant comparative method (Bogdan, 1992, pp.72-5). Supporting the Gupta & Jain (1997) premise, the data collected suggests

that a number of user interface features are required to support VQE. The three user groups proposed a number of features to support non-lexical, visual query expression: a scanning tool, a free-hand drawing tool, a visual browsing tool, and a visual building tool. Contrary to current VIR user interfaces which only support visual browsing this data suggests that end users have a range of query needs, which should be supported by a range of visual query expression tools. Similarly, the data also suggest that no single interface feature would support all the activities and tasks of this end user population. For known queries, all twenty-three interviewees suggested a *scanning tool* as their primary and preferred tool for VQE. This feature would allow users to scan an image directly into the system to use as the basis of their search. While the three end-user groups have a common interest in the effective identification of similar images from the dataset, the findings highlighted a dichotomy between the activities of trademark agents and those of PIN information officers and patent service personnel.

This is reflective of the activities of the three user groups and can be attributed to the type of client and nature of the service they provide. For example, trademark agents have specific requests for known item queries. The data suggests that trademark agents would only currently require a scanning facility to accurately capture the clients proposed device mark. In contrast, PIN information officers and patent service personnel have a broader range of enquiries that encompass both known and partially known queries. As a result, these two groups proposed a broader range of facilities to assist in VEQ: a *visual query building tool*, a *structured visual browsing tool*, and a *free hand drawing tool*. The visual query building tool would allow end users to select predefined shape features e.g. circles, squares, triangles, rectangles to use as the basis of their query. The structured visual browsing tool would allow end users to scroll through visual surrogates and select an image on the basis of its visual properties to use as their query. The free-hand drawing tool would allow end-users to construct their queries by free-hand drawing.

3 Future Work

Future work will focus on the evaluation of the proposed user defined user interface to assess whether the suggested tools enhance VIR interaction. For comparative purposes the user defined user interface will be evaluated alongside an interface that supports QPE. Usability will be measured using a combination of both objective and subjective measuring instruments: specification metric, critical incidents, and the QUIS questionnaire. The evaluation, analysis and interpretation of the data collected at this stage will determine the usability of the user defined user interface module. This will provide an understanding of how well the user interface module supports the activity of non-lexical, VQE and if the module improves the quality of the HCI within a VIR domain.

References

Batley, S. (1989), Visual Information Retrieval: Browsing Strategies in Pictorial Databases, *in Proceedings of the 12th Online Information Meeting*, Learned Information Ltd, pp.373–81.

Bogdan, R. (1992), *Qualitative Research for Education*, second edition, Simon and Schuster.

Eakins, J. P. (1996), Retrieval of Trademark Images by Shape Feature, Technical Report BLR&IC Report 26, British Library Research and Innovation Centre.

Ford, J. (1975), *Paradigms and Fairytales: An Introduction to the Science of Meanings*, Routledge and Kegan Paul.

Gecsei, N. & Martin, D. (1989), "Browsing Access to Visual Information", *Optical Information Systems* **9**(5), 237–41.

Gupta, A. & Jain, R. (1997), "Visual Information Retrieval", *Communications of the ACM* **40**(5), 71–9.

Mostafa, J. & Dillon, A. (1996), Design and Evaluation of a User Interface Supporting Multiple Image Query Models, *in* S. Harden (ed.), *Proceedings of the 59th Annual Conference of the American Society for Information Science*, Information Today Inc, pp.52–7.

Author Index

Keyword Index